Encyclopedia of
Rural America
The Land and People

Encyclopedia of Rural America

The Land and People

Second Edition

Volume 2

N–Z

Gary A. Goreham

Editor

Grey House
Publishing

PUBLISHER:	Leslie Mackenzie
EDITORIAL DIRECTOR:	Laura Mars-Proietti
EDITORIAL ASSISTANT:	Jael Bridgemahon
MARKETING DIRECTOR:	Jessica Moody

EDITOR:	Gary A. Goreham
COPYEDITOR:	Elaine Alibrandi
COMPOSITION & DESIGN:	ATLIS Systems

Grey House Publishing, Inc.
185 Millerton Road
Millerton, NY 12546
518.789.8700
FAX 518.789.0545
www.greyhouse.com
e-mail: books @greyhouse.com

Publisher's Cataloging-In-Publication Data
(Prepared by The Donohue Group, Inc.)

Encyclopedia of rural America : the land and people / Gary A. Goreham, editor.
  – 2nd ed.

    2 v. : ill. ; cm.

  Includes bibliographical references and index.
  Content: v. 1. A-M – v. 2. N-Z.
  ISBN: 978-1-59237-115-0

1. Country life–United States–Encyclopedias. 2. United States–Rural conditions–Encyclopedias. 3. United States–Geography–Encyclopedias. I. Goreham, Gary. II. Title.

E169.12 .E53 2008
973/.09173/4

CONTENTS

Preface, ix
Introduction, xiii

Encyclopedia of
Rural America
The Land and People

VOLUME 2

Encyclopedia of
Rural America
The Land and People
Volume 2

Natural Resource Economics

The quantity, quality, conservation and sustainability of natural resources in rural America. Natural resources have played a pivotal role in the long and checkered evolution of the rural economies of the U.S. This article is a brief survey and synthesis of the economics of natural resources use in rural America and its evolving future directions. The first part of the article provides a glimpse at major natural resource concerns from a historical perspective and sets the stage for the discussion that follows. The second part presents a survey of use of specific natural resources in rural America. The third part discusses the philosophical change that is transforming the allocation and management of natural resources. The final part sets forth future directions for natural resource policy in rural America.

Historical Setting

Natural resource problems have been a source of serious concern among economists and non-economists for nearly two centuries in the U.S. and abroad. These concerns, for analytical purposes, can be grouped into three main categories: quantity (resource scarcity), quality, and conservation. A sketch of some representative thinking on these issues is presented as a backdrop for the following discussion.

Early concern about the adequacy of natural resources to support human life if resource use and population growth continued undiminished at the then-prevailing rate was expressed by British classical economists Thomas Malthus in the late eighteenth century and David Ricardo in the early nineteenth century. According to Malthus, population tended to increase far more rapidly (in "geometric progression") than agricultural production and the supply of food, leading inevitably to economic disarray. The relatively fixed quantity of land was considered largely responsible for this situation. Malthus discounted technological improvement and factor substitution as possible means to correct the situation.

Ricardo theorized that soil quality differences largely accounted for land rent. He held the view that the most productive land was cultivated first, followed by land of progressively decreasing quality, resulting in an increasing scarcity of high-quality land and eventual resource exhaustion. Ricardo extended his analysis to natural resources in general, although empirical evidence was lacking in other areas, for instance, mining. Nevertheless, this was an important insight into the pattern of natural resource utilization, as subsequent experience has shown.

John Stuart Mill struck a more positive note about the future of natural resources in the mid-nineteenth century. Mill differed from Malthus and Ricardo in an important respect; he argued that the margin of productivity could be extended without limits extensively and intensively. Mill, however, was deeply concerned about the possible deterioration in the quality of natural resources due to overcrowding caused by rapid population growth—a first glimmer of "congestion externalities" (deleterious external effects of overcrowding).

The most comprehensive recent analysis of natural resource scarcity in the U.S. was published by Simpson, Toman, and Ayres (2005). This volume, based on a review and synthesis of theoretical and empirical investigations, concludes that fundamental changes have occurred in the outlook on natural resource scarcity. Unlike the previous concern about the adequacy of fuel, mineral and agricultural resources and their efficient allocation, this study states that the concern today has shifted to "the Earth's limited capacity to handle the environmental consequences of resource extraction and use." The authors advocate major changes in the economic, legal and institutional dimensions of natural resource allocation and use to effectively address pressing issues of resource scarcity.

Natural resource conservation has been a source of concern in the U.S. Marsh, as far back as 1865, expressed concern about human activities and their impact on ecological balance. Later, Pinchot (1910), often noted as the founder of the American Conservation Movement, wrote extensively about the need to conserve "wood, water, coal, iron, and agricultural products" which he considered indispensable for human survival.

Ciriacy-Wantrup (1952) in his seminal book explored the economic and policy dimensions of resource conservation from a largely institutional perspective. He identified the following key economic forces as shaping the decisions of resource users: prices, property rights, tenancy, credit, taxation and market form. He effectively articulated the need to establish a Safe Minimum Standard of conservation to prevent resource depletion and exhaustion. More recent conservation studies extended the analysis through economic modeling and econometric and other quantitative studies.

Natural Resource Use in Rural America

Natural resource use in rural America was primarily rooted in the philosophy of production agriculture embodied in profit maximization through output expansion. The notion of sustainable agriculture and resource use was not an integral or important part of the commonly held agricultural creed. The discussion that follows focuses on problems of quantity, quality and conservation in the context of specific natural resources: water, land, forest and energy.

Water. Water consumption in rural America increased substantially as a result of the dramatic increase in irrigated agriculture, especially in the Western U.S. Expansion of crop production to arid and semiarid regions through extensive water storage and transfer systems, as in California, significantly added to the demand for limited water resources over the years. Irrigation currently accounts for 74 percent of the West's total freshwater withdrawal and 90 percent of its consumptive use. Market sales of crops from the 43 million irrigated acres in the 19 states comprising the United States West account for almost $32 billion, representing one-third of the United States' total crop sales.

Quality of both ground and surface waters deteriorated due to salinization and contamination from pesticides, nitrates and selenium. Rachel Carson's (1962) chilling account of the consequences of organic pesticide use in agriculture drew national attention and created a new awareness of its hidden dangers. The

The environmental movement has heightened awareness of noneconomic considerations in natural resource management. Preservation of the environment for recreational uses is a factor that needs to be balanced against the financial concerns of natural resources industries such as logging and mining. © *Bettmann / Corbis Philip Gendreau.*

comparative abundance and cheapness of water in many areas of rural America in the past accounted for the slow adoption of water conservation technologies such as drip irrigation. The market for and pricing of water were seldom considered seriously in the planning and allocation of water. Quantity, quality and conservation surfaced today as issues of paramount importance in the effective planning, management and allocation of the dwindling surface and groundwater supplies in rural America.

Land. Soil erosion continues to be a major source of concern. The productivity of land in rural America has been severely impacted as a result of unabated soil loss. Over the years, several techniques have been developed to keep soil in place such as reduction or elimination of tillage, reduction of runoff through irrigation management, and the covering of soil with plants and mulch. However, the problem of soil erosion is far from contained.

Soil quality is another important issue in land management. It is a key element in the sustainability of agricultural production. Over the years, soil quality suffered irretrievable losses in many areas of rural America due to monoculture and other crop management systems. Such systems use large quantities of inputs to maintain output.

Soil conservation assumed a new prominence in the context of land management in rural America because of pervasive soil erosion and soil quality losses. Soil conservation is intended to help soils retain their productive capacity by preventing depletion and limiting average soil losses from erosion ideally to a maximum of four tons per acre.

Forests. Forestry or forest resources figured prominently among America's natural resources. It represents an early U.S. example of the application of science to natural resources management. Major issues center on the multiple uses of the public forest lands and timber harvesting practices. The former include disparate uses, such as wilderness, mining, recreation and timber. The latter deal with a panoply of problems, among them, optimum rotation and clear cutting. Rapid deforestation resulting from unchecked cutting of trees for lumber has been and continues to be a source of serious conflict. Another issue that is adding to the problem is the extraction of non-timber forest products in the rural areas adjoining the forests. The impact of the greenhouse gases (chloro-fluoro-carbons) on the forests is an area of looming concern.

Energy. Energy use in U.S. agriculture has been the subject of intense scrutiny, especially in the wake of the Organization of Petroleum Exporting Countries (OPEC) oil embargo of 1973 and the natural gas shortages in the winter of 1976-1977, because of the highly energy-intensive nature of agriculture. Gasoline, diesel oil, fuel oil, LP gas and natural gas traditionally accounted for a significant part of energy use in agriculture. In addition to direct use in agricultural and livestock production, large quantities of petroleum products go into the production of embodied energy such as chemicals and fertilizers.

This traditional pattern of energy use is now changing. Recent studies suggest a reduction in the energy intensity of Western U.S. agricultural production. Gopalakrishnan (1994) points out that energy used to produce a dollar's worth of agricultural output registered an almost 9 percent decrease between 1974 and 1978. Energy-non-energy substitution and adoption of various energy conservation measures such as tillage and weed control, fertilizer management, better irrigation practices, optimal tractor performance, efficient feed handling, and processing and distribution practices contributed to substantial energy savings. The conclusion is that U.S. agriculture has become less energy-intensive in the wake of sharp energy price escalations.

Although U.S. agriculture over the past several decades has become increasingly capital-intensive, the potential for capital-energy substitution still exists in the U.S. farming sector. Along with capital, there exist some possibilities of land and labor substitution for energy in the agricultural sector. Efforts could be made to implement fewer energy-intensive farming techniques, which in turn might require more labor-intensive farming. These possibilities have to be vigorously explored, given the recent phenomenal increase in oil prices, with a barrel of oil costing in excess of $100.

Sustainability: The Guiding Principle

Recent years, roughly the last two decades, witnessed a major change in the philosophy underlying natural resource use in America. This philosophical change is embodied in what has come to be widely known as sustainable resource use. The focus is on keeping the natural resource bounty of a country intact by regulating its rate of use on a sustained basis so that its depletion or exhaustion is averted. The key to such regulation is to ensure that the rate of resource replenishment matches or exceeds the rate of depletion of the natural resource. This marks a distinct departure from the production-oriented resource use approach that was in vogue for many years in America.

Sustainable agriculture is gaining widespread acceptance within mainstream agriculture. The environmental costs associated with many of the earlier agricultural practices are addressed by sustainable agriculture with its focus on the avoidance of air, water and land pollution. Sustainable agriculture views natural resources from a functional approach as living, vital, dynamic entities integrally intertwined with the environment, as opposed to independent free-floating resource commodities. Sustainable resource use thus encapsulates a dynamic vision of natural resources use which will ensure continued availability of resources, uncompromised in quantity and quality, to future generations. (For a detailed discussion of the concept of sustainability, see Edwards, 2005.)

Natural Resources in Rural America: Future Directions

Major changes that should occur in the formulation of a natural resources policy for rural America reflecting the tenor of the times are briefly touched on under four broad categories: economic, institutional, technological and ethical-environmental. Economic changes would encompass the more vigorous use of market and price to allocate increasingly scarce resources among competing demands in an economically sustainable fashion. A case in point is water. Water market and water pricing will take on new importance, especially in the water-short Western U.S. as is evident from the recent experience of Arizona and Colorado, among others. Key issues associated with water transfer, water pricing and water marketing are explored in Brewer et al. (2007). Fuller use of input substitution possibilities in response to relative price changes, as in the case of energy use in agriculture discussed earlier, is another likely economic change. Regulation of the rate of resource use through the rigorous enforcement of quotas, standards, zoning and taxes represents another economic change. An aspect of water resources management that will assume major importance in the years ahead is related to the catastrophic consequences of water disasters and the consequent need to craft creative solutions to effectively address them (Gopalakrishnan, 2007).

Institutional changes connote broad and sweeping changes in natural resources policy stemming from or instigated by shifts or variations in the sociocultural milieu. (See Gopalakrishnan, 2005, for a comprehensive discussion of the role of institutions in water allocation and management.) Modifications in current natural resources laws are also an integral part of such change. Resource conservation, sustainable resource use, and resource quality will assume a new importance in shaping rural America's natural resources policy. Pollution-abatement policies will be more widely accepted and adopted. Water, land and forestry resources will be directly impacted by the broad sweep of these changes.

Technological changes will address resource scarcities of the Ricardian variety in an attempt to extend the margin of resource use to ever-further limits. Changes in technology, for instance, could make an increasing array of renewable energy sources such as biomass, solar, wind and waves cost-effective and well within the reach of large segments of population. Water-conserving irrigation technologies and other resource conserving and sustaining techniques will become far more common in the rural America of the twenty-first century.

Perhaps the most important group of changes affecting the quantity, quality and sustainability of resource use in rural America will be the upshot of altered environmental and ethical perceptions. The view of natural resources as impersonal resource commodities, and thus economic production inputs, is being steadily replaced by a notion of resources as an integral part of the larger environment. There is growing recognition today that resources must be used with great care as to their possible environmental impacts. Biodiversity preservation, maintenance of environmental quality, sustainable resource management, and the assurance of intergenerational equity are the core elements of this evolving philosophy. In brief, this signals a distinct shift in the underlying resource use philosophy from the economics of the marketplace to the moral standing of the marketplace.

— *Chennat Gopalakrishnan*

See also

Agricultural and Applied Economics; Agriculture, Alternative; Conservation, Energy; Conservation, Soil; Conservation, Water; Environmental Protection; Ethics; Forests; Future of Rural America; Land Stewardship; Policy, Environmental; Soil; Water; Water, Value of

References

Brewer, Jedidiah, Robert Glennon, Alan Ker and Gary D. Libecap. *Water Markets in the West: Prices, Trading and Contractual Forms*. Washington DC: National Bureau of Economic Research, 2007.

Carson, Rachel. *Silent Spring*. Boston, MA: Houghton Mifflin, 1962.

Ciriacy-Wantrup, S.C. *Resource Conservation*. Berkeley, CA: University of California Division of Agricultural Sciences (originally published in 1952), 1963.

Edwards, Andres R. *The Sustainability Revolution: Portrait of a Paradigm Shift*. Gabriola Island, BC, Canada: New Society Publishers, 2005.

Gopalakrishnan, Chennat. *The Economics of Energy in Agriculture*. Aldershot, UK: Avebury, 1994.

Gopalakrishnan, Chennat, Cecilia Tortajada, and Asit K. Biswas, eds. *Water Institutions: Policies, Performance and Prospects*. Heidelberg: Springer, 2005.

Gopalakrishnan, Chennat and Norio Okada. *Water and Disasters*. London: Routledge, 2007.

Marsh, George P. *Man and Nature: or Physical Geography as Modified by Human Action*. New York, NY: Charles Scribner, 1865.

Pinchot, Gifford. *The Fight for Conservation*. New York, NY: Doubleday, Page and Co., 1970.

Simpson, David R., Michael A. Toman, and Robert U. Ayres. *Scarcity and Growth Revisited: Natural Resources and the Environment in the New Millennium*. Washington DC: Resources for the Future (RFF) Press, 2005.

Natural Resources Engineering*

The study of natural resources engineering begins with study of the primary physical forces operating in the environment and extends to biological and chemical forces. Since the dawn of history men and women have been cultivating food and fiber, domesticating animals, and developing resources as portrayed in the book of Genesis. The natural resources engineer works with strategies and techniques to manage or cope with nodes of the hydrologic cycle. Rainfall, runoff, erosion, bioremediation and conversion are some of the operations that come under the purview of the natural resources engineer. The provision of tools facilitating "dressing and keeping" while engaging in economic activities defines our overarching vision for the natural resources engineer.

Defining Natural Resources Engineering and Related Terms

Natural resources engineering—the design of planned activities complementary to or in opposition to natural and societal forces leading to modifications of the soil, water, biota and/or air environment. The natural forces arise from the hydrologic cycle, whereas societal forces stem from the desires of people. The problem space is the farm or field scale, while the purpose is resource development and/or environmental management.

Bioremediation—biological remediation; the application of plant, biological amendments or microbial organisms toward the sequestering, removal or transformation of chemical or biologicaltoxins from a soil body or air environment.

Bioconversion—the biologically mediated physical and chemical conversion of municipal, agricultural and industrial organics and other byproducts to useful products such as biofuels.

Extensive agriculture—traditional agricultural enterprises where we measure production with yield units per hectare (e.g., field scale) and environmental controls are minimal. Examples include forage production, row crops, forest systems and some animal production systems.

Farm, field and factory scale—refers to typical problem size; different from industrial, regional and global scales on one hand and greenhouse, room scale and microbial scales on the other hand. Natural resources engineers manage soil and water at the farm and field scales.

Intensive agriculture—agricultural enterprises where we measure production or yield in units per meter² (e.g., room or greenhouse scales) and environmental controls are considerable. Examples include greenhouse production systems and concentrated animal production systems. Natural resources engineers will increasingly work in this domain.

Urbanization—the land transformation from natural or agricultural use to intensive commercial, residential, mining or industrial uses. For example, urbanization occurs when natural forest, grasslands and managed forest are displaced by anthropocentric development. Problems arising from intensive agricultural enterprises and urbanization are very similar.

The Hydrologic Cycle and the Water-Soil-Air-Biotic Continuum

Water and wind are the driving forces for production and pollution. Thus, we must be concerned with the hydrologic cycle. For example, consider the continental United States. The equivalent depth of water passing over the U.S. in the atmosphere is 300 in. Average precipitation over the U.S. land mass is about 30 inches (762 mm), partitioned as follows: 26 inches (660 mm) as rain and four inches (102 mm) as snow, sleet, hail. Of the received precipitation, approximately nine inches (229 mm) goes to groundwater or runs off; 21 inches (533 mm) returns to the atmosphere; and 0.73 inches (18.5 mm) is consumptively used.

Agriculture consumes 83 percent of the consumptively used water; agricultural irrigation requires about 40 percent of consumptively used water, and of this, 40 percent is lost due to inefficient irrigation and to seepage below the root zone.

Corresponding partitions for the world are 31 inches (800 mm) fall as precipitation; 12 inches (320 mm) runs off to land; and five inches (130 mm) runs off and is distributed to oceans (Maidment, 1993).

The hydrologic cycle is shown pictorially in Figure 1 with data typical of the Southeast U.S. A visit to the United States Geological Survey (USGS) home page at http://www.usgs.gov will provide much information relating to runoff and groundwater levels at sites around the U.S.

* This material is abstracted from the following work, for which permission is granted to use: Tollner, E.W. *Introduction to Natural Resources Engineering*. New York: Blackwell Scientific, 2002.

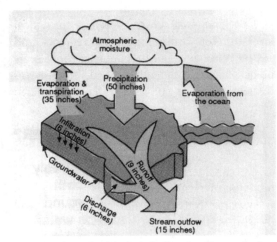

Figure 1. *Schematic of the hydrologic cycle with magnitudes representative of the Southeast U.S.*

Worldwide, social forces consisting of population increase, desire of developing countries to catch up with developed countries' standard of living, increasing environmental awareness in developed countries, and the desire of people to improve their living situation merge in various combinations to drive land use change. Changes in land use reflect the most succinct reason for the problem areas summarized in the previous section. Trends listed in Table 1 suggest opportunities for natural resources engineers (NRCS, 1985; NRCS,1998). These trends include outward expansion of the rural-urban "fringe," the increasing concentration of animal production, and the applications of agricultural and municipal wastes to land. An evaluation of land use and trends motivated the USDA Soil Conservation Service to change its name and focus. The Soil Conservation Service is now the Natural Resources Conservation Service (NRCS).

Natural Resources Engineering Scope

Major topic areas of natural resources engineering include flooding, drainage, erosion control, irrigation, drought, aesthetics, water quality renovation and management, and air quality, bioconversion, and biofuels.

Table 1.
Synopses of U.S. land use changes over the last 40 years.

Land use category	Change from 1958 to 1977	Trend from 1977 to 1997
Cropland	−8 percent	continued decrease
Pasture land, etc.	+12 percent	leveled off since
Forest land	−18 percent	some increase
Urban land	+76 percent	accelerating increases
Open water	+27 percent	leveled off

Flooding: Flooding becomes more problematic as urbanization occurs. Flooding in upstream watersheds is one of the most significant natural phenomena as it causes loss of life, property damage, crop loss, health hazards, loss of ecological services, and reduced access to remote areas. Flood damage in rural areas is an estimated $2 billion annually in the U.S. (See figure 2.)

Drainage: The need for drainage frequently results from excess rainfall. Drainage can be a surface or subsurface issue. Agricultural drainage is often necessary (see Figure 3) for high levels of production and timely field operations. In arid areas, salinity considerations also demand subsurface drainage. Of 260 million irrigated hectares worldwide, 60 million hectares suffer from salinization (Jensen, 1993). The International Commission on Irrigation and Drainage (ICID) reported that 40 million hectares in the U.S. were protected by drainage works, accounting for nearly half of the total drained (surface and subsurface) area of the world (ICID, 1965). Drainage is important both in crop production and in many remediation projects.

Erosion control: Erosion occurs when rainfall dislodges soil particles and excess rainfall (runoff) transports the particles off-site. Figure 4 is an example of extensive rill erosion. Terracing, conservation tillage, and application of soil stabilizers are erosion control strategies. Control of erosion caused by wind and water is necessary to maintain high levels of production. Wind erosion control reduces sediment and chemical pollution. Croplands in the U.S. produce approximately 4,800 tons of soil per square mile annually. Urbanization related construction sites produce 48,000 tons of soil per square mile annually (USEPA, 1973). The annual erosion from agricultural fields and pastures is about 1 m from one thousand 200-ha farms. ($\approx$3,800,000,000,000 kg at density of 1,900 kg/m^3 or 4,189,500,000 tons). Erosion from cropland and construction is declining due to control measures (NCSS, 1998). The eroded material contains higher proportions of fine particles, organic matter and chemicals than the original soil which affects soil productivity and runoff water quality. Erosion by wind can also create air quality problems. Worldwide, of the six billion hectares of arable land, water erosion affects approximately 1.1 billion hectares and wind erosion affects 0.5 billion hectares. Estimates of global soil loss rates range from 0.09 mm/year to 0.3 mm/year (Lal, 1994). A loss rate of 0.1 mm/year from six billion hectares is 1.14×10^{14} kg.

Figure 2. Flooding: Farm surrounded by flood water. © *Bettmann / Corbis.*

Figure 3. Tractor in a water laden field.

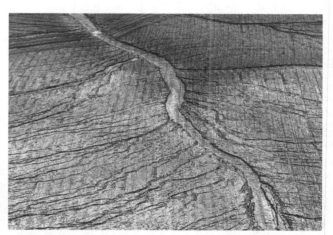

Figure 4. Photograph of sheet, rill and gully erosion occurring in Iowa (Courtesy of NRCS).

Irrigation: Crops and turf frequently need irrigation for reliable crop production even in humid areas. Irrigation is employed to compensate for a lack of timely rainfall. Managed irrigation increases crop yields, enhances germination and emergence, moderates air temperatures, and applies agronomically appropriate levels of nutrients and pesticides. Figure 5 shows a center pivot system using sprinklers. Arid ar-eas require supplemental irrigation to produce high yields. The 8 percent of cropland in the U.S. irrigated produces 25 percent of the total value of farm crops.

Drought: Historically, natural resources engineers in the Southeast U.S. have been mainly concerned with how to manage the effects of too much water with per-haps some supplemental irrigation to avoid water stress. However, engineers are recently becoming cog-

Figure 5. Center pivot irrigation system over corn in Georgia (Courtesy of Mr. Calvin Perry).

nizant of the effects of too little rainfall for prolonged times. For example, federal reservoirs in Georgia have been operated to cause record flows even while reaching record low levels in an attempt to provide adequate

Figure 6. Stream restoration in North Carolina (Courtesy of Dr. Greg Jennings).

flows downstream to maintain ecological preserves at the river discharge into the Gulf of Mexico. Engineers become concerned with water harvesting in times of drought and look to understand water yield probabilities with precipitation probabilities. (See Saxton et al., 2006 and Tollner, 2004). The current water "war" among Georgia, Florida and Alabama points out the extreme complexity of water management, with competing demands of agriculture, urban water use, electric power plant cooling and ecological services.

Aesthetics: The urban sprawl near many urban areas has prompted an interest in restoring many streams to a state that supports a full range of ecological services. There has been a surge in revisiting a channel design methodology classically known as the regime theory approach but now known as the Rosgen method based on Rosgen (1996). This approach attempts to mimic geomorphology found in designated reference reaches for the area. Figure 6 shows a stream undergoing restoration. Natural resources engineers

Figure 7. Windrow composting pad with a windrow turner in the background.

work closely with landscape architects in land design projects.

Water quality renovation and management: Researchers (Leeden et al., 1990) detected at least 16 different pesticides in the ground water in 26 different states. Pollution constituents are chemical elements in undesirable places and are a sign of inefficiency (Risse and Cheadle, 1996). Animal waste constituents, pesticides and other water quality problems will continue to grow due to urbanizationand concentrated animal production. Applying erosion control plans, imposing stream stabilization and improvement practices may partially offset adverse effects of urban development. Waste bioconversion is one strategy toward recovering value returnable to the land.

Air quality, bioconversion and biofuels: Odor and particulate pollution is a major public problem associated with intensive animal crop production, bioremediation and waste treatment. Particulate pollution is a major issue in some countries such as China. Odor is the number one issue with respect to intensive animal production. Odors are also the number one issue with composting facilities. We consider some atmospheric phenomena that can aggravate or attenuate odor-related problems. We define bioconversion as the biologically mediated conversion of municipal, agricultural, industrial waste organics, and other residues to useful products. Many ancient societies practiced composting (Epstein, 1997). Composting, shown in Figure 7, is an example of a field scale bioconversion process. Environmental issues related to bioconversion may intensify as bioconversion technology is used in biofuel production.

Natural Resources Engineering and Ecology

The natural resources engineer will frequently work with ecologists and other professionals in developing environmentally sustainable systems. Natural resources engineering can also be cast in ecological terms. The ecologist frequently views field scale environmental problems through the lens of a macroscopic control volume with somewhat indistinct boundaries. Consider a control volume with the bottom boundary at some soil depth, the top boundary at some aerial height, and the other boundaries facing north, east, south and west. Property lines or problem extent dictates the problem space. Our inability to draw clear distinctions between resource management issues and environmental management issues may make the problem boundaries fuzzy. Air, water, soil and biotic material represent states within the volume. Theoretical ecologists use differential equation nomenclature to describe the natural resources engineering space. The initial condition represents the state of the water-soil-air-biota system at Time Zero, the time we engage the problem. Often, sites require preliminary work to define the relevant states and their initial condition. Fluxes through any of the boundaries result from various gradients or levels of the state variables existing around the boundaries. A suite of generalized, yet unspecified, differential equations (or chaotic functional forms) describe the constituent movements within the volume. Humankind's activities represent forcing functions varying both temporally and spatially. An earthquake or other natural catastrophe is considered a forcing function which demands additional activities.

Truly sustainable agricultural and urban development requires systems-based planning in the light and understanding of the hydrologic cycle (Hes and van Lier, 1999) and ecological pulsing (Jorgensen and Mitsch, 1989). The current state-of-the-art of natural resources engineering is rapidly moving forward as is our knowledge of ecological processes. Pollution is becoming recognized as a significant contributor to inefficiency and is causing forfeiture of profits (see Tibor and Feldman, 1997). This paradigm is becoming accepted both in agriculture and manufacturing. Natural resources engineers will find employment with firms involved in natural and increasingly urban environmental management systems, risk assessments and quality audits.

— *Ernest W. Tollner*

See also

Agricultural and Biological Engineering; Conflict, Water; Environmental Protection; Environmental Regulations; Natural Resources Management; Water Policy; River Engineering; Water, Value of; Watersheds

References

Epstein, E. *The Science of Composting*. Lancaster, PA: Technomic Press, 1997.

Hes, M.B.A. and H.N. van Lier. "Land and Water Use Planning." In *CIGR Handbook of Agricultural Engineering: Land and Water Engineering*. St. Joseph, MI: American Society of Agricultural Engineers, 1999.

International Commission on Irrigation and Drainage (ICID). *Annual Bulletin*. New Delhi, India: International Commission on Irrigation and Drainage, 1965.

Jensen, M.E. *The Impacts of Irrigation and Drainage on the Environment*, 5th ed. Gulhati Memorial Lecture. The Hague, Netherlands: International Commission on Irrigation and Drainage, 1993.

Lal, R. "Soil Erosion by Wind and Water: Problems and Prospects." In *Soil Erosion Research Methods*, 2nd ed. Edited by R. Lal. Ankeny, IA: Soil and Water Conservation Society, 1993.

Leeden, F. van der, F.L. Troise, and D.K. Todd. *The Water Encyclopedia*. Chelsea, MI: Lewis Publishers, Inc., 1990.

Jorgensen, S.E. and W.J. Mitsch. "Ecological Engineering Principles." In *Ecological Engineering: An Introduction to Ecotechnology*, Edited by W.J. Mitsch and S.E. Jorgensen. New York, NY: John Wiley & Sons, 1989.

Maidment, D.R. "Hydrology." In *Handbook of Hydrology*. Edited by D.R. Maidment. New York, NY: McGraw-Hill, 1993.

Natural Resource Conservation Service (NRCS). *America's Soil and Water: Conditions and Trends*. Washington, DC: U.S. Department of Agriculture, Natural Resources Conservation Service, 1985.

Natural Resource Conservation Service (NRCS). *Stream Corridor Restoration: Principles, Processes and Practices*. Washington, DC: U.S. Department of Agriculture, Natural Resources Conservation Service, 1998. Available online at: http://www.usda.nrcs.gov.

Risse, L.M. and S.A. Cheadle. "Pollution Prevention in Agricultural Livestock Production." Report submitted to the Georgia Pollution Prevention Assistance Division, Georgia Department of Natural Resources, Atlanta, GA, 1996.

Rosgen, D. *Applied River Morphology*, 2nd ed. Pagosa Springs, CO: Wildland Hydrology Press, 1996.

Saxton, K. E. and P. H. Willey. "The SPAW Model for Agricultural Field and Pond Hydrologic Simulation." Chapter 17 (pp. 401-435) in *Mathematical Modeling of Watershed Hydrology*. Edited by V. P. Singh and D. Frevert. CRC Press, 2006.

Tibor, T. and I. Feldman. *Implementing ISO 14000*. New York, NY: McGraw-Hill, 1997.

Tollner, E.W., D. Meyer, S. Triminio-Meyer, B. Verma, G. Pilz and J.J. Molnar. "Spreadsheet tools for developing surface water supplies for freshwater fish in developing countries." *Journal of Aquacultural Engineering* 31, nos. 1-2 (2004):31-49.

Tollner, E.W. *Introduction to Natural Resources Engineering*. New York, NY: Blackwell Scientific, 2002.

Natural Resources Management

An expansive interdisciplinary concept, having a wide-ranging view on the sustainable utilization, conservation and preservation of natural capital for the highest and best uses for society without degrading the resources being utilized.

Management of these uses entails sustained utilization of renewable resources, conservation of non-renewable resources, and preservation of threatened or endangered resources. The emphasis is fundamentally on managing and mitigating human impacts on the environment. This management approach requires an all-encompassing perspective taking into account the complex interactions of biotic and abiotic environmental factors, economic and other social factors, human impacts such as pollution, and the sustainability of ecosystem diversity and viability on planet Earth. Natural resources management is an applied science, putting into practice current research findings of the basic sciences for sustained utilization of scarce natural resources. An underlying tenet of natural resources management is an understanding of our human role and responsibility as sentient and rational components of the natural world.

Humans have always used natural resources starting with the first hunters and gatherers, but *management* of natural resources has its origins in humans' use of fire. While early European explorers to North America accepted the surrounding landscapes as pristine, these areas were impacted and modified repeatedly with fires purposefully set by Native Americans (Krech, 1999). These people changed, modified and maintained landscapes by controlled use of fire as a powerful management tool. Application of fire use by Native Americans, to enhance their economic well-being, is documented as follows: hunting, crop management, insect collection, pest management, range management, fireproofing, warfare and signaling, economic extortion, clearing areas for travel, tree felling, and clearing riparian areas (William, 2000). When European settlers arrived, their concerns focused on farming, ranching and constructing permanent homesteads which necessarily suppressed the use of fire. Fire suppression also had environmental impacts such as allowing trees to encroach onto prairie landscapes.

Fire suppression and plowing the soil for agriculture reduced native ecosystems such as the tallgrass prairie to less than 2 percent of pre-settlement areas. The tallgrass, mid-grass and shortgrass prairies were ecosystems that once covered more than 3.5 million square kilometers (1.4 million square miles) of the North American heartland, comprising the largest ecosystem on the continent (Savage, 2004). The prairie grasses and forbs were nurtured by some of the richest and most productive soils on Earth. But, nutrient rich prairie topsoil held in place by an immeasurable network of tightly interwoven plant roots and fungi was destined to undergo an unprecedented human impact. European homesteaders were bringing agriculture and the mold-board plow to the prairie landscape; cultivation replaced native prairie grasses and forbs with domestic crops. During the wet cycle, these former prairie landscapes produced an incredible bounty of grains and row crops. As the 1930s approached and the rainfall lessened in the natural prairie climate wet/dry cycle, the plowed and dried black soil stood bare, no longer held in place by the roots of prairie plants. Topsoil that had taken 300-1,000 years per inch to form was turned to dust and carried away by wind erosion. The "Dust Bowl" was a tragic display of human misery resulting from soil mismanagement.

The foundation of civilization is agriculture (Brown, 2006) and the foundation of agriculture is management of the soil. The living soil is one of our most valuable natural resources. Management of soils as productive, living ecosystems is one of our greatest challenges. Erosion of fertile topsoil by wind and water is a destructive force that renders productive agroecosystems worthless. Overgrazed rangelands and poorly managed agricultural sites are the major causes of desertification, devastating human communities and local economies in erosion-prone "hot spots" worldwide. Wind erosion devastated vast areas of the continental United States during the 1930s, but soil loss via water erosion is our modern-day problem. Overland flow of eroded soil from farmlands is a major non-point source pollutant, causing pesticide toxicity and sedimentation in water channels.

There is no life without water on our planet, and over 96 percent of this water is saltwater. Surface waters such as freshwater lakes and rivers provide most of our day-to-day water needs, yet these water resources account for less than 1 percent of Earth's total water (Gleick, 1996). We use approximately 1,545 billion liters (408 billion gallons) of water per day for all uses in the continental United States (Hutson et al., 2004). Yet, this vital natural resource is impacted by pollution from pesticides, nutrients (fertilizers), volatile organic compounds, trace elements and raw sewage. Agriculture is faulted for 70 percent of water pollution. Our lakes have been designated as 48 percent eutrophied by nutrient additions contained in overland flow from farmland and 40 percent of all surface waters have been described as unfit habitats for fishing or human recreational use. Hundreds of chemicals have been detected in our drinking water (Johns Hopkins, 1998): The hackneyed phrase "the solution to pollution is dilution," is no longer the tongue-in-cheek answer for managing our water supply. Fresh, clean water is a scarce natural resource and pollution carries many costly economic externalities.

Management of this vital natural resource in the continental United States is not so much a problem of scarcity as it is a problem of mal-distribution; California, Florida and Texas account for 25 percent of our water usage. Irrigation systems for agriculture constitute the major use of surface water and groundwater withdrawals. California, Texas and Nebraska are the highest users of groundwater for irrigation. Irrigation accounts for approximately 65 percent of total water use. Groundwater such as is found in the High Plains Aquifer, also known as the Ogallala Aquifer, is a water resource several million years old. A gift from the Miocene and Pliocene epochs, this ancient water is held in an underground water table underlying portions of Colorado, Kansas, Nebraska, New Mexico, Oklahoma, South Dakota, Texas and Wyoming. While water in this aquifer is theoretically renewable, more water is pumped out annually for irrigation than could possibly be replaced by natural means, and this water table is being depleted. In 2005, total water storage for the aquifer was estimated at 3,608 km^3 (866 mi^3, a 9 percent decrease since the 1950s when pumping groundwater for irrigation was first implemented at a significant level (McGuire, 2007). Since this valuable natural resource lies beneath our richest area of agricultural production, managing it will require readdressing agricultural practices. Planting crops that require less water and improvements in irrigation (such as drip irrigation and micro-irrigation systems) are our best natural resource management tools for conserving this invaluable and virtually irreplaceable resource of ancient water.

While land and water are tangible natural resources protected by law and bought and sold in the market place, breathable air has only recently become marketable. Industrial pollution turns breathable air into a valuable commodity, offering a market solution to pollution. The concept of *emissions trading* provides an economic incentive for industries to pollute less by allowing them to sell their emissions credits to indus-

tries that continue to pollute the atmosphere (Stranlund et al., 2002). A regulatory agency determines the appropriate emissions standards in a cap-and-trade emissions market. Emissions credits are allocated to polluters who can sell their unused credits if their emissions are lower than the set cap or buy unused credits from other companies if they are exceeding their emissions cap. This system offers a market-based monetary inducement for limiting emissions and is successfully working in reducing SO_2 and NO_x emissions, two of the main pollutants causing acid rain. Those industries that can control their emissions at low cost will theoretically do so, enabling them to sell their unused emissions credits to higher polluting industries at a profit. The Chicago Climate Exchange specializes in trading CO_2 emissions credits. This cap-and-trade effort is being effectively applied to other pollutants such as fine particulates (<2.5 μm), organic volatile compounds, and other greenhouse gas emissions. This may prove to be a successful natural resources economics approach to managing an intangible natural resource, such as the air we breathe (Farrell and Lave, 2004). Critics of emissions trading view it as a license to pollute and instead advocate reducing pollution at its source.

Carbon sequestration offers another alternative to reducing CO^2 in the atmosphere by allocating carbon credits to farmers and ranchers for engaging in specific land use management practices. No-till agricultural systems eliminate the need for plowing. No-till systems reduce erosion and maintain the underground portions of harvested crops which remain beneath the soil surface available for recycling into valuable nutrients for future crops and for holding the topsoil in place. Carbon credits can also be earned by seeding unused farmlands to grass or reforesting cleared areas. These practices create habitat for many species of mammals, birds, invertebrates, reptiles and amphibians. Management of native rangelands with appropriate grazing systems also qualify for carbon credits as well as prevent soil erosion, maintain habitat for wildlife, and allow for the sustainable production of cattle and other livestock. This is another example of natural resources management economics in action, whereby landowners can trade their carbon credits to supplement their income and help our planet contend with global warming.

The state of our food supply, availability and quality of our water, and condition of our air are all reflections of our ability or inability as rational beings to sustainably manage our natural resources. Civilization's foundation is agriculture, and agriculture is founded on the soil and timely availability of water. Without soil and water there is no plant life and without plant life, there is no breathable air. Plants utilize CO_2 in the process of photosynthesis to create oxygen, a component of the air we breathe. As primary producers, plants represent the first trophic level upon which other living organisms depend. Wildlife, fish, birds, invertebrates, people and plants are the biotic components of natural resources management. Water, minerals and air are the abiotic components. Deforestation, desertification, urbanization, industrialization and increasing human population are civilization's components. But, without civilization there is no need for natural resources management. Not all natural resources are renewable, but all natural resources can be managed sustainably. Civilization has given us research and educational tools to do this. For example, the Natural Resources Management Interdisciplinary Program at North Dakota State University implements both these tools very successfully in our undergraduate and graduate degree programs. The mission of this program is to educate people in the sustainable management of scarce natural resources. The program offers a management-oriented academic program that emphasizes problem-solving and prepares students to address environmental issues extending beyond a single discipline or subject area. Students enroll in a wide array of courses that allow them to integrate the biotic, abiotic and social aspects of natural resources management into one program of study.

Earth's rapidly increasing human population necessitates innovation in the management of finite natural resources. Graduates of programs, such as the Natural Resources Management Interdisciplinary Program at North Dakota State University, are people who make a difference, inspired with a mission to succeed in managing our natural resources for their highest and best uses for society without degrading the natural systems upon which all life on Earth depends.

— *Carolyn Grygiel*

See also

Biodiversity; Conservation, Soil; Conservation, Water; Environmental Protection; Environmental Regulations; Environmentalism; Environmental Sustainability; Natural Resource Economics; Policy, Environmental; Wilderness; Wildlife Value Orientations; Wildlife Management

References

Brown. L.R. *Plan B 2.0: Rescuing a Planet Under Stress and a Civilization in Trouble.* New York: W.W. Norton & Co., 2006.

Farrell, A.E. and L.B. Lave. "Emission Trading and Public Health." *Annual Review of Public Health* 25 (2004): 119–138.

Gleick, P. H. "Water Resources." Pp. 817-823 in *Encyclopedia of Climate and Weather, Volume II.* Edited by S. H. Schneider. New York: Oxford University Press, 1996.

Huston, S.S., N.L. Barber, J.F. Kenny, K.S. Linsey, D.S. Lumina, and M.A. Maupin. *Estimated Use of Water in the United States in 2000.* USGS Circular 1268. U.S. Geological Survey, 2004.

Johns Hopkins School of Public Health. *Population Reports.* Baltimore, MD: Population Information Program, Center for Communication Programs, The Johns Hopkins School of Public Health. 25:1 (1998).

Krech III, S. *The Ecological Indian: Myth and History.* New York: W.W. Norton and Co., 1999.

McGuire, V.L. "Changes in Water Level and Storage in the High Plains Aquifer, Predevelopment to 2005." P. 2 in *U.S. Geological Survey Fact Sheet 2007—3029,* 2007.

Savage, C. *Prairie: A Natural History.* Vancouver, B.C., Canada: Greystone Books, 2004.

Stranlund, J. K., C.A. Chavez, and B.C. Field. "Enforcing Emissions Trading Programs: Theory, Practice and Performance."*Policy Studies Journal 30 (2002),* 343–362 2002.

William, G.W. "Introduction to Aboriginal Fire Use in North America." *Fire Management Today.* 60(2000), 8–12.

Neoliberal Economics

A means of using government to enhance business interests through limited intervention and market self-regulation. This entry describes the tenets and salient aspects of neoliberal economics and its effects on economic sectors of rural America, agriculture, manufacturing and commerce. Neoliberal economic policies create the capacity for businesses to search for low-cost environments and internalize profits; critics counter that negative externalities are pushed onto vulnerable communities. The entry concludes with the likelihood of reformed public policies for the social welfare of rural America.

Historical Background

Neoliberalism emerged as a political movement in the 1970s in the United States and Great Britain with claims to restore the principles of the liberal market economy first articulated by Adam Smith, David Ricardo, and John Stuart Mill. According to classical liberal economic theory, markets function best and yield necessary social benefits when allowed to self-regulate. Government interventions to regulate markets in response to the Great Depression of the 1930s, such as the New Deal in the U.S. and Keynesianism in Great Britain, represented a departure from liberal economic principles. Neoliberal economists at the University of Chicago, most notably Milton Friedman, argued that government regulation was interfering with the proper functioning of the market and hampering the economy's capacity to contribute to social welfare.

Critical observers counter that neoliberal theorists make misleading claims in their efforts to restore liberal economic principles. First, the classical liberal assumption of Adam Smith and his contemporaries is that markets are nested within a sociocultural context; neoliberal economists of today replace that with the assumption that sociocultural outcomes are produced by markets (Bonanno, 1998). Second, although proponents of neoliberalism might claim to be liberating markets from government protectionism, neoliberalism is more accurately described as policy reforms that shift responsibility for governance from national governments to international and local governing institutions and the private sector. Ironically, such theoretical and empirical critiques indicate that neoliberalism represents a stark contrast to liberal economics. In practice, neoliberalism requires an enhanced role for various levels of government to foster privatization and the expansion of market forces.

Despite the misleading claims, Friedman's neoliberalism became influential in the U.S. and abroad. President Ronald Reagan (1981-1989) forcefully believed that government intervention was a drag on the economy, and he promoted deregulation based on Friedman's work. Prime Minister Margaret Thatcher pushed similar policies in Great Britain. By the end of the 1980s, the "Washington Consensus," which refers to the assumption that developing countries can best address economic development by deregulation and free trade, became the central dogma of Washington-based institutions, like the International Monetary Fund, the World Bank and the U.S. Treasury Department. Through these global economic institutions, neo-liberalism was exported to Latin America, Asia and other parts of the world (Krugman, 2007).

Neoliberal Markets and Global Sourcing

When considering the impacts of neoliberalism on rural America, it is necessary to understand the connections between neoliberalism and global sourcing. Global sourcing refers to the business strategy of searching the globe for favorable business conditions. Favorable conditions for production include proximity to raw materials and other essential inputs. Favorable business conditions also tend to include weak labor and environmental regulations, which allow companies to keep production costs low. Neoliberalism is linked to global sourcing to the extent that deregulation by national governments enhanced the capacity of giant international corporations to take advantage of weaker labor and environmental regulations around the globe.

In the U.S., neoliberalism was initiated through a decision not to enforce antitrust laws, which has led to the concentration of economic activity by fewer corporations and enhanced their capacity to employ global-sourcing strategies. Global economic institutions, such as the Global Agreement on Trade and Tariffs (GATT) and the World Trade Organization (WTO), facilitated the globalization of neoliberalism by securing the commitment of member countries to reduce trade barriers and improve market access. The North American Free Trade Agreement (NAFTA), launched in 1994, was particularly successful in instituting a neoliberal economic platform for Canada, the U.S. and Mexico. Other regional trade agreements continue to reach into Central and South America and across the Pacific.

The business strategy of seeking favorable sources for production is an old one, and in the past provided modest economic benefits to rural America. Throughout most of the twentieth century, rural areas held the advantage of lower costs for land and labor compared to cities. For many decades, manufacturing plants and other economic activities moved out of urban areas to take advantage of cheaper, non-union rural workers and less strict environmental regulations. However, as neoliberal restructuring of national economies enabled sourcing to go global, economic activities shifted from the rural United States to less developed or newly industrialized nations. As a result, there was a marked relocation of industrial investment from the First World to the Third World (McMichael, 2004). The consequences of free trade agreements like NAFTA and

WTO affected rural America in its impacts on agriculture, manufacturing and labor displacement.

Neoliberal Impacts on Agriculture

The combination of neoliberalism and global sourcing has made rural areas vulnerable to agribusiness exploitation. Agri-food corporations seek areas of lax regulatory regimes, low taxes, low wages, and weak unions; these correspond to areas with high poverty rates, large minority populations, and relatively little political power. The poultry growing and processing industries throughout the South and Mid-Atlantic states illustrate this situation. Besides labor concerns, neoliberal economic trends can also lead to pollution havens or areas of high concentrations of dirty industries, such as concentrated animal feeding operations for hogs and cattle. Vulnerable rural areas, usually low-income and often minority populations, are less able to resist an industry that tends toward negative externalities.

Case studies of livestock operations in the Midwest and Plains states also illustrate how agribusiness companies exploit policies that allow them to pit one locale against another (Bonanno, 1998). Processing companies have relocated their headquarters from one state to avoid tougher regulations, even after state governments have offered subsidies to retain them. Local communities are pitted against each other to get subsidies and weak regulations. In areas where local citizens were able to mobilize to establish regulations on odor or waste management, livestock processors would respond by relocating to other areas.

Under international trade agreements, impacts for rural America have been uneven. The North American Free Trade Agreement provided some opportunities for agricultural export expansion, but NAFTA also provided the opportunity for agribusiness companies to expand or relocate across borders. This free flow of capital, together with agricultural imports from Canada and Mexico, challenged the livelihoods of farmers and producers in the United States. Federal farm policies, such as contained in the U.S. Farm Bill, are criticized for not fully addressing the complexity of issues facing rural economies and populations in a neoliberal environment.

In other extraction sectors of the rural economy, namely mining and fishing, rural communities face job losses when their natural resources are depleted. Companies using a global sourcing strategy are able to move to new locations, whereas resource-dependent rural communities are challenged to attract new industry or businesses. Rural areas with natural amenities, such as attractive topography or agreeable climates, can draw tourists and potentially improve local incomes and social conditions. Given the loss of agricultural jobs, new skills training is often required.

Neoliberal Impacts on Manufacturing

Just as some types of manufacturing previously relocated from urban to rural areas in the U.S., this phenomenon continues from rural America to nations like Mexico or China. Rural regions are squeezed between low-cost developing nations and high-cost U.S. metro areas with skilled workers and knowledge-based firms. Since the late 1990s, rural manufacturing jobs have decreased at a faster rate than urban manufacturing jobs.

Some industries are associated with more undesirable social and environmental outcomes than others. For example, the apparel and textile industries once prevalent in the rural U.S. South tend to use global sourcing to find the weakest regulatory environments for their manufacturing and assembly sites. As developing countries and poor regions within industrial countries strive to attract or retain employment opportunities in the apparel and textile industries, there is a resulting downward spiral in labor and environmental conditions. In contrast, corporations in the personal computer industry tend not to be part of the race-to-the-bottom, because they are more focused on minimizing risks of interruptions in the commodity chain than in finding the weakest regulations (Kenney and Florida, 2004).

In anticipation of job losses due to competitive markets and international trade, federal policies seek to mitigate the effects through reeducation and transition services. These are generally referred to as "trade adjustment assistance" programs. However, two factors limit the relevance of these policies for rural people. First, the rural economy often depends on one industry rather than a set of diverse industries in urban economies. Second, even when there are other employment opportunities in rural communities, they often require retraining and skill upgrades. Training and education institutions are rare in rural areas.

Neoliberal Impacts on the Retail Sector

Global sourcing changes the commercial retail sector which, besides distributing goods and services, provides employment opportunities and generates tax revenue for local economies. The neoliberal assumption is that within a competitive business environment, businesses will generate public benefits as they strive to maximize profits. However, when neoliberal policies enable a corporation to develop a monopolistic business model, the competitive environment is undermined, thereby invalidating the public-benefits assumption. As a consequence, public benefits will be replaced with negative outcomes.

Wal-Mart, the leading employer in the U.S., adopted a monopolistic business model when it began locating its stores in rural areas and severely impacting small businesses in surrounding towns and small cities. Studies indicate that Wal-Mart is increasingly generating net public losses instead of benefits. For example, in a nationwide study of the effects of Wal-Mart on county-level well-being indicators, Goetz and Swaminathan (2006) found that higher rates of family poverty were associated with Wal-Mart stores. A staff study conducted at the behest of Congressman George Miller (D-California) found that the typical Wal-Mart store with 200 employees cost the nation's taxpayers $420,750 a year. Such studies show that Wal-Mart passes its costs on to the public when, instead of meeting the needs of its employees by paying a livable wage and offering affordable health care, it leads them to take advantage of social services. This in turn leads to increased burdens on taxpayers for health care, food stamps and other services.

Civil Society Responses

Neoliberal economists stake their claim on the efficiency of self-regulating markets, and critics respond with the accusation of unfairness in such markets. Civil society groups express this criticism through calls for fair trade, not free trade, and in anti-WTO and anti-globalization movements. These claims call for an important distinction between neoliberalism and globalization; the self-regulated market of neoliberalism is not to be confused with the greater flows of people, goods, services and information across borders under globalization.

Research on international trade indicates that different industry characteristics, as well as characteristics of locales, may have an interactive effect. As Kenney (2004) argues, a firm may "interact with those places to evolve positive externalities such as improved skill levels in the workforce, the creation or attraction of suppliers, and an infrastructure of collective goods such as universities, research institutions and transportation or communication facilities." However, the capacity of a locale to promote positive externalities might be dependent upon relative wealth and political power. In a neoliberal political-economic environment, those locales

may have diminished negotiating capacity when they are pitted against other locales.

Research on uneven effects of globalization suggests that it can be promoted without compromising livable wages, environmental protection and social welfare provisions, as long as national and international policies and treaties are in place to promote the positive externalities. There are indications that the neoliberal ideology is declining in rhetorical prominence. Although public sentiment may be turning, it will not necessarily translate into more favorable policies. As Giddens (2000) poses, citizens will need to mobilize in creative ways and across national boundaries to counter the economic and political power of large companies. Whether such civil society movements will emerge in the near future remains an open question requiring more social scientific research.

— *Leland Glenna and Robert Gronski*

See also
Civic Agriculture; Agriculture, Structure of; Community Economics; Corn Economy; Policy, Agricultural; Policy, Economic; Sustainable Rural Economies

References
Bonanno, Alessandro. "Liberal Democracy In The Global Era: Implications For The Agro-Food Sector." *Agriculture and Human Values* 15(2)(1998): 223-242.
Friedman, Milton. *Capitalism and Freedom*. 40th Anniversary edition. University of Chicago Press, 2002.
Giddens, Anthony. *The Third Way and Its Critics*. Massachusetts: Blackwell Publishers, 2000.
Goetz, Stephan and Hema Swaminathan. "Wal-Mart and County-Wide Poverty." *Social Science Quarterly* 87(2)(2006): 211-225.
Kenney, Martin and Richard Florida, eds. *Locating Global Advantage: Industry Dynamics in the International Economy*. Palo Alto, CA: Stanford University Press, 2004.
Krugman, Paul. *The Conscience of a Liberal*. New York: W.W. Norton and Company, 2007.
McMichael, Philip. *Development and Social Change: A Global Perspective*. 4th ed. Thousand Oaks, CA: Pine Forge Press, 2007.
Stiglitz, Joseph E. *Globalization and Its Discontents*. New York: W.W. Norton and Company, 2002.

Nursing and Allied Health Professions

Non-physician health care providers. This article addresses the shortage of nurses and allied health professionals in rural areas and means by which they are being recruited to rural areas. The practices of rural nursing and allied health, along with legislative initiatives that support rural health care practices, are discussed.

Rural Shortage of Nurses and Allied Health Professionals

A shortage of nurses and allied health professionals exists in rural America. Numerous factors have been cited as to why rural areas may be less attractive practice sites. Governmental agencies, educational institutions and professional health organizations are pursuing strategies to increase the recruitment and retention of nurses and allied health professionals in rural areas.

There has been concern for a number of years regarding the provision of health care to populations in rural areas. A rural shortage of nurses and allied health professionals is a major factor related to the lack of optimal health care service provision. Other factors that contribute include a rural-urban maldistribution of physicians and, in some instances, a lack of rural health care facilities. According to an American Hospital Association survey, 36 percent of hospital closings in the 1980s were in rural areas (Burke et al., 1994). Certain types of health problems are more prevalent in rural settings, and this different health problem profile may influence the practice decisions of health care professionals. Rural areas generally have higher rates of chronic disease and more problems related to maternal and child health. Agricultural work presents a higher risk for health problems and injury than work in other sectors.

Studies that focus on reasons why rural areas fail to recruit and retain adequate numbers of nurses and allied health professionals identify contributory factors. These include a perception of limited recreational and family educational opportunities; a lack of ready access to state-of-the-art health information and professional continuing education opportunities; heavier patient/client demands; lack of prescriptive privileges; limited ability to consult with colleagues or professional specialists; higher numbers of patients with less ability to pay for health care; and difficulties encountered with reimbursement (Travers and Ellis, 1993; Willis, 1993; Price, 1993; Muus et al., 1993; Straub and Wright, 1993). In some instances, salaries in rural areas may be less competitive than those in urban areas (Bigbee, 1993). Lack of employment opportunities for spouses in rural areas may also play a role.

Statistics concerning the precise nature of the nursing and allied health professional shortage in rural America are limited (Office of Technology Assessment, 1990). According to government statistics, 17 percent of the country's registered nurses (RNs) in 1988 worked in rural areas. Of those, the majority were based in the more populated rural counties. Only 8.7 percent were employed in counties of less than 50,000 residents, and most were employed in counties of greater than 25,000 residents. When compared to urban RNs, rural RNs were "more likely to work full-time, more likely to work in nursing home or public health settings, less likely to work in hospitals, and less likely to have a baccalaureate degree" (Office of Technology Assessment, 1990). Counties with small populations were more likely to have nurses prepared at the minimum of a baccalaureate degree level. The conclusion can be drawn that more remote areas perhaps required higher levels of nursing expertise.

Statistics on numbers of allied health professionals in rural areas are even more scarce than those for nursing. To some extent, this reflects lack of consistency in use of the term "allied health professional" and the large number of health professionals considered under the umbrella of allied health. Available evidence and anecdotal reports support the concept of rural shortages.

Nursing and Allied Health Professional Recruitment to Rural Areas

Efforts are currently underway to recruit and retain more nurses and allied health professionals in rural practice. In part, efforts have been driven by a lack of physicians in rural areas and insufficient numbers of nurses and allied health professionals. Nurse practitioners (NPs) and physician assistants (PAs) received particular attention in attempts to increase health care delivery services to rural areas. This focus resulted from recognition that these health care practitioners can provide basic health care services to areas that lack direct physician coverage. In the arena of primary care, NPs and PAs can accomplish 75 to 90 percent of physician duties (Osterweis and Garfinkel, 1993).

The NP is generally an RN with a graduate degree. There are some NPs, however, who obtained their education through certificate programs. According to a 1990 survey, NPs who obtained their credential through a certificate program were more likely to work in rural settings. The movement away from granting the NP credential through certification and solely through graduate programs has been defined as a potential obstacle for the production of rural NPs. The PA generally holds a minimum of a baccalaureate degree. There are PA programs, however, that are certificate, associate degree, or master's degree programs. The practice of PAs is legally linked with physician practice, while NPs are trained to work in an independent practice.

The professions of NP and PA both emerged in the 1960s in response to concerns about shortages of physicians. Both of these practitioners are now in high demand in both urban and rural areas.

Nurse practitioners located in rural areas are more frequently specialists in family health employed in primary care clinics. Nurse practitioners in rural areas are more likely to have admitting privileges for both hospitals and nursing homes. An analysis of 1991 surveys of migrant and community health centers found that NPs and certified nurse midwives (CNMs) were more likely to serve as physician substitutes in rural settings than were PAs (Shi et al., 1993). The majority of NPs are based in counties with higher population bases. In 1988, 85 to 91 percent of NPs practiced in counties with greater than 50,000 population (Fowkes, 1993).

In 1990 only 12.9 percent of PAs practiced in rural areas (Travers and Ellis, 1993). Rural PAs differ from their urban counterparts in that they are more frequently primary care specialists. The majority of rural PAs (83 percent) are located in states that give PAs the authority to write prescriptions (Willis, 1993). Cawley (1993) noted a trend for fewer PAs to practice in rural areas and cited factors contributing to this decline as increased numbers of females in the profession, retirement of rural PAs, and the increased demand for PAs in specialty practices and in the hospital setting.

Community and migrant health centers are major organizations employing both NPs and PAs in rural settings. Such clinics on average employ 2.2 full-time equivalent NPs or PAs per site (Fowkes, 1993).

Certified nurse midwifes (CNMs) and certified registered nurse anesthetists (CRNAs) are also important health professionals in the rural setting. Appropriately trained CNMs manage uncomplicated pregnancies. CRNAs provide anesthesia services and may be the sole providers of such services in rural areas. There is concern that CNMs and CRNAs practice in less than optimal numbers in rural settings. Of the 42 CNMs certified in Arizona, only 10 were found to practice in rural areas (Gordon and Erickson, 1993). These investigators found that Arizona CNMs practicing in rural areas

were less likely than their urban counterparts to be prepared at the master's degree level and had fewer years of practice experience.

The 1990s' phenomenon of downsizing caused the nursing shortage to diminish in many urban areas. Some urban professionals who saw their jobs disappear decided to relocate to rural areas to practice. Any shift toward rural areas as the result of urban downsizing may be influenced by future patterns of rural hospital closure and by the presence in rural communities of clinics, offices, home health services and long-term care facilities. One scenario foresees the change from acute care beds to long-term care beds in rural hospitals coupled with the development of rural emergency care clinics serving as feeders to urban hospitals (Rubenstein, 1989).

The managed care movement will influence patterns of rural health care practice. Rural practitioners will need to be in alliances that allow them to benefit financially. The tendency of managed care to use more technician-level allied health practitioners may be felt in rural areas. Managed care should promote increased use of NPs and PAs. This may benefit rural areas because of increased pressure for adequate NP and PA reimbursement under the rubric of cost-effectiveness.

Rural Practice of Nursing and Allied Health

Rural practice has advantages. For example, nurses and allied health professionals working in rural areas tend to have greater and more diverse responsibilities and have greater freedom in the work environment. The rural environment provides opportunities for greater recognition and appreciation from members of the community. In some instances, rural health care facilities offer higher base salaries and salary bonuses in an attempt to attract non-physician health care providers. Organizations of allied health professionals in some states are active in rural recruitment and retention.

Telemedicine and other uses of computer technology such as tele-education and teleconferencing make health information and access to specialists more of a reality for the rural nurse or allied health care worker. These technologies may overcome the perceived rural practice barriers of information and professional colleague isolation. Other innovations that should help enhance the ability of rural health practitioners to communicate are the increasing availability of medical and health care resource software, the Internet, CD-ROMs and fax machines.

Educational programs find that allowing students to train in rural areas is beneficial in expanding the numbers of students who choose to enter rural practice upon graduation. In 1991, the Committee on Allied Health Education and Accreditation (CAHEA) of the American Medical Association (AMA) collected and analyzed data concerning rural training. The survey found that training for the following allied health occupations was offered in 150 or more rural locations: radiographic technician, respiratory therapy technician, medical record technician, occupational therapy, physician assistant and medical assistant. Rural allied health training was more likely to occur in more populated rural areas and was more likely to occur in professions of allied health with a primary care focus as opposed to professions that are most specialized and equipment intensive (Gupta and Konrad, 1992). A 1992 survey of all programs accredited to train PAs found that 58 percent of programs offered practice experience in rural counties and two accredited PA programs were based in rural counties (Hooker et al., 1994). Scholarships for those willing to serve in medically underserved rural areas after graduation is another strategy being used to recruit allied health professionals into rural locations.

Some programs target high school students in rural areas in an attempt to develop interest in and provide academic preparation for health care careers. These programs operate under the premise that individuals who come from a rural environment are more likely to return to that environment to practice. Walker (1991) emphasized that local training in health care will enable rural residents to help meet their own health care workforce needs.

A new health educational model relevant to preparing individuals to work in rural health is the cross-training or multi-skilling approach that educates allied health professionals and nurses in multiple areas outside of their traditional scope of practice. The Agency for Health Care Policy and Research of the U.S. Public Health Service described models for rural health care using a single class of allied health worker trained to accomplish tasks in radiology, laboratory science and emergency medicine. This agency also says nurses can be cross-trained to perform therapy services and other non-nursing functions (Agency for Health Care Policy and Research, 1991).

Legislative Initiatives Supporting Rural Health Care Practice

State legislative initiatives and federally funded programs actively promote rural nursing and allied health practices. For example, Nebraska and Kentucky funded programs to increase the number of rural students entering health programs (Straub and Wright, 1993). Texas embraced the concept of using cooperative programming and distance learning to bridge health science centers with rural academic universities. Texas funded Rural Health Outreach programs to provide continuing education to nurses in rural areas. In addition to education on technical topics, the Rural Outreach Program provides stress reduction and burnout prevention programming (Okimi et al., 1992). Federally funded Area Health Education Centers (AHECs) played a major role in supporting rural health practice through both pre-professional and continuing education programs.

Legislative initiatives, other than those dealing with education, play an important role in encouraging nurses and allied health professionals to practice in rural areas. Legislative initiatives that allow for more independent practice and greater reimbursement potentially support rural health care practice by non-physician providers.

Government health care reimbursement policies have been revised to include coverage for more services offered by NPs and PAs. Services of NPs and PAs in designated rural health professional shortage areas are now eligible for Medicare reimbursement. PAs and NPs in rural areas are eligible in many states to receive Medicaid reimbursement. The Rural Health Care Services Act, passed originally in 1977, was modified to aid in recruitment and retention of non-physician health care providers through revision of provisions related to reimbursement. Problems with both governmental and non-governmental health insurance coverage, however, still exist with regard to these and other allied health care practitioners.

Another legislative prerogative is defining scope of practice. States that allow nurses and allied health professionals, particularly NPs and PAs, to expand practice scopes are more conducive to rural practice and primary care. Areas covered under scope of practice legislation include type of required physician supervision, types of procedures that can be performed, and medication authority.

Legislative initiatives that permit Medicare to allow for options related to on-site time commitments for rural health facility personnel are another strategy to aid in providing nursing and allied health care. For example, allowing rural hospitals to deviate from the requirement that a RN be present on-site for 24 hours per day is one strategy being considered.

Non-physician health care providers (nurses and practitioners in allied health) are critical to provide appropriate health care services in rural America. Attempts will continue to recruit and retain these individuals in rural settings.

— *Judy E. Perkin*

See also

Rural Health Care; Injuries; Policy, Health Care

References

Agency for Health Care Policy and Research. *Delivering Essential Health Care Services in Rural Areas: An Analysis of Alternative Models.* AHCPR Pub. No. 91-0017 (May). Washington, DC: U.S. Department of Health and Human Services, Agency for Health Care Policy and Research, 1991.

Bigbee, Jeri L. "The Uniqueness of Rural Nursing." *Nursing Clinics of North America* 28 (1993): 131-144.

Burke, George C. III, Grant T. Savage, Kelly C. Baird, Veronda L. Durden and Robert A. Pascasio. "Stakeholder Impact on Two Rural Hospital Closures." *Texas Journal of Rural Health* 8 (1994): 5-13.

Cawley, James. "Physician Assistants in the Health Care Workforce." Pp. 21-39 in *The Roles of Physician Assistants and Nurse Practitioners in Primary Care.* Edited by D. Kay Clawson and Marian Osterweis. Washington, DC: Association of Academic Health Centers, 1993.

Committee on the Future of Rural Health Care. *Quality through Collaboration: The Future of Rural Health.* Washington, DC: Institute of Medicine of the National Academies, 2004.

Fowkes, Virginia. "Meeting the Needs of the Underserved: The Roles of Physician Assistants and Nurse Practitioners." Pp. 69-84 in *The Roles of Physician Assistants and Nurse Practitioners in Primary Care.* Edited by D. Kay Clawson and Marian Osterweis. Washington, DC: Association of Academic Health Centers, 1993.

Gordon, Ilene and Julie R. Erickson. "Comparison of Rural and Urban Certified Nurse-Midwives in Arizona." *Journal of Nurse Midwifery* 38 (1993): 28-34.

Gupta, Gloria C. and Thomas R. Konrad "Allied Health Education in Rural Health Professional Shortage Areas of the United States." *Journal of the American Medical Association* 268 (1992): 1127-1130.

Hooker, Roderick S., Gloria C. Gupta, and Thomas, R. Konrad. "Rural Health Training Sites for Physician Assistants." *Journal of the American Academy of Physician Assistants* 7 (1994): 353.

Murphy, John. "Taking the Less-Traveled Road." *Advance for Physical Therapists* 6 (1995): 8-9.

Muus, Kyle J., Terry D. Stratton, and Kazi A. Ahmed. "Medical Information Needs of Rural Health Professionals." *Texas Journal of Rural Health* 1st Quarter (1993): 10-15.

Office of Technology Assessment. *Health Care in Rural America*, OTA-H-434 (September). Washington, DC: U.S. Congress, Office of Technology Assessment, 1990.

Okimi, Patricia H., John C. Reed, and Jacqueline E. Bernhardt. "Continuing Education for Rural Nurses: A State Funded Program." *Texas Journal of Rural Health* 2nd Quarter (1992): 7-12.

Osterweis, Marian and Stephen Garfinkel. "The Roles of Physician Assistants and Nurse Practitioners in Primary Care: An Overview of the Issues." Pp. 1-9 in *The Roles of Physician Assistants and Nurse Practitioners in Primary Care.* Edited by D. Kay Clawson and Marian Osterweis. Washington, DC: Association of Academic Health Centers, 1993.

Price, Diane. "PAs in Rural Practice." *Journal of the American Academy of Physician Assistants* 6 (1993): 423-427.

Rubenstein, David A. "The Rural Hospital in the Year 2001." *Texas Journal of Rural Health* 2nd Quarter (1989): 29-34.

Shi, Leiyu, Michael E. Samuels, Thomas R. Konrad, Thomas C. Ricketts, Carleen H. Stoskopf, and Donna L. Richter. "The Determinants of Utilization of Nonphysician Providers in Rural Community and Migrant Health Centers." *Journal of Rural Health* 9 (1993): 27-39.

Straub, La Vonne A. and W. Russell Wright . "Preparing Rural Students for Health Careers." *Texas Journal of Rural Health* 1st Quarter (1993): 16-27.

Travers, Karen L. and Robert B. Ellis. "Why PAs Leave Rural Practice: A Study of PAs in Maine." *Journal of the American Academy of Physician Assistants* 6 (1993): 412-417.

Walker, Mary. "Non-Physician Health Professionals and Rural Health Care." *Texas Journal of Rural Health* 2nd Quarter (1991): 8-12.

Willis, Judith B. "Barriers to PA Practice in Primary Care and Rural Medically Underserved Areas" *Journal of the American Academy of Physician Assistants* 6 (1993): 418-422.

Wright, Kathleen A. "Management of Agricultural Injuries and Illness." *Nursing Clinics of North America* 28 (1993): 253-266.

Nursing Homes

Licensed health care facilities that provide long-term care services to chronically impaired people of all ages.

The older adult population (those aged 65 or older) makes up 12 percent of the U.S. population, and approximately one-fifth of this group lives in rural areas (Coburn, 2002). Fifteen percent of individuals living in nonmetropolitan areas are aged 65 or older (USDA, 2007). As we can see, there is a higher proportion of elders living in rural areas who may need nursing home care. Therefore, nursing homes in rural America are an important source of long-term care. Unlike many forms of formal health and long-term care, access to nursing homes may be better in rural than in urban areas. The conversion of small rural hospital beds to skilled nursing beds has improved access to skilled nursing care in rural areas. Findings regarding the quality of care in rural facilities suggest that they may provide better care for pressure ulcers, tube feeding and incontinence, but are less adequate at providing aggressive rehabilitative services (Phillips et al., 2004). There is clear, although limited, evidence that nursing homes in rural areas can be highly integrated into their local communities. In order for rural nursing homes to be successful in the future, it will be important that they assure quality care, maintain community integration, and serve as catalysts for related home and community services.

Important Source of Care

Nursing homes are an important source of long-term care services in rural areas. Long-term care services include assistance with activities of daily living (ADLs), such as help with feeding, dressing, toileting, bathing and transferring. Such assistance may be needed by people of any age, but older people are more likely than others to require it. There is some evidence that rural older Americans have higher levels of chronic impairment than other elders, which could lead to a greater need for long-term care services, especially nursing home care, due to the limited availability of other sources of care. However, rural elders are more likely to rely on their family or other informal supports to help with their needs (Coburn, 2002).

Access

Although access to many kinds of health and long-term care services may be more limited to elders in rural areas, this situation is not generally true of nursing home care. Nationally, nonmetropolitan areas tend to have substantially more nursing home beds relative to their populations (70 beds per 1,000 elders versus 47.6 beds per 1,000 elders in metropolitan settings), even though metropolitan areas tend to have larger facilities (Coburn, 2002). However, the demand for nursing home

care has been changing. The effect of this trend on nursing homes in rural areas where there is limited availability of other sources of long-term care is not currently known.

Characteristics of Residents

There is some evidence that residents of rural nursing homes are younger and somewhat less functionally impaired than urban nursing home residents. In fact, newly admitted residents tend to be less impaired with their ADLs than those admitted to urban nursing homes, though they are more likely to be cognitively impaired (Bolin et al., 2006). Greene (1984) hypothesized that this difference may be the result of limited community services in rural areas, leading to the premature institutionalization of rural elders. Rural nursing homes have a higher proportion of residents aged 85 years or older than urban facilities and rural nursing home admissions are more likely than urban admissions to enter a nursing home from a private home. Those who enter a rural nursing home are also more likely to have lived alone prior to admission (Phillips et al., 2001).

Development of Swing Beds

Rural NHs may not be able to provide the range of special services required by many current admissions (Phillips et al., 2004). On the other hand, hospital swing beds in rural areas may be able to provide post-acute and rehabilitative care to patients who would otherwise be admitted to nursing homes having special services (Shaughnessy, 1994). Swing-bed care has been called "short-term long-term care" or "sub-acute care." The development of rural hospital swing beds was supported by the Omnibus Budget Reconciliation Act of 1980 as a way to improve the financial viability and financial resources of rural nursing homes and extend access to cost-effective nursing home care in rural areas.

Slightly over 60 percent of rural hospitals participate in swing-bed agreements (Begley, 2003). Swing-bed care is less expensive than skilled nursing home care, but offers similar or better overall quality (Begley, 2003). The rural hospital swing-bed program appears to have increased access to long-term care services without increasing costs. The overall success of rural hospital swing beds has led to similar programs in urban areas.

Quality of Care

There is limited research regarding quality of care in rural nursing homes. Research findings suggest that nursing homes in isolated areas (population less than 2,500 people) provide better long-term and chronic care than those in urban areas, though facilities in isolated areas provide worse post-acute care (Phillips et al., 2004). It is interesting that as the level of rurality increases, nursing home staffing levels tend to decrease but there is also a decline in the number of deficiencies identified through the annual certification and licensing survey data (Phillips et al., 2001). Although the low number of deficiencies would suggest a higher quality of care in rural settings, rural nursing homes have been found to have more potential quality-of-care problems than urban facilities (Phillips et al., 2001). There is some anecdotal evidence (Shaughnessy, 1994) that staff in rural nursing homes are more mindful of their patients' functional and support needs than is typical in urban facilities. The difference may be due to lower staff turnover in rural facilities or because the smaller size of rural communities and facilities promotes continuing social interaction between nursing home staff and administration with family members and friends of patients both within and outside the facility. However, there may be some quality-of-care problems in rural facilities, such as poor training and the over-provision of assistance with ADLs, which could limit rehabilitation or even hasten functional decline of some nursing home residents. The quality of care in nursing homes remains a complex issue.

Community Ties and Permeability

In an in-depth, multi-method study of one 90-bed rural nursing home in Kentucky, Rowles (1996) identified a high level of economic, social, psychological and historical integration between the nursing home and the rural community, leading to a sense of community ownership and support for the facility. Rowles also discovered a high level of permeability, or consistent exchange, of people and communication between the nursing home and the community. This high degree of permeability made it possible for many patients in the facility to continue to feel that they were residents of the rural community as well as experience an improved quality of life, even among those highly impaired.

Issues for Assuring Success

The nursing home is likely to be a continuing component of long-term care in rural areas because institutional care is the best alternative for a select portion of chronically impaired individuals. Several related issues must be addressed in order to assure that rural nursing homes operate successfully and support the long-term

care needs of impaired rural residents. These issues include 1) how to assure the quality of rural nursing home care; 2) how to ensure that rural nursing homes and their residents manage to maintain, to the fullest extent possible, their ties with the community; and 3) how to enhance the role of rural nursing homes as catalysts for improved community-based and home care services, which are frequently limited in rural areas.

— *William J. McAuley and Megan E. McCutcheon*

See also
Elders; Rural Health Care; Mental Health of Older Adults; Policy, Rural Family; Policy, Health Care; Senior Centers

References
Begley, S. "The Swing-Bed Program." In *The Robert Wood Johnson Foundation Anthology*, 2003. Available online at: www.rwjf.org/files/publications/books/2003/chapter¢fl_11.html.

Bolin, J.N., C.D. Phillips, and C. Hawes. "Differences Between Newly Admitted Nursing Home Residents in Rural and Nonrural Areas in a National Sample." *The Gerontologist* 46 (2006): 33-41.

Coburn, Andrew F. "Rural Long-Term Care: What Do We Need to Know to Improve Policy and Programs?" *The Journal of Rural Health* 18 (2002): 256-269.

Hawes, C., C.D. Phillips, S. Holan, and M. Sherman. *Assisted Living in Rural America: Results from a National Survey. Report to the Office of Rural Health Policy.* Bryon, TX: Southwest Rural Health Research Center, School of Rural Public Health, Texas A&M University System, 2007.

Greene, V.L. "Premature Institutionalization among the Rural Elderly in Arizona." *Public Health Reports* 99 (1984): 58-63.

Phillips, C.D., W.S. Holan, M., Sherman, M.L. Williams, and C. Hawes. "Rurality and Nursing Home Quality: Results from a National Sample of Nursing Home Admissions." *American Journal of Public Health* 94 (2004): 1717-1722.

Phillips, C.D., C. Hawes, and M.L. Williams. *Nursing Home Residents in Rural and Urban Areas, 2001: Report to the Office of Rural Health Policy in the Department of Health and Human Services.* Bryon, TX: Southwest Rural Health Research Center, School of Rural Public Health, Texas A&M University System, 2004.

Rowles, G.D., J.A. Concotelli, and D.M. High. "Community Integration of a Rural Nursing Home." *The Journal of Applied Gerontology* 15 (1996): 188-201.

Shaughnessy, P.W. "Changing Institutional Long-term Care to Improve Rural Health Care." Pp. 144-181 in *Health Services for Rural Elders*. Edited by R.T. Coward, C.N. Bull, G. Kukulka, and G.M. Galliher. New York, NY: Springer, 1994.

U.S. Department of Agriculture. "Rural Population and Migration: Trend 6—Challenges from an Aging Population," 2007. Available online at: www.ers.usda.gov/Briefing/Population/Challenges.htm.

Source: USDA www.mypyramid.gov

Nutrition

The interaction between food and living things, encompassing physiological and biochemical processes, and influenced by psychological, social, economic, environmental and technological factors. Most rural Americans have an adequate intake of essential nutrients but need help to improve their diets to meet recommendations that will promote health and reduce the risk for chronic diseases. Balancing energy intake with physical activity to maintain a healthy weight, increasing intake of fruits, vegetables and whole grains, and decreasing intake of fat, *trans* fat, saturated fat, and sodium are primary recommendations. Food access, delivery of nutrition education and other preventive and emergency feeding programs for the rural poor may be more difficult than in urban settings due to the logistical realities of rural living.

Nutrition Recommendations for Rural Americans

Most rural Americans understand that diet plays an important role in both causation and prevention of chronic diseases. Consensus exists, based on ongoing diet and health surveillance of the U.S. population, about the urgent need for all Americans to avoid overweight and obesity, to increase fruit and vegetable consumption, and to decrease intake of fat, *trans* fat, saturated fat and sodium. As recommended by the 2005 Dietary Guidelines for Americans, and in order to insure adequate intake of the Dietary Reference Intakes (commonly known as the Recommended Dietary Allowances) for essential nutrients, all Americans are urged to eat a variety of foods. They are especially encouraged to increase consumption of fruits, vegetables, and to choose whole grains, low-fat or non-fat dairy products and lean meats. Less than 25 percent of Americans eat the recommended amounts of fruits and vegetables, and rural residents are no different. For a 2,000-calorie reference diet, the Dietary Guidelines recommend two cups of fruit and two and a half cups of vegetables every day. But, according to statistics, Americans eat, on average, only about 0.83 cups of fruit and 1.72 cups of vegetables. The national campaign, Fruits and Veg-

gies—More Matters, which replaced the widely recognized 5 A Day Program, promotes fruit and vegetable intake for all Americans. The United States Department of Agriculture (USDA) MyPyramid Food Guidance System integrates the 2005 Dietary Guidelines and provides practical, food-based recommendations, encouraging balance, variety and moderation. MyPyramid allows people to design a plan that meets their individual energy requirements, nutritional needs and food preferences. The U.S. Department of Health and Human Services' Healthy People 2010 Nutrition Objectives address these nutritional concerns and additionally target iron deficiency and anemia in some population groups and the need for adequate calcium intake across the lifespan.

The Dietary Guidelines for Americans and other recommendations apply to rural and urban dwellers alike since the diets of the two groups are quite similar. The major source of information about diets of Americans comes from the "What We Eat in America Survey," the dietary interview component of the National Health and Nutrition Examination Survey (NHANES), which is an ongoing and comprehensive health and nutrition monitoring survey across the U.S. population. Many Americans fail to meet the Dietary Guidelines and MyPyramid recommendations and are below recommended levels in some nutrients. Recent data have shown that most Americans had inadequate intakes of vitamin E; there is also potential concern for dietary fiber, vitamins A and C, and minerals magnesium, calcium and potassium. Some nutrients may be a problem for specific population groups including vitamin B6 for adult females, phosphorus for adolescent females, and zinc for teenage girls and older adults.

The widespread prevalence of overweight and obesity, including in rural America, is at an all-time high. Obesity is a major risk factor for cardiovascular disease, certain types of cancer, and type 2 diabetes. Although dietary intake does not appear to differ significantly between rural and urban Americans, there is evidence that overweight and obesity may be higher among people living in rural settings than in urban areas. A primary focus of the Healthy Rural People 2010 (HRP2010) report is overweight and obesity. The HRP2010 goal of reducing obesity to 15 percent is not close to being achieved. Recent statistics place the obesity rate for rural adults at 23 percent, compared to 20.5 percent for urban adults. Rural residents of Mississippi, Texas and Louisiana, and African Americans and American Indians, had the highest obesity prevalence rates of rural groups. Some studies also found obesity more prevalent in rural women.

Cultural and structural features of the traditional rural lifestyle may present challenges to maintaining a healthy weight. Cultural factors include less compliance with dietary recommendations, higher dietary fat and calorie consumption, decline in the frequency of physical activity and exercise, more sedentary work lifestyles, and increased television watching, including computer and video games. Structural and "built environment" factors in rural areas contributing to overweight and obesity include increasing portion sizes and widespread inexpensive, calorically dense foods, lack of nutrition education, low access to dietitians/nutritionists, fewer physical education classes in schools, and fewer facilities for exercise. Successful programs and methods to combat the increasing overweight and obesity concerns in rural areas are critical and rural health care practitioners and health educators may be key resources.

Nutrition and Rural Elderly

Older adults living in rural communities are thought to be more vulnerable to nutritional inadequacies, although this is based on research that has tended to target specific rural populations and not national samples. Adequate nutrition is important as it can help promote independence and maintenance of functional health status. Rural elderly may not meet the Dietary Guidelines for Americans and MyPyramid Food Guidance System recommendations. They have been reported to have low consumption of fruits, dark green and yellow vegetables, whole grains, and low-fat dairy foods, and to have less desirable intakes of fats and oils, sweets and snack foods. Diets of some rural elderly segments have been evaluated as "poor" or "needed improvement." A number of factors, including social and geographic isolation, transportation limitations, store availability and distance, low incomes and low educa-

tional status, and limited availability of nutrition-related services may all contribute to the challenge of maintaining a healthy diet in older rural adults.

Nutrition and Rural Children

Overweight is a serious health and nutrition concern for children and adolescents, including those living in rural areas. Comparison of two national surveys (NHANES 1976-1980 and 2003-2004) has shown increasing prevalence of overweight in children aged two to five years (from 5.0 to 13.9 percent), 6-11 years (from 6.5 to 18.8 percent), and 12-19 years (from 5.0 to 17.4 percent). Research has indicated that rural children have higher body mass indexes (BMI) and higher prevalence of overweight than the national average. Rural youth are about 25 percent more likely to be overweight or obese than metropolitan counterparts. Similar to rural adults, possible "obesogenic" factors for rural children include less physical activity (including environmental challenges such as limited park access and exercise facilities, fewer sidewalks, lack of public transportation, and limited school physical education classes), more television watching and computer use, and increasing portion sizes, among others.

Food intake trends by children 6-11 and 12-19 years of age, based on three nationally representative surveys (the Nationwide Food Consumption Survey, 1977-78; the Continuing Survey of Food Intakes by Individuals, 1994-98; and the What We Eat in America, NHANES, 2001-2002), indicated that dietary patterns and the types and amounts of foods children consume have changed considerably over the last 25 years. While some changes were positive (decreased intake of whole milk), more of the changes were not. The mean daily energy intake increased; the proportion of children eating breakfast decreased; and the number of children snacking and number of snacks increased. Children consumed fewer vegetables and consumed more carbonated beverages, fruit drinks, savory snack foods, pizza and candy. Nutritional guidance and education targeted to children and their caregivers and access to healthier food choices are critical.

Nutrition Programs for Rural Residents

A variety of nutrition programs that provide food and nutrition information and education is available to rural residents, primarily targeting those socioeconomically disadvantaged, or children. The USDA is responsible for the Food Stamp Program and associated Food Stamp Nutrition Education Program (FSNE), the National School Lunch and Breakfast Programs, the Child and Adult Care Food Program (which serves child and adult day care sites), the Special Supplemental Nutrition Program for Women, Infants, and Children (WIC), and Commodity Food Distribution programs such as The Emergency Food Assistance Program (TEFAP) and Food Distribution Program on Indian Reservations. Nutrition programs for older adults such as home-delivered meals and congregate meals are provided through authorization of the Older Americans Act and often through non-government organizations including religious organizations. The USDA also administers the WIC and Senior Farmers' Market Nutrition Programs.

Nutrition education and health promotion information and services may be less available to rural people due to long travel distances to programs and providers, health insurance coverage issues, weather, and availability of health agencies and professionals, although increasing digital and electronic access to information via the Internet and World Wide Web, and satellite technologies may be helping to bridge this gap. The Cooperative Extension Service, community education programs, local hospitals and clinics, government food programs such as WIC and FSNE, some television and radio programming, printed materials, and the Internet are all potential sources of credible nutrition and health information. Government requirements for nutrition labeling on food products is also useful if the rural consumer is interested in and aware of how to use the labels.

Food Cost and Availability

People living in rural areas can face "food deserts"— large and isolated geographic areas where mainstream grocery stores are absent or distant, creating areas where it is difficult to find healthful foods at affordable prices. Living in a food desert may impact the diet quality of rural residents and put them at risk for poor dietary intake, including being less likely to consume the recommended servings of fruits and vegetables. The relationship of food deserts to obesity has also been hypothesized. Rural areas tend to have a greater percentage of convenience stores, small supermarkets, and "mom and pop" type stores which offer fewer fresh fruits and vegetables, and fewer foods such as whole grain breads and cereals, low-fat or non-fat dairy products, and lean meats. If healthier foods are available, these are often at higher prices. Grocery store consolidation has resulted in the loss of many rural small town grocery stores, increasing distance up to 30 miles or more. This is especially of concern for elderly rural

residents who may not have transportation. Rural households can face higher prices than those available to suburban households, and studies in states from across the country have found the highest grocery prices in some of the poorest rural areas, and for those that might least be able to afford it such as WIC participants. Rural residents in some areas routinely spend a higher percentage of their income on food than those living in more urban areas. These factors may influence nutritional adequacy and the ability of rural residents to follow recommended dietary guidelines.

Food Insecurity

Food insecurity is the mental and physical condition that comes from not eating enough food due to insufficient economic, family or community resources. It is more problematic for Americans living in rural areas and large cities compared to suburban areas. In 2006, 12 percent of rural households (10.9 percent nationally) reported they were food insecure at least sometime during the year. Of these rural households, 4.4 percent (4.0 percent nationally) were classified as having "very low food security"—meaning that the food intake of one or more adults was reduced and their eating patterns were disrupted sometime during the year due to lack of money or other resources. Food insecurity is more prevalent in areas of the South, and the national rate is doubled for households with children. Rural residents also rely disproportionately more on the USDA Food Stamp Program (FSP). About 16 percent of the U.S. population lives in rural areas but 21 percent of the FSP participants live there. Overall, about 10 percent of rural residents rely on food stamps compared to about 7 percent in urban areas. Data also show that about 35 percent of those eligible to participate don't, which may be due to challenges of transportation, lack of information, uncertainty about eligibility, the time and effort to apply, or unwillingness to take government assistance. Food security surveys also have shown that about 4.4 percent of rural households (compared to 3.3 percent nationally) accessed emergency food from food pantries or food shelves one or more times during a 12-month period in 2006.

In summary, many rural Americans, and those who serve them, face numerous challenges in achieving diets consistent with recommendations for overall good health and chronic disease risk reduction. Chief among these are improved access to healthful, affordable food and improved nutrition literacy.

— *Joyce M. Merkel and Susan J. Crockett*

See also
Food Safety; Policy, Food

References

Jackson, J. Elizabeth, Mark P. Doescher, Anthony F. Jerant, and Gary L. Hart. "A National Study of Obesity Prevalence and Trends by Type of Rural County." *Journal of Rural Health* 21 (2005): 140-148.

Joens-Matre, Roxane R., Gregory J. Welk, Miguel A. Calabro, Daniel W. Russell, Elizabeth Nicklay, and Larry D. Hensley. "Rural-Urban Differences in Physical Activity, Physical Fitness, and Overweight Prevalence of Children." *The Journal of Rural Health* 24 (Winter 2008): 49-54.

Lutfiyya, May N., Martin S. Lipsky, Jennifer Wisond-Behounek, and Melissa Inpanbutr-Martinkus. "Rural Residency a Risk Factor for Overweight and Obesity in US Children?" *Obesity* 15 (2007); 2348-2356.

Nord, Mark, Margaret Andrews, and Steven Carlson. *Household Food Security in the United States, 2006.* ERR-49. Washington, DC: U.S. Department of Agriculture, Economic Research Service, November 2007.

Ogden, Cynthia L., Margaret D. Carroll, Lester R. Curtin, Margaret A. McDowell, Carolyn J. Tabak, and Katherine M. Flegal. "Prevalence of Overweight and Obesity in the United States, 1999-2004." *Journal of the American Medical Association* 295 (2006): 1549-1555.

Smith, Kristin and Sarah Savage. *Food Stamp and School Lunch Programs Alleviate Food Insecurity in Rural America. Summer 2007 Fact Sheet.* Durham, NH: Carsey Institute, University of New Hampshire, 2007.

Tai-Seale, Tom and Coleman Chandler. "Nutrition and Overweight Concerns in Rural Areas: A Literature Review." Pp. 115-130 in *Rural Healthy People 2010: A Companion Document to Healthy People 2010.* College Station, TX: Texas A&M University System Health Science Center, School of Rural Public Health, Southwest Rural Health Research Center, 2003.

U.S. Department of Agriculture. "What We Eat In America, NHANES 2001-2002: Usual Nutrient Intakes from Food Compared to Dietary Reference Intakes." Washington, DC: U.S. Department of Agriculture, Agricultural Research Service, 2005. Available online at http://www.ars.usda.gov/research/publications/publications.htm?SEQ_NO_115=184176. Accessed March 1, 2008.

U.S. Department of Health and Human Services and U.S. Department of Agriculture. *Dietary Guidelines for Americans, 2005.* 6th ed. Washington, DC: Government Printing Office; 2005.

Vitolins Ara Z., Janet A. Tooze, Shannon L. Golden, Thomas A. Arcury, Ronny A. Bell, Cralen Davis, Robert F. Devellis, and Sara A. Quandt. "Older Adults in the Rural South Are Not Meeting Healthful Eating Guidelines." *Journal of the American Dietetic Association* 107 (2007): 265-272.

Recommended Websites

2005 Dietary Guidelines for Americans: http://www.health.gov/dietaryguidelines/

MyPyramid Food Guidance System: http://www.mypyramid.gov/

Fruit and Veggies—More Matters: http://www.fruitsandveggiesmatter.gov/

Healthy People Rural 2010: http://srph.tamhsc.edu/centers/rhp2010/

C.D.C. Overweight and Obesity http://www.cdc.gov/nccdphp/dnpa/obesity/

USDA Food and Nutrition Assistances Programs: http://www.fns.usda.gov/fns/services.htm

Organic Farming

The process of producing wholesome crops and livestock without synthetic fertilizer or pest controls through the creation of healthy soil and complex biological systems. Organic farming was the first type of farming practiced, and as such has a history stretching back many centuries. In the last 200 years, synthetic fertilizers and pest controls were developed, and the methods of organic farming were gradually phased out. Sixty years ago, J.I. Rodale reintroduced organic farming to the U.S., with the intent of maintaining healthy soil, food, and people. Today, many in the farming industry have returned to organic methods in response to a world deeply concerned about the health of its people and environment.

Building the Organic Movement from the Ground Up

The development of industrialized farming in the U.S. began in colonial times. Farming was the basis of the colonial economy, and most of the expansion and settlement was done by farmers. Some settlers formed friendships with the Native Americans who showed them how to grow native crops like corn, squash, beans, and herbs. By the late 18th century, wealthy landowners, such as George Washington and Thomas Jefferson, saw farming as a way to show that the newly formed U.S. was a successful nation. This political motive, along with the need to feed a growing population, led to the development of industrialized farming, or the creation of farms modeled after factories.

Further technical developments continued this pattern. In Germany, the chemist Justus von Liebig discovered that adding mineral nutrients to the soil helped plants grow more abundantly. This was the beginning synthetic fertilizer use, and with the introduction of the first chemical pesticides shortly thereafter, many traditional agricultural practices were abandoned. In 1859, the first steam powered tractor went on display, further reinforcing the move from traditional practices. Even then, there was concern for the new methods. President Lincoln questioned the direction farming was taking and warned that, in the future, large industrial farms may not be sustainable.

J.I. Rodale Introduces Organic Farming

After World War I, industrial farming methods were expanded and intensified through the introduction of single crop plantings and synthetic fertilizer. By the beginning of World War II, industrialized farming was standard. In 1940, J.I. Rodale bought a run-down farm in Pennsylvania and decided to grow food for his family in the healthiest way possible. Rodale was concerned that many members of his family died at an early age, almost all from heart attacks. He read the works of Sir Albert Howard, who had done scientific research in India. Sir Howard had recognized the value of returning good nutrients to the soil by using compost and the possibility of poor soil affecting the health of the lands, and consequently, the human body. Rodale came to believe that the relationship of soil to healthy plants was the missing link to healthy people. Rodale was also inspired by F.H. King's *Farmers of Forty Centuries* and Lord Walter Northbourne's *Look to the Land*, who first used the term "organic farming." Rodale started to publish *Organic Gardening and Farming* magazine in 1942, and wrote *Pay Dirt* in 1945 and *Organic Front* in 1948.

Using the word "organiculture," Rodale began to spread his ideas. Initially, organic farming was not accepted by farmers, the government, or the academic community. By the 1950s and 1960s, however, a growing band of gardeners, farmers, and traditionalist communities, such as the Amish, had adopted organic methods. In 1962, Rachel Carson's consciousness-raising *Silent Spring* alerted people to the effects of agricultural chemicals on environment and human health. The week before Rodale died in 1971, the *New York Times* carried a cover feature story about him. His ideas and the organic movement were beginning to gain recognition.

Establishing Scientific Credibility

J.I. Rodale's son, Robert, realized the need for greater scientific credibility in organic farming. Central to this was a strong research program. He founded the Rodale Research Center in 1971 on a 305 acre farm in Maxatawny, Pennsylvania. The Research Center is now called the Rodale Institute. The farm, like most in the area, had been chemically treated for many years, and the research program was to study the introduction of organic methods. To do this, a partnership was formed with a neighbor, who agreed to farm according to the methods set out by the Center. The neighbor was initially skeptical, however within a few years, he saw yields of corn on the farm equal or exceed those of neighboring farms, his costs were lower, and the methods were safer because of the reduced use of chemicals. He then changed his own farm to an organic one. This success and the growing popularity of organic farming led to the need to provide specialized information to the growing number of organic farmers. The needs were met in 1979 with the publication of the *New Farm* magazine, which grew out of *Organic Gardening*.

In 1980, a U.S.D.A. team under the Carter administration gave the first official governmental recognition to organic gardening's merit. The team's report stated that the soil is a living system and must be fed so that the activity of beneficial organisms in the soil will not be restricted. Team members discovered organic farms of all sizes were productive, efficient, and well-managed, and that their practices controlled soil erosion, minimized water pollution, and conserved energy. The report praised organic farmers for their unique, innovative methods of soil management for pest control. It concluded that much could be learned from these farmers and that research and educational programs should be developed to serve the needs of these farmers.

The "Farming Systems Trial" was started in 1981 at the Rodale Institute, and continues today. It is the longest-running side-by-side comparison of organic versus conventional corn and soybean production systems in the United States. It develops scientifically reliable statistics showing that organic farming can be as productive and profitable as conventional farming. At this time, Robert Rodale coined the term "regenerative agriculture." This meant that soil could be regenerated when farmers break the bonds of solidified thinking and become fluid in their ability to adapt, and so through chaos find a new, regenerated way of being. Just as a forest regenerates after a forest fire, so too do farmers need to keep regenerating soil; it needs to be continually reborn and revitalized.

U.S. Government Supports Sustainable Agriculture

In 1985, Congress authorized the Low Input Sustainable Agriculture program, or LISA. Funds were provided for projects to answer questions of farmers and researchers searching for ways to reduce off-farm inputs. Appropriations climbed from nearly $4 million in 1988 to more than $115 million in 1996.

Several events occurred in 1990 relating to organic farming. First, the National Academy of Sciences report on alternative agriculture concluded that alternative farming systems are practical and provide economical ways to maintain yields, conserve soil, maintain water quality, and lower farm operating costs. Second, part of the Farm Bill called for federal organic certification standards. The U.S.D.A. appointed a Standards Board, whose recommendations were implemented in 2002. Third, the non-profit Rodale Institute was officially formed. The Institute expanded beyond research to include outreach. Programs in Senegal, Guatemala, Russia, and China helped farmers to regain what they lost through the years when they attempted to industrialize.

Today's Organic Farmers

Many farmers who market their crops and livestock conventionally use some regenerative practices to cut input costs, increase biodiversity, clean land and water, protect the health of their families and earn the respect of their communities as careful stewards of natural resources. They take special care to encourage good physical properties of the soil with abundant populations of microbes, earthworms, and other soil life. This helps to protect the environment and prevent erosion among its many benefits.

Organic farmers use complex crop rotations that alternate row crops with close-growing crops, such as small grains or forages. They rotate crops such as corn and other grains that remove nitrogen from the soil with legumes that add free nitrogen from the air to the soil. Between cash crops, organic farmers often grow cover crops and "green manure" crops that are soil-improving crops; they are not harvested, but plowed under to feed the soil. These diverse rotations help to control weeds, insects, diseases, and other pests.

Livestock are an integral part of an organic farm because animals consume forages grown in complex rotations and help to recycle the nutrients to the fields through the manure they produce. The manure is managed carefully, often composted before it is applied to the fields so that the nutrients are not washed into ground water or surface water causing pollution. Composted soil has more stable nutrients, holds water better, encourages abundant root growth, and protects crops from soil disease. Leaves collected from municipalities are another source of organic matter, which are turned into compost to improve the soil.

Organic farmers often sell their produce directly to the consumer to eliminate the middle person. The challenge for the future is to grow the produce as closely as possible to the consumers. Consumers are willing to pay a higher price for their produce because of the high quality, better taste, and freedom from pesticides. The concern for a healthier lifestyle is gaining momentum.

Today there is a network of farmers helping each other to recapture the best that was lost through the years before the introduction of chemical fertilizers. They are refining traditional practices by what is being learning today in studies the soil and surroundings. They are learning how to close the circle that moves to the rhythm of life as it describes the harmonious whole.

— *Ardath Rodale*

See also

Agrichemical Use; Agriculture, Alternative; Biodiversity; Conservation, Soil; Cropping Systems; Farm Management; Groundwater; Land Stewardship; Organic Foods Industry; Pest Management

References

Howard, Sir Albert. *An Agricultural Testament*. London, UK: Oxford University Press, 1940; Emmaus, PA: Rodale Press, 1979.

King, F.H. *Farmers of 40 Centuries, or Permanent Agriculture in China, Korea, and Japan* London, UK: Cape, 1928; Emmaus, PA: Rodale Press, 1979.

Lampkin, Nicolas. *Organic Farming*. Ipswich, UK: Farming Press Books, 1980.

National Research Council. *Alternatives Agriculture*. Washington, DC: National Academy Press, 1980.

Northbourne, Walter Ernst Christopher James, Baron. *Look to the Land*. London, UK: J.M. Dent and Sons, Ltd., 1940.

Organic Trade Association, Greenfield, MA. Available online at: www.ota.com.

Rodale, J.I. *Pay Dirt*. Emmaus, PA: Rodale Press, Inc., 1945.

Rodale, J.I. *The Organic Front*. Emmaus, PA: Rodale Press, Inc., 1948.

U.S. Department of Agriculture, National Agriculture Library. *Sustainable Agriculture in Print: Current Books*. Beltsville, MD: Alternative Farming Systems Information Center, 1993.

U.S. Department of Agriculture, National Agriculture Library. *Periodicals Pertaining to Alternative Farming Systems*. Beltsville, MD: Alternative Farming Systems Information Center, 1993.

Organic Foods Industry

The sector of the U.S. foods industry involving the production, marketing, distribution and sales of organic products. This article provides a summary of some of the major production, market, policy and institutional issues affecting the organic sector and its dynamics within the U.S. food industry. It offers an overview of organic business trends, research and institutions across the U.S.

Organic farming is recognized as one of the fastest-growing segments of U.S. agriculture and food marketing. Organic sales in the U.S. are estimated to have been $16 billion in 2005 and up to $17.8 billion by 2007 (private market data cited by USDA-ERS, 2007). On the supply side, U.S. producers are turning to certified organic farming systems for numerous reasons including: capitalizing on new markets with higher cash returns, lower input costs, personal goals to decrease reliance on nonrenewable resources, and in the end, boosting farm income. On the consumer side, perceptions that organic foods enhance food safety and support sustainable production practices has gained a wider set of consumers' attention (e.g., Huang, 1996; Kuchlar, et al., 2000; Bond, et al., 2006). The market has responded and an increasing number of manufacturers, distributors and retailers specialize in growing, processing and marketing an ever widening array of organic food and fiber products.

Organic farming and food handling in the U.S. have been regulated by federal law since 1990. By the late 1980s, a large segment of organic producers and food manufacturers believed that implementing a national organic standard would greatly advance the industry and help convert many more acres into organic production. In 1990, the Organic Foods Production Act was passed which mandated the United States Department of Agriculture (USDA) to establish a set of national standards for organic production and processing. Up to this point, organic certification was being performed by dozens of independent certifiers using their own sets of standards. It took seven years for the USDA to release its first proposed set of the National Organic Standards (NOS), and when it did in 1997, several standards drew criticism during public comment. Subsequently, in 1999, the revised version of the NOS released was more in line with established organic standards. The federal standards were fully implemented in October 2002.

In order to legally sell a fresh or processed product as organic in the U.S., the grower and handler/processors must be certified organic. Producers with sales below $5,000 annually are exempt from the certification requirement. Certification is an auditing service that is provided to farmers and handlers/manufacturers by entities that are accredited by the USDA. Certification involves submission of an annual organic system plan to the certifier, payment of fees, and an annual inspection of the facility with an eye toward mitigating potential sources of contamination by non-organic inputs.

The year 2005 was the first time in which all 50 states had some certified organic farmland. The impact of organic agriculture varies significantly across rural America when one explores acreage in production, levels of sales or types of organic products being sold (National Agricultural Statistics Service). The organic farming sector is quite diverse, with holdings ranging from very small acreages marketing a wide variety of organic food products directly to consumers through farmers' markets and CSAs; to mid-sized farms which manage larger CSAs and market at numerous regional outlets; to large-scale organic operations whose scope of production compares with that of the largest conventional producers. In addition, organic handlers and processors are responsible for packing, shipping and otherwise processing prepared organic foods. A number of large-scale conventional food companies have developed their own organic product lines, including Kraft and General Mills, partly to source large-scale grocery stores, thus extending the reach of organic food into rural America.

Organic Food Production in Rural America

Between 2002 and 2006, organic sales in the U.S. almost doubled, with the most recent estimate of total sales being $17.8 billion in 2007. As the organic market matures, there may be some shifts in the types of products, volumes and major organic trading partners, all of which will influence the competitiveness and potential growth of organics in rural America. USDA ERS reported that U.S. producers managed four million acres of farmland organically in 2005, including 1.7 million acres of cropland and 2.3 million acres of rangeland and pasture. Acreage statistics clearly reflect the incredible growth of organic production in the early part of this century. Between 1997 and 2005, there was a 200 percent increase in organically certified farmland in the U.S. Organic poultry holdings increased by 1,623 percent and numbers of organic livestock gained almost 1,000 percent growth over the same period. As of 2005, there were 8,493 farm operations with some certified production, a 69 percent increase over 1997. (This estimate may be biased downward because of the $5,000 exemption in the national standards.)

While organic farming systems have become far more prevalent over the past 15 years, in 2005 certified organic production was practiced on only about 0.5 percent of all U.S. cropland and pasture. Obstacles to adoption by farmers include lack of access to markets during the three-year transition period; high managerial costs; the paperwork burden and cost of organic certification; and risks of shifting to a new way of farming. Lack of access to appropriate markets and inability to grow to the scale preferred by many marketing partners also represent barriers driven by the industry beyond the farmgate.

Figure 1 shows that California remains the leading state in certified organic cropland, mostly invested in fruit and vegetable production. North Dakota, Montana, Minnesota, Wisconsin, Texas and Idaho were also top organic states, producing a far larger share of field crops. Over 40 states also had some certified organic rangeland and pasture in 2005, although only four states—Alaska, Texas, California and Montana—had relatively large tracts of organic rangelands (more than 100,000 acres each). A source for production data is http://www.ers.usda.gov/Data/Organic.

While there is much good news about the growth in organic production across rural America, it is important to note that a supply shortage of raw organic food materials is a reality that has slowed down some industry growth. An additional challenge to U.S. producers is the organic trade deficit. The USDA Foreign Agricultural Service (FAS) found that the import share of the organic market in 2002 was approximately 17 percent of the $8.6 billion spent on organic products. Imports of

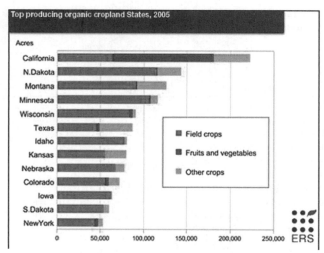

Figure 1. Note: *Field crops include grains, beans, oilseeds, and hay/silage. Fruits and vegetables also includes organic herbs/nursery/greenhouse. "Other crops" are cotton, peanuts, potatoes, green manure cover crops, trees for maple syrup, fallow and unclassified. Source: USDA/ERS Organic Production database.*

relatively cheap organic commodities can enhance accessibility of organic products to rural consumers, but can also increase competition with domestic organic producers.

A Global Market Assessment for Rural U.S. Organic Producers

There are a number of major competitors for the world organic food dollar. Australia has the world's largest number of certified organic acres in absolute terms, mostly in pasture. Between 2003 and 2006, China moved from the country with the eleventh largest acreage under organic management to second largest in the world (Willer et al., 2008). Argentina has been displaced to third place and the U.S. is fourth (Willer et al., 2008).

Countries in the European Union (EU) saw growth in consumer demand earlier than the U.S. and subsequently mounted significant supply responses both from private producer responses and based on significant policy incentives given by some countries. EU countries also explicitly acknowledge the environmental benefits that organic farms provide and have established a program of incentives to encourage organic production. Such incentives include:

- conversion and support payments for organic lands (62 percent of organic lands received some level of support in 2001);
- targets for land under organic management (ranging from 3 percent in France to 20 percent in Germany and Sweden);
- marketing programs; and
- support for organic research and education (estimated at 70-80 million euros annually (Dimitri and Oberholtzer, 2005).

Collectively, this acknowledgement of the multiple benefits of organic agriculture and grower incentives, including national targets for organic acreage, is known as the EU Action Plan (Commission of the European Communities, 2004).

There are many quickly emerging competitors in the organic sector. India and Thailand export moderate amounts of organic spices, fruits and vegetables, tea, coffee, cotton, cereals and honey. China and Southeast Asia have positioned themselves to be major players in global organic trade because of their comparative advantage in inexpensive labor relative to high-input production systems. In South America, Argentina is second only to Australia in absolute land area certified as organic. Approximately 90 percent of the production is oriented toward the export market. Brazil ranks fifth internationally in total area under organic management with increasing amounts of production in coffee, bananas, soybeans and corn (Yuseffi, 2004).

The Canadian General Standards Board adopted voluntary standards for organic production in 1999 and codified their organic standards into law in 2006, which will likely strengthen the role of Canada in organic trade. While demand for organic food in Canada has grown at rates comparable to those in the U.S., 85-90 percent of the market is supplied by the U.S., making Canada the largest market for U.S. organic exports (USDA-FAS, 2005). The Canadian federal government has established the Organic Agriculture Center of Canada as a research and education facility and provided other financial support for certification and promotion.

In Japan, diverse alternative food production and distribution systems have developed, and consumers, heavily influenced by recent food scares, have increased emphasis on "local" and "natural" food products. The market was estimated at $3 billion in the late 1990s, but the 2001 introduction of stringent Japan Agricultural Standards created an apparent shrinkage of the market to around $350 million.

Organic Demand, Marketing and the Supply Chain

In recent years, consumer demand for organic products has grown steadily. Sales were estimated at $1 billion in 1990 and have increased at approximately 20 percent per year since then to reach $16 billion in 2005 or almost 3 percent of the total U.S. food market. The *Nutri-*

Table 1.
Organic Food Sales in the U.S. by Food Category
2005, in millions of dollars, from OTA (2006)

2,140	Dairy
1,360	Bread/Grains
1,940	Beverages
5,369	Fruits/Vegetables
667	Snack Foods
758	Packaged/Prepared Foods
341	Sauces/Condiments
256	Meat/Fish/Poultry

Source: OTA (2006).

Table 2.
Organic Supply Chain Participants

Purchasing characteristics of handlers

Geography of purchasing	All handlers	Manufacturer/ processor	All other functions
	Percent of handlers		
Buys locally (within one jour's drive) (any amount)	38%	38%	40%
Buys locally (more than half)	23%	22%	20%
Buys regionally (within the State or surrounding States) (any amount)	50%	55%	51%
Buys regionally (more than half)	31%	32%	28%
Buys nationally (any amount)	46%	49%	45%
Buys nationally (more than half)	29%	28%	27%
Buys internationally (any amount)	35%	35%	42%
Buys internationally (more than half)	20%	19%	26%

Operational characteristics

	All handlers	Manufacturer/ processor	All other functions
Converted or expanded to organic from conventional	77%	76%	69%
Began as an organic facility	23%	24%	31%
Handles both organic and nonorganic products	83%	80%	79%
Handles only organic products	17%	20%	21%

Source: USDA-ERS, 2007

tion Business Journal estimates that sales growth will continue at 9-16 percent through 2010, when over 3 percent of U.S. food sales will be organic (Oberholtzer et al., 2005).

Table 1 shows that fruits/vegetables remains the highest sales category among organic foods, but dairy, breads/grains and other beverages are significant shares as well. Nondairy livestock products have lagged significantly in sales, but USDA lifted restrictions on organic meat labeling in the late 1990s, and the organic poultry and beef sectors are now expanding rapidly.

Still, the organic food supply chain is facing an increasingly complex landscape of consumer interests. Most notably, the public awareness of global climate change has dramatically increased, with the social and environmental effects of the global food system and food miles becoming hot topics for public discussion. Pirog et al. (2005) found that consumers are generally interested in buying locally grown food and, holding everything else constant, they are more likely to choose locally grown conventional products than organic products from other states or countries. In a 2006 national consumer study focused on local foods, direct marketing and organic produce, Bond et al. (2008) found that local foods rated similarly to organics, and among some consumers were more highly valued. Moreover, when asked, many consumers responded that the premia they would pay for organic produce was because of their perceptions that they would support local agricultural production. Although there are not documented numbers on the premium for organics, there are some representative numbers that show consumers' willingness to pay more. According to the USDA-ERS (2000-01) Boston wholesale markets reported 10-20 percent premia for various vegetables, and premia for grain crops ranged between 35 and 220 percent between 1995 and 2001. This is a crucial distinction in

how important organic production will be to rural America. Many market opportunities presented by the growth in organic food demand might be most effectively exploited by producers directly marketing to their surrounding consumer base and urban markets.

According to the USDA-ERS, the vast majority of organic commodities pass through the hands of at least one middleman, also called a handler, on the way from the farmer to the consumer. Examining organic supply chain participants reveals trends in the organic industry. Most of the handlers and manufacturers converted or expanded into the business from conventional food businesses, and only 17 percent handle exclusively organic products. These responses signal that organics are becoming a mainstream sector of the food industry. Of interest to local and regional food systems, many of these handlers report that almost a quarter buy more than half of their products locally and another third buy regionally, even though international procurement is clearly a significant share of their businesses (USDA-ERS, 2007).

Organic Stakeholders, Institutions and Emerging Issues

The EU Commission estimated that the government support is a major factor in explaining the significant share (3.5 percent) of total agricultural land in the EU that was certified organic in the early 2000s, and recent estimates suggest another 500,000 hectares were added in 2006. Organic acreage is highest in the Alpine countries; 12 percent in Switzerland, and 13 percent in Austria (EU Commission). Many believe these growth goals have been a direct result of the policy initiatives put forth among the countries (overviewed earlier in this chapter). Compare with the 0.5 percent of all U.S. cropland and pasture that is certified organic.

In the U.S., industry experts surveyed by the Organic Trade Association expect U.S. organic production to reach 5-10 percent of the U.S. food market within 10-20 years with expanding sales of non-food organic products such as clothing, personal care products, and pet food (OTA, 2005). However, many believe the United States' ability to meet this growth will be heavily dependent on whether research, education and policy initiatives continue to remove barriers to organic agriculture. An overview of the support for the organic industry, including roles of stakeholders, government and nonprofit initiatives, is key to understanding the future of organic agriculture in rural America.

The first identifiable USDA activity in organic agriculture was the 1980 *Report and Recommendations on Organic Farming* (USDA Study Team on Organic Farming, 1980), produced under the direction of Agriculture Secretary Bob Berglund. This report concluded that organic farming was viable and warranted increased institutional support; however, it was released in an election year and the new administration ignored its suggestions.

In the U.S., the government has not been as proactive in providing incentives and other support to the organic sector as the support provided by the EU. An early assessment of federal investment in organic research was published by the Organic Farming Research Foundation (OFRF) in 1997. The report, *Searching for the "O-Word,"* documented that less than one-tenth of one percent of the USDA's research funding was directed toward organic agriculture (Lipson, 1997). This publication has been frequently cited as evidence of the federal government's lack of support for the organic industry. More recent estimates by the OFRF indicate that organic represents almost 4 percent of U.S. food spending, but that organic research funding is less than 1.5 percent of the USDA's research and education budget.

Follow-up reports published by the OFRF in 2001 and 2003 provide an inventory of Land Grant organic

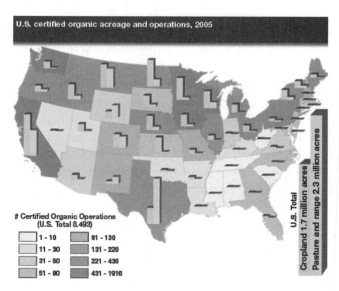

Note: Alaska and Hawaii are not shown; organic pasture/range in Alaska accounts for 60 percent of the U.S. total.
Source: USDA, Economic Research Service, based on information from USDA-accredited State and private organic certifiers.

activity in each state, documenting organic research, extension and education. The 2003 edition reported that the number of organic research sites is still far below that of conventional agriculture but that organic research acreage is growing rapidly. The OFRF estimated that 0.13 percent of the 885,863 acres in the U.S. Land Grant system were dedicated to organic research in 2003 (Sooby, 2003).

Thilmany (2006) reported that a broad set of U.S. Land Grant institution projects invested $23.2 million in organic activities, of which only $9.4 million was directly from the USDA's Cooperative State Research, Education and Extension Service (CSREES), which provides formula funding to universities and competitive funds to support agricultural research. The remainder of support was provided by state and local partners. Thilmany reported 219 projects in 46 states with 63 different partners. While many of the projects involved research, she found increasing investment in higher education, small business innovation and extension/outreach programs. In addition, the USDA's Agricultural Research Service (ARS) invested over $15 million in research that directly addresses organic agriculture, with over half of this work conducted under organic production conditions. The USDA's Economic Research Service also has a significant and increasing organic program. ERS has published ongoing estimates of organic acreage and production and many reports on economic issues related to the organic industry.

Finally, the USDA's Foreign Agricultural Service, Agricultural Marketing Service, Risk Management Agency, National Agricultural Statistics Service, and National Resource Conservation Service all have increased their attention to and support of the sector in various ways. The U.S. organic industry will be best positioned to grow and compete globally for the growing consumer dollars directed to organic food and fiber products with better marketing and production information, trade and technical assistance, conservation and risk management programs.

Implications for Rural America

Organic agriculture and foods are arguably among the most dynamic aspects of production agriculture, the food marketing chain and forces affecting rural America. Rural America has, and should continue to see, great opportunities in the interest and development of organic food systems. This is especially true in light of emerging interests in sourcing organics locally by consumers, and subsequently, some marketing channels. However, the support of public institutions that have historically been instrumental in the development of the agricultural sector is essential to the organic sector's viability in a global marketplace.

— *Dawn Thilmany and Jane Sooby*

See also

Agrichemical Use; Agriculture, Alternative; Agriculture, Sustainable; Biodiversity; Biotechnology; Farm Management; Genetically Modified Organisms; Organic Farming; Pest Management

References

Bond, C., D. Thilmany and J. Keeling-Bond. "Understanding Consumer Interest in Product and Process-Based Attributes for Fresh Produce." *Agribusiness: An International Journal* (2008, in press).

Commission of the European Communities. European action plan for organic food and farming. Commission Staff Working Document. Brussels, 2004. Available online at: http://europa.eu.int/comm/agriculture/qual/organic/plan/workdoc_en.pdf.

Huang, C.L. "Consumer Preference and Attitude Towards Organically Grown Produce." *European Review of Agricultural Economics* 23 (1996): 331-342.

International Federation of Organic Agriculture Movements (IFOAM). *Global Organic Farming: Continued Growth*, 2008. Available online at: www.ifoam.org. Accessed February 2008.

Kuchler, F., K. Ralston and J. Robert. "Do Health Benefits Explain the Price Premium for Organic Foods?" *American Journal of Alternative Agriculture* 15, no. 1 (2000): p. 9-18.

Lipson, M. *Searching for the "O-Word": Analyzing the USDA Current Research Information System for Pertinence to Organic Farming*. Santa Cruz, CA: Organic Farming Research Foundation, 1997. Report available online at http://ofrf.org/publications/o-word.html.

Lohr, L. *Factors Affecting International Demand and Trade in Organic Food Products: Changing Structure of Global Food Consumption and Trade* (WRS-01-1). Washington, DC: U.S. Department of Agriculture, Economic Research Service, 2001.

National Agricultural Statistics Service. 2002 Census Publications. http://www.agcensus.usda.gov/Publications/2002/index.asp, accessed February 2008.

Pirog, R., T. Van Pelt, K. Enshayan, and E. Cook. *Food, Fuel, and Freeways: An Iowa Perspective on How Far Food Travels, Fuel Usage, and Greenhouse Gas Emissions*. Ames, IA: Iowa State University, Leopold Center for Sustainable Agriculture, 2001. Available online at: http://www.leopold.iastate.edu.

Pirog, R. and B. Andrew. *Checking the Food Odometer: Comparing Food Miles for Local versus Conventional Produce Sales to Iowa Institutions*. Ames, IA: Iowa State University, Leopold Center for Sustainable Agriculture, 2003. Available online at: http://www.leopold.iastate.edu.

Oberholtzer, L., C. Dimitri, and C. Greene. *Price Premiums Hold on as Organic Produce Market Expands*. Outlook Report VGS-308-01. Washington, DC: U.S. Department of Agriculture, Economic Research Service, 2005.

Organic Trade Association (OTA). *The Past, Present and Future of the Organic Industry: A Retrospective of the First 20 Years, A Look at the Current State of the Organic Industry, And Forecasting the Next 20 Years*, 2005. Available online at: http://www.ota.com/pics/documents/Forecasting2005.pdf.

Sooby, J. *State of the States: Organic Farming Systems Research at Land Grant Institutions 2001-2003*, 2nd edition. Santa Cruz, CA: Organic Farming Research Foundation, 2003. Report available online at: http://ofrf.org/publications/sos.html.

Thilmany, D. *Integrating Organics into CSREES and Broader USDA Programs: Organizational and Leadership Alternatives*. White paper for the USDA-CSREES (Spring), 2006. Available online at: http://dare.agsci.colostate.edu/csuagecon/extension/docs/agbusmarketing/abmr06-01.pdf .

U.S. Department of Agriculture, Economic Research Service. "Organic Agriculture: Consumer Demand Continues To Expand," 2007. Available online at: http://www.ers.usda.gov/Briefing/Organic/Demand.htm#farmmarketdemand. Updated: August 22, 2007.

U.S. Department of Agriculture, Economic Research Service. Various Figures, Tables and Data downloaded from the Organic Agriculture Briefing Room, 2008. Available online at: http://www.ers.usda.gov/Briefing/Organic. Accessed January 2008.

U.S. Department of Agriculture, Foreign Agricultural Service. *U.S. Market Profile for Organic Food Products*, 2005. Available online at: http://www.fas.usda.gov/agx/organics/USMarketProfileOrganicFoodFeb2005.pdf.

U.S. Department of Agriculture, Study Team on Organic Farming. *Report and Recommendations on Organic Farming*. Washington, DC: U.S. Department of Agriculture, Study Team on Organic Farming, 1980. A copy of this report is available for free from the Alternative Farming Systems Information Center. Send an e-mail to afsic@nal.usda.gov with the subject line "Publication request-free organic report CD."

Willer, Helga, Minou Yussefi-Menzler, and N. Sorensen, eds. *The World of Organic Agriculture—Statistics and Emerging Trends 2008*. Bonn, Germany and Frick, Switzerland: International Federation of Organic Agriculture Movements and FiBL, 2008

Yuseffi, Minou. "Development and State of Organic Agriculture Worldwide." Pp. 13-20 in *The World of Organic Agriculture—Statistics and Emerging Trends 2004*. Edited by Helga Willer and Minou Yussefi. Bonn, Germany: International Federation of Organic Agriculture Movements, 2004. Available online at: https://www.fibl.org/english/shop/show.php?sprache=EN&art=1298.

Parks

Areas of open space available for public use and enjoyment. Parks come in all shapes and sizes and can be found in the smallest villages or the largest cities. Parks and open space are integral parts of a community and provide opportunities to enjoy the rural outdoors and our natural resources.

Community and Rural Parks

Throughout the history of the United States, parks and recreation lands played an important role in the cultural and social growth of its citizens. From the earliest settlements in the Eastern part of the country there were lands set aside as commons for general public use. The community parks of today evolved from the commons or village square of the past as the concept spread westward.

The village square often was located in the center of a small rural community and was the focal point of social activities. The village bandstand was used not only for band concerts, but was also the platform from which great political and philosophical speeches and debates emanated. Special events, such as ice cream socials, community picnics, family reunions and various contests were held and continue to be held in the village park or square. The business district often grew up around the commons or square, and the communities continued to grow in ever expanding circles around the square. Many larger cities can trace their origins to such a starting point.

Another derivation of this concept was the courthouse square in the county seats of rural America. Many classic architectural masterpieces are preserved throughout the country in the courthouse squares which, in many cases, also functioned as community parks. Many old courthouses ceased to be functional and have been converted into historical museums. Because of this change in usage, the structures and park-

like settings take on a different cultural character, but are still there for public enjoyment.

The community school also was a focal point in rural areas. If enough land is associated with the school to provide facilities such as playgrounds, ball fields, tennis courts, and if there is a gymnasium, the school functions as the community park and recreation center for the rural school district. Small rural communities and the surrounding agricultural area tend to provide park areas and recreation facilities on a less formal basis (i.e., no special park district or village park department). Instead, these communities tend to rely on ad hoc committees and volunteer participation to provide these amenities and activities.

With the demise of rural school systems through consolidation of districts and other mechanisms for efficiency, the older schools and associated land became surplus to the educational needs. However, from the viewpoint of the community and rural areas, the structures and grounds are important elements to sustain a quality of life in these rural settings. Sometimes the buildings or parts of the buildings can be retained for community use, while in other instances the structures are razed and the land retained as a village or township park. Thus, these facilities, paid for by local taxes, continue to benefit the people or their descendants who initially paid for them. It is important for the viability of rural areas and communities to have parks close to residents' homes, in the neighborhood or the township.

In the hierarchy of parks and park systems in the U.S., most lands committed to parks and designated open space are found in rural or remote areas. This article initially focused on the commons or village square because these areas were the basis for the park system concept. They were the precursors of our city, county, regional, state and national park systems. With the exception of the city and urban park systems, all the other systems are located primarily in rural areas. The parks are found in rural areas because they are the primary locations for natural resources and provide the necessary land base.

National Parks

The U.S. has not been very progressive in land use policies, but has originated two land policies of worldwide significance: the creation of a national park system policy and the Tennessee Valley Authority policy. The national park system policy has not only attracted the attention of natural resource leaders throughout the world, but has been copied or adapted in various ways by many foreign countries.

The creation of the national park system came about as the result of the rapid westward expansion of the U.S. after the Civil War. Thoughtful leaders advocated conservation practices to insure the protection of suitable lands and waters for future public enjoyment. The influence of these leaders may have seemed quite small when the store of these natural resources appeared inexhaustible at the time; however, it was far-sighted, to say the least (Wirth, 1980).

Congress acted as early as 1832 to reserve acreage in the Hot Springs, Arkansas, area for public use, but the first area to be designated as a national park was Yellowstone in 1872. This was the first national park in the world, the epitome of park designations. Yellowstone National Park was in the first group of worldwide areas to be designated as World Heritage Areas in 1972, 100 years after its founding.

Until the early 1960s almost all of the areas operated by the National Park Service were in rural areas, readily accessible to rural people. However, the reasons for establishing the national parks and related areas in the system were not compatible with the recreational needs of rural citizens. Although established in mainly rural areas, the primary intent of the national parks was to preserve areas of outstanding scenic beauty and cultural value available to urban and rural, domestic and foreign visitors alike.

County and Metropolitan Park Systems

The success of the national park concept led to establishing county and state park systems throughout the country. The first county park systems to be established included Essex County, New Jersey, in 1895; Milwaukee County, Wisconsin, in 1897; and Nassau County, New York, in 1898. Today there are hundreds of county-level systems around the country with titles such as County Park Department, County Park and Recreation Commission, County Forest Preserve District, County Conservation District, or County Forestry

and Park Department. Whatever the title, they all serve the citizens of a particular county and local visitors by helping meet their park, recreation and open space needs (Weir, 1928).

Most of the county park and open space lands are in rural settings and therefore are readily accessible to rural residents in a county. Rural residents often relate more directly to county park systems. Since these residents are not a part of an incorporated area, they do not find it convenient to use facilities or participate in programs offered by these systems. In some areas, if families are not taxpayers in a particular jurisdiction, they are precluded from participation in recreation activities or must pay a registration premium for participation.

The county park and open space areas in many metropolitan areas that were once in rural settings are now "green oases in the urban desert." These areas can still be used by the rural population, but are not as accessible or inviting as they once were. Many choice county areas with outstanding natural resource attributes have been severely and adversely impacted by an increased use load of a burgeoning and encroaching population around them.

The rapidly expanding metropolitan areas led to the establishment of multi-county or metropolitan park systems around a few major population centers. This concept provides a broader tax base than is possible from a single county and allows the purchase of choice natural resource lands out in the more rural counties where such land is still available. Examples of this type of system are the Huron-Clinton Metro Park System, a six-county system around Detroit, Michigan; the Maryland-National Capital Park and Planning Commission, on the north and west sides of Washington, D.C.; the Oakland Bay Regional Park District, on the east side of San Francisco Bay; and the Hennepin Regional Park System, in the Minneapolis, Minnesota, area. This type of system should be more prevalent in the major metropolitan areas to serve both the rural and urban populations.

State Parks

Another step up the ladder in the hierarchy of park systems is the state park systems. There were a scattering of individual state parks in the 1860s, when California set aside Yosemite as a state park and later transferred it to the U.S. Government as a national park. Examples of other state parks established before 1900 include the Adirondack State Park in New York; Interstate Park, jointly established by Wisconsin and Minnesota; and Mackinac Island State Park, Michigan. All of these early parks were located in very remote rural areas, in some cases almost wilderness, so they were not much more accessible to rural populations than to urban areas.

The state park movement had its greatest boost as a result of the 1908 White House Conference on Conservation called by President Theodore Roosevelt, well known for his interest in conservation of natural resources. This conference led to the creation of formal state park agencies in about one-third of the states over the next 15 years. This growth continued slowly until today, when every state in the country has a state park system. The state parks are unique natural, cultural or historic resources, and are predominantly located in rural settings where these unique sites are found. Therefore, the surrounding rural population has the easiest access to these sites. In some areas the surrounding rural communities benefit substantially from the influx of visitors and the money that visitors are willing to spend in and near the parks.

Forests and Special Use Areas

Other natural resource-based lands, such as county, state, national and industrial forest lands, provide over 300 million acres of land, most of which are open for a wide variety of recreational uses. Many of the outstanding scenic and recreation areas of these forests rival the parks operated by companion park agencies. Rural communities surrounded by public lands depend on sustainable use of these areas to maintain their economies. Recreational uses bring in visitors from urban areas and are an important source of revenues for rural counties. One of the values of this public/private sector partnership is managing the natural resource base to maintain the economic and intrinsic values derived from these resources.

The Greenway Concept provides opportunities to connect rural areas with urban areas. The relatively recent focus on buying up abandoned railroad rights-of-way and converting them to trails of various types provides one of the best examples of connecting rural areas to the urban environment. Linear patterns such as drainways, stream corridors, power line easements, and canals present opportunities to create Greenways that cut across rural-urban imaginary boundaries. Trail systems developed in conjunction with Greenways can connect urban areas through the pastoral rural scene so that recreationists in both areas have mutual enjoyment.

Although financial return is not the basic intent of most trail systems, there can be an economic benefit to people living near a trail. They have the opportunity to provide services to trail users, such as bike, snowmobile or horse rentals, camping, bed and breakfast, food, or other types of supplies. Some rural communities and individuals capitalized on such opportunities and benefited substantially. For example, a 1992 study by the National Park Service and Penn State University, *The Impacts of Rail-Trails*, examined three trails: the Heritage Trail in Iowa, the St. Marks Trail in Florida and the Lafayette Trail in Louisiana. The study found that "use of the sample trails generated significant levels of economic activity...the amount of 'new money' brought into the local trail county was $630,000, $400,000 and $294,000 annually for the respective trails."

All citizens benefit to some degree from the very diverse park systems of the country. All major cities and most smaller communities and villages have parks, if not extensive park systems available to residents. Rural residents can benefit from the various parks and park systems to the same degree, or possibly greater than urban residents because usually they are in closer proximity to the resource-based areas operated by township, county, state and national agencies. These areas have a wide array of facilities and activities readily available to rural citizens.

Therefore, rural residents have the most outstanding natural and cultural resources of the U.S. accessible in every state through the noted governmental agencies. There is no shortage of parks and open space in rural areas in general, although there may be certain locations in this country where parks and open space may still be at a premium. Continued planning to obtain and develop rural park and recreation areas is still badly needed in many areas because land use planning has been tagged with an unfair connotation and felt to be undemocratic. If the parks and recreation needs of rural citizens are to be met in the future there must be better land use planning today.

— *Robert D. Espeseth*

See also
Camps; Development, Community and Economic; Environmental Protection; Land Stewardship; Regional Planning; Tourism, Ecotourism; Wilderness; Wildlife

References
Compton, J.L. 2001. "The impacts of parks on property values." *Parks and Recreation* (May 2001): 90-95.

Lapping, Mark B., Daniels, Thomas L., and Keller, John W. *Rural Planning and Development in the United States.* New York, NY: Guilford Press, 1989.

Machlis, Gary E. and Donald R. Field. *National Parks and Rural Development: Practice and Policy in the United States.* Washington, DC: Island Press, 2000.

Miller, S. *The Economic Benefits of Open Space.* Portland, ME: Maine Coast Heritage, 1992.

National Park Service and Pennsylvania State University. *The Impacts of Rail-Trails: A Study of Users and Nearby Property Owners from Three Trails.* Washington, DC: Government Printing Office, 1992.

National Park Service. *Economic Impacts of Protecting Rivers, Trails and Greenway Corridors.* Washington, DC: Government Printing Office, 1990.

Nicholls, Sarah. "Measuring the impact of parks on property values." *Parks and Recreation* (March 2004): 24-32.

Weir, H. L. *Parks: A Manual of Municipal and County Parks.* New York, NY: A.S. Barnes and Co., 1928.

Wirth, Conrad. *Parks, Politics and People.* Norman, OK: University of Oklahoma Press, 1980.

Pasture

A grazing management unit separated from other units by fencing and devoted to forage production for harvest by grazing animals (Barnes et al., 1995). This article addresses the differences in the two main types of pastures found in America, management inputs required for each, and grazing management systems used in pastures.

Types of Pastures

Pastures are broadly divided into two categories: rangelands and pastureland. Rangelands are lands on which the native vegetation (climax or natural potential) is predominantly grasses, grass-like plants, forbs and shrubs suitable for grazing. Rangelands are the primary land type found in the world and comprise 70 percent of the land surface area of the earth (Holechek et al., 1989). Most rangelands in the U.S. are located west of the Mississippi River and account for 62 percent of the total land area in the U.S.

Most rangelands are unsuitable for cultivation due to their semi-arid nature, excessive relief, and lack of soil fertility. Because of the inability to cultivate rangelands, their primary use is to convert solar energy captured by native plant species into red meat, milk, and fiber via the grazing ruminant.

Immediately west of the Mississippi River, there is adequate precipitation to support the rangeland ecotype classified as tall grass prairie. The predominant forage species are little bluestem, big bluestem, indiangrass and switchgrass. Available moisture declines from east to west and the tall grass prairie gives way to the short grass prairie of the western Great Plains. The predominant forage species of this ecosystem are buffalograss and blue grama, whereas in the intermountain region, wheatgrasses and fescues are prevalent. In arid country typical of west Texas, New Mexico, Arizona and Nevada, or in the intermountain desert country of Utah, various shrubs such as mesquite, sagebrush and junipers predominate. Many of the shrubs are classified as weed species with little value for livestock grazing because of unpalatable compounds or defensive mechanisms such as spines. These same shrubs, however, may play an important role as wildlife food and cover.

Grazing systems commonly used on rangelands include continuous or season-long, deferred-rotation, seasonal-suitability, best-pasture, rest-rotation, high intensity-low frequency, and short-duration (Holechek et al., 1989). Range grasses should be allowed to rest between grazing events. Rest allows plants to mature and build an adequate supply of carbohydrates in root systems for subsequent growth. When plants do not receive adequate rest from grazing events, desirable species decline in number and are replaced sequentially by species of reduced palatability and eventually by weed species with little or no nutritive value for grazing animals. Likewise, adequate stubble height should be maintained so that enough photosynthetic material remains for the plant to carry out basic metabolic life processes. The stubble height required is species dependent.

Prescribed burning and proper grazing management are used to encourage persistence and productivity of desirable forage species. Although there are other interrelated factors, absence of fire combined with overgrazing degraded many rangelands to brush communities with little or no grazing value. Fire is a natural part of the rangeland ecosystem and is a useful management tool to control brush encroachment and release grass species from competition.

When grazing management alone will no longer improve rangeland condition, herbicides are often used to reduce the number of weed species and encourage production of desirable forage species. Proper grazing management and prescribed burning are then used as management tools to extend the treatment life of the herbicide application.

Pasturelands are distinguished from rangelands by the periodic use of agronomic inputs to maintain introduced forage species. These species typically have the potential for increased dry matter production relative to rangeland species, tolerate close or continuous grazing, and respond well to fertilization. Examples of popular introduced species are bermudagrass in the Southern U.S. and tall fescue in the Midwest.

Precipitation

The most limiting factor to forage production is moisture. With the exception of the coastal areas of Washington, Oregon and northern California, most of the annual precipitation occurs east of the Mississippi River in the continental U.S. Long-term annual mean precipitation levels for the Eastern U.S. approach 16 cm, and areas along the Gulf Coast and Atlantic seaboard routinely receive in excess of 20 cm per year (Martin et al., 1976). Not surprisingly, most pastureland is found in areas where precipitation is adequate to support increased levels of forage production. These areas include the Southeastern states from east Texas to the Atlantic seaboard, the Midwest along both sides of the Ohio River, and the Northeast.

Soil Fertility

High levels of precipitation associated with the Eastern U.S. resulted in the formation of acid soils of reduced fertility due to leaching of basic cations from the upper soil horizons. Thus, where most of the pastureland is located, lack of soil fertility, not moisture, is a common limiting factor to forage production. Unlike precipitation, however, this factor is under direct control of the manager.

The first step in amending a deficiency in the soil nutrient status is to obtain a soil analysis. The soil analysis is used to determine levels of nitrogen, phosphorus and potassium in the soil and soil pH (soil acidity). Under certain circumstances, analyses for other micro-nutrients may be required. Written recommendations for the level of each fertilizer nutrient required, based on the yield goal for specific forage crops, are furnished to the producer by the laboratory conducting the analysis.

Nitrogen is an important element required for optimum plant growth and is positively correlated with the crude protein content of the forage. Unfortunately, soil nitrogen is usually very low and generally ranges from 0.03 to 0.4 percent in the top 30 cm of cultivated soils (Tisdale et al., 1985). Industrially supplied sources of nitrogen (e.g., ammonium nitrate, urea ammonium nitrate, ammonium sulfate and urea) are common forms of nitrogen fertilizer used in agriculture.

An alternative method to supply nitrogen is through the use of legumes. Legumes are plants that have a symbiotic relationship with host-specific *Rhizobia* bacteria. In the symbiotic relationship, the legume serves as a host plant for the bacteria, while the bacteria fixes atmospheric nitrogen into a form readily used by the plant. Forage legumes have the ability to provide the equivalent of 56 to 224 kg ha^{-1} of actual nitrogen to other non-nitrogen-fixing plants under good growing conditions, thus reducing the need for nitrogen fertilizer.

Other nutrients such as phosphorus, potassium, sulfur and boron are applied as required based upon the soil test recommendations. Only a soil analysis will provide this critical information.

Acid soils generally do not have direct negative effects on plant growth; however, indirect effects can hamper plant production. Soil nutrients, particularly phosphorus, are most available at near-neutral pH levels. Many producers, therefore, apply crushed limestone to increase soil pH to enhance nutrient availability for optimum forage production.

Recent dramatic increased costs in inorganic fertilizer have prompted many producers to examine alternative forms of fertilizer materials. Where available, poultry litter is a suitable alternative source of fertilizer nutrients for pasture production systems. Many times the litter contains nutrients in nearly a 1:1:1 ($N:P_2O_5:K_2O$) ratio, which over time may lead to a buildup in soil test phosphorus. Thus, soil test values for phosphorus must be monitored closely to ensure that the buildup does not exceed state recommendations.

Additionally, waste water treatment sludge (biosolid) is also utilized as a source of fertilizer nutrients. Unlike broiler litter, the typical analysis of the biosolid is 6 percent N and 3 percent P_2O_5. Additional potassium will likely be required depending on soil test recommendation. Biosolids may receive different class designations depending on whether there are heavy metal or pathogen issues. The best of the biosolids do not have heavy metal or pathogen issues and are completely safe to use in pasture systems. Biosolids, like litter, usually are very competitively priced relative to inorganic fertilizers.

Pasture Use

Forages produced in pastures are used in one of three methods: conserved forage (either hay or silage), green chop, or direct harvest by grazing animals. Regardless of how forage is used, two aspects of forage production remain under direct control of the manager: the fertility program (previously discussed) and the stage of maturity of the forage at harvest.

Forage maturity and nutritive value are inversely correlated; that is, as the forage increases in maturity, the nutritive value declines. Thus, immature plants are highest in both nutritive value and digestibility. Obviously, dry matter production increases with stage of maturity, and a balance between nutritive value and production must be achieved. Harvest schemes for hay, silage or green chop should be timed to obtain an optimum quantity of forage of high nutritive value. Grazing systems should likewise attempt to maintain forage in a relatively immature stage to enhance animal performance.

Hay for livestock is second only to corn as the most important U.S. agronomic crop in many years. Hay is produced on 25 million hay acres and is valued at over $11 billion to U.S. agriculture (Albrecht and Hall, 1995). Species used as hay include alfalfa, timothy, orchardgrass, wheat, oat, rye, annual ryegrass, tall fescue, wheatgrass, bermudagrass, bahiagrass, dallisgrass, sorghum-sudan hybrids, forage legumes and native species.

Silage is another form of conserved forage, but unlike hay, is stored in airtight containers (silos, bunkers, trenches or individual large round bales) at higher moisture levels, generally 65 to 70 percent. The forage undergoes a reduction in pH due to anaerobic bacteria and stabilizes at a pH level between 3.6 to 4.2. Under this acid condition, forage nutritive value remains constant indefinitely. The most common forage utilized as silage is corn, but sorghums, alfalfa, cereal grains and even bermudagrass have been conserved as silage.

Green chop is a system in which forage is harvested mechanically and brought to the livestock for consumption. The use of green chop increases forage harvest efficiency and reduces forage waste. In some cases, despite increased equipment costs, some producers find the use of green chop to be an economically viable use of higher-quality forages.

Grazing Management

The manipulation of the grazing animal by the manager with a defined goal or objective in mind is known as grazing management. Proper grazing management should match forage nutritive value and availability with the nutrient requirements of grazing livestock. In many cases, the only management change required for improved efficiency is to develop a controlled breeding season that matches seasonal forage availability with nutrient requirements of gestating or lactating females or that of growing animals.

There is no single grazing system that will meet the requirements of all producers. Certain parcels of land lend themselves better to one type of grazing system than others. Management philosophies and experience levels of producers will likewise dictate how livestock will be manipulated. Generalized grazing systems that facilitate livestock movement, however, have been developed that enable producers to have improved control over the forage allocation process and are discussed below. A critical point to remember is that grazing systems generally have less impact on animal performance than do stocking rate or soil fertility.

Continuous Stocking

Continuous stocking is popular because it requires the least level of input from the livestock producer and, when moderately stocked, generally results in the highest individual animal performance when compared with rotational stocking systems. Improved individual animal performance associated with continuous stocking is due to increased diet selectivity by the animal. Grazing systems that involve livestock movement between pastures force animals to consume forage that they might not otherwise select and performance may be reduced.

The major disadvantage of continuous stocking relates to the variable growth rate of forages. For example, during early spring, warm-season grasses experience rapid growth rates that necessitate a relatively heavy stocking rate for proper harvest efficiency. Later, during periods of reduced precipitation levels associated with summer, growth rate declines, and a reduction in stocking rate is required. If a variable stocking rate that matches varying forage levels is not used, pastures will either be overstocked or understocked. Overstocking combined with poor soil fertility can result in weed invasion, a reduced carrying capacity of the pasture, and decreased profitability of the enterprise.

Conversely, understocking results in patch (or spot) grazing. Patch grazing occurs when animals repeatedly graze the same area because the immature regrowth is more palatable and of higher nutritive value.

Ungrazed areas increase in maturity, decline in nutritive value, and become increasingly less palatable. The wasted forage reduces the potential profit from the livestock operation.

To optimize forage use under continuous stocking, a variable stocking rate should be used and may be accomplished by adjusting either livestock numbers or pasture size. The use of inexpensive electric fencing allows producers to rapidly adjust pasture size and maintain the proper stocking rate relative to the forage growth rate. Simply opening or closing gates of a multi-paddock operation will accomplish the same result. Excess forage from the portion of the pasture not grazed during the rapid-growth phase should be cut as hay. Cutting excess forage for hay or silage is one of the best methods to incorporate the variable stocking rate pasture management scenario.

One variation of continuous stocking involves installation of a creep gate. With a creep grazing system, younger animals have free access to separate pastures planted to forage species of higher nutritive value, but size of the creep gate opening prevents entry into the pasture by mature animals. Forage species typically used in creep grazing systems include small grains, ryegrass, and clovers for fall and winter grazing. Sorghum-sudan hybrids, pearl millet, annual lespedezas, and cowpeas are used in summer programs.

Rotational Stocking

Rotational stocking requires that a single pasture be subdivided into two or more smaller units, although not necessarily equal in size, and livestock are moved from one paddock to another for short periods of time. The concentration of livestock results in a temporarily overstocked condition and allows for increased forage harvest efficiency.

The optimum time to move livestock from one paddock to another is critical in rotational stocking and requires considerable management expertise. Tenure in a paddock may vary from one to 10 days per paddock depending on climatic conditions and forage growth rate. Rotational stocking systems where livestock are moved on a calendar basis will not achieve optimum animal performance or forage use. Varying forage levels may require producers to skip one or more paddocks in the grazing rotation and harvest skipped units for hay during periods of excess forage production.

Rotational stocking allows for better control of livestock. Potential health problems may be observed at an earlier stage since the producer spends more time

with the livestock. Rotational stocking early in the spring may help to control early weed species.

The primary disadvantage of rotational stocking is reduced individual animal performance because of reduced diet selectivity. Another disadvantage of rotational stocking relates to the expense of additional fence construction, although this may be offset by the use of low-cost electric fencing. Additional water development may be necessary, and labor costs associated with routine movement of livestock are additional considerations.

Some forage species may warrant the use of rotational stocking. For example, weeping lovegrass, if not rotationally stocked, is patch grazed by livestock and quickly becomes excessively mature and unpalatable. Reseeding annual clovers should be rotationally stocked to promote seed production and stand persistence. The use of rotational stocking may also help to maintain the nutritive value of warm-season perennial grasses, thus improving animal performance somewhat. Rotationally stocking cool-season forages may not be as important to the grazing animal, but rest between grazing events may allow for increased dry matter production.

A modification of rotational stocking known as forward creep grazing may enhance growing animal performance. The livestock herd is split into two groups: "first and last" grazers. The first grazers are usually younger animals with a higher nutritive requirement compared with mature animals. The leaders graze a paddock first and obtain forage of the highest nutritive value. When approximately one-third of the forage has been consumed, the first grazers are rotated to a new paddock. The last grazers are then rotated into the paddock just vacated by the first grazers. The last grazers are generally mature animals with lower nutritive requirements.

Strip grazing is another technique that uses two portable fences (typically electric) to allot a small area of pasture for grazing. As with other rotational stocking systems, the temporarily overstocked condition associated with strip grazing results in increased forage harvest efficiency, although animal performance is typically reduced. Strip grazing allows forage to be consumed with a minimum amount of trampling of the remaining forage.

One final grazing system to be considered is limit grazing. With limit grazing, separate pastures are generally planted to annual species of high nutritive value. Livestock are allowed to graze the pastures on a limited basis, either a few hours per day, or a few days per week. This system typically is used during the winter when forage growth is limited. Allowing livestock to have adequate quantities of good hay or dormant standing forage and limited access to pastures planted to cereal grains or ryegrass enables spring-calving brood cows to maintain their body condition at a reduced cost. Fall-born calves experience improved weight gains compared to calves wintered on hay only. Weight gains are achieved at less cost than for cattle wintered on concentrates.

The key to proper grazing management is to think through the process with respect to expectations and the inputs required for each system. The manager should seek an optimum balance between harvest efficiency, resource conservation, individual animal performance, and, most importantly, the economic returns from the totalenterprise. Using either a continuous or rotational stocking system can result in a profitable livestock operation depending on the managerial expertise.

Good management is an essential element of a sound pasture program. Close attention to soil fertility, forage stage of maturity at harvest, and grazing management will enhance the probability for maximum economic return, and thus the sustainability, of the forage production system.

— *Larry A. Redmon*

See also

Agronomy; Biodiversity; Dairy Farming; Livestock Production; Ranching; Regional Diversity; Soil; Specialized Livestock Production; Wool Industry

References

Albrecht, Kenneth A. and Marvin H. Hall. "Hay and Silage Management." Pp. 155 in *Forages. Volume I: An Introduction to Grassland Agriculture.* 5th ed. Edited by Robert F. Barnes, Darrell A. Miller, and C. Jerry Nelson. Ames, IA: Iowa State University Press, 1995.

Heitschmidt, Rodney K. and Jerry W. Stuth, eds. *Grazing Management: An Ecological Perspective.* Portland, OR: Timber Press, Inc., 1991.

Hodgson, John. *Grazing Management Science into Practice.* New York, NY: John Wiley and Sons, Inc., copublished with Longman Scientific and Technical, 1990.

Holechek, Jerry L., Rex D. Pieper, and Carlton H. Herbel. *Range Management: Principles and Practices.* Englewood Cliffs, NJ: Prentice Hall, 1989.

Martin, John H., Warren H. Leonard, and David L. Stamp. *Principles of Field Crop Production.* 3rd ed. New York, NY: Macmillan Publishing Co., Inc., 1976.

Tisdale, Samuel L., Werner L. Nelson, and James D. Beaton. *Soil Fertility and Fertilizers.* 4th ed. New York, NY: Macmillan Publishing Co., Inc., 1985.

U.S. Department Of Agriculture. *Agricultural Statistics.* Washington, DC: US Government Printing Office, 1993.

Permaculture

The combination of permanent agriculture and permanent culture as defined by the Australian, Bill Mollison (1990) and colleagues. This article describes the design of perennial agricultural systems, with focus on their structure and function, using natural systems as a guide to understanding complex plant interactions and complementarities, as well as the human designs of sustainable and productive plant and animal systems in addition to cultures.

Permaculture: Systems That Mimic Nature

A popular conception of permaculture is the planting of perennial species along with some annuals in special designs that mimic natural systems and provide a permanent agriculture. Although this is the basis for planting tree and crop species plus integrating animals into the system, the proponents of permaculture see the concept as far broader. Their vision is to extend the idea of diversity and permanence in agriculture to creating a durable and sustainable society (Mollison, 1990). Here are the principles, as summarized by Holmgren (2002), a long-time collaborator with Mollison:

- Observe and interact, recognizing designs and learning through experience in the field.
- Catch and store energy, including water, solar gain, carbon, and soil organic matter.
- Obtain crop yields, through conversion of energy and materials, and measure extraction.
- Recognize self-regulation and feedback, to achieve resilience and self-reliance in systems.
- Use renewable resources and services, to design and maintain sustainable productivity.
- Produce no waste, recycle all materials and energy back into production and environment.
- Design from patterns toward details, from society and landscape down to ecosystems.
- Integrate components, recognize multiple functions, and build cooperation.

- Use small and slow solutions, with optimum scale and efficiency of perennials.
- Value, conserve, and apply diversity to balance production with sustainability.
- Create edges and work at the margins of systems, with maximum biological activity.
- Build creative response to change, with flexibility in biological, economic, social succession.

Anyone reading this list is immediately impressed by the lack of any formula or menu for farming, nor for design of the agricultural landscape. Rather, the permaculture concept provides a series of guidelines for first envisioning and then implementing systems that will prove appropriate to a given location and set of environmental conditions. Those systems will take into account the topography, the soils and annual rainfall and its distribution, the temperature patterns through the year, and the types of perennial and annual crops as well as the animal species that are adapted to that place. Beyond the biological potentials and characteristics of the environment, systems must reflect the philosophy and goals of the land managers who live there, the natural and economic resources available, and the long-term sustainability of the system to succeed based on contemporary resources. All of this management must take place within the context of a human activity system that has certain goals of producing crops and animals, preserving a livable environment, and not exhausting non-renewable natural resources. It will be helpful to describe examples of how permaculture leads to design of specific agroecosystems.

Structural Design of Permaculture Systems
The principal challenge in the structural design of permaculture systems is to utilize the physical properties of the land, while closely mimicking the patterns and functions of natural ecosystems. The rationale is that these ecosystems have evolved in certain conditions to optimize survival of the majority of their component species. Bill Mollison provides a number of applications of the major principles listed above to consider when designing a permaculture system; unless otherwise cited, the ideas here are from his primary text (Mollison, 1990).

Working with nature rather than against it may seem like common sense, but it has become increasingly uncommon in modern agriculture. The current trend in our industrial agriculture is to create biotechnology that will allow us to defy or dominate nature, and to simplify management by homogenizing the production environment and making fields ever larger for mechanical efficiency. Another unusual strategy is recognizing that encountering a problem may actually be the solution, once that problem is adequately defined and understood. According to the proponents of permaculture, problems only arise when we refuse to work with nature. For example, a problematic land situation becomes an asset if this is seen as an opportunity to include new species in the system that utilize the given resources.

Another important concept is to make as little change as possible in the natural system that will still allow managers to meet their goals. This further emphasizes the importance of working with nature. If one assumes that the greatest possible effect is the greatest possible yield, then it would require a close relationship with nature to achieve this without heavy reliance on external inputs. When considering the greatest possible yield, it is interesting that Mollison considers system yield to be theoretically unlimited. He maintains that the yield of the system is only limited by the imagination of the designer. A permaculture system may not match the conventional monoculture system in yield of grain, but depending on imagination the permaculture system may yield byproducts that would otherwise be squandered in a conventional system. Overall, Mollison emphasizes the utilization of the physical landscape and its diversity of ecological niches in order to create a greater potential for total sustainable yield of the entire system.

Once the landscape and its resources have been considered, the permaculture system is divided into several zones. At the core of the system is the family house, the core of labor, energy and maintenance (Nugent and Boniface, 2004). Permaculture promotes smaller operations that require close stewardship of the land, which is something modern agricultural systems cannot achieve due to their large size and industrial management style. System zoning begins with the house as zone zero and moves outward. Zone one is generally reserved for the permaculture garden including horticultural crops that require frequent attention. The next zones are for animals that need daily attention or cereals and intercrops with products that are harvested frequently. The zone farthest from the house is then reserved for trees, which serve several purposes such as wood, fruits, and nuts. These trees can be used as a windbreak and may also provide shade from the sun as it moves through the day and defines and main-

Bioswales are important components of permaculture systems. Photograph by Courtney Taylor.

tains the different zones in the system. The zones established in permaculture systems are much different from the zones of conventional agricultural systems. Quarter sections and county roads often define rectangular fields, but the local landscape and microclimate are far more complex, and permaculture recognizes this (Bell, 2004). The utilization of zones and respect for the unique characteristics of the land are essential to any permaculture system.

Close relationship with the land allows for informed decisions on which plant species to include in the system. There are many species that can occupy almost any set of conditions in a system, including alkaline-tolerant plants, salt-tolerant plants, and water-tolerant plants (Nugent and Boniface 2004). It is not uncommon for farmers to repeatedly plant the same plant species on areas of their land with salty soils or areas that frequently flood. In a permaculture system, this is seen as a potential waste of resources and an effort to defy nature. When a close relationship with the land is

established and so-called problem or unique areas are identified, there are many alternative plant species to choose that will yield some type of benefit to the larger system. There may not be an economic market for a mature salt-tolerant plant species or its byproducts, but if chosen well that species may provide benefits to the whole system in terms of beneficial insect habitat, wildlife habitat and overall biodiversity. Structural design of a permaculture system promotes efficient use of the land and its resources that lead to a functionally productive agroecosystem.

Function of Permaculture Systems

Proper function of permaculture systems is rooted in diversity. However, just any collection of randomly assorted plants and animals does not guarantee a functionally diverse agroecosystem. The permaculture system must be designed so that the diversity of species utilizes beneficial relationships within the system. If these beneficial relationships are ignored, the result is a potentially diverse, but chaotic ecosystem with minimal resource use efficiency (Whitefield 2004). Mollison states as a principle of ecosystem stability that the simple number of species in a mixture in the design does not necessarily provide stability, but rather it is the complementarity of the elements and their positive or beneficial interactions that contribute to agroecosystem function and stability. When an efficient link is made in a permaculture system, the output of one species becomes the input for another species. The greater the number of beneficial links in the system, the more independent it becomes of external inputs. Many species, such as walnut trees, provide multiple benefits to the system in the form of nuts, timber, and effect on microclimate through windbreak and shading capacities (Whitefield 2004). These types of multiple use species are ideal for permaculture systems.

The permaculture system will function to maximize resource uses within the system as is found in natural ecosystems. Diversity of species in the system maximizes resource use efficiency because each species will contribute unique nutrient, water and light demands to the system, thus maximizing light in each dimension of the canopy as well as nutrients and water in each soil horizon. Monoculture systems waste resources as they only fill one ecological niche. Including a large diversity of species in the system also minimizes risk to the farmer. For example, if one resource such as water is in excess or becomes limiting it may ruin an entire season in a monoculture system. This is unlikely in a permaculture system, because while some plant species may suffer, others will flourish and the whole system will still produce substantial yields. Diversity provides stability and resilience in permaculture agroecosystems, while monoculture systems rely on heavy external inputs to provide minimal levels of stability and resilience.

When selecting functional species for the permaculture system, it is important to search for species complementation and to reduce interspecific competition. It is important to discover the right level of competition in the agroecosystem by maximizing the number of plant species that compete efficiently for the same resources and convert them to a useful product. It is useful to select species for the permaculture system that will not unduly compete spatially or temporally for essential resources. This can be achieved by selecting and combining multiple species with different root morphologies or time of emergence and maturation (Francis 1986).

Similar to the design, the function of species in a permaculture system is dependent on the local environment. While diversity is essential, a given species will not fully benefit the total system productivity and sustainability if its demands are not provided for by local environmental resources. Like natural ecosystems, a permaculture system may require establishment through the use of pioneer species. Pioneers are generally short-lived, nitrogen-fixing and fast-growing species that will eventually be outcompeted by primary species, but the pioneers provide a good growing environment by shading out grasses and providing nutrient-rich mulch for subsequent crops (Nugent and Boniface 2004). Overall, species diversity provides ecosystem stability, succession and resource use efficiency that will yield high levels of net productivity desired in functional permaculture systems.

Environmental Impacts of Permaculture Production Systems

It is apparent from this discussion that permaculture systems properly designed for a given niche or location will use resources efficiently, maximize production, and balance useful product with what remains to sustain the system. A key factor is the combination of multiple species with different plant morphology, different cycles of growth and reproduction, and different nutrient use patterns. A well-designed system will intercept sunlight, absorb water and nutrients, and continue primary productivity through as much of the year as possible. Because there are roots at different strata in the soil, a permanent mulch of leaves and crop debris on the soil surface, and multiple layers of leaves in the canopy above, the impact of heavy rain is attenuated and the energy is dispersed, allowing most or all of the precipitation to infiltrate to the root zone and below, and there is little or no erosion. Most permaculture systems are designed to work without chemical pesticides and with minimal added chemical fertilizers, making these environmentally sound systems that do not leak undesirable chemical residues into waterways or the soil profile. Well-designed systems may be among the most environmentally friendly of all agroecosystems, compared only with permanent pastures and silvo-pastoral systems.

Economics and Future Applications of Permaculture

It is both different and difficult to assess the economic viability of permaculture systems, because unlike monocultures of annual plants all of the benefits are not observed or measured in single seasons and such rewards as improved soil quality may not be manifested in crop or tree performance for many years. In addition, there are multiple ecosystem services provided by permanent plantings that are not recognized or rewarded in our current short-term economic system that only pays for immediate crop yields. It is important in evaluating the economics of permaculture to be sure that all benefits are adequately accounted for, that intangible outputs and those difficult to measure are recognized, and that systems are sought that will take into account both short-term returns as well as long-term benefits to the farm manager and family as well as to society.

The long-term potentials for permaculture systems will depend on a number of factors, including the amount of research and promotion that is done, the progress that can be made in further design and adoption of systems, and the recognition of the multiple outputs or services that the systems provide. This will require a broader appreciation of ecosystem services, beyond the current payments for carbon sequestration, and their entry into the marketplace. Such a change will not occur without a broader appreciation of the role of rural landscapes in cleaning water and air, dispersing the power of strong winds and rain storms, holding back water to prevent flooding, and other mitigating functions that often are not understood by society. When these functions are taken into account, measured, and rewarded locally or through federal programs, there will be more encouragement financially for farmers to explore the application of permaculture principles and the planning and planting of more diverse mixtures of species in carefully designed systems that are appropriate to each set of conditions. It is only through such a process that permaculture, perennial systems are likely to become more a part of the agricultural landscape.

— *Charles Francis and Sam Wortman*

See also

Agriculture, Alternative; Sustainable Agriculture; Agroecology; Conservation, Soil; Conservation, Water; Environmental Sustainability; Wildlife Value Orientations

References

Bell, G. *The Permaculture Way: Practical Steps to Create a Self-Sustaining World.* East Meon, UK. Permanent Publications, 2004.

Francis, C.A. *Multiple Cropping Systems.* New York: Macmillan Publishing Company, 1986.

Holmgren, D. *Permaculture: Principles and Pathways beyond Sustainability.* Victoria, Australia: Holmgren Design Services, 2002.

Mollison, B.C. *Permaculture: a Practical Guide for a Sustainable Future.* Washington, DC: Island Press, 1990.

Nugent, J. and J. Boniface. *Permaculture Plants: a Selection.* Hampshire, UK: Permanent Publications, 2004.

Whitefield, P. *The Earth Care Manual: a Permaculture Handbook for Britain and Other Temperate Climates.* Portsmouth, UK: Permanent Publications, 2004.

Pest Management

An ecological approach to insect control. Although dictionaries define pests as "any destructive insect," the term pest has no ecological validity. Any organism that competes with humans for available resources of food and fiber is both destructive and pestiferous. Thus, weeds, fungi, microorganisms, rodents and birds can also be categorized as pests. Insects and related arthropods, however, comprise more than three-quarters of all animal species and are by far the most numerous of pest species. The concept of pest management was first developed as an ecological approach to insect control. This will be the frame of reference in this article, although the principles emphasized can be applied equally well to other pest organisms.

Integrated Pest Management

Pest management is philosophically similar to the more familiar concepts of forest, game and fisheries management, and is an effort to optimize pest control tactics in an ecological and environmentally sound manner. Integrated pest management (IPM) has been variously defined as: 1) a system where all available techniques are evaluated and consolidated into a unified program to regulate pest populations so that economic damage is avoided and environmental disturbances are minimized, and 2) intelligent selection and integration of pest control actions that ensure favorable economic, ecological and sociological consequences.

IPM has three primary goals. The first goal is to determine how the life system of the pest needs to be modified to reduce its numbers to tolerable levels, that is, below the economic threshold. The second goal is to apply biological knowledge and current technology to achieve the desired modification, or applied ecology. The third goal is to devise pest control procedures compatible with economic and environmental quality constraints, or economic and social acceptance (Metcalf and Luckmann, 1994). Thus, IPM procedures rely on protection and conservation of natural enemies: parasites, predators and diseases that regulate the biological balance of pest populations. IPM rejects the regular or preventive use of broad spectrum insecticides and the general philosophy of species eradication, which generally is unworkable.

The establishment of IPM programs is based on identifying the pests to be managed in the agroecosystem, defining the economic injury level as that pest population density which causes enough injury to justify the cost of treatment, and establishing the economic threshold as that pest damage where control measures should be applied to prevent an increasing pest population from attaining the economic injury level.

Although the IPM philosophy is equally applicable to vast agricultural operations or to the home garden, and the insect pests that are economically important may be the same for each crop, the methods of pest control that are optimal in the home garden are often impractical for the commercial grower. There are important differences in the cosmetic requirements for production of fresh fruits and vegetables from those of the cannery industry. In general, labor-intensive procedures such as hand worming and picking of pests that are highly useful in small-scale production are completely impractical for production of row crops or in commercial fruit orchards.

Components of Pest Management Programs

IPM is a system to minimize pest damage through a combination of compatible tactics that make life difficult for the pest and that are economically, environmentally and socially acceptable. Although it is the pest that is to be managed, pest management is people-oriented. As long as the pest manager accepts the ecologically oriented philosophy of IPM, many old practices of pest control are acceptable components of pest management systems. Doing nothing is a valid IPM alternative, as time often will restore ecological balance between the pest and its environment.

There are several widely used insect control components that almost invariably form the framework for successful IPM programs. These should be considered in the order presented to develop a successful program.

Ecosystem Planning. The most appropriate way to avoid major insect pest control problems is through careful choice of the crops to be planted and of the genetic varieties to be produced. To grow highly suscepti-

ble plant species having major insect enemies, one must be prepared for the annual battle with pests and for the necessity of frequent use of insecticides. Examples include home growing of cabbage, cauliflower, broccoli and eggplant; growing apples and peaches; and landscaping with white birch, honey locust and sycamore. The tactic of cultivar choice is an especially important one for the arborist, landscaper or house gardener who is often not equipped philosophically or strategically for cosmetically unsightly or unpalatable pest damage. Often the most appropriate answer is to plant only species of garden plants, shrubs and trees that are of high tolerance.

Plant species can be systematically rated for susceptibility to insect pest damage according to the following five categories: 1) are practically immune; 2) have few and minor problems; 3) have a single important pest; 4) have a devastating enemy; and 5) have several important pests (see Table). In general, for the home garden, it is prudent to consider cultivating plants at the top of the line. These ratings apply to insect and mite problems encountered in the Midwest. Other factors such as aesthetics, taste, food quality, and susceptibility to climate and plant diseases must also guide the choice. A large number of vegetables belonging to categories 1 and 2 can be grown without problems from insect pests and diseases. Troubles can be expected with the higher categories 3, 4, and 5 (Metcalf et al., 1994).

Resistant Varieties. For most commercially grown crops, specific varietal cultivars differ considerably in their degree of susceptibility to attack by insect pests and plant diseases. This tactic of host plant resistance is a basic component of IPM, and the commercial planting of resistant varieties is of major importance to suppress insect pests such as those of corn (corn earworm and European corn borer), sorghum (chinch bug), barley (greenbug), wheat (Hessian fly and wheat stem sawfly), alfalfa (spotted alfalfa aphid), and cotton (lygus bug). There is a continuing struggle between plant breeders developing such resistant varieties and insect pests evolving resistant biotypes to overcome the varietal resistances. New techniques of transgenic biology are already producing new varietal cultivars incorporating major host-resistant factors, and these may become important in IPM programs. However, the struggle between plants and pests will always represent a series of genetic accommodations leading to both new and superior cultivars and more vigorous insect pests.

Susceptibility of Selected Plants to Insect Pest Damage

Plant Type	Insect Pest Damage Categories				
	(1) Practically immune	2 Few, minor problems	3 Single important pest	4 A devastating enemy	5 Several important pests
Vegetables	beets, chard, Chinese cabbage, lettuce, radishes, peas	mustard, spinach, sweet potatoes	asparagus, corn (early), onion, tomatoes	beans, broccoli, cauliflower, cucumbers, eggplant, squash	cabbage, corn (late), melons, potatoes
Fruits	strawberries	blackberries, cherries, raspberries	apricots, currants, grapes, plums	nectarines, pears, quince	apples, peaches
Shade trees	sweet gum, tree of heaven	burr oak, gingko, Norway maple, Oriental plane, scarlet, red, and white oak, sugar maple, tulip tree	American plane, Blue ash, Chinese elm, hickory, mountain ash, red maple, spruce, white pine	box elder, buckeye, catalpa, European linden, hackberry, honey locust, horse chestnut, Scotch pine, walnut, willow	American and European elm, black ash, black locust, cottonwood, green ash, Lombardy poplar, Scotch elm, silver maple, white birch

Source: Metcalf et al., 1994.

Biological Control. The greatest single factor in keeping plant-feeding insects from overwhelming the rest of the world is that they are fed upon by other insects (Metcalf and Metcalf, 1993). Such entomophagous insects are considered in two groups: predators that catch and devour smaller or more helpless creatures, and parasites (sometimes called parasitoids) that live in or on the bodies of other animals, the hosts.

The science of biological control is little more than 100 years old, dating from the successful importation in 1888 of the Australian lady bird beetle, *Rodolia cardinalis,* to control the cottony cushion scale, *Iceya purchasi,* that was destroying California citrus groves. Recent estimates indicate that at least 70 species of important insect pests of the U.S. are partially or completely controlled by establishment and manipulation of parasites and predators.

There are several categories of biological control that are important to agriculture. First, classical biological control involves the importation and establishment of foreign natural enemies to control exotic pests which they preyed upon in the original area of endemicity. Second, augmentation of natural enemies involves efforts to increase populations of parasites and predators through periodic releases into the environment of the pest. Third, conservation of natural enemies involves efforts to preserve and maintain existing populations of natural enemies through altering pesticide use patterns or changing crop management practices. Biological control is totally compatible with the use of resistant crop varieties and the two tactics, which are relatively inexpensive and have high benefit/risk ratios, serve as the foundations of modern IPM.

Chemical Control. The use of insecticides has been the major tactic for insect pest control for well over 100 years. Insecticides are the only tool for IPM that is reliable for emergency action when pest populations approach or exceed the economic threshold. "Chemical pesticides will continue to be one of the most dependable weapons of the entomologist for the foreseeable future…. There are many pest problems for which the use of chemicals provide the only acceptable solution. Contrary to the thinking of some people, the use of pesticides is not an ecological sin. Their use is indispensable to modern society" (National Academy of Sciences, 1969). However, much of the use of insecticides has been ecologically unsound and their misuse, overuse, and injudicious use have been the major factors in the growth of interest in IPM. The IPM concept seeks to maximize the advantage of their use and to minimize the disadvantages.

As a general principle, the use of insecticides in IPM should be as a means of last resort when other carefully planned control measures failed and emergency intervention is necessary. This use should be thoroughly integrated into the IPM program by choosing an insecticide least likely to seriously damage beneficial insects, to pose unacceptable health hazards to the user and the consumer of treated produce, and to adversely affect environmental quality. Another important factor to be considered is the effect of the insecticide application in the presence of insect pest populations that are genetically resistant to one or more of the major classes of insecticides, i.e., organochlorines, organophosphates, carbamates and pyrethroids.

Ready-to-use (RTU) insecticide products that are formulated in both pressurized and pump dispensers provide a very appropriate way to deal with thousands of relatively minor insect pest problems. These RTU formulations are precisely prepared as to components and concentrations of active ingredients that provide insecticidal efficiency against specific groups of pests of home and garden, greenhouses, warehouses, markets, restaurants, animal quarters, and institutions. Thus, the IPM practitioner must be particularly knowledgeable about insecticide management, which is a recognized component of integrated pest management (see Metcalf and Luckmann, 1994).

Insecticides composed of microbial toxins (e.g., *Bacillus thuringiensis* or Bt) and viruses that are almost totally specifically toxic to small groups of insect pests are a rapidly growing addition to the armamentarium of the pest management specialist. Their use is compatible with all other IPM tactics.

Practical Pest Management

To practice IPM on any scale, whether as a home gardener, family farmer, commercial grower or IPM specialist in agribusiness, it is necessary to proceed through a series of common steps. These differ only in the way the required information is obtained and in the complexity and sophistication of the specific procedures employed.

Potential Pest Problems. The crop being raised has its specific set of potential pests; infestations by each of these results in characteristic crop damage and in predictable crop loss. The required information to address these is obtainable from reference books in local libraries or bookstores, through county extension agents and in experiment station bulletins and circulars, or by consulting a professional entomologist or IPM specialist. There are advantages to becoming an IPM expert, so one should be aware of what to look for in anticipating the initial indications of pest problems and the methodology to deal with it.

Scouting. Individual gardeners should check their plants for the presence of damaged leaves and fruits, and of insect eggs, larvae and adults as they work in the garden or admire the plants. When dealing with larger plots or fields, subsampling of discrete areas on a quantitative basis (e.g., so many insects per leaf, fruit, plant or foot of row) will be necessary to relate pest populations to their economic thresholds. The use of other quantitative sampling methods, such as the sweep net or with sticky traps baited by volatile lures, is most useful in orchards and row crops. In large com-

mercial operations, employment of professional scouts is an important part of IPM.

Management Decisions. The economic injury level (EIL) for each specific crop is the key to implementing IPM decisions. The EIL is defined as that pest population where damage is tolerable and above which economic loss occurs. The action threshold for pest control interventions is the economic threshold (ET) that is the pest density at which control measures should be applied to prevent an increasing pest population from reaching the EIL.

For practical use there are four categories of economic threshold. First, non-thresholds are where the pest population is always greater than the EIL, as is typical in vegetable and fruit crops where a premium is paid for cosmetic appearance, or where applied control is used as a form of crop production insurance. Second, nominal thresholds are where the exact relationships between pest injury and crop damage are undetermined so that EIL values can only be approximated based on experiment station and producer experience. This is the present situation on the majority of small vegetable and fruit crops. Third, simple thresholds are where ET values are calculated from EIL values based on long-term study of generalized insect injury and crop response. These values represent the best current practices for commercial insect control on important crops. And fourth, comprehensive thresholds are where ET values are computed from EILs developed for major crops after extensive research relating pest injury, crop phenology and economics.

Many factors and attitudes also affect individual grower decisions about the level of damage or crop loss that growers are willing to accept. The garden hobbyist is unwilling to accept the slightest trace of insect injury to prized blossoms or fruits. On the other hand, the organic farmer often accepts damage that would make produce unmarketable in normal channels. The pest losses incurred can be partially offset by the organic premium that some consumers will pay to avoid residues of chemical insecticides on edible produce.

Treatment Decisions. Control interventions are needed only when the scouting data indicate that the population of the pest exceeds the ET. At this point, the grower must optimize the type of treatment based on personal experience, extension service recommendations, prevailing market prices and resources available. Each individual manager must make this decision based on personal philosophy, economics and environmental impacts. From these factors, appropriate treat-

This mechanical sprayer dusts vines with fungicide at the Buena Vista Winery in Sonoma, California. In addition to pest control, the sprayer also fertilizes and waters the grapevines. © *Bettmann / Corbis*

ment interventions will be selected from an array of pest management tools. Rescue treatments with chemical or microbial insecticides provide the only certain remedy when the economic threshold is breached, and will be employed mostly as the last resort.

These decisions and the control actions that follow comprise integrated pest management, and although the process may seem complex, there is an immense amount of relevant information available from state and federal experiment stations and extension services (see Flint and Van den Bosch, 1981; Davidson and Lyon, 1987; Pedigo, 2001; Olkowski et al., 1991; Metcalf and Metcalf, 1993). Practicing IPM specialists are available to provide the expert knowledge required and to assume the responsibilities for applied control.

Tools of Pest Management. The specific ways in which pests can be abated, controlled and managed are outlined as follows, but limitations of space preclude their specific discussion. Consult the references cited for additional information. First, cultural methods in-clude agronomic practices such as use of resistant crop varieties, crop rotations, crop refuse destruction, soil tillage, variations in timing of planting and harvest, and pruning and thinning. Second, mechanical methods involve hand destruction, exclusion by screens or barriers, and trapping and collecting. Third, physical methods make use of heat, cold and radiant energy. Fourth, biological methods include protection and encouragement of natural enemies, introduction and artificial increase of specific parasites and predators, and propagation and dissemination of insect diseases. Fifth, chemical methods make use of attractants, repellents and insecticides. Sixth, genetic methods involve propagation and release of sterile or genetically incompatible pests and genetically engineered crop plants. Finally, regulatory methods involve plant and animal quarantines, eradication and suppression programs.

Combining these tools into a set of tactics for IPM that are applicable for one's pest control problem, commensurate with the scope of one's operation, feasible with the means at one's disposal, and in accord with one's philosophy is what pest management is all about.

— *Robert L. Metcalf and Lesley Deem-Dickson*

See also

Agrichemical Use; Agriculture, Alternative; Biodiversity; Cropping Systems

References

Davidson, Ralph H. and William F. Lyon. *Insect Pests of Farm, Garden, and Orchard.* 8th ed. New York, NY: Wiley, 1987.

Flint, M.L. and R. Van den Bosch. *Introduction to Integrated Pest Management.* New York, NY: Plenum Press, 1981.

Metcalf, Robert L. and Robert A. Metcalf. *Destructive and Useful Insects: Their Habits and Control.* 5th ed. New York, NY: McGraw-Hill, 1993.

Metcalf, Robert L. and William H. Luckman. *Introduction to Insect Pest Management.* 3rd ed. New York, NY: Wiley, 1994.

Metcalf, Robert L., B.M. Francis, D.C. Fischer, and R.M. Kelly. *Integrated Pest Management for the Home and Garden.* 3rd ed. Urbana-Champaign, IL: Institute for Environmental Studies, University of Illinois, 1994.

Norris, Robert F. Edward P. Caswell-Chen, Marcos Kogan. *Concepts in Integrated Pest Management.* Upper Saddle River, NJ: Prentice Hall, 2002.

Olkowski, William, Sheila Daar and Helga Olkowski. *Common-sense Pest Control.* Newton, CT: Tauton, 1991.

Pedigo, Larry P. *Entomology and Pest Management,* 4th ed. New York, NY: Macmillan, 2001.

Pedigo, Larry P. and Marlin E. Rice. *Entomology and Pest Management,* 5th ed. Upper Saddle River, NJ: Prentice Hall, 2005.

Petroleum Oil Industry

The economic system that produces, refines, markets and transports petroleum products. This article provides a brief overview of the petroleum industry and reviews available data on oil activity in the U.S. The economic impact of the industry on local areas is reviewed including boom-bust cycles that strained some oil-dependent regions. Finally, environmental considerations related to the oil industry are discussed.

Overview

The petroleum industry played a central role in the development and evolution of many rural areas in America. Resource extraction is usually located in rural areas, thus extraction often provides jobs and income for the local economies of these areas. The structure of the petroleum industry includes four components: production, refining, marketing, and transportation. Production involves the location and extraction of oil and natural gas from underground reservoirs. Refining involves the manufacturing of finished products (e.g., gasoline and jet fuel) from the crude oil. Marketing includes the distribution of finished products to consumers including both wholesale and retail efforts. Finally, transportation includes the pipelines, tankers, barges, and trucks that move crude oil to refineries and on to markets. Production activities have been tied most closely to rural areas but the other components of the industry also impact many rural areas. See Measday and Martin (1986) for an overview of the evolution of the petroleum industry including a history of the world market and key corporate and governmental players.

The U.S. petroleum industry provided $219 billion in annual shipments and employed about 101,000 people in 2001 (Energy Information Administration). The industry has been impacted significantly by world wide political changes and volatile oil prices. The U.S. does represent about 29 percent of global production with 150 operating refineries according to Energy Information Administration statistics. Positive factors influencing the domestic oil industry include advances in technology (e.g., drilling), strong industry survivors, and more effective firms operating at lower costs. U.S. industry policy will play a key role in future developments in the industry. Võ (1994) examined the global oil industry and U.S. relations with the international community. Võ indicated future relations would be complex and unpredictable given the political complications of past years. What an understatement that turned out to be. The war in Iraq and other world-wide events have had impacts felt around the world. In 2004 there was a surge in oil demand that drained excess capacity (IPAA 2005-2006). Fears about future energy security and China's surging oil demand led to rising oil prices. Rural areas dependent upon the oil industry are impacted directly as the domestic petroleum industry is affected.

Data on Oil Activity in the U.S.

Oil production is concentrated geographically in specific states and regions throughout the country. Data published by the Independent Petroleum Association of America (IPAA 2005-2006) presents a useful picture of petroleum oil activities. State rankings for crude oil production are provided and the top ten states are: Federal off shore, Texas, Alaska, California, Louisiana, New Mexico, Oklahoma, Wyoming, Kansas, and North Dakota. These states tend to be located in the Southwest and the West. Other states also are impacted by crude oil production and data for each state are included. Natural gas production is somewhat similar with the following ten states being ranked highest: Texas, Texas, Federal off shore, Oklahoma, New Mexico, Wyoming, Louisiana, Colorado, Alaska, Kansas, and California. The IPAA publication provides historical data (production, imports, supply, demand, reserves, and price) in addition to the state rankings. Each state is profiled including wells drilled and production, and a list of petroleum associations and state agency contacts is provided.

Economic Impact on Local Areas

Oil extraction played a key role in the economy of many regions. Oil extraction is one of the natural resource based activities that helped to shape rural America. Castle, et al. (1988) reviewed the performance of natural resource industries (forestry, energy, mining, and fishing) and the resulting impacts on rural America. The key factor identified is instability, and currently these areas are adjusting to decline, lower incomes, and higher unemployment. As natural resource based industries downsize, the impacts are relatively greater in nonmetropolitan areas where a larger contribution to employment in natural resources is observed.

Regional impact patterns exist both for oil extraction and natural resource activities. Most areas specializing in energy extraction are the coal or natural gas producing areas of the Rocky Mountains, the oil producing areas of Texas, Oklahoma, and the Gulf Coast, and the coal fields of Southern Illinois, Kentucky, and the Appalachian Mountains. The more remote the location of these resources, the greater the impact of resource extraction. This is because these remote economies tend to be highly dependent on extractive activities with few economic alternatives. According to Castle, et al. (1988), major influences that impact resource-dependent economies are international events (e.g., Middle Eastern politics and the price of oil), environmental policies (the Clean Air Act and resulting impacts on production), and industry structure (deregulation of the natural gas industry and large oil firms). These macro issues and trends ultimately impact the local economies where oil extraction and other natural resource based activity occur.

Energy development had significant impacts on regions in the western U.S. Murdock and Leistritz (1979) reviewed the impacts of activity with oil, natural gas, oil shale, coal, and uranium. Many of these resources are indirectly related to oil; oil shale and coal are alternatives to petroleum and mining of these products results from high oil prices. Murdock and Leistritz presented an overview of energy technology and energy needs, a thorough literature review, and the effects of energy development on agriculture and local business. They discussed policies to provide impact information and deal with appropriate growth management options. They identified housing and community facility needs as results of economic development and resource extraction in many Western regions.

Oil extraction activities also have indirect impacts. Platt and Platt (1989) noted that service industries often are linked to the oil and natural gas production industries. Whereas production is sensitive to general economic condition, the service industries are most sensitive to growth or decline in oil production, which demonstrates the linkages other sectors of the economy have to oil extraction.

Natural resource extraction often causes gains and losses not evenly distributed to all groups. Oil and natural gas extraction often occurs in remote areas with an indigenous population. McNabb (1990) noted how the off-shore oil and gas activities in Alaska impacted the native Eskimo population. The Eskimo population depends on fishing harvests that are negatively impacted by oil exploration. The alternatives for the native population are few, and lower living standards result. McNabb argues that whereas Alaska is a major exporter of oil, the Eskimo population benefits little.

Boom and Bust Cycles

With each oil price cycle or industry restructuring, the changes have caused a boom and bust cycle for communities dependent upon petroleum for economic well being. Rising prices bring growth and increased economic activity. Often this growth is faster than local infrastructure can support. Frequently, there have been shortages of housing, retail services, and other goods as economic booms occur in communities and regions with petroleum resources during times of rising oil prices. Investments in public and private infrastructure are made to respond to the rapid rise in demand. Eventually, oil prices decline and excess capacity exists in the community. Morse (1986) reviews the history of the oil market and the resulting boom-bust cycles. He notes this cycle impacts the industry itself, the end users of oil, and the macro economy of the world. Detomasi and Gartrell (1984) edit a text that contains eleven papers surveying the state of the art in research regarding specific problems faced by resource communities. Issues related to community services, housing, impact on income distribution, and impact on indigenous people are reviewed. Models and methods of analysis to better understand and predict impacts are reviewed and evaluated.

Leistritz and Murdock (1981) examined alternative methods to model the economic, demographic, public service, and fiscal impacts of major resource development projects. Projects other than oil and gas are included as examples of projects, but the approach and methodology are similar. They reviewed each component of impact analysis (economic, demographic, public services, fiscal, social) and discussed how to interface these components through computerized models. Since each component is related and linked, this is a critical concept. For example, new jobs in the economic sector often bring new people and create new demands for public services such as schools and health care. Tax revenues often are not collected in the appropriate jurisdiction or during the right time period to pay for needed services. These types of impacts often occur during the boom or rapid growth periods of resource extraction communities.

Brabant (1983) explored the ways in which communities respond to needs for basic services. The impact of resource extraction varies across time, space, and type of impact. There is a strong need for development planning and community organization. Community leaders need to anticipate the changes that will occur as the community experiences the boom-bust cycle.

Specific examples of the local impact of petroleum boom-bust cycles are presented by Harrop (1990) regarding the Anadarko Basin in Oklahoma. Prior to 1980, oil was $15 per barrel; it rose to $35 per barrel in 1980-1981, but fell back to $15 by 1986. During that time period, population almost doubled for some cities and counties in Western Oklahoma. Following the bust in the late 1980s, there were tremendous levels of excess capacity in commercial and industrial properties. The boom of 1980 made the front page of the *Wall Street Journal* where shortages of housing and strained infrastructure were noted (Padilla 1982). The real estate market was reported to be thriving although one local leader interviewed noted that any potential crash would not be a pleasant fall.

Boyd (2005) describes the history and recent events related to oil production in Oklahoma. The oil industry experienced large increases in prices from 1973 to 1979. This was the beginning of the oil boom. Prices then began to decrease after the boom. From 2000-2005, the state average per barrel of oil was around $30. This number has since increased. In 2005, prices were anticipated to stay well above $30 a barrel. This is due to a decline in production. Also, new discoveries of oil have not replaced what has already been produced. China and India are also demanding larger amounts of oil. A disruption in Venezuela, Nigeria, Russia, and the Middle East can increase the price of oil.

Along with the importance of oil to Oklahoma's economy, natural gas is just as if not more important to the Oklahoman economy. The geology of Oklahoma is more inclined for gas production. The oil industry is expected to remain volatile in the future.

Environment and Oil

Conflicts between production, economic growth, and environmental protection have become an important factor (Gilbert 1993). Oil is used primarily as a transportation fuel, and the U.S. continues to rely on the automobile with little potential shown for mass transit. Due to concern with air pollution, emissions, and rising gasoline fees or emission taxes there is strong incentive to identify alternatives to oil. If shifts in demand occur, rural areas dependent on oil extraction will be impacted. However, Gilbert noted that most environmental impacts occur during transportation of crude oil to refineries.

The Exxon Valdez oil spill is a notable example of an environmental impact occurring during transportation of crude oil. This oil spill greatly impacted communities of Southcentral Alaska. In 1989, the Valdez super-tanker was involved in an oil spill off Alaska's Prince William Sound, and the results devastated wildlife (Cohen 1993). The long-term damage to the local resource base was significant. Concern with environmental accidents and laws like the Clean Air Act of 1990 will encourage increased reliance on alternative fuels (Kezar 1994-1995). Alternative fuel options, such as natural gas, will possibly cost more. Environmental concerns must be balanced with economic efficiency to determine the most effective choices.

Natural gas has been called an under-utilized energy and chemical feedstock (Hall, Hay, and Vergara 1990). The base or supply of natural gas is abundant.

Obstacles to using this resource include a lack of knowledge about gas valuation and pricing. Specific uses for natural gas include power for transportation and the production of fertilizer. Hall, et al. describes the historical development of the natural gas industry.

Finley (1993) assessed the U.S. natural gas resource base and concluded it was an abundant, moderately priced resource. Natural gas may serve as a bridge alternative to coal and oil. This will depend on a viable producing industry and efficient delivery system. Natural gas plays an important role in many rural areas; it serves as a power source for irrigation systems operating in the Great Plains. Large geographic areas converted from dry land farming to irrigated farming, thus increasing output and income levels. Barkley (1988) noted that deregulation of the natural gas industry impacts rural areas. The average price of natural gas went down but became more volatile. This instability may create changes in farming patterns, which will ultimately impact the economies of towns in the Plains region.

Oil and the petroleum industry played a central role in many rural locales' economies. The nature of the industry led to boom-bust cycles that impacted rural areas where oil is produced. Predicting the magnitude of these impacts and identifying appropriate planning responses is a critical component of rural development efforts. The future impact of oil will depend on worldwide consumption, market trends, and environmental considerations.

— *Mike D. Woods*

See also

Conservation, Energy; Development, Community and Economic; Employment; Environmental Protection; Impact Assessment; Income; Mining Industry; Natural Resource Economics

References:

Barkley, Paul W. "The Effects of Deregulation on Rural Communities." *American Journal of Agricultural Economics* (December 1988): 1,091-1,096.

Boyd, D.T. Oklahoma Oil and Gas Production: Its Components and Long-Term Outlook, *Oklahoma Geology Notes* 65, no. 1 (2005): 4-23.

Brabant, Sarah. "From Boom to Bust: Community Response to Basic Human Needs." *Journal of Applied Sociology* 10 (1993): 23-47.

Castle, Emery N., Ann L. Shriver, and Bruce A. Weber. "Performance of Natural Resource Industries." Pp. 103—133 in *Rural Economic Development in the 1980's*. Washington, DC: U.S. Department of Agriculture, 1988.

Cohen, Maurie J. "Economic Impact of an Environmental Accident: A Time-Series Analysis of the Exxon Valdez Oil Spill in South Central Alaska." *Sociology Spectrum* 13 (1993): 35-63.

Detomasi, Don D. and John W. Gartrell, eds. *Resource Communities: A Decade of Disruption*. Boulder, CO: Westview Press, 1984.

Energy Information Administration, Office of Industrial Technologies. "Petroleum Industrial Technologies. Petroleum Industry Analysis Brief." February 2004. Available online at: http://www.eia.doe.gov/emeu/mecs/iab98/petroleum/profile.htm.

Finley, Robert J. "A Positive Assessment of the U.S. Natural Gas Resource Base." Pp. 1—7 in *The Role of Natural Gas in Environmental Policy*. Austin, TX: Bureau of Business Research, University of Texas, 1993.

Gilbert, Richard, J., ed. *The Environment of Oil*. Norwell, MA: Kluwer Academic Publishers, 1993.

Hall, Carl W., Nelson E. Hay, and Walter Vergara. *Natural Gas: Its Role and Potential in Economic Development*. Boulder, CO: Westview Press, 1990.

Harrop, Paul S. "The Life and Death of an Oil Field Boom Town: An Appraisal Profile of Elk City, Oklahoma." *The Real Estate Appraiser and Analyst* (Spring, 1990): 4-10.

Independent Petroleum Association of America. "The Oil and Natural Gas Producing Industry in Your State, 2005-2006." Available online at: http://www.ipaa.org/reports/econreports/IPAAopi.pdf.

Kezar, Michelle L. "New Law, New Fuels." *Cross Sections* 11, no. 4 (Winter 1994-1995): 1-5.

Leistritz, F. Larry and Steven H. Murdock. *The Socioeconomic Impact of Resource Development: Methods for Assessment*. Boulder, CO: Westview Press, 1981.

McNabb, Steven. "Impacts of Federal Policy Decisions on Alaska Natives." *Journal of Ethnic Studies* 18, no. 1 (1990): 111-126.

Measday, Walter S. and Stephen Martin. "The Petroleum Industry." Pp. 38-73 in *The Structure of American Industry*. Edited by Walter Adams. New York, NY: MacMillan, 1986.

Morse, Edward. "After the Fall: The Politics of Oil." *Foreign Affairs* (Spring 1986): 792-811.

Murdock, Steve H. and F. Larry Leistritz. *Energy Development in the Western United States: Impact on Rural Areas*. New York, NY: Praeger Publishers, 1979.

Padilla, Maria. "Oklahoma's Oil and Gas Boom Brings Cash, People, Problems." *The Wall Street Journal* (March 16, 1982): 1.

Platt, Harlan and Marjorie Platt. "Failure in the Oil Patch: An Examination of the Production and Oil Field Services Industries." *The Energy Journal* 10, no. 3 (July 1989): 35-49.

Võ, Hân Xuân. *Oil, the Persian Gulf States, and the United States*. Westport, CT: Praeger, 1994.

Plant Diseases

Like humans and animals, all species of plants are subject to disease. Diseases that affect plants can be grouped into one of two categories: abiotic (noninfectious) or biotic (infectious). Abiotic diseases are caused by non-living factors such as adverse weather conditions, nutrient imbalances or chemical toxicities in the soil, or air pollution. Biotic diseases are caused by living organisms, usually microbes, which establish a parasitic relationship with a plant. These microbes, whether fungal, bacterial, viral or animal, are commonly called pathogens.

Plant Pathology and Its Beginning

Plant pathology studies the interaction between plants and pathogens, the development of disease (epidemiology) and the influence of environmental factors on disease incidence. It encompasses basic biology as well as applied agricultural sciences. Plant pathology involves the study of plants and pathogens at the genetic, biochemical, physiological, cellular, population and community levels. The knowledge derived from these studies is then integrated into agricultural practice.

Scientists who study plant pathogens and plant diseases are called plant pathologists. Plant diseases were observed and questioned during the domestication of plants. The discipline of plant pathology arose during the nineteenth century after a scientific approach was used to investigate the cause of a catastrophic disorder of potatoes that today is know as late blight. This disorder directly led to the Irish Potato Famine of the 1840s. Early plant pathologists were often medical doctors that took an interest in the health of plants. Plant pathologists of the time were guided by accounts of disease epidemics and famine recorded by the early Greeks, Romans, Egyptians and ancient scripture. Since that time plant pathology has evolved with the general advancement of science. Although plant pathology has its beginnings in botany, it additionally requires knowledge in chemistry, physics, genetics and meteorology, to name a few. By applying knowledge from many scientific disciplines, plant pathologists strive to understand and ameliorate the threat of pathogens of plants to the quantity, quality and security of our food supply. Although the national food supply has always been a concern to the federal government, the events of September 11, 2001, have heightened concern on this topic. Several plant pathogens are now covered by the Homeland Security Act because of the potential threat of agroterrorism.

The discipline of plant pathology has made monumental contributions to the knowledge of crop production and crop health that are essential to meet the future demands and challenges of rural America and world agriculture. Agriculture is vital to the future of America and must remain intensive and productive, but do so in a manner that will enhance its economical, environmental and social appeal. Through education, research and extension, plant pathologists contribute to the future of agricultural science and its application toward improved and sustainable agricultural production systems. The Morrill Land Grant Act of 1862 (Experiment Station research) and the Smith-Lever Act of 1914 (Cooperative Extension Service) paved the way for public universities to have a significant role in the advancement of agriculture in the United States. Plant pathology has been a vital part of each Act since its conception. In addition, the United States Department of Agriculture (USDA) employs scientists in many areas of study including plant pathology. The combined effect of both Acts of the U.S. Congress provided a structured system for university faculty to engage in scientific discovery and information transfer to farmers and other members of the agribusiness community. Furthermore, plant pathologists are employed by commercial seed and agricultural chemical companies.

Diseases of Historic Importance

Similar to the black plague of fourteenth century, the influenza pandemic of 1918, and the AIDS pandemic of today, plant diseases had and continue to have a significant impact on society, politics and economics. The Irish Potato Famine of the mid-1800s is one such example. The oomycete pathogen *Phytophthora infestans* thrived during a time when environmental conditions favored disease development and political issues made the potato the main food staple of the Irish. The famine resulted in the deaths of over a million people and the emigration of more than 1.5 million to the United States.

The southern corn leaf blight (SCLB) epidemic, which occurred throughout the central United States from 1970 to 1972, was the result of a new strain of the fungal pathogen *Cochliobolus heterostrophus*, favorable environmental conditions, and the uniform planting of susceptible corn hybrids containing the Texas male-sterile cytoplasma. Before 1970, SCLB was a disease of minor importance causing less than 1 percent yield loss in the southern regions of the Corn Belt. In 1970, the combination of an aggressive strain of the fungus and

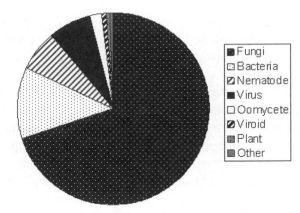

Figure 1. *Graphic representation of the number of each pathogen type causing disease in plants.*

susceptible hybrids resulted in the loss of 710 million bushels of corn, equaling $1 billion. Grain reserves in the U.S. eased the impact of this loss on food supplies, but the epidemic illustrated the need to enhance the genetic diversity of agricultural crops. Today, pathogens like *Ralstonia solanacearum* race 3 biovar 2, a causal agent of bacterial wilt, and *Xanthomonas oryzae* pv. *oryzicola*, the causal agent of bacterial leaf streak of rice, are listed as select agents by the USDA because of their potential threat to food safety.

Types of Pathogens

Pathogens of plants can be found in all kingdoms of life. They can be fungal, bacterial, animal and even plant. Similar to medical science, determining the type of pathogen responsible for the disease is critical to its management. Pathogen type is generally determined by the symptoms they cause or signs (the visible structures of the pathogen) they produce.

Fungi comprise the majority of plant pathogens (Figure 1) and are the causal agents for economically significant diseases like Dutch elm disease, southern corn leaf blight, Asian soybean rust and white mold. Fungal plant pathogens are divided into three groups: the deuteromyces (asexual fungi), the ascomycetes (sac fungi), and the basidiomycetes (rusts and smuts). Signs indicating a fungal pathogen include mycelium (a mass of thread-like strands), spores (reproductive structures analogous to seeds), and fruiting bodies (structures that house spores i.e., mushrooms).

Though fungal-like in appearance, members of the kingdom Chromista are more closely related to plants than to fungi. Plant pathogenic members of this kingdom are classified as oomycetes and include those pathogens responsible for late blight of potatoes, damping-off and root rots, and downy mildew of grapes.

Signs for diseases caused by oomycetes are similar to those observed for true fungi.

Bacterial plant pathogens, like all bacteria, are single-celled organisms that lack a true nucleus (prokaryotic). Bacteria are responsible for diseases like Steward's wilt of corn, fire blight of apple and pears, and soft rot of potatoes. Plant pathogenic bacteria can be classified as gram negative or gram positive, based on the chemical composition of their cell walls or as mollicutes (wall-less). Bacterial oozing and streaming of cells are two signs indicative of a bacterial pathogen. Oozing is usually seen around wounds, exuding from surface tissues like the skin of apples, or as sticky strands between two pieces of cut tissue. Bacterial streaming is observed when diseased tissue is cut and placed into water. A cloudy stream, composed of millions of bacteria, can then be observed coming from the cut end.

Insects and nematodes are both animal plant pathogens. Insects are often vectors (an organism that can carry a pathogen and introduce it into a plant) but can also cause damage on their own (i.e., thrips). Insects, however, are studied predominately by entomologists. Nematodes are one of the most abundant organisms on earth. They are microscopic, non-segmented worms capable of living in soil or water and under the most extreme environmental conditions. Many nematodes are beneficial to the health of the environment. However, plant pathogenic nematodes are responsible for some of the most economically significant diseases. The soybean cyst nematode, for example, is the most yield-limiting disease of soybean, costing American farmers an estimated $1.5 billion annually. Observable signs of nematode infection are galls and cysts. Plant galls, which occur from infection by the root-knot nematode, are cellular outgrowths that result in swelling or knotting of the roots. Cysts, which can be found protruding from the surface of roots, are the dead bodies of female cyst nematodes like soybean cyst or potato cyst nematode.

Although it is debated whether or not they are living or non-living, it cannot be debated that viruses and viroids are both pathogens of plants. Viruses are classified by the type of nucleic acid they contain (DNA or RNA), which is covered by a protein coat. Viroids, however, consist solely of RNA and do not have a protein coat. These pathogens have only been discovered within the last century, yet several important plant diseases such as potato spindle tuber, tomato spotted wilt, and barley yellow dwarf are known to be caused by viruses and viroids. Unlike other pathogens of plants, there are no signs of virus or viroid infection that can be observed without the aid of a microscope. Inclusion bodies, or crystalline clusters of virus particles, can be seen with a light microscope and can be diagnostic of the infecting virus.

Plants themselves can also take on a parasitic habit. These parasitic plant species are those that must rely on another plant for nutritional needs. There are several thousand parasitic plants distributed among several plant families. All parasitic plants lack roots and possess haustoria, which are specialized feeding structures allowing them to obtain nutrients from other plants. Two common parasitic plants are mistletoe, a hemiparasite that requires water and minerals from its host plant but is capable of photosynthesis, and dodder, a holoparasite that requires water, minerals and photosynthates from its host.

Symptoms of Diseases and Effect on Productivity and Quality

Diagnosis of a plant disease and the causal pathogen starts with characterizing the symptoms of the disease. Symptoms are changes in the external or internal tissues that result from pathogen infection. They can be localized (occurring in a small area) or systemic (occurring throughout the plant). Symptoms can also be described as necrotic (death or discoloration of tissues), hypertrophic (overdevelopment/accelerated growth), or hypotrophic (underdevelopment/halted growth).

Though plant pathologists use these symptoms to diagnose a disease and to recommend management strategies to the grower, they also indicate yield loss, reduced storage time, a change in end use, or an unmarketable product. For example, lesions on the surface of an apple from an infection by *Venturia inequalis*, the pathogen that causes apple scab, could force growers to sell their crops to a juicing company for a lower cost rather than sell them as fresh market. Potatoes latently infected by the late blight pathogen, *Phytophthora infestans*, can become focal points for infection of healthy tubers, leading to rot in storage.

Plant diseases can also lead to further economic loss beyond the sale of a crop. Infection by toxin-producing pathogens, like *Fusarium graminearum*, the causal pathogen of Fusarium head blight of wheat, can result in abortions, vomiting or death of livestock fed the infected grains.

Table 1.
Common symptoms of plant disease.

Symptom	Description	Disease Example
Blasting	Failure to set seed or fruit	Blast of oats
Blight	General, rapid death of tissues	Late blight of potatoes
Canker	Dead, sunken tissue on stems, branches, or twigs	Citrus bacterial canker
Chlorosis	Yellowing	Barley yellow dwarf
Damping-off	Decay of seedlings	Pythium damping-off
Dieback	Death of tissues starting at the tips	Diplodia tip blight of pines
Flagging	Wilt occurring on one side	Fusarium wilt of tomatoes
Galls/Knots	Swelling of root or stem tissue	Bacterial crown gall
Leaf retention	Incomplete abscission of leaves	Brown stem rot
Lesion	Localized area of dead tissue	Early blight of tomato
Mosaic	Patchy areas of yellow and green	Alfalfa mosaic virus
Mottle	Patchy areas of light and dark green	Bean pod mottle virus
Rot (Dry)	A dry, crumbling decay of tissues	Fusarium dry rot of potatoes
Rot (Soft)	A slimy decay of tissues	Soft rot of potatoes
Rugosity	Small, irregular bumps in leaf tissue	Soybean mosaic virus
Streak	Elongated areas of chlorosis or necrosis	Wheat streak mosaic virus
Stunting	Reduced size or vigor	Soybean cyst nematode
Water-soaking	Wet, sunken areas that appear translucent	Common blight of beans
Wilt	Drooping of tissues due to water loss	Steward's wilt of corn
Witches-brooming	Massed proliferation of stems or roots	Aster yellows

Management of Diseases

The goal of plant disease management is to keep disease below an economic threshold. This is the level where the cost of controlling the disease equals the market value of the crop. However, the acceptable amount of damage can vary by disease and by crop. A grower may be more inclined to aggressively control Apergillus ear and kernel rot than northern corn leaf blight (*Exserohilum turcicum*), which does not affect the edible part of the plant.

By understanding the aspects of the disease triangle, pathologists can develop and implement effective disease management strategies. The disease triangle, an essential tool for plant pathologists, allows them to visualize the interactions among plant, pathogen and the environment that lead to disease (Figure 2).

In plant pathology, methods for controlling plant diseases can be broadly grouped into one of six categories, **Resistance**, **Eradication**, **Protection**, **Exclusion**,

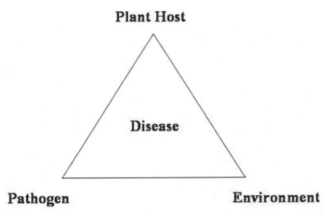

Figure 2. *The disease triangle.*

Avoidance and Treatment (**REPEAT**). Resistance involves the selection of varieties within a plant species that can prevent the pathogen from infecting or prevent disease from developing. Red Delicious apples, for example, are resistant to the disease fire blight, while the apple variety Gala is susceptible. Eradication methods attempt to remove or destroy diseased plants or a pathogen from a given geographical area. These methods rarely eliminate a pathogen or a disease from an area but can effectively reduce disease potential. Protection methods utilize cultural practices and protective pesticides to protect a susceptible plant from pathogen infection. Exclusion methods attempt to prevent introduction of a pathogen into a given area and include quarantine and certified seed programs. Avoidance methods are designed to keep a susceptible plant away from a pathogen or disease environment. Treatment methods are intended to reduce disease damage to already infected plants. In contrast to human and animal medicine, chemical treatments seldom effectively cure a plant infected by a pathogen.

Cultural practices, chemical controls, biological controls and plant resistance are the weapons available to combat plant disease. However, there is no "silver bullet," and sustainable disease management requires a multi-tactic approach. Integrated Pest Management (IPM) is a disease control strategy that coordinates the management of pathogens, weeds and insects while maintaining profitability and minimizing risks to the environment.

Biotechnology and Plant Diseases

Technical advances in United States agriculture, as with genetically modified organisms (GMOs), have provided growers with alternatives to pesticides. Two well-established examples are crops with herbicide and insecti-

cide resistance. Resistance to the herbicide glyphosate in corn and soybeans has made production of these crops more convenient, simpler and safer. Resistance to insects found in BT (*Bacillus thuringiensis* toxin) producing crops provides similar benefits.

Today, there is only one example of a commercially available crop genetically engineered to express genes for resistance to pathogen infection or disease development. As early as the 1980s, Hawaiian papaya plantations have gradually increased the planting of GMO papaya, which has saved the industry from devastation by the papaya ringspot virus. In the future, as consumer acceptance of GMOs increases and technology continues to improve the efficacy, stability and potential environmental effects of GMOs, it is likely that biotechnology will provide more options for managing pathogens and diseases of plants.

— *Teresa J. Hughes and Craig R. Grau*

See also

Biotechnology; Corn Industry; Cropping Systems; Genetically Modified Organisms; Grain Farming; Horticulture; Organic Farming; Temperate Fruit Industry; Vegetable Industry; Wheat Industry

References

Agrios, George N. *Plant Pathology*, 5th ed. Burlington, MA: Academic Press, 2004.

The American Phytopathological Society website, www.apsnet.org.

Holiday, Paul. *Dictionary of Plant Pathology*, 2nd ed. New York: Cambridge University Press, 1998.

Marra, Michelle C., Nicholas E. Piggott, and Gerald A. Carlson. *The net benefits, including convenience, of Roundup Ready® soybeans: Results from a national survey*. NSF Center for IPM Technical Bulletin 2004-3. Raleigh, NC: NSF Center for Integrated Pest Management., 2004.

Schumann, Gail. and Cleora J. D'Arcy. *Essential Plant Pathology*. St. Paul, MN: American Phytopathological Society, 2006.

Shurtleff, Malcolm C. and Charles W. Averre III. *Glossary of Plant Pathological Terms*. St. Paul, MN: American Phytopathological Society. 1997.

Plantations

Large areas of land on which a dominant set of crops is grown under a hierarchical social structure. The common meaning of the word *plantation* arose during the

Men with hoes on a plantation. Boyd-Walters Collection, courtesy of Delta State University, Cleveland, MS.

European colonization period in the tropics and subtropics of the New World. Plantations were self-sustained communities where political and economic institutions were monopolized by the authority of the planter. This organizational structure became prevalent in the American Old South, where the plantation was often the center of commercial and social life. In this part of the country, the plantation has been one of the main history-making entities. The ideals of this system were incorporated into the dominant agents of social control at the time, such as the family, church, school, state and the system of racial subjugation through slavery. Today, the term *plantation* is used in reference to a wide variety of agricultural and forestry systems. This article reviews the social history of plantations, with particular emphasis on the social structure of plantation systems.

Brief History

Plantations did not come into widespread existence in what was to become the U.S. until the 1600s. By this time Spain and Portugal had established large plantations in Central and South America, and these systems were used as models by the English in the newly developed colonies. The tobacco trade is considered by many historians to have built the foundation of the Southern planter. While tobacco farms were widespread throughout the states of the Southeast, Virginia was the most successful in farming tobacco. The Carolina area became a large producer of rice, and Georgia

planters farmed indigo. In time, the strongest Southern crop associated with the plantation system was to become cotton.

The true planters in the U.S. were the plantation owners. A person had to own at least 20 slaves to be considered a true planter, and very few of the planters had plantations this large. In fact, it is estimated that as the Civil War approached, only one in 500 planters owned a plantation with more than 100 slaves (Stone, 1993). Planters occupied the top of the hierarchy, followed by overseers who managed field operations, and then there were indentured servants, slaves or other laborers (Trotter, 2001).

Plantations were not unique to the U.S.; they developed in other parts of the world as well. Plantations were prevalent in Barbados, Jamaica and Brazil, among many other places. Slave labor was also used in these areas, where sugar became the staple crop. The plantation system largely shaped future underdevelopment in these areas as well as in the United States (Beckford, 1999).

Plantations and Place

By the 1720s, the agricultural economy experienced significant growth with the formation of cotton and sugar cane plantations, which subsequently fueled enormous increases in wealth in the plantation regions. With this wealth came the determination of each plantation owner to construct immaculate mansions. When possible, plantation mansions, with their long-sloped roofs and hand-carved colonnades, faced the waterways, which were crucial to the success of the plantations because they provided the basis of transport for commodities produced on the plantations. With westward expansion, the waterway that was increasingly in view from plantations was the Mississippi River.

The number of labor-intensive plantations in the U.S. abruptly declined following the abolition of slavery, causing many of the existing large-scale plantations to be broken into smaller farms operated by individual owners. Some plantations, however, did continue to operate and even prosper, using wage-laborers and then tenants or sharecroppers instead of slaves. During the Civil War years, many grand plantation homes were destroyed or simply deteriorated. Some of these mansions were restored during Reconstruction; others have been restored in recent decades.

One of the greatest misconceptions regarding plantations in the U.S. is that there were a large number of them. This misconception was most common about the Old South. In fact, during the days before the Civil War the typical Southerner rarely visited a plantation, much less owned one. Only a small proportion of people enjoyed the lifestyle of a plantation owner. Still, given elite power and their scale, plantations occupied a central force in the economy and social control of labor.

The Structure of Work on Plantations

Behind the facades of the elegant mansions and beneath the superstructure were the indentured servants, slaves, and later tenants/sharecroppers (for a critical account, see Genovese, 1974). Life on the plantation was a struggle both spiritually and physically. Indentured servants provided the main source of labor on many plantations up through much of the 1600s. Poor Europeans who wanted to go to the colonies received passage if they agreed to become a servant for a specified number of years to pay their transportation debt. Criminals were also sent to the colonies and, in most cases, were forced to be servants. Some Europeans were even kidnapped and taken to the colonies as servants. Indentured servants were often, but not always, treated harshly, and usually were not granted freedom until after their contracted time was completed.

Beginning in the 1500s, Spain and Portugal led in the slave trade and development of plantation systems for sugar production. The Dutch soon followed as their major competitor in the slave trade. African life in British-controlled North America is often traced to the early 1600s. Africans primarily occupied a position of subordination with Whites as indentured servants. Over time, through the overlapping inequality of servitude and race, Blacks were to be defined as slaves for life, starting with Virginia and Maryland in the 1660s. With an active international slave trade, they were brought to White America in chains and forced to live under a system of oppression. This behavior by White America is often referred to as one of history's greatest crimes.

Slaves were forced to make a livable world for themselves and their children while enduring the harshest of conditions. Travelers to the South created a popular image of the living quarters of slaves as that of a one-room log cabin, commonly housing more than six slaves. Although there was some stability in the life of slave families, most families experienced disorganization and instability. Slave families who experienced a relatively cohesive life were those who worked on large plantations.

Plantation owners, especially those with larger plantations, paid special attention to the physical condition of their slaves. Many looked upon their slaves as they did their livestock, breeding them thoughtfully and selectively. Plantation owners allowed their physically superior male slaves to move freely among their female slaves, thus, providing larger and healthier children for future field hands.

On the more aristocratic plantations, masters instilled a pride of caste among their house servants, creating a sharp social line between the slaves of the Big House and those of the quarters. The Big House referred to the living quarters of the planter on a plantation. Historical records show that the idea of the Big House reaffirmed the image of the master/planter as being a very powerful and wealthy figure. For example, a cook in the Big House may not let her child play with the children of the field slaves. This expression of contempt for field slaves was an attempt by the house servants to raise their own image in society. Although the effort was at the expense of other slaves, it narrowed the distance between White and Black (Genovese, 1974).

Post-Civil War, control over labor switched from slavery to sharecropping, tenant farming, and the crop-lien system as planters attempted to keep plantations in production (Fite, 1984). Responding to Blacks' new freedom, another set of social control mechanisms, the Black Codes, were used to control labor. This mechanism created a dual legal system in the South, pitting Blacks and Whites against each other. The tension between races stemmed from Blacks being forced to work for low wages with limited mobility because of their skin color. Poor Whites were denied jobs because planters felt justified to pay Black workers less than White workers. This post-Civil War racial divide continues to maintain tension in race relations throughout much of the Southern region.

With mechanization of plantation agriculture, especially during the post-World War II years, and as cotton prices began to fall, other crops, including soybeans and catfish, began to replace it. In places such as Sunflower and Humphrey Counties, Mississippi, catfish became an important product. Although catfish farming brought millions of dollars to the Delta in the 1990s, much of the profit went to the largest of White landowners and supervisors, epitomizing how catfish farming strengthened the plantation mentality in the Delta (Schweid, 1991).

Plantations in the Modern World

Plantations exist in our modern world both domestically and internationally at the intersection of traditional and new economic interests in agriculture. These plantations produce agricultural and other goods, with ownership and control arrangements including family, company, tenant/sharecropper and state enterprises (Beckford, 1999). Still, they all share a hierarchical social structure.

Other plantations supply historical landmarks for tourists interested in rural heritage. These plantations can be visited, and although their romantic charm is easily embraced, historic and present-day labor-controlling systems perpetuate the Old South's paternalistic mentality of the plantation system. Tourists continue to be drawn from around the world to the plantations and mansions. Many states restored mansions and plantations, which are now open to the public. The Waverly Plantation is a favorite in Columbus, Mississippi; Franklin, Tennessee, is home to the Carnton House; the Astabula Plantation is in Pendleton, South Carolina; and the John Dickinson Mansion is in Dover, Delaware. The South has many plantations, mansions, and other historic sites that give visitors a glimpse of what used to be.

Plantations in rural America played an important part in shaping the nation. Although many overlook their historical importance, one must only refer to the colonial, Antebellum, Reconstruction, and Great Depression eras to witness their impact. Mansions and Southern belles are depicted in the romance of the plantation era, but slavery and its defenders will always be remembered for making the plantation an unjust system.

— *John J. Green and Terri L. Earnest*

See also
African Americans; Agriculture, Structure of; Architecture; Culture; Forestry Industry; History, Rural; Inequality; Land Ownership; Social Class

References
Beckford, George L. *Persistent Poverty: Underdevelopment in Plantation Economies of the Third World*, Second Edition. Kingston, Jamaica: The University of the West Indies Press, 1999.

Fite, Gilbert C. *Cotton Fields No More: Southern Agriculture 1865-1980*. Lexington, Kentucky: The University Press of Kentucky, 1984.

Genovese, Eugene D. *Roll Jordan Roll: The World the Slaves Made*. New York, NY: Vintage Books, 1974.

Schweid, Richard. "Down on the Farm." *Southern Exposure* Fall (1991): 15-21.

Stone, Lynn. *Old America Plantations*. Vero Beach, FL: Rourke Publishing, Inc, 1993.

Trotter, Joe William, Jr. *The African American Experience*. Boston, MA: Houghton Mifflin Company, 2001.

Policing

That component of the law enforcement community which serves and protects the rural regions and small towns which dot the national landscape. Commonly, this refers to the policing of sparsely populated counties and also those towns with 2,500 or fewer residents. The purpose of this chapter is to review five important aspects of small-town and rural police: 1) their scope of responsibilities, 2) police-community relations, 3) distinct aspects of stress among rural police, 4) budgetary constraints and challenges, and 5) educational and training issues. Unlike many other research reviews, this discussion highlights the conditions and challenges of rural policing.

Introduction

Sociological and criminological research focuses disproportionately on policing in urban areas, with the result that important issues in rural policing largely remain a noticeable gap in our police research inventory. This is in spite of the fact that rural America is an important segment of our country; i.e., it includes more than 80 percent of the national land and houses 67.5 million (21.9 percent) of our citizens. (U.S. Census Bureau, 2006). Furthermore, extant research on police departments documents that of over 17,800 agencies studied across the country, 9,001 (50.4 percent) employ fewer than 10 sworn officers with an additional 6,517 of these (36.5 percent) characterized by a range of 10 through 49 licensed officers (Reaves, 2007). When researchers do study rural police departments and their personnel, there exists a tendency to generate comparative rural-urban profiles which, in effect, reinforces the salience of urban organizations, their challenges, conditions and constraints. This imbalance neglects vital needs of rural police departments (Cebulak, 2004) and, in addition, impedes a more informed understanding of policies and programs which assist in the control of crime and improved law enforcement protection and services (Weisheit et al., 2006).

Scope of Responsibilities

Numerous law enforcement agencies have authority and responsibilities in rural regions. Citizens of rural America are served and protected by small town police and sheriff's departments, state police and highway patrol units, state conservation units, and some federal agencies such as the United States Forest Service. The county sheriff's department continues as the primary means of service and law enforcement protection in rural areas. Of the approximately 3,000 counties in the U.S., most law enforcement units which serve the public at this level are independent county agencies, and the senior administrator is the elected county sheriff. This reflects the design of our colonial founders who structured the primary means of law enforcement at the local level and wanted it overseen by locally elected officials.

County sheriff's departments have a wide scope of responsibilities. These involve law enforcement, processing criminal and civil court orders, county jail administration, courtroom safety, property seizure, and the collection of fees and taxes. Many rural county sheriff's departments employ only a handful of deputies, several of whom work part-time, none of whom are specialists, and as a result, expertise in any single aspect of policing is virtually nonexistent. Congruent with this profile of wide responsibilities performed by a small labor force of generalists is the conclusion that per-capita costs of rural law enforcement agencies tend to be lower than larger, urban-based agencies where

the staff are more highly specialized and salaried (McDonald et al., 1996).

Citizen expectations of rural law enforcement personnel are higher than in the urban domain. This is handled by rural agencies through heavy reliance on interagency cooperation and interpersonal dynamics rather than a show of numerical and specialized technical force. Thus, the community policing concept has a long-standing acceptance and reliance in rural America compared to urban areas where it is a much more recently adopted police strategy of public service (Weisheit et al., 2006).

Police Community Relations

Whereas Wilson's (1968) threefold typology of legalistic, service and watchman police styles is recognized as a beginning point to understand rural policing and its relationship with communities, Klonski and Mendelsohn (1970) long ago noted that the communal system of justice aptly describes and explains the cultural context in which rural police function. In this cultural milieu, rural law enforcement personnel rely heavily on informal rules of control as a foundation to conduct their work. As a result, local community standards, as compared to the content of legislatively established official standards of behavior, tend to influence decisions as to who will and will not be subject to the official actions of police and the related criminal justice bureaucracy. This sociocultural standard generates a partnership between the citizens and police in many rural areas, i.e., the conceptual core of community policing. Sociologists, criminologists and police administrators have come to realize that this partnership produces a flow of information from the public to the police that contributes significantly to the ability of police to serve and protect the public more effectively. This is especially noticeable when compared to the conditions of alienated police-community relations found in urban America.

The rural ethos appears to connect to the higher rate of crimes which are cleared by arrest in rural as compared to urban jurisdictions. Weisheit et al. (2006) point out that for seven of the eight FBI index crimes (rape being the exception), the clearance rate is noticeably higher in rural than it is in urban areas. More specifically, they report that the overall clearance rate for felony violence in rural areas to be at 60 percent (59.9 percent) and for urban areas it is barely 40 percent (40.2 percent). For property crimes, the rural clearance rate is 17.8 percent and in urban America this performance barometer is found to be 12.8 percent. These statistical differences, used in gauging law enforcement effectiveness, seem to correlate with the sociocultural environment in which rural agencies function. This may reflect the conceptual proposition that rural police are more a part of the community than urban police who may be more apart from their local constituents.

Job Stress among Rural Police Officers

The wide, open geographical terrain, extensive scope of functional responsibilities, and the importance of police-community relations combine to generate distinct conditions that foster stress among rural police. Sandy and Devine (1978) describe four factors that are unique to rural policing. The first of these is personal security. Rural patrol officers are keenly aware that security through backup may be an hour or more wait. Second, social factors contribute to the level of stress among rural officers. In a sheriff's department, for example, the patrol deputies are usually residents of the county which employs them. Whereas this benefits them insofar as they know their constituents on a personal basis, this condition produces a lack of anonymity and the resulting loss of personal privacy. More recently Bartol (1996) underscores that this "fishbowl factor" intensifies existing levels of stress caused by other job-related factors. A third factor contributing to stress is the working conditions found in rural policing. Budgetary constraints, limited opportunity for vertical promotion, and challenges related to lateral movement to another agency (such as to an urban department which places a premium on specialization) contribute to the stressful nature of rural police work. Finally, inactivity leads to inadequate sensory stimuli, which impacts an officer's self-esteem.

Interesting gender differences appear in research on police stress in rural areas. Compared to officers who are male, females employed in rural law enforcement report much more task-related stressors. For example, women in rural policing indicate that they are more intensely impacted by the personal tragedies they encounter and that they feel more stress related to their responsibilities for the public's safety (Bartol, 1996). Unfortunately, administrators of rural departments recognize little if any need to confront stress, preferring instead to prioritize direct services to the public.

Budgetary Constraints and Challenges

Rural law enforcement agencies budget for service to the public more than protection of the public through rigid enforcement of criminal laws. As suggested earli-

Clay County, MN is well respected for its collaborative service efforts, including Family Services. Photograph by Tom McDonald.

er, this generates a composite economic evaluative profile which is cost-effective in the use of taxpayer resources. Estimates from the Bureau of Justice Statistics indicate that *per-officer* expenditures for rural police departments serving fewer than 2,500 residents is $42,000 and the comparable figure for urban departments serving one million or more residents is better than double the rural level, i.e., $85,700 per sworn officer. For those departments serving fewer than 2,500 people, the annual *per-resident* expenditure is $156 and the estimate for those agencies serving one million people or more is $262 (Hickman and Reaves, 2003).

Many rural regions are constrained by population decline and a shrinking tax base. This challenges the rural county sheriff's ability to adequately finance the full range of services which remain a priority for the public. The trends in economic restructuring and persistent poverty in rural America do not appear to bode

Service vehicle from the Sheriff's Department of Clay Count, MN. Photograph by Tom McDonald.

well for rural law enforcement. Possible changes in federal economic policies that have supported rural regions will apparently intensify this difficulty. As nothing is inevitable, creative policy makers in rural regions have the opportunity to respond to these local and national changes through imaginative management strategies such as the consolidation of public services. Adjustments in economic and policing policy priorities must be designed to satisfy the needs and wishes of the local constituency. Agreements about multi-county jails are a step in this direction. Collaborative community responses via leadership from rural county law enforcement and county prosecutors offer impressive potential in addressing economic constraints and improving services. An example is found in rural Utah, namely Latah County, where creative leadership from the county sheriff's department and prosecutor's office organized other stakeholders in confronting the problem of domestic violence and responding to it with increased cost-effective services (Hochstein and Thurman, 2006). Other rural counties have successfully responded to challenges in juvenile justice through collaborative partnerships including law enforcement, family court services, corrections and community-based service providers (Bergseth and McDonald, 2007; Bouffard and Bergseth, in press). Since much heterogeneity within rural America now exists, considerable variance in changes is quite likely.

Education and Training in Rural Policing

Education and training needs of rural law enforcement personnel have been a low priority among administrators who work with town managers or chairs of county commissions. In this rural context, the education and training of personnel are sometimes not viewed as a high priority or a wise use of the budget. Thus, recruiting well-educated, highly trained law enforcement personnel in rural regions is noticeably difficult. Releasing rural officers to attend educational programs and training workshops involves registration, lodging and meal costs that are often viewed as prohibitive.

Technological developments, however, appear to be a means to adapt to economic constraints. Federal funding incentives provide Internet access to rural law enforcement agencies allowing access to online training materials. Congressional legislation has been proposed to create a "Rural Policing Institute" as an office within the Federal Law Enforcement Training Center (GovTrack.us, 2007). In addition, the National Center for Rural Law Enforcement provides an electronic information resource center with valuable technical assistance and coordinated listserv communication among rural agencies (http://www.ncrle.net). Interactive video could allow educational programs to be delivered to rural agencies, thereby avoiding the costly necessity of releasing staff to attend workshops. Similar innovations for training purposes are available through the Law Enforcement Training Network (http://www.twlk.com/

law/letn_home.aspx). As a result, training resource opportunities are readily available, economically priced and updated regularly. This permits budget managers to purchase a range of programs and build an impressive training library.

These and other technological innovations bode well for access to and the use of distance educational and training programs. Accessing this array of technological resources allows law enforcement administrators to maintain staff development, to do so in a way which avoids the disruption of policing services necessitated by attending programs offered in urban areas, and accomplishes this agenda with cost-effective results.

Whereas education and training for rural police have been low priorities at the local rural level, state laws increasingly mandate minimum standards on both of these items. Innovative technologies and creative law enforcement administration can assist small departments in responding to changes in state requirements regarding educational and training standards. Police leaders of rural law enforcement departments are now required and able to note these changes.

Conclusion

Rural law enforcement agencies are responsible for more than 80 percent of our territory and close to 22 percent of our citizens. Therefore, attention to this segment of U.S. law enforcement is warranted. Many conditions, constraints and challenges exist. Much more rural-specific research is needed; it deserves a higher priority than has been the traditional work of sociologists and criminologists. This chapter focused on the sociocultural milieu in which rural policing operates. While it may seem that the rural context is small and more easily managed than the challenges of the urban context, researchers need keen alertness to the subtle complexities required by such endeavors in our rural areas. Theoretical models and methodological designs used successfully for research in urban areas are of questionable and uneven value for research on rural policing. Attention to the complexities of rural research is essential if our inventory of knowledge about policing is to be useful for political and agency leaders. This is particularly true as rural policing enters the culturally complex and politically volatile changes that will challenge it in the twenty-first century.

— *Thomas D. McDonald and Kathleen J. Bergseth*

See also

Crime; Domestic Violence; Gambling; Marijuana; Substance Abuse

References

Bartol, C.R. "Police Psychology: Then, Now, and Beyond." *Criminal Justice and Behavior* 23, no. 1 (1996): 70-89.

Bartol, C.R. (1996). "Stress in Small-Town and Rural Law Enforcement." In *Rural Criminal Justice: Conditions, Constraints, & Challenges*. Edited by T.D. McDonald, R. A. Wood, and M.A. Pflug. Salem, WI: Sheffield Publishing Co., 1996.

Bergseth, K.J. and T.D. McDonald. *Reentry Services: An Evaluation of a Pilot Project in Clay County, MN*. Report submitted to the Minnesota Department of Public Safety. Fargo: North Dakota State University, Department of Criminal Justice and Political Science, 2007.

Bouffard, J.A. and K.J. Bergseth. "The Impact of Reentry Services on Juvenile Offenders." *Youth Violence and Juvenile Justice*, in press.

Cebulak, W. "Why Rural Crime and Justice Really Matter." *Journal of Police and Criminal Psychology* 19, no. 1 (2004): 71-81.

GovTrack.us. H.R. 1028-110th Congress. "To Create a Rural Policing Institute as Part of the Federal Law Enforcement Training Center." GovTrack.us (database of federal legislation), 2007. Available online at: http://www.govtrack.us/congress/bill.xpd?bill=h110-1028. Accessed March 7, 2008.

Hickman, M.J. and B.A. Reaves. *Local Police Departments, 2000*. Washington, DC: U.S. Department of Justice, Office of Justice Programs, Bureau of Justice Statistics, 2003.

Hochstein, L.E. and Q.C. Thurman. "Assessing the Need for Domestic Violence Victim Services in One Rural County." *Police Quarterly* 9, no. 4 (2006): 448-462.

Klonski, J.R. and R.I. Mendelsohn. *The Politics of Local Justice*. Boston, MA: Little Brown and Co., 1970.

McDonald, T.D., R.A. Wood, and M.A. Pflug, eds. *Rural Criminal Justice: Conditions, Constraints, & Challenges*. Salem, WI: Sheffield Publishing Co., 1996.

Reaves, B.A. *Census of State and Local Law Enforcement Agencies, 2004*. Washington, DC: U.S. Department of Justice, Office of Justice Programs, 2007.

Sandy, J.P. and D.A. Devine D.A. "Four stress factors unique to rural patrol." *The Police Chief* 45, no. 9 (1978): 42-44.

U.S. Bureau of the Census. *American Community Survey*. Washington, DC: U.S. Bureau of the Census, 2006. Available online at: http://www.census.gov/acs/www. Accessed March 13, 2008.

Weisheit, R.A., D.N. Falcone, and L.E. Wells. *Crime and Policing in Rural and Small Town America, 3rd Edition*. Long Grove, IL: Waveland Press, 2006.

Wilson, J.Q. *Varieties of Police Behavior: The Management of Law and Order in Eight Communities*. Cambridge, MA: Harvard University Press, 1968.

Policy, Agricultural

The range of actions taken by government and other public bodies to influence the people, economy, and course of events in agriculture, and through these to have an impact on rural America. At the founding of the country, agriculture and rural were synonymous. The course of agricultural policy in rural America has been one of increasing disassociation, especially in the last 100 years. Today, agricultural policy is no longer rural policy, and sectors other than agriculture are the major influences on rural people. This article will examine three major epochs of agricultural policy with special emphasis on the period since 1933.

First Epoch: Land and Settlement Policy

There are three major epochs of agricultural policy. The first from the American revolution until the beginning of the 20th century. The land was opened and the landscape was peopled during this period. Agricultural policy was land policy and settlement policy. From 1900 until 1933, the second major epoch, government took the role of supporting infrastructure and resource conservation. Starting in 1933, the third major epoch, government became directly involved in agriculture and the decisions made on the farm. These changes mirrored the national trends in government's role in the life of its citizens.

Opening the land and peopling the landscape took over a century to accomplish. There are almost 2 billion acres in the lower 48 states, and roughly 400 million are cropland base. Another 200 million acres of lower quality land could be brought into production. By 1956, the federal government distributed the public domain as follows:

In the early days of the American republic, there was pressure to use land distribution to earn revenues and pay off the debt of the new nation. Thomas Jefferson's view prevailed, however, and land was sold or granted on more favorable terms to create a nation of small yeoman farmers central to Jefferson's notion of agriculturally based democracy. In this phase of settlement, the fertile land was seemingly endless. It was cultivated extensively as people moved westward—extensively in terms of cultivating more land to produce more and extensively in terms of moving on to better lands at the frontier when old land lost fertility.

Second Epoch: Indirect Role of Government

The transition to the 20th century and a different role for the federal government is best illustrated by the rec-

ommendations of the Country Life Commission shortly after 1900. The Commission, appointed by Theodore Roosevelt, looked into the conditions of rural life and made recommendations about what government might do to improve it. The Commission was led by Liberty Hyde Bailey and included Gifford Pinchot among its members. It held hearings around the country and surveyed the rural populace, receiving over 100,000 responses to a national questionnaire.

The conclusions of the Commission were that the Federal Government should improve the environment for farmers and the infrastructure for rural life. Among its recommendations were to create a postal savings banks, institute a rural free postal delivery, conduct extensive applied research and extension education from the Land Grant Colleges, and improve health education and transportation in rural areas. Over the next several decades, almost all of the recommendations were put into action. The focus was both rural and agricultural–they were still synonymous. None of the recommendations involved government actively in the decisions of individual farmers or rural people, but the message of a positive role for government in rural affairs was real, even if it was an indirect one.

The Agricultural Depression and the Agricultural Adjustment Act

The role of government changed completely in 1933 (Rasmussen 1985). The early 1900s had been the "golden age" of agriculture. The notion of parity for agriculture was based on the experience of 1910 through 1914 when farmers had low costs for inputs and good prices for farm products. Agriculture boomed during World War I and the immediately succeeding years. But in the early 1920s, foreign agricultural markets collapsed and agriculture entered a depression that was ended only by World War II. Farm incomes and land values plummeted. A farm selling in Northern Indiana in 1919 at

Millions of Acres in the Original Public Domain as of 1956

Recipients	Millions of Acres
Sales and Grants Largely to Private Individuals	455.5
National Forests, Parks, Wildlife, Military Reservations	187.8
Unreserved and Unappropriated Public Domain	170.6
Homestead and Related Grants	147.0
Railroads	131.0
States to Support Transportation and Other Infrastructure	125.0
States to Support Education	99.0
Military Land Bounties	73.5
Indian Tribal and Trust Lands	52.8
GRAND TOTAL, Original Public Domain	1,442.2

Source: (Cochrane 1993, 175)

the end of the boom did not regain its nominal dollar purchase price until after World War II. Farms were lost and there was severe economic distress in rural areas long before the stock market crash of 1929. When Franklin Roosevelt took office in 1933, incomes in rural areas were only 40 percent of incomes in urban areas, and unemployment in urban areas was around 30 percent.

The Roosevelt administration's mandate was to tackle this problem, and the Agricultural Adjustment Act of 1933 was enacted. The task was to get cash into rural areas, and the tactic was to raise farm prices. Production was restricted to raise prices on basic commodities important to farmers' incomes. Prices were also supported through non-recourse loans on crops, which brought the federal government into the commodity storage business if farmers turned over the crop rather than pay back the loan. Direct payments were made to farmers in some cases; marketing orders were set up to manage the supplies of specialty crops and dairy products; and new credit institutions were set up appropriate for agricultural needs. The government purchased worn out or non-productive farms and, under the 1937 and 1938 Acts, paid farmers to adopt conserving practices, make physical improvements to their lands, or hold fragile land out of production. These provisions also helped to restrict supply and raise prices. These basic components of agricultural policy were still in effect through the early 1990s in rural America.

Most remarkable was the Roosevelt administration's willingness to try many new measures, jettison those that did not work, and move on to new measures that may work. Did these policies achieve their goals? In 1940, George Tolley, the USDA's chief economist under Secretary of Agriculture Henry A. Wallace, wrote that the policies of the New Deal had three objectives. One objective was to improve the viability of commercial agriculture; second, to enhance the life of the subsistence farmer, the rural poor, or the migrant laborer; and third, to protect the land and enhance conservation and the more productive use of resources. Tolley commented that the first task of underpinning commercial agriculture had been accomplished, but the tasks of helping those less fortunate and enhancing conservation and resource stewardship had not been accomplished (USDA, *Farmers in a Changing World* 1940).

Today, USDA income statistics show that farm family incomes are on a par with non-farm family incomes. Thus, the severe disparity between farm and non-farm average income is no longer evident. Although most farm families achieve this equality with additional off-farm income just as non-farm families also have more than one wage earner. However, the equality of income and living conditions for commercial farmers sought by the New Deal has been largely achieved.

Which Policy Matters?

To what extent does agricultural policy impact rural areas? Chester Davis, an early Agricultural Adjustment Act administrator, understood that agricultural policy was not necessarily the main influence on either the farmer or the rural populace. What really affected agriculture and rural areas was "expressed in a complexity of laws and attitudes which, in the importance of their influence on agriculture, shade off from direct measures like the Agricultural Adjustment Act through the almost infinite fields of taxation, tariffs, international trade, and labor, money, credit, and banking policy" (USDA, *Farmers in a Changing World* 1940, 325). Then, as today, Davis saw that much of what moves rural America does not come from agricultural policy.

Agriculture and rural America have been affected greatly by monetary and credit policy. The Farm Credit Banks, Resettlement Administration, Farm Security Administration, and finally the Farmers Home Administration increased the availability of credit to the sector at critical times. The easy credit policy of the late 1970s followed by the restrictive monetary policy of the Federal Reserve and the collapse in exports in the early 1980s were factors in the farm financial crisis that proved disastrous for farms and for rural areas. Massive agricultural price support expenditures were made in the last half of the 1980s to counter the hardship from the boom and bust of the 1970s and 1980s.

Tax policy influenced the returns to agriculture and the size of firms. Cash accounting, special depreciation rules, and special inheritance provisions tended to increase the size of firms. (USDA *A Time to Choose* 1981). Other public policies coupled with economic forces are capable of unleashing drastic economic change within agriculture. "We have credit policies that cheapen the cost of credit for large borrowers. We have tax policies that encourage vertical integration, agglomeration, and farm size enlargement." (Raup 1978, p.305). One of the problems that many see is a synergism of agricultural and non-agricultural policies that both depopulate rural America and decrease the economic linkages between the farm and its local community. There are trade-offs between the resiliency of the moderate-size family farm and the greater efficiency of larger, more integrated units. And there are trade-offs between the positive economic and social role of many family farms in a rural community and the cost savings and improved efficiency of larger farms in obtaining inputs and capital from outside the rural area.

Technology and Productivity

The 1930s ushered in an era of increasing productivity and intensification in agriculture and direct government involvement in farming. The closing of the frontier was one factor in this change. Productivity was relatively stagnant from 1900 to the 1930s as was the size of the farm population. From 1940 to 1990, farm population went from about 30 million to 4 million whereas input productivity more than doubled. "Postwar farm policies continued to support farm income, making more capital available for the purchase of new farm machines and, thereby, more labor available for other parts of the economy" (Mayer 1993, 82). World War II, the flow of public technology available from the Land Grant institutions, and the building of the interstate highway system led to farm consolidations, out-migration of labor from agriculture, and increasing proportions of farm inputs coming from large, off-farm, centralized suppliers. An engine of growth dominated and drove the structural changes in the agricultural sector.

Self-Perpetuating Programs

Why was there little change in American agricultural policy? When the federal government became actively involved in agriculture in the 1930s, the farming landscape was more homogeneous. It was believed that programs based on subsidizing farm products would be fair because the public perceived a large mass of small-to-mid-sized farmers having similar output, productivity, and needs for support. However, "through a process of uneven consolidation, U.S. farm structure became increasingly skewed, and a wealthy minority of large-sized farmers eventually came to produce the majority of all supported farm products, thus capturing the majority of all support benefits" (Paarlberg 1989, 1161-1162). In essence, policies were initiated and continued whereby large operations obtained more program benefits and smaller firms remained more vulnerable to failure. The very characteristic of family farms–that they fail with relatively low cost to society as a whole–allowed a transition to occur with rapid farm consolidation almost unnoticed by many because the

social costs were borne quietly, primarily by those involved.

Especially today, after farm consolidation and the changed relationship between farms and their communities, agricultural policy is not rural policy. There is increasingly a disconnection between agriculture and rural areas. Agricultural production enterprises are a shrinking part of rural economic activity. But, for better or worse, agriculture, forestry, and other rural-based industries have been major factors shaping the institutions and norms of rural areas (Castle 1993). It is in this sense that agriculture remains most important to rural areas today, not because of its economic activity or the impacts of agricultural programs. Conditions in rural areas are different from the 1930s, yet the same norms, institutions, and policy devices persist.

The stresses of the 1980s illustrated the problems for both agriculture and for rural areas. Both suffered more from macroeconomic policy, deregulation, changes in international markets, and increased international competitiveness than many other sector or region. The question becomes one of how rural areas adapt to the changing circumstances around them, including the budget-driven changes in agricultural policy that eventually will further diminish the transfer of income to rural areas that exists today. To what extent will diminished agricultural programs increase the risk level for the farming community and add instability to the rural community? If much of the relative decline of rural economies since the 1930s has been due to successful adoption of labor-saving technology in agriculture and other rural pursuits, where will a future take rural America that promises more of the same?

In the past, a rural area with a strong agricultural base could be an economic entity unto itself. This is no longer the case. Industrialization has "peripheralized the role of rural areas ... Most rural areas now constitute specialized components of larger regional economies, supplying a particular industry and/or factor of production" (Cooper 1993, 38). Agriculture is one of many in such a context. The old notion was that a rural place or region was related to an accompanying immobility of capital and labor, but this is no longer the case. Agriculture is no longer a core. Agricultural policy held a static view of place for agriculture. If the infusion of cash from agricultural programs in the late 1980s solved the farm crisis, it did not solve the rural crisis. Most rural employment is in other sectors such as forest products, mining, manufacturing, and producer services. It is here that agricultural policy has not been able to address the sluggish rural economies that persisted since the Reagan recession of the early 1980s. What we have seen recently is "a long term decline in the relative importance of resource industries as employers, the pressures of technology and foreign competition on employment in low-wage rural manufacturing industries, the endemic liabilities of small population concentrations and distance from major urban centers, and chronic weaknesses in the rural labor force due to lower education and poorer skills" (Reid 1989, 358). This can not be turned around only with agricultural policy.

Where is agricultural policy likely to go, and what will be its likely impact on rural America? Over the next decade large income transfers to agriculture on the basis of one's specific crop or scale of production may well cease. If a successful argument is made that agriculture is more subject to and especially damaged by income volatility, then some sort of income insurance or other risk reducing program to lower potential vulnerability may be seen. However, international competition, market specialization, technology and the imperative of its early adoption, tax measures, and credit policy are likely to continue to encourage consolidation and vertical integration of agriculture irrespective of the 1996 Farm Bill. A shift from the historic participation-based payments program to something like income risk insurance or needs-based transfers will not halt the drift of agriculture toward something less important and less central to rural America. The basic political tenant of agricultural programs has been more toward income redistribution than productivity and capacity enhancement. Agricultural programs used by large producers and landowners have been skewed to favor income transfers to these effective interest groups. Little has been done to ease the adjustment of those leaving agriculture. To impact rural America, it is not just agricultural policies, but policies that affect the other components of the rural economy, that must be geared toward productivity, capacity enhancement, and easing the transition of people from one sector to another.

— *Otto C. Doering III*

See also

Agricultural Prices; Agricultural Programs; Agriculture, Structure of; Development, Community and Economic; Farms; Policy, Economic; Policy, Food

References

Castle, Emery N. "Rural Diversity: An American Asset." *Annals of the American Academy*, 529 (September 1993): 12-21.

Cochrane, Willard. D. *The Development of American Agriculture; A Historical Analysis.* 2nd ed. Minneapolis, MN: University of Minnesota Press, 1993.

Cooper, Ronald S. "The New Economic Regionalism: A Rural Policy Framework." *Annals of the American Academy* 529 (September, 1993) 34-47.

Eidman, Vernon R. *The 2002 Farm Bill. a Step Forward or a Step Backward?* St. Paul, MN: University of Minnesota, Center for International Food and Agricultural Policy, 2002.

Hayenga, Marvin, James MacDonald, Kyle Steigert, and Brian L. Buhr. *The 2007 Farm Bill: Policy Options and Consequences; Concentration, Mergers and Antitrust.* Oak Brook, IL: Farm Foundation, 2007.

Mayer, Leo V. "Agricultural Change and Rural America." *Annals of the American Academy*, 529 (September, 1993): 80-91.

Paarlberg, Robert. "The Political Economy of American Agricultural Policy: Three Approaches." *American Journal of Agricultural Economics* 71, no. 5 (December, 1989): 1,157-1,164.

Rasmussen, Wayne D. "Historical Overview of U.S. Agricultural Policies and Programs." *Agricultural-Food Policy Review: Commodity Program Perspectives.* Agricultural Economic Report No. 50 (July). Washington, DC: U.S. Department of Agriculture, Economic Research Service, 1985.

Raup, Philip M. "Some Questions of Value and Scale in American Agriculture." *American Journal of Agricultural Economics* 60 (May 1978): 303-308.

Reid, J. Norman. "Agricultural Policy and Rural Development." *Emerging Issues*, Agricultural Economic Report No. 620. Washington, DC: U.S. Department of Agriculture, Economic Research Service, 1989.

U.S. Country Life Commission. *Report of the Commission on Country Life.* Chapel Hill, NC: University of North Carolina Press, 1944.

U.S. Department of Agriculture. *A Time to Choose: Summary Report on the Structure of Agriculture.* Washington, DC: U.S. Department of Agriculture, 1981.

U.S. Department of Agriculture. *Farmers in a Changing World; 1940 Yearbook of Agriculture.* Washington, DC: U.S. Department of Agriculture, 1940.

Yeutter, Clayton. *U.S. Farm Policy—At a Crossroads? The 2007 Farm Bill and the Doha Round.* St. Paul, MN: University of Minnesota, Center for International Food and Agricultural Policy, 2005.

Policy, Economic

The set of laws, programs, and administrative rules that guide, encourage, or constrain economic activity. Reed and Long (1988) define policy as a "guiding and consistent course of action," and emphasize the importance of policy decisions being guided by selection of a consistent set of policy objectives. They refer to the set of programs selected to advance the chosen policy objectives as a "policy strategy" which is roughly equivalent to the way the term "policy" is used in this article.

Federal, state, and local governments, through tax, spending, and regulatory actions, create economic policy. National policy designed to support the economies of urban areas (where three quarters of Americans live) may work to the disadvantage of rural areas, which are sparsely populated, isolated, and often dependent on a narrow economic base. This led some to suggest the creation of an explicit national or state rural policy.

The first section of this article provides three reasons why governments have economic policies. This is followed by a discussion of the rural context for economic policy—the distinctive characteristics of rural areas and the forces leading to rural change. The next two sections describe the economic policies of the federal government and of state and local governments and their impacts on rural areas. The final section is a discussion of the idea of comprehensive national policy to address the needs of rural areas.

Why Economic Policy?

First, national governments enact monetary, fiscal, and trade policies to establish the legal and monetary framework necessary for an economy to function smoothly. This framework provides security in trade and a basic social and physical infrastructure (e.g., schools, water, and sewer systems). A certain level of taxes is necessary to support these activities.

Second, governments often enact policies to correct market inefficiencies and undesirable social, economic, or environmental effects of private decisions. Within a basic market framework, firms and individuals often make decisions that are either economically inefficient or have undesirable side effects. For example, because of imperfect information, urban banks may reject a loan for a credit-worthy rural business in favor of a loan to a risky urban venture. Or, a farm decision to apply pesticide may harm the habitat of an endangered species. The decisions of manufacturing firms to locate overseas may increase poverty and worsen the distribution of income in this country. Sub-

sidized loan programs, pollution taxes, and welfare and job training programs are examples of economic policies that address these concerns.

Finally, in addition to providing a framework and correcting the negative impacts of market decisions, governments attempt through policy to affect the overall level of economic activity, the health of certain sectors and regions, and the achievement of certain social goals.

The Rural Context for Economic Policy

Rural America is becoming increasingly similar to urban America in population and economic characteristics, values, and the availability of services and amenities. There are at least four characteristics, however, that distinguish rural areas, and that cause rural areas to be affected differently from urban areas by economic policy and global economic and social forces. First, rural areas tend to have a narrower economic base than urban areas, and specialize in the natural resource industries of agriculture, forestry and wood products, energy extraction, and mining. Almost half of the rural counties in the U.S. depend on one of these industries for 20 percent or more of their labor and proprietor income; 30 percent of these counties depend on agriculture (farming, food processing, and agricultural services); and 14 percent depend on the other three natural resource industries.

Second, rural areas are isolated. They are, for the most part, distant from economic and political centers, and do not have ready access to the economic and political discussions that shape policy decisions.

Third, rural areas are sparsely populated. Nonmetropolitan counties average 19 people per square mile whereas metropolitan counties have 332 people per square mile. Low population densities hinder the attainment of economies of size and concentration possible in urban areas.

Fourth, rural people are more involved in local self-governance than urban people. Although they have only 24 percent of the population, rural areas have 75 percent of the local government units. This places more demands on rural people for leadership roles, often in volunteer positions, and gives them more experience in self-governance (Weber, et al. 1989).

There are at least four sets of forces that are changing the economies of rural and urban areas and are providing new constraints and opportunities for rural areas. First, technological change led to new production processes and dramatic reduction in the cost of transportation and communication. While these changes reduced the need for firms to be close to markets or firm headquarters, they also tended to reinforce urban concentrations because technological change tends to proceed faster in areas with denser concentrations of similar businesses.

Second, corporate organizational structures are moving toward flexible multi-source international production and away from vertically integrated structures in which a single firm is involved in all aspects of production, marketing, and distribution. Firms are coming to rely more on "strategic alliances, short-term contracts, and the shipment of components from many different international sources to as many different markets" (Glasmeier and Conroy 1994:6).

Third, increasing global competition has come, in part, from technological changes and corporate restructuring. It resulted in a rapid increase in multinational firms, foreign direct investment, and international strategic alliances and production networks. Globalization provides opportunities for new foreign investment in U.S. rural areas so that foreign firms can have better access to U.S. markets. It also has the potential to lead to more rural branch plant closures by U.S. firms as they seek markets and lower production costs overseas.

Fourth, the American population is aging; people live longer and the Baby Boom generation (people born between 1946 and 1964) moves toward retirement. Retirees generally do not move from where they spend their adult lives, but an increasing number of elderly people are seeking the amenities and low living costs of rural areas. During the 1990s rural retirement counties grew faster than other types of rural counties. Rural areas had a larger share of the population over 65 years of age (14.7 percent) than urban areas (11.9 percent). Rural areas also have a larger share of personal income (18.8 percent) in retirement-related transfer payments (social security and government pensions) than urban areas (13.5 percent). Retirees generate both income and demand for unique health care, housing, transportation, and recreation services.

Federal Policy

The federal government attempts to affect economic activity both through national economic policies and through policies directed at narrower aspects of the public interest—the vitality of specific economic sectors or regions and the attainment of specific social goals, such as the maintenance of minimum health and income standards (Reid and Long 1988).

The federal government has three sets of national economic policies through which it attempts to affect the overall level of economic activity in the country: monetary policy, fiscal policy, and trade policy. Through monetary policy, the federal government attempts to influence the money supply, the availability of loanable funds, and the interest rate. The principal tools of monetary policy are the discount rate (the interest rate charged by the Federal Reserve System on loans to banks), the reserve requirement (the amount of reserves a bank must have on deposit with the Federal Reserve), and the open market operations (purchases and sales of government securities) of the Federal Reserve System. Changes in the money supply, the availability of loanable loans, and the interest rate affect the rate of investment (an important component of gross national product and a determinant of future economic health) and the rate of inflation (which affects the value of the dollar in international trade as well as the domestic standard of living).

Through fiscal policy, the federal government attempts to affect the overall level of national income and employment. The principal tools of fiscal policy are the level of taxes and the level of spending. By changing tax policy, the federal government can affect levels of savings and consumption; and by changing spending, it can affect the level of overall demand and employment in the economy.

Through trade policy, the federal government can affect the level of imports and exports, and thus, national income and employment. The main tools of trade policy are tariffs (taxes on imports, making them less attractive to American consumers), import quotas (which restrict the supply of imports), non-tariff barriers (such as requirements that imports pass certain tests or meet certain standards), and export embargoes (prohibitions of certain exports).

Monetary, fiscal, and trade policies are interrelated and work together to move the nation toward its economic goals of full employment, long-term economic growth, and price stability. The health of the rural economy clearly depends on the health of the national economy, and thus, the success of the federal government in advancing national economic goals is critical to the overall well being of rural America.

Because of the characteristics of rural industries and population, however, the effects of changes in national economic policy may be felt disproportionately in rural areas. An increase in the interest rate reduces construction activity, which hurts rural economies dependent on wood products. It also increases interest income, which helps rural areas with large concentrations of retirees. Cuts in the federal defense budget that lead to military base closings hurt rural areas dependent on those installations. The reduction of trade barriers under the North American Free Trade Agreement and the General Agreement on Trade and Tariffs encourages the movement of low-wage, low-productivity manufacturing plants out of the rural areas of the U.S. (where they have gone in past decades) to other countries with lower labor costs (Glasmeier and Conroy 1994).

Some economic policies of the federal government are directed toward specific sectors, regions, or social objectives. These also affect rural economic activity.

Sectoral policies attempt to improve the health of individual economic sectors. Agricultural policy, for example, regulates the supply, demand, and price of important farm commodities. Forest policy controls allowable harvest and reforestation on federal timberlands. Fishing policy determines the access to, and allowable harvest from, fisheries. By affecting the production and income of businesses in the natural resource industries on which many rural economies depend, these policies affect the economic health of rural America.

Regional policies attempt to stimulate economic development in specific well-defined regions (such as the Tennessee Valley, Appalachia or the Upper Great Lakes) or in non-contiguous areas with similar characteristics (rural and urban areas). The Appalachian Regional Commission, which administers a range of programs that fund infrastructure investments in Appalachia, is an example of the first kind of policy. The programs of the former Farmers Home Administration, that help finance housing, water, and sewer systems in rural areas, are examples of the second.

Social programs such as Medicaid, Social Security, and Aid to Families with Dependent Children also affect rural economic activity. With higher poverty rates and higher proportions of the population over 65 years of age than urban areas rural areas can be greatly affected by national or state social program changes.

State and Local Economic Policy

State and local governments spend, tax, and regulate economic activity, and can affect the economic health of their regions. In recent years, as economic competition between nations intensified and corporate structures have become more multinational, states and localities have become much more aggressive in offering incentives to businesses for locating plants in their areas. The state of Oregon, for example, enacted a Strategic Investment Program in 1993, which allows local government to substantially reduce property taxes on large new industrial investments. This program is credited with inducing several large semiconductor plants to locate in the Portland metropolitan area in the past several years. The size of the minimum investment that qualifies for this program ($100 million) makes it more likely to be attractive in urban than rural areas. In 1995, the neighboring state of Washington enacted its own tax concession plan to attract high technology investments across the Columbia River into Washington.

In a recent survey, Glasmeier and Conroy (1994: 11) found that rural communities offer "wide ranges of subsidized sites, training services, and plant construction, as well as abatement of taxes for long but varying periods of time [in spite of] a relatively strong consensus among both location theorists and development practitioners that the incentives now being offered by local governments may never be recouped in terms of direct and indirect benefits to the communities".

A National Rural Policy?

Many rural areas are economically healthy, but the average rural American has less income, a higher probability of being unemployed or in poverty, and receives less health care and schooling than the average urban American.

This led some to suggest that the nation must develop a comprehensive rural policy that attempts to reinvigorate rural economies, taking into account the unique characteristics and problems of rural areas. Others, pointing to the diversity of rural areas, the economic interdependence of rural and urban areas, and the increasing importance of state and local leadership in economic development, argue for a federal role limited to creating a healthy macro-economy, fostering economic cooperation among jurisdictions, and insuring adequate investment in people (Deavers 1989).

All Americans have a stake in the economic vitality of both urban and urban areas. Rural people depend on urban economies for many specialized goods and services and often move to urban areas in search of jobs and urban amenities. Rural areas are a source of much of the food, fiber, minerals, and water consumed in urban areas and are the places many urban workers were raised. Urban residents recreate in rural places and often retire to rural communities.

People will continue to live in rural areas. Economic policy should recognize, therefore, that "it is in the nation's best interest to insure that those who do, and their children, do not become second-class citizens" (Stinson 1989: 7).

— *Bruce A. Weber*

See also

Agricultural and Applied Economics; Development, Community and Economic; Employment; Farm Finance; Foreclosure and Bankruptcy; Fringe Benefits; Income; Financial Intermediaries; Marketing; Natural Resource Economics; Taxes; Trade, Interregional; Trade, International; Workers' Compensation

References

Browne, William P. and Louis E. Swanson. "Living with the Minimum: Rural Public Policy." Pp. 481-492 in *The American Countryside: Rural People and Places*. Edited by Emery N. Castle. Lawrence, KS: University Press of Kansas, 1995.

Deavers, Kenneth L. "Choosing a Rural Policy for the 1980's and '90's." Pp. 17/1-17/17 in *Rural Economic Development in the 1980's: Preparing for the Future*. Rural Development Research Report No. 69 (September). Edited by David Brown, et al. Washington, DC: U. S. Department of Agriculture, Agriculture and Rural Economy Division, Economic Research Service, 1988.

Flora, Cornelia B. and James A. Christenson, eds. *Rural Policies for the 1990s*. Boulder, CO: Westview Press, 1991.

Glasmeier, Amy K. and Michael E. Conroy. *Global Squeeze on Rural America: Opportunities, Threats, and Challenges From NAFTA, GATT, and Processes of Globalization*. A Report of The Institute for Policy Research and Evaluation, Graduate School of Public Policy and Administration. College Park, PA: Pennsylvania State University, 1994.

Kruege, Anne O., ed. Economic Policy Reform: The Second Stage. Chicago, IL: University of Chicago Press, 2000.

Persson, Torsten and Guido Enrico Tabellini. Political Economics: Explaining Economic Policy. Cambridge, MA: MIT Press, 2002.

Reid, J. Norman and Richard W. Long. "Rural Policy Objectives: Defining Problems and Choosing Approaches." Pp. 9/1-9/16 in *Rural Economic Development in the 1980's: Preparing for the Future*. Rural Development Research Report No. 69 (September). Edited by David Brown, et al. Washington, DC: U.S. Department of Agriculture, Agriculture and Rural Economy Division, Economic Research Service, 1988.

Stinson, Thomas F. "Toward a Federal Rural Policy." *Minnesota Agricultural Economist* 659 (October 1989): 5-7.

Weber, Bruce, Ron Shaffer, Ron Knutson, and Bob Lovan. "Building a Vital Rural America." In *Options in Developing a New National Rural Policy*, proceedings from four regional Rural Development Policy Workshops, Reno, Nevada, 1989.

Weber, Bruce A. "Extractive Industries and Rural-Urban Economic Interdependence." Pp. 155-179 in *The American Countryside: Rural People and Places*. Edited by Emery N. Castle. Lawrence, KS: University Press of Kansas, 1995.

Policy, Environmental

The set of laws, programs and administrative rules that guides the nation's environment-related issues. Many of the more controversial issues in rural America are in the area of environment. This article examines at a select number of critical areas of environmental concern, and the policies and programs which impact them. While not comprehensive these issues form a framework under which most environmental problems facing rural America fall.

Historical Background

In the last century rural America saw tremendous environmental change. Much of that change took place after the depression of 1897. These changes were accelerated by the development and use of the automobile. America was expanding in the period prior to 1897. Increased natural resource exploitation, agricultural development, and the establishment of regional community centers occurred, but in most cases, environmental change during this period was local. Regional environmental concerns, which are the bases for modern day environmental policies, did not begin to emerge until the latter part of the nineteenth century.

As American society emerged from the depression of 1897, farmers began to realize increased prices for their goods, industries increased demand for raw materials, and home construction expanded increasing demand for wood products and materials. With the onset of the twentieth century came mass production. Electrical energy came into being and with it increased demands for coal and oil. Agriculture began its transition from single-family farms to what became industrial agriculture—large-scale crop production. With the industrialization of agriculture and the chemical revolution of the mid- to late nineteenth century came a new generation of environmental concerns—non-point source pollution and chemical contamination.

Land

The American landscape is a dynamic landscape. Throughout the nation's history, people reworked, altered, and in many instances, permanently changed the character of the lands of rural America. Perhaps the most pronounced environmental change in rural America was with the land. This change came in the form of conversion from one use to another (development) and in the recognition of impacts associated with current management and use of the land (soil loss).

The rate of conversion of agricultural lands in rural America remained under debate. In 1981, the National Agricultural Lands Study reported that three million acres of agricultural land were being lost to urbanization each year. In 1992, the Soil Conservation Service estimated a rate of conversion of two million acres per year. The true impact of this change has yet to be realized, but because much of these lands are highly productive, such conversions impact our ability to produce food and fiber. Moreover, because the lands being converted are highly productive, agriculture is forced to bring marginally productive, environmentally sensitive lands into production. The net result is poor yields with increased environmental impacts.

2007 Farm Bill

At present, Congress devotes billions of dollars each year to subsidies that result in farmers applying large doses of pesticides and chemical fertilizers to their crops. Such practices contribute substantially to the contamination of drinking water supplies, result in unnecessary pesticide residues on foods, and degrade the environment. At this writing, the 2007 Farm Bill is still being debated in Congress, and several major changes are being considered. What appears below is a brief summary of the major conservation elements of the current 2002 Farm Bill.

2002 Farm Bill

The Farm Security and Rural Investment Act of 2002 (Farm Bill) is a landmark piece of legislation for conservation funding and for focusing on environmental issues. The conservation provisions assist farmers and ranchers in meeting environmental challenges on their land. This legislation simplified what were existing programs and created new programs to address high priority environmental and production goals. The 2002 Farm Bill is intended to enhance the long-term quality of our environment and conservation of our natural resources. There are a number of conservation programs authorized under this law.

The Conservation of Private Grazing Land Program is a voluntary program that helps owners and managers of private grazing land address natural resource concerns while enhancing the economic and social stability of grazing land enterprises and the rural communities that depend on them. The Conservation Security Program is a voluntary program that provides financial and technical assistance for the conservation, protection, and improvement of soil, water, and related resources on Tribal and private lands. The program provides payments for producers who historically have practiced good stewardship on their agricultural lands and incentives for those who want to do more.

The Environmental Quality Incentives Program is a voluntary conservation program that promotes agricultural production and environmental quality as compatible national goals. Through EQIP, farmers and ranchers may receive financial and technical help to install or implement structural and management conservation practices on eligible agricultural land. The Farmland Protection Program is a voluntary program that helps farmers and ranchers keep their land in agriculture. The program provides matching funds to state, tribal, or local governments and nongovernmental organizations with existing farmland protection programs to purchase conservation easements or other interests in land.

The National Natural Resources Conservation Foundation promotes innovative solutions to natural resource problems and conducts research and educational activities to support conservation on private land. The NNRCF is a private, nonprofit 501(c) (3) corporation. The foundation builds partnerships among agencies and agricultural, public, and private constituencies interested in promoting voluntary conservation on private lands. The Resource Conservation and Development Program (RC&D) encourages and improves the capability of civic leaders in designated RC&D areas to plan and carry out projects for resource conservation and community development. Program objectives focus on "quality of life" improvements achieved through natural resources conservation and community development. Such activities lead to sustainable communities, prudent land use, and the sound management and conservation of natural resources. The Wetlands Reserve Program is a voluntary program that provides technical and financial assistance to eligible landowners to address wetland, wildlife habitat, soil, water, and related natural resource concerns on private land in an environmentally beneficial and cost effective manner. The program provides an opportunity for landowners to receive financial incentives to enhance wetlands in exchange for retiring marginal land from agriculture. The Wildlife Habitat Incentives Program (WHIP) is a voluntary program that encourages creation of high quality wildlife habitats that support wildlife populations of National, State, Tribal, and local significance. Through WHIP, NRCS provides technical and financial assistance to landowners and others to develop upland, wetland, riparian, and aquatic habitat areas on their property.

The Conservation Reserve Program (CRP) is a voluntary program that pays farmers to retire environmentally sensitive lands from production for 10 years. These lands include highly erodible areas, farmed wetlands, flood plains, and areas next to streams. Participating farmers receive an annual payment, plus cost-sharing to establish a permanent cover of grass, trees, or shrubs. CRP was designed to reduce surplus production and to provide important environmental benefits, including soil erosion control, improved water quality, wildlife habitat enhancement, and increased recreational opportunities. Since its authorization in 1985, nearly fifty million acres have been enrolled in the CRP.

CRP is largely a grassland restoration program because most environmentally sensitive, marginal cropland was converted from native prairie in the Great Plains and prairie region. CRP provided a stewardship opportunity to move away from farming unnecessarily on highly erodible, environmentally sensitive lands. Approximately 87 percent of CRP was restored to grassland habitat, and about two-thirds is located in prairie regions.

Wetlands

There are roughly half as many wetlands in the contiguous 48 sates as 200 years ago. The rate of conversion was about 105,000 acres per year between 1987 and 1991, down from 500,000 acres annually between 1954 and 1974. Six federal agencies are primarily responsible for about 25 laws that regulate, acquire, or use incentives to protect wetlands.

The current distribution and quality of wetlands in rural America is the product of ever-changing wetland policies. These policy shifts are the result of increased understanding of the importance of viable wetlands in the landscape.

Wetlands were initially viewed in America as wastelands. These areas were believed to be unproductive, a nuisance, and a health hazard. In the Swampland Acts of 1849, 1850, and 1860, Congress granted 64.9 million acres of wetlands to 15 states in exchange for state promises to drain and convert them to farmland. The Reclamation Act of 1902 and the 1944 Federal Flood Control Act involved USDA and the U.S. Army Corps of Engineers, respectively, in programs to promote wetland conversion. Other federal policies provided USDA cost-sharing for drainage, tax laws allowed expensing drainage costs, and farm commodity programs encouraged expansion of production.

During the 1940s and into the 1970s, messages to swampland owners became mixed following adoption of policies that encouraged wetland protection. By 1962, USDA cost-sharing was eliminated for certain classes of wetland. The Water Bank Program (implemented in 1972 in 10 states) was the first USDA effort to encourage protection of wetlands.

Federal Water Pollution Control Act Amendments in 1972 regulated discharge of dredge and fill material into navigable waters. Executive Order 11990 (1972) stated that U.S. agencies should not be involved in any development activities that encouraged wetland conversion and by 1978, drainage cost-sharing had been eliminated.

Swampbuster provisions of the 1985 Food Security Act eliminated U.S.D.A. farm program benefits for crops grown on wetland converted after 1985 by tying farm program benefits to compliance with wetland protection measures. Swampbuster was continued by the 1990 farm bill with modifications including: changing the swampbusting initiation from the time the crop was planted to the time when conversion makes crop planting possible; expanding program benefits lost with swampbusting; and allowing mitigation in certain circumstances.

Much of the recent wetland controversy focused on definition and delineation. Mainly there is disagreement concerning evidence of three wetland characteristics (soils, hydrology and vegetation) needed to identify an area as a wetland. Wetlands regulated under sections 401 and 404 of the Clean Water Act (see below) were identified using technical criteria in the 1987 Corps of Engineers Wetland Delineation Manual.

The Clinton administration embraced the concept of no-net-loss as an interim goal in wetland protection with the long-run goal of increasing the quality and quantity of the nation's wetland resource base. No-net-loss of wetlands is not a policy per se but is a policy goal specifying that loss of wetlands be balanced with a gain in wetlands elsewhere. The Natural Resource Conservation Service (NRCS) of the USDA has the responsibility to determine the extent of swampbuster and Clean Water Act jurisdiction on agricultural lands.

Wetlands will continue as an important and controversial environmental arena in rural America. The unprecedented floods in the Midwest in 1993 inundated millions of acres of farmland, and led to an increased emphasis on the need for floodplain management. As a result, flood relief and floodplain management are used as the rationale to fund wetland restoration in the Mississippi Valley.

Section 404 of the Clean Water Act

The primary goal of the Clean Water Act (CWA), 33 U.S.C. §1251 et seq., is to "restore and maintain the chemical, physical, and biological integrity of the Nation's waters." In keeping with that goal, Section 404 of the CWA regulates the disposal of dredged and fill material into U.S. waters, including wetlands. Other activities that destroy wetlands, such as drainage, flooding, pumping, and burning are not regulated under the CWA unless they entail discharges of dredged or fill material into U.S. waters.

Section 404 is administered jointly by the U.S. Army Corps of Engineers (Corps) and the U.S. Environmental Protection Agency (EPA). The Corps is authorized to issue or deny permits for fill activities into U.S. waters. Section 404(b) (1) of the CWA directs the EPA to develop guidelines for the Corps to use in assessing environmental impacts of proposed projects. The EPA also has veto authority over Corps permits. In addition, the EPA, the U.S. Fish and Wildlife Service (FWS), and the National Marine Fisheries Service (NMFS) may review and comment on permit applications, provide technical assistance to protect fish and wildlife resources, and mitigate project impacts.

Under §404(e) of the CWA, the Corps has authority to issue general permits on a state, regional, and nationwide basis for any category of activities involving discharges of dredged or fill material if the activities are similar in nature and will cause only minimal, individual and cumulative adverse environmental impacts. General permits constitute an alternative to individual §404 permits. When a landowner applies for an individual §404 permit, the Corps gives each permit application case-specific review. A general permit, on the other hand, operates like an exemption. If the proposed activity fits into the category of activities authorized under a general permit, it is automatically authorized.

The Corps authorizes approximately 90 percent of proposed activities, or about 90,000 activities annually, through general permits. Only about ten percent of projects or activities that impact wetlands are regulated through individual permits.

To date, the Corps issued 39 nationwide general permits and many more state and regional general permits. Typical projects covered under general permits include navigation markers, utility line structures, bank stabilization projects, minor dredge and fill projects involving less than 10 cubic yards of fill material (not in wetlands), boat docks, and certain federally approved and funded projects.

Probably the single most controversial general permit is Nationwide Permit 26 (NWP 26), which authorizes discharges of dredged or fill material into wetlands that are either isolated or above the headwaters of a river or stream with average annual flow of five cubic feet per second or less. Isolated wetlands are these that are not adjacent to water bodies such as lakes or streams. An estimated 10,000 wetland acres are lost through Nationwide Permit 26 alone.

Under NWP 26, activities that fill less than one acre of wetlands are automatically authorized without any meaningful environmental review. For fills between 1 and 10 acres in size, NWP 26 requires the discharger to notify the Corps before discharging by submitting a pre-discharge notification. The Corps will consider the proposed fill action and send a notice to EPA, FWS, and NMFS to allow them an opportunity to comment. The agencies have 30 days in which to notify the discharger of any additional restrictions in the NWP 26 authorization. Otherwise, the discharger may proceed in compliance with the general conditions of the NWP 26 regulations. For fill activities that would destroy 10 or more acres of isolated wetlands or headwaters, an individual §404 permit is required.

Water

Water in rural America has been overused and misused. America's surface-water resources are truly immense. There are over a million miles of rivers and streams in America. The nation's inland water bodies encompass over 61,000 square miles, and there are an additional 94,000 square miles in the Great Lakes.

Surface water bodies serve as the drinking water supply for half of America's population. These systems are also the repository for wastes from 64,000 factories and sewage treatment plants. Of these dischargers, about 7,000 are considered major dischargers under federal legislation. As a result, billions of pounds of pollutants are released into the nation's waters every year from these point sources.

Groundwaters of America face similar problems. Since 1985, America, and in particular rural America, increased its use of groundwater. Contamination of groundwater also increased. Much of this contamination came from chemical pollution: heavy metals, such as mercury or cadmium; pesticides, such as DDT and 2,4,5-TP; and organic chemicals, such as PCBs and dioxins.

Water Policy

The national goal of the Clean Water Act is that all waters should be safe for fishing and swimming. To date, only 66 percent of the nation's waters meet this goal. To achieve this ambitious goal, Congress enacted a variety of programs to attack the many types of pollution entering the waters.

The Clean Water Act established a federal-state partnership to control the discharge of pollutants from large point sources. The EPA develops national guidelines to control industrial pollution discharges that are based on the Best Available Technology that is economically achievable. These national standards regulate and apply to entire industrial categories.

Sewage treatment plants must meet basic levels of secondary treatment that use biological processes to transform disease-causing organisms into harmless matter. The federal government provided billions of dollars in grants and loans to state and local governments to construct sewage treatment plants to meet this standard.

All industrial and sewage treatment plants must obtain a permit that specifies the type and amount of pollutants they may discharge. The permits specify industry-wide technology standards, state water quality standards, and sewage treatment standards that apply to that source. They are reviewed and renewed every five years to account for improvements in technology. Thirty-nine states run this type of permitting program. It is this permitting system that holds dischargers accountable. The federal government, the state governments, and citizens can sue sources that violate their permits.

To ensure that waters stay safe for fishing and swimming, new sources of pollution are carefully reviewed to ensure they will not degrade the water body.

Pristine waters, such as headwaters in our national parks or wilderness areas, can be designated by states to receive special protection.

Polluted runoff from agriculture, forestry, mining and other sources is the largest remaining source of water pollution. Under current law, states are required to plan and use cost-effective best management practices by landowners at the earliest practical date. Requirements for individual landowners who cause pollution are weak and unenforceable.

One source of water pollution that is becoming increasingly significant is the growth of large feedlots and factory farms. These concentrated animal feeding operations are responsible for phosphorus, pathogens, and nutrients from animal waste seeping into surface and ground water. The EPA regulates these operations as point sources, but enforcement has been minimal.

Habitat and Species Loss

The rate of species extinction, although a natural process, has reached epidemic proportions in recent years. It is currently estimated that between 1 to 100 species are lost each day. By comparison, the rate of extinction before the appearance of humans was only about one species every 100 years.

Protecting the existence and variety of species (biological diversity) is essential to life on Earth since all species, including humans, are dependent on each other for survival. An astounding number of species provide over 40 percent of prescription drugs, including a possible cure for threatening diseases like AIDS and cancer. They provide sustainable food crops and consumer products like cotton and paper, clean the air and water, and give invaluable esthetic and recreational experiences.

The acceleration of the extinction rate is directly linked with the human population explosion and the increased demands humans place on the environment. More people mean more trash, buildings, roads and highways, all factors that increase the difficulty for species to survive. People alter or destroy habitats through drilling for oil, strip mining for minerals, or logging for timber, which often conflicts with species ability to find food and shelter and raise their young. Wildlife trade, pollution, and introduction of non-native species take their toll on the ecosystems native to many species.

The Endangered Species Act of 1973 attempts to counteract the alarming rate of species extinction. The Act provides a mechanism to conserve plants and animals in danger of extinction and protects the ecosystems necessary for their survival. Once a troubled species is identified, it is placed on a threatened or endangered species list. Either the U.S. Fish and Wildlife Service or National Marine Fisheries Administration is then responsible to develop a plan to recover it, and insure that government and citizen actions do not further harm the species. The Act requires that a recovery plan be written for each listed species.

Despite the continued overwhelming support of U.S. citizens, there are growing pressures from special interests groups to weaken the Endangered Species Act. These groups, representing some members of the oil, timber, mining, livestock and real estate development industries, see environmental laws as blocking their ability to do business.

Future Challenges

The future environmental challenges that stand before rural America are global in scope. The responsibility to protect and preserve a quality environment belongs to both individuals and communities. That said, long-standing environmental problems continue to plague many rural areas. Industrial agriculture and forestry have taken a toll on the integrity of large ecosystems and the future productivity of the land. New environmental challenges, such as sprawl and land fragmentation, are increasing with rapid population growth and new ownership and land use patterns.

Overshadowing all other issues is climate change, which is introducing unprecedented stress on ecosystems and the communities that depend on them. From impacts on overall ecosystem health to changes in sea-level and storm impacts, to consequences for agriculture, forestry, recreation, and tourism, climate change is a growing concern for rural America.

Ecological interdependence exists among nations; there is no boundary to our environment, so the issues facing rural America will involve individuals and communities from many nations and regions. How the rural American environment is treated ultimately impacts other parts of the world and can be expected to haunt those guilty of its mistreatment. Future environmental concerns will truly require residents to think globally when acting locally. In agriculture, for example, cropping practices should be adopted that minimize the contaminants produced while providing sinks for those

that are contaminating. There is a continuing need to merge environmental considerations with those of economics in decision making at the local and international levels in order to provide equitable solutions to problems. For agriculture, this implies providing technology, where appropriate, to assist other nations overcome their problems. At the same time, social and cultural differences must be respected while attempting to improve the human condition. For rural America, future environmental challenges have a global meaning.

— *William W. Budd*

See also

Agricultural Programs; Biodiversity; Conservation, Energy; Conservation, Soil; Conservation, Water; Environmental Protection; Environmental Regulations; Forestry Industry; Groundwater; Land Stewardship; Mining Industry; Natural Resource Economics; Parks; Policy, Agricultural; Soil; Water; Weather; Wetlands; Wilderness; Wildlife

References

Petulla, Joseph M. *American Environmental History,* 2nd edition. Columbus, OH: Merrill Publishing Co., 1988.

Plater, Zygmunt J.B., Robert H. Abrams, and William Goldfarb. *Environmental Law and Policy: A Coursebook on Nature, Law, and Society.* St. Paul, MN: West Publications, 1992.

Steiner, Frederick R. *Soil Conservation in the United States: Policy and Planning.* Baltimore, MD: Johns Hopkins University Press, 1990.

Valente, C. and W. Valente. *Introduction to Environmental Law and Policy.* St. Paul, MN: West Publications, 1995.

Policy, Food

Government programs and regulations designed to help assure that all Americans have access to an adequate diet of safe food at a reasonable price. Food policy is consistent with investing in the health and productivity of the people in the Untied States, especially its poor. It is designed as a safety net for those who cannot afford adequate nutrition to sustain a healthy lifestyle. This chapter looks at the nature and extent of poverty in rural America,[1] food programs available to those in pov-

---

[1]Rural is defined herein as the non-metro areas that contain no cities with population over 50,000. Metro (urban) is defined as having cities of at least 50,000 residents or with an urbanized area of 50,000 or more and total area population of at least 100,000. Fringe counties that are tied economically to core counties are also classified as metro areas.

erty and how well they are served by these programs. Originally, food policy upheld the income of farm families by stabilizing commodity prices through the government purchase of surplus commodities. In the early part of twentieth century, it was perceived that rural people could grow their own food and that the distribution of food to alleviate hunger and help poor people maintain their health and lead productive lives was largely an urban poverty program. However, since seventeen percent of the U.S. population lives in rural America and sixteen percent of them live in poverty, the poverty rate is actually three percentage points greater than in metro areas. In modern times, rural residents are little more likely to grow their own food than metropolitan dwellers; food assistance programs are at least as important for the rural poor as for the non-rural poor in America.

The Poor and the Rural Poor in America

A lack of food and adequate nutrition are almost always a result of inadequate income. The poverty level income in America is defined by a construct based on the ability to purchase a minimally nutritious diet, originally the 1961 Economy Food Plan designed by USDA. "The poverty thresholds are updated every year to reflect changes in the Consumer Price Index. The following technical changes to the thresholds were made in 1981: (1) distinctions based on sex of householder were eliminated, (2) separate thresholds for farm families were dropped, and (3) the matrix was expanded to families of nine or more persons from the old cutoff of seven or more persons" (U.S. Census Bureau 2008: 428) The number of Americans living below the official poverty level income changed little between 1960 and 1993 (39.9 to 39.3 million) but fell to 32.9 million by 2001. The poverty rate declined from 22.2 percent of the population (30.0 percent of the rural population) in 1960 to 15.1 percent of the population (16.8 percent of the rural population) in 1993 to 13.1 percent in 2005 (16 percent in rural areas). Nineteen percent of rural children (15 percent of metro children) lived in poverty in 2000, down from 24 percent (22 percent of metro children) in 1993.

For a frame of reference, a family of four was considered to live in poverty in 1993 if they had an annual earned income of less than $14,763. In 2006 the com-

parable poverty level was $20,444. After adjusting for inflation, this represents a one percent decline in real income. The median U.S. family income was $31,241 in 1993 and $59,894 in 2006 in current dollars. Median rural family income was $25,256 in 1993 and $38,293 in 2006. This is a 40 percent increase in real medium family income in both urban and rural areas. The lack of a gap between the growth in rural and urban median family incomes can be accounted for by a more than four percent annual rise in the average farm household income between 1990 and 2004. Average farm household income was $38,237 in 1990 and $81,420 in 2005. This represents a real increase of 42 percent in real dollars.

There is still a gap in real earnings per nonfarm job which grew at an annual rate of 0.5 percent between 1990 and 2004 (1.4 percent between 1970 and 1986) in rural areas compared to 1.2 percent in metro areas (4 percent between 1970 and 1986). Nonfarm job earnings in rural America were 72 percent of metro earnings in 1993 and 67 percent in 2004. Incomes are lower in rural areas primarily because wages are lower. Over half of workers in rural areas earn low wages, defined as wages that yielded an annual income less than the poverty level for a family of four.

As industry has moved out of rural areas over the past half century, workers also moved out, leaving behind housing that depreciated in value. This relatively inexpensive housing became attractive to the poor from other areas where housing costs can take more than 50 percent of their income. This type of in-migration tends to concentrate poverty in pockets of rural areas where people are poorer, older, less well-educated, and less connected to the labor force than those who moved out. In general, the lower the population density, the higher the poverty rate in rural areas. These tend to be people who are persistently poor, with long term needs for food assistance and other poverty programs.

The elderly in rural areas are also more likely to be poor than the elderly in metropolitan areas. Twenty-six percent of the elderly (over age 65) live in rural areas. Within rural areas fourteen percent of the population is elderly and thirteen percent of the rural elderly are poor. In three hundred out of 2,259 rural counties, more than twenty percent of the residents are poor compared to only two percent of the 826 metro counties. Almost half of these rural-elderly counties are in the center of the United States; they have "aged in place." That is, the preponderance of elderly poor in these counties is due to the shrinking of agriculture and an out-migration of youth leaving the older residents behind. Seventeen percent of the rural-elderly counties are so designated because on in-migration of retirees. In these rural-elderly counties 8.4 percent fewer dollars were spent on food stamps, school lunches and Women-Infants and Childrens' programs than in metro counties. However, seventeen percent of the rural-elderly counties were "transfer-dependent" receiving at least one-quarter of their income from government transfer payments including social security and farm supports.

Twenty percent of the rural population are children, and a quarter of them are living in poverty. States that have pockets where more than half of the children living in poverty are South Dakota, Texas, Louisiana, and Mississippi. Forty-five percent of the poor children live in the south. One quarter of poor children live in mother-only families. The working poor are found in both rural and metro areas. More than seventy-five percent of parents of poor children are in the labor force, yet over half of the children in rural working households live in poverty.

Although 20 percent of farmers reportedly live in poverty, rural poverty is not an agricultural problem. It is a problem for a broad range of people who do not earn sufficient income to be able to purchase enough food to have a nutritionally adequate diet on a regular basis.

Food Programs and Rural People

The first government food assistance programs were started during the Depression of the 1930s. Since hunger is largely caused by a lack of income, enhancing the incomes of farmers (25 percent of the population then) was one way to alleviate their hunger. Distributing food to non-farmers was a way to invest in the human capital of the country by trying to prevent hunger. Thirteen million people (five percent of the population) received food supplements by 1939. An early version of the Food Stamp Program was initiated at that time, but most of these early food programs were discontinued during World War II.

Increased demand for agricultural products and a strong economy brought food policy back to the political foreground in the late 1960s. At that time, a book titled *Let Them Eat Promises: The Politics of Hunger in America*, a CBS television documentary, "Hunger, U.S.A.," Congressional fact-finding trips to the rural South, and other political protests focused attention on the pressing problems of the poor. Although many food assistance programs, including the current Food Stamp Program, already had been established by the late 1960s, a White House conference was held in 1969 in which former President Nixon said it was time to end to hunger in America once and for all. A Senate Select Committee on Nutrition and Human Needs was established; spending on food programs reached $1.1 billion by 1969. During the 1970s a major expansion took place in the Food Stamp Program and federal expenditures on food assistance programs. Table 1 provides a list of the many food and nutrition assistance programs with their dates on initiation and total expenditures since 1980 in current dollars. Table 2 provides the constant (inflation adjusted) 2007 dollars. For example, the food stamp program cost $34.6 billion in 2007 and $23.2 billion in 1980 in real 2007 dollars—a 49.3 percent increase. Government spending for most programs rose in real terms over the 27 year period between 1980 and 2007. This is partly due to increased food costs and partly due to more eligible people using these programs. In addition, there have been some absolute increases in the value of food stamps and in dollars allocated to Women Infants and Children (WIC).

A decline in real expenditures between 1990 and 2000 in the Food Stamp Program was due to a new social welfare program called the Personal Responsibility and work Opportunity Reconciliation Act (PRWORA) of 1996. This act replaced an entitlement program Aid to Families with Dependent Children (AFDC). PRWORA is funded through block grants to States and seeks to move people from welfare to work by imposing a five-year lifetime limit on receiving Federal welfare benefits and requiring recipients to participate in work activities within two years of receiving benefits. Able-bodied adults without dependents face a three-month limit on receiving food stamps, unless they are working or in a job-training program. Most non citizens cannot receive food stamps until they become citizens or worked for at least 10 years. After 1996 the food stamp rolls fell substantially. Rural residents faced extra challenges with PRWORA due to fewer available jobs and greater need for private transportation. Nevertheless, the greatest declines in food stamp participation were in metro areas where both the size of the eligible population and the participation rates declined. In rural areas only the size of the eligible population de-

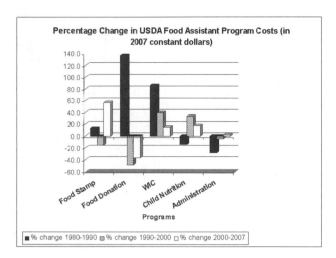

Percentage Change in USDA Food Assistant Program Costs (in 2007 constant dollars)

Programs: Food Stamp, Food Donation, WIC, Child Nutrition, Administration

■ % change 1980-1990 ▨ % change 1990-2000 □ % change 2000-2007

clined. About 25 percent of food stamp recipients are in rural areas. Overall, only about 65 percent of eligible individuals participate in the Food Stamp Program (Whitener, et al. 2002).

Food Programs that declined in real terms throughout the period 1990–2007 are food donation programs and special milk where the allocations have declined in real terms. Program administration also declined.

Food programs serve rural people at least as well as those in metropolitan areas. Food program participants are over-represented in rural areas. For example, seventeen percent of all households are in rural areas where twenty-five percent of the households receiving food stamps reside. Reports about the participation rates in the food stamp program vary by research organization or agency; but there seems to be a consensus that about two-thirds of eligible individuals and 59 percent of eligible families participate in both rural and urban areas.

Food stamps are, however, a relatively less important source of food aid in rural areas. Ignorance and pride often prevent people from using food stamps and pride related to self-sufficiency is allegedly greater in rural areas, especially among farmers. Transportation to apply for, pick up, and use food stamps is a greater problem in rural areas. Confounding this is that many of the rural poor are elderly and may need to hire someone to drive them to a county office to obtain food stamps and that may cost more than the value of the stamps. The shift away form actual stamps to a credit card-like system (electronic benefits transfer) has alleviated some of the problems of mobility and embarrassment.

Mobility of rural poor may make it difficult for them to receive food aid in each new location without reestablishing their eligibility. Other problems include a lack of literacy required to fill out forms and an asset base that may be needed to do business (e.g., farm equipment or more expensive vehicles) but that disqualifies a family for food assistance. Case workers who do not understand the different financial resources and assets in rural areas, or who insult applicants, may preclude some from participating when they are eligible. Additionally, case loads can run over 250 per case worker, making it very difficult to serve all clients well.

About the same percent of poor children in rural and urban areas receive a school lunch (74 percent); rural poor children are more likely to be in families receiving food stamps (52 percent vs. 48 percent in metro areas. The variety of food aid programs for the elderly such as Senior Nutrition sites where hot meals are served five days a week and food packages are provided for them to take home or, meals are delivered to their doors, make it relatively easy to participate. In many communities the Senior Citizen Center has become a noontime social event.

Food banks and other food distribution centers in rural areas are frequented by elderly. Many report preferring to obtain actual food than food stamps. The food shelves are easier to access on an ad hoc basis, serving temporary food needs without much eligibility screening. Since many food stamp recipients run out of food before the end of the month, they also supplement their food supply with food from food shelves. It has become an important part of the food and nutrition safety net.

Food assistance is not designed to lift people out of poverty. The monetary value of food stamps provides about 20 to 30 percent of a poverty level income for a family of four. In combination with other food and welfare programs it provides between 45 and 90 percent of the value of a poverty level income. It does, however, provide basic nutrition and food for those who would otherwise go hungry. Most studies found that those who receive food stamps increase their overall food spending by about 20 to 30 percent (e.g., Senauer and Young 1986; Fraker 1993). One dollar's worth of food stamps frees 70 to 80 cents of cash that was previously used for food and that can then be spent on other goods and services. Food stamp recipients also eat more nutritious diets than non participants who are eligible for the program.

Table 1
United States Food Assistance Programs (Expenditure in current dollars—millions)

Program	Year Program Initiated	1980	1990	2000	2007	Participation
Food Stamp[1]	1961	9,206.5	16,431.6	18,335.1	34,584.3	26.5 million participants per month
Nutrition Assistance	1975-1982				1,566.8	n/a
Food Donation Program[2]	1936	172.9	646.6	436.4	333.0	n/a
Nutrition Services Incentive Program	1965				2.6	n/a
Food Distribution on Indian Reservation	1976				77.0	86.6 thousand participants per month
Disaster Feeding (by FEMA)					7.1	
TEFAP	1981				246.3	n/a
WIC[3]	1972	749.2	2,207.6	4,065.8	5,610.7	8.3 million participants per month
Commodity Supplemental Food	1982				141.0	466.1 thousand participants per month
Child Nutrition[4]		4,033.9	5,496.2	9,670.7	13,640.4	
National School Lunch	1946	2,279.4	3,213.9	5,492.9	7,704.2	28.3 million daily lunches served (average)
School Breakfast	1966	287.8	596.2	1,393.3	2,163.3	9.4 million daily breakfasts served (average)
Child and Adult Care	1968				2,232.3	1.8 billion total meals and snacks served
Summer Food Service	1969				288.9	120.3 million total meals and snacks
Special Milk	1955	145.2	19.2	15.4	13.6	91.4 million total half pints served
Food Program Administration[5]		80.4	92.0	114.9	140.5	n/a

Source: USDA, Food and Nutrition Service. Data as of November, 2007.

[1]Food stamps includes the Food Stamp Program and the Nutrition Assistance Programs in Puerto Rico, the Northern Marianas, and starting in FY 1996, American Samoa

[2]Food donations includes the Food Distribution Program on Indian Reservations, the Nutrition Services Incentive Program, the Disaster Feeding Program, the Emergencey Food Assistance Program, and the Food Distribution Programs for Charitable Institutions and Summer Camps

[3]WIC includes the Special Supplemental Nutrition Program for Women, Infants, and Children (WIC) and the Commodity Supplemental Food Program

[4]Child nutrition includes the National School Lunch, School Breakfast, Child and Adult Care, Summer Food Service, and Special Milk Program

[5]Food program administration includes administrative expenses

[6]All percentage changes are calculated based on 2007 constant dollar values

The impact of food programs on farm incomes is negligible, even though initially many food programs were implemented to save farm incomes. Farm prices have been estimated to rise less than one percent and farm income less than 1.8 percent for every dollar spent on food aid. Total food expenditures on food to be eaten at home increased less than three percent as a result of domestic food aid. Whereas the impact of food programs on individual recipients' health and well-being can be dramatic and society's investment in its human capital is rewarding on both productive and humanitarian grounds, food policy, as implemented in the U.S., has little impact on agricultural producers. Food policy graduated from distributing surplus commodities that supplemented individuals' diets to a program of providing whole, nutritious meals, nutritional education and, in some cases, cash with which poor consumers can purchase whatever they deem the most important to their livelihood. Recipients tend to prefer cash with as little administrative regulation as possible. Taxpayers tend to prefer highly targeted and monitored programs that ensure that their dollars are spent on nutritious food. This long-standing tension will play out in political and economic decisions as long as there are food and other welfare programs for people with low incomes.

— *Jean D. Kinsey*

See also

Consumerism; Food Safety; Home Economics; Homelessness; Nutrition; Policy (various); Poverty; Welfare

References

Devaney, B. and R. Moffit. "Dietary Effects of the Food Stamp Program." *American Journal of Agricultural Economics* 73 (1991): 202-211.

Duncan, Cynthia M. *Rural Poverty in America.* New York, NY: Auburn House, 1992.

Fraker, Thomas. "The Effects of Food Stamps on Food Consumption: A Review of the Literature." *Mathematica Policy Research.* Washington DC: U.S. Department of Agriculture, Food and Nutrition Service, 1993.

Isaacs, Julia and Margaret Andrews, "The Cost of Benefit Delivery in the Food Stamp Program," Contractor and Cooperator Report No. 39. Washington, DC: U.S. De-

Table 2
Unites States Food Assistance Programs (Expenditures in constant 2007 dollars—millions)

Program	Year Program Initiated	1980 in constant 2007 $	1990 in constant 2007 $	2000 in constant 2007 $	2007	% change 1980-1990	% change 1990-2000	% change 2000-2007	% change 1980-2007
Food Stamp[1]	1961	23,161.5	26,061.8	22,072.4	34,584.3	12.5	−15.3	56.7	49.3
Nutrition Assistance	1975-1982				1,566.8				
Food Donation Program[2]	1936	435.0	1,025.6	525.4	333.0	135.8	−48.8	−36.6	−23.4
Nutrit. Serv. Incent. Pgm.	1965				2.6				
Food Dist. Indian Res.	1976				77.0				
Disaster Feeding (by FEMA)					7.1				
TEFAP	1981				246.3				
WIC[3]	1972	1,884.8	3,501.4	4,894.5	5,610.7	85.8	39.8	14.6	197.7
Commodity Suppl. Food	1982				141.0				
Child Nutrition[4]		10,148.4	8,717.4	11,641.9	13,640.4	−14.1	33.5	17.2	34.4
National School Lunch	1946	5,734.5	5,097.5	6,612.5	7,704.2	−11.1	29.7	16.5	34.3
School Breakfast	1966	724.0	945.6	1,677.3	2,163.3	30.6	77.4	29.0	198.8
Child and Adult Care	1968				2,232.3				
Summer Food Service	1969				288.9				
Special Milk	1955	365.3	30.5	18.5	13.6	−91.7	−39.1	−26.6	−96.3
Food Program Administration[5]		202.3	145.9	138.3	140.5	−27.9	−5.2	1.6	−30.5

Source: USDA, Food and Nutrition Service. Data as of November, 2007.

[1]Food stamps includes the Food Stamp Program and the Nutrition Assistance Programs in Puerto Rico, the Northern Marianas, and starting in FY 1996, American Samoa

[2]Food donations includes the Food Distribution Program on Indian Reservations, the Nutrition Services Incentive Program, the Disaster Feeding Program, the Emergency Food Assistance Program, and the Food Distribution Programs for Charitable Institutions and Summer Camps

[3]WIC includes the Special Supplemental Nutrition Program for Women, Infants, and Children (WIC) and the Commodity Supplemental Food Program

[4]Child nutrition includes the National School Lunch, School Breakfast, Child and Adult Care, Summer Food Service, and Special Milk Program

[5]Food program administration includes administrative expenses

[6]All percentage changes are calculated base on 2007 constant dollar values

partment of Agriculture, Economic Research Service, March 2008.

Jolliffe, Dean, "Nonmetro Poverty: Assessing the Effect of the 1900s," *Amber Waves*, September, 2003.

Kinsey, Jean D. and David M. Smallwood. "Domestic Food Aid Programs." Pp. 135-152 in *Food, Agricultural and Rural Policy Into the Twenty-first Century*. Edited by M. Hallberg, B. Sptize, and D. Ray. Boulder, CO: Westview Press, 1994.

Lane, Sylvia, John Kushman, and Christine Ranney. "Food Stamp Program Participation: An Exploratory Analysis." *Western Journal of Agricultural Economics* 8 (1983): 13-26.

Physicians Task Force on Hunger in America. *Hunger in America: The Growing Epidemic*. Middletown, CT: Wesleyan University Press, 1985.

Reeder, Richard J. and Samuel D. Calhoun, "Federal Funding in Nonmetro Elderly Counties," *Rural America* 17, no. 3 (Fall, 2002): 20.

Rogers, Carolyn C. *Rural Children at a Glance*. Economic Information Bulletin No. 1. Washington, DC: U.S. Department of Agriculture, Economic Research Service, March 2005.

Senauer, Ben and Jean Kinsey, eds. *Final Report by the Food and Consumer Issues Working Group, 1995 Farm Bill Project*. Washington DC: National Center for Food

and Agricultural Policy and St. Paul, MN: University of Minnesota, Hubert H. Humphrey Institute of Agricultural Policy, March 1995.

Senauer, Benjamin and Nathan Young. "The Impacts of food Stamps on Food Expenditures: Rejection of the Traditional Model." *American Journal of Agricultural Economics* 68 (1986): 37-43.

"(The) Socioeconomic Well-Being of Rural Children Lags that of Urban Children" *Rural conditions and Trends* 9, no. 2 (2006): 85.

Stewart, James B. and Joyce E. Allen-Smith, eds. *Blacks in Rural America*. New Brunswick, NJ: Transaction Publishers, 1995.

U.S. Census Bureau. Various pages on income and households. Available online at: http://www.census.gov/compendia/statab

U.S. Congress. *Hunger in Rural America, Hearing before the Subcommittee on Domestic Marketing, Consumer Relations, and Nutrition of the Committee on Agriculture House of Representatives*, 101 Congress, May 17, 1989, Serial No. 101-15. Washington, DC: Government Printing Office, 1989.

U.S. Department of Agriculture. *Rural American at a Glance: 2007 Edition*. Economic Information Bulletin No. 31. Washington, DC: U.S. Department of Agriculture, Economic Research Service, October, 2007.

U.S. Department of Agriculture, Economic Research Service. Various pages with search with rural and poverty. Available online at: www.ers.usda.gov.

Whitener, Leslie A. Greg J. Duncan and Bruce A. Weber, "Reforming Welfare: What Does It Mean For Rural Areas?" Food Assistance and Nutrition Research Report No. 26-4. Washington, DC: U.S. Department of Agriculture, Economic Research Service, June, 2002.

Policy, Health Care

The constellation of public actions and decisions, especially at the federal level, that influences the ability of rural people to receive needed health care services. Federal policies that influence the development and sustainability of rural health care delivery in the U.S. Three major themes have influenced rural health care policy in the U.S. First, the federal government enacted policies from the 1940s through the 1960s to build a physical infrastructure and attract health professionals to rural communities. Since that time, policy makers have worked to sustain access to services in the communities that benefited from that initial effort. Second, because of who they serve, the services they offer, and the local resource base, rural health care providers are particularly vulnerable to the unintended consequences of swings in payment policies that are designed to squeeze savings from the system. Third, rural health care systems may benefit from policies that emphasize quality improvement and cost effective investments in health care.

Health care has emerged as a top priority domestic issue (flip-flopping with the economy) in public opinion polls, primarily because of increased costs. Health care expenditures are expected to account for 19.5 percent of the gross domestic product by 2017, up from 16.3 percent in 2007. Individual consumers feel the pain of cost increases in annual increases in insurance premiums that exceed increases in income, even though the pace of premium increases has moderated. For many insured consumers, out-of-pocket expenses have increased as employer-sponsored insurance plans have increased deductibles and copayments (Keehan, et al. 2008). Issues in health policy include concerns about quality of care being delivered, with the Medicare program publishing data comparing quality of services among hospitals, nursing homes, and physicians. Current and impending shortages of health care profes-

sionals have been used as evidence of problems in assuring access to health care services. For the first time, US policy makers now confront the challenge of resolving serious issues, if not crises, in all three cornerstones of health policy—cost, quality, and access—at the same time. The health care needs of rural America have to be considered in that context.

Sustaining Services in Rural Areas

The national government began investing heavily in access to health care in rural America with the Hospital Survey and Construction Act of 1946, which channeled billions of dollars into the construction or modernization of rural hospitals during the subsequent two decades. The national government has invested in personnel as well, primarily through payments embedded in the Medicare and Medicaid programs (for graduate medical education provided in teaching hospitals), research programs at academic health centers (especially funds from the National Institutes of Health), and health services grants for professional training (such as special programs for family medicine and nursing). Programs have also been developed to provide assistance directly to health professionals to encourage them to practice in certain professions (e.g., primary care) and in certain areas (e.g., federally designated shortage areas).

In the last three decades (from 1980 to 2008, the time of this writing), federal policies have targeted investment in rural health systems, most often as titles in legislation intended to have broad impact on health care costs and access. In 1983, a major shift in Medicare policy from retrospective pricing for hospital care to a prospective payment system allowed special categories of rural hospitals to be paid differently than all other hospitals: sole community hospitals (isolated facilities), rural referral centers (large regional hospitals) and Medicare dependent hospitals (60% or more of their inpatient revenue derived from Medicare). In 1997, when Congress extended the prospective payment methodology to virtually all providers, special provisions were made for critical access hospitals (CAHs, a new category of facilities with 25 or fewer beds and located at some distance from other hospitals), rural home health agencies, and rural health clinics (primary care clinics using non-physician providers). In 2003, when Congress enacted major changes in the Medicare program, special payment provisions were created for physicians practicing in rural scarcity areas and for managed care organizations enrolling rural residents.

The national government will at times invest more directly in rural facilities and providers. The Medicare Rural Hospital Flexibility Grant Program provides grants to states for that purpose, focused on CAHs and their communities. Health professions loans and loan repayments are available through the National Health Services Corps for persons who agree to start their careers in rural underserved areas. The US Department of Agriculture provides loans and loan guarantees to some rural institutions providing health care (hospitals and nursing homes). Other grants are available to rural communities and providers to build provider networks, adopt electronic records systems, provide special services, and demonstrate innovative approaches to health care delivery.

Unintended Consequences of Payment Policies

The special efforts to sustain rural health services described above were needed because well-intentioned policies to control costs are often based on statistical models that assume substantial volumes of business and an ability to use capital reserves. From 1983 through 2003, the prospective payment system for inpatient care in hospitals most clearly illustrated this problem. That system assumes hospitals can recover their costs by gaining sufficient revenue from patients who need fewer than predicted services to balance those who need more. For low-volume hospitals (predominantly rural) that approach is not effective. The policy response is to use special adjustments (hence different categories of hospitals), including adjustments based on low volume (a proposal currently being considered). A current example of unintended consequences is the effect of the new Medicare drug benefit on rural independent pharmacies. The new benefit pays private insurance carriers to make drug benefits available to Medicare beneficiaries, which shifts the source of payment to pharmacies from either out-of-pocket or Medicaid (the new Medicare benefit supplants Medicaid as the drug benefit for low-income elderly and disabled). Private insurance payment has been lower than previous payment, and independent pharmacies are unable to negotiate the lowest prices possible on their purchases of pharmaceuticals and/or best possible prices from insurers. In both examples, hospitals and pharmacies, if economic circumstances became extreme for rural providers, local access to services would be imperiled.

Congress appears to be ready to change payment policies again, this time to build into payment formulas an element based on the quality of care provided. The Centers for Medicare and Medicaid Services (CMS) in 2008 presented Congress with a white paper describing the implementation of "value based purchasing" (VBP) as a payment methodology. CMS has developed measures that it reports regarding quality provided by hospitals, nursing homes, and physicians. To create incentives for all hospitals to perform well, CMS currently pays more to hospitals that report data for all CMS quality indicators (which include consumer satisfaction) and that make the data publicly available. A similar approach is being suggested for physicians, again using indicators by CMS. Many policy makers would like to change the payment systems to be based eventually entirely on performance. The unintended consequences for rural providers would once again be related to volume of services and available capital for investment. Service volume is already an issue for small rural hospitals, because the current reporting system shows "insufficient data" when publishing indicators for those hospitals, which to patients could imply suboptimal care. Data published as averages or rates may be biased by one adverse admission. The lack of capital could affect the ability of rural providers to develop reporting systems needed to participate in new VBP programs.

Rural Health Care Systems Leading in Quality Improvement

In November 2004, the Institute of Medicine (IOM) released the report *Quality through Collaboration: The Future of Rural Health*. As part of an IOM series that pushed a policy agenda to improve quality of American health care services and protect patient safety, the rural report broke new ground by advocating a focus on community health and care of individuals. The report also inspired rural advocates to push a policy and practice agenda that would feature rural providers and systems as innovators in quality improvement. The National Rural Health Association (NRHA) created a quality initiative in 2005 that it continues to support. The initiative currently supports use of the Agency for Healthcare Research and Quality survey on patient safety culture in small rural hospitals as a means of implementing data-driven improvements in organization culture that will in turn improve patient safety and quality.

Three general strategies for improving quality of care could be initiated in rural areas as primary demonstrations. The first strategy is to improve communications among health providers treating the same patient during the same episode of illness. Because rural health care organizations are smaller than their urban counterparts, particularly in small rural hospitals, improving inter-personal communications should be a simpler task. Communication with providers outside the community is more challenging, but rural primary care physicians are likely to have well-established relationships with such providers because they are involved in patient care across the primary physician's patient population. The second strategy is to improve adherence to standard protocols. Again, the small scale of rural health care should make this task less onerous than in urban areas, both because of the fewer number of patients and because of the more narrow range of functions, particularly in small rural hospitals. Early comparative data is in fact showing that small rural hospitals score above the national average on those indicators for which they are likely to see a high proportion of patients. The third strategy is perhaps the most promising for rural health system leadership. Many proposals for reforming the health care system start with a foundation of a patient-centered medical home (PCMH). Rural primary care physicians are ideally suited to establish PCMH's in their clinics, serving the functions of care coordination, comprehensive care, and continuous care. Physicians may need to improve information systems, including adopting electronic medical records, to accomplish everything expected of a PCMH, but they begin with an advantage in physician-patient relationships that includes an appreciation of all circumstances affecting patient health and already being the provider of first choice for nearly all of their patients.

Rural Health Policy in the Larger Rural Policy Context

Both individual and community health improvement will require consideration of health policy within a broader community context. Many factors other than services provided by the medical community affect health care—the quality of the environment, the quality of housing, education achievement, and income to name a few. Seeing health care as a continuum beginning with health behavior and environmental conditions affecting the onset of adverse health conditions and ending with palliative care at the end of life, there are many dynamic interactions between health care services and other policy choices affecting the community, which in turn affect everyone's health. Thus, there are reasons for health care providers and advocates for

rural health to broaden their activities beyond clinical health care to include becoming involved in improving the quality of life in rural places more broadly.

Conversely, rural decision makers focused on community development and sustaining the viability of rural places should look to health care as a vital ingredient in any strategy. There are at least five dimensions to the role of health care in community sustainability. First, health care services can influence health status, which in turn influences labor productivity, absenteeism, and quality of life. Second, high quality services make a community more desirable and effective in its ability to attract and retain people and businesses. Third, the skills and abilities of health professionals and other health service workers are available to the community to enhance the local pool of leadership talent. Fourth, the health services sector needs cash and short-term investments to meet payroll and other needs. Typically these funds are held in local financial institutions and become available for investment purposes by others. Finally, the health services sector is an important local employer and purchaser of local goods and services.

Although the health care sector can legitimately be viewed as a growth industry, it is not likely that all locales will benefit. Those communities that are best positioned and most responsive in anticipating structural and policy changes will capitalize on the potential of the health service sector as a growth industry. Conversely, those communities and areas that cannot compete effectively in tomorrow's challenging environment will likely sustain economic losses.

— *Keith Mueller and Sam Cordes*

See also
Addiction; Dental Health Care; Food Safety; Insurance; Rural Health Care; HIV/AIDS; Mental Health; Nursing and Allied Health Professions

References
Committee on the Future of Rural Health Care, Institute of Medicine. *Quality through Collaboration: The Future of Rural Health.* Washington, DC: National Academies Press, 2004.

Geyman, John P., Thomas E. Norris, and L. Gary Hart, eds. *Textbook of Rural Medicine.* New York: McGraw-Hill, 2001.

Glasgow, Nina, Lois Wright Morton, and Nan E Johnson, eds. *Critical Issues in Rural Health.* Oxford: Blackwell Publishing, 2004.

Keehan, Sean, Andrea Sisko, Christopher Truffer, Sheila Smith, Cathy Cowan, John Poilsal, and M. Kent Clemens. "Health Spending Projections Through 2017:

The Baby-Boom Generation is Coming to Medicare." *Health Affairs* 27, no 2 (2008): 2145-2155. Published online at: http://content.healthaffairs.org/cgi/content/full/27/2/w145.

Loue, Sana, and Beth E Quill, eds. *Handbook of Rural Health*. New York: Kluwer Academic/Plenum Publishers, 2001.

McBride, Timothy D. and Keith J. Mueller. "Effects of Medicare Payment on Rural Health Care Systems." *Journal of Rural Health* 18 (2002): 147-163.

Mueller Keith J. and A. Clinton MacKinney. "Care Across the Continuum: Access to Health Care Services in Rural America." *Journal of Rural Health* 22 (2006): 43-49.

Ricketts, Thomas C. III, ed. *Rural Health in the United States*. New York: Oxford University Press, 1999.

Policy, Rural Development

The range of efforts such as the creation of wealth, conservation of natural resources, enhancement of the capacity of rural people to identify and address their basic goals and needs, the provision of basic social service, and other activities aimed at improving personal and community quality of life. With the notable exception of the farm commodity and conservation programs rural policy tends to be minimal in its assistance to rural areas and fractured in its goals. There has never been a coherent federal policy for the economic and social development of rural people and their communities. However, during the past two decades, this minimalist approach to rural development has shifted toward a greater emphasis on economic and social infrastructure development through federal programs that give greater emphasis to local decision-making and funding.

Twentieth Century Rural Policies

Public and private sector development policies vary from active intervention to intentional neglect. The historic emphasis of federal rural development policies has been on assistance to farming enterprises characterized by much local input. An argument can be made that the New Deal agricultural policies coupled with rural electrification, the Tennessee Valley Authority (TVA), Civilian Conservation Corps, and the Works Project Administration represented an interventionist federal rural development policy. However, as the economic crisis of the Great Depression waned and as the economic base of rural America shifted from extractive industries such as farming, mining, forestry, and fishing toward manufacturing and service sector employment there was not a corresponding shift in emphasis among the myriad rural development policies until the mid-1990s when fundamental changes in rural policy seemed to be underway.

Historically, federal rural development has not been the battlefield for partisan political party debates, but has been subject to the institutional political tensions between the legislative and executive branches. Congress determines the general guidelines for rural development programs and appropriates funds. The Executive branch agencies interpret and manage these programs within the guidelines of congressional intent. In recent decades, Congress has been more likely to assign greater responsibilities to the states instead of to federal agencies.

Federal rural development policy has long been identified with the USDA, particularly with farm programs born during the New Deal when a majority of rural Americans earned their livelihood directly from agriculture or other natural resource-based industries. American rural communities historically displayed great diversity in their economic activities, geography, culture, ethnicity, and other socioeconomic characteristics. Whereas some communities in the Plains continue to depend on farming, southern and Midwestern communities tend to depend on manufacturing and service jobs.

The development of broad-based national social policies during the New Deal, World War II, and the Great Society profoundly altered the relationship of rural citizens' with the federal government. Rural people became reliant on social security, health, welfare, and other federal social services. Other notable national programs had great impacts on rural socioeconomic development include the Eisenhower interstate highway system, social welfare programs of the New Deal and the Great Society, and national credit policy. If total federal expenditures are used as indicators of policy emphasis, then rural America may be more affected by policies administered by non-USDA federal agencies. These would include Health and Human Services (HHS), Housing and Urban Development (HUD), Small Business Administration, Economic Development Administration, and even the Department of Defense. Federal regional agencies, such as Tennessee Valley Authority and the Appalachian Regional Commission, provide direct assistance to rural people. It is important to understand that rural public policies are much more than the programs authorized by the succeeding Farm Bills and administered by USDA.

Agricultural and Urban Biases for Rural Policy

The historic target of rural public policy has been the farm population. Ranching and other enterprises have received less support. Approximately two-thirds of rural people were engaged directly in farming in 1935, the peak year for American farm numbers. Agricultural policy was a rural development policy. By the 1990s less than 10 percent of rural people were directly employed in farming, though many communities in the High Plains continue to primarily depend upon farming. During the mid-decades of the twentieth century, rural America experienced a dual transformation with profound implications for economic and social well-being. The economic base of most rural communities shifted from extractive industries to manufacturing and the service sector. This shift in economic base was accompanied by a change in social class. Whereas most farm families owned some part of the farming operation and were therefore to some degree self-employed, most rural people now work for someone other themselves. Rural poverty continues to rival poverty rates in the inner cities. The jobs created during this transformation, on average, have not closed the income gap between metropolitan and nonmetropolitan counties. Yet, farm policy continues to be thought of as rural policy by agricultural legislators.

Political science studies of agricultural policy and the U.S. Congress (Browne 1995) emphasize a lack of interest by members of the Senate and House Agricultural Committees in non-farm rural development. A policy consequence has been for federal rural development policy to reflect the interests of more politically powerful non-farm groups such as the rural banking and credit interests, rural electric cooperatives, and the rural housing industry. This pluralist political process yielded very specific categoric grant programs (e.g., water and sewer projects) that were distributed across USDA agencies. There was no coherent USDA policy to coordinate these categoric grant programs.

An ancillary consequence has been for USDA rural policies to be characterized by an emphasis on physical infrastructure (water and sewer) and employment (rural credit and economic development) with little emphasis given to enhance social infrastructure and the capacity of rural communities to manage self-development efforts. The lack of coordination of USDA rural development programs led policy analysts to label federal rural development policy as minimalist or as de facto community triage. The harsh criticisms implied by these labels are not without considerable validity.

Rural social policy was relegated to other federal agencies such as HHS and HUD. If the amount of funds transferred from the federal government to rural areas is used as a measure of policy importance, individual entitlement programs, such as Social Security, Medicare, and other social welfare programs, account for the great bulk of federal assistance and policy to rural people. But, there are few, if any, of the non-USDA programs designed specifically for the diverse experiences and needs of rural people. Although there is evidence that non-USDA agencies have begun to recognize the need for programmatic adaptations to rural experiences, it is unlikely these agencies will alter existing urban biases in the near future. Therefore, where an agricultural bias existed for USDA administered rural development program, other federal programs have been characterized by a marked urban bias.

The Devolution of the Federal Government and Block Grants

Current and future rural development policy at the federal level is shaped by national political economic forces. Whereas the 1930 to 1970 period was characterized by the rapid expansion of interventionist federal programs and authority, the succeeding decades focused on the devolution of the federal government. That is, national public policy recently attempted to reduce both the size and authority of federal agencies. This movement toward a more restricted role for the federal government is referred to as the devolution, as opposed to the evolution, of government. The primary policy vehicle for the devolution of the federal government are block grants rather than more restricted categoric grants.

Block grants represent generic policy formulas that offer a framework to transfer some measure of authority and resources from a higher to a lower level of government. In the case of rural development, this was principally a transfer from the federal to state and local authorities. Whereas categorical grants target funds to specific types of assistance (e.g., sewer and water lines and telecommunications), block grants funnel money to state and local authorities who then have considerable program authority. Three specific policy goals are often cited as favoring the use of block grants. First, is the general concern to reduce the federal budget deficit. Block grants provide the option of reducing program funds (including administrative funds) while passing along much greater flexibility to the state governors. This permits a substantial reduction in budget. And, if the history of community block grants is followed, most if not all of the funds can be eliminated in future sessions of Congress since members will receive little if any political benefits from the block grant programs. Second, block grant programs require less federal bureaucracy to administer. Ironically, block grants can increase the total size of government by requiring states to increase their administrative bureaucracy. But this may be considered by members of Congress to be an acceptable political consequence. Third, it proponents of block grants claim that by increasing the flexibility of the states to administer a federal program there are substantial gains in program efficiency and effectiveness. However, this claim is unlikely to be universal among the states. Some states indeed may increase the efficacy of their programs, but there is no inherent guarantee.

There are three types of block grants. First, restricted block grants funnel funding and some authority to the states, but with specific regulations and guidelines for program expenditure. States are given some leeway to adapt programs to their special circumstances. Second, unrestricted block grants, similar to the Community Development Block Grant program of the 1980s, have far fewer guidelines for state and local program targeting and expenditure. Both restricted and unrestricted block grants have been used with varying degrees of success in rural areas.

Third, competitive block grant programs have been used less, but recently gained considerable policy legitimacy. Unlike many other block grant programs, competitive block grants do not necessitate either an entitlement or a guaranteed formula under which funding moves to the states or rural communities. Funding is based on a competitive process where states or communities develop proposals. The Enterprise Community and Empowerment Zone (EC/EZ) program is a competitive grant program. Competitive block grant programs permit rural communities to create rural development programs that fit both their specific circumstances and general federal rural development guidelines. In doing so, such programs promote federal and local development partnerships. The role of state government, subregional development organizations, private foundations, and other rural development providers are determined by the local grant proposal. However, competitive block grants are likely to be pursued by communities that are already well-organized and have access to the necessary technical assistance to write a competitive grant.

Renewed Interest in Local Self-Development
The political movement to restrict the authority of the federal government is often tied to a desire to make public policy more relevant to local circumstances. The U.S. has a long-term cultural suspicion of large centralized government and a belief in local self-determination. The policy dilemma is the institutionalization of federal and local partnerships where one partner has such superior resources and political power. This is not a new policy dilemma. USDA farm programs historically required much local input and even governance. Since USDA farm programs historically were tied to local boards, USDA administrators may be able to draw on local-federal institutional partnerships to create new rural development programs.

The past emphases on local development was far less the will of a grand development model than on political realities. These partnerships reflected the great diversity of characteristics and needs of farm groups and their communities. This has been particularly true for agricultural commodity policies. American farm entitlement, conservation, and extension programs derived much of their political legitimacy by institutionalizing federal-local partnerships through local boards. The Agricultural Adjustment Administration Boards (later the Agricultural Stabilization and Conservation Service Boards, and now the Farm Services Administration Boards), the Soil and Water District Boards (now the Conservation District Boards), and the county-level extension councils are historic examples of rural federal and local partnerships.

Transformations in Rural Development Policy
The 1995 congressional reorganization of USDA, coupled with the rural development title of the 1996 Farm Bill, may fundamentally alter USDA's rural development initiatives. The most innovative Congressional initiatives are the establishment of Rural Community Action Program (RCAP) and the Fund for Rural America (FRA). RCAP provides a framework for restrictive block grant programs to the states that are administered by the USDA Rural Development State Directors, but mandates considerable local input aimed at social and economic strategic planning and development. FRA represents the first time funding has been transferred from farm commodity programs to a very general rural development fund. FRA funds will be used primarily for

rural development programs that enhance the creation of value-added agricultural industries and agricultural research and development. However, a portion of these funds will be applied to rural economic and social development.

The reorganization of USDA in the twenty-first century may have even greater implications for defining the federal role in rural development. For the first time, rural development has an agency status similar to the farm programs, Rural Development (RD). This agency is instructive as an case study of the difficulties for USDA in engaging rural non-farm goals. USDA-RD has primary responsibility for non-farm rural credit programs. However, since other USDA agencies retained rural development programs, program coordination was necessary. A memorandum of understanding was signed by the Undersecretaries for Research, Education, and Economics (REE), Natural Resources (NR), and RD that established the Rural Economic Development Action Team (REDAT) to identify and address overlapping program areas. Unfortunately, inter-agency turf struggles may reduce the effectiveness and eventually the life of REDAT. In addition, Congress provided a general policy framework for the National Rural Development Partnership for Rural America to provide institutional links among USDA and other federal programs and state rural development efforts. These legislative and bureaucratic transformations raised two unresolved critical policy questions. First, will these changes make the USDA's role in rural development more relevant for rural communities? Second, how will these changes affect other rural development providers? As the first decade of the twenty-first century may indicate, USDA continues to wrestle with rural development as a mission area.

The late twentieth century reorganization required USDA administrators to create new bureaucratic protocols for inter-agency cooperation (e.g., REDAT), and generate performance criteria in an uncertain political environment (e.g., Government Performance Review Act). The challenges of these new missions may be far greater for USDA than for other federal agencies since the USDA administrators must enhance USDA's capacity to manage rural development programs, while both redefining its expanded rural development mission and downsizing its professional work force. All of these new demands on a reorganized federal bureaucracy pose both liabilities and opportunities to achieve their new missions.

The early twenty-first century may witness the emergence of a renewed commitment to rural America and its communities. A constraint will be funding. It is unlikely more federal funding will be assigned to USDA in general and to rural development programs specifically. Rather, the goals and outcomes are likely to become more targeted. This opportunity will be greatly determined by how visions of cooperation and commitment are articulated and applied to institutional relationships.

The irony of this opportunity is that the fractured and generally disarticulated federal rural policies of the past are seen by many as part of the rural policy dilemma, thus begging the question of how to coordinate and administer programs that foster partnerships between diverse rural communities and rural development providers. In essence, the present opportunity will be shaped by new programs and policy initiatives and on the restructuring of USDA to provide a minimal but coherent rural policy rather than historically fractured policy initiatives. This future will be equally dependent on enhancing human capacity, local economies, and basic physical infrastructure support. The focus will be on rural communities and their citizens.

The devolution of the federal government generally has been characterized by a downsizing of federal agencies and a transfer of some administrative authority to the states. For most federal agencies this meant a movement from more centrally controlled and cohesive regulatory and funding programs and toward more minimal roles. This movement toward a more minimal role is consistent with their bureaucratic downsizing. However, USDA is in something of a paradox in the case of rural development. Historically, rural development at USDA has been characterized by fragmented programs (primarily categorical grant programs) scattered across several agencies. There was no coherent rural development policy tying these efforts together. Therefore, for rural development at USDA the devolution of government required a reorganization of programs that yield a much more cohesive policy. USDA is attempting to become more involved in rural development at the very time its bureaucracy is being both downsized and reorganized.

The programmatic consequences for these changes will not be fully understood for years to come. The questions confronting rural development policy are impressive. Liabilities may reside in the inability of USDA agencies to overcome bureaucratic turf tussles, both within USDA and with other federal agencies. Other liabilities may appear in the reorientation of USDA personnel to qualitatively different assignments as professionals. Still others may occur in how USDA field offices, those USDA professionals who work directly with the public, make the transition from treating the public as clients to working with rural communities and citizens as partners. Can sufficient authority be passed along to field office personnel to make USDA's considerable resources effectively available at the local level? A great concern is whether or not liabilities will cause opportunities to be missed.

Although federal rural development policy never achieved a sustained presence at the local level, the New Deal farm and resource conservation programs were based on a federal and local partnership. This experience of more than a half century of working with local boards can provide clues to make the newly emerging rural development initiatives locally relevant. Certainly the Resource Conservation and Development program within the National Resource Conservation Service offers a readily available institutional example. What seems apparent is that the opportunities to make USDA a key player are greater now than at any other time this century. At the time of publication of this book, rural public policies were undergoing their greatest changes since the New Deal.

— *Louis E. Swanson*

See also

Community; Development, Community and Economic; Economic Development; Decentralization; Government; Infrastructure; Public Services; Policy (various); Regional Planning; Sustainable Rural Economies; Taxes; Trade Areas; Urbanization

References

Brown, David L. and Louis E. Swanson (eds). *Challenges for Rural America in the Twenty-First Century*. University Park, PA: The Pennsylvania State University Press, 2003.

Browne, William P. *Cultivating Congress*. Lawrence, KS: University Press of Kansas, 1995.

Browne, William P., Jerry Skees, Louis E. Swanson, Paul B. Thompson, and Laurian J. Unnevehr. *Sacred Cows and Hot Potatoes: Agrarian Myths in Agricultural Policy*. Boulder, CO: Westview Press, 1992.

Castle, Emery N. *The Changing American Countryside: Rural People and Places*. Lawrence, KS: University Press of Kansas, 1995.

Policy, Rural Family

Those public policies that impact quality of family living for rural residents. This article provides a brief overview of the diversity of lived experiences of rural residents. Selected research findings and quotes provide evidence of diversity and issues. The article is intended to provoke thought about the inter-relationship between the private lives of families and the public policies that impact families and how family members can be included in public policy decision-making.

Beyond the confines of city limits and suburban sprawl lies rural America—home to about 20 percent of the U.S. population. From here, natural resources are extracted to fuel and feed the greater majority of the U.S. or for export to other countries. Here visitors come seeking recreation. And to here, many are moving as they return to rural roots, to find a perceived safe place to raise children, or to retire. It's also rapidly becoming home to recent immigrants. Rural America has appeal for its beauty, heritage, mythology and ties to generational homes of many Americans.

In the small towns and countryside, residents live and work for a living and frequently struggle to do so with limited local resources. For while the country holds appeal, it also holds challenges. Understanding those challenges as they affect families is worth investigation.

The body of knowledge about challenges affecting the well-being of rural families is not extensive. It is especially limited on the topic of low-income families. To expand the understanding of the well-being of rural families, especially low-income families, the communities in which they live, and the public policies that impact their lives, a 17-state longitudinal study was launched in 1998 and will continue through 2013. Many papers and reports have been published from that study known as *Rural Families Speak* (see Reference section below) and a related study *Engaging Unheard Voices* (2006). The study was undertaken to address important public policy questions about the role of federal, state and local government and the private sector in relationship to rural families.

In addition, many descriptive details and statistics are widely available both in U.S. Government documents and studies from institutes, rural development centers and land-grant or other universities. Some are cited in the bibliography. They provide information that frames life in rural America—information that can be used to set and change policies affecting rural families. But what they do not do is provide an understanding of the lives lived by rural residents so that public policy takes into account the diversity of families.

A few words of mothers from the *Rural Families Speak* study will be incorporated throughout this article with the intent of making real the conditions described. At stake is quality of living for rural families whose well-being is vital to the health of the economy and society.

Rural Family Matters

Families are the basic unit of the economy and of society. How well they function as consumers, producers of household goods and services, workers, family caregivers, citizens and taxpayers affects the quality of community life and local economies. And how well the physical, social, political, technological and economic environments function affects families, particularly in rural areas where the nature of society is so influenced by the context where it exists. There is a symbiotic relationship between rural families and these environments which should be considered and understood during public policy decision-making.

Physical environments are changing. With urban sprawl, land once supportive of a making a living or for recreation is converting into housing, roads and other public uses to service an influx of residents and business, bringing both opportunities for employment and costs in terms of congestion, air and water quality and demands on local services such as schools. In more isolated areas, people leave because the environment does not support livelihoods.

With physical change comes social change. Social environments are affected as family members move out of communities, new families move in and the population ages. And with social change comes political change as those in positional and elected power change over time along with the ideologies that infuse their decisions and actions.

Technologically, just as rural electrification changed the way people lived and worked, so, too, is digital technology influencing education, recreation and commerce in rural areas, putting some areas in the forefront of going global and leaving others behind. And the economic fortunes of communities are reflected in the family economy as employers come and go, construction waxes and wanes, the housing and financial markets fluctuate. These changes affect the ability of families to fully function as well as to achieve and maintain desired quality of living.

Families vary in their response to systems changes, in part by the variation in their makeup and resources. Not all families are equally impacted by change. Just as their urban counterparts, they are diverse in family structure, composition and relationships, age, education, race and ethnicity, disabilities, income, beliefs, behaviors and values. Some are families by blood, some by marriage and some by choice or chance. All move through life with a mix of resources and factors that protect them and put them at risk. Depending on the communities in which they reside, rural families may or may not be supported in their functions as providers for, and protectors of, family members.

But with all their diversity, rural families have some matters in common—health, employment and income. They also share dreams and aspirations. The mothers we interviewed consistently described theirs as the American dream: a good education, job security, home ownership, good health and happiness. And the extent to which those dreams are realized depends on both internal and external factors as individual family members and families interact with each other and with the communities in which they live and work.

Health Matters

If health is part of the American dream and "Health is the First Wealth," as Emerson is to have said, then health matters to rural families and pays off in terms of employment and quality of living—a key finding from our study. Yet, rural families have higher rates of infant, child and adolescent deaths, and among adults, of suicide, motor vehicle accidents and cardiovascular disease-related deaths. Rates of obesity and tooth loss are greater than among their urban counterparts.

Surprisingly, rural areas have lower levels of food security than do urban areas. Food security means that families have an adequate daily food intake to meet their nutritional needs. Lack of adequate food is associated with physical and mental health problems and the inability of children to develop and grow into healthy adults. When children are not adequately nourished and nurtured, they cannot learn. When they cannot learn, as adults, they can't adequately earn. When they can't adequately earn, they can't become productive workers and citizens.

For rural families, poor mental health is a risk factor for substance abuse. For those who are screened, the odds of having depressive symptoms are about 50-50. Depressive symptoms affect the ability to work. As one unemployed mother in the *Rural Families Speak* project said, "I left because depression set in. And I started having a lot of crises in my life, so I just couldn't handle the work." Another risk factor for substance abuse among mothers is working multiple jobs in addition to caring for their children. Among our families, many worked multiple jobs.

Drugs, alcohol and tobacco are used by rural residents to cope with life. Once considered an urban problem, substance abuse is now as common in rural areas as in cities. While rates of drug, alcohol and nicotine use for adults are about the same in rural towns, mid-size cities and large urban centers, the rates for teens are higher in rural areas. Teenage substance abuse affects adulthood. As one of the interviewed mothers said, "And then as I got older, I didn't keep a lot of jobs as I got from 18 to 24 maybe because I became an alcoholic."

Poor physical health, of adults and/or children, affects employment such that chronic health conditions are found more frequently among unemployed women. One said that, "[from] September to February we're in the hospital at least three times a month... I can't hold a job because I've got to be in the hospital with her." Lack of health insurance, tied to jobs without benefits, is often the difference between accessing health services and forgoing doctor visits or filling prescriptions, affecting the ability to be employed as told by one mother working three jobs: "I put off going to the doctor for nine months. I dragged myself to work. Finally the pain was too much and I couldn't work. I had a growth. Once it was removed, I got back to work but not before we went without income for two months. We had to go ask for medical cards and public assistance to get by. Maybe others need public help because they don't have health insurance."

Rural families of all races, ethnicity, ages and most income levels have limited community resources with which to address their health problems which include availability, accessibility and affordability of care due to: 1) shortage of qualified mental health, medical, pharmaceutical and dental health providers and facilities and services; 2) distances to services; and 3) the high cost of treatment. Lack of preventative, primary and specialty care is detrimental to the health of children, affecting their performance in school and causing problems into adulthood. Adults struggle to be effective parents, employees and citizens when dealing with health problems. Lack of health care is detrimental to the local economy as employers and retirees resist lo-

cating in areas without such care. Federal policy acknowledges that addressing rural health disparities is the number one priority for research and policy, and yet health care remains a challenge for the twenty-first century.

Income and Employment Matters

Earning a living is a challenge for rural families. Participation in the labor force is the basis for family economic self-sufficiency. However, rural families face barriers that include availability of jobs and jobs with benefits; the health of wage earners, children and elder members of the family; availability, accessibility and affordability of care-giving, especially for children; reliable transportation; and the cost of living, especially for basics like housing, utilities and food.

Consistently, poverty rates are higher in rural than in urban areas. The reality for rural families is framed by their local economy. In many rural areas, there are limited employment opportunities that pay living wages and benefits and few opportunities for training and advancement. For many workers, the work is seasonal, resulting in underemployment among willing workers. Conditions in rural areas are not the same as those in urban areas and require customization of policies for rural areas so that the business and community resources upon which rural families draw are strengthened.

Quality, available and affordable childcare is a barrier to employment for families with children. For those with schoolchildren, lack of after-school care is problematic as is the lack of night, weekend and holiday care for families working shifts. Making sure that registered childcare facilities meet high standards of care and creating comprehensive childcare subsidies allows rural women to seek and maintain employment.

Transportation is another major challenge for rural families. With distances between home and worksite, grocery outlets, schools, and health care and few public transport options, a personal vehicle is nearly a must. Personal vehicles are costly, especially with the costs of repairs and the rising price of gas. One mother said, "So when the car goes, then the whole life goes down the tubes."

Protective Factors

The conditions affecting families in rural areas are not all detrimental. There is hope. In fact, many of the families who spoke with us are amazingly resilient. Some of their resilience is internal—they acknowledge coming from families that are hardy and pull together during tough times. There is a pride in being self-sufficient or getting by with the help of family and friends who are part of their network and support them emotionally, physically and/or financially. Attitude was a factor in even the presence of depressive symptoms among some of the mothers. Depressive symptoms were less frequent among those who perceived that their economic situation wasn't so bad, that their income was adequate, that they had support in their parental roles and who found support from religious practices. For some, having community resources to draw upon got them through periods of particular challenge. Drawing on neighbors for assistance is a hallmark of most rural areas, as is the expectation of reciprocity.

The role of community and public policies is a protective factor. For many of the families, community resources such as education, transportation, health care services, social services and recreational facilities complemented and supplemented their personal and family resources. But in some communities, resources were scarce, leaving families without the benefit of a supportive environment. For some of those families, the lack of support from the public arena was frustrating. Desire for change motivated some to become engaged in matters of public policy to address their needs.

Civic Engagement

Rural communities vary in how they approach public problems and issues and make public policy affecting families. Some are run by an elite few; some are more open. Mothers often had ideas about how to make conditions better for their families but also found barriers to engaging in public problem solving. Among the families, such barriers as divisions by social class; lack of knowledge about issues or how to get involved; the way groups are organized and led; lack of childcare; and sometimes, perception that the issues are not personal kept people from engaging in public policy. Such barriers are consistent with those described in literature on life in rural areas and are illustrated by the following comments from three rural mothers' interviews: 1) "Here it's all what your name is and how much money you have depending on if they'll listen to you." 2) "The town pretty much don't want any input." 3) "Everybody's afraid they are going to step on somebody's toes

and they don't want to do anything to make anybody look at them. They are afraid to talk out."

Yet, under the right conditions, these mothers can and will participate in civic problem solving. They will when issues are dear to them and affect their families. They can when meetings are open and welcoming and childcare is available. They will when the methods of hearing from citizens are inclusive such as deliberative forums. They can and will because they did after we listened to them, convened and moderated a forum designed to consider three approaches to a pressing issue—recreation for youth and adults in a rural county with limited recreational options for the locals yet extensive recreation for tourists. They did when encouraged to tell their stories and barriers were removed.

Policies affecting rural families are too vital both to localities and families to be crafted by policy makers alone. When done well, the likelihood increases that families will obtain and maintain desired quality of living. Engaged citizens are key to identifying and working through tensions and tradeoffs of rural family policy.

— *Bonnie Braun*[1]

See also
Adolescents; Family; Policy, Health Care; Policy, Social; Rural Women

References
Bauer, J.W. and M.J. Katras. *Rural Prosperity: A Longitudinal Study of Rural Communities and Rural Low-Income Families*. St. Paul, MN: University of Minnesota, 2007. National Research Initiative Competitive Grants Program final report (pdf) available online at: http://fsos.cehd.umn.edu/projects/rfs/publications. html.

Berry, A. *The Relationship between Selected Housing and Demographic Characteristics and Employment Status among Rural, Low-Income Families*. Unpublished doctoral dissertation, Louisiana State University, Baton Rouge, 2003.

Braun, Bonnie, Elaine A. Anderson, and Joanna Waldman. *Engaging Unheard Voices in Public Policy*. Minneapolis, MN: National Council on Family Relations, 2006.

Dolan, Elizabeth M., Leslie Richards, Yoshie Sano, Jean Bauer, and Bonnie Braun. "Linkages between employment patterns and depression over time: The case of

[1]The research for *Rural Families Speak*, upon which this article is based, was supported in part by USDA/CSREES/NRICGP Grant 2001-35401-10215, 2002-35401-11591 and 2004-35401-14938, the University of Maryland Agricultural Experiment Station and the American Association of Family & Consumer Sciences and for *Engaging Unheard Voices* by the Charles F. Kettering Foundation.

low-income rural mothers." Pp. 225-229 in *Consumer Interests Annual, Volume 51*. Milwaukee, WI: American Council on Consumer Interests, 2005.

Duncan, Cynthia. *Worlds Apart: Why Poverty Persists in Rural America*. Yale University Press, 1999.

Economic Research Service. *Rural America at a Glance*. Economic Information Bulletin No. EIB-31. Washington, DC: U.S. Department of Agriculture, 2007.

Gamm, Larry D., Linnae L. Hutchison, Betty J. Dabney, Alicia M. Dorsey, eds. *Rural Healthy People 2010: A Companion Document to Healthy People 2010. Volume 1.* College Station, TX: Texas A&M University Health System Health Science Center, School of Rural Public Health, Southwest Rural Health Research Center, 2003.

Greder, Kimberly and William D. Allen. "Parenting Issues in Culturally Diverse Families." In *Cultural Diversity and Families: A Family Science Perspective*. Edited by Bahira Sherif Trask & Raeann R. Hamon. Thousand Oaks, CA: Sage Publishing, 2007.

Greder, Kimberly and Jeanne Warning. "Involving Marginalized Families in Shaping Policies: Roles for Cooperative Extension." *Marriage and Family Review* 38, no. 2 (2006): 77-95.

Huddleston-Casas, Catherine, Bonnie Braun, Elizabeth, Dolan, and Jean Bauer. "An Ecology of Economic Vulnerability among Rural, Low-Income Families." Paper presented at the annual meeting of the National Council on Family Relations, Pittsburgh, PA, November 2007.

Katras, Mary Jo, Virginia S. Zuiker, and Jean W. Bauer. "Private Safety Net: Childcare Resources from the Perspective of Rural Low-Income Families." *Family Relations* 53 (2004): 201-209.

Mammen, S. and F.C. Lawrence. "How Rural Working Families Use the Earned Income Tax Credit: A Mixed Method Analysis." *Financial Counseling and Planning* 17 (2006): 51-63.

Maring, Elizabeth F. and Bonnie Braun. "Drug, alcohol and tobacco use in rural, low-income families: An ecological risk and resilience perspective." *Journal of Rural Community Psychology* 9, no. 1 (2007). Available online at:http://www.marshall.edu/jrcp/Maring%20and%20Braun.pdf

Meit, Michael. *Bridging the Health Divide: The Rural Public Health Research Agenda*. Bradford, PA: University of Pittsburgh Center for Rural Health Practice, 2004.

National Center on Addiction and Substance Abuse. *No Place to Hide: Substance Abuse in Mid-Size Cities and Rural America*. New York: Columbia University, 2000.

National Center on Health Statistics (NCHS). *Health, United States, 2001 with Urban and Rural Health Chartbook*. Hyattsville, MD: Centers for Disease Control, 2001.

National Issues Forums. Available online at: http://www.nifi.org.

Nord, Mark, Margaret Andrews, and Steven Carlson. *Household Food Security in the United States, 2006*: Economic Research Report, 2007.

Olson, Christine M., Kendra Anderson, Elizabeth Kiss, Frances C. Lawrence, and Sharon B. Seiling. "Factors protecting against and contributing to food insecurity in rural families: A mixed-methods analysis." *Food Economics and Nutrition Review* 16 (2004): 12-20.

Reschke, Kathy L. and Susan K. Walker. "Mothers' Child Caregiving and Employment Commitments and Choices in the Context of Rural Poverty." *Affilia: The Journal of Women and Social Work* 21 (2006): 306-319.

Simmons, Leigh Ann, Elaine Anderson, and Bonnie Braun. "Health Needs and Health Care Utilization among Rural, Low-Income Women." *Journal of Women and Health*. (2008).

Simmons, Leigh Ann, Bonnie Braun, Richard Charnigo, Jennifer R. Havens, and David W. Wright. "Depression and Poverty Among Rural Women A Relationship of Social Causation or Social Selection?" *Journal of Rural Health* (2008).

U.S. Department of Health and Human Services. *One Department Serving Rural America: HHS Rural Task Force Report to the Secretary*. Rockville, MD: U.S. Department of Health and Human Services, 2002. Available online at: http://ruralhealth.hrsa.gov/PublicReport.htm.

Policy, Socioeconomic

Policy relating to the conditions in a variety of dimensions of social life—economic dimensions (such as employment, income and poverty); physical and mental health status; educational attainments; social disorganization (teenage fertility, substance abuse, accident rates and crime); quality and quantity of local services, infrastructure and housing; and environmental preservation and natural resource sustainability. Each dimension of socioeconomic well-being has its own literature and research traditions attached to it, so specific works on each topic should be consulted. Causes, consequences and policies affecting socioeconomic well-being depend on the particular indicator used to define it. This article gives an overview of the umbrella topic of socioeconomic well-being and the policy interventions that address it. Policy interventions can be seen as derived from underlying assumptions about the causal factors involved in socioeconomic well-being. For researchers, these causal factors are derived from theory and research findings, but for policymakers, interventions may be driven also by political exigencies and ideological stance. Contrasts between rural and urban areas with regard to interventions to improve socioeconomic well-being are discussed.

Background to Research on Socioeconomic Well-Being

Several issues should be noted about research on this topic. The first is the analytical level to which studies refer. Studies examining socioeconomic well-being typically use individuals, households or locales, such as counties and communities, as the unit of analysis. Contrasts between rural/nonmetropolitan and urban/metropolitan individuals, households and locales are often made. Second, the topic of socioeconomic well-being is derivative of an older research tradition: the social indicators school, popular in the social sciences through the 1980s. This research tradition was concerned with developing quality-of-life indicators by which populations in different geographic locations could be compared. Research on quality of life and the social indicator school itself were later subject to criticisms of being atheoretical, ignoring the broader political-economic context, and imposing external, normative standards on local populations. The result is that contemporary researchers analyzing socioeconomic well-being are more aware of and often directly concerned with remedying these past problems.

The extent to which rural individuals, households and communities experience poorer socioeconomic well-being is still an empirical question, the answer to which depends on the type of well-being considered, time period, region of the country, and how comparisons are made with metropolitan populations. Extensive empirical work tends to confirm the generalization that nonmetropolitan people, households and places have poorer economic conditions, lower income and higher poverty rates than metropolitan people (Brown and Swanson, 2003; Rural Sociological Task Force on Persistent Rural Poverty, 1993; USDA, 2007. Educational attainments among rural people also have been historically lower. Beyond, educational and economic indicators are less clear. Some health status indicators, such as age-adjusted death rates from heart disease and stroke, suicide rates for males, and deaths from motor vehicle accidents, reveal higher rates for rural areas. Certain types of substance abuse, such as alcoholism and methamphetamine use, and crime, such as trespassing, are thought to be higher in rural areas. The quality of rural infrastructure and housing is generally poorer.

Provision of social, educational and health services is generally considered more problematic in rural as compared to urban areas for several reasons. Rural areas have lower population density, which complicates service delivery and makes it more expensive. Service organizations and agencies tend to be fewer. Staffing is more problematic due to greater difficulty of attracting skilled professionals. A long-standing problem has been attracting physicians, whose training on high-technology medical equipment is difficult to transfer to rural practice, and whose lifestyle interests often center on urban amenities. The composition of rural populations, with a higher proportion of aging, less educated and poorer people further present barriers to service outreach.

Variations among Rural People

Any generalizations about the socioeconomic well-being of rural people need to be tempered with a consideration of the extensive variations within rural areas and populations and between them and metropolitan areas and population. Nonmetropolitan people residing in counties adjacent to metropolitan counties tend to have better socioeconomic conditions than their more remote rural counterparts. Rural people are differentiated by class, gender, race and ethnicity, so that those higher in the stratification order experience a better quality of life. Finally, rural people are not the only ones whose residence location jeopardizes life chances. Comparisons of nonmetropolitan people with those of the urban core reveal striking similarities in terms of poorer economic conditions.

Policy Interventions: Overview

Policy interventions flow from assumptions about how differences in well-being are created. Following are two poles of a continuum in which interventions may be introduced. The first is from the supply side and involves human capital; it is motivated by the desire to empower rural people and upgrade their personal and community lives. To the extent that poorer well-being of rural people is due to their compositional characteristics (such as age, education, skill levels and other personal attributes), interventions may be human-capital focused. Such interventions are typically centered on upgrading labor market quality through education, job training programs and health care, providing services for working people such as child and elder care, and through improving quality of life through social welfare interventions. Other supply-side interventions may take the form of improving local social capital or participatory initiatives that enhance community capacity for self-development.

The contrasting pole of intervention is on the demand side. It assumes that well-being is increased through altering the economic and social institutions that surround rural people. Most economic development programs take this approach. They center on improving the quality of local industries and firms and expanding employment in them. Improving local infrastructure and social institutions (e.g., schools) and access to local services also can be seen as attempts to stimulate demand aspects of social and economic structure, which in turn may filter down to human capital upgrades.

Sociologists generally recognize the interrelationships between demand- and supply-side improvements, but caution that enhancing human capital upgrades in education and skills is not sufficient to improve well-being unless accompanied by demand-side expansions in local employment and wages. Also problematic in rural areas is local investment in education. Relative to urban areas, rural tax bases, and hence local property tax support for schools, are typically lower. People with higher education are more likely to out-migrate. Urban areas thus capture rural investment in education.

Another way that policy interventions have been understood is through place- or person-based policies. Person-based policies involve portable investments in people such as welfare and education. Place-based policies center on investment in local business, infrastructure and community institutions. These policy contrasts overlap with the supply-demand distinction noted above.

Policy Interventions: Issues and Problems

Analysts raise several policy intervention issues when considering rural areas. An important issue is the degree to which national policies are spatially biased. National policies are formulated in four major ways and each has outcomes that affect rural and urban people differentially (Rural Sociological Task Force on Rural Poverty, 1993).

First, macroeconomic policies designed in response to global or national economic trends, such as deregulation or monetary and trade policy, differentially affect rural well-being. For example, deregulation of the transportation industry curtailed bus and air service to remote rural areas. The North American Free Trade Agreement (NAFTA) has tended to have a more negative impact on rural employment in that it has af-

fected lower wage or routine manufacturing industries which are traditionally rural-based.

Second, sectoral policies, such as farm commodity programs, are designed to affect specific industries, and thus have direct spatial effects. Farm policies have been considered major strategies of national government intervention in rural development, although promoters rarely make this intent explicit.

Third, policies and programs may also be directly earmarked for rural development or attached to highly rural regions, such as those administered by the Appalachian Regional Commission and the Tennessee Valley Authority. These programs have centered historically on upgrading rural infrastructure.

Finally, national social welfare policies and programs have spatially varying effects. Rural people are more likely to be working poor than their urban counterparts. As a consequence, a lower proportion of rural people's incomes has historically come from means-tested income transfer programs such as social welfare programs. There is also some evidence that when rural people make use of social programs such as welfare and food stamps, they experience greater stigmatization than do urban people. A large amount of work has been directed to the impacts of 1996 welfare reform legislation and the TANF (Temporary Assistance to Needy Families) on rural populations. There is some evidence that rural people fare worse under welfare reform. The supply of jobs in rural areas is less, making it more difficult for the rural poor to fulfill employment requirements. Under welfare reform, local governments have assumed a greater role in administration of social programs. But rural local governments face greater barriers in terms of less staff and resource capacity to administer these programs.

Another issue affecting the performance of policy interventions in rural areas is the extent to which they are fragmented across policy domains and administrative units. Policies designed to improve the environment, for instance, may conflict with local employment goals, as illustrated by the case of Northwest logging. Local services for solid waste disposal, fire protection, ambulance services and other types of social provisions may be supplied by multiple, overlapping administrative units, including a mix of public and private providers. Policies and programs set at the national or state level may be administrative differentially by lower levels of government. For example, state and federal guidelines for TANF may be interpreted and applied informally in different ways by county social welfare service offices. Although urban areas face similar issues, coordination, coverage and consistency are particularly problematic for smaller, rural communities. Decentralization of federal and state programs appears to have more negative consequences for rural people. Local governments in rural areas tend to have less administrative capacity overall and fewer resources. These governments may also have less political desire to help the poor because their constituents favor limited government and lower taxes.

Delivery of social, health, employment, educational and other services designed to improve local socioeconomic well-being is considered more complex for rural areas due to lower population density, smaller tax base, more limited infrastructure, and the general characteristics of rural people. Multi-community or county collaborations have been implemented particularly in the consolidation of local schools and hospitals. These types of collaborations have been increasing over time and offer a potential direction for improved service delivery in rural areas.

The characteristics of rural people make service outreach more problematic. A higher proportion of elderly and poor complicates service delivery. Farmers and other small business owners often fall outside eligibility requirements for means-tested programs. Less formal-sector employment creates health insurance and retirement savings barriers. Some analysts argue that farmers and other rural people have more individualistic attitudes about seeking help and are less likely to use formal mental health and other social service interventions. However, the extent to which rural people have different attitudes than their urban counterparts regarding use of social services is still not clear. Use of social services is related to both the social, economic and demographic characteristics of rural residents and the conditions by which services are made accessible to rural people.

— *Linda M. Lobao*

See also

Decentralization; Dependence; Elders; Government; Housing; Policy (various entries); Public Services; Quality of Life; Rural Demography; Spatial Inequality; Welfare

References

Brown, David L. and Louis E. Swanson, eds. *Challenges for Rural America in the Twenty-First Century*. University Park, PA: The Pennsylvania State University Press, 2003.

Flora, Cornelia Butler, Jan L. Flora, and Susan Fey. *Rural Communities: Legacy and Change*. (second edition). Boulder, CO: Westview Press, 2004.

Glasmeier, Amy. *Poverty in America: One Nation Pulling Apart*. New York: Routledge, 2006.

Lobao, Linda M., Gregory Hooks, and Ann R. Tickamyer, eds. *The Sociology of Spatial Inequality*. Albany: The State University of New York Press, 2007.

Lobao, Linda M. *Locality and Inequality: Farm and Industry Structure and Socioeconomic Conditions*. Albany, NY: State University of New York Press, 1990.

Rural Sociological Task Force on Persistent Rural Poverty. *Persistent Poverty in Rural America*. Boulder, CO: Westview Press, 1993.

U.S. Department of Agriculture. *Rural America at a Glance*. Washington, D.C: U.S. Department of Agriculture, Economic Research Service, Economic Information Bulletin Number 31, October 2007.

Weber, Bruce, Greg J. Duncan, and Leslie A. Whitener, eds. *Rural Dimensions of Welfare Reform*. Kalamazoo, MI, 2002.

Policy, Telecommunications

Public programs, laws, actions, and decisions, especially at the federal level, that influence the use of technology to communicate over long distances. Advances in technology and changing regulatory policies provide opportunities for rural communities to overcome the disadvantages of time and space, and to become more integrated into the global, information economy.

Advances in communication and information technologies and radical changes in the way these technologies can provide services have occurred along with the shift toward a more service-oriented economy. These developments hold considerable promise for rural areas. They reduce the importance of distance and space, two factors that typically have disadvantaged rural areas in the past. Equally important, they can provide the economic infrastructure that will allow rural communities to participate in, and reap the benefits of, an increasingly knowledge-based and electronically networked global economy.

For rural communities to benefit from these developments, however they will need access to a modern network infrastructure. Ironically, just at the moment when communication and information technologies are beginning to play such a critical role, the regulatory structure that once assured rural access to communication technologies is rapidly coming unraveled. Under these circumstances, new and creative approaches to promote network deployment in rural communities must be found.

Barriers to Network Deployment

Rural communities typically lagged behind urban areas in the deployment of communication technologies because of the high costs involved in providing service. Costs are higher in rural areas not only because of difficult terrain, but also because, with low-density populations and low-volume traffic dispersed over large areas, costs are much harder to share. High costs, in turn, serve to increase the price of access, and thus reduce demand. They undermine the incentives that vendors and service providers may have to extend service to these areas.

Consider basic telephony, for instance. In rural areas, about one-half of all voice telephone service is provided by small independent telephone companies, with the Bell Operating Companies providing the other half. Few, if any, of the larger, more specialized providers are trying to enter or develop rural markets. Given a highly competitive, post-divestiture environment, they are focusing their efforts on the more lucrative domestic and increasingly global business markets. With this goal in mind, for example, U.S. West, which services the largest number of remote areas and users, has begun to de-invest in some of them.

To appreciate the problem of rural deployment, one need only compare the average costs of providing urban and rural telephone service. For example, the Bell Operating Companies (BOCs), which service mostly urban areas, have approximately 10,000 lines per central office; their average costs are much lower than those of small, rural independent companies, which average about 2,500 lines per central office. Similarly, the BOCs have, on average, almost 130 subscribers per route mile of outside plant, whereas the small independents average only six. Equally important in terms of costs, the average length of a large company's subscriber loop (the wire between the central office and the user's premises) is about half that of the small independents (Office of Technology Assessment 1992).

Urban markets are also more lucrative than rural markets because they are comprised of a greater number of high-paying customers. Not only are per capita incomes generally lower in rural areas than in urban areas, so too is the density of business customers. Thus, whereas 33 percent of the BOCs' access lines serve business customers, only about 18 percent of small rural companies' access lines (using Rural Utilities Service borrowers as a measure) are dedicated to business usage.

A comparable situation can be found in the case of cable television, which provides the major source of video entertainment in rural areas. Most rural residents gain access to cable television through a head-end receiving station, which receives video signals from satellites, and distributes them via coaxial cables to receivers' homes. Although the cost of the head-end is fixed, that of installing and maintaining the cable is generally proportional to distance, and thus to the number of houses receiving service. Cable penetration rates reflect this cost relationship; rates range from 60 percent in high density areas to 46 percent in communities with less than 3,000 residents. Where subscriber density falls below 10 percent, rural communities will unlikely be served (National Telecommunications and Information Administration 1995).

Rural users can also gain access to television programming directly via satellite, but only if they are willing to bear most of the distance-related costs. To receive satellite signals, they must buy a television receive only (TVRO) satellite dish, which until recently might cost between $750 to $1,800. Thus, the number of TVRO owners is relatively few, ranging from six percent in the open country to 11 percent in rural mountain areas (Office of Technology Assessment 1992).

The deployment of modern information technologies and networked applications is likely to repeat this pattern, not only because of high costs and low demand, but also because the rural infrastructure as it presently exists is unable to support a number of them, especially those at the high end. The poor quality of rural networks stems, in part, from the number of multiparty lines that can still be found in rural areas. Multiparty lines are unsatisfactory to transmit data because of interruptions. Long local loops diminish the quality of rural access. Loops exceeding 18,000 feet, for example, require special treatment, such as loading coils and range extenders, to maintain the quality of voice transmission. These treatments, however, can also introduce distortions in data transmission.

Recent studies show that the demand for many information-based services is quite high. Rural users are willing to pay as much as, if not more than, their urban counterparts for equivalent services because they view them as essential. Networking technologies most in demand include telephone answering machines, fax machines, computers, cellular phones, and computer modems (Alle, et al. 1996). Rural users are also interested in Internet access. In one recent study, four to six percent of those polled wanted to subscribe to Internet services, and 14 to 17 percent wanted additional information (Curran 1995).

In many of the more populated rural areas, the public switched telephone network (PSTN) can support such low-to-mid speed data transmission services and some low speed video services. However, accessing high speed circuit switched or fast packet switched computer networks is impossible for the most part. High speed networks require high quality digital circuits that can support transmission at speeds of 56 kilobits or more. Such circuits are generally not found in rural areas (National Telecommunications and Information Administration 1995).

The lack of high-speed networks is a major shortcoming. Although many individual users may not need such high capacity, rural communities as a whole are increasingly likely to do so. Without high bandwidth facilities, rural communities will be less able to take advantage of the growing number of community-based and business services such as electronic commerce, distance learning, and tele-medicine, which can help them to better compete in a knowledge-based global economy. As a result, rural communities may lag behind urban areas not only with respect to technology deployment but also in terms of overall competitiveness and economic growth.

The Impact of Technology Advance

The technical performance of all network components greatly increased, but costs fell precipitously. These advances can improve the economic viability of providing advanced communication services to rural areas. New technologies, however, are not a panacea. Although technology advance allows for enhanced services at lower costs, it also raises the standards that rural networks must meet just to keep up.

Technological advances in wireless systems, long the mainstay in rural telecommunications, are perhaps the most significant. Taking advantage of digitization and compression, wireless technologies can now provide services that are increasingly comparable to wire-line services. In areas where wire-line costs are prohibitive, microwave, radio, and satellite can provide access.

Microwave can deliver high capacity long haul and short haul analog and digital services. One of its major advantages is its relatively low construction costs. Unlike terrestrial, wire-line technologies, microwave does not require placement of physical cable plant; rooftops, hills, and mountains often provide an inexpensive base for microwave towers. Today, unit costs of microwave service are falling as more high-powered systems expand the usable spectrum.

Like microwave, specialized mobile radio (SMR) can provide a variety of telecommunications and broadcasting services. However, its use for rural service has only recently been approved by the Federal Communications System (FCC). Providing short-haul telecommunication services, SMR can be used for the local loop in remote areas, greatly reducing access costs. Enhanced specialized mobile radio (ESMR) technology, which can provide video, voice, and data services, is also now available.

Advance satellite technology can similarly reduce the costs of providing rural service. Because satellite-based signals are broadcast over a wide area, virtually any user within the satellite's "footprint" can access the network at the same cost. Moreover, mobile satellites now have sufficient power to enable the use of a larger number of small, mobile terminals on the ground. Portable units are self-contained and lightweight, capable of fitting on a company or family car. With these terminals, users can connect with private networks or the public telephone network for a variety of services, including fax, data, facsimile transmission, and computer-to-computer communications.

The cost of providing wire-line services is likewise declining due to technology advances. Most important has been the introduction of loop carrier systems and digital remote electronics and switching technology. Loop carrier systems concentrate access lines by combining many customers into one or more shared trunks, reducing the need for each customer to have a dedicated loop. Digital switching reduces the amount of dedicated loop plant by allowing remote nodes to be connected to the host digital switch. Moreover, with remote digital switching, carriers can now use fewer expensive host switches to provide advanced intelligent services such as access to 1-800-number databases.

Notwithstanding these technology advances, it is likely that telecommunication deployment in rural areas will continue to lag behind. One recent analysis suggest that, assuming a cost of $1,000 per subscriber, it will be 10 to 20 years before narrowband digital service can be delivered to rural areas. Broadband capabilities could be available to business subscribers within two to 10 years, at a cost of $5,000 per subscriber. But it would take 10 to 20 years for residential users to receive broadband services, assuming the same per-subscriber costs. Achieving parity with urban areas will be even more difficult in the future, given deregulation and an increasingly competitive industry environment (Office of Technology Assessment 1992).

Deregulation: The Challenge of a New Regulatory Environment

Telecom deregulation, initiated in 1984 with the divestiture of the Bell system, culminated in January 1996 with passage of the Telecommunications Reform Act. The implications of deregulation for rural telecommunications are twofold. Competition and the loss of subsidies in rural areas may undermine the economic basis upon which rural networks traditionally have been deployed. At the same time, however the regrouping of the communication industry in the wake of competition may afford rural providers new opportunities to share their costs across a larger number of providers, users, and applications.

In the past, government regulatory policy played a major role in assuring that communication technologies were deployed to rural areas. One major aspect of this policy was price averaging and cross subsidization; another was the provision of low cost loans to small, independent, and cooperative telephone companies through the government established Rural Electrification Administration (REA), now the Rural Utilities Service (RUS).

Deregulation undermined the pricing structure that traditionally supported rural communication services. In a fully competitive environment, differences between costs and prices are untenable. When prices are kept artificially high to maintain subsidies, users will seek alternative, private solutions to meet their communication needs. Thus, to survive, communications providers must continue to price access close to real costs. Many subsidies are eliminated as a result.

The Federal Communication Commission (FCC) encouraged this development by shifting costs from interstate interexchange service to local exchange service. At the same time, it tried to ensure affordable rural services by subsidizing some providers, using revenues drawn from a Universal Service Fund. Under the new communications act, price averaging is mandated, and the FCC, together with the states, is charged to develop a plan to finance universal service in a competitive era.

The Communication Act of 1996, which significantly deregulates all segments of the communications industry, is intended to eliminate the remaining barriers to competition. Accordingly, the Regional Bell Companies are now permitted to enter the long distance market, with FCC approval. Likewise, all cable rates are to be deregulated in the next three years, and in small communities, regulation ends immediately. Moreover, broadcasters are now permitted to enter a greater number of markets.

The new law poses a major challenge for rural providers. Not only must rural telephone companies operate at costs that are high relative to urban areas; they must also contend with potential competition. Providers that typically served urban areas may now find it profitable to extend service to many, and especially the most populated, rural areas. Free to provide voice, video, and data services, these competitive providers can now benefit from greater economies of scale and scope, and thereby more easily spread their costs.

On the other hand, under the new law, existing rural telephone companies can take similar steps. They can enter new business areas, join together to provide advanced services, and develop joint ventures, thereby extending their reach and sharing their costs more broadly. Many have already begun to do so.

Thus, for example, a number of rural telephone companies are beginning to provide Internet access as well as cable services. Working jointly through the National Rural Telecommunications Cooperative (NRTC), others arranged with the Direct Broadcast Satellite (DBS) consortium Sky Cable to distribute its basic programming, using relatively low-cost, fixed, 18-inch satellite dishes (Murphy 1995). In like fashion, ComNet, a consortium of 19 independent telephone companies in Ohio, cooperate to provide toll-free access to e-mail, bulletin boards, information services, and the Internet (Wetli 1994).

Even more promising for the future, a growing constituency is emerging to promote the deployment of advanced technologies in rural networks. Looking to communication technologies to support education, health care, and economic development, many state and local governments, community groups, and non-profit organizations are getting involved. California State University, at Chico, for example, linked-up with a broad-based community partnership and Pacific Bell to establish the Northern California Regional Computer Networks. In another effort, the International Internet Association (IIA) arranged with its partner, International Discount Telecommunications, to offers unlimited rural access to the Internet via a low-cost 1-800 dial-up number.

— *D. Linda Garcia*

See also

Electrification; Infrastructure; Technology; Technology Transfer; Telecommunications

References

Allen, John C. and Johnson Bruce B. "Telecommunications and Economic Development: A Study of 20 Rural Communities." *Rural Telecommunications* (July/August 1996): 28-33.

Curran, Steve. "Why Your Telco Can't Ignore the Internet." *Rural Telecommunications* (September/October 1995): 30-38.

Federal Communications Commission. Website available at: http://www.fcc.gov.

National Telecommunications and Information Administration. Website available at: http://www.ntia.doc.gov.

National Telecommunications Information Infrastructure. *Survey of Rural Information Infrastructure Technologies*. Washington, DC: U.S. Department of Commerce, September 1995.

Mayo, John W. and William F. Fox. "State Level Telecommunications Policy in the Post-Divestiture Era." *Survey of Business* (Fall 1992): 10-19.

Murphy, Beth. "Rural Americans Want Their DirecTV." *Satellite Communications* (March 1995): 30-32.

Nuechterlein, Jonathan E. and Philip J. Weiser. Digital Crossroads: American Telecommunications Policy in the Internet. Cambridge, MA: MIT Press, 2006.

Parker, Edwin B., Heather Hudson, and Don A. Dillman. *Rural America in the Information Age*. Boston, MA: University Press of America, 1989.

U.S. Congress, Office of Technology Assessment. *Rural America at the Crossroads: Networking for the Future*. Washington DC: U.S. Government Printing Office, 1992.

U.S. Congress, Office of Technology Assessment. *Wireless Technologies and the National Information Infrastructure*. Washington DC: U.S. Government Printing Office, August 1995.

Wetli, Patty. "Rural Telcos Launch Subscribers From Main Street to Cyberspace." *America's Network* (December 15, 1994): 46-47.

Politics

Everyday public activities in which citizens and their formal and informal leaders address problems or issues and establish common goals and rules that often shape the direction of local governments. This entry examines rural issues at the national and local level. It explores the capacity of rural political communities to address their issues. The diffusion of power and role of local political units in decision making are discussed.

Introduction

Politics in rural areas is more than what government and politicians do. It is everyday public activity that involves local citizens and nonelected leaders who attempt to address problems and issues, establish common goals and rules, and shape direction for local units of government. Rural politics is influenced by external forces from the region, state, national, and international arenas. These influences have economic, legal, environmental, and social components.

Rural politics in America has democratic roots that usually involve four major ideals. First, deliberation and debate are the ways that public issues and the trade-offs associated with choices are examined before a conclusion is reached about the common good or a common sense of direction. Second, elections are viewed as the proper means to select governmental leaders. Third, power is diffused. And fourth, the local unit of government is an instrument for the public to act collectively. The practice of these democratic ideals varies according to the issue, the external influences, the type of local government that predominates at the local level, and the people themselves.

Rural Issues at the National Level

Rural politics is extremely diverse and dynamic. However, state and national portraits of rural America often equate it with the business of agriculture and family farms or project an image of poverty and stagnation. Critics argue that these stereotypes do not portray rural issues accurately. Ninety percent of rural residents earn their livelihood from nonagricultural activities. The widely admired family farmer of today is more likely to own a million dollars in capital and be incorporated. Although poverty exists, it is no more representative of rural life than of urban life. Rural residents have lower income levels than urban residents but also have lower indices of inequality. Rural poverty is concentrated among the elderly, who live in disproportionately large numbers in rural areas.

The farm bloc, a potent bipartisan assortment of commodity organizations and other farm-related groups, received historically more national attention than any other rural group. The farm bloc has linked "rural" with family farming. National farm policy and expensive farm entitlement programs were justified on the grounds that they assisted financially strapped farmers and provided a cheap food supply for urban consumers. Other portions of rural America's heterogeneous economic base traditionally have received less national attention.

In recent years there has been an increase in nonfarm interests in agriculture and rural America. Environmental organizations and representatives of hired farm labor and other groups entered the fray with their concerns for environmental issues, worker and food safety, food distribution, sustainable agriculture, and rural development. Agroenvironmentalism emerged as a movement to address high rates of soil erosion and evidence of surface and groundwater pollution from chemicals used in farming. The rapid loss of medium-sized family farms led to questions about who benefits from farm policy.

Federal legislators view rural America as the source of the nation's food supply and as an incubator for American values such as self-reliance and stewardship of the land and faith. However, they also see rural communities as places with declining job opportunities, environmental problems and limited access to health care, broadband Internet access and inadequate transportation. They believe rural constituents have less influence in the House of Representatives because of population shifts to urban and suburban areas. Partisan and ideological differences among rural and non-rural legislators make it difficult to build coalitions. The declining influence of the farm bloc and growing interest in nonfarm rural issues and corresponding legislation at the national level have been fragmented and disjointed. Rural America is not guided by a comprehensive federal rural development policy.

Politics at the Local Level

Some observers believe that rural politics is shaped by two different political economics, local and external. In the first, there is a distribution of power and wealth among local residents with minimal outside control. Politics is guided by ideological or economic interests. Some communities or key actors in this first situation have been fatalistic and unwilling to change, or they have been divided internally. However, other rural communities have mobilized grassroots support to establish collective visions and carry out community-based agendas for action. Most of the available literature about local political economies is focused on the diffusion of power in them.

Diffusion of power in the local political economy. There is a history of disagreement about whether shaping local rural community policies and decisions involves a relatively diffuse power structure or whether that power is concentrated in the hands of a few elites. Pluralists tend to view politics as relatively open. From their perspective, people choose to get involved or not because of some grievance or issue; the interests of economic classes do not permanently dominate the agenda. Pluralists tend to see a fluidity of groups and classes non-participating or not participating in decision making.

The elitist argument suggests power is distributed hierarchically. The elitist school of thought sees power as a pyramid with key decision makers representing the needs of the wealthy families and businesses. The elites tend to belong to the same clubs and social circles and serve on key boards. They may not be directly involved in partisan politics but work with elected leaders to avoid government interference in their affairs. The Growth Machine school is a variation of elitism in which the elites are described as those who receive their income from property. They promote population growth and construction because they make money from providing the foundation for manufacturing, retail and services. This group is well organized to seek zoning variances, tax abatements and public investments for manufacturing sites even though the empirical evidence indicates these incentives provide limited community benefits and the costs of development is paid by local citizens.

Another perspective, the interactional approach (Wilkinson 1991), suggests that leadership is multifaceted. There is a spectrum ranging from highly specialized leadership to more generalized community leadership. For example, highly focused economic activities are likely to be influenced by businesspeople, whereas more general activities, such as local government, are guided by generalized leaders with backgrounds that reflect local diversity. Some specialized leaders mature into generalized leaders over time. The number of generalized leaders varies from community to community. Openness to participation in community affairs is mixed and varies among localities. Several studies suggest that race may be a barrier to participation in leadership in many rural settings.

The pulls of the external political economy. In recent years, social scientists noted the external barriers to a cohesive local political economy. They asserted that there is more external influence from corporations, national and international markets, or government and external communication networks. Hence, rural politics is pulled and tugged by competition between the interests of local residents and external factors.

Most state legislators are unified in their belief that rural America's challenges are primarily economic. They tend to rely on tax breaks and other incentives to attract businesses to rural areas such as increasing access to broadband, healthcare and improving educational opportunities. Rural state legislators are more likely to propose policies that involve monetary investments in rural areas. According to a recent Kellogg Foundation report, state legislators are at the forefront of innovation and experimentation in developing economic opportunities for rural areas.

Rural politics are also influenced by external trade. For example, major coal, oil, or mineral interests in Appalachia, Wyoming, and western Colorado are dominant local employers and are more likely to influence rural political decision than communities where power and wealth are relatively diffused. At times, higher prices for rural-produced grains and energy products allow rural residents more purchasing power, but the cyclical nature of markets can also decrease rural incomes. Federal deregulation of the banking industry and the move toward bank consolidation in the 1980s opened up opportunities for urban-based banks to enter rural financial markets or to strengthen their presence there significantly. This trend may create new opportunities for rural communities, but it also may limit credit to credit-starved regions. These relationships influence how politics is discussed and carried out at the local level.

Federal and state governments play a significant role in rural politics. Unfunded state and federal mandates have strained local budgets and the problem-solving capacities of rural communities run by volunteer leaders. Federal rural development programs also have influenced rural political agendas and goal-setting because of the attractiveness of external funds. Federal investments during the 1960s through the 1980s led to improved transportation and communication systems for rural communities, which encouraged more interdependence between rural and urban areas. With improved access to major highways, many rural communities developed planning strategies to diversity their local economies in order to minimized economic and political dependence on external forces. In other cases, federal deregulation of transportation industries led to a cutback in bus, air, and railroad transportation.

Another force shaping rural politics is urban America. Urban dwellers often have moved into rural areas because they perceived a better environment and a higher quality of life. The urbanites tend to bring a high demand for public services that rural residents are often reluctant to fund. Urbanites view rural areas as prime recreation areas, where they often compete with rural recreation seekers or resource industries. Urban demand for water, energy, and other resources has contributed to environmental changes in rural America. Rivers are dammed and rural power plants are built to satisfy urban consumers' needs. Strip mining changes the landscape, and rural sprawl infringes on natural areas and wildlife habitats.

The global economy is also influencing rural politics. Corporations are shifting manufacturing jobs from rural areas to developing countries where labor costs are lower. Consequently, rural jobs are moving to the service sector where pay tends to be lower and benefits are limited. Multilateral agreements such as the North American Free Trade Agreement (NAFTA) and the World Trade Organization have led to the continued industrialization of agriculture. There is an opposing trend among American consumers who are concerned about the quality and safety of food they eat and preserving the quality of rural life and the environment which also influences rural politics.

Another force is the changing function of rural communities and the sense of place. Rural communities are not necessarily fully functioning service, retail, and employment centers. In many cases, retail downtowns have been replaced by regional shopping centers or major discount chains. In some rural economies, the majority of workers commute to urban or other rural areas. Rural residents may identify with groups and organizations outside their community. Thus, politics takes on unique dimensions in these changing rural settings.

Most of the nation's environmental resources are in rural areas. Hence, growing environmental movements and federal environmental regulations often are aimed at rural communities. Conflicting environmental demands require communities to make trade-offs. Local decision makers question who will pay the costs of environmental stewardship or cleanup. Local firms and governments may wish to relax environmental regulations in order to create economic development opportunities for rural residents. In other cases, environmental protection is viewed as a necessity for rural viability. Competition for control of land resources among corporations, environmental groups, recreation users, government and other organizations often dominates rural political agendas. Some communities may be poorly equipped to handle these conflicts, and so community fragmentation is likely to occur.

Rural politics is also influenced by growing public concerns about farmland protection, historic preservation, main street revitalization, and maintaining viable rural communities. Land trusts and preservation groups have emerged in rural areas. Zoning and other types of local legislation are implemented to control the direction of rural growth.

Capacity to Address Rural Issues

Rural political communities tend to have a wide variation in their capabilities to address issues. However, they have some commonalities. Rural peoples have many of the same problems as urban residents, such as poverty and environmental change. However, the scale of the problem and cultural traditions of problem solving may increase the potential for solving problems in rural areas if there are adequate resources and favorable policies. Rural communities face several unique obstacles to solving their problems. Rural leaders often serve in a volunteer capacity and lack the large, specialized technical support staffs found in urban areas. They must draw on technical expertise from outside their communities or in many cases, they have limited access to such knowledge bases. In contrast to urban areas, rural political communities tend to engage competitively rather than cooperate through inter-rural governmental units. As a consequence, rural communities find it difficult to benefit from economies of scale. Unrestricted intrarural competition leads to less effective and less efficient service delivery.

Modern politics changed rural areas. In the recent past, rural areas tended to dominate state legislatures when representation was based on areas rather than population. However, the Supreme Court's 1963 one-person, one-vote decision (*Gray v. Sanders*) lessened the legislative influence of rural areas in states where urban dwellers predominate. State and federal mandates tended to force rural communities to provide highly specialized services over more generalized, locally based services. The problem is exacerbated by rural citizens who are tied to unidirectional metropolitan communication linkages. As a result, rural communities find it difficult to communicate with each other. Some national and state policy-makers have attempted to address these issues through incentives for locally based intercommunity cooperation in rural areas, or through inter-rural regional institutions, such as non-metropolitan regional planning commissions. Cooperative extension services and major U.S. foundations have launched educational initiatives to strengthen the capacity of rural communities to address these issues and other complex problems.

Intellectual shifts in community development practices have influenced the capacity of rural communities to define their desired future. In the past, the deficit approach focused on problems and needs. This concentration on the negative aspects of the community overwhelms citizens and leads to a victim mentality. In contrast, the asset based approach focuses on community strengths to bring about the kind of changes which citizens desire. Communities can discover their unique cultural, financial, human, environmental and infrastructure assets that can be leveraged with external assets to bring about desired changes.

Social capital can positively or negatively impact community goals of prosperity, better health or a sustainable environment. Social capital is defined as those interactions which lead to mutual trust and cooperation for mutual benefit. It is manifested in networks and organizations. The community development literature suggests that communities can bring about desired changes if they have strong social capital within the community and foster interaction with external groups. Communities can strengthen their social capital if they build shared visions and strengthen relationships and communication patterns. It is more than a bond among elites but involves interaction among diverse groups within the community and linkages with others outside the community. Social capital is part of the political dialogue and is influencing how rural leaders and groups behave because it allows communities to control their social and economic development efforts more effectively.

Political Units

Rural politics shapes and is shaped by local political institutions. Counties are the primary level of government in 48 states. In Louisiana, the place is filled by parishes, equivalent to counties. Local government in Alaska is still evolving; settlements there can request the kind of government they want. Cities in Alaska, as elsewhere, are responsible for police and fire protection and sewer and water services. However, boroughs—which are equivalent to other states' counties—focus on planning and zoning, parks and recreation, tax collection, and schools. Rural Alaska also has "unorganized burroughs," where government functions are performed by the state.

County governments throughout the United States perform a number of important functions: law enforcement, judicial administration, road and bridge construction and maintenance, supervision of legal documents, and social welfare. State legislators tend to grant counties relatively broad powers, with anticipated supervision of smaller municipalities. However, whenever towns or cities win greater home rule (local political autonomy), power is counterbalanced with that of the counties.

Townships also may play a role in rural politics, depending on the region. Some states have townships while others do not. Most of the six New England states are divided into townships of about 20,000 acres, which perform traditional county functions. The government structure of these townships varies from direct democracy to representative town meetings to a council manager. Other townships have little local power. For example, townships in the Midwest only maintain small-town roads, provide fire protection, and serve as voting districts. In a few states, townships may provide for their own planning and zoning, whereas this function is confined to the counties and cities in most states.

Special purpose governments are another type of rural government. If school districts are counted among them, special purpose districts make up over half of the 88,000 governments in the United States. Special purpose governments can be described as unifunctional, whereas counties, towns, cities, and townships are multifunctional in the services they provide. Each special governmental district provides unique services such as water, sewers, roads or drainage to small towns and unincorporated areas. Some are designed to protect lakes or other natural or human-made resources.

The American Indian Self-Determination Act of 1975 allowed federally entrusted tribal governments to become more independent. Tribal governments can impose taxes, create corporations, establish hunting and fishing regulations for their own members within their reservations, and regulate zoning and land use. They have the ability to develop their own community regardless of state and local regulations. Their autonomy is greater than that of other rural government entities, leading occasionally to disputes. For example, the creation of gaming and bingo parlors by tribal governments has been a source of friction between some rural municipalities and rural residents and the reservations. Others find that tribal self-determination offers limited resources and may lead to factional politics within the tribe.

After the September 11, 2001 terrorist attacks on the World Trade Center Towers in New York City and the Pentagon, U.S. federal government agencies have provided significant funds, information and training for local governments to protect water and food supplies and to prepare for bioterrorism and other emergency attacks. Rural governmental units are being engaged to upgrade security at dams, power plants, weapon stockpiles and chemical plants and are provided with resources for planning, implementing and managing higher security and emergency responses.

Rural politics at the national level is diverse and fragmented, and it no longer concentrates exclusively on agricultural issues. Rural politics at the local level could be characterized as a tug-of-war between external factors and local perspectives. Rural communities, like urban ones, vary in their capacity to address their issues and problems.

— *Ronald J. Hustedde*

See also

Decentralization; Development, Community and Economic; Government; Spatial Inequality; Leadership; Policy, Rural Development

References

Brown, Ralph. "Rural Community Satisfaction and Attachment in Mass Consumer Society." *Rural Sociology* 58 (Fall 1993): 387-403.

Brown, David L. and Louis E. Swanson, *Challenges for Rural America in the Twenty-First Century,* 2nd edition. University Park, PA: The Pennsylvania State Press, 2005.

Flora, Cornelia Butler and Jan L. Flora. *Rural Communities: Legacy and Change,* 3rd edition. Cambridge, MA: Westview Press, 2008.

Howarth, William, "The Value of Rural Life in American Culture." *Rural Development Perspectives* 12, no. 1 (1997): 5-10.

Korsching, Peter F., Timothy O. Borich, and Julie Stewart, eds. *Multicommunity Collaboration: An Evolving Rural Revitalization Strategy.* Ames, IA: North Central Regional Center for Rural Development, 1992.

Logan, John R., Rachel Bridges Whaley and Kyle Crowder, Pp. 603-630. "The Character and Consequences of Growth Regimes: An Assessment of 20 Years of Research," *Urban Affairs Review* 32 (May 1997).

Perceptions of Rural America, Battle Creek, MI: W.K. Kellogg Foundation, Nov. 1, 2002.

Perceptions of Rural America: National State Legislator Survey, Battle Creek, MI: W.K. Kellogg Foundation, Nov. 19, 2002.

Perceptions of Rural America: Views from the U.S. Congress, Battle Creek, MI: W.K. Kellogg Foundation, May 1, 2002.

Wilkinson, Kenneth P. *The Community in Rural America*. Westport, CT: Greenwood Press, 1991.

Poultry Industry

An important year 'round source of reasonably priced quality egg and poultry meat products.

The industry is one of the most efficient in agriculture, and is often studied by other animal industries for its innovations and structure. The industry is highly integrated and concentrated. Both production and marketing costs remain low, contributing to the growth in use particularly of broiler and turkey meat.

History and Status

The industry experienced many changes as it evolved into its present form. Chickens were brought to America with the first settlers, but they were not the primary poultry meat source, and were depended upon mainly for seasonal egg supplies. Wild fowls abounded. As settlements grew, chicken production was encouraged and turkeys were domesticated. The development of transportation encouraged the long-distance movement of eggs and live poultry. Later, refrigeration provided more help to the movement of eggs. Grain production in the Midwest led to development of a large poultry production region, and that area remained the primary surplus region until well after World War II. Poultry production expanded in earlier days close to large consuming centers, and for many years there was a substantial amount of slaughtering and egg packing close to consuming centers. New York dressed poultry (blood, feathers and feet removed) was shipped in volume in frozen form from distant areas until about the last four decades. Then, the eviscerated form, first frozen and then fresh, began to replace the New York dressed form. Rapid truck movement from country points now permits quick delivery of poultry of higher quality. Egg quality is much higher than it once was because of efficient cage operations and technology, which permits widespread country packing of eggs in consumer-ready form.

Today's poultry industry is commercialized, high-technology, large-scale, specialized, and vertically and horizontally integrated. The number of producing, marketing and input-supplying units declined for several decades. Major items produced by the industry today are from large egg-laying flocks, year 'round broiler enterprises, and single- to multiple-batch turkey enterprises. Resulting consumer products appear as shell eggs, egg-containing manufactured products, whole and cut-up fresh and frozen broilers, roasters and turkeys, and further-processed products made from poultry meat. Only a small amount of non-commercial production is left to meet limited demand for local or specialized items carrying price premiums. Production of ducks, geese and game birds is highly specialized and localized, and sold as higher-priced luxury items. Ducks are by far the most important of the latter group.

Consumption and Uses

The consumption of eggs and poultry is substantial and the choice of diverse products. Per-capita annual consumption of broilers and turkeys more than doubled over the last two decades, broilers reaching 80 pounds per capita per annum, and turkeys 18 pounds, ready-to-cook weight. Consumption of other mature chicken is two pounds per capita; all other poultry is less than one pound per capita. Egg consumption per capita per annum fell from nearly 300 to 234 over the last two decades. This decline was in consumption of shell eggs due to changes in eating habits and to concerns with cholesterol and salmonella. Through 1993, the American Egg Board spent $94 million to counter adverse publicity, promote egg nutrition, and develop new products. "Bad" cholesterol levels in eggs are lower than earlier claimed, according to the latest government data.

Important shares of egg, broiler and turkey production are used in manufactured or further-processed products, and by the away-from-home market (restaurants, fast-food outlets, hospitals, schools and other institutions). A quarter of egg production goes into manufactured products, and a quarter of shell egg consumption is consumed away from home. About half of broiler sales are to retail outlets, and about a third to institutional market outlets. Nearly half of the turkey output is used in further-processing, and much of this, as well as some whole and cut-up turkey, goes to the away-from-home market. Over the last two decades, the proportion of broilers sold in cut-up form increased from one-third to over half, and nearly a third of turkey output is now sold in cut-up form. The use of broiler meat in further-processed products remained at 7 to 8 percent of output, since broiler meat tends to cost more than meat from mature chickens.

Inedible eggs and poultry are used in pet food production. Poultry byproduct meal is manufactured from inedible carcasses and parts, offal, and some spent hens. Feathers from poultry-processing are converted into feather meal. Both meals are recycled through poultry feeds. Some of the feathers from chicken processing are used in pillows, and most waterfowl feathers and down in expensive insulated sleeping bags and jackets.

Consumer Protection

The high quality of edible egg and poultry products is sustained by the federal and state system of inspection and grading. Mandatory inspection exists in slaughtering, eviscerating and further-processing poultry plants and in plants producing liquid, frozen and dried egg products. Nominal inspection exists in egg packing plants, and grading of both eggs and poultry can be carried out under federal and state supervision. The USDA has federal responsibility for inspection and grading programs up to the retail and institutional levels. At those levels, responsibility rests with the Food and Drug Administration and various state and local agencies.

Efficiency and Costs

One reason poultry and eggs remain competitive is that growing efficiency in production and marketing keep prices low in comparison to other animal proteins. Laying hens, broilers and turkeys are efficient converters of feed into finished products. It takes 3.75 pounds of feed to produce a dozen eggs. For broilers, two pounds of feed are required per pound live weight, and for turkeys, three pounds or less of feed per pound live weight. There have been substantial declines in the feed/product ratios over the last few decades due to improved breeding and feeding and management. Additionally, the number of birds that can be handled per person employed more than quadrupled because of mechanization and better housing and the realization of substantial economies of scale. There have been substantial gains in productivity in marketing due to simplified marketing channels, economies of scale, and mechanization. Over two decades, productivity in egg marketing increased 80 percent, 50 percent on broilers, and over 60 percent on turkeys. Intermediaries declined in importance; there is now more direct plant-to-retailer or warehouse movement, and less jobbing activity.

During 1994, the average cost to produce a dozen Grade A Large eggs was 46.8 cents per dozen, and the industry net return was 3.8 cents. The cost to produce a pound of live broiler during 1994 was 27 cents, and the net return was 6 cents ready-to-cook equivalent. The cost to produce a pound of live turkey in 1994 was 37.5 cents, and the net return was 2.8 cents per pound, ready-to-cook equivalent. The net return has been positive for each commodity for the last several years. In the longer run, broiler returns remained consistently positive, whereas returns from eggs or turkeys varied from positive to negative.

It cost 19 cents in 1994 to move eggs from the farm to the retail store level. About a cent of this was for assembly and procurement. A unique feature of the egg industry has been the growth of "in-line" complexes. With production and packing at the same geographic location, eggs are conveyed from cages to the packing room by belts. Currently, over half of commercial production is of the "in-line" type, and this materially lowers average industry assembly costs. Nearly 2 cents are required for long-distance hauling of eggs; 12 cents for grading, packing and cartoning; with the balance of 4 cents for wholesaling. The average annual retail markup on eggs ranges between 17 and 21 cents.

Costs of moving ready-to-cook broilers from producing areas to retail were about 20 cents per pound in 1994. Nearly 4 cents were for assembly and hauling; 11 cents for processing; and about 5 cents for wholesaling. Retail markups range from 20 to 26 cents. For turkeys, costs from producing areas to the retail level were 24 cents per pound ready-to-cook equivalent. Retail markups range from 20 to 26 cents.

Production and Pricing

Production of eggs and poultry is relatively widespread, but tends to be concentrated more heavily in those states that have a comparative advantage or where individual entrepreneurs have been most persistent. Sixty percent of the nation's broilers are produced by the five leading states (Arkansas, Georgia, Alabama, North Carolina and Mississippi); 82 percent by the top 10; and 95.5 percent by the first 20. Only California, Missouri and Pennsylvania outside the South rank in the top 15. The five leading turkey-producing states (North Carolina, Minnesota, Arkansas, California and Missouri) produce nearly 54 percent; the first 10 states over 75 percent; and the 20 leading states, 85 percent. The five leading states in egg production (California, Georgia, Arkansas, Indiana and Pennsylvania) account for about 36 percent of output; the first 10 states produce nearly 60 percent; the 20 leading states over 80 percent.

Basic price levels on broilers, turkeys and other poultry are determined primarily by sales to volume buyers in large consuming centers, with returns to plants and producers largely reflected by intervening costs of transportation. Sales to manufacturing of further-processed poultry products and institutions relate to basic price levels. Trading between producers and packing plants of Gradable Nest Run and Graded Loose eggs provides a base to which cartoning and movement costs to large markets can be added to fix prices to volume buyers. Trading of Nest Run Breaking Stock between producers, packers and egg breakers and dryers largely determines the input costs for liquid, frozen and dried egg products. In addition to current sales of these products to food manufacturers, long-term price contracts are common.

Market Movements

The bulk of poultry industry products go to domestic outlets, and the market for these is nationwide. While the local needs for each commodity often may be produced within a few hundred miles, large quantities are required to move greater distances to balance supplies with demand. The interregional movement of broilers and turkeys has trended upward for many years, and it may now be increasing on eggs. Only 14 Southern states are surplus on broilers; all others are deficit, with as much as 40 percent moving interregionally. Less than 20 percent of turkey output moves interregionally. Long-distance hauling of eggs is increased by the need to obtain particular grades and sizes, even though eggs are produced to some extent in all states. In total, about a fifth of egg output moves interregionally.

Recent-year strong domestic price levels have been supported by growing and substantial export markets for broilers and turkeys, and, to a lesser extent, for eggs. The major increases in exports began about 1990, with broiler exports rising from 4 to 10 percent of output, and turkeys from 2 to 11 percent of output. Egg exports rose from 2 to about 3.5 percent of output. Asia is our major export market for broilers, but Russia and Eastern Europe have been increasing rapidly in recent years, supplementing continuing increases in the Western Hemisphere and the Middle East. Mexico is our largest export market for turkeys, followed by Korea,

Europe, the Far East, and lately, Russia and Eastern Europe. The most important egg markets are Japan, Hong Kong, Canada and Mexico, with the balance widely scattered geographically. The competitiveness of U.S. poultry and egg production, export promotion, and the Export Enhancement Program has helped in expanding our export markets, as may recent trade pacts. But export sales remain vulnerable to political developments abroad.

Integration and Concentration

The poultry industry exhibits a high and unique degree of vertical and horizontal integration, and is increasingly concentrated in fewer and fewer hands. Vertical integration began in the industry with various types of contractual arrangements between producers and packing plants, feed dealers, and some who were marketing-oriented. Over the years, contractual arrangements have been increasingly replaced by processor-owned farms, and the number of independent producers declined drastically. Currently, only about 1 percent of broiler output is from fully independent farms. The proportion of non-commercial turkeys is estimated at 3 to 4 percent, whereas the volume of eggs being produced by independent farmers or marketed through true cooperatives is at 6 percent. Many large firms engaged in the egg, broiler or turkey business are also involved with feed milling and distribution, further-processing, long-distance transportation, and wholesaling. Some are part of large conglomerates or have international branches.

There has also been a growing degree of concentration. The top 10 broiler firms accounted for 59 percent of output in 1994; 52 firms for 99 percent. Many firms have more than one plant, and are also engaged in further-processing. The top five turkey firms account for 48 percent of output; the top 10 for 74 percent; and 28 for virtually all of the commercial production. In 1994, 57 firms owning more than one million laying hens accounted for 72.5 percent of the total. And 380 firms having 75,000 or more layers accounted for 94 percent.

Employment

The poultry industry furnishes substantial employment opportunities to rural America. But because of the decline in small independent output, employment in today's commercial egg and poultry enterprises is likely to be as a contractual or salaried worker. Even to become a commercial grower on the scale demanded by present companies requires capital investments of many thousands of dollars. Traditionally, catching and hauling live birds had low status appeal, as did killing, picking and eviscerating operations. Mechanization alleviated this to some extent. Nevertheless, poultry processing plants employing several hundred to a few thousand workers are valuable to local economies. Egg packing and further-processing jobs are more rewarding, but relatively fewer people are required. Related input-supplying and construction also helps local employment. From the processing and packing operations forward, marketing activities tend to be more urban-associated, except for local retailing and away-from-home facilities, and local-based hauling companies. Additional information is available from the Poultry Science Association, which publishes *Poultry Science* and the *Journal of Applied Poultry Research* (http://www.poultryscience.org).

— *George B. Rogers*

See also

Agricultural Prices; Animal Rights/Welfare; Livestock Industry; Livestock Production

References

American Poultry Historical Society. *American Poultry History, 1823-1973.* Madison, WI: American Printing and Publishing, 1974.

American Poultry Historical Society. *American Poultry History, 1974-1993.* Mt. Morris, IL: Watt, 1996.

Barbut, Shai. *Poultry Products Processing: An Industry Guide.* CRC, 2001.

Benjamin, E.W. and H.C. Pierce. *Marketing Poultry Products.* 3rd ed. New York, NY: John Wiley, 1937.

Benjamin, E.W., J.M. Gwin, F.L. Faber, W.D. Termohlen. *Marketing Poultry Products.* 5th ed. New York, NY: John Wiley, 1960.

Lasley, F.A. *The U.S. Poultry Industry: Changing Economics and Structure,* A.E. Report No. 502 (July). Washington, DC: U.S. Department of Agriculture, Economic Research Service, 1983.

Lasley, F.A., W.L. Henson, and H.B. Jones. *The U.S. Turkey Industry.* A.E. Report No. 525 (March). Washington, DC: U.S. Department of Agriculture, Economic Research Service, 1985.

Lasley, F.A., H.B. Jones, E.E. Easterling, and L.A. Christensen. *The U.S. Broiler Industry,* A.E. Report No. 591 (November). Washington, DC: U.S. Department of Agriculture, Economic Research Service, 1988.

Rogers, George B. *Historical and Economic Development of the Poultry Industry, 1517-1950.* Beltsville, MD: National Agricultural Library. Unpublished manuscript in ""Personal papers of George B. Rogers," 1951.

Rogers, George B. "Poultry and Eggs." In *Another Revolution in U.S. Farming?* A.E. Report No. 441 (December).

Edited by Lyle Schertz. Washington, DC: U.S. Department of Agriculture, E.S.C.S., 1979.

Sams, Alan R., ed. *Poultry Meat Processing.* CRC, 2000.

Sawyer, Gordon. *The Agribusiness Poultry Industry: A History of Its Development.* New York, NY: Exposition Press, 1971.

Sykes, Geoffrey. *Poultry: A Modern Agribusiness.* London: Crosby, Lockwood and Sons, 1963.

U.S. Department of Agriculture. *Poultry Situation, Livestock and Poultry Situation, Poultry Outlook,* and *Poultry* (various issues). Washington, DC: U.S. Department of Agriculture.

Poverty

The lack of income or other resources needed to achieve a minimally acceptable standard of living. In the U.S., poverty often is perceived as a principally urban problem, yet historically and today it is more prevalent in rural areas. Compared to the urban poor, the rural poor have somewhat different characteristics, face unique macroeconomic circumstances, and exhibit dissimilar economic survival strategies. Nevertheless, popular perception and political concern about the poor often are shaped by images of inner city poverty. The unique nature of rural poverty needs to be better understood if we are to tailor realistic policy options for rural areas. This entry seeks to provide a rudimentary understanding. First, the definitions of and trends in poverty are detailed. Then, to help explain the rural disadvantage in poverty, the individual-level and structural causes of poverty are reviewed. Finally, rural-urban differences in the survival strategies of the poor are considered.

Absolute Poverty

Poverty can be defined in many ways. *Absolute poverty* occurs when people and their families lack the income or resources necessary to maintain a subsistence-level standard of living. The official definition of poverty in the U.S. follows this absolute approach. Developed in the early 1960s, poverty thresholds were set at three times the cost of a minimally adequate diet. To account for variation in needs across families of different types, multiple poverty thresholds were specified to adjust for family size, number of children, gender of family head, whether the head was elderly, and whether the family lived on a farm. Farm families were assigned lower poverty thresholds because it was assumed they produced some of their own food and therefore needed less income to get along. Other than adjusting annually for inflation, recent decades have seen only slight modifications to the official poverty thresholds (e.g., the farm/non-farm distinction is no longer made). In 2006 a family of four was defined as poor if their annual pre-tax income was less than $20,614.

The official poverty thresholds have come under criticism over the years. Reasons include being insensitive to geographic differences in cost of living, not counting in-kind income (e.g., food stamps) as income, and ignoring disproportionately rapid increases in the costs of non-food necessities since the thresholds were developed. A National Academy of Sciences panel developed an alternative set of thresholds to correct for these problems and that are uniformly higher than the official ones that remain in use today (Citro and Michael 1995). The application of the proposed new measure would result in higher poverty rates.

Relative Poverty

Whereas absolute poverty exists when a family has less than subsistence-level income, *relative poverty* is defined as having an income that is much less than average. A typical relative definition is annual family income that is less the one-half the median annual family income. Trends in relative poverty rates are especially sensitive to changes in the equality of income distribution and these rates tend to be higher than the absolute poverty rates. Perhaps as a result, relative poverty has never been seriously considered as an alternative to the official (absolute) measure of poverty in the United States.

Trends in Absolute Poverty

The figure shows absolute poverty rates among metropolitan (metro) and nonmetropolitan (nonmetro) individuals for the period 1959 to 2006. The 1960s typify the post-war years as a period of steadily declining poverty rates, especially in nonmetro areas. Since the early 1970s poverty rates have been rising and falling in response to economic cycles, but generally trend upward; in both metro and nonmetro areas poverty rates were higher in 2006 than they were three decades prior. In every year, the nonmetro poverty rate was higher than the corresponding metro rate, and the gap widened in the most recent period observed. The poverty rate in 2006 was 15.2 and 11.8 percent in nonmetropolitan and metropolitan areas, respectively. Thus, poverty remains more prevalent in the nonmetro areas, dispelling the myth that it is a principally urban phenomenon.

Poverty rates by residence, 1959-2006

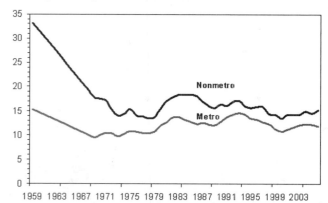

Note: Metro status of some counties changed in 1984, 1994, and 2004. Metro and non-metro rates are imputed for 1960–1968, 1970 and 1984. *Source:* Economic Research Service using data from the U.S. Census Bureau's Current Population, Annual Social and Economic Supplement, 2007.

The enduring nature of rural poverty distinguishes it from poverty in metro areas. The USDA defines persistent poverty counties as those that have had 20 percent or more of their residents living in poverty for the last four census years (1970, 1980, 1990, and 2000). Of the 386 persistent poverty counties in 2004, 340 were nonmetro. The map shows that persistent poverty counties are concentrated in Appalachia, an arc stretching from the rural Carolinas into the Mississippi Delta region, the Rio Grande Valley and southwest, and the northern plains. The spatial distribution of persistent poverty counties corresponds with the spatial distribution of racial and ethnic minorities in rural America: African Americans in the South, Hispanics and Native Americans in the Southwest, and Native Americans in the Central Plains. Poverty rates also are higher in more remote nonmetro counties. The 1999 poverty rate for residents of nonmetro counties adjacent to metro areas was 13.3 percent (or little different from the U.S. rate), but 16.8 percent were poor in nonmetro counties that were not adjacent and had no city of at least 10,000 residents (U.S. Department of Agriculture 2004).

As noted, the official poverty thresholds do not adjust for geographic differences in the cost of living. Some assert this cost is lower in rural areas. Correcting for metro/nonmetro differences in the cost of housing, Joliffe finds poverty rates to be higher in metro than nonmetro areas (Joliffe 2006). However, the costs of other necessities (e.g., transportation, food), which are often higher in nonmetro areas, are not taken into account. While residential differences in living costs should be recognized, a full accounting is needed be-

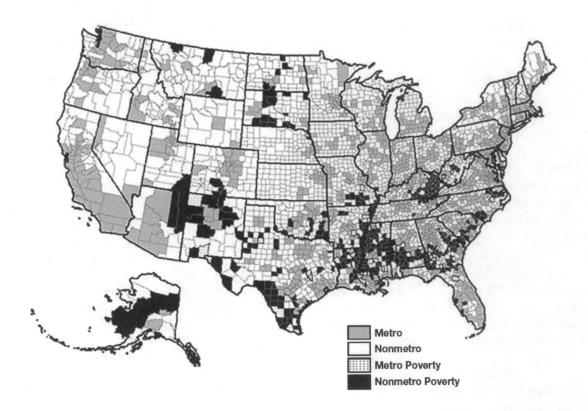

Metro
Nonmetro
Metro Poverty
Nonmetro Poverty

fore implications for metro/nonmetro differences in poverty can be made.

Explaining Rural Poverty

Studies of the causes of poverty differ in their emphasis on individual and family characteristics versus structural characteristics of place of residence. Both kinds of studies are helpful to understand why poverty rates are higher in nonmetro America.

Individual-level Explanations. At the individual level, the set of factors that influence poverty status is highly similar in rural and urban areas. In both places, for example, those with little education are more likely to be poor than those with more, as are Blacks or Latinos when compared to Whites. In seeking to understand and explain the higher poverty rate in rural America, social scientists have explored rural/urban differences in both population composition and in the effects of specific variables on the likelihood of being poor.

Some differences in population composition work in favor of rural residents which makes their higher poverty rate seem puzzling. Nonmetro individuals are less likely to be members of racial or ethnic minority groups known to suffer much higher risks of poverty. When residential differences in poverty rates are exam-

ined within categories of race and ethnicity, the nonmetro disadvantage appears that much worse. In fact, 2004 Current Population Survey data show that the nonmetro poverty rates for Whites, Blacks, Latinos, and Native Americans were even higher than those for their counterparts living in the central cities of metropolitan areas. An implication is that rural minorities rank among the poorest of all Americans. Compositional differences in family structure also benefit rural residents. Nonmetro residents are more likely than metro residents to be residing in families headed by a married couple, and they are less likely to be in female-headed families. Working against nonmetro residents is the fact that they are more likely to be elderly, a compositional difference that is consistent with their higher poverty risks.

An important correlate of poverty is human capital. According to human capital theory, workers are remunerated in direct proportion to the bundle of skills they bring to the labor force. Those with human capital deficits—indicated often by low levels of education or labor force experience—are at greater risk of poverty. Nonmetro adults have fewer years of completed education on average, and are more likely to have dropped out of high school than their metro counterparts. There also is evidence that rural schools are of lower quality, and that rural high school students score lower on standardized tests of scholastic aptitude. There is less empirical support for a rural human capital disadvantage in work experience. In fact, when human capital is measured as total years of full-time work experience and the percent of adult years worked full-time, rural household heads are relatively advantaged compared to urban heads.

The returns to human capital for rural workers are less than those for workers in urban areas. In 2003, the weekly earnings for wage and salary workers with some college were 5 percent lower for nonmetro than metro workers and this disparity increases to 10 percent for workers with a college degree. Poverty rates could be higher in rural areas partly because additional years of education are less effective in keeping adults and their families out of poverty.

Structural Explanations. In addition to the attributes of people and families, individual well-being will be shaped by structural characteristics of the places in which they live. These include the abundance and quality of surrounding economic opportunities and the permeability of local socioeconomic hierarchies. When rural poverty has reached the national spotlight, structural explanations—most notably dependence on extractive industries—are often invoked. It remains true that poverty rates are higher in counties dominated by farming and other extractive industries. For example, in 1999 the poverty rate for farming-dependent and mining-dependent nonmetro counties was 16.5 percent compared to only 13.7 percent for other nonmetro counties. Often such places lack diversified economies making them highly vulnerable to macroeconomic slumps and international competition. The farm crisis of the early 1980s, for example, contributed to the rise in rural poverty by hurting both farmers and ancillary businesses that depend on a healthy farm sector.

Today only about three percent of all nonmetro workers are in agriculture-related industries, while less than one percent are in other extractive industries. In trying to understand the structural causes of rural poverty, it is important to look beyond agriculture to other aspects of industrial structure. Local economies dominated by manufacturing tend to have lower poverty rates. While metro and nonmetro areas are roughly equivalent in the percent in manufacturing, nonmetro workers are more likely to be in the less lucrative nondurable manufacturing sector. Moreover, the slowly rising poverty rates in nonmetro America over the past quarter-century can be attributed partly to the continued industrial restructuring away from manufacturing and toward services. Current Population Survey data indicate between 1980 and 2006, the percent of the nonmetro workforce employed in manufacturing declined by 20.1 percent, while that in services grew by 18.3 percent.

Local industrial structure provides some clues to differential opportunity between places, however analyses that control for it are still unable to completely explain the rural disadvantage in poverty (Brown and Hirschl 1995). And while controlling for prevailing wages can greatly explain the nonmetro disadvantage in poverty risks, this begs the question of why their wages are lower in the first place. While speculation includes smaller firm size, lower unionization rates, different phases of production that concentrate in rural areas, and lower costs of living, there are no firm explanations.

In addition to industrial structure, individual opportunities are shaped by the permeability of local social hierarchies. In some instances the persistence of rural poverty has been linked to highly ascriptive stratification systems. Certain families within rural communities might become pejoratively labeled and encounter blocked access to educational and occupational opportunities (Duncan 1999). Similar arguments explain persisting poverty among rural minorities. Minority individuals within communities can experience prejudice and discrimination in the pursuit of economic goals, just as minority communities as a whole can experience blocked access to societal resources.

An important reason to study structural determinants of poverty is that they can help account for individual-level disadvantages. For example, the comparatively low education of rural residents has been linked to (1) poorer quality schools, (2) a rural 'brain drain' where the best students migrate to opportunities found in more urban locales, and (3) the possibility that rural residents, sensing a local economy that yields a low payoff to education, rationally under-invest in their own human capital. Similarly, whereas the increase in rural poverty in recent years might be blamed partly on the rise in female-headship and family instability, both seem to result from industrial restructuring and constrained opportunities. The point is, seemingly individual-level explanations for poverty may have important structural roots. Another way this conundrum has been posed has been to question whether rural residence is endogenous to factors that cause poverty (Weber, et al. 2005). In other words, through a process of residential sorting, people of limited income generating capacity "choose to" move to or stay in rural areas; it's not the place, it's the people. Research has discounted this residential sorting hypothesis (Fisher 2007).

Rural Economic Survival Strategies

The uniqueness of rural poverty is evident also in the economic survival strategies used by the rural poor. These strategies are consistent with the strong sense of individualism and self-reliance said to distinguish many rural areas. For example, compared to their metro counterparts, poor nonmetro families rely more on earnings from labor force participation, and less on Public Assistance and other means-tested transfer programs (i.e., they are more likely to be among the working poor). The higher labor force participation of the rural poor, along with difficulties of availability and accessibility to assistance programs generally, helps explain the lower rates of welfare use among the rural poor. There also is evidence that a greater sense of individualism in rural areas lowers welfare receipt both by making the rural poor themselves more averse to relying on the government, and by making the negative stigma associated with welfare receipt stronger in rural America (Rank and Hirschl 1993).

Besides formal work and welfare, recent years have seen growing interest in informal or underground economic activities as household survival strategies among the poor. The informal economy consists of unregulated economic activities which generate real or in-kind income. Such activities include, for example, under-the-table work for cash or other things of value, selling rummaged goods, and selling home-produced food or crafts. Several studies have shown that informal work is common in rural areas, and can be critical for helping poor rural families survive through difficult periods (Slack 2007).

Conclusion

In this entry we have highlighted the distinctive nature of rural poverty and argued that its uniqueness needs to be borne in mind when dealing with the rural poor. Poverty policy proposals designed to strengthen the family and move the poor off of welfare and into the workforce make somewhat less sense in rural areas where the poor already are more likely to work and live in intact families. Instead, rural poverty would be ameliorated more by programs designed to generate employment opportunities and make work pay a living wage.

At the same time, significant areas of convergence need to be recognized. First, as figure 1 revealed, the nonmetro disadvantage is not nearly as great today as it was 40 or more years ago. Second, recent decades have witnessed a substantial increase in the prevalence of single-parent families in rural areas, eroding the rural advantage in this regard, and giving rise to an increase in rural child poverty. Third, over the past decade there has been a significant rise in earnings and decline in Public Assistance as a percent of poor family income, especially in urban areas. While rural families still rely more heavily on earnings and less on government transfers than the urban poor, the residential differences are much less stark today. Moreover, rural areas are not immune to many of the regrettable correlates of poverty including drug and alcohol abuse, domestic violence, and homelessness, which is disturbing since services often are lacking or inaccessible in rural areas.

— *Leif Jensen and Eric B. Jensen*

See also

Employment; Homelessness; Income; Inequality; Policy, Socioeconomic; Policy, Rural Family; Underemployment; Welfare

References

Brown, David L. and Thomas A. Hirschl. "Household Poverty in Rural and Metropolitan-Core Areas of the United States." *Rural Sociology* 60 (1995), 44-66.

Citro, Constance E. and Robert T. Michael. *Measuring Poverty: A New Approach*. Washington, DC: National Academies Press, 1995.

Duncan, Cynthia M. 1999. *Worlds Apart: Why Poverty Persists in Rural America*. New Haven, CT: Yale University Press, 1999.

Duncan, Cynthia M., ed. *Rural Poverty in America*. New York: Auburn House, 1992.

Fisher, Monica. 2007. "Why Is U.S. Poverty Higher in Nonmetropolitan than in Metropolitan Areas?" *Growth and Change* 38, no. 1 (2007): 56.

Fitchen, Janet M. *Poverty in Rural America: A Case Study*. Boulder: Westview, 1981.

Jensen, Leif and David J. Eggebeen. "Nonmetropolitan Poor Children and Reliance on Public Assistance." *Rural Sociology* 59 (1994), 45-65.

Jensen, Leif and Diane K. McLaughlin. "Human Capital and Nonmetropolitan Poverty." Pp. 111-138 in *Investing in People: The Human Capital Needs of Rural America*. Edited by Lionel J. Beaulieu and David Mulkey. Boulder, CO: Westview Press, 1995.

Jolliffe, Dean. "Poverty, Prices, and Place: How Sensitive Is the Spatial Distribution of Poverty to Cost of Living

Adjustments?" *Economic Inquiry* 44, no. 2 (2006): 296-310.

Lichter, Daniel T. and David J. Eggebeen. "Child Poverty and the Changing Rural Family." *Rural Sociology* 57 (1992): 151-172.

Rank, Mark R. and Thomas A. Hirschl. "The Link between Population Density and Welfare Participation." *Demography* 30 (1993): 607-622.

Rural Sociological Society. *Persistent Poverty in Rural America*. Rural Sociological Society Taskforce on Persistent Rural Poverty. Boulder, CO: Westview Press, 1993.

Slack, Tim. "The Contours and Correlates of Informal Work in Rural Pennsylvania." *Rural Sociology* 72, no. 1 (2007): 69-89.

U.S. Department of Agriculture. "*Rural Poverty at a Glance.*" Rural Development Research Report Number 100. Washington DC: U.S. Department of Agriculture, 2004.

Weber, Bruce, Leif Jensen, Kathleen Miller, Jane Mosley, and Monica Fisher. "A Critical Review of the Rural Poverty Literature: Is There Truly a Rural Effect?" *International Regional Science Review* 28, no. 4 (2005): 381-414.

Private Property Land Ownership Rights

Socially protected streams of benefit associated with land in rural areas. Property rights enumerate the multitude of ways that land may be used and thus help determine its value. When compared with urban land, rural land will be associated with fewer specifically defined rights but also fewer formal restrictions. Hence, rural landowners enjoy many privileged uses of land, which are known as presumptive rights. Rural land also has two important characteristics that limit value. First, rural land is farther from urban infrastructure and markets, making it difficult to capture returns at the level of urban land. Second, rural land generally contains larger quantities of natural resources and environmental amenities. To the extent that federal and state policies affect these resources, rural landowners may take advantage of these policies and have their land uses restricted in ways that differ from urban landowners.

Private Property Rights in Rural Land

Private property rights have been defined in various ways. Many economists and lawyers view a property right as socially protected access to a benefit stream (Bromley, 1989) or as a legally protected expectation of deriving certain advantages from a thing (Powell, 1998). Although brief, such definitions employ several complex concepts. The term "property" does not refer to "land" directly—land is "real" property—but instead involves a relationship between a person and a thing. "Benefits" and "advantages" are most usefully thought of as accruing over time. For instance, rural landowners can use a lease to transfer temporary benefits to another individual. In the U.S., "social" or "legal protection" means that local, state or federal governments have sanctioned, or authorized, a specific use of property. It also means that if someone takes a landowner's property, he or she can call upon the power of the state to return it. Governments can take property from individuals unilaterally using the Constitutional power of eminent domain. However, property rights ensure that governments must also pay just compensation. Just compensation, in effect, is the market value of the private property rights associated with a given land parcel.

Ownership is a surprisingly confusing term, and it is generally advisable to refer to the "holder" of specific property rights (Demsetz, 1998). In brief, landownership must include the right to possess, or exclusively physically control, land. Fuller ownership will include more complete rights to use and manage land, to earn income from and to transmit land to others (Bromley, 1989). Although this entry maintains the "landownership" language for ease of comprehension, the "holder of rights" terminology is more appropriate in advanced discussions.

Property rights in land are viewed by lawyers using the "bundle of sticks" analogy. There are innumerable ways in which land may be used, and there are other valuable legal attributes of land, such as how and to whom it may be transferred. Each of these beneficial uses and legal attributes can be viewed as a right, or a "stick," associated with a land parcel. Landownership thereby becomes a bundle of sticks, and land value increases with the number and economic importance of the sticks. Examples of property rights in rural land might include the ability to use it to grow a crop, harvest trees, or hunt some animals. Landowners may pursue all three, some, or none of the activities at a given time, but the rights exist regardless of whether they are exercised. Most rural land will contain these common use rights and many other use rights.

Some property rights may not be in the bundle of sticks, however. For instance, the rural landowner may not be able to fill wetlands or develop residential housing in violation of zoning codes. A key to understanding the legal interpretation of private property rights is that landowners cannot "do whatever they want to do" with their land. Some uses are permitted and some are prohibited.

Extent and Limitations on Property Rights

But what about activities that are not permitted and not legally prohibited? Many uses of rural land fall into this category. Demsetz (1998) refers to these as "unarticulated rights" under the presumptive control of a landowner. It helps to distinguish formal property rights regimes from informal, or presumptive, regimes. Formal rights mean that a government body has specifically allocated a property right to a holder. In presumptive rights regimes, however, a landowner may use land as if he or she held a property right. For instance, in some rural areas there are no prohibitions about types of domestic wastewater treatment, allowing landowners to use cesspools or septic systems on land with poor percolation. It is not that landowners have private property rights to these forms of wastewater treatment. Rather, until restrictive regulations are adopted, landowners in these areas can make sewage treatment decisions as if they had the right. Presumptive rights might be altered in the future as local ordinances or state regulations specify standards for domestic wastewater treatment.

Even without governmental restrictions, presumptive rights regimes may not persist. Neighbors may be harmed when a landowner exercises presumptive rights. Economists define these situations as negative externalities, describing instances where a presumptive land use harms another party but where the landowner does not offer compensation. This is the essence of land-use conflicts and is common in rural settings. There exists a common law standard that owners may not use their land in ways that substantially interfere with another's use of property. The harmed party has the option of using civil law to have a court declare the offending use a "nuisance"—a common law ruling that compels the landowner to stop pursing the activity (injunction) and/or compensate the victim (damages).

Another important aspect of private property rights in land is the concept of legal duty and its use in resolving land-use conflicts. Governments bear many costs associated with property rights, including the costs of adopting rules, operating legal systems, and enforcement. As such, governments tend to select only the most important types of property for formal protection. These are typically those land uses most likely to cause conflicts. If rights are allocated to the landowner, the neighbor becomes the "duty" bearer, meaning that one has a duty to bear the external costs of the landowner's exercise of the property right. In other conflicts, the landowner becomes the duty bearer and the neighbor, or society in general, becomes the property right holder.

Characteristics of Rural Landownership Rights

Rural areas create special opportunities and challenges for rural landowners. Foremost, rural areas tend to have less restrictive zoning than urban areas and may even have no zoning. Zoning is the principal tool used by local governments prevent land-use conflicts, protect land values, and to protect the health, welfare, morals and safety of local communities. One reason rural areas have less zoning is that they have lower population densities and larger parcel sizes, which means that landowners will be less likely to come into conflict because of physical proximity. In addition, the health and safety regulations needed to allow high densities in urban areas are not as essential in rural areas because behavior below standards affects fewer people. A second reason is that local governments have fewer resources to enforce rigorous zoning in rural areas. In many ways, rural landowners enjoy more freedom in their land-use decisions, though many of these uses are associated with presumptive rights.

Rural landowners also may face different land market challenges than the typical urban landowner. Since rural areas have lower population densities, the amount of government service per unit of area is much less than in urban areas. Many rural landowners, therefore, will have more difficulty enforcing exclusive use—i.e., preventing trespass—because they have more land on which trespass may occur and fewer police services to enforce their rights. These geographical realities also limit opportunities to develop land intensively. Central sanitary sewers, high-capacity roads, schools and convenient shopping are less likely to be near a rural land parcel. These challenges will tend to lower rural land values.

With respect to natural resources and environmental amenities, rural areas have more federal and state restrictions. Rural landowners enjoy opportunities associated with extraction (mineral, timber), agriculture and outdoor recreation that are not available to urban landowners. These natural opportunities are some of the most valuable rights (formal and presumptive) associated with rural landownership. However, natural amenities have increased in value to urban populations, too, and recently adopted statutes tend to preserve current natural uses. In addition, federal policy has affected agricultural land use since the Great Depression and, in the past four decades, also restricted land-use options in the name of environmental quality. Some people view these restrictions as uncompensated, "regulatory takings" of private property rights. Others perceive the end of presumptive rights such that landowners are assigned duties.

Federal and State Policies

Many policies promote development of rural areas and help subsidize agricultural and forest uses. Governmental efforts to provide services such as rural electrification, economic development and highways are more costly in rural areas. On a per-capita basis, the urban population subsidizes these efforts and thereby raises the value of some property rights associated with rural landownership. Similarly, policies promoting agriculture, forestry, mineral extraction and other primarily rural land uses increase the returns to rural landownership. Although many federal policies benefit rural areas, agricultural landowners may be the largest beneficiaries. An investigative series in the *Washington Post* on farm subsidies found that agricultural landowners receive approximately $20 billion per year and argues that many payments are made to landowners who do not need them or who do not farm. Nevertheless, an important political question arises when these policies change. Should rural landowners be compensated when beneficial policies are discontinued?

Rural landowners also face considerable constraints from federal and state policies. Throughout U.S. history, rural landowners have disproportionately borne the burdens of eminent domain, particularly for road building. Although all benefit from roads, only the owners in the path of a new road are forced to sell. Many believe that the market price used to determine just compensation does not accurately reflect the costs to the landowner of the disruption. In addition, since the 1970s flagship federal environmental statutes have been adopted and revised, often accompanied by similar state legislation. Several of these statutes constrain the activities of rural landowners disproportionately because they manage most of the natural resources and environmental amenities. The land-use constraints created by federal policies alone are so great that some

have argued that these statutes constitute federal land-use planning (Babbitt, 2005). Among these statutes, the Federal Water Pollution Control Act of 1972, also known as the Clean Water Act (CWA), and the Endangered Species Act (ESA) of 1973 are viewed as particularly restrictive for rural landowners.

These federal statutes empower agencies, such as the U.S. Army Corps of Engineers and the U.S. Fish and Wildlife Service, to write and adopt regulations that shape rural land use. Landowners with water bodies or wetlands on or adjacent to their land are constrained by the CWA, among other state and federal statutes. For instance, if a landowner has a wetland that is not isolated (i.e., within approximately 100 feet of a water body), he or she may not discharge dredged or fill material into the wetland without a permit from the U.S. Army Corps of Engineers. This requirement sometimes surprises landowners who do not recognize that, legally, a wetland may be land that is covered by water for only a short time each year.

Typical ESA constraints involve private land that is designated "critical habitat" for an endangered or threatened species. This often occurs in rural areas and limits landowners' land-use options because they are prohibited from harming the protected species and degrading its habitat. As was seen in the spotted owl conflict in the Pacific Northwest, the constraints are considerable—a landowner may not be able to harvest timber on private land. Another example is the red wolf reintroduction to North Carolina (Duke and Csoboth, 2003). The U.S. Fish and Wildlife Service identified a rural area in eastern North Carolina to reintroduce red wolves after years of captive breeding. Although red wolves had long been eradicated from eastern North Carolina, the affected counties were an attractive site for reintroduction because they contained a national wildlife refuge and had low population densities. Despite laudable efforts to ease the impact of reintroduction, rural landowners were constrained and negatively affected by the reintroduction. They bore risks of attacks on humans, livestock and pets, and they could not "take" the species—where "take" is defined, at minimum, as to harass, harm, pursue, hunt, shoot, wound, kill, trap, capture or collect the protected species.

In the future, rural landowners should expect federal and state policies to continue to constrain land-use options and, in areas experiencing population growth, new or expanded zoning rules. Beneficial policies, especially at the federal level, are likely to continue, also.

New opportunities are likely to arise in the growing land preservation movement, which is led by nonprofit groups like the Nature Conservancy and state and local governments. Land preservation programs offer payments to rural landowners who maintain, in perpetuity, natural and/or agricultural uses. In terms of property rights, rural landowners who preserve their land can earn cash for the value of their presumptive and formal rights to develop land.

— *Joshua M. Duke*

See also

Agricultural Law; Land Ownership; Land Reform; Values of Residents

References

Babbitt, Bruce E. *Cities in the Wilderness: A New Vision for Land Use in America*. Washington, DC: Island Press, 2005.

Bromley, Daniel W. *Economic Interests and Institutions: The Conceptual Foundations of Public Policy*. New York: Basil Blackwell, 1989.

Demsetz, Harold. "Property Rights." In *The New Palgrave Dictionary of Economics and the Law*. Edited by Peter Newman. New York: Stockton Press, 1998.

Duke, Joshua M. and Laura A. Csoboth. "Increased Scientific Capacity and Endangered Species Management: Lessons from the Red Wolf Conflict." *Drake Journal of Agricultural Law* 8 (2003):539-590.

Hohfeld, W.N. "Fundamental Legal Conceptions as Applied in Judicial Reasoning." *Yale Law Journal* 26 (1917):710-770.

Manning, Richard. *Grassland: The History, Biology, Politics and Promise of the American Prairie*. Penguin, 1997.

Powell, Frona M. *Law and the Environment*. San Francisco: West Educational Publishing Company, 1989.

Washington Post. *Harvesting Cash: A Yearlong Investigation by the Washington Post*. http://www.washingtonpost.com/wp-srv/nation/interactives/farmaid/ last accessed, January 11, 2008.

Public Housing Authorities

Quasi-governmental, nonprofit, tax-exempt organizations that govern various aspects of an area's housing (Northeast Washington Housing Solutions 2005). This article will provide information on Public Housing Authorities and their growing importance to rural communities. Many rural communities are faced with two demographic trends related to migration: a growing se-

nior citizen population and out-migration of young professionals. Folts et al. (2005) state, "Housing for elderly is most adequate in urban metropolitan areas, less adequate in towns outside metropolitan areas, and least adequate in rural areas." In response, some of rural communities have created much-needed housing without waiting for outside assistance from government agencies. They formed Housing Authorities as a tool to address their communities' housing shortages.

Public Housing Authorities as a Mechanism to Meet Rural Housing Needs

Some senior citizens may be interested in downsizing from their multi-level homes to a residence that requires less labor to maintain. Options could include town-home-style residences or multiplex units with no steps, lawn care, or snow removal.

However, new construction in many rural communities has come to a virtual standstill because it is cost prohibitive for building contractors or developers to construct multi-family unit dwellings. For construction of housing units to be profitable, rental rates would be unobtainable for most middle- and low-income families. But, if housing units could be built by a Housing Authority, rental rates could be kept at a more affordable level. Housing Authorities are nonprofit, tax-exempt agencies which have greater latitude to offer affordable rental rates with adequate living space.

Such facilities would be intended as senior-friendly, but not senior exclusive. Housing Authority residences could meet the needs of young professionals, such as educators, health care specialists, or law enforcement officials, who are new to the community. Or, if seniors had adequate housing options to which they may transition, they may be able to sell their homes to the new-to-the-community families or households.

Creating Public Housing Authorities

Rural communities interested in establishing Public Housing Authorities to construct public housing typically follow a series of steps. First, the town's government officials must consult with state laws to determine if state statutes allow rural communities to form a Public Housing Authority. For example, the North Dakota Century Code was amended in 2005 authorizing all communities, regardless of population size, to form Public Housing Authorities and construct low- to moderate-income housing units (Tweeten et al., 2007).

Second, the town government must certify that a housing shortage exists. Public hearings may be needed to ensure that building low- to moderate-income hous-

Public housing four-plex developed by Housing Authority, Finlay, ND, 2007. Photograph by Gary Goreham.

ing is a project to which the private construction sector is unable to respond.

Third, a Public Housing Authority is formed. Housing Authority members are appointed by the town's mayor. In most cases these individuals are volunteers, not paid contractors or construction experts. They serve on the Housing Authority as a service to their community.

Fourth, funding for the project is sought. Essential Function Bonds are one financial mechanism utilized for Public Housing Authority building projects (Apgar and Whiting, 2003). This form of financing requires state-level enablement legislation for the Public Housing Authority to acquire financing for housing projects. Finally, a building contractor is contracted, and construction of the housing project begins.

The goal of Public Housing Authorities has been to fill the housing gap in a growing number of rural communities. The anticipated result is that these housing projects, once expenses have been paid, will be sold to the private sector and the property placed back on the tax rolls. The creation of Public Housing Authori-

ties has given many rural communities a powerful tool to secure their future.

— *Jodi Burkhardt Bruns and Gary A. Goreham*

See also
Development, Community and Economic; Economic Development; Elders; Government; Housing; Migration; Policy, Social; Public Services

References
Apgar, W. and E.J. Whiting. "Essential Function Bonds: An Emerging Tool for Affordable Housing Finance." White Paper W03-2. Prepared for the National Association of Local Housing Finance Agencies, 2003. Available online at: http://www.innovations.harvard.edu/showdoc.html?id=5055.

Folts, W. Edward, Kenneth B. Muir, and Bradley Nash, Jr. "Housing and the Older Rural Population." *Journal of Housing for the Elderly* 19, no. 1 (2005): 41-52.

Northeast Washington Housing Solutions. "Definitions and Powers of a Housing Authority." Spokane, WA: Spokane Housing Authority, December 2005. Available online at: http://www.spokanehousing.org/about/powers.htm.

Tweeten, Kathleen M., Jodi Burkhardt Bruns, Gary A. Goreham, and F. Larry Leistritz. "Rural Community

Housing Authority Public Housing Projects."
(EC-1345). Fargo, ND: North Dakota State University
Extension Service, September 2007.

Public Libraries

Locally funded institutions that serve as the community's information center, by acquiring, organizing, and disseminating information to meet customers' demands. This article considers the nature of rural and small public libraries in the U.S. in light of the present existing opportunities to provide for adult lifelong learning. Not reviewed is the active role played by the library in providing services to children or bookmobile and books-by-mail services which are also currently very popular strategies to serve rural constituents.

Rural Libraries

To discuss public librarianship in the U.S. is to realize the fact that 80 percent (7,118) of these institutions are located in population centers serving up to 25,000 people. Of this 80 percent, or 2,656 libraries, may be found providing services in places up to 2,500 individuals. The majority of rural libraries are staffed by one full-time person, have a collection of fewer than 10,000 books and serial volumes, and operate within a total budget of $21,000 (Chute 1994). This situation prompted at least one author to write about the "genteel poverty" of the library. For emphasis, total budget addressed previously, means exactly that—the funds available for everything from paying the utilities to staff salaries. This is unlike a situation in a school library where salary costs come from a line item in the school's budget for personnel, and the librarian's allocation is primarily for materials. Parenthetically, some rural libraries in the U.S. have no line item in their budgets for book purchases. In these instances, a variety of different means are used to raise funds, including donations for memorials for those who are deceased, or living memorials in recognition of someone in the town. Rural libraries have used the latter approach to obtain children's books donated by children themselves.

In comparison to the basic model of rural (population less than 2,500), in service populations up to 25,000, the typical public library has from two-to-four full-time staff persons available, the book and serial volume collection numbers 24,000, and the total operating budget is $117,000. While an improvement over the conditions facing smaller libraries, one will recognize that these are not luxurious factors of support (Chute 1994).

Information Needs

As our country adjusted to the nature of its institutions to accommodate the waves of immigrants in the 19th and 20th centuries, the same challenges exist for the rural towns and townships which today are faced with new accelerated demands for a wide variety of social and cultural services. Further, because the new rural residents brought with them expectations nurtured by urban living, unavoidable conflicts arise because of urban-acquired value systems that cannot presently be supported by existing rural infrastructures. There is deep concern, for instance, that may not be sufficient to meet these new needs and a complete reworking may be necessary. While the dichotomy of rural and urban is closing, politically and culturally, nonmetropolitan America continues to lag behind in relation to its economic base, health support, social services, and educational institutions.

Rural America faces many additional problems that are inextricably related to satisfying information needs. Included are local governmental officials, rural planners, and decision makers. Also included are those who transform the rural economy from its agrarian and extractive beginnings to its current dependence on manufacturing and service industries. Information needs must be satisfied for both the private and public sector as they develop new job training alliances, individuals and agencies responsible for the future of the rural family, and those who develop and execute telecommunications policy. Those involved in developing efficient ways to disseminate agriculture-related information need information, as do those who develop agribusiness near the place of farm production and those who live in rural America and wish to maintain a better life by access to timely information.

Planning Considerations

As decision makers contemplate avenues for lifelong learning at the community level, the following comments about rural library services must be considered. First, surveys among library managers about their most pressing issues would show finances as a leading concern. Throughout the country, some communities can provide a working budget for services and activities, and others cannot. Per capita expenditures range from a high of over $30 to a low of $7 (Chute 1994).

Taxpayers often oppose raising assessments to pay for services, and prefer institutional activities to remain at present levels. Community leaders have been flexible in attempting to raise sufficient funds to support the local library. Fund raisers previously used to enhance endowments or provide for special programming are now used to raise working capital to enable daily library functioning. As a result, a wide-range of fund raising activities are used, ranging from selling stationery and used books to wine and cheese parties, dances, and direct solicitations to local community groups such as the Rotary and Women's Club. At issue is the question of who is responsible to adequately fund America's rural and small libraries. The answer has many parts. Because of its varied services the public library is one of the best economic values, which has not been emphasized enough.

Second, rural and small towns are traditionally conservative institutions. The statement, "we never did it that way before" is an important attitude to recognize. Unfortunately, this attitude may also be shared by the library personnel and trustees/board members who see no reason to change the library's routines. The typical librarian lived in his or her community an average of 17 years, and has been the librarian for 10 years (Vavrek 1989).

Third, the most important factor limiting the present and future development of rural information services is the lack of academically trained staff. Only about 34 percent, or 3,452, of the full-time librarians in libraries in communities of less than 25,000 people have an American Library Association's (ALA) master's degree; in communities of less than 2,500 people, the incidence is five percent (86) (Chute 1994).

Reasons for this educational situation include attitudes such as: "we've never had a trained librarian; why do we need one now? "or "What's the matter with a salary of $13,000?" Additional reasons include: the relatively few schools of library and information science serving a geographically dispersed population; the inability of individuals to leave their positions to participate in classroom coursework; and the attitude of some staff persons who do not recognize their need to pursue formalized education. Some of these problems are being mitigated by enterprising institutions that aggressively offer long-distance educational opportunities to students in person or by satellite or cable.

The problems of providing training and education is not only limited to the formal, credit generating, degree awarding programs, but also to continuing educa-

tion. In addition to the schools of library and information science, library cooperatives, systems, regional libraries, and state library agencies are providing consumers with their wants and needs. Unfortunately, there are too many library staff and trustees in need of continuing education, particularly technology, than providers. Frequently, there is little offered systematically. Training is immensely significant small towns become virtual communities in cyberspace (Rheingold 1993).

Fourth, not only is trustee development key to future planning, it is a topic waiting for action. States such as Nebraska have gone further than most to establish certification requirements for trustees to remain active. But, anecdotal information from trustees and librarians around the country suggest that "me versus them" mentality may prevail. If libraries in rural communities are to prosper, it cannot be at the expense of rolling over trustees, who hire and fire the librarian and are responsible for the library's financial solvency. Development needed to insure that the library plans for the future, uses its resources wisely in consort with other agencies, and becomes a true community information center, begins with mutual trust between library staff and trustees/directors.

Fifth, planners must be aware that typical rural public libraries probably have not conducted user surveys. Vavrek (1989) reported that only 22 percent, or 81, of libraries conducted a community analysis over the last five years, and 23 percent, or 86, of them had multi-year plans. In the absence of data describing the library's use and the attitude of clients toward available services, planning is done in an ad hoc manner. Substituted for survey data, library personnel use interpersonal methods to gather information under the impression that they are familiar with community members who use the library.

Sixth, despite the age of electronic access to information through a variety of networks, rural libraries are perceived primarily as a place of books. Despite the wide variety of resources available in rural libraries, user studies suggest that requests for bestsellers and leisure reading materials outstrip the demand for informational and reference material (Vavrek 1990; Estabrook 1991; Vavrek 1993). Additionally, one must consider the tradition of libraries as repositories of books. Librarians were brought up in this cultural environment. Although things are changing, the typical rural library has little money to invest in alternative technological. Little time is spent marketing or advertising the diverse services available. As a result, while about 70 percent of library users heard or saw advertisements about the library over the last year, over 40 percent of the general public had not (Vavrek 1990; Vavrek 1993).

Seventh, 70 percent of rural public library users are women (Knight and Nourse 1969; Doremus, Porter, and Novelli 1987). Analysts have spent little time considering why the tendency of use has been this way and what it means. It is the author's impression, that women read more than men, and that despite an increasing number of women working outside of the household and a growing number of men staying at home, the female member has the continuing responsibility to educate children, which includes trips to the library with the children for activities like storyhours. When the Center for the Study of Rural Librarianship (CSRL) at the Clarion University of Pennsylvania reported that 70 to 80 percent of rural library users were women, some attributed this to women obtaining library items for members of the household. But, in only 28 percent of the cases were women in the library for reasons other than their own (Vavrek 1990).

It is likely to assume that women will support their local public libraries. Whether this situation continues in the future is a matter of concern to library planners. With more women working outside of the home, their level of library use may diminish because of a lack of time. It is crucial that services be targeted to men as well.

Eight, technology ranges on a continuum; to some it means that the library has a phone or conventional typewriter. Most librarians wish to use technology, but providing sufficient funds to accomplish this is a concern. The situation is improving. Because of the influence of cooperative library ventures, many libraries are included in online catalog access, statewide data bases, and Internet connections. About 30 percent of small libraries are connected to the Internet. Inhibiting growth of the newest technology is a matter of education and training. Typically, the infrastructure to support the daily use of new technology does not exist. To illustrate, a recent CSRL study of 317 libraries in populations of less than 25,000 found that each library had at least one personal computer, fax machine, and CD-ROM workstation. The computer was used for a variety of tasks, but word processing was the most popular. Most libraries reported that they spend less than $500 annually to purchase technology-related items such as software, CD-ROM applications, and hardware.

The ninth topic relates to library and information services for Native Americans. The Strategic Plan for the Development of Library and Information Services to Native Americans indicates that the lack of coordination among diverse Federal agencies, and the lack of overall coordinating leadership impeded development of Native American library programs. Most states do not include tribal libraries in their statewide library network plans (U.S. National Commission on Libraries and Information Science [USNCLIS] 1992). This situation is unfortunate because reservation libraries are one of the best examples of multi-function facilities. For example, the community college libraries at the Standing Rock Sioux Reservation and the Devil's Lake Sioux Reservation in North Dakota function both as public and tribal libraries. Similar facilities are in South Dakota and Montana.

The USNCLIS (1992) recommended several challenges. First, develop consistent funding sources to support improved Native American library and information services. Second, strengthen library and information services training and technical assistance to Native American communities. Third, develop programs to increase tribal library material holdings and to develop relevant collections in all formats. Fourth, improve access and strengthen cooperative activities. Fifth, develop state and local partnerships. Sixth, establish Federal policy and responsibilities. Seventh, identify model programs for Native American libraries and information services. Eight, develop museum and archival services to preserve Native American cultures. Ninth, encourage adult and family literacy programs, basic job skills training, and strengthen tribal community colleges. And tenth, encourage application of newer information network technologies.

Rural Public Library and Adult Services

Rural public libraries provided three types of products and services: educational, recreational, and informational. Although the public library always recognized the adult client as a major benefactor of activities, services for children received the highest priority. The library came to be perceived as a place for children and women. Summer story hours for kids and programs for children usually generate enthusiastic lines of young users.

Whereas services for children are burgeoning, programs for adults frequently generate few takers. As a consequence, librarians schedule few adult programs. When library staff examine marketing techniques to identify constituencies and their needs, they frequently lack the skills to conduct marketing programs. They develop sporadic efforts at public relations, and many staff members never organize any programs. Programming costs vary, and rural librarians have become adept at budget programming. However, objectives cannot be accomplished with no money for programming.

Despite limitations, adult education is blooming. Public librarians recognize the need to expand adult programming and services. Activities range from great book discussions to computer classes, business programs, health services, higher education programs, co-incidental activities with Black History Month, literacy services, travel-related events for retired persons/seniors, and genealogy. There are lifelong learning services offered in public libraries for support staff through teleconferencing.

There are incidences of adult services offered in conjunction with other community agencies (e.g., literacy agencies, Small Business Development Centers, Cooperative Extension Services), however few libraries have local action plans for these services. One example of cooperation was stimulated by the Arizona State Library that helped to develop Economic Development Information Centers (EDICs) in public libraries. These, in turn, initiated cooperative projects with other groups.

The present and future role of the rural public library as a source for lifelong learning, ongoing development, and application of technology must be assessed. The Internet is developing at such a pace that many people want access to it, including residents of the most rural communities. Wilkinson (1992) believes that technology has both the potential to rescue geographically remote areas from economic and social problems and to break their backs. Rural towns may cease being communities with the capacity for development and growth and instead, become nodes on a network.

As the countryside merges with urban America, models of rural and small libraries will continue to change. Maintaining and supporting community libraries is not an act of romanticism or kindness. It is a means to support the American dream.

— *Bernard Vavrek*

See also

Education, Adult; Educational Facilities; Literacy; Literature; Technology; Telecommunications

References

Canepi, K. 1997. "Information Access through Electronic Databases for Rural Public Libraries." *Rural Libraries* 17, no. 1 (1997): 7-33.

Chute, Adrienne. *Public Libraries in the United States: 1992.* Washington, DC: Government Printing Office, 1994.

Doremus Porter Novelli. *Life Style Profile of the Library User.* Chicago, IL: American Library Association, 1987.

Estabrook, Leigh. *National Opinion Poll on Library Issues.* Champaign-Urbana, IL: Graduate School of Library and Information Science, Library Research Center, University of Illinois, 1991.

Heuertz Linda, Andrew C. Gordon, Margaret T. Gordon, and Elizabeth J. Moore. "The Impact of Public Access Computing on Rural and Small Town Libraries." *Rural Libraries* 23, no. 1 (2003).

Knight, D.M. and Nourse, S., eds. *Libraries at Large: Tradition, Innovation, and the National Interest.* New York: R.R. Bowker Company, 1969.

MacDonald B. "The Public Image of Libraries and Librarians as a Potential Barrier to Rural Access." *Rural Libraries* 15, no. 1 (1995): 35-57.

Rheingold, Howard. *The Virtual Community: Homesteading on the Electronic Frontier.* Reading. MA: Addison Wesley, 1993.

U.S. National Commission on Libraries and Information Science. *Pathways to Excellence: A Report on Improving Library and Information Services for Native American Peoples.* Washington, DC: Government Printing Office, 1992.

Vavrek, Bernard. "The Rural Library: Some Recent Research." *Rural Libraries* 9 (1989): 85-95.

Vavrek, Bernard. *Assessing the Information Needs of Rural Americans.* Clarion, PA: College of Library Science, Center for the Study of Rural Librarianship, Clarion University of Pennsylvania, 1990.

Vavrek, Bernard. *Assessing the Role of the Rural Public Library.* Clarion, PA: Department of Library Science, Center for the Study of Rural Librarianship, Clarion University of Pennsylvania, 1993.

Vavrek, Bernard. 1995. Rural Information Needs and the Role of the Public Library. *Library Trends* 44, no. 1 (1995): 21-48.

Wilkinson, Kenneth. P. *Social Forces Shaping the Future of Rural America.* Clarion, PA: Information Futures Institute. Unpublished manuscript, 1992.

Public Services

Public goods that modern societies have evolved to improve quality of life, which are provided or controlled by local, state or national governments, and which are paid for by taxes, such as schools, roads, and police protection or provided on a fee-for-service basis, such as electricity, telephone, water, and health services.

Discussed below is the role of government in providing services, the emergence of new governments created to provide new services, and methods service providers are using to provide services to dispersed rural populations at an affordable cost. Over time the number of services has grown in response to new technologies and complexities of modern living. Providing and paying for the growing number of services has become a major challenge for rural governments.

Rural Demand for Services

Rural dwellers face the same issues faced by most people anywhere—housing, education, health care, transportation—problems that are sometimes complicated and sometimes simplified by the relatively low population density of rural areas. The challenges became greater, however, as many rural areas lost population whereas the demand for services grew at a pace at least equivalent to the growth in American real income and standard of living over the past several decades.

Americans expect a wide range of services. Along with income, American quality of life increasingly came to be defined in terms of the quality and quantity of public and private services available to meet the needs and desires of citizens. Citizens with access to quality services at a reasonable cost generally are considered to have a better quality of life than citizens who do not. Although rural residents today generally have access to the same range of services as urban residents, they may, because of lower population density, have to travel further, pay more, or receive services of somewhat lower quality and sophistication.

Rural public services range across a wide spectrum from electricity, safe drinking water, telephones, and other services that reach the home to the roads people take and the bridges they cross to reach the schools, hospitals, and other human services that have become necessities of life. A part of the value of services is that they have traditionally been provided close enough to home to enable rural consumers to have reasonable access at an affordable cost. Consequently the number of rural service providers is numerous and they are dispersed in accord with the population. It would not be unusual in a typical rural county to find as many as 50 different agencies and organizations responsible for providing public services.

Rural public services exhibit characteristics of a public good. Public goods are characterized by joint consumption and exclusivity. Joint consumption implies that consumption of the good by one person does not preclude its consumption by others. Many community services such as schools, parks, sewer systems, and roads fit that description, whereas others such as electricity, water services, telephone, and health care are provided on a fee-for-service basis. Exclusivity means that most services are provided by a sole local supplier.

Role of Government

The public generally relies on the political process to determine the type and extent of services offered. Local governments (e.g., counties, municipalities, townships, school districts, special districts) serve as the political mechanism to make decisions about which type and quantity of services are provided. They also either serve as the direct provider of many of those services or contract with other organizations to provide them. Providing the services that each locality has grown to need and want, or that have been mandated by state or federal government, is a major reason for the existence of more than 83,000 local governments in the U.S., 65 percent of which are located in rural (nonmetropolitan) areas. Because rural America includes 81 percent of the nation's land area but only 20 percent of the population, a much larger number of governments is required to serve the population. The population per government is only one-fifth as great in rural than in urban areas.

Because rural local governments and other service providers serve fewer people scattered over a larger space, it typically is more costly per person to provide services. The smaller size, depending on the service, can affect the quality of services provided. Because of the smaller rural economic and population base, paying for services places an added strain on rural local governments and consumers alike.

Adaptations to Provide Rural Services at an Affordable Local Cost

Until about 1920 most rural services were provided by general local governments. That was largely because few services were provided. Until then federal and state governments played a minimal role in rural service delivery. Since then technology changed and made new services available; concurrently providing services to rural populations has come to be thought of as serving the national interest. As more services were offered and new technologies made more services possible, the number of providers of rural services grew and various policies for sharing costs were adopted. In addition rural populations adopted new strategies to provide services. Following are some of the adaptations that were made to provide accessible and affordable services.

Consolidations

Generally the costs of providing public services are sensitive to economies of scale—the larger the number of consumers served, the lower the cost per consumer of providing the service. A U-shaped cost curve has been found for many public services such as police and fire protection and public education. It is more expensive per person to provide the service to both extremely small and extremely large populations. Since the size of the population influences costs and the ability to provide a service, rural government officials and other decision makers employed various strategies to take advantage of economies of scale. Significant among those has been consolidation—joining two or more service providers into a single organization to lower costs and expand services. The most widespread use of that strategy has been consolidation of public school districts. In 1930 there were 128,000 school districts in the U.S. with a high percentage located in rural areas. Many of the rural districts offered only elementary education in one room schools. By 1990 all but 14,000 of the school districts had been consolidated out of existence. Of the remaining districts just over 7,000 are located in rural areas. The larger consolidated schools also offer a much greater array of educational services because of their greater size and the corresponding economic efficiencies. However, size alone does not affect the quality of service. Recent research showed that many small rural schools offer high quality education, in part, because their small size provides a supportive social environment including involvement of parents and community (Hobbs 1995).

A concomitant change in public policy greatly affected rural education. Until about 1920 virtually all the cost of public education was borne by the local school districts. Since an educated population is considered in the state and national interest, state governments began to share educational costs with local school districts. Today an average of more than 50 percent of the cost of public education is borne by state governments (more in some states, less in others). Local school districts and the national government bear about 45 percent and 5 percent, respectively.

Although health care services generally are offered by private providers, there has been great consolidation of rural health care services into larger regional towns and small cities, leaving most small rural communities without a physician. Population per physician is 2.5 times greater in rural areas than urban. Consolidation forced most rural residents to travel greater distances for health care services, adding to the cost they pay for the service. Despite this handicap, recent research finds little or no difference between rural and urban residents in number of physician visits per year (Hart, et al. 1994).

Despite extensive consolidation of education and health care services there has been little consolidation of local governments. Virtually all the town and county governments of decades past remain in existence. Some towns and counties, in an effort to lower costs and improve services, share the provision of some services with other units of local government.

A Federal Role in Providing Services

Rural Americans today enjoy most of the same kinds of services available to urban people, but many changes were required to achieve that. As new technologies emerged, new and popular services became available such as electric power, sewer and water systems, telephones, and motor vehicle travel. Urban consumers were usually the first to enjoy these benefits, largely because of the economic efficiency in providing services to more densely populated areas. Consequently rural areas usually lagged behind. Extending those services to rural areas often necessitated the creation of new methods and forms of organization. For example, early electrical services generally were provided to larger towns and cities by private, profit-making companies or municipalities. Rural electrification was initiated through the federal government with the establishment of the Rural Electrification Administration (REA) in the 1930s because it was much more expensive, if not unprofitable, to extend electric power lines to individual farms. The REA facilitated the formation of consumer-owned (rather than investor-owned) local Rural Electric Cooperatives to provide service to rural areas through the provision of low interest loans. There are nearly 1,000 local rural electric cooperatives in existence today that provide about 10 percent of the electrical power consumed in the U.S.

The federal government began to establish agency offices in rural areas to provide direct services to farmers including farm loans, soil conservation, commodity programs, and research and information services during this era. These agencies have since expanded to provide loans for rural housing, community facilities, and rural development.

Special Districts

One reason for the large number of governments in rural areas is that many are recently created, special-purpose governments organized by groups of citizens to provide a single service. This strategy has been used widely by rural populations seeking to provide services not offered through other local governments. Among the most numerous types of rural special districts are those organized to provide fire protection, road extensions, parks, public water and sewer, and ambulance and emergency medical services. State regulations govern the establishment of such districts. Thus, there is organizational variation among the states. Some special districts affiliate with other local governments, have independent taxing authority, and have the power to elect their own governing officials. The service is usually provided by a fee-for-service when not supported by a taxing authority. There are nearly 30,000 special districts in the U.S. with more than half located in rural areas.

Human Services Expansion and Delivery Methods

The federal and state role in human service delivery at the local level increased significantly in the 1960s. Dozens of programs providing funds to establish services, such as manpower training, Head Start centers, and environmental, mental health, nutrition, transportation and other services for the elderly, Small Business Development Centers, and family services, have been enacted. The development of new local organizations provided the service. Many of the new organizations were operated as non-profit agencies. The funds to support these services were allocated either by state or federal government or a combination of the two. Local governments frequently played a role in awarding contracts to provide those services. The effect has been to greatly expand the number of services and service-providing organizations in rural localities.

New Technologies and New Possibilities for Delivering Services

Just as vehicle travel opened the practical possibility of consolidating of rural services, new developments in telecommunication technologies made it possible to reconsider how some services will be delivered in the future. Many rural services depend on the exchange of information such as health care and education. In the past, that exchange occurred by having the consumer travel to more distant schools or health care services. An increasing number of rural schools now offer a part of their curriculum through various forms of distance learning. A widely used practice involves the use of interactive television to provide specialized education services to clusters of small rural schools. Similar developments occur in telemedicine. It is cheaper and faster to transport information than to transport people. This causes rural officials and leaders to develop new approaches to service delivery.

The requirement for an information infrastructure limits the use of telecommunication technologies. Many rural areas lack the telephone and other information technologies needed for new methods of service delivery. The current situation for rural areas is somewhat similar to the situation that existed with electricity 70 years ago.

Complexity of Organization Delivering Rural Services

The complex structure of overlapping local, state, and federal agencies and public utilities provided rural people with an equality of services. Most service providers have funding sources and are associated with different lines of authority. Each service has its own constraints and limitations. A wide range of services may be grouped under the same broad heading. However, they have different management and delivery problems because they are specialized and require different technical delivery capabilities.

Although the many services have produced great benefits for rural localities, the array of organizations that provide them has produced new challenges for rural leaders and decision makers. It is difficult for rural consumers to avail themselves of the combinations of services they need because services are so dispersed among so many different organizations and agencies. The task of directing, managing, and providing public input for the service providers places a strain on limited rural leadership. It is not unusual to find rural leaders serving on many, different service provider boards and commissions. One future challenges facing rural service delivery will be to provide better integration of services so that they may more effectively serve the cause of retaining and strengthening rural communities.

— *Daryl Hobbs*

See also

Education, Youth; Electrification; Government; Infrastructure; Municipal Solid Waste Management; Policing; Quality of Life; Taxes; Telecommunications

References

Brown, David L. "Is the Rural-Urban Distinction Still Useful for Understanding Structure and Change in Developed Societies?" Pp. 1-7 in *Population Change and the Future of Rural America: Conference Proceedings.* Edited by D. Brown and L. Johnson. Washington, DC: U.S. Department of Agriculture, 1993.

Brown, David L. and Nina L. Glasgow. "A Sign of Generational Conflict: the Impact of Florida's Aging Voters on Local School and Tax Referenda." *Social Science Quarterly* 73 (1991): 786-797.

Dillman, D.A., D.M. Beck, and J.C. Allen. "Rural Barriers to Job Creation Remain, Even in Today's Information Age." *Rural Development Perspectives* 5, no. 2 (February 1989): 21-27.

Dooley, F.J., D.A. Bangsund, and F.L. Leistritz. "Regional Landfills Offer Cost Savings for Rural Communities." *Rural Development Perspectives* 9, no. 3 (June 1994): 9-15.

Fox, William F. *Relationships between Size of School Districts and the Cost of Education,* TB-1621 (April). Washington, DC: U.S. Department of Agriculture, Economics, Statistics, and Cooperatives Service, 1980.

Hart, L. Gary, Michael J. Pirani, and Roger A. Rosenblatt. "Most Rural Towns Lost Physicians After Their Hospitals Closed." *Rural Development Perspectives* 19, no. 1 (October 1994): 17-21.

Hobbs, Daryl. "Social Organization in the Countryside." Pp. 369-396 *The Changing American Countryside: Rural People and Places.* Edited by Emery Castle. Lawrence, KS: University Press of Kansas, 1995.

Jansen, Anicca. "Rural Counties Lead Urban in Education Spending, but Is That Enough?" *Rural Development Perspectives* 7, no. 1 (October-January 1991): 8-14.

Oarkerson, Ronald J. "Structures and Patterns of Rural Governance." Pp. 397-418 in *The Changing American Countryside: Rural People and Places.* Edited by Emery Castle. Lawrence, KS: University Press of Kansas, 1995.

Reeder, R. J. and A.C. Jansen. "Government Poverty Declines, But Spending Disparity Increases." *Rural Development Perspectives* 9, no. 2 (February 1994): 47-50.

South, S.J. "Age Structure and Public Expenditures on Children." *Social Science Quarterly* 72 (1991): 661-675.

Zimmerman, Joseph F. "The State Mandate Problem." *State and Local Government Review* 19 (1987): 78-84.

Quality of Life

The degree to which human multifaceted potentials are reached on the individual, community and societal levels. Individual- and societal-level measures of quality of life are discussed in this article, as are objective versus subjective measures of the concept.

Origins of Quality of Life Research

Much of the quality of life research on the individual level came from the medical and health community. Decisions about health care are often made based on the anticipated impact on the patient's future quality of life. The Centers for Disease Control and Prevention (CDC) tracks health-related quality of life (see http://www.cdc.gov/hrqol). A series of survey questions is used to look at healthy days, including 1) Would you say that in general your health is: Excellent, Very good, Good, Fair or Poor? 2) Now thinking about your physical health, which includes physical illness and injury, for how many days during the past 30 days was your physical health not good? 3) Now thinking about your mental health, which includes stress, depression, and problems with emotions, for how many days during the past 30 days was your mental health not good? 4) During the past 30 days, for about how many days did poor physical or mental health keep you from doing your usual activities, such as self-care, work, or recreation?

They have a five-question protocol on activity limitations and five questions on healthy day symptoms. The availability of this data in the U.S. and other countries over time has led to led to the journal, *Quality of Life Research*, and two professional organizations, the International Society for Quality of Life Research and the International Journal for Quality of Life Studies.

For non-scholarly audiences, quality of life has been popularized into "happiness," with analyses by a variety of variables (Pew Research Center). Some of these studies confounded quality of life (intangible) with standard of living (material/tangible), asking people if they were better or worse off than in a previous time period.

Quality of life among the elderly and ill was studied intensively because these groups were the target populations of many large-scale government programs. This may explain the focus on the physical ability to do for one's self in many of the quality of life studies (Schuessler and Fisher, 1985).

Morreim (1992) points out two types of quality of life research. He calls the first "consensus quality of life," which is composed of shared societal values about what comprises the good life and what life conditions are to be pursued or avoided. Such measures yield terms like "quality adjusted life years" or "well years," which are used in economic analysis to rate the cost effectiveness of proposed public policies. These measures are gathered from what healthy individuals view as important aspects of quality of life, and are used to forecast what might decrease it.

Another set of measures, "personal quality of life," focuses on individuals' judgments about their own life quality, particularly the effects of disease and therapy on ill persons. Thus, quality of life publications tend to focus on an individual's ability to tie one's shoe, bathe oneself, fix one's own meals, and feed oneself, which relate physical condition to personal self-sufficiency in a very basic sense. The self-sufficiency notion of providing for oneself is a basic aspect of quality of life measures implied in alternative agriculture and community development.

Personal quality of life is difficult to operationalize since such measures are very difficult to validate. Yet quality of life research is important despite methodological difficulties; it is the ultimate aim of much scientific advancement. In medicine, for example, the health care agenda is not simply to keep people alive, but to keep them alive with a good quality of life. Medicine's central goal has been quality of life: easing pain, ameliorating handicaps, and providing reassurance and support. Many clinical trials measure changes in health quality of life.

It could be argued that the goal of economics is not simply to increase income, but to increase the means by which people increase their quality of life. Quality of life research is essential but difficult, since the material end of technology is but a means to a human end. Measures that come from the affected populations themselves are probably the most important and most accurate, as suggested by John Eyles (1990) who links quality of life to environmental quality.

Societal Level Measures of Quality of Life

A range of aggregate measures of quality of life using secondary data sources with such things as infant mortality and per-capita income divided by infant mortality was developed in the 1970s. A variety of secondary data sources were used to construct measures of quality of life for nations or states. Quality of life was examined in various dimensions, primarily based on spatial distribution, including physical and material well-being, social relations, social activities, personal development and recreation. Research by geographers suggests that environmental quality and quality of life may be two sides of the same coin.

The Economic Intelligence Unit (see http://www.eiu.com) in 2005 developed a quality of life index for nations based on national surveys and differential weights. The highest weight went to political freedom and security, followed by health, family relations, job security, material well-being, gender equality, and social and community activities.

Subjective versus Objective Quality of Life

Not all researchers are comfortable with self-reported quality of life. Moum (1988), for example, believes that both systematic and random errors (e.g., daily moods) may suppress, mask or wash out statistical associations between objective, sociologically relevant indicators of well-being and self-reported quality of life. His data include Norwegian quality of life health measures, which he found are overestimated among older respondents, underestimated among well-educated respondents, and unstable among young female respondents. Some of his quality of life measures (e.g., satisfaction with oneself, lack of faith in oneself, a life worth living, a meaningless life, very good spirits, feeling depressed, and depression fact score) were in terms of how respondents felt during the last two weeks. They were also asked questions about their use of sedatives and sleeping pills, trouble with sleep, and nervousness or fidgetiness in the last two weeks. In contrast, research with sustainable farmers in the Midwest uses a much richer, complex set of dimensions to measure quality of life that included spirituality, communication, work, nature, love and health.

Most research since 1975 about the content of quality of life examines differences between objective and subjective indicators of quality of life. Objective quality of life indicators reflect observable environmental conditions such as per-capita income and average daily temperature. These qualities are presumed to be causes of quality of life. Subjective quality of life indicators consist of responses to survey items measuring feelings of satisfaction (e.g., general feeling about life as a whole), happiness, and domain-specific feelings (e.g., feelings about one's job). There is a certain tautology in some economic models of quality of life. It is assumed that higher per-capita income automatically increases quality of life without looking at a wide variety of other factors. Various dimensions of quality of life may not necessarily be correlated with each other.

Schuessler and Fisher (1985) point out that the measurement problems related to quality of life exist because quality of life is a latent trait, not subject to direct observation. There is no clear consensus on which indicators to use. Many studies suggest that interpersonal relations are an important aspect, if not the most important aspect, of quality of life. For example, Wilkening and McGranahan (1978) found that change in interpersonal relations contribute more heavily to satisfaction with quality of life than does either socioeconomic status or social participation.

Schuessler and Fisher (1985) discuss various criticisms of quality of life measurement, but find that each can be adequately addressed. Quality of life measures must be examined at different levels of aggregation. Quality of life measures can have policy implications. This highlights the need to develop consistent, locally meaningful measures of the various dimensions of quality of life on the individual level as they relate to rural issues such as community development and adoption of alternative agricultural practices. Although secondary data and surveys have been the main tools, focus groups are increasingly employed to gather quality of life indicators for special populations (Leung, 2004).

Rural-Urban Differences in Quality of Life

There are many stereotypes that state the quality of life in rural areas is superior to that of urban areas. However, very few subjective measurements support that stereotype. Using objective measurements, whether rural quality of life is better than urban depends on the specific measurement and area being studied. For example, air quality, which is assumed to be associated with quality of life, is generally, but not always, better in rural areas. Poverty rates in rural areas are similar to those in central cities, although rural areas have a slight edge when the rural South is removed from the calculation. The terms "slower pace" and "less stress" are often, although not always accurately, related to rural areas. Some research has examined the difference among rural places and quality of life, finding that the presence of amenities in terms of natural capital was associated with higher perceived quality of life (Deller et al., 2000).

Another set of stereotypes holds that urban quality of life is higher because of the ability to purchase a wider variety of goods and services. Rural development for many people has been oriented toward making rural areas more like urban areas by recruiting industry. The wide variation among rural areas makes it difficult to generalize about rural-urban differences in quality of life. Greater differences are found in both objective and subjective quality of life measures between rural places and rural people than between rural and urban places and people.

— *Cornelia Butler Flora*

See also
Elders; Rural Health Care; Income; Mental Health; Mental Health of Older Adults; Policy, Rural Family

References

Cobb, C. W. 2000. *Measurement Tools and the Quality of Life.* San Francisco, CA: Redefining Progress. Available online at: http://www.progress.org.

Deller, S.C., T. Tsai, D.W. Marcouiller and D.B.K. English. "The Role of Amenities and Quality of Life in Rural Economic Growth." *American Journal of Agricultural Economics* 83 (2001): 352-365.

Economic Intelligence Unit. "The Economist Intelligence Unit's Quality-of-Life Index," 2005. Available online at: http://www.eiu.com.

Eyles, J. "Objectifying the Subjective: The Measurement of Environmental Quality." *Social Indicators Research* 22 (1990): 139-153.

Leung, K.E. Wu, B. Lue and L. Tang. "The Use of Focus Groups in Evaluating Quality of Life Components among Elderly Chinese People." *Quality of Life Research* 13 (2004): 179-190.

Morreim, E.H. "The Impossibility and the Necessity of Quality of Life Research." *Bioethics* 6, no. 3 (1992): 218-232.

Moum, T.. "Yea Saying and Mood of the Day Effects in Self-reported Quality of Life." *Social Indicators Research* (1988): 117-139.

Pew Research Center. "Are We Happy Yet?" February 13, 2006. Available online at: http://pewresearch.org/pubs/301/are-we-happy-yet.

Schuessler, K.F. and G.A. Fisher. "Quality of Life Research in Sociology." *Annual Review of Sociology* 11 (1985): 129-149.

Wilkening, E.A. and D. McGranahan. "Correlates of Subjective Well Being in Northern Wisconsin." *Social Indicators Research* 5 (1978): 211-234.

Ranching

A social structure that evolved with unique economic and environmental conditions for large-scale herding following its inception during the mercantilist period (Galaty and Johnson, 1990).

Ranching was initiated as and remains a system of large animal production for economic exchange. The term derives from *rancho*, Spanish for small farm. The earliest ranches in North America were initiated in the Southwest out of colonial Spanish land grants of more than one million acres. Small agricultural operations, villages and towns were scattered throughout the land grants. Properties belonged to their users and were administered by the land grantee. Almost synonymous with cattle raising in the West, sheep and horse ranches are operated independently or as integral components in some outfits. The application of principles of private property govern American ranches. Some, like the fabled King Ranch, are multigenerational dynasties of huge disparate properties (Slatta, 1989).

Ranching occupies a specialized economic and environmental niche. It can be interpreted from a variety of sociological perspectives. While facing environmental threats and social criticisms, its mythos survives among the small number of remaining ranchers and symbols of their way of life. Ranching can best be interpreted from a variety of sociological perspectives: functional, human ecological, interactional, and as a way of life.

Structures and Functions of Ranching

Understanding the economic and environmental characteristics of ranching is essential since they provide the parameters for the social systems. It is a major form of land use between the Mississippi and the Pacific, from Canada to Mexico. Early ranching resembled a plantation in its production of a single product—sheep, cattle, horses—with the intention of profit based on export. It relied, as it still does, on cheap local labor.

It also requires massive shipping, initially along trails, like the Chisolm, the Santa Fe, and the Bozeman (Wellman, 1939). Operations were largely self-sufficient since little assistance for immediate difficulties was available. Raising herds of large animals requires large acreages. Forty acres per animal unit (cow/calf) may be required. As a modern stage of pastoral herding, it relies on naturally growing or at least minimally attended pastures or range.

Ranching can provide relatively low-impact sustainable food production from land unsuitable for other agricultural uses, especially non-irrigated mountain and arid areas (Savory, 1988). It is a viable and efficient use of marginally tillable or untillable land so long as there are no more profitable uses. Hay operations and some seasonal and supplementary feeding are nearly universal. As population increases and technologies become more sophisticated, there is continual pressure to convert ranch land to other uses, particularly agricultural, residential, recreational and mining. Ranching may be regarded as a transitional stage, occupying the primary economic production in areas only until more profitable uses of the land displace it.

The earliest ranching was on open range, made possible by few residents, few alternative uses, and seemingly boundless range. As neighbors increased, property lines became clearer and fencing became increasingly common. Simultaneously, it was discovered that fencing was essential for more efficient production, because it allowed rotation of pastures and seasonal breeding. Open range, such as on grazing associations and reservations, connote stock on the highways rather than totally unrestricted pasture. The disastrous winter of 1888, immortalized by Charlie Russell's *Last of the Five Thousand*, which shows a single emaciated survivor from a large herd, signaled the end of the open range (Russell, 1890). Ranchers, too, have been decimated since the early twentieth century. Census data do not accurately distinguish farmers from ranchers. Many are both, arbitrarily calling themselves one or the other. A crude estimate is that of the roughly four million farmers who earn more than half of their income from agriculture, about 2 percent (80,000) own and operate a ranch.

Ranch work gradually has become less labor intensive than in its formative years (Gray, 1968). Handling large animals from birth through shipping or slaughter remains difficult and dangerous work. Branding, docking, castrating, inoculating, dehorning and other jobs requiring directly handling animals typically are performed with immobilizing chutes and other mechanical assistance. Less traumatizing techniques, such as elastrators replacing knives for castrating and docking, are common. Motorized vehicles are usually used to drive and haul animals between ranches and markets. Horses and stock dogs are essential for broken terrain and rough ground surfaces. Mixed animal operations are common, although the hierarchy is clear in the folk phrase "sheep for profit, cattle for prestige, and horses for pleasure."

Human Ecology of Ranching

Ranching from a human ecological perspective follows directly from attendant environmental and economic conditions. The social structure that evolved on the frontier—first ranches, then towns—existed primarily, if not solely because of the production, sale and transportation of animals with their service institutions and markets. Small towns grew and prospered during the era of settlement while work was labor intensive and expanding. Homesteading, often into areas unsuitable for farming, further stimulated growth. Between 1920 and 2000, most counties in ranch area continually lost population as homesteaders discovered making a living was impossible on their land and as technology gradually replaced labor. A bar, gas station and a few houses are all that remain of once-prosperous towns with schools, churches and main streets. The few remaining towns serve large trade areas. County seats commonly have fewer than 2,500 residents and serve areas the size of small Eastern states. Even so, their markets have largely been replaced by the few metropolitan areas in the region that increasingly are where ranchers purchase machinery, vehicles and household items.

Social Conflict and Ranching

The stratification system can as easily be understood from a conflict perspective as from a structural functional perspective. Social class, prestige and power overlap; they differentiate the haves from the have-nots and their position in the division of labor that persists from generation to generation. At the top of the stratification system are large, long-time owners and operators of ranches and businesses. The middle class comprises full-time employees with moderate wages and salaries and smaller operators. The lowest class is largely unemployed or seasonally employed laborers.

Across this spectrum, property ownership and residential stability are very important. Large, multi-generational ranches are landed elites who exert local political, cultural and economic influence. Some occupations are seasonal, such as sheep shearers or custom cutters. Others, like veterinarians, are local specialists. Their positions in the stratification system are commensurate with their skills, training and earnings. Residents in ranch country frequently are residuals from a winnowing process that led most former residents to migrate. Those who remain often perform a variety of functions. Successful ranchers are trustees of financial institutions and members of influential committees. Professionals and business owners often own agricultural land. Conversely, lower class residents are likely to be excluded from participation in formal organizations or voluntary associations. Rural stratification expands upon itself. Outside ownership of ranches has always been common, both as an investment and as a place for escape. Outside owners, while a topic of conversation, are not part of the local stratification system, despite their obvious influence of the local economy.

Symbolic Interaction and Ranching

The realities described through the human ecological and structural functional perspectives become more subjective when taken from a symbolic interaction orientation. The meaning of ranching, both to ranchers and outsiders, is a composite, partially idealized and partially factual. Ranchers personify Frederick Jackson Turner's "rugged individualist." Survival in remote and challenging environments requires independence, self-sufficiency and the ability to make do. Ironically, that very individualism makes ranching vulnerable, both directly and indirectly, to outside forces. Extra-locally, commodity markets and corporations determine much of the profits and losses on ranches. Locally, their opposition to collective activities such as planning and zoning made them vulnerable to land developments, resource extraction, even religious cults.

The Mythos of Ranching as a Way of Life

A subjective mythos surrounds ranching. "Are you a real cowboy?" Debra Winger asks John Travolta in *Ur-*

ban Cowboy. The question is about the authenticity of a role type that captured imaginations internationally for over a century (Jobes, 1986). As opposed to phony drugstore cowboys, a real cowboy can do the tasks of ranching. Moreover, real cowboys have a mythical common character: soft-spoken, succinct, serious but of good cheer, and competent. They are husbands of the land (husbandry), frequently glorifying their concern with the environment. They are expected to believe in a Great Creator while acknowledging human weakness. Believing in God while occasionally acting like the Devil are not mutually exclusive, especially for the young and single. The roles are similar, yet distinguishing between men and women. There are single woman and man ranchers. The role convention, however, is of the ranch family. Women are more responsible for early child care and food preparation. Men primarily perform machine maintenance. Beyond these, tasks frequently require the entire family to participate, making ranch life relatively egalitarian related to gender. Small operations increasingly require husbands and especially wives to work off the ranch for supplementary income.

The mixing of reality and fantasy, mythos is especially evident when friends and neighbors join together in ranch work that formerly was accomplished by the hand labor of large crews. Round-up presents such an occasion in some areas. Neighbors, remote family members and friends converge to assist each other, whether they are really needed or not. Skilled hands are able to demonstrate their camaraderie and competence. *Gemeinschaft* is recollected. Tales of prior experiences are warmly shared. Copious amount of food and hospitality further show the special skills of women. When the cap is removed from a whisky bottle, it often is symbolically tossed away. Round-up is but one of several such events that consciously demonstrate a way of life that all present universally agree is without equal, in part because of its historical, almost atavistic, origins.

Ranching has its own unique recreation, based largely on the mythical perpetuation of such skills and values. In concept, rodeo events are created around the practical essential tasks of being a cowboy. In fact, they are extremely specialized events, performed at the highest levels by trained athletes, who rarely, perhaps never, use their skills on a ranch for practical purposes. Many events, such as bull riding and bull fighting, have no practical functions. Women's events, particularly goat roping, have been established to demonstrate compe-

tence, although such activity may not exist on a ranch. Much of rodeo is a caricature of the noble qualities of ranch life, unabashedly glorifying it. Participants, whether from Texas or Montana, California or New Jersey, dress, speak and generally act in a single genre, again, reflecting the ideals of the way of life. Men and women are, deliberately and visibly, easy to distinguish as men and women. Deference is paid to God, Free Enterprise, Family and Nature. Competitors help each other and share ideas and experiences. Competition is entirely individual, except for team roping and occasional idiosyncratic events held at few rodeos. Winning, determined by time and style, is paid off directly in cash. No remuneration occurs for failure.

The mythos of ranching is currently under attack. Environmentalists concerned with overgrazing of range and destruction of riparian areas challenge ranchers' identity as husbands of the land. Animal rights activists such as Jeremy Rifkin (1992) criticize the basis of their livelihood, claiming that killing is inhumane and that red meat is unhealthy. Recreationists treat ranchers as irrelevant or intrusive, since livestock interfere with recreational uses for the environment. The issues and problems delineating ranchers from others are more than a symbolic challenge to their way of life, although those are genuine and serious. They affect food consumption, the very livelihood of ranchers.

Contemporary Problems of Ranching

Ranching is increasingly encountering complicated issues and problems, in large part because of the transitional stage it implies between early and later stages of environmental development. Restrictions concerning land and water uses continually pit outside interests against ranchers. In the West, where water is a particularly scarce and precious commodity, alternative uses of water allocations constantly are being proposed. Residential and industrial developments, frequently in distant states, may be the sources of such conflicts. Similarly, the availability of leased lands from government agencies such as the Bureau of Land Management and the Forest Service are sources of contention. Free-market advocates, symbolized by the Sage Brush Rebellion, call for the privatization of public lands. Other interests advocate establishing new priorities for water and land use that usurp the management prerogatives of ranchers. Rules controlling irrigation and noxious plants are obvious examples of very complex phenomena.

The control of land itself presents an overt threat to ranching. In some areas land claims remain under dispute, particularly in traditionally Hispanic areas and Indian reservations. The position of ranchers as a cherished elite is challenged. From the perspectives of both users and ranchers, changing rules previously governing accessible public and semi-public lands are problematic. Ranchers who previously allowed hunting increasingly do not, or do so for a fee. Government leases previously closed to the public now are open to them. The strains between ranchers and outsiders, recreationists, minorities and government are extreme.

The transfer of land from one generation to the next presents a final problem to the ranchers. Decisions governing ranch operations generally are controlled by the older generation. Younger family members usually contribute increasingly disproportionate amounts of work with marginal increases in income or influence over the operation. This is a phase that is particularly vexing for spouses. The problem emerges in part because of the limited capacities of ranches to expand profits that could be redistributed to the younger generations. It also is a function of different notions of how the ranch should be run and who has the right to implement decisions.

In spite of contemporary pressures to undermine ranching, ranching will persist into the long foreseeable future. The human ecological foundations, established social structures and identifiable interaction systems and way of life combine to create a persistent social system, in spite of both internal and external conflicts. Ranching will also capture the imagination of outsiders, as it has for over a century.

— *Patrick C. Jobes*

See also

Cowboys; History, Agricultural; Horse Industry; Intergenerational Land Transfer; Land Ownership; Livestock Production; Pasture; Policy, Environmental; Social Class; Values of Residents; Wool Industry

References

Galaty, John G. and Douglas L. Johnson, eds. *The World of Pastoralism: Herding Systems in Comparative Perspective.* New York, NY: Guilford Press, 1990.

Gray, James R. *Ranch Economics.* Ames IA: Iowa State University Press, 1968.

Holechek, Jerry L. "Western Ranching at the Crossroads." *Rangelands* 23, no. 1 (February, 2001): 17-21.

Jobes, Patrick C. "Social Structure and Myth: Content and Form in Ranchland." *Studies in Popular Culture* 9, no. 2 (1986): 51-64.

Knight, Richard L., Wendell C. Gilgert and Ed Marston, eds .*Ranching West of the 100th Meridian: Culture, Ec-*

ology and Economics. Washington, DC: Island Press, 2002.

Rifkin, Jeremy. *Beyond Beef: the Rise and Fall of the Cattle Culture.* New York, NY: Dutton 1992.

Russell, Charles M. *Studies of Western Life, with Descriptions by Granville Stewart.* New York, NY: Albertype Company, 1890.

Savory, Allan. *Holistic Resource Management.* Washington, DC: Island Press, 1988.

Slatta, Richard W. *Cowboys of the Americas.* New Haven, CT: Yale University Press, 1989.

Starrs, Paul F. *Let the Cowboy Ride: Cattle Ranching in the American West.* Baltimore, MD: Johns Hopkins University Press, 2000.

Sayre, Nathan Freeman. *Ranching, Endangered Species, and Urbanization in the Southwest: Species of Capital.* Tucson, AZ: University of Arizona Press, 2006.

Sayre, Nathan Freeman. *The New Ranch Handbook: A Guide to Restoring Western Rangelands.* Santa Fe, NM: Quivira Coalition, 2001.

Wellman, Paul I. *The Trampling Herd.* Philadelphia, PA: J. B. Lippincott, 1939.

Recreation Activities

Leisure activity engaged in for the attainment of personal and social benefits. This chapter begins with the definition of recreation and a short history of recreation in rural America, followed by a classification system for grouping rural recreation activities and some of the common benefits of recreation. The article concludes with an overview of some of the current issues and trends in rural recreation activities.

Consideration of recreation activities in rural America invokes a variety of images associated with both social and natural landscapes. These images range from the traditional social orientated recreation activities associated with small town life—church socials, country fairs, picnics, family reunions—to outdoor recreation activities of hunting, fishing, camping, hiking that depend on the natural resource base of rural America. Recreation activities in rural America, like other aspects of rural life and human behavior, is constantly changing. Attitudes and participation patterns continually evolve.

Defining Aspects of Recreation

Recreation is leisure or free time activity that is engaged in for the attainment of personal and social benefits. Rural recreational activities should include doing something desirable for participants and for society. Recreation is viewed as restoration from the toils of work. The word "recreation" comes from the concept of creating again, recollecting, or reforming in the mind. The idea of refreshment of spirit and strength after toil led to the word being used to mean diversion, play, or amusement. Recreation is instrumental to work because it enables individuals to recuperate and restore themselves in order to accomplish more work. Recreation is related to an individual or group choice taking place during discretionary time.

Historical Perspective of Recreation in Rural America

Foster Rhea Dulles' (1965) classic, *A History of Recreation: America Learns to Play,* compared the growth of recreation in the U.S. to a river; its course adapts itself to the nature of the country through which it flows. As the U.S. evolved from a largely rural country to a largely urban country, recreational choices have evolved and been adapted based on changing technology. Dulles identified two factors that shaped recreation in America. The first factor is the continuing influence of Puritanism, both rising from and enforcing a dogma of work born in economic circumstance, which can be traced from the 17th to the 20th century. Until recently, Puritanism devalued any activity that could be viewed as a waste of time. Some rural communities passed laws to prohibit activities on Sundays except those that were spiritual or essential for basic subsistence, and others forbade participation in specific activities such as card games, mixed dancing, and theatrical performances.

The degree to which Puritan taboos were observed and the nature of these restrictions varied considerably from rural area to rural area. The growing number of non-Puritan rural peoples became increasingly discontent and viewed the restraints place on them as intolerable. Worn out by the endless work on their little farms, discouraged by poor harvests, fearful of famine and plague, they found release for pent-up emotion in drinking. Taverns sprang up as naturally as the meeting-house, and the festive nature of the tap-room met a genuine need. Taverns were well patronized, and often provided opportunities to play cards or watch cockfighting, bear baiting, or boxing. Aside from the tavern sports, most rural recreation engagements made at least some pretense of serving socially useful ends. Rural residents commonly participated in hunting and shooting contests, in simple country sports, and in the communal activities of training days and barn raisings. Women took part as spectators, if not as participants, in farm festivals and holiday celebrations, or in whatever amusements were available.

Contemporary observers agreed that there was a general lack of amusements in rural America in the late 19th century. Farm life varied greatly in different parts of the country, but in general life in rural America could not offer recreational opportunities comparable to those in urban America. However, the isolated rural family may have had more enjoyment than did their urban counterparts in their passive commercialized amusements. Many farm organizations, such as the Grange, fulfilled many recreation needs and became the principal social gathering of the farm community. Women were admitted for the first time into full memberships. The Grange organized lectures, concerts, held young people debates and spelling bees, promoted singing school, and arranged evenings of general entertainment. The annual state or county fairs that originated as educational vehicles, quickly were transformed into recreation opportunities. The annual county fairs and other special events (e.g., socials at the local schoolhouse, square dances, 4th of July picnics, and circuses) were anticipated for months and remembered long afterward with continuing pleasure.

The second factor Dulles identified as of paramount influence on recreation was the gradual transformation of the economy from the simplicity of the agricultural era to the complexity of the machine age. By 1880, railroad fares decreased to the point that railroads provided rural residents an inexpensive form of recreational travel. New methods and machinery provided rural people with more free time and better access to city amusements. Five years after the appearance of the nickelodeon in 1905, there were over 10,000 theaters around the country. Automobile ownership expanded dramatically in the 1920s and also revolutionized transportation in rural America. Automobiles provided the opportunity for most rural residents to drive to a movie house or a community center for entertainment. The transition to the machine age also included the first major boom in the production and sales of manufactured items used primarily for recreation. Radio ownership went from 5,300 in 1920 to more than 5 million in 1924.

The stock market crash of 1929 and President Roosevelt's subsequent New Deal programs changed the number and types of rural recreation opportunities.

Massive federal funding supported the design and construction of a wide range of public recreation facilities at all levels of government. The years following World War II brought widespread changes to rural recreation opportunities. The use of regional, county, state, and national parks and forests increased dramatically. The war effort developed four-wheel drive and off-road vehicles that became major forms of recreation for rural people. Car camping became popular during this period with the development of thousands of campsites. Innovations in small engine technology have increased the use of personal individual vehicles such as all-terrain vehicles, snowmobiles, and personal water craft in the last two decades. The transition to the computer age is leading to many changes in recreation opportunities for recreation in rural America today. Video stores replaced theaters in rural towns and villages. Other developments in communication technology, including electronic bulletin boards, -CDs, DVDs, and the Internet, are changing the range of passive and educational recreation opportunities available to rural people. The opportunity to participate in a broad array of recreational pursuits requires a classification system of the different forms of recreation.

Classification of Rural Recreation Activities

Dumazeider (1967) developed a comprehensive classification with five major divisions, each with two subdivisions. This classification system identifies and specifies the more visible aspects of the rural recreation experience and how one uses free time. Physical recreation includes: (a) physical activities, such as taking part in hunting and fishing, softball leagues, bridge club, etc.; and (b) travel activities, such as bus tours, Sunday drives, or driving for pleasure. Intellectual recreation includes: (a) intellectual understanding, such as obtaining knowledge through formal or informal education programs, how to manuals, books or field studies, television programs, or lectures; and (b) intellectual production, such as being creative as an amateur writer, scientist, or philosopher. Artistic recreation includes: (a) artistic enjoyment, such as listening to music; attending concerts; operas; plays; visiting museums, traveling art shows, and reading about arts; and (b) artistic creation, such as taking lessons in the arts, singing, playing an instrument, painting, writing poetry or prose, dancing, acting, taking part in crafts as an amateur, or participating in community arts programs and organizations. Sociable recreation includes: (a) sociable communication, such as oral communication for plea-

sure between two or more people in person, on the telephone, or through written communication such as letters or the Internet; and (b) sociable entertainment, such as one-way communication from performers or the mass media to the consumer, as in the movies, newspapers, television and magazines and books. Practical recreation includes: (a) practical collection, such as personal hobbies that result in something to show for the effort of involvement in community collecting, preserving farm machinery and sharing, such as at museums, art galleries, historical homes; and (b) practical transformation, such as activities that seek to change a thing (do-it-yourself projects), a person (gossips, advisors, amateur psychiatrists) or social institutions (political or service organization participants).

This classification system can be useful to group rural recreation participation activities and follow patterns. Another approach is to examine the benefits of participation in recreation in rural America.

Benefits of Recreation

Assessing the benefits of participation in recreation activity is a very complex process. The benefits vary with the kinds of activity, the participants, the environment and others. Kelly (1983) groups benefits of recreation participation into three overlapping categories: personal benefits, societal benefits, and economic benefits.

Personal benefits are those benefits associated with the individual. These have been inferred from studies of past rural recreation experiences and include excitement and relaxation. Many rural recreation activities are associated with environmental appreciation and immersion, learning and testing competence, familiarity and exploring what is either new or old, and stimulation of the mind and body. More long-term benefits may result from these experiences such as self-enhancement through improved mental and physical health.

Societal benefits are outcomes that are related to social groups or collectives. These benefits relate to the support or enhancement of communities, families, and friendship groups that are central to life. Rural people's involvement with rural-based organizations and events are partially an extension of personal benefits, but in the long run the benefits of recreational involvement associated with social institutions—family, church, government, school, and community—are societal rather than personal. They lead to increased social cohesion. Through recreation activities, rural people realize that they are part of a larger collective. County fairs and involvement in Grange activities do more than provide personal benefits; they reinforce the idea that rural people are part of a larger collective. It reduces the feelings of isolation that many rural people may encounter.

Economic benefits are outcomes of participation in rural recreation that contribute to economic well-being of rural America. These benefits include the contribution of resources to employment opportunities for rural peoples. The benefits may be primary, such are income-producing employment, or secondary, such as demand for goods and services in communities. A growing number of people in rural America depend on tourism and recreation for their livelihood. Given this wide range of benefits associated with participation in various recreation activities, it is important to consider recreation participation patterns of rural Americans relative to persons living in urban and suburban areas.

Rural Recreation Activity Participation Patterns

Rural Americans entertain themselves to a considerable degree with the same leisure time and recreation activities as urban and suburban counterparts. They watch many of the same television programs, read the same books, and watch the same movies that their city and suburb counterparts do. They, too, follow professional and college sports, and go to conventions and maybe save for a charter flight to Europe or Hawaii. Yet there are differences in their circumstances and environments. The country dweller lacks easy access to metropolitan museums, theaters, and concerts halls, but the advent of cable and satellite antennas bring many of the cultural events into their living rooms. The rural resident has easy access to many opportunities associated with undeveloped and abundant natural resources. It may be possible to fish or hunt close to home. Lower land prices may allow people to keep horses or other large pets, and grow most of their own fruits and vegetables. Many rural residents find it easy to have large pieces of recreation equipment on their land such as motors homes, big boats, workshops, or horse trailers. Rural people have higher participation rates than urban and suburban residents in camping, hiking, hunting, horseback riding, freshwater fishing, and snowmobiling.

Ruralness is an identity, a way of life, and a state of mind, but it is also about the pace of life. Residents of small places continually refer to themselves as rural people and their communities as rural places. Those who move from urban to rural places often state they have escaped the "rat race." Ruralness and recreation in rural areas has a great deal to do with the pace of life. Recreation remains an important defining characteristic of what it means to be rural. Rural people still participate in traditional rural recreation activities, and these activities will continue to contribute to the physical and social landscape of rural areas.

— Robert A. Robertson and Rodney B. Warnick

See also
Arts; Camps; Community Celebrations; Gambling; Games; Music; Parks; Public Libraries; Restaurants; Senior Centers; Sport; Theatrical Entertainment; Tourism, Ecotourism; Wildlife

References

Chubb, Michael and Holly R. Chubb. *One Third of Our Time? An Introduction to Recreation Behavior and Resources.* New York, NY: John Wiley and Sons, Inc., 1981.

Dulles, Foster R. *A History of Recreation: America Learns to Play,* 2nd edition. New York, NY: Meredith Publishing Company, 1965.

Dumazeider, Josef. *Towards a Society of Leisure.* New York, NY: Free Press, 1967.

Fisher, Ronald M. "Leisure Time: The Sharing of Happiness." Pp. 124-151 in *Life in Rural America.* Washington, DC: National Geographic Society, Special Publication Division, 1978.

Hortz, B. and R. Petosa. "Impact of the 'Planning to be Active' Leisure Time Physical Exercise Program on Rural High School Students." *Journal of Adolescent Health* 39, no. 4 (2006): 530–535.

Kaplan, Max. *Leisure Theory and Policy.* New York, NY: John Wiley and Sons, Inc., 1975.

Kelly, John R. "Social Benefits of Outdoor Recreation: An Introduction." Pp. 3-15 in *Recreation Planning and Management.* Edited by Stanley R. Leiber and Daniel R. Fesenmaier. State College, PA: Venture Press, 1983.

Reeder, Richard J. and Dennis M. Brown. *Recreation, Tourism, and Rural Well-being.* ERS Report No. 7. Washington, DC: U.S. Department of Agriculture, Economic Research Service, August 2005.

Roberts, Leslie and Derek Hall. *Rural Tourism and Recreation: Principles to Practice.* Oxfordshire, UK: CABI Publishing, 2001.

Yu, Jih-Min. "The Congruence of Recreation Activity Dimensions among Urban, Suburban, and Rural Residents." *Journal of Leisure Research* 17, nc. 2 (1985): 107-120.

Regional Diversity

The spatial mosaic of complex and varied natural and cultural environmental features, conditions and patterns that gives character to America's distinctive regional landscapes. This entry defines the concept of region and illustrates it with selected examples from both the natural and human environments. Many natural and cultural regional transitions may be imperceptible to the casual observer because they often occur on a macro-, rather than a micro-, scale. Within the nation's 3.8-million-square-mile area can be found rural regional diversity unsurpassed by that of any other country.

Nature of Regions

Rather than being random in their nature and distribution, America's rural features, conditions and resulting landscapes lend themselves well to regional expression, classification, distribution and delineation. A region is an area of Earth's surface that differs from other portions by virtue of possessing one or more homogeneous features, conditions or other characteristics. Regions serve the same purpose for geographers and others that various time periods do for historians; they function as convenience packages for organizing and analyzing information spatially. The regional concept facilitates communication about places, their locations and their characteristics. *Middle West*, for example, evokes a mental image of a specific spatial location (where it is), unique characteristics of a place (what is there), and spatial distribution (area). Important information is communicated about both place and space, yet details are vague. Geographers continue to argue about those features that make the Middle West and many other regions unique and where their boundaries should be drawn.

All regions are abstract; they are based on arbitrarily selected criteria. Some regions exhibit relative homogeneity of a single feature. Examples include a river drainage basin, soil type, area of single crop dominance, the marketing area of a product, or a ZIP code. Others, such as ecosystems, economic regions and vernacular regions (e.g., "Dixie," the "Corn Belt," or the "Sun Belt") are multiple-feature regions with many traits that set them apart from other areas within the country.

Geographers recognize three types of regions: formal, functional and popular (vernacular or perceptual). Formal regions are areas with one or more traits in common, such as landforms, climate, ecosystems, crops and/or cultural practices. Boundaries usually are poorly defined and their locations may vary greatly from map to map. This occurs because the criteria used in identifying regional boundaries often vary, as do the cutoff points. Further, rather than being defined by sharp lines, most formal regions are separated by broad transitional zones. The problem can be illustrated by the lines that separate the Middle West and West, the Humid Continental and Dry Continental climates, or the grassland and desert ecosystems.

Functional regions are those organized around some function. They are recognized both by the function that they perform and the node or control point from which their functions are coordinated. Examples include political units, infrastructure (e.g., transportation, utility or irrigation systems), economic networks and social units (e.g., clubs, church parishes and schools) in small town America. Finally, popular regions are those widely recognized and used by the general population. Examples include Dixie, Washington's Palouse Country, the Panhandle (several states), East River/West River in South Dakota, and Delmarva or Eastern Shore for the peninsula lying east of Chesapeake Bay. Organizing geographic features and conditions, both physical and human, in a regional context can enhance understanding of their characteristics, distributions and relationships.

Natural Regions

Because of its broad latitudinal range, from Hawaii's humid tropical conditions to Alaska's polar ice cap at high elevations, the U.S. includes within its territory all of Earth's climates and ecosystems. It is the only country to possess such tremendous regional diversity. Landforms range from mountains to interior plains and coastal lowlands, with hills and plateaus also contributing to the country's varied terrain. Water features (rivers, lakes and groundwater) vary greatly from place to place in both quantity and quality. America's vast and diverse store of mineral resources (energy, metals and nonmetallic) are distributed in countless regional patterns. Soil types and fertility also occur in marked patterns of regional variation.

Landforms are the most visible natural features. Most major physiographic provinces in the U.S. trend in a north-south axis. The Pacific Mountain system includes California's fault block Sierra Nevada (including 14,494 foot Mt. Whitney) and the volcanic Cascades that extend from northern California northward into Washington. An Intermontaine Plateau province extends from western New Mexico northward into eastern Washington, with chief subregions that include the Basin-and-Range of the Southwest, the Great Basin, and the Colorado and Columbia plateaus. The Rocky Mountains extend from northern New Mexico northward to Idaho and western Montana. Interior Plains extend from the Rockies to the Appalachians; sub-provinces include the Great Plains and Interior Lowlands. The Gulf-Atlantic Coastal Plain is a low-lying region with little surface configuration that extends from southern Texas to southern New Jersey. The Black Hills (South Dakota), Ozark-Oachita Highlands (Arkansas, Missouri and eastern Oklahoma) and folded Appalachian Highlands (Alabama to Maine) contribute to the landform diversity of the Central and Eastern U.S.

Atmospheric conditions are the primary key to regional diversity within the natural environment. Weather and climate influence plant life, animal habitat, the weathering and subsequent erosion of landforms, soil characteristics and water features. Elements such as temperature, precipitation, growing season and storms also present opportunities and challenges to human cultural adaptation, land use and settlement.

Tropical climates occur in Hawaii (including the world's wettest spot, Mt. Waialeale, which receives an annual average 472 inches of rain), southern Florida (Wet and Dry Tropical), and the southern margins of the desert Southwest (Dry Tropical). Subtropical climates occur in the Southeast (Humid Subtropical), the southern Great Plains and Southwest (Dry Subtropical), and coastal California (Mediterranean Subtropical, unique because of its intense summer drought). Coastal Oregon and Washington experience a moist, mild climate (Temperate Marine). Much of the northern half of the country experiences a Dry Continental (west) or Humid Continental (east) climate, divided by the 20-inch precipitation line that coincides roughly with the 100th meridian. Most of Alaska lies within the Subarctic and Polar climate regions.

Because of its varied climates, the U.S. includes all major ecosystems within its territory. Such diversity is significant because it contributes to diverse biomes, wildlife habitats, natural landscapes and economic opportunities. Even the nation's history was somewhat influenced by natural vegetation. European settlers nurtured in woodland areas were unfamiliar with the vast grasslands of the country's interior. This region was the last to be settled and developed within the conterminous 48 states. Ecosystem diversity (climate, vegetation, soil and animal life) also is an important factor in cultural ecology, how humans use the land and re-

sources. All of the world's crops and livestock, for example, can be raised someplace in the U.S., and relatively large areas are well suited to growing such essential crops as grains, fruits and vegetables, oilseeds and cotton.

Desert vegetation is dominant in the Southwest and portions of the western interior. Steppe (short) and prairie (tall) grassland ecosystems dominate the non-desert western interior and central plains regions of the country. Savanna grasslands occur in southern Florida. Needleleaf evergreen forests dominate the coastal lowlands of the Southeast, higher elevations of the western U.S., the Pacific Northwest, and the taiga forests of Alaska. Broadleaf deciduous forests extend throughout much of the area drained by the Mississippi and Ohio rivers. Mixed forests dominate the vegetation pattern in the Ozarks, Appalachians and New England.

Climates and ecosystems occupy large areas, and the transition from one region to another often is both gradual and nearly imperceptible. Mountainous regions are an exception. High mountains in tropical Hawaii, for example, include nearly all of Earth's climates and ecosystems, in micro-scale, from Humid Tropical to Polar, with corresponding changes in natural vegetation. Similar diversity, though not as extreme, occurs throughout the mountainous West. Diverse ecosystems create the varied natural habitats that support the country's abundant wildlife.

Soils are formed by a number of factors that include parent material, climate, vegetation, slope and time. Diverse geologic, climatic and vegetation conditions have contributed to both a diverse array of soil types and vast areas of extremely fertile soils that constitute the natural foundation of the nation's unsurpassed agricultural productivity.

Water features also contribute to rural regional diversity. Facing upon three oceans, the Atlantic, Pacific, and in Alaska the Arctic, contributed greatly to the nation's regional diversity. The sea served both as a protective barrier and as an avenue of migration and trade. It exerts a major influence on weather and climate, modifying temperatures and serving as the chief source of moisture. Many coastal areas turned to the sea for wealth, whether by fishing, exploiting off-shore petroleum resources, or tourism, and developed a unique regional character in the process.

River valleys and fertile alluvial flood plains long have been choice sites for human settlement. The nation's heartland is drained by the Mississippi River and its many tributaries, including the Ohio and Missouri, which combine to create one of the world's most extensive waterway transportation networks. The Colorado River and Rio Grande of the Southwest are of tremendous regional importance for power, recreation, irrigation and urban water supplies. In the Pacific Northwest, the Columbia River is a source of energy, domestic and irrigation water, and salmon. Countless other streams and their associated valleys, such as the Hudson, Delaware and Tennessee rivers, played a vital role in the historical settlement, development and character of their basins.

Most of the country's natural lakes occur in the glaciated area north of the Missouri and Ohio rivers. The Great Lakes (Superior, Michigan, Huron, Erie and Ontario) were created by the vast continental ice sheets that covered northern portions of the continent during the Ice Age. They form the greatest system of fresh water lakes in the world. With several engineering assists in the forms of locks, canals and channel improvement, the lakes form a shipping outlet that links the nation's agricultural and industrial heartland to the Atlantic Ocean.

Culture Regions

Regional diversity based on cultural patterns—differences in the way people live, what they build, and what they do, how they speak and worship, and so forth—is every bit as pronounced as are regional variations that exist within rural America's natural environment. Within any natural region, a variety of human differences can be found. Whether economic, social, political, religious or ethnic, or some other trait, these human practices contribute to a diverse mosaic of culture traits and cultural landscapes. Regional differences are so great, even on a micro-scale, that a thriving service industry developed around the organization and use of demographic, economic and social data identified by ZIP code areas.

Culturally, America's "melting pot" of racially and ethnically varied peoples and ways of life continues to diversity. Rural America has always been ethnically diverse. The Middle West, for example, is rich in ethnic islands often identified by town names that commemorate the founders' place of origin. Each such settlement contributed to the quilted mosaic of rural American settlement. Today ethnic diversity continues to reach into and affect much of rural America. It is not uncommon to find exotic foods on the shelves of rural or small town grocery stores, available in response to the tastes of an ethnically changing population. Certain economic opportunities (e.g., agriculture and agricultural processing, fishing and mining) attracted ethnic populations to many parts of the U.S., and their cultural imprint has become increasingly evident in many rural areas.

Demographic patterns of rural America also are changing. Some regions are experiencing sharp population decline, whereas others are undergoing explosive population growth. Generally, recent movement has been from north to south ("Rust Belt" or "Snow Belt" to "Sun Belt"), from interior to coastal, and from urban to suburban and exurban. Composition of the rural population also is changing. An aging population characterizes many agrarian areas that experience out-migration of the young, and areas that attract retirees.

Rural population decline in the U.S. has been widespread, but in terms of contemporary impact is restricted primarily to some farming regions. Factors contributing to the decline (e.g., the "Buffalo Commons" of the Great Plains region) include increased mechanization that vastly reduced the need for human labor, lower fertility rates and smaller family size, and increasing farm size. The last factor substantially reduced the number of rural families and, in so doing, reduced the market for goods and services formerly provided by small rural communities. Improved transportation facilities made it possible to conduct business in what became thriving regional centers that offered a greater variety of goods and services at a lower cost.

Much of the rural population growth of recent decades occurred in areas that formerly were negatively perceived and subject to out-migration. Examples include the Ozark and Appalachian highlands, many former mining camps turned ghost towns in the Mountain West, the Sun Belt where effective air conditioning made living comfortable, and much of the coastal zone. Many urban residents found rural America to be an attractive alternative to city living. The resulting urban-to-rural migration, with its concomitant economic, social and political changes, can overwhelm small, homogeneous, traditionally conservative rural communities.

In terms of demographic, social and economic change, a region that appears to be quite homogeneous can, in reality, be extremely diverse. For more than 300 years, perhaps the most distinctive and homogeneous rural cultural region in America has been northern New Mexico's Hispano homeland. During much of the twentieth century, small, economically impoverished rural communities in the region experienced population decline. Today, they are thriving, but for a variety of reasons.

As land and housing values skyrocketed in Taos, Los Alamos, and Santa Fe, many local residents found themselves unable to afford living in their own home community. Surrounding towns grew as bedroom communities for now displaced commuters. Others became amenity centers and grew because they attracted affluent residents seeking a serene, culturally exotic, country life. Elsewhere, a heterogeneous social mix of "New Agers," mainstream dropouts, religious cultists and right-wing militants settled in communities shared by those of similar interest. Finally, many rural communities have begun to grow as Hispanic Americans, many of whom left the area decades ago but never sold their property, returned to retire in their ancestral homeland. Each of the disparate groups imprints its own experience, interests and values on the community in which it resides. In this way, a number of small microregions evolved in what was once perhaps the nation's most homogeneous culture region, the Hispano Heartland of northern New Mexico.

Economic areas are among the best known and most widely recognized rural regions. The Corn Belt, Cotton Belt, Napa Valley, and Yakima Valley are examples of well-known formal culture regions based on a particular economic activity. Less well recognized, but equally common and important, are thousands of functional areas, each of which can be recognized by its node or function control center. Examples include trade or marketing areas, service areas and transportation or communication networks. These can be based on a variety of factors, including the spatial distribution of a particular grocery, fast-food or gasoline chain; the area from which an enterprise draws its customers; the area served by an electrical or natural gas company; the route map of an airline, or the broadcast area served by a radio or television station. Most functional areas begin and are controlled from urban centers. Gradually, during the twentieth century, much of rural America was integrated into the majority of essential functions, hence, functional regions.

Finally, rural America includes a great number of popular economic regions. These regions, illustrated by Washington state's Inland Empire; the Metroplex of Dallas, Fort Worth, and environs; North Carolina's Research Triangle Park; and northeast Mississippi's Golden Triangle, often are created and perpetuated by Chambers of Commerce. Strictly rural vernacular regions, emanating from traditional cultural roots, include the Mississippi Delta culture region of northwestern Mississippi, and Alabama's fertile Black Belt.

Primary industries dominate the rural environment where agriculture mining, logging, and fishing contribute immeasurably to the nation's regional character and diversity. Each of these activities, in turn, has its own peculiar regional subtypes. In terms of rural landscape imprint, socioeconomic integration and economic infrastructure, the wine industry of California's Napa and Sonoma valleys, southern Florida's truck farming of vegetables for northern markets, and the flue-cured tobacco belt of the Carolinas and Virginia are three extremely distinctive and diverse regions. Yet each specializes on a particular horticultural crop. Animal industries, such as cattle ranching, dairying, hog production and poultry raising, also contribute to regional diversity.

Regional Change

Regions are fluid. Most, if not all of them, change through time. Change generally occurs most rapidly in regions delineated on the basis of such human characteristics as demographic, economic, political, ethnic or social homogeneity. Natural regions also change, although generally at a much slower and less perceptible rate than do human regions. Few areas in America's contemporary rural environment remain stationary. An ability to adapt to changing conditions and regional affiliations is essential to the future well-being of rural America.

— *Charles F. Gritzner*

See also

Biodiversity; Culture; Desert Landscapes; Hydrology; Mountains; Settlement Patterns; Soil; Weather; Wetlands

References

Allen, James P. and Eugene J. Turner. *We the People: An Atlas of America's Ethnic Diversity*. New York, NY: Macmillan, 1988.

Garreau, Joel. *The Nine Nations of North America*. Boston, MA: Houghton Mifflin Company, 1981.

Gastil, Raymond D. *Cultural Regions of the United States*. Seattle, WA: University of Washington Press, 1975.

Gerlach, Arch C., ed. *The National Atlas of the United States of America*. Washington, DC: U.S. Department of the Interior, Geological Survey, 1970.

Glassborow, Jilly and Gilliam Freeman, eds. *Atlas of the United States*. New York, NY: Macmillan, 1986.

Graf, William L., ed. *Geomorphic Systems of North America*. Boulder, CO: The Geological Society of America, 1987.

Hart, John Fraser, ed. *Regions of the United States.* New York, NY: Harper and Row, 1972.

Rooney, John F. Jr., Wilbur Zelinsky, Dean R. Louder, eds. *This Remarkable Continent: An Atlas of the United States and Canadian Society and Cultures.* College Station, TX: Texas A&M University Press, 1982.

Weiss, Michael J. *Latitudes & Attitudes: An Atlas of American Tastes, Trends, Politics, and Passions.* Boston, MA: Little, Brown and Company, 1994.

Zelinsky, Wilbur. *The Cultural Geography of the United States.* Englewood Cliffs, NJ: Prentice-Hall, 1992.

Regional Planning

Future-oriented studies and action programs undertaken by groups of sub-state local governments, and/or sub-national state governments. This article provides an overview of the regional planning experience in rural America. The first section discusses historic trends and their effects on planning. The second section summarizes the current status of various approaches to regional planning. The third and final section speculates on the future of regional planning in light of a broader set of social and technological trends.

Historical Experiences

There are really two rural Americas in the U.S. There is the rural America that is declining and the rural America that is growing. The former tends to be distant; that is, it lies beyond and between metropolitan influences. The latter is typically located on either the fringes of the cities or is distant but has amenities, often recreational, that attract urban residents to it. Each of these types of rural regions has its own sets of planning problems and challenges. Distant areas need regional planning, but engage in little of it because of disincentives to cooperate. The regional planning in growing areas seeks to centralize authority for land use and environmental management in order to promote efficiency, conservation and social equity. But the future of regional planning of all types is uncertain. It is derivative of the larger political dialogue, and influenced by social forces such as renewed citizen activism and heightened conflict over private property.

The relationship of urban America to its rural regions might be characterized best as ambiguous. On the one hand, there is the doctrine, traceable to neoclassical economic theory, that little, if anything, can or should be done to try to alleviate rural decline. Such decline is viewed as a product of powerful, rational economic and demographic forces that are beyond policy influence. Where public effort is expended, it is targeted to the development of selected growth centers where manufacturing opportunities can congregate and to which rural residents can migrate. On the other hand, there is the view that rural regions are declining as a function of market failure. This view suggests that it is necessary and appropriate to intervene via regional planning and directed policy assistance. From this perspective, rural regions serve a social, economic and cultural role for the nation, and their impoverishment is dysfunctional from the perspective of a larger, long-term economic calculus.

The U.S. first ventured into widespread experiments in regional planning during the 1930s. The rapidly changing conditions of rural America, as a function of the economic Depression and widespread natural resource depletion (such as the "Dust Bowl" conditions of the Plains states), called forth creative responses by the national government. It was during this period that large-scale regional planning projects were implemented, the most well known being the Tennessee Valley Authority (TVA). While ultimately the TVA became a power generation agency for the region, its original concept was to provide rural-based modernization throughout the Southeast. Also during the 1930s the only national planning agency the U.S. has ever had, the National Resources Planning Board (NRPB), undertook several pioneering studies on the regional character of America and possible structures for regional planning. But little actually came of all this. The NRPB was disbanded, and the TVA and its cousins became agencies for the generation of inexpensive power on the theory that this would attract economic enterprises to growth centers in distressed rural regions.

Regional planning for rural areas re-emerged in the 1960s in two guises. As part of the social planning of the period, programs were developed to address the social and economic disadvantages of rural places relative to urban areas. These programs were regional in nature because it appeared administratively easier and more cost-efficient to provide services on this basis. Few of these programs endured.

Contemporary Programs

The regional planning efforts that endured grew out of the need to manage rapid growth in urban fringe rural areas and in those distant areas with recreational amenities. The tradition in these areas was one of fragmented, decentralized local control over growth and natural resources. In a selected set of states, such as Vermont, New York, Florida, Wisconsin, California and Oregon, legislation was passed reasserting the state's authority over growth and natural resource management. This was reinforced by efforts at the federal level for selected natural resources such as those along the coastal zones. The rationale in all of these cases was that the existing system of local control in rural regions was characteristically and inherently parochial, discriminatory, destructive of ecosystems, and socially irresponsible. Also, the tradition of local control, dating back to the turn of the twentieth century, was perceived as inefficient as local administrators had neither the technical knowledge nor the administrative capacity to respond to the complex problems of growth. In order to achieve greater rationality in land use and natural resource management and meet a greater public good, it was proposed that more centralized administrative structures were necessary.

This approach to more centralized regional planning has expanded into the present. There are now about 12 states that have one or more programs for their rural areas oriented to control and contain urbanization or preserve land uses that are considered to have social significance, such as farmland and environmentally sensitive areas. These programs all share the characteristic of reducing the autonomy and authority of local government. For example, in Oregon a set of state goals exist that must be met in all local planning efforts. Local plans are reviewed at the state level for consistency with these goals. In Florida, environmentally sensitive areas must be identified in local plans, and local zoning is required to protect the integrity of such areas. Plans in one locality must be coordinated with the plans of adjoining localities, and efforts to provide public services must be organized consonant with the plans. As in Oregon, there is also a state-level review of local plans for consistency with these requirements. New Jersey's approach emphasizes local areas developing plans and then meeting with each other to develop a consistent approach to land use and natural resource management. In all cases, local efforts to act autonomously have been preempted, and plans for rural locales have to be coordinated with those of related rural places, and the region, and often state, as a whole.

While these comprehensive-style approaches at more centralized planning are generally lauded by planning professionals, environmental protection advocates, and good government reformers, they have been adopt-

ed by only about a dozen states, and the majority of these states are on the East and West Coasts where most of the rural growth areas can be found. While that has recently begun to change somewhat, with high-growth rural areas emerging in some interior states such as Colorado, Texas and Minnesota, in general, the middle part of the U.S. either has not experienced the same types of growth pressures that prompted the centralized efforts, or has experienced actual population decline and severe economic restructuring.

As a result, regional planning between the coasts has taken one of two forms. Some states have examined a form of rural triage. Prompted by concerns for the continued viability of all rural places, triage-style rural regional planning entails identifying those places with enough comparative advantage to survive successfully in the twenty-first century and then targeting centralized infrastructure and social investments toward these places. This is a continuation of what became of the TVA-style approach to regional planning.

The second approach is related, though more radical in concept. Known as the "Buffalo Commons" concept, it is regional planning writ large. The Buffalo Commons is a proposal for the future of the Great Plains, an area covering parts of 10 states. It argues that the original settlement of this region was a historical error. Ecologically, the region is ill adapted to extensive human settlement and intensive land use activities such as agriculture. Instead, the best use of the region is as prairie grazing ground and national recreation area. The advocates of the proposal do not suggest the literal evacuation of towns, villages and cities in the Great Plains region. Instead, they call for no extraordinary counter-measures to prevent what seems to be occurring as a result of economic, social and demographic transition, and conscious attention to reshaping the region as these transitions occur.

Because of the controversial nature of both of these approaches, neither has been adopted, and no alternative has emerged to fill the gap. As a result, little regional planning of substance occurs in rural areas between the coasts. In these places, the management of natural resources, such as farmland, forests and wetlands, and the future structure of the economy continue to be the domain of market forces and local planning, when such planning exists at all.

The Future of Regional Planning

The future of regional planning is murky. All efforts to undertake public planning in the U.S., regardless of geographic level or specific place, often become caught in the larger political dialogue. To the extent market-oriented forces command the rhetoric of politics, then public planning of all types is viewed with disfavor. It is seen as interventionist, disruptive, inefficient and unproductive. To the extent markets are perceived to fail, and the public interest and public benefits are depicted as explicitly threatened, then public planning can be undertaken, and is often viewed as a possible solution.

The future of regional planning in those parts of rural America that are growing, or likely to grow, could continue along the route of centralization. But even this is uncertain given the renewed sense of localism across the country. While citizens can rationalize the basis for centralization, they are increasingly concerned about ceding control for land use and environmental management decisions to levels of government that can be difficult for them to access and influence. It appears that there are instances where they prefer the anarchy of fragmented local control to the bureaucratization of centralized control.

With respect to the distant rural areas, there is reason to expect that most will continue to decline. This will be especially true to the extent that their fate is left to market forces. In places where planning does exist, it will be local rather than regional in structure. In part this will be due to the predominant underlying political and fiscal structure that favors inter-jurisdictional competition rather than cooperation.

Planning of all types is likely to be shaped by several social trends and forces throughout the U.S. In addition to a renewed sense of localism, these include widespread citizen activism, the impact of new information technology, and heightened conflict over private property rights.

Citizen activism brings more people with more types of articulated interests into the policy and planning process. Increasingly, citizens are convinced that their perspective on the public interest is the correct one, and they seem less willing to compromise, especially in an era of tight fiscal resources. The new information technology decentralizes access to specialized information resources. This allows citizen activists to develop more sophisticated analyses to support their positions, and to challenge the official positions put forth by planning agencies. Together, widespread citizen activism and the new information technology make planning processes less and less dependent upon experts and more overtly political.

Heightened conflict over private property rights may be the most prominent social trend to impact regional planning into the future. Proposals for regional planning are increasingly portrayed as attempts to diminish the private property rights of individual landowners. In turn, this is characterized as a threat to liberty, the structure of American democracy, and what citizenship means in the U.S. To the extent that this representation of regional planning prevails, it will be difficult to undertake any planning of any substance anywhere in the country. Unless the concept of regional planning can be reinvented to position it as a defender of private property rights and a contributor to liberty and democracy, it may have little future in the U.S. in general, and rural America in particular.

— *Harvey M. Jacobs and Edward J. Jepson, Jr.*

See also

Community; Community Capitals; Development, Asset-based; Development, Community and Economic; Sustainable Development ; Future of Rural America; Government; Policy, Rural Development; Settlement Patterns; Urbanization

References

Clawson, Marion. *New Deal Planning: The National Resources Planning Board*. Baltimore: Published for Resources for the Future by the Johns Hopkins University Press, 1981.

DeGrove, John M. *Planning Policy and Politics: Smart Growth and the States*. Cambridge, MA: Lincoln Institute of Land Policy, 2005.

Friedmann, John and Clyde Weaver. *Territory and Function: The Evolution of Regional Planning*. Los Angeles and Berkeley, CA: University of California Press, 1979.

Friedmann, John and Robin Bloch. "American Exceptionalism in Regional Planning, 1933-2000." *International Journal of Urban and Regional Research* 14 (1990): 576-601.

Jacobs, Harvey M., ed. *Who Owns America?: Social Conflict Over Property Rights*. Madison, WI: University of Wisconsin Press, 1998.

Jacobs, Harvey M., ed. *Private Property in the 21st Century: The Future of an American Ideal*. Northampton, MA: Edward Elgar Publishing, 2004.

Lapping, Mark B., Thomas L. Daniels, and John W. Keller. *Rural Planning and Development in the United States*. London, UK and New York, NY: Guilford Press, 1989.

McGranahan, David A. and Timothy R. Wojan. "The Creative Class: A Key to Rural Growth." *Amber Waves* 5: 2 (2007): 16-21.

Popper, Deborah E. and Frank J. Popper. "The Great Plains: From Dust to Dust." *Planning* (December 1987): 12-18.

Seznick, Philip. *TVA and the Grass Roots.* New York: Harper Torchbook, 1966.

Religion

"A unified system of beliefs and practices relative to sacred things" (Durkheim, 1947). Rural religion has been significantly altered by the general movement of American society to the city and the suburb. This change resulted in a precarious situation for the rural church. Nonetheless, rural religion survives in a somewhat unique form, perhaps to witness a revival as post-industrial society deconcentrates into nonmetropolitan areas.

The Uniqueness of Rural Religion

Religion takes many varied forms in the countryside from denominations to sects to cults. Rural religion and its varying forms have all been greatly impacted by the transition of American society from an agrarian to an industrial one in the nineteenth century, and now from an industrial to a global-oriented, post-industrial society. Rural religion must continuously adjust to these far-reaching changes. After reviewing the existing body of literature on rural religion, Goreham (1990) calls attention to the following themes into which this body of knowledge falls.

The economic, political and social dislocations brought about by the industrial and urban upheavals in the U.S. had a profound impact resulting in the decline of the rural church and its congregations. However, various denominational polities, theologies and congregational leaderships mediated this change from the broader society to the local country religious group.

The responses rural churches made to this massive social change varied along ideological fault lines present in these religious groups. Some groups advocated an activist position in the face of negative change, whereas others called for a renewed evangelistic fervor. The growth in consciousness that came about in reaction to these social changes led churches to define themselves in terms of their distinctiveness. Some have been content to see themselves simply as the "church in the country," but others noted their responsibility for stewardship of natural resources and the environment, responsibility to provide food to the hungry throughout the world, and responsibility to minister to a unique clientele.

Where this consciousness led to a unique role for the rural church, an accompanying development in a theology and philosophy of the rural church, the land, agriculture and rural life followed. These formulations ranged from seeing the land as a sacred trust to a need to protect and steward the land or to reduce world hunger and rural poverty.

Much of the writing on the rural church is devoted to the methods and techniques of ministering to people in a rural setting. As such, this body of thought and research has been concerned with how to conduct worship and liturgy, education, youth programs and the like.

A Short History of American Rural Religion

Religion was established in the U.S. basically as a small town and rural phenomenon. Although Europeans came to seek religious freedom, it was not long until they had established North American versions of the European theocratic states. The War of Independence and the creation of the American constitution set in motion forces that led to a struggle for souls largely fought on the emerging frontier. Thousands of open-country and small-town churches sprang up along the paths of exploration and settlement. After the home and family, religion and the church became the most influential components of the rural community.

While Protestants were establishing and re-establishing their denominations on the frontier, the Catholic Church was having a slow beginning in erecting its ecclesiastical structures in New England. However, Catholics following the Maryland model organized into house churches, stations and chapels. When priests could be secured, a central parish became established with an itinerant circuit-riding priest. As did Protestants, Catholics moved onto the frontier of Kentucky and beyond after independence from England. Here they came in contact with faith communities already established by the French and the Spanish.

With the Civil War, both Protestantism and Catholicism had to brace themselves for the onslaught of urbanization, massive immigration, and the depletion of the countryside of its population and resources. By the turn of the century, both were ripe for a rural church movement.

As the 1880s arrived, American denominations were becoming aware of the problems of doing church in the countryside. An impetus in doing something about them came from President Theodore Roosevelt's *Commission on Country Life*. This group felt that the problems of the country were basically moral and religious in nature and that the churches had a great potential power to deal with them. By the early twentieth century, the denominations began to organize themselves into a movement at the national and local levels cooperating with each other and with governmental, agricultural, community and educational institutions to become change agents of a spiritual, economical, social, political and educational sort. The agricultural landgrant colleges and rural sociology, as an applied academic discipline, were enlisted as trusted allies to remake the countryside. Various national organizations were formed to address rural concerns. For example, under the leadership of Bishop Edwin Vincent O'Hara, Catholics founded their own country church movement in the form of the National Catholic Rural Life Conference. This group worked to strengthen rural parishes and to keep Catholics on the family farm.

Change in American Society—Change in Rural Religion

All the while, the nation and the church were becoming more and more urban and suburban in orientation and approach. Huge numbers of immigrants swelled the urban population of Catholics well beyond their Protestant counterparts. This migration of peoples left the Catholic Church, more than ever, with a greater need to attend to and to focus on the churches of town and countryside.

More specifically, rural religious groups have been reacting for nearly a century to trends toward less and less retail and service activities in local villages and towns as shopping centers emerged in nearby cities and metropolitan areas. While the retail and perhaps manufacturing functions of the village declined, residential functions increased. Outside of these villages in the open country, there was a long-term trend for rural neighborhoods to disappear in the face of improved transportation, and for open-country churches, schools and stores to consolidate. Increasing standards of living, needs and wants turned the ruralite to the outside world. Forms of association in the countryside changed from simple to more complex ones where wider contacts and interests are fostered through a broad variety of special-purpose organizations. The family evolved such that its members participate as much with non-family as with family. There was, likewise, a movement toward community segmentation and away from community wholeness. Although neighborhoods in the vicinity of villages and towns tend to disappear first, new neighborhoods appear near cities and large towns, taking on a semi-suburban, more heterogeneous lifestyle enclave form of existence. And although rural communities were once villages with attached, interdependent neighborhoods, today these communities tend to have ill-defined boundaries and often blend in with the surrounding city. The development of modern transportation systems accelerated the tendency for rural religious organizations to become centralized in village or town.

Rural Religion in Decline?

As the rural population decreased in proportion to the urban population, a decline in the rural church has been a constant threat for rural people. The open-country churches died more rapidly than the village and town churches. Changes in transportation and social organization of the countryside have made it more difficult for the open-country church to survive. Where open-country and hamlet congregations do survive, they tend to exist in stable farming neighborhoods and where population shifts have been minimal.

Today the overwhelming numbers of people in rural churches are non-farmers. Non-farm rural persons do not always hold the same views as the farmer-members. There is thus a trend toward more heterogeneity among the membership, and frequently conflict develops between the traditional country churchgoer and the newcomers. Factors involved in the relative decline of the rural church are declining and shifting rural populations, overchurching, a declining sectarianism, a competing urban culture, and the loss of financial support from rural people. However, the long-term trend supports deconcentration of metropolitan population into nonmetropolitan areas. It is likely that two rural churches will emerge: one in areas of rural out-migration which will be driven by the "politics of decline" and the other in areas of rural in-migration which will be propelled by the "politics of growth."

Chronic Problems of the Rural Church

Typical problems encountered by rural and small-town churches have been the inability to maintain adequate programs. There has been a strong small church movement in recent times to provide knowledge and help to these churches in providing and maintaining adequate programs. However, rural churches tend to do many things in informal ways. This often looks like inadequate programming to city and suburban denominational counterparts. Consolidation of churches and programs between congregations often has been the solution to this problem. This is, however, not always a realistic possibility.

Another common problem encountered in rural churches has been inadequate financing. Small numbers and inconsistency of farm income make this a real problem for most religious communities. The every-member canvas and the Lord's Acre Program, allotting some portion of the crop or livestock to the church, are examples of attempted solutions.

Rural churches wrestled with getting, keeping and training ministers knowledgeable and sensitive to rural culture. Agricultural colleges, departments of rural sociology, town and country church departments of denominations, and sensitive seminary education have been used to overcome this difficulty in rural religious life.

A final problem most religious groups in the country dealt with has been adjustment to change. The continuing movement of rural people to metropolitan, city or town areas left these groups in a state of near-constant change. Likewise, more recent movement of urban/exurban populations into formerly country congregations leads to a new round of adjustments.

Roman Catholics and Protestants in the Countryside

The Roman Catholic Church in nonmetropolitan areas has been called an "overlooked giant." Such a phrase seems to apply also to the rural and small-town sector of Protestantism. Between 40 and 50 percent of all Catholic parishes, and 25 to 40 percent of all Catholics live outside cities of 50,000 or their incorporated suburbs. A study by the United Methodist Church (United Methodist Church, 1992) reveals that nearly two out of three Methodist congregations are small, and most are from rural and small town areas. The same is true of many other Protestant denominations that are generally more rural than Catholics.

A study of Roman Catholic parishes and their parishioners by Burkart and Leege (1988) revealed the general tendency for congregational life, in whatever locale, to be affected by the culture of the surrounding area. While noting that rural church members tend to be increasingly heterogeneous, other surveys still reveal ruralites, particularly those who farm, to be different in orientation and lifestyle. Their closeness to the land affects values about work, commitment, exercise and health, and religion. The Notre Dame Study, generaliza-

ble to rural and small-town Catholics in the U.S., probably applies also to Protestants in arguing that rural religious people tend to be more moralistic in the way that they view God, God-given laws, human nature, morals and ethics. This greater moralism, correlated with a greater conservatism, is reflected in attitudes toward change, the church and its policies and positions, and social issues. This would seem to indicate a greater religious orthodoxy as conceived by the sociologists of religion, Charles Glock and Rodney Stark. Data from the Notre Dame Study suggest that rural and town Catholics tend to view God more as a judge, unapproachable, mysterious and strict, a God that is creative but has also given humans clear-cut rules to follow. These same rural churchgoers are more inclined to relate directly to God as Father than to other mediators such as Christ, the Church, or their fellow Christians. The greater presence of Protestant groups such as Baptists and Methodists in the countryside perhaps predisposes Catholics to view God in this fashion. The tendency to avoid open conflict and a greater propensity to focus on tradition and the past means the rural person is less disposed to be high in Glock and Stark's social activism. Finally, these data on rural and small-town Catholics show individuals who say they experience God less directly in their lives than do their urban/suburban counterparts. It is not known if this would also apply to rural Protestants as their religious ideology would more predispose them toward the validity of religious experience. It is perhaps true that rural religious individuals place more emphasis upon religious codes rather than in experiencing God in deeper, more exotic ways.

Likewise, rural churchgoers probably experience a greater community through friendliness. The community may be a part of their religious experience or may be a part of their larger rural society. The closeness of their communities may account for a greater tendency toward ecumenism and boosterism.

This greater presence of community in the life of the rural resident usually manifests itself in a greater experience of informal social control. The impact of extended family and friends is stronger in the religious experience of ruralites.

Rural and town dwellers are less patient with any form of human mediation in their lives. This manifests itself in less tolerance for any hierarchical structures (ecclesiology) in their religious life and a greater informality in leadership patterns and parish programming.

Rural congregations or parishes approximate the sociological type of small-scaled organization. As such, tasks are less differentiated and structures of accountability less distinct. There are fewer positions and staff of all kinds, fewer formal programs, and a higher reliance on voluntarism.

Rural religion is somewhat unique with a different culture and a different set of social dynamics. As such, it is not just a smaller version of the urban or suburban church. As people of the country are more affected by the seasons and by events that are closer to nature, they traditionally have been interested more in integrating with nature than in using it. Persons from small-scaled communities have been nourished on stable and mutual relationships. Frequently, functional and personal roles overlap in the countryside. Relationships involve many segments of life; they are broad in scope. Rural residents are different from their urban counterparts, and their religious expression likewise differs.

Lastly, rural religion functions somewhat differently than religion in the city and suburb. It serves to integrate the ruralite into an already strong local non-religious community. However, there is evidence of not only anomic rural communities but demoralized congregations. To the degree that a strong rural community already exists, those in the country use religion less for community-building functions than do their urban and suburban counterparts who are more inclined to join religious organizations in an attempt to create a sense of community in an environment largely void of real community.

In a similar fashion, religious meaning is less salient to the person of town and countryside as it traditionally has been supplemented by a secular culture that values most of the same things found in religion. This does not imply that religious meaning and belonging are unimportant to individuals who live in the country. As rural dwellers can find meaning and belonging more readily in their secular environments, rural religion functions more to underpin rural community life. With the spread of urbanism, the functions of religion in the countryside more closely approximate those of the urban-global citizen, a fact that sometimes gives rise to a fundamentalist backlash.

Rural Religious Fundamentalism

Rural religion often has manifested itself in movements, sects and cults of various forms. One of the reactions to the late nineteenth-century integration of the country into the city and its industrial life has been religious fundamentalism. Fundamentalism is reinforced through reactions to the trend toward integration of the rural economy into the world economy. As noted above, rural religion tends to be conservative. But there has been a greater secularization and liberalization of urban religious groups. Accordingly, the strongholds of fundamentalism have generally been in rural areas and cities with a strong rural influence. To these groups the growth of science is often seen as developing at the expense of the Bible. The alleged evils of the city, and more recently, the perceived dangers of a global economy, tended to foster a more fundamentalistic view of religion. An additional factor would seem to be the longing for a more rural, community-based approach to religion found among many anomic urbanites transplanted from the country. Finally, as rural places tend to have less educated inhabitants than do urban places, fundamentalism is further reinforced. Contemporary groups such as state militias, the Posse Comitatus, agricultural "fundamentalists," and other apocalyptic groups often merge a religious fundamentalism with a strong political, economic and social conservatism.

Rural Religious Sects

Elmer Clark (1949) studied American religious sects, producing seven types of sectarian groups in his analysis. Various sect groups shall be mentioned here that have been prominent in rural American religion using David Moberg's (1984) classification of religious groups. First, the charismatic or Pentecostal sects seek special blessings and believe in manifestations such as speaking in tongues, visions, trances, dancing before the Lord and other experiences. Mormons would fit into this category. The Mormons and their splinter groups have had a significant impact on various regions of rural America. They are today one of the fastest growing religious groups in the U.S. Perhaps the "snake handling" religious groups of the Appalachian region of the U.S. would be a further manifestation of this religious tendency.

Second, Clark's communistic sects are religious groups that have withdrawn from society to practice some esoteric religious and economic ideologies. Often such sects are possible only if removed to the country. The Oneida Perfectionists, the Shakers, and the Amana colonies are representative rural groups.

A final category of Clark's typology of sects relevant to our discussion of rural religion is the legalistic or objectivist sects. These groups stress some definite rites or taboos, usually derived from the Bible, around which the life of the religious group forms. Some rural representatives of these groups would be the Mennonites, the Amish, and the Hutterites. These groups in varying degrees managed to preserve the rural way of life and religious expression.

Rural religion is different from urban religion. It conforms, at least in part, to the dictates of rural culture and life, and manifests itself in a religious organization with smaller social scale and a personal religiosity that is less differentiated. Rural religion enriches rural culture and diversity with yet another variation on the theme.

— *Gary Burkart*

See also

Agrarianism; Churches; Culture; Ethics; History, Rural; Jews in Rural America; Land Stewardship; Music; Social Movements; Theology of Land; Values of Residents

References

Andrews, David. *Ministry in the Small Church*. Kansas City, MO: Sheed and Ward, 1988.

Burkart, Gary, and Patricia O'Connell Killen. "A History of the Rural Catholic Church in the U.S." In *The Rural Parish: Retrieving Our Future*. Los Angeles, CA: Franciscan Communications, 1992.

Burkart, Gary, and David Leege. "Parish Life in Town and Countryside." Pp. 1-13 in *Report 13, The Notre Dame Study of Catholic Parish Life*. Notre Dame, IN: University of Notre Dame, 1988.

Clark, Elmer T. *The Small Sects in America*. Nashville, KY: Abingdon, 1949.

Durkheim, Emile. *The Elementary Forms of the Religious Life*. Glencoe, IL: Free Press, 1947.

Dudley, Carl and Douglas Walrath. *Developing Your Small Church's Potential*. Valley Forge, PA: Judson Press, 1988.

Goreham, Gary A. *The Rural Church in America: A Century of Writings—A Bibliography*. New York, NY: Garland, 1990.

Richard T. Schaefer and William N. Zellner. *Extraordinary Groups: An Examination of Unconventional Lifestyles*, 8th ed. Worth Publishers, 2007.

Judy, Marvin. *From Ivy Tower to Village Spire*. Dallas, TX: Southern Methodist University Printing, 1984.

Moberg, David. *The Church as a Social Institution*. Grand Rapids, MI: Baker Book House, 1984.

Quinn, Bernard. *The Small Rural Parish*. New York, NY: Glenmary Home Missioners, 1980.

U.S. Catholic Historical Society. "Catholic Rural Life." *U.S. Catholic Historian* 8, no. 3 (1989).

United Methodist Church Report. *Strengthening the Church with Small Membership*. New York, NY: General Board of Global Ministries, 1992.

Weissbach, Lee Shai. *Jewish Life in Small-Town America: A History*. New Haven, CT: Yale University Press, 2005.

Restaurants

Eating and drinking establishments that do business in communities with less than a population of 5,000 across the U.S. Restaurants in rural America historically played an important part in the social life of the community. They served as a place to provide nourishment for residents and travelers, and as a place where residents convened to share informal news and events of the community. Today rural restaurants serve vital economic and social roles in their communities. Many of these communities owe their survival to the existence of their restaurants. Although economic survival is often difficult for the restaurants, they continue to dot the landscape in communities across the country.

History

From the largest metropolitan area to the smallest unincorporated town, almost all will feature some type of restaurant. Americans seem to have a special relationship with their restaurants. The restaurant industry is resourceful (Anonymous, 1988). Diners will travel great distances to go to great restaurants, no matter where they are located (Anonymous, 1994). Restaurants have been, currently are, and will continue to be an important part of the American social experience.

Restaurants historically played an important part in the founding of America. Eating and drinking places were among the first businesses to appear in early settlements. These early restaurants, although far different from today's establishments, served an important role in the social life of the community. Friends and neighbors gathered for social interaction and to exchange news. These early restaurants were a focal point for the operation of the early community. They brought people together to share topics of importance to the whole community.

When Americans began to move West, restaurants again played an important part in communities (Katsignis and Porter, 1983). Inns and taverns developed along trails and rail lines that were used to open the country to westward migration. These establishments' immediate role was to provide meals and lodging to early pioneers. However, they also served as focal points to spread important social events and news.

Roles in Today's Society

Restaurants today look much different from their predecessors. They now are part of a large industry that supports the economic base of American society. Some establishments focus on quality food and quick service. At the other end of the spectrum are restaurants that provide a high level of personalized service and gourmet dining experiences. They focus on a leisurely pace that pampers their guests. Between these two extremes are a multitude of other types of restaurants.

Today's restaurants play differing roles based on their location. Large city restaurants and rural restaurants are similar in providing basic product and service to their guests, even though the primary reason for going to a restaurant is to eat. However, beyond this, the roles played by the restaurants vary greatly. The remainder of this article will examine the role that restaurants play in rural society.

Role of Rural Restaurants

Why are restaurants present in rural communities? Why do restaurants prevail and grow in a community where many retail segments have ceased to operate? There are at least three important reasons rural restaurants exist: economic, social and survival.

Economic. The most obvious role of rural restaurants is based on the economic impact for several constituents: restaurant owner/operators, restaurant employees, the community at large and other retail outlets. First, many restaurants in suburban and metropolitan areas are owned by one party and operated by a separate manager. Whereas the manager derives his or her economic well-being from a particular restaurant, the owner is involved in more than one restaurant operation. Their economic base is diversified so that the success of one restaurant is not as significant for economic survival. Rural restaurants generally are owned and operated by the same people. The owner/operator may be a husband and wife team, or may be either or one singularly. Where either the husband or wife operate the restaurant, the other generally holds other employment. The economic success of the operator is directly tied to the restaurant. The operators are in business to make money. The restaurant's success will determine the economic level of its operators.

Second as the operators make a living from the restaurant, the same is true for restaurant employees.

This is not universal to all rural restaurants since some may be operated solely by the owners or in conjunction with nonpaid family members. However, for those who use paid employees, employees count on the restaurant for economic success. If the restaurant ceases to exist, their place of employment ceases to exist. With a chronic shortage of job opportunities, the economic impact may go beyond the individual employee to the community at large.

A third area of economic impact of a rural restaurant is the community in which it exists. The restaurant pays taxes to the community and helps support the economic infrastructure of the community.

Fourth, a rural restaurant impacts the economic health of other retail establishments in the community. Many rural people have the unique characteristic of tending to support local businesses first. So, any other retail business that provides necessary products and services to the restaurant is economically impacted by the presence of that restaurant.

Restaurants play a significant role in the economic health of an area. Although a rural community is not totally dependent on a restaurant, blending its business with other rural businesses can enhance the economic well-being of the community. It can be argued that all restaurants play the same role in any community; however, the importance of this particular type of business is what sets it aside. Restaurants come and go in cities with little effect on the economic condition of the city. However, in a rural setting the presence or absence of a restaurant has a larger economic impact.

Social. One of the most unique roles of restaurants in rural settings is the social role.

Although groups of friends may gather for social occasions in any restaurant, the social role of rural restaurants goes far beyond this function. Restaurants serve as the social "nerve" center of rural communities. Groups of rural people discuss in the local restaurant all aspects of community life. From political situations to social or personal situations, all topics may be covered in these groups. Although these groups' discussions may be dismissed as local gossip, a closer examination reveals at least two important functions for this activity. First, rural residents may be more independent and individualistic; they often shun organized meetings. Many of the formal meetings used to conduct the city's business will not work in a rural community. Their informal gatherings serve as substitutes to inform and involve town members in town operation. Second, informal social groups serve as forums to exchange personal information among the residents. The rural community disseminates information through local newspapers and media and through conversation. Rural people are genuinely concerned about their neighbors, but may not see them on a regular basis. The social activities that occur in the restaurant can fill the role of providing this information.

It is unlikely that another business could fill this role as well as the rural restaurant, given people's nature. Many people converse more freely if food and drink are involved. Nearly all social meetings center around eating. The rural restaurant is the only business that can naturally fulfill this important function.

Survival. The third role of a rural restaurant is closely associated with the preceding two. Restaurants provide survival to many segments of the community. Older patrons frequent the restaurant on a daily basis because they depend on the food for physical survival. Political rallies, field trips and other formal social activities often are held in or in conjunction with the local restaurant. These formal functions are important to the survival of the subgroups in the community. The survival of these groups would be made more difficult if the restaurant was not there.

The community's survival itself may be jeopardized without the presence of a restaurant in that the restaurant contributes to community financial survival. Restaurants attract visitors and guests to the town, thus amplifying the economic benefits. A more important survival role of the restaurant is the continued presence of community organization. The restaurant serves as a place of centered focus for the community, a place where individuals gather informally and formally to reaffirm their existence within the community.

The roles of restaurants are varied; they contribute to their rural community in numerous and important ways. Continual financial pressures are exerted on these businesses. They are not easy to operate, yet are essential to community survival. Without restaurants, the quality of rural life most certainly would be diminished.

— *James L. Groves*

See also

Community; Community, Sense of; Culture; Employment

References

Anderson, Joanne M. *Small-Town Restaurants in Virginia.* Winston-Salem, NC: John F. Blair Publisher, 2004.

Anonymous. "Out-of-the-way Restaurants Have to Try Harder." *Nations Restaurant News* 28, no. 44 (1994): 11, 84.

Baraban, Regina S. and Joseph F. Durocher *Successful Restaurant Design*, 2nd ed. Hoboken, NJ: Wiley, 2001.

Katsignis, C. and M. Porter. *The Bar and Beverage Book.* New York, NY: Wiley and Sons, 1991.

Lundberg, D.E. *The Hotel and Restaurant Business.* 4th ed. New York, NY: Van Nostrand Reinhold, 1984.

Lundberg, D.E. and J.R. Walker. *The Restaurant From Concept to Operation.* 2nd ed. New York, NY: Wiley and Sons, 1993.

Miller, Daniel. *Starting a Small Restaurant*, Revised Edition. Boston, MA: Harvard Common Press, 2006.

Mixon, J.M. *Hotel & Restaurant Industries: An Information Sourcebook.* Phoenix, AZ: Oryx Press, 1988.

Powers, Tom, Jo Marie Powers, Clayton W. Barrows, and National Restaurant Association Educational Foundation. *Introduction to the Hospitality Industry*, 5th ed. Hoboken, NJ: John Wiley & Sons, 2002.

Retail Industry

Establishments engaged in selling merchandise and service for personal or household consumption. Migrations and changes in the age distribution are processes that influence the evolution of rural retailing. Historically, in- and out-migration flows affected the viability of retailing in rural communities by changing the threshold level of demand for rural businesses. Currently, changes in the age distribution of the population affect the structure of retailing in rural communities by changing the composition of the consumption bundle.

Introduction

Rural America is continually adjusting to new circumstances and conditions in an evolutionary process. Much of rural America's history is a story of population movement—immigrants coming to America, people migrating to the new Western frontiers, communities growing from the perpetual procession of new farms, and then community decline as rural peoples migrated into urban areas in search of opportunity. The perpetual shifting of population into and out of rural America affected the occupational mix, age composition, family organization, political character and structure of retailing in rural communities.

The ever-changing nature of rural America is part of a natural progression of events that continues to affect the character of retailing in rural America. Improved transportation made possible by hard-surfaced roads, trucks and automobiles increased rural mobility and affected rural shopping patterns. More recent changes in the retail distribution system, exemplified by Wal-Mart, mark a trend toward larger retail outlets offering a broader array of goods at one store. The post-World War II changes in mobility and the retail distribution system are important recent supply factors that coincide with a longer-run demographic process affecting the demand for retailing in rural America.

Two pre-eminent demographic processes affecting rural communities are migration patterns and transitions in the age distribution. Both processes greatly affect the growth, stability and decline of retailing activity in rural communities. Historically, in- and out-migration flows affected the aggregate level of demand for retailing in rural communities. Currently, changes in the age composition of the rural population are a principal demand factor affecting the structure of retailing in rural communities.

Historical Process

Two distinct periods characterized by diametrically opposed demographic processes can be identified in rural America. The initial period was one of a massive in-migration of a relatively young, child-bearing aged population into rural America. The subsequent period was one of a substantial out-migration of child-bearing aged peoples from parts of rural America.

The initial period gave rise to a classic community in rural America. The Classic Era lasted from the mid-nineteenth century to about 1940. The subsequent period, or Post-Classic Era, began about 1940 and has persisted into current times. The diametric migration patterns and age compositions between the two eras greatly affected the structure of retailing in rural communities.

The Classic Era was stimulated by the 1862 Homestead Act and other land laws designed to develop the largest portion of rural America. The total rural population in the country increased from 25.2 million to 56.5 million between 1860 and 1935. The increasing rural population provided the threshold level of demand necessary to develop thousands of viable downtown family retail businesses. The Classic Era featured a viable rural economy with thousands of intact communities of all sizes performing a total array of social and economic functions, including a bustling family-owned and -operated retail business district.

The Post-Classic Era began with the Great Depression and was accelerated during the post-World War II urban boom. The simultaneous rapid capitalization of rural agriculture and urban manufacturing stimulated a massive out-migration of the farm population, resulting in the number of farm operators decreasing from 6.8 million in 1935 to less than two million in 1992. Although, the total rural population stabilized at about 60 million, the spatial and demographic distributions of the rural population changed dramatically during the period.

Spatially, the apparent stabilization of the rural population occurred adjacent to urban areas. The total rural population in the U.S. increased by three million persons during the 1980s. Over one-third of the increase (896,805 persons) occurred in the 10 most urban states, as opposed to a 1 percent increase in the 10 most rural states.

Demographically, whereas the total number of persons defined as rural changed very little, there has been a significant change in the age distribution of the rural population. The number of children living in rural areas decreased by 25 percent from 23 million to 17 million during the Post-Classic Era. Concurrent with the decrease of school-aged children, the elderly population increased 70 percent from 4.4 million to 7.5 million in rural areas. The tremendous exodus of child-bearing adults and children from rural America profoundly impacted the social and economic functions of rural communities.

The Post-Classic Era for rural America is a period of sustained stagnation or deterioration for thousands of small communities. Two of the most obvious consequences have been school consolidations and stressed downtown retailing sectors. The rural population no longer provides the threshold level of demand necessary to sustain viable small local schools or retail businesses in many communities. The Post-Classic Era features rural communities that no longer contain the total array of social and economic functions performed during the Classic Era.

Implications for the Future

One of the most obvious national demographic trends is the growth in the number of elderly Americans. The number of persons 65 years of age and older increased from 3.1 million at the turn of the twentieth century to 31.1 million in 1990. The Census Bureau predicts a 14 percent increase in the number of persons 65 years of age and older by the year 2010.

The national trend toward an older population is accelerated in rural America. Nationally, 34 states gained rural population (2.7 million) and 18 lost rural population (.5 million) during the last decade. In the 18 states that continue to lose rural population, the population of persons over the age of 65 increased from 11 to 14 percent. Rural communities already reached the projected increase for the county in 2010 (14 percent), implying that rural communities are leading the nation in the demographic transition to an elderly population.

Not only is the elderly population rapidly increasing in rural areas losing population, but the spatial distribution of the elderly population is becoming more concentrated in smaller communities. The proportion of elderly population is inversely related to city size, with urban places containing the lowest percentage, 14.8 percent, and the smallest of communities, 1,000 or less total population, housing the highest percentage, 22.3 percent.

The continuing demographic transition to an older population will continue to affect communities in rural America throughout the century. Less than 2 percent of all elderly are expected to move out of the county of current residence and less than 1 percent are expected to move out of the state of current residence (Taeuber, 1992). The expected increase in the elderly population in rural America will have a fiscal impact on local tax revenues and consequently an impact on local public service expenditures (Glasgow and Reeder, 1990; Hoppe, 1991).

Personal consumption expenditures among the aging population in rural areas will have a significant impact on the retail sector of community (Heinte, 1976; Happel et al., 1988; Hass et al., 1990; Miller, 1993). The evidence indicates that as the rural population continues to age, the propensity to shop locally will increase in smaller communities (Henderson, 1994). The result implies less relative retail and service business decline among the smallest communities (total population less than 1,000) in the future than during the initial phase of the Post-Classic Era.

The impact on rural retailing can also be expected to differ by type of business. The relative frequency of different types of retail establishments within the retail distribution system will continue to adjust as the level and source of income (retirement versus wage and salary) continues to adjust in rural areas (Henderson, 1990). Some rural business types (e.g., drugstores) could flourish in the future, whereas others (e.g., building materials) could continue to decline (Henderson, 1994).

Implications for Retailing in Rural Communities

Historically, population size and age distribution influenced retail business activity in a community. All rural retail businesses have a threshold customer base necessary to cover costs and maintain a profit. During the Classic Era, in-migration translated into an increased customer base, excess demand, the creation of new retail businesses, and the growth of viable downtown retail business districts. During the Post-Classic Era, out-migration rendered a decreased customer base, insufficient demand, the dissolving of existing retail businesses, and the stagnation or decline of downtown retailing in many rural communities. Both processes continue in numerous contemporary rural communities.

Currently, the continuing demographic transition away from a family-based consumer patronage to an elderly consumer base is causing a change in the composition of the consumer shopping bundle demanded from rural retailers. The transformation in the consumption bundle directly affects the viability of the existing rural retail sector by changing the mix of goods and services demanded. Shifts in the total amount spent on each good in the consumption bundle and changes in the relative proportion of income spent on a particular good in the consumption bundle affect the viability of specific retail businesses offering the goods.

The table illustrates the difference between the consumption bundle across various age groups for selected goods. The consumption bundle varies by age cohort, which implies that a change in the age distribution of the consumer base affects the sales and profit level for individual rural businesses. Changes in sales and profits for individual businesses eventually will alter the structure of the rural retail sector by making some business types more profitable than others. Preliminary research implies that grocery stores, eating places, drugstores, home furnishing stores, and building material stores will be especially affected (Henderson, 1994).

One conspicuous difference in the consumption bundle by age is that persons between the ages of 35 and 54 spend nearly twice as much per year as do persons 65 years of age or older. The rural cohort between the ages of 35 and 54 are predominately families, complete with dependent children, which require a higher level of aggregate family spending. The age cohort of persons over the age of 65 are typically smaller households, two or less, with a lower level of aggregate household spending. As rural America becomes an older population with smaller household sizes, the total

Age Comparisons of the Consumption Bundle, in Dollars (2006). Based on Consumer Expenditure Survey. Data are averages for the non-institutional population and are out-of-pocket expenditures.

	Age					
	Under 25 years	25-34 years	35-44 years	45-54 years	55-64 years	65+ years
Total	28,181	47,582	57,476	57,563	50,789	35,058
Food	3,919	6,104	7,331	7,328	6,132	4,319
Food at home	1,946	3,186	4,128	4,036	3,518	2,659
Food away from home	1,973	2,918	3,203	3,292	2,613	1,659
Alcoholic beverages	473	657	496	612	477	263
Housing	9,355	17,139	20,303	18,377	16,529	11,787
Shelter	5,923	10,725	12,445	10,896	9,199	6,281
Owned dwellings	1,405	6,132	8,965	8,024	6,866	4,210
Rented dwellings	4,315	4,286	2,938	2,064	1,460	1,630
Other lodging	203	307	541	807	873	441
Utilities, fuels, & public services	1,781	3,093	3,854	3,912	3,640	3,008
Natural gas	186	421	559	598	563	507
Electricity	693	1,133	1,419	1,445	1,362	1,154
Fuel oil & other fuels	30	73	157	150	167	176
Telephone	722	1,129	1,271	1,269	1,115	770
Water & other public services	150	337	449	449	433	400
Household operations	374	1,130	1,380	793	934	720
Personal services	213	706	811	192	221	105
Other household	161	424	569	601	714	615
Housekeeping supplies	295	531	761	727	739	554
Laundry & cleaning supplies	83	155	189	160	165	112
Other household products	149	266	413	369	369	290
Postage & stationery	64	111	159	198	205	153
Household furnishings	982	1,660	1,864	2,050	2,017	1,224
Household textiles	56	124	140	175	207	1,663
Furniture	350	510	536	569	462	274
Floor coverings	24	35	40	48	80	47
Major appliances	104	194	272	285	295	208
Small appliances, misc. wares	52	109	113	149	111	79
Misc. household equipment	396	687	762	824	862	454
Apparel and services	1,464	2,152	2,368	2,176	1,892	930
Men and boys	294	544	575	538	400	207
Women and girls	554	737	922	913	835	416
Children under 2	130	187	128	72	66	20
Footwear	251	371	404	343	288	133
Other apparel and services	234	313	338	311	303	154
Transportation	5,667	9,047	9,977	10,111	8,676	5,658
Vehicle purchases (net outlay)	2,396	3,912	4,057	3,983	3,165	2,301
Gasoline and motor oil	1,637	2,346	2,636	2,693	2,288	1,359
Public transportation	221	448	559	616	584	414
Health care	706	1,652	2,284	2,757	3,556	4,331
Entertainment	1,348	2,237	2,966	2,770	2,666	1,584
Personal care products & services	348	547	688	696	586	475
Reading	46	82	112	133	147	136
Education	1,259	710	857	1,736	662	219
Tobacco products, etc.	286	318	354	433	370	171
Miscellaneous	388	615	943	971	1,105	762

Source: U.S. Bureau of Labor Statistics, Consumer Expenditures, 2006.

expenditures per household can be expected to decrease. Less aggregate spending per household means decreased aggregate retail sales, declining retail business numbers, and continued stagnation or decline of downtown retailing in some rural communities. The negative effect of decreased aggregate household spending will be offset by the positive effect of the expected increase in local spending associated with elderly populations in the smallest of rural communities.

Differences in the consumption bundle by age vary by category of consumption. Health care is the one part of the consumption bundle where the proportion of total expenditures increases with age. The proportion of the consumption bundle spent on health care monotonically increases from a low of 2.4 percent for persons under the age of 25 to a high of 12 percent for persons over the age of 65. Conversely, the proportion of the consumption bundle spent on transportation decreases from a high of 20.9 percent for persons under the age of 25 to a low of 15.6 percent of the budget for persons over the age of 65.

The total cumulative effect on retailing in rural communities will be significant with millions of additional dollars being spent on goods in some sectors (e.g., health care) and millions less being spent on goods in other sectors (e.g., transportation). Continuing changes in the age composition of the rural population can be expected to change the composition of the consumption bundle of the consumer base, and continue to affect the sales and profit levels for particular rural businesses.

The future distribution of retail businesses by type in rural America can be expected to continue to adjust to the changes in consumer expenditures and demands of rural consumers. At the regional level, the dynamic nature of the consumer base will continue to affect the choice of shopping destination, further supplementing the growth of larger rural retail centers adjacent to other stagnating or declining smaller communities (Henderson, 1992). At the community level, some business types will do better than others as the configuration of retail outlets in rural communities continues to adjust to the changing rural market conditions. At the individual retail business level, the product mix of individual retailers can also be expected to adjust in accordance with changes in the rural consumption bundle associated with the aging rural population.

— *David A. Henderson*

See also

Consumerism; Development, Community and Economic; Entrepreneurship; Policy, Economic; Service Industries; Settlement Patterns; Taxes; Trade Areas; Urbanization

References

Bureau of Labor Statistics. "Table 3. Age of Reference Person, Average Annual Expenditures and Characteristics, Consumer Expenditure Survey, 2006." Washington, DC: U.S. Department of Labor, Bureau of Labor Statistics, 2006. Available online at: http://www.bls.gov/cex/2006/Standard/age.pdf.

Glasgow, N. and R. Reeder. "Economic and Fiscal Implications of Nonmetropolitan Retirement Migration." *The Journal of Applied Gerontology* 9 (1990): 433-451.

Happel, S., T. Hogan, and E. Pflanz. "The Economic Impact of Elderly Winter Residents in the Phoenix Area." *Research on Aging* 10 (1988): 119-123.

Heinte, K. *Retirement Communities for Adults Only*. New Brunswick, NJ: State University of New Jersey, 1976.

Henderson, D. "Rural Retail Sales and Consumer Expenditure Functions." *Journal of Agricultural Economic Research* 42 (1990): 27-34.

Henderson, D. "Estimates of Retiree Spending in Retail and Service Sectors of Community." *Journal of the Community Development Society* 25 (1994): 259-276.

Henderson, D., L. Tweeten, and M. Woods. "A Multicommunity Approach to Community Impacts: The Case of the Conservation Reserve Program." *Journal of the Community Development Society* 23 (1992): 88-102.

Hoppe, R. *The Role of the Elderly's Income in Rural Development*. Rural Development Research Report 80. Washington, DC: U.S. Department of Agriculture, ERS, 1991.

Miller, Nancy J., Terry L. Besser, LuAnn R. Gaskill, and Stephen G. Sapp. "Community and Managerial Predictors of Performance in Small Rural US Retail and Service Firms." *Journal of Retailing and Consumer Services* 10, no. 4 (July 2003): 215-230.

Miller, W.P. *Economic and Fiscal Impacts of Bella Vista Village, Arkansas*. Fayetteville, AR: University of Arkansas, Cooperative Extension Service, 1993.

Taeuber, C. "Sixty-five Plus in America." *Current Population Reports*, Special Studies P23-178. Washington, DC: Bureau of the Census, 1992.

Vias, Alexander C. "Bigger stores, more stores, or no stores: paths of retail restructuring in rural America. *Journal of Rural Studies* 20, no 3 (July 2004): 303-318.

Rice Industry

Individuals and firms involved in the production, distribution, marketing, processing, and sale of rice and rice by-products to domestic and international consumers. This article provides an overview of the rice industry. The key components of the rice industry discussed are production, government programs, marketing, economic impacts on rural economies, and current industry trends.

Introduction

Rice is one of the most important foods because it accounts for over 22 percent of global caloric intake.

World per capita consumption averages approximately 140 pounds annually, but exceeds 300 pounds in some Asian countries. Rice is consumed primarily as a white milled grain but is also used in a variety of other forms (e.g., flour, noodles, breakfast cereals, beer, and animal and pet feed). The U.S. produces less than two percent of the world's rice but has been the third largest rice exporter over the past decade. China and India produce approximately 68 percent of the world's rice and all Asian countries account for 92 percent of the world's production and consumption.

Rice production ranks as the seventh highest value field crop in the U.S., but it ranks in value among the top three field crops in Arkansas and Louisiana. Other states that produce rice include California, Mississippi, Texas, Missouri, and Florida. Both long grain (indica type) and medium/short grain rice (japonica) are produced in the U.S. U.S. rice consumption increased rapidly in recent years from 14 pounds per capita in 1984 to 30 pounds per capita in 2006. This growth has been driven by increasing dietary and nutritional concerns, and rapidly growing Asian and Hispanic populations who have a strong preference for rice. Higher-valued uses of rice and rice co-products (e.g., starch, proteins, oil, and fiber) are expanding rapidly. The baking industry uses rice starch, oil, and stabilized rice bran as food ingredients. Oil extracted from rice bran makes a superior cooking oil. Farmers use rice bran for animal feed, and rice hulls are used as fuel fodder to generate energy or for poultry litter. Rice hull ash can be made into an excellent absorbent (used in cleaning oil and chemical spills) and kitty litter.

Only seven percent of rice production is traded internationally compared to 18 percent for wheat. Thailand, the U.S., Vietnam, China, India, and Pakistan are typically the major exporters of rice, and together account for 85 percent of all rice exports. Major rice importers are the European Union, Saudi Arabia, Iran, Iraq, Brazil, Mexico, and Sub-Sahara Africa. The U.S. exports about 50 percent of its rice and consequently, U.S. rice prices are primarily determined by global supply and demand conditions. Important customers for U.S. rice exports are Saudi Arabia and other Middle-Eastern countries, Canada, Mexico, and Europe. The U.S. imports about thirty percent of its total food rice consumption, of which most is scented or aromatic rice (jasmine or basmati).

U.S. long grain rice. Photograph by Keith Weller. Source: USDA-ARS

Production

The location of rice production in the U.S. is primarily influenced by climatic and topographical requirements. Ideally, these requirements include adequate water, relatively high air and soil temperatures, adequate solar radiation, the absence of destructive storms, a moderately long growing season, relatively dry conditions during the ripening season, and land whose grade does not exceed one degree with a subsoil hardpan that inhibits percolation. The latter facilitates uniform flooding and drainage as required during the growing season. The plentiful availability of either surface or ground water for maintaining flood conditions on the rice land is the most important factor influencing the location of rice production. Flooded conditions provide benefits of weed control, improved water and air microclimates, and a root zone environment well-suited for rice culture. Rice typically needs 110 to 150 growing days with abundant sunshine and average temperatures between 68 and 100 degrees Fahrenheit. Temperatures below 59 degrees Fahrenheit retard seedling development, slow tiller formation, delay reproductive growth, and consequently reduce grain yields.

From its beginning in the early 17th century Virginia, U.S. rice production slowly spread along the southern Atlantic coastal plain, across the Appalachians into Kentucky and Tennessee, along the Gulf Coast, and up the lower Mississippi River (Mississippi Delta). In the Antebellum Period, most slave-holding states grew some quantities of rice, with South Carolina accounting for the bulk of production. By the end of the 19th century, the Mississippi Delta, the prairies of southwest Louisiana, and the Gulf Coast of Texas produced the bulk of U.S. rice. Louisiana become the largest rice producer in 1890. Rice production began in the Central Valley of California in 1912. During much of the 20th century, Arkansas, California, Louisiana, and Texas produced similar quantities of rice. Since the early 1970s, however, Arkansas became the largest producer with about 42 percent of production. Nearly all current production is located in California (Sacramento Valley) and the five southern states of Arkansas, Louisiana, Mississippi, Missouri, and Texas.

Rice has relatively high production costs per acre compared to other grains. The national average cost per acre in 2006 was $755, of which $415 was operating cost. Considerable differences exist for total costs across the production regions from a high for California of $977 per acre to $622 for the non-delta Arkansas region. However, yields in California are typically 5 percent higher than the U.S. average. This yield advantage helps California to be competitive on a per hundredweight (cwt) cost basis. Much of the higher production cost for rice compared to other crops is associated with irrigation, especially creating and maintaining levees for continual flooding. In addition to equipment normally used for soybean production, a common rotation crop in the South, rice production requires a levee plow, levee gates, a landplane, grain carts, and additional trucks for hauling. Disease control is also a major cost because of the humid conditions caused by continual flooding. Aside from production costs, profitability or competitiveness is also determined by yields, prices, and alternative crops. Some areas, such as Texas and about 400,000 acres of land in California, have such impermeable soils that they are only suitable for rice production. Most southern states have a good alternative crop in soybeans.

Returns to rice producers have included market sales and direct government payments. Between 2002 and 2006, annual average market prices have fluctuated between $4 and $10 per cwt. Producers also received government deficiency payments (the difference between a target price of $10.71 per cwt and the higher of the market price or the government loan rate of $6.50 per cwt plus a direct payment of $2.35 per cwt). Gross returns, excluding government payments have fluctuated between $281 to $647 per acre for the period between 2002 and 2006. Differences in gross returns result from different yields and prices received. Within any marketing year, prices received by individual farmers vary considerably depending on the rice type (long, medium, and short grain), rice grade, and quality characteristics. Traditionally, long grain rice received a premium over medium and short grain rice due to stronger market demand. However, the price premium favored medium grain over the past several years because of increased demand for japonica rice by Japan and South Korea as a result of the WTO agreement to liberalize global rice trade. Quality attributes of rice affect its price. Rough rice (rice in hulls) grades are adjusted based on foreign matter, heat damage, red rice (weed), and chalky kernels. Milled rice is graded on the basis of the percentage of broken kernels, foreign matter, red rice, chalky kernels, and color.

Government Rice Programs

The U.S. rice farm program for the period of 2002 through 2007 contained three sets of policy instruments to support prices and incomes of rice producers. These included price supports through a price floor, known as the nonrecourse loan rate, and income supports through direct payments and counter-cyclical payments. Due to relatively favorable target prices compared to market prices, participation in the rice program typically attracted over 94 percent of eligible rice production. The average annual cost since 2002 has been approximately $920 million. This accounted for approximately 16 percent of the gross income of U.S. rice producers since 2002.

Marketing and Consumption

Rice is harvested in the U.S. between August and November. The grain at harvest typically has a moisture content of 16 to 24 percent and must therefore be dried to a desired level of 13 percent. The harvested rough rice grain is dried in either on-farm drier facilities or in large commercial drier elevators. Rough rice remains in storage until mill orders are received. Rice must be milled before it can be consumed. The dried rough rice is processed at the mill by cleaning, sorting by size, and removal of the hull and the bran layers. White milled rice is the most common form of processed rice, however it can also be parboiled, precooked, or left as brown rice with the bran layer intact. Once milling is complete the rice and by-products (hulls and bran) enter domestic and export market channels.

Producers have several alternative pricing methods for their rough rice: cooperative pooling, private auction, direct contracting, and hedging on the futures market. Each producer chooses the pricing mechanism that best suits his or her payment and risk preference. Farmer cooperatives represent a significant segment of the U.S. rice industry. They are particularly important in Arkansas and California and are fully vertically integrated from the farm to the domestic and export distribution channels.

Domestic use of U.S. rice flows through three distinct channels. Direct food use by households, restaurants, and institutional kitchens in marketing year 2004-2005 accounted for 53 percent of domestic use. Processors of breakfast cereals, baby foods, package mixes, rice cakes, pet foods, soups, and candy used 30 percent of the domestic shipments. The third domestic use is by the beer industry, which incorporates rice as a fermentable carbohydrate adjunct. The brewery industry purchased 17 percent of the domestic market. The domestic processor and direct food use segments grew consistently over the past decade whereas beer use has declined. Dietary changes in the U.S. that favor complex carbohydrates such as rice, a growing demand for ethnic foods, and convenience in preparation are expected to be factors that contribute to further growth in the domestic rice market.

Exports of U.S. rice are important to the global supply and demand balance. Whereas the U.S. produces less than two percent of the world's rice, it accounted for 12 percent of world rice exports since 2000. The U.S. ranked fourth, behind Thailand, Vietnam and India as a leading rice exporter since 2000. U.S. export shipments are made to over 80 countries but the dominant customers include the Middle East countries, the European Union, Canada, Central America, the Caribbean and Mexico. As a result of the Uruguay Round WTO agreement on rice trade liberalization, Japan has also become an important buyer of U.S. rice. The world rice trade is a relatively small percent of world rice production and consumption compared with other grain markets. Total world rice trade accounts for only seven percent of world production and consumption. Therefore year-to-year shortfalls and surpluses can result in extreme swings in the quantity traded and prices. For instance, a shortfall in the global rice crop in 2007 marketing year has caused U.S. long grain export prices to move quickly from $395 per metric ton in August 2007 to over $750 per metric ton by April 2008. The volatility of rice trade and prices is caused by several key factors, including: (1) the concentration of production in Southeast Asia, which is subject to an unpredictable monsoon climate, (2) protectionist trade policy for rice production to achieve food security in countries where rice is the main staple food, and (3) market segmentation based upon differences in rice types and qualities.

Economic Impacts of Rice Production

The concentration of rice production in the U.S. means that adjustments by the industry are vitally important to the local input markets, land prices, labor markets, and related marketing industries. Because rice production and processing is highly capital intensive and specialized, changes in production can have pronounced effects on the local economies that depend on the rice industry.

Estimates of the economic impact of rice for the State of Arkansas were developed in 1994 (Department of Commerce). Since Arkansas production accounts for approximately 49 percent of the total U.S. output, these estimates are likely to represent the entire industry. The annual farm level value of rough rice sales in Arkansas averaged $750 million. Additional economic activities associated with the input, milling, wholesale, and retailing of the rice industry accounts for an additional $1,150 million for a total economic impact on the state economy of $1.9 billion.

Trends in the Industry

The U.S. rice industry is dynamic, highly integrated, and specialized. Significant changes in government programs, international competition, and changes in U.S. consumer diets bring about changes in the location, size, and economic characteristics of the rice industry. The rice sector has been relatively more dependent on government price and income supports. Due to the high cost of producing rice relative to alternatives, notably soybeans and feed grains, a reduction in rice production is expected in areas where these alternatives are competitive.

The domestic market is expected to grow and compete for the reduced domestic rice supply, thereby reducing U.S. rice exports. The competitive position of U.S. rice on world markets will be expected to remain strong in high quality markets such as Europe, the Middle East, Central America, Mexico and Japan. The

World Rice Exports

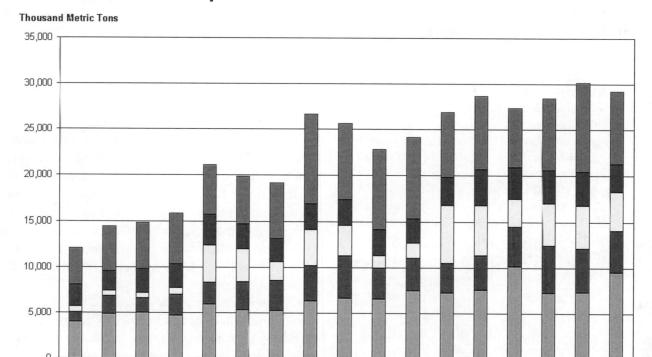

expected downsizing will impact not only on farm input markets, which are oriented to rice production, such as specialized equipment, but the U.S. rice milling industry will also be expected to adjust. The U.S. rice milling industry operated in a very dynamic environment over the past two decades. It experienced a period of expansion during the 1970s, followed by a period of down-sizing in the 1980s and ownership restructuring in the 1990s. As the rice industry moves into an environment of even greater market-orientation and less government intervention, the U.S. rice industry will experience further elimination of existing mills and a trend toward greater market concentration as fewer firms survive the challenges ahead. The industry must continue to improve efficiency if it is to maintain its share in the domestic and international markets.

— *Eric J. Wailes*

See also

Agricultural Programs; Cooperatives; Irrigation; Marketing; Policy, Agricultural; Soil; Trade, International

References

Childs, N. and Janet Livezey. *Rice Backgrounder*. Outlook Report No. (RCS-200601), December 2006.

Department of Commerce. "Fact Sheet–Value of Rice Production to Arkansas." Mimeo. 1994.

Dethloff, Henry C. *A History of the American Rice Industry, 1685-1985*. College Station, TX: Texas A&M University Press, 1988.

Food and Agriculture Policy Research Institute (FAPRI). *FAPRI 2008 U.S. and World Agricultural Outlook*. FAPRI Staff Report 08-FSR 1. Iowa State University and University of Missouri-Columbia. Ames, IA 2008. Available online at: http://www.fapri.iastate.edu/outlook2008.

Luh, Bor S., ed. *Rice: Production and Utilization*, 2nd edition. Volume 2. New York, NY: Van Nostrand Reinhold, 1991.

Setia, Parveen, Nathan Childs, Eric Wailes, and Janet Livezey. *The U.S. Rice Industry*. Agricultural Economic Report No. AER-700. Washington, DC: U.S. Department of Agriculture, Economic Research Service, Commodity Economics Division, 1994.

Smith, R.K., E.J. Wailes, and G.L. Cramer. *The Market Structure of the U.S. Rice Industry*. Bulletin 921. Fayetteville, AR: University of Arkansas, Arkansas Agricultural Experiment Station, 1990.

Salassi, M. *Characteristics and Production Costs of U.S. Rice Farms, 1988*. AIB-657, Washington, DC: U.S. Department of Agriculture, Economic Research Service, 1992.

USA Rice Federation. *U.S. Rice Domestic Usage Report MY 2004-2005*. Arlington, VA: USA Rice Federation, 2005. Available online at: http://www.usarice.com/industry/2005milledricesurvey.pdf.

Wailes, Eric J. "Rice." In *Quality of U.S. Agricultural Products*. Task Force Report No. 126. Ames, IA: Council for Agricultural Science and Technology, 1996.

Wailes, Eric J. "Rice Global Trade, Protectionist Policies, and the Impact of Trade Liberalization." In *Global Agricultural Trade and Developing Countries*. Edited by M. Ataman Aksoy and John C. Beghin. World Bank, 2005.

River Engineering

The building of dams and other projects that facilitate navigation, flood control, pollution control, irrigation, recreation and water supply.

Introduction

The U.S. is an amazing hydrological system of more than 300 major rivers with tributary streams that extend about 3.6 million miles. Rivers are the lifeblood of the rural economy. Dredged and impounded for navigation, rivers are highways of commerce, the nation's first interstate transport system. Vital to agribusiness, rivers nationwide reclaim almost 58 million acres of farmland. Rivers are open sewers for agricultural runoff. They are hydro factories that produce a tenth of America's electrical power. Rivers are fisheries and habitat for about 75 percent of the American desert's animal species. Rivers are also wilderness areas, boating facilities and rampaging floods. In these ways, and many others, the story of rural America and the development of its rivers are inextricably intertwined.

Early River Projects

Construction in America's rivers long predated the civil engineering profession. About 700 years before Columbus, Hohokama Indians of the desert southwest pioneered irrigation with extensive networks of ditches and dams. Prehistoric peoples in the Columbia basin narrowed large rivers with stones to harvest the salmon migration.

Europeans regarded rivers as thoroughfares of empire, yet the hazard of interior navigation—the sandbars, shoals, snags (dead trees), rapids and falls—were impediments to colonization. By the time of the American Revolution, the British army had drawn detailed maps of the most dangerous rapids. Builders aided navigation with dockyards, beacons, ice piers and stationary winches to "warp" boats through gravel and mud. In 1785, George Washington organized a stock company that cleared rocks from the Potomac and canalled around Great Falls. Ambitious projects also developed the Santee, James, Delaware, Susquehanna, Schuylkill, and Merrimack rivers. New York's Erie Canal, opened in 1825, was a 364-mile engineering sensation that made the Hudson-Mohawk a conduit of the western trade.

The success of the Erie Canal fueled a pro-business, pro-union campaign to build a vigorous maritime economy through federal public works. Encouraged by the Supreme Court's outspoken nationalism in *Gibbons v. Ogden* (1824), a case that confirmed the federal jurisdiction over interstate river commerce, Congress pieced together omnibus waterway legislation with projects for every state. The U.S. Army Corps of Engineers supervised the largest federal projects. Ably assisted by steamboat pilots and the U.S. Topographical Bureau, the Corps and its contractors developed a fleet of machine boats to clear the log-infested Ohio-Mississippi system. In 1832 snag boat inventor Henry Miller Shreve, a federal river superintendent, cleared a 100-mile logjam on the Red River that blocked American access to Texas. Army builders and contractors also aided attempts to canal around treacherous rapids at Louisville on the Ohio, Des Moines on the Mississippi, Muscle Shoals on the Tennessee, and Sault Ste. Marie.

Federal Programs after the Civil War

After the Civil War the river program expanded with strong support from the South and the West. It was an age of innovation—of suction dredging, underwater explosives, steel lighthouses, concrete dams and motorized locks that made rivers work likes canals. One project dear to the heartland was the deepwater shipping channel that opened the Mississippi below New Orleans. In 1885 a movable dam at Davis Island below Pittsburgh became the first of the Ohio River's 46 locks and dams.

Dredging opened a 30-foot channel to Philadelphia and a 20-foot channel to Portland. Serious flooding in Louisiana, meanwhile, led to the establishment of a levee oversight bureau called the Mississippi River Commission, founded in 1879. That year John Wesley Powell of the U.S. Geological Survey advocated a public system of ditches and dams in a report that became a blueprint for reclamation in the 17 Western states.

Powell preferred small government and local control but recognized, nevertheless, that large-scale reclamation would require federal aid. Although Mormon irrigators had built impressive church-sponsored projects without public assistance, state initiatives were rarely successful. Cautiously at first, Congress aided farmer cooperatives and irrigation districts through water and land-grant programs such as the 1877 Desert Land Act and 1894 Carey Act. In 1902 Congress extending federal financing through the U.S. Reclamation Service, later renamed the Bureau of Reclamation. Soon the bureau had astonished the nation with a string of spectacular projects: Roosevelt Dam on the Salt (1911), Arrowrock on the Boise (1915), and Elephant Butte on the Rio Grande (1916). Financial setbacks, however, crippled some grandiose projects. At Uncompahgre in Colorado, for example, a $1 million dam proposal ultimately cost three times that amount. Seldom in the history of federal dam-building have farm payments covered the cost of construction. Congress, according to a 1986 U.S. Department of the Interior estimate, has footed the bill for 86 percent of the $19.6 billion appropriated for reclamation (Wahl, 1989).

Hydropower

Hydroelectric power sales helped the financially troubled projects recover some of the loss. Pioneered by the Edison Electric Company, the use of impounded water to generate electricity came of age in the 1880s and 1890s with American innovations such as power plants, voltage regulators and long-distance transmission lines. Intense competition among private and public purveyors prompted Congress to coordinate hydro development through the Federal Power Commission, established in 1920. Federal activity increased with Wilson Dam and power house at Muscle Shoals on the Tennessee River, a Corps project completed in 1925. Wilson Dam touched off a fiery debate between private power utilities and water conservationists such as Senator George W. Norris of Nebraska, a crusader for public power. In 1933, Norris sponsored the legislation that became a controversial experiment in federal planning,

the Tennessee Valley Authority (TVA). Serving a seven-state region hard hit by the Great Depression, the TVA made the Tennessee River the most dammed and developed stream in the nation. Electricity, by 1950, reached 80 percent of the region's farms.

Hydropower also reached America's farms through the dams and power lines authorized by the Rural Electrification Administration (REA), an agency that began as a relief operation in 1936. By 1941 the REA served more than a million consumers.

Rural demand for electricity helped justify massive construction. One engineering triumph was Boulder Dam (renamed Hoover Dam in 1947) on the Colorado River, finished in 1935. At 726 feet the gravity-arch dam was the height of a six-story office building, nearly twice as tall as any existing dam. Federal engineers also broke construction records on the Columbia River at Bonneville Dam (completed in 1937) and Grand Coulee Dam (1941). Shasta Dam with its giant power plant, authorized by Congress in 1935, became the centerpiece of California's Central Valley Project, a vast network of dams and canals. With 475 miles of pipelines, 20 miles of tunnels, 22 pumping stations and seven power plants, the Central Valley Project became the largest water conveyance system ever undertaken by a state.

Flood Control and Multipurpose Projects

Another catalyst to rural development has been the federal attempt to contain raging floods. For many years the Corps of Engineers believed that flood levees were the most effective way to control inundation, but catastrophic flooding along the Mississippi in 1927 shattered that conventional wisdom, forcing engineers to consider flood reservoirs and dams. The 1936 Flood Control Act greatly expanded the Corps' jurisdiction with $310 million for some 250 projects. By 1952, Congress had spent more than $11 billion on flood control levees and dams.

Flood control became a primary justification for basin-wide dam and canal projects that also developed rivers for hydropower and navigation. Disastrous flooding along the Missouri in 1943 interrupted the war effort and launched one of the Corps' most ambitious multipurpose projects, the Pick-Sloan Plan. The first large dam in the system was the $183 million project at Fort Randall that created a giant slackwater channel for navigation, backing up the Missouri for 150 miles. Corps engineers also designed the 434-mile multipurpose McCellan-Kerr waterway along the Arkansas River

Mississippi River 9-Foot Channel, Lock & Dam No. 1, Saint Paul, Minnesota. Courtesy of the Historic American Engineering Survey, National Park Service.

to Tulsa. Featuring three large flood reservoirs and the Dardanelle Lock and Dam, completed in 1969, the waterway with its heavy barge traffic benefited farmers directly by dramatically cutting freight rates on fertilizers and grain.

The Mississippi system, meanwhile, has became one of the world's most sophisticated networks of multipurpose flood, hydro and navigation projects with more than 200 major dams. One critical part of the system is a navigation lock in the right bank of the Mississippi about 300 miles upstream from the mouth of the river. Built by the Corps in 1963, the lock prevents the river from shifting into the Atchafalaya floodway, bypassing New Orleans. In 1963 the Corps also completed the slackwater dam at the Chain of Rocks near St. Louis that removed one of the last great hazards to barge navigation.

In all, about 75,000 large dams had been built in the nation's rivers. The Corps of Engineers has turned about 26,000 miles of river into channelized highways for barges. The Bureau of Reclamation has built at least 16,000 miles of canals, 1,500 miles of pipeline, and 355 storage reservoirs. Along the Colorado the volume of stored water for irrigation is six times the river's annual flow. Outside Alaska, only 42 rivers run free for more than 120 miles without locks or dams.

Opposition to River Projects

Even as engineering transformed the nation, there was seldom a time in the nation's history when dam builders worked in a vacuum without facing stiff opposition. Soon after the Civil War the Corps was widely denounced as a pork barrel organization, extravagant and corrupt. Again in 1951, the New Dealer Harold Ickes

called the Corps "the most powerful and pervasive lobby in Washington, ...our highest ruling class" (Maass, 1951). Meanwhile, the Bureau of Reclamation was a target of an angry campaign to save part of Dinosaur National Monument from a high dam at Echo Park.

The Echo Park controversy built a nationwide base of support for anti-dam legislation such as the 1964 Wilderness Act and the 1968 Wild and Scenic River Act. Perhaps the most significant challenge to dam building was the 1969 National Environmental Policy Act, a law that required engineers to see rivers not only as plumbing but also as parkland, raft runs, scenic vistas and complex ecosystems. With the 1972 Clean Water Act came the recognition that slackwater projects often promote the swamp-like eutrophication that clogs rivers with algae and pollutes drinking supplies. Although a few threatened streams have recovered—the Cuyahoga at Cleveland, for example, is no longer a fire hazard—the U.S. Environmental Protection Agency (EPA) estimates that one-third of America's river mileage does not meet federal clean water standards.

The twenty-first-century fear of habitat loss and water pollution has seeded the engineer's search of nonstructural "green" approaches to river design. Rivers have been "remandered" to braid and twist through prairie wetlands. Parklike urban greenways pass high water through subdivisions. Dam removal, although controversial, is increasingly common. From 1999 to 2007, American engineers removed more than 250 hydropower impoundments and mostly small irrigation dams.

Recent disputes over river construction often have a rural-urban dimension that forces government to make difficult choices. On the Columbia and Snake rivers, where sockeye and Chinook salmon are dangerously close to extinction, the attempt to save fish by releasing reservoir water pits irrigators against urban-centered industry and water conservation groups. Meanwhile, the thirsty consumers in Las Vegas, Phoenix, Los Angeles, Albuquerque, Salt Lake City, and Denver tap into the Colorado, challenging the "first-in-time, first-in-line" doctrine of prior appropriation, a bedrock of Western law. Thus, the rivers that touch every part of the nation are battlefields of raging debate over the human encounter with nature and the role technology plays in shaping American life.

— *Todd Shallat*

See also

Conservation, Water; Environmental Protection; Groundwater; Hydrology; Impact Assessment; Natural Resources Engineering; Watersheds

References

Armstrong, Ellis L. *History of Public Works in the United States, 1776-1976.* Chicago, IL: American Public Works Association, 1976.

Bartlett, Richard A. *Rolling Rivers: An Encyclopedia of America's Rivers.* New York, NY: McGraw Hill, 1984.

Maass, Arthur. *Muddy Waters: The Army Engineers and the Nation's Rivers.* Cambridge, MA: Harvard University Press, 1951.

Palmer, Tim. *Lifelines: The Case for River Conservation.* Washington, DC: Island Press, 1994.

Shallat, Todd. *Structures in the Stream: Water, Science, and the Rise of the U.S. Army Corps of Engineers.* Austin, TX: University of Texas Press, 1994.

Wahl, Richard W. *Markets for Federal Water: Subsidies, Property Rights, and the Bureau of Reclamation.* Washington, DC: Resources for the Future, 1989.

Wilkinson, Charles F. *Crossing the Next Meridian: Land, Water, and the Future of the West.* Washington, DC: Island Press, 1992.

Rural Church Movement

Organized, collaborative action by denominations, congregations and church-related agencies on behalf of rural churches and their communities during the twentieth century. This article addresses the rural church movement in the U.S. starting in the early twentieth century with specific emphasis on the mid-1960s through the present. The rural church was affected by the social, demographic and economic changes that took place in the U.S. during the second half of the twentieth century. Some of the key concerns of the rural church movement are the need for a trained supply of clergy, rural parish life, community economic development, social justice concerns, and agricultural concerns. The words church, congregation and parish will be used interchangeably throughout the article.

Roots in the Early Twentieth Century

The American church in the early 1900s was a *rural* church in that the majority of the American population and churches were located in rural areas. As such, the economic and social challenges affecting rural communities were reflected in those communities' churches. Rural sociologist Edmund deS. Brunner noted that as the community goes, so goes the church.

The rural church movement had parallels with the country life movement, which began in 1908 with President Theodore Roosevelt's Country Life Commission. Under the leadership of Liberty Hyde Bailey, the Country Life Commission was the catalyst for rural reform from 1908 through 1917. The country life movement was formalized into the American Country Life Association, in which the emphasis on technology and modernization helped to establish the direction that rural development policy took throughout the century. Many of the individuals involved in the country life movement were also prominent in the rural life movement, such as Kenyon L. Butterfield, David E. Lindstrom, E.W. Mueller, Edwin V. O'Hara, and Warren H. Wilson.

Edwin Lee Earp was among the first of these church leaders to use the term "rural church movement" in his 1914 book entitled, *The Rural Church Movement.* By mid-century, a growing literature had emerged describing the rural church movement, including books like Mark Rich's *The Rural Church Movement* (1957) and Charles McBride's *An Introduction to the Rural Movement* (1954), and periodicals like the *Christian Rural Fellowship Bulletin* and the *Town and Country Church.* Currently, various denominations offer publications related to rural life, such as the *United Methodist Rural Fellowship Bulletin,* the *Rural Messenger,* and *Catholic Rural Life.*

Players in the Rural Church Movement

Champions of the rural church cause have been found at the national denominational and regional judicatory levels. Despite multiple reorganizations and mergers during the twentieth century, many denominations maintained a department designated to work with their rural churches. Current examples include the Rural/Small Community Ministries Office of the Episcopal Church, the Rural Ministry Resources and Networking (Rural Desk) of the Evangelical Lutheran Church in America, the General Board of Global Ministries of the United Methodist Church, the Small Church and Community Ministry of the Presbyterian Church USA, the Commission for Town and Country Ministry of the Evangelical Covenant Church, and the National Catholic Rural Life Conference.

Other champions of the rural church were found among land-grant university and seminary faculty. These individuals, along with denominational officials, met to explore ways to address the concerns both of the rural church and rural communities. The American Country Life Association served as a key forum for the rural church movement leaders for over five decades. Other rural church-related organizations emerged during the second half of the twentieth century. The Joint Strategy and Action Committee (JSAC) was organized by various denominational social action groups in conjunction with the National Council of Churches in the late 1960s. JSAC published the *JSAC Grapevine* for nearly 20 years and addressed topics such as eco-justice, food stewardship, and global economic disparities.

The Rural Church Network (RCN) of the U.S. and Canada emerged out of the Joint Strategy and Action Committee in the 1980s, initially for denominational officials with rural church portfolios to share programs their denominations had devised to serve rural churches affected by the farm crisis. The RCN currently meets twice per year and is attended by denominational officials with rural ministry portfolios, seminary and land-grant university faculty, rural church-related agencies, and U.S. Department of Agriculture representatives. A variety of denominations participate in RCN activities including Roman Catholics and Mainline and Evangelical Protestants. The RCN's purpose is to develop strategies for ministry in town and rural areas and to share ministry resources "in areas of interest including evangelism, clergy and lay leadership, contextual training for ministry, church development, community economic development, and town and rural research" (http://www.ruralchurchnetwork.org/).

The Rural Church Movement's Response to National and Rural Events

Those involved in the rural church movement responded to transitions in the national and rural levels by developing educational programs, publishing materials, convening conferences, and advocating for rural legislation. The thrust of their efforts fall into several categories, but five stand out: the need for a trained supply of clergy, rural parish life, community economic development, social justice concerns, and agricultural concerns.

Need for Rural Clergy and for Rural Clergy Education and Training. One perennial concern that occupied the country life movement was the need to recruit and retain quality, trained pastors and priests. Churches typically desire resident, full-time clergy, but not all congregations are financially positioned to provide pay and benefits for staff, and many denominations faced clergy shortages. One strategy to provide clergy despite shortages was to merge or yoke congregations into multiple-point parishes that could be served by circuit-riding clergy, a clergy couple, or a pastoral team. Another response to the clergy shortage was the bivoca-

tional pastor or "tent-making" model, whereby the pastor's time would be split between the church and a secular occupation.

Seminaries were requested by their constituency churches to provide rural training experiences for the seminary students preparing to serve rural parishes. Some seminaries provided pastoral training programs specifically for the rural context. Several seminaries offered "rural plunge" experiences, rural internships, or opportunities to participate in church-related organizations like the Appalachian Ministries Educational Resource Center. Others provided an occasional contextualized course in rural ministry or formed consortia with other seminaries to expand their rural ministry offerings.

Some church leaders questioned whether the "general practitioner" Master's of Divinity seminary programs could truly be structured to provide training for any specialized context. They suggested that continuing education programs be devised to augment seminary courses. Post-seminary continuing education programs were offered to meet clergies' need for rural contextual training. Additionally, state Conferences of Churches offered ecumenical programs for clergy new to rural ministry. Land-grant universities introduced rural clergy to teaching, research and extension facilities and recognized the clergies' outstanding accomplishments.

Parish Life and Care for Small Congregations. A second issue addressed by the movement's leaders was leading and operating the rural parish itself. Church administration, conflict management, project management, church landscaping, parsonages, leadership training and organizational survival were examined. Church attendance was an important topic to rural church leaders, particularly in regions with declining populations. Materials were developed for strategic planning, such as Harold Huff's *Planning for Action: Aids for Leaders in Church Planning* (1968) and Bernard Quinn's *Mission, Missions and the Creative Planning Process* (1968).

With America's population migrating to urban areas, memberships fell in a substantial proportion of rural churches. By the second half of the twentieth century, the majority of church *members* in most denominations were urban, whereas the majority of their *congregations* were rural and small. The recognition that the majority of congregations were small led many denominations to form departments that emphasized the "small" church rather than the "rural" church, assuming that small church programs and materials would be applicable both in rural and urban contexts. In 1973, the United Methodist Church published *Ways of Learning in Small Churches*, followed by the 1975 Presbyterian Church USA's *Learning in the Small Church*. Newsletters on small churches in the 1980s included Anthony Pappas's *The Five Stones* and the *Small Church Newsletter* of the Missouri School of Religion's Center for Rural Ministry.

Pastoral leadership was an ongoing concern. Some rural churches needed clergy to help them rebuild their corporate self-esteem, having been described as "problem," "survival-oriented," and "marginal." Pastoral materials were developed for preaching, administering sacraments and conducting weddings and funerals in a rural context. Other materials were developed on how to minister to and evangelize the urban-to-rural migrants.

Community Economic Development. Denominational leaders, often in conjunction with land-grant university faculty, actively encouraged rural churches to participate in community development efforts. For example, a 1964 conference to address the churches' role in community economic development was co-sponsored by the University of Wisconsin, National Catholic Rural Life Conference, National Lutheran Council, and Wisconsin Council of Churches. Victor Klimoski and Bernard Quinn's edited book, *Church and Community: Nonmetropolitan America in Transition* (1970), offered examples of the church's and clergy's roles in rural development.

Some church leaders believed that community involvement was instrumental to the church's vitality. For example, Bernard Evans asked, "Can rural churches survive?" in a 1988 *USA Today* article. He described the impact of declines in rural America on the churches. James Cushman's (1981) *Beyond Survival: Revitalizing the Small Church* suggested that, in the face of rural decline, community ministry was one way to achieve church revitalization. Other church leaders believed that community involvement was an expression of the church's mission. In so doing, the church could address the needs of people in the community.

Social Justice Concerns. Justice concerns were woven through the discussions of church leaders. The first issue was the recognition that dramatic social, economic, demographic and cultural changes were affecting the rural U.S. The impact of social change on rural churches and communities was described both by state Conferences of Churches, such as Stanley Voelker's "Ef-

fects of Population Trends on Churches in the Northern Great Plains" (North Dakota, 1965), and by land-grant universities like North Carolina State University's *Religion and Social Change* (1969).

A second issue—poverty—was a concern both for the nation and for rural churches. After President Johnson declared a "war on poverty" in 1964, Lyle Schaller and James Cogswell enlisted the church to "the war" in *The Churches War on Poverty* (1967) and *The Church and the Rural Poor* (1974), respectively. Pastors' conferences addressed poverty. In 1965, the Illinois Cooperative Extension Service annual rural pastors' short course was entitled, "The Church Faces Poverty," and Mississippi State University's annual church leadership institute was entitled "The Less Fortunate in Our Midst."

Third, regional concerns were addressed, such as those in Appalachia. Both the Appalachian Regional Commission and the Coalition for Appalachian Ministry (CAM) were started in 1960 to address poverty and development concerns. The Commission on Religion in Appalachia (CORA) was started in 1965. The goals of both CAM and CORA were for the churches in the Appalachian region to address the "war on poverty."

A fourth issue was ecumenical ministry. Ecumenical efforts had been underway throughout the century, and ranged from shared or cooperative ministry to multi-denominational yoked congregations. Edmund deS. Brunner and Marvin Judy had addressed ecumenical action in *The Larger Parish, a Movement or an Enthusiasm?* (1934) and *The Larger Parish and Group Ministry* (1959), respectively. However, with Vatican Council II (1962-1965) came a new surge of ecumenical writings, such as Harold McSwain's 1955 *The Cooperative-type Ministry and Renewal in Town and Country Churches*; *Ecumenical Designs: Imperatives for Action in Non-metropolitan America* by Dave Bell et al. in 1967; Horace Sill's 1967 *Grassroots Ecumenicity*; and Bernard Quinn's 1968 *Ecumenical Planning for Mission in Town and Country America.*

Agricultural Concerns. Agriculture experienced dramatic changes that were both labor- and land-saving and held demographic and economic implications for rural communities. Mechanical technologies involved larger, self-propelled equipment; confined livestock operations proliferated for poultry, beef, hogs and dairy; chemical and biological technologies were widely adopted; and new, high-yielding varieties of crops were introduced. As a result of these changes, agriculture became more productive and efficient. Legislation was passed to maintain a steady, reasonably priced food supply—hence the "cheap food policy"—and yet provide a livable income for the producers of that food. Several publications exemplified the rural churches' concern for farms, farmers and rural communities given the broader issues in agriculture—the National Council of Churches' *Ethical Issues in Commercial Agriculture* (1970) and Elwin Mueller's *New Landmarks: A Series of Papers Dealing with Some of the Economic, Social, and Spiritual Interests of the American Farmer* (1970). Soon to follow were Walter Brueggemann's *The Land: Place as Gift, Promise, and Challenge in Biblical Faith* (1977).

One of several jolts to the rural economy occurred in 1972 with the "Russian grain deal." Grain prices, land prices and interest rates spiked. However, a grain embargo was imposed on the Soviet Union in 1979 when it invaded Afghanistan. The result was a drop in land values, which ushered in the "farm crisis" of the early 1980s. The farm crisis dominated rural church leaders' conversation both at the denominational level and the congregational level, particularly by congregations in the Midwestern states. The farm crisis became a concern of nearly every denomination in the U.S. as church leaders wrote materials to inform the urban public about the plight facing rural America and prepared programs to assist rural residents affected by the farm crisis. They recognized the farm crisis as an extension of a long-term, chronic "rural crisis."

A second agricultural topic addressed by the rural church during this era was sustainable (environmentally regenerative, financially profitable and socially just) agriculture. The Catholic bishops issued a powerful statement on land issues that addressed agricultural sustainability in *Strangers and Guests: Toward Community in the Heartland* (1980). *Sustainability in Agriculture: Challenge for the Church* (1990) was a joint publication by the Evangelical Lutheran Church in America, the Presbyterian Church USA, and the United Methodist Church.

Rural church leaders worked to formulate a theology of the land and the environment to undergird its praxis. Churches of various denominations were concerned about the biblical and theological mandate to care for creation. Many tangled questions emerged that pertained to the environment and the land and those who live on the land. An ecumenical conference was held in the mid-1980s at St. John's University and Seminary in Collegeville, Minnesota, to address these questions (Leonard Weber et al., *Theology of the Land*,

1987). Other topics addressed during the last two decades of the twentieth century were changes in federal farm policy, consolidations within the agri-food system, corporate concentration of the agri-food system, globalization, and the advances and challenges of biotechnology.

Edmund deS. Brunner had pointed out early in the century that as the community goes, so goes the church. The leaders of the rural church movement additionally emphasized that as the church goes, so goes the community.

— *Gary A. Goreham and Courtney E. Taylor*

See also

Agricultural and Farmworker Unions; Churches; Country Life Movement; Environmental Movements; History, Agricultural; History, Rural; Jews in Rural America; Religion; Social Movements; Sustainable Agriculture Movement

References

Earp, Edwin Lee. 1914. *The Rural Church Movement*. New York: Associated Press.

Goreham, Gary A. *The Rural Church in America: A Century of Writings: A Bibliography*. New York: Garland Publishing Co., 1990.

Judy, Marvin T. *From Ivy Tower to Village Spire: A History and Contemporary Appraisal of the Role of the Theological Seminary in the Small Membership Church in Town and Rural Areas*. Dallas, TX: Perkins School of Theology, Southern Methodist University Printing Office, 1984.

Jung, Shannon, Pegge Boehm, Deborah Cronin, Gary Farley, C. Dean Freudenberger, Judith Bortner Heffernan, Sandra LaBlanc, Edward L. Queen II, and David C. Ruesink. *Rural Ministry: The Shape of the Renewal to Come*. Nashville, TN: Abingdon Press, 1998.

Klimoski, Victor J. And Bernard Quinn, (eds.). 1970. *Church and Community: Nonmetropolitan America in Transition*. Washington, DC: Center for Applied Research in the Apostolate.

McBride, Charles Ralph. 1955. *An Introduction to the Rural Church Movement*. Kansas City, KS: Central Seminary Press.

Rich, Mark. 1957. *The Rural Church Movement*. Columbia, MO: Juniper Knoll Press.

Rural Church Network of the U.S. and Canada. David Ruesink, Executive Secretary. Available online at: http://www.ruralchurchnetwork.org.

Rural, Definition of

Tracing the source of the word "rural" to its historical origins leads to the Latin word *rus*, which is interpreted as meaning "the country," the Indo-European word *rewos* meaning "space or wide," and the Gothic word *rums* meaning "room or space." Other words that often are used to specify rural areas or people include bucolic, pastoral, rustic, and provincial. Although the idea of "rural" has widespread intuitive understanding, as with many scientific concepts, attempts at articulating a precise meaning have led to a tangle of arguments and counter-arguments concerning the utility of a given definition. The major point of agreement among those involved in the debate has been that there is no singular or multifaceted definition that will suffice to satisfy the research, programmatic, and policy communities that employ the concept. With this unsettled situation in mind, this discussion summarizes the origins of the concept, the interface of the concept of rural with the concept of urban, and, finally, the issue of the dimensions of rurality and the current efforts to articulate the meaning of the concept.

The Rural-Urban Dichotomy and Continuum

A key consideration in the concept of rural is the recognition of an explicit or implicit definition or a delineation of the concept of urban. Louis Wirth's (1938) classic work *Urbanism as a Way of Life* is perhaps the most widely cited binary juxtaposition of urbanism and ruralism. In this work, the rural way of life was characterized by stability, integration, and rigid social stratification. Urbanism, on the other hand, was seen as dynamic and unstable, fluid in terms of social stratification, impersonal, with specialized social interaction, and compartmentalized employment and family. Wirth's perspective was one of many that used societal level studies to describe and explain social changes as the country and the world became more industrialized and urbanized in the late nineteenth and early twentieth centuries. Other perspectives, including the societal contrasts of Emile Durkheim (mechanical and organic solidarity), Ferdinand Tönnies (*Gemeinshaft* and *Gesellschaft*), Georg Simmel (emotional and blasé), Max Weber (rational and traditional), Pitirim Sorokin (familistic and contractual), and Ernest Becker (sacred and secular) have been used to differentiate rural and urban ways of life.

Attempts to use rural and urban ways of life as empirical illustration of these grand theories of societal change quickly proved that such binary juxtopostions were overly reductionist and inadequate to capture the diversity that exists within a society. Thus, led by the work of Redfield (1947), researchers proposed a continuum that arranged communities according to levels of rurality and urbanity. At one end of the continuum were very isolated, remote rural areas, and at the other extreme were large cities, with transitional areas in between. The idea of the continuum provided a useful mechanism to empirically document differences and similarities between people and places in the U.S. However, the findings have been mixed in documenting meaningful differences and, while the corporeality of the continuum is generally accepted, some regarded the importance of the differences as trivial (Dewey, 1960) or incontinuously distributed across population aggregates (Duncan, 1957).

Dimensions of Rurality

Inherent in the efforts to contrast rural and urban life has been the need to identify the dimensions along which distinctions are made. Although the specific delineation of rural populations varies depending on the research topic or the agency or institution that gathers the data, three dimensions—ecological, occupational and sociocultural—have been core to both historical and more contemporary definitions of rural (see Sorokin and Zimmerman, 1929; Bealer et al., 1965).

The ecological component points to relatively sparse populations and relative isolation from urban areas. This spatial apportionment of the population has been the foundation of most academic and policy designations of rural and urban. The importance of rural as an ecological characteristic lies in the cost of space (Kraenzel, 1980), where distance and population sparsity are extraordinary factors in the availability and access to and costs of needed services and goods. Further, smaller size and relative isolation impact both inter- and intra-locality personal contacts.

As for the occupational dimension, rurality historically has been associated with the predominance of extractive and production-type industries, including agriculture and ranching, forestry, mining, oil and gas extraction, and natural resource-based tourism. This dimension then has focused on the articulation of distinct occupational and economic activities that occur outside of urban areas. Whereas the rural areas of the U.S. have a diverse occupational structure when considered in the aggregate, local economies of rural areas are likely to be much less diversified.

The sociocultural dimension of rurality, the most complex and least well articulated, generally refers to value structures or shared ideals that serve as the fundamental underpinnings of patterned interactions. Rural culture has been variously described as socially conservative, provincial, fatalistic, traditional, hesitant to change, independent, prejudiced, ethnocentric and intolerant of heterodox ideas (England et al., 1979; Glenn and Alston, 1967; Loomis, 1950). However, empirical research has not served to substantiate these elements of the sociocultural domain as capable of distinguishing between rural and urban populations, and has shown that heterogeneity of values rather than homogeneity characterizes rural America.

The matter of the dimensions of the rurality concept has a temporal aspect. It can be argued that development and population increases and dispersal limited the utility of certain components of the concept of rurality, particularly when time is included as a variable. When time is considered, the ecological approach to defining rural has proven the most enduring in research and policy matters in that distance and relative isolation, unlike the occupational and sociocultural components, are less temporal-centric. In the past, rurality may have been highly correlated with such sociocultural characteristics as traditionalism and social conservatism, but changes in society, such as improved telecommunication and transportation and greater homogeneity in education, weakened the association. Similarly, in the past, rurality was highly correlated with an agrarian/extractive occupational structure. However, decentralization of industry and mechanization and concentration of agriculture weakened the epistemic correlation between the rurality concept and an agricultural occupation structure. Although some sociocultural differences may remain and agricultural occupations still employ rural residents, some argue that the most salient contemporary differences in rural and urban areas are primarily a consequence of the spatial organization of the U.S. population (Wilkinson, 1984). The implied correlate of a temporal dimension of the concept relates back to efforts to articulate the societal continuum(s) between rural and urban components. Specifically, the applicability of the dimensions of rurality (ecological, occupational and ecological) may prove effective in delineating populations in areas that have not experienced the same level of development in contact technologies and socioeconomic change as has been seen in Western societies. Thus, while occupational and sociocultural dimensions have diminished definitional utility in more technologically advanced regions of the world, they may remain valid in less technologically advanced areas of the world.

While the utility of the multidimensional conceptualization of rural has been the source of substantial debate in scholarly and policy applications, this is not the case in the mind's eye of the general public. Research has indicated there are general images that are conjured up when people are asked about their perception of rurality. In general, the research shows that "rurality" invokes highly positive images of areas that are distinct from urban areas. The image of rural areas are characterized by being places with agriculture dominating the economy, it being family oriented with strong religious founding and self reliance, set in a bucolic environment with beautiful vistas, and generally being better places to raise families in a friendly and relaxed atmosphere (Kellogg, 2002). This positive constructed image of rural America has been variously termed as the rural mystique (Willits and Bealer, 1992), the rural sentiment (Park and Coppack, 1994), and the rural idyll (Bunce, 1994). Thus, much of recent effort directed toward understanding rurality in contemporary society has not focused on trying to identify certain sociocultural characteristics, economic or occupational structures, or spatial distinctiveness. Instead, it takes a social construction approach that examines the images, ideas and symbols that are developed when people think about "the rural." This social representativeness implies that there is not a singular rural place or people or characteristic, but rather a broad array of constructed or imaginary rural places and social conditions (Wood, 2005). From this perspective, "what or who is rural" is a function of the forces that shape an individual's formation of the concept. As individuals are exposed to images of "rural" through the mass media, literature, poetry and individual experience, the idea is constructed. These images then are filtered through the individual's values, beliefs and knowledge to define rurality. Heuristically, this approach stresses the primacy of examining the symbolism representing rurality, the sociocultural import attached to perceived dynamics in aspects related to the concept, and perhaps most importantly, the value structure within society that serves to reinforce the symbols and meanings attached to the idea of "rural."

— *Frank L. Farmer*

See also

Community; Rural Demography; Rurality, Measures of; Rural Sociology; Town-Country Relations; Urban-Rural Economic Linkages; Urbanization

References

Bealer, Robert C., Fern K. Willits, and William P. Kuvelsky. "The Meaning of 'Rurality' in American Society." *Rural Sociology* 30 (1965): 255-266.

Bunce, M. *The Countryside Idyll: Anglo-American Images of Landscape*. London: Routledge. 1994.

Dewey, Richard. "The Rural-Urban Continuum: Real but Relatively Unimportant." *American Journal of Sociology* 66 (1960), 60-66.

Duncan, Otis Dudley. "Community Size and the Rural-Urban Continuum." Pp 35-45 in *Cities and Society*. Edited by Paul K. Hatt and Albert J. Reiss, Jr. Glencoe, IL: Free Press, 1957.

England, J. Lynn, W. Eugene Gibbons, and Barry L. Johnson. "The Impact of a Rural Environment on Values." *Rural Sociology* 44 (1979): 119-136.

Glenn, Norval D. and Jon P. Alston. "Rural-Urban Differences in Reported Attitudes and Behavior." *Social Science Quarterly* 47 (1967): 381-400.

Halfacre, Keith. "Rethinking Rurality" Pp 285-306 in *New Forms of Urbanization*. Edited by T. Champion and G. Hugo. Hampshire, England: Ashgate, 2004.

Kellogg Foundation. 2002. *Perceptions of Rural America*. Battle Creek: Kellogg Foundation.

Kraenzel, Carl. *The Social Cost of Space in Yonland*. Bozeman, MT: Big Sky Press, 1980.

Loomis, Charles P. "The Nature of Rural Social Systems: a Typological Analysis." *Rural Sociology* 15 (1950): 156-174.

Park, Deborah Carter and Phillip Coppack. "The Role of Rural Sentiment and Vernacular Landscapes in Contriving Sense of Place in the City's Countryside." *Geographiska Annalar* 76b, (1994): 161-172.

Redfield, Robert. "The Folk Society." *American Journal of Sociology* 52 (1947): 294-308.

Sorokin, Pitirim and Carle Zimmerman. *Principles of Rural-Urban Sociology*. New York, NY: Henry Holt, 1929.

Wilkinson, Kenneth P. "Rurality and Patterns of Social Disruption." *Rural Sociology* 49, no. 1 (1984): 23-36.

Willits, Fern K. and Robert C. Bealer. *The Rural Mystique*. The Pennsylvania State University Agricultural Experiment Station Bulletin No. 870. University Park, PA: Pennsylvania State University, 1992.

Willits, Fern K., Robert C. Bealer, and Vincent L. Timbers. "Popular Images of 'Rurality': Data from a Pennsylvania Survey." *Rural Sociology* 55 (1990): 559-587.

Wirth, Louis. "Urbanism as a Way of Life." *American Journal of Sociology* 44 (1938): 1-24

Woods, Michael. *Rural Geography*. London: Sage Publications, 2005.

Rural Demography

The study of the changing population and composition of rural areas. Rural demography is a specialization within a much broader field of social demography. It is an applied, policy-oriented approach that takes its roots from early research for the U.S. Department of Agriculture (USDA) back in the early 1900s (Kandel and Brown, 2006). At that time, policymakers were interested in social and demographic research on rural America. They established the Division of Farm Population and Rural Life within the USDA in 1919. Since that time rural demographers have been chronicling the changes that have taken place in rural areas and their resultant consequences.

Population change is one of the central themes within demographic analysis. It comprises three basic components: births (fertility), deaths (mortality) and migration. Other emphasis is placed on shifts in population composition, which is less focused and encompasses a broad array of social and economic indicators (Shryock and Siegel, 1976). This discussion of rural demography begins with the debate over the term "rural." Attention is directed first at differing interpretations of the term and then to analysts' contributions to its refinement. A brief history of population change in rural America follows. The remainder of the article centers on the three key components of population change.

What is "Rural"?

The term "rural" has multiple meanings. In an extensive literature review, Halfacree (1993) found 34 different definitions used between 1946 and 1987 which he grouped into six broad categories: statistical, administrative, built-up area, functional regions, agricultural, and population size/density. Not surprisingly, many of these definitions are time sensitive and the circumstances surrounding their construction have since been altered. The shifting social, geographic and cultural landscape that creates the need for such a definition requires a constant reformulation of the term. This is the case even for "official" definitions of rural used by federal statistical providers. For example, the formal definition coined by the fact-finders at the U.S. Census Bureau has changed multiple times. These changes began in earnest after 1910. At that time, "urban" was defined as inhabitants living in cities of at least 2,500 people, while "rural" was viewed as the remainder of the population. In 1900, the rural population accounted for 60.4 percent of the U.S. population and declined to 54.4 percent by 1910. A slight modification was made in the 1920 Census to take into account the practice among some Northeastern states that required incorporated cities to have at least 10,000 residents. Cities in these states with a population base between 2,500 and 10,000 were referred to as towns (or townships). Thus, the urban definition was expanded to encompass these territories. In 1930, a density dimension was added. Territory (either incorporated or unincorporated) with at least 10,000 people and a density of 1,000 persons per square mile was defined as urban. Other minor modifications were made to the density ruling as suburban sprawl pushed housing developments outside city limits, requiring the concept of rural to take on a slightly different meaning. In the 2000 Census, advancements in technology (particularly Geographic Information Systems, GIS) allowed Census Bureau analysts to jettison the use of place boundaries and concentrate solely on population density to differentiate urban from rural. Rural now is defined as all territory, population, and housing units located outside of urban areas (UAs) and urban clusters (UCs). Urban areas are contiguous census blocks encompassing populations of over 50,000, while urban clusters encompass populations from 2,500 to 50,000. A sequencing algorithm is used to select UAs and UCs by first starting with core blocks that have a population density of 1,000 persons per square mile and extending out to contiguous blocks with a density exceeding 500 persons per square mile. This density-based definition uniquely characterizes the relationship between people and space and avoids artificial classifications due to political boundaries. This means that large but sparsely populated places (i.e., 2,500 persons or more) may have both urban and rural populations within their city boundaries. For example, in 2000, there were 9,063 census designated places and incorporated places in the U.S. with a population of at least 2,500 people (the previous threshold for urban). Slightly over 2 percent of this population base, or nearly 4.1 million people, within these cities were classified as rural. In contrast, 37.3 percent of the population living outside the city limits of a place of at least 2,500 people (nearly 32.7 million) was defined as urban in 2000.

This reveals the growing importance of suburbanization among American communities and the need for constant revisions of the definition of urban versus rural.

A second federal statistical definition that frequently is used interchangeably with rural is nonmetropolitan. This concept and its counterpart—metropolitan—were first introduced in 1949 to capture suburbanization for policy development. The concept is defined by the Office of Management and Budget (not the Census Bureau), and its definition also has been altered numerous times in an attempt to adjust for urban sprawl. The major distinction, however, is that the definition is county-based (except in New England, where it is town-based). For example, prior to 2000, nonmetropolitan meant residence in a county that does not contain either a place with a minimum population of 50,000 or a Census Bureau-defined urbanized area that has a total population of at least 100,000 (75,000 in New England). The definition was significantly altered in 2000 to include micropolitan areas. Micropolitan areas are county or county groupings (if they meet specified requirements of commuting to or from the central county) that have at least one urban cluster with a population base between 10,000 and 50,000. In 2000, there were 370 metropolitan statistical areas in the U.S. which housed 82.6 percent of the total population or nearly 232.6 million people. In addition, there were 565 micropolitan statistical areas accounting for 10.3 percent of the population or nearly 30 million people. This means only 7.1 percent of the U.S. population, not quite 20 million people, lived outside either a metropolitan or micropolitan area in 2000 (referred to as noncore counties). This county-based definition creates some confusion. For example, one can live in an urban city and still be defined as nonmetropolitan. Likewise, a farmer living in the countryside can be defined as metropolitan. Nonetheless, this definition is useful because it is not restricted to city boundaries. Modern commuting changed the pattern of living in rural areas, and this definition allows for a more accurate classification of residents. Unfortunately, because the definition of nonmetropolitan changed over time, longitudinal comparisons are difficult.

Analysts continue to refine the term "rural." The Economic Research Service of the U.S. Department of Agriculture (USDA-ERS) provides comparisons among nine representative rural definitions. Among the most popular are the following:

USDA Definitions

Rural-Urban Continuum Codes

David Brown and his colleagues at the USDA-ERS expanded the dichotomous definition of metropolitan/nonmetropolitan to include nine categories to explore more effectively the influence of urban areas on residential movement. Metropolitan counties were subdivided into three categories based on size of population. Nonmetropolitan counties were subdivided in two ways. First, they were classified as adjacent or nonadjacent to a metropolitan area. Second, within the adjacency classification, they were subdivided by population size of largest city. This modification, known as the Beale Codes or the Rural-Urban Continuum Codes, shows the strong pull of large urban places. In 2000, two-thirds of the nonmetropolitan residents in the U.S. lived in counties adjacent to metropolitan centers. Furthermore, only 16.6 percent of those living in nonadjacent counties lived in a county that had an urban population of less than 2,500 people.

Urban Influence Codes

The Rural-Urban Continuum Codes noted above were refined in 2003 to incorporate micropolitan areas. This resulted in what is known as the Urban Influence Codes. Similar to their predecessor, these codes were subdivided into metropolitan and nonmetropolitan groupings. Metropolitan counties were split into two groups, large and small, with the cutoff at one million people. The nonmetropolitan counties were subdivided into 10 categories based on size and adjacency. Three of the nonmetropolitan categories were micropolitan and subdivided based on whether they were adjacent to a large, small, or no metropolitan county. These first three nonmetropolitan categories, along with the two metropolitan groups, were labeled core categories. The remaining seven nonmetropolitan categories were labeled noncore and were similarly subdivided based on their adjacency to either a metropolitan or micropolitan county.

County Typology or Dependency Codes

Another contribution to the term rural came from Lloyd Bender and his colleagues at the USDA-ERS They categorized rural counties by their major economic base, commonly called the E.R.S. Typology or Dependency Codes. Seven distinct types of rural counties were identified including counties depending heavily on farming, manufacturing or mining; counties specializing in government functions; persistent poverty coun-

ties; federal land counties; and retirement settlements (Bender et al., 1985). These codes were more recently expanded and revised (Cook and Mizer, 1994) to incorporate categories with special relevancy for rural policy such as commuting and transfers-dependent counties. The most recent revision was in 2004, which added additional policy-relevant categories for counties including housing stress, low-education, low-employment, population loss, nonmetropolitan recreation, and retirement destination.

Population-Interaction Zones for Agriculture (PIZA)

The rapid spread of rural land conversion has created a growing political debate, most of which is controversial. Analysts at the USDA-ERS developed a system to classify rural farmland into "population-interaction zones for agriculture" (PIZA). Zones were identified that represent transitional lands where urban activities (residential, commercial or industrial) impact agriculture. The interaction between urban and rural populations in these transition areas typically increases the value of farmland, changes production or farm enterprise practices, or elevates the probability of farmland conversion. The PIZA index classifies areas into four categories: 1) rural with little or no urban-related population interaction, 2) low population interaction, 3) medium population interaction, and 4) high population interaction.

Other Definitions

Other rural definitions developed by the USDA-ERS focus on commuting and labor markets. In addition to the statistical definitions generated by federal statistical agencies, there are a number of notable examples produced by other researchers. Perhaps one of the most known is the rurality codes generated by Professor Charles Cleland from the University of Tennessee.

Rurality Codes

Charles Cleland from the University of Tennessee at Knoxville further refined the definition of rurality by adding a new dimension: connectedness (1994). The term attempted to capture the degree of isolation or limited access rural areas have to other areas. A connectedness index was constructed to rank counties on a scale from 0 to 20. He labeled this a rurality index. Indicators that comprise the scale encompass not only measures of physical isolation such as low density, but also economic factors that act as barriers to accessing the larger society. The most recent update of these codes occurred in 2000.

Rural Population Change

The population of rural America declined systematically since 1900. Technological advancements, especially in farming, are a major reason for the exodus. Larger equipment, new seed varieties, and advances in chemicals, for example, expanded production capabilities of farmers. Agricultural output per hour of farm work rose roughly 1,300 percent between 1940 and 1990 (Beale, 1993). Productivity more than doubled per acre, whereas harvested cropland remained fairly constant. As a result of economies of scale, farm labor dropped dramatically. In the past four decades alone, farm employment declined from eight million to slightly more than three million. Currently, farmers account for less than 8 percent of the rural workforce. This proportion was nearly twice that level in 1970. This translates into large rural population losses. For example, in 1940, the U.S. farm population topped 30 million, or one in four residents. At present, fewer than six million people live on farms, accounting for less than 2 percent of the total population. Neighboring rural towns have witnessed a similar population free fall. Residential losses in rural communities between 1940 and 1970 exceeded 50 percent, due largely to lack of employment opportunities. Even greater losses occurred in the 1980s. Population decline in nonmetropolitan counties still continues. Between 2000 and 2005, half of the 2,051 nonmetropolitan counties lost residents (Beale and Cromartie, 2007).

The diversity of rural America is reflected in very different population changes. Whereas farm-dependent counties continue to lose population, many other rural areas enjoy significant population gains. For example, more than half of the 565 farm-dependent counties lost population between 1990 and 2000 (McGranahan and Beale, 2002). In contrast, during this same time period, natural amenity counties were rapidly growing. Most of these counties are located in the intermountain West and the Southwest, upper Great Lakes, Missouri Ozarks and along the Gulf Coast.

Migration

Migration is the major reason for shifts in residential patterns. When people move, the place they move from loses population while the place they go to increases population. In contrast, births and deaths, the other two main components of population change, affect the population size only of the place of residence. The U.S. has become a very mobile society. Nearly 40 million Americans moved between March 2005 and March 2006, which is about 14 percent of the total population.

Estimates indicate that the average American will move nearly 12 times in his/her lifetime (Hansen, 1994). However, the migration experience is very selective. Nearly 29 percent of the 40 million U.S. residents who moved between March 2005 and March 2006 were in their twenties. This is largely due to employment or educational reasons. In addition, the West had the highest rate of mobility (16 percent) and the Northeast the lowest (10 percent). Also, Hispanics had the highest moving rate (19 percent) followed by Blacks (18 percent), while non-Hispanic Whites had the lowest moving rate (12 percent).

Net migration is determined by subtracting natural increase (births minus deaths) from the difference in the base population between two time periods. In general, nonmetropolitan areas have been net exporters of population. There have been notable exceptions, especially the decade of the 1970s. This period of rural revival was marked by widespread movement of people from large cities to rural areas, including areas most remote from metropolitan counties. Nonmetropolitan counties grew at twice the rate of metropolitan areas, expanding by three million people from net migration alone. The influx of metropolitan movers accounted for nearly half the population growth of nonmetropolitan counties between 1970 and 1980. Numerous reasons have been cited for this unique change in the historical pattern including quality-of-life factors, decentralization of manufacturing, modernization of rural communities, retirement and recreational movement, and a general increase in rural employment (Fuguitt et al., 1989). However, the decade of the 1980s quickly reversed the short-lived trend. Between 1980 and 1990, net migration losses in nonmetropolitan counties topped half a million. The latest *Current Population Survey* data indicate that between 2005 and 2006, the nonmetropolitan areas had net out-migration of 155,000 people, while the suburbs gained 2.2 million people through in-migration.

Fertility

Women in rural areas historically have had higher rates of fertility than women in urban areas. An analysis of the Census of 1800 shows the ratio of children to women of childbearing age was more than 50 percent higher in rural areas compared to urban places (Grabill et al., 1958). The gap between urban and rural childbearing, however, declined dramatically over time. The cumulative fertility of women 35 to 44 years old in 1980 was only 11 percent higher among rural women compared to urban women. In 1992, the rate of births per 1,000 nonmetropolitan women was 1,590 compared to 1,459 for metropolitan women. However, the expected number of lifetime births for nonmetropolitan women was lower than it was for metropolitan women (2,231 and 2,253, respectively) (Bachu, 1992). Although differences exist in childbearing among rural women in nonmetropolitan areas versus metropolitan areas, the reversal in the long-term trend is notable. For example, data from the most recent *American Community Survey* show that the rate of births to women ages 15 to 50 in 2006 was very similar between urban and rural areas, 55 per 1,000 compared to 54 per 1,000, respectively.

The out-migration of young adults from nonmetropolitan areas creates a dramatic decline in births in rural areas. As more young adults in their prime childbearing ages leave rural areas, fewer people are left to have children. For example, there were 25,648 fewer births in nonmetropolitan counties in 1999 relative to 1990 based on Census Bureau estimates.

The composition of rural families has also changed. In 1990, the number of nonmetropolitan children living in homes without both parents reached nearly four million, an increase of one million just between 1970 and 1990 (Ghelfi, 1993). Data from the March 2002 *Current Population Survey* show 4.2 million nonmetropolitan children under the age of 18 living in homes without both parents or 32 percent. Racial disparities were also apparent in these data. For example, 27 percent of children in nonmetropolitan White families were living in homes without both parents, compared to 65 percent of children from nonmetropolitan Black families.

Mortality

One of the plaguesome factors in rural American population is natural decrease. Natural decrease occurs when deaths outnumber births. Historically, natural decrease seldom occurred in the U.S. However, since the Baby Bust years of the late 1960s, a growing number of counties experienced natural decrease. By 1970, nearly 20 percent of all U.S. counties experienced at least one year of natural decrease (Johnson and Beale, 1992). Less than 10 years later, that proportion had jumped to 32 percent.

Natural decrease is predominately a nonmetropolitan phenomenon; over 95 percent of the counties experiencing natural decrease are nonmetropolitan. Many of the most rural counties are plagued by persistent decline. For example, nearly 46 percent of the nonmetropolitan counties that experienced natural decrease in the late 1960s had at least 10 years of natural decrease by 1990. Recent data indicate that 839 of the 2,051 nonmetropolitan counties, or 41 percent, experienced natural decrease between 2000 and 2005. This is up from 610 natural decrease counties between 1990 and 1999 (Beale and Cromartie, 2007).

The major cause of natural decrease is protracted out-migration of young adults. This creates an imbalance between the young and old. The out-migration of those in their prime childbearing ages reduces the likelihood of new births, while the corresponding increase in the proportion of elderly heightens the likelihood of increased deaths. The result is natural decrease. An example of the imbalance is best illustrated by the magnitude of loss of young adults. Between 1960 and 1970, nearly 40 percent of nonmetropolitan young adults in their twenties moved to metropolitan areas. Even during the turnaround decade of the 1970s, there was a net loss of nearly 300,000 young adults from nonmetropolitan counties. Recent data from the 2006 *Annual Social and Economic Supplement to the Current Population Survey* indicates that 686,000 young adults in their twenties and thirties moved from nonmetropolitan counties to metropolitan counties between 2005 and 2006. This represented 46.5 percent of all nonmetropolitan to metropolitan movers during this time period.

— *Richard Rathge*

See also

Elders; Marriage; Migration; Rural, Definition of; Rural Women; Urbanization

References

Bachu, Amara. "Fertility of American Women." *Current Population Reports*, P20-470 (June). Washington, DC: U.S. Bureau of the Census, U.S. Government Printing Office, 1992.

Beale, Calvin L. "Salient Features of the Demography of American Agriculture." In *The Demography of Rural Life*. Edited by D.L. Brown, D.R. Field, and J.J. Zuiches. University Park, PA: Northeast Regional Center for Rural Development, 1993.

Beale, Calvin L. and John Cromartie. "Rural Population and Migration." Briefing Rooms, Economic Research Service, Washington, DC: U.S. Department of Agriculture, 2007.

Bender, Lloyd D., Bernal L. Green, Thomas F. Hady, John A. Kuehn, Marlys K. Nelson, Leon B. Perkinson, and Peggy J. Ross. *The Diverse Social and Economic Structure of Nonmetropolitan America*, USDA-ERS. Rural Development Research Report No. 49. Washington, DC: U.S. Government Printing Office, 1985.

Cleland, Charles L. "Measuring Rurality." Paper presented at the annual meeting of the Southern Demographic Association, Atlanta, GA, October 1994.

Cook, Peggy J. and Karen L. Mizer. *The Revised ERS County Typology: An Overview*, USDA- ERS. Rural Development Research Report No. 89. Washington, DC: U.S. Government Printing Office, 1994.

Fuguitt, Glenn V., David L. Brown, and Calvin L. Beale. *Rural and Small Town America*. New York, NY: Russell Sage Foundation, 1989.

Ghelfi, Linda M., ed. *Rural Conditions and Trends: Special Census Issue* 4(3). Economic Research Service, Washington, DC: U.S. Department of Agriculture, 1993.

Grabill, Wilson H., Clyde V. Kiser, and Pascal K. Whelpton. *The Fertility of American Women*. New York, NY: Wiley, 1958.

Halfacree, K.H. "Locality and Social Representation: Space, Discourse, and Alternative Definitions of the Rural," *Journal of Rural Studies* 9(1):23-37, 1993.

Hansen, Kristin A. "Geographical Mobility: March 1992 to March 1993." *Current Population Reports*, P20-481. Washington, DC: U.S. Bureau of the Census, 1994.

Johnson, K. and Calvin L. Beale. "Natural Population Decrease in the United States." *Rural Development Perspectives* 8:8-15, 1992.

Kandel, William and David L. Brown. *Population Change and Rural Society*. The Netherlands: Springer, 2006.

McGranahan, David A. and Calvin Beale. "Understanding Population Loss." *Rural America* 17(4):2-11, 2002.

Shryock, Henry S. and Jacob S. Siegel. *The Methods and Materials of Demography*. New York, NY: Academic Press, 1976.

Rural Emergency Management Programs

Programs that "coordinate and integrate all activities and organizations necessary to build, sustain, and improve the capability to prepare for, protect against, respond to, recover from, or mitigate against threatened or actual natural disasters, acts of terrorism, or other manmade disasters" (DHSb, 2008). The specific responsibilities involved in running an emergency management program include developing and maintaining plans; working with, providing information to, and training all stakeholders involved in disaster management (see Figure 1); ensuring all federal policies and mandates are implemented; applying for grant funding; and completing grant-related reports. These basic activities are virtually the same for rural and urban areas, although the challenges associated with executing these activities are often distinct in rural versus urban emergency management programs. The U.S. Department of Homeland Security's list of fundamental emergency management program functions are displayed in Figure 2.

Introduction

To understand rural emergency management programmatic structure, we need to begin with an analysis of the historically complex federal/rural emergency management relationship. Prior to 1950, there was little systematic policy-making or program-building at the federal level with respect to disasters (Rubin, 2007). Major disasters such as the Galveston Hurricane of 1900 and the San Francisco Earthquake of 1906 triggered the involvement of various federal agencies, but the pattern of policy and program development was reactive and focused on addressing the response needs of specific events. This episodic response of the federal government to local disasters began to change forever with the passage of the Civil Defense Act of 1950, the Federal Disaster Act of 1950, and later, the major, Robert T. Stafford Act of 1974 (Canton, 2007; Rubin, 2007). These acts placed the primary responsibility for emergency management program functions at the local level, but the legislation also moved toward a more coordinated, centralized role for the federal government in assisting with disasters.

These changes at the federal level affected local emergency management programs and policies in both urban and rural settings. Thus, the discussion of rural emergency management programs will begin with a broad discussion of the evolving federal/local emergency management relationship without specific discussion of urban/rural differences. However, there are significant urban/rural differences in the fit between federal programmatic structures and local realities, so the dis-

---

STAKEHOLDERS

Elected Officials
Local Area Planning Committees
Fire Department
Hazardous Materials Response
Search and Rescue
Police Department
Emergency Medical Services
Hospitals and Health Care Systems
Public Health Department
Public Works/Utilities Department
Schools, Colleges, Universities
Animal Care and Control Agency

Figure 1. *Stakeholders in Rural Emergency Management*

Function	Description
1. Laws and Authorities	The emergency management program must have a legal basis for the establishment of the emergency management organization, the implementation of an emergency management program, and continuity of government that exists in local law/ordinance and is consistent with State statutes concerning emergency management.
2. Hazard Identification and Risk Assessment	The program must identify and evaluate natural and technological hazards within its jurisdiction and update its evaluation periodically.
3. Hazard Mitigation	The jurisdiction must establish a pre-disaster hazard mitigation program.
4. Resource Management	The program must ensure that it has the human resources required to carry out assigned day-to-day responsibilities and has identified and trained the human resources necessary to respond to and recover from disasters.
5. Planning	The program must develop and maintain plans for mitigation, response, and recovery to disasters.
6. Direction and Control	The program must develop and test Emergency Operations Center operating procedures. The program must adopt, train in, and implement the National Incident Management System.
7. Communication and Warning	The program must evaluate communications system capabilities and develop communication and warning procedures.
8. Operations and Procedures	The program has to develop procedures for conducting needs and damage assessments, requesting disaster assistance, and conducting a range of disaster response functions.
9. Logistics and Facilities	Programs must ensure that Emergency Operations Centers have the capability to sustain emergency operations for the duration of an emergency or disaster and have developed logistics management and operations plans.
10. Training	The program must conduct training needs assessment, incorporate courses from various sources, and provide/offer training to all personnel with assigned emergency management responsibilities.
11. Exercises, Evaluations, and Corrective Actions	The program must establish and maintain an emergency management exercise program that includes exercises of the Emergency Operations Plan on an annual basis, and incorporates an evaluation component and corrective action component.
12. Public Education and Information	The program must develop an emergency preparedness public education program, establish procedures for disseminating and managing emergency public information in a disaster, and establish procedures for initiating and operating a Joint Information Center (JIC).
13. Finance and Administration	The program must establish and maintain an administrative system for day-to-day operations.

Figure 2. Emergency Management Program Functions (Adapted and modified from DHSb 2007)

cussion will later turn to examination of the challenges facing rural emergency management in implementing federal mandates. Finally, the discussion will conclude with a brief examination of future trends in rural emergency management programs.

The Federal/Local Emergency Management Programmatic Relationship

The federal/local emergency management relationship is programmatically complex and constantly changing. Numerous legislative bills and amendments to bills have shaped and re-shaped federal policy since the initial pieces of major, federal emergency management legislation were passed in the middle of the twentieth century. Any effort to summarize this recent history would require a lengthy and convoluted discussion covering a mind-numbing progression of program and agency changes and a multitude of confusing acronyms (Rubin, 2007).

Instead, understanding both the past and the likely future can be expedited by identifying the underlying dynamics and dimensions of change. The underlying dynamic of change has been reactive rather than proactive. Different disasters have revealed different preparedness, mitigation, response and recovery problems creating limited windows of opportunity for programmatic change (Birland, 1997; Rubin, 2007). This reac-

tive dynamic has triggered shifting emphases along each of the following dimensions of change: 1) the allocation of responsibility for disaster management (changing emphasis on local responsibility); 2) threat prioritization (terrorism vs. natural disaster); 3) how best to organize for disaster response (top/down vs. bottom/up); and 4) multiple organization coordination (network vs. command and control). The history of change in the federal/rural emergency management relationship has been and will likely continue to be one of episodic, reactive shifts in emphasis along each of these dimensions prompting the federal government to develop polices and mandates directing local and state programs to emphasize certain hazards, utilize specific strategies and tactics for dealing with disasters, and fulfill planning and reporting requirements of various types.

However, there have been overall trends in the federal/local relationship. Throughout the latter half of the twentieth century the number of major, costly disasters has continually increased while after-action assessments of organizational response reveal a consistent litany of basic problems with coordination and communication. Increasingly, the federal government has attempted to institute standardized structures, processes and plans for intergovernmental coordination and communication to overcome issues in the management. These programmatic transformations have often significantly altered the organizational mandates facing local emergency managers.

The most recent re-specification of the federal/local emergency management relationship was triggered by the terrorist attack on the World Trade Center Towers and Pentagon on September 11, 2001, and the devastation from Hurricane Katrina in 2005. These two events led to major revisions in federal emergency management policy and the restructuring of emergency management programs with substantial implications for rural emergency management. Much of the restructuring was associated with the newly established National Incident Management System (NIMS). "NIMS is a systematic, proactive approach guiding departments and agencies at all levels of government, the private sector, and nongovernmental organizations to work seamlessly to prepare for, prevent, respond to, recover from and mitigate the effects of incidents, regardless of cause, size, location or complexity, in order to reduce the loss of life, property and harm to the environment" (DHSa, 2007). Many of the components of NIMS have been incorporated in federal policy before, but never before have all of these components been brought together in such a comprehensive programmatic effort to integrate emergency management, both public and private efforts, from the national to the rural level.

Specifically, NIMS constitutes a standardized set of concepts, principles, procedures, organizational processes, terminology and standards for preparedness, resource management, communications, command and ongoing maintenance related to the management of emergencies and disasters *at all levels*. Most of the emergency management programmatic issues discussed earlier are addressed by NIMS. NIMS provides a standardized framework specifying who should be involved in disaster management and what their responsibilities are; NIMS creates a uniform structure with the expectation that this structure should be used for any type of disaster; NIMS consists of standardized procedures, communication protocols, equipment, resource terminology, etc., to be implemented in all organizations that are involved in disaster response; and NIMS is based on a top/down, military-style incident command structure (ICS) with unified command similar to that used by many fire departments when responding to emergencies. If NIMS were fully implemented, then all levels of government (federal, state, county, city and rural) across all agencies and all private sector organizations at all levels would work together in a well-coor-

dinated, standardized environment in virtually any disaster situation.

Rural Emergency Management Programs

So, have rural emergency management programs become mere cogs on the well-oiled gears of NIMS? No, at least, not yet, and the reasons reveal much about the nature of rural emergency management programs. Cogs must be standardized, but research by Quarantelli (1988) and Leifeld (2007) found considerable variation in rural programs. These variations included the status of the emergency manager position (full-time vs. part-time, paid vs. volunteer), the use of local volunteers as staff and/or first-responders, a self-determination ethos, significant resource limitations, different program locations in local organization charts, and considerable variation in missions, task responsibilities and funding levels (Leifeld, 2007; Quarantelli, 1988).

Particularly significant variations are associated with the nature of the emergency manager's position in many rural areas and with access to resources. All counties in the United States are mandated to have a designated emergency manager, but the federal government does not fully subsidize the cost of employing people for the position. Most rural emergency managers are part-time. To achieve a full-time status, some emergency managers serve two or more counties, while some emergency managers hold more than one position (e.g., auditor, assessor, deeds, veteran's affairs, sheriff, 9-1-1 coordinator, fire chief, or head of emergency medical services). Such dual positions can be stressful, particularly given the increase in federal emergency management mandates.

In addition, there are sometimes dramatic variations in access to resources. Rural resource challenges include out-migration, marginal businesses, few well-paying jobs, loss of young people, increase in elderly, and a decrease in the tax base. Such resource limitations lead to a heavy reliance on volunteers. In urban areas first responders are typically paid, whereas in rural areas first response functions often have been provided through a small contingent of paid law enforcement with fire and EMS services delivered by volunteers. Depending on the discipline they serve, volunteers face numerous training requirements just to be able to perform basic service for their community. And, it is increasingly difficult for counties to provide basic services, much less prepare for disasters, because of a decline in volunteers in first response. Those who are willing and able to volunteer are often leaving rural areas. This means that many emergency managers are hesitant to add any additional burden, such as training in NIMS, onto their already taxed volunteer responders. In sum, rural emergency management programs face numerous everyday challenges, so an environment of shifting federal mandates can make these rural programs even more challenging to manage.

The Future of Emergency Management Programs

What does the future hold for rural emergency management programs? Rural areas often cannot afford to fund the equipment and training needs much less a position to coordinate emergency management. The demands of implementing top/down protocols can be overwhelming. One structural consequence of increased demands without increased resources is increased regionalization of emergency management. Today, rural emergency management is, for the most part, organized and coordinated at the county level. The organization of emergency management at the county level makes emergency managers responsible for large geographic areas with, oftentimes, diverse needs and characteristics. This can increase efficiency, but can also increase the separation between the emergency manager and the public (Murty, 2001).

Meanwhile, there are likely to be continued pendulum swings in emergency management with each swing affecting rural emergency management, but the long-term programmatic trends do suggest a future of fewer resources, increased demands in the face of increasingly costly disasters, and a continued push toward standardization of emergency management programs across all levels of government. Perhaps some balance can eventually be achieved between the twin demands of standardization and flexibility. As described in Caruson and MacManus (2006), intergovernmental and interorganizational relationships in emergency management have shown some overall improvement as a result of recent federal mandates, including NIMS, despite the challenges we have described—two steps forward for every one step backward? To follow the continuing development of emergency management programs, consult www.fema.gov, www.ready.gov and the many excellent state emergency management websites.

— *Jessica Leifeld and George A. Youngs, Jr.*

See also

Department of Homeland Security and Rural America; Disaster Preparedness and Mitigation; Rural Emergency Response and Recovery; Emergency Management Pro-

fessionals; Firefighters; Government; Injuries; Terrorism; Weather

References

Birkland, Thomas A. *After Disaster: Agenda Setting, Public Policy, and Focusing Events*. Washington D.C.: Georgetown University Press, 1997.

Canton, Lucien G. *Emergency Management: Concepts and Strategies for Effective Programs*. Hoboken, NJ: Wiley, 2007.

Caruson, K. and S. MacManus. "Mandates and Management Challenges in the Trenches: An Intergovernmental Perspective on Homeland Security." *Public Administration Review* 66 (2006): 522-536.

Department of Homeland Security (DHSa). *The National Response Framework*. Washington, DC: Department of Homeland Security, 2008. Available online at: http://www.fema.gov/emergency/nrf/glossary.htm#E.

Department of Homeland Security (DHSb). *IS-230: The Principles of Emergency Management*. Washington, DC: Department of Homeland Security, 2007. Available online at: http://training.fema.gov/EMIWeb/IS/is230lst.asp.

Leifeld, J. *An Exploration of the National Incident Management System (NIMS) Mandate in Rural America: Through the Eyes of Emergency Management Practitioners*. Master's Thesis. Fargo, ND: North Dakota State University, 2007.

Lindell, M., C. Prater, C., and R. Perry. *Introduction to Emergency Management*. Hoboken, NJ: Wiley, 2007.

Murty, S. "Regionalization and Rural Service Delivery." Pp. 199-216 in *The Hidden America: Social Problems in Rural America in the 21st Century*. Edited by R. Moore. Cranbury, NJ: Associated University Presses, 2001.

Quarantelli, E. *Local Emergency Management Agencies: Research findings on their progress and problems in the last two decades*. Preliminary Paper #126. Newark, DE: Disaster Research Center, University of Delaware, 1988.

Quarantelli, E. *Catastrophes are Different from Disasters: Some Implications for Crisis Planning and Managing Drawn from Katrina*, 2006. Available online at: http://understandingkatrina.ssrc.org/Quarantelli.

Rubin, C., ed. *Emergency Management: The American Experience 1900-2005*. Fairfax, VA: Public Entity Risk Institute (PERI), 2007.

Rural Emergency Response and Recovery

"Activity in the immediate aftermath of a disaster to protect life and property . . . [and] activity to return the affected community to pre-disaster or preferably, improved conditions" (McEntire, 2007). Rural emergency response and recovery are the responsibility of the local area where a disaster has hit (Rubin, 2007). If a rural area is hit by a tornado, flood, hurricane, earthquake, terrorist event or some other type of natural or human-made disaster, rural emergency management personnel must first assess their ability to respond and only ask for outside help if the event overwhelms local capacity. Requests for outside help follow pre-set procedures moving from one level of government to the next as the size of the disaster demands.

This distribution of responsibility suggests the need for a three-part discussion of rural emergency response and recovery. First, it is important to understand the challenges and responsibilities of rural emergency management itself. Second, it is equally important to see rural emergency management in the context of a national emergency management system, the rules and resources of which both support and constrain local response and recovery. Third, while these twin perspectives on the local and national contexts of rural emergency management reveal significant challenges ahead, many of these challenges are being met, so the final section will discuss how rural emergency management is moving forward. The discussion below begins with a focus on local rural emergency management.

Local Rural Emergency Management

Rural areas face a variety of unique challenges in disaster response and recovery (Flint and Brennan, 2007). These challenges are primarily associated with low population density and limited resources. Low population density means that victims, first responders, and response equipment are likely to be widely dispersed and therefore are unlikely to be in the same place at the same time. In addition, low population density typically

Figure 1. Greensburg, KS, on May 16, 2007, 12 days following a tornado that virtually destroyed this entire community. Source: www.fema.gov, photographs, ID 30066. Photograph by Greg Henshall.

means limited resources—a small tax base trying to support significant, everyday infrastructure demands. The rural reality of limited resources means that even a fully coordinated response (all available responders and equipment actually arriving in the same place at the same time) may be insufficient to handle major disasters.

Limited resources are a concern for rural households as well as rural response agencies. Following Hurricane Katrina in 2005, much attention was given by the national news media to the urban poverty existent in pre-disaster New Orleans. The urban poverty had been there for everyone to see, but its depth and breadth had not been fully appreciated by the nation nor fully incorporated into local emergency response planning. If the clearly visible problems of the urban poor can be overlooked, then the rural poor may be in even more jeopardy of being missed by those in power doing emergency response planning. Following Hurricane Hugo in 1989, researchers (Miller and Simile, 1992) found that many of the widely dispersed rural poor hidden down country roads outside Charleston, South Carolina, had not even been noticed prior to the disaster, much less made part of emergency response plans, by potential help-givers including government agencies (also see Tootle, 2007). Furthermore, many researchers (e.g., Bolin and Klenow, 1983) have called attention to the special needs during disaster response of vulnerable groups such as the elderly whose presence in rural areas will increase.

The impact of low population density and limited resources on rural response and recovery can best be understood in the context of a famous typology describing the various types of organizations that are likely to assist in a disaster (Dynes, 1970). The four types of organizations in this typology are established, expanding, extending, and emergent, and each type responds differently following a disaster. Established organizations, such as fire departments and hospitals, help by performing many of the functions that such organizations already have been trained to provide with existing personnel. Expanding organizations, such as the Red Cross and Salvation Army, routinely prepare for disaster but must add trained volunteers to their normal staff in order to accomplish disaster-related goals. Extending organizations, such as local businesses and churches, do not routinely prepare for disaster, and therefore, must move beyond their normal functions in order to provide support during a disaster. Finally, emergent organizations, such as neighborhood search and rescue groups, develop on the spot without prior organizational structure and dissipate as response efforts decrease. The unique challenges faced by each of these four types of organizations in rural emergency response and recovery will be discussed below.

Established Organizations. Established organizational response in rural areas including rural emergency medical service (EMS), fire, police and rural hospitals often have limited revenue streams, personnel and resources. Such organizations may be effective in addressing everyday emergencies, but are unlikely to have the surge capacity to respond adequately in the face of a major disaster. Rural medical clinics and hospitals are likely to be smaller, fewer in number, and less prepared for multiple victims with major injuries. Rural EMS and rural fire departments often must rely on volunteers. Such organizations typically are not staffed around the clock; they are limited in the training that they can impose on their volunteers; they have limited equipment; and the equipment that they do have is often out-of-date. Even rural emergency managers may be volunteers or if paid, may be serving as an emergency manager while also serving in some other capacity such as sheriff or fire chief. Thus, established, first-responder organizations in rural areas often work with limited resources, training and staff.

Expanding Organizations. Similarly, expanding organizations can find it challenging to respond effectively in rural areas. In many disaster situations, the assistance of expanding organizations such as the Red Cross or Salvation Army can be integral in addressing immediate needs for food and shelter. However, these agencies can only expand when there are the people, equipment and resources for expansion. In rural areas, especially areas far away from a sizable urban area, such expansion may absorb precious time.

Extending Organizations. Extending organizations in rural communities include local churches and businesses. A great deal of help is likely to be expected and offered from these organizations, but not without draining already limited resources. Rural churches and businesses often operate on the margins and run the risk of being overwhelmed by a community's disaster-related needs. A recent study of rural versus urban ministers (Echterling et al., 1988) found that rural ministers were more likely to burn out during a disaster than do urban ministers. Rural ministers could not help their church members, as urban ministers often did, by simply referring members to local bureaucratic agencies professionally trained to provide the needed

help—such agencies are not available in rural areas. Furthermore, rural ministers were more likely than urban ministers to be considered close friends by church and community members and to be expected to provide the personal, home-based, around the clock help that close friends provide to each other. Thus, rural extending organizations and their leaders may find that their resources fail to match community needs.

Emergent Organizations. While the disaster response of established, expanding, and extending organizations is hampered by the limited resources of rural areas, the disaster response of emergent organizations may be uniquely strong. Rural residents value self-sufficiency, but they are also quick to help when a neighbor's need is clearly perceived as legitimate and his or her plight is perceived to be beyond the victim's control (Schmidt and Weiner, 1988). A disaster creates such perceptions. Furthermore, research on helping behavior (Latané and Darley, 1970) shows that potential helpers are more likely to assume responsibility when there are fewer people present. This general phenomenon is called the bystander effect, and it may explain why studies have shown that people in need of help are more likely to receive it in small towns than in larger, urban areas (Levine et al., 1994). These social psychological processes, along with rural cultural values of neighborliness, encourage the development of emergent organizations in rural areas for such disaster-related needs as search and rescue even before established, expanding, and/or extending organizations begin to help.

The common focus by all the various types of organizations on immediate response needs can trigger a brief honeymoon period of consensus and mutual support sometimes referred to as a "therapeutic community" (Miller, 2007). Victims are taking collective action to protect life and property, and this collective action can trigger a heightened sense of community morale. A common refrain during this period is, "We are a great community, and when we are done with recovery, we will be even bigger and better than before." Then, collective action declines post-disaster, personal losses become more salient, overlooked conflicts emerge, community morale sinks, and response has become recovery.

Just as response is first and foremost a local responsibility, so is recovery. Several realities face rural areas as they try to recover. First, low population densities may become even lower. People forced to evacuate during a disaster—especially those who have lost all of the very little they previously had—are sometimes re-

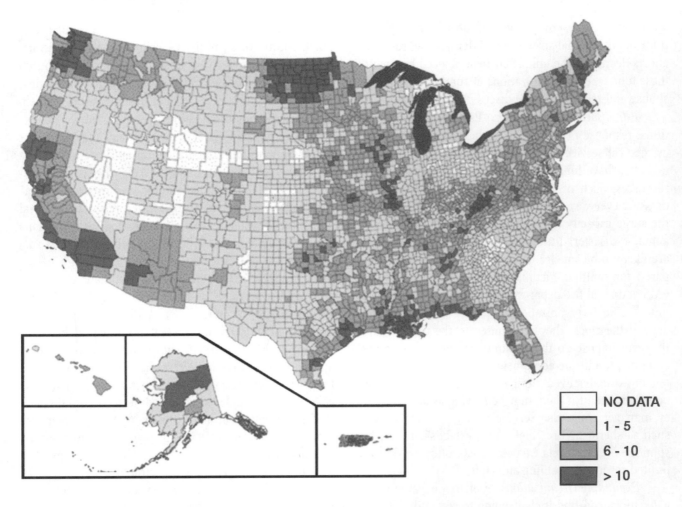

Figure 2. *County-by-county Presidential Disaster Declarations in the United States and Territories from 1965 through 2003 (Map not to Scale. Source: FEMA).*

luctant or unable to return (Rubin, 2007). Second, already limited resources must be stretched even further to cover disaster-related expenses. Third, the acute disaster of a flood or tornado may exacerbate an already chronic disaster of long-term economic decline. And, finally, residents in rural areas may be hesitant to ask for outside help. When 30 community leaders in two small, disaster-impacted communities where recently asked what advice they would offer other leaders facing disaster, nearly all of the 30 leaders advised their colleagues to be humble and ask for help—do not try to go it alone (Youngs and O'Neill, in press). Most of the 30 leaders pressed this point even while these leaders wished to prepare their colleagues for the complex and demanding world of national, help-giving agencies.

Rural Emergency Management in a National Context

The latter half of the twentieth century saw the emergence of an increasing role for the federal government in disaster response and recovery. It has been a very bumpy road, but federal policies and programs have become increasingly centralized, and some would argue that these policies have actually become too centralized (Rubin, 2007). While ultimate responsibility for rural emergency response and recovery still resides at the local level, the expectation that the federal government will help in major disasters has created a largely top/down emergency management structure with a significant impact on how emergency management is expected to be done at the rural level. The FEMA map shown in Figure 2 displays the pattern of Presidential Disaster Declarations from 1965 through 2003, highlighting the impact of federal involvement in major disasters in both urban and rural areas throughout the U.S. Thus, the second part of this paper will briefly examine the national context of rural emergency management response and recovery.

Four aspects of the national context deserve special attention including resources, complexity, centralization and change. First, increasing federal resources to assist with disasters is associated with an increasing role for the federal government in rural disaster response and recovery. Much is expected of those who have much, and the federal government has access to expertise, personnel, equipment and money that far outstrips the resources of local responders, especially in many rural areas. The presence of federal resources during disaster response can mean the difference between life and death for rural disaster victims.

Second, the national context of emergency management is one of great organizational complexity. A hint of this complexity is provided by the following summary of the key agencies with disaster responsibilities in a major disaster (Waugh, 2003):

FEMA [the Federal Emergency Management Agency] and its state, county, and city counterparts and the agencies that have disaster-related responsibilities ... the U.S. Army Corps of Engineers, the U.S. Forest Service, the Nuclear Regulatory Commission, and the Environmental Protection Agency and their state counterparts [have disaster-related responsibilities as do] major nonprofit participants ... [including] the ARC [the American Red Cross],... the Salvation Army, and the hundreds of international, national, regional, and local faith-based and secular nonprofit organizations that volunteer their time and resources prior to, during and after disasters [as well as] major for-profit participants ... from engineering firms specializing in seismic safety to consultants who assist with emergency planning and critical incident stress debriefings to debris management firms that remove the physical evidence of disaster.

Third, the U.S. Department of Homeland Security has adopted a centralized, standardized National Incident Management System (NIMS) and mandated all levels of government, nonprofit agencies and private organizations to do emergency management within this system (see www.fema.gov/emergency/nims/index.shtm). The goal of NIMS is to standardize roles, structures and terminology with the hope that such standardization will reduce the organizational confusion and miscommunication frequently found during disaster response. As an incentive to cooperate, emergency managers including rural emergency managers must be "NIMS compliant" in order to be eligible for

various sources of federal funding. While federal policy makers have tried to combine standardization with flexibility, many critics of NIMS question the extent to which NIMS permits flexibility. Recent research (Leifeld, 2008) suggests that rural emergency managers may be resistant to fully implementing NIMS because its formality clashes with the informal understandings and emergent organizational relationships that make local response work. These results reflect what is likely to be a never-ending tension between legitimate heterogeneity in rural emergency management agencies based on unique local history and organizational environments versus the value of standardization for efficiency and a research-based realization that some models for doing emergency management at the local level are indeed better (Quarantelli, 1988).

Finally, a fundamental aspect of the national context facing rural emergency managers is change. Birkland (1997) has suggested that federal policy-making is largely event driven, and Rubin (2007) has documented this reactive relationship between major disasters and emergency management policy in a history of emergency management in the U.S. from 1900 to 2005. NIMS is the most recent example of a response triggered by major disasters, in this case, the World Trade Center and Pentagon attacks in 2001 and Hurricane Katrina in 2005. As new events occur and national policies change, rural emergency managers must adapt as best they can or risk access to federal funding and support.

Thus, rural emergency managers face challenges associated with both the local and national contexts of their agencies. These challenges must be addressed by personnel who may be volunteers or part-time emergency managers relying on other volunteers and/or part-time staff. The rural emergency manager may only face one to three disasters in his or her career (Fischer, 1998), but he or she must be prepared to make life and death decisions when such events transpire. Are there sources of help to support rural emergency response and recovery in the future?

Efforts to Address Rural Recovery and Response Concerns

The future effectiveness of rural emergency response and recovery may be enhanced by three relatively recent and emerging developments. First, FEMA has supported the creation of citizen responders trained to help family, neighbors and local citizens during the first few critical hours following a disaster. The organizational framework for this effort is CERT, Community

Emergency   Response   Teams (https://www.citizencorps.gov/cert/). These teams offer an important response capability while first responders and equipment try to converge on the disaster site from across the rural area (Brennan and Flint, 2007) . Second, improved communication technology and access to tremendous Internet resources for officials and residents   (e.g.,   www.fema.gov;   www.ready.gov; www.redcross.org/services/disaster;   and www.eden.lsu.edu) may promote more effective response efforts. And, third, recent trends toward the regionalization of emergency management, especially at the county or multi-county level, may strengthen local response even though it simultaneously obfuscates the meaning of local (Murty, 1994). Thus, the future of rural emergency response and recovery includes a diversity of demanding challenges along with promising supportive developments for the future.

— George A. Youngs, Jr. and Jessica Leifeld

See also

Department of Homeland Security and Rural America; Disaster Preparedness and Mitigation; Emergency Management Professionals; Firefighters; Government; Injuries; Rural Emergency Management Programs; Terrorism; Weather

References

Birkland, Thomas A. *After Disaster: Agenda Setting, Public Policy, and Focusing Events.* Washington, DC: Georgetown University Press, 1997.

Bolin, Robert and Daniel J. Klenow. "Response of the Elderly to Disaster: An Age-Stratified Analysis." *International Journal of Aging and Human Development* 16 (1983): 83-96.

Brennan, Mark A. and Courtney G. Flint. "Uncovering the Hidden Dimensions of Rural Disaster Mitigation: Capacity Building through Community Emergency Response Teams." *Southern Rural Sociology* 22 (2007): 111-126.

Dynes, Russell. *Organized Behavior in a Disaster.* Lexington, MA: Lexington Books, 1970.

Echterling, Lennis G., Cecil Bradfield, and Mary L. Wylie "Responses of Urban and Rural Ministers to a Natural Disaster." *Journal of Rural Community Psychology* 9 (1988): 36-46.

Fischer, Henry W., III. *Response to Disaster: Fact versus Fiction and its Perpetuation: The Sociology of Disaster.* Lanham, MD: University Press of America, 1998.

Flint, Courtney G. and M.A. Brennan. "Rural Communities and Disasters: Research from the Southern United States." *Southern Rural Sociology* 22 (2007): 1-5.

Latané, B. and J.M. Darley. *The Unresponsive Bystander: Why Doesn't He Help?* NY: Appleton-Century-Crofts, 1970.

Leifeld, Jessica A. "An Exploration of the National Incident Management System (NIMS) Mandate in Rural America: Through the Eyes of Emergency Management Practitioners." Master's Thesis. Fargo, ND: North Dakota State University, 2007.

Levine, R. V., T. S. Martinez, G. Brase, and K. Sorenson. "Helping in 36 U.S. Cities." *Journal of Personality and Social Psychology* 67 (1994): 69-82.

McEntire, David A. *Disaster Response and Recovery: Strategies and Tactics for Resilience.* NJ: Wiley, 2007.

Miller, Lee M. "Collective Disaster Responses to Katrina and Rita: Exploring Therapeutic Community, Social Capital and Social Control." *Southern Rural Sociology* 22 (2007): 45-65.

Miller, Kristen S. and Catherine Simile. "'They Could See Stars from their Beds': The Plight of the Rural Poor in the Aftermath of Hurricane Hugo." Paper presented at the Society for Applied Anthropology annual meetings, Memphis, TN, 1992.

Murty, Susan. "Setting the Boundary of an Interorganizational Network: An Application." *Journal of Social Service Research* 24 (1994): 67-82.

Quarantelli, E.L. "Local Emergency Management Agencies: Research Findings on Their Progress and Problems in the Last Two Decades." Preliminary Paper # 126, Newark, DE: Disaster Research Center, University of Delaware, 1988.

Rubin, Claire B., ed. *Emergency Management: The American Experience, 1900-2005.* Fairfax, VA: Public Entity Risk Institute, 2007.

Schmidt, G. and B. Weiner. "An Attribution-Affect-Action Theory of Behavior: Replications of Judgments of Help-Giving." *Personality and Social Psychology Bulletin* 14 (1988): 610-621.

Tootle, Deborah M. "Disaster Recovery in Rural Communities: A Case Study of Southwest Louisiana." *Southern Rural Sociology* 22 (2007): 6-27.

Waugh, William. "Terrorism, Homeland Security and the National Emergency Management Network." *Public Organization Review: A Global Journal* 3 (2003): 373-385.

Youngs, George A., Jr. and H. Katherine O'Neill. "Strategies for Resilience: A Qualitative Analysis of Rural Community Leaders' Advice on Disaster Recovery." *Journal of Emergency Management,* in press.

Rural Delivery Service

The daily delivery of mail to rural farm residents by the U.S. Postal Service (formerly Rural Free Delivery, or

RFD). This article addresses the establishment of city free delivery of mail, the farmers' mail system before RFD of mail, experimental RFD, and RFD expanded and made permanent. It describes RFD under the postal corporation, the effect of RFD on rural America, the development of good roads on RFD, and the beginnings of rural parcel post. The article concludes with a discussion of efforts to change Rural Delivery Service (RDS), and RDS as an obstacle to privatizing the U.S. Postal Service.

Emergence of Rural Free Delivery

Congress authorized the Postmaster General to establish free delivery of mail in cities in 1864. The next year, it restricted this delivery to cities of 50,000 or more inhabitants, but gradually expanded the service until it reached towns of 10,000 in 1887. Yet during that time, the postal system in rural America remained much as it had been before the Civil War.

Until the establishment of RFD, farmers received their mail from more than 70,000 small, Fourth Class Post Offices to which Star Route mail carriers, under contract to the Post Office, brought the mail from rail or stagecoach centers, usually no more often than two or three times per week. Although this system provided farmers with an opportunity to visit neighbors, it often deprived them of postal services that their post offices were too small to offer. Moreover, it made impractical a subscription to a daily newspaper. In 1896, however, the Post Office Department inaugurated an RFD service to alleviate rural isolation and help revolutionize farm life.

RFD of mail was not easily established. John Wanamaker, President Benjamin Harrison's energetic Postmaster General, proposed creating an RFD service for farmers in 1891, but his term of office expired before his proposal reached further than the establishment of a village free delivery experiment. Nevertheless, members of the Grange and Farmers' Alliance clubs, enthused by the publicity he generated for the proposal, seized on the idea, and arguing that the government's mail service discriminated against them in favor of the cities, swamped Congress in 1892 with petitions demanding an RFD of mail service.

Confronted by their demands, Congress appropriated $10,000 for an RFD experiment. Tom Watson, a Populist Congressman from Georgia, was responsible for this small appropriation and ever after claimed to be the "Father of the RFD."

In 1893, however, Grover Cleveland, the first Democratic President between the Civil War and 1900, returned to office and appointed William Bissell, his friend from Buffalo, as Postmaster General. Conservative and obdurate, Bissell refused to begin an experiment that he believed would bankrupt the government. But Congress, unwilling to accept this decision, continued to appropriate money for the experiment until 1896 when William L. Wilson, former Congressman from West Virginia, replaced Bissell as Postmaster General, and promised to begin the RFD experiment. On October 1, 1896, at Charles Town, Uvilla, and Halltown, in his home state, he established the first of what, by the spring of 1897, became 82 experimental mail routes in 28 states and the Territory of Arizona.

The experiment had scarcely begun before the Republicans, less cautious about expanding the power of the national government than the Democrats had been, returned to control both houses of Congress and the presidency in 1897. The fledgling RFD experiment fell into the hands of two politicians: Perry Heath, President McKinley's First Assistant Postmaster General, and August Machen, Superintendent of Free Delivery. Driven as much by possible political advantage, perhaps, as by concern for the farmers, they saved RFD from an early death by cleverly inviting farmers to petition their congressman for a rural mail route if they wished to have their mail delivered to their farms. The farmers responded to this invitation with thousands of petitions, which led to the establishment of hundreds of rural mail routes and virtually forced Congress to make the experiment permanent, which it did in 1902.

Political pressure, combined with a growing emphasis on saving farms and farmers in the period, forced the rapid expansion of the service until 1926 when there were 45,318 rural mail routes. After this, because of improved country roads and the mail carriers' substitution of the automobile for the horse and buggy, rural mail routes were gradually lengthened and reduced in number to 31,346 in 1970, the year Congress converted the Post Office to a government corporation.

Rural Free Delivery under the Postal Corporation

Virtually compelled to be self-sustaining by 1984, the new Postal Service's management sought to reduce expenses by replacing many small town and village post offices with "heavy duty" rural mail routes on which carriers served large clusters of mail boxes. The reduction of post offices, however, necessitated an increase in the number of rural mail routes and mail carriers. In September 1995, there were 54,442 rural mail routes, 46,163 rural mail carriers, and 53,634 replacement carriers.

Until its establishment in the early 1900s, the national government had developed few programs for farmers that had a more powerful effect upon rural America than the free delivery of mail. It raised land values, eroded farm isolation, erased the discrimination between the urban and rural mail service, and became a daily reminder to farm families that the national government had not forgotten them. It gave farmers the daily market quotations and swelled the profits of publishers of daily newspapers as thousands of farmers subscribed to their papers. True, RFD eliminated many little post offices that were the hubs of small communities, but it also made two inestimable contributions to rural life: good roads and a bona fide parcel post.

Because postal regulations required farmers to keep their roads passable if they wished to have their mail delivered, farmers began to improve their roads in the early 1900s as they never had before and became a vital part of the good roads movement of the era. Rural delivery also played a key role in the enactment of the Federal Highway Act of 1916. Because each road over which a rural route ran was obviously a post road, which Congress had the right to establish, members of Congress found in rural delivery the constitutional authority to give money to the states on a dollar matching scheme to build roads over which the mail was carried or might be carried.

When rural delivery began, only packages weighing no more than four pounds were mailable. But when rural mail carriers began to pass farms with the mail each day, they themselves began to carry packages to farmers outside the mails for a small fee. When the Post Office Department stopped this service, parcel post enthusiasts argued for a parcel post that would permit the sending of large packages through the mails. Small town merchants, who feared farmers would use the parcel post to purchase their goods from mail order stores, and the express companies wary of this postal competition, fought bitterly against an enlarged parcel post. But Congress, unable to ignore the practical use of RFD, created the present parcel post system in 1912, which began on January 1, 1913. With the introduction of the 911 emergency system, the method used to address mail changed from rural route numbers to house and street numbers. The National Rural Letter Carriers'

Association represents rural letter carriers with the U.S. Postal Service.

Rural Delivery Service an Obstacle to Privatizing the Post Office

Rural Delivery Service has been a costly service, but efforts to cheapen the service by contracting the routes to the lowest bidders failed, largely because Congress refused to give one kind of postal service to cities and another to farmers. Even the new Postal Service was unable to change the basic structure of rural delivery, although it substituted contract post offices for post offices that formerly had postmasters and established highway contract routes, somewhat akin to the old Star Routes, in some areas.

Rural Delivery Service recently has been the one greatest obstacle to privatizing the Post Office. Private contractors may be able to deliver the mail in cities more cheaply than the Postal Service can and still make a profit. But this would be more difficult in rural America where the mail service has never paid its way.

— *Wayne E. Fuller*

See also
Government; History, Rural; Infrastructure; Media; Public Services; Quality of Life; Town-Country Relations

References
Aaberg, Gwendolyn M. *The R F D: Golden Jubilee, 1896-1946*. Washington, DC: np, 1946.
Fuller, Wayne E. *R.F.D.: The Changing Face of Rural America*. Bloomington, IN: Indiana University Press, 1964.
Greathouse, Charles A. "Free Delivery of Mails." In *U.S. Department of Agriculture Yearbook*. Washington, DC: GPO, 1900.
Kernell, Samuel. "Rural Free Delivery as a Critical Test of Alternative Models of American Political Development." *Studies in American Political Development* 15 (2001): 103-112.
May, Earl. "The Good Roads Train." *World's Work* 2 (July 1901): 956-960.
May, Earl. "Parcel Post At Last." *The Outlook* 102 (December 1912): 872-873.
Scheele, Carl. *A Short History of the Mail Service*. Washington, DC: Smithsonian Press, 1970.
Thorbahn, M. "100 Years of Americana: Rural Free Delivery Celebrates a Milestone." Available online athttp://www.usps.com/history/plife/pl091096/american.htm. Accessed February 2008.
Thrasher, Max Bennett. "Thirty Miles with a Rural Mail Carrier." *The Independent* 55 (February 5, 1903): 311-317.

Rural Health Care

The organization and provision of services meeting the preventative, acute, chronic and long-term care health-related needs of the rural population. The organization of this entry is as follows: changes in the health care industry; the distribution and adequacy of rural health care providers; the viability of rural hospitals; the viability of rural community pharmacies; rural mental health; telemedicine; rural health networks and the future of rural health care.

Changes in the Health Care Industry

As the pace quickens in the twenty-first century, significant change is being experienced in many, if not most industries. However, few industries are changing faster than the health care industry. Since the 1960s, an explosion of medical technology has continually reshaped the way medicine is practiced in the U.S. and throughout the world. Equally important are changes in the way medical care is financed and delivered. With the introduction of Medicare in the 1960s, the federal government not only became a major financing agency for health care, but in many ways became the leading force in health care policy reformation.

An example of Medicare's influence occurred in 1983 when the federal government changed its payment methodology to providers from cost-based reimbursement to prospective payment. With this shift, health care providers no longer received payment for services based upon the costs of treating an individual patient. Rather, they received a fixed average cost for treatment of a specific diagnosis (known as a Diagnostic Related Group, or DRG). With the introduction of a fixed payment, the incentive to control resource utilization was now placed on the health care provider organizations. By the end of the 1980s virtually all private insurance companies had followed the government's lead by introducing some form of prospective payment in their own reimbursement methodologies. The influence of Medicare and federal policy in the development and transformation of health policy for the future cannot be overstated. This is especially true given that the leading edge of the disproportionately large Baby Boom cohort will be eligible for Medicare benefits starting in 2010.

Another leading force of change in the health care industry has been the introduction and proliferation of managed care organizations. With the advent of managed care and all its variations (e.g., Health Maintenance Organizations, Preferred Provider Organizations, and Independent Practice Associations), provider organizations assume a much greater level of financial risk in the delivery of health services. This risk is greatest when provider organizations, usually health maintenance organizations, accept a fixed capitated payment for each plan subscriber (usually known as a "per member per month" payment). Provider risk is assumed in less restrictive plans where physicians and other providers discount their services to insurers in return for these plans, encouraging their members to use providers who offer discounts.

As these industry changes occur, the impact on rural areas and the ability of rural health care delivery systems to adapt is often left out of the national discussion. The following discussion examines some of the more salient characteristics and issues surrounding rural health delivery systems.

Distribution and Adequacy of Rural Health Care Providers

Concerns about having an adequate supply of health professionals in rural areas are not new. The supply of primary care physicians continues to be of specific concern. While the definition of a primary care physician has been somewhat flexible, most definitions include general practitioners, family physicians, general internists, general pediatricians and sometimes obstetrician/gynecologists. In addition to the undersupply of primary care physicians in rural areas, the nationwide shortage of dentists, nurses, pharmacists, physical and occupational therapists, laboratory technicians and medical technologists disproportionately impacts rural communities.

In 1978 the federal government designated 1,209 Health Professional Shortage Areas (HPSAs) nationwide. These are contiguous geographic service areas (usually a county) with a population-to-primary-care-physician ratio of 3,500-to-1 or greater. In 1978, of those 1,209 designated shortage areas, 73 percent were located in rural areas. In spite of the large increases in the physician supply since, the number of shortage areas has continually grown, while the distribution of these shortage areas has remained rather stable. Today the federal government reports that there are 5,735 designated shortage areas and includes shortages of mental health professionals and dentists, in addition to primary care physicians. Examining the location of these HPSAs reveals that 67 percent of the primary care and dental shortage areas are located in rural areas, as are 64 percent of the mental health shortage areas.

Dr. Lee Mizrahi, with his wife, baby and staff at the free medical clinic he runs for migrant farm workers near Delano, California. © *Ted Streshinsky / Corbis*

While the maldistribution of primary care physicians and other health care professionals in rural areas is generally recognized, there has been considerable debate regarding potential solutions. Initially, the purpose of designating HPSAs was twofold: first, physicians practicing within these shortage areas received a reimbursement bonus by the federal government for the Medicare beneficiaries they treated. This, of course, was viewed as an incentive to practice in these shortage areas. Second, programs such as the National Health Service Corps (NHSC) were created to require health professionals with a federal service obligation to practice within these designated shortage areas. Today, the NHSC programs provide scholarships for students enrolled in medical or dental school, or in primary care nurse practitioner, nurse midwife or physician assistant programs. The NHSC and several states also make available educational loan repayment for graduates of the health professions programs named above, as well as to dental hygienists and several categories of mental

health professionals in return for two years of service in these health professional shortage areas.

Rather than a government solution, others suggested that "market forces" would eventually correct the maldistribution of health professionals. In the early 1980s the Graduate Medical Education National Advisory Committee issued a report that many interpreted as a prediction of a national oversupply of physicians, suggesting that physicians would be forced to diffuse into rural areas and lessen the maldistribution (DHHS, 1981). Today, however, it is generally recognized that there is little evidence that the market will correct the maldistribution of health care professionals. In spite of all of these efforts, the reality today remains that while approximately 20 percent of Americans live in rural areas, only 10 percent of all physicians practice in rural areas.

Viability of Rural Hospitals

There is little question that the hospital is the hub of the health care delivery system in rural communities. Besides serving as the focal point for health care delivery, rural hospitals are often important providers of social services; serve as an important asset in the recruitment of new businesses to the community; and are themselves often one of the largest employers in the community. In every sense, rural hospitals are institutional and economic anchors in their communities.

Unfortunately, during the 1980s the viability of many rural hospitals began to steadily erode, and during that decade rural hospitals failed in unprecedented numbers. Between 1980 and 1983, an average of 12 rural hospitals closed each year. However, between 1984 and 1986 that annual average increased to 25, and by the end of the decade (1987 to 1989) an average of 42 rural hospitals closed annually (American Hospital Association, 1994).

The reasons for this unprecedented failure of rural hospitals in the 1980s are multiple. First, while a significant rural-to-urban migration has been a historical reality since the 1930s, the 1980s was a particularly difficult decade, highlighted by a major recession and farm crisis. Accordingly, the resulting decrease in rural residents reduced the demand for all rural services (including hospital services). Between 1980 and 1990, rural hospitals experienced a 17 percent reduction of their certified beds and a 16 percent decrease in occupancy rates (AHA, 1992).

Second, as the practice of medicine advanced, many procedures that were routinely performed in the hospital were now being performed in outpatient settings. Clearly, these changes affected both rural and urban hospitals; however, the magnitude of change impacted rural hospitals disproportionately. For example, between 1980 and 1990 rural hospital admissions declined 37 percent, while rural outpatient visits increased 36 percent. During the same period of time, urban hospital admissions declined only 6 percent, while outpatient visits increased 52 percent (AHA, 1992).

Third, given the demographic reality that rural communities have a disproportionately high percentage of elderly residents, the changes in Medicare reimbursement to hospitals noted earlier were particularly devastating to rural hospitals. Recall that in the 1980s Medicare began paying hospitals a fixed average payment for a specific diagnosis instead of the traditional reimbursement based upon costs. For larger urban hospitals this change in reimbursement was less of a problem due to their high volume. Accordingly, urban hospitals might have lost money on this fixed payment for some patients while making a sizeable profit on other patients. But due to their higher volume, on average their costs equaled Medicare's new payment rate. For many small rural hospitals with very low volume, however, one or two Medicare patients who experienced complications from surgery could create a financial crisis. The lesson learned was simply that averaging works well when there is sufficient volume to average out; but where there is low volume, averaging does not work nearly as well.

In response to the unprecedented closures of rural hospitals across the country, state and federal officials began to realize that rural hospitals were unique and different unto themselves, and not just like urban hospitals "shrunk to size." As a result, state legislatures as well as federal officials began to experiment with the development of a new type of hospital. designed to meet the unique needs of rural communities. It began in 1987 when the Montana Legislature authorized the Medical Assistance Facility (MAF) demonstration project (Office of the Inspector General, 1993). To provide continued access to health care in Montana's frontier communities, full-service hospitals were converted into low-intensity, short-stay health care facilities. MAFs had to be located more than 35 road miles from the nearest hospital or be located in a federally designated frontier county (population density of six residents or fewer per square mile). These new facilities were allowed to provide up to 96 hours of inpatient care, and were allowed to offer any health service for which they were adequately equipped and staffed to perform. These early demonstration projects proved so successful that they served as the blueprint for Critical Access Hospitals in the 1997 federal Rural Hospital Flexibility Program ("Rural Flex" or "Flex Grant" Program), which created and authorized these smaller and more appropriate types of hospitals nationwide.

Today a large majority of small rural hospitals in the U.S. are designated as Critical Access Hospitals and it has made a positive difference in the outlook of these facilities. And while much of that is due to the program rules that allow these Critical Access Hospitals to return to cost-based reimbursement, it is far from the only reason. In fact, multiple evaluative reports by the national "Flex Monitoring Team" document that these right-sized rural facilities are now more financially sound; have witnessed significant expansions of their service capabilities; have an easier time securing needed capital; and are more likely to be involved in a variety of organizational networks to improve their operational efficiencies (Casey and Klingner, 2004).

Viability of Rural Community Pharmacies

While the financial stability of rural hospitals has improved, the closure of independent retail pharmacies in rural communities has become an increasing concern. Between 1996 and 1998, 46 rural pharmacies closed in North Dakota, South Dakota and Minnesota (Casey et al., 2002), about five pharmacies per state per year. In 2005, 12 pharmacies closed in rural Minnesota communities; in two instances these were the only pharmacies in town (Traynor et al., 2005). Many rural pharmacy closures arise when the pharmacist-owner wishes to retire and is unable to sell the pharmacy to a younger pharmacist. This trend is expected to continue: the average age of pharmacists practicing in rural northern Minnesota and rural Texas at the time of this writing is greater than 50 years old.

The majority of retail pharmacy businesses in rural communities are independently owned pharmacies. Economic pressures are making many previously viable independent pharmacies less attractive business ventures (Stratton, 2001). The customer base is shrinking in rural communities where populations are decreasing. To make matters worse, rural pharmacies face increasing competition from out-of-town chain pharmacies and pharmacies located within mass merchandisers where rural residents might travel to shop, and by mail order or out-of-town "click and brick" pharmacies (where patients request a prescription refill via the Internet and the pharmacy mails the prescription to them). The margins on prescription drugs have also been eroding since the late 1980s as Pharmacy Benefit Managers (PBMs) and other third-party payers (including Medicaid and Medicare Part D) have reduced payments to pharmacies (Radford et al., 2007). In contrast, Medicare Part D and other payers now reimburse pharmacists for providing Medication Therapy Management services, where the pharmacist works with the patient and the patient's other health care providers to optimize the patient's drug therapy as part of the patient's overall treatment plan. Rural pharmacists are well positioned to offer these services because of their familiarity with their patients.

Rural Mental Health

The economic uncertainties of farming, mining, forestry and fishing-dependent occupations can induce chronic stress in rural families. The farm crisis of the

Mobile unit used in a mobile pharmacist-conducted wellness clinic for rural Montana communities. Photograph by Timothy P. Stratton. Copyright, American Pharmacists Association (APhA). Reprinted by permission of APhA.

1980s was not only a crisis in economic terms, but in sociological, psychological and emotional terms as well (NRHA, 1999). Although the prevalence of clinically defined mental health problems and alcohol and substance abuse among rural and urban adult populations appear to be similar, substantial evidence suggests that the number of mental health providers in rural America remains inadequate (Pion et al., 1997; NRHA, 1999).

Based solely on the distribution of psychiatrists, as of 2005, 64 percent of the designated Mental Health Provider Shortage Areas in the United States were located in rural areas. This lack of professionals often prevents rural hospitals from providing emergency psychiatric services—18.6 percent compared with 37.4 percent of metropolitan hospitals (NRHA, 1999). Because of the scarcity of trained mental health providers in rural areas, primary care physicians are the dominant providers of mental health care in rural communities despite a lack of specific mental health training. Confounding this role is the stigma attached to having a mental disorder in rural areas which causes patients to often seek treatment under the guise of a physical complaint, which in turn contributes to under-diagnosis and under-treatment of mental disorders among rural residents. To surmount this challenge, mental health services are increasingly provided from distant communities using telecommunications technologies (Smith and Allison, 1998).

Among telemedicine programs (discussed later in this entry), telemental health services have consistently been one of the top three most frequently provided health services using telehealth technologies. Telemental health services are delivered in rural primary care clinics, hospital emergency rooms, community mental health centers, schools, long-term care facilities and directly into patient homes.

Telemedicine

Telemedicine is the practice of health care delivery, diagnosis, consultation, treatment and transfer of medical data and education, using interactive audio, visual and data communications. Telemedicine has become a critical tool for the direct care of rural patients and for the development of rural health systems. Telemedicine affords rural residents ready access to medical specialists and sub-specialists without the inconvenience of traveling to urban centers.

The most sophisticated, costly telemedicine projects use interactive two-way video technology, enabling medical specialists in urban settings to see, hear and examine rural patients who are referred by their local physician. Other telemedicine projects use modern telecommunications technologies to digitize and forward radiologic film (x-rays), cardiac strips, and other diagnostic data for review by urban specialists (American Telemedicine Association).

Applying telemedicine technology to a rural pharmacy practice has enabled North Dakota pharmacists to supervise pharmacy technicians who are working in distant rural communities which no longer have their own pharmacist (NDSU). Similar technology enables rural Critical Access Hospitals (CAHs) to have pharmacists at urban hospitals review new medication orders written for CAH patients in the middle of the night or at other times when the rural hospital's pharmacist is not on-site, improving patient safety and job satisfaction of CAH nurses and pharmacists (Stratton et al., 2008).

Rural Health Networks

While the idea of establishing rural health provider networks is not new, it is, however, changing. For many years rural hospitals came together under the organizational umbrella of a rural hospital alliance, cooperative or network. Members of these organizations often found efficiencies of participation in areas such as joint purchasing, joint marketing and common political advocacy. However, the common feature of these organizational structures was the homogeneity of its members (i.e., rural hospitals).

More recently, there have been significant interest and activity in the development of vertically integrated networks (Moscovice and Elias, 2003). Unlike previous rural health networks, these vertically integrated networks are characterized by their heterogeneity of participants (i.e., rural clinics and hospitals, urban providers and nursing homes). Consequently, when autonomous organizations agree to participate in a vertically integrated network, access to a broader range of services for residents in the service area often occurs. As various providers affiliate with the network, the actual service area increases as well; the community expands and is redefined.

The Future of Rural Health Care

The future of health care delivery in rural communities is somewhat mixed. Providing health care services to rural communities will always remain challenging due to geographic isolation and sparse population densities. Recruiting health professionals to rural communities becomes more difficult as nationwide shortages of primary care physicians, dentists, nurses, medical technologists and pharmacists deepen in both urban and rural communities. These recruiting challenges are addressed to some extent by increasing the use of health information technology and electronic medical records to connect rural patients with specialists in urban centers. Cuts in federal funding to support rural health training programs are offset somewhat by increased state support for loan forgiveness programs for health care providers willing to work in underserved rural communities. The numbers of rural uninsured and underinsured patients will increase as rural economies shrink and local businesses close, relocate or drop their employee health coverage—a trend being addressed by federal investment in "safety-net" providers such as Rural Health Centers.

On the other hand, funding of the Rural Hospital Flex Program and the creation of rural health networks has improved the financial stability of rural hospitals, dramatically reducing the rate of rural hospital closures and improving the quality of patient care. On balance, the environment for rural health care providers is considerably better than it was 20 years ago.

— *Jack M. Geller and Timothy P. Stratton*

See also

Addiction; Dental Health Care; Mental Health; Mental Health of Older Adults; Methamphetamine Use; Nursing and Allied Health Professions; Policy, Health Care

References

American Academy of Family Physicians. "Keeping Physicians in Rural Practice: Position Paper," 2002. Avail-

able online at: http://www.aafp.org/online/en/home/
policy/policies/r/ruralpracticekeep.html

American Hospital Association (AHA). *AHA Hospital Statistics: A Comprehensive Summary of U.S. Hospitals, 1991-92 Edition.* Chicago, IL: American Hospital Association, 1992.

American Telemedicine Association. Available online at: www.atmeda.org.

Bureau of Health Professions. "The Pharmacist Workforce: A Study of the Supply and Demand for Pharmacists," December, 2000. Washington, DC: Bureau of Health Professions. Available online at: ftp://ftp.hrsa.gov/bhpr/nationalcenter/pharmacy/pharmstudy.pdf.

Casey, M.M., J. Klingner, and I. Moscovice. "Access to Rural Pharmacy Services in Minnesota, North Dakota, and South Dakota." Working Paper #36 (July), 2001. Minneapolis, MN: University of Minnesota Rural Health Research Center. Available online at: http://www.hsr.umn.edu/rhrc/pdfs/wpaper/working%20paper%20036.pdf.

Casey, M.M. and J. Klingner. "2004 CAH Survey National Data," 2004. Minneapolis, MN: University of Minnesota Rural Health Research Center. Available online at: http://www.flexmonitoring.org/documents/CAHSurvey-National.pdf.

Center for Policy Studies, AAFP. "The Effect of Accredited Rural Training Tracks on Physician Placement." *American Family Physician* 62, no. 1 (2000): 22.

Chou A. "Healthcare Workforce Summary." Montana Office of Rural Health AHEC. Available online at: http://healthinfo.montana.edu/Workforce%20Summary.doc.

Department of Health and Human Services (DHHS). *Report of the Graduate Medical Education National Advisory Committee (GMENAC) to the Secretary of the Department of Health and Human Services, Vol. I: Summary Report.* DHHS Pub. No. (HRA) 81-651. Washington, DC: Department of Health and Human Services, Office of Graduate Medical Education, 1981.

Department of Health and Human Services, Centers for Medicare and Medicaid Services. Medicare website. Available online at: http://www.medicare.gov/medicarereform/drugbenefit.asp.

Egan, T. "Amid Dying Towns of Rural Plains, One Makes a Stand." *The New York Times*, December 1, 2003. University of California, Davis: *Rural Migration News.* Available online at: http://migration.ucdavis.edu/rmn/more.php?id=836_0_2_0.

General Accounting Office. "Rural Development: Profile of Rural Areas," April, 1993. Washington, DC: General Accounting Office. Available online at: http://archive.gao.gov/t2pbat6/149199.pdf.

General Accounting Office. "Nursing Workforce: Recruitment and Retention of Nurses Aides Is a Growing Concern," May, 2001. Washington, DC: General Accounting Office. Available online at: http://www.gao.gov/new.items/d01750t.pdf.

General Accounting Office. "Health Workforce: Ensuring Adequate Supply and Distribution Remains Challenging," August 1, 2001. Washington, DC: General Accounting Office. Available online at: http://www.gao.gov/new.items/d011042t.pdf.

General Accounting Office. "Physician Workforce: Physician Supply Increased in Metropolitan and Nonmetropolitan Areas but Geographic Disparities Persisted," October, 2003. Washington, DC: General Accounting Office. Available online at: http://www.gao.gov/new.items/d04124.pdf.

Government Accountability Office. "Health Professional Shortage Areas: Problems Remain with Primary Care Shortage Area Designation System," October, 2006. Washington, DC: Government Accountability Office. Available online at: http://www.gao.gov/new.items/d0784.pdf.

Moscovice, I.S. and E.S. Elias. "Using Rural Health Networks to Address Local Needs: Five Case Studies," July, 2003. Academy Health/Robert Wood Johnson Foundation. Available online at: http://www.academyhealth.org/ruralhealth/casestudies.pdf.

National Rural Health Association (NRHA). *Study of Models to Meet Rural Health Care Needs Through Mobilization of Health Professions Education and Services Resources. Volume I.* Washington, DC: Health Resources Services Administration, 1992.

National Rural Health Association (NRHA). "Mental Health in Rural America: Issue Paper," 1999. Available online at: http://www.nrharural.org/advocacy/sub/issuepapers/ipaper14.html.

North Dakota Telepharmacy Project (NDSU). "What is Telepharmacy?" Fargo, ND: North Dakota State University, North Dakota Telepharmacy Project. Available online at: http://telepharmacy.ndsu.nodak.edu.

Office of the Inspector General. "Medical Assistance Facilities: A Demonstration Program to Provide Access to Health Care in Frontier Communities," July, 1993. Washington, DC: Office of the Inspector General. Available online at: http://oig.hhs.gov/oei/reports/oei-04-92-00731.pdf.

Office of Rural Health Policy. "Facts About... Rural Physicians." Chapel Hill, NC: University of North Carolina, Cecil G. Sheps Center for Health Services Research. Available online at: http://www.shepscenter.unc.edu/research_programs/rural_program/phy.html.

Office of Technology Assessment. *Nurse Practitioners, Physician Assistants, and Certified Nurse Midwives: A Policy Analysis.* Washington, DC: U.S. Government Printing Office, 1986.

Pion, G.M., P. Keller, and H. McCombs. *Mental Health Providers in Rural and Isolated Areas.* October, 1997; Rockville, MD: U.S. Department of Health and Human

Services—Substance Abuse and Mental Health Services Administration. Available online at: http://mental-health.samhsa.gov/publications/allpubs/SMA98-3166.

Radford A., R. Slifkin, R. Fraser, M. Mason, and K. Mueller. "Experience of Rural Independent Pharmacies with Medicare Part D: Reports from the Field." Journal of Rural Health 23, no. 4 (2007): 286-93.

Smith, H.A. and R.A Allison. "Telemental Health: Delivering Mental Health Care at a Distance," 1998. Rockville, MD: U.S. Department of Health and Human Services. Available online at: ftp://ftp.hrsa.gov/telehealth/mental.pdf.

Stratton, T.P. "The Economic Realities of Rural Pharmacy Practice." *Journal of Rural Health* 17, no. 2 (Spring, 2001): 77-81.

Stratton T.P., M.M. Worley, M. Schmidt, and M. Dudzik. "After-Hours Pharmacy Coverage for Critical Access Hospitals in Northeast Minnesota: The Wilderness Health Care Coalition Health Information Technology Project." (Submitted, 2008).

Traynor, A.P. and T.D. Sorensen. "Assessing Risk for Loss of Rural Pharmacy Services in Minnesota." *Journal of the American Pharmaceutical Association* 45 (2005): 684-693.

Rural Preservation

The preservation and maintenance of historic farmhouses, barns, outbuildings, country churches and schools, fraternal lodges, general stores and other buildings that embody the character of rural life in America's past at different times and in all parts of the country.

Introduction

These places enrich our understanding and appreciation of one of the most important themes in our national experience. Building preservation is closely related to the conservation of farmland and natural areas that provide the historic settings for such places. And like land conservation, preservation of historic rural buildings faces tremendous challenges from demographic, economic and technological forces that have been transforming the American countryside since World War II. There is no single best tool for promoting rural preservation, but rather a variety of programs and initiatives at all levels of government and in the private sector that will vary in their availability, applicability and effectiveness from place to place. Where historic farms and rural buildings are preserved, it is often simply due to the owners' continued care and maintenance of lands and buildings that remain useful or meaningful to them.

In 1950 there were over five million farms in the United States; today there are under two million, with the number declining annually. The disappearance of the small family farm and loss of population from the countryside meant the abandonment of countless farmhouses and outbuildings, accompanied by the decline of rural institutions and the buildings that sheltered them. In the meantime, urban sprawl from growing metropolitan areas has absorbed many millions of acres of formerly productive farmland nationwide and obliterated associated agricultural buildings. Recent surveys of historic properties in the counties around the growing cities of Raleigh and Winston-Salem, North Carolina, revealed that 33 percent of the rural properties first recorded in the 1980s, primarily old farm complexes, have vanished in the wake of new suburbs and commercial centers. Even where the agricultural economy has remained stable, changes in agricultural technologies and governmental policies have shifted populations, altered landscapes, and rendered traditional farm buildings obsolete. Automated systems for harvesting and curing tobacco, combined with the end of the tobacco allotment program, led to the obsolescence and abandonment of tens of thousands of traditional flue-cure barns in North Carolina and other tobacco-growing states in the last quarter of the twentieth century. With few prospects for adaptive use, these and other special-purpose farm buildings vanish by the thousands every year.

Several public, nonprofit and private programs and options are frequently brought into play to promote preservation in rural areas. Success often depends on several being employed simultaneously.

National Register of Historic Places and State Registers

Established in its present form with the National Historic Preservation Act of 1966, the National Register is the cornerstone of the historic preservation movement in the United States. It is the nation's official list of buildings, structures, objects, sites and districts worthy of preservation for their significance in American history, architecture, archaeology and culture. The National Register is a federal-state partnership administered by the National Park Service, with nominations submitted by the states through state historic preservation offices. All states and territories participate in the program, and some also have separate state landmark and district designation programs. There are currently over 80,000 National Register listings nationwide, including many thousands of historic farms, plantations, ranches, churches, schools and other rural historic properties. Many states have nominated rural historic districts of adjoining historic farms encompassing thousands of acres of agricultural landscape.

Besides documenting and recognizing places of historical significance, the National Register provides special consideration for listed properties and districts in the planning of potentially harmful federal undertakings such as highway construction and some types of development requiring federal permits. Many states have laws protecting National Register properties in the planning of state undertakings. National Register listing is often an important element in any rural preservation plan, whether individual farm or district. But listing incurs no obligations or restrictions on private activities, and is no guarantee of protection or preservation. It has had limited effect against urban sprawl and the degradation of rural landscapes where other preservation mechanisms are not also in place.

One of the chief benefits of National Register listing for private owners is eligibility for a 20 percent federal investment tax credit for a qualifying rehabilitation of an income-producing historic structure, augmented with similar state credits for both income-producing and non-income-producing buildings in many states. The National Park Service reports that between 1979 and 2006, nearly 34,000 buildings listed in the National Register of Historic Places or located within National Register districts have been rehabilitated under the federal preservation investment tax credit program, representing private investment of $40 billion in our nation's historic buildings. But this activity has been concentrated in commercial, industrial and residential historic districts in large and mid-size towns. Figures do not exist that quantify this activity in rural areas nationwide, though in North Carolina, historic farm structures account for only 3 percent of the number of projects and only 1 percent of the total investment. Thus, the program has functioned largely as an incentive for urban preservation and revitalization, with modest impact in most rural areas.

Federal grants for rehabilitations of National Register properties are extremely limited. Some states have dedicated enhancement grant programs for properties listed in the National Register or state register, though most limit eligibility to public and nonprofit organizations. While direct grant assistance is rarely available from either source for private property owners, both the National Park Service and state preservation offices provide free technical advice about best rehabilitation practices and referrals to specialty artisans and contractors.

Local Preservation Commissions

Local preservation commissions established by county and municipal governing boards under the authority of state enabling legislation (which differs from state to state) have been an important mechanism for historic preservation in both urban and rural areas. Such commissions study and recommend selected properties and districts for designation as historic by local ordinance, sometimes with property tax relief for the owners, and with varying degrees of oversight over changes proposed by owners. Most of the nation's 3,000-plus commissions operate in municipalities, though there are a growing number of county preservation commissions with jurisdictions in rural areas. County governments uncomfortable with zoning and facing pressure from property rights advocates may decline to establish a commission that property owners might consider a regulatory threat, or may limit a commission's activities even if one is established. However, such commissions are effective in counties with strong public and landowner support for the preservation of historic rural places.

National Preservation Advocacy Organizations

The National Trust for Historic Preservation is the primary nonprofit preservation advocate in the United States and directs a number of preservation initiatives. In cooperation with *Successful Farming* magazine, the Trust operates a program called Barn Again! to encourage the rehabilitation and continued productive use of historic barns on farms and ranches. The program provides technical assistance, publishes rehabilitation guides, sponsors workshops and presents annual awards for barn rehabilitations. It is most active in the Midwest and other areas where large historic barns suitable for adaptive use remain on productive farms. The National Barn Alliance, originally associated with several Midwestern land grant colleges, is a network of agricultural extension educators and historic preservationists with a similar advocacy program. The Alliance and Barn Again! are cooperatively sponsoring a national barn survey to record historic barns.

State and Local Preservation Advocacy Organizations and Revolving Funds

Besides being a voice for the importance of historic places, many of these nonprofit organizations operate revolving funds for the purchase of endangered historic buildings and their resale to new owners who are willing and able to preserve them with protective covenants attached to the properties in perpetuity. Some have had notable success creating a niche market for rural properties of historic and architectural significance. Of the 500 properties saved by the Historic Preservation Foundation of North Carolina, Inc., a great many have been abandoned farm and plantation houses, some of which were once considered hopeless cases, that are now enjoying new life with new owners. The success of a revolving fund depends on the cooperation of the properties' original owners and their willingness to sell at least part of their land. In some cases buildings may be moved for restoration at a location nearby.

Some nonprofit preservation advocacy groups accept preservation easements, which are private legal interests conveyed by property owners that bind both current and future owners to protect the historic character of the property. By this means a rural family may benefit from a tax deduction for the donation of the easement while continuing to enjoy use of the property, with assurance that it will continue to be preserved by future owners. Public preservation agencies and preservation commissions in some states also hold easements. Qualifications for an easement-holding organization are generally defined by state law, and eligibility for tax deductions is governed by IRS regulations.

Most traditional county historical societies, of which there are several thousand nationwide, do not operate revolving funds or hold easements, but many take a preservation advocacy role, and many own and maintain historic properties or operate museums.

Land Conservancies and Farmland Trusts

Land trusts are nonprofit organizations that protect natural areas and productive farmland through acquisition of the land or the rights to develop it. The preservation of historic and cultural features on the land is not the priority of these organizations, though they sometimes work in tandem with preservation nonprofits, public preservation agencies, and preservation commissions to protect historic features as well as their natural or agricultural surroundings. Lands preserved in this way also often provide a protected setting for adjacent historic properties not managed by the land trust. In additional to national land trusts like the Nature Conservancy and the American Farmland Trust, there are many state land trusts and over 1,300 local land trusts.

Museums

Museums are a small but highly visible and accessible facet of rural preservation with an important role in educating new generations about our agricultural past. Farm and rural life museums are operated by all levels of government and by nonprofit organizations from coast to coast. Many offer living history demonstrations showing past agricultural practices. Examples range from the federally owned Mountain Farm Museum in the Great Smoky Mountains National Park and the Grant-Kohrs Ranch National Historic Site in Montana, to state museums such as Old World Wisconsin, to locally owned museums such as the Queens County Farm Museum in New York City and the Carroll County Farm Museum in Maryland, to nonprofit museums such as the Garfield Farm Museum in Illinois and the Tobacco Farm Life Museum in North Carolina. There is no single clearinghouse for information about all farm and rural life museums nationwide, but the Association for Living History, Farm, and Agricultural Museums serves as a network for many such museums.

Unassisted Preservation

All of these programs can have a positive influence on rural building preservation, and their importance will grow in years to come. But in vast sections of rural America, they are thus far almost unknown. Travelers on country roads in many parts of America see old houses and farm buildings in various states of repair amid the fields and woodlands. Most of those that are maintained are kept in stewardship by their owners because they remain useful to them as their homes or in their farm operations or businesses, or because they see them as historically important to their families or communities, or both. Continued economic change and development pressures may in time make it difficult for these private stewards to keep things as they are, but in the meantime we have them to thank for preserving much of historic rural America.

— *Michael T. Southern*

See also

Architecture; Barns; Churches; Culture; History, Agricultural; History, Rural

References

Brewer, Richard. *Conservancy: The Land Trust Movement in the United States.* Hanover, New Hampshire: The Dartmouth College Press and the University Press of New England. 2003.

Stipe, Robert E., ed. *A Richer Heritage: Historic Preservation in the Twenty-First Century.* Chapel Hill: University of North Carolina Press, 2003.

————, and Antoinette J. Lee, eds. *The American Mosaic: Preserving a Nation's Heritage.* Washington, D.C.: The United States Committee of the International Council on Monuments and Sites, 1987.

Stokes, Samuel N., et al. *Saving America's Countryside: A Guide to Rural Conservation.* Baltimore: The Johns Hopkins University Press and the National Trust for Historic Preservation in the United States, 1989.

Rural Sociology

The study of social organization and social processes characteristic of communities and regions where population sizes and densities are relatively low. This article begins with the history of rural sociology. Current research emphases, the organization of academic departments, and professional associations of rural sociologists will then be discussed.

Introduction

While rural sociologists emphasize the study of social structures and processes of rural societies, they also recognize the fact that these structures and processes do not exist in isolation or a social vacuum. "Rural" is, in part, a reflection of the larger processes of the regional differentiation and allocation of populations, economic activities, and other human activities within a society as a whole, or increasingly within global economy and society. Rural social structures and well-being are greatly influenced by the formation and implementation of public policies in regional, national, and global political systems.

Rural sociology is predominantly an academic profession, with the bulk of its members being university faculty or researchers in government or private organizations. Rural sociologists serve rural areas and peoples through research and outreach in rural population, rural community, rural social stratification, natural resources and environment, sociology of agriculture, and sociology of agricultural science and technology.

Rural sociologists are actively involved in international development and related work.

History

While rural sociology for most of its history has been closely associated with the land-grant university system, America's pioneering rural sociologists largely worked outside of the land-grant system. Notable examples of early rural sociological research included the work of W.E.B. DuBois of the U.S. Department of Labor on the well-being of Black sharecroppers in the Cotton Belt in the late 1890s, and that of F.H. Giddings of Columbia University during the first decade of the 20th century on agricultural communities in the Northeast.

There were two major impetuses to the establishment of rural sociology in the land-grant system. The first was the Country Life Commission, which was appointed in 1908 by President Theodore Roosevelt and chaired by Liberty Hyde Bailey of Cornell University. The Commission *Report*, published in 1909, was based, in part, on studies of 12 American rural communities, which taken together constituted the first nationwide survey of rural communities in the U.S. The *Report* stressed that many of the problems of rural America were socioeconomic problems (e.g., speculative landholding and single-crop plantation agriculture in the South), and recommended that the land-grant system invest in social science expertise to better understand and provide solutions to these problems.

The second, and ultimately the most significant, impetus to the establishment of rural sociology programs was the Purnell Act of 1925. The land-grant universities and the state agricultural experiment stations–institutions with which the majority of rural sociology programs have been affiliated–had been established through the Hatch Act of 1862 and the Hatch Act of 1887, respectively. Until the 1920s, however, federal agricultural research funding was very limited, and did not involve social science research at all. The Purnell Act of 1925 significantly expanded the federal commitment to experiment station research, and for the first time allocated federal funds to agricultural economics, rural sociology, and home economics research. Within 15 or so years of passage of the Purnell Act, most of the land-grant rural sociology programs that exist today were founded.

While the Purnell Act ultimately proved to be the principal stimulus to university-based rural sociology programs, government rural sociological research, particularly that in the U.S. Department of Agriculture

(USDA), was the single most important component of the profession's work until the late 1930s. Spearheaded by the efforts of prominent rural sociologists such as Charles Galpin and Carl Taylor, rural sociology became institutionalized in federal agencies such as the Division of Farm Population and Rural Life of the USDA's Bureau of Agricultural Economics (BAE). Rural sociologists working in USDA and elsewhere in government pioneered many of the research methods, such as rural community surveys, that became the standard approaches in the profession as a whole. Government rural sociological research came to be particularly important in generating national-level data on social trends in and the condition of rural America.

Rural sociology in its early years had a strong social reform ethic, and rural sociologists tended to be supporters of the New Deal. Rural sociologists played a pivotal role in conducting research in the Rural Population Division that was drawn on in the design and administration of New Deal programs. Rural sociologists also played prominent roles in New Deal agencies such as the Farm Security and Resettlement Administrations. Rural sociology's role in government, however, would ultimately be substantially diminished. Conservative opposition to the New Deal led to dismantling many New Deal agencies and abolishing the BEA in the 1940s.

During the 1970s and 1980s there was a renaissance of the role of rural sociology in government, particularly within the Economic Research Service of USDA. USDA rural sociologists play a particularly important role in analyzing disseminating aggregate data on rural social trends and issues.

Contemporary Rural Sociological Research

Modern rural sociology has seven major branches: rural population, rural community, rural social inequality and social policy, natural resources and environment, sociology of agriculture and agrofood systems, sociology of agricultural science and technology, and sociology of international development. Each of these areas has active theoretical and empirical research wings as well as applied research and practice wings (e.g., community development, technology assessment, social impact assessment, and rural poverty alleviation).

From the very inception of rural sociology, sociological analysis of rural population and rural community dynamics through census and social survey data has been central to the field. DuBois' early work on Black farming, for example, was based largely on population census data. The work of the Division of Farm Population and Rural Life of the BAE was pivotal in providing basic descriptive data about the rural population and in establishing rural population studies as one of the pillars of the field. Today virtually every major rural sociology program has one or more experts in rural demography or rural community sociology.

Since the time of ancient societies and empires, there has been a tendency for rural people to suffer disproportionately from poverty, disadvantage, and political subordination. In modern industrial societies, rural people in aggregate tend to be poorer than urban-metropolitan people. The fact that rural people are particularly likely to experience poverty and inequality has made analyses of rural social stratification and inequality an important dimension of rural sociology. Studies of regional and labor market inequalities, rural gender inequality, and rural racial inequalities have been among the most important recent focal points of rural stratification research. These analyses have been extended to the global level and to metropolitan-corporate forces such as trade liberalization agreements and the globalization of agriculture and finance. Thus, rural sociologists who study dimensions of inequality often focus on the social policies that exacerbate or alleviate the disadvantage experienced by rural peoples.

There has been a long, significant tradition of rural sociological scholarship on the relations among people, communities, and natural resources (Field and Burch, 1988). Rural sociologists were thus well positioned to play a prominent role in the emergence of environmental sociology during the 1970s and 1980s. Rural sociology continues to provide particularly strong leadership in applied areas of environmental sociology such as social impact assessment.

The sociology of agriculture and agrofood systems and the sociology of agricultural science and technology are both new labels for subject matters that have been studied by rural sociologists for some time. Early 20th century rural sociology focused on the social structures of farming and rural communities. During the 1930s and 1940s there was considerable rural sociological research on the implications of mechanization for rural farm people and rural communities, and in the 1950s and 1960s the adoption and diffusion of agricultural innovations was the single, most important area of rural sociological research. These two areas have been revitalized in the 1980s and 1990s. In addition to studying the social forces that affect family farming and farm labor utilization, the sociology of agriculture now places major emphasis on the globalization of agro-industrial systems. The sociology of agricultural science studies the social and economic influences on new technologies such as biotechnology, as well as the social significance of indigenous or local agricultural knowledge.

Many of the most prominent American rural sociologists of the post-World War II period devoted major segments of their careers to encourage the diffusion of rural sociology across the globe, particularly in the developing world. The post-War period was an emerging era of developmentalism (i.e., an era of faith in the efficacy of planned social change and development in the decolonizing world). Rural sociologists made significant contributions to international development, but they were also among the early critics of the Green Revolution. Documentation of the shortcomings of the Green Revolution, particularly its tendency to exacerbate rural inequalities, proved to be very influential in spearheading rural sociological specialties in the sociology of agriculture and agrofood systems and the sociology of agricultural science and technology.

Academic Departments

About 28 states have a university rural sociology program of some type, although almost half of these programs are very small, essentially confined to one or two staff members. Most universities with rural sociology programs are land-grant universities, although there are several public and private non-land-grant universities that teach courses and train students in the profession. There are several different modes of organization of rural sociology programs. The most common structure, which characterizes about 15 universities, is for rural sociologists to be members of a larger department of sociology or sociology and anthropology. In addition, there are four departments of agricultural economics and rural sociology and eight universities in which rural sociology programs exist within multidisciplinary departments that often contain "community development" in their names. Stand-alone departments of rural sociology are increasingly rare—only six survived the budget crisis that hit many colleges of agriculture in the 1990s. Several departments with long traditions have changed their names from rural sociology to a range of names that often include "community" in the title.

Training, Extension, and Public Service

Rural sociology traditionally has not been a significant undergraduate university major. Some university undergraduates, particularly in colleges of agriculture, receive some exposure to rural sociology through a lower-division course. But rural sociology, much like sociology, is an area in which one must complete a Ph.D. to be considered a practicing professional. About 20 universities offer graduate degrees, usually both master's and Ph.D. degrees, with the opportunity to specialize in rural sociology or its major substantive areas.

Many land-grant rural sociologists have appointments, either part-time or full-time, in Cooperative Extension. Most Extension rural sociologists are in community development or applied demography. Rural sociology tends to place a major emphasis on applied research and service, and thus rural sociologists regardless of whether they have formal Extension appointments tend to give high priority to public service and policy involvement.

Rural Sociological Society (RSS) and International Rural Sociology Association (IRSA)

During the first two decades of American rural sociology, rural sociologists looked mainly to the American Sociological Society (later renamed the American Sociological Association) as their principal professional association, and were members of the Rural Section of the society. By the mid-1930s, however, rural sociologists began to feel the need for a separate organization and publication outlet. In 1936, the journal, *Rural Sociology*, was founded. *Rural Sociology* today remains the flagship journal of the profession in North America. In 1937, Rural Section members voted to establish an independent professional association and founded the Rural Sociological Society (RSS). RSS today has about 800 members from 28 countries, is the publisher of *Rural Sociology*, and holds an annual meeting. Most of its members are either in academic positions or engaged in graduate studies.

The International Rural Sociology Association (IRSA) was founded in 1966, mainly at the initiative of rural sociologists in the U.S. and Europe. IRSA is a federation of regional rural sociological societies, including RSS, and groups from Latin America, Africa, Asia, and Europe. IRSA holds a World Congress for Rural Sociology every four years.

— *Frederick H. Buttel and Leann M. Tigges*

See also

Careers in Agriculture; Cooperative State Research, Education, and Extension Service; History, Rural; Land-Grant Institutions, 1862, 1890, and 1994

References

Brown, David L., and Louis Swanson, eds. *Challenges for Rural America in the 21st Century*. University Park, PA: Penn State Press, 2003.

Buttel, Frederick H. and Howard Newby. *The Rural Sociology of the Advanced Societies: Critical Perspectives*. Montclair, NJ: Allenheld Osmun, 1980.

Field, Donald R. and William R. Burch, Jr. *Rural Sociology and the Environment*. New York: Greenwood Press, 1988. Middleton, WI: Social Ecology Press, 1993.

Firey, Walter. *Man, Mind, and Land: A Theory of Resource Use*. Glencoe, IL: Free Press, 1960. Middleton, WI: Social Ecology Press, 1999.

Goldschmidt, Walter. *As You Sow: Three Studies in the Social Consequences of Agribusiness*. Montclair, NJ: Allenheld, Osmun, 1978.

Nelson, Lowry. *Rural Sociology: Its Origin and Growth in the United States*. Minneapolis: University of Minnesota Press, 1969.

Newby, Howard. "Rural Sociology: A Trend Report." *Current Sociology* 28, no. 1 (1980): 3-109.

Sachs, Carolyn. *Gendered Fields: Rural Women, Agriculture and Environment*. Boulder, CO: Westview Press, 1996.

Wilkinson, Kenneth P. *The Community in Rural America*. New York: Greenwood Press, 1991. Middleton, WI: Social Ecology Press, 1999.

Rural Women

Women who live on farms and in nonfarm residences in the open countryside and in villages and towns in nonmetropolitan counties. This article presents a snapshot of the diversity of rural women. It pays attention to research on women and farming because of farm women's longstanding vital role in agriculture and rural community life. It considers the lives of rural nonfarm women, who make up the majority of women in nonmetropolitan areas. It places women in families, in jobs, and in their communities.

Throughout human history, women have been associated with food production. In the indigenous horticultural societies of the U.S., women were often principal food producers. During U.S. history, women owned agricultural land and often farmed it. Today, a small, shrinking number of rural people in the U.S. are engaged in farming. But the percent of female farmers in both globalized capital-intensive agriculture and in locally oriented direct market agriculture is rising. These women are joined along country roads and interstate highways by women who manage corporate offices; drive school buses, gravel trucks and snow plows or serve as police officers for local governments; work as nurses and physicians at local hospitals and retirement centers; and serve as local attorneys and veterinarians. While rural women own and manage service sector firms and retail businesses, more women are wage laborers in low paying retail sales, service jobs and light manufacturing. In fact, there are few occupations where rural women are not found. And more and more rural women do not work in their local communities. Instead, they commute long distances, often to urban areas in adjacent counties, to work. At the same time, more and more urban and suburban born women who can afford to live in rural places commute to work elsewhere, even in other states and nations. Most women are married, but it includes women who, as single parents, work to support their children while studying at local colleges, and those who depend solely on public assistance. Throughout rural areas across the country, an increasing number of rural women are immigrants. Accompanying the increased variation in the work of rural women are differences in educational and income levels, access to education and health care, and level and type of community participation.

Women and Farming

The transition of rural America during the 20th century from a predominantly rural farm to a rural nonfarm population was an uneven process resulting from the penetration of capitalist relations in agriculture and spatial decentralization of industrial capital. Traditionally, a web of community ties connected farms and families together in rural neighborhoods. These patriarchal family farms depended on unpaid family labor and community-exchanged labor of women and men. Women played a vital role in rural survival through community building, home production, and making do, and in this manner not only increased their share of farm resources but also communal resources available to farm men (Neth 1995).

However in the 20th century, mechanization and agricultural policy led to farm consolidation, rural depopulation, and displacement of farm labor. As consumption replaced home production, the need for cash increased. Modern agriculture fostered a gendered set of economic and social concerns. The business of farming was elevated as efficiency of production took center stage, and family and community needs traditionally associated with women were devalued. Initially, families blended modern and traditional patterns.

Capital penetration in farm input and product markets created business cycles that concentrated and differentiated farm structure (Buttel, et al. 1990). In the last half of the 20th century, the number of farms declined from six million to just over two million, while the farm population decreased from 30 million to just under four million. Today, the number of farms and the total land in farms continues to fall as the average farm size rises. Land in farms with sales less than $100,000 declined in the last intercensual period, while land in farms with over one-half million in sales increased. As farm numbers shrank and average farm size increased, the number of women principal farm operators showed double digit increases in the intercensual periods of the past decades (USDA 2004). In 2002, USDA reported 847,832 women were farm operators; 237,819 women were principal farm operators.

Farm Women and Women on Farms

Farm Operators/Partners and Business Managers. In the U.S. in 2002, women ran one in every ten farms. Instead of assuming one operator per farm as had been done in the past, the 2002 Census of Agriculture collected information on the total number of self-classified farm operators and demographic information on up to three operators per farm. Eleven percent of the principal farm operators were women; 27 percent of all individuals identified as farm operators were women. The highest percent of women principal farm operators was in the Northeast, along the Atlantic coast, in the Southwest, and along the coastal Northwest. In these areas, 20 percent or more of the principal farm operators were women. Most women principal farm operators were full owners who lived on small farms with very modest farm sales. For just over half of these women, farming was their principal occupation; the comparable percent for all farm operators was 46 percent. Nearly one-half of the female farm operators did not work off farm, but just over one-third worked 200 days or more off farm. Among farms reporting multiple operators, about two-thirds listed men as principal operator and women as second operators; age and other family data suggest that most of these were spouses. Women farm operators, principal and secondary, were younger than their male counterparts (USDA 2004; USDA 2005).

A 2001 national survey asked 2,661 farm women to identify themselves as principal operators, agricultural partners, business managers, agricultural helpers, or not involved in the farm. Ten percent identified as principal farm operators, one-fourth of whom were widows. Women who were principal farm operators seem to be from two distinct backgrounds: women who grew up on farms and those who chose farming after living in urban/suburban areas. These "independent farmers" more likely live in the Northeast, Southeast, Great Lakes and the West Coast and operate farms that produce more diverse and less commoditized farm products; they are less likely to use chemical intensive practices (Sachs, et al. 2008). Nearly a third of the farm women surveyed self-identified as full agricultural partners and seven percent as business managers. In short, just over one-half of the farm women surveyed provided labor and made management decisions on the farms. Indeed, 87 percent of these women reported their name was on the farm deed and 81 percent that they were involved in farm operations, including fieldwork, making major purchases and supervising hired labor. Overall, about one-third of the women who had production responsibilities and owned land did not see themselves as farm operators. Indeed, self-classification varied by region, with women in the Midwest least likely to see themselves as a main operator. The wide range of farm household tasks surveyed were gendered with most of the women reporting they did recordkeeping, gardening, "go—phering," and caring for the farm household; fewer did fieldwork and farm management tasks (Willits and Jolly 2002). A decline in farm women's reported supervision of family and hired labor may be related to smaller families and fewer children at home as well as a change in the hired labor pool; throughout the country farm laborers are increasingly young immigrant males, especially Latinos. Supervision of hired labor was greatest for farm women surveyed in the heartland.

The majority of the women surveyed lived on medium and small farms. These farm women are increasingly involved in farm decision-making, particularly decisions about land and other capital investments (e.g., equipment); about production issues like changes in the product mix and the use of machinery and agricultural chemicals in fieldwork, about marketing issues like timing of commodity sales, and about hiring decisions. When intergenerational transfer of the farm is through the farm woman's family, she is very likely to be involved in the range of farm production and management decisions. Farm women are much less likely to be involved in farm decision-making when the farm was inherited or purchased through the husband's family (Findeis and Swaminathan 2002).

Over the past half century, study after study found that farm women are slightly better educated than their husbands/partners and that farm women are most likely to keep financial and production records. As computers became important for farm record keeping and management, farm women often adopted the new technology. The 2001 survey shows farm women continued that trend and now are most likely to use the internet and e-mail to access production, marketing, and other financial information and to communicate with educators, consultants, and other farmers. Statewide studies also show the importance of the internet and computer technology for women farmland owners' decision-making and the use of electronic spaces where farm women can communicate with each other, especially in planting and harvesting seasons and when child care is an issue for face-to-face meetings (Bregendahl, et al. 2007).

Beginning in the last decades of the 20th century, commodity groups and cooperative extension developed workshops and seminars to train farm women in day-to-day production tasks and decision-making. Women-focused agricultural production and management programming expanded under the direction of women agricultural specialists (e.g., Heart of the Farm — Women in Agriculture, University of Wisconsin-Extension); farm women's organizations (e.g., American Agri-Women); and activist groups concerned with food, nutrition, and environment (e.g., Food and Agriculture Network). These groups do both traditional and alternative programming, in small and large groups, using interactive sessions with women presenters and informal mentoring by women with practical experience. Though still underrepresented in the agricultural production sciences, women agricultural scientists in land grant universities are more likely to value research on environment, agricultural sustainability, consumer health, and preserving small farms and to be concerned about university links to private industry (Buttel and Goldberger 2002).

Women who choose farming as a profession encounter gender-specific barriers especially in capital-intensive agriculture. In response, some say, women farmers have moved toward sustainable agriculture that tends to be more land and labor intensive. Some scholars (Feldman and Welsh 1995) believe that women's role in decision-making on small farms may explain why small farm owners choose to adopt alternative ag-

ricultural technologies and techniques. Women farmland owners (includes operators and landlords) surveyed in Minnesota and Iowa stressed values associated with alternative agriculture — independent self-sufficient communities built around family farms whose operators have the personal knowledge and skills to grow a diverse range of food for the local and regional market. They favor conservation practices to protect the health of the land and ensure its long-term sustainability (Chiappe and Flora 1998; Bregendahl, et al. 2007).

In the last decades of the 20th century, there was a rebirth of locally oriented agriculture and food systems. Farms that sell directly to the public are especially prevalent in metropolitan areas and nonmetropolitan counties adjacent to metro areas and particularly in the Northeast (Lyson and Guptill 2004: 380). Among direct market farmers, a much higher percent are women primary operators than for agriculture in general; 36 percent of the primary operators were women and around 60 percent of the second and third farm operators were women. Direct market farm operators compared to farm operators in general, are younger and more highly educated, with nearly three-fourths having a college and one-fourth a graduate degree. Direct market farms are small, most of their farm income comes from the sale of full shares of their products, and they have greater gross income than most U.S. farms; they appear less likely than other farmers to rely on nonfarm income (Lass, et al. 2003).

Agricultural Laborers. As classic family farming is replaced, the switch to industrialized agriculture has been selective by commodity, geography, and the gender and type of labor supply (Padavic 1993). Corporationization of agriculture has had variable impacts on women's participation in the agricultural wage labor force. Mechanization of several commodity systems decreased the demand for low-wage, low-skill labor of African Americans in much of the South in the 1970s. Women employed as farm laborers declined sharply as markets for labor-intensive crops employing women collapsed or the work of women was mechanized. Many of these women shifted to jobs in the newly-arriving light manufacturing industries or the service sector (see below). In the West, a supply of undocumented immigrant Latino labor in a labor market offering few alternatives favored industrial production of vegetables and fruit, often using sex segregated wage labor. When growers needed to recoup capital investments through lower wages, they could hire women at less than half the going wage of male workers who had performed the task before mechanization. Immigrant Latino women spend long hours in the fields and have sole responsibility for housework and family care; they live in some of the worse conditions for raising a family (Valle 1994). African American and Latino women are also employed in poultry, meat and other food-processing industries.

Rural Women and Nonfarm Employment

Marriage is still the most common marital status in rural farm and nonfarm households, but rural family structure increasingly mirrors that in metro areas, urban and suburban. In two decades, married-couple households declined from 86 to 79 percent of nonmetropolitan households. Single parent families grew, in part because of rising divorce rates in rural areas. In 2000, single mothers headed one in ten nonmetropolitan households. Rural families also became smaller. In 2000, rural families averaged 3.02 persons per household, a figure below that for urban families. In rural areas, the child dependency ratio fell in the past two decades, but unlike in urban and suburban areas, the elderly dependency ratio rose (MacTavish and Salamon 2003: 74-81).

Farm Women. Structural changes in agriculture in the last decades of the 20th century were accompanied by greater nonfarm employment of farm women. By the early 1990s, nonfarm labor force participation by farm women approached that of rural nonfarm and urban women. The impact of globalization on economic restructuring in rural areas means more married nonfarm women with children and single mothers actively balancing demands of the labor market with activities of the household and family. Today, 60 percent of rural women and 62 percent of urban women are in the labor force. Whether living on farms, in the open country or in small villages and towns, the majority of rural households have multiple income earners; in perhaps a quarter of these households, at least one wage earner holds multiple jobs. In addition, there is increasing evidence of widespread participation across income categories in multiple informal work activities to supplement income and cut costs.

Nonfarm income exceeds farm income on a majority of U.S. farms today; women's income is an important part of that nonfarm income. Sixty-two percent of working age farm women surveyed in 2001 reported a nonfarm related wage or salaried job off farm. Farm women in the Northeast and the Central regions reported more off-farm employment than those in the West

and South. Women are also involved in the nonfarm businesses operated by about 15 percent of the farms. Numerous studies show that farm women's off-farm employment not only supplies a stable income for household needs, but also provides health and life insurance and funds for retirement for the farm family. To a lesser extent, her earnings support farm expenses as well.

Among farm couples with husbands not employed off farm, farm women are more likely to be multiple job-holders — both farm and off farm, especially those who grew up on a farm and have their name on the farm deed. Farm women with higher levels of education and older children in the household more likely contribute off-farm earnings to the farm household, perhaps helping to finance children's college education. When farm husbands work off farm, farm women's age is an important influence on multiple job-holding; in this case, farm women's work patterns follow a typical life-cycle effect (Findeis and Swaminathan 2002).

Rural Nonfarm Women. Relative declines in traditional manufacturing activities accompanied the lost of farms. Public and private services, heavily dependent on population and income levels, became the dominant industry in many rural communities. But the economic bases of rural labor markets differ, as do job opportunities and wage rates. Traditional rural industries like mining and lumbering typically still employ primarily men, while industrial capital that relocated to rural areas in search of cheaper labor employs women as well As in urban areas, women often find themselves in women-dominated occupations: as office assistants, tellers, nurses, primary school teachers, retail sales clerks, medical and dental assistants, guidance counselors, and social workers. For both women and men, human capital investments like education and skill development have an important impact on work stability and income. But the return on the same investment is often greater for men; that is, earnings are lower and work less stable for women with the same education and skill levels as men.

Most rural nonfarm women rely on employment in low-paying jobs with few fringe benefits, typically in nondurable goods manufacturing or the service sectors, and often in urban areas outside their county of residence. Hence, more and more rural women spend increased hours in daily commutes. Many of these women are part of dual-earner families for whom nonfamily child care is often costly and can be difficult to find. Because more cars are needed for the commute, transportation costs also eat into earnings. In rural areas with amenities attractive for recreation and retirement, nonfarm women are concentrated in jobs in the hospitality and health industries. The movement from local independent businesses to large chain stores resulted in regional concentration of retail establishments. Rural women are an important part of the labor force of these regional retail chain stores. Most husbands work in wage labor jobs as well, though men's jobs typically pay more than women's (Struthers and Bokemeier 2003). In perhaps as many as one in four rural families, one of the spouses moonlights (Ziebarth and Tigges 2003).

Rural communities with manufacturing firms established in the late 1800s and early 1900s have been the victims of plant closings and job transfers to lower wage areas outside the U.S. In several communities, women were a major part of the labor force. Like men, these women are now employed in lower-paying jobs with fewer benefits (Glasgow and Barton 2003). For example, when rural communities lose low-skilled manufacturing firms (e.g., apparel production) and gain information-intensive service firms (e.g., apparel catalog sales call center), rural women typically trade full-time, secure jobs with higher hourly wages, health insurance, and other union-negotiated benefits for seasonal and part-time jobs with lower hourly wages and less generous benefits (Collins and Quark 2006).

Historically, most rural black women worked in domestic service jobs in private homes and as agricultural laborers. Though also found in significant numbers in low-wage nondurable good manufacturing and retail sales, today, rural black women are concentrated in hospitality services as low-wage, unskilled workers in hotel/motel housekeeping, laundry, kitchen, and in fast food establishments. In effect, it continues the longstanding pattern of domestic service to whites. Often these rural black women have long commutes of two to four hours per day using public transportation (Webb 2003).

Although employed at about the same rate as urban women, rural women have had difficulty finding stable, good-paying jobs commensurate with their education and skill. Like urban women, an increasing number of rural women established small-businesses. But studies show that small business is another area where rural women are disadvantaged in earnings and job security. The gender gap in small-business sales has prompted some researchers (Tigges and Green 1994) to argue that women may be financially better off in management than self-employed. But management posi-

tions are less often an option in rural areas, unless one commutes or telecommutes–an alternative that continues to multiply.

Rural Women and Family Economics. A frequently reported strategy among rural families is to focus on cost-cutting rather than income-raising. Common practices include do—it—yourself housing projects (e.g., home building, remodeling, and repairs) and other self-provisioning (e.g., gardening, hunting, fishing, and food preservation), and barter (e.g., exchanging skilled labor—weekend carpenter/plumber, handmade gifts, child care). Barter is the least reported of these activities, but perhaps as many as a third of households report doing one of these activities for money (Tickamyer and Wood 2003). While men are more likely to report working in the informal labor market for money, cash work is also important to rural women. Home child care arrangements and household cleaning are perhaps the most common source of unreported cash for rural women. Running a very small home business may be important to both men and women. But, increased time spent commuting and increasing exurban sprawl seem to be decreasing the extent of self-provisioning while creating greater dependency on supermarkets, convenience stores, and large box retailers, perhaps especially for those who can least afford to be drawn into the cash economy (MacTavish and Salamon 2003).

Emphasis remains strong in rural areas on women's responsibilities for family and household. Rural mothers believe it is important to raise children in rural areas even if they spend many hours in day care, commute across the county to school, and sometimes return before their parent(s). Daily lives that necessitate traveling to dispersed places for work, school, child care, shopping, and other services create patterns for rural families that increasingly resemble the lifestyle of suburban families rather than that of rural families in the past. These patterns leave less time for elements central to the rural childhood ideal: daily chores, shared family time, and intergenerational activities (MacTavish and Salamon 2003). But, about a third of rural nonfarm women are stay-at-home mothers by choice or circumstances (Ziebarth and Tigges 2003). In families where women make this choice, shared family time is emphasized and children may be involved in some of the self-provisioning that supports the household. These rural women may provide more personal care to elderly parents. Other stay-at-home mothers are single and have disabilities and/or very young children. They are likely to live in poverty.

Limited job opportunities, job instability, and low wages in rural labor markets can account for poverty among rural women; a history of discrimination adds to these factors for nonwhite rural women. A greater percentage of the rural poor than urban poor are employed steadily, although often at minimum wage service jobs that, even if full-time or in combination are more than full-time, do not provide incomes above the poverty line. Displaced homemakers often have limited job histories and job skills needed to acquire steady employment. For others, disabilities, poor health, alcoholism, low self-esteem, and the need to care for other family members make getting a job difficult. Single mothers without a high school diploma have the most difficulty meeting economic needs and family responsibilities in these low-wage labor markets that have limited possibilities for advancement without more education or training (Struthers and Bokemeier 2003). Single mothers in nonmetropolitan areas follow similar livelihood strategies (e.g., "doubling-up" or co-residence, cohabitation) as single mothers in metro areas. But nonmetropolitian single mothers experience higher poverty rates, higher barrier to welfare receipt, and lower economic returns on their livelihood strategies (Brown and Lichter 2004). Older rural women also have higher poverty rates than their counterparts elsewhere, in part because of lower lifelong earning and limited access to pension benefits. Poverty rates are especially high among African American, Latino and Native American rural women (Jenson, McLaughlin and Slack 2003: 120-125).

Fitchen (1991) reported a pattern of redistribution of poverty from urban and rural areas to depressed rural areas largely because of inexpensive rental housing that became available after plant closings and the loss of farms prompted a middle class exodus. Run-down farmhouses in the countryside and older housing stock in villages and small towns were bought for back taxes by landlords, subdivided, and sold on contract or rented to low-income families. Manufactured homes located in mobile home parks on rented land house pockets of the rural poor, including the growing number of rural women who are single, divorced, or in fluid and fragile family situations (Fitchen 1991). Mobile homes now represent one in five new homes in nonmetropolitan areas and one in eight existing homes (MacTavish and Salamon 2003).

Rural Women and Community

Rural women's unpaid activities contribute to production and social reproduction. Traditionally, it was women's work to care for household members too young and too old to meet their own needs, and for those who were ill. They also provided for the daily needs of able-bodied adult members of the household and directed the education of the children. Laws and customs forbid their participation in the formal political process, but through church and family activities they built the networks of mutuality and reciprocity that undergirded rural communities fostering the successful socialization of generation after generation of children and youth and long-term in-home care of its elderly and disabled. Over time these networks were formalized in women's organizations that tended to the general welfare of the community and its members.

Farm women joined agrarian movements (e.g., the National Farmers' Alliance) and many political parties, skillfully popularizing the plight of farm families through their poems, songs, and stories. In early surveys and public discourse, they advanced the relationship between the welfare of the family and the farm. Some farm organizations like the National Farmers Union, the Grange, and the Non-Partisan League integrated men and women into one organization; women were members of an auxiliary of the American Farm Bureau and many commodity organizations (Haney and Knowles 1988).

In the 1980s and 1990s, farm women founded their own organizations: American Agri-Women, Women in Farm Economics (WIFE), and Women for the Survival of Agriculture. Their approaches, policy positions, and the characteristics of their membership varies, but their primary focus has been to improve farm income and to bolster family-based traditional agriculture (Haney and Milller 1991). The 2001 national survey shows that farm women have a higher level of participation in farm organizations than in the past, but agricultural policy—making is still primarily the domain of men.

Given the patterns of earning a living and cutting costs discussed above, for many rural women where is limited time and energy for participation in community organizations and engaging in other community-sustaining activities. Local schools, churches, government, and community organizations may face a shortage of volunteers for activities that bind communities across income and other social lines, that support neighbors in need, and that enrich the lives of its children and adult and elderly citizens. At the same time, there is evidence of increasing community leadership roles among rural women: more rural women are elected leaders in their communities, for example. Some chair county boards, serve as mayors of small towns, are presidents of formerly all-male service organizations, and of school and hospital boards; business women head the Chambers of Commerce and other local economic development efforts.

Case studies suggest that leadership of community organizations may fall to a few volunteers who may become overloaded and on the shoulders of those from the wealthier segments of the community that have time for community roles. Consequently, they argue, poorer and working class women and their families are less likely to have their concerns become part of the discourse and less likely to receive assistance or advocacy for policies that address their needs (Ziebarth and Tigges 2003). Others argue the twin forces of globalization of markets and suburbanization of small towns and the countryside converged to transform rural communities from relatively homogeneous locally-focused "hometowns" to generic "nontowns" where people have limited sense of place or community identity and children are no longer raised by "the village" as "parental civic engagement and adult watchfulness decline" (Salamon 2003).

— *Wava G. Haney*

See also

Careers in Agriculture; Community; Domestic Violence; Elders; Employment; Family; Labor Force; Land Ownership; Rural Demography; Underemployment; Voluntarism; Poverty; Welfare

References

Bregendahl, Corry, Carol R. Smith, Tanya Meyer-Dideriksen, Beth Grabau, and Cornelia Flora. *Women, Land, and Legacy*sm*: Results from the Listening Sessions*. Ames, IA: North Central Regional Center for Rural Development, 2007. Available online at: http://www.ncrcrd.iastate.edu.

Brown, J. Brian and Daniel T. Lichter. "Poverty, Welfare, and the Livelihood Strategies of Nonmetropolitan Single Mothers." Rural Sociology 69 (2004): 282-301.

Buttel, Frederick H., Olaf F. Larson, and Gilbert W. Gillespie, Jr. *The Sociology of Agriculture*. Westport, CT: Greenwood Press, Inc., 1990.

Buttel, Frederick H. and Jessica Goldberger. "Gender and Agricultural Sciences: Evidence from Two Surveys of Land-Grant Scientists." *Rural Sociology* 67 (2002): 24-45.

Chiappe, Maria B. and Cornelia Butler Flora. "Gendered Elements of the Alternative Agriculture Paradigm." *Rural Sociology* 63 (1998): 372-393.

Collins, Jane L. and Amy Quark. "Globalizing Firms and Small Communities: The Apparel Industry's Changing Connection to Rural Labor Markets." Rural Sociology 71 (2006): 281-310.

Feldman, Shelley and Rick Welsh. "Feminist Knowledge Claims, Local Knowledge, and Gender Divisions of Agricultural Labor: Constructing a Successor Science." *Rural Sociology* 60 (1995): 23-43.

Findeis, Jill L. and Hema Swaminathan. "Multiple Job-holding among U.S. Farm Women: Off-farm Work and On-farm Decision-making Using a Bargaining Approach." Paper presented at the American Agricultural Economics Association Annual Meeting, 2002.

Findeis, Jill L. and Hema Swaminathan. "Off-farm Work and Non-farm Businesses." In *Farm Women in the United States*. Edited by Carolyn Sachs, Fern Willits, and Jill L. Findeis. University Park, PA: Penn State University Press, forthcoming.

Fitchen, Janet M. *Endangered Spaces, Enduring Places: Change, Identity, and Survival in Rural America*. Boulder, CO: Westview Press, 1991.

Glasgow, Nina and Alan Barton. "Older Workers and Retirement in Rural Contexts." In *Communities of Work: Rural Restructuring in Local and Global Contexts*. Edited by William W. Falk, Michael D. Schulman, and Ann R. Tickamyer. Athens, OH: Ohio University Press, 2003.

Haney, Wava G. and Jane B. Knowles, eds. *Women and Farming: Changing Roles, Changing Structures*. Boulder, CO: Westview Press, 1988.

Haney, Wava G. and Lorna Clancy Miller. "U.S. Farm Women, Politics and Policy." *Journal of Rural Studies* 7 (1991): 115-121.

Jensen, Leif, Diane K. McLaughlin, and Tim Slack. "Rural Poverty: The Persisting Challenge." In *Challenges for Rural America in the Twenty-First Century*. Edited by David L. Brown and Louis E. Swanson. University Park, PA: Penn State University Press, 2003.

Lass, Daniel, Ashley Bevis, G.W. Stevenson, John Hendrickson, and Kathy Ruhf. "Community Supported Agriculture Entering the 21st Century: Results from the 2001 National Survey." Madison, WI: Center for Integrated Agricultural Systems, 2003. Available online at: http://www.cias.wisc.edu/pdf/CSA_survey_01.pdf.

Lyson, Thomas A. and Amy Guptill. "Commodity Agriculture, Civic Agriculture and the Future of U.S. Farming." Rural Sociology 69 (2004): 370-385.

MacTavish, Katherine and Sonya Salamon. "What Do Rural Families Look Like Today?" In *Challenges for Rural America in the Twenty-First Century*. Edited by David L. Brown and Louis E. Swanson. University Park, PA: Penn State University Press, 2003.

Neth, Mary. *Preserving the Family Farm: Women, Community, and the Foundations of Agribusiness in the Midwest, 1900-1940.* Baltimore, MD: Johns Hopkins University Press, 1995.

Padavic, Irene. "Agricultural Restructuring and the Spatial Dynamics of U.S. Women's Employment in the 1970s." *Rural Sociology* 58 (1993): 210-232.

Sachs, Carolyn, Atsuko Nonoyama , Amy Trauger, Hema Swaminathan, and Latika Bharadwaj. "Gender and Technologies on the Farm." In *Farm Women in the United States.* Edited by Carolyn Sachs, Fern Willits, and Jill L. Findeis. University Park, PA: Penn State University Press, forthcoming.

Salamon, Sonya. "From Hometown to Nontown: Rural Community Effects of Suburbanization." *Rural Sociology* 68 (2003): 1-24.

Struthers, Cynthia and Janet Bokemeier. "Stretched to Their Limits: Rural Nonfarm Mothers and the "New" Rural Economy." In *Communities of Work: Rural Restructuring in Local and Global Contexts.* Eds. William W. Falk, Michael D. Schulman, and Ann R. Tickamyer. Athens, OH: Ohio University Press, 2003.

Tickamyer, Ann R. and Teresa A. Wood. "The Social and Economic Context of Informal Work." In *Communities of Work: Rural Restructuring in Local and Global Contexts.* Eds. William W. Falk, Michael D. Schulman, and Ann R. Tickamyer. Athens, OH: Ohio University Press, 2003.

Tigges, Leann M. and Gary P. Green. "Small Business Success Among Men- and Women-Owned Firms in Rural Areas." *Rural Sociology* 59 (1994): 289-310.

U.S. Department of Agriculture (USDA). "Quick Facts: Women in Agriculture." Washington, DC: U.S. Department of Agriculture, National Agricultural Statistics Service, 2004. Available online at: http://www.agcensus.usda.gov/Publications/2002/Quick_Facts/womens-quickfact.pdf.

U.S. Department of Agriculture (USDA). "What We Know about the Demographics of U.S. Farm Operators." Prepared by Rich Allen and Ginger Harris. Washington, DC: U.S. Department of Agriculture, National Agricultural Statistics Service, 2005. Available online at: http://www.agcensus.usda.gov/Publications/2002/Other_Analysis/index.asp.

Valle, Isabel. *Fields of Toil: A Migrant Family's Journey.* Pullman, WA: Washington State University Press, 1994.

Webb, Susan E. "The Bus from Hell Hole Swamp: Black Women in the Hospitality Industry."

In *Communities of Work: Rural Restructuring in Local and Global Contexts.* Eds. William W. Falk, Michael D. Schulman, and Ann R. Tickamyer. Athens, OH: Ohio University Press, 2003.

Willits, Fern and Natalie Jolly. "Changes in Farm Women's Roles: 1980-2001." In *Farm Women in the United States.* Edited by Carolyn Sachs, Fern Willits, and Jill L. Findeis. University Park, PA: Penn State University Press, forthcoming.

Ziebarth, Ann and Leann Tigges. "Earning a Living and Building a Life: Income-Generating and Income-Saving Strategies of Rural Wisconsin Families." In *Communities of Work: Rural Restructuring in Local and Global Contexts.* Edited by William W. Falk, Michael D. Schulman, and Ann R. Tickamyer. Athens, OH: Ohio University Press, 2003.

Rural-Urban Economic Linkages

Economic structural connections that center on the question as to whether urban growth is beneficial or detrimental for rural areas (from the viewpoint of rural development economics). Although Bell and Korsching discussed some of the negative impacts of urban growth on rural communities, rural development and regional economists emphasize that rural areas can also benefit from urban growth (see article, *Town-Country Relations*). Economists base their analysis of this issue on an urban core and rural periphery framework. The question hinges on whether spillover effects (beneficial impacts of urban growth on rural areas) outweigh backwash effects (negative impacts of urban growth on rural areas). Key theoretical concepts that underlie rural-urban linkages include central place theory and agglomeration economies.

Core-periphery models are based in part on central place theory, where the ability of a place to provide a particular set of goods and services is determined by the local population base. For example, a major metropolitan area would have the population base to support the provision of advanced medical services (such as a major heart center) or a local opera company. These so-called higher-ordered services would not be found in smaller, rural communities. Agglomeration economies, where firms benefit from cost reductions because of their close proximity to each other and to urbanized services (such as dense transportation systems) also play a key role in such models.

The central place and agglomeration concepts form the basis of a model where an urban core is surrounded by a peripheral, largely rural region. The rural region purchases higher-ordered goods and services from the core. The rural region also specializes in producing goods based on local natural resources or low-cost labor in routine manufacturing in which it holds a competitive advantage. While trade can flow into the core, such products can also have external national or international markets. Krugman (1991) discusses the model in dynamic and cumulative terms by claiming that interactions between increasing local (core) consumer demand and agglomeration-based increasing returns in producing and transporting manufactured products in the core can lead to a core-periphery economy.

Economic growth in the urban core is detrimental for periphery (rural) economic development through backwash effects (Barkley and Henry, 1997). Backwash effects have an important trade element, such as growth in lucrative core service sectors replacing the same in nearby or even remote rural communities. One backwash effect that Bell and Korsching discuss is the migration of workers from rural to urban areas. Another key (albeit difficult to quantify) backwash effect is the transfer of financial capital from rural areas to urban communities, thus resulting in a possible shortage of financial capital in many rural communities. In this regard, one is left to wonder if the major restructuring of the banking community through a wave of mergers has harmed rural economic development efforts. Arguably, such restructuring has resulted in a reduction in local decision-making concerning local rural financial investments.

Economic growth in the urban core is beneficial for periphery (rural) economic development through spread effects (Barkley and Henry, 1997). An example of a quantifiable spread effect is the set of backward linkages from core economy sectors to periphery input suppliers. The possible diffusion of financial capital from the core to the periphery is more difficult to quantify spread effect. Potentially important but difficult to objectively evaluate spread effects include the diffusion of innovation and growth attitudes from core to periphery areas.

Some analysts emphasize how urban growth tends to harm rural areas. For example, Mydral (1957) argued that backwash effects tend to dominate, and Bell and Korsching heavily emphasize such impacts. The most recent empirical literature indicates that backwash effects are generally larger, but there can be exceptions where spread effects are more important (for example, for urban/metropolitan-influence counties closer to urban growth centers). Hirschman (1958) argued that backwash effects will initially dominate as urban growth pulls in rural resources. Eventually, how-

ever, such effects ebb, resulting in a decentralized spatial distribution of economic activity. One argument (Krugman, 1991) is that a core-periphery economic structure, with backwash effects tending to dominate, can hold for a long time. (An example is the past, but long-standing, dominance of the Midwest manufacturing belt). However, seemingly small changes in economic structure can set off a fast-paced, cumulative process of periphery economic growth, in part based on import substitution.

Research conducted in the 1990s that employed multiregional input-output models provided detail concerning rural and urban trade in a core-periphery framework. Evaluated economics included the Washington State economy (Seattle as the core; the rest of the state as the periphery) (Hughes and Holland, 1994); the Portland metropolitan area and periphery (Holland et al., 1996); a study by of the northern Nevada economy (Harris et al., 1996); and the Monroe, Louisiana Functional Economic Area (FEA) (Hughes and Litz, 1996). The consensus is that urban cores dominate terms of trade, especially in providing higher-ordered services to their periphery regions. Further, smaller urban centers appear to be the most highly integrated with their periphery.

Spatial econometric models have driven conclusions in the most recent studies (Henry et al., 1997, 2001; Partridge et al., 2005). The consensus of this research is that spread effects are usually larger than backwash effects for rural areas closer to urban cores. For more distant rural communities, backwash effects tend to dominate. Work by Glaeser and Kohlhase (2004) concerning manufacturing also supports this contention. Their analysis reveals a peaked relationship between manufacturing's share of local economic activity and local population density. Up to a point, manufacturing tends to be increasingly important as the degree of urbanization declines. Beyond that point, however, the contribution of manufacturing declines for less populated rural areas. A cursory examination of a recent county level population loss map, where the depopulation of remote areas in the western High Plains and rural Appalachian is evident, also confirms the observation that backwash effects predominate for more remote places. In the final analysis, support is given to the Partridge et al. (2005) statement that the predominance of backwash versus spread effects differs across rural communities or that the relative power of such effects are location specific. They state that "the optimal policy mix for governance and rural development would be informed by delineating the geographic range over which" backwash or spread effects dominate or cancel each other out.

Further, several observers, such as Weiler et al. (2006) and Hughes (forthcoming), discuss the advantages of regional cooperation and governance. They argue that economic development efforts where regional subunits of government cooperate have numerous advantages over efforts by single locations, such as an individual city or county. Relating this concept to rural-urban linkages, concrete examples could include urban centers that emphasize linkages to nearby rural communities as a quality-of-life argument for attracting affluent in-migrants and developing capital resources. Rural areas can tout the nearby presence of urban amenities and higher-ordered services (such as medical services) in attracting outside investment and in-migrants. Interesting questions that could be evaluated within such a context include how rural areas could exploit the growing interest in organic products (Holland and Weber, 1996) or local food systems (Brown, 2003) in facilitating agricultural-based rural development.

— *David W. Hughes*

See also

Community Capitals; Community Economics; Economic Development; Policy, Economic; Town-Country Relations

References

Barkley, D. and M. Henry. "Rural Industrial Development: to Cluster or Not to Cluster." *Review of Agricultural Economics* 19 (1997): 308–25.

Bell, Michael M. and Peter F. Korsching. "Town-country Relations." In *Encyclopedia of Rural America: The Land and the People,* 2nd edition. Edited by Gary A. Goreham. Millerton, NY: Grey House Publisher, 2008.

Brown, C. "Consumers' Preferences for Locally Produced Food: a Study in Southeast Missouri." *American Journal of Alternative Agriculture* 18 (2003): 213–24.

Glaeser, E. and J. Kohlhase. "Cities, Regions and the Decline of Transport Costs." *Papers in Regional Science* 83 (2004): 197–228.

Harris, T.R., K. McArthuer, and S.W. Stoddard. "Effects of Reduced Public Land Grazing: Urban and Rural Northern Nevada." Pp. 41-54 in *Rural-Urban Interdependence and Natural Resource Policy.* WRCD 42. Corvallis, OR: Western Rural Development Center, May, 1996.

Henry, M.S., D.L. Barkley, and S. Bao. "The Hinterland's Stake in Metropolitan Area Growth." *Journal of Regional Science* 37 (1997): 479–501.

Henry, M.S., B. Schmitt, B., and V. Piguet. "Spatial Econometric Models for Simultaneous Systems: Application to Rural Community Growth in France." *International Regional Science Review* 24 (2001): 171–93.

Hirschman, A.O. *The Strategy of Economic Development.* New Haven, CT: Yale University Press, 1958.

Holland, D.W. and B.A.Weber. "Strengthening Economic Linkages: a Policy for Urban and Rural Development." In *Rural-Urban Interdependence and Natural Resource Policy.* WRCD 42. Corvallis, OR: Western Rural Development Center, May, 1996.

Holland, D.W., B.A. Weber, and E.C. Waters. "Modeling the Economic Linkage between Core and Periphery Regions: the Portland, Oregon Trade Area." In *Rural-Urban Interdependence and Natural Resource Policy.* WRCD 42. Corvallis, OR: Western Rural Development Center, May, 1996.

Hughes, D.W. and D.W. Holland. "Core-periphery Economic Linkage: a Measure of Spread and Possible Backwash Effects for the Washington Economy." *Land Economics* 70 (1991): 364–77.

Hughes, D.W. and V.N. Litz. "Measuring Rural-Urban Economic Linkages in the Monroe, Louisiana, Trading Area through an Interregional Input-Output Model," Louisiana Agricultural Experiment Station Bulletin Number 856. Baton Rouge: Louisiana State University, 1991.

Hughes, D.W. "Rural-Urban Economic Linkages: Implications for Industry Targeting Recommendations." In *Targeting Regional Economic Development.* Edited by S. Goetz, S. Deller, and T. Harris. Philadelphia: Taylor & Francis (Forthcoming).

Krugman, P. *Geography and Trade.* Cambridge: MIT Press, 1991.

Myrdal, G. *Economic Theory and Underdeveloped Regions.* London: Gerald Duckworth & Co. Ltd., 1957.

Partridge, M., R.D. Bollman, M.R. Olfert, and A. Alasia "Riding the Wave of Urban Growth in the Countryside: Spread, Backwash, or Stagnation," Paper Presented at the North American Regional Science Association International meetings, Las Vegas, NV, 2005.

Weiler, S., J. Henderson, and K. Cervantes. "Innovative Regional Partnerships in the Rural Tenth District." *The Main Street Economist, Kansas City Federal Reserve, Center for the Study of Rural America* 1, no. 5 (2006): 1–5. Available online at: http://www.kc.frb.org/RegionalAffairs/Mainstreet/MSE_5_06.pdf.

Sawmilling

The conversion of logs into lumber. Sawmilling is an important national industry supplying large amounts of wood to construct houses, furniture and other products. Softwood and hardwood sawmills differ considerably in raw materials processed, end products, capitalization and size. Competition among sawmill firms, coupled with timber price increases, has led to rapid improvements in sawing technology and application of computer technology in the lumber manufacturing process. There are important regional differences in ownership of timberlands by forest products companies that impact these companies greatly. Wood products are an important part of life, and wise management of timberlands will allow use of these products without reducing the wildlife or recreational value of the timberland.

Industry Structure

Sawmilling is an industry that supports the economy of many rural areas. Most sawmills are located in rural areas close to the timber resource on which they depend. In many Western and Southern states, forestry and the production of forest products are the leader or among the leaders in total dollar sales and employment. U.S. sawmills employed a total of 118,000 workers with sales of $23.4 billion in 2000. As will be discussed below, competitive factors and structural changes in domestic and international wood markets have reduced sales of U.S. lumber, and past markets were more vigorous with $25 billion of lumber sales in 1999. Peak U.S. lumber prices were experienced in mid-1996 at $480 per thousand board feet but declined to $340 per thousand board feet in 1999, again as a result of market factors to be discussed below. Nationally, about 38 billion board feet of softwood lumber and nearly 11 billion board feet of hardwood lumber are produced annually.

The sawmilling industry is composed of a large number of firms and is characterized by a high level of inter-firm competition. This competition resulted in a steady decline in the number of sawmills in the years following World War II. For example, there were 16,859 sawmills and planing mills in the U.S. in 1958. These decreased in number to 9,000 by 1977 and to 6,196 by 1992. Sawmill numbers continue to decline with the number of U.S. sawmills reported to be 4,400 in 1997. Sawmill size has increased at the same time that sawmill numbers have declined; the total U.S. annual production volume increased from about 35 billion board feet in 1958 to 49 billion board feet in 2006. The increase in total production is, therefore, spread over many fewer sawmills as sawmill numbers contract. However, increased sawmill size has resulted in the ability to use increased amounts of capital to more efficiently manufacture lumber from logs.

Recent Market Factors Reducing Demand for U.S. Lumber

Over the last decade global competition in world lumber markets and domestic substitution have reduced U.S. lumber market share. A major factor is the high productivity of plantation softwoods, mainly pine species, in the Southern Hemisphere. In the Southern Hemisphere, timber reaches sawlog maturity in about 18 years, nearly one-half the time required even in the warmer climate of the U.S. South. In addition, areas of new timberlands are opening up as transportation infrastructure is developed in previously virgin forests. The best example is in Russia which holds 25 percent of the world timber supply that is gradually rendered more accessible to harvest.

Domestic innovations in substituting composite products for lumber have also reduced demand for U.S. timber in the home building industry. I-beams that comprise a composite product of plywood or oriented strand board in a wide central web with 2x4s on its two edges have replaced a significant share of wide lumber in the home building market. The same is true for substitutes for wide lumber such as laminated veneer lumber, glulam and other similar products.

Increased international production of lumber and substitutes explains the previously described flat demand and decreased prices for U.S. lumber in recent years.

Sawmilling Terminology

The forest products industry has traditionally segregated the wood it processes into the two broad categories of hardwood and softwood species. Unfortunately, these two terms are somewhat misleading to those outside of the industry. The term *hardwood* does not mean that the wood is physically harder than that of a softwood, although this is often the case. The term *hardwood* refers to wood obtained from broadleaf deciduous trees (angiosperms) such as oak, elm, ash, hickory and aspen. *Softwood* refers to the wood of coniferous trees (gymnosperms) that usually have leaves in the shape of needles. Examples are pine, spruce, hemlock, Douglas fir and true fir. Note that the hardwood, aspen, is considerably softer than hemlock, Douglas fir and most pine species, and is equivalent in hardness to the spruce and fir species.

Also confusing to those first exposed to sawmilling is the practice of measuring lumber in units termed board feet. A board foot is defined as a solid one-foot by one -foot square piece of wood that is one -inch thick.

Hardwood Sawmills

Hardwood sawmills tend to be relatively small firms, with most producing less than 15 million board feet of lumber annually. The lumber sawn at hardwood sawmills is marketed primarily to furniture and pallet manufacturers. With the increase in the volume of goods shipped on pallets, the demand for pallet lumber grew to more than 50 percent of total hardwood lumber production.

Hardwood lumber is graded into quality classes by appearance because historically a large percentage of hardwood lumber was destined for furniture production. Consumers traditionally placed a high value on clear, defect-free parts on the exposed surfaces of wood furniture. For this reason the hardwood lumber appearance grades primarily measure the percentage of clear area available to produce clear, defect-free parts.

Softwood Sawmills

Softwood sawmills differ considerably from hardwood sawmills in processing methods and size. The softwood timber resource is usually more concentrated geographically, and trees require considerably fewer years to reach maturity. This decreases the haul distance to sawmills for softwood sawlogs and results in larger sawmills with higher capitalization. Most softwood sawmills produce between 100 and 200 million board feet annually.

Most softwood sawmill lumber production is consumed by the large U.S. housing market. Depending on the state of the economy, about one million single-family dwellings, half a million multiple-family dwellings, and one-quarter of a million mobile homes are produced annually. Preservative-treated wood for outdoor structures is another large softwood market. Southern sawmills supply nearly all of the treated wood market because the southern yellow pine that they process is more easily treated with preservatives compared to other species. Slightly less than 50 percent of softwood lumber produced by Southern sawmills becomes a treated wood product.

To remain competitive, nearly all softwood sawmills use computer automation in the lumber manufacturing process. Sophisticated scanners view the size and shape of tree-length logs, and computers determine the optimal short-log lengths to which to cut the tree-length logs. Scanners and computer solutions are also applied to maximize lumber yield during the log sawing and lumber edging and trimming. Hardwood sawmills adopted some aspects of this computer technology. Many hardwood sawmills, however, are too small to devote the capital required to computerize to the same degree as have softwood sawmills.

Improved Sawing Systems

Reduction in saw thickness for both hardwood and softwood sawmills occurred in the U.S. since the first sawmill was built on Manhattan Island in 1633. Early saws removed 0.5 to 0.75 inch of wood to produce each board. Kerf is the term used to describe the width of the sawpath in cutting wood. By 1840 sawing machine kerfs had been reduced to about 0.313 inch.

When the circular saw was introduced in the U.S. in 1814, its circular cutting action increased sawing speed, but kerf widths remained about the same. Bandsaw use began in the U.S. shortly after the Civil War. Advantages of bandsaws were reduced kerf width and the ability to saw logs of greater diameter. By the 1970s the typical circular saw kerf width was 0.250 to 0.280 inch, while the typical bandsaw kerf was about 0.180 inch. Sudden increases in U.S. stumpage prices in the 1970s stimulated efforts to reduce sawing machine kerf. Bandsaw kerfs on some machines were reduced to 0.125 to 0.140 inch, while kerfs on small-diameter circular saws were reduced to 0.140 to 0.160 inch.

The continuing computer automation of softwood sawmills and kerf reductions on sawing machines in both softwood and hardwood sawmills during the 1970s and 1980s resulted in a significant increase in sawmill log-to-lumber conversion efficiency. U.S. Forest Service studies show that lumber conversion increased by about 16 percent between 1952 and 1985.

The reduction in lumber prices due to increasing international competition and substitution of composite products for wide lumber has resulted in intense pressure on the U.S. sawmilling industry to innovate. Since 1985 additional innovations have increased lumber conversion efficiency.

Curve sawing systems are softwood sawmill sawing machines that are able to follow the curve (usually termed crook or sweep by sawmillers) in sawlogs that inevitably fail to grow straight. These systems saw two faces of a log flat to produce a 2-sided cant that contains most of the crook that was present in the log (Figure 1). This cant is then scanned by lasers to define the crook present in the cant, and a computer solution is generated that provides the highest-yielding sawing solution (Figure 2). The cant is then fed to a sawing machine that saws parallel to the crook in the log, producing lumber that includes the crook (Figure 3). The crook in the lumber largely relaxes after sawing and disappears completely during drying as lumber is restrained from bending when dried at high temperature. The lumber actually dries straighter with a higher value return when produced by a curve sawing system due largely to increased strength when graded by machine. In addition, lumber is longer as the saws remain in the log for a longer distance before running out of the log taper when the curve is followed by the saws. For machine-graded lumber the value increase was shown by research to be $5 per thousand board feet in 2004 dollars.

Conversion improvement percentages obtained by curve sawing are a subject of some secrecy by sawmilling companies and are hotly debated in the absence of hard data. Conversion value increases of about 2 to 16 percent have been reported with total value increase somewhat higher due to reduced drying degrade and

Figure 1. *Top view of two-sided cant produced on first sawing machine in a curve sawing system.*

increased value for higher-strength lumber processed by machine grading systems. Highest conversion values are for small diameter logs where failure to follow log curve with the saws has a larger impact. The actual conversion improvement from a curve sawing system depends, therefore, on several factors, including the specific amount of crook and sweep in a region's timber, the efficiency of the specific curve sawing system, the diameter of the timber processed, whether lumber is machine graded and whether decrease in drying degrade is actually captured by the sawmill as increased value.

Variable pitch saws are another innovation introduced to the sawmilling industry in the 1980s. These saws vary the distance between teeth (this distance is termed "pitch" by sawmillers) for the purpose of dampening harmonic saw blade vibration. The variable distance results in the reduction of the natural oscillation that occurs in blades during sawing. When this natural vibratory oscillation is reduced by use of variable pitch saws, the lumber surface is smoother and less planing depth is needed to remove the surface unevenness produced by these vibrations. This, in turn, allows for a reduction in the lumber thickness sawn with a direct increase in log-to-lumber conversion efficiency. Sawmillers have also found that the reduced saw vibration provided by variable pitch saws allows faster feeding of

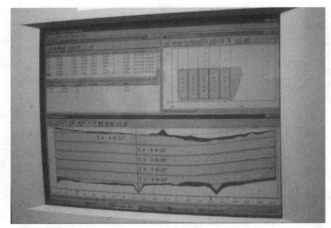

Figure 2. Computer image of curve sawing solution of two-sided cant: top view.

Figure 3. Curve sawn cant exiting the gang-saw outfeed.

logs during sawing with a consequent increase of lumber production.

It was also during the 1980s that Canadian sawing machinery manufacturers began to develop ultra high-speed sawmills. Because of the slower growth rate of timber in the cooler climate of Canada, much of the timber not grown in the rainforest conditions in the Pacific Northwest is of relatively small diameter. Therefore, it was a priority for Canadian conditions that sawing systems be developed for processing this small timber rapidly. The key to the economic success of these systems is a high feed rate with more modern systems capable of processing more than 20 pieces per minute of logs that may average six inches in diameter. These high production rates make timber, that may previously have been suitable only for economic processing into pulp wood for paper production, suitable for production of lumber. These Canadian-designed ultra high-speed sawmills have been installed in the U.S. in re-

gions where small diameter softwood timber is available.

The innovations described above are not a complete list of those developed for U.S. sawmills over roughly the last two decades but are three of the most significant. It is these innovations that have kept U.S. sawmills from losing more market share than has been lost in recent years. In addition, these improvements are beneficial to the environment. Higher conversion efficiency allows more lumber to be produced from the same volume of trees cut. Less land can, therefore, be devoted to timber production and more to such uses as forest recreation and wildlife habitat. Increased processing speed allows more lumber to be produced with the same amount of equipment, thereby reducing capital cost per production unit. This assists in keeping U.S. sawmills competitive with sawmills located in warmer regions where timber grows at a much faster rate.

Sawmilling: A Cyclical Industry

Both hardwood and softwood sawmilling are cyclical industries whose fortunes are closely tied to the vigor of the construction industry. When the economic cycle is at its peak and the housing industry builds many units, there is high demand, and prices are higher for softwood lumber. When the economy is slow, the softwood lumber industry faces depressed markets and lower prices.

The hardwood lumber industry also follows the economic cycle, but the economic peaks and valleys it faces lag behind those of the softwood lumber industry. This is because hardwood furniture to furnish the new homes and offices is built some months following the new construction.

The U.S. is both an importer and exporter of significant volumes of lumber. In 2000 the U.S. imported 45 million cubic meters of lumber, about 30 percent of total U.S. production, while only three million cubic meters were exported. This is a sharp difference compared to the U.S. import and export situation in 1993 when 35 million cubic meters were imported and 5.5 cubic meters were exported. This change in the import and export picture for U.S. lumber indicates the substantially changed market conditions for U.S. produced lumber in the last 20 years. The large volume of imported lumber flowing into the American market increases the domestic lumber supply and acts to reduce prices to the consumer. Over 90 percent of U.S. imported lumber comes from Canada. Therefore, U.S. sawmills are under competitive pressure from Canadian sawmills in addition to the intense competition existing among domestic sawmills.

Ownership of Timberland

The pattern of ownership of timberland in the U.S. has a great impact on the forest products industry. The forest industry owns a relatively minor portion of the nation's timberland holdings, ranging from 11.6 to 15.7 percent depending on the region. The ownership patterns between public and private holdings differ considerably by region, however, with private holdings in the East at 69.8 percent compared with 24.1 percent for the West. Public holdings in the East are relatively minor with 14.5 percent of the timberland being publicly owned compared with the major public holdings of 64.3 percent in the West.

A result of these regional differences in timberland holdings between public and private owners is that Western sawmills must obtain most of their sawtimber from public lands, and Eastern sawmills need to obtain most of theirs from private owners. Thus, Western sawmills are more influenced by public policy issues concerning the management of public lands than are Eastern sawmills. In recent years, changes in public policy have had a dramatic impact on the Western sawmilling industry.

In the East, sawmillers are much less subject to shifts in public policy regarding timberland management because they purchase their timber mostly on the open market from private timberland owners. Dependence on private timberland owners for sawtimber brings with it some problems for Eastern sawmillers. Private owners may have goals other than timber production for their lands. An owner interested only in managing for wildlife or for recreation may not be interested in selling sawtimber. In addition, even those owners interested in timber production may lack forestry management skills themselves or the motivation to obtain professional forestry management advice. Thus, a significant portion of Eastern private lands may be undermanaged for timber production and sawtimber supplies may be less assured than the Eastern sawmill industry finds desirable.

Since 1987 the harvest of softwood timber from national forests has decreased dramatically, from nearly 13 billion board feet to just under two billion board feet in 2007. This reduction occurred due to popular concern regarding environmental damage from harvesting operations. In addition, several wildlife species with ranges on national forest lands have required endangered species protection with set-asides of large acreage blocks for land for their welfare. The reduced timber harvest on national forest lands affected mainly the Western U.S., where a large percentage of total land is owned by the federal government. The reduction of harvest on national forest lands in the Western U.S. shifted considerable lumber manufacturing share to the Southern U.S., where ownership of public lands is a fraction of that in the Western U.S. Over 50 percent of U.S. lumber is produced by Southern sawmills. The reduced harvest of timber in the West resulted in many sawmills being closed and caused layoffs of large numbers of forest products employees. In addition, reduced timber supplies resulted in significant, but temporary, lumber price increases.

Many rural Americans own small, portable sawmills to produce lumber from trees harvested on their own land. The lumber produced is used for construction and other projects on their property or is marketed locally. Home sawmilling provides lumber at reduced prices for rural Americans. These small, portable sawmills typically use small bandsaws that are miniature versions of the large bandsaws in large sawmills. The kerf widths of these bandsaws are very thin, in the 0.040- to 0.060-inch kerf width range.

Wood Products Are Part of Our Lives

Almost all U.S. houses are of wood-frame construction. Writing paper, computer paper, tissues and hand towels are wood products, many of which are manufactured from sawmilling residue. Recent studies of substitute materials for wood (steel, aluminum, concrete and oil-based products such as plastics) have shown that production of these products has considerably more potential for environmental harm than that of wood products. This is due to the very large energy requirements needed to produce these substitute products. Wood products are also renewable resources, while steel, plastic and other substitutes are from non-renewable sources.

Waste disposal has become a problem for many industrial enterprises. For most sawmills this problem is less serious. Sawmills that dry their own lumber use the sawdust and bark to produce steam heat for their lumber dry kilns. Many sawmills market their planer shavings, log slabs, and board edgings for paper and composite board production. Charcoal and mulch are other products often produced from sawmill residue.

Although improper and indiscriminate timber harvesting can harm the environment, proper harvesting can enhance the use of forested areas by wildlife. Harvesting increases the use of forested areas by wildlife when timber diversity is maintained. Many rural families enjoy hunting, and most game populations benefit from proper harvesting. When harvesting is totally prohibited, the diversity of tree species is reduced. Shade-loving tree species replace sun-loving species. The shade-loving tree species are often not those that people and wildlife prefer most. For example, sugar maple and beech trees will predominate in our Eastern hardwood forests if cutting is prohibited for long periods. Both people and wildlife appear to prefer a high proportion of oak trees in the forests. People like the oaks for aesthetic reasons and wildlife like the acorns they produce.

— *Philip H. Steele*

See also

Forest Products; Foresters; Forestry Industry; Forests; Natural Resource Economics; Parks

References

Bedard, Pierre and C. Tremblay. "Impact of Curve Sawing on Kiln-Drying and MSR Grading." *Forest Products Journal* 54, no. 9 (2004): 69-76.

Brown, T.D. *Quality Control in Lumber Manufacture*. San Francisco, CA: Miller Freeman Publications, Inc., 1982.

Denig, J. *Small Sawmill Handbook*. San Francisco, CA: Miller Freeman Publications, Inc., 1993.

Steele, P.H., F.G. Wagner, and R.D. Seale. "An Analysis of Sawing Variation by Machine Type." *Forest Products Journal* 36, no. 9 (1986): 60-65.

Steele, P.H., F.G. Wagner, R.D. Seale, F.W. Taylor, and R. Bennett. "Kerf Width by Machine Type." *Forest Products Journal* 37, no. 3 (1987): 35-37.

Steele, P.H., F.G. Wagner, and R.D. Seale. 1988. "Comparison of Sawing Variables for Softwood Sawmills by Region of the United States." *Forest Products Journal* 38, no. 4 (1988): 19-24.

Steele, P.H., F.G. Wagner, Y. Lin, and K. Skog. "Influence of Softwood Sawmill Size on Lumber Recovery." *Forest Products Journal* 41, no. 4 (1991): 68-73.

Steele, P.H., M.W. Wade, S.H. Bullard, and P.A. Araman. "Relative Kerf and Sawing Variation Values for Some Hardwood Sawing Machines." *Forest Products Journal* 42, no. 2 (1992): 33-39.

Tooch, D.E. *Successful Sawmill Management*. Old Forge, NY: Northeastern Loggers Association Inc., 1992.

U.S. Department of Agriculture, Forest Service. *An Analysis of the Timber Situation in the United States: 1989-2070*. General Technical Report RM-199. Ft. Collins, CO: Rocky Mountain Forest and Range Experiment Station, 1990.

Wang, S.J., Munro, B.D. Giles, D.R., Wright, D.M. "Curve Sawing Performance Evaluation." *Forest Products Journal* 42, no. 1 (1992):15-20.

Williston, E.M. *Saws—Design, Selection, Operation, Maintenance*. San Francisco, CA: Miller Freeman Publications, Inc., 1978.

Williston, E.M. *Small Log Sawmills*. San Francisco, CA: Miller Freeman Publications, Inc., 1978.

Williston, E.M. *Computer Control Systems*. San Francisco, CA: Miller Freeman Publications, Inc., 1978.

Williston, E.M. *Lumber Manufacturing*, revised edition. San Francisco, CA: Miller Freeman Publications, Inc., 1978.

Senior Centers

Community focal points on aging where older adults come together for services and activities that reflect their experience and skills, respond to their diverse needs and interests, enhance their dignity, support their independence and encourage involvement in and with the community.

As part of a comprehensive community strategy to meet the needs of older adults, senior centers offer services and activities within the center and link participants with resources offered by other agencies. Center programs consist of a variety of individual and group services and activities. The center also serves as a resource for the entire community for information on aging; support for family care givers; training professional and lay leaders and students; and for development of innovative approaches to addressing aging issues (National Council on Aging, 1991).

Rural senior centers play important roles for older persons, their families and the community. This article provides an overview of the nature, operation and programming of rural senior centers. It focuses on the availability of such centers, their resources, the activities they provide and the characteristics of older persons who utilize them. We also consider the importance of such centers for the community at large and for serving elders with unmet health and social needs.

Senior Center Availability

The number of senior centers has grown steadily since their inception in the 1940s, spurred by federal, state and local funding and the interest of older adults in center programming (Gelfand, 2006; Krout, 1989). The definition of the term "senior center" is not consistent through time and place, and the federal government does not keep an inventory of these organizations, but recent estimates place the number between 10,000 and 16,000 (Miltiades et al., 2004). Diversity is a key characteristic of senior centers. They span the gamut from small, volunteer-run programs to large, multipurpose and comprehensive service agencies. This diversity is found within as well as between rural and urban senior centers. Large urban areas often have many centers, each with its own racial, cultural and economic make-up. Many rural communities pride themselves on having a local place that provides activities for elders.

Few studies have been conducted on rural senior center availability, but at least one indicates that a sizeable number of senior centers can be found in rural areas across America. Krout (1983) used a 1982 National Council on the Aging senior center list and found that many small towns and villages have a place that is referred to as a senior center or club, and one-half of the 4,000 centers from a 33-state listing were located in non-metropolitan counties. The author is not aware of any current national statistics on the number of rural senior centers. It seems logical to think that, in the aggregate, rural areas undergoing growth in their older population either through in-migration of elders or retention of older adults as they age in place have experienced an expansion in the number of senior centers.

Senior Center Resources

National surveys conducted in the 1970s and 1980s found that rural senior centers have smaller facilities, lower budgets, and smaller numbers of volunteer and paid staff than urban centers. In the late 1980s, the majority of rural senior centers reported budgets of less than $20,000, although this figure may be misleading as space and even some staff are sometimes provided by outside organizations such as Area Agencies on Aging. Additionally, Krout (1990) found that rural centers were less likely than urban ones to have experienced budget increases during the 1980s.

Traditionally, senior centers in rural areas have been located in separate facilities, oftentimes one or two main rooms with bathroom facilities. Sometimes they utilize space in community centers, churches, even fire halls, but centers without their own facility often serve largely as nutrition sites. Even so, some rural senior centers occupy over 5,000 square feet of space and have facilities that can accommodate a wide range of programming.

The importance of adequate and affordable transportation for senior centers in rural areas cannot be stressed enough. Whether this transportation is provided by seniors themselves, relatives, friends or neighbors, or by transportation programs funded by federal, state and/or local dollars, it is essential for the survival of a community-based program such as a senior center. Some senior centers are integrated with or administer and provide transportation systems of one kind or another. Affordable and convenient access to rural senior centers is a key ingredient for success, and the ability of a center to provide transportation in one form or another to rural seniors is a real advantage.

Senior Center Activities

The nutrition (or congregate/in-home meal) function is very important for senior centers and often serves as an anchor for other programming (Gelfand, 2006). Many times this other programming consists of socialization, recreation (card playing, bingo, trips) and education on a range of topics. However, some rural senior centers offer a much richer mix of services including adult day care, case management, health screening, care giver support and housing assistance. It is important to recognize that many rural elders attend centers mainly for social, recreational and volunteering opportunities and because the center serves as a place where they can stay connected with others and their community (Krout, 1988). The number and nature of programs offered by rural senior centers are closely related to the availability of financial resources and professional staff. However, even though rural senior centers support a smaller number of activities and services than urban centers, they still offer a wide range of programming. The author's research has found that even senior centers in communities of less than 2,500 persons report offering an average of a dozen activities and services (Krout,1990). A center's role in providing activities is partly determined by the presence or lack of other service sites and providers in the community. The lack of other services or sites can heighten the importance of even a small number of rural senior center activities.

Community Roles and Relationships

The relationships between rural senior centers and other community agencies are extremely important. Some rural centers are closely connected administratively and through planning and funding to Area Agencies on Aging (AAAs), while others have minimal contact with these organizations. Some rural senior centers have a fairly high degree of interaction through referral and other activities with AAAs, hospitals, home health agencies, legal services and other components of the community-based care system. These rural senior centers often are designated as official "focal points" by local AAAs. They can benefit from mutual marketing, referral of potential participants, transportation services and funding for services. These factors enhance the center's ability to attract a greater number of seniors and to provide a wider variety of programming.

Since service providers and sites are generally lacking in rural areas, senior centers are often a small community's only service/information and referral point for elders, and they serve as a key link to the larger health and human services network. They also can serve as a resource for the entire community as well as older adults and provide opportunities for residents to empower themselves and their communities. Senior centers provide a setting for rural elders not only to receive services and social support, but also to contribute their skills and leadership qualities to other elders and the community. For example, the Nebraska Department on Aging has developed a process by which rural senior centers work with an array of community interest groups to serve as focal points for community service development, not just for elder services. Although the degree of interaction with other agencies can be influenced heavily by factors such as financial and staff resources, terrain, population density and availability and distance to service providers, it also reflects the orientation of center staff and participants. A rural center that is fairly isolated in terms of distance need not be isolated from other community-based services.

Characteristics of Senior Center Use and Users

Senior centers are well known to older persons, and research has shown that between 15 and 20 percent of older adults in this country participate in center activities (Krout, 1989).

The general lack of availability and accessibility of rural services would suggest lower utilization rates for rural centers. However, research findings on this issue have been equivocal. Some rural community studies have found rates of as high as 25 percent, while others have rates of less than 10 percent (Krout et al., 1994). As Reinke (2001) notes, senior centers reflect the demographics, culture and resources of the community in which they are located. Data have not been collected that allow an unequivocal statement about who attends senior centers. Krout et al. (1990) found center participants had higher levels of social interaction, lower incomes, were more likely to live alone and were in slightly better health than non-participants. In general, research indicates that the participants of rural centers are somewhat older, poorer and more likely to be white than are the participants of urban senior centers. Again, the make-up of senior centers reflects geographic differences, so poor areas of the country or states will find a more economically disadvantaged center population just as an area with a high proportion of non-whites will see the same in its senior center users. In addition, survey data suggest that rural centers are more likely to have experienced an "aging in place" as indicated by increases in the ages of rural center user populations (Krout, 1994). That is, fewer numbers of the "young-old" are utilizing centers, and their user population is increasingly made up of "older-old" seniors who have been participants for many years. Rural centers, like senior centers everywhere, are examining their program offerings to better appeal to "baby boomers."

Conclusions

Rural senior centers provide a place where older adults go for meals, recreation, socialization, education and more specialized services. They often provide a link to other aging services in and near the local community. With relatively few resources, many rural senior centers also utilize volunteers on a regular basis. The limited data available on rural senior center participants suggest a need for resources for income support programs (e.g., Supplemental Security Income, food stamps, home heating assistance, tax reductions and income supplement opportunities). With these additional resources, rural centers could better assist participants in identifying and becoming involved in these programs through education and referral activities. Health and wellness education and promotion (e.g., nutrition, exercise and stress reduction) as well as a wide variety of regularly scheduled health screening activities (e.g., dental, blood pressure, vision, diet and diabetes) also appear to be particularly salient for rural senior center populations.

Unfortunately, many of the program needs noted above are often less likely to be met adequately in rural areas because senior centers and the aging services network in general lack the dollars and health and social service professionals to provide them. Resource and training materials can and should be developed to more adequately meet the needs of rural center participants and build the capacity of rural centers to meet them. Finally, linkages with other agencies and the adoption of communication technology (e.g., remote broadcast and videos) can also serve to overcome rural senior center resource gaps and accessibility problems.

— *John A. Krout*

See also

Elders; Mental Health of Older Americans; Nursing Homes

References

Gelfand, Donald. *The Aging Network.* New York, NY: Springer Publishing, 2006.

Krout, John. *The Organization, Operation, and Programming of Senior Centers: A National Survey. Final Report to the AARP Andrus Foundation.* Fredonia, NY, 1983.

Krout, John. "Community Size Differences in Service Awareness Among the Elderly." *Journal of Gerontology* 43 (1988): 528–530.

Krout, John. *Senior Centers in America.* Westport, CT: Greenwood Press, 1989.

Krout, John. *The Organization, Operation And Programming Of Senior Centers In The America: A Seven Year Follow-Up.* Fredonia, NY: Unpublished, 1990.

Krout, John. "Community Size Differences in Senior Center Programs and Participation: A Longitudinal Analysis." *Research on Aging* 16 (1994): 440–462.

Krout, John, Peggy Williams, and Ollie Owen. *Senior Centers in Rural Communities: Providing Community-Based Services to the Rural Elderly.* Thousand Oaks, CA: Sage Publications, 1994, pp. 90–110.

Krout, John, Stephen Cutler and Raymond Coward. "Correlates Of Senior Center Participation: A National Analysis." *The Gerontologist*, 30, (1990): pp. 72–79.

Miltiades, Helen B., Sara Grove and Cynthia Drenovsky. *Understanding The Impact Of Senior Center Participation On Elder's Health And Well-Being.* Harrisburg, PA: Commonwealth of Pennsylvania-Department of Aging, 2004.

National Council on the Aging, Inc. *Senior Center Standards: Guidelines for Practice.* Washington, DC: The National Council on the Aging, Inc., 1991.

Reinke, Candis. *Senior Centers: Where Do We Go From Here?* Arrowhead Area Agency on Aging, 2001, pp. 39-91.

Service Industries

A diverse set of industries that includes business services, finance and real estate, health services, transportation services, retail trade, and private household services. This article presents definitions and classification schemes used to characterize service industries. Trends in the level and location of service industry employment are reviewed. The quality of service industry jobs and the implications of service sector growth for economic development are discussed.

Definitions and Trends

Over 65 percent of the employment in nonmetropolitan areas is in service industries—markedly less than that in metropolitan areas (Smith, 1993). The quality of service industry jobs in nonmetropolitan areas is highly variable. The extent to which service industries can serve as a source of economic development for nonmetropolitan areas is still being debated.

Service industries traditionally have been classified as the tertiary sector to distinguish them from the goods-producing industries (agriculture, forestry, fisheries, mining, construction and manufacturing) that comprise the primary and secondary sectors of the economy. However, collapsing a wide array of industries into a single residual group is unsatisfactory because of the considerable diversity among service industries with respect to activities, markets and capacity for sustaining local and regional economies.

Fortunately, several classification schemes have been developed to characterize types of service industries. One useful categorization distinguishes producer from consumer services. Producer services provide inputs to other industries as an intermediary step in the production of a final good or service. These include finance, insurance and real estate (FIRE), business services, legal services, and other professional-related services. Typically, producer service industries serve government agencies and business and manufacturing firms, and provide economic value by contributing to the competitiveness of another industry (Marshall, 1988; Smith, 1993).

Producer services typically locate in metropolitan areas that offer access to a skilled and educated labor force, a centralized location, and cost efficiencies associated with agglomeration (that is, cost efficiencies because a larger market permits greater economies of scale in production and greater specialization among firms). Data from the first half of the 1980s indicate that between 12 and 17 percent of metropolitan workers were employed in producer service industries, while less than 10 percent of nonmetropolitan workers were employed in this sector (Hirschl and McReynolds, 1989; Miller and Bluestone, 1988).

Nonmetropolitan areas are more likely to attract back-office than front-office facilities in producer services. Work production in back-office facilities tends to be routinized and labor-intensive, and to have a preponderance of low-wage jobs. This contrasts with the less routinized, more administratively based activities in front-office facilities that tend to locate in more urbanized areas (Glasmeier and Borchard, 1989). Such a propensity promotes a spatial division of labor within the service sector, particularly in producer services. However, some evidence indicates that certain producer service industries, such as data processing facilities, are decentralizing to a limited extent by locating in smaller population centers (Noyelle, 1986).

On the other hand, consumer services typically serve private individuals, and their distribution across space follows the population distribution. Consumer services include retail trade, repair services, entertainment, recreation and personal services. About one-fifth of nonmetropolitan workers are employed in consumer-related industries, with the majority in retail trade (Kassab and Luloff, 1993; Miller and Bluestone, 1988).

In addition to producer and consumer services, other types of services can be delineated based on the market or function served by the industry. These include distributive, social, educational, health and government services.

Distributive services include transportation, communications, public utilities, sanitary services and wholesale trade. These industries distribute goods and services within or among organizations, such as businesses and government agencies, as well as between organizations and consumers. Hence, distributive service industries are connected to the goods-producing sector since they help sustain a network of organizations engaged in producer-related activities. Like producer services, distributive services tend to locate in more urban locations; fewer than 10 percent of the workers in nonmetropolitan areas are employed in this sector (Kassab and Luloff, 1993; Miller and Bluestone, 1988).

The market for social, educational and health services includes both government agencies and individuals. This sector constitutes a relatively important source of employment in nonmetropolitan areas. Of the 20 percent of nonmetropolitan workers employed in this sector, the majority are in education and health ser-

vices (Kassab and Luloff, 1993). The health sector is composed of hospitals, nursing homes, personal care facilities, and offices of physicians and other health care providers. The social services are a diverse group that includes job training and vocational rehabilitation, child day care, and residential care not involving nursing services. Educational services include elementary, secondary, trade, business and vocational schools, as well as colleges, universities and libraries.

The political process is a major factor affecting the level of employment in government services. Industries within this category include general government offices, justice, public order, and safety organizations. About 6 percent of nonmetropolitan workers are employed in this sector (Kassab and Luloff, 1993).

Job Quality

Research indicates that discrepancies in job quality, particularly with respect to monetary compensation, are contributing to an increased polarization in the quality of jobs between metropolitan and nonmetropolitan areas. Average earnings for workers in nonmetropolitan areas tend to be lower than those for metropolitan workers employed in the same industry. For instance, average yearly wages for metropolitan workers employed in FIRE were estimated at nearly $17,000 per year (in 1982-1984 constant dollars) but only $12,000 for nonmetropolitan workers. Metropolitan workers employed in wholesale trade earned nearly $6,000 more than nonmetropolitan workers, while metropolitan workers employed in health and social services earned about $5,000 more than nonmetropolitan workers. Nonmetropolitan wages in retail trade came the closest to meeting metropolitan wages, although a gap of about $1,000 was evident (Kassab, 1992). Furthermore, the financial status of households in nonmetropolitan areas has declined over time, compared with the status of households in metropolitan areas (Kassab et al., 1995).

The quality of jobs in nonmetropolitan service industries varies widely in terms of monetary compensation and benefits. Research indicates that the highest paid nonmetropolitan service workers tend to be in distributive services. Wage and salary earnings for public utility workers averaged nearly $32,000 in 1990, and about $25,000 for transportation and communication workers. Average earnings in these industries were higher than those for nonmetropolitan workers employed in the goods-producing industries and government. For instance, employees in mining averaged $30,000 in 1990 while those employed in government and high-wage manufacturing industries, such as electronics, or stone, clay, glass and concrete products, only averaged about $22,000 in 1990 (Kassab and Luloff, 1993).

Wholesale trade is one of the lower paying industries within distributive services, with workers averaging $21,000 per year (1990 dollars). Even so, these relatively lower paid distributive service workers earned on average more than workers in low-wage manufacturing industries, such as textiles or apparel ($16,000). Whereas the level of pay in distributive services tended to exceed or be comparable with that offered in manufacturing, jobs in transportation and wholesale trade were less likely to offer health insurance benefits than jobs in either low- or high-wage manufacturing. About two-thirds of the nonmetropolitan workers employed in distributive services were employed in transportation or wholesale trade (Kassab and Luloff, 1993).

The earnings distribution for nonmetropolitan producer service workers is bifurcated. Those employed in legal services, insurance, banking and other finance services reported 1990 wages and salaries in the $20,000 to $26,000 range, but average annual earnings of those employed in real estate, business services, and other professional-related services were in the $13,000 to $17,000 range. The greater prevalence of part-time workers in this last group of industries contributes significantly to the bifurcated earnings structure (Kassab and Luloff, 1993).

Similarly, the quality of jobs within social, educational and health services tends to be bifurcated. Whereas average earnings for workers in the hospital and education industries ranged from $18,000 to $19,000 in 1990, average earnings for workers in nursing, personal care facilities and social services were $11,000. Moreover, hospital and education workers were more likely to have health insurance benefits than workers in the latter group.

Research indicates that, compared with households in which the head is employed in traditionally higher paying industries (such as manufacturing, mining or government), families whose heads are employed in higher paying service industries (such as the producer or distributive services) are more likely to experience economic hardship. Children in the household are less likely to have health care insurance coverage. These differences most likely reflect the wide variability in earnings and the presence of marginal positions within these service industries, as contrasted with the relative homogeneity of traditional higher wage industries (Kassab et al., 1995).

Jobs in the consumer, health, education and social services constitute an integral component of the nonmetropolitan economy, with about 40 percent of nonmetropolitan workers in 1990 employed in these sectors (Kassab and Luloff, 1993). These industries continued to add workers (i.e., jobs) to the nonmetropolitan economy, as indicated by research covering the 1981-1986 period. Moreover, these sectors are expected to continue to grow at least until 2000. However, many of these new jobs require relatively few skills and, consequently, pay low wages (Porterfield, 1990; Smith, 1993). For instance, retail trade, entertainment and recreation service employees averaged between $11,000 and $12,000 per year in 1990. Furthermore, workers in consumer services are among the least likely to have health insurance benefits. Two factors contributing to the low level of compensation are the prevalence of lower level service occupations and part-time employment. However, discrepancies in job quality between these industries and traditional nonmetropolitan industries (e.g., agriculture, forestry and fishery) are not large; workers in traditional nonmetropolitan industries earned about $13,000, on average, in 1990 (Kassab and Luloff, 1993).

Implications for Economic Development

The promotion of jobs in higher paying service industries, particularly in producer services, has been a focus of economic development efforts. In metropolitan areas, evidence indicates that this sector can constitute part of the economic base and as such, serve as an autonomous force for generating economic growth. Services that are sold or exported outside of the local area to another region or city result in an influx of outside income (i.e., basic income). In addition, job growth in producer services has exceeded that in the goods-producing sector for some time (Smith, 1993).

However, in nonmetropolitan areas, evidence regarding the capacity of service industries to grow independently of goods-producing industries is in conflict (Hirschl and McReynolds, 1989; Miller and Bluestone, 1988; Smith, 1993). Furthermore, nonmetropolitan growth rates in the producer services and in many of the other service industries, lagged behind those in metropolitan areas. In 1969, for instance, 68 percent of the wage and salary employment in metropolitan areas was in service industries; this increased to 80 percent by 1989. In contrast, nonmetropolitan employment in service industries increased only from 63 to 66 percent during this period. Continued gains in the complement of service industries within nonmetropolitan areas would help diversify the local economy and promote economic stability (Smith, 1993).

Disparities between metropolitan and nonmetropolitan areas with respect to the types of service industries comprising the local economy may mean that the mechanisms influencing service sector growth and development differ. Social, educational and health services are more concentrated in nonmetropolitan than metropolitan areas. These industries may be growing in nonmetropolitan areas in response to non-work basic income, particularly income associated with the elderly, such as pensions and Social Security. In metropolitan areas, gains in service industries are more closely associated with basic income derived from work sources (Hirschl and McReynolds, 1989). All the same, the predominance of low-wage/low-skill jobs in nonmetropolitan areas raises concerns about the capability of these jobs to adequately sustain the economic well-being of nonmetropolitan households.

— *Cathy Kassab*

See also

Employment; Home-based Work; Income; Labor Force; Policy, Economic; Work

References

Glasmeier, A. and G. Borchard. "Research Policy and Review 31. From Branch Plants to Back Offices: Prospects for Rural Services Growth." *Environment and Planning* 21 (1989): 1565-1583.

Henderson J. "Building the rural economy with high-growth entrepreneurs." *Federal Reserve Bank of Kansas City Economic Review*, 2002. Available online at: http://www.kansascityfed.org.

Hirschl, Thomas and Samuel A. McReynolds. "Service Employment and Rural Community Economic Development." *Journal of the Community Development Society* 20 (1989): 15-30.

Isserman A.M. "Competitive Advantages of Rural America in the Next Century." *International Regional Science Review* 24, no. 1 (2001): 38-58.

Kassab, Cathy. *Income and Inequality: The Role of the Service Sector in the Changing Distribution of Income.* New York, NY: Greenwood Press, 1992.

Kassab, Cathy and A.E. Luloff. "The New Buffalo Hunt: Chasing the Service Sector." *Journal of the Community Development Society* 24 (1993): 174-195.

Kassab, Cathy, A.E. Luloff, and Fred Schmidt. "The Changing Impact of Industry, Household Structure, and Residence on Household Well-being." *Rural Sociology* 60, no. 1 (1995): 67-90.

Marshall, J.N. *Services and Uneven Development.* New York, NY: Oxford University Press, 1988.

Miller, James P. and Herman Bluestone. "Prospects for Service Sector Employment Growth in Nonmetro America." *Review of Regional Studies* 18 (1988): 28-41.

Noyelle, Thierry J. "Advanced Services in the System of Cities." Pp. 143-164 in *Local Economies in Transition.* Edited by Edward M. Bergman. Durham, NC: Duke University Press, 1986.

Porterfield, Shirley. "Service Sector Offers More Jobs, Lower Pay." *Rural Development Perspectives* June-Sept. (1990): 2-7.

Smith, Stephen M. "Service Industries in the Rural Economy: The Role and Potential Contributions." Pp. 105-126 in *Economic Adaption: Alternatives for Nonmetropolitan Areas.* Edited by David L. Barkley. Boulder, CO: Westview Press, 1993.

Settlement Patterns

The spatial arrangement of people, enterprises and infrastructure in the open countryside and in places of various sizes. The diversity of current settlement patterns grows out of human interaction with the physical landscape. Early settlers exploited geographical advantages and took advantage of federal land disbursement initiatives to lay out property boundaries, town locations and transportation networks. The regionally distinctive configurations that emerged are still with us today despite major economic and technological changes. In the twentieth century, decreasing farm employment, increasing concentration of population and economic activity in metropolitan centers, and a near-total reliance on the automobile for work and shopping lessened the importance of villages and towns as retail centers, although many continue to grow and thrive as residential communities.

Diversity of Current Settlement Patterns

Rural and urban settlement patterns are highly integrated and cannot be viewed in isolation. Almost half of the 62 million rural Americans in 1990 lived in metropolitan areas, consisting of counties with urbanized cores of 50,000 people or more and suburban fringes. Even though they live in rural settings, defined as open countryside or places of 2,500 people or fewer, the vast majority of metropolitan-rural people lead lives that are better characterized as suburban. Because the U.S. settlement system is largely organized around metropolitan areas, the territory falling outside the range of daily metropolitan commuting, labeled nonmetropolitan, came to be equated with rural in the eyes of many researchers and policy makers (see "Rural, Definition of" and "Rural, Measurement of").

In that context, the roughly 50 million nonmetropolitan Americans live in a diverse and regionally varying settlement structure. In 1990, half of them lived outside of nonmetropolitan places (including people living in unincorporated villages with less than 1,000 residents), 15 percent lived in villages with fewer than 2,500 people, and another 15 percent lived in towns with populations between 2,500 and 10,000. The remaining 20 percent lived in cities ranging in size from 10,000 to 50,000. Combining the first two categories above shows that almost two-thirds of nonmetropolitan residents lived in rural areas, with the remainder in urban towns and cities.

Nonmetropolitan territory averaged 18 persons per square mile in 1990, but wide regional diversity exists in both the number and arrangement of people on the landscape. Nonmetropolitan population densities range from 800 persons per square mile in parts of the highly industrialized Northeast to less than one in sections of the arid West. Ranching and mining in Western states support a much smaller population in the open countryside, so that 132 counties lie beyond the frontier line of two people per square mile (Duncan, 1993). Fifty percent of nonmetropolitan residents in the West are urban, compared to just 30 percent in the Northeast. The South and Midwest fall in between these extremes.

Settlement patterns are determined by physical environment, historical events, economic processes and human initiative. Climate, topography, geology and soils provide a framework within which economic, social and technological factors operate to distribute and connect populations. The semi-arid climate and flat topography of the Great Plains favor an economy of large-scale farms employing relatively few people; the population density in such farming-dependent counties is down to 10 people per square mile and two-thirds of such counties are entirely rural, containing no town larger than 2,500 people. Mining-dependent counties, found largely in the Appalachian and Rocky Mountains, are more densely settled (30 people per square mile) and more concentrated into towns along valley floors separated by uninhabitable slopes and peaks. Density is highest where manufacturing prevails, such as near textile and furniture plants in Piedmont regions of the Southeast; counties dependent on manufacturing contain 60 people per square with 80 percent of the population living in urban settings (Cook and Mizer, 1994).

Early Settlement

Much of U.S. history is embedded in the landscape, because basic patterns of public and private ownership (e.g., land boundaries, town locations, street patterns) are hard to change once they are established. Rural settlement patterns in the U.S. are largely Northern European in origin (Meinig, 1986). Spanish influences prevail in the Rio Grande Valley and other subregions, but during initial exploration and settlement Spain favored strictly commercial enterprises in the New World with small, mostly male populations. At first greatly influenced by Native Americans, settlers blazed trails, built roads, followed watercourses, surveyed and cleared land, laid out towns, established plantations and smaller homesteads, and built fortifications at strategic sites. The location and layout of these first settlements, and the farming and building methods initially employed, became the foundations for future expansion (Meinig, 1993).

Colonial settlement was highly dispersed and lacked towns in many areas. Plantations along the rivers in Virginia did not depend on towns for marketing their agricultural products, and decentralization defined much of the rural South where towns were difficult to establish. Authorities encouraged and sometimes required settlement in towns, to promote town-based commerce and to ease protection and taxation, but settlers hungered for land and rejected town living for individual farms (Lingeman, 1980).

The Puritans of New England, whose settlement patterns reflected their religious purpose, followed a different scheme. Land was granted as a town to a group, which was responsible for distributing land to individuals and also keeping part of it as town land. Members lived in an organized community setting centered on the town and symbolized by the commons (large greens that still grace New England towns), but they owned their own land and valued enterprise and self-sufficiency. New towns were formed when older towns grew too large and needed to "halve off." Puritan town development ended in New England by the time of the Revolution, but these religious communities determined the pattern of rural settlement in much of the Northeast and sent their ideas about how a town should look and be organized west in subsequent migrations.

New England towns were irregular in shape as were most rural parcels laid out along the Eastern Seaboard during the Colonial Period. Survey techniques employing "metes and bounds" created inexact boundaries that have been carried down to the present. The distinctive rectilinear settlement pattern west of the Appalachian Mountains began with the Land Ordinance of 1785, a federal effort to ensure an orderly system of land distribution. Legal problems that plagued landowners in the East were lessened by sending surveyors to plot the six-square-mile townships and their component one-square-mile sections, often before settlement occurred. This township-and-range system was carried into most settled areas of the U.S. all the way to the Pacific, and was even employed in mountainous landscapes where such grids were impractical.

Regional Diversification

Settlement proceeded unevenly from several Atlantic core areas (New England, Pennsylvania, Virginia and South Carolina), each imprinting distinctive patterns on western lands. Settlers went first to high-quality land near transportation routes. Islands of settlement developed around mining and logging camps and army posts, but dispersed, agricultural homesteads and trade centers were most prevalent. Cities grew up at strategic physical locations, such as the confluence of major waterways (Pittsburgh), where portage was necessary around falls (Louisville), or in the center of rich agricultural districts (Lexington). In the northern tier of states destined to become the country's industrial heartland, investments in transportation (first roads, then canals, then railroads) lowered physical restrictions early on and bound the Midwest to Atlantic port cities in an integrated economic network.

Important insights into U.S. settlement geography come from central place theory, the predicted outcomes of which are most clearly seen in the Midwest. Settlements exist for their functions, many of which are ubiquitous (providing goods, services and administration). Central place theory predicts the size and spacing of places based on thresholds (the minimum size of the trade area needed to support a given function) and ranges (how far people travel to obtain these functions). In the nineteenth century, grocery stores, saw mills and churches were lower-order functions with small thresholds found in hamlets spread thickly across the landscape, often at six-mile intervals in compliance with township-and-range geometry. People traveled farther to larger central places, fewer in number, to ob-

tain higher-order goods and services, such as hardware, clothing, financial help and legal services. Assuming entrepreneurs located to minimize distance traveled by their customers, a nested hierarchy of hexagonal trade areas resulted, with higher-order centers containing all functions found in those of a lower order.

Physical barriers such as mountains and lakes, variations in climate and soils, and other environmental factors affecting the location of non-ubiquitous functions such as mining, manufacturing and transportation account for much of the deviation from central place patterns. Also, central place dynamics were weaker in different regional economic systems. Southern plantations (large, commercial enterprises dependent on the exploitation of large numbers of slave laborers) produced staples principally for export, and thus did not support complex patterns of commerce and trade. The planters themselves often lived in nearby cities such as Charleston, Natchez or Memphis, for comfort, security and socializing, while Black slaves and overseers lived in concentrated rural settlements on the land being farmed. The majority of White Southerners ran small farms, lived and worked on their land, often alongside the few slaves they may have owned. Stark economic and social contrasts developed between wealthy planter towns and most of the countryside. Towns serving small farmers were often meager, operating as seasonal marketplaces or county seats and providing the few services (e.g., blacksmithing) that farmers did not perform themselves.

The Civil War changed settlement in the South. A plantation-like economic system survived in the form of sharecropping, but Black families moved from clustered slave quarters to widely dispersed tenant farmsteads (Aiken, 1985). Railroad expansion brought industry in the form of textile mills in the Piedmont and lumber camps throughout the Coastal Plains. Towns and cities grew up around these activities and alongside the tracks every six to 10 miles to serve as distribution and marketing centers.

The distinctly linear pattern of settlement associated with railroads can still be found throughout the country, perhaps most clearly on the Great Plains, where towns were laid out like beads on a string, often named in alphabetical order. East of the Mississippi River, settlement preceded the railroads and later conformed to it. In much of the West, railroads preceded settlement and railroad companies operated as real estate speculators, dispensing millions of acres of land

and actively recruiting settlers from the U.S. and Europe to guarantee profits.

Like the mining towns in the Rocky Mountains and Sierra Nevada that instantly sprang to life and just as quickly disappeared, Great Plains settlements suffered from volatile international markets and natural resource depletion. Railroad boosterism, aided by the Homestead Act of 1862, pushed population densities above the long-run carrying capacities of fragile, prairie ecosystems. Many Great Plains towns disappeared shortly after being founded and much of the area has experienced steady population loss since the late nineteenth century.

Twentieth Century Changes

On the eve of the Automobile Age, Charles J. Galpin conducted a landmark study depicting the small scale of rural society in one Midwestern county (Galpin, 1915). Community life centered on one of 12 trade centers, "within which the apparent entanglement of human life is resolved into a fairly unitary system of interrelatedness (p. 18)." Ranging in size from 500 to 2,500 people, most of these centers contained their own bank, newspaper, milk delivery service, high school and one or more churches. The average size of their trade areas, about 50 square miles, conformed to the speed of the horse and wagon, the dominant mode of transportation at the time. Such communities were the home to most Americans born before 1920, the year in which urban residents outnumbered rural residents for the first time.

Since then, the automobile and other technological advances rearranged settlement patterns, community life and society in general. In moving from a rural to a metropolitan economy, the single, most transforming element was the displacement of farm labor. With productivity increasing 1,200 percent, the number of farm residents fell from 30 million in 1940 to five million in 1990 despite expanding farm output. During the same 50-year period, the number of farms dropped from six to two million and average farm size tripled. The proportion of farmers living off the farm jumped from five to 20 percent (Beale, 1993). Few Black farmers had the financial resources or access to credit needed to mechanize and consolidate; thus, the rural Black population in the South re-clustered into subdivisions and towns.

The automobile helped to trigger a convergence of rural and urban economic and social conditions, so that today's rural settlement patterns conform more to job commuting, retirement and recreational businesses than to farming, mining or logging. Many areas once entirely rural have been absorbed into metropolitan regions through suburbanization. Industrial deconcentration and growth in the service sector, including a growing number of information-oriented jobs that can be performed anywhere, greatly expanded rural commuting patterns.

Six-mile agricultural communities with 50-square-mile trading areas have been replaced by 30-mile "Wal-Mart" towns serving 5,000 square miles. Towns and villages left behind often continue to function and even thrive as residential centers. However location within municipal boundaries seems to have become a disadvantage. Retail centers are moving to outskirts where large tracts of undeveloped land allow larger stores and parking lots. Housing is following the same pattern, especially among higher-income populations.

Retirees and other migrants, many escaping urban ills, now populate former fishing villages, lakeside resorts, mountain hideaways and other rural settings prized for their natural amenities. Such growth creates much-needed employment at the same time that rising property values push many long-term residents out and force lower-income workers to commute long distances. In amenity-rich areas such as the intermountain West and the South Atlantic coast, development spread far beyond the confines of earlier settlements and increasingly consists of second homes, which stand empty much of the time. Such development increases the difficulties of preserving the amenities—unspoiled scenery, pristine air and water, rural ambience—that attract newcomers in the first place.

— *John B. Cromartie*

See also
Community; History, Rural; Migration; Plantations; Regional Diversity; Regional Planning; Rural, Definition of; Rural Demography; Spatial Inequality; Trade Areas; Urbanization

References
Aiken, Charles S. "New Settlement Patterns of Rural Blacks in the American South." *Geographical Review* 75 (1985): 383-404.

Beale, Calvin L. "Salient Features of the Demography of American Agriculture." In *The Demography of Rural Life*. Edited by David L. Brown, Donald R. Field, and James J. Zuiches. University Park, PA: Northeast Regional Center for Rural Development, 1993.

Cook, Peggy J. and Karen L. Mizer. *The Revised ERS County Typology: An Overview*. Rural Development Research Report 89. Washington, DC: Rural Economy Division, Economic Research Service, U.S. Department of Agriculture, 1994.

Duncan, Dayton. *Miles from Nowhere: Tales from America's Contemporary Frontier*. New York, NY: Viking, 1993.

Fuguitt, Glenn V., David L. Brown, and Calvin L. Beale. *Rural and Small Town America*. New York, NY: Russell Sage, 1989.

Galpin, Charles J. *The Social Anatomy of an Agricultural Community*. Wisconsin Agricultural Experiment Station Research Bulletin Number 34. Madison, WI: University of Wisconsin, Madison, 1915.

Kandel, William and John Cromartie. *New Patterns of Hispanic Settlement in Rural America*. Rural Development Research Report No. (RDRR99), May 2004. Available online at: http://www.ers.usda.gov/publications/rdrr99.

Lichter, Daniel T. and Kenneth M. Johnson. "Emerging Rural Settlement Patterns and the Geographic Redistribution of America's New Immigrants." *Rural Sociology* 71, no. 1 (March 2006): 109-131.

Lingeman, Richard. *Small Town America: A Narrative History, 1620-The Present*. Boston, MA: Houghton Mifflin, 1980.

Meinig, Donald W. *The Shaping of America: A Geographical Perspective on 500 Years of History. Volume 1: Atlantic America, 1492-1800*. New Haven, CT: Yale University Press, 1986.

Meinig, Donald W. *The Shaping of America: A Geographical Perspective on 500 Years of History. Volume 2: Continental America, 1800-1867*. New Haven, CT: Yale University Press, 1993.

Sexuality

The experiences of sexuality and sexual identity of individuals living on farms and in non-metropolitan areas. This entry provides insight into the diverse expressions of sexuality in rural America. Tracing the roots of this body of research through its intersection with rural gender studies, the entry emphasizes the development of this emergent area in rural studies. It pays particular attention to the experiences of minority sexualities, including gay, lesbian, bisexual and transgender (GLBT) individuals and communities. At the same time, it addresses the significance of heterosexuality to rural communities. The scholarship on both the marginalized sexualities and heterosexuality produces a rich and fertile body of research that will continue to develop within the area of rural studies.

Rural Lesbian and Gay Lives

Questions and concerns about gay and lesbian experiences of rural life are an outgrowth of both gender research in rural studies and an interest in rural marginality (Bell and Valentine, 1995). In the last 10 years, the study of gender and rural life has grown in depth and breadth. During this time, an outgrowth of research on gendered experiences in rural communities and work emerged along with a growing interest in the impact of the rural environment on the formation of gendered identity. The newest area to emerge out of rural gender studies is the interconnection between gender and sexuality.

Scholarship in rural sexuality seeks to fill the gap in knowledge surrounding the experiences of gay and lesbian lives and communities in rural areas. This absence is due not only to rural studies not addressing the experiences of sexual minorities, but also the bias in GLBT studies toward urban issues and experiences (Bell, 2006 and Halberstam, 2003). Scholarship on rural sexuality includes research on gay and lesbian communities in rural areas, representations of rural gay and lesbian individuals, and efforts to unravel the diversity of rural life.

Gay and Lesbian Communities. New research on the life histories of marginalized communities in rural areas provides a great deal of insight into the ways in which lesbians and gay men build community and integrate into rural life. Research reveals the diversity of experiences among these communities. This scholarship provides insight into the ways sexual minorities organize and develop community in rural settings (see Bonfitto, 1997; Cody and Welch, 1997; McCarthy, 2000). Some communities openly express their homosexuality, while others get along by keeping their sexual orientation private. Cody and Welch (1997) outline "coping styles" adopted by gay men in rural New England to manage their experiences with intolerance in the community and their feelings of isolation and invisibility.

Another component of rural gay and lesbian communities involves the assumption that lesbians and gay men who live in rural areas migrate to cities to escape the intolerance in rural areas. Bell (2006) asserts that, although there is some degree of reality to this migration, there are recent trends in rural migration that need to be more thoroughly researched. The first involves the disillusionment experienced by many lesbians and gay men upon their move to urban centers that are supposedly more accepting of diversity. Some research indicates that those individuals migrating from rural to urban cities experience bias from those within urban gay communities, who consider them to be backward and unsophisticated (Berube, 1996). This sometimes leads to a return migration to their rural home, which can be difficult, especially if the separation from home was the result of tensions regarding their sexual orientation.

A second important trend is that a growing number of sexual minorities born in rural areas choose to stay and build a life and community for themselves in their rural hometowns. Choosing to stay in rural communities often means that lesbians and gay men must manage their sexuality in ways that can leave them isolated and vulnerable in the rural community. A final point raised by Bell (2006) is that there is a growing movement of lesbians and gay men to rural areas. This migration is not necessarily tied to their sexual identity but reveals an important counter trend that raises many questions about the stereotypical urban gay life.

In addition, concern for rural gay men involves their support network and how that relates to those men diagnosed with HIV/AIDS. Research has shown that rural gay men diagnosed with HIV/AIDS face even greater challenges than urban gay men in receiving medical and social services (Shernoff, 1997). Although there seem to be trends that demonstrate a stronger presence of minority sexualities in rural areas, significant stigmas still exist for these individuals and groups.

Representations of Gay and Lesbian Life. Another area of research in rural gay and lesbian lives includes scholarship on representations of homosexual life in rural areas. Increasing attention to minority rural sexualities in popular media, including films such as *Boys Don't Cry* (directed by Kimberly Peirce) and *Brokeback Mountain* (directed by Ang Lee), provides greater awareness of these populations. Coupled with the media interest in cases such as Matthew Shepard, who was murdered in Laramie, Wyoming, after leaving a gay bar, these popular images of what it means to be a GLBT individual in rural America are often underscored by the challenges of surviving as a sexual minority in an intolerant community.

Judith Halberstam (2003) examines representations of queer rural life in her analysis of representations of the murder of Brandon Teena. A female-to-male transsexual who was raped and murdered in rural Nebraska, Teena became part of popular culture and knowledge in the film, *Boys Don't Cry*. Her story is also the subject of the documentary, *The Brandon Teena*

Story (directed by Susan Muska and Greta Olassdottir). The importance of this strand of research is that it reveals the way these high-profile cases complicate what is considered normal both within rural life as well as within GLBT communities (Halberstam, 2003). In addition, cases like those of Teena and Shephard can take on an iconic status, which can lead to equating the experiences of all sexual minorities in rural communities with these iconic figures. Halberstam (2003) asserts that many more studies need to be conducted to better understand the diversity within rural gay and lesbian lives.

A final significant contribution to this area of rural studies involves including multiple and diverse experiences of rural lives as well as the lives of those within GLBT communities. There is no universal or singular rural experience. For example, what rural means to a gay man in the rural American Northeast will be different from what rural means to a lesbian woman living in the rural American upper Midwest. In fact, the experiences of formal and informal social networks in rural areas can vary between lesbian and gay communities within the same geographical location. For example, Kirkey and Forsyth (2001) found that, in rural western Massachusetts, gay men constructed a lifestyle that was centered within the home, yet integrated into the broader community. This was in contrast to a large lesbian community, which was more active and visible within the public sphere. Similarly, what it means to be gay may vary dramatically between a gay man who was born and raised in the upper American Midwest than from a gay man who moved to the upper American Midwest in his late 40s. The point here is that research in rural sexuality concerns itself with the diversity of lifestyles at work within both rural life and sexual identity.

Rural Heterosexuality

A second key area of rural sexuality involves research on the ways in which heterosexuality is constructed in rural life. Scholarship in this area seeks to unravel the relationship between heterosexual identity and the social construction of the rural (Little, 2003). This departs from research on rural life as experienced within GLBT communities by focusing, not on marginal sexualities, but on heteronormative practices in rural areas. It also complements the work done on homosexuality in rural areas, because it examines how traditional and stereotypical notions of masculinity and femininity, and their ties to heterosexuality, inform dominant notions of gender and sexual identity. Because heterosexuality is the dominant and normal sexual identity, it has not been the focus of attention for many scholars in the area of rural gender studies (Little, 2003). For this reason, the way heterosexuality impacts notions of proper masculinity and femininity in rural life is a small but growing body of scholarship.

The research on heterosexuality that is currently available examines its relationship to both the constitution of traditional gender identities and idyllic notions of rural life (Little, 2003; 2007). Little lays the groundwork for this area of study. By analyzing the behaviors and activities taken for granted in everyday rural life, she argues that rural heterosexuality is represented as reassuring and safe, which underscores the belief in the traditional family as foundational to the maintenance and survival of rural communities (Little, 2003; 2007).

Scholarship on sexuality in rural America reveals a diverse set of experiences that expose a variety of assumptions about not only the lives of lesbians and gay men, but also stereotypes of rural life in contemporary America.

— *Christina D. Weber*

See also
Family; Marriage; Policy, Rural Family; Policy, Health Care; Rural Women

References
Bell, Derrick. "Queer Country Revisited." Pp. 345-358 in *Rural Gender Relations: Issues and Case Studies*. Edited by Bettina Bock and Sally Shortall. Nosworthy Way, Wallingford, Oxfordshire, UK Cabi Publishing, 2006.

Bell, Derrick and Gill Valentine. "Queer Country: Rural Lesbian and Gay Lives." *Journal of Rural Studies* 11, no. 2 (1995): 113-122.

Berube, Allan. "Intellectual Desire." *GLQ: A Journal of Lesbian and Gay Studies* 3, no.1 (1996): 139-157.

Bonfitto, Vincent. "The Formation of Gay and Lesbian Identity and Community in the Connecticut River Valley of Western Massachusetts." *Journal of Homosexuality* 33, no. 1 (1997): 69-96.

Cody, Paul and Peter Welch. "Rural Gay Men in Northern New England: Life Experiences and Coping Styles." *Journal of Homosexuality* 33, no. 1 (1997): 51-67.

Halberstam, Judith. "The Brandon Teena Archive." Pp. 159-169 in *Queer Studies: An Interdisciplinary Reader*. Oxford: Blackwell Publishers, 2003.

Kirkey, Kenneth and Ann Forsyth. "Men in the Valley: Gay Male Life on the Suburban-Rural Fringe." *Journal of Rural Studies* 17, no. 4 (2001): 421-441.

Little, Jo. "'Riding the Rural Love Train': Heterosexuality and the Rural Community." *Sociologia Ruralis* 43, no. 4 (2003): 401-417.

Little, Jo. "Constructing Nature in the Performance of Rural Heterosexualities." *Environment & Planning D: Society & Space* 25, no. 5 (2007): 861-866.

McCarthy, Linda. "Poppies in the Wheat Field: Exploring the Lives of Rural Lesbians." *Journal of Homosexuality* 39, no. 1 (2000): 75-94.

Sherhoff, Michael. "Gay Men with AIDS in Rural America." *Journal of Gay & Lesbian Social Services* 7, no. 1 (1997): 73-85.

Signs
Devices, fixtures, placards or structures that use any color, form, graphic, illumination, symbol or writing to advertise or announce the purpose of a person or entity, or to communicate information of any kind to the public. This article discusses the purposes and common uses of both public and private signs. It reviews the different types of signs. Public efforts to regulate private signs and the practical and legal issues involved in such regulation are examined.

Context and Types of Signs
Signs—sources of valuable information, essential tools of commerce, or blights on the landscape? They can be all of those. The answer depends in part on the nature and location of the sign. To some extent, however, the answer depends on the perspective of the viewer. The fast food restaurant operator and the environmentalist have different views on the subject. The environmentalist with a screaming child in the back seat who can be calmed only by a special meal served under golden arches may have quite a different perspective from that of the same environmentalist in a more abstract discussion about signs.

Although signs can be intrusive in an urban environment, they are more noticeable in rural areas where they amount to a larger percentage of the human-built landscape. Advertising and other private signs are the subject of the most public concern involving signs. Through appropriate sign regulation, local governments can and do manage the number, size, height and location of such private signs.

Most signs in the rural U.S. are oriented to roads. Although there are small signs in store windows, signs inside shopping malls, and signs in locations to identify restrooms, such signs are beyond the scope of this discussion. Signs along bicycle and hiking trails are similar in purpose to the road-oriented signs described below, although the signs aimed at bicyclists and pedestrians are generally smaller than those intended for high-speed traffic and thus less intrusive.

There are three basic categories of signs in the rural U.S.: public signs, quasi-public signs, and private signs. Public signs are those determined by public agencies to be essential or at least important to the functioning of society or to governmental operation. Such signs include speed-limit and other traffic regulation signs; signs giving distances to the next city and other important travel information; signs identifying historic landmarks, scenic overlooks and other points of interests; and official notices announcing elections, public hearings and other formal matters.

Quasi-public signs include street addresses and other signs necessary or useful for public purposes but generally placed on private property. Street numbers are required by many local governments to assist public safety officials. Other quasi-public signs may identify driveway entrances and exits, public telephones, handicapped parking spaces, and other directions and facilities on private property. Although these signs are not as essential to public business as street addresses and speed limits, they are a great convenience to the public and fulfill public purposes. For these reasons, local governments often require some quasi-public signs (particularly street numbers) and allow or encourage others without much public regulation.

Private signs include everything from the smallest "for rent" sign to the largest billboard. The most numerous private signs are those located on business properties, identifying those businesses and advertising their services and goods. Private signs also include non-commercial signs, such as those urging the reader to vote for a particular candidate or to support a particular cause or issue. Most controversy and serious public discussion about signs involve such private signs.

Regulation of Sign Placement and Design

Some signs are clearly essential to the life of a complex society, particularly one that moves on four wheels at high speed. Questions involving signs focus on how many signs of what size and design should be allowed where.

Most public signs providing traffic directions, warnings and information conform to U.S. Department of Transportation standards, which are based on considerations of safety and visibility. Such signs are a familiar part of the highway landscape, and their design is likely to remain unchanged except as these national standards evolve. Other public signs, such as official notices, are typically so non-intrusive on the visual environment that they are often not even noticed by their intended audiences.

Quasi-public signs vary somewhat by region, but they are generally relatively small and nondescript. Occasionally a rural subdivision may be identified by a large structural entrance marquee, or a family farm may be identified with a barn-sized sign painted on the roof, but those are atypical. Quasi-public signs erected by private individuals become most problematic when erected in the public right-of-way, interfering at times with road maintenance and even with visibility and highway safety.

Most of the actual and perceived intrusion of signs on the rural landscape involves private signs, erected to attract the business or attention of the motoring public. Burma Shave pioneered the use of such signs, placing catchy verses on series of small signs along highways in rural areas. Other early signs in rural areas consisted of metal logo signs, often located at businesses, and advertisements for soft drinks and tobacco painted on the sides of barns.

As highway traffic grew, so did the advertising directed at it. Signs grew both in number and size. The increase in the number of signs is in part a function of an increase in population and the related increase in business activity. It is also a function of the significant increases in the number of miles that people drive. As people drive more, they spend more time in their car, and that time becomes a sort of prime time for advertisers in a different medium.

Billboards initially proliferated along major highways. One policy aimed at controlling the impact of billboards succeeded in reducing their numbers but increasing their size. Under the Highway Beautification Act adopted during the 1960s, new billboards were significantly restricted within a specified distance of federally subsidized highways. The result of that program was a gradual reduction in the number of billboards, as old signs were removed and not replaced. Because of the restrictions on new signs near the highways, however, the billboard industry developed super-sized billboards, designed to be located outside the federally regulated zone of 660 feet from the paving and easily read from that greater distance. The other significant change in sign design along rural roadways was the effort of some businesses, notably fast food franchises, to reach highway traffic with very tall signs located at the site of the business but designed to be read or recognized from a highway many hundreds of feet away.

Local governments can and do regulate sign numbers, size, height and location. Most local governments that adopted zoning also have sign regulations of some sort. Typical local sign regulations specify the number of free-standing signs to be located on a single property, the size of individual signs, the height of signs, and the distance that signs must be set back from a roadway or property line.

Some communities also regulate sign lighting and even the colors and materials used in signs. Lighting restrictions are common, particularly on signs in or near residential areas. Regulation of colors and materials is most common in historic districts, but such regulations are also found in a number of tourist communities and exclusive suburbs. Other communities have the legal authority to regulate sign design, but many choose not to expend the political capital necessary to regulate business beyond basic standards on number, size, height and location.

Often much of the visual impact of signs comes from sign clutter, a proliferation of different types of signs in front of one or more businesses. A convenience store may have a professional pole sign with its name and logo, a changeable marquee with gas prices, a banner announcing a new food special, a sandwich board promoting a brand of cigarettes, and several paper window signs promoting food specials. Communities address this visual clutter both with limits on the number of signs and with significant restrictions on such temporary signs as banners and sandwich boards. Several communities ban trailer-mounted readerboards with flashing lights that may confuse motorists, although some allow that type of sign without the lights. Some communities prohibit or severely restrict such promotional devices as beacons, spotlights, large balloons, flapping pennants and moving signs.

Many local ordinances regulate on-premise signs (advertising goods and services offered on the same property) and off-premise signs (which are usually but not always billboards) differently. That distinction raises some significant constitutional and other legal problems. The safer approach to sign regulation is to regulate signs based on their location and physical characteristics, not on their messages. In many communities sign regulations vary by zoning district, imposing the most restrictive regulations in residential areas and the least restrictive ones in some commercial areas, with industrial and agricultural areas falling somewhere between the two.

Small paper signs, often used to promote political candidates or issues or to advertise yard or tag sales, pose interesting practical and theoretical challenges in sign regulation. Users often place those signs in the public right-of-way. Such use of public property for private activity typically requires complex lease negotiations and extensive bonding, insurance and indemnification arrangements. Unwilling to confront good-hearted citizens who are simply trying to empty their attics or promote good government, many local governments look the other way and tacitly allow such signs to exist, even on the right-of-way. A few communities developed regulatory schemes specifically to allow such signs for limited periods of time. Others have aggressive enforcement programs and regularly remove such signs, even on weekends.

Regulating signs is one of the most significant political challenges that a community can face. Consideration of a new sign ordinance is often contentious, even dividing the business community. Only a community-wide re-zoning is likely to be more hotly debated. Thus, adopted local sign regulations may start from sound planning suggestions, such as those outlined here, but evolve through the planning process into something much more complex and much less ideal. Anyone attempting to evaluate local sign regulations should always recognize the political and legal context in which they were adopted.

Just as the flashing lights, neon tubing, and readerboard marquees of 42nd Street are an integral part of that urban streetscape, so are signs part of the rural landscape. Increases in the number and size of signs made them more intrusive on the rural landscape and thus the subject of greater public concern. The greatest intrusions are by the very large signs that are targeted at distant or high-speed roads. Although some people may propose banning many signs as a solution to visual blight, the more appropriate response is typically to use sign regulations to manage the number, size, height and location of signs. Through such regulations, local governments can keep signs in scale with the buildings and activities of a particular streetscape, thus making them again a vital part of the rural community, rather than an intrusion on it.

— *Eric Damian Kelly*

See also
Environmental Regulations; Government

References

Fleming, Ronald Lee. *How Corporate Franchise Design Can Respect Community Identity*, rev. ed. Planning Advisory Service Report No. 452. Chicago, IL: American Planning Association, 2002.

Fraser, James. *The American Billboard: 100 Years.* Darby, PA: Diane Publishing Co., 2004

Greene, Frederick Stuart, Robert Moses, Lithgow Osborne, and Rexford Tugwell. *The Billboard: A Blot on Nature and a Parasite on Public Improvements.* New York, NY: New York Roadside and Safety Improvement Committee, 1939.

Kelly, Eric Damian and Gary J. Raso. *Sign Regulation for Small and Midsize Communities.* Planning Advisory Service Report No. 419. Chicago, IL: American Planning Association, 1989.

Mandelker, Daniel R. and William R. Ewald. *Street Graphics and the Law*, rev. ed. Chicago, IL: American Planning Association, 2004.

"Signs of the Times." *Planning* 57, no. 11 (November 1991): 32.

Venturi, Robert, Denise Scott Brown, and Steven Izenour. *Learning from Las Vegas.* Rev. ed. Cambridge, MA: MIT Press, 1977.

Williams, Norman. "Scenic Protection as a Legitimate Goal of Public Regulation." *Washington University Journal of Urban and Contemporary Law* 38 (1990): 3-24.

Social Class

A categorization of people based primarily on their occupation or similar economic positions in a stratified social system. The discussion of social class in rural America may be described in terms of two distinct approaches. First, there are analyses that focus on gradations within the social hierarchy. These are social strata, and the study of such strata is social stratification. Second, there are analyses that focus on the social relationships that people enter into during the process of economic production. These are more strictly understood as social classes. Both types of analyses will further vary depending on whether the population in question is composed entirely of farmers or encompasses a broader rural community.

The following discussion will refine this definition of class and stratification analysis, then turn to an examination of trends in this tradition within rural sociology. Finally, some basic characteristics of rural class and stratification structures, drawn from the U.S. Census, will be presented.

Rural Stratification

Stratification analyses of rural communities or regions follow largely the same pattern as stratification analyses of society as a whole. There are exceptions, however, stemming from the fact that the assignment of status in the everyday lives of rural people is bound less tightly to occupation than is that of their urban counterparts. Since anonymity is less prevalent in rural communities, the assignment of status is, on the one hand, more likely to be grounded in individual achievement (within a particular occupation). On the other hand, status is also based on ascribed characteristics derived from the individual's association with family (nuclear and extended), when the latter are known to the community. Apart from these differences, the study of stratification in rural communities examines all the same factors that would be examined in any stratification study of the larger society: occupational status, income, education and wealth. However, even within each of these categories variations between rural and urban values might be observed. For example, some occupations, such as farming, might be assigned a higher status by rural residents than by urban ones.

Attempts at analyzing the stratification of the farm population raise unique challenges that distinguish this group from rural non-farm residents. For instance, stratification analyses of the farm population may include specific indicators or combinations of indicators to determine the number of strata. Farm size in acres or sales volume, net farm or family income, net worth, educational attainment and tenure status are common variables used to determine an individual's location within a particular stratum among a farming population.

Rural Class

The analysis of class focuses on social relationships constructed in the production process, especially relationships between direct producers and non-producers. For example, analyses of class in antebellum America would involve study of the relationship between plantation owners as non-producers and slaves as producers. Under modern capitalism, it would involve study of the relations between, for instance, farm wage workers and farm owners. California fruit and vegetable production exemplifies a historical dependence on this type of class structure. Similarly, to the extent that a rural region has undergone an industrialization process, a class analysis examines the relationship between owners of rural industries and wage workers.

A rural class analysis is rather indistinct from the study of class in urban settings. More distinctive is the relationship between producers and non-producers in what often appears as "the family farm." Most family farmers engage in social relationships with non-producers in the process of production. Many borrow heavily from banks or other credit institutions. Others rent land, making payments to landowners in the form of cash or a share of the crop. In some commodities, especially where there is a regional monopolization on processing facilities (e.g., hog or chicken production), farmers sign contracts with processors that rather strictly specify labor and price conditions. These relationships can, at times, approximate those of wage workers and limit the autonomy of the farmer. Each of these cases can constitute class relationships insofar as control over production and the distribution of economic returns (value) to labor and capital are contested.

Bankers, landlords or agricultural processors do not represent the extent of non-production social relations into which farmers enter. Commodity systems and value chain studies from the 1990s have drawn our attention to the role of consumers in the production process. The changing role of consumers has yielded a new set of relationships that has significant impacts for rural class relations. Since the early 1990s, changes have occurred between farmers and consumers, bringing them closer together. These new social relationships between producer and consumer may be cultivated in the context of farmers' markets, community supported agriculture, u-pick farm stands, or other direct buying venues, but the key is that these historically economically antagonistic groups have found common interest in promoting non-economic values in farming. These values are often driven by aesthetics, environmental protection, recreation or animal welfare and are often referred to as "post-productionist." As a result, farmers who engage in post-productionist farming practices have been the beneficiaries of a newfound "status" within their rural community and sometimes on the national stage. Such farmers have assumed minor celebrity status, in part, due to agrofood writers who tout their agro-ecological vision (e.g., Michael Pollan) or local chefs who are drawn to them for high-quality or organic produce. Increasingly, farming practices are becoming a foundation for differentiating the agriculture producing class (Wright and Middendorf, 2007). This is

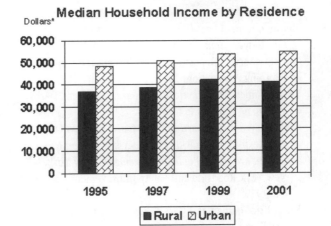

Median Household Income by Residence

Comparison of Rural and Urban Income Levels

Note: Incomes reported in 2001 dollars
Source: Adapted from U.S. Department of Agriculture, Economic Research Service, (ERS),
http://www.ers.usda.gov/Briefing/incomepovertywelfare/RuralIncome/.

not just a matter of status, as economic returns often follow visibility. Likewise, when farmers lose status, value can be diminished. For example, the public intolerance to cigarette smoking and ensuing policy have cast a shadow over tobacco farming as an occupation and denigrated markets for producers.

Farmers have historically engaged in a similar practice among themselves. Status, however, has been attributed to technologically aggressive individuals or to farmers renowned as "good farmers." What distinguishes this newer phenomenon is that, increasingly, those from the non-farm population are influencing farm class relations.

The Study of Rural Class and Stratification

Early twentieth-century studies in rural sociology focused on class and stratification issues in the context of a community studies orientation. These studies focused on the overall stratification structure of rural communities. For example, were they "diamond-shaped" (that is, having a large middle class with a small elite and small, impoverished lower strata) or were they "triangular" (with a small elite and a large underclass)? During and after the Great Depression, rural sociological studies of class structures sometimes met with political opposition. Now-classic studies, such as Goldschmidt's (1947) research on class structure in post-World War II California, met with attempts at suppression, while others, such as an analysis of sharecropping conditions in the South, were completely censored (Hooks, 1986). Some of these studies have been lost altogether.

Sewell (1965) wrote that rural sociology maintained consistent interest in stratification issues throughout the mid-twentieth century, although he noted that these interests were generally subordinated to other concerns of the discipline. In the post-World War II era, stratification variables were often embedded in the study of the diffusion and adoption of agricultural innovations. In the late 1960s and early 1970s, rural sociologists and the mass media increasingly examined issues related to rural poverty and to migratory farm labor.

By the late 1970s, a qualitative shift had emerged in rural sociology that made class analysis a focal point of the discipline, especially in what came to be labeled the new sociology of agriculture (Buttel et al., 1990). The first wave of these concerns was associated with the study of the relationships between family farms and capitalist enterprises at the input and output levels. These studies tended to reflect both a populism and a functionalism, or a grounding in the literature on complex organization. Heffernan (1972), for instance, studied vertical integration, emphasizing the contractual relationship between poultry producers and processors. Rodefeld (1974) developed a typology of farmers based on categories associated with ownership and control of land, labor, capital and management within agricultural production.

A more explicit class analysis of agriculture in the advanced capitalist societies developed in the late 1970s and early 1980s, fueled by an infusion of interest in Marxist theory. Initially, many of these studies took a rather orthodox or structuralist Marxist approach. This view contended that agricultural class structures would eventually come to parallel the class structures of the larger capitalist society. Mann and Dickinson (1978), for instance, followed Marx in contending that the transformation of the class structure of agriculture was dependent on the specific logic of capital. This logic was said to be shaped by the distinctive nature of agriculture. It was contingent, first, on the perishability of agricultural commodities and, second, the disjuncture of labor time and production time in the production of agricultural commodities. These obstructed capitalist penetration, or transformation, but eventually the obstacles would be overcome.

Other forms of class analysis took a more historical orientation. By examining specific agricultural regions, a number of scholars demonstrated the necessity of developing a historically informed analysis of U.S. agriculture. Pfeffer's (1983) study of regional variations in agricultural class structures examined corporate farming in California, sharecropping in the South, and family farming in the Great Plains. This study illuminated the role of land tenure and labor relations in the emergence of diverse class structures. Pfeffer showed the inadequacy of linear models. Rather, distinct class structures emerge from historical struggles over the distribution of wealth between producers and non-producers.

Adapting Wright (1978) to an exploration of agricultural class structure, Mooney (1983, 1988) focused on the contradictory class location of many farmers. Mooney challenged the view that agriculture must be eventually transformed into wage labor. He showed that instead, capital might continuously and more effectively appropriate surplus value from agricultural producers in the form of rent, interest, contract production and part-time farming. This left control over the agricultural production process socially contested between farmers on the one hand and landlords, bankers and processors on the other. The strength of cooperatives in the agricultural economy was a manifestation of this contest for control of capital and surplus value between farmers and non-producers. Further, cooperatives reflected an institutionalized form of this contradictory class position of farmers. The class analyses performed by scholars like Pfeffer and Mooney thus emphasized regional traditions, social structures and historical legacies over the abstract logic of capital.

A more concrete and historical analysis is also seen in Friedland, Barton, and Thomas's (1981) analysis of agriculture (see also Thomas, 1985). Their commodity systems approach contains a class analysis embedded within their attention to social relations of production in any given commodity production and distribution chain. As this approach diffused within the sociology of agriculture, attention to class and status variables varied considerably with the particular focus of individual researchers. The most recent developments in the field have blurred the boundaries between agriculture and food systems and turned their attention to issues associated with globalization processes and alternative, or "shorter," agri-food networks, which include post-productionist values and relocalization. Most of this research, though non-systematic, does retain analytic interest in class and equity issues. However, there has been considerable distancing from a Marxist perspective.

The Class and Stratification Structure of Rural America

Although official data reflecting urban and rural differences are often inadequate (and government sources increasingly neglect this variable), it is possible to describe, with some basic information, stratification as it varies within the rural population and between urban and rural populations. Data on class categories are much more difficult to obtain, outside of specific surveys generated to analyze class structure (e.g., Mooney, 1988). Such surveys often are limited to single points in time and specific regions. The following discussion provides some basic data on the issues of self-employment, income distribution, poverty and educational attainment.

Self-employment. Rural America has long been perceived as a haven for the self-employed, whether in town or on the farm. This popular image is a fiction insofar as there always has been more use of wage labor and the presence of absentee capital than it acknowledges. Self-employment declined in rural areas considerably over the last half of the twentieth century. A process of rural industrialization has taken place largely in the 1970s and 1980s in many parts of rural America. Small, family-owned, non-farm enterprises have given way to regional or national retail chains in hardware stores, groceries and restaurants. As for family farmers, the industrialization of agriculture has facilitated the consolidation and concentration of holdings, forcing many self-employed operators off the farm. Yet, agriculture retains a large number of self-employed (41.8 percent) compared to 6.9 percent in non-agricultural industries (U.S. Department of Labor). Since the 1980s self-employment in rural areas has once again begun to grow, even though earnings for those self-employed lag behind those in wage and salary jobs (Goetz, 2008). In 2003, 5.3 million rural (non-farm) workers were self-employed. Average earnings for the typical self-employed rural worker were only $16,851 in 2005, whereas the average annual earnings for a rural wage and salary worker were almost twice that amount at $31,596 (Goetz, 2008). Whether the recent upswing in rural self-employment is a result of a unique entrepreneurial ethos or a lack of viable employment alternatives continues to be debated.

Income. The use of income data can be problematic in comparing rural and urban standards of living since certain costs of living, such as housing, can be much lower in rural areas (see figure). On the other hand, expenses for transportation are often higher given the lack of public transportation. In 2006, the median income for all U.S. households was $48,201. The disparity between rural and urban median income has increased considerably since 1990. Inside metropolitan areas, the median income was $50,616 in 2006 (1990, $32,002), while the total rural median income was $38,293 (1990, $27,460). Household income varies by region of the country with the highest median income in the West ($52,249), followed by the Northeast ($52,057), and Midwest ($47,836). The South had the lowest median household income at $43,884. Household incomes can also vary based on race and age. Asian households have the highest median income ($64,238), followed by white, non-Hispanic households ($52,423). Greater differentiation can be found by examining income distribution within the rural population. Farm income is more variable than non-farm income, but since the early 1990s farm operator households have experienced higher average incomes than all U.S. households. In 2000, average farm household income was $62,019. This is explained in part by the impact of off-farm income to the household economy.

Poverty. The percentage of people living in poverty in rural areas has outpaced that in urban areas. Throughout the U.S., approximately 12 percent of individuals lived below the poverty level in 2002. In urban areas, 11.6 percent live below the poverty level, whereas in rural areas the percentage below poverty level is higher (14.2 percent). However, there is considerable variation in poverty among rural areas with regional pockets of persistent poverty (RSS Task Force, 1994). Much of the persistent poverty is concentrated in the rural South and regions historically populated by racial and ethnic minorities. Within rural counties not adjacent to metropolitan areas, the poverty rate is the highest at 16.8 percent. This was comparable to the 11.5 percent of persons who lived in the largest metropolitan areas. The percentage of people below poverty level among the rural farm population was 14 percent. Race and gender are also significant variables that are linked to a higher incidence of poverty. Female-headed households in rural areas were considerably more likely to live below poverty level than their urban counterparts (37.1 percent and 27.1 percent, respectively). The rate of poverty for African Americans and Native Americans is more than three times higher in rural areas than in urban areas. A third of the rural poverty population is made up of children (35 percent) (USDA, ERS, 2004).

Education. The gap between the educational attainment of rural and urban populations (25 years and over) has narrowed. The percentage of rural residents with less than a high school education (13.9) is virtually the same as urban Americans who have not completed high school training (13.8). However, there remains significant difference among those receiving a college education. Even though the gap closed somewhat during the 1990s, members of the urban population were more likely (29 percent) to have completed a bachelor's degree than rural residents (17 percent) (USDA, ERSa). No progress has been made within the rural Latino population. This group is especially disadvantaged with 45.1 percent reporting less than a high school education in 2000. This is due in part to the recent influx of new immigrants who possess lower levels of formal schooling. For rural African Americans, significant improvements have been made at the elementary and secondary levels, achieving parity with whites. Rural African Americans continue to lag behind rural whites in higher education. Only 8.1 percent of rural African Americans have received a college degree compared to 19.5 percent of urban African Americans (RSS, 2006).

Conclusion

The above statistics are intended as a general profile of trends in rural areas and distinctions between rural and urban places. It is important to remember, however, that stratification and class structures of rural communities vary considerably by region and sometimes even by the predominant commodity mix in either agriculture or in the other rural resource-based extractive economies of lumbering, fishing and mining. Such variations might often be more significant than differences between urban and rural populations. There is a need for government agencies to be more aware of urban-rural differences when collecting data on many of these variables related to class and stratification.

— *D. Wynne Wright and Patrick H. Mooney*

See also

Homelessness; Income; Inequality; Migrant Agricultural Workers; Plantations; Poverty; Quality of Life; Social Movements; Underemployment

References

Buttel, Frederick, Olaf Larson, and Gilbert Gillespie. *The Sociology of Agriculture.* Westport, CT: Greenwood Press, 1990.

Friedland, William H., Amy E. Barton, and Robert J. Thomas. *Manufacturing Green Gold.* New York, NY: Cambridge University Press, 1981.

Goetz, Stephan J. "Self-Employment in Rural America: The New Economic Reality." *Rural Realities* 2 no. 3 (2008). Retrieved February 4, 2008. Available online at: http://www.ruralsociology.org/pubs/RuralRealities/Volume2Issue3.html.

Goldschmidt, Walter. *As You Sow.* New York, NY: Harcourt, Brace and Co., 1947; reprinted Montclair, NJ: Allanheld, Osmun and Co., 1978.

Heffernan, William D. "Sociological Dimensions of Agricultural Structures in the United States." *Sociologia Ruralis* 12 no. 3/4 (1972): 481-499.

Mann, Susan A. and James M. Dickinson. "Obstacles to the Development of a Capitalist Agriculture." *Journal of Peasant Studies* 5, no. 4 (1978): 466-481.

Mooney, Patrick H. "Toward a Class Analysis of Midwestern Agriculture." *Rural Sociology* 48, no. 4 (1983): 563-584.

———. *My Own Boss? Class, Rationality and the Family Farm.* Boulder, CO: Westview Press, 1938.

Pfeffer, Max J. "Social Origins of Three Systems of Farm Production in the United States." *Rural Sociology* 48, no. 4 (1983): 540-562.

Rodefeld, Richard. *The Changing Organizational and Occupational Structure of Farming and the Implications for Farm Work Force Individuals, Families and Communities.* Unpublished Ph.D. dissertation. Madison, WI: University of Wisconsin-Madison, 1974.

Rural Sociological Society Task Force on Persistent Rural Poverty. *Persistent Poverty in Rural America.* Boulder, CO: Westview Press, 1993.

Rural Sociological Society (RSS). *Improving Educational Attainment: Issue brief: Challenges for Rural America in the 21st Century.* No 5, 2006. Retrieved February 2, 2008. Available online at: http://www.ruralsociology.org/briefs/brief5.pdf.

Thomas, Robert. *Citizenship, Gender and Work.* Berkeley, CA: University of California Press, 1985.

U.S. Department of Agriculture, Economic Research Service (USDA, ERSa) "Rural Poverty at a Glance." Washington, DC: U.S. Department of Agriculture, Economic Research Services, 2007. Retrieved February 2, 2008 Available online at: http://www.ers.usda.gov/publications/rdrr100/rdrr100.pdf.

U.S. Department of Agriculture, Economic Research Service (USDA, ERSb). "Rural Poverty at a Glance." Washington, DC: U.S. Department of Agriculture, Economic Research Services. 2004. Retrieved February 2, 2008. Available online at: http://www.ers.usda.gov/publications/rdrr100/rdrr100.pdf.

U.S. Department of Agriculture (USDA). "Accessing the Economic Well-being of Farm Households." *Agricultural Outlook.* Washington, DC: U.S. Department of Agriculture, Economic Research Services (USDA, ERS), 2002. Retrieved February 2, 2008. Available online at:

http://www.ers.usda.gov/publications/agoutlook/
aug2002/ao293i.pdf.

U.S. Department of Labor. "Self-Employment Rates,
1948-2003." Washington, DC: U.S. Department of Labor, Bureau of Labor Statistics. Retrieved February 3,
2008. Available online at: http://www.bls.gov/opub/ted/
2004/aug/wk4/art02.htm.

Wright, Erik Olin. *Class, Crisis and the State*. London, UK:
New Left Books, 1978.

Wright, Wynne and Gerad Middendorf. *The Fight Over
Food: Producers, Consumers, and Activists Challenge the
Global Food System*. University Park, PA: Pennsylvania
State University Press, 2007.

Social Movements

"Collective challenges by people with common purposes and solidarity in sustained interaction with elites,
opponents, and authorities." (Tarrow, 1994). Definitions of social movements vary from subtle variations
within a certain perspective to strong differences
among perspectives. One particularly important difference lies in the degree to which the role of ideology is
emphasized versus the role of material resources. A related distinction has to do with the degree of emphasis
on informal association as opposed to formal organization. This discussion emphasizes social movements that
tend toward more formal organization and focuses on
the resource mobilization and political process models
of social movements.

Specifically, three types of social movements in
rural America will be analyzed and compared, giving
special attention to the history of each. Changes in the
character of U.S. agriculture have led to and have been
caused by historical changes in the nature of rural social movements. The basic forces of technology and
market conditions in interaction with the interests of
rural people will continue both to shape and be shaped
by rural collective action (Mooney, 2000).

Types of Social Movements

Social movements in rural America may be divided into
three distinct types. The first two types are associated
with agricultural production, specifically, either with
the interests of family farmers (the first type) or with
the interests of hired farm workers (the second type). A
third type of movement involves the more general pursuit of rural interests rather than of specific agricultural
interests.

Farmers' movements in the United States have a
long and fascinating history. In some ways, these
movements can be said to differ from one another
across time as the nature of agriculture changed. In
other ways, however, the elites, opponents and authorities that farmers challenged in their mobilizations have
been somewhat constant. Bankers, landlords, middlemen, government officials and land-grant colleges most
often have been identified by farmers' movements as
antagonists. Although the specific persons involved
may have changed, their roles and the conflict generated by such roles lends some continuity to agrarian mobilization in the United States.

Historical Overview of Farmers' Movements

As early as the colonial period, farmers mobilized to
pursue specific interests in a variety of conditions. The
Hudson River Valley of New York State has a long history of rebellion by farm tenants against their landlords
that stretches from the colonial era to the mid-nineteenth century. The North Carolina Piedmont region
was home to the colonial-era Regulator movement that
sought greater political representation (and less taxation) for farmers as against the interests of the coastal
elite. Shortly after the Revolution, Shays' Rebellion was
fought against the creditors and courts that sought to
collect cash payments on debts in a rural economy that
was still largely based on barter. This rebellion, centered in Massachusetts, helped sway elites to adopt the
Constitution as it demonstrated the need for a centralized army, given the inability of local militia to put
down the rebellion. The Whiskey Rebellion involved
Pennsylvania farmers' opposition to a tax on the sale of
the whiskey that they distilled from their corn crops as
a means to produce a less perishable and more easily
transportable commodity.

However, after mass migration westward over the
Appalachian Mountains began, agrarian discontent was
more likely to lead to individual or familial geographic
mobility than to collective action. The exception to this
was the existence of localized squatter associations protecting their claims to land they developed. Throughout
all this period there were also hundreds of relatively
isolated rebellions staged by slaves engaged in agricultural production across the South (Aptheker, 1988).

The closing of the frontier and the end of slavery
corresponded with a new wave of farmers' movements.
Two elements stand out with respect to the post-Civil
War farmers' movements: the development of pressure
on political parties to better represent the interests of

farmers and the emergence of cooperatives to meet the economic needs of farmers in the face of what were seen as increasingly monopolized markets. Depending on the relative competitiveness of the party structure, farmers' tended to engage in either pressure on the hegemonic party, to take over and strengthen the weaker party, or to develop a third party. The farmers' movements of the late 1800s are the most well-known attempts to challenge the American party system, although the culmination of this effort in the elections of 1896 often is seen, perhaps incorrectly, as an example of cooptation and ultimate failure of the farmers' movement. In addition to pursuing a political agenda, the movements also experimented with formal economic cooperation.

The Grange, founded shortly after the Civil War, and modeled largely after the Masonic Order, engaged in political activity largely oriented to reform and regulate the railroads. The Grange developed several cooperative enterprises that, even if often failing, served to teach valuable lessons to future generations of cooperators.

The Northern and Southern Alliances turned to political solutions in the form of populism, but in many regions sub-alliances formed the basis of a cooperative movement. The apparent failure of most efforts to build agricultural cooperatives in the late nineteenth century may have been largely due to a lack of capital needed to withstand the opposition mustered by private sector agribusiness firms. For example, when tobacco producers in Kentucky and Tennessee attempted to organize cooperatives, they were met with competition from the Duke and Regie Tobacco Companies. The firms sent buyers into the countryside offering farmers quick cash if they would sell their tobacco to the monopoly and bypass the farmers' cooperative. The temptation to sell outside the co-op and "free-ride" on the collective efforts of their neighbors was a temptation too great to withstand for desperately poor farmers, who, in some cases, had not seen income in more than a year.

Conditions changed in the early twentieth century for two reasons. First, nearly two decades of relative prosperity provided the producers of some commodities with the capital resources to firmly establish cooperative economic institutions as a mainstay of the American agricultural economy. The National Farmers' Educational and Cooperative Union (Farmers' Union) and the Society of Equity were key farmers' movements that built cooperative enterprises in the early twentieth

century. Yet others were not so fortunate. For example, the producers of cotton and tobacco were forced to rely upon state intervention to stabilize their efforts at cooperation. New Deal agricultural policy infused the needed capital to farmer cooperatives to provide stability and reduce the economic necessity of free-riding, a dilemma with which many cash-poor farmers were faced.

A more radical strand of the cooperative movement was embodied in an agrarian socialism that became quite strong in the upper Midwest and Great Plains in the early twentieth century. The Nonpartisan League of North Dakota is the most famous and successful manifestation of this cooperative socialism. The Nonpartisan League temporarily gained control of the government of North Dakota between 1916 and the late 1920s and continued to influence politics in the Northern Plains for decades. The success of farm cooperatives in this era and the threat from these more radical socialist movements facilitated the passage of the Capper-Volstead Act in 1922, which more firmly secured agricultural cooperation in law. The threat of these agrarian socialist movements stimulated counter-movements by elites designed to co-opt or preempt the organization of farmers around leftist ideology, politics and economics. The most important of these counter-movements is the American Farm Bureau Federation. The Farm Bureau was organized through the efforts of USDA personnel with the financial resources of agribusiness interests such as banks, railroads, Sears, International Harvester, and the U.S. Chamber of Commerce (all of which, up to that point, had been seen traditionally as the opponents of most farmers' movements). Using cooperative enterprises as the basis of selective economic incentives toward membership, the Farm Bureau pushed an increasingly conservative ideology and by the post-World War II era had become a powerful political and ideological opponent of the Farmers' Union in advocating a laissez-faire orientation toward agricultural production at the farm level (as distinguished from government subsidization of research and development projects through the USDA and the land-grant college complex).

The Depression era generated important mobilizations of farmers. In the Midwest, the Iowa-based Farmers' Holiday Association sought to engage in a farm strike to obtain better prices. This movement provided the networks of farmers that served as the basis for the famous "penny auctions" in which farmers forcefully disrupted the sale of foreclosed farms. In the South, the

Southern Tenant Farmers' Union, centered in Arkansas and Delta cotton regions, sought greater rights for both Black and White sharecroppers, such as entitlement to a share of the crop subsidies provided by New Deal agricultural policy. Founded in the last days of the old cotton South sharecropping system, which soon would be replaced by mechanization, chemicalization and, to some extent, soybeans, this latter movement in a way established a precedent for the Civil Rights movement that later blossomed in the South.

In the post-World War II era, the National Farmers' Organization (NFO) emerged out of the Iowa-Missouri region as a movement to develop collective bargaining for farmers. As had groups that previously attempted to control farm production, the NFO often found itself confronting the use of violence against free riders who benefited from price increases without bearing any of the costs incurred by those engaged in farm commodity holding actions. The shift to the use of economic rather than political power may be seen as a function of the dramatic demographic declines in farm population after World War II. The NFO remains, along with the Farm Bureau and the Farmers' Union (and the Grange in some regions), one of the more influential general farm movement organizations.

The most recent specifically farmers' movement is the American Agricultural Movement (AAM). Centered in the Wheat Belt, the AAM talked of a farm strike during the "farm crisis" of the 1980s, but primarily engaged in political protest activity to increase the federal government's support of farm prices. The AAM was, for a short time, successful in manipulating media (especially television) coverage. Otherwise, the legacy of the AAM may lie primarily in its networking function in relationship to the broader rural social movements that coincided with the agricultural and rural crisis of the early 1980s. More recent opposition has departed considerably from exercises in producer activism. Again, in part due to the changing demographic nature of the farm population, activism is more likely to be a joint endeavor between producers, consumers and others concerned with the environment and issues of distributive justice.

Activism in agriculture re-emerged in the 1990s and onward following a period of political quiescence. This resurgence reflects an unlikely coalition of producers and consumers and can be thought of as an extension of the larger sustainability movement that gained momentum in the late twentieth century. These new movements, like early twentieth-century efforts at agricultural cooperation, attempt to use the market as an instrument of change, but they are much less organized than activism in the late nineteenth and twentieth century. New alliances between producers, consumers and environmentalists are attempting to create new markets outside the mainstream commodity-driven network (Allen, 2004; Henderson, 1999) infused with non-economic, or post-productionist, values. Growth in interest and activity around food security, organic foods, eco-labeled foods, direct marketing, fair trade, local foods, community kitchens and gardens, community-supported agriculture, cow-shares and farmers' markets collectively evidence the emergence of new agricultural movements that are having a more significant impact on the structure of U.S. agriculture than any grassroots collective mobilization since the cooperative movement.

At the same time, the current commodity-driven food system has become an arena of contest. Just as the economic structure of the eighteenth century catalyzed resistance on the part of farmers and slaves, the global restructuring of agricultural markets has also created the conditions for unrest. Struggles over genetically modified organisms (GMOs), bio-piracy, and dissent targeted at transnational regulatory bodies such as the World Trade Organization (WTO) are illustrative of this resistance. Discontent with the structure of the agri-food system on the domestic front is also increasingly contentious as evident in food anti-disparagement laws, the backlash against confined animal feeding operations (CAFOs), aquatic "feedlots," and periodic outbreaks of mad cow disease, and E. coli contamination.

This more recent wave of resistance signifies a mounting reflexivity and new modes of action among producers, consumers and activists in the production and consumption of food. Food, along with its attendant production processes, is moving to the forefront of our value system with conventional production and consumption cultures under reconsideration (Wright and Middendorf, 2007). These new agrarian movements cannot fully be explained by resource mobilization and political process theories, necessitating a turn to culture, values and ideology.

The New Rural Social Movements

Perhaps the most important precursor to more broadly based rural social movements, as distinct from farmers' movements, was the Country Life Commission of the early twentieth century. Danbom (1979), among others, contends that the Country Life Movement, which derived from the more general progressive movement of the early twentieth century, was primarily urban-based and "concerned with the social and economic difficulties an unindustrialized agriculture created for urban-industrial society, identifying them as rural problems despite the fact that farmers did not see them as such."

More recently there have been new movements associated with the interests of the broader rural society. Many of these movements may deserve the label "new social movements." Although the notion of new social movements is heavily contested with respect to its most useful definition, in general new social movements tend to exhibit a greater concern with broader cultural or lifestyle issues than with merely economic or production matters. In this sense they strive to change values, norms and beliefs in civil society, rather than invest all of their resources into traditional forms of political influence via governmental action. There is also a conscious effort to resist formal and hierarchical organizational structures and to incorporate strong democratic participation from the grassroots upward. Many of the new agri-food movements share these characteristics, which makes labeling them as "rural life" movements or "agri-food" movements difficult. They blur conventional boundaries and span the reach of both sectors.

Most of the research on new social movements focused on urban manifestations. However, by the early 1970s several local groups coalesced to form a coalition known as Rural America. New Deal agricultural policy, formulated around specific commodities, led to the rise of commodity associations as particularly powerful players in the formulation of agricultural policy. This piecemeal approach impeded the development of a holistic policy attending to the total fabric of rural life. Rural America represented an attempt by rural citizens to develop such a policy. The primary drive behind Rural America came from rural churches, cooperatives, the Farmers' Union, and especially younger rural residents, many of whom constituted a portion of the rural population turnaround of the early 1970s, returning to or staying in rural communities after attending college or serving in the Vietnam War in the 1960s. This organization provided important networks to develop the multiplicity of local movement centers that arose during the farm crisis of the 1980s. These later movements tended to be concerned about rural society as a whole even though the crisis itself was grounded in the credit-based agricultural economy. Most striking about these newer rural social movements was the explicit incorporation of strong elements of environmentalism, feminism and civil rights issues (Mooney and Majka, 1995). The traditional dichotomy between farmers and environmentalists was eroded, giving way to a movement focused around the development of a sustainable agriculture coincident with the family farm and similar types of agriculture. Women took much stronger leadership roles in these newer rural social movements and facilitated the development of this broader, more inclusive agenda. These movements expressed more concerns with civil rights issues (such as access to land by minorities and Native American rights) than had been characteristic of farmers' movements in the past.

Farm Workers' Movements

Farm workers' movements have been largely a twentieth-century phenomenon, generally corresponding to the development of large, capitalist agricultural production. These movements primarily have originated in California and the Southwest, although more recently a mobilization of farm workers has taken place in the so-called eastern stream (i.e., migrants from the Southeastern U.S. who travel to Michigan, Ohio, Wisconsin, etc.). Many obstacles impede the mobilization of farm workers. First is the often abundant labor supply for farm work, leaving workers very little leverage for the sale of their labor. This impedes their ability to strike, a weakness that is exacerbated by the succession of various ethnic groups one after another to farm in the West (e.g., Chinese, Japanese, Filipinos, Mexicans and Anglos). Ethnic identity has fostered solidarity within each ethnic group but often has been the basis of conflict among these workers as a class.

This problem, in turn, reflects the relative lack of resources available to farm workers for mobilization. Sometimes these workers do not even have citizenship to use as political clout. The conditions of migratory labor obstruct the building of ties and networks with other members of communities and political representatives. The fact that agricultural labor has not been covered by basic labor legislation can be seen as both a cause and a consequence of farm workers' lack of resources for political mobilization. These conditions force farm workers to depend on external resources to support their movements. But even here, what would seem to be likely allies, such as organized labor, have proven highly unreliable and even antagonistic at times. Thus, the fortunes of farm workers' movements depend largely on the political opportunities offered by periods or cycles of protest that are generated in the larger society. Not surprisingly, the Depression and the late 1960s and early 1970s have been their moments of greatest success. The 1970s, for example, saw the United Farm Workers (UFW) rely heavily on the support of consumers in the form of boycotts of certain growers to exert pressures they could not bring on their own.

The organization of the UFW itself depended on the political opportunity afforded by the termination of the U.S.-sponsored Bracero Program (1942-1964). Under the Bracero Program, the state organized the importation of five million guest workers from Mexico, thwarting the tactical efficacy of the labor strike as a means to improve wages or working conditions. The UFW emerged subsequent to the end of the Bracero Program and borrowed heavily from the ideology and practices of the larger Civil Rights movement taking place in the society. It is unclear (and often debated) whether the death of Cesar Chavez (1927-1993), the longtime charismatic leader of the UFW, will deepen the deterioration that the movement has suffered in the 1980s and 1990s or provide opportunity for a resurgent mobilization generated by a new leadership. Consideration of migrant guest worker programs re-emerged in the early part of the twenty-first century.

The Farm Labor Organizing Committee (FLOC) spun off the UFW efforts but focused on negotiating contracts primarily in Ohio and Michigan. The relative success of this movement perhaps hinged on the triadic, rather than dyadic, nature of the negotiations. These farm workers engaged in negotiations with both processors (such as Campbell's or Heinz) and smaller, family-type producers. This is a different situation from that in California, where grape growers, for example, are also the producers of wine.

Both the UFW and the FLOC focused on issues of wages, but also on issues of control over the labor process. The latter included hiring criteria, methods of pesticide application, grievance procedures, rest breaks, access to cool drinking water, and the use of various tools or machinery to reduce the drudgery of the labor.

The Near Future

The influence of social organizations on the direction of change will likely continue to be determined largely by the relative power of the commodity associations to influence governmental policy with respect to specific commodities. Trends toward government downsizing may mitigate this latter effect to some extent. Two particular developments will shape the character of future rural social movements: globalization and biotechnology. Although rural America has always been embedded

in a global market, the recent acceleration of the process of globalization (e.g., General Agreement on Trades and Tariffs and the North American Free Trade Agreement) will demand that farmers and other rural people think in global terms, even if they are only capable of acting at the local level. Similarly, technological development has also long driven the structure of agriculture and rural society. However, recent developments in genetic engineering promise revolutionary changes in the production and marketing practices of farm and rural people. Control over the uses and abuses of this technology will certainly be a focus of rural social movements in the future. In much the same way, it is expected that the adoption and diffusion of nanotechnology in the food system will also lead to differential benefits for some groups, and therefore, produce grievances that may fuel mobilization.

The growing movement for sustainable development, including sustainable livelihoods, must contend with opposing elites and authorities whose interests do not coincide with local or regional sustainability. In this sense, rural movements will demand external alliances with sympathetic consumers and environmentalists in order to challenge these powerful opponents in an increasingly global and high-technology market for both agricultural commodities and rural labor.

— *D. Wynne Wright and Patrick H. Mooney*

See also

Agricultural Law; Cooperatives; History, Agricultural; History, Rural; Latinos; Country Life Movement; Environmental Movements; Rural Church Movement; Sustainable Agriculture Movement; Agricultural Organizations; Town-Country Relations

References

Allen, Patricia. *Together at the Table: Sustainability and Sustenance in the American Agrifood System*. University Park, PA: Pennsylvania State University Press, 2004.

Aptheker, Herbert. *Abolitionism: A Revolutionary Movement*. Boston, MA: Twayne Publishers, 1988.

Danbom, David B. *The Resisted Revolution: Urban America and the Industrialization of Agriculture, 1900-1930*. Ames, IA: Iowa State University Press, 1979.

Friedmann, Harriet. "From Colonialism to Green Capitalism: Social Movements and Emergence of Food Regimes." Pp 227-264 in *New Directions in the Sociology of Global Development: Research in Rural Sociology and Development, Vol. 11*. Edited by Frederick H. Buttel and Philip McMichael. Amsterdam: Elsevier, 2005.

Henderson, Elizabeth. 1999. "Rebuilding Local Food Systems from the Grassroots Up." Pp 175-188 in *Hungry for Profit: The Agribusiness Threat to Farmers, Food and the Environment*. Edited by Fred Magdoff, John Bellamy Foster, and Frederick H. Buttel. New York: Monthly Review Press, 2000.

Juska, Arunas and Bob Edwards. "Refusing the Trojan Pig: The Trans-Atlantic Coalition Against Corporate Pork Production in Poland." Pp. 187-207 in *Coalitions Across Borders: Transnational Protest and the Neo-Liberal Order*. Edited by Joe Brandy and Jackie Smith. Lanham, MD.: Rowman & Littlefield Publishers, 2004.

Majka, Linda C. and Theo J. Majka. *Farm Workers, Agribusiness and the State*. Philadelphia, PA: Temple University Press, 1982.

McConnell, Grant. *The Decline of Agrarian Democracy*. Berkeley, CA: University of California Press, 1953.

Mooney, Patrick H. "The Specificity of the Rural in Social Movement Theory." *Polish Sociological Review* 1, no. 129 (2000):35-55.

Mooney, Patrick H. and Scott Hunt. "Repertoires of Interpretation: Master Frames and Ideological Continuity in U.S. Agrarian Mobilization." *Sociological Quarterly* 37, no. 1 (1996):177-197.

Mooney, Patrick H. and Theo J. Majka. *Farmers' and Farm Workers' Movements: Social Protest in American Agriculture*. New York, NY: Twayne Publishers, 1995.

Saloutos, Theodore and John D. Hicks. *Twentieth Century Populism: Agricultural Discontent in the Middle West, 1900-1939*. Lincoln, NE: University of Nebraska Press, 1951.

Schurman, Rachel. "Fighting Frankenfoods: Industry Structures and the Efficacy of the Anti-Biotech Movement in Western Europe." *Social Problems* 51, no. 2 (2004): 243-268.

Tarrow, Sidney. *Power in Movement: Social Movements, Collective Action and Politics*. Cambridge, UK: Cambridge University Press, 1994.

Taylor, Carl C. *The Farmers' Movement: 1620-1920*. Westport, CT: Greenwood Press, 1953.

Wright, Wynne and Gerad Middendorf. *The Fight Over Food: Producers, Consumers, and Activists Challenge the Global Food System*. University Park, PA: Pennsylvania State University Press, 2007.

Social Services, Faith-based

Services provided to individuals, families, and communities by faith-based organizations that range from social welfare to health care, financial aid, housing, disaster relief, and more. This article provides an historical overview of the role played by religious organizations throughout the nation's history in offering social services. It discusses the unique way faith-based organizations partner with other community organizations to provide these services. The federal policy of faith-based initiatives is described as it has been applied in rural America.

Historical Overview

Since the sixteenth century, churches and faith-based services have been an important part of the U. S. landscape, particularly the service delivery system. Such involvement in health and social services by the religious sector dates back to English Poor Laws. In particular, England's Speenhamland Act of 1795, a publicly funded, national initiative that used churches to deliver services to the poor, influenced U.S. social policy (De Schweinitz 1947). In pre-revolutionary Virginia, Anglican Church officials cared for the old, the sick, the deserted, and the illegitimate children of their communities (Coll 1969). During the colonial era, the Philadelphia Quakers developed the Friends almshouse for poor relief (Compton 1980), the Episcopalians established the Boston Episcopal Society (Axinn and Levin 1992), and the government used Baptist, Jesuit, Presbyterian, Moravian, and Congregationalist churches to educate and train Native Americans (Nichols 1988). To the extent that churches had the membership base and financial resources, they continued to develop programs and serve the broader community. Rural congregations constitute the roots of American religion's orientation toward social service and action.

By the early twentieth century, the U.S. was quickly shifting from a rural –centered nation to an urban-centered nation. This transformation left rural areas and their institutions overshadowed by their urban counterparts. Today, rural America's diversity includes different norms, cultures, economies, and institutions. In most rural communities, congregations are the most prominent and pervasive institutions. Often the declining number of community residents and leaders and the dwindling membership of many rural congregations have left many rural congregations and communities struggling to survive. These facts create a marginality and invisibility that should be viewed as problematic. However, some rural communities remain stable while others attract new residents; and hence rural congregations continue to play a role in shaping the public sphere. Rural congregations are also far more diverse than generally expected. For example, the Missouri Rural Churches Project found that in townships with declining population there are congregations with stable membership (13%) and those with growing membership (15%). Conversely, in townships with growing populations there are churches with declining membership (5%) and those with stable membership (11%). Even in rural churches were membership decline is evident there can also exist a faithful remnant and vibrant fellowship. In general, rural congregations remain open and active in spite of periods of residential loss (Rathge and Goreham, 1989).

By the 1930s, the economic downturn caused by the 1929 stock market crash called for more government involvement in social service delivery. Under President Roosevelt, the New Deal policies, namely the Social Security Act of 1935, established large government social programs. The 1962, 1976, and 1974 amendments to the Social Security Act formalized public financing with nongovernmental social service organizations including faith-based agencies like Salvation Army (Lynn 2002). In many rural and small town communities, the state and federal governments provided limited services and funding, hence, local congregations and other religious organizations did not forfeit their social responsibilities.

Rural Congregations as a Valued Community Partners

According to the 2000 census, 19.7 percent of the population lives in rural (non-metropolitan) communities; 14.5 percent of the population live in non-metropolitan communities and 11.9 percent live in metropolitan communities (U.S. Census 2000). The mandate of many communities of faith gives priority to serving the poor, particularly feeding the hungry, clothing the poor, and caring for the sick, widows, and children. Therefore, it is not surprising that previous studies of rural congregations document that these congregations primarily provide basic needs such as food, clothing, emergency financial assistance as well as pastoral counseling (Bartowski and Regis 2003; Boddie 2002; Cnaan, Boddie, Handy, Yancey, and Schneider 2002).

Rural congregations typically organize their services in a variety of ways including informal services offered upon request to more formal mutual aid and self help to formal, institutionalized projects and programs sponsored by congregations and ministerial coalitions as well as nonprofit and for profit organizations. In rural and small town churches, a small membership and modest budget make it difficult for churches to sponsor large programs. In many cases, rural and small congregations provide more informal services through members and clergy support as well as volunteers to other groups or agencies like local hospitals and prisons (Boddie 2002; Cnaan, Boddie, Handy, Yancey, and Schneider 2002). Swierenga (1997) described rural congregations as cultural nests that bring families, social classes, and nationalities together to share beliefs, values, and rituals. Rural congregations often function as extended families; and hence many rural congregations offer social support and coping to assist those confronting personal and family crisis, illness, disability, chronic pain, serious accidents, disaster, caregiving, loss of loved ones, and substance abuse. Many rural church community activities center around fellowship during holidays such as Easter, Christmas and Thanksgiving or church anniversary days.

Few rural congregations (4-in-1,000, provide the kinds of social and community services urban congregations provide (Billingsley, 1999). For example, the following rural churches go beyond the charity type services most rural churches provide.

The 1,000-member, Holy Ghost Roman Catholic Church in Opelousas, Louisiana provided GED preparation, a food program, a fitness center, a counseling program, a foundation to promote community economic development, and a non-profit organization to stimulate business development.

The 200-member, Greater Christ Temple Church in Meridian, Mississippi purchased three restaurants, a bakery, an auto-repair shop, and a 400-acre farm with 700 head of cattle and two meat-processing plants.

Mendenhall Bible Church, Mendenhall, Mississippi established a corporation that built a business complex that brought more jobs in the community.

The 200-member, Valley Queen Baptist Church, in Marks, Mississippi provided a feeding program, a homeless shelter, a nursing home program, an economic development project, and a community economic

Congregations are also regarded as a primary source of charitable giving, particularly in rural communities. Estimates of the total giving to U.S. congregations range from $82.83 to $86.28 billion (Brown, Harris and Rooney 2004). However, in rural communities, congregations offer opportunities and limitations with respect to the financial capital they can attract and invest in social service provision. The assets most needed and often lacking in rural and small town congregations are property owned by the congregation, as well as inventory, equipment and weekly bank deposits and other investments and savings. Rural congregations generally support programs that had been established by one of the other congregations as well those needed by the local public school system and Department of Human Services. Volunteers from the congregations often support a range of activities sponsored by the local hospital, local prison, local hospice, senior center, mental health care facility, and/ or child welfare and adoption agency. Rural congregations often form cooperative ministry structures such as ministerial and other coalitions such as hospitality, nursing home, or thrift shops to maximize congregational resources while serving the broader community.

Another way to consider the financial contribution of congregations is to measure the value of the public goods produced by congregations – the average financial value of a congregation-based program. One such measure is called replacement value for service programs (Cnaan, Boddie, Yancey, Handy, and Schneider 2002). To calculate this value, respondents were asked to report their five flagship programs and the total value of their operating cost including direct and indirect expenses. This value captured the financial support by the congregation, in-kind support, value of utilities, estimated value of congregational space, clergy, staff, and volunteer hours, and external funding/ income. A conservative estimate was derived by totaling the estimated value reported for all programs and dividing the result by the total number of programs including programs with no reported values. For a rural community, Council grove, Kansas, this value was $1,066.46 much less than the reported value for urban congregations ($4,285.78). However, on average, rural congregations in this town allocated 27.8 percent of their annual budget to social services as compared to 22.6 percent for the 251 urban congregations (Cnaan, Boddie, Yancey, Handy, and Schneider 2002).

A New Policy Context

Politics and policies have largely shifted greater attention to congregations and faith-based providers as viable partners in social service provision. This swing toward private sector provision of services responds to increased opposition to big government and increased spending on social programs in the late 1970s through the late 1980s. Under the Reagan administration (1981-1989), welfare policies were under attack and faith-based organizations became one option for securing a US safety net. Following the same course, the George H.W. Bush administration (1989-1993) endorsed expanding the reach and responsibility of faith-based organizations through their compassionate care. Under the Clinton administration (1993-2001), Congress passed the Personal Responsibility and Work Opportunity Reconciliation Act of 1996 dismantling 60 years of entitlement programs. This legislation also included section 104, also known as the Charitable Choice provision, which allowed pervasively sectarian organizations like congregations to compete for government contracts. Under the Clinton Administration, Charitable Choice enjoyed bi-partisan support. Established by laws during the period of 1996-2000, Charitable Choice was applied to several programs: Temporary Assistance to Needy Families (TANF), Community Services Block Grant (CSBG) programs, programs for substance abuse and mental health, and the Welfare-to-Work program. When President Clinton promoted faith-based initiatives emphasizing a local approach to the issue of poverty, he spoke of the church as a potential catalyst for sparking a vision for other institutions in society to help the poor. With cuts in welfare assistance, food stamps, Medicaid, supplemental social security insurance, and child welfare programs, many more people are expected to turn to congregations for stop aid. Rural and small town congregations share greater responsibility to care for their community and its residents given the limited local government agencies and resources available.

President George W. Bush (2001–2008), shared Reagan's vision of congregation-based social service providers as influential agents that could bring about greater responsibility, better discipline and work ethics among the poor caring for the poor. He viewed faith as a missing element in effective social service delivery (Bush 2001a). To institutionalize a National Faith-based policy, President Bush exercised his authority to use executive orders, regulations, and discretionary grants to broaden the National Faith-based agenda. First, he instituted six executive orders to provide infrastructure to facilitate the funding for faith-based and community-based organizations and eliminate regulatory, contracting, and programmatic barriers for faith-based and community-based organizations (see http://www.whitehouse.gov/government/fbci/news_archive.html).

In 2002, the Bush administration established the Compassion Capital fund (CCF), a discretionary grant program designed to increase the effectiveness of faith-based and community organizations to serve those most in need by providing technical assistance though intermediaries as well as distributing small grant awards. In the following year, the Compassion Capital Fund expanded to include a Targeted Capacity-Building program that awards $50,000 to FBOs and CBOs. To date, this fund has expanded the funding of grants to larger faith-based organizations including those serving rural communities. Since the inception of the Compassion Capital Fund, $148 million has been given to more than 3,000 organizations including sub-awards from intermediary grantees (Health and Human services/ Govnews, 2005). This fund has provided incentives for community and faith-based organizations to spur new types of partnerships and build local capacity among grassroots organizations. Over 90 percent of the Compassion Fund grants have been dispersed to organizations in metropolitan areas. Given the great social needs of rural communities, the Faith-based initiatives could have potential benefit for enhancing the local service infrastructure. One among rural grantees charged with capacity building and sub-granting for local agencies was the Montana Office of Rural Health (MORH). In 2002, MORH received a grant for three years to fund the Montana Faith-Health Demonstration Project. Like most CCF projects, this project enhanced and expanded the role of faith-based organizations (FBOs) and community-based organizations (CBOs) providing health and social services to the underserved and most needy individuals and families. Health and social service organizations received technical assistance and sub-grants. One of MORH's foundational programs was the Parish Nurse Center at Carroll College. The Parish curriculum included prayer, worship and religious training. On this basis, the Freedom from Religion Foundation, Inc., and several Montana taxpayers asserted that administration of state and federal funds by MORH was a violation of the First Amendment's Establishment Clause, particularly the preferential funding of such a religiously explicit parish nursing program. The federal district court ordered MORH to withdraw the government funding from the parish nursing programs.

Challenges and Opportunities

Congregations are found to be valuable and trustworthy by those seeking help with emotional and spiritual distress related to financial and health problems (Wuthnow 2004). On the other hand, the good intention of faith-based providers often outweigh their financial resources and administrative expertise (Sinha 2007). Overall, rural congregations represent an important part of the system of private- and public sector social services, particularly in communities with great need and limited public services (Chaves 2004; Smith and Sosin 2001; Wuthnow 2004).

— *Stephanie Clintonia Boddie*

See also

Churches; Community Capitals; Culture; Development, Asset-based; Jews in Rural America; Rural Chruch Movement; Policy, Rural Family; Poverty; Policy, Socioeconomic; Religion; Welfare

References

Axinn, J. and H. Levin. *Social Welfare: A History of the American Response to Need.* New York: Longman, 1992.

Billingsley, A. *Mighty Like a River: The Black Church and Social Reform.* New York: Oxford University Press, 1999.

Brown, M.S., J.C. Harris, and P.M. Rooney. *Reconciling Estimates of Religious Giving.* Indianapolis, IN: Center on Philanthropy at Indiana University, 2004.

Chaves, M. *Congregations in America.* Cambridge, MA: Harvard University Press, 2004.

Cnaan, R.A., R.J. Wineburg, and S.C. Boddie. *The Newer Deal: Social Work and Religion in Partnership.* New York: Columbia Press, 1999.

Cnaan, R.A., S.C.Boddie, F. Handy, G. Yancey, and R. Schneider. *The Invisible Caring Hand: American Congregations and the Provision of Welfare.* New York, NY: New York University Press, 2002.

Coll, D. *Perspectives in Public Welfare.* Washington, DC: U.S. Social and Rehabilitation Services, 1969.

De Schweinitz, K. *England's Road to Social Security: From the Statute of Laborers in 1349 to 1947.* Philadelphia, PA: University of Pennsylvania Press, 1947.

Lynn, L.E. "Social Services and the State: The Public Appropriation of Private Charity." *Social Service Review* 76 (2002): 58-92.

Nichols, J.B. *The Uneasy Alliance: Religion, Refugee Work, and U.S. Foreign Policy.* New York: Oxford University Press, 1988.

Rathge, R.W. and G.A. Goreham. "The Influence of Economic and Demographic Factors on Rural Church Vitality." *Journal for the Scientific Study of Religion* 28 (1989): 59-74.

Sinha, J.W. "A Faith-Based Alternative Youth Education Program: Evaluation a Participatory Research Approach." *Journal of Religion and Spirituality in Social Work* 25, nos. 3/4 (2007): 197-221.

Smith, S.R. and S. Sosin "The Varieties of Faith-Related Agencies." *Public Administration Review* 61 (2001): 651-657.

Swierenga, R.P "The Little White Church: Religion in Rural America." *Agricultural History* 71, no. 4 (1997): 415-441.

Wuthnow, R *Saving America? Faith-based Services and the Future of Civil Society.* Princeton, NJ: Princeton University Press, 2004.

Social Work

Professional engagement in understanding the causes of and solutions to social problems. The social work profession is committed to meeting human needs, promoting social justice, enhancing quality of life, and developing the full potential of individuals, families, groups and communities in society. Social work in rural America presents both special challenges and unique opportunities to the professional practitioner. Special considerations are, however, often necessary when doing social work in rural communities in terms of the demographic profiles of the clients and patients served, skills employed, resources available, and the ethical and value dilemmas likely to be confronted.

Given the emergence of social work in the nineteenth century during a period of rapid industrialization, it is not surprising that much of professional practice has been associated with urban needs and problems. It was not until the mid-1970s with increased concern over rural areas by the federal government that the idea of rural social work practice as a specialized field began to attract attention. The unique needs of rural communities and the importance of developing helping strategies that respond specifically to the issues of rural life have been emphasized by those who advocate for the importance of rural social work practice (Lohman and Lohman 2005).

In July 2002, Tommy Thompson, then Secretary of the United States Department of Health and Human Services, launched the *Initiative on Rural Communities.* After talking with people all across the country he came to the realization that "we had to change the way we thought about rural communities—we could no longer just think of them as small 'cities.' Rural communities have unique challenges that bring with them unique opportunities" (Health Resources Services Administration 2002). Unfortunately, the presence of social workers in rural communities has remained limited and there continues, to this day, to be a serious shortage of such professionals in nonmetropolitan areas. Recruitment and retention of social workers in rural communities are major challenges and have contributed in part to the declassification of positions such that jobs formally requiring professional social workers are now being filled by those with little or no professional training. Social workers with specialized training, who are better prepared to work with particular subgroups of rural citizens and those persons with unique needs, are particularly limited in number in rural communities. Rural-based social service organizations are considerably more likely than urban-based agencies to employ personnel without formal social work training and are more likely to hire individuals with bachelor's level social work education (BSWs) as compared to master's level training (MSWs).

The National Association of Social Workers (NASW), the largest membership organization of professional social workers in the world, with 150,000 members, has issued a policy statement on social work in rural areas. NASW recognizes that while increasing numbers of social services are available in rural communities, their design and administrative operation is heavily influenced by an urban bias or a skewed representation of rural life. The NASW policy statement emphasizes that most of rural America is either unserved or underserved in terms of health care, transportation systems, and mental health programs. Services that focus on mental health issues and other illnesses traditionally responded to by social workers need to be particularly sensitive to differences in the emotional experience of psychological illness in a rural area which, in turn, requires a different type of helping response than in urban communities. For example, recognition of the importance of natural helping networks (i.e., family, friends, and neighbors) as resources in such situations is particularly important in rural social work practice.

Schools of social work, like human service organizations situated in rural states and regions, tend to be smaller and fewer in number. They are also more likely to prepare their students for careers in generalist social work practice rather than offering curriculum focusing on specialized forms of practice. Bachelor's level students (BSWs) prepared in generalist practice are trained to apply multilevel, multi-method approaches to the resolution of the problems of persons in their environments, while master's program students (MSWs) are educated for social work as advanced generalist practitioners prepared to work as clinicians, consultants, supervisors, and administrators.

To maximize their effectiveness, rural social workers must be able to: 1) understand the connectedness of individual, family, collective, and institutional levels of practice; 2) incorporate cultural competence in their practice; 3) use multiple methods to understand multiple levels of analysis and practice; 4) understand the impact of being an "actor" within the community; 5) focus on redressing disadvantage; 6) utilize collaborative approaches where possible; 7) redress the negative effects of distance on service provisions; 8) understand and work within dense social networks; 9) develop strategies to access scarce resources; 10) manage personal and professional issues when high visibility in a community can impact personal privacy; and 11) juggle multiple roles with integrity and awareness of potential role conflicts (University of Minnesota Duluth 2008).

Social workers in rural communities need to be ready to modify their traditional (urban-based) approaches to working with clients. It is particularly important for rural social workers to be flexible in terms of their practice philosophy, appreciate a multidisciplinary orientation, and be comfortable with role ambiguity. Social workers also need to make special efforts to understand the culture, concerns, and needs of those who reside in rural communities. Rural citizens are inclined to display a relatively independent character. They may be hesitant to ask for help from community social workers even if such assistance is needed, available, and affordable (Kaye 2002). Rather, rural residents may tend to rely on themselves to resolve problems, valuing highly their autonomy and preferring informal (i.e., family and friends) to formal community agency resource systems when helped is needed (University of Minnesota Duluth 2008). Such cultural tendencies are not universal in rural communities and should be seen as shaping but not necessarily interfering with efforts on the part of the profession to help.

Special obstacles for rural versus urban social workers and others who serve the health and human service needs of rural residents include the likelihood of: higher levels of poverty, illness, and disability; fewer and less easily accessible health and human agencies and organizations; and clients or patients living in geographically isolated communities with poor roads and a lack of public transportation. Because of low population density, fragile tax bases, scarce resources, and the shortage of health, mental health, and other human service personnel, poor, aged, and isolated groups in rural communities experience disproportionately burdensome transportation and home heating energy costs compared to their urban counterparts.

Higher proportions of rural residents are in poor health compared to their urban counterparts. Even so, medical, dental, psychiatric, home care, nutrition and other health services are less accessible to rural residents than in metropolitan areas. Furthermore, in a rural community, fewer numbers of alternative living arrangements and family respite or relief services may force relatives to consider institutionalizing their incapacitated relatives sooner than otherwise required. Existing housing in rural communities is frequently older and in greater need of repair and renovation compared to urban-situated housing stock.

Younger people living in rural communities tend to be more mobile, having an inclination to eventually leave their rural birthplaces for increased job opportunities and the attractiveness of the "bright lights" of the urban centers. On the other hand, older adults tend to age-in-place, remaining in rural communities for extended periods of time, frequently until death. And older adults not uncommonly look to retire to less populated regions of the country attracted by the beauty of the landscape, less crime, and lower cost of living. As a result, the size of the older adult population (65 years and older) in rural communities continues to grow at a particularly fast pace. Older adults make up a larger proportion of the population in rural areas (20 percent) than in urban areas (15 percent). Social workers who serve rural elders experience individuals tending to be less educated, having lower incomes, more chronic health conditions, and greater limitations in activities of daily living. They are also more likely to be obese, have poorer self-rated health, lower amounts of physical activity, poorer nutrition intake, and higher mortality (death) rates. On the other hand, rural elders have higher rates of marriage, more involvement in community activities, more support from local organizations, less fear of crime, less abrupt retirement, greater feelings of open space and freedom of self, and greater life satisfaction than their urban counterparts.

The scarcity of particular kinds of social work and related human services in rural communities is notable. The result is that in many cases individuals and families will rarely have a full spectrum of health and human service options available to them as they would in a more densely populated metropolitan area or even in suburban communities. Particularly scarce services in local communities include mental and behavioral health services, home health and other home-based services, hospice or end-of-life care services, adult day care, substance abuse and alcohol treatment services, and domestic abuse protection services. Preventative services are in scarce supply as well.

It is especially important that rural social workers be willing to reach out actively to those they wish to help. The most successful rural social worker will spend little time in the office and considerable time traveling to those in need of assistance. Rural social workers should also consider making use of the latest technology available to them that allows the establishment and maintenance of worker-client communications by any means necessary to get the job done. Seeing clients at centralized office locations has limited value in many instances. The value of decentralized and mobile social services is high although it can result in increased time and costs associated with serving rural citizens.

Social workers need to be especially cognizant of the social characteristics of rural communities including clearly defined boundaries and respect for privacy, high levels of interaction among confidant(e)s and significant others, and a shared or common sense of identity among residents. These characteristics can reflect themselves in the close-knit nature and an apparent lack of heterogeneity in rural communities. These characteristics can consequently result in increased time and effort required by professional social workers who are not originally from a particular rural community to build trust and become accepted by its residents.

Given the scare resource environment in which rural social workers practice, important working principles include a willingness to collaborate with other health and human service providers. As has been suggested, it is also important to make maximum use of available technology in designing and delivering services including Internet-based communication and information sharing, and remote video conferencing and tele-health services. Practice flexibility is preferred—rural social work providers benefit most from being generalists, wearing multiple hats in delivering services. To understand their clients and patients, social workers need to make special efforts to become versed in the culture, concerns, and needs of rural residents. This is crucial, as are special efforts to become trusted members of the community in which they live and work.

Because they are such integral members of the rural communities in which they live, social workers can expect to be confronted by particular ethical challenges regarding privacy, confidentiality, and managing dual relationships in their daily work. Dual relationships refer to the multiple relationships that can exist in which one is clearly a professional relationship while the others are of a nonprofessional nature. The dense, close-knit, and complex nature of interactions in rural communities create special challenges for ensuring confidentiality and privacy rights for clients, colleagues, and organizations (Galambos et al. 2006). Quite commonly, social workers in rural communities may know clients or come into contact with clients in another setting outside of their professional role as a social worker, such as when they meet in grocery stores, restaurants, and at school functions and community events. It is very important to maintain confidentiality and professional boundaries in these situations. While dual relationships may be impossible to always avoid, establishing boundaries is essential. Organizations that social workers work for in rural communities should have policies on confidentiality and clients should be informed about those policies. The NASW has published a formal code of ethics that provides detailed guidelines for maintaining professional behavior when working in situations that can give rise to dual relationships between worker and client. NASW recognizes that few settings in which social workers find themselves expose them to greater risk of violating the NASW code of ethics around issues of boundary setting than rural communities.

Social workers who practice in rural communities are more likely to have difficulty locating a wide range of job advancement opportunities or jobs in specialized areas of interest. They also tend to receive lower salaries and experience some risk in terms of feeling a sense of professional isolation and opportunities for continuing specialized education.

Rural Americans deserve access to the skills and expertise offered by trained social work professionals. Social workers engaged in advocacy, legislation, and policy formulation that strengthens the rural infrastructure in the areas of economic development, health and social services, education, and transportation are also badly needed. If more professional social workers were both willing to establish residence in rural communities and had jobs available to them at salaries comparable to urban-based social workers, they would more likely capitalize on the need for their expertise and enjoy the quality of life that a close-knit and caring rural community can offer. In rural America social workers can expect to experience fewer degrees of professional turf protection because levels of competition are less severe. Rural practice also provides excellent opportunities to mentor the next generation of social work professionals as the current corps of rural social work professionals are aging themselves.

— *Lenard W. Kaye*

See also

Adolescents; Mental Health; Mental Health of Older Americans; Poverty; Policy, Rural Family; Policy, Health Care; Welfare

References

Butler, Sandra.S. and Lenard W. Kaye. *Gerontological Social Work in Small Towns and Rural Communities.* New York: The Haworth Press, Inc., 2003.

Contemporary Rural Social Work—A journal devoted to the development of knowledge and promotion excellence in rural social work. *Contemporary Rural Social Work* is an online journal that provides a forum for the intellectual exchange of ideas that advance rural practice and promote excellence in rural social work. Available online at: http://www.ruralsocialwork.org/journals/RSWC_Joural_vol1.pdf.

Galambos, Colleen, Watt, J. Wilson, Anderson, Kimberly, and Fran Danis. "Ethics Forum: Rural Social Work Practice." *Journal of Social Work Values & Ethics.* Available online at: http://www.socialworker.com/jswve/index2.php?option=com_content&do_pdf=1&id=23.

Ginsberg, Leon H., ed. *Social Work in Rural Communities*, 4th edition. Alexandria, VA: Council on Social Work Education, 2005.

Health Resources and Services Administration (HRSA). "Secretary Thompson Remarks—Summit on Rural America." Washington, DC: U.S. Department of Health and Human Services. Available online at: http://ruralhealth.hrsa.gov/RuralAmericaSummit.htm.

Kaye, Lenard W. "Case Management and Rural Health Care Delivery." *Geriatric Care Management Journal* 12(1) (Winter 2002):2-3.

Lohman, Nancy and Roger A. Lohman. *Rural Social Work Practice.* New York, NY: Columbia University Press, 2005.

National Association of Social Workers. "Rural Social Work Policy Statement Abstract." Washington, DC: National Association of Social Workers, 2008. Available online at: http://www.naswdc.org/resources/abstracts/abstracts/rural.asp.

National Association of Social Workers. "Rural Social Work." *Social Work Speaks Abstracts.* Washington, DC: National Association of Social Workers, 2008. Available online at: http://www.naswdc.org/resources/abstracts/abstracts/rural.asp.

Rural Social Work. A refereed journal devoted to issues of welfare practice and service delivery in rural and remote areas. The journal seeks to foster analysis comment and debate about issues of importance to rural welfare practitioners, administrators, and service users. Available online at: http://www.latrobe.edu.au/socialwork/rsw.html.

Scales, T.Laine and Calvin L. Streeter, eds. *Rural Social Work: Building and Sustaining Community Assets.* New York: Wadsworth Publishing Company, 2003.

Soil

Naturally weathered earth, including inorganic and organic matter, that supports the plant growth by supplying elements, water and a medium for anchorage. Despite this definition, soil means different things to different people. Some define soil as a medium for plant growth, but this tells little of its nature. Others say that soil is weathered rock, but a good definition needs to include the strong impact living things have on the nature of soil. Soil has been studied extensively both because plants grow in it (the field of edaphology) and for its own nature (pedology). An edaphologist may define soil as a mixture of mineral and organic materials capable of supporting plant growth. A pedologist may say that soil is a natural product formed by biochemical weathering acting on mineral and organic materials. Many qualifications could be added to either definition. This article will consider the physical, chemical and biological nature of soil, and how these properties influence its use for growing plants.

Soil covers nearly all of the earth's land surface. Soil and plants rooting in it are almost everywhere unless human efforts have displaced them with buildings, roads or other structures. People grow plants in soil, dig in soil, walk on soil, build on soil, and sometimes build with soil. Some soil gets in the wrong place and is called "dirt." Hands, clothes, houses and machines get dirty. Soil is so prevalent and commonplace in life that it often is ignored, but it is vital to Earth's life support system.

Soil Profiles and Pedons

Soil is extremely variable. Farmers know that sandy soils store less water and nutrients for plant growth than loamy soils, and that clay soils are harder to work than other soils. They also know that erosion changes the nature of soil by exposing subsoil layers. The layers that occur in a soil are often so distinct that an engineer considers them to be different soil materials for construction purposes. For example, a subsoil layer may be suitable for holding water in a pond, whereas the topsoil above it would be too porous for this purpose.

The soil layers at a particular site are so related to each other that a soil scientist considers the assemblage as a soil. A vertical section through these layers is called a soil profile. Each profile includes some combination of the following.

O (organic) horizons:

I. A horizons that are generally higher in organic matter and therefore darker colored than the deeper-lying layers.
II. E horizons with lighter colors because eluviation (loss of small solid particles) and leaching have removed materials from them.
III. B horizons that contain a higher percentage of clay than the rest of the profile (partly because of illuviation, deposition of the particles eluviated from above).
IV. Transitional horizons.

Whatever combination of these horizons happens to be present is called the solum (meaning true soil). Underlying unconsolidated material lacking the influence of living things is called parent material or C horizon, and bedrock is designated as the R layer (see table).

A soil profile with enough surface area to grow a medium-sized plant (usually about one square meter) is called a pedon. A contiguous group of similar pedons is called a polypedon. Soil surveyors name, classify and map soils in the field. Soil maps accompanied by descriptive and interpretive materials are published in soil survey reports.

Plant Growth Media

Plants can root in many kinds of media, including water cultures and various mixtures of solid materials, but no other medium competes with soil for the amount and variety of plants grown. Food and fiber products that support human life are grown mostly in soil.

Soil is versatile, but it is seldom a perfect growth medium. Plant growth can usually be increased and improved in quality by adding fertilizer and either adding water to a dry soil or removing water from a wet soil. Soil amendments, such as lime to neutralize excessive acidity or gypsum applied to remedy alkalinity, can dramatically improve plant growth. Organic materials, such as plant residues or manure added to soil, are generally favorable for plant growth. Microbes decomposing organic materials may tie up nitrogen for a time, but they make the soil more porous and workable, and they ultimately release plant nutrients. Tillage or other manipulations can alter the soil structure and pore space, and thus influence water and air movement, seed germination and root growth.

Varieties of Soil

Soil scientists have described and named thousands of different soil series, each of which has its own set of profile characteristics. Five factors influence the nature of the soil that forms in any particular place. These are climate, living organisms, topography, parent material, and time. Climate and living organisms are active factors, providing the weathering environment that converts rock into parent material and parent material into soil. Topography exerts a strong local effect by influencing water movement both on and in the soil and affecting temperature through the angle of the sun's rays. Weathering processes are slow but persistent, so changes continue over long periods of time.

Climate and living organisms are interrelated because certain types of plants and animals live in certain climates, but their actions are too varied for these two factors to be combined. In general, the large-scale soil patterns of the world are controlled by the climatic factor, and the local soil patterns are strongly influenced by topography. For example, a particular group of soils commonly occurs repeatedly in a geographical area with each soil occupying a specific topographic portion of each hill and valley in the area.

Soil Classification

Several systems have been devised to arrange the thousands of known soil series into higher units of classification analogous to those used for plants and animals. The current U.S. system is known as Soil Taxonomy. It has six categorical levels; soil series are classified into families, subgroups, great groups, suborders, and orders. Soil series are most useful when detailed soil information is needed, usually at a local level. Higher levels are useful when more generalized information is needed, such as the preparation of a world or national soil map. At its highest level, Soil Taxonomy groups all soils into 11 orders (see table).

Physical Properties of Soil

The usefulness and behavior of a soil depends greatly on its physical properties. Depth, texture, structure, porosity, color and temperature are all significant physical properties. Soil depth represents the zone from which plants can extract water and nutrients. Depth is simple where the solum directly overlies bedrock, gravel or some other contrasting layer, but it is less precise where the underlying material is loess, alluvium or other material that resembles soil. The solum still coincides with the root zone, but the bottom of the root zone can be diffuse and difficult to identify precisely.

Soil texture characterizes the sizes of mineral particles in the soil. A textural analysis begins by either measuring or estimating the percent by weight of sand, silt and clay in the soil. The USDA divides mineral material into clay particles less than 0.002 mm in diameter, silt particles between 0.002 and 0.05 mm in diameter, and sand particles between 0.05 and 2 mm in diameter. Particles larger than 2 mm in diameter are called gravel and stones. Laboratory measurements are made with sieves to separate the very coarse, coarse, medium, fine and very fine sand sizes, and settling rates in water are used to separate the silt and clay. Field estimates are made by feeling the hardness, grittiness, stickiness and plasticity of the soil. Texture names such as silty clay loam include various combinations of sand, silt, clay and loam. The word loam represents a mixture exhibiting the properties of all three size ranges approximately equally. It should be noted that a loam soil contains less clay than sand or silt; clay exhibits its properties very strongly because clay particles have a very large surface area per gram.

Soil structure is the arrangement of individual soil particles into aggregates and peds. Soil tilth, the ability of a soil to be tilled easily, is related to structure. Small, loosely packed clumps of soil forming granular structure give good porosity, permeability and tilth to the surface horizons of many soils. Denser peds that fit more tightly together form blocky structure that may occur at any depth. Many subsoils have cracks that bound the vertically oriented peds of prismatic structure. The E horizons of some soils have platy structure with horizontal surfaces. Each kind of structure influences the movement of water and air and the growth of plant roots.

Soil structure may be disturbed by tillage. For example, working a wet soil may produce clods, and traffic can compact the soil. Compaction is favorable for building a roadbed or a dam, but it is generally unfavorable for plant growth and soil tilth. Fortunately, natural forces such as freezing and thawing and the activity of living things tend to regenerate soil structure and tilth.

A favorable soil for plant growth has a wide range of pore sizes. The continuity of the pores larger than 0.1 mm is important for aeration and soil permeability. Microscopic pores hold water against gravity, but plant roots can withdraw roughly half of this water for plant use. Water available to plants may occupy 15 to 20 percent of the volume of a porous soil with loamy texture, but the percentage decreases in sandy soils as the surface area of the particles decreases. Some dense clay soils have no large pores and therefore may be permanently saturated with water.

Soil color has little importance of its own, but it indicates other properties such as organic matter content that darkens soil color, the presence of excess salts or free lime that may lighten soil color, or of oxidized iron coatings that redden soil color. Poor soil drainage is indicated by rust mottles in the soil, and long-term saturation is indicated by bluish-gray colors of reduced iron compounds.

Cool soil temperature may slow or prevent seed germination, and hot temperatures may cause soil water to evaporate rapidly. Temperature also influences the rate of weathering of soil minerals, the decomposition of organic materials, and the release of plant nutrients.

Chemical Properties of Soil

Sand and silt are chemically inert, but clay and humus (the organic matter remaining after decomposition slows) have electrical charges that attract ions to their surfaces. The large surface area of these small particles makes colloidal chemistry very important in soils. The ions held in temperate regions are dominantly calcium and magnesium, but lesser amounts of potassium, sodium and micronutrient cations are also held. The attraction is strong enough to resist leaching but weak enough to permit exchanges to occur and for plants to obtain nutrient ions. Plants often exchange hydrogen ions for nutrient ions, thus causing the soil to become more acid.

Weathering and leaching cause the soils of humid regions to lose fertility over long periods of time. Highly weathered tropical soils lose cation exchange capacity as well as plant nutrients, so it is more difficult to maintain good soil fertility in the tropics than in temperate regions. Crop removal and nitrogen fertilizers cause soils to acidify much more rapidly than they would naturally. The remedy is to apply lime periodically to keep the soil pH suitable for the crop being grown.

Inadequate leaching causes salinity in some soils of arid environments, especially where a water table provides upward moving water carrying soluble salts toward the surface. This condition applies to many house plants as well as to arid climatic regions. Excess salts form a white crust on the high points of the soil whenever it dries out. The remedy is to increase downward movement by drainage and leaching. A soil amendment such as gypsum must be applied before leaching if the accumulated salts are high in sodium. Otherwise, leaching can produce a sodic soil that is too alkaline and impermeable to grow plants.

Biological Properties of Soil

Soil supports a remarkable population of living things. Plant roots constitute the largest living mass in the soil, and bacteria are the most numerous inhabitants. A single gram of fertile topsoil may contain billions of bacteria. Fungi, actinomycetes, protozoa, nematodes, insects, earthworms, rodents, snakes and many other living things are also at home in soil. Decomposing the dead remains of plant and animal life is an important activity in soil. Plant nutrients are recycled thereby for future generations of plants.

Soil is made porous by the tunneling of earthworms, insects and other animal life, and by the growth of plant roots. Gummy substances produced during decomposition processes improve structural stability that keeps it porous. Materials such as cellulose and protein are decomposed in a few weeks or months of warm weather, but more resistant materials are left to accumulate as soil humus that takes years or even centuries to decompose. Prolific plant growth, cool temperatures and wet conditions that reduce soil aeration favor the accumulation of several percent of organic matter in the upper part of a soil. Dominantly organic peat and muck soils are produced in saturated bogs or in cold climates such as in Alaska. Organic matter contents are usually less than 1 percent in tropical soils because the organic matter decomposes rapidly there, in desert soils because little organic matter is produced there, and in subsoils because plant roots diminish with depth.

Using Soil for Growing Crops

Annual crops will be emphasized here, although perennial grass and trees also can be crops. Until recently, annual cropping began with tillage to eliminate weeds and produce a seedbed. The current trend is toward less tillage, the ultimate being "no-tillage" in which the only soil disturbance is that caused by planting. Pesticides can control weeds and other pests, and many soils make suitable seedbeds without tillage. Fertilizer is still needed to make up for nutrient deficiencies caused by crop removal. Also, the soil pH should be monitored and lime or gypsum applied when needed.

Soil conservation efforts have benefited greatly from reduced tillage. Undisturbed soil is less easily eroded, and crop residues left on the surface absorb the impact of raindrops and wind. Even so, proper management of sloping soils involves choosing crops that provide good cover and/or mechanical practices such as terracing or contour tillage to reduce runoff.

Soil organic matter contents usually decline in cropped soils, and practices such as reduced tillage that cause slower decomposition are generally beneficial. It is important to return as much organic matter to the soil as possible, especially if the soil tilth needs to be improved. Crop residues, manure and green manure all provide beneficial organic matter. Gardeners have found compost to be good for improving both fertility and tilth. The composition of compost varies, but it generally includes layers of soil, manure and grass clippings or other organic materials. Nitrogen fertilizer and lime are often added. The mass is kept moist so that microbes will decompose (compost) the organic materials. The pile may be mixed and turned periodically, and applied to a garden after some weeks or months of composting (the process is generally too labor intensive for use on field crops).

— *Frederick R. Troeh*

See also

Agriculture, Hydroponic; Conservation, Soil; Cropping Systems; Regional Diversity; Tillage

References

Brady, Nyle C. and Ray R. Weil. *The Nature and Properties of Soils*, 14th ed. Englewood Cliffs, NJ: Prentice Hall, 1997.

Eswaran, H., T. Rice, R. Ahrens, and B.A. Stewart, eds. *Soil Classification: a Global Desk Reference*. Boca Raton, Fla.: CRC Press, 2002.

Fanning, D.S. and M.C.B. Fanning. *Soil Morphology, Genesis, and Classification*. New York, NY: Wiley, 1989.

Foth, H.D. *Fundamentals of Soil Science*. 8th ed. New York, NY: Wiley, 1990.

Soil Survey Staff. *Keys to Soil Taxonomy*, 10th ed. Washington, DC: U.S. Department of Agriculture, Natural Resources Conservation Service, 2006. Available online at: http://soils.usda.gov/technical/classification/tax_keys/keys.pdf.

Troeh, Frederick R., Roy L. Donahue, and J. Arthur Hobbs. *Soil and Water Conservation: Productivity and*

Environmental Protection, 4th ed. Englewood Cliffs, N. J: Prentice-Hall, 2003.

Troeh, Frederick R. *Soils and Soil Fertility,* 6th ed. Hoboken, NJ: John Wiley and Sons, 2005.

The 11 Soil Orders in Soil Taxonomy

Order	Abbreviated Description
Alfisols	Soils with grayish brown colors and significant clay accumulation in their B horizons; most Alfisols form under forest vegetation.
Andisols	Soils containing high contents of glass and/or extractable iron and aluminum compounds; most Andisols form in young volcanic ash materials.
Aridisols	Light-colored soils that generally have alkaline reactions; Aridisols form in arid regions.
Entisols	Soils that have little or no horizon differentiation; Entisols are very young soils, at least in appearance.
Histosols	Soils whose properties are dominated by organic matter (>20 to 30 percent o.m.); Histosols form in wet and/or cold conditions.
Inceptisols	Soils with some soil profile development but without significant clay illuviation; Inceptisols form in humid climates under forest vegetation.
Mollisols	Soils with thick, dark-colored upper horizons; Mollisols form in temperate climates under grass vegetation.
Oxisols	Soils that are very highly weathered and low in natural fertility; Oxisols form in tropical climates.
Spodosols	Intensely leached soils with bright colors, strong acidity and low fertility; Spodosols form under evergreen trees in cool, humid climates.
Ultisols	Strongly weathered soils with redder or yellower colors and more acidity than Alfisols; Ultisols form under forest vegetation in warm, humid climates.
Vertisols	Soils with high clay contents that form deep cracks at least 1 cm wide when dry; Vertisols form in high-clay parent material in climates with wet and dry seasons.

Solar Energy

Harnessing the sun to heat homes, heat water, and produce electricity. Energy from the sun provides warmth, helps plants grow, and drives the weather. Today, solar energy is also used to heat homes, heat water, and generate electricity. After a brief discussion of the solar resource, the basic solar energy technologies are described along with information on how they operate.

A Useful and Abundant Resource

The solar resource is huge. Each day approximately 87,000,000,000,000,000 watts or 87,000 Terawatt (TW) of solar energy strikes the earth's atmosphere. In comparison, the world's energy consumption in 2006 was approximately 16 TW. This annual total could be provided from an area the size of West Virginia (54,000 km^2 covered with solar cells.

To make use of the solar resource it is necessary to understand variability and reliability of the resource. For example, solar energy is unavailable at night and very little energy is available when it is mostly cloudy and/or raining.

Sunlight is composed of a spectrum of wavelengths from short wavelength ultraviolet light to long wavelength radio waves. As sunlight passes through the atmosphere some of it is absorbed, reflected, or scattered. Much of the ultraviolet radiation is absorbed by the ozone in the atmosphere and a good deal of the long-wavelength infrared irradiance is absorbed by the atmosphere. The atmosphere is largely transparent to the visible portion of the spectrum. Approximately 50 percent of the energy from the sun is radiated in the visible wavelengths.

Harnessing Solar Energy

Three general areas of solar technologies are covered: passive solar, solar thermal collectors, and solar electricity.

Passive Solar. Passive systems use conduction, convention, or radiation to move heat from one area to another. A purely passive system does not use fans or pumps to move heat, but occasionally mechanical systems are combined with passive designs to improve overall efficiency. Passive systems require thoughtful design based on an understanding of how heat is transported or stored.

Conduction is the transfer of heat through a medium. A metal spoon in a hot cup of coffee conducts heat from the coffee to the handle of the spoon. Different materials conduct heat at different rates. Metal is good conductor of heat; rock or stone are fair conductors of heat; and wood and plastic are poor heat conductors. **Convection** is the transfer of heat in a gas or liquid by the circulation of the medium from one area to another. **Radiation** is electromagnetic energy that can be thought of as consisting either of waves or of particles called photons. Ultraviolet radiation is composed of waves with short wavelengths and infrared radiation is composed of waves with long wavelengths. Visible light has wavelengths between 400 and 800 nanometers. Infrared radiation is emitted from sources considered hot, such as a fire, and when the photons are absorbed by the skin, the radiation heats the skin.

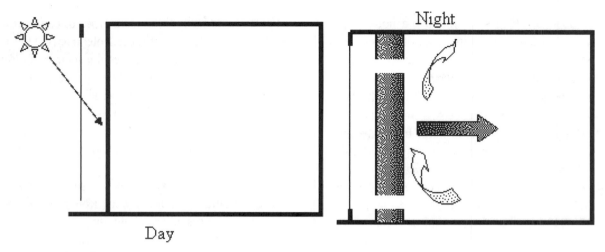

Figure 1. *Trombe Wall—operation during the day and night.*

A Trombe Wall demonstrates three modes of heat transfer in its design. A Trombe Wall is a concrete or brick wall behind a glazing with vents on the top and the bottom to allow air circulation. During the day the sunlight heats the wall and cool air enters the lower vent, is heated by the wall, and flows out the upper vent. The glazing keeps this air from mixing with the outside air and keeps the outside air from cooling the Trombe Wall. At night, the vents are shut and the heat that has been slowly conducting through the Trombe Wall is radiated into the room and air circulating against the wall heats the room through convection.

A Trombe Wall's efficiency depends on the thickness of the wall and it can be improved by putting a selective coating on the exterior face of the wall to enhance the absorption of solar radiation and minimize radiation to the outside.

Some surfaces, such as black surfaces, will absorb solar radiation in the visible wavelengths better than others, such as white surfaces. A material that is a good absorber is also a good emitter. Absorptive properties are dependent on wavelength of light. Solar collectors use materials, called selective surfaces, which are good absorbers in the visible portion of the spectrum and poor absorbers (poor emitters) in the infrared portion. Selective surfaces enhance the absorption of solar radiation and help prevent re-radiation from the heated surface.

Another passive solar technology is daylighting. Daylighting designs allow sunlight to enter deeper into the work space and reduce the need for electric lighting. Light shelves by the exterior windows bounce sunlight on a lightly colored ceiling and reflect sunlight deeper into the room while shading the lower window area from the glare of direct sunlight. Skylights can also be incorporated into daylighting schemes.

Solar Thermal Collectors. Solar thermal collectors have a window that lets sunlight strike an absorber plate. The glass or plastic glazing prevents outside air from blowing against the absorber plate. Collectors use a selective surface to minimize the amount of heat radiated from the hot absorber plate. Metal pipes are attached to the back of a metal absorber plate and fluid in the pipes transfers the heat in the absorber to the fluid through conduction. A good collector is also well insulated to minimize heat loss through conduction. There are three type basic types of domestic solar water heaters: a batch system, a passive system, and an antifreeze system.

The **batch** system consists of a tank that is painted black with or without a selective surface. It is housed in an insulated box with a transparent cover. The sun heats the tank and the water inside. Water is pumped through the tank to an existing water heater. Batch water heaters are simple and relatively inexpensive, but they also are not very efficient.

Passive or thermo-siphoning solar water heating systems are more efficient than batch heaters and are common in warmer climates. A thermo-siphon system has the hot water tank above the solar collectors. A thermo-siphon system uses the principle that hot water rises to circulate the water through the collector and into the storage tank. The storage tank can be well insulated as opposed to the tank in the batch system that must be able to collect the incident solar radiation. The water tank can be heated by an auxiliary source and act as the water heater or it can be used to preheat the water for a standard water heater.

Active water heating systems have a pump that circulates a fluid through the collector and transfers the heat to a storage tank by use of heat exchanger. The storage tank can either be the water heater or an auxiliary tank that preheats water entering the water heater. In most cold climates an **antifreeze solution** is used as the transfer fluid and this prevents water from freezing in the pipes. When water freezes it expands and this can break the pipes. In an antifreeze system, the antifreeze is circulated through the solar collector and back to a heat exchange. A controller monitors the temperature difference between the storage tank and the outlet from the solar collector. When the temperature difference is great enough, the controller turns on the pump to circulate the fluid. If the storage tank gets too hot, the controller will also turn off the pump.

The heat exchanger warms water in the water heater or an auxiliary tank that feeds the pre-heated water directly into the regular water heater saving the energy needed to raise the inlet water from ground temperature to the temperature in the solar heated tank. Often in the summer the temperature in the solar storage tank will exceed the outlet temperature of the water heater.

Although a standard flat plate solar collector reduces radiative losses with a selective surface and reduces conductive losses with insulation, convective losses resulting from air carrying the heat away is not well addressed. To eliminate the convective losses, some companies manufacture evacuated tubes with the fin and pipe inside the tube. Removing the air eliminates the convective losses inside the collector. Evacuated tube collectors are more efficient when the collector inlet temperature is about 35° C above ambient temperature.

Typically solar water heating collectors are between 30 and 40 percent efficient. In theory, the optimum orientation of a fixed flat plate collector is to have the collector face the equator tilted at latitude. In practice, weather affects the solar resource and the optimum orientation. For instance, areas with a lot more summer sun and cloudy winters will have an optimum tilt around latitude minus 10 degrees.

Solar Electricity. There are two ways of generating electricity from solar radiation. One method is to use solar energy to heat a fluid that turns water into steam to drive a steam generator (solar thermal electricity). The other method is to turn solar radiation directly into electricity using photovoltaic (PV) cells.

There are basically three main types of concentrators used to generate **solar thermal electricity**. One is a parabolic trough that concentrates the solar radiation on a tube running down the focal plane of the trough. A second type is a dish, similar to a large TV satellite dish that concentrates sunlight at a focal point. A third type is called the solar tower where a field of mirrors, or heliostats, concentrates the solar radiation on a tower near the center of the field.

A parabola, when pointed at the sun, will focus sunlight at a point. When a parabolic trough is pointed at the sun, it focuses the sunlight on a line. A tube, with oil as a heat transfer fluid, is placed on the focal line. The fluid will be heated to around 400° C. The oil is pumped to a hot oil storage tank or to the boiler where steam is created. The steam is either superheated by natural gas or the solar heated oil. The steam runs a standard turbine to generate electricity. Afterwards the remaining steam is condensed and cooled as it passes through a cooling tower.

Trough systems built in the 1980s run in size from about 30 megawatts (MW) to 80 MW. In 2007, a 64 MW solar electric trough system was installed in Nevada.

A variant on the parabolic though system is a system that uses **linear Fresnel lenses** to reflect light onto a linear tube in a collector running parallel to the lenses. The Linear Fresnel design enabled higher concentrations (~60-80 suns) to be reach than available with the Parabolic Trough because the system could be scaled up with numerous smaller lenses that did not have to be constructed as one large unit that tracked the sun. In the 1990s, Compound Parabolic Concentrators (CPC) were used for the collector carrying the evacuated tube collector to improve efficiency.

A **parabolic dish**, looks like a giant television satellite dish, focuses light at a point. The dish reflects sunlight to the focal point and a heat engine is mounted at the focal point. The heat engine generates electricity and thus avoids the necessity to transfer heat via pipes. On the other hand, each dish requires its own engine. Sterling engines are typically used because they are fairly efficient for small size engines. This combination is often referred to as a Dish/Sterling system.

Solar thermal electricity may also be generated through a **central receiver/power tower system.** By using a large field of mirrors mounted on trackers (heliostats), sunlight is reflected onto a central receiver mounted on a large tower. Oil or molten salt is pumped through and heated in the central receiver. This fluid is then feed to a storage tank. A heat exchanger in the tank is used to create steam to drive a steam turbine. Power tower systems raise the fluid to higher temperatures than a parabolic trough system and hence can operate at higher thermodynamic efficiencies.

Photovoltaic (PV) cells, also called solar cells, act much like batteries except they are powered by sunlight instead of chemical reactions as in lead acid batteries. Each silicon solar cell has a voltage of approximately 0.5 volts.

The current or amperage of the solar cell is dependent on the number of electrons that are knocked into the conduction band. This current is proportional to the amount of solar radiation incident on the solar cell and the area of the solar cell. The product of the current and the voltage is the power produced by the solar cell. As with batteries, when solar cells are connected in series, the voltage increases and when solar cells are connected in parallel, the current increases.

A PV panel or module is a group of solar cells connected together in a hermitically sealed enclosure. An array is formed when these panels are connected together. A photovoltaic system consists of one or more arrays.

Photovoltaic panels produce direct current that is used to power the "load." This can range from charging a battery in a calculator to powering a satellite to powering a building or a city. When a PV system is connected to the utility grid, it must first be connected to an inverter. An inverter changes the direct current from the array to alternating current used by the utility grid. Inverters connected to the utility grid are designed to stop the flow of electricity to the grid if power from the utility fails. This prevents injury to those working to restore power.

The IV curve is a plot of current verses voltage of a solar cell or module. Over much of the voltage range, the current is proportional to incident energy (sunlight). As the voltage approaches the open circuit voltage the current begins to fall to zero. The open circuit voltage is the voltage across the cell or module that occurs if there is no circuit to conduct electricity.

To obtain the most power from the solar cell array, inverters contain a maximum power point tracker that monitors the voltage and current from the array and makes adjustments to the load seen by the array to maximize the energy output from the array. The DC to AC conversion efficiency of an inverter is about 90 percent or more.

Photovoltaic systems operate independently (stand alone systems) or connected to the utility grid (grid-tied systems).

Stand alone PV systems are connected to charge controller that regulate the charging and operating of batteries. The batteries can be used to power DC systems or go through an inverter to run an AC powered system. For remote homes, stand along PV systems are often combined with other charging systems such as a propane generator to charge the batteries at night or prolonged periods with little sunlight.

Grid-tied photovoltaic systems come in all sizes from kilowatts (kW) to megawatts (MW). This means that they can be generating electricity near where the electricity is used or remote locations with an exceptional solar resource. A one kW PV array occupies about ten square meters (roughly 100 square feet) and produces between 1,000 to 2,000 kilowatt hours of electricity per year, depending on the solar resource.

— *Frank Vignola*

See also

Electrification; Natural Resources Engineering; Technology; Technology Transfer; Wind Energy

References

Duffie, John A. and William A. Beckman. *Solar Engineering and Thermal Processes*, Hoboken, NY: John Wiley and Sons, 2006.

Gordon, Jeffrey, ed. *Solar Energy—The State of the Art.* London, UK: James and James, 2001.

Mazria, Edward. *The Passive Solar Energy Book: A Complete Guide to Passive Solar Home, Greenhouse and Building Design.* New York, NY: Rodale Press, 1979.

Gore, Al. *An Inconvenient Truth.* New York, NY: Rodale Press, 2006.

Home Power. Ashland, OR: Home Power Magazine.

McDaniels, Dave. *The Sun Our Future Energy Source.* Hoboken, NY: John Wiley and Sons, Inc., 1979.

Perlin, John. *From Space to Earth, the Story of Solar Electricity.* Ann Harbor, MI: AATEC Publications, 1999.

Ramlow, Bob and Benjamin Nusz. *Solar Water Heating.* Gabriola Island, BC: New Society Publishers, 2006.

Solar Today. Boulder, CO: American Solar Energy Society.

Strong, Steven J. with William G. Scheller. *The Solar Electric House.* Still River, MA: Sustainability Press, 1987.

Tackling Climate Change in the U.S. Boulder, CO: American Solar Energy Society, 2007.

Useful websites:

"Solar radiation basics." Available at: http://solardata.uoregon.edu/SolarRadiationBasics.html.

"View the earth's orbit around the sun." Available at: http://www.sciences.univ-nantes.fr/physique/perso/gtulloue/Sun/motion/Declination_a.html.

"Plot sun's path across the sky." Available at: http://solar-data.uoregon.edu/SunChartProgram.html.

"How solar cells work." Available at: http://solardata.uoregon.edu/download/Lessons/PVLessonPlan1SolarCells.pdf and http://www.nrel.gov/learning/re_photovoltaics.html.

Spatial Inequality

The distribution of different forms of inequality across geographic territory. This topic addresses two central questions. First, how and why do markers of stratification such as reflected in economic status, race/ ethnicity, gender, health, education and other statuses vary across places and their populations? Second, how do places themselves become markers of stratification? That is, how do uneven development processes give rise to distinct places such as prosperous or poor communities and regions?

This entry provides a general overview of the topic of spatial inequality. It discusses bodies of social science research addressing this topic and outlines factors identified by analysts that create variations in poverty and prosperity across places. Attention here is to spatial inequality at the subnational scale or across regions within the U.S., which is most pertinent to rural places and people.

Examples of Spatial Inequality

Spatial inequality at the subnational scale can be illustrated by the following examples. One is persistent disadvantages faced by regions such as the rural South, U.S.-Mexican border locales, Appalachia and rural Native American locales. These regions continue to lag behind others, as particularly seen in their high poverty rates.

A second example of spatial inequality involves recent development patterns where rapid economic growth is combined with income polarization, producing inequality "hot spots." These patterns are illustrated in the cases of Denver and Aspen, where high-growth culls the middle and working classes, pushing the latter group into rural hinterlands where housing costs are lower; and remote, rural Midwestern communities, where the growth of industrialized agriculture and processing facilities creates regional clusters of lower wage labor pools. A third example concerns the contemporary rural Midwestern manufacturing belt. In

this region, relatively once prosperous communities have increasingly lost employment in the wake of global competition.

A general illustration of spatial inequality at the subnational scale is shown in maps, below, using data on family poverty rates from the last four Censuses of Population for U.S. counties. The maps highlight trends whereby northern and western counties historically have had lower poverty rates. The maps show high poverty remains in much of the South and Appalachia and appears to have expanded across the southwest.

The previous examples illustrate the topic of spatial inequality. They are all linked by raising fundamental questions about the manner by which poverty and prosperity are produced across territory.

The Development of Research on Spatial Inequality

The study of inequality spans geography, sociology, economics, political science and other disciplines. However, only sociology is foremost characterized by its core interest in the topic, seen in its vast literature on the allocation of resources reflecting material privilege, social prestige and political power. Common forms of inequality studied are material resources or economic conditions indicating poverty and prosperity, educational attainments, health status and political power. Sociologists typically study the allocation of forms of inequality across social groups such as class, race/ethnicity and gender groups. In principle, all the previous forms of inequality can be studied across places at different scales, with places ranging from micro-level units like the individual and household to the macro-level nation-state and the entire global system. Spatial inequality refers to the study of inequality across places at all these different scales—as well as across scales, so, for example, communities might be studied as embedded in the nation-state or broader global system.

As an umbrella term for this topical area of research, "spatial inequality" has come into relatively recent usage, although the topic itself has been addressed at least implicitly since the inception of the social sciences. That is, the classical founders of social science disciplines often were concerned with how the movement from agrarian to industrialized societies created variability in life changes populations across nations and regions, a general example of spatial inequality. However, for the most part, explicit coverage of the topic still remains limited. In sociology, for instance, well-developed bodies of inequality research are found

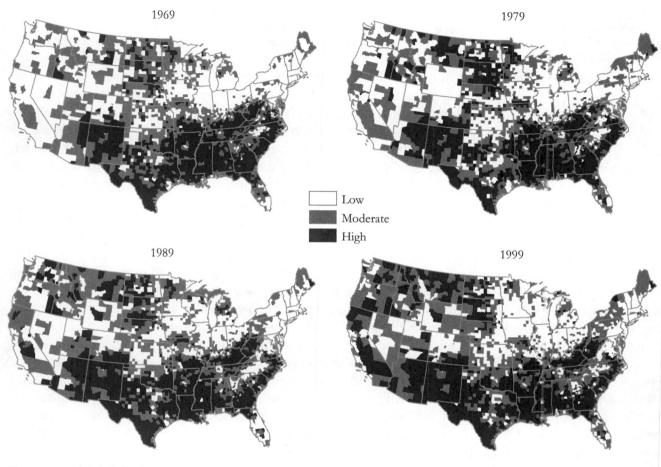

1969

1979

Low
Moderate
High

1989

1999

Maps courtesy of Linda Lobao.

mainly at two opposing scales, the city or local level and across the global system of nation-states. At these two scales, coherent theoretical and methodological literatures on inequality exist, literatures recognized by virtually all sociologists and familiar to other social scientists as well. By contrast, sociology has given much less attention to inequality at the middle-scale, the area between the nation-state and the urban or local scale. This scale can be considered as area extending regionally beyond the city, potentially spanning both urban and rural areas and the nation as a whole.

In terms of the study of different forms of inequality across the subnational scale and particularly U.S. rural areas, rural sociologists probably have made the greatest inroads. The field has a longstanding tradition of analyzing urban and rural regions jointly and comparatively. Several research areas within rural sociology that have contributed to the study of spatial inequality are delineated by Lobao (2004). These include the rural inequality tradition, which focuses on rural poverty as well as on labor market and demographic processes contributing to different forms of inequality

across geographic territory; the rural spatial segregation tradition, where researchers have studied the Southern black belt, Native American rural areas, U.S.-Mexican border areas, and newer areas of Latino or other ethnic in-migration; the sociology of agriculture literature, where researchers have examined the effects of large-scale industrialized farming versus family farming on regional and community well-being; environmental and/or natural resource sociology, which have attended to the impacts of the extractive sector on community well-being; and the comparative community tradition, where recent research casts a critical eye on race/ethnic, class and gender inequalities.

Determinants of Spatial Inequality

Different theories exist about why inequality varies by geographic location. These theories differ depending upon social science discipline and by type of inequality examined. In the discussion below, I focus on inequality in economic well-being, outlining some of the major determinants of poverty and prosperity at the subnational scale. Theoretical interpretation of these determinants draws largely from sociology.

Economic Structure. Most attention to determinants of subnational inequality is given to the structure of the economy. In studying economic structure, researchers usually focus on industrial sectors (sectors of economic activity), which vary by quality and quantity of employment generated. Higher-wage industries, such as durable manufacturing and producer services, are usually contrasted with lower wage industries, such as consumer services and agriculture. Economic structure influences income levels and distribution across regional populations in direct and indirect ways. Primary impacts are through earnings and occupational structures. Secondary impacts occur through economic multiplier effects in which employees and firms purchase local goods and services. Higher-wage employment tends to create regional wage spreads, driving up labor costs as employers compete for labor. Insofar as higher-wage sectors depend on skilled labor and generate relatively greater profits, employers also may support a stronger social safety net that can enhance regional well-being. Finally, economic structure may affect well-being indirectly via family structure. Areas more dependent on lower wage industries are likely to have greater social disruption due to poor-quality employment, and in turn, to have a higher proportion of single-family households, a known correlate of poverty.

Empirical studies thus tend to find that regions with greater wage service sector and durable manufacturing employment have better well-being: family incomes are higher, and poverty rates and income inequality tend to be lower. By contrast, areas with greater mining and agriculture, which tend to generate lower wage and/or unstable employment, are usually found to have poorer conditions. Public employment also varies in quality, affecting regional fortunes in a similar manner. For example, federal employment tends to generate higher earnings than do state/local government, so the former has more beneficial effects on regional incomes. In sum, where higher-quality employment is present, there tends to be a shadow effect on the population at large—poverty rates are lower and economic well-being of all residents is higher.

Regional Institutional Arrangements. Spatial disparities in economic well-being also arise from institutionalized arrangements between capital, labor, the state and citizens. By institutionalized arrangements, I mean established power relationships, reflected in social practices, resources, laws and organizations. Where

these arrangements tend to favor workers, the poor and civic society as a whole, economic well-being should be higher. Several examples of how institutional arrangements affect subnational inequality follow.

First, regions vary by the degree to which workers are advantaged in securing material demands from employers. Researchers have given most attention to education, arguing that it increases the bargaining power of labor vis-à-vis employers. Greater years of schooling are almost always highly related to higher income levels and lower poverty. Labor unions and professional associations further increase laborers' bargaining power. Where unionization is higher, median family income tends to be higher and poverty and income inequality lower. Bargaining power of all workers is also thought to be higher where race/ethnic and gender labor market inequalities are lower, as measured by labor force participation rates, earnings gaps and relative group size.

Second, regions vary by the degree to which the state protects the livelihood of citizens and the poor. Government policies and programs have spatially uneven impacts due to their target populations and the nature of the U.S. federalist system, where federal and state programs are often administered through county offices with different political cultures. Decentralization also allows state and local governments to act more autonomously, creating greater spatial variation in the degree to which interests of citizens and the poor are served. Where the state provides a stronger social safety net, populations benefit and aggregate economic well-being tends to be higher.

Third, regions vary in their legacy of racial/ethnic subordination, where state and market forces combine to disadvantage areas with higher proportion of African Americans, Latinos, and Native Americans. Persistent poverty is found in regions with high minority populations, and recent immigration has created new pockets of poverty.

Fourth, regions vary in the degree to which a civic society has developed. Researchers measure civic society through the presence of small businesses and other indicators of an independent middle class, voting rates and church attendance. Where civic society is more developed, economic and other well-being tend to be higher.

Internal and External Location-specific Attributes. Another set of determinants involves internal attributes of places and external location. Internal attributes of places include populations' demographic characteristics, ecological features of the built and natural environment, and specific history. Infrastructure, such as interstate highways and airports, and natural amenities are usually found to be more important in the fortunes of rural places than urban ones. External factors involve the location of places in the broader political economy. Places vary in socioeconomic conditions in part due to their location relative to neighboring places and because they are nested in territorial units, such as states, nation and global economy. Closer proximity to metropolitan centers continues to be associated with better well-being. Places located in a particular state may gain or lose relatively as federal policy is deployed to benefit some states over others. Position in the global economy affects variations in regional well-being through trade and regulatory changes.

In sum, the determinants of spatial inequality at the subnational scale, including differences between urban and rural regions, can be viewed related to economic structure, institutional arrangements, and location place-specific attributes.

— Linda M. Lobao

See also

Government; Housing; Policy (various entries); Public Services; Quality of Life; Rural Demography

References

Chakravorty, Sanjoy. *Fragments of Inequality*. New York: Routledge, 2006.

Cotter, David A. "Poor People in Poor Places: Local Opportunity Structure and Household Poverty." *Rural Sociology* 67, no. 2 (2002): 534-555.

Falk, William, Michael Schulman, and Ann Tickamyer, eds. *Communities of Work: Rural Restructuring in Local and Global Contexts*. Athens OH: Ohio University Press, 2003.

Glasmeier, Amy. *Poverty in America: One Nation Pulling Apart*. New York: Routledge, 2006.

Lichter, Daniel and Diane K. McLaughlin. "Changing Economic Opportunities, Family Structure, and Poverty in Rural Areas." *Rural Sociology* 60 (1995): 688-706.

Lobao, Linda M. "Continuity and Changer in Place Stratification: Spatial Inequality and Middle-Range Territorial Units." *Rural Sociology* 69 (2004): 1-30.

———. *Locality and Inequality: Farm and Industry Structure and Socioeconomic Conditions*. Albany, NY: State University of New York Press, 1990.

Lobao, Linda M., Gregory Hooks, and Ann R. Tickamyer, eds. *The Sociology of Spatial Inequality*. Albany: The State University of New York Press, 2007

McCall, Leslie. *Complex Inequality: Gender, Class and Race in the New Economy*. New York: Routledge, 2001.

Partridge, Mark D. and Dan S. Rickman. *The Geography of American Poverty: Is There a Need for Place-Based Policies?* Kalmazoo, MI: Upjohn, 2006.

Specialized Livestock Production

Production of animals other than from traditional livestock species including species such as deer, elk, llama, alpaca, bison, ratites, bees, rabbits, mink, aquaculture, etc. As traditional livestock production (i.e., beef and dairy cattle, swine, poultry, sheep and goats) becomes more intensively managed and competitive, interest has grown in raising exotic or wild species. These operations range from small-scale hobby farms, where the primary income is not from the farm, to larger operations from which the sole income is derived from the production of non-typical agricultural animals. Individuals operating such enterprises do not attempt to directly compete with conventional livestock production, but rather seek to develop niche markets for their product. Specialized livestock production is a growing force in rural America as many try to find creative methods to profit from their acreage.

Deer Production

Perhaps the most economically viable of these operations is the farmed deer enterprise. In the most recent United States Census of Agriculture, conducted in 2002, there were a reported 286,800 deer on farms in the United States, and 97,900 elk. The North American Deer Farmers Association (NADeFA) today represents over 385,000 animals with an estimated livestock value of $111 million. Common species represented by this association include axis, fallow, red, sika, whitetail, elk (wapiti) and others. All of these animals are members of the family cervidae and are collectively referred to as cervids. The Agriculture and Food Policy Center at Texas A&M University recently completed a survey of the Economic Impact of the United States Cervid Farming Industry, which surmised that "cervid farming" generates $3 billion a year in economic activity, based on numbers from 2006 and early 2007 (Anderson et al., 2007).

The industry is regulated by both federal and state entities, and laws are not consistent across the United States. There are several components to the farmed cervid industry, including markets for breeding stock, venison, velvet antler for traditional Asian medicine, hides and antler sheds, hunting, and urine collection as a hunting attractant. The growth of this industry has spawned creation of industry-specific careers such as nutritional or reproductive consultants and manufacturers of deer-specific fencing and equipment. According to NADeFA's website, the consumption of venison (including elk meat) in the United States has more than doubled since 1992, and the product is marketed as being leaner and having less cholesterol and fewer calories than other red meats. Currently, much of the venison consumed in the United States is imported from New Zealand; therefore, potential exists to expand venison production in the United States. Regulations regarding the sale of venison vary, but venison sold to the public should be processed in an approved facility under government inspection. There are not many facilities offering such services at this time, and this is an area which may see future growth.

Deer require less labor than cattle, in part because they are generally disease-resistant and self-sufficient, but labor inputs vary depending on the intensity of management. More deer can be sustained on an acre of land than cattle, making the initial investment of land per animal less; however, fencing requirements differ greatly from cattle in both material and investment. To maintain deer in fenced paddocks, woven fencing is required with a minimum height of six and a half feet. Depending upon the type of deer, often fences are eight to 10 feet high. This prevents deer from escaping and decreases predation, but also makes the initial investment much higher. Handling facilities for deer also differ from cattle, and at some point, deer must be handled for veterinary procedures, the removal of velvet antler, urine collection, marketing of breeding stock, collection of semen from males, or artificial insemination of females. While some of these procedures can be done through darting or tranquilization, it is less expensive, less stressful for the animal, less time consuming, and safer to install proper deer handling facilities. The initial investment for such a facility is high, but in time the facility pays for itself due to not having the cost of tranquilization and risks associated with tranquilizing animals. Handling facilities for deer consist of runways and alleys, holding pens with solid walls, and typically a drop floor chute in which the animal's weight assists in restraint for procedures. The layout of the handling facility should allow deer the illusion of escape from humans. Facilities for elk are slightly different, with construction consisting of open walls and squeeze chutes more similar to those used with cattle.

In addition to the high investment for fencing and handling facilities, breeding stock can be very expensive, with the average cost of whitetail breeder bucks being close to $21,000 per animal (Anderson et al., 2007); however, when managed correctly, deer farmers are seeing good returns on the investment.

Raising or purchasing farmed deer for hunting purposes is an important component of the industry, and individual states have varying requirements for licensing such operations regarding the total land mass required, the stocking density, times at which hunts are allowed, etc. While most deer hunting still occurs in the more traditional manner, individuals who travel to hunting preserves that release deer raised or purchased from breeding operations contribute an estimated $757 million to the total economic impact of the cervid farming industry (Anderson et al., 2007). These dollars are not limited to the individual deer operations, but are spread throughout the overall economy as money is spent on food, lodging, hunting supplies, transportation, etc.

Cervid farming is an important and viable industry in rural America. The activity of this industry supports a total of 29,200 jobs, with the vast majority of these being located in rural communities (Anderson et al., 2007). As further evidence, of the estimated 7,800 operations in existence today, 1,600 are Amish operations (Anderson et al., 2007). The deer farming industry allows people in rural communities to diversify their agricultural enterprises with a relatively small acreage investment and creates valuable job opportunities.

Llama and Alpaca Production

Llama and alpaca production is another area seeing some popularity for smaller enterprises. Initial investment in breeding stock for both llamas and alpacas is high, and only two products are produced, fiber and the live animal. Llamas have not been specifically bred for fiber production, and their coats contain stiff guard hairs in addition to fine wool fibers. These guard hairs must be removed unless the product to be produced is a rug or a rope. Alpacas, in contrast, have been bred specifically for fiber production and their coats do not contain these guard hairs. Both llamas and alpacas are shorn once a year, and the price for fiber varies depending upon quality.

Typically llama and alpaca enterprises are viewed as high-risk by financial institutions, and it can be challenging to find the funds to get started in these

Photograph courtesy of Andrew W. Lewis Research Associate at the Texas AgriLife Research and Extension Center at Overton, TX.

ventures. However, aside from the cost of breeding stock, llamas and alpacas do not require much acreage per animal (2.5 acres can support 10 animals in most locations), can perform well on marginal pasture with some supplemental feed, and do not require special fencing or facilities for handling. Barbed wire is not recommended, and if threatened these animals can jump over five feet. According to the International Llama Registry website, there are over 159,000 llamas registered in the United States to 28,000 owners, indicating that relative animal numbers per operation are low. Figures from the 2002 United States Census of Agriculture show a total of just under 145,000 llamas owned by 18,000 operations; therefore, the industry is seeing growth in numbers. Numbers of llamas were not individually reported in the 1997 Census of Agriculture, thus demonstrating the increasing popularity of these animals. The Alpaca Registry, Inc. website states that in the 1980s, the first 10 alpacas to reside outside of zoos were imported to North America, and by 2005, there were around 80,000 alpacas in the United States. Today there are 102,000 registered alpacas in the United States; therefore, alpacas are becoming a more common

agricultural enterprise, and have been included in the 2007 United States Census of Agriculture, results from which are not currently available.

While both llama and alpaca meat is consumed for human food in their native South America, there is no market for this type of meat in the United States. These animals are viewed as companion animals; therefore, there are negative feelings regarding such consumption. This leaves a void for animals that are not suitable for breeding. While alpacas are only used for fiber production or breeding purposes, llamas are also utilized as pack/cart-pulling animals, companion and pet therapy animals, and as guardians of other livestock such as sheep and goats; however, there are still limited numbers of animals needed to perform in these capacities, and the marketing of animals not suitable for breeding is an issue which these industries must face. Nevertheless, llama and alpaca enterprises are experiencing growing popularity in rural America, and allow individuals to produce a livestock product on limited acreage.

Bison Production

Bison production is seen as a sustainable agriculture practice, especially in the rangelands of western North America where they once roamed as enormous herds. Production of these animals in their native range and as antibiotic- and hormone-free animals is a niche in which some producers are finding a suitable market. In 2002, there were an estimated 232,000 bison farmed in the United States. Since then the number of bison processed under federal inspection has increased (up 21 percent in 2006), and consumer demand for bison meat grew by 17 percent in 2005, as stated on The National Bison Association's website. In 1993, the North American Bison Cooperative was formed, and this cooperative operates the only USDA and EU approved processing plant for bison. While federal inspection of bison meat for public sale is not mandatory, there is a voluntary program in which producers can participate. Meat that is state inspected is allowed to be sold interstate, but local and state laws may limit the number of markets in which it can be sold. Therefore, an advantage exists when producers market federally inspected bison meat products.

Bison require more acreage per animal than deer, llamas or alpacas. Beginning producers should stock bison in numbers comparable to beef cattle. In time, producers may find that the acreage will support more animals and can subsequently increase the stocking density. Fencing for bison does differ from that used for cattle. While some individuals use very sturdy cattle fencing, most prefer a taller, stronger fence to maintain bison. This is of particular importance with perimeter fencing, as bison are not as easily herded and returned to their home pastures as are cattle. Fences for bison should be at least six feet high, and are often electric. It is important to remember that bison are not domestic animals, do not behave as domestic animals, and must be handled with care. Handling facilities, therefore, differ from those utilized to work cattle, and must be stronger and taller than even the pasture fences used to contain the bison. Recommended handling facilities consist of solid, seven-foot-high sides, and must allow handling to occur with people on the outside. Further recommendations for bison handling can be reviewed on Dr. Temple Grandin's website.

Other Specialized Livestock Production

A variety of other animals are represented in specialized livestock production including ratites (ostrich, emu and rhea), bees, rabbits, alligators and other forms of aquaculture, muskoxen and yak. All of these animals will be included as individual entities in the final report of the 2007 United States Census of Agriculture. Some animals, such as muskoxen and reindeer are reported only regionally for several states in the Northwest, including Alaska. Production of these animals is limited, but regionally important enough to be included in the census. In other states, reindeer are included with other deer. Production of ratites is reported along with poultry. This industry has suffered from high expenses to purchase breeding stock without a well-developed market for the subsequent product (eggs, meat and oil). Emu and ostrich numbers were 48,000 and 20,500, respectively, in the 2002 United States Census of Agriculture after being included in an "other poultry" category in 1997. Prices for breeding stock have dropped considerably, and ratites slaughtered and processed for human consumption must be processed under federal inspection if sold through interstate or international markets. As such, there has been an increase in the number of slaughtering facilities. Colonies of bees maintained in 2002 were 2,300,000, down from 2,500,000 in 1997, with a subsequent drop seen in the pounds of honey sold. Similarly, there was a drop in the number of rabbits from well over 500,000 in 1997 to just over 400,000 in 2002. While rabbit meat can be very popular in upscale restaurants, there is not a large market established for the commodity product, and processing of meat for public sale can be a challenge as regulations vary depending upon the individual state, and in some cases, county. Production of mink and their pelts also decreased slightly during this period.

The aquaculture industry is increasing in the United States, and in 2005 the second United States Census of Aquaculture was conducted. At that time, there were a reported 4,300 operations, up from just over 4,000 in 1998. These operations were reported in 49 states, and had estimated sales in 2005 of over $1 billion. While not typically thought of as an agricultural enterprise, aquaculture is a real, farmed industry, and is making an impact in rural communities. To be considered an aquaculture enterprise, there must be some form of control over the rearing process of the animals, some inputs must be made, animals must be individually owned, and harvesting must occur in a controlled environment; therefore, animals that are wild-caught from neutral waters are not considered an aquaculture product. Animals produced in these enterprises range from food to sport to bait fish, include crustaceans, mollusks, alligators, turtles, snails, etc., and are sold at all sizes. Therefore, this industry involves a variety of animals and is seeing popularity as an alternative animal enterprise.

Many options exist for livestock production in rural America that differ from the traditional forms of livestock production. In some cases, these markets are emerging and high-risk; therefore, producers must be well-informed and prepared to withstand some hardships on the way to building a successful enterprise. These specialized production systems offer those living in rural America, who do not want to be involved in traditional livestock production, an opportunity to earn some income from their land while maintaining a close affiliation with animals. Finding suitable uses for acreage in rural communities will be vital to protecting the acreage from development and maintaining the rural landscape. While specialized livestock production will likely never play a primary role in animal agriculture, it will remain an important and viable option for producers considering alternatives to producing commodities from traditional animal species.

— *Trista A. Strauch and Ronald D. Randel*

See also

Dairy Farming; Livestock Industry; Livestock Production; Ranching

References

Anderson, David P., Brian J. Frosch, and Joe L. Outlaw. 2007. *Economic Impact of the United States Cervid Farming Industry.* Research Report 07-4. Agricultural and Food Policy Center, Texas A&M University, 2007.

Gegner, Lance E. *Llama and Alpaca Farming.* Fayetteville, Ark.: ATTRA, 2000.

Gegner, Lance E. 2000. *Bison Production.* Fayetteville, Ark.: ATTRA.

Gegner, Lance E. 2001. *Ratite Production: Ostrich, Emu, And Rhea.* Fayetteville, Ark.: ATTRA.

Grandin, Temple. *Buffalo Handling Requirements.* Temple Grandin. http://www.grandin.com/behaviour/tips/buffalo.html.

Lanier, Jennifer L. and Temple Grandin. *The Calming of American Bison (Bison Bison) During Routine Handling.* Temple Grandin. http://www.grandin.com/references/bison.paper.html.

United States. *2002 Census of Agriculture. 1, Geographic Area Series.* Washington, D.C.: U.S. Dept. of Agriculture, National Agricultural Statistics Service.

United States. [2004-]. *2002 Census of Agriculture. Volume 3. Special Studies, Part 2.* Washington, DC: U.S. Dept. of Agriculture, National Agricultural Statistics Service.

Sport

A competitive physical activity guided by established rules and motivated by a combination of intrinsic and extrinsic rewards. The history of sport in America is examined from the colonial era through the 1800s and into the modern age. Particular attention is given to rural America's historical contributions to sport and the importance of sport for modern rural communities.

Introduction

Sport is a pervasive part of American society. Three levels of sport—informal, organized and corporate—can be distinguished. Informal sport is primarily for the enjoyment of the participants who determine and enforce the rules. Organized sport involves formal organizations (e.g., leagues, teams and sponsors) and a regulatory agency that establishes and enforces rules. The manifest function of organized sport is to benefit participants by promoting physical and mental health and instilling core cultural values. Corporate sport is dominated by economics and politics. Organizations at this level of sport are less concerned with the participants' interests and more concerned with benefiting the consumer (e.g., fans, owners and alumni), generating profits and maintaining a high concentration of power. In general, rural communities are directly involved in informal sport and organized sport and indirectly involved in corporate sport.

Sport can be viewed as a mirror of society that reflects the social structure and the changes society experiences. This is evident in the history of American sport from colonial times to the present as society shifted from a rural, agricultural context to an urban, industrialized context. Guttman (1978) maintains that modern sport did not come into existence until the late 1800s as a result of the industrial revolution and urbanization. Although colonial sport was primarily a rural activity, the evolution of American society shifted the predominate context of sport to urban centers. Nevertheless, sport continues to play an integral role in rural America.

Sport in the Colonial Era

Sport in the colonial era reflected religious influences and living conditions of the colonists. Puritan and Protestant religious influences inhibited sport participation. Lucas and Smith (1978) note, "That everyone should have a calling and work hard at it was a first premise of Puritanism.... Not leisure and enjoyment but activity only served to increase the glory of God." As a result, local laws prohibiting many sporting activities were enacted. The struggle for survival and severe living conditions of the colonists left little time for leisure activities. Further, the sparse population of the frontier inhibited the pursuit of many of the folk games that were part of European culture.

Although officially prohibited in most colonies, certain sporting activities took place during this period. Popular sports included horse racing, footraces, jumping contests, fistfighting, wrestling matches, eye-gouging, shooting matches (rifles and pistols) and hunting contests. The Dutch introduced kolven, a game similar to golf, and gander pulling, a contest in which participants attempted to jerk the head off a live goose. Other sporting activities involving animals were cockfighting and rat baiting (dozens of rats were placed in a ring with a ratting dog and spectators wagered on the number of rats the dog would kill in a specified period of time). Bear baiting (large dogs turned loose on a chained bear) and dog fights were also common recreational sports during this era. Taverns often served as social centers where sporting activities, such as cards, dice, billiards, skittles (a precursor to bowling) and shooting matches took place.

Sport activities were more frequent in areas less influenced by Puritan religious traditions, such as the Southern colonies and the frontier. Sport activities increased during the later years of the colonial period. Most of the sports were informal activities or organized by sponsors such as county fairs, communities and taverns. Sport activities often occurred as part of holiday festivals or during militia training. In the South, the gentry established jockey clubs for thoroughbred horse racing. The wealthy had more time for recreation and could afford to engage in more expensive sports.

Sport in Nineteenth-century America

Sporting activities of the colonists continued after they gained independence. In rural and frontier areas, sport continued to be informal or loosely organized around community festivals. However, American society and sport began to change during this period. Racing became a popular mass entertainment sport with horse racing as one of the biggest attractions. Other racing activities involved trains, sailing boats and steamboats. Promoters, such as railroad companies, organized races to increase profits. Racing events were often scheduled in remote places accessible by rail. Spectators not only paid admission to the event, but also paid to travel on the trains carrying them to the event. Although it was illegal, rail and steamboat companies promoted prize-fighting. Sporting activities increasingly catered to an urban clientele and focused on making profits from sporting activities.

American society experienced a transformation during the mid-1800s as industrialization and urbanization increased. During this transformation, the focus of sport moved from rural areas to urban centers. Informal sport dominated in rural America, but an urban-based corporate sport emerged to dominate the nation's attention.

Baseball epitomized this transformation. Baseball emerged from a variety of games, such as town ball, rounders, and "One Old Cat," played in urban areas like New York City and Boston. Formal rules of baseball became established in 1845 by Alexander Joy Cartwright. Although formal baseball began as an urban, upper-class activity, it soon spread to middle and working classes and rural areas. Professionalism in baseball gradually developed and became concentrated in urban areas. However, many rural communities sponsored baseball teams that played in loosely organized leagues.

Other sports, such as football and basketball, followed a development path similar to that of baseball. They were primarily urban in origin, initially played by middle- and upper-class athletes, and spread to rural areas. However, football and basketball were more strongly linked to college sports. Like baseball, these sports became professionalized around the late 1800s. They were eventually dominated by a corporate sports orientation, and sport organizations and universities increasingly concentrated on the commercial aspects of the activity.

Sport in the Modern Age

The twentieth century witnessed the emergence of the sport hero in American culture, and rural sports made significant contributions by providing many star athletes. Examples of athletes with rural backgrounds starring in baseball include Grover Cleveland Alexander, Ty Cobb, Dizzy Dean, Lefty Grove, Gil Hodges, Carl Hubbell, Walter Johnson, Connie Mack, Mickey Mantle, Roger Maris, Jackie Robinson, and Cy Young. Football stars, such as Red Grange, and famous Olympians, such as Jessie Owens and Jim Thorpe, came from rural areas. Boxing stars, like Jack Dempsey and Joe Louis, had rural origins. Legendary coaches hailing from rural areas include Paul Bear Bryant, John J. McGraw, Branch Rickey, and Adolph Rupp.

The linkage of sport with secondary public education was an important component of rural sport. This linkage developed at the turn of the twentieth century and was aided by two major factors. First, popular collegiate sports were diffused to high schools, first in metropolitan areas, then in rural areas. Second, the population shift from rural to urban areas accelerated during the 1900s, causing disruptions and crisis in rural communities. Local high school sports programs became a source of community identity and cohesion during this period. School sport in rural communities promoted parental, alumni and community support for the school.

Since the 1970s high school sports programs faced numerous issues involving gender equity in boys' and girls' sports programs, pay equity between men and women coaches, rising costs of equipment and travel, and increasing commercialization. The organization of high schools within each state also has been an issue as smaller rural schools were pitted against larger, urban schools in state tournaments. Most states resolved this equity issue by instituting a classification system based on school size. As late as 1996, however, Indiana high school basketball still operated under a single class system.

Little league baseball was established in 1939 with roots in rural America. Carl Stolz of Williamsport, Pennsylvania, organized the league with initial support from Floyd A. Mutchler of Lycoming Dairy Farms. Little league grew from its humble beginnings to sponsor a national tournament in 1948 (Lock Haven, Pennsylvania, defeated St. Petersburg, Florida). Stolz received corporate support for the tournament from the United States Rubber Company, which made a long-term commitment to support the organization after receiving positive publicity. Presently, Little League Baseball, Inc. has more than $11 million in total assets and consists of more than 7,000 leagues with more than 48,000 teams. Most rural communities have a Little League team. Further, there are more than 8,000 international leagues in over 40 countries that are affiliated with Little League Baseball, Inc.

Currently, corporate sport dominates athletics. However, informal sport can be found throughout the nation. Rural areas continue to produce athletes who gain national recognition and superstar status. Although the future of sport will most likely continue to be dominated by urban-based corporate sport organizations, rural sport will continue to be an important component of rural communities. From high school sports to Little League, community-based softball leagues, Pop Warner League football, tennis, swimming and other athletic activities, sport will continue to provide recreation opportunities in rural areas and serve as a source of rural community identity and pride.

— *Duane A. Gill*

See also
Community, Sense of; Culture; Educational Curriculum; Gambling; Games; History, Rural; Horse Industry; Recreational Activities; Stock Car Racing

References

Eitzen, D. Stanley and George H. Sage. *Sociology of North American Sport*. Dubuque, IA: Wm. C. Brown, 1993.

Fine, Gary Alan. *With the Boys: Little League Baseball and Preadolescent Culture*. Chicago, IL: University of Chicago Press, 1987.

Guttman, A. *From Ritual to Record: The Nature of Modern Sports*. New York, NY: Columbia University Press, 1978.

Krout, John Allen. *Annals of American Sport, The Pageant of America Series*. New Haven, CT: Yale University Press, 1929.

Lucas, John A. and Ronald A. Smith. *Saga of American Sport*. Philadelphia, PA: Lea and Febiger, 1978.

Radar, Benjamin G. *American Sports: From the Age of Folk Games to the Age of Televised Sports*. Englewood Cliffs, NJ: Prentice-Hall, 1990.

Nover, Douglas A. and Lawrence E. Ziewacz. *The Games They Played: Sports in American History, 1865-1980*. Chicago, IL: Prentice-Hall, 1983.

Spears, B. and R.A. Swanson. *History of Sport and Physical Activity in the United States*. Dubuque, IA: Wm. C. Brown, 1979.

Twombly, Wells. *200 Years of Sport in America: A Pageant of a Nation at Play*. New York, NY: McGraw-Hill, 1976.

Stock Car Racing

A form of automobile racing using modified standard American cars on oval, usually paved, tracks. Beginning as speed competitions among moonshine runners, stock car racing developed into a nationally recognized American sport in the middle of the twentieth century. Bill France spearheaded the National Association for Stock Car Auto Racing in 1948, organizing and legitimizing the races. Professional drivers make it a family affair, involving several generations. The mostly Southern sport courted corporate sponsorship from the beginning and attracts fans from throughout the country.

From Moonshine Runs to Race Tracks

Stock car racing, born in the delivery of moonshine liquor in the 1930s and raised by Bill France in the National Association for Stock Car Auto Racing (NASCAR), brought the thrill of driving fast cars to rural southeasterners. Using only American-made standard or stock cars modified for racing, the blue-collar, predominantly Southern drivers prove which car is fastest on dirt and paved race tracks. Corporate sponsors watch the cars circle the track as rolling advertising billboards for their products. Stock car racing became the fastest growing spectator sport, encompassing drivers and fans from other regions and economic classes.

On the back roads of the Deep South and mountain roads of Appalachia, young men delivered moonshine liquor to the Piedmont and Tidewater Flatlands during the 1930s. The hardscrabble existence in the mountain regions afforded the residents few opportunities. The soil supported few cash crops besides corn and grain. Converting them into moonshine liquor made these crops easier to haul to market than the bulky harvest. Despite the federal government's insistence on controlling liquor production through taxation, the local, independent-minded moonshiners continued to produce their wares with a free-enterprise mentality; they believed it their right to make a living as they had been for years. To outrun and outmaneuver local sheriffs and the federal revenue agents determined to stop the flow of untaxed alcohol, the drivers modified and improved their cars' performance. Junior Johnson and Curtis Turner became legends for their skill in implementing a "bootleg turn"—rapidly reversing the direction of their speeding car. Johnson once commented, "I always think someday I'm gonna look in my mirror on the race track and see a flashing blue light. I got caught at the still [in 1955]. I never got caught on the road. They never outrun me" (Wilkinson, 1983; Bledsoe, 1975). The competitive daredevil drivers, proud of their driving ability and cars, inevitably began to race each other to prove who had the fastest car.

From one-on-one speed contests on back roads, in cow pastures, and clearings, the participants moved to old fairgrounds and horse racing tracks. Throughout the 1930s and early 1940s, racing remained a local event, often disorganized and run by shady promoters who sometimes absconded with the gate receipts before the race ended. The racing boom exploded with returning World War II veterans. The red clay in the foothills of the Appalachian and Blue Ridge Mountains offered an excellent natural racing surface. Farmers easily cut out a quarter- or half-mile oval, hammered together wooden grandstand seating, and created a racetrack.

Bill France Creates NASCAR

The home of land-speed racing, Daytona Beach, Florida, became the site of the first organized and sanctioned stock car race in March 1936 when the American Automobile Association, the owner of the timing equipment, sponsored a race of a specified length and specific purse. Sig Haughdahl, a motorcycle and car racer, cut two passes through the sand dunes to form an oval beach road course for the race. Although it failed because of the deep sand and infighting among the local politicians, one of the drivers, Bill France, Sr., saw the potential; within two years he promoted races over the beach course. Drivers from as far away as the red clay ovals of Atlanta, Georgia, traveled to Daytona Beach to race, often generating more excitement along the way than when they arrived. France continued to hold weekend races; his vision, along with several other racers and promoters, created NASCAR in the 1940s to bring the sport respectability and profit.

In December 1947, Bill France, Sr. and Bill Tuthill, a promoter of midget car and motorcycle races, called a meeting with other promoters in the lounge of the Streamline Hotel in Daytona Beach, Florida, to discuss organizing stock car racing. Within two months, France and Tuthill drafted the plan for NASCAR, a name suggested at the December meeting by Red Voght, an early builder of some of the fastest Atlanta stock cars. France brought in one of his service station's customers, attorney Louis Ossinsky, to handle legal issues and problems. They incorporated NASCAR on February 21, 1948, with France holding 50, Tuthill 40, and Ossinsky 10 shares of stock. NASCAR set and enforced rules, ensured that promoters paid purses, paid bonuses to top drivers based on a points-earned system, and sought insurance for drivers. The first year began slowly with only nine races, mostly promoted by France. The following year France's novel idea to hold a new car race catapulted stock car racing into the popular sport for which he had hoped.

The new race used regular cars directly from the showrooms, thus the term *stock*. Spectators finally were able to see which American-made cars that the average person drove were the fastest. The fans could more easily identify with the Fords, Chevrolets, Pontiacs, Hudsons, and Plymouths, among others, than the nondescript modified lightweight cars with big engines previously run in stock car races. The June 19, 1949, race on a Charlotte, North Carolina, 0.75-mile dirt track attracted over 13,000 paying fans and instituted NASCAR's Grand National Division. This track evolved into the Charlotte Motor Speedway, a 1.5-mile track completed in 1960. In neighboring South Carolina, Harold Brasington, a construction worker and heavy-equipment owner, built an Indianapolis 500-type oval, 1.25-mile speedway for stock cars in Darlington in the summer of 1950. To overcome the deep sand that bogged down the cars on the Daytona Beach course, France built a 2.5-mile triangular oval off the beach where he staged what would become, after the Indianapolis 500, the second most-attended car race—the Daytona 500.

Bill France, as president of NASCAR, made stock car racing a national sport. To protect his brainchild, France courted politicians to prevent interference with his tracks and to thwart unfavorable legislation that might ban racing. As a self-styled, benevolent dictator, he kept the reputation of the sport uppermost, often to the disgruntlement of owners and drivers seeking an edge. When one car manufacturer modified a model to gain an advantage, France placed restrictions on it to bring all cars back to parity. Driver Bobby Allison, often frustrated with constantly changing rules, recognized that "Big Bill knew there were a lot of people who wanted to see those cars on the track, and he knew that having them look like the ones at home in the driveway was important. He made the rules where there wasn't anyone who could run away and hide. Another thing he did was keep the rules where it didn't take a young fortune to get started." But France also ruled with an iron fist. Allison remarked, "There were no arguments, no back talk, no nothing. If you were going to race in NASCAR, you were going to do it his way and not say anything until you were asked" (Glick, 1992). In the 1950s when Curtis Turner and Tim Flock tried to form a drivers' union, France suspended them from NASCAR racing for four years. When France retired as president of NASCAR in 1972, his son Bill France, Jr. assumed control of the organization. The elder France continued as the head of International Raceway Corporation that operates Daytona International Speedway and Alabama International Motor Speedway at Talladega (the 2.66-mile track constructed in 1969) until his death in 1992. When Bill France, Jr. died in June 2007, his son, Brian, became chairman and CEO, continuing the family dynasty.

The Drivers

Until stock car racing succeeded in Daytona when blue-collar, working-class White men entered stock car racing as owners, drivers, mechanics and fans, upper-class men dominated motor sports in America. As the sport branched out from the South, drivers from Northern and Western states began to win their share of races. Except for Wendell O. Scott, who raced full-time between 1949 and 1973, African Americans lack a presence in NASCAR. Women remain on the sidelines, unlike drag racing's driver Shirley Muldowney and Indy Racing League's Danica Patrick, as relatives or race queens; the male network does not support women drivers or mechanics.

The mainstay of NASCAR remains the tiers of racing which bring the sport to short dirt tracks (for the Modified, Sportsmen, and other lesser divisions) near small, rural towns in the South (like the old three-eighths-mile clay Lanier Raceway in north Georgia), short paved tracks under one mile (like Richmond), and to the speedways of Charlotte and Atlanta for the Winston Cup Grand National Circuit. From more than 50 races a year, NASCAR pared down the annual races to 30 to 33 in 11 divisions. Fans in Martinsville, Virginia; Jennerstown, Pennsylvania; Loudon, New Hampshire; and Indianapolis, flocked to what NASCAR claims is the fastest growing spectator sport in America. The France family-run organization fosters loyalty from the drivers who earn bonuses in special NASCAR programs. Successful drivers such as Richard Petty and Darrell Waltrip never considered racing Formula One cars in the Indianapolis 500; Cale Yarborough and Bobby Allison briefly attempted to cross over to Formula One but soon returned to stock car racing.

NASCAR is a family affair in more than its organizational control. Three generations of the Petty family—father Lee, his son Richard, and grandson Kyle—successfully raced stock cars. Other racing families include the Bodine brothers (Geoff, Brett and Todd), fathers and sons Ralph and Dale Earnhardt, Ned and Dale Jarrett, and brothers Terry and Bobby Labonte, Dale and Michael Waltrip, and Rusty and Mike Wallace. Kyle Petty remarked that since racing is a time-consuming sport, with racing from February through the middle of November and building and testing cars in January, "If you're going to hang out with your family, you have to hang out at a racetrack. So when you grow up in that environment and look for something for your children, you say: 'Well, it wasn't too bad when I was growing up; it can't be too bad for them, either.' So you bring them along" (Denlinger, 1995).

The sport also attracts families as fans. As the race car craze outgrew its Southeastern roots, Northern, Midwestern, and Western middle-class families flocked to the racetracks and televised coverage. Compared with other sports heroes, stock car drivers make themselves accessible to their fans for autographs, pictures and personal contact. The fans, in turn, root not for a particular car, but its driver. They identify with the human in control rather than the brand-name of the car or its sponsors.

Sponsors

Long before baseball erected billboards or colleges sought corporate tie-ins, stock car racing depended on sponsors to underwrite the costs of running the expensive machines. In exchange for financial support, the owners emblazon corporate logos on the cars and drivers' uniforms. Initially supported by beer and tobacco companies such as R.J. Reynolds, which lends its product name to NASCAR's primary series, the Winston Cup, stock car racing appealed to other corporate sponsors who recognized the advertising potential in having their product visible on every lap of a televised race. Sponsors include McDonald's, Budweiser, Valvoline, and their product competitors Burger King, Miller Genuine Draft, and Pennzoil. Even country music performers see the benefit of sponsoring a rolling billboard.

When R.J. Reynolds backed the sport in 1971, Bruton Smith saw a wise investment future in stock car racing. He developed the Charlotte Motor Speedway into a well-respected, and perhaps the finest, racing oval in the country. Smith constructed condominiums overlooking the track in 1984. When he purchased the Atlanta Motor Speedway in 1990, he vowed to convert it into a world-class speedway and attract fans from the over three million people in the countryside surrounding Atlanta and return NASCAR to its roots in the Atlanta area.

— *Susan Hamburger*

See also
Community Celebrations; Recreational Activities; Sport; Tourism, Ecotourism

References
Black, James T. "The South's Fastest Sport." *Southern Living* (May 1990): 12-14.

Bledsoe, Jerry. *The World's Number One, Flat-Out, All-Time Great, Stock Car Racing Book.* Garden City, NY: Doubleday, 1975.

Chapin, Kim. *Fast as White Lightning: The Story of Stock Car Racing.* New York, NY: Dial Press, 1981.

Denlinger, Ken. "NASCAR and the Crew." *Washington Post* (August 1, 1995): C1 and 3.

Glick, Shav. "France: Benevolent Dictator." *Los Angeles Times* (June 12, 1992): C2.

Pillsbury, Richard. "A Mythology at the Brink: Stock Car Racing in the American South." *Sport Place International* 3 (1989): 2-12.

"Scott Legacy: Overcoming Racism." *Atlanta Journal and Constitution* (December 25, 1990): E-12.

Wilkinson, Sylvia. *Dirt Tracks to Glory; The Early Days of Stock Car Racing as Told By the Participants.* Chapel Hill, NC: Algonquin Books, 1983.

Substance Abuse

Use of a substance that produces impairment or distress; can result from the use of illicit (e.g., cocaine, heroin) or licit (i.e., prescribed sedatives, stimulants, opioids) substances. This article overviews the epidemiology of substance abuse in rural areas and highlights two substances that currently present specific and substantial threats to rural areas: methamphetamine or "meth" and prescription opioids, particularly OxyContin® or "Oxy." Specific aspects that contribute to or protect from substance abuse in rural areas will also be briefly discussed.

There has been an increase in focus on substance abuse in rural America in recent years. This focus has been driven largely by reports in the popular media surrounding "epidemic" levels of substance abuse, particularly methamphetamine and prescription opioids, in rural areas. While data from the Substance Abuse and Mental Health Services Administration (SAMHSA) indicate that prevalence of substance abuse is lower in non-metropolitan areas than in metropolitan areas, dramatic increases in the incidence of reported substance abuse as well as in substance abuse treatment admissions have been observed in rural areas of the United States. SAMHSA data also indicate that substances are more likely to be injected in non-metropolitan areas than in metropolitan areas. Rural drug abusers entering treatment report high rates of lifetime alcohol use (which exceeds 80 percent by some estimates) and unacceptably high rates of other drug use, particularly opioids (which exceeds 25 percent by some estimates) and amphetamines (which exceeds 15 percent by some estimates). These data suggest that substance abuse is a growing rural problem, which may be associated with increased risk for disease transmission *via* injection drug use.

Methamphetamine or "Meth"

Methamphetamine is a psychomotor stimulant that produces its effects by promoting the release of dopamine, serotonin and norepinephrine in the brain. When abused, methamphetamine is generally taken intranasally, smoked or injected. The prevalence of methamphetamine abuse nationwide has been increasing, progressing from Western states into the East, with rural areas showing particular susceptibility to methamphetamine abuse. While it was initially smuggled into the United States from Asia to Hawaii and from Mexico to California, it is now commonly "cooked" or made locally, most often using a hazardous and dangerous process called "pseudoephedrine reduction." This methamphetamine production technique is passed on from one person to the next and/or using reference sources such as books or the Internet. This "cooked" methamphetamine is often called "crank." Although pharmaceutical-grade methamphetamine is available by prescription to treat narcolepsy, obesity and attention-deficit hyperactivity disorder, the large majority of methamphetamine abused comes from these cooking techniques or is smuggled into the United States. The active ingredient in both pharmaceutical and "cooked" methamphetamine is the same; however, "cooked" methamphetamine is also likely to contain toxic adulterants, which may lead to other physical health complications.

The proliferation of local production techniques has likely contributed to the increased prevalence of methamphetamine abuse in rural America. "Cooking" methamphetamine may be easier in rural than urban areas and bypasses the need for transportation of the drug into rural areas. Methamphetamine can be "cooked" in homes or vans, on farms, or in small spaces using common household items like iodine, lye, anhydrous ammonia and pseudoephedrine. These ingredients are available in rural areas, particularly anhydrous ammonia, which is an agricultural fertilizer. Consequently, rural areas are particularly well suited for manufacturing "meth" inexpensively in small, clandestine labs, although specific point-prevalence data are not available regarding levels of methamphetamine use in rural America.

Three recent developments may have discouraged the prevalence of methamphetamine production, although their influence on methamphetamine abuse is not known. First, enforcement activities have increased for locating and closing local methamphetamine laboratories. The number of "busts" of methamphetamine laboratories increased sharply with resource allocation. Currently, though, it is important to note that the number of "busts" has actually decreased, giving the impression that local "meth" production and use are also decreasing. Second, production of methamphetamine has shifted from local laboratories that are only capable of producing small batches of "meth" to "superlabs" that can produce much more in a single reaction. These "superlabs" may decrease local production, but may actually increase availability of "cooked meth." Third, legislation has been passed to limit the availability of a key ingredient in the methamphetamine production process, pseudoephedrine. This legislation was aimed at decreasing local production; however, methamphetamine can be manufactured using another reaction with phenylactone and methylamine, which was the original production method before pseudoephedrine reduction became popular. Researchers have also speculated that it is only a matter of time before creative "cookers" develop a chemical reaction to manufacture methamphetamine using unregulated ingredients.

Regardless of the influence of these factors on "meth" availability and abuse, recent research has highlighted the prevalence and impact of methamphetamine use in rural America (Booth et al., 2006; Garrity et al., 2007; Grant et al., 2007; Sexton et al., 2006; Stoops et al., 2005). For example, Stoops and colleagues found that non-urban drug court clients are over two times more likely than urban drug court clients in Kentucky to report methamphetamine abuse in their life. In a study of rural stimulant users, Booth and colleagues and Garrity and colleagues demonstrated that rural "meth" users in a number of states are more likely to have criminal justice involvement but may have fewer physical health complications compared to rural cocaine users. Grant and colleagues extended these findings and showed that rural individuals reported earlier initiation of regular methamphetamine use, more alcohol use disorders, more intravenous methamphetamine use, and greater methamphetamine-induced psychotic symptoms than urban individuals. Each of these factors is associated with poor treatment outcomes and may complicate treatment processes. This is particularly important because, as described in the final section below, treatment for substance abuse in rural areas is limited and may not be suited to address the complications associated with methamphetamine abuse in rural individuals.

A final important consideration is the great hazard posed by "cooking" methamphetamine; a report by Sexton and colleagues shows that the process is often associated with accidents that may be exacerbated by "cooking" while high and results in multiple toxic waste products. So, while "meth" abuse presents a significant problem to rural areas, production also can have a devastating effect.

Prescribed Opioids or "Oxy"

Prescribed opioids, including OxyContin®, Lortab®, Vicodin®, or Dilaudid®, are analgesic drugs that are scheduled by the U.S. Food and Drug Administration because of their significant potential for abuse. Although the active ingredients vary, prescription opioids are generally a combination of a synthetic, semi-synthetic, or natural opioid (e.g., oxycodone, hydrocodone or codeine) and a non-steroidal anti-inflammatory drug (e.g., ibuprofen, acetaminophen or naproxen). One exception to this combination is OxyContin®, which is a controlled-release formulation of oxycodone alone that has received particular attention for its abuse in rural areas. When abused, prescription opioids are generally taken orally, intranasally or intravenously. It is important to note that a significant number of individuals who abuse prescription opioids started out with a legitimate prescription or got their prescribed opioids from a family member or friend with a legitimate prescription before developing prescription opioid abuse.

Prescription opioid abuse is an increasing problem in the U.S. Data from the 2006 National Survey on Drug Use and Health indicate that 5.2 million Americans had illicitly used a prescription opioid in the past month. This number represents an increase of 500,000 people from 2005, and data from individuals aged 18-25 indicate that the number reporting illicit use of prescription opioids in the past month increased from 4.1 percent in 2002 to 4.9 percent in 2006, a faster rate than for the population in general. Importantly, national rates of illicit prescription opioid use are higher than those for heroin, cocaine or methamphetamine and are exceeded only by marijuana. Moreover, the number of individuals initiating illicit use of prescription opioids was greater than that for marijuana in 2004 and 2005. As with "meth," specific point-prevalence data are unavailable regarding prescription opioid use in rural America, but these drugs have been cited as threats in rural states by both the popular media and the National Drug Intelligence Center.

Several efforts have been made to decrease the level of prescription opioid abuse. For example, states have begun limiting the availability of online pharmacies that provide prescription opioids to reduce supply. Another way to limit supply is electronic prescription reporting programs. These electronic programs identify physicians who commonly prescribe drugs of abuse or patients who inappropriately fill prescriptions for drugs of abuse. One such program is the National All Schedules Prescription Electronic Reporting System (NASPER). Formulations that limit misuse can also be developed to prevent and decrease prescription opioid abuse and dependence. For example, oral prescription opioid tablets could be formulated with naloxone, an opioid antagonist with limited absorption following oral administration. When taken as prescribed, naloxone would remain inactive. However, if the prescription opioid were used by a route other than oral (e.g., injected), the naloxone would block the abuse-related effects and could precipitate withdrawal in individuals who are physically dependent. This formulation approach has been used for buprenorphine (Suboxone®), a drug used in the treatment of opioid dependence, to prevent misuse. Lastly, therapy for prescription opioid abuse has been developed specifically for use in rural areas using a multimodal treatment regimen that relies on rural traditions of oral history by using "talking" to develop solutions to problem situations that might result in drug use or risky behavior.

Like methamphetamine, recent research has also examined the prevalence and impact of prescription opioid abuse in rural America (Leukefeld et al., 2007; Havens et al., 2007a; Havens et al., 2007b). This series of studies has demonstrated that opioid abuse is highly prevalent in rural areas relative to urban areas, that opioids are commonly taken intravenously by rural individuals, and that rural individuals begin abusing opioids from both recreational and legitimate entry points (i.e., starting with a prescription for pain).

Factors That Affect Rural Substance Abuse

It is apparent that substance abuse in rural areas is associated with factors that complicate treatment. For "meth" and "oxy," abuse of these drugs by rural individuals is associated with other drug use and psychological disorders. "Meth" and "oxy" abuse treatment vary, but both require a considerable amount of time and resources. For example, if an individual who abuses opioids is physically dependent, he or she must undergo detoxification. Detoxification can be costly and may require hospitalization for three to seven days, presenting an onerous burden on rural individuals who may not have the money to pay, may not be able to take time off from work, or may not have transportation or the ability to travel to treatment. Both methamphetamine and opioid abuse have been shown to benefit from various counseling techniques like cognitive-behavioral therapy, which can also be expensive, and counselors may not be geographically close to individuals who need them. Finally, medications (pharmacotherapies) have been developed to treat opioid abuse. These pharmacotherapies all require monitoring by a physician, who, like counselors, may not be geographically close.

Access to treatment for substance abuse like detoxification, counseling or pharmacotherapy is already insufficient in rural areas due to cost and geography; when complicated by psychological disorders, other substance abuse, or risky drug use practices, treatment requirements for substance abuse in rural areas overtax the options that are available. Limited law enforcement resources in rural areas may also result in an inability to control the sales and production of abused substances, making these areas targets for those individuals who would seek to sell drugs in an environment with decreased risk of criminal justice intervention.

The characteristics of rural areas are not solely contributors to risk for substance abuse, however. Rural areas also have characteristics that may protect against substance abuse. For example, the close-knit nature of rural communities, focus on family life, and increased levels of religiosity can serve to discourage substance abuse. Moreover, the isolated nature of certain rural areas may prohibit availability of substances of abuse. Unfortunately, as technology and development have made rural areas more accessible and provided a number of opportunities to rural America, the impact of these protective characteristics on substance abuse may have eroded.

Summary

Substance abuse is a grave problem facing rural areas of America. Substance abuse is increasing in rural areas and certain substances, methamphetamine ("meth) and prescription opioids ("oxy"), create particular concern. Methamphetamine and prescription opioid abuse are associated with other rural problems like polysubstance abuse (i.e., combining drugs), risky drug-taking behaviors associated with HIV and Hepatitis C, and psychological disorders. Rural characteristics may complicate substance abuse even further because of limited treatment and law enforcement resources. Other rural characteristics may serve to "combat" substance abuse, however. Treatment options and enhanced law enforcement as well as community resources are needed to address the growing substance misuse in rural areas.

— *William W. Stoops, Jamieson L. Duvall, and Carl G. Leukefeld*

See also

Addiction; Adolescents; Marijuana; Mental Health; Methamphetamine Use; Policy, Health Care; Public Services

References

Booth, Brenda M., Carl G. Leukefeld, Russel Falck, Jichuan Wang, and Robert Carlson. "Correlates of Rural Methamphetamine and Cocaine Users: Results from a Multistate Community Study." *Journal on Studies of Alcohol* 67 (2006): 493-501.

Garrity, Thomas, F., Carl G. Leukefeld, Robert G. Carlson, Russel S. Falck, Jichuan Wang, and Brenda M. Booth. "Physical Health, Illicit Drug Use, and Demographic Characteristics in Rural Stimulant Users." *Journal of Rural Health* 23 (2007): 99-107.

Grant, Kathleen M., Stephanie Sinclair Kelley, Sangeeta Agrawal, Jane L. Meza, James R. Meyer, and Debra J. Romberger. "Methamphetamine Use in Rural Midwesterners." *The American Journal on Addictions* 16 (2007): 79-84.

Havens, Jennifer R., Carrie B. Oser, Carl G. Leukefeld, J. Matthew Webster, Steven S. Martin, Daniel J. O'Connell, Hilary L. Surratt, and James A. Inciardi. "Differences in Prevalence of Prescription Opiate Misuse Among Rural and Urban Probationers." *The American Journal of Drug and Alcohol Abuse* 33 (2007a): 309-317.

Havens, Jennifer R., Robert Walker, and Carl G. Leukefeld. "Prevalence of Opioid Analgesic Injection among Rural Nonmedical Opioid Analgesic Users." *Drug and Alcohol Dependence* 87 (2007b): 98-102.

Leukefeld, Carl, Cynthia Brown, James Clark, Theodore Godlaski, and Ron Hays. *Behavioral Therapy for Rural Substance Abusers.* Lexington, KY: University Press of Kentucky, 2000.

Leukefeld, Carl, Robert Walker, Jennifer Havens, Cynthia A. Leedham, and Valerie Tolbert. "What Does the Community Say: Key Informant Perceptions of Rural Prescription Drug Use." *Journal of Drug Issues* 37(2007): 503-524.

Robertson, Elizabeth B., Zili Sloboda, Gayle M. Boyd, Lulu Beatty, and Nicholas J. Kozel. *Rural Substance Abuse: State of Knowledge and Issues. NIDA Research Mono-*

graph 168. Rockville, MD: United States Department of Health and Human Services, 1997.

Sexton, Rocky L., Robert G. Carlson, Carl G. Leukefeld, and Brenda M. Booth. "Patterns of Illicit Methamphetamine Production ('Cooking') and Associated Risks in the Rural South: An Ethnographic Exploration." *Journal of Drug Issues* 36 (2006): 853-876.

Schoeneberger, Marlies L., Carl G. Leukefeld, Matthew L. Hiller, and Ted Godlaski. "Substance Abuse among Rural and Very Rural Drug Users at Treatment Entry." *American Journal of Drug and Alcohol Abuse* 32 (2006): 87-110.

Stoops, William W., Michele Staton Tindall, Allison Mateyoke-Scrivner, and Carl Leukefeld. "Methamphetamine Use in Nonurban and Urban Drug Court Clients." *International Journal of Offender Therapy and Criminal Counseling* 49 (2005): 260-276.

Sugar Industry

The production of raw sugar cane and sugar beets and its transformation into marketable sweeteners. This entry will address international and U.S. governmental issues related to the sugar industry before focusing on production and processing of sugar cane and sugar beets in the United States. Implications of the industry for labor and the environment are discussed.

Sugar and International Relations

Most sugar produced worldwide is consumed domestically, often at government-controlled prices. A large portion of world sugar trade is conducted under bilateral agreements and preferential terms, such as the European Community's Lomé Convention with ex-colonies in Africa, the Caribbean and Pacific (1975-2000) and currently the Cotonou Convention (2000-2020). As a result, slight shifts in total world production or government policy can have substantial impacts on prices. Governments can block exports in times of scarcity and dump surpluses in times of excess production. Price variability, in turn, increases risk, particularly to producers who do not have mechanisms to smooth price variations. The North American Free Trade Agreement and other free trade agreements in theory have opened up national markets to sugar from treaty signatories, but in fact, U.S. sugar producers strive to export high fructose corn syrup, block sugar imports, and work with corn interests to keep out sugar ethanol from Bra-

zil and other countries that can produce ethanol more cheaply than in the U.S.

The U.S. maintained domestic sugar prices both for producers and consumers at or above world market prices since the mid-1930s, a practice followed in many countries due to the great fluctuation annually in sugar production worldwide. Price maintenance has been accomplished by limiting sugar supplies domestically (through acreage allotments) and internationally.(through tonnage quotas).

U.S. Sugar Legislation

Until the 1900s, sugar tariffs were a major source of revenue for the federal government. Refiners wanted to import raw sugar as cheaply as possible, but imports provided competition for U.S. growers. The Sugar Act of 1934 (also known as the Jones-Constigan Act) was intended to isolate domestic U.S. sugar production from price depressing conditions. The Secretary of Agriculture determined the U.S. sugar consumption requirements each year. Those requirements were divided among U.S. production areas and foreign countries by assigning a quota to each. The 1937 Sugar Act added an import tax. Non-quota sugar, raw or processed, could not be imported. The quota provisions were suspended with World War II and the disruption of normal agricultural production, but were reintroduced after the war through the Sugar Act of 1948. The Act was similar to previous legislation, but provided greater detail; the 1948 Act was amended in 1951, 1956, 1962, 1965 and 1971.

The Food and Agriculture Act of 1977 provided support for the 1977 and 1978 sugar cane and sugar beet crops through loans or purchase over twice the world market price. These loan provisions helped to shift power within the industry from the growers, which was favored under the initial New Deal legislation, to the processors. Loans are made to processors rather than to growers.

The Food Security Act of 1985 mandated a price support program for domestically produced sugar cane and sugar beets at not less than 18 cents per pound. However, the Dole Amendment to the 1985 Farm Bill stipulated that the sugar program must be conducted at no cost to the U.S. Treasury, which meant that no Commodity Credit Corporation (CCC) forfeiture was permitted. The 1996 Farm Bill continued to protect sugar growers, with domestic sugar prices still protected above world market prices. NAFTA, which went into effect January 1, 1994, meant that the protection for sugar was gradually decreased, but not eliminated.

The sugar title in the 2008 Farm Bill determines how U.S. sugar policy is to be conducted. Previously, the U.S. sugar program uses domestic marketing allotments, price supports and tariff-rate quotas to influence the amount of sugar available to the U.S. market. The program's effect has been to support U.S. prices of sugar at levels above world market levels. U.S. sugar users maintain that keeping U.S. sugar prices higher than world levels has made U.S. sugar manufacturers increasingly uncompetitive in domestic and export markets. The U.S. sugar program's effectiveness will be challenged in 2008 when all sweetener trade restrictions with Mexico are removed as part of the North American Free Trade Agreement. A provision in the House version of the 2008 Farm Bill would require the government to buy surplus sugar and sell it to ethanol producers for conversion into fuel alcohol.

Growing Sugar

The majority of sugar production in the U.S. comes from sugar beets, with the proportion from sugar beets increasing from 52 percent in 1980-1981 to 60 percent in 2005-2006. Since 1980, sugar beet production has increased in the upper Midwest—North Dakota and Minnesota—(from 30 percent to 48 percent of all production) and Pacific Northwest (from 17 percent to 20 percent) and declined in the Great Plains (from 20 percent in the early 1990s to 13 percent) and in California and Arizona (from 24 percent to 7 percent). The Great Lakes region's share of an increasing total production has held steady at 10 percent. While sugar beet production increased, the number of farms producing sugar beets declined 29 percent between 1997 and 2002.

Sugar cane is grown in primarily in Florida and Louisiana, with minor sugar cane production in Texas and Hawaii. While sugar cane production has grown in the first three states, in Hawaii, high costs and high land costs led to a reduction in sugar cane production from 8.8 million tons in the early 1980s to two million tons in the 2000s. Sugar cane is now grown on only two islands, Kauai and Maui. Puerto Rico stopped producing sugar cane for sugar in 2002. Sugar cane farms are much larger than sugar beet farms: on average 3.75 times larger in 2002.

The number of farms producing sugar cane declined steadily, particularly in Louisiana. The largest farms are in Florida, averaging 3,339 acres compared to the national sugar cane farm average of 765 acres.

Ownership of sugar cane production is highly concentrated, particularly in Florida, where relatively few landowners, who are also processors, control most of the sugar cane production.

The number of small farms producing sugar cane and sugar beets declined between 1997 and 2002, while the number of large farms increased.

Both sugar beets and sugar cane must be processed immediately after harvest or sucrose content decreases. Thus, sugar beet and sugar cane production is dependent on the presence of processing plants. The total number of sugar beet processing facilities in the U.S. declined from 36 in 1992 to 24 in 2006, leaving Texas, Ohio, Kansas, Washington and Oregon without any sugar beet processing capacity, Nebraska and Colorado with just one plant, and California, which was the major sugar beet producing state in 1992, with two plants. Sugar cane milling capacity has decreased 12 percent since 1992. In 1992-1993, there were 44 sugar cane processing plants on U.S. territory. In 2006, there were 20. Louisiana has the greatest number of processing plants.

Sugar Processing

Sugar processing requires enormous capital investments. Growers cannot process sugar individually except at very inefficient levels. Both cane and beet growers depend on processors not only to add value to their crop, but to sell it as well. Thus, power in the sugar industry is centered in the hands of the extractors and processors. While many growers can produce sugar cane or sugar beets, such production is worthless unless there is a nearby processor. For example, in the Red River Valley of North Dakota and Minnesota, those who are not members of the sugar beet processing cooperative are totally shut out of the profitable sugar beet production.

While the beet sugar that comes from sugar beet processing is refined and ready for use as a food product, U.S. raw cane sugar must be further refined for use as a food ingredient. The number of sugar refiners in the U.S. declined drastically to only eight in 2005. Refining volume declined as the amount of raw sugar imported declined. The major reason for the decline in number of sugar refiners is increasing use of high fructose corn syrup in baking and soft drinks.

U.S. cane costs of production are at least twice as high as the world's lowest cost producers. U.S. beet sugar costs of production are below the world average of all beet sugar-producing countries. However, the world's average beet sugar cost of production is about 75 percent above the average cane sugar cost of production. These sugars remain competitive because of supply limitations. As a result, U.S. costs of producing high fructose corn syrup (HFCS) have been much lower than U.S. sugar production costs.

Labor

Both cane and beet sugar in the U.S. have been labor intensive, although there is increased mechanization to harvest and planting sugar cane and to thin sugar beets. In a few parts of Louisiana and most of Florida, sugar cane is harvested by hand due to the composition of the soil, which will not support large harvesting machinery, such as the combines used in Texas or the bulldozers and cranes used in Hawaii. Cane cutting is dirty, hot, dangerous work. Almost all of the labor used to cut sugar cane is brought into the U.S. by a contractor under special agreement with the Immigration and Naturalization Service using specific laws passed for that purpose. Sugar growers provided powerful pressure in the face of congressional investigation to maintain an immigrant labor stream. Either the contractor or the plantation owner must provide housing for the workers, who must leave the country when their contract is complete or their work is terminated. Workers are reportedly charged for a bewildering number of goods and services provided by their contractors and employers, often reducing their paychecks to nearly nothing.

From 1967 to 2002, cane industry employment dropped by 54 percent and beet processing employment by 50 percent. In 1967, employment in cane refining was 45 percent larger than employment in cane processing; by 2002 employment in the two sectors was about equal. The same trends are seen for production workers and for the annual number of hours for workers engaged in production. Total real wages in 2002 for beet and cane processing were about 57 percent to 59 percent of their level in 1967, while total real wages paid in the refining industry in 2002 were only about 35 percent of their 1967 level. Hourly real wages increased in the beet and cane processing industries but not in the sugar refining sector from 1967 to 2002.

The Environment

Sugar cane is grown in monoculture. This has implications for biodiversity and increased input use; pests become resistant and soils exhausted. Sugar cane is therefore a major user of chemical inputs. Sugar cane monoculture has had negative environmental impacts in the U.S. However, some argue that it is the best agricultural use for the Everglades.

Agricultural pollution as a result of sugar cane production brought about major destruction of the Florida Everglades. There has been excessive phosphorus runoff. Also, the capture of water from the Everglades for sugar cane production decreased the flow of water through the Everglades. The consequences of the externalized environmental impact of sugar cane production threaten many plant and animal species, South Florida's water supply, tourism and fishing. Genetically modified sugar cane is produced in Brazil for use in ethanol production.

Sugar beets, in contrast to sugar cane, are grown in three- to five-year rotations with other crops, reducing their vulnerability to pests. Newly developed genetically modified sugar beets are available, but U.S. sugar beet growers delayed in planting them due to bans in Europe and other countries where the sugar would be exported. The major environmental impact of sugar beets is that they encourage intensive use of inputs. Because they are much more profitable than other crops that can be grown in the area, land prices are driven up. High land costs, in turn, encourage high input use to recoup the increased investment in purchase or rent necessary to gain access to land. As U.S. sugar prices dropped in response to NAFTA, sugar beet farmers decreased their rotations in order to maximize short-term earning.

— *Cornelia Butler Flora*

See also

Labor Force; Trade, International; Genetically Modified Organisms; Corn Industry

References

Alvarez, José. 2005. "Sweetening the US Legislature: The Remarkable Success of the Sugar Lobby." *The Political Quarterly* 76: 92-99.

Economic Research Service. 2008. *Sugar and Sweetener Yearbook*. Tables. http://www.ers.usda.gov/Briefing/Sugar/data.htm (accessed January 27, 2008).

Economic Research Service/USDA. 2006 *Sugar and Sweeteners Outlook*/SSS-245 http://www.ers.usda.gov/Briefing/EuropeanUnion/PDF/EU25SugarPolicySSS245.pdf (accessed January 27, 2008)

Economic Research Service/USDA. 2006 *Sugar and Sweeteners Outlook*/SSS-246. http://www.ers.usda.gov/Briefing/Sugar/sugarpdf/SSS246Mexico.pdf (accessed January 27, 2008)

Flora, C.B. and G. Otero. 1995. "Sweet Neighbors? The State and the Sugar Industries in the United States and Mexico under NAFTA." Pp. 63-74 in *Mexican Sugar-*

cane Growers: Economic Restructuring and Political Options. P. Singelmann (ed.) San Diego: Center for U.S.-Mexican Studies, University of San Diego, Transformation of Rural Mexico, Number 7.

Haley, Stephen and Mir Ali. 2007. Sugar Backgrounder. Washington, D.C.: Economic Research Service/USDA SSS-249-01.

Haley, Stephen and Andy Jerardo. 2007. Sugar and Sweeteners Outlook. Economic Research Service/USDA SSS-250.

Higman, B.W. 2000. "The Sugar Revolution." *Economic History Review.* 53:213-236.

Messina, William A. Jr. and James L. Seale, Jr. "U.S. Sugar Policy and the Caribbean Basin Economic Recovery Act: Conflicts Between Domestic and Foreign Policy Objectives." *Review of Agricultural Economics* 15, no. 1 (January 1993): 167-180.

Wilkinson, Alec. *Big Sugar: Seasons in the Cane Fields of Florida*. New York, NY: Alfred A. Knopf, 1989.

Sustainable Agriculture Movement

Social movements to improve the food and agriculture system. The movement for agricultural sustainability in the U.S. began in the 1970s. However, its origins can be found in movements that began a century earlier, addressing food and farming issues. This article looks at the history of those movements and highlights the most important issues of the sustainable agriculture movement.

Role of Social Movements

Social movements are collective efforts of people to change what they perceive to be a society-wide problem. Throughout human history, change has been brought about by people organizing themselves to correct a perceived injustice or inequity. Social movements are crucial for creating social change by providing analysis of current problems, offering alternatives and mobilizing people to act. For people who do not control major economic resources or have access to formal political power, social movements are crucial for defining how issues and solutions are conceptualized.

The power of social movements lies in their ability to challenge dominant perspectives and priorities by raising new issues and ideas, changing popular consciousness and opening new arenas of public policy. In the U.S., food safety laws, the right to vote, the abolition of slavery, workers' rights to unionize, anti-hunger programs all were brought about by the collective actions of ordinary people working through social movements to solve social problems.

Movement for Agricultural Sustainability

In the case of agriculture, these problems have included pollution of the environment from agricultural practices, poor wages for food and farm workers, and hunger in the midst of plenty of food. The U.S. Department of Agriculture (USDA) recognizes that the problems facing rural America are largely due to social, economic and cultural conditions and cannot successfully be addressed solely through science. This shows the importance of a social movement for sustainable agriculture, since sustainability cannot be achieved through science alone, but requires people acting together to create social change.

Agricultural sustainability is important to all people, regardless of their economic or social class. Because food is essential for human survival—everyone needs to eat to live—the movement for sustainable agriculture is among the most important of our time. The sustainable agriculture movement is a global movement, with groups working toward sustainability in nearly every country of the world. The United Nations' Agenda 21, adopted at the Earth Summit in 1992, promoted sustainable agriculture to meet food needs without further degrading natural resources.

In the U.S., interest in a better food and agricultural system has been featured in the civil rights, free speech and anti-war movements. Food movement activism has included fasts against wars, interracial dining at segregated restaurants and consumer boycotts in support of agricultural workers. More recently the movement for sustainable agriculture has emerged. Initially referred to by different names such as "low-input agriculture," "ecological agriculture," and "organic farming," the term "sustainable agriculture" has emerged as the most prevalent and accepted. Sustainable agriculture means a food and agriculture system that meets people's needs and sustains the environment. It is safe, fair and sound.

Goals of the U.S. Movement for Sustainable Agriculture

In the U.S., the sustainable agriculture movement comprises consumers, farmers, students, researchers, educators, environmentalists, food security activists, policy makers and nongovernmental organizations working together to create a food and agriculture system that is both socially just and environmentally sound. The sus-

Jason Mark, apprentice at the Center for Agroecology & Sustainable Food Systems, harvests crops from organic fields at the University of CA-Santa Cruz. Photo courtesy of the Center for Agroecology & Sustainable Food Systems.

tainable agriculture movement advocates environmentally sound farming methods such as organic farming, which avoids the use of chemical fertilizers and pesticides. It also promotes direct farmer-to-consumer marketing systems such as farmers' markets, community-supported agriculture, and farm-to-school programs. The movement asserts the right of all individuals to eat safe, healthy food regardless of their income. It therefore supports both public programs that support food provision for low-income people and the development of opportunities for people to produce their own food, such as urban agriculture.

Today's sustainable agriculture movement grew from early engagements and concerns about the food system in the U.S. dating back to the 1800s (see Allen, 2004, for a comprehensive history of the movement). These concerns include environmental issues, economic issues, food safety issues and worker issues. These challenges had a social as well as environmental dimension in that they also involved the need to recognize and address the implications of poverty and racism in the production and consumption of food.

Environmental Issues and the Movement for Sustainable Agriculture

As early as the 1800s, the U.S. conservationist movement raised concerns about artificial fertilizers and soil depletion. The impacts of agricultural practices became a concern of the modern environmental movement with the 1962 publication of Rachel Carson's *Silent Spring*, which raised previously unasked questions about harmful effects of pesticides. The organic farming movement, which advocates farming without the use of chemical pesticides and fertilizers, developed rapidly in the 1970s. In the U.S., organizations such as California Certified Organic Farmers, and later the Organic Farming Research Foundation, took on a leading role in promoting both organic practices and certification. Internationally, the International Federation for Organic Agriculture Movements (IFOAM) took the lead.

Interest in and activities around sustainable agriculture grew in the early 1980s, fueled by concerns about resource depletion (such as groundwater overdrafts and soil erosion), environmental contamination (such as pesticides in groundwater), water quality damage through sedimentation, and the loss of wildlife habitat. People became increasingly concerned that the industrial system of agriculture was so damaging to the environment that the ability to produce food at all would be threatened over time.

Although many felt that USDA policies and programs had contributed to environmental problems in agriculture, it was a USDA report on organic farming that provided an important catalyst for the sustainable agriculture movement. This 1980 report showed that food could be produced effectively using organic methods, an assertion that had been contested within the USDA.

Economic Issues and the Movement for Sustainable Agriculture

Another aspect of the agricultural sustainability movement is economic. The sustainable agriculture movement builds on the agrarian populist movement, which addressed issues of the survival of family farms in an era of economic concentration that followed the Civil War. Agrarian populism was revived in the late 1960s in defense of the family farm and rural communities, in opposition to the technological, public-policy and market advantages that large-scale, industrialized agriculture enjoyed over small-scale farming. Then, in the 1980s there was a major economic crisis for farmers. For example, although U.S. farm production was at its highest level in history, 1982 was the worst year for farm income since 1932. Many farmers could not make ends meet and lost their farms. For many years, farmers' share of the food dollar has been decreasing. For every dollar spent on food in the supermarket, farmers receive about 25 cents. The rest goes toward labor, packaging, transportation, processing, advertising and other costs.

Health Issues and the Movement for Sustainable Agriculture

The sustainable agriculture movement advocates healthy and safe food. Movements for healthy and safe food and health also have a long history in the U.S. As early as the 1830s, for example, vegetarians protested public health recommendations for a heavily meat-based diet, and at the end of the nineteenth century, consumers protested the food adulteration that had become part of the industrialization of the food system. Upton Sinclair's 1906 graphic account of the meat-packing industry in his novel *The Jungle* caused an outcry that led to regulations aimed at improving food safety and controlling fraud.

No health issue is more important than having access to food in the first place. Yet many people in America, particularly children and people of color, regularly do not have enough food to eat, much less healthy food such as fresh fruits and vegetables. It was not until the Depression that federal food assistance programs were developed in an attempt to reconcile the paradox of large surpluses of food due to productive agriculture on the one hand and rampant hunger on the other .(Poppendieck, 1995). These early programs focused primarily on the disposal of agricultural surpluses.

Contemporary efforts to end hunger in the U.S. began in the late 1960s when hunger was discovered in America by the Citizen's Crusade Against Poverty's inquiry into the incidence of hunger and malnutrition. Federal "Great Society" programs, beginning with President Johnson's "War on Poverty," provided support for organizing urban communities around basic needs (such as food) and community empowerment. At this time, social programs such as food stamps, school lunches, and supplemental food for women, infants, and children (WIC) were initiated to combat hunger.

Still, in the 1990s many people still did not have enough good food to eat. A group of researchers and food activists got together and came up with the idea of a new approach called "community food security." This is defined as a condition in which, "all persons" obtain "at all times a culturally acceptable, nutritionally adequate diet through local non-emergency sources" (Community Food Security Coalition, 1994). To achieve this goal, community food security efforts focus on a diverse set of strategies that include community food planning, direct marketing, community gardening and urban food production, strengthening food assistance, farmland protection, food retail strategies, and community and economic development. This approach has become part of the movement for sustainable agriculture.

Worker Issues and the Movement for Sustainable Agriculture

Worker rights and safety are also key issues in the sustainable agriculture movement. Agriculture is among the top three most dangerous industries for workers in the U.S. Farm workers are at risk from fatal or disabling injuries from machinery, falls and livestock. Exposure to pesticides can cause acute conditions such as respiratory conditions and flu-like symptoms as well as chronic conditions such as cancer and Parkinson's disease. Injuries and illnesses are compounded by lack of adequate health care amongst farm worker populations. The earliest agricultural labor movements, of course, were the anti-slavery movements. These were followed by movements focusing on migrant workers during the Great Depression. During the Civil Rights movement, struggles for farm worker justice involved a successful inter-ethnic coalition that became the United Farm Workers (UFW) union. In 1962 Cesar Chavez and Dolores Huerta, coming out of backgrounds as community organizers, co-founded the National Farmworkers Association, which would later become UFW. During the 1970s consumers supported the union through a boycott of table grapes and head lettuce, designed to apply pressure for legislation that would give farm workers the right to organize without threat of retaliation. The UFW was successful in part because it was able to organize for justice among urban consumers as well as workers in the fields.

Sustainable Agriculture Movement Organizations

While anyone who advocates and practices eating and farming in ways that are environmentally sound, healthy and socially just is part of the sustainable agriculture movement, there are a number of organizations directly involved in promoting sustainability in the American food and agriculture system. The National Campaign for Sustainable Agriculture is a nonprofit organization created in 1994 to coordinate unified action within the sustainable agriculture movement. The organization is "dedicated to educating the public on the importance of a sustainable food and agriculture system that is economically viable, environmentally sound, socially just, and humane." The Campaign works with regional organizations to analyze policy problems and solutions, increase public participation in sustainable agriculture concerns, and educate the general public about how agriculture is affected by federal policy. The National Campaign is a networking organization, the 113 member organizations of which include family farmers, environmentalists, consumers, and social and economic justice advocates.

Success of the Sustainable Agriculture Movement

Reforming traditional institutions is the primary focus of many social movements, and the sustainable agriculture movement is no exception. One measure of the success of social movements is the extent to which they are able to influence existing authorities and institutions. By this gauge, the movement for sustainable agri-

culture has been extremely successful. Sustainable agriculture programs have been established in the U.S. Department of Agriculture as well as at many of the largest American agricultural universities. For example, over 150 American agricultural universities now have sustainable agriculture programs, while there were very few even a decade ago. In addition, the U.S. Department of Agriculture has a Sustainable Agriculture Research and Education Program and a Community Food Projects Program.

Members of the sustainable agriculture movement also helped to develop a law to label organic food in the U.S. The National Campaign for Sustainable Agriculture and the Community Food Security Coalition joined forces with organic food interests to organize for a Federal Organic Rule. As a result of their efforts, the National Organic Standards Board solicited and received more public input on the organic standards than any previous federal rule (Guthman, 1998). During the four-month public comment period, the U.S. Department of Agriculture received more than 220,000 comments on the rule from producers, consumers, environmentalists and others—the largest public response USDA had received to any proposal in the memories of the people at the USDA. The sustainable agriculture movement led the USDA to develop an organic rule that was palatable to organic farmers and consumers rather than one that catered to industrialized agribusiness.

In addition to working within existing institutions, social movements also work to construct new social forms outside existing institutions that can facilitate the achievement of social-movement goals. These include food policy councils, new marketing forms (e.g., community-supported agriculture and farmers' markets), and new modes of food production (e.g., urban agriculture and organic farming).

The Future of the Sustainable Agriculture Movement

Both the problems in the American food and agriculture system and the social movements meant to ameliorate them have had a long and continuing presence in the U.S. Beginning in the 1800s and culminating in the contemporary sustainable agriculture movement, efforts to collectively resolve problems in the food and agriculture system are gaining in momentum. A government report framed sustainable agriculture as the fourth major era in agriculture (following the horsepower, mechanical, and chemical eras), stating that the effects of this new era could be more profound than those of previous agricultural revolutions.

Agricultural sustainability problems are growing in scale and scope. Global warming in the future will likely exacerbate environmental problems associated with agriculture, and may lead to an even more skewed distribution of food resources between the rich and poor. In response, more and more people are taking leadership in solving these problems through the sustainable agriculture movement and supporting institutions. For example, there are 10 times as many CSAs (community-supported agriculture) today as there were in 1990, and there was a fourfold increase in the number of certified organic crop acreage from 1992 to 2005. The sustainable agriculture movement is essential for the creation of an environmentally sound and socially just U.S. agricultural and food system.

— *Patricia Allen*

See also

Agriculture, Alternative; Agriculture, Sustainable; Agroecology; Sustainable Development; Environmental Sustainability; Social Movements; Organic Farming; Organic Foods Industry; Agricultural Organizations; Permaculture; Sustainable Rural Economics

References

Allen, Patricia. *Together at the Table: Sustainability and Sustenance in the American Agrifood System.* University Park, PA: Pennsylvania State University Press, 2004.

Belasco, Warren J. *Appetite for Change: How the Counterculture Took on the Food Industry, 1966-1988.* New York, NY: Pantheon Books, 1989.

Carson, Rachel. *Silent Spring.* Boston, MA: Houghton Mifflin, 1962.

Gottlieb, Robert. *Environmentalism Unbound: Exploring Pathways for Change.* Boston, MA: MIT Press, 2001.

Poppendieck, Janet. *Sweet Charity? Emergency Food and the End of Entitlement.* New York, NY: Penguin Books, 1998.

Sinclair, Upton. *The Jungle.* New York, NY: Doubleday, Page, and Company, 1906.

Sustainable Development

A normative concept referring to the type of economic, social and environmental change that ought to occur now and in the future. This entry describes the fundamental normative ideas or models guiding sustainable development and discusses them in the context of rural America. The proverbial definition of sustainable development was proposed in 1987 by the World Commission on Environment and Development known as the "Brundtland Report," named after the Commission's Chair Gro Harlem Brundtland. However, this definition is one of myriad definitions often in conflict with each other. To clarify confusion in sustainable development language, it is now customary to differentiate between weak and strong sustainability. These terms are described here in reference to the ecological critique of modern consumer society and reviews the resulting rural sustainable development formulations.

Introduction

Throughout the 1970s and 1980s the term *sustainable development* grew in popularity as a response to the global ecological crisis understood as the problem of sustaining the impact of the world's growing human population on a finite Earth. The international and environmental communities rallied behind this concept, which was defined by the 1987 United Nations' World Commission on Environment and Development (WCED) or Brundtland Report as "development that meets the needs of the present without compromising the ability of future generations to meet their own needs." Subsequently, this definition received global endorsement in 1992 at Rio's Earth Summit through the signing of the United Nations Conference on Development and the Environment (UNCED) Agenda 21 by 178 nations. Signatory nations pledged to implement the action plan at every level (local, regional, national and international), and to assess progress towards sustainable development every five years. Since then, the concept gained worldwide acceptance and adoption by the private, public, nonprofit and non-governmental sectors as well as by regional and multilateral institutions such as the World Trade Organization and the World Bank.

The WCED formulation of *sustainable development* stresses the principle of intergenerational equity, which exhorts current generations to judiciously use natural resources and to care for the environment so that our children and grandchildren may enjoy similar opportunities for development in the future. However, despite its vast acceptance, the ambiguity of the definition leaves room for a great variety of competing and contradictory "green" approaches. It also explains why a wide array of individuals and organizations with seemingly dissimilar interests such as rural residents, ecotourism entrepreneurs, organic farmers, agribusiness and biotechnology corporations, the U.S. Department of Agriculture or even the World Trade Organization make claim to embracing sustainable development. To clarify this paradox, it is necessary to identify the the degree—strong or weak—to which sustainable development formulations buy into and respond to the ecological critique of modern consumer society.

The Ecological Critique of Modern Consumer Society

The ecological critique of modern industrial society and conventional economics rejects equating development with economic growth and places the economy within Earth's biophysical limits. This critique, elaborated in 1989 by Herman Daly and John Cobb in *For the Common Good: Redirecting the Economy toward Community, the Environment and a Sustainable Future*, singles out the rural community and the decline of the family farm as an emblematic casualty of modern economics and agricultural industrialization.

Referring to Walter Goldschmidt's 1946 classic study of two rural California communities—Dinuba, a vibrant community of small farms, and Arvin, a disintegrating rural community dominated by large agribusiness—Daly and Cobb endorse the study's indictment of agricultural industrialization as the annihilator of family farming and the vitality of rural communities.

> Policies following from present [economic] theory work in three interrelated ways: The commitment to productivity reduces the need for farmers and depopulates the rural area. The commitment to profit maximization, with prices not including social and ecological costs, leads to unsustainable use of the land. The commitment to free trade leads to specialized production for export, especially in the tropics, and to inability of rural peoples to feed themselves (Daly and Cobb, 1994)

The critique calls for rethinking traditional economic theory in the service of community and the environment. The resulting alternative economics would aim at generating local, basic self-sufficiency delinked from international trade and focused on the preservation and rebuilding of the American rural community of small family farms (Daly and Cobb, 1994). New economic policies would favor the regeneration of family farms by ending federal agricultural subsidies to agribusiness. To encourage careful husbandry, taxes would shift from income to pollution taxes of ecologically destructive farming practices impacting land, air and water sources.

Strong Sustainable Development

The aforementioned ecological critique is based on a model of *strong sustainability* and steady-state economics, which stresses that humanity cannot be sustained beyond the bounds of nature and that to be sustainable, high resource consumption and waste producing societies must radically restructure their economies to operate within ecological means. This model also rejects the substitutability of nature for manmade goods. It underscores the uniqueness of life-supporting services (i.e., carbon absorption and climate regulation) provided by ecosystems (i.e., forests), which can yield marketable goods (i.e., wood fiber). Instead of seeing these natural assets as substitutable, it sees them as irreplaceable complements of economic assets. Thus, strong sustainable development involves preserving intact for the next generation an undiminished stock of these critical, non-substitutable ecosystems on which human life depends (Rees, 1997). Strong sustainable development is communitarian and democratic in political outlook and emphasizes small scale in settlement, production, technology and leisure. It entails also an ethical commitment to ecological principles and social justice. A strong sustainability approach to rural development fully embraces the ecological critique and the alternative self-reliant community vision.

Although there are formidable challenges to the implementation of a comprehensive rural sustainable development agenda, as envisioned in the strong ecological critique, several think tanks, not-for-profit and non governmental organizations collectively known as third sector organizations (TSOs)—representing coalitions of family farmers, urban consumers and rural communities—have come together to leverage resources aimed at changing Farm Bill public policy. Rather than benefitting primarily large-scale farmers and agribusiness, farm policy shifts pursued by these coalitions entail supporting a new generation of sustainable family farmers, lobbying for fair prices for family farm products, and advocating for health and food safety policies, land and water stewardship and conservation, and rural community regeneration.

The North American *permaculture* (a contraction of permanent agriculture), which is an ecologically principled system of food production, land use and community design for sustainable living, and the *ecovillage movement*, whose members share ecological and spiritual values about living in small-scale communities with minimal ecological impact, are to this day the most salient examples of communitarian strong sustainability approaches. They form part of a larger movement coded "eco-localism." This development approach involves the creation of local, self-reliant, sustainable rural economies involving such activities as food co-ops, micro-enterprises, farmers' markets, community supported agriculture (CSA), community-based renewable energy projects, car sharing and barter systems, co-housing, mutual aid, home-based production, community corporations and banks, and locally-based business alliances (Curtis, 2003; Weinberg, 2000).

Weak Rural Sustainable Development

At the opposite end of the radical ecological critique lies a free-market view of sustainable development, which is fundamentally technocentrist. It subscribes to *weak sustainability's* premise that ecological limits and natural resource scarcities have been historically overcome through technology and trade. For instance, under this view, corn-to-ethanol production is a technological solution to fossil fuel scarcity, and natural resource-poor populations have been able to sustain their economies beyond ecological limits by acquiring natural resources through international trade. Embracing the technological substitutability of natural capital for manufactured capital, weak sustainable development involves passing a non-diminishing stock of both natural and manmade capital from one generation to the next. This is the 1987 WCED's perspective of sustainable growth, which deemed necessary a five- to 10-fold increase in world manufacturing output to alleviate present development inequities between developed and developing nations. Thus, rather than rethinking conventional economics and restructuring the rural economy toward local self-sufficiency, weak sustainable development advocates the greening of economic development through ecological modernization. Ecological modernization is precisely the process that will usher a green industrial revolution. Key elements include: the radical minimization of resource use and pollution and waste generation, the redesign of industry mimicking biological models, and the adoption and diffusion of green technologies that are both profitable and environmentally friendly (Hawken et al., 1999). In addition to transforming business models and production, educating consumers toward adopting green consumption patterns and lifestyles is at the core of this development approach.

Promoting "ecological entrepreneurship" is one goal of rural sustainable development under this perspective. It seeks to minimize the community's ecological footprint by growing a local economy of green business incubators. In addition to promoting sustainable agriculture, key green development strategies pursued in small towns and rural communities include attracting green start-ups from a variety of industries such as construction, energy generation (e.g., wind, solar, biodiesel, biomass) and waste reduction and recycling (e.g., waste-water bioremediation services and new rural recycling businesses).

Sustainable Development at the Rural-Urban Fringe

Protecting the community's environment and quality of life is an equally important goal of sustainable development. While strong sustainability favors a "no growth" approach to rural-to-urban land conversion, weak sustainability adheres to "smart growth"—a catch-all term encompassing a variety of land use policies intended to influence the pattern and density of urban development. It typically favors a growth management approach to rural-to-urban land conversion at the urban fringe. Rural municipalities and counties adopting smart growth initiatives usually include farmland, forestland and watershed protection packages, which utilize zoning, urban growth boundaries and land trusts as means to preserve rural productive landscapes and to protect them from urban encroachment.

These farmland and forest protection schemes have been more successful in strong farming communities than in weak ones. However, given the rapid conversion of farmland to urban land occurring over the last 30 years, local, state and federal governments have started to explore the feasibility of financial incentive programs designed to keep land in agriculture. In theory, these programs pay farmers and landowners for ecological services associated with their operations, such as removal of atmospheric carbon and greenhouse gases absorbed (sequestered) in the soil via conservation tillage or by converting cropland to forest and grassland. Rural amenities, such as scenic beauty, open space and preservation of the "farming way of life," are additional ecological services explored by this type of farmland preservation program, which are popular in fast-growing urban areas of highly urbanized states.

Criticism and Debate

Since 1992, the idea of sustainable development has won almost universal acceptance. However, implementation has been slow and controversial. This is in part due to the debate between weak and strong sustainability proposals, but also to criticism from inside and outside the sustainable development community (Audirac, 1997).

Skeptics of environmental limits dismiss sustainable development altogether as flawed and unnecessary. They see sustainable development as eco-imperialism imposed upon poor people and nations, particularly when activists from industrialized nations, invoking sustainable development and environmental protection, block economic development initiatives, such as needed hydroelectric projects in developing nations. Similarly, southern nations resent sustainable development positions limiting international trade as "green" barriers erected against their exports. They contend that the greatest ecological reforms would need to be made first by the wealthiest countries, since more than 200 years of unsustainable industrial development and consumption patterns of the world's industrialized nations is to blame for the present ecological crisis. Advocates of this view defend the right of developing countries to repeat what today's industrialized nations see as yesterday's mistakes. Others charge that sustainable development policies should emphasize sustainable livelihoods and poverty eradication over environmental protection.

Inside the sustainable development community, critics of weak sustainability, who assert that global limits to growth have been reached and that the present scale of industrial growth is unsustainable, charge that WCED sustainable development policy is oxymoronic. Multiplying the present scale of world industrial output five or 10 times, as proposed by the WCED, would move the planet from current unsustainability to imminent collapse (Daly, 1991). Deep Ecology critics, the most radical ecologists, complain that weak sustainable development does not go far enough in challenging consumer culture and in advocating social equity. At the other extreme, free-market environmentalists, the most conservative devotees of weak sustainability, argue that strong sustainable development policies are unsound. Free markets rather than government regulations are better options to effectively deal with pollution and resource depletion.

Global climate-change science and politics have recently energized sustainable development policy with an emphasis on greenhouse gas emission reduction. The Kyoto Protocol's market in tradable carbon dioxide (CO_2 allowances permits developed countries to meet their emissions reduction commitments by investing in sustainable development projects in developing countries or at home. This is a global green market scheme enjoying growing popularity primarily among utility companies and other high greenhouse gas emitters, who, to offset their greenhouse emissions, are investing in climate-friendly sustainable development programs. Organic farming, which is apparently more climate-friendly than industrial agriculture, along with bio-fuel production (i.e., corn-based ethanol), and methane-capture projects from farm waste are expected to get a boost from carbon trading schemes. However, climate-change science is not unanimous on the causes and effects of global warming, and some scientists who have recently reversed themselves, becoming climate skeptics, have furthered the controversy about global climate and related sustainable development programs.

Conclusion

Two basic types of sustainable development can be identified depending on whether they subscribe to strong or weak sustainability models. Strong sustainable development is inspired by a radical critique of modern economics, industrialization and international trade. It defines development as community-based qualitative change that is socially just and contained within biophysical limits. It focuses on promoting small, ecological self-reliant communities. In contrast, weak sustainable development is free market-oriented and relies on international trade and technological and managerial solutions to natural resource scarcity. The greening of industry, business and consumers through innovations that are ecological friendly and profitable is the aim of this brand of sustainable development.

In practice, strong sustainable development in rural America is primarily a grassroots movement centered on regenerating the local community from within. While it attempts to integrate social, ecological and economic objectives, weak sustainable development, on the other hand, is the predominant green business approach to economic development. Dubbed "smart growth" in matters related to rural-to-urban land conversion, it emphasizes the management of community growth rather than slow growth or no growth favored by strong sustainable development. Stimulating green entrepreneurship and attracting green start-ups are key economic development strategies that rural towns and municipalities practice under the banner of sustainable development. However these green development practices give priority to ecological and economic objectives over social ones.

Although two decades have passed since sustainable development permeated everyday language, the concept itself and the policies promoting it have remained controversial. This is partly due to the conceptual tensions between weak and strong sustainability, but also due to the development issues that both sustainable development versions evoke between developed and developing nations. Nevertheless, sustainable development is unquestionably a global and local outlook on ecology, economy and society that will engage rural and non-rural America for generations to come.

— *Ivonne Audirac*

See also

Environmentalism; Environmental Sustainability; Environmental Movement; Natural Resources Management; Permaculture; Sustainable Rural Economics

References

Audirac, Ivonne. *Rural Sustainable Development in America*. New York: John Wiley & Sons, 1997.

Curtis, Fred. "Eco-localism and Sustainability." *Ecological Economics* 46 (2003), 83-102.

Daly, Herman E. "Sustainable Growth: A Bad Oxymoron." *Grassroots Development* 15, 3 (1991): 39.

Daly, Herman E. and John B. Cobb. *For the Common Good: Redirecting the Economy Toward Community, the Environment and a Sustainable Future*. 2nd edition. Boston, MA: Beacon Press, 1994.

Hawken, Paul, Amory B. Lovins, and L. Hunter Lovins. *Natural Capitalism: Creating the Next Industrial Revolution*. Boston, NE: Back Bay Books, 1999.

Lewandrowski, Jan, Mark Peters, Carol Jones, Robert House, Mark Sperow, Marlen Eve, and Keith Paustian. "Economics of Sequestering Carbon in the U.S. Agricultural Sector." Technical Bulletin No. TB1909. Washington, DC: USDA, Economic Research Service, March 2004. Retrieved January 15, 2008. Available at http://www.ers.usda.gov/Publications/tb1909/

Melzer, Graham. *Sustainable Community: Learning from the Cohousing Model*. Victoria, BC: Trafford, 2005.

Mol, Arthur P.J. and David A. Sonnenfeld, eds. *Ecological Modernisation Around the World: Perspectives and Critical Debates*. London and Portland: Frank Cass, 2000.

Rees, William E. "Ecological Footprints and the Imperative of Rural Sustainability." Pp. 41-78 in *Rural Sustainable Development in America*. Edited by Ivonne Audirac. New York: John Wiley & Sons, 1997.

Weinberg, Adam S. "Sustainable Economic Development in Rural America." *The Annals of the American Academy of Political and Social Science* 570 (2000): 173-185.

Sustainable Rural Economies

Self-renewing, regenerative local economies that are holistic, diverse and interdependent. The development of sustainable economies in rural communities presents some uniquely difficult challenges. Over the span of the industrial era, the ecological, social and economic resources of rural America have been systematically extracted and exploited in the pursuit of greater wealth and material well-being. Even the natural productivity of agricultural land has been depleted as the industrial model of economic development has been applied to farming. Industrial economic development strategies are inherently incapable of sustaining rural economies. This is not a matter of personal opinion but a reflection of the most fundamental principles of science. Economic incentives are inherently individualistic and thus too "shortsighted" to value the regeneration of ecological and social resources needed to sustain rural economies.

For rural Americans to restore and sustain the economic wealth of their communities, they must adopt a fundamentally different approach to economic development. They must find ways to renew and regenerate the natural and social capital of rural areas—the ultimate sources of all economic capital and wealth. Living systems are self-renewing and regenerative. Thus, the development of sustainable rural economies must be guided by the ecological, social and economic principles of *living* systems. The stages of sustainable development must mimic those of living organisms: conception, early development, growth and maturity. Sustainable rural economies must rely on local people who have reached social and ethical maturity to accept responsibilities for creating local economies capable of meeting the needs of the present without compromising the future. Promising approaches to sustainable economic development are being tried and tested by a growing number of progressive rural communities all across America.

History

Rural communities were established for a purpose. The indigenous people of North America congregated in rural areas in specific places where they were able to hunt and gather food and materials for clothing and shelter. They lived sustainably, in harmony with the nature of the places where they lived. European immigrants brought a distinctly different culture but settled rural areas for the same basic purposes to realize the inherent value of natural resources located in specific places. Those resources included not only wildlife, but also timber and minerals, and perhaps most important, fertile farmland. European settlements sprang up on the American frontier to support fur trading, logging, mining and farming. Unlike the indigenous villages of hunters and gatherers, the European settlers produced large surpluses of fur, lumber, minerals and food for economic gain. These surpluses supported not only the rural settlements but also growing urban centers which were linked economically, but not geographically or socially, to America's rural communities.

The productivity of *local* resources has remained the most important purpose for most rural communities. As the fur-bearing animals were killed off, the timber logged off, and the minerals mined out, the most persistent of America's rural population centers proved to be in its farming communities. A few logging and mining communities remain, and some rural communities today are supported by recreational or residential developments, linked to local natural attractions. Most rural American communities are the remnants of previously healthy and vibrant farming communities. However, like many fur trading, logging and mining communities before them, the remaining farming communities are being used up, or "farmed out," leaving rural residents with no sustainable source of economic development, or in many cases, even economic survival.

Historically, rural communities have employed the same model or paradigm of economic development as those used in developing the industrial sectors of the economy. In fact, the transition from an agrarian to urban society was made possible by the industrialization of rural, natural resource-based enterprises. Specialization, standardization and consolidation of control within natural resource industries made it possible for fewer people to meet the food, clothing, shelter and basic material needs of the nation, freeing workers for employment in the factories and offices of the growing manufacturing and distribution sectors of the economy.

As agriculture adopted the same industrial strategies of mining and manufacturing, agricultural productivity increased, but rural communities eventually were left in decline and decay, their economic resources used up or farmed out. Industrial economic development is very efficient in extracting economic value from both natural and human resources, but does nothing to renew or regenerate the ecological or social resources, the ultimate sources of all economic wealth. Most rural American communities are rapidly depleting and degrading the natural and human resources needed to sustain both current and future generations of rural

people. The continued extraction and exploitation of the natural and social capital of rural communities quite simply is not sustainable.

Industrial Versus Sustainable Development

The lack of sustainability of industrial development is derived from the most fundamental laws of science: the laws of thermodynamics. Every activity of benefit to humans involves the use of energy, including energy expended by humans. Houses, cars, clothes, food all require energy to make and energy to use; in fact, materials are simply highly concentrated forms of energy. Working, managing and creating all require human energy, which comes from various forms of physical energy. The first law of thermodynamics states that energy can be neither created nor destroyed, but the second law, the law of entropy, states that whenever energy is used or reused, some of its *usefulness* is lost. Even when energy is used most efficiently, when all wastes are reused or recycled, some usefulness is inevitably lost to entropy.

Industrial development is driven by the economic motives of maximum profits and growth, at least in capitalist economies. These motives provide strong incentives to use and even reuse energy to produce things of economic value, but provide no incentive to do anything to offset the inevitable loss of energy to entropy. Economic value is inherently individualistic in nature and thus must accrue to the individual investor or decision maker within his or her lifetime.

The diminishing time-value of economic benefits is clearly reflected in market rates of interest, which result in heavy discounts for future values. For example, economic benefits expected to accrue a decade in the future typically are worth less than fifty cents today for each dollar expected later. This explains why few corporations make decisions based on anything longer than five- to 10-year planning horizons. It makes no economic sense to invest in either nature or society for the benefit of someone in some future generation. There is no economic incentive to maintain the productivity of natural resources or rural society for the benefit of some unknown rural residents of future generations (Ikerd, 2005).

Sustainable rural economies must be built using a very different development model or paradigm. Sustainable development must mimic the processes of living, biological systems. Living plants have the capacity to capture and store solar energy to offset the energy lost to entropy. In fact, all living things have both a natural capacity and a natural tendency for renewal and regeneration, with or without any economic incentive to do so. Obviously, an individual life is not sustainable because every living thing eventually dies. But communities of living individuals clearly have the capacity to be productive and, at the same time, devote a significant part of their life's energy to conceiving and nurturing the next generation, thus sustaining the life of the community. People have the capacity to collect solar energy with windmills, dams and photovoltaic cells, and they have the natural tendency to reproduce, even though for most people there is little if any economic incentive to raise children. Living things—plants, animals, families, communities, societies—are clearly capable of permanence as well as productivity. Sustainable rural communities must utilize their inherent capacities for both production and regeneration.

Principles of Sustainable Rural Community Development

The principles of sustainable economic development can be derived from the ecological, social and economic principles of sustainable living systems. The guiding principles of healthy, productive natural ecosystems include *holism*, *diversity* and *interdependence*. The natural ecosystems of rural areas are far more than collections of individual physical and biological elements. Relationships among the individual elements are as important as the individual elements to the sustainability of natural ecosystem as wholes. Diversity also is an essential characteristic of sustainable natural ecosystems. Diversity is necessary for regeneration and renewal, resilience and resistance, and for adaptation and evolution to accommodate inevitable changes in the natural environment. Interdependence transforms the potential benefits of holism and diversity into positive ecological reality. Interdependent relationships are neither extractive nor exploitative but are mutually beneficial. Ecologically sustainable rural ecosystems must be managed holistically to maintain interdependent relationships among the diverse physical and biological resources of rural areas.

The guiding principles of healthy, productive human communities include *trust, kindness* and *courage*. These basic principles of social relationships arise from a set of common core values, which transcend religion, philosophy, race, nation and culture (Kidder, 2005). Trusting relationships are built on the core values of honesty, fairness and responsibility. When trusts are validated, social relationships grow stronger and social capital is accumulated. When trusts are violated, social relationships grow weaker and social capital is depleted. Relationships of kindness are built on the core values of empathy, compassion and respect. Impartiality, dependability and honesty are necessary but are not always enough. Sustainable relationships sometimes require mercy rather than justice. Finally, trust and kindness accomplish little without the courage to act. Courage requires self-confidence, discipline and perseverance. It takes courage to reject deception, inequity, irresponsibility, ruthlessness and disrespect—to be trusting and kind. Sustainable rural economies must be built on a foundation of trust, kindness and courage.

The guiding principles of healthy, productive economies include *value, efficiency* and *sovereignty*. Economic value is determined by scarcity, meaning the quantity of something available, relative to quantity of money people are willing and able to spend to get it. Economic value differs from *intrinsic* value in that the economy often places little value on things of great intrinsic value, such as air, water, friendships or ethics. Sustainable communities produce things of great intrinsic value, but they also must produce things of economic value. Economic efficiency reflects the economic value of something that is produced relative to the value of the natural, human and economic resources used to produce it. Sustainable communities must make productive use of their land, people, intellect, energy and money. Economic sovereignty is the freedom to make informed choices, free from coercion or persuasion. Local economies cannot create economic value efficiently, for the good of the community, unless people are free to make their own choices.

The integrity of a community, meaning its completeness, strength and soundness, depends on the extent to which the principles of sustainability permeate all aspects of the community. The social community must be more than a collection of people. The relationships among individuals must be holistic, diverse and interdependent. Its social and cultural resources must be used wisely, not just to create economic value but to create things of intrinsic social value. Social integrity depends on ecological and economic integrity.

Sustainable relationships between a community and its natural environment can be derived directly from the principles of social relationships. Environmental pollution and degradation violate the principles of kindness or trustworthiness in relationships among people, both within or among generations. And natural resources must be used not just to create economic value but also to maintain the intrinsic value of living in a clean and healthy natural environment. Ecological integrity depends on social and economic integrity.

Finally, a sustainable economy also must be holistic, diverse and interdependent. A degree of specialization and standardization may be necessary for efficiency, but a sustainable economy must maintain a measure of diversity and its economic relationships must be mutually beneficial, rather than extractive or exploitative. Economic relationships must be based on trust, not just contracts and laws, and must reflect a sense of kindness toward others, including those of the future. Economic integrity is inseparable from ecological and social integrity.

Processes of Sustainable Rural Economic Development

The *process* of sustainable rural economic development also must be based on the processes of living systems. Living organisms are first conceived by mature adults. After conception come birth, early development and growth to maturity. Industrial organizations are built rather than born, and are "full-grown" when they begin operation. Their economic benefits are realized almost immediately. However, outside investors in rural industries have no natural ties to the rural communities where they invest. They have no commitment to contribute to the local community in any way that does not support their short-run economic interests. Rural economic ventures are far more likely to be sustainable if they originate with local people, are nurtured by local people, and grow to maturity under the direction of local people who are committed to the future of their community.

Support for local ventures during the stages of early development should focus on creation and dissemination of knowledge, to empower people to solve their own problems and to realize their unique opportunities. The knowledge provided must be appropriate for sustainable, living processes. Public institutions should be redirected to creating and disseminating information and technologies appropriate for sustainable rural economies. Public policies for sustainable rural economic development should be fundamentally different from the industrial development policies of the past. The economic developmental stages of growth and maturity require little more than encouragement. Access to financing, appropriate marketing infrastructure, accommodative laws, and facilitating regulations are examples of the types of encouragement that local

entrepreneurs need to grow, develop and become mature, productive members of their communities.

The key to success in the living systems approach to development is to focus on people rather than production and profits. Once people have achieved maturity—economically, socially and ethically—they are then capable of making meaningful commitments to the well-being of others. Mature members of sustainable rural communities recognize their responsibilities of caring for others and for stewardship of nature as privileges, not as sacrifices. They become not only the most productive members of the local economy but also the self-renewing and regenerative forces that create sustainable local economies.

Several specific programs are available to guide rural communities through the sustainable economic development process. The Natural Step is a nonprofit organization founded in 1989 by Swedish scientist Karl-Henrik Robèrt. A number of rural *eco-municipalities* across Canada and the United States are working to develop "ecologically, economically, and socially healthy communities for the long term" by using the Natural Step framework (James and Lahti, 2004). The Natural Step seeks to minimize the accumulation of wastes from both naturally occurring and manufactured substances while maintaining the productivity of natural ecosystems and sustaining a healthy, productive local society. The Business Alliance for Local Living Economies is an international alliance of more than 50 independently operated local business networks dedicated to building local living economies (BALLE, 2007). A *living economy* is defined as one in which economic power resides locally, for the purpose of sustaining healthy community life and natural life as well as long-term economic viability. There is no shortage of programs to guide sustainable rural economic development. The key to success, however, is widespread local commitment to the purpose and principles of sustainable rural economic development.

— *John E. Ikerd*

See also
Agriculture, Sustainable; Community Economics; Development, Community and Economic; Sustainable Development; Environmental Sustainability; Sustainable Agriculture Movement; Policy, Rural Development

References
Business Alliance for Local Living Economies (BALLE). "Mission and Principles Statement," Available online at: http://www.livingeconomies.org/aboutus/mission-and-principles-1. Accessed December 2007.

Ikerd, John. *Sustainable Capitalism: A Matter of Common Sense*. Bloomfield, CT: Kumarian Press, Inc., 2005.

Kidder, Rushworth M. *Moral Courage*. New York: William Morrow, HarperCollins Publishers, 2005, p 43.

James, Sarah and Torbjorn Lahti. *The Natural Step for Communities: How Cities and Towns Can Change to Sustainable Practices*. Gabriela Island, BC: New Society Publishers, Inc., 2004.

Swine Industry

Production of swine in America. Pork makes up 23 percent of the United States' meat and poultry supply. Pork ranks third behind chicken and beef in per-capita consumption. Swine farms produce 110 million pigs annually, which amount to 22 billion pounds of meat. Consumption of pork has been relatively stable for several decades, in contrast with chicken which has been increasing and beef which has declined (USDA/NASS, 2007; USDA/ERS, 2008).

Swine production involves a breeding herd of males and females. Females that have given birth to at least one litter of baby piglets are called "sows." Immature females are referred to as "gilts." Males used for breeding purposes are "boars." Baby male pigs are normally castrated at a few days of age, because meat from uncastrated males can have an unpleasant odor and taste when cooked. Castrated males are called "barrows" (University of Minnesota Extension, 2008).

Sows are housed in a special area when giving birth or "farrowing" where the piglets are kept warm and protected from crushing by the sow. The piglets are weaned from the sow at a few weeks of age and moved to a nursery. At around 45 pounds and three months of age, the piglets are moved to a grower-finisher building until they reach market weights of around 270 pounds at about six months of age.

Pigs in the U.S. are fed a diet that is mostly corn, for energy. The rest of the diet is mainly a protein source such as soybean meal, with a small amount of other ingredients such as vitamins and minerals to balance the diet. Modern swine feeding programs are closely geared to animal needs during specific growth phases, and respond quickly to changes in ingredient availability and cost. The pigs are usually fed a number of different diets as they grow larger. Barrows and gilts are usually housed and fed separately because their feed requirements are different.

Swine Health and Diseases

Pigs are subject to a number of diseases which can kill the pigs outright or cause breeding problems or reduce growth rates. Producers minimize disease risk by restricting human entry into facilities, isolating new breeding stock before introduction to the herd, vaccinating, administrating antibiotics, and separating pigs of different ages in different facilities so that a disease outbreak at one facility doesn't spread to other locations. Swine diseases commonly vaccinated against include erysipelas, leptospirosis, parvovirus, mycoplasma, rhinitis, and porcine reproductive and respiratory virus (PRRS) (USDA/NAHMS, 2001).

"Industrialization" of the Swine Industry

Recent decades have seen changes in the technology and business organization of the swine industry that some have described as "industrialization". (Reimund et al., 1981). These changes have trailed similar changes in poultry and beef feeding, and have coincided with similar changes in the dairy industry. Prior to the 1980s, pigs in the U.S. Corn Belt were commonly farrowed and raised to market weights at the same location. This "farrow-to-finish" system had labor requirements such that a herd of around 100 sows kept the farm operator fully employed along with operating a corn-soybeans crop enterprise that supplied corn for the pigs and some for sale. The hogs and inputs were usually bought and sold on "spot" markets where prices and other terms of trade were decided on the spot rather than negotiated in advance and spelled out in contracts of various kinds.

Some pigs are still produced in farrow-to-finish systems, but today it is more common to locate the grow-finish facilities some distance away from the breeding facilities so that a disease outbreak at one location is less likely to spread to other locations. The grow-finish facilities are operated "all-in/all-out" and are washed between groups to minimize disease risk. The nursery is also often located at a third location, although more recently a trend is to combine the nursery and grow-finish phases in one location to eliminate the need to move the pigs between those two facilities. Health-enhancing technologies such as all-in/all-out rearing and early weaning improve performance and reduce dependence on antibiotics.

Separating the breeding herd from the market animals makes it possible to increase the size of the breeding herd, which improves labor efficiency. Increased operation size has been accompanied by technological improvements in areas such as ventilation and manure handling systems. In general, more careful facility design and better information systems improve throughput of animals from a given investment in land and buildings.

Swine genetics have changed along with the rest of the industry. While the traditional swine breeds such as Yorkshire, Duroc, Landrace, and Berkshire still exist, production of replacement breeding animals has largely moved to specialized swine genetics companies that use breeding systems which utilize crosses of specialized sire and dam lines to achieve desirable traits, and artificial insemination and related technologies which allow elite lines to be utilized more widely to meet particular goals and needs of their customers who produce the market animals for slaughter.

As swine production technology has changed and operations have grown in size, contractual arrangements and vertical ownership integration have emerged as ways to capture added value and reduce risks. Marketing contracts between the pork producer and the slaughtering firm reduce price risks while assuring supplies. Production of the animals themselves has been segmented into various functions linked by production contracts. Production contracts commonly link one business entity (known as the "integrator" or "contractor") that produces piglets and feed to "contractees" that supply labor and facilities. Contractee swine finishing is popular with crop producers who do not wish to devote the time to manage a breeding herd but who see swine finishing as a sideline income source which also produces manure to fertilize crops.

The swine industry structure has been characterized in terms of a bifurcated production channel, with one side being a producer-centered, commodity hog side dominated by independent producers and a few large production contractors, along with a specialty hog side dominated by the industrialized producers with packing and processing facilities (Ginder, 1998). Branding of pork products is becoming popular as processors seek to produce more consistent, higher-quality products for which consumers will pay higher prices. Many of the changes in genetics and feeding systems are intended to increase uniformity as well as quality, in order to reduce processing costs through automation while increasing the proportion of product that meets branding criteria.

Alternative Swine Production Systems

Pork "quality" is perceived differently by different consumers. Physical and chemical characteristics such as leanness, color and firmness are a few quality attributes that are widely valued in the marketplace. Other attributes that are increasingly valued by certain demographic consumer segments include antibiotic-free, pasture-raised, locally grown, and breed-specific (Iowa State University Extension, 2003). The pork industry is segmenting to some degree as some farms and processors adopt alternative swine production systems to appeal to these various consumer groups. When a production system is "alternative" rather than in the mainstream, the reason probably is that relatively few consumers have to date been willing to pay higher prices to compensate producers for higher costs involved in that system. Over time, consumer preferences change such that some of these "alternative" attributes come to dominate the mainstream pork marketplace.

Geographic Location

Iowa is the number one swine producing state and had 28 percent of the hog inventory in December 2007. Other states in the top five for hog inventories are North Carolina (15 percent), Minnesota (11 percent), Illinois (6 percent), and Indiana (5 percent). Swine production is generally located in states that produce large amounts of corn and soybeans, which are the most important feed crops for pigs. Iowa produced 23 percent of the nation's corn in 2007. The top five corn producing states are Iowa (19 percent), Illinois (18 percent), Nebraska (11 percent), Minnesota (10 percent), and Indiana (8 percent). This is nearly the same ranking as for swine, except that North Carolina swine production edges out Nebraska despite producing only around 1 percent of the nation's corn.

North Carolina's position as the second-ranked swine state illustrates the fact that feed availability is not the only factor affecting where hogs are produced. One factor thought to have contributed to the North Carolina swine industry's growth was the elimination of government support for tobacco production, which led to a search for alternative employment opportunities for tobacco farm workers. North Carolina in the 1980s was also the home of several firms that were early adopters of an industry model where the swine farrowing and finishing facilities and supporting facilities such as feed mills were located and sized to coordinate material flows for maximum efficiency. This allowed the efficient use of unit trains of corn from the Midwest, for example, to minimize the cost disadvantage of not being in a major corn-producing area (Purdue Cooperative Extension Service, 1995). North Carolina's situation also illustrates that when an innovative production system is developed in a given industry, the innovation is often adopted first outside the main production area and only later moves into the mainstream industry. This phenomenon may be because the main area's previous infrastructure competes with the new one and makes it more difficult for the industry to visualize and accept the "creative destruction" involved with the new system.

Swine manure can give off odorous gases such as hydrogen sulfide, especially when stored in liquid form, and can pollute water supplies if applied at excessive rates. Plans for new or expanded swine operations have often been met by opposition from neighbors concerned about such risks. Aside from North Carolina, some other sparsely populated states on the periphery of the Corn Belt such as Oklahoma and Colorado have also seen the development of large swine operations in recent years. Large land parcels are available there that make it easier to establish buffers between the swine operations and neighboring homes and businesses.

Economics of the Industry

Profitability of swine production tends to be somewhat cyclical due to the time lag involved in expanding or contracting the swine breeding herd in response to market signals. Feed makes up around half of the cost of producing pigs. Market signals often come in the form of prices of corn and other feeds, hence the term "hog-corn cycle." An analysis of the 10-year period 1996-2005 found that monthly profits in a typical Iowa farrow-to-finish swine operation would have ranged from $-64 to $+45 per market hog as hog and feed prices varied over the period (Lawrence, 2008). Production contracts and marketing contracts often pay producers based on formulas that dampen this short-term price volatility, although highly leveraged producers still sometimes encounter financial difficulty when longer-term price swings occur.

Challenges Faced by the Swine Industry

One challenge faced by the American swine industry is how to adjust when prices rise for corn, soybeans and other feeds. Demand from the emerging biofuel industries generated sharp price increases in late 2007 and 2008. For example, monthly corn prices averaged near $2.00 per bushel between 2002 and 2006. The highest price reached in that four-year period was $3.03. The price was over $3/bushel in every month of 2007, and had exceeded $5/bushel on a fairly sustained basis in 2008. Economic models suggest that when costs rise, then over the long run livestock producers tend to cut back on production. The cutbacks reduce retail meat supplies and drive up retail prices. The higher meat prices return pork production profits to where they were before feed prices increased. In the short run, however, there may be shifts in market share among livestock species if, for example, forage-based livestock such as beef and dairy production are less affected than pork and poultry industries where the diets are almost entirely grain-based. There may also be winners and losers within the swine industry if some producers or processors are more highly leveraged and unable to weather cash flow shortfalls resulting from the feed price increases.

Other challenges and implications for the future include the following:

- Continued challenges related to environmental and odor problems will affect facility size and location, unless technological fixes are developed.
- Food safety risks may lead to trace-back systems from final product to genetics to quickly and easily identify sources of contamination.
- Heightened risk from new sources such as shutdown of large plants or disruption of contracts, globalization, and more specialized production units could disrupt supplies.
- Decisions concerning new production, processing and distribution centers will tend to be made in a more coordinated fashion than in the past, when they were made relatively independently.
- Pork's competitive position could improve relative to beef and possibly even relative to poultry.
- Finally, ownership of world pork production and processing could become more globalized with more firms investing across national boundaries.

— *William Lazarus*

See also

Commodity Inspection; Livestock Industry; Livestock Production; Marketing; Policy, Agricultural

References

Ginder, R.G. "Alternative Models for the Future of Pork Production." In *Industrialization of Agriculture: Vertical Coordination in the U.S. Food System*. Edited by J.S. Royer and R.T. Rogers. Aldershot, England; Brookfield, Vermont: Ashgatge, 1998.

Iowa State University Extension. *Community Agriculture and Food Industries Part II: Training for New Food and Farming Ventures, Resource Manual and Workshop*. Ames, IA: Iowa State University Extension, September 2003.

Lawrence, John. *Monthly Swine Farrow to Finish Returns*. 2006. Available online at: http://www.extension.iastate.edu/agdm.

Purdue Cooperative Extension Service. *Positioning Your Pork Operation for the 21st Century*. 1995. West Lafayette, IN: Purdue Cooperative Extension Service, 1995.

Reimund, Donn A., Martin, J. Rod, and Moore, Charles V. *Structural Change in Agriculture: The Experience for Broilers, Fed Cattle, and Processing Vegetables*. Technical Bulletin 1648. 4/1981. Washington, DC, USDA Economics and Statistics Service.

University of Minnesota Extension. *Introduction to Animal Agriculture, Swine*. St. Paul, MN: University of Minnesota Extension, 2008. Available online at: http://www.manure.umn.edu/animalag.html.

U.S. Department of Agriculture, Economic Research Service (USDA/ERS). *Food Availability (Per Capita) Data System*. Washington, DC: U.S. Department of Agriculture, Economic Research Service. Available online at: http://www.ers.usda.gov/data/FoodConsumption/, 2008, accessed 3/25/2008.

U.S. Department of Agriculture, National Agricultural Statistics Service (USDA/NASS). *Quarterly Hogs and Pigs*. Washington, DC: U.S. Department of Agriculture, National Agricultural Statistics, December 2007. Available online at: http://usda.mannlib.cornell.edu/usda/current/HogsPigs/HogsPigs-12-27-2007.pdf.

U.S. Department of Agriculture, National Animal Health Monitoring System (USDA/NAHMS). *Swine 2000 Part I: Reference of Swine Health and Management in the United States*. Washington, DC: USDA Animal and Plant Health Inspection Service, Veterinary Services, August 2001.

Taxes

Mandatory payments to governments which are unrelated to the amount or value of government services received by the taxpayer. This article discusses elements of the property tax and the individual income tax that have distinct implications for rural America.

Introduction

Rural residents pay property taxes, sales taxes, income taxes, and a host of other minor taxes and fees to support local, state, and federal governments. Most tax issues are national and of equal importance to rural and urban taxpayers, but some concerns have a distinct rural focus. Much of the local tax base in rural America is land used in resource based activities, and this property (farmland, forests, and mineral deposits) poses particular assessment problems. Special income tax provisions for defining farm income also disproportionately affect rural residents.

Property taxes are the most important source of tax revenue for rural America's local governments. The individual income tax provides the bulk of rural revenues for the federal government, whereas state receipts come in varying proportions from sales and income taxes.

In counties with populations below 50,000 the property tax is the most important local tax, accounting for $27 billion (nearly 78 percent of local tax revenues) in 2002. Local governments in more populated counties, where local income and sales taxes are more widely used, obtained about 72 percent of their tax revenues from property taxes. Although the use of other local revenue sources including fees and local sales and income taxes has grown over the past two decades the property tax remains the primary source of local government tax revenue in rural counties.

Property Tax

The tax levied on each piece of property is computed by multiplying the taxable value of that property by a tax rate. Tax rates are set locally by each of the local governments with authority to tax property located within its boundaries. Historically tax rates have been expressed in mills (dollars per thousand dollars of taxable value), but more recently there has been a tendency to express the tax rate as a percentage of taxable value. Individual property tax bills reflect the sum of the property taxes levied by all local governments with power to tax that particular parcel. Thus, properties located outside the city limits pay less in property taxes than identically valued properties inside city boundaries since no city taxes are levied on that property. Typically, property owners receive a single tax bill for each parcel of property. Local tax revenues are usually collected at the county level then distributed to the appropriate local governments.

Real property (land and buildings) is the largest component of the local property tax base. In some states personal property (equipment, farm machinery, breeding stock, and inventories) is also subject to the property tax. Motor vehicles may also be subject to a personal property tax at the state and, sometimes, local levels.

The fair and true market value, or estimated market value, of each piece or parcel of property subject to tax is determined by local assessors. State officials then compare local assessments against actual market values determined by recent sales of property and adjust or equalize assessed values to ensure a consistent ratio of assessed value to market value across the state. Without this check localities could systematically under-assess property and unfairly increase the amount they receive from state aids, such as school aid, which depend on the value of the local property tax base.

Taxable property value, the value actually subject to tax, is computed in one of two ways. In most states taxable value is established by law at a single, fixed, uniform percentage of the estimated market value for all types of property. That percentage is often less than 100 percent of market value. In these uniform property tax systems, $100,000 of commercial property and $100,000 of agricultural property would each have a taxable value of $100,000, assuming an assessment rate of 100 percent. If the local tax rate were 15 mills, ($15 per $1000 or 1.5 percent) both the agricultural and commercial property would face a tax levy of $1,500.

In some states the statutory ratio of a property's taxable value to its full and true value depends on the type, or class of property under consideration. In states with classified property tax systems the effective tax rate, the tax as a percentage of full and true value, varies depending on the type of property. For example, if the class rate for commercial property were 100 percent and the class rate for agricultural property 50 percent, the taxable value for the commercial property in the example used above would remain at $100,000, but that for the agricultural property would fall to $50,000. With this classified system and assuming the same 15 mill rate as above, the tax levied on the commercial property would continue to be $1,500, but that on the agricultural property would fall to $750. The effective tax rate on agricultural property would be one-half that on commercial property, even though the tax rates set by local governments were the same. Owners of residential homesteads and agricultural property are the most frequent beneficiaries of a classified property tax system.

Assessors set the fair and true market values for most types of real property by comparing sales prices of similar properties or by capitalizing expected net income from the property. Much land in rural America, however, requires special treatment. Sales of farmland, timberland, and mineral rights often are insufficient to support use of the comparable sales method. Capitalizing net income can be inconclusive or misleading due to problems in determining the true income producing potential of the property.

States have responded by adopting alternative methods to assign assessed values for these resource based properties. For mineral lands the full extent and value of deposits are unknown, so accurate assessments of fair and true property values are impossible. Most states where mineral values are important replaced the property tax on mineral lands with a severance tax levied at a fixed rate on either the quantity or value of the mineral extracted each year.

Timber land creates a different problem for the property tax. Levying an annual tax on the value of an unharvested forest resource creates a cash flow problem for the owner, encouraging premature harvest and conversion to other land uses. Privately owned timber land is exempted from the property tax in some states, and replaced with a severance tax levied at the time of harvest.

By 1988 all states had provisions allowing assessment of farm lands at their agricultural value, and not at their value for alternative uses. Some states went further, basing their assessment of farm land on soil quality indices or other measures of farm land productivity, and not on estimates of market value or comparable sales.

Assessing farmland in areas on the fringe of residential development poses additional challenges since the farmland in question may have a higher value for residential development, but the owner may wish to continue farming the land. In extreme cases valuing the land for tax purposes at its highest and best use could drive that land out of agriculture. States developed several alternative approaches to deal with that problem while limiting windfall gains to real estate speculators.

One approach requires that any land currently used for agriculture be assessed only on its agricultural value until the land is converted to a non-agricultural use. Other states require establishment of a dual assessment roll, with all farmland assessed at its value for both agriculture and its highest and best use. Taxes are levied only on the agricultural value of the parcel, but at the time of sale and conversion to non-agricultural uses, foregone taxes plus interest for a pre-determined number of past years comes due.

In some states restrictive zoning agreements are used to reduce tax pressure for development of agricultural land. By definition, when zoning prohibits non-agricultural uses, the land has no value other than for agriculture, so assessments must be based solely on the parcel's agricultural value. Properties zoned agricultural typically cannot be converted to non-agricultural uses for several years after a change in zoning is approved. During those intervening years assessments may be gradually increased to reflect the non-agricultural value of the land. In some states, notice of intent to change zoning classifications must be given as much as 10 years in advance.

Census of Agriculture data show farm real estate taxes averaged $5.70 per acre in 2002. There is wide variation in the average tax rate among states due to the degree of local reliance on the property tax and to the value of farmland. Taxes per acre are much higher in New England and the mid-Atlantic states and lower in western states where a larger proportion of the farm land is low valued grazing land. Although annual estimates of farm real estate tax levies at the state level are no longer reported by USDA some state level information continues to be gathered by the Department. However, data is not reported for all states and personal and real property taxes paid are not separately identified making the data non-comparable to that collected prior to 1995.

Total property taxes levied on farm real estate and personal property are estimated by USDA to have totaled $9.5 billion in 2007.

Income Taxes

The income of individuals actively participating in farming is reported for federal income tax purposes on Schedule F. In 2005 1,981,250 filers reported income on that schedule. Not all of those filing F Schedules live in rural areas. There is agricultural activity in all but the most densely settled urban counties. Income from farming is also received by individuals who lease land to others on either a cash or a crop share basis, and take no active role in the production of crops or care of livestock. That income is reported on Form 4835. In 2005 592,528 filers reported farm rental income and many of those receiving farm rental income live outside rural areas.

Farmers reported a net loss for federal income tax purposes of $12.2 billion in 2005. Much of this loss was reported by filers with large non-farm incomes. Individuals whose federal adjusted gross income (AGI), after their farm loss, exceeded $100,000 reported net farm losses of just over $3 billion. An additional $3.2 billion of net farm losses were reported by filers with negative adjusted gross income (AGI). Some of those reporting negative AGI may have offset relatively large non-farm incomes with even larger farm losses. The importance of off-farm income to farm households is shown by the fact that while 1.37 million of the 1.98 million Schedule Fs filed showed a loss, all but 104,000 of those filers reported positive AGI.

Income reported on Schedule F is not considered a good measure of farm income. Federal tax law allows farmers to use cash basis accounting rather than accrual accounting for tax purposes, so reported income does not reflect changes in farmer-owned inventories of products and inputs. In addition, since sales of breeding stock are considered to be sales of capital assets and reported on Schedule D as a capital gain, F Schedule income understates actual farm income. The combination of cash basis accounting and capital gains treatment for some forms of farm income made it possible to create tax shelter investments offering large, currently deductible operating losses, offset by future capital gains taxable at a lower tax rate. The tax reform act of 1986 eliminated much of the tax benefit available for agricultural investments.

— *Thomas F. Stinson*

See also

Agricultural and Applied Economics; Agricultural Law; Farm Finance; Government; Income; Land Value

References

Aiken, David. *State Farmland Preferential Assessment Statutes*. RB31. Lincoln, NE: Department of Agricultural Economics, University of Nebraska, 1990.

DeBraal, J. Peter. *Taxes on U.S. Agricultural Real Estate, 1890-1991, and Methods of Estimation*. SB-866. Washington, DC: U.S. Department of Agriculture, Economic Research Service, 1993.

Stinson, Thomas F. and George Temple. *State Mineral Taxes, 1982*. Rural Development Research Report No. 36. Washington, DC: U.S. Department of Agriculture, 1982.

Wunderlich, Gene and John Blackledge. *Taxing Farmland in the United States*. Agricultural Economics Report No. 679. Washington, DC: U.S. Department of Agriculture, 1994.

Technology

The tools, knowledge, skills, and procedures to create, utilize, and accomplish useful things. Although technology pervades all aspects of life, this entry specifically addresses technologies used in rural America's production systems, that is, the extraction of raw materials, and the production and distribution of food, fiber, manufactured goods, and services. The discussion includes the nature of technology, how technology is developed, the use of technology in the production and distribution of goods and services, the social and economic impacts of technology on rural society, the movement toward development and use of more sustainable forms of technology, and the importance of assessing the potential impacts of new technologies.

The Nature of Technology

Human populations use technology to adapt to the environment, to modify the environment to make it more hospitable, and to obtain the means of existence from the environment. Although technology usually is thought of as the physical or hardware aspect of culture—that is, the tools, implements, instruments, and machines—in a broad sense technology also includes the software or the knowledge needed to apply the technology toward practical ends. This software includes the social organization necessary for the use of complex technologies. The useful trait is not inherent in the technology but is socially defined by the members of each specific culture. Rural technologies range from the mammoth earth moving equipment used in strip mining, to the computer expert systems used by farmers to make decisions on crop and livestock production, to sonar systems used by fishing trawlers to locate schools of fish, to scouting systems for insects by grape growers for vineyard integrated pest management, to the basic shovel, hoe, and rake used to cultivate home gardens.

Technology Development

Traditionally technologies were developed through trial-and-error and the accumulated experiences of users in crafts and trades. Over the last two centuries, however, the development of new technology became closely associated with progress in science. America's strong faith in science and science's perceived efficiency to address and solve society's problems, augments its perceptions of the usefulness and benefits of technology.

America's faith in science and technology is evident in the primary institution that develops and disseminates production-oriented technology in rural areas, the Land grant university system. Congress established the land grant system with the Morrill Acts of 1862 and 1890 to provide states with resources to teach the agricultural and mechanical arts. The system was developed further through the Hatch Act of 1886 and the Smith-Lever Act of 1914 which established state agricultural experiment stations and state extension services, respectively. The work of this system is funded by the states and by other federal agencies within and outside of the U.S.D.A. Much of the new technology research and development of private industry is accomplished through private industry's grants to scientists in the land grant universities.

Land grant university scientists shared America's faith in science and technology and saw their products as overwhelmingly positive. The leaders of those institutions pressed forward with programs based on scientific knowledge to improve the conditions and welfare of rural people, especially in production agriculture. Much scientific research during the first half of the 20th Century resulted in technologies that greatly increased agricultural production, but few concerns were raised about the decreasing farm population and the declining rural communities.

Technology and Production

Agricultural technologies and the technologies of other extractive industries (fishing, forestry, mining, oil extraction, quarrying) are part of the treadmill of production. The treadmill involves two processes: first, expansion of technological capacity resulting from reinvestment into the production system of surplus values (profits) from previous production, and second, the preference for economic growth even when decision makers know that adverse effects will result (Schnaiberg and Gould 1994). To maintain the accelerating treadmill, technology increases in size, power, capacity, and speed. The pulpwood industry uses a large tractor-like machine with a hydraulically powered clipper to harvest pulpwood trees quickly, strip miners use gigantic excavating and earth moving equipment with many cubic yards capacity to move overburden and extract coal, and farmers use combines to harvest grain such as corn, soybeans, or wheat that can cut a swath 36 feet wide.

Some new technologies have the potential to affect the structure, organization, and operation of entire industries or all of rural society. Two such technologies are biotechnology and computer/telecommunications technologies. Biotechnology is any technique to improve plants or animals by changing their genetic structure, or to use living organisms to make or modify products. It includes the artificial production of enzymes necessary to produce hormones, vaccines, and feed additives; artificial reproduction or growth of cells such as cloning or growing tissue cultures; and genetic engineering, altering the genetic structure of the cell. Genetically modified food products are controversial. Consumers are concerned about the safety of genetically modified foods, and countries vary in regulations on importing and growing such products. The European Union is very restrictive requiring an assessment of potential cumulative and long-term effects of genetically modified foods on human health and the environment. In the United States much controversy has centered around one biotechnology product known as recombinant bovine somatotropin (rBST), a hormone that substantially increases a cow's milk production. One issue of the rBST controversy is public concern over the hormone's potential presence in milk from rBST-injected cows, and thus the milk's safety for human consumption. Despite extensive educational programs by the dairy industry, consumers have not accepted milk from cows treated with rBST, so more dairies and grocery chains are providing consumers the rBST-free milk they want. A second issue is that increased milk production may lead to a further decrease in the number of dairy farmers, with impacts on the viability of rural communities and the milk processing industry.

The telecommunications technology complex joins computer technologies with telecommunications and broadcast media into a single infrastructure. It has the potential to break down distance barriers in the production and delivery of goods and services, and is seen as a tool to return isolated rural areas to mainstream American social and economic activity. Expanding the telecommunications infrastructure to rural areas is particularly cogent in a society with an increasing role for information and its storage, retrieval, and transmission in social and economic functions. Jobs, such as credit card account processing, telemarketing, data entry and processing, and copy and manuscript editing all can be done through telecommuting from a computer cottage. Will rural areas benefit significantly from telecommunications? The outcome is uncertain. Much of this type of work can be transferred from rural America to other places having the infrastructure and also having lower labor costs such as Latin America or the Far East.

Some recent technological advances include precision agriculture and biofuel production. Precision agriculture uses global positioning systems (GPS) linked to computers built into farm machinery. Data on in-field variability such as soil types, soil fertility, and past productivity is programmed into the computers and guided by GPS to apply the optimum amounts of fertilizer, seeds, and other inputs in the field. The computer-GPS systems can even steer the tractor requiring the farmer only to turn the equipment at the end of rows. Biofuels include ethanol and biodiesel. Plants for producing biofuels, especially ethanol, have been built in the corn growing regions of the United States and Canada, with Brazil also being a major producer. Because of concerns about the impact of corn ethanol production on the environment and on food prices, many scientists and industry leaders see the future in cellulosic ethanol, that

is, ethanol produced from plant materials such as corn stalks, tall grasses like switch grass, and fast-growing trees.

Impacts of Technology

Impacts of technology and the technology treadmill on rural people and communities are profound. Advancements in technology relieve much of the drudgery and long hours related to extractive occupations. But rural areas also suffer from the negative effects of technological advancement. One potential impact is a restructuring of industrial sectors. Implementation of advanced technology creates the need for increased income to pay for the investments in the technology. Existing production units (e.g., farms, fishing fleets, and logging firms) are reorganized and consolidated into larger operations to compensate for declining prices resulting from increased production. The investment in technology and formation of larger operations renders much of the labor and management surplus, creating a stream of rural outmigration. The loss of population in turn leads to the restructuring of rural communities' commercial and institutional sectors, as there are fewer individuals, families, businesses, and organizations requiring their goods and services. Thus, businesses close, schools and churches consolidate, and many rural towns become virtual or actual ghost towns.

A second negative impact of the technological treadmill is on the rural environment, especially owing to the growth in size, power, and capacity of the technology. Larger and heavier farm machinery increases soil compaction affecting plant growth. Demands for corn for ethanol production results in farmers raising continuous crops of corn rather than rotating corn with crops that restore soil fertility. Continuous corn cropping requires greater input of chemical fertilizers that pollute streams, lakes, and groundwater. Strip mining for coal in the Southern Appalachian region has reached new heights in environmental degradation through a technique called "mountaintop removal." The increasing size and scale of mining equipment have made it more economically efficient to remove the top of a mountain to access a coal seam than to use traditional shaft mining. Dust from blasting creates health problems for residents of nearby communities, and the removed overburden is pushed into the valleys where it pollutes streams and creates flood hazards. Regulations on land restoration are either not observed, or, if restoration is accomplished, it does not approximate the pre-mining ecological soundness.

Another technological treadmill impact on rural areas is that technology tends to benefit urban areas over rural areas. Most new technology has urban origins. Research and development, whether conducted by private corporations or public educational institutions, tend to be urban activities. Examples of urban research and development centers are the high-technology research parks such as North Carolina's Research Triangle (North Carolina State University in Raleigh, Duke University in Durham, and University of North Carolina in Chapel Hill) or Massachusetts' Route 128 in and around Boston. Initial new technology beneficiaries are urban areas, with rural areas benefiting as the technologies diffuse, a process sometimes called the trickle down effect. Some rural areas cannot take advantage of new technologies for lack of the supporting infrastructure. The information highway bypasses many rural communities because local telephone companies lack fiber optic lines and digital switching. At times rural areas actually are on the technological forefront. The early establishment of telephone and electric services in the 1930s is a prime example. However, these services were promoted by a specific government policy through the Rural Electrification Administration. Generally, early rural implementation of technology is atypical.

Not only do urban areas reap early benefits of technological advancement, but the externalities, the indirect and long-term costs of using technologies, often fall to rural areas. The dumping grounds for waste materials of the technological treadmill, including nuclear and other hazardous waste, are primarily rural. Rural communities with no other prospects for economic prosperity may accept such wastes in local dumps for a fee. Some rural communities have land fills and hazardous waste sites thrust upon them with little or no local involvement or control in the siting decision. Other rural communities have their landscapes ravaged and soil and water polluted from strip mining that provides raw materials for industrial growth.

Sustainable, Appropriate, and Indigenous Technology

In reaction to problems created by the technological treadmill, sustainable technology has emerged as part of the larger sustainability movement. The values of sustainability promote technologies that are ecologically sound, economically viable, socially just, and humane. One major component of sustainable technology is appropriate technology. "Appropriate" indicates a favorable judgment as to the effects of a technology on its social, cultural, and environmental context. Barbour (1980) suggested five characteristics of appropriate technology. First, intermediate scale technology is more efficient than traditional tools or methods, but sufficiently inexpensive to promote wide adoption and use. Second, to promote retention of a gainfully employed population, technology should be labor intensive rather than capital intensive. Third, a relatively simple technology promotes easy adoption, self-help in operation and maintenance, and thus independence. Fourth, a technology that is relatively simple, small in scale, and does not rely on outside experts or large supporting organizations or infrastructure promotes self-reliance, self-determination, and local control. And finally, a technology that is environmentally compatible promotes low-energy use, minimal pollution, renewable resource use, and the integration of functions.

Although any specific technology considered appropriate may not embody all of these characteristics, some examples of rural appropriate technologies are wind and solar electricity generators, hedgerows to prevent soil erosion and block heat-robbing wind, and a simple kit that allows farmers to test fields for the amount of nitrogen fertilizer required. Wind generators are increasingly common sights in farmers' fields in the Western Corn Belt and Plains States. As a practice for ecologically sound farming, sustainable agriculture also is becoming more common. Definitions of sustainable agriculture usually include lower chemical inputs, reduced soil and water degradation, greater diversification and self sufficiency, family-based labor, appropriate scale of technology, and production for the local market.

Indigenous knowledge, a concept closely related to sustainable technology and appropriate technology, is knowledge unique to a given society or culture. It is the information base for decision making, sometimes simply called local knowledge. Research and development involving indigenous knowledge reverses the roles of technology developers and technology users. Technology users share their fund of viable traditional tools and methods with the technology developers. Minimum tillage, a cultivation practice that retains protective amounts of residue on the soil's surface to prevent erosion, was first used by farmers who often also built their own special tillage equipment. The practice was later embraced and promoted by university scientists and government agencies. Often spurned in the past as being outdated, unproductive, or unscientific, indigenous technologies and methods are being reevaluated.

Organizations of users have emerged that conduct their own research and work collaboratively with scientists to merge the best of new and traditional technologies.

Much of the impetus for incorporating indigenous knowledge comes from Third World areas. Lacking scientific methods and sophisticated instruments, technology users develop their fund of knowledge based upon what they observe and the meaning they attach to it. Therefore, indigenous knowledge tends to be organized around that which is conspicuous and culturally important. This provides the basis for a strategy for incorporating indigenous knowledge into technology development (see Bentley 1992 for additional information). For phenomena both important and conspicuous, the technology developer can learn from the user. For phenomena either not important or not easily observed the developer and user work cooperatively to learn together. And for phenomena neither easily observed nor important and thus ignored by the user, the user can learn from the developer.

Technology Impact Assessment

Potential impacts of new or emerging technologies on rural people or communities can be examined through technology assessment. Although benefits of new technologies are often evident immediately, technology assessment can provide an early warning system for potentially negative impacts which may be delayed, remote, and cumulative. Technology assessments helped to raise the public consciousness and affected state and federal policy on new technologies such as bovine somatotropin, large-scale confinement operations for raising hogs, the siting of nuclear waste facilities, and the development of off-shore fisheries.

Although technology is pervasive in all aspects of life, it does not in itself determine the direction of change and development in rural America. The creation, development, and use of technologies is based on choices made by government, scientists, engineers, manufacturers, marketers, users, and benefiters, and these choices, in turn, are determined by society's values. The benefits received and cost incurred are trade-offs resulting from these choices.

— *Peter F. Korsching and Michael M. Bell*

See also
Agriculture, Alternative; Bioeconomy; Biotechnology; Computers; Cropping Systems; Electrification; Genetically Modified Organisms; Land-Grant Institutions, 1862, 1890, and 1994; Mechanization; Policy, Telecommunications; Technology Transfer; Telecommunications; Tillage

References
Altieri, M.A. *Agroecology: The Science of Sustainable Agriculture*. Boulder, CO: Westview, 1995.

Barbour, Ian G. *Technology, Environment, and Human Values*. New York, NY: Praeger, 1980.

Bentley, Jeffrey W. "Alternatives to Pesticides in Central America: Applied Studies of Local Knowledge." *Culture and Agriculture* (1992): 10-13.

Burns, Shirley Stewart. *Bringing Down the Mountains: The Impact of Mountaintop Removal on Southern West Virginia*. Morgantown, WV: West Virginia University, 2007.

DeGregori, Thomas R. *Agriculture and Modern Technology*. Ames, IA: Iowa State University Press, 2001.

Korsching, Peter F., Patricia C. Hipple, and Eric A. Abbott, eds. *Having All the Right Connections: Telecommunications and Rural Viability*. Westport, CT: Praeger, 2000.

Schnaiberg, Allan and Kenneth Allan Gould. *Environment and Society: The Enduring Conflict*. New York, NY: St. Martins, 1994.

Weber, David J., ed. *Biotechnology. Assessing Social Impacts and Policy Implications*. New York: Greenwood, 1990.

Technology Transfer

An exchange of information between technology developers and technology users that involves identifying and using new tools to solve new problems or to address existing problems more effectively. This article summarizes traditional models of technology transfer and presents new network and community approaches to transfer. People once believed technology transfer was like going to the store; they looked over available products and processes and decided what to buy (i.e., what to adopt). Technology is the source or hub from which spokes, or transfer agents, diffuse information to independent adopters. But this understanding of technology accounts for only part of technology transfer in rural communities. In particular, many technologies require the direct involvement of participants working in informal networks. The transfer of such system technologies involves more complexity, beyond that of one-on-one contacts between technology sources and independent adopters.

Promoting Adoption and Diffusion Through Information Access

The traditional adoption and diffusion perspective promoted a five-stage model of technology transfer (Rogers, 1983): 1) awareness; 2) interest; 3) evaluation; 4) trial; and 5) adoption. Although the progression of technology transfer stages is not always completely linear, the order of the stages is approximately accurate. For example, a user must first become aware of and interested in a new tool in order to evaluate it, and subsequently try it and decide to adopt it. Therefore, from the user's perspective, each successive stage of the model provides additional information about the new technology or tool. However, virtually no technology is universally acceptable or accepted at the adoption stage since additional modifications are often necessary long after adoption.

This model emphasizes education and the flow of information to rural communities. Progress occurred in both channels to disseminate information and the type of information needed for adoption decisions.

Channels for Technology Transfer. Media (advertising on new machinery, extension circulars on health hazards, and videos on waste management systems) make rural communities aware of new ideas. Impersonal channels (radio reports on endocrine disruptors and magazine coverage of aquifer problems) and interpersonal sources (field days on calf management and satellite conferences on market opportunities) help deepen an interest in technologies and their impact.

An enduring approach used with increasing creativity is the demonstration project, a hands-on way to evaluate a technology through a local trial. Mobile vans have been used to demonstrate technologies to farms or communities, like Pennsylvania's forage testing program. Permanent training sites combine seminars, field visits and experimental use of new systems, like Texas' Stiles Farm Computer Training Center. Joint programs of public agencies and farm associations use multiple sites to systematically adapt and demonstrate new technologies, like Michigan's program on the new system of high-density fruit production. In short, when rural people get together to define and directly contribute to their goals, field trials can be very useful.

Type of Information Needed for Technology Transfer. In the traditional literature, the type of information needed for technology transfer is described with such concepts as profitability, compatibility and trialability. These three concepts state that information on a new technology should describe the technology, relate each of its components to existing practice, and explain how the components interact in producing an overall benefit. The description should be complemented with thorough statements of the resources (capital, time and management effort) required and benefits accrued from implementing each component as well as the entire system. Decision makers need to know of difficulties and failures encountered by other adopters and the extent of continued interest among their peers.

Technology transfer has been studied by experts from several disciplines (see Gold et al., 1980, economics; Tornatzky and Fleischer, 1990, technology management; and Saltiel et al., 1994, sociology). Profitability plays a central role in the findings of most such studies. For example, Griliches (1960) determined that profitability explained much of the variation in adoption rates for hybrid corn.

However, predicting the profit to be gained is often complicated by factors outside the technology itself. Government programs and economic wherewithal can constrain or add to the profit from a technology. New technologies often replace existing methods, and it is a principle of technological change that new technologies stimulate improvements in old ones. The most reliable vacuum tubes ever made were developed after the invention of transistors (Cooper and Schendel, 1976). Changes in the prices of economic factors and the availability of ancillary technologies may also affect the profitability of old and new technologies. For example, the profitability of the tractor was sharply increased by increased labor costs and the invention of a universal hitch that allowed tractors to pull carts, spreaders and reapers (Sahal, 1981).

Social Interaction and Technology Transfer

It is often true that the best way to move technology is to move people. Therefore, most studies of technology transfer emphasize interaction between adopters in complex social networks. At times, opinion leaders influence a wide segment of their community. In other cases, people are informally allied with competing subgroups (like diversified, mono-crop and organic advocates) which favor alternative technologies. The behavior of leaders in encouraging bridges between competing subgroups can determine whether this competition is productive or adversarial. In still other cases, intermediaries play a strong role, such as an irrigation association that aided in the formulation and dissemination of safety standards for irrigation systems. The basic message is that people need to interact with others who have accumulated experience and data on a technology and its impact.

Interaction Between Technologists and Adopters. The more technology developers, such as corporations, agencies and universities, know about the needs of rural communities, the better they can help them. Technology management studies have shown that technology transfer works best when developers and users: 1) mutually define a problem; 2) interact to interpret data from pilot programs and share in defining next steps; and 3) disseminate information and the technology through pre-existing networks of users (Wolek, 1985).

Rural communities will benefit from knowing their needs and cooperating to satisfy them. This means that rural communities face the challenge of building a capability to define problems in technical terms and to lobby technologists to work on solutions.

Systems Technologies and the Creation of Community Infrastructure

Technologies, such as Integrated Pest Management (IPM), dairy herd management, soil and water conservation, and sustainable agriculture, have multiple components. We call such technologies "systems" (see *Agriculture* article).

Local Situation Requires Systems. Albrecht and Ladewig (1985) documented the impact of local soil and water quality on the value of a technology. They showed that irrigation technologies (e.g., furrow diking, soil moisture detection, center pivot, and return pits) are more readily adopted on farms having lower lifting costs because more ground water is available. Generalizing, technologies must be adapted to local application. In this sense, the totality of the adaptations reflect essential parts of the system being adopted. In some situations, like growing early market cantaloupes in Texas, the local adaptations are extensive. Such adaptations will not occur and there will be nothing of value to transfer unless local people play a strong role.

The components of a system generally interact to provide a greater total impact; they are synergistic. People can adopt some components and not others as they have with IPM and soil conservation (Nowak, 1987). Ridgely and Brush (1992) showed that fruit farmers adopted relatively low-cost components of IPM technology before adopting the more costly components like insect monitoring and using economic thresholds before orchard treatment. IPM components, such as using beneficial insects as substitutes for insecticides, were less adopted since the market placed a high price on blemish-free fruit. In short, "whatever works for you" seems to be a rule in system transfer.

Building Innovative Communities. Most technological systems require action on the part of a supporting infrastructure. For example, although air transport existed for several decades, it was not until the mid-1950s that volume exploded. Aircraft technology had improved, but even more important was the existence of an infrastructure of trained pilots, mechanics, airports, a supply system and experienced air travelers brought about by World War II.

Systems innovation may be conceived as three stages: 1) initial application of the technology to existing tasks (early movies were of familiar images such as plays); 2) development of an infrastructure to service the technology (mobile camera crew); and 3) expansion into new applications by the people staffing the infrastructure (action movies filmed on location).

The importance of building a supporting infrastructure presents a challenge for communities. That challenge is to cooperate in building community supports for systems that have a favorable impact on the community. An infrastructure was what a group of citrus farmers in Arizona developed when they sought to raise the price of their fruit through higher quality. They had to commit to public standards of quality, support an independent testing organization, find and negotiate with a market outlet (a California cooperative grocer), and employ a fruit shipper that would maintain the quality fruit they grew. In summary, the two commitments essential for rural communities interested in transferring useful technologies are to develop local networks to adapt technologies to local conditions, and to build the infrastructure required for complete and practical operation of the needed system.

Power Structures and Technology Transfer

Models of technology transfer are politically potent. In the 1700s, Dutch farms were the leading source of red dye (madder) used in Europe. By the 1800s, their market was under serious attack from a French factory technology. The Dutch refused to transfer the new technology because they saw the central issue as one of who was going to control the dye industry (manufacturers or farmers). For a while, the Dutch lost market share, but farmers and government cooperated to develop a new technology that not only kept farmers in charge, but provided significantly better quality at lower cost.

A central issue in rural technology transfer is whose future welfare is primary—rural communities, academics, government policymakers or agribusiness (Heffernan, 1984). Rural people who cooperate to form innovative communities will establish the conditions they need to make their own futures.

— *Francis W. Wolek and Cathy A. Rusinko*

See also

History, Agricultural; Land-Grant Institutions, 1862, 1890, 1994; Technology

References

Albrecht, D.E. and H. Ladewig. "Adoption of Irrigation Technology: The Effects of Personal, Structural, and Environmental Variables." *Southern Rural Sociology* 3 (1985): 26-41.

Cohen, G. *Technology Transfer: Strategic Management in Developing Countries.* Thousand Oaks, CA: Sage Publications, 2004.

Cooper, A.C. and D. Schendel. "Strategic Responses to Technological Threats." *Business Horizons* (February 1976): 61-69.

Gold, B., G. Rosseger, and M.G. Boylan. *Evaluating Technological Innovations.* Lexington, MA: Lexington Books, 1980.

Griliches, Zvi. "Hybrid Corn and the Economics of Innovation." *Science* 132, no. 3422 (July 29, 1960): 275-280.

Heffernan, W.D. "Constraints in the U.S. Poultry Industry." *Research in Rural Sociology and Development* 1 (1984): 237-260.

Kline, R.R. *Consumers in the Country: Technology and Social Change in Rural America.* Baltimore: Johns Hopkins University Press, 2000.

Nowak, P.J. "The Adoption of Agricultural Conservation Technologies." *Rural Sociology* 52, no. 2 (1987): 208-220.

Ridgely, A. and S.B. Brush. "Social Factors and Selective Technology Adoption: The Case of Integrated Pest Management." *Human Organization* 51, no. 4 (1992): 367-378.

Rogers, E. *Diffusion of Innovations.* New York, NY: The Free Press, 1983.

Sahal, D. *Patterns of Technological Innovation.* Reading, MA: Addison-Wesley Publishing, 1981.

Saltiel, J., J.W. Bauder, and S. Palakovich. "Adoption of Sustainable Agricultural Practices: Diffusion, Farm Structure, and Profitability." *Rural Sociology* 59, no. 2 (1994): 333-349.

Wilkins, G. *Technology Transfer for Renewable Energy: Overcoming Barriers in Developing Countries.* London: Royal Institute of International Affairs, Chatham House, 2002.

Wolek, F.W. "The Transfer of Agricultural Technology." *Journal of Technology Transfer* 9 (1985): 57-70.

Telecommunications

The communication of any single or mix of message forms in text, graphics, images, moving images, computer code or a variety of command signals over an electrical conduit, fiber optic strands, or in a variety of electromagnetic broadcast forms such as microwave, television, radio, cellular telephone, or satellite. Telecommunications has a special role in rural America— or in any rural environment—because it overcomes distance and the other challenges of the lack of population density. The public often associates telecommunications with the public telephone system, radio, or television. Less visible to the public are data networks such as in the linking of banks, large corporations, military installations, and university computer centers, to name a few. The Internet is an amalgam of computer-based telecommunications data networks that are able to communicate with one another.

"Distance Penalty" in Rural America

Rural sociologists or economists note the "distance penalty" of living or doing business in a rural area. Because distributing telephone or broadcast or data services over the relatively greater distances involved in rural as compared to urban areas, and because less densely populated markets offer less potential for return on investment, rural areas traditionally have been underserved in many types of business or public services.

As compared to their urban counterparts, many rural retail businesses are fewer, further apart, and carry less inventory, which is among the reasons for the early growth of catalog marketing. Rural schools typically are underfunded and offer far fewer educational opportunities. Rural physicians tend to be general practitioners rather than specialists, often must serve patients over large geographic areas, and do not have the services of nearby modern clinics or hospitals. Although rural manufacturers may have lower labor and land costs, this is often offset by the penalties of distance to gather raw materials or ship finished products. Emergency medical, fire, or police services either have far longer response times or are virtually non-existent.

Many people accept the challenges of these distance penalties in order to enjoy the space, natural environment, lack of congestion and crime, and other benefits of the rural lifestyle. Fortunately, advances in telecommunications may lessen these penalties as more alternatives are offered for information, education, entertainment, and economic development.

Improvements in Rural Telephone Services

Telecommunications in rural America benefited greatly from the U.S.'s tradition of promoting inexpensive, quality access to public telephone service. Whereas many small or isolated rural communities traditionally depended on small, independent or cooperative telecommunications utilities, since the World War II services from these groups have improved remarkably. A major reason is the expansion of the Rural Electrification Administration (REA) into low interest loans for rural telephone development. In some instances this gave small independents or cooperatives an edge over the Bell System or larger independents because of low interest financing. There was also the development of high cost pools, whereas funds were drawn from more lucrative parts of the telephone business to subsidize the relatively high costs of low-density networks. This kept basic telephone rates reasonable for the rural customer. REA funds have been very much a part of the development of American rural telephony from the 1950s through the 1980s.

Multiparty lines have been steadily reduced, line quality increased, and local calling areas expanded. Finally, rural telephony leaped with the arrival of cellular services, which greatly expanded in the 1990s. Ironically, many regulators thought that cellular telephones would be of no particular interest to the rural areas, and less profitable, so the designation of rural service areas for cellular phones was slower in coming than to urban areas. On the contrary, there was remarkable growth in rural cellular usage, and much of it could have been forecasted by common sense. For example, farmers are not usually at desks where there are telephones, so they see great advantages to telephones that can be accessed from different farm buildings, or from the tractor while plowing or harvesting.

Radio was a communications staple for the rural household, particularly from stations that could greatly extend their broadcast range ("clear channel") during the evening hours. Beginning in the late 1950s when television stations became economically feasible in the smaller cities or towns of America, their range also extended to the rural dweller. The greatest expansion in broadcast communication services to rural America came with the availability of the home satellite dish. Satellite-delivered broadcast services freed the rural consumer from the penalty of distance. Practically speaking, the satellite makes distance largely irrelevant. In the 1980s and 1990s, the number of broadcast alternatives that can be received from the transponders of a single satellite expanded. In 1995, digital satellite broadcasting exploded onto the scene for all of the U.S. It offered more channels, better fidelity, and eventually lower costs than the larger satellite dishes that can be seen in the yards adjacent to country homes.

Telecommunications and Rural Businesses and Farms

Telecommunications has been a boon to many types of rural American businesses. In the heyday of catalog sales, particularly in the years after World War II, it became much more common to order merchandise by telephone, than by mail. It became especially convenient for farmers to order feed grain, seed, fertilizers, equipment repair parts, or to get help from a dealer or repair station for equipment problems. Small businesses in rural America found the telephone an increasingly handy means to communicate with their wholesalers or suppliers, or in the case of franchisees, their supervising offices.

After the breakup of AT&T in 1984, states realized that they had more control over the destiny of intrastate telecommunications regulation and soon saw the relationship of activities in this area to aspirations for economic development. Many arguments regarding revisions of state telecommunications regulation in the late 1980s and early 1990s were cast with goals in economic development. The strategy was that enhanced telecommunications capabilities, less regulation, and low tariffs made it possible for many rural businesses to expand. Small manufacturers, for example, could stay in touch with their suppliers and their customers through use of telephone and data communications. Studies in the 1980s showed the rise of businesses that were developed in rural areas that could not exist but for telecommunications. This included businesses that conducted wide area marketing through long distance telephone, businesses that were small scale suppliers of subcomponents for large manufacturers, and even marketing businesses that made exclusive use of the telephone for customer contact ("telemarketing" and "1-800" numbers).

During the 1980, the rise of the personal computer that could be linked through a modem to the telephone system greatly enhanced many of these capabilities. Complex inventory of retail businesses, like drugstores or hardware outlets, could maintain inventories on their local personal computers, and then, with the use of special software, call their suppliers and automate the restocking process. Service and transportation businesses could better plan their schedules by use of computer software and connections, and many kept in touch with their moving units through cellular telephone. The remarkable growth of Wal-Mart is due in part to their innovative uses of telecommunications for inventory management.

In the 1980s and 1990s, small businesses, farms, and cattle operations with access to data networks found themselves in a newly advantageous position to solicit bids for cattle feed, seed, fertilizer, or other supplies. Many rural feedlots (where cattle are brought to fatten for market) have management offices that look like computer centers. Managers track the feeding schedules of cattle, check on weight gains, survey wholesale feed availability for the best prices, and examine their own marketing possibilities to get the highest price for the cattle. The value-added chain is made much more productive and profitable through rural information services.

Although for small businesses to acquire data communications services has often been an expensive step, the coming of the Internet promised to open a new range of possibilities for rural dwellers and business persons. The Internet makes it possible for the resident or client not only to have better access to financial acquisition and marketing services, but promises to extend some of this reach globally. It is possible for the farmer to check grain production, say in Russia, in order to estimate if weather conditions may make it attractive to import or export grain to that market. New data on global commerce or services appear monthly on the Internet.

Telecommunications and Rural Social Service and Medicine

Telecommunications continue to benefit social service delivery in rural America. Distance education can bring highly skilled classroom lectures via satellite to the rural school. This is complemented by two-way video systems that link schools and classes, for example a high school calculus class from a rural school to one in a nearby city. Telecommunications can be used to download new curriculum materials to rural schools, to support voice calling or electronic mail for troubleshooting, and can allow rural schools to integrate their administration much more closely with their school district and state education agencies. There are numerous examples of how rural teachers have been able to confer with one another, thus a biology teacher in a remote rural school can confer with biology teachers in other rural schools and even with experts at the state university.

Distance education systems offer many continuing education alternatives to farmers and rural business persons. There exists a variety of opportunities for individuals to upgrade their education on new farming methods, to participate in small business seminars, or for individuals to improve their technical education for manufacturing jobs.

Rural medicine benefited from telecommunications. Called telemedicine, there are increasing opportunities for rural health care providers to exchange diagnostic information with urban clinics or hospitals. There are types of telemedicine where a rural patient might be seen by a physician in an urban clinic. Telecommunications is used extensively by rural clinics and physicians to take and analyze electrocardiograms. Medical applications of radiology are an accepted part of telemedicine. More diagnostic and medical advice services can be expected not only to link rural and urban medical facilities in the years to come, but also with directly with rural homes on demand.

There are many social implications that modern telecommunication brings to rural America. Some of the previously penalizing aspects of rural living have been eliminated or partly alleviated by the availability of telecommunication services. Rural dwellers no longer need to be in isolation from neighbor to neighbor, from town to town, or from rural area to the city. Connection is as close as a phone call. Rural dwellers in the U.S. watch much of the same television fare as do their urban counterparts. In many cases, rural dwellers with satellite services have more television program alternatives than urban residents have over their cable or over-the-air broadcasting. Perhaps most intriguing is the concept of the "new rural society" as envisaged by Peter Goldmark (1972), the inventor of one form of color television and the long-play record. Goldmark thought that by using telecommunications to "stretch the links," many of the services available to the urban dweller could be delivered to the rural business or household. As this becomes possible, people have more choice as to where they can live or do business. It may no longer be necessary to give up fresh air, clean water, and a beautiful environment for the problems of the city in order to make a good living and have access to social services. So, too, could the child of the rural dweller have access to the state-of-the-art educational services as expanded by distance education.

— *Frederick Williams*

See also

Computers; Development, Community and Economic; Electrification; Education, Youth; Rural Health Care; Infrastructure; Media; Policy, Telecommunications; Technology

References

Bollier, D. *The Importance of Communications and Information Systems to Rural Development in the United States. Report of an Aspen Institute Conference.* Turo, MA: Aspen Institute for Humanistic Studies, 1988.

Dillman, D.A. "The Social Impacts of Information Technology in Rural North America." *Rural Sociology* 50, no. 1 (1985): 1–26.

Dillman, D.A. and D.M. Beck. "Information Technologies and Rural Development in the 1990s." *Journal of State Government* 6, no. 1 (1988): 29–38.

Glasmeier, A.K. The High-Tech Potential: Economic Development in Rural America. New Brunswick, NJ: Center for Urban Policy Research, Rutgers University Press, 1991.

Goldmark, P.C. "Communication and the Community." In *Communication: A Scientific American Book*. San Francisco, CA: W.H. Freeman, 1972.

Goldmark, P.C. "Tomorrow We Will Communicate to Our Jobs." *The Futurist* 6, no. 2 (April 1972): 55-58.

Hudson, H. E. "Ending the Tyranny of Distance: The Impact of New Communications Technologies in Rural North America." In *Competing Visions, Complex Realities: Social Aspects of the Information Society*. Edited by J.R. Schement and L. Lievrouw. Norwood, NJ: Ablex, 1987.

National Rural Telecommunications Cooperative. Herndon, VA. Website available at: http://www.nrtc.coop/us/main/index.

Office of Technology Assessment. *Critical Connections: Communications for the Future.* Publication OTA–CIT–407. Washington DC: U.S. Congress, Office of Technology Assessment 1990.

Parker, E.B., H.E. Hudson, D.A. Dillman, S. Strover, and F. Williams. *Electronic Byways: State Policies for Rural Development through Telecommunications*, 2nd edition. Washington, DC: The Aspen Institute, 1995.

Schmandt, J.F. Williams, R.H. Wilson, and S. Strover, eds. *Telecommunications and Rural Development: A Study of Business and Public Service Applications*. New York, NY: Praeger, 1991.

Strover, S. and F. Williams. *Rural Revitalization and Information Technologies in the United States*. Report to the Ford Foundation. New York, NY: Ford Foundation, 1990.

U.S. Department of Agriculture, Rural Development Telecommunications Program. Website available at: http://www.usda.gov/rus/telecom/index.htm.

Williams, F. *The New Telecommunications*. New York, NY: Free Press, 1991.

Temperate Fruit Industry

Production, marketing, sales and related businesses associated with fruit grown in temperate climates. The fruit industry in recent years has grown substantially, changing products and production and marketing practices, becoming an intensively managed, highly technical enterprise. This article addresses each of these issues.

Temperate Fruit Production

Commercial temperate fruit and nut production in the U.S. ranged from 13 to 15 million metric tons/year in the past decade, and with a record farm gate value of $16.7 billion in 2006 (NASS). These figures do not include many locally grown and consumed products, nor do they include citrus or other subtropical crops. However, in 2007, of the temperate fruit crops, wine, juice and table grapes represented (percent of total tonnage) 41.2 percent; apples, 30.3 percent; peaches and nectarines, 8.6 percent; pears, 5.1 percent; plums and prunes, 3.1 percent; sweet cherries, 1.7 percent; strawberries, 6.8 percent; and cranberries 2.0 percent. Small fruits, other than grapes and strawberries, accounted for less than 1 percent. All these fruits, including grapes and apples, are considered minor crops compared to corn, wheat and soybeans. Although total acreage has decreased a little in the past decade, and total production is down for apples, peaches, pears and apricots, in some cases crop increases have been dramatic, e.g., nearly 70 percent for sweet cherries, 100 percent for strawberries, and over 60 percent for wine grapes. And, over the longer term, 30 years, per-capita fresh fruit consumption has increased substantially.

Temperate Fruit Crops

Before Europeans arrived, Native Americans cultivated some native fruits, but mostly harvested wild fruits. These included raspberries, blackberries, dewberries and strawberries in many parts of North America. Wild grapes grew throughout Eastern America; blueberries and cranberries grew in the North, mulberries and per-simmons in the South, and plums, crab apples and cherries in every part of the country from Canada to the Gulf. Like the natives, early settlers frequently used indigenous plants, and some of these, including corn, soon became dietary and economic mainstays. In the case of fruits, however, settlers more often relied on European introductions, making little effort to domesticate and improve native species.

Most of the deciduous tree fruits now common in America such as apple, pear, quince, peach, sweet and sour cherry, plum (both European and Asian), and apricot are Old World species cultivated there since ancient times. All are native to temperate regions, which provide an essential winter chilling period (extended exposure to temperatures of 4 to 7 degrees C, and where most can withstand mild to moderate, if not severe, winters. These species came to North America with the Europeans and were common features of colonial farms and settlements. They were quickly adopted by Native Americans who relied extensively on cultivated fruits and vegetables in their diets. As American agriculture developed, fruit orchards of all types were soon planted, and nearly every early farmer in the Northern U.S. maintained an apple orchard. Apples were grown for cider, a common drink of the rich and poor. Cider was as much a local agricultural mainstay as butter and eggs, and was, along with applejack and peach brandy, a commodity exported to Southern states and the West Indies.

Grapes, the most widely planted deciduous fruit crop in the world, were not important in the Eastern U.S. until attempts to cultivate relatively cold-tender and disease-susceptible European *Vitis vinifera* varieties were abandoned in favor of more cold-tolerant and pest- and disease-resistant American varieties from *V. labrusca* and *V. rotundifolia*. European grapes did well in California and continue there as the mainstay of table grape, raisin and wine production. Large-scale wine and sparkling wine production did not become important in either the East or California until after the Civil War, and then grew steadily until Prohibition. Since then, per-capita wine consumption, especially of California-grown *V. vinifera* products, has increased, particularly in the past 10 years.

Commercial fruit production, which initially followed settler populations, has more recently expanded where favorable climates provide advantages. Significant production is limited to relatively few areas where latitude, elevation or proximity to large bodies of water result in appropriate climatic conditions. California

New varieties of fruit are being developed for northern climates, such as the HoneyCrisp apple. Photograph courtesy of Maple Hill Orchards, Frazee, Minnesota.

with its moderate winters accounts for half of U.S. deciduous fruit production, including over 90 percent of the grapes. Other important areas are the Pacific Northwest, the eastern shores of the Great Lakes, a narrow belt along the eastern slopes of the Appalachians, and some areas in the Northeast and the Southwest. Since the continental U.S. has few frost-free areas, subtropical species, including those only slightly frost-tolerant (e.g., citrus, olive, pomegranate, avocado and fig) are restricted to the milder climatic regions of California and Florida.

Growing, Propagating, Grafting

Cultivars or named varieties (the result of vegetative propagation from cuttings or grafting) were uncommon in colonial America. Early settlers and missionaries distributed seeds and seedlings that were not likely to come true to type. In the late 1700s, budded and grafted apples and pears became familiar in New England,

and nursery-grown trees were available. In Virginia most trees were grafted. Some early varieties remain in cultivation. The Montmorency tart cherry is several hundred years old, as are several common European pears and wine grapes. The native cranberries and blueberries underwent little improvement since their prehistoric use by Native Americans. However, although more than 2,000 apple varieties have been developed in America, and over 100 have been imported from Europe, few remain in cultivation. Only 13 relatively recent varieties now account for 90 percent of the apples grown in America, but the relative popularity of the most commonly grown cultivars was beginning to change 20 years ago (O'Rourke, 1994), and this continues.

The use of vegetatively propagated rootstocks is now nearly standard in tree fruit production. There are several reasons: growth control (dwarfing effects), induction of precocious (early) flowering, disease and pest resistance, anchorage, lack of suckering (root sprouts) and resistance to drought and flooding. Unfortunately, although some rootstocks are widely used, none provides all these characteristics, and some tree fruits are still grown on rootstocks that lack many of these characteristics.

Trees

Orchard practices have changed dramatically over the last 100 years. Pruning and training were rare practices in early America, except to keep fruit out of the reach of livestock. Johnny Appleseed (John Chapman), an early American nurseryman, reportedly believed that pruning and grafting were wicked. Orchardists now endeavor to develop maximum bearing potential per unit land area in a minimum of time, and to expedite pest control and harvesting. To achieve these goals, orchards are planted at much higher densities than even a generation ago. Density is obtained by using dwarfing (growth controlling) rootstocks coupled with extensive pruning and training (sometimes relying on support with posts and wires) to drastically limit overall tree size. For example, apples previously grown on non-dwarfing rootstocks at a density of 70 or fewer trees per acre may now be on fully dwarfing rootstocks at 1,000 or more trees per acre.

Trees are trained to improve light interception, distribution and penetration into the leaf canopy. Shaded leaves are inefficient; a shaded interior produces inferior fruit of poor color. Efficiency requires maximizing light interception. Balancing these requirements

while considering spray coverage for pests and diseases and convenience in harvesting to reduce labor costs results in a wide variety of highly specialized training methods and cropping systems for nearly all deciduous fruit crops. Barritt and van Dalfsen (1992) referred to this as the orchard system puzzle where tree arrangement, spacing and density, variety selection, tree quality, support system, pruning, training and site selection must all fit together.

Pest and Disease Control

There were no effective disease and pest controls until the late 1800s. When diseases and pests threatened, crop loss, tree removal and orchard abandonment were the alternatives. Life histories of insect pests only began to be understood early in the 1800s. Even less was known about diseases. Early settlers, however, did not have as many problems. Fruit growing was less concentrated, and, consequently, so were the pests. Many of today's most serious diseases and insects are relatively recent introductions from other parts of the world, and in colonial times, fresh market quality was less important. Consumers were less demanding and faulty fruit still made good cider and brandy.

Fruit growers now rely extensively on a variety of chemical and biological controls. Broad spectrum chemicals are still the control mainstays, but chemicals for insect mating disruption (pheromones), "soft" pesticides (insect growth regulators), biopesticides (biologically derived chemicals) and releases of insect parasites (e.g., wasps) are becoming more common. The efficacy of these alternatives often remains to be determined, and both the technical expertise required for implementation and costs are higher.

Pest resistance to conventional chemicals is a continuing problem, and, as alternatives are developed to handle single pests, non-target species may become problems that require more conventional controls. New sprayer designs eliminate drift and are much safer for applicators, but their use is confined to high-density orchards and vineyards where trees and canopies are limited in size. Organic production, using only natural pesticides, is being tested, but will be difficult to achieve in perennial crops that cannot be rotated to new fields as high pest and pathogen populations develop.

Currently, regulatory agencies debate how to implement programs that reduce pesticide risk or use. Technological advances, mainly better understanding of pest biology coupled with research to conserve beneficial insects and mites in apple orchards, enabled some reductions in pesticide rates. Just as significantly, with development of smaller trees and widespread adoption of dwarfing rootstocks, spray coverage is now more efficient, requiring less water and less pesticide. Pest management builds on improvements in both biological understanding and orchard technology. Pesticide policy makers must recognize the importance of such relationships between understanding pest ecology and the ability of growers to adopt new technology if the industry is to progress in pest management.

Fruiting and Harvesting

Most fruit crops will set more fruit than necessary for a full crop. Thinning (partial removal of fruits by hand or chemically) is often essential for quality purposes, to increase average fruit size, and to improve color. Thinning is often necessary to stimulate flower initiation for the next year to avoid alternate bearing (heavy crops alternating with no or light crops).

Harvesting deciduous fruits may be highly mechanized, as in the case of grapes, cherries, blueberries, raspberries and some cling peaches destined for processing, but fruits intended for fresh markets are usually hand harvested to avoid surface damage and bruises that reduce consumer acceptance and accelerate deterioration and decay. Hand harvesting, however, presents problems that increase costs and social issues associated with availability and use of migrant labor.

Grading, Packing, Storage and Processing

New equipment, technology and computers now allow packing houses to sort fruit efficiently by grower source, cultivar, size (weight) and color. The entire packing process is highly automated. Fruit may be graded for firmness and sugar and acid content. These factors relate to maturation or degree of ripening, which affects potential for long-term storage. Harvest quality affects quality after storage, and if picked at the right stage of maturity, some apple varieties may be stored for 6 to 12 months with no loss of fresh market quality. Some pear varieties require an extended chilling period before they can complete maturation and ripening.

Controlled atmosphere (CA) storage, which relies on modifications of the humidity, carbon dioxide and oxygen in the air surrounding stored fruit, can extend the storage life of some fruit. Most apple growers rely on CA technology to market a high-quality product well beyond harvest. Although nearly all major apple growing areas have expanded CA capacities, the technology is not yet applicable to most other fruit species. Nonetheless, advances in storage, shipping and handling transformed much of the industry, with the trend often being concentration of production where growers have climatic advantages.

As indicated, apples and other tree fruits were once grown predominantly to produce ciders and brandies. Fresh products could not be shipped, and processing technology had not developed except for dried products. Use of apples for processing grew steadily between World War II and the early 1970s. Total apple production, which dropped sharply after World War II, began a long-term upward trend in 1952. But, in the mid-1970s, per-capita consumption of almost all processed fruits and vegetables began to decline. Sliced products are still important in processing, especially for pies, but apple processing and juice markets today generally offer relatively low profits, especially with a fivefold increase in the 1980s of imported concentrated frozen juice. Processing is often only a means to salvage otherwise low-value (cull) fruit. Grapes, however, are primarily grown for juice and wine production; many other fruits are grown predominantly for processing into jams and juices.

Regional Differences

Consumer preferences in the past varied significantly from region to region. Varieties grown and marketed locally often reflected these preferences. Today these differences are frequently offset by consumer preference for fresh products year 'round and centralization of marketing by chain stores. Other factors include growers who have regional climatic advantages and are located some distance from markets. They tend to rely on fresh market varieties that can be stored and shipped without significant loss of quality. Processing quality, however, is a different marketing consideration. It is often difficult to substitute fruit varieties and maintain processing quality. With grapes, for example, varietal characteristics are critically important in determining wine quality and type.

Economics

Trends in orchard and vineyard numbers and acreages generally reflect trends in agriculture. Total fruit production is up, although acreages have stabilized or even declined. However, in Washington state, which leads in apple production, acreages increased continuously over the last 30 years, but even there, orchard numbers declined, especially in the 1960s. Small orchards (less than 25 acres) have been declining steadily since the

1970s almost everywhere, but corporate operations remain rare. Although most of the acreage is managed by full-time producers, many orchards and vineyards are operated part-time. The number of young people in the fruit industry, either part-time or full-time, is quite small. Studies in both Michigan and Washington have shown that 50 percent or more of full-time operators are over 55.

Other economic factors include changing consumer preferences, demographics and lifestyles. These have increased per-capita consumption and also demand for greater variety and novelty of fresh fruits and vegetables. Items almost unknown in 1980, such as kiwifruit, star fruit, or Granny Smith apples, were known to most consumers by 1990. Retailers responded by devoting an increasing share of ever-larger stores to fresh produce. Keeping shelves stocked on a 12-month basis requires retailers to draw supplies from many parts of the world. European and Eastern U.S. wholesalers are now as likely to negotiate for fresh apples with suppliers in Chile or New Zealand as in nearby producing regions. The entire fruit industry is responding by learning to identify markets and consumer preferences.

Demands by retailers place pressure on warehouses to carefully monitor their product composition. Larger orchard operations with more available fruit and the potential for more consistency, grades, sizes and varieties have distinct advantages over smaller operators. Consequently, demand for locally grown products from small growers often becomes insignificant in marketing channels.

Import/Export

Over half the apples in New Zealand are exported to compete in the off-season with U.S. and other Northern Hemisphere fruit from storage. Air transportation means that sweet cherries harvested in New Zealand and blueberries from Chile are only one or two days from U.S. markets, just as U.S. producers ship sweet cherries to Tokyo and blueberries to Europe.

Although only 3 percent of U.S. apple production is exported, this is changing. With approval of the North American Free Trade Agreement (NAFTA), apples are now exported to Mexico. An agreement signed in 1993 allows import of U.S. apples into China if exporters meet phytosanitary requirements (certifications that fruit is free of pests and diseases). So far, few growers and shippers are part of such certification programs. Phytosanitary measures became a major impediment to U.S. apple and other fruit exports over the past decade as barriers, import quotas, bans and high tariffs are reduced or eliminated by trade agreements such as NAFTA and the General Agreement on Tariffs and Trade (GATT).

Although consumption of fresh fruit and fruit products is increasing, production has more than kept pace, especially in the past decade. With more domestic and foreign competition, more fruit products, and an increasingly demanding consumer, America's fruit industry is changing. It is more integrated, has larger operators, and places more focus on promotion, quality, product image and export market development. Efficiencies are increasing, and the entire industry is far more mechanized and computerized. Access to quality and diversity of fruit and fruit products throughout the year has never been better.

— *Wayne Loescher*

See also

Aquaculture; Commodity Inspection; Food Safety; Greenhouses; Horticulture; Organic Foods Industry; Plant Diseases; Policy, Agriculture; Trees; Vegetable Industry

References

Barritt, Bruce H. and K. Bert van Dalfsen. *Intensive Orchard Management: A Practical Guide to the Planning, Establishment, and Management of High Density Apple Orchards.* Yakima, WA: Goodfruit Grower, 1992.

Faust, Miklos. *Physiology of Temperate Zone Fruit Trees.* New York, NY: John Wiley and Sons, Inc. 1989.

Hedrick, Ulysses P. *A History of Horticulture in America to 1860.* Portland, OR: Timber Press, 1950.

Kader, Adel A., ed. *Postharvest Technology of Horticultural Crops* Oakland, CA: University of California, Division of Agriculture and Natural Resources, 1992.

O'Rourke, A. Desmond. *The World Apple Market.* Binghamton, NY: Haworth Press, 1994.

Otto, S. *The Backyard Orchardist.* Maple City, MI: Otto Graphics, 1993.

Phillips, M. *The Apple Grower: A Guide for the Organic Orchardist.* White River Junction, VT: Chelsea Green Publishing, 1998.

Ryugo, Kay. *Fruit Culture: Its Science and Art.* New York, NY: John Wiley and Sons, Inc., 1988.

U.S. Department of Agriculture, National Agricultural Statistics Service. Available online at: http://www.usda.gov.

Webster, A.D., and N.E. Looney, eds. *Cherries: Crop Physiology, Production, and Uses.* Oxon, UK: CAB International, 1996.

Westwood, Melvin N. *Temperate-Zone Pomology, Physiology and Culture,* 3rd edition. Portland, OR: Timber Press, 1993.

Terrorism

The use or threatened use of certain unlawful acts by individuals or groups of people with the intention to intimidate or coerce people, societies and governments, to spread propaganda, to erode public confidence in government, or to bring about large-scale losses of life, the destruction of property, widespread illness and injury, the displacement of large numbers of people, and devastating economic loss, often for political or ideological reasons. This paper discusses terrorism risks and security vulnerabilities in rural areas. While rural communities may seem to be at a lower risk to terrorism threats compared to their urban counterparts, many rural and agricultural interests may be easier and more appealing targets for terrorists. An examination of rural communities, their vulnerabilities and capacity to respond to terrorism plays an important role in strengthening rural preparedness.

Introduction

Rural America faces challenging terrorism risks and security vulnerabilities. Rural communities are in several unique ways more vulnerable than their urban counterparts to terrorism, communicable disease outbreaks and natural disasters. While urban areas present complex security problems, given their high population densities and vital assets and infrastructure, the rural sector poses significant security challenges because of the unique threats to agriculture, food and water supplies, nuclear plants and the fragile infrastructure within vast and often desolate areas. Although the potential of terrorism threats in rural areas has been recognized for many years, until recently attention has mostly been focused on America's metropolitan areas resulting in disparities between rural and urban readiness.

Defining Rural

To analyze the issue of terrorism on rural America, it is important to describe what is meant by rural. Defining "rural" is not a simple task. The perception of rurality is multidimensional and its characterization is attached to particular objectives and views. Rural areas have been defined as particular types of regions and communities according to some objective measures, such as population density, commuting patterns, poverty or unemployment rates, extent of wild areas and farmland. There is no one standard definition of rural which can satisfy all stakeholders or their goals. It is difficult to arrive at a single definition as the classification has to suit different purposes. There is nevertheless a need

Table 1.
Rural/Urban—Land and Population
(Source: Shambaugh-Miller, 2007)

Definition	Percentage Classified as Rural/Non-Metropolitan	
	Land (Percent)	Population (Percent)
U.S Census Bureau: Urban and Rural Areas	97.4	19.7
Economic Research Service, U.S Department of Agriculture & WWAMI: Rural-Urban Commuting Areas (RUCA)	78.8*	19.6*
U.S. Office of Management and Budget (OMB): Metropolitan and non-metropolitan areas	74.5	17.4

*RUCA codes used to calculate percent of land and people classified as rural: 4.0, 4.2, 5.0, 5.2, 6.0, 6.1, 7.0, 7.2, 7.3, 7.4, 8.0, 8.2, 8.3, 8.4, 9.0, 9.1, 9.2, 10.0, 10.2, 10.3, 10.4, 10.5, 10.6

to arrive at adequate definition(s) of rural that would capture the diverse characteristics of rurality. Table 1 shows the percentage of land and people classified as rural under the most common definitions.

The population in rural America is smaller and more dispersed than in urban America. However, rural America is not only home to nearly one-fifth of the nation's population but also extends over more than three quarters of America's total land area (Table 1 and Figure 1).

Terrorism and Rural Vulnerabilities

Terrorists use threats to cause fear and a feeling of vulnerability among the public to get attention to their political or ideological agenda. Terrorist acts bring about large-scale losses of life, the destruction of property, widespread physical and psychological illness and injury, the displacement of large numbers of people, and devastating economic loss. Terrorism threats can originate locally or from foreign countries. Many rural and agricultural interests may be easier and more appealing targets for terrorists, given the risks and possibilities of widespread economic damage. Threats in rural settings may be the outcome of opportunistic acts, as there might be inadequate security systems, low vigilance and alert, and lower risks of being detected. Acts of terrorism may include bombings, cyber attacks, hijacking and the use of chemical, biological and radiological weapons. Examples of chemical agents are ricin, mustard gas, cyanides, sarin and arsenic. Biological agents include anthrax, smallpox, salmonella, *E. coli* and Hantavirus. Instances of radiological terrorist events include the introduction of radioactive material into a food or water supply, use of dirty bombs, the destruction of a nuclear facility, and the explosion of a nuclear device near a population center.

Although this paper discusses only terrorism risks, we need to point out that the rural areas are very vulnerable to other types of disasters, including natural disasters such as floods, fires, snowstorms, earthquakes and communicable disease outbreaks. In the rural areas the major points of vulnerability lie within the agricultural sector: food supply, livestock, crops, agricultural chemicals, and chemical and storage facilities. Rural areas support the country's agricultural industry and produce the nation's food. Much of the nation's water supply and nuclear plants are also located in rural areas. Other potential targets include the transportation infrastructure, utilities, sensitive government installations, unprotected country borders, limited healthcare infrastructure and other isolated targets of opportunity. The rural infrastructure might also be overwhelmed if there is a mass exodus from the urban areas under terrorist attack or other mass emergency events.

Potential Rural Targets

Farming and Agriculture. The food and agriculture industry in the United States is highly effective and productive, and plays a very important role in the economic sector. Its productivity allows Americans to spend less than 10 percent of their disposable income on food, compared to a global average which is two to three times higher. Farming and ranching are the basis of the $1 trillion food and fiber industry with nearly $60 billion in annual exports. According to the National Association of State Department of Agriculture (NASDA), this industry generates almost 15 percent of the total economic activity in the nation, as well as providing almost 18 percent of the country's jobs. Figure 2 shows the average size of farms and the market value of agricultural products sold.

Agroterrorism is an intentional release of a disease to livestock or crops or into the food chain and is often considered as a form of bioterrorism. An agroterrorist attack may not create the psychological shock and trauma factors of other more "instantaneous and visible" terrorist acts such as bombings and explosions; nevertheless, it is a potentially appealing terrorist act because of the disastrous consequences to which it may lead. Damage from an agroterrorist incident can be widespread, and can include loss of lives, economic loss, and collapse of public confidence in authorities. The protection of this important industry is crucial given its significant vulnerabilities stemming from concen-

trated and intensive farming practices, susceptibility of livestock to disease, lack of farm and food-related security and surveillance, inadequate disease-reporting systems, insufficient veterinarian training, unavailability of countermeasures or quarantines and incident response plans, and a focus on aggregate rather than individual livestock statistics (Chalk, 2004; Monke, 2004). The potential of terrorist acts against the food and agricultural industry is increasingly being acknowledged as a national security concern. The National Homeland Security Strategy recognizes the importance of this industry and in 2003 designated agriculture as a critical infrastructure as per Homeland Security Presidential Directive 7 (HSPD-7). The agroterrorism issue has received increased attention over the past few years, including two bills which have been introduced in the 108th Congress to improve preparedness for agroterrorism. In 2004 HSPD-9 was released to establish a national policy to protect against terrorist attacks on agriculture and food systems.

Energy Facilities and Nuclear Plants. Terror acts in rural areas can go beyond agroterrorism. Rural communities are vulnerable to nuclear terrorism (Stamm, 2002). Many nuclear plants and energy facilities (Figures 3 and 4) are located in rural settings. Additionally, the U.S. Air Force missile launch facilities are located in rural areas (HRSA, 2002). These can be targeted causing great human and economic loss.

Road Networks and Transport. Roads and bridges, which are fundamental forms of infrastructure for any community, may be targeted, thereby demolishing the crucial communication network for connecting people, goods and critical services. The road network in rural America is vital for the nation's transportation system, providing links between rural-to-rural and rural-to-urban places. Rural roads account for 80 percent of the total U.S. road mileage and 40 percent of the vehicle miles traveled (Quiros et al., 2003). Hazardous materials which are located in or are transited via rural settings may also be potential targets. Hazardous materials, or dangerous goods, include explosives, gases, flammable liquids and solids, oxidizing substances, poisonous and infectious substances, toxic chemicals and pesticides, radioactive materials, corrosive substances and hazardous wastes. Major highways and hazmat routes are shown in Figure 5.

Water Supply. The headwaters for a great part of America's water supply are located in rural areas. With the rise in urban population, many municipalities face growing water demand and increasing competition for

Figures 1–7 appear in color at the end of this volume.

declining water supplies. Water rights are increasingly being purchased from rural areas to satisfy the urban demand (NREL, 2006). Traditionally, water infrastructure was overlooked as a potential terrorism target; mostly, contamination of water was caused from natural or unintentional accidents. It has now become apparent that intentional contamination of water is a possible public health hazard. The Environmental Protection Agency (EPA), with other federal agencies, has worked with water utilities and state and local governments to improve the drinking water security. Congress has appropriated funds for the EPA to work with states and the water sector to improve the security of water supplies. Figure 6 shows the major rivers and dams in the U.S.

Rural Healthcare. The public healthcare system is a crucial component of the nation's preparedness against terrorism and natural disasters. Reports on rural healthcare system preparedness have emphasized the limited capabilities and capacities of rural hospitals. While both urban and rural healthcare systems are confronted with many barriers to preparedness, rural healthcare facilities face additional unique challenges (Stamm, 2002). The rural healthcare setting is characterized by geographic constraints and weather extremes, long distances between facilities and supporting organizations, and long transport times, challenges to professional quality of life (Stamm, 2006), and an increasing number of underinsured and uninsured rural communities. Most rural hospitals are small and have limited human and financial resources and insufficient surge capacity. They have deficiencies in emergency and hazmat equipment, in decontamination and critical care capacity and in communications systems. Rural healthcare facilities face healthcare workforce shortages and place heavy reliance on volunteer first responders. Although 20 percent of Americans live in rural areas, only some 9 percent of the nation's physicians practice there (AHRQ, 2005). Hospitals have limited personnel with expertise and/or experience in surveillance or outbreak monitoring, in mental health issues, in infectious diseases, and in mass emergency events. There has been a relative lack of attention on the psychological consequences and the manifestation of physical problems as a result of terrorist events in rural communities.

Large-scale mass casualty events will quickly overwhelm rural healthcare facilities. Building capacity and capability to respond to mass casualty events are difficult for the best of hospitals that have access to resources and are a particularly overwhelming challenge for the nation's approximately 2,000 rural hospitals. Figure 7 shows the locations of hospitals in the U.S.

Rural Readiness. Are rural communities ready and prepared to identify, respond to and mitigate terrorism threats and acts? Strategies have been set up at federal, state and local levels to prepare the rural areas for intentional or natural disasters. Several studies on rural readiness indicate that the rural communities are not as ready as they could or should be. The disparities between rural and urban preparedness are largely attributed to insufficient funding, limited access to training, and a lack of human resources and infrastructure. The inherent characteristics of rurality such as weather extremes, geographic inaccessibility and low population play a role in these challenges. Many planning guidelines and recommendations have focused mostly on urban and suburban regions and may not have considered variances in rural communities. In its Ready or Not? 2006 report (TFAH, 2003-2007), the Trust for America's Health observes that each state has different strengths, weaknesses and unique challenges that impact its ability to prepare for and respond to public health emergencies that have to be taken into account.

Strengthening Rural Preparedness

To strengthen rural preparedness, these areas need further consideration:

- Identification and assessment of all vulnerabilities and risks in rural areas
- Leadership and coordinated planning at the local, regional and state levels
  - Participation of all stakeholders in preparedness programs
  - Setting up and clarification of roles, relationships and responsibilities
- Acquisition, improvement and maintenance of equipment and infrastructure
- Improvement of telecommunication infrastructure
- Training of all stakeholders using traditional and novel distance learning technologies
- Implementation of new surge capacity approaches and shifting away from isolated hospital preparedness to collaborative preparedness with several entities including community and other hospitals
- Strengthening the quality of the disaster response by supporting professional and volunteer responders who are themselves at risk

Figures 1–7 appear in color at the end of this volume.

- Availability and accessibility of financial support for rural preparedness activities
- Establishment of rigorous accountability procedures and performance measures in all preparedness programs as a condition of their funding

— *Jaishree Beedasy, Ramesh Ramloll, B. Hudnall Stamm*

See also

Department of Homeland Security and Rural America; Disaster Preparedness and Mitigation; Emergency Management Professionals; Military Personnel and Industry; Policing; Rural Emergency Management Programs; Rural Emergency Response and Recovery

References

Agency for Healthcare Research and Quality (AHRQ). *Health Care Disparities in Rural Areas: Selected Findings from the 2004 National Healthcare Disparities Report Agency for Healthcare Research and Quality.* AHRQ Pub No. 05-P022 (May). Rockville, MD: Agency for Healthcare Research and Quality, 2005.

Association of State and Territorial Health Officials (ASTHO). *Rural Public Health Preparedness Challenges: An Ongoing Dialogue Issue.* ASTHO Report (June) 2006. Arlington, VA: Association of State and Territorial Health Officials, 2006. Available at www.astho.org/pubs/RuralPublicHealthPreparednessChallenges.pdf.

Campbell, Paul, Joshua Frances, and Michael Meit. *Preparing for Public Health Emergencies: Meeting the Challenges in Rural America.* Conference proceedings and recommendations, Saint Paul, MN, September 27-28, 2004. Available at: www.prepare.pitt.edu/pdf/crhp_agenda.pdf.

Chalk, Peter. *Hitting America's Soft Underbelly: The Potential Threat of Deliberate Biological Attacks Against the U.S. Agricultural and Food Industry.* Santa Monica, CA: RAND Corporation, 2004.

Gursky, Elin A. *Hometown Hospitals: The Weakest Link? Bioterrorism Readiness in America's Rural Hospitals.* ANSER Institute for Homeland Security. Report Commissioned by the National Defense University, Center for Technology and National Security Policy, 2004. Available at www.ndu.edu/ctnsp/Hometown_Hospitals.pdf.

Health Resources and Services Administration (HRSA). *Rural Communities and Emergency Preparedness.* Washington, DC: Office of Rural Health Policy, HRSA, U.S. Department of Health and Human Services, 2002 . Available at: ftp://ftp.hrsa.gov/ruralhealth/RuralPreparedness.pdf.

Monke, Jim. *Agroterrorism: Threats and Preparedness.* Washington, DC: Library of Congress, Congressional Research Service, CRS Report RL32521, 2004. Available at: www.fas.org/irp/crs/RL32521.pdf (2004); www.law.umaryland.edu/marshall/crsreports/crsdocuments/RL32521_08252006.pdf (updated 2006); www.nationalaglawcenter.org/assets/crs/RL32521.pdf (updated 2007).

National Renewable Energy Laboratory (NREL). *The Wind/Water Nexus: Wind Powering America.* Report # DOE/GO-102006-2218 (April). Washington, DC: NREL, U.S. Department of Energy, 2006.

Niska, Richard W. and Catherine W. Burt. "Emergency Response Planning in Hospitals, United States: 2003-2004." *Advance Data* no. 391 (2007): 1-13.

Quiros, Lesliam and Barrett Shaver. *Rural Road Links: A Review on Current Research Projects & Initiatives Aimed at Reducing Vehicle Crash Fatalities on Rural Roads.* UC Berkeley Traffic Safety Center Paper UCB-TSC-TR-2003-10. Berkeley, CA: University of California, Berkeley, 2003.

Shambaugh-Miller, Michael. *Development of a Rural GIS Typology for Policy Makers.* RUPRI Center for Rural Health Policy Analysis, 2007. Available at: www.unmc.edu/ruprihealth/presentations/6th%20Quadrennial%20BCA%20Symposium%20Presentation.pdf.

Stamm, B. Hudnall. "Terrorism Risks in Rural and Frontier America." *Engineering in Medicine and Biology Magazine.* 21, no.5 (2002): 100-111.

Stamm, B. Hudnall. *Recruitment and Retention of a Quality Health Workforce in Rural Areas.* National Rural Health Association, Issue Paper Number 14: Issues of Preserving Rural Professional Quality of Life, May 2006.

Tiemann, Mary. *Safeguarding the Nation's Drinking Water: EPA and Congressional Actions.* Congressional Research Service (CRS) Report RL31294 (March 13). Washington, DC: CRS, 2007. Available at: www.ncseonline.org/NLE/CRSreports/07Apr/RL31294.pdf.

Trockman, Steven, *Rural Emergency Preparedness: What All Rural Responders Must Know About Public Health Emergencies.* Text book sponsored by the University of Pittsburg Graduate School of Public Health Center for Public Health Preparedness and the University of Pittsburg Center For Rural Health Practice, 2005. Available at: www.prepare.pitt.edu/pdf/crhp_textbook.pdf.

Trust for America's Health (TFAH). *Ready or Not? Protecting the Public's Health from Disease, Disasters, and Bioterrorism.* TFAH Annual Reports 2003-2007. Available at: http://healthyamericans.org/reports/bioterror07.

Willis, Henry H., Jamison Jo Medby, Andrew R. Morral, and Terrence K. Kelly. *Estimating Terrorism Risk.* Santa Monica, CA: RAND Corporation, 2005.

Figures 1–7 appear in color at the end of this volume.

Textile Industry

The manufacture of yarns and woven, knitted, and non-woven fabrics for apparel, home furnishings, automobiles, hospitals, and industrial end uses; broader usage denotes the complex of industries producing fibers for textiles, the textiles themselves, and apparel and other end products made from textiles. This article reviews the historical development and current state of the textile industry in relation to its role in the rural economy.

History of the Rural Textile Industry

In the 17th and 18th centuries, needed textiles often were produced at home. Fluctuating availability and cost contributed to the home manufacture of cloth, which was typically made with homegrown flax or wool. Yarn spinning was the most likely process to be undertaken at home. Rural women and children spun for their families. Yarn and cloth could be bought from local women, and in prosperous areas consumers could order textiles from local craftspeople or acquire imports. Weaving operations were less likely to be undertaken in the home. Looms were larger and more expensive than spinning wheels. Paying skilled weavers yielded products of higher quality and greater complexity. The services of water-powered mills might be purchased to complete the necessary cleaning, shrinking, and felting of home-produced wool fabrics. Such mills operated in sparsely populated areas throughout the U.S. well into the 19th century.

However secured, textiles were needed for household linens and to be transformed into functional garments or other constructed items for the home. Within a home economy, sewing was women's work, requiring some knowledge of how to cut and join pieces to fit them to a body. Coarser or cheaper fabrics, looser styling, and poorer fit indicated lower economic status. Clothing might be patched, remade, and passed to others until it was worn out. Tailors were employed by those with the financial means to create custom fit, fashionable garments of finer fabrics.

Commercial manufacture of common textiles was not a reality in North America until the late 1700s and early 1800s, and then was limited. Access to imported textiles varied at first with the arrival of ships and later with transportation and distribution networks. As the 19th century progressed, more factory-made textiles became available from growing industries. Home production declined most slowly in rural areas. The expanding U.S. cotton and wool textile industries focused on producing commonly used fabrics for consumers in rural and urban settings and for manufacturers of ready-to-wear garments. Rural Americans with access to stores or itinerant merchants could purchase woven textiles such as sheeting, shirting, duck, flannel, cassimere, and jean.

New England companies led textile industrialization. Large mills turned first to young farm women to supply much of the labor. Textile workers coming off the land were significant sources of labor for Southern textile mills. Many Southern cotton mills became part of the rural landscape when built in small towns. Small Midwestern woolen mills often were located at rural sites with the intent of selling locally (Dublin 1979; Hall, et al. 1987).

By the 1850s, men's apparel was being manufactured for the marketplace as ready-to-wear, and men could purchase any necessary clothing item. Reliance on construction of men's wear by family members lessened; custom production by tailors remained for the wealthy. Industrial development in menswear was urban-centered, but basic sewing tasks sometimes were put out to rural seamstresses, and small merchant tailoring businesses in frontier areas offered ready-mades.

Only limited types of ready-made items were marketed for women until the late 1800s to early 1900s. Before then, women had to sew or find a dressmaker or seamstress. Many women who earned a living or augmented family income through sewing resided in rural areas. They and women sewing for their families were aided by the availability of full-sized garment patterns, first marketed in the 1860s. Broad distribution of sewing machines by the 1870s made construction much easier, and relieved some of the tedium of the mending or restyling required to make continued use of items.

Garment patterns, women's magazines, and catalogs provided fashion information in rural areas. By 1900, the expansion of mail-order catalogs targeted rural Americans and substantially increased access to textile products. Two companies, Montgomery Ward and Sears Roebuck, expanded to offer all kinds of merchandise. The advent of rural free delivery by the U.S. Postal Service at the turn of the century helped distribution. The timing corresponded with the expansion of women's ready-to-wear apparel manufacturing, and rural women could purchase a broad assortment of garments. Expanded availability of ready-to-wear in the early 20th century led to a decline in the number of tailors, dressmakers and seamstresses. As cars and roads proliferated, stores in larger towns became more accessible. With the advent of rayon fabrics by the 1920s and the post-World War II addition of nylon, polyester, and other synthetic fibers, textile and apparel product variety increased, and rural-urban access differences lessened.

The U.S. Textile Industrial Complex Today

In 2006, the industrial sectors that produce textiles, textile products, and apparel employed approximately 595,000 people; 33 percent of them worked in textile mills, 27 percent in textile product manufacturing, and 40 percent in apparel production. Natural fibers (e.g., cotton) from the agricultural sector and synthetic fibers (e.g., polyester) from chemical corporations provide the primary raw materials for textile and apparel products. Cotton has long been grown in the American South; now new fibers made from cultivated plants such as corn and bamboo from different locations are becoming available. From fiber to apparel, many factories have been located in towns and small to medium size cities adjacent to rural areas. Textile and textile product manufacturing is centered in the Southeast. Apparel production is most concentrated in the Northeast, California, and the Southeast. Although 88 percent of textile and apparel facilities are small, having fewer than 50 employees, 72 percent of all workers are located in establishments with 50 or more employees (BLS 2008).

Textile manufacturers execute yarn spinning, weaving, knitting, and finishing (e.g., dyeing, bleaching, and stonewashing). Textile product companies include makers of carpets, rugs and other goods for residential and nonresidential interiors, as well as a broad assortment of industrial uses. Apparel companies design garments for production and distribution. Some companies have their own factories manufacture the garments, but many contract with facilities that provide cutting and sewing operations.

Textile manufacturing relies increasingly on a skilled workforce to operate new technologies that include automated processes, promote efficient production, and control quality. Apparel manufacturing remains labor intensive because of the need for many workers to cut and sew garment parts that vary with changing styles. Since the 1970s, retail price competition in the American marketplace has led many retailers and apparel companies to produce or buy garments in lower wage countries outside the U.S. Foreign apparel producers often use foreign textiles. Since 1994, 362,200 textile jobs and 638,200 apparel jobs have disappeared, and a continuing decline in textile and apparel manufacturing workers is predicted into the 2010s. In the many cases where a textile mill or apparel factory was the major employer in a small town, rural areas frequently have been hard hit by this economic transition. Although there are many fewer production jobs, the product development, manufacturing, and distribution functions remain centered in the U.S., but typically in urban locations (BLS 2008; Home Textiles 2007).

World Production and Trade

From 1974 through 2004, U.S. textile and apparel manufacturing was partially protected by the Multi-Fiber Arrangement (MFA), an international trade agreement that set quotas to govern the quantity of products that could be imported from developing countries. In 2005, the World Trade Organization's (WTO) Agreement on Textiles and Clothing replaced the MFA and eliminated quotas (USDA 2004). Since then, U.S. producers and workers that were already affected by rising levels of imported goods, have experienced the more damaging impact of a heightened surge of apparel made in Asia, particularly China. The movement of a significant portion of production to low labor cost areas overseas has benefitted American consumers as it has kept retail prices relatively low, but it has hurt domestic, particularly small rural, manufacturers. Because large retailers can easily go outside the U.S. to obtain goods and keep prices low while maintaining the flexibility they need to satisfy rapidly changing consumer desires, they can make demands on U.S. producers regarding quality standards, prices, and delivery times. Lack of the financial and technological resources to meet the demands has resulted in plants being closed and jobs lost.

In 1994, the North American Free Trade Agreement (NAFTA) was implemented to create a freer trade environment between the U.S., Canada, and Mexico by reducing tariffs and restrictive practices. The U.S. is a leading exporter of cotton, and NAFTA expanded the cotton trade level among its members. The elimination of quotas in 2005, however, adversely affected the U.S. cotton market, resulting in a significant decline in demand for U.S. cotton (USDA 2005). Trade liberalization has led to increases in overall textile and apparel exports, but larger increases in imports. In 2006, the U.S. hit a record trade deficit of $86.5 billion, a nearly 154 percent rise from 1994 (USITC 2007). Further globalization and trade liberalization will continue to affect the viability of U.S. textiles and apparel sector, especially producers and workers in rural communities.

The Role of Unions

Although a small proportion of textile and apparel workers are members today, the labor unions that developed historically with the textile and apparel industries still play a role in supporting industrial production in the U.S. UNITE HERE, formed in 2004, is the composite union that includes several formerly separate labor organizations. The Union of Needletrades, Industrial and Textile Employees (UNITE) was created in 1995 through the merger of the International Ladies' Garment Workers' Union (ILGWU) and the Amalgamated Clothing and Textile Workers Union (ACTWU). The latter had evolved from 1965-1983 combinations of the Amalgamated Clothing Workers of America, the Textile Workers Union of America, the American Federation of Hosiery Workers, the United Shoe Workers, and the United Hatters, Cap and Millinery Workers' International Union (UNITE HERE 2008).

Beginning in the early 1900s, the ILGWU and ACWA worked to improve poor working conditions, stabilize wages, and improve manufacturing efficiencies to service their members and the companies they organized. Over the years, they established adult education programs, health centers, day care facilities, and pension and welfare funds in rural and urban areas. In the 1970s, the ACTWU sponsored major organizing drives for textile and apparel plants in the rural South. In the same period, the ILGWU launched a major advertising campaign, "Look for the Union Label," that aimed to raise Americans' awareness of the impact on jobs of purchasing imported textile and apparel products. Both unions worked individually, together, and with businesses to seek legislation restricting imports to protect industry jobs (Douglas 1986; Ulrich 1995; UNITE HERE 2008).

Consumers and the Environment: Issues and Legislation

Federal laws directly target the textile industrial complex in relation to consumer product knowledge and protection. From 1939-1971, four laws were passed to govern consumer product labeling: Wool Products Labeling Act (1939), Fur Products Labeling Act (1952), Textile Fiber Products Identification Act (1958/2006), and Care Labeling (1971/2000). The Flammable Fabrics Act (1953/1990) and Federal Hazardous Substance Act (1960/1995) provide rules to protect consumers from potentially harmful situations involving textile products.

In relation to the environment, the textile industrial complex is guided by legislation drafted for agriculture and all industries to address the issues of clean air and water, pollution and toxic substances, and solid waste disposal. For legal, environmental, and economic reasons, companies making or finishing textiles spend large sums of money to make the manufacturing adjustments necessary to reduce water and energy consumption and control polluting emissions. Some companies are developing, producing, or adopting materials that are environmentally friendly; examples include bamboo, corn, naturally colored and organically grown cotton, and fibers made from recycled soda bottles. Cultivation of natural fibers as renewable resources particularly affects the rural U.S. Companies that dye, bleach, or complete finishes like stonewashing jeans work to clean, recycle, and retain water within factories. Some carpet and apparel producers have taken responsibility for dealing with discarded products' contributions to land fills by taking them back and finding environmentally positive ways to reuse or redistribute them.

— *Pamela V. Ulrich and Sang-Eun Byun*

See also

Employment; Labor Unions; Manufacturing Industry; Trade, International; Wool Industry

References

Bureau of Labor Statistics (BLS). "Textile, Textile Product, and Apparel Manufacturing." Washington, DC: U. S. Department of Labor, Bureau of Labor Statistics, 2008. Available at http://www.bls.gov/oco/cg/cgs015. htm.

Burns, L.D. and Bryant, N.O. *The Business of Fashion*. New York: Fairchild Publications, 2007.

Douglas, S.U. *Labor's New: Unions and the Mass Media*. Norword, NJ: Apex Publishing Co., 1986.

Dublin, T. *Women at Work: The Transformation of Work and Community in Lowell, Massachusetts, 1826-1860*. New York, NY: Columbia University Press, 1979.

Hall, J.D., J. Leloudis, R. Korstad, M. Murphy, L. Jones, and C.B. Daly. *Like a Family: The Making of a Southern Cotton Mill World*. Chapel Hill, NC: University of North Carolina Press, 1987.

Home Textiles Today. U.S. Job Loss Breaks 1 Million Mark for Textiles and Apparel Since NAFTA, 2007. Available at http://www.hometextilestoday.com/article/CA6448940.html.

Kidwell, C.B. and Christman, M.C. *Suiting Everyone: The Democratization of Clothing in America*. Washington, D.C.: Smithsonian Institution Press, 1974.

Textile World. "US/China Textile Trade Deficit Hits New High," 2008. Available at http://www.textileworld.com/

Articles/2008/February_2008/Textile_World_News/ Textile_Trade_Deficit_Hits_New_High.html.

Ulrich, P.V. "Look for the Label"—The International Ladies' Garment Workers' Union Label Campaign, 1959-1975. *Clothing and Textiles Research Journal* 13, no. 1 (1995): 49-56.

UNITE HERE, 2008. Available at http://www.unitehere. org/about.

U.S. Department of Agriculture (USDA). "Bilateral Fiber and Textile Trade Database." Washington, DC: U.S. Department of Agriculture, Economic Research Service, 2004. Available at http://www.ers.usda.gov/Data/Fiber-TextileTrade.

U.S. Department of Agriculture (USDA). "Cotton: Market Outlook." Washington, DC: U.S. Department of Agriculture, Economic Research Service, 2005. Available at http://www.ers.usda.gov/briefing/cotton/2005baseline. html.

U.S. International Trade Commission (USITC). Shifts in U.S. Merchandise Trade 2006, 2007. Available at http:// www.usitc.gov/tradeshifts/2007/tradeshifts_textiles. htm.

Wilson, K. *A History of Textiles*. Boulder, CO: Westview Press, 1979.

Theatrical Entertainment

Dramatic presentations ranging from melodramas and Shakespeare's plays to the non-scripted events, such as vaudeville, medicine shows and Chautauqua. This article examines the variety of theatrical and related entertainment performance events found in rural America during the rapid expansion of the country following the Civil War. An explanation of likely performance spaces and the variety of events that used the expanding railroad system shows a breadth of experiences beyond the legitimate drama from the 1870s into the 1920s, such as tent rep (drama in a tent), Chautauqua, medicine shows, variety and vaudeville. When the single auditorium in a rural community had to accommodate all these events, the entertainment calendar was a mosaic of events filling the social and cultural needs of a community. The impact of mass entertainment forms, such as film, radio and television, and the loss of the road (chains of theaters networked across the country), meant the almost complete loss of live entertainment to rural America by World War II.

The Development of Theater in Rural America

In the later part of the nineteenth century, an increasing number of performance entertainments followed the rail lines out of the large cities. A large population base, needed to repeatedly fill a theater, could be obtained by moving the performers from location to location. The economic incentive of developing the road was enhanced by communities including a performance space for use by these troupes of entertainment early in town construction. This is particularly evident in the Western development of the country following the Civil War, whereas in Eastern states, theatrical sites became additions to a community. Glenn and Poole (1993) documented over 300 existing structures in Iowa and estimate four times that number originally existed. This author located over 400 sites in North Dakota; only 5 percent of the structures survive.

Active construction of theaters from the 1870s into the 1910s resulted in distinct types of construction that often reflected the increasing success of the community. Some of these included 1) a general utility hall on the second floor of a commercial establishment, 2) a second-floor theatrically equipped space with specific theater seating and support areas, often becoming very elaborate, 3) a single-story building with a stage and flat floor for multiple uses, and 4) large, multi-floor, ornate grand opera houses. Because these buildings became gathering places for the community, they served many social functions. It was not uncommon to find kitchens and reports of meals served in conjunction with a performance. Schools rarely had auditoriums, and churches often had proscriptions about entertainments, so the immediate community could converge on the opera house for more than a cultural experience. The buildings became the hub of many fraternal, religious, business, athletic, and a wide assortment of professional and amateur entertainments. As communities grew, often so did the number and size of these spaces. Local and regional historical societies and museums continue to document and preserve mementos of these cultural and social centers.

Community leadership wished to emulate the cultural values of the legitimate theater found in larger cities. As the railroads spread, so did the touring companies, taking large and small troupes doing Shakespeare, *The Count of Monte Cristo*, or *Ten Nights in a Bar Room*, and stars such as Sarah Bernhardt to all stops along the rails. These troupes were booked across national circuits from New York City and smaller regional circuits developed from important regional cities such as Chicago. In the first decade of the twentieth century, there were between 230 and 420 troupes on the road (Poggi, 1968). Of the some 3,000 theaters and a national population around 76 million at the time, over 1,000 theaters were adequate for the top touring productions (Lewis, 1973). Resident acting companies in larger cities (Durham, 1987) had smaller counterparts throughout the country, which brought most Americans into contact with mainstream theater. In examining cultural concerns about leisure time during the nineteenth century, even the highest pretensions of culture had to deal with the sentiments expressed in "A Lecture on Amusements"—"It is a fair objection to the theater, that, as an amusement, it is too exciting.... To older persons it may not be so hurtful; but for the young man, I do not know of any habit…which is more injurious, or more fraught with serious danger, than that of theatergoing. It stimulates the imagination too strongly" (Lewis, 1973). Such attitudes, then and now, drive discussions about the role of entertainment in the value system of a small community. The movement in documenting the history of popular culture has revealed additional entertainment forms that contributed to the discussion about appropriate entertainments for American audiences.

Beyond the Drama

Paralleling the legitimate theater was the development of troupes of variety and vaudeville performers into circuits. Although not bound by a dramatic script, these entertainments often repeated a similar pattern of acts. A combination of performers with physical skills such as juggling or knife throwing, comic patter such as George Burns and Gracie Allen, singing by the likes of Al Jolson, or trained animal acts gave a predictable evening of entertainment. The earlier form, variety, though similar to vaudeville, often carried a tarnished image and appealed to a rougher, predominantly male crowd. Vaudeville's claim to wholesome family entertainment meant easy booking into the opera house. Another social hub in many communities was the saloon. Less refined performances could move from specialized saloon theaters in large cities into a circuit of performances in smaller cities. Other troupes, such as companies of British Blondes, could perform their musical numbers, with high stepping chorines, in the largest opera house in the county or be forced into one of the less desirable saloon theaters in a battle of community standards. These minimally scripted spectacles and troupes of specialty performers became enormously popular, as did

the omnipresent minstrel company. The musical and dance numbers of the minstrel show, the racy song-and-dance couple of variety, and the trained pig act opening a vaudeville evening meant live entertainment to audiences of merchants and farmers everywhere. Another of the entertainments that moved into town for a day or two would be the medicine show. Sometimes done in the opera house, this combination of performance and salesmanship often came in a vehicle that allowed a quick setup and takedown. The entertainment, a small troupe doing comedy and music routines, was geared to assembling a crowd to sell the merchandise—patent medicine.

While not theatrical in nature, cultural and refined presentations were available through lyceum circuits and speaker's bureaus devoted to all forms of education and self-improvement. The Boston Lyceum Bureau (later the Redpath Lyceum Bureau), booked such luminaries as Mark Twain and Julia Ward Howe. In summers in the 1910s and 1920s, tent Chautauqua was a principal source of edification to communities throughout the country. National and regional circuits, as well as independent Chautauqua sites, kept a high moral tenor of religious and political speakers, musical performers, inspirational messages from the Women's Christian Temperance Union, elocution and dramatic readings, and addresses by the likes of William Jennings Bryan.

The Decline of Hometown Entertainment

The delivery of entertainment to rural America significantly changed following World War I. The impact of film, radio and improving highways began to erode at the core social function of meeting at the opera house. The number of legitimate theater companies on tour went from 339 in 1900 to 22 in 1935 (Lewis, 209). In large part, only the largest theaters could generate the income needed to maintain the costs of touring companies. Improving highways meant the small-town opera house closed down when the audience drove to larger cities for theatrical entertainment. National weekly radio shows and a motion picture distribution system brought the best vaudeville stars and stage stars into the home or the movie house (usually the old opera house with a screen and a balcony converted into a projection booth). The mass distribution of entertainment was not necessarily tied to live performers and a community center in every town. New school auditoriums often provided better spaces for theater and musical events and served community talent needs as the professional entertainers were seen or heard via the new technologies.

Tent Entertainments

"Ladies and gentlemen, children of all ages!" and similar bombast was heard throughout the land by the late nineteenth century when circus troupes of all sizes traversed the countryside. Designed to enthrall the spectator, not all of these skilled entertainments were housed in large tents at major cities. Smaller troupes, often dog and pony shows, played in smaller tents, in the open air, on theater stages, and did not require the large entourage associated with Barnum or Ringling Brothers circuses. The carnival, a commercial venture engaging its patrons in activities of thrill-seeking rides and games of skill and chance, also made the rounds of communities, mostly in tents. The circus tent virtually disappeared in lieu of the large arenas in mid-size and large cities. Now, carnivals mostly follow the state and county fair circuit.

A unique form of tent show, begun in the last half of the nineteenth century, continued into the 1950s. Prior to World War I, acting troupes, carrying all the needed staging paraphernalia, brought their tent theaters to communities to present what William Slout called rep shows, tent rep, rag opries and tent shows. Over 400 tent shows crossed the U.S. by the mid-1920s. In part, the tents allowed companies to go to communities without theaters and to places where indoor theater was impossible with the heat of summer. Often bound to specific regions, hundreds of tent shows returned year after year bringing most of the dramatic forms found on the indoor stages. Interrupted by World War I, the tent show continued into the 1930s, while an offshoot of the form called the Toby Show continued into the 1960s. Toby, the freckle-faced yokel with red hair and many rural manifestations in dress and demeanor, would be figured in performances and playlets as the tent show played several nights in one community before moving on. Caroline Schaffner, a driving force in preserving the heritage of Toby and the tent repertoire tradition, established the Museum of Repertoire Americana in Mount Pleasant, Iowa, which preserves this uniquely rural entertainment form.

Today's Venues

Although the decline of the road meant an increasing loss of professional entertainers, many communities created their own little theater or community theaters. By 1910 the Drama League was born with the stated desire to bring better plays to small towns. Leaders in theater higher education across the country, such as Frederick Koch at the University of North Carolina, Hubert Heffner at Stanford, E.C. Mabie at the University of Iowa, and others linked their expertise to the increasing numbers of small-town drama clubs. Today most states have their own community theater associations. There are regional affiliations such as the Southeastern Theater Conference, Inc.'s Community Theater Festival each year and the national American Association of Community Theaters. The latter provides connections between community theaters across the country, linking large and small communities in the production of dramatic works.

Currently there are nearly 100 outdoor companies affiliated with the Institute of Outdoor Drama at the University of North Carolina-Chapel Hill, many of which are major summer tourist venues that impact rural economies. The Institute's affiliates participate in historical performances such as *Unto These Hills* in Cherokee, North Carolina, religious performances such as the Passion play in South Dakota's Black Hills, and Shakespearean Festivals such as those held in Cedar City, Utah. There is no agency to determine the impact of the revenues produced with the hundreds of summer stock theater companies found in tourist sites across the country, but the Institute of Outdoor Drama estimates that its nearly 100 outdoor affiliates employ about 5,000 people and have an annual economic impact on the U.S. travel and tourism industry of approximately $500 million.

Local pride was evident in other civic, social and fraternal festivities. Glassberg (1990) studied the evolution of the historical pageant at the turn of the twentieth century, which celebrated national and local interpretations of the American experience. If the local historian views the construction of the opera house and the attempts to draw entertainment, local events and professional touring troupes as a manifestation of civic pride, the broad view of entertainment history shows a diverse range of cultural and popular presentations. Distribution circuits of a wide variety of entertainments followed the rail system throughout the country as it developed from the 1860s into the 1920s. While mass-produced entertainments and newer technologies have reduced the live professional troupes to a trickle, there are many thriving locally produced theaters, pageants, festivals and summer stock companies that still bring rural communities a cultural identity, a reminder of an earlier, more abundant tradition.

— *Lawrence J. Hill*

See also

Arts; Community Celebrations; Culture; Films, Rural; History, Rural; Music; Recreational Activities

References

DiMeglio, John E. *Vaudeville U.S.A.* Bowling Green, OH: Bowling Green University Popular Press, 1973.

Durham, Weldon B. *American Theater Companies, 1888-1930.* New York, NY: Greenwood Press, 1987.

Glenn, George D. and Poole, Richard L. *The Opera Houses of Iowa.* Ames, IA: Iowa State University Press, 1993.

Hoh, Lavahn. *Step Right Up: The Adventures of Circus in America.* White Hall, VA: Better Way, 1990.

Institute of Outdoor Drama "What Is the Institute of Outdoor Drama?" North Carolina-Chapel Hill, Institute of Outdoor Drama. Accessed February 2008. Available at http://www.unc.edu/depts/outdoor/about/index.html.

Lewis, Philip C. *Trouping: How the Show Came to Town.* New York, NY: Harper & Row, Publishers, 1973.

McNamara, Brooks. *Step Right Up.* New York, NY: Doubleday, 1976.

Morrison, Theodore. *Chautauqua: A Center for Education, Religion, and the Arts in America.* Chicago, IL: University of Chicago Press, 1974.

U.S. Outdoor Drama (Summer 1995): 1-4.

Poggi, Jack. *Theater in America: The Impact of Economic Forces, 1870-1967.* Ithaca, NY: Cornell University Press, 1968.

Slout, William L. *Theater in a Tent: The Development of a Provincial Entertainment.* Bowling Green, OH: Bowling Green University Popular Press, 1972.

Wilmeth, Don B. *Variety Entertainment and Outdoor Amusements: A Reference Guide.* Westport, CT: Greenwood Press, 1982.

Theology of Land

An effort to describe land in relationship to God, which implies that human beings should relate to the land in a way appropriate to God's relationship to, and purposes for, land. Such a theology bears on ecological, economic, globalization and immigration issues. In this postmodern world, land and other physical concerns go strangely neglected.

This entry identifies four conceptions of land; offers an overview of the biblical and theological themes by which the Judeo-Christian tradition has understood land in relation to God; and describes the way land enters into some contemporary issues.

Theology is a human effort to understand aspects of life from the perspective of an ultimate center of value. Thus, a theology of land is subject to all the contingencies that influence men and women. A theology of the land written by theologians in some lands, say Iraq, or South Africa, or Brazil, will be very different from that written in the rural U.S. It will also differ by time period; imagine, for example, how much more complex such a theology would have been in 1900 when many U.S. citizens had a visceral appreciation of how their lives and that of the land were interdependent.

Conceptions of Land

Consider such current issues as political conflicts between ethnic and national groups over land issues, population and development pressures, and the ecological destruction that accompanies present life styles in affluent countries. These are vitally affected by an understanding of land and by the empirical facts of land dynamics. The way in which land is conceived in public policy and church debates will determine whether the health of the earth community can be restored and sustained.

Theology has intersected with several definitions of land. First, land can be defined scientifically as earth—topsoil, subsoil, bacteria, water drainage, grub worms, humus, and tilth—all very concrete ingredients of land. Second, land can be used in a socio-political sense to indicate boundaries and geographic borders. That carries two connotations: one is merely geometric; the other includes the full range of values and identifications that accompany ethnic and national loyalties. A third definition looks at land as a possession or commodity. Land in this sense can symbolize all of one's material properties and even status. Fourth, land can be defined as nature and the environment itself (the earthly habitat) and thus, as a component of every human activity and choice. Although each of these conceptions of land adds its weight to a more complete picture of land, this entry will focus on the fourth, more holistic one.

Judeo-Christian Themes for Interpreting Land

One metaphor comes close to comprehending the themes by which the Hebrew Scriptures, the New Testament, and the Christian theological tradition interpreted land as environment or earthly habitat. The earth is **home**, God's home, home for humankind, and homes for animals and otherkind. Such a theocentric perspective implies that the earth is the place where human beings find their identity and purpose. God does not dwell only in the heavens; the incarnation of God becoming human in Jesus Christ establishes that God's home is also with humankind. This theme suggests that, while the land is not itself sacred, it is intrinsically valuable to God and is essential to human, animal, and plant life. The incarnation of Jesus Christ adds another spectrum to the meaning of this earth as being God's home and home for humankind. The Christian faith affirms that the whole creation is full of God (see McFague, 2000).

The theme of land as God's home carries three other, more explicitly Biblical themes: the land is God's **gift** to all living things; the land is God's **covenantal promise** to human and otherkind (plants, animals); and the land is God's **challenge** to humans. (The best summary of these themes is Brueggemann 1977.)

The land is God's gift to all living things. The Christian and Jewish faiths affirm as one of their cornerstones the fact that "God created the heavens and the earth" (Genesis 1:1), and that the whole earth continues to be God's (Psalm 24:1). Throughout Scripture the entire cosmos that God created is described as "very good." God gives the land to human beings to care for and to enjoy. This is one clear source of the stewardship of creation ethic.

The Hebrew author, called the Deuteronomist, sees land as a gift fromYahweh (God), the same Yahweh that delivered the slave band from Egypt, the same Yahweh who promised land to Abraham and Sarah, and the Creator. This gift implies accountability to the Creator. Similarly Jesus Christ over and over again in his parables and natural metaphors points to the giftedness of nature. Over and over he praises the beauty and fittingness of the land as a gift from God. Jesus Christ expresses the incarnational love of God in the same way, although to a greater degree, as the gift of God to human and otherkind in the land.

The centrality of the Creator image of God is evident in its placement as the First Article in the Apostles and Nicene creeds. Most traditions maintain that the creativity of God continues today in the natural and human world. Rural peoples find this cyclical and continual creativity easy to understand and see in their fields and countryside.

Several characteristics with clear moral import are evident in the theme of land as gift: the life of the world as God's life; the interconnection of all life; the land as a living creative organism; and the limitations of creat-

edness. These understandings find expression in many farmers feeling that they have the land "on loan," as they say. The world and all that is in it remain God's but some farmers and other rural residents feel their interconnection with God through the land. Because of God's gift, they have gifts to pass on.

The land is God's covenantal promise to human beings and otherkind. One series of concrete Biblical events that enable Jews and Christians to see the land as God's promise are the covenants Yahweh made with Hebrew leaders. These covenants involve the promise of land, indeed, a Promised Land. The covenant God made with Noah after the flood was also made with "every living creature;" especially mentioned are "the birds, the cattle, and every beast" (Genesis 9:10). These covenants underscore God's love and care for God's home.

Jesus Christ is often seen as the culmination of the promise/covenant tradition. There is considerable debate about whether the new covenant in Jesus Christ totally supersedes the older covenants involving land. Another Biblical theme expresses God's promise in a way that can reconcile such debate. the blessing tradition. This tradition emphasizes the more everyday, routine way God is active in cosmic history.

Jesus Christ is portrayed as the reconciler who articulates God's continuing love for the people and the whole creation. "For in him the fullness of God was pleased to dwell, and through him to reconcile all things..." (Colossians 1:19-20). The most compelling vision of land is one that is crystallized in Jesus Christ as the carpenter of Nazareth/Son of God. In bringing together the images of creation and redemption, Jesus Christ expresses the concrete intention of God to produce *shalom*. *Shalom* refers to the way the whole created order functions in symbiotic interdependence; it implies an ecological smoothness, harmony, or enjoyment in which there is an abundance for all.

Characteristics with clear moral implications emerging from the theme are: the redemption of the land along with humankind; a presumption in favor of solutions that benefit all life rather than only human life; a view of the world as a kinship system; and a warning not to forget that land is always populated, and that humankind counts as part of the whole. Humankind is called to find ways to live that respect, and indeed restore, all other life forms. There is a hint that only in this way can the human species find the fullness of *shalom*.

The land is God's challenge to men and women to work for justice in the whole creation. This theme should be understood in the context of the other two, as all three are interrelated. The land is a gift from God and a covenant with God, and as such it involves human responsibility. God challenges human beings to care for the land as part of the task of sustaining God's home in a way that will allow all life to flourish. The way that men and women respond to God's goodness is through worship and responsibility.

God, as Scripture points out, is present in land, actively delighting in the created order, watching out for the sparrow and lily, as well as enjoying the whales and mountain goats. God calls humans to live with *sadek*, righteousness. Humans are to embody justice by maintaining the right relationship or balance that God created between human need, plant life, and animal flourishing. Humans have the land only in trust; they are shop stewards.

This challenge is directed not only to ecological health, but also and interrelatedly to political and economic health for people. Humankind is one of the species for whom the land was created. God challenges them to create structures that enable all peoples to realize justice, to participate in shaping their future, and to live so as to sustain an equitable and sufficient distribution of the earth's bounty among all creatures.

The land is home for all life. There is something wrong, from God's point of view, when political, economic, and environmental structures prevent the land from being a good home for every species. Thus, world hunger violates God's design. The land seen as God's challenge expresses the moral vision of the earth as being one community. It is intended to foster communion among all beings. The only way that can happen is through establishing structures that make for justice; furthermore, the more just those structures are, the more likely the possibility of communion. (For examples of how human beings can "live lightly on the land" in ways that can be sustained even in the midst of great pressures, see McKibben 1995).

Emerging Theological and Social Issues

The press of environmental degradation and the specter of global conflicts has made Christian theologians and ethicists aware of the need to understand land issues and to incorporate a sympathy for the land and other beings into our way of life. What is emerging is an appreciation of the physical and material roots of life. Theology is overcoming its dualistic treatment of

A pulpit and communion table as typically decorated for Thanksgiving with local produce of the land. Kresge Chapel, Kansas City. Photograph by Heather Chamberlin.

bodies as inferior to minds/spirits and is balancing its appreciation of history with an appreciation of nature.

Church-based Response. In the last 30 years, there has been a torrent of books and articles on the environment. Many denominations have social statements on the need to attend to ecology, among them Lutherans, Methodists, Presbyterians, Roman Catholics, and the World Council of Churches. After all, a majority of Protestant and Roman Catholic churches are still located in rural areas.

The rural base of many of these issues stimulated a collaborative text on *Rural Ministry: The Shape of the Renewal to Come* in which a team of nine construct a theology of rural life and ministry for local congregations. That book takes land issues as a central concern. Some of the theological themes lifted up there are the presence of God, a sense of place, a love of community, dealing with suffering and decline, and reclaiming power.

Unless concern about land becomes translated into an appreciation of land locally—the quality of the places where people live, those concerns will remain general and abstract. Theology has not yet de-universalized its message. Definitely moving in that direction have been feminist, African American, Latino/a, and Asian calls for contextual theology, a recognition of social context. That context frequently recognizes land and environmental issues; this is especially the case in developing countries. (May 1991)

A systematic theology of land would to recognize the interconnection of human and ecological issues in a way that also comprehends political and economic structures and the power relations contained in any system of land distribution. I think Wendell Berry, Aldo Leopold, Larry Rasmussen, and Sallie McFague come close to formulating such a theology. They all start with a theory of how human beings are themselves spatial, physical beings and interpret that theologically. They see land issues as part of the agenda of every contextual theology. They leap the gap between individual physicality and corporate, socioeconomic structures.

Societal issues. Societal issues provoke theological response. Among those issues that are emerging in rural America, one that has quite pernicious consequences is growing concentrations in the food supply system. For example, many rural communities are experiencing the placement of large-scale hog production facilities in their backyards. The hog production industry is concentrated at 66%: beef packers at 83.5%, and broilers at 58.5%. (The top four companies control these percentages of each market.) It is the same eight or ten companies that control most of the agricultural commodity markets. This has implications for democratic participation in rural areas; economic implications for all food eaters; destructive consequences for rural community life in towns where production is located; and very negative environmental impacts. It threatens to erode democratic participation throughout the U.S. It fails to recognize the "giftedness" of land. (Statistics available from HendricksonM@missouri.edu.) The date of this research is April 2007. CR4—the percentages we quote—are "the concentration ration (relative to 100%) of the top four firms in a specific food industry.")

Tied into this issue (and one that we readily identify) is the cost of our "cheap food" policies in the U.S. There are significant health issues (obesity, type 2 diabetes, respiratory illnesses) as well as costs to rural communities, farmers, and farmworkers. One is tempted to say that the American way of eating is a problem. (On this front , see Jung 2004 and Pollan 2008.)

A second issue is the lack of any serious attention to rural development policy and funding. In contrast to many developing countries, the U.S. continues to neglect its rural communities. Economic policy disadvantages small and medium sized farmers, and the effect of that has been a shrinking of the number of farms and the quality of life in rural America. The "farm crisis" of the 1980s became a community crisis in the 1990s. Both farm land and community land are fragile. Like other centers of community life, many rural churches are finding it difficult to afford a minister. While there are instances of amazingly creative local efforts at revitalizing their communities, many other local efforts will fail for lack of assistance. Rural areas do not receive services in proportion to the taxes they pay; one impact of this is the rate of poverty found in rural communities which now exceeds the rate in center-cities. That can have an impact on land issues, especially if low cost labor attracts industries and businesses that exploit both the land and rural people without returning community or individual benefits. Such destruction of community and impoverishment is not in keeping with the covenantal promises of Yahweh.

A third land issue connects the sort of conflict that afflicts U.S. urban centers and also international and intranational relations. Group violence and conflict has a physical or land basis that is intermixed with racial, ethnic, religious, and class differences. The immigration issue has many facets related to land and place. The society needs designs that reinforce mutual, reciprocal benefit and neighborliness rather than adversarial, competitive relations. Land issues are not only rural; they include the design of cities and interior layout of institutions. The theology and ethics of land remain God's challenge to all people; it is now gaining considerably more attention.

— *L. Shannon Jung*

See also

Agrarianism; Animal Rights/Welfare; Churches; Community; Community, Sense of; Culture; Environmental Protection; Ethics; Future of Rural America; Land Stewardship; Rural Church Movement; Religion; Values of Residents

References

Berry, Wendell. *The Unsettling of America: Culture and Agriculture*, rev. ed. San Francisco, CA: Sierra Club Books, 2004.

Brueggemann, Walter. *The Land: Place as Gift, Promise, and Challenge in Biblical Faith*. Philadelphia, PA: Fortress Press, 1977.

Evans, Bernard and Greg Cusack, eds. *Theology of the Land*. Collegeville, MN: Liturgical Press, 1987.

Jung, Shannon, Pegge Boehm, Deborah Cronin, Gary Farley, Dean Freudenberger, Judy Heffernan, Sandy LaBlanc, Ed Queen, and Dave Ruesink. *Rural Ministry: The Shape of the Renewal to Come*. Nashville, TN: Abingdon Press, 1998.

Jung, Shannon. *Food for Life: The Spirituality and Ethics of Eating*. Minneapolis, MN: Fortress Press, 2004.

Leopold, Aldo. *A Sand County Almanac*, rev. ed. New York: Oxford University Press, 2001.

McFague, Sallie. *The Body of God: An Ecological Theology*. Minneapolis, MN: Fortress Press, 1993.

McFague, Sallie. *Life Abundant: Rethinking Theology and Economy for a Planet in Peril*. Minneapolis, MN: Fortress, 2000.

May, Roy. *The Poor of the Land: A Christian Case for Land Reform*. Maryknoll, NY: Orbis Books, 1991.

McKibben, Bill. *Hope, Human and Wild: True Stories of Living Lightly on the Earth*. Boston, MA: Little, Brown, and Co., 1995.

Rasmussen, Larry. *Earth Community, Earth Ethics*. Maryknoll, NY: Orbis Books, 1997.

Warren, Karen. "The Power and the Promise of Ecofeminism." *Environmental Ethics* 12, no. 2 (Summer 1990): 125-146.

Tillage

Any one of several types of mechanical manipulation of soil primarily for seedbed preparation and weed control.

Historical Perspective

Historical evolution of tillage systems provides modern civilization learning opportunities to cope with future challenges to sustainable management of natural resources. Lal et al. (2007) discuss how agriculture originated 10 to 13 millennia ago in the Fertile Crescent of the Near East, mostly along the Tigris, Euphrates, Nile, Indus and Yangtze River valleys and was introduced into Greece and southeastern Europe about 8,000 years ago. Sumerian and other civilizations developed a wide variety of simple tools (digging sticks) to place and cover seed in the soil that led to more complex paddle-shaped spades or hoes pulled by humans or animals. A wooden plow, called an "ard," was developed in Mesopotamia about 4000 to 6000 BCE that led to the "Triptolemos ard" named after the Greek god and hero. Historical documents and archaeological evidence illustrate

the "mystique" of tillage implements that were thought to "nourish the earth" and to "break the drought" as is evidenced in several ancient scriptures. The ard evolved into the "Roman plow," with an iron plowshare, described by Vergil around 1 CE, and was used in Europe until the fifth century. The plow further evolved into a soil inverting tool during the eighth to the tenth century. In the U.S., a moldboard plow was designed by Thomas Jefferson in 1784, patented by Charles Newfold in 1796, and marketed in the 1830s as a cast iron plow by a blacksmith named John Deere. Use of the plow expanded rapidly with the introduction of the "steam horse" in 1910 that led to widespread severe soil erosion and environmental degradation culminating in the Dust Bowl of the 1930s. A transition from moldboard plow to various forms of conservation tillage began with the development of herbicides after World War II. No-till or conservation tillage technologies are very effective in minimizing soil and crop residue disturbance, controlling soil evaporation, minimizing erosion losses, sequestering carbon in soil and reducing energy needs. However, no-till is effective only with the use of crop residue as mulch, which has numerous competing uses. Replacement of plow tillage by conservation agriculture, based on crop residue management and use of leguminous cover crops in the rotation cycle, can achieve positive nutrient balance by using manures and other biosolids, and increase carbon storage in soil and terrestrial ecosystems. The no-till soil and crop residue management system promotes soil carbon storage and long-term sustainable agriculture that provides food, feed, fiber, biofuels, ecosystem services and environmental benefits for all of society.

Tillage has been an integral part of U.S. agricultural production. As the technology evolved, tillage expanded to include many aspects of soil and crop residue management and evolved into different tillage systems, each with its own objectives. This review is intended to show what we have learned from the past and the need for a smooth transition toward less intensive tillage to maintain sustainable production. Equipment presently used in these systems is briefly described. Improved soil management practices related to less intensive tillage are described that minimize agriculture's impact on environmental quality while maintaining the soil resource.

Introduction

Agriculture is one of the foundations of rural America and has a major influence on components of industry, world trade and global ecology. Traditional agricultural production involves at least five separate operations: 1) tilling or preparing the soil; 2) planting; 3) cultivating; 4) harvesting, and 5) processing, transporting and storage before consumption. Tillage is first on this list because it has been an integral part of the production process. New technology is redefining and combining some of these operations where tillage and planting are combined (no-till) and where mechanical cultivation is being replaced by herbicides.

The moldboard plow, historically, was an essential tool used by the early pioneers to settle the prairies of the Central and Western U.S. From its rudimentary origins as a glorified hoe many years ago, the plow has been the principal tool to open land to plant and destroy weeds and bury crop residue. The moldboard plow allowed farmers to create a soil environment in which grain crops could thrive. The use of the plow was unquestioned and the ritual performed every year shaped the culture and rhythm of the rural community. The moldboard plow left a clean, neatly furrowed field that reflected farmers' pride in their property and management skills. The plow has been a significant symbol over the last 150 years and now is being reevaluated as new, conservation tillage techniques are developed and researched. Tillage practices evolved continually around the best crop systems limited by soil and water resources for a given geographical location. Tillage is thought of as the mechanical manipulation of the soil. Tillage is needed to prepare the seedbed, that is, to develop an area where crop seeds can be planted, sprout, take root and grow to produce grain. Tillage loosens the soils, kills the weeds that compete with crop plants for needed water and nutrients, and improves the circulation of water and air within the soil. Tillage can increase mineralization and release soil nutrients that enhance crop growth for a short time. It can enhance pest and disease control by covering or stirring crop residues. Tillage can be used to enhance soil temperature and is often the main reason for clean tillage and moldboard plowing dark soils of the Northern Corn Belt. Tillage covers the reflective residues and increases the solar heat absorption in the cooler seasons.

While tillage has been used to create the"ideal environment" for plant establishment and productivity, intensive tillage is the major factor that sets a soil up for all types of erosion including water, wind and tillage. Most people understand soil degradation and sediment deposition caused by water and wind erosion; however, few people understand soil degradation caused by tillage erosion. Tillage erosion refers to the down-slope movement of soil caused by tillage operations (Lobb et al., 2007). The amount of soil that will move down-slope when tilling the soil varies with the implement used, the direction of the tillage operation (down-slope, up-slope or cross-slope), the speed of tillage and the slope of the field. The net impact of tillage erosion is the loss of topsoil from uplands and knolls which as a result become unproductive. As agriculture proceeds to meet the food security needs of an expanding population, it is essential that we understand all impacts of tillage on food production capacity and for maintaining environmental quality. A portion of the driving force to transition from intensive tillage to forms of conservation tillage is being driven by continued erosion problems directly related to intensive tillage.

Description of Tillage Systems

The concept of tillage systems combines various aspects of the tilling, planting, managing residue, and applying pesticides and fertilizers. Because of the number and diversity of the tillage systems components, it is difficult to give any one system a meaningful name or very precise definition. Systems can be identified according to their ultimate objective, whether it is conventional or conservation tillage, and sometimes they are described by the primary tillage implement used (e.g., whether it is a moldboard plow or a chisel plow). The name problem often is compounded because the definitions differ among geographic regions. Different names may be used to identify a similar tillage system in different parts of the country. Listing all the operations in the system results in the most accurate description as described in Reicosky and Allmaras (2003).

Conventional Tillage. Conventional tillage is a sequence of operations most commonly used in the given geographic area to prepare a seedbed and produce a given crop. Because the operations vary considerably in the different climatic, agronomic and other field conditions, the definition of conventional tillage varies from one physiographic region to another. Conventional tillage is often thought of as two major operations: primary tillage and secondary tillage. Primary tillage is more aggressive, deeper, and leaves a rougher surface relative to secondary tillage operations. Primary tillage tools are the moldboard plow, chisel plow and various types of subsoiler implements designed to disturb the soil to greater depths.

Figure 1. *Modern no till seeder spring planting corn directly into winter rye stubble harvested for silage. Photo credit: Don Reicosky.*

Secondary tillage varies widely in the type and number of operations and generally works the soil to a shallower depth, provides additional soil breakup, levels and firms the soil, closes some of the air pockets, and kills some of the weeds. Secondary tillage equipment includes disk harrows, field cultivators, spring- and spike-toothed harrows, levelers, drags and various types of packers.

Conservation Tillage. Conservation tillage is a general term that encompasses many different types of tillage and planting that maintain at least 30 percent or greater residue cover after planting. The objective is to provide a means of profitable crop production while minimizing soil erosion caused by wind and water. Although specific operations may vary, the emphasis is on conserving soil, water, energy, labor and equipment.

No-till (Slot Planting, Zero Till, Direct Seeding). The soil is left undisturbed from harvest to planting except for fertilizer nutrient injection. Planting or drilling is accomplished in a narrow seedbed or a slot created by a coulter, row cleaner, disk opener, in-row chisels, and sometimes small rototillers. Weed control is accomplished primarily with herbicides.

Ridge-till. The soil is left undisturbed from harvest to planting except for nutrient injection. Planting is completed in a seedbed prepared on ridges four to six inches higher than the middles built the previous season with an aggressive cultivation. About one-third of the soil surface is tilled with various types of sweeps, disk openers, coulters or row cleaners. Weed control is accomplished with a combination of herbicides and cultivation.

Strip-till. Similar to the ridge-till, strip-till leaves the soil undisturbed from harvest to planting except for nutrient injection. Tillage in the row is done by in-row chisel, a row cleaner or a rototiller that disturbs about one-third of the soil surface. Weed control is accomplished with a combination of herbicides and cultivation.

Mulch-till. The total soil surface is disturbed prior to planting to various depths. Tillage is accomplished by chisels, field cultivators, disks, sweeps or blades to varying depths and degrees of mixing. Generally, there is more than 30 percent residue cover after planting. Weed control is accomplished with a combination of herbicides and cultivation.

Reduced-till. Less intensive tillage types are accomplished with various tillage tools that leave 15 to 30 percent residue cover after planting and during critical

Figure 2. A strip tillage implement with localized soil disturbance in the row and undisturbed surface in the interrow. Photo credit: Don Reicosky.

erosion periods. Weed control is usually accomplished with a combination of herbicides and cultivation.

General Description of Tillage Implements

Moldboard Plow. The moldboard plow has been used extensively in the U.S. since about 1775. Many other tillage tools were invented to replace them but the moldboard plow is still used by many farmers as the primary tillage tool in areas receiving medium to high rainfall. The moldboard plow cuts, lifts, shears and inverts the furrow slice to break up tough sod and turn under green manure crops on heavier soils. Moldboard plows are equipped with one or more bottoms of various cutting widths.

Chisel Plow. The chisel plow is a primary tillage implement that breaks or shatters the soil, leaving it rough with residue on or near the surface. Its general operating depth ranges from six to 12 inches. It consists of multiple rows of staggered curve shanks mounted either rigidly or with spring cushions or spring resets. Their interchangeable sweeps with chisel spikes and shovel tools are attached at each shank. Working width is increased by adding wings to the main unit.

Subsoiler. The subsoiler is a primary tillage tool similar to a chisel plow in that it is typically designed to operate from 12 to 22 inches deep. Subsoilers are used primarily to alleviate soil compaction and therefore are used when the soil is dry for maximum effectiveness. The subsoiling leaves as much or more of the residue on the surface as does the chiseling. Coulters are often used to cut residue to minimize clogging.

Blade or Sweep Plows. The blade plow or sweep plow is used primarily in the drier areas of the Great Plains to cut the roots of the weeds and leaves most of the residue on the soil surface. The V-shaped sweeps range from 2.5 to six feet wide and are mounted on standards attached to a toolbar. The typical operating depth varies from two to five inches. The wider the sweep, the greater the soil depth needed to operate the equipment.

Rotary Tiller. Rotary tillers are used as once-over tools designed to produce a finished seedbed in one operation. These are operated by the power takeoff from the tractor, and simultaneously till the soil and incorporate fertilizers and pesticides. Planter units occasionally are attached to the rotary tiller, making tillage and planting a one-pass operation. Some rotary tillers only till narrow strips, whereas others till the entire surface area. Residue remains on the surface between the strips for erosion control, and herbicide can be incorporated within the strip.

Rod Weeder. Rod weeders are used in the Western Great Plains and the Pacific Northwest primarily for weed control and the summer fallow and prior to seeding. A rod shaft is mounted on bearings and either rotated by ground-driven wheels or left free to turn due to soil forces acting on it. The rotating rod is operated just under the surface to pull the weeds by the roots and flip them onto the soil surface to dry them out. Most of the residue remains on the surface after the rod weeder.

Disk Harrow. The disk harrow is used as a primary or secondary tillage implement. When used as a primary instrument, its large-diameter, concave disks mounted on a common shaft form a gang that is used as an offset disk harrow to turn soil. The tandem disk harrow has two opposite gangs that throw the soil outward from the center of the implement followed by two gangs that throw the soil back towards the center. The disk cuts, throws and loosens the surface soil three to six inches deep, and is used primarily to break up large clods and cut some residue into the surface. The result is a rougher surface than other forms of secondary tillage, but multiple passes can result in a fine surface for seedbed preparation.

Field Cultivator. A field cultivator is a secondary tillage tool that is similar to a chisel plow but lighter in construction and designed for less severe conditions. Field cultivators generally have three or four ranks of equally spaced, flexible shanks. The shanks are spaced

Figure 3. *Modern 10-bottom moldboard plow that results in nearly complete soil inversion in corn stalks. Photo credit: Chris Wente.*

24 to 40 inches apart and provide effective soil disturbance from the depths of three to five inches.

Harrows. Harrows are used as a secondary tillage operation to level the soil surface, redistribute surface residue to enhance moisture retention, pulverize the clods and disturb the germinating weed seeds. Harrows can be considered a spring-tooth harrow or spike-tooth harrow with round, wire teeth. Harrows often are attached to the rear of the disk harrows. These are often the final operations prior to planting.

Culti-packer. The culti-packer is especially useful to compact and level freshly plowed soil. It pulverizes the clods, firms up the surface two to four inches, but has little effect on the lower half of the furrow slice. The surface is ridged rather than smooth as a smooth roller presses stones into the soil surface. Rollers and packers can consist of one or two smooth or shaped in-line gangs of rollers.

Combination Implements. Combination implements consist of a wide variety of components commonly found as part of other tillage tools that are adjustable to vary the residue cover left after tillage to fit the definition of conservation tillage. For example, a combination implement may have two single-acting disk gangs in front, followed by three or four rows of field cultivator shanks and shovels, followed by a multi-row, spike-tooth harrow or possibly subsoiler shanks. Combination implements often are used for one-pass incorporation of chemicals. Most combination implements operate in heavy residue conditions without clogging and often require the larger horsepower available in today's modern tractors.

Tillage and Environmental Issues

Concern over soil erosion and increased pressure to farm land too steep or dry for conventional practices led to the development of reduced tillage and residue

Figure 4. *A modern chisel plow implement that tills the soil to about 6 inches deep. Photo credit: Don Reicosky.*

management systems that conserve crop residues on the soil surface. Within the past three decades the merits of reduced or no-tillage management systems have been recognized throughout the U.S. Increased interest in conservation tillage arises from advantages these systems offer over conventional tillage practices.

Surface residue prevents erosion by absorbing raindrop impact and by slowing both water runoff and wind erosion. Conservation tillage techniques reduce soil erosion losses and increase use of land too steep to farm by conventional tillage methods. Other advantages include improved timing of planting and harvesting, increased potential for double-cropping, conservation of soil water through decreased evaporation and increased infiltration, and a reduction in fuel, labor and machinery requirements. With conservation tillage most residues are left on the soil surface, and only a small portion is in intimate contact with the soil moisture unavailable to the microorganisms. As a result, the residue decomposes more slowly. These advantages occasionally are offset by several disadvantages that limit crop production when compared with conventional systems. Disadvantages include cooler soil temperatures, which in temperate and cold climates, impede the germination and early crop growth. Other management

concerns are increasing the potential of insect and disease damage to crops and increased need for more precise management of soil fertility and weed control.

Although moldboard plowing and other forms of intensive tillage have done much to increase crop production in the last 150 years in the U.S., the increase in production has not been without some unseen costs in decreased soil quality and environmental impact (Schlesinger, 1985). The unseen, unmeasured costs that result from intensive tillage includes loss in soil organic matter due to enhanced oxidation and depletion of soil fertility reserves. The organic matter of many of the prairie's soils declined from 40 to 60 percent of that present under virgin conditions. The magnitude of these effects depends primarily on the intensity of tillage, that is, the type and frequency of tillage and the quantity and quality of crop residue returned to the soil. Intensive tillage, primarily moldboard plowing, decreases soil carbon in virtually all crop production systems. Differences in soil carbon decrease were related to various crop rotations and residue return in a given management system.

Recent studies involving tillage methods indicate major loss of gaseous soil carbon immediately after intensive tillage (Reicosky and Lindstrom, 1993) that may

Figure 5. A combination tillage implement with discs and subsoil shanks in the upper Midwest, locally referred to as a "deep ripper" in corn stalks. Photo credit: Don Reicosky.

contribute to global climate change. They measured the effects of fall tillage methods on carbon dioxide flux in the Northern Corn Belt. Measurements immediately after tillage showed differences in the carbon dioxide loss were related to soil fracturing that facilitated the movement of carbon dioxide out of and oxygen into the soil. The moldboard plow treatment buried nearly all the residue and left the soil in a rough, loose, open condition, and resulted in the maximum carbon dioxide loss. Considerably more carbon was lost as carbon dioxide from the plowed plots than from the area not tilled. Moldboard plowing now appears to have two major effects: to loosen and invert the soil and allow a rapid carbon dioxide loss and oxygen entry, and to incorporate and mix residues to enhance microbial attack. These tillage-induced gaseous losses are exacerbated with high wind speeds over the tilled surface of muck soils relative to non-tilled conditions (Reicosky et al., 2008). Tillage-induced change in soil air permeability enabled wind speed to affect the gas exchange and soil carbon dioxide concentration at 12 inches deep, literally drawing the carbon dioxide out of the soil, resulting in a rapid decline in the soil carbon dioxide concentra-

tion. The moldboard plow perturbs the soil system and causes a shift in the gaseous equilibrium by releasing carbon dioxide, enabling oxygen to enter the soil to oxidize soil organic matter more rapidly. Continued research has shown the cumulative loss of carbon dioxide was directly proportional to the volume of soil disturbed. These results suggest that to minimize carbon dioxide loss related to tillage requires minimizing the volume of soil disturbed in the tillage operation. A second confounding factor is that the fossil fuel requirement increases proportional to the volume of soil disturbed in the tillage operation. The combination of large amounts of carbon dioxide lost from tillage and large amounts of diesel fuel used in tillage places a priority on forms of conservation tillage that minimizes both of these components.

Today, society faces important decisions regarding climate change mitigation as related to tillage. The soil is the fundamental foundation of our economy and our existence. Soil organic matter is the foundation of sustainable agriculture and highly dependent on tillage management decisions that influence intensity of tillage and the amount and placement of residues. While soil erosion continues to be a major problem, we must expand our thinking to address tillage-related soil quality issues controlled by soil carbon. Conservation tillage or no-till systems have shown an increase in soil organic matter within 10 to 12 years of consistent use. The increase in the soil organic matter depends on a delicate balance between the quality and quantity of residue inputs of the previous crops and the tillage intensity associated with establishing the next crop. Interest in bio-energy production is increasing exponentially across the U.S. and around the world. Biomass removal for bio-energy will require better management of the carbon cycle. We must place more emphasis on conservation of all natural resources and additional emphasis on carbon as a key component in maintaining ecosystem stability. The degradation of soil quality results from biomass removal and subsequent soil carbon and plant nutrient loss associated with bio-energy production. Farmers are faced with serious decisions managing this delicate balance with respect to tillage and biomass removal impacts and environmental consequences of maintaining sustainable production of food, feed, fiber and fuel.

— *Don C. Reicosky*

See also

Agricultural and Biological Engineering; Agriculture, Alternative; Agronomy; Conservation, Soil; Cropping Systems; Land Stewardship; Mechanization

References

Alimaras, R.R., P.W. Unger, and D.W. Wilkins. "Conservation Tillage Systems and Soil Productivity." Pp. 357-411 in *Soil Erosion and Crop Productivity*. Edited by R.F. Follett and B.A. Stewart. Madison, WI: American Society of Agronomy, 1985.

American Society of Agricultural Engineers, Cultural Practices Equipment Committee. "Terminology and Definitions for Agricultural Tillage Implements." Pg. 310-319 in *ASAE Standards, 1986*. Edited by R.H. Hahn and E.E. Rosentreter. St. Joseph, MI: American Society of Agricultural Engineers, 1986.

Carter, M.R. *Conservation Tillage in Temperate Agroecosystems*. Baco Raton, FL: Lewis Publishers, CRC Press Inc., 1994.

Griffith, D.R., J.F. Moncrief, D.J. Eckert, J.B. Swan, and D.D. Breitbach. "Crop Response to Tillage Systems." In *Conservation Tillage Systems and Management, Crop Residue Management with No-till, Ridge till and Mulch till*. Midwest Plains Service, MWPS-45, First Edition. Ames, IA: Agriculture and Biosystems Engineering Department, Iowa State University, 1992.

Lal, R., D.C. Reicosky and J.D. Hanson. "Evolution of the Plow over 10,000 Years and the Rationale for No-till Farming." *Soil Tillage Research* 93 (2007):1-12.

Lobb, D.A., E. Huffman, and D.C. Reicosky. "Importance of Information on Tillage Practices in the Modeling of Environmental Processes and in the Use of Environmental Indicators." *Journal of Environmental Management* 82 (2007): 377-387.

Phillips, R.E. and S.H. Phillips, eds. *No-Tillage Agriculture: Principles and Practices*. New York, NY: Van Nostrand Reinhold Co., Inc., 1984.

Reicosky, D.C. and R.R. Allmaras. "Advances in Tillage Research in North American Cropping Systems." Pp. 75-125 in *Cropping Systems: Trends and Advances*. Edited by A. Shrestha. New York: Haworth Press, Inc., 2003.

Reicosky, D.C. and D.W. Archer. "Moldboard Plow Tillage Depth and Short-Term Carbon Dioxide Release." *Soil Tillage Research* 94 (2007): 109-121.

Reicosky, D.C., R.W. Gesch, S.W. Wagner, R.A. Gilbert, C.D. Wente, and D.R. Morris. "Tillage and Wind Effects on Soil CO_2 Concentrations in Muck Soils." *Soil Tillage Research* 99, no. 2 (2008, in press).

Reicosky, D.C. and M.J. Lindstrom. "The Effect of Fall Tillage Methods on Short-term Carbon Dioxide Flux from Soil." *Agronomy Journal* 85 (1993): 1,237-1,243.

Reicosky, D.C. and M.J. Lindstrom. "Impact of Fall Tillage and Short Term Carbon Dioxide Flux." Pg. 177-187 in *Soil and Global Change*. Edited by R. Lal, J. Kimble, E. Levine, and B.A. Stewart. Chelsea, MI: Lewis Publishers, 1995.

Reicosky, D.C., W.D. Kemper, G.W. Langdale, C.L. Douglas, Jr., and P.B. Rasmussen. "Soil Organic Matter Changes Resulting from Tillage and Biomass Production." *Journal of Soil and Water Conservation* 50, no. 3 (1995): 253-261.

Schlesinger, W.H. "Changes in Soil Carbon Storage and Associated Properties with Disturbance and Recovery." Pp 194-220 in *The Changing Carbon Cycle: A Global Analysis*. Edited by J.R. Trabalha and D.E. Reichie. New York, NY: Springer-Verlag, 1985.

Soil Science Society of America, Terminology Committee. *Glossary of Soil Science Terms*. Madison, WI: Soil Science Society of America, 1987.

Journal of Soil and Water Conservation 32, no. 1 (1977): 3-65. Special issue on conservation tillage in different geographic regions of North America.

Tobacco Industry

A complex, tumultuous, long-term relationship among farmers, leaf dealers and manufacturers that contributed significantly to the development of the nation. Since the earliest settlements, development of the tobacco industry paralleled the development of the U.S. Tobacco production is very labor intensive, but the high value per acre contributes significantly to farm income in tobacco-producing states. Government policy toward the industry has been to raise revenue from excise taxes on the sale of tobacco products and to make the growers and leaf buyers responsible for all financial interactions.

Development

Tobacco, *Nicotiana tabacum*, has a deeply rooted and storied history in the U.S. and contributed much to the latter's cultural and monetary development. The recorded history of tobacco in the U.S. began with a related species, *Nicotiana rustica*, grown by Native Americans when European settlers first arrived. This high-nicotine-content, harsh-tasting tobacco was smoked, chewed and used as snuff for medicinal, religious and ceremonial purposes. The Spanish introduced the milder *N. tabacum* from South America into the Caribbean Islands. John Rolfe obtained seed of this species from Cuba and planted it at Jamestown in 1612. The first shipment of tobacco leaf from the colonies went to England in 1613. The demand for tobacco grew rapidly in England, and the tobacco economy of the colonies provided an impetus for development of lands west of the eastern seaboard. Tobacco was an instant source of income for the British government and became a surrogate currency in the colonies. Tobacco served as collateral for loans for the colonies to help finance the American Revolution and has been a significant part of American culture and source of government income ever since.

Today tobacco is grown in at least 21 states and Puerto Rico. However, North Carolina and Kentucky produce 71 percent of the total with Georgia, South Carolina, Tennessee and Virginia producing another 24 percent. The high per-acre value of tobacco, averaging $3,580 in 2006, makes it significant to the growers and to the economies of the producing areas. Tobacco is the nation's seventh largest cash crop with an annual farm value of $1.2 billion from only 300,000 acres of cropland. Historically, in most of the tobacco-producing areas, tobacco has been produced on relatively small farms with small tobacco production per farm; thus, tobacco often was the major cash crop from the farm. With the recent changes that have occurred in the tobacco program, the number of growers has decreased

Photographs courtesy of the Department of Plant and Soil Sciences, University of Kentucky.

and the amount of tobacco produced per farm has increased significantly. If this trend continues, U.S. tobacco will become more competitive in world markets.

Production

Tobaccos in the U.S. are grouped into seven kinds, each with different types and many grades. The most significant are the flue-cured, light air-cured and fire-cured types. Burley tobacco is the most important of the light air-cured group. Flue-cured tobacco production is centered around North Carolina, and Kentucky produces the majority of burley tobacco. Flue-cured and light air-cured tobaccos are used primarily in cigarette production and account for the vast majority of total production and value of U.S. tobacco. The other kinds are used mostly for cigar manufacture and smokeless tobacco products.

Tobacco production requires 130 to 250 hours of labor per acre. The lower end of the range is for flue-cured tobacco with much more mechanization in the harvest and curing process, and the high end is for

Photographs courtesy of the Department of Plant and Soil Sciences, University of Kentucky.

stalk-cut, fire-cured tobacco. The very small seed and slow seedling development necessitate transplanting young plants to the field. Traditionally, seeds were sown on top of soil beds three months prior to transplantation. This early seeding requires the seedbeds to be covered with cotton cloth to protect the young seedlings from freezing temperatures that occur in early spring. At transplanting time, individual plants were pulled from the seedbeds and transplanted to the field. More recently the seeds are sown in multi-celled trays

Photographs courtesy of the Department of Plant and Soil Sciences, University of Kentucky.

that can be handled as multiple plant units in greenhouses. Each cell is filled with a soilless medium and the trays are floated in nutrient solution. Advantages of the greenhouse system include faster plant development and reduced labor requirement. Transplants may be set by hand, but most often it is done mechanically with the aid of a one- to four-row transplanter. These operations may require 50 hours of labor per acre.

When the plants begin to flower, the entire apical meristem is removed (topping) to allow desirable development of leaf yield and quality. Topping also allows

growth of axillary buds to form suckers that must be removed or inhibited. Suckers may be removed from the plants by hand, or more commonly the plants are treated with a growth modifier that prevents development of the axillary buds. Tobacco harvesting is a physically demanding task, especially for air-cured tobacco, which requires about 65 hours of labor per acre evenly divided among cutting the plants, impaling them on a stick, and hanging the sticks in the curing barn.

Growing tobacco is a management-intensive process, but curing the leaf is the most important operation in production of quality product. Flue-cured tobacco is so called because it describes the heating system used in early curing barns. Bulk-curing barns with forced-air heat replaced the older barns with flues and convection heat. The initial step in curing is harvesting the ripe leaves. Flue-cured leaves are primed, removed individually from the stalk, starting at the bottom of the plant as the leaves ripen. At each harvest three to five leaves are removed from the stalk at approximately weekly intervals. Leaves are placed into bulk-curing barns in racks or boxes directly from a mechanical harvester, thus greatly reducing labor input. During the first stage of curing, conditions are maintained at approximately 95°F and 85 percent relative humidity to cause yellowing, destruction of the chlorophyll, and simultaneous hydrolysis of many leaf constituents. After yellowing is completed in 36 to 48 hours, the temperature is raised to about 125°F to dry the leaf lamina and allow oxidation of constituents formed in the first phase of curing. The temperature is further raised to 160°F to dry the leaf midrib and stop any remaining biological reactions. The entire process takes about five to seven days, then the leaves must rehydrate to become pliable for preparation and transport to market.

Air-cured tobaccos are harvested by cutting the stalk and hanging the whole plant in a curing barn; consequently, all the leaves are harvested at the same time. Barns for air-curing tobacco have large vents on the sides to allow for humidity control around the leaf during curing. The best curing conditions are when the temperature ranges between 60° and 90°F and the relative humidity averages between 65 and 70 percent. Relative humidity is the critical factor because if it is too low, the leaves dry too fast and the biological and chemical changes that are required for high-quality cured leaf do not occur. If the relative humidity is too high, microorganisms begin to grow on the tobacco and damage the leaf. Air-curing is dependent upon the ambient conditions, but is usually completed in eight to 10 weeks.

Dark fire-cured tobaccos are stalk-cut and air-cured through the yellowing process and drying of leaf lamina, then the barn is filled with wood smoke to put a finish on the leaf. Loss of barns and tobacco to fire is a hazard of this curing process. This tobacco type is in demand for use in smokeless tobacco products, and is produced mainly in western Kentucky and western Tennessee.

After the curing process is completed, the leaves must be separated into grades, usually two to four grades based on color and visual assessment of quality. Prior to grading leaves of stalk-cut, air-cured tobacco, the plants must be taken down from inside the curing barn and leaves removed from the stalk. These tasks require an additional 85 hours of manual labor. The leaf is now ready for market. Most market packages are now large, 550-pound bales.

Manufacture

Approximately 95 percent of the tobacco produced in the U.S. is flue-cured and burley for use in cigarettes. U.S. consumption of cigarettes has declined over the last 40 years, yet about 484 billion cigarettes were manufactured in the U.S in 2006. Of this total, over 24 percent is exported, making the U.S. the world's largest exporter of manufactured tobacco products. Tobacco leaf production for domestic consumption has been adjusted not only to the decreased per-capita use, but decreased weight of leaf used per cigarette. Reduced amount of tobacco in each cigarette occurred because of decreased cigarette size and change in technology. Cigarette circumference decreased and with the shift to filter cigarettes, the portion containing tobacco decreased. Improved technology to make sheet tobacco from leaf midribs and scrap pieces of leaf and the expansion or puffing of the leaf also decreased the amount of tobacco required to fill a cigarette. Retail product sales generated over $25 billion in local, state and federal taxes in 2006.

Prior to 1890 the manufacture and sale of tobacco products were largely done by small, local companies using locally produced tobacco. Standard manufacturing and marketing techniques were begun in the later half of the nineteenth century, and Bull Durham® brand was one of the first widely recognized brand names in America. In 1883 James Bonsack patented a cigarette-making machine that allowed mass production of uniform quality cigarettes. James Duke obtained

exclusive use of this machine for what eventually became the American Tobacco Company. By 1910 American Tobacco controlled 86 percent of the cigarette market and cigarettes quickly became the primary tobacco product sold. Farm prices of tobacco plummeted during this time, and the battle of words and violence between growers and manufacturers were known as the Tobacco Wars or Black Patch Wars. In 1911, the Supreme Court ruled that the American Tobacco Company was in violation of the Sherman Anti-Trust Act and the company was divested. Dominance of cigarettes as the product of consumer choice was greatly enhanced by the development of the blended cigarette, Camel®, introduced in 1913. The blended cigarette contained about 60 percent flue-cured tobacco, 30 percent burley, a small amount of Turkish tobacco to enhance flavor, and light, air-cured Maryland tobacco for better burning quality. Burley tobacco has the unique property among tobaccos of absorbing and holding additives such as sweeteners and flavorings. The use of additives in the manufacturing process allows more stringent quality control for each cigarette brand as taste and aroma are not dependent entirely on the raw leaf used.

Policy

Attempts to regulate supply and price have been initiated by growers since the beginning of tobacco production in the early 1600s. In the long term, these actions were unsuccessful. The federal government initiated a price support program to the farmers in return for regulation of production quantity in the Depression of the early 1930s and the program continued through 2004. Thus, there is now no federal tobacco program for growers and tobacco may be produced without government geographical restriction. In the later years of the federal program it was a no-net-cost to the taxpayers. To finance the no-net-cost program the producer and the purchaser were required to pay equal amounts toward expenses incurred to operate the program, plus the expense to purchase the tobacco that was not sold to a primary purchaser. Beginning in 1998 the tobacco industry began to change rapidly. The tobacco Master Settlement Agreement (MSA) was negotiated between the large cigarette manufacturing companies and state attorneys general. The MSA required the companies to make payments to the states and to limit certain marketing and advertising activities, especially to youth. The companies received relief from the states for liability of health care costs associated with smoking. Payments by the tobacco companies were based on market share and are projected to be over $200 billion during first 25 years. This is the largest civil settlement in U.S. history. Associated with the MSA was a plan for the tobacco companies to provide about $5 billion over 12 years to growers and rural communities impacted by any decline in tobacco sales due to the MSA. The MSA was known as Phase 1 and the payments to growers as Phase II. In 2004 Phase II was replaced by the Tobacco Transition Payment Program (TTPP) or so-called tobacco buyout. The TTPP provides payments from the tobacco companies to original tobacco quota owners and tobacco producers to transition to a free market situation from the federally regulated program of quotas of the past. Tobacco quota owners and tobacco growers will be paid over a 10-year period ending in 2014 for their quota or tobacco production. In exchange, growers will have no regulation on amount of tobacco they may produce, but there is increased risk as there is no price support for tobacco sold. Tobacco production has changed to production contracts between the grower and the buyer. The buyer agrees to purchase the tobacco at a predetermined price for grade and quality as long as the grower fulfills the terms of the growing contract. The buyer determines the grade and thus the price to the grower. The TTPP has resulted in fewer, but larger, tobacco growers and the MSA has reduced tobacco consumption and thus production in the U.S.

— *Lowell Bush*

See also

Agricultural Programs; History, Agricultural; Greenhouses; Policy, Agricultural

References

Akehurst, B.C. *Tobacco*. 2nd ed. New York, NY: Longman, 1981.

Axton, W.F. *Tobacco and Kentucky*. Lexington, KY: University Press of Kentucky, 1975.

Bush, L.P. and M.W. Crowe. "Nicotiana Alkaloids." Pp. 87-107 in *Toxicants of Plant Origin*. Edited by P.R. Cheeke. Boca Raton, FL: CRC Press, 1989.

National Association of Attorneys General. *Master Settlement Agreement*. Available online at: http://www.naag. org/backpages/naag/tobacco/msa/msa-pdf. Last modified July 02, 2007

Tobacco Institute. *Tobacco—Deeply Rooted in America's Heritage*. Washington, DC: Tobacco Institute, no date.

Tobacco Transition Payment Program: http://www.fsa. usda.gov/FSA/webapp?area=home&subject=toba&topic=landing

Tso, T.C. *Production, Physiology, and Biochemistry of Tobacco Plant*. Beltsville, MD: Ideals, Inc., 1990.

Tourism, Ecotourism

In the United States and globally "rural areas have long provided the settings for recreation and tourism" activities and experiences (Roberts and Hall, 2001). With the decline of long-established rural industries (e.g., agriculture, mining and forestry) in recent decades, many rural communities have begun to explore tourism development as a means to strengthen their economy (Busby and Rendle, 2000). Rural tourism can be defined as any type of tourism activity that takes place in a rural area (Roberts and Hall, 2001). Rural tourism may range from typical mass tourism (e.g., amusement parks, commercial retail shopping) to very specialized forms of alternative tourism (e.g., vacation farms, backpacking). Rural tourism can be divided into various categories including agritourism, farm tourism, naturebased tourism and ecotourism, just to name a few. The purpose of this paper is to focus on ecotourism in rural communities.

To aid in understanding ecotourism in rural areas, it is important to define certain terms. The first is rural tourism which was discussed above. A specific type of rural tourism is nature-based tourism, which involves tourism activities and experiences that are dependent upon the natural resource base, such as all-terrain vehicle riding, hunting, bird watching, canoeing and hiking (Roberts and Hall, 2001). A specific segment of naturebased tourism is ecotourism (see Figure 1).

Ecotourism, in some form, has existed throughout history. However, the term ecotourism was first made popular by Ceballos-Lascurain in the 1980s. Ceballos-Lascurain defined ecotourism as "traveling to relatively undisturbed or uncontaminated natural areas with the specific objective of studying, admiring, and enjoying the scenery and its wild plants and animals, as well as any existing cultural manifestations (both past and present) found in these areas" (Ceballos-Lascurain, 1990, as cited in Juric et al., 2002). Since its inception, many professionals, academics and organizations have modified this definition (Fennell, 2003). Common themes found in many definitions indicate that ecotourism involves small-scale and locally owned tourism opportunities in natural areas, an education component, and a management strategy that revolves around sustainability (Beeton, 1998; Blamey, 2001; Diamantis, 1999; Fennell, 2003, Weaver, 2005). These commonalities are what distinguish ecotourism from the more generic nature-based tourism.

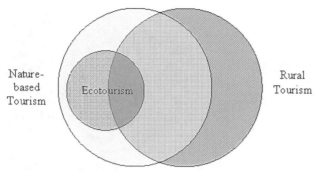

Figure 1. Conceptual Relationship of Ecotourism, Nature-based Tourism and Rural Tourism

Nature-based Tourism

The nature-based component of ecotourism is its most distinguishing characteristic (Blamey, 2001). Ecotourism is tourism which takes place within an ecological setting (Beeton, 1998, Weaver, 2005). The nature-based experience may encompass an entire ecosystem such as snorkeling at a coral reef, exploring a marshland, or hiking in an alpine tundra, or it may be specific to one element in the natural environment, such as specific flora, fauna or geographic formations (Beeton, 1998, Weaver, 2005). Examples of specific fauna include viewing big horn sheep in the Rocky Mountains, the red wolf in eastern North Carolina, and sea turtles on the Atlantic Coast. While ecotourism experiences usually involve areas in their natural state, they may also occur in environments that have been modified by humans (e.g., a boardwalk over marshland) (Beeton, 1998). Most people can easily identify with the nature-based component of ecotourism as it is often featured in the media, as well as used to promote and market many businesses. Unfortunately, many groups and organizations have solely focused on this facet of ecotourism and therefore do not possess a complete understanding or appreciation of ecotourism (Beeton, 1998).

Education

A second characteristic of ecotourism that clearly differentiates it from nature-based tourism is education. Providing learning opportunities and experiences which enhance the visitor's understanding and appreciation of the natural environment is a fundamental tenet of ecotourism (Beeton, 1998; Blamey, 2001; Weaver, 2005). Such an educational experience should include a sound plan, the development of goals and objectives specific to the site, and the use of effective teaching techniques. It addition, it should focus on information about the natural environment, as well as any cultural aspects that are related to humanity's interaction with the local ecosystem (Blamey, 2001). Common techniques used to educate the visitor about a particular ecotourism site include interpretative tours, signage, brochures, guidebooks, as well as many forms of technology (Weaver, 2005). For example Clemmons Educational State Forest in North Carolina developed a "Talking Tree" Trail and a "Talking Rock" Trail. On the "Talking Tree" Trail, through the use of recordings, specific trees "talk about themselves" (e.g., characteristics of that species of tree). On the "Talking Rock" Trail, visitors learn about the geology of the area from the actual rocks, also through recordings.

Sustainability

A third component of ecotourism is the concept of sustainability (Beeton, 1998; Blamey, 2001; Weaver, 2005). The basic premise of sustainability is to ensure today's use of the natural environment for tourism purposes and not compromise the use of these same resources by future generations. Ecotourism endeavors to preserve and conserve the natural environments in which the experience occurs. To accomplish this requires a deliberate plan which takes into account the natural, economic, social and cultural environments of the destination.

Small Scale and Locally Owned

The last component of ecotourism focuses on how the benefits of ecotourism are distributed throughout the community. This implies that the local community (businesses, residents and governments) should be the primary recipients of the benefits (e.g., economic) produced through tourism. In most cases this only occurs when there is strong local leadership coupled with control over ecotourism sites, visitors, businesses and endeavors (Weaver, 2005). Examples of such control mechanisms or techniques include the use of governmental permits and access to natural areas, the development of voluntary standards by local business owners, and the formation of local community environmental groups.

Ecotourism Principles

Just as there are numerous definitions of ecotourism, various groups and individuals have developed "principles" for ecotourism. It is important to understand the key principles that distinguish ecotourism from other forms of tourism. The two most prominent sets of principles for ecotourism were developed by the United Nations Environment Programme (UNEP)/ World Tourism Organization (WTO) and the International

Photograph by Erick Byrd.

Ecotourism Society (IES). The UNEP/WTO (2002) principles from the Quebec Declaration on Ecotourism state that ecotourism should:

- contribute actively to the conservation of natural and cultural heritage;
- include local and indigenous communities in its planning, development and operation, and contribute to their well-being;
- interpret the natural and cultural heritage of the destination to visitors; and
- lend itself better to independent travelers, as well as to organized tours for small-size groups.

The International Ecotourism Society's (2008) principles state that ecotourism should:

- minimize impact;
- build environmental and cultural awareness and respect;

- provide positive experiences for both visitors and hosts;
- provide direct financial benefits for conservation;
- provide financial benefits and empowerment for local people; and
- raise sensitivity to host countries' political, environmental and social climate.

Whereas the previous two sets of principles are most recognized, Patterson's (2007) list of principles have a more pragmatic focus which may be more easily operationalized by business owners. Patterson's (2007) principles are:

- use low-impact camping and recreation techniques;
- limit visitation to areas, either by limiting group size and/or by the number of groups taken to an area in a season;

Table 1.
Potential Ecotourism Activities and Businesses in Rural Areas

Activities	Businesses/Attractions
Camping	Bed and Breakfast
Boating	Outfitter
Backpacking	Cabins
Farm Stays	Sanctuaries
Sightseeing	Outdoor Museums
Wild Flower Viewing	Education Centers
Bird Watching	Marinas
Stargazing	Aquariums
Bike Tours	Zoos
Wine Tourism	Boardwalks
Photography	National Parks
Catch and Release Fishing	National Forests
Mountain Biking	State Parks
Rafting	State Forests
Horseback Riding	Local Parks
Skiing	
Canoeing, Kayaking, Rafting	
Hiking	

(Beeton, 1998; Roberts and Hall, 2001)

- support the work of conservation groups preserving the natural area on which the experience is based;
- orient customers on the region to be visited;
- hire local people and buy supplies locally, where possible;
- recognize that nature is a central element to the tourist experience;
- use guides trained in interpretation of scientific or natural history;
- ensure that wildlife is not harassed; and
- respect the privacy and culture of local people.

Examples of Ecotourism in Rural Areas

There are many ecotourism activities that take place in rural areas, and subsequently, businesses that cater to the needs of the visitors (see Table 1). The primary characteristics that differentiate an ecotourism activity from other tourism activities are the components of ecotourism previously discussed. For example, Beeton (1998) stated that "photography could be a part of any tourism activity, but when it is combined with information on what is being photographed and opportunities to experience the environment it becomes an ecotour activity."

Benefits and Costs

Ecotourism has the potential to positively and negatively impact a local community. Economic benefits could include diversification of the local economy, addition of

"new" money into the local economy, creation of new jobs, and infrastructure development (Diamantis, 1999; Beeton, 1998). Potential negative impacts may include increases in local property taxes and an increase in unskilled, low-paying jobs.

Environmental benefits include the idea that ecotourism places an economic value on the natural resources. The natural resources are viewed as an attraction that must be managed in order to preserve them for future use (Diamantis, 1999; Beeton, 1998). This view can, in turn, provide motivation for the restoration, protection and conservation of other areas within the local community (Diamantis, 1999). In addition to being a strong force for rural economic regeneration, tourism is also associated with the conservation of rural landscapes. In many cases ecotourism uses revenues to encourage conservation of the natural resources. Some of the potential undesired or negative environmental impacts include extreme stress on the natural resources due to rapid business growth and the increased numbers of visitors which may damage or destroy the very thing that is attracting them to the area (Diamantis, 1999).

Some of the social/cultural benefits of ecotourism to a local community include an increased community pride and quality of life. Increased civic pride can lead to opportunities to share and protect the local culture and history. Local residents are also able to have access to these ecotourism sites for their recreational use. Negative impacts may include resentment and antagonism about visitors and tourism for the locals.

The impacts (economic, environmental and social/cultural) of ecotourism are unique to each area. Certain activities that may have a positive impact in one area may have a negative impact in another. For example, Buckley (2001) explains that "damage to plants by hikers' boots is far more significant on an alpine meadow than in subtropical rainforest, but weed seeds and soil pathogens in mud on hikers' boots are more significant in rainforest than alpine environments." Therefore, each unique area will require a unique management plan and strategy. Variables that managers need to include in such a plan involve activity choice, manner in which the activity is carried out, equipment that will be used or needed (both by the visitors and the managers), location (e.g., trail heads, parking and viewing sites) and timing (e.g., seasons and hours), group size, education of the visitor, education of the local community, training of staff, and environmental management (Buckley, 2001). As much as one would like to minimize the negative impacts that tourism has on the natural environment, once visitors step into the natural environment to interact and enjoy it, they will have an impact that cannot be changed. Responsible ecotourism should include planning, management and practice, which maximize the positive impacts of ecotourism, while at the same time minimizing the potential negative impacts.

— *Erick T Byrd, Lauren Duffy, and Nancy J Gladwell*

See also

Agritourism; Environmental Ethics; Environmental Movements; Environmental Sustainability; History, Environmental; Sustainable Development

References

Beeton, Sue. *Ecotourism: A Practical guide for Rural Communities*. Collingwood, Australia: Landlinks Press, 1998.

Blamey, Russell. "Principles of Ecotourism." Pp. 5-22 in *The Encyclopedia of Ecotourism*. Edited by David Weaver. Wallingford: CABI, 2001.

Buckley, Ralf. "Environmental Impacts." Pp. 379-394 in *The Encyclopedia of Ecotourism*. Edited by David Weaver. Wallingford: CABI, 2001.

Diamantis, Dimitrios. "The Concept of Ecotourism: Evolution and Trends." *Current Issues in Tourism* 2 (1999): 93-122.

Fennell, David. *Ecotourism*, 2nd ed. New York: Routledge, 2003.

The International Ecotourism Society. "Definitions and Principles." Available online at:http://www.ecotourism.org.

Juric, Biljana, T. Bettina Cornwell, and Damien Mather. "Exploring the Usefulness of an Ecotourism Interest Scale." *Journal of Travel Research* 40 (2002): 256-269.

Patterson, Carol. *The Business of Ecotourism: The Complete Guide for Nature and Culture-Based Tourism Operators*, 3rd ed. Victoria, BC, Canada: Trafford Publishing, 2007.

Roberts, Lesley and Derek Hall. *Rural Tourism and Recreation: Principles to Practice*. New York: CABI Publishing, 2001.

United Nations Environment Programme and World Tourism Organization. "Quebec Declaration on Ecotourism." Available online at: http://www.uneptie.org/pc/tourism/ecotourism/documents.htm

Weaver, David. "Comprehensive and Minimalist Dimensions of Ecotourism." *Annuals of Tourism Research* 32 (2005): 439-455.

Town-Country Relations

The forms of conflict and cooperation between, and contrasting attitudes towards, town and country. These relations constitute a spatial opposition of deep economic and cultural significance, one of the great axes along which social life is organized and understood. This entry describes how this axis is manifested in the images, social identities, communities, patterns of migration, economic development, and power relations of rural and urban America.

Images of Town and Country

"Fuscus, who lives in town and loves it, greeting from one who loves the country, and lives there!" With these words, written in the year 20 BCE, the Roman poet Horace began one of his many works advocating country living (Raffel 1984: 215). Horace's writings, along with Aesop's ancient fable of the town mouse and the country mouse, show that relations between town and country have been an issue for 2,000 years at least. Probably for as long as there have been towns and surrounding countryside, the residents of both have pondered their attitudes towards each other and the interests and sentiments that sometimes unite and sometimes divide them.

Yet for all their ancient significance, town and country are notoriously ambiguous terms. In America, "town" can refer to a city—an urban settlement. It can as well refer to a "small town"—a settlement perceived to be culturally and economically rural, despite its concentration of population and businesses. By contrast, British usage see "town" as clearly urban and use the term "village" for most of the places Americans call "small towns." Americans also use the term "village" at times, but for them the term "town" can cover both a village and a city—and sometimes even the "country," as in the use of "town" and "township" to demarcate local political boundaries in rural areas. The term "country" is no less indefinite. English speakers use it to refer to the open country of the wilderness, the farms and small towns of the rural countryside, and sometimes the quasi-rural landscape of exurbia and suburbia.

Despite these spatial and conceptual ambiguities, town and country do have distinct meanings, ultimately drawn from the opposition between culture and nature so central to Western thought. This distinction, imprecise and contradictory as it may often be, has been a central prop for many moral arguments. "Those who labour in the earth," wrote Thomas Jefferson (1984

[1787]: 290), "are the chosen people of God...whose breasts he has made his peculiar deposit for substantial and genuine virtue." The Jeffersonian faith in the pastoral, natural, and democratic virtue of country folk has, however, often jostled uneasily against what Raymond Williams (1973) in *The Country and the City* called the "counter-pastoral" image of the countryside. Rather than a deposit of genuine virtue, the counter-pastoral sees the countryside as a repository of backwardness, isolationism, and small-mindedness.

Like country life, the values of town life have been both elevated and denigrated in American thought. The town has been praised as the seat of progress, civilization, and a sophisticated and open-minded lifestyle. And from Thoreau onward, it has also been regarded as a constraining jungle of laws, rules, greed, and competitiveness. Both town and country have been seen as the true site of individual freedom, freedom from social convention on the part of the country, and freedom from country gossip on the part of the town. As well, both have been seen as the essential condition for real community, from the ethnic solidarity of "urban villages" to the helpfulness and neighborliness of country life.

Social Identity and Community

Given this range of available meanings, the distinction between town and country remains a valuable boundary upon which to establish a sense of identity. Many Americans continue to identify themselves as a "small town person" or a "city person," and to take pride in the distinction. Part of the power of this distinction derives from people's sense of its naturalness. The sheer physicality of place makes the country-town distinction an appealingly authoritative one. Moreover, the widely held notion that country places are closer to nature than urban areas, combined with the increasingly positive associations given to being closer to nature, makes a country identity especially secure and sought-after.

This spatial identification is central to what Hummon (1990: 11) called community ideologies, "systems of belief that legitimate the social and psychological interests of community residents." For example, a person who can claim to be "a local" may gain both a rooted sense of self and greater political legitimacy in local conflicts. A commitment to a spatial locale also may serve as the principle around which an economic and social solidarity may be constructed. As Allen and Dillman (1994) in *Against All Odds* document for the small town of Bremer, Washington, a strong local community

is possible even in an age in which information technologies shattered so many spatial boundaries.

Many scholars, however, have argued that the distinction between country life and town life in the modern world is, in the oft-quoted words of Richard Dewey (1960: 60), "real, but relatively unimportant." Earlier scholarship argued for the existence of a rural-urban continuum, using Ferdinand Tönnies's famous distinction between Gemeinschaft (communities based upon shared sentiments) and Gesellschaft (communities based upon interdependent interests). A host of studies have challenged the idea that Gemeinschaft is more typical of rural communities and Gesellschaft of urban ones. William Friedland (2002) has also argued that the industrialization of agriculture is now so complete that it has become mainly an open-air assembly line, and that we are now seeing the "final separation" of agriculture and rurality. But despite these scholarly challenges, the American popular imagination still finds the distinction between country life and town life a fruitful one to make. To the extent that people still act on this distinction as a source of identity and ideology, it remains both real and important, at least in its consequences. In any event, commitment to the local community remains high in many rural and urban locales.

Migration

With these commitments has come population growth in both town and country. The twentieth-century decline in the US rural population reversed itself beginning about 1970, and with some ups and downs has continued since then. The rural population grew by 1.4 percent per year in the 1970s, fell back to 0.3 percent per year during the 1980s and the troubling years of the "farm crisis of the early 1980s," gained back to 1.0 percent per year in the 1990s, and at this writing is seeing growth of about 0.4 percent in the 2000s. But urban growth has been far faster than rural growth, aside from the 1970s, and is now running at about 3 times the rate of rural growth, leading to a steady decline in the percentage of Americans in rural areas, even as rural population has grown.

Moreover, the majority of rural growth since the "turn-around" in rural population began has been due to in-migration, not natural increase among those already residing in rural areas. Typically, the rural growth is in those areas closest to centers of urban growth, as urbanites seek rural amenities within commuting distance of cities and suburbs. Consequently, two-thirds of the non-metropolitan population in the

US now lives in counties adjacent to metropolitan counties. Many rural counties with special scenic value have also experienced a significant influx of retirees and other originally urban people not so spatially tied to metropolitan workplaces.

Consequently, the Economic Research Service (2007) of the US Department of Agriculture reports that the category "rural" has become "harder to define." Even where the rural population is growing, their employment is increasingly urban, as good roads and electronic media have increased the ease of commuting. Plus much of the rural population now lives in the remoter sections of counties that the Census defines as metropolitan overall, due to the presence of a significant urban center. Sonya Salamon's 2002 *Newcomers to Old Towns* traces this process of rural suburbanization in central Illinois, and finds that the urban migrants are changing social relations as well. Increasingly, she writes, these areas are best described as "post-agrarian" in their values, sense of more far-flung community ties, and sources of income.

Town and Country as an Isolated State

These changing trends in America's rural population show how crucial the patterns of economic development and technological change are to understanding town-country relations. In 1826 in *The Isolated State*, Johann Heinrich Von Thünen suggested a simple but powerful thought experiment about these patterns. Imagine an isolated world in which a single city sits in the midst of the hinterland from which it draws its resources. Such a city would be surrounded by concentric circles in which "with increasing distance from the Town, the land will be progressively given up to products cheap to transport in relation to their value" (Von Thünen 1966 [1826]: 8). Perishable products (such as dairy, fruit, and vegetables) are expensive to transport, and so must command a high price and be produced close to town. This will raise the value of the land (what Von Thünen called "land rent") on which these products are produced. Cheaper products easier to transport will be produced on lower valued land farther from the town.

The real world, of course, is more complex. Cities and towns are not isolated from each other. Moreover, modern transportation technology greatly changed the economics of moving goods from Von Thünen's day, resulting in inter-regional agricultural specialization. A ham-and-cheese sandwich with lettuce and tomato served in New York City might have cheese from Duchess County, some 50 miles away, as Von Thünen would have expected. The ham, however, probably came from Iowa, the wheat for the bread from South Dakota, and in an inversion of Von Thünen's zones of production and land rent, the lettuce and tomato from California. The cheese might have come from California too. Yet understanding the origin of real-world departures from an isolated state remains a valuable way to understand the dynamics of inter-regional competition and cooperation, the growth and decline of urban and rural populations, and the direction technological change has followed in the industrial period. Town-country relations have been greatly affected by efforts to get around the economic realities Von Thünen's model pointed out.

Yet despite these efforts, the general pattern of primary production (that is, agriculture, forestry, and quarrying) still follows Von Thünen's model. Eighty-six percent of America's fruits and vegetables and 63 percent of its diary products are produced in metropolitan or metropolitan-influenced counties (American Farmland Trust 2002). Goods like grain and timber (which are relatively non-perishable, and therefore easier to transport) remain lower valued and produced further from cities on lower valued land, such as the grain land of Iowa, the Dakotas, and Nebraska, and the forest land of Montana, Oregon, Alabama, and Maine. The frequently depressed rural economies and continued rural population decline of these states reflects these lower values. In 1987, Deborah and Frank Popper made the highly controversial suggestion, still under vigorous discussion, that in some Western states, this amounts to a re-creation of the frontier, in which there is little population or economic activity.

Von Thünen's model, however, presupposes the existence of a town. Walter Christaller sought to explain the town's origin with his Central Place Theory. A town, said Christaller (1966 [1933]: 19), derives from the need for central goods and central services, goods and services "produced and offered at a few necessarily central points in order to be consumed at many scattered points." These goods and services are mainly those provided by government, industry, marketplaces, and the media. Christaller argued that there is a regional hierarchy of higher-order and lower-order central places, like satellites around a great planet. William Cronon's 1993 book *Nature's Metropolis* explores the history of these interconnections between Chicago and its hinterlands.

This sense of a world on the move is at the heart of the new "mobilities" and "flows" perspectives gaining interest among scholars, and largely based on the work of the British sociologist John Urry and the Spanish sociologist Manuel Castells. "Global fluids" of materials, ideas, and people are transforming the old "moorings" of place, as we develop into a single, global "network society." Increasingly, because of these changes in technologies, economies, and cultures, we must recognize that few places, in the town or the country, can be deemed isolated anymore.

Power Relations between Town and Country

These flows are "becoming the dominant spatial manifestation of power and function in our societies," writes Castells (2000: 409). Moreover, the hierarchy of places and differentiation of function described by Christaller goes on, and promotes urban dominance over the countryside. Consequently, wealth tends to flow from periphery to center, argues the urban growth machine theory of Logan and Molotch and the world systems theory of Emmanuel Wallerstein. In order to maximize return on fixed capital, such as buildings and machines and the relatively fixed capital of human resources, urban economic and political elites advocate pro-growth policies that circulate as much mobile capital as possible through cities and towns. The size and centrality of cities gives urban elites a political advantage when lobbying to create economic structures that will direct capital flows in their direction. The result is that, despite the frequent objections of local citizens, elites operate cities and towns as economic vacuum cleaners, drawing capital and population from each other and from the hinterlands.

Industrializing the countryside is one way that urban interests gain control over rural capital, with important consequences for rural areas. In one of the most famous works of rural sociology, *As You Sow*, Walter Goldschmidt (1947) argued that the structure of agriculture has a large impact on poverty and community life in farming-dependent counties. Based on a case study comparison of two California farming communities, Goldschmidt developed what has come to be called the "Goldschmidt hypothesis": That industrial farming leads to the deterioration of community well-being. Subsequent research generally upheld this conclusion, with the important caveat that rural poverty, the retention of rural social institutions, such as churches and schools, and rural depopulation depend on other factors as well.

Given these economic patterns, it is perhaps unsurprising that country people often feel a general hos-

tility to town people and town things. These tensions emerge in the century-long debate over whether the structure of the U.S. political system gives too much power, or not enough, to rural interests. These tensions are probably also largely responsible for the continued salience many people find in claiming a town or a country identity. As well, there is now a resurgence of rural social movements around the world, from the Confédération Paysanne (Peasants Confederation) of France, to the Landless Rural Workers Movement of Brazil, to the sustainable agriculture movement of the U.S.

But these new rural movements often draw strength from linking rural and urban concerns. The distinction between town and country is, in the final analysis, a mental construction that people choose to make, with real consequences for how they act. The likely persistence of economic tensions between central places and their hinterlands suggests that this is a construction that many people will continue to find significant to their lives, but perhaps also to reconfigure in ways that are beneficial to us all.

— *Michael M. Bell and Peter F. Korsching*

See also

Community; Community, Sense of; Development, Community and Economic; History, Rural; Rural Demography; Rural, Definition of; Settlement Patterns; Trade Areas; Urbanization

References

American Farmland Trust. *Farming on the Edge: Sprawling Development Threaten's America's Best Farmland.* Washington, DC: American Farmland Trust, 2002.

Dewey, Richard. "The Rural-Urban Continuum: Real but Relatively Unimportant." *American Journal of Sociology* 66 (1960): 60-66.

Castells, Manuel. *The Information Age: Economy, Society and Culture. Volume 1. The Rise of the Network Society*, 2nd edition. Oxford: Blackwell 2000.

Christaller, Walter. *Central Places in Southern Germany.* Carlisle W. Baskin, trans. Englewood Cliffs, NJ: Prentice-Hall, (1933) 1966.

Economic Research Service. "Rural Population and Migration: Trend 1 — Harder to Define 'Rural.'" Washington, DC: U.S. Department of Agriculture, Economic Research Service, 2007. Available online at: http://www.ers.usda.gov/Briefing/Population/Rural.htm.

Friedland, Williams H. "Agriculture and Rurality: Beginning the Final Separation?" *Rural Sociology* 67, no. 3 (2002): 350-371.

Hummon, David M. *Commonplaces: Community Ideology and Identity in American Culture.* Albany, NY: State University of New York, 1990.

Jefferson, Thomas. *Writings*. Edited by Merril D. Peterson. New York, NY: Literary Classics of the United States, 1984.

Raffel, Burton. *The Essential Horace*. San Francisco, CA: North Point Press, 1983.

Von Thünen, Johann Heinrich. *Von Thünen's Isolated State*. Peter Hall, ed. Carla M. Wartenberg, trans. Oxford: Pergamon, (1826) 1966.

Trade Areas

The geographical areas from which residents are attracted to shop at a trade center. Trade centers are locations with an assortment of businesses that sell goods and services to consumers. Early trade areas in the U.S. originated with Native American settlements, but changed over the years as non-natives settled the country. As the country become more mechanized, local residents gained mobility and started shopping farther from home, thereby changing the size and shape of trade areas. Academics developed theories of trade areas and various methods of measuring them. Individual merchants can determine the size of their own trade areas by analyzing data gathered from consumers. Regional variations of trade area size and shape are brought about by differences in topography and population density. Dominant businesses within a community can enlarge the trade area for a community, whereas weak businesses can decrease it.

History

The first trade areas in what is now the U.S. were developed by Native Americans who lived primarily in tribes. Tribes in different parts of the country had access to various raw materials and natural resources and developed an array of handicraft skills. Tribal members could improve their well-being by trading with members of neighboring tribes—thus, the beginning of trade areas. The early non-native settlers in the U.S. tended to settle in the vicinity of streams and wooded areas since they needed the streams for transportation and water, and the wood to construct buildings and provide fire. Consequently, the early businesses in the country consisted of trading posts around these settlements, and they became trade centers for the newly settled territories.

In the mid- to late 1800s, railroads played a large role in settling the rest of the country. Railroads provided a leap over horses and oxen in the transportation of both people and goods. There was great competition to entice the railroads to come through various settlements. The lucky settlements that got a railroad station tended to become trade centers and their populations grew rapidly. Meanwhile, transportation for pioneer farmers was poor, consisting primarily of horses and oxen traveling over rough trails. For many pioneer farmers, making trips to the railroad trade centers was a formidable task. Therefore, intermediate trade centers sprang up between the railroad stations, and initially were successful because of the immobility of the rural residents.

Despite their limited mobility, some early settlers made occasional trips to larger towns and cities by animal power or later by train to shop for items not locally available. However, the first major challenge to rural retailers occurred in the late 1880s when Montgomery Ward and Sears Roebuck began mail order operations. At its peak, Sears Roebuck offered over 100,000 items through its catalog. Mail order firms offered great convenience to rural residents by allowing them to order by mail and receive shipment within several weeks. The mail order companies captured trade from many rural retailers.

Automotive vehicles appeared in the early 1900s. However, it was some time before roads and highways were sufficiently developed to allow easy travel to larger trade centers to shop. By the end of the 1930s, both motor vehicles and highways had been improved considerably, but the Great Depression of the 1930s kept most rural residents shopping close to home because they did not have the money to travel or shop.

The U.S. mobilized for World War II from 1941 to 1945. Severe rationing of retail goods and gasoline caused most rural residents to stay close to home to shop. After World War II, the combination of relative prosperity and great pent-up demand caused rural consumers and others to go on shopping sprees, creating the first widespread migration from rural areas to larger trade centers to shop. At about the same time, rapid mechanization of farms meant that fewer and fewer people were needed in agriculture, thus causing many people to leave the rural areas and seek opportunities elsewhere. This out-migration was the beginning of severe depletion of the trade areas of rural retailers.

Shopping malls began to appear in larger trade centers in the 1950s and 1960s, and spread rapidly across the country in the 1970s and 1980s. Consumers were attracted to shopping malls in large numbers be-

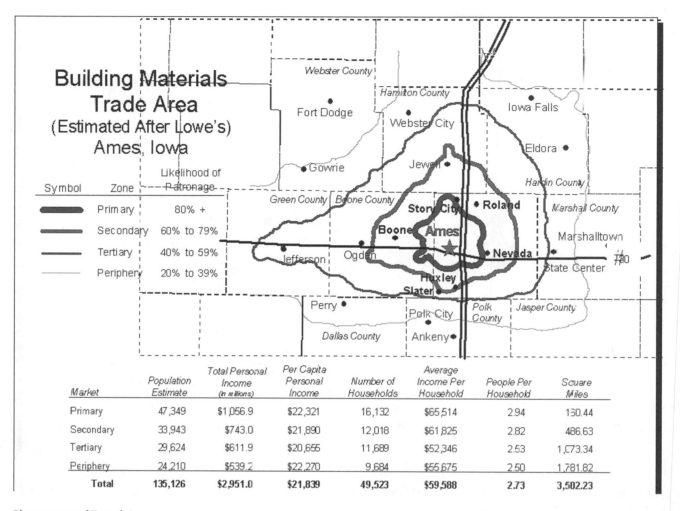

Building Materials
Trade Area
(Estimated After Lowe's)
Ames, Iowa

Symbol	Zone	Likelihood of Patronage
	Primary	80% +
	Secondary	60% to 79%
	Tertiary	40% to 59%
	Periphery	20% to 39%

Market	Population Estimate	Total Personal Income (in millions)	Per Capita Personal Income	Number of Households	Average Income Per Household	People Per Household	Square Miles
Primary	47,349	$1,056.9	$22,321	16,132	$65,514	2.94	130.44
Secondary	33,943	$743.0	$21,890	12,018	$61,825	2.82	486.63
Tertiary	29,624	$611.9	$20,655	11,689	$52,346	2.53	1,073.34
Periphery	24,210	$539.2	$22,270	9,684	$55,675	2.50	1,781.82
Total	**135,126**	**$2,951.0**	**$21,839**	**49,523**	**$59,588**	**2.73**	**3,502.23**

Photo courtesy of Kenneth Stone.

cause of their wide selections, ease of access, free parking, controlled climate and extended shopping hours. Rural residents flocked to the malls, thus further eroding the trade areas of rural retailers. The 1980s and 1990s saw the expansion of many mass merchandiser chains such as discount general merchandisers and specialty super stores. These chains have increasingly congregated around larger trade centers and accelerated the capture of retail trade from the rural areas.

The trends of continual consolidation in farming and retailing continue today; they are responsible for shrinking rural trade areas and have caused major problems for small town retailers. For example, studies in Iowa show that towns of 500 to 1,000 population lost over 45 percent of their retail trade between 1983 and 1993.

Theories of Trade Areas

Central Place Theory. In the early 1900s, sociology, geography and economics scholars began to express interest in the theory of trade areas and the measurement of their size. Two German scholars, Walter Christaller and August Losch, were responsible for the first major developments of a theory of retail trade, called Central Place Theory, although some believe that the French scholar J. Reynaud originated the idea in the mid-1800s.

Central Place Theory is the theory of the location, size, nature and spacing of business communities. It seeks to explain the function and spacing of different size trade centers and to develop a hierarchy. In more recent times, various researchers designated the hierarchy of central places with such names as minimum convenience, partial shopping, complete shopping, and primary regional. For example, a minimum convenience trade center may have only a convenience store, service station, hair salon, and restaurant, and draw customers from a five-mile radius. Conversely, a primary regional trade center may have a complete assort-

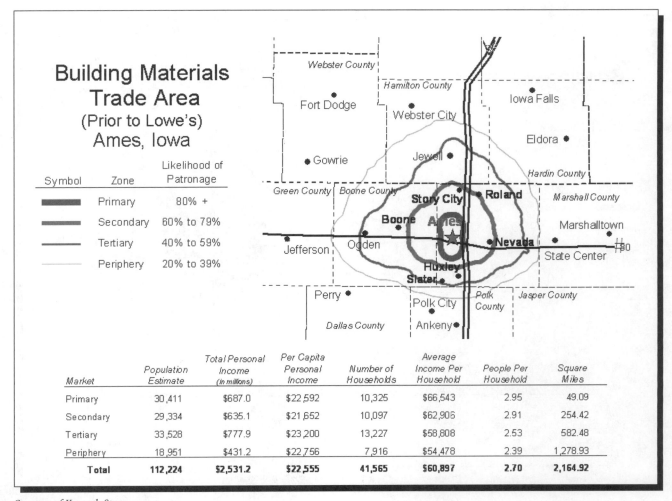

Building Materials Trade Area
(Prior to Lowe's) Ames, Iowa

Symbol	Zone	Likelihood of Patronage
	Primary	80% +
	Secondary	60% to 79%
	Tertiary	40% to 59%
	Periphery	20% to 39%

Market	Population Estimate	Total Personal Income (in millions)	Per Capita Personal Income	Number of Households	Average Income Per Household	People Per Household	Square Miles
Primary	30,411	$687.0	$22,592	10,325	$66,543	2.95	49.09
Secondary	29,334	$635.1	$21,652	10,097	$62,906	2.91	254.42
Tertiary	33,528	$777.9	$23,200	13,227	$58,808	2.53	582.48
Periphery	18,951	$431.2	$22,756	7,916	$54,478	2.39	1,278.93
Total	**112,224**	**$2,531.2**	**$22,555**	**41,565**	**$60,897**	**2.70**	**2,164.92**

Courtesy of Kenneth Stone.

ment of businesses and draw customers from a 100-mile radius.

Early researchers experimented with several variables to explain the relationship between trade center size and spacing. For example, the number of telephones in a community was used to designate a place in the hierarchy when mainly businesses had telephones. In later years, nearly everyone had a telephone. It became obvious that variables such as this could quickly become obsolete. Others used the number of businesses and the relative size of the businesses in formulae designed to develop a ranking of central places. Most of these variables were difficult to acquire and impractical to use. This led to the use of a simpler, generalized theory, called Reilly's Law of Retail Gravitation.

Reilly's Law of Retail Gravitation. In 1929, William J. Reilly of the University of Texas developed a simple equation to determine the breaking point between two competing trade centers where consumers theoretically would be indifferent as to which trade center they pa-tronized. In other words, the boundaries of a trade center's trade area could be derived by computing various points of indifference. In general, the model found what we intuitively know; that the larger the trade center, the farther the locations from which it draws customers.

The Huff Model. The Huff Model was introduced by David Huff in 1963. It has become a very popular model to use in delineating trade areas. It is a gravity model that has several advantages over Reilly's model. In particular, it can consider multiple competitors (stores or towns) simultaneously in evaluating the trade area for a given store or town. It can assign probabilities that shoppers in various outlying areas will shop in the subject town. The probability surfaces can then be used to construct a trade area map, essentially showing the primary trade area and secondary trade areas.

GIS (Geological Information System). GIS is sophisticated computer software that can analyze various

Basic Trade Area for Emmetsburg, Iowa
Using Reilly's Law of Retail Gravitation
FY97

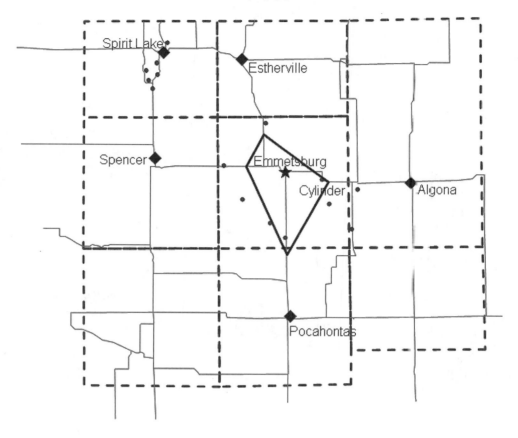

Scale Legend
0   6

Courtesy of Kenneth Stone.

databases connected with geographic locations on the earth. In trade area applications, it can analyze both theoretical and actual data depicting customer locations and generate a map that delineates the trade area. For example, GIS can use inputs for the Huff Model to draw a theoretical trade area. In addition, it can take actual customer location data to draw a firm's actual trade area or it can use town data to draw a town's actual trade area map.

Regional Variations

Many of the studies on trade areas have occurred in the Midwest where the terrain is fairly uniform and where there are few barriers to transportation. In these areas, it is easy to predict trade area size for various trade centers.

Geographical Differences. In mountainous areas where travel is very difficult, it is possible for smaller trade centers to pull trade from a large geographical area and to remain viable. Certain parts of the High Plains and Desert Southwest have very sparse populations. Small trade centers remain robust because it is simply too far to travel to a larger trade center.

Dominant Businesses. There are many small trade centers across the country with one or more superior businesses. For example, it is common to see an outstanding restaurant in a small town that draws business from a large area. Other towns may have an outstanding furniture store, a large building materials store, or a large automobile dealer, any of which can draw an inordinate amount of traffic to the respective towns.

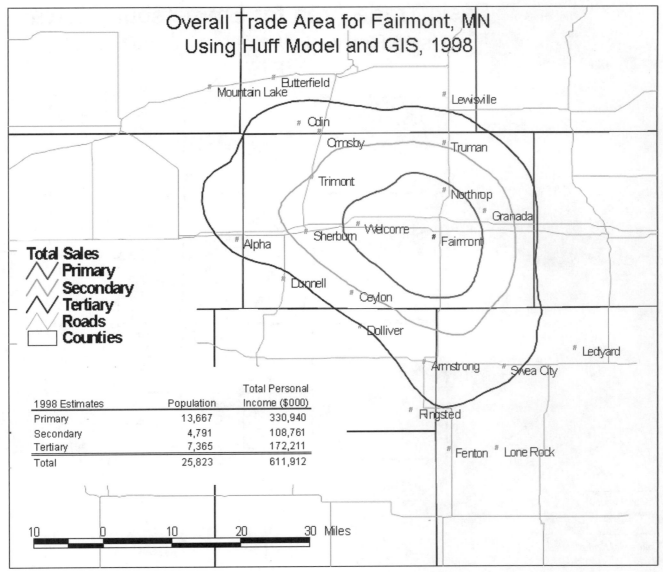

Overall Trade Area for Fairmont, MN
Using Huff Model and GIS, 1998

1998 Estimates	Population	Total Personal Income ($000)
Primary	13,667	330,940
Secondary	4,791	108,761
Tertiary	7,365	172,211
Total	25,823	611,912

Courtesy of Kenneth Stone.

In recent times, factory outlet malls have been opening in some small towns along major highways. These centers draw traffic, not only from the highway, but sometimes become shopping destinations for customers from 100 or more miles away.

Measurement of Actual Trade Area Size

Researchers discovered ways to measure the theoretical size of trade areas, but business people needed practical ways to determine the size of their trade areas. Some of the more common ways included consumer surveys, check and credit card receipts, and pull factor analysis.

Consumer Surveys. Trade areas can be delineated fairly well by conducting a consumer survey. A random sample of consumers within a generous radius of a trade center is selected and respondents are queried about where they shop for various goods and services. The approximate trade area then can be defined based on consumer responses.

Check, Credit Card Receipts and Zip Codes. Individual merchants can determine their own trade area by analyzing their checks and credit card receipts periodically. Some stores may also ask all customers for their postal zip codes from time to time. The findings can be plotted on maps to show primary and secondary trade areas.

Pull Factor Analysis. Pull factor analysis is a precise way to show the relative size of a trade area, but not the exact geographic boundaries. The pull factor was developed by Stone and McConnon (1980) and is

Story City, Iowa, a progressive small town. Courtesy of Kenneth Stone.

derived using sales data, usually gathered from state sales tax reports. A pull factor is merely a town's per-capita sales divided by the state per-capita sales. For example, if a town had per-capita sales of $15,000 and the state per-capita sales were $7,500, the pull factor would be $15,000 divided by $7,500 = 2.0. The interpretation is that the town is selling to 200 percent of the town population in full-time customer equivalents (the amount customers would have spent if they made all their purchases in that town). The pull factor is very useful in comparing trade area size over time since it adjusts for price inflation, population change, and changes in a state's economy.

Loyalty Cards. Some larger retail stores issue loyalty cards to customers. On receipt of the loyalty card, customers fill out a personal information form, listing address, age, gender, occupation, etc. Each time a customer makes a purchase, the loyalty card is scanned and discounts are given on selected merchandise. The database developed from these sales data is invaluable in plotting the actual trade area for a business. With the aid of a GIS system, very precise trade area maps can be produced. Furthermore, the trade area pur-chases can be correlated with socioeconomic factors and even the day of the week and the time of day. In practice, however, most retail stores do not insist that the customer fill out the personal information form. Also, very few stores actually analyze this valuable data. It is more difficult for small stores to implement such a system, but it is possible, usually with the help of a third-party vendor.

The Future

The continued concentration of large mass merchandiser stores in larger trade centers and the persistent outmigration of people from rural areas do not bode well for most small trade centers. The residents of these smaller towns are greatly inconvenienced in that they must travel somewhere else to transact a large share of their business.

The development of electronic interactive mail order (Internet shopping), along with the tremendous improvement in delivery services, holds some promise for changing the retail equation in the future so that place no longer matters. People in the most rural areas may be able to shop for virtually anything in the world from the comfort of their homes. Conversely, small-town merchants with unique products will not be constrained to their local trade areas, but will be able to market to the world.

— *Kenneth E. Stone*

See also
Community; Community, Sense of; Development, Community and Economic; History, Rural; Rural Demography; Regional Planning; Settlement Patterns; Town-Country Relations; Trade, Interregional; Urbanization

References
Anding, Thomas L., John S. Adams, William Casey, Sandra de Montille, and Miriam Goldfein. *Trade Centers of the Upper Midwest: Changes from 1960 to 1989.* CURA 90-12. Minneapolis, MN: University of Minnesota, Center for Urban and Regional Affairs, 1990.

Berry, Brian J.L. *Geography of Market Centers and Retail Distribution.* Englewood Cliffs, NJ: Prentice-Hall, Inc., 1967.

Bolstad, Paul. *GIS Fundamentals: A First Text on Geographic Information Systems.* White Bear Lake, MN: Eider Press, 2002.

Borchert, John R. and Russell B. Adams. *Trade Centers and Trade Areas of the Upper Midwest.* Minneapolis, MN: Upper Midwest Research and Development Council, 1963.

Fox, Karl A. *Urban-Regional Economics, Social System Accounts, and Eco-Behavioral Science.* Ames, IA: Iowa State University Press, 1994.

Huff, D.L. "A Probabilistic Analysis of Shopping Center Trade Areas." *Land Economics* 39 (1963): 81-90.

King, Leslie J. *Central Place Theory.* Beverly Hills, CA: Sage Publications, 1984.

Mahoney, Tom. *The Great Merchants.* New York, NY: Harper and Brothers, 1955.

Martin, Paul S., George I. Quimby, and Donald Collier. *Indians before Columbus.* Chicago, IL: University of Chicago Press, 1947.

Stone, Kenneth E. *Competing With the Retail Giants: How to Survive in the New Retail Landscape.* New York, NY: John Wiley and Sons, 1995.

Trade, International
The commercial exchange of goods or services across national frontiers. Continued growth in international trade is having a significant impact on all human communities, including those in rural areas. The extent of that impact, and whether it is positive or negative, varies by product, region and point in time.

Introduction
International trade is one of the various forms of cross-national human interaction that increasingly are being viewed as linked to, or an expression of, globalization. International trade is connected with, but often distinguished from, international capital movement and cross-national labor migration. Like foreign investment and labor migration, international trade is not a new phenomenon. For example, obsidian, which was prized in the production of scythes, and thus was important in the development of the agricultural revolution, was traded from present-day Turkey to peoples throughout the Mediterranean and Levant more than 8,000 years ago. However, the frequency, speed and breadth of international trade, including the variety of goods and services traded, have grown rapidly in recent decades. Consequently, the various configurations that international trade can take, and the ways in which it integrates with local social, economic and political activities, is becoming more complex. The challenge of conducting assessments of international trade is made difficult by the need to investigate the short-term and the long-term economic, political and cultural impacts on people at national, regional and local levels. The study of the role of, and impacts on, rural communities in international trade is further complicated by the fact that a great deal of economic activity in local communities (e.g., teaching, health services, construction, etc.) remains local. Nonetheless, it is possible to identify some of the agreed-upon general impacts that international trade appears to be having on rural people and communities.

Trade and Prices
One of the more direct impacts that the expanding volume of international trade has had on rural areas has been a general decline over the past several decades, relative to the price of manufactured goods, in the prices paid for primary commodities, particularly agricultural commodities. Simultaneously, as primary commodities and raw materials from extractive industries are traded more on global markets, they become increasingly subject to price fluctuations. When global supplies of a commodity are in short supply and/or experience heavier demand, rural areas that produce these commodities can experience jumps in income. At the same time, when more regions around the world produce and market the same or substitutable com-

modities, or as demand for a commodity falls due to changes in tastes or declines in purchasing power, prices for these commodities can fall. Thus, whether a community benefits or not from growth in international trade will depend in part on whether its residents produce and consume commodities and products that are in short or abundant supply and demand in world markets, as well as the actions of governments and firms. A current example of the complexity and unpredictability of these processes is the current volatility in corn prices that some observers attribute to increased demand for ethanol, and the varying effects this volatility appears to be having on corn growers, ethanol producers and feed grain prices, all of which is having dissimilar impacts on associated rural communities.

Trade and Labor

Another impact of expanding international trade on rural America has been to place people within global labor markets. As international movement of goods and services becomes easier due to improved transportation and telecommunication technologies, firms are increasingly able to locate production facilities in whatever country provides them with the least expensive labor force of a particular quality. Thus, just as the prices of commodities produced in rural America have become increasingly coupled with global prices for comparable commodities, wage rates in the rural U.S. are being affected directly by overseas wage rates. This can serve to suppress wage rates for jobs that can be exported while also creating new employment opportunities for individuals and firms that have a competitive advantage in the production of a particular good or service. This leads to challenges for many communities as they struggle with decisions over whether to engage in economic development strategies that are focused on encouraging local entrepreneurism or industrial recruitment.

Some rural communities in the U.S. have been adversely affected by shifts in where multinational firms source labor because they had become dependent on low-skill manufacturing jobs. During this century, and especially after the end of the Second World War, many U.S. rural areas became less dependent on agriculture and more dependent on manufacturers relocating from urban areas for employment. This was made possible by the fact that rural labor was less organized and less expensive than urban labor. Thus, many rural communities became an attractive place for firms to relocate,

particularly those that depended on cheap labor. However, many of these same firms have found it profitable to leave rural America and relocate to overseas locations where labor is relatively plentiful and inexpensive.

Trade opportunities can contribute to the creation of jobs in rural areas of the U.S. as well. For example, increased food product exports, particularly of processed and semi-processed foods, contribute to the growth of food processing firms, many of which are located in rural regions of the U.S. that are centers of agricultural commodity production. However, these employment opportunities often are not found in the same communities that have experienced job losses due to the overseas transfer of jobs. In addition, many of the new jobs serve as a magnet for attracting in-migrants into communities, which can have both positive and negative political, economic and social impacts on local communities. Positive and negative impacts are often more acute in nonmetropolitan communities because they have smaller populations and thus the start-up or closure of a single enterprise will directly affect a larger percentage of the local population.

Estimating the number of jobs generated or lost due to changes in trading patterns is extraordinarily complicated. Economists do generate "multipliers" that can be used to estimate the number of jobs generated by an increase in exports of a particular good or commodity. However, these figures are often based on broad assumptions, and do not always capture the complexity of the economic situation facing particular firms. Often, firms are not able to achieve the efficiency levels they need to stay in business without both domestic and overseas orders. In other words, it is difficult to claim that particular jobs are attributable to domestic or overseas sales because many firms sell the same products or services to local as well as global markets.

Finally, it is important to note that job generation can result from increased *imports* of capital investments, finished goods or product parts that are used or sold in domestic markets. An interesting example of such a case is the economic growth experienced by rural regions that have become home to Japanese automobile manufacturers. Certainly, the continued viability of many rural firms, and of the socioeconomic well-being of the communities where they are located, is dependent on international trade activity, just as many communities have experienced socioeconomic decline as a result of international trade.

Trade and Environment

Research on the environmental impacts of international trade has grown significantly in the past 10 to 20 years, perhaps reflecting increased public consciousness about global, as well as national and local, environmental issues. As is the case with prices and labor, the environmental impacts of trade are difficult to identify because of the complexity of trade patterns. These include what is being produced, how it is being produced, the technologies involved, and the extent of local environmental regulations. Thus, it is impossible to make a definitive statement on whether trade is, on the whole, having more of a detrimental or beneficial impact on the environment. However, some positive impacts of trade on the environment include trade in environmentally sound production inputs and technologies, as well as the strong association that has been observed between increasing incomes and environmental quality. Some of the negative impacts that have been found are trade in dangerous chemicals, hazardous wastes and endangered species, as well as faster depletion of natural resources. Arguably, the negative environmental impacts of increased international trade are falling disproportionately on poorer countries. Just as low wage rates have compelled many firms to relocate some of their manufacturing facilities overseas, less stringent environmental regulations may compel some companies to move plants outside of the U.S. Indeed, a recent popular book written by a U.S. economist argues that the United States-based manufacturers cannot compete with Chinese counterparts due in part to lax environmental regulations, as well as lower wage costs and other factors, in China.

Conclusion

Undoubtedly, international trade is growing and is affecting rural America. Although one can find examples of year-to-year growth as well as decline, the overall trend in recent decades has been for expansion in both exports and imports around the world. This trend is being experienced in rural and urban areas throughout the world and is likely to continue.

Whether this growth will, on balance, be a positive influence on rural life will not only vary by region and community, but will depend on how local people adjust to the challenges and opportunities presented by international trade. National governments continue to be under pressure to lower trade barriers and permit a freer exchange of goods, services and capital throughout the world, just as local communities are under pressure to attract internationally competitive businesses that can promote economic growth. A difficulty that local communities face as this situation develops is that their residents tend to be inwardly focused, while firms, particularly multinational firms, have the ability to organize and act globally. It is important to remember that, despite the reporting of export and import statistics by country, virtually all international trade is managed by, takes place between, and is for the benefit of, private firms. Understanding how rural communities can respond to the changing conditions associated with an increasingly integrated global political-economy will be crucial for determining whether and how rural residents will prosper in the twenty-first century.

— *Raymond A. Jussaume, Jr.*

See also

Agricultural and Applied Economics; Manufacturing Industry; Marketing; Markets; Policy, Economic; Trade Areas; Trade, Interregional; Value-added Agriculture

References

Broadway, Michael. "Meatpacking and the Transformation of Rural Communities." *Rural Sociology* 72 (2007): 560-582.

Chanda, Nayan. *Bound Together: How Traders, Preachers, Adventurers and Warriors Shaped Globalization.* New Haven, CT: Yale University Press, 2007.

Copeland, Brian R. and M. Scott Taylor. "Trade, Growth and the Environment." *Journal of Economic Literature* 42 (2004): 7-71.

Crowe, Jessica. "Development Strategies in Rural Washington." *Rural Sociology* 71, no. 4 (2006): 573-595.

Falk, William W. and Thomas A. Lyson. *Rural Labor Markets. Research in Rural Sociology and Development.* Greenwich, CT: JAI Press, Inc, 1989.

Freudenburg, William R. "Addictive Economies: Extractive Industries and Vulnerable Localities in a Changing World Economy." *Rural Sociology* 57 (1992): 305-332.

Gaston, Noel and Daniel Trefler. "The Role of International Trade and Trade Policy in the Labor Markets of Canada and the U.S." *The World Economy* 17 (1994): 45-62.

Leach, Belinda and Anthony Winson. "Bringing 'Globalization' Down to Earth: Restructuring and Labour in Rural Communities." *Canadian Review of Sociology and Anthropology* 32 (1995): 341-364.

Mollick, André Varella, João Ricardo Faria, Pedro H. Albuquerque, and Miguel A. León-Ledesma. "Can Globalisation Stop the Decline in Commodities' Terms of Trade?" *Cambridge Journal of Economics* 19 (2008).

Navarro, Peter. *The Coming China Wars.* Upper Saddle River, NJ: Pearson Education, 2007.

Sharp, Jeff, Kerry Agnitsch, Vern Ryan and Jan Flora. "Social Infrastructure and Community Economic Development Strategies." *Journal of Rural Studies* 18 (2002): 405-417.

Stevens, Candice. "The Environmental Effects of Trade." *The World Economy* 16 (1993): 439-451.

Williamson, Thad, David Imbroscio, and Gar Alperovits. *Making a Place for Community: Local Democracy in a Global Era.* New York: Routledge. 2003.

Trade, Interregional

The exports and imports of a region. Measurement and meaning confound the use of the term interregional trade: first, the measure of gross exports, the out-shipments of goods and services to producers and consumers outside a region; second, the measure of gross imports, the in-shipments of goods and services for the use of economic units inside the region. Apropos to both measures is the concept of the region itself. In an economic sense, a region is a collection of local labor market areas or the commuting areas of central places that are the areas' trade centers. Further distinctions refer to rural versus urban and metropolitan regions.

The trading region includes the infrastructure of commerce as well as the export-producing businesses, their workers and production facilities, and a host of residential activities catering to these businesses and their workers and households. All are important participants in the initiation and support of interregional trade, the inevitable result of businesses and workers exercising their particular competitive advantage through remunerative product specialization. We therefore address the topic by defining and identifying interregional trade within and between trading regions and, finally, accounting for the variability and value of interregional trade arising from the product specialization of its export-producing businesses and industries.

Trading Regions and Local Labor Markets

A trading region is a mixture of urban and rural areas—metropolitan and nonmetropolitan—that transcends state boundaries. Each region has a center, or core area, and a periphery. Core areas of the largest metropolitan regions are also air nodes in the U.S. air transportation network of connecting cities within each region. Core areas include micropolitan areas with resident populations of 10,000 to under 50,000 and metro-politan areas with resident populations of 50,000 and above.

Rural, nonmetropolitan areas have dropped steadily in resident population to less than 17 percent of the total in 2005, including the micropolitan areas that account for slightly more than 10 percent of the total. Value added by nonmetropolitan area industry is about 10 percent also, with commodity-producing industries—farming, mining, forest products and commodity processing rather than service—accounting for the larger share of the total (Panek et al., 2007). Both interregional and intraregional trade moves the excess production of the core areas to a variety of domestic markets that arise from the production imbalances. The domestic exports are several times larger than the total foreign exports, given the product diversity of the regional economies, along with their cross-border industry clustering, that generates new markets for producer goods.

Even a region like Minneapolis-St Paul, with a majority of counties in entirely rural Labor Market Areas (LMAs), forms a highly integrated trading region with much internalization of trade between metropolitan and nonmetropolitan areas (Tolbert and Sizer, 1996). The metropolitan core area is of critical importance to the rural areas with an expanding industrial base because of its linkages to the core area producer services and transportation infrastructure. Also important are the secondary core areas—the micropolitan core areas. The commuting areas of both the primary and the secondary core areas serve as economic communities for solving area-wide problems by strengthening and extending the networks that facilitate the flows of information about technological developments, employment and entrepreneurial opportunities, and related factors affecting the competitive position of export-producing businesses.

An excess of local jobs over resident job holders identifies the central place of a labor market area (Maki and Lichty, 2000). This definition of a central place focuses on the critical resource of most regional economies, a diverse and dynamic labor market and its daily commuting area. The in-commuting of non-resident job holders overcomes the deficit in resident job holders for the central places. This accounts for the varying concentrations of economic activity, depending on type and size of the LMAs and their location relative to the metropolitan core area (Maki and Reynolds, 1994). The regional database includes a common data set of industry and commodity exports and imports, as well as in-

Table 1.
Industry location quotient ranking, Minneapolis-St. Paul-Bloomington MSA, 2002 and 2005.

		Employment		Earnings	
	2002		2005	2002	2005
Sector	(thou.)	LQ	LQ	LQ	LQ
Total (excluding proprietors)	2,014	1.05	1.04	1.06	1.06
Excess employment:					
Management of companies and enterprises	58	2.49	2.47	2.72	2.63
Finance and insurance	136	1.34	1.35	1.28	1.32
Wholesale trade	98	1.25	1.24	1.37	1.39
Arts, entertainment, and recreation	51	1.19	1.19	1.02	0.99
Information	55	1.16	1.09	0.87	0.88
Professional and technical services	149	1.11	1.09	1.04	1.02
Manufacturing	219	1.08	1.12	1.07	1.13
Educational services	44	1.08	1.09	0.78	0.83
Health care and social assistance	207	1.01	1.04	0.89	0.92
Deficit employment:					
Other services, except public administration	119	0.99	0.95	0.98	0.97
Retail trade	228	0.96	0.96	0.89	0.87
Administrative and waste services	117	0.95	0.93	0.92	0.90
Real estate and rental and leasing	68	0.93	0.94	1.01	0.99
Accommodation and food services	128	0.91	0.92	0.78	0.78
Construction	112	0.91	0.88	1.00	0.94
State government	54	0.83	0.86	0.84	0.85
Local government	140	0.80	0.79	0.79	0.77
Federal, civil	20	0.59	0.61	0.55	0.56
Military	13	0.47	0.56	0.22	0.34

*Four industry groups—forestry, fishing, related activitries; mining; utilities; transportation and warehousing—are omitted due to lack of data. Total employees for the four industries were 117,000 in 2002.
Source: Regional Economic Information System, BEA, U.S. Department of Commerce, 2007

dustry and commodity sales and industry employment and value added, for all U.S. counties.

Table 1 lists industries in the 13-county Minneapolis-St. Paul-Bloomington MSA according to their employment Location Quotient (LQ) values for 2002. Nine of the 10 industries with LQ values greater than 1.00 are services producing. Manufacturing, the only commodity-producing industry with an above-average LQ, improved its ranking in both employment and earnings as the nation's economy improved. A majority of the top-ranking services-producing industries experienced lower earnings LQ values than employment LQ values—another indicator of below average earnings per worker in the Twin Cities MSA.

The Minneapolis-St. Paul-Bloomington, or Twin Cities, MSA, along with the St. Cloud and Rochester MSAs, forms the metropolitan core of the 83-county Minneapolis-St. Paul-St. Cloud Economic Area (EA). This EA also includes the Mankato Micropolitan Statistical Area (MSA). It is the nearby export market and service area for the Twin Cities economy depicted above (Johnson and Kort, 2004). The extended domestic export market and service area is the combined Upper Midwest and Pacific Northwest Regions, once served by numerous railroads stretching from the Canadian border to the Pacific Ocean. An extensive transportation, communications and information infrastructure, coupled with an early start and an ambitious and innovative people, explains much of the Twin Cities economic success.

Much of the old Manufacturing Belt covering the Great Lakes, Mideast and New England regions experienced a sharp downturn in Gross Domestic Product from 2004 to 2005, largely the result of a declining auto manufacturing industry (BAE, 2007). Michigan, for example, faces severe problems in financing state and local governments that ultimately impact on its ability to support much needed infrastructure replacement.

Product Specialization and Localization

By definition, a positive balance of trade exists when gross commodity exports exceed gross commodity imports. Interregional trade is, thus, a measure of the competitive advantage of a region's export-producing industries. A region may experience a positive balance of trade, however, and lag in economic growth, compared to another region that is experiencing a negative balance of trade. For example, a disproportionately large share of the export earnings may leave the first region immediately without benefiting regional residents. On the other hand, a large share of the gross imports of the other region may be capital goods. These could be purchased by local private investors acquiring financial resources from outside the region. The first region, with positive exports, lacks profitable investment opportunities, while the second region at least has the expectation of profitable investment opportunities. A region consisting largely of declining rural areas typically falls into the first category of a positive trade balance. A region consisting largely of rapidly growing urbanizing areas falls into the second category. Interregional trade has various measures each with its particular meaning for the two types of trading regions.

A leading measure of gross exports is the propensity to purchase locally produced goods and services, that is, goods and services produced within the area or region of measure. A leading measure of gross imports is the propensity to import. The primary difficulty in the use of these two measures is the lack of any accurate monitoring of commodity or product flows from one area or region to another. We have only indirect measures of these two indicators of actual shipments from a variety of data sources, including the U.S. Censuses of Transportation that show the gross out-shipments and in-shipments of industries in each state. Once we have the estimates of gross out-shipments using the indirect measures, we can then estimate gross in-shipments, given the total production in the area or region.

Construction and the services-producing industry groups consistently show net in-shipments of goods and services for the industry clusters outside the core area. Construction, of course, is the most highly import-dependent industry group. However, the aggregation of many individual industries into the broader categories, like manufacturing, obscures the sharply contrasting composition of exports of the core area and its surrounding LMAs. The additional data would more clearly identify opportunities for the internalization of interarea trade within the region.

Applying the share of total employment engaged in producing the exports of each industry to the industry's total employment yields a measure of the industry's contribution to the local economic base. Using this measure, manufacturing accounts for 50 percent or more of the economic base of all but the North Central and the North West LMAs of Minnesota and North Dakota (Tolbert and Killian, 1987). Agriculture is dominant in the North West LMAs, accounting for 46 percent of the sub-region's economic base. Exports thus become the means to acquire an in-flow of dollars into the area for purchasing from its own metropolitan core area the many goods and services sought by local producers and consumers. Earnings per worker—employees and proprietors—are sharply higher in the core areas than the periphery of the metropolitan-centered labor market areas (LMAs).

Each industry produces one or more commodities. Use of commodity, rather than industry, measures of exports and imports reveals the balance of trade among individual commodity groups for each of the combined LMAs. Measures of net commodity exports, for example, would show the excess of individual commodities produced within the area over their total imports. They would show the purchases of commodity imports by individual producing and consuming sectors and the extent to which each sector contributes to any trade deficits. The proportion of net exports accounted for by each locally produced commodity is,

also, an alternative measure of an area's economic base.

As an area grows and diversifies, import replacement occurs for both intermediate inputs and final purchases. Imported finished goods and services dominate total imports in the periphery of an economic region, while imported intermediate goods and services are dominant in its core area. Again, the import dependencies of the core area contrast sharply with those of the periphery, which, of course, is a measure of the opportunities for internalizing the export trade of individual LMAs within the region.

We validate the indirect measures of gross exports and gross imports with a variety of auxiliary measures of local economic activity and structure. First, product specialization and localization measures show the relative importance of the product in the region and the nation and its geographic distribution within a region. Second, the central place and its local labor market measures link the geographic localization of production within a region or area to its industry structure. Third, regional advantage measures show the propensities to trade, both export and import, of the individual, geographically differentiated regional industries.

An additional measure of product specialization is the localization index, also referred to as a location quotient. A ratio of one for all regions would mean that the industry is ubiquitous on a regional scale of measurement, a possibility only for the frequently purchased items that lack large economies of scale in their production and distribution. An alternative form of the localization index is its absolute value. If the industry measure were employment, the absolute measure would show the excess employment for the region, that is, the employment in excess of the amount based on a localization index of one. For both measures, the most detailed industry and geographic breakdown of the regional economy yields the most accurate representation of product specialization and localization.

— *Wilbur R. Maki*

See also
Agricultural and Applied Economics; Marketing; Markets; Trade Areas; Trade, International

References
Bureau of Economic Analysis (BEA). "News Release: BEA Introduces New Measures of the Metropolitan Economy." *BEA Regional Economic Accounts*, September 26, 2007.

Johnson, Kennth P. and John R. Kort. "2004 Redefinition of the BEA Economic Areas." *Survey of Current Business,* November 2004.

Maki, Wilbur R. and P.D. Reynolds. "Stability Versus Volatility, Growth Versus Decline in Peripheral Regions: A Preliminary U.S. Application." Pp. 27-42 in *Northern Perspectives on European Integration.* Edited by Lars Lundqvist and Lars Olof Persson. Stockholm, Sweden: Nordiska Institutet for Regionalpolitisk Forskning, 1994.

Maki, Wilbur R. and Richard W. Lichty. "Exports and Economic Base." Chapter 4 in *Urban Regional Economics: Concepts, Tools, Applications.* Ames, IA: Iowa State University Press, 2000.

Panek, Sharon D., Frank T. Baumgardner, and Mathew J. McCormick. "Introducing New Measures of the Metropolitan Economy; Prototype GDP-by-Metropolitan-Area Estimates for 2001-2005." *Survey of Current Business* (November, 2007): 79-87.

Tolbert, Charles M., and M. S. Killian."Labor Market Areas for the United States." Staff Report No. AGES870721. Washington, DC: U.S. Department of Agriculture, Agriculture and Rural Economy Division, Economic Research Service, 1987.

Tolbert, Charles M. and Mary Sizer. *Labor Market Areas for the United States: A 1990 Update.* Staff Report 9614. Washington, DC: U.S. Department of Agriculture, Economic Research Service, Rural Economy Division, 1996.

Trailer Parks

Common name for a neighborhood form that emerges when trailer homes are clustered densely on a single site; often used as a derogatory term for mobile or manufactured home communities.

Trailer parks, more properly known as *mobile* or *manufactured home communities*, emerged in the rural U.S. during the last 80 years. Almost half of the nation's 8.9 million mobile homes are situated in an estimated 50,000-60,000 communities, mostly located in rural places. Mobile home parks vary in size from as many as 600 units to only a few units lining a single lane. Most typically, trailer parks have fewer than 200 units. While newer, upscale manufactured home communities resemble suburban developments, older, shabbier trailer parks persist wherever the need exists for cheap housing.

As a neighborhood, a rural trailer park differs fundamentally from other communities of place because it is the private property of a landowner who runs it as a profit-making enterprise. As private property, community governance is not democratic; those who own the land or those who manage the park for the owner make and enforce the rules by which residents must live. Other social, economic, and structural concerns specific to trailer park residence emerge that diminish the residential experience. Despite these limitations, mobile home communities or trailer parks are a popular choice among rural households of modest means because residents obtain a stand-alone house, albeit on rented land.

Whereas communities and many housing advocates typically have opposed trailer parks, recent shifts have led to a call for the preservation of parks as few other affordable housing options exist. The conversion of parks of resident-owned communities appears to hold promise to redefine the place of trailer parks in the rural landscape.

The Emergence of Trailer Parks in the Rural U.S.

Historically, trailers and trailer parks are seen as major housing innovations instrumental in meeting the chronic national demand for affordable homeownership. Trailers first appeared in the United States in the early 1920s as temporary housing for vacationing families and itinerant workers. Early "trailer courts" provided the needed places for "tin can" travelers to park their homes. Like those in the vintage film *The Long, Long Trailer,* these early trailer courts were akin to campgrounds based around a small store, restrooms, and a filling station. Since the 1930s trailer parks have carried the stigma of group housing for those down on their luck. The negative stereotypes that became associated with mobile homes and trailer parks emerged in part because the federal government used them for temporary housing: for New Deal workers involved in large construction projects; for defense plant workers during WWII; and for housing emergencies created by natural disasters (e.g., post-Katrina). After World War II, trailer parks rapidly developed near universities to house returning veterans taking advantage of their G.I. Bill educational benefits. While these early trailers and mobile communities were considered temporary, by the 1950s both had earned a "fixed" place in the rural landscape.

Today, among low and moderate income rural households in particular, mobile homes provide a significant source of housing. Between 1990 and 2000 the number of manufactured homes in non-metro places grew by 25 percent to represent one in six of all owner-

Trailer park in rural Oregon. Photograph by Katherine MacTavish.

occupied rural homes. Not all mobile homes are situated in parks. Rural areas, in particular, are characterized by individual mobile homes scattered alone or next to a "stick" house, typically owned by a relative who owns the land. Still, half of the nation's 8.9 million mobile homes are sited in an estimated 50,000-60,000 parks with over half of these located in non-metro places.

Mobile home parks in the U.S. remain more common to rural areas because either urban zoning excludes them or rural zoning is more lax. Many rural parks are starkly utilitarian in comparison to modern suburban-like manufactured home communities. Filled with older homes and few amenities, these rural trailer parks persist wherever the need exists for cheap hous-

ing; on the urban fringe, the edge of small towns, or to house migrant populations.

Types of Communities

While there is increasing variation in quality, most mobile home parks in the United States fit into one of four different types: seasonal, land-lease, rental, and resident-owned. *Seasonal communities*, most common to the Sun Belt region, are populated largely by retired people seeking warmer winter climates in states like Arizona or Florida. Residents of these communities, often termed *Snowbirds*, travel an annual north-south migration route in recreational vehicles or with vehicle-pulled trailers to rental sites in parks that may offer minimal to extravagant amenities. Some seasonal parks also house permanent residents.

In *land-lease communities*, residents own their unit, but rent the land on which their home sits from the park owner. These parks may have large lots for newer, double-wide homes or older, single wide units on smaller lots. Some cater to specialized populations as *Adult Only* or *55 and Older* parks. Others mix retired households, singles, and families with children.

In *rental parks*, the landlord owns the land as well as the homes and rents both to tenants. This type of settlement perpetuates the negative stereotypes for mobile home parks as transient places. Such communities, by virtue of social and economic realities, often house a fair share of a community's "hard living," poor, and less well-educated residents. Located on the edge of town adjacent to railroad tracks, junkyards, or industrial operations, rental parks are often the kind of shabby places negatively portrayed in the popular media.

Finally, a newer variation is a form of cooperative or subdivision community where residents own both their home and the land, or at least a share in the land on which their home sits. These *resident-owned communities* have emerged in an effort to ensure greater equity and increased stability. Resident-owned communities operate much like other owner-occupied or collectively governed neighborhoods.

Trailer parks that operate as land-lease, rental, or a combination of the two are those most common in rural places. These also remain in many ways the most troubled and troubling for small towns and residents alike. Whereas a mobile home offers rural households of modest means instant access to the American dream of owning a stand-alone home, specific social, economic, structural concerns emerge that diminish the residential experience when that home is placed in a trailer park.

Social Stigmatization and Small Town Trailer Parks

Despite their apparent consumer appeal, as a housing form trailers and trailer parks remain controversial, often marked as "bad" places filled with "bad" people. This stigmatization, together with issues much like those in low-resource urban neighborhoods—a lack of trust, a diminished sense of community, residential segregation, and a sense of transience—combine to intensify the vulnerability of rural poor families in both land-lease and rental trailer parks.

For park residents of modest means, the stigma of poverty or low earnings is often compounded by residence in a disparaged neighborhood. For families with children, social stigma based on place of residence creates specific challenges. Parents struggle to manage their identity within a small town when park residence brings with it a label as "trailer trash." Children are excluded from social and educational opportunities important to their development because of where they live. In the end, parents often question their choice of moving into a park and dream of the day they can get the kids out. Trailer parks of retired people are not stigmatized, as those that house working-poor families with children, and are more likely to have residents who perceive a sense of community.

The segregation of trailer parks to edge of town or the wrong side of the tracks further limits rural trailer park residents' access to the potential social benefits of small town life. Ghettoized within a neighborhood that densely concentrates poorer households, residents are often unwilling to forge strong ties with neighbors who they expect will soon move on. When a park is highly transient, issues of trust and the need to protect privacy limit social interactions among neighbors who are virtual strangers.

A mobile home park is by its nature a place of transience. While mobile homes are far less mobile, residents who share a cultural ideal of social mobility continue to see their mobile home as only temporary; home until they can move up to a 'stick built" house. A sense of impermanence and rootlessness can mean that park residents miss out on a strong identity to place and attachment typical to rural people that comes from generation after generation of families sharing a history and culture.

The Economics of Small Town Trailer Parks

Owning a home is in all likelihood the largest investment most Americans make. A mobile home offers rural households of modest means affordable access to the dream of owning a stand-alone home in a small town setting. Yet lending practices, investment markets, and community opposition often prevent rural mobile homeowners from realizing the full potential of their investment, particularly when that home is placed in a park on rented land.

Unlike conventional homes, most mobile homes (85 percent) are purchased with chattel loans rather than mortgages. These personal property loans, financed by sub-prime lending or finance companies, are easier for those of modest means to obtain and require no upfront costs, but they carry higher interest rates (up to 13.4 percent and higher). Because mobile homes depreciate rapidly much like a vehicle, after 20 years a family has accrued little value on its investment in a mobile home while paying more proportionately than a conventional homeowner. Further, despite federal efforts to develop equitable financing for mobile homes, lending tends to be predatory. U.S. repossessions climbed as high as 20 for every 100 sold in 2001 according to the industry, which acknowledges that loans were made to those who could not afford them.

During the 1990s especially, mobile home parks were touted as a highly profitable investment with few upkeep costs aside from driving around each month collecting rent checks. Parks once owned by local families were bought up by non-local investors or traded among Real Estate Investment Trusts (REITs) who had little stake in park upkeep or resident life. A fair share of non-local park owners is known to dramatically increase lot rents and institute extra fees for children, pets, and parking that present a significant additional draw on low-income household budgets. Because these communities are private property and few states have statutes regulating evictions, residents are subject to displacement without due process. More recently, as markets have shifted, parks have been sold to make way for more profitable types of real estate development. The prohibitive moving costs and a national shortage of trailer sites mean that residents have little choice but to relinquish their home when a park is sold.

Communities are just beginning to realize the cost of absorbing and somehow housing displaced park residents.

Local and small town governments continue to oppose trailer parks for a variety of reasons. First, the concentration of low-income households in a trailer park is considered a significant draw on local police, education, medical, and fire protection services, while in return is seen as generating insufficient property taxes. The tax issue is a complex one as mobile home parks may actually save a local government money by assuming the costs of sewage, water, trash collection, road maintenance as well as the provision of affordable housing options not otherwise available. Finally, having a park nearby is thought to lower the property values of a community's conventional housing.

Home Construction, Zoning, and Tornadoes

Health and safety issues having to do with threats from water, wind, fire, air pollution, and overcrowding re-

main significant in mobile home parks, particularly in those containing older units. HUD codes passed by the U.S. Congress in 1974 have been touted as a major step in improving the construction and safety of modern mobile homes. Design changes and significant enlargements through double and even triple-wide construction mean that today's manufactured homes bear little resemblance to earlier trailers. Residents in a rural trailer park, however, are more likely to own and occupy older, lower-end units. Many owner-occupied units in the U.S. (average constructed in 1984) are approaching or surpassing the estimated 22-year median mobile home life span.

Although owners readily express satisfaction with their mobile homes, many also report the need for significant repairs associated with leaking doors, windows, roofs, and failing particle board subflooring. A concentration of flammable materials makes the likelihood that a fire will be fatal high in a mobile home, particularly in older units termed "matchsticks" or "firetraps" among firefighters. Elevated formaldehyde levels from the pressed wood products used in mobile home construction have been linked to chronic respiratory and allergy problems, particularly in children. Doubling or even tripling up is a cost savings strategy common among poor households. Yet in older single wide units so common to rural trailer parks with half the living area of a conventional home, overcrowding (less than one room per person) can be severe. Further, zoning practices typically marginalize mobile home parks into places that due to weaker building codes and regulations create undesirable residential environments and foster class segregation. In fact, trailers parks are often zoned commercial-industrial and are not regulated as are residential areas in or near the same town. Maintaining a safe, healthy living environment in such conditions is challenging.

The notion that trailer parks or mobile home communities attract tornadoes is common but inaccurate for several reasons. The National Weather Service even makes explicit note of trailer parks as being vulnerable to overturning during strong winds, yet when trailers are secured with "tie downs" or cables anchored in concrete footing, they are less likely to sustain wind damage. Regulations requiring tie downs, however, do not exist or are not enforced in all locations. Further, tornadoes are more prone to occur in states such as Florida, the Carolinas, Oklahoma, or Missouri that are both highly rural and have a higher proportion of trailer use.

Future Prospects for Rural Trailer Parks

In recent decades two destinies appeared as prospects for rural trailer parks. When marginalized to undesirable locations, rural trailer parks evolved as ghettos for the rural poor, urban immigrants and other adults living on lower and fixed incomes. The aging nature of many rural parks as well as the transition of parks to investment properties and non-local ownership has propelled this prospect. Alternatively, parks were eliminated through land sales and redevelopment that led to closures. Older mobile home communities situated on the urban fringe are those most threatened by upscale or suburban developments. Because local governments do not consider mobile home communities the highest use for the land, these parks have few advocates, and are vulnerable to development interests that want to close them and displace the poor and working-poor residents.

Communities and affordable housing advocates are, however, beginning to look anew at mobile home parks. The costs to communities for housing displaced low-income residents when a park is closed are proving significant. Further, the lack of other suitable affordable housing options (parks currently represent the largest source of unsubsidized affordable housing in the U.S.) encourage the reexamination of mobile home parks as a viable housing solution. A movement to preserve mobile home parks is afoot. The conversion of parks to resident-owned communities led by nonprofit groups like the New Hampshire Community Loan Fund and Resident Owned Communities-USA holds promise as both a means to hang on to this housing form while eliminating some of the social, structural, and economic concerns detailed above. State legislation establishing first right of refusal, wait times, and compensation protections when parks are sold is appearing. All such efforts forge the way for a new future for rural trailer parks that might help realize the potential these neighborhoods might hold for offering rural poor and working-poor access to a home.

— *Katherine MacTavish*

See also

Homelessness; Housing

References

Hart, John, Michelle Rhodes and John Morgan. *The Unknown World of the Mobile Home*. Baltimore, MD: The John Hopkins University Press, 2002.

Hurley, Andrew. *Diners, Bowling Alleys and Trailer Parks: Chasing the American Dream in Postwar Consumer Culture*. New York: Basic Books, 2001.

MacTavish, Katherine. "The Wrong Side of the Tracks: Social Inequality and Mobile Home Park Residence." *Community Development* 38 (2007): 74-91.

MacTavish, Katherine and Sonya Salamon, S. "Mobile Home Park on the Prairie: A New Rural Community Form." *Rural Sociology* 66 (2001): 487-506.

MacTavish, Katherine and Sonya Salamon. "Pathways of Youth Development in a Rural Trailer Park." *Family Relations* 55 (2006): 163-174.

MacTavish, Katherine, Michelle Eley, and Sonya Salamon. "Housing vulnerability among rural mobile home park residents." *Georgetown Journal of Poverty Law and Policy* 13 (2006): 95-117.

Manufactured Housing Institute. Available online at: http://www.manufacturedhousing.org.

New Hampshire Community Loan Fund. Available online at: http://www.nhclf.org.

Salamon, Sonya. Mobile Home Communities. *Encyclopedia of Community: From the Village to the Virtual World*. Karen Christensen and David Levinson (Eds.) Sage 2003 (3): 925-929.

Wallis, Allan D. *Wheel Estate: The Rise and Decline of Mobile Homes*. New York: Oxford University Press, 1991.

Transportation Industry

The collection of firms that move goods from one location to another, including railroads, truck lines, airplanes, barge lines, and pipelines. A series of Congressional Acts in the late 1970s and early 1980s deregulated the transportation industry. This article discusses the events leading to transportation deregulation, the subsequent adjustments made by the transportation industry and their customers in rural areas.

Importance of the Rural Transportation Industry

Transportation is very important to the economic well-being of rural America. Rural areas generally ship a relatively limited range of goods that are dependent on the mix of available regional resources. Typical shipments from rural areas include crops, processed foods and other agricultural products, forest products, mine and quarry products, and products of light manufacturing. Modern rural communities require a full range of consumer goods and manufactured and raw materials such as fertilizers and fuels. Because of the volumes and distances involved, low-cost, reliable transportation is critical to rural communities. From the passage of the Interstate Commerce Act in 1887 until transportation deregulation in1980, rural residents depended on government, primarily the Interstate Commerce Commission, to ensure adequate and reliable transportation from the transportation industry. Recently the increased use of agricultural crops and forest products for biofuels and biofuel feedstocks have added to the transportation requirements needed to connect rural areas with local and distant markets.

The transportation industry in rural areas, as elsewhere, is comprised of different methods or modes, including rail, motor vehicles, air, water, and pipelines. Railroads were the primary method of rural transportation of both goods and people from the Civil War until the widespread adoption of automobiles when improved highways and vehicles enabled motor carriers to increase their share of intercity freight traffic. By 1980, prior to deregulation, rail's share of intercity ton-miles had declined to 37.5 percent compared to 56 percent in 1950. However, since deregulation rail's share increased and has exceeded 40 percent since 1995.

Barges on inland waterways, although not serving most rural areas directly, are very important as they are generally the low cost mode of transportation Excluding seacoasts and the Great Lakes, there are over 26,000 miles of navigable rivers and canals in the U.S. The Mississippi River and its tributaries make up about half of the navigable waterway mileage. Barges are used to move bulk commodities, such as grains and feeds, coal, fertilizer, chemicals, petroleum products and biofuels, at least part of the way to and from rural areas. The waterways are especially important to move grain and agricultural products to export ports.

In recent years, intermodal transportation, which uses two or more modes for a single shipment, increased in importance. Examples of intermodal movements include trailers on flat cars (TOFC), other containers on flatcars (COFC), or trucks. Air cargo has grown rapidly but remains a specialized market. Pipelines are very important in transporting natural gas, petroleum, and petroleum products to rural areas. The transportation industry has undergone significant changes in recent years resulting from deregulation and technological changes in transportation and the general economy and the widespread adoption of just-in-time inventory control methods.

The Regulatory Era

The Interstate Commerce Commission (ICC) played a major role for many years to ensure that rural areas received fairly priced and reliable transportation service from railroads and eventually from trucking and busing firms. The ICC was established by the Interstate Commerce Act of 1887 in response to pressures from rural shippers and communities. When the Interstate Commerce Act was passed, railroads were the dominant and often the only means of passenger or freight transportation throughout much of America. Congress desired to protect the public from monopoly abuses and discriminatory practices used by the railroads at the time.

The Interstate Commerce Act made explicit legal principles already embedded in common law. It required that rates be reasonable and just, prohibited discrimination against shippers and undue preferences among regional areas, and charging more for a short haul than a longer haul. The ICC established numerous precedents as it was the first independent federal regulatory agency established to enforce the law on a continuing basis. It had to develop the procedures for economic regulation almost on a trial and error basis. The ICC eventually was given regulatory power over rail mergers and the control of entry and exit of both routes and service into and within the industry.

Concurrent with the development and evolution of the ICC, the motor vehicle industry was developing. Roads and highways were built to accommodate this new and highly flexible mode. By the 1930s, the monopolistic power and financial health of the railroads had been severely eroded by competition from trucks and passenger vehicles. Partly to protect the railroads from motor competition, Congress passed the Motor Carrier Act of 1935 that gave the ICC broad powers over interstate shipments and rates by the motor carriers. Similarly, with the Civil Aeronautic Act of 1938, Congress created the Civil Aeronautics Authority (CAA) that had powers similar to the ICC to make rates and control entry and exit of routes in the airline industry. The CAA eventually became the Civil Aeronautics Board (CAB) and then part of the Federal Aviation Administration in 1967.

Increased regulation was unable to ensure both reliable, low-cost transportation service and financial health for all modes of rural transportation. Competition from trucking and barges reduced or eliminated railroad profits. Trucking firms were able to selectively capture the rail traffic with profitable rates, whereas barges successfully competed for low-valued commodities on the basis of cost.

The interstate highway project and other federal expenditures on highways encouraged trucking expansion and the use of automobiles for passenger traffic.

The federal government paid the capital costs to develop the modern inland waterway system by the Army Corps of Engineers (COE) during the 1930s. The federal government continued to finance waterway improvements and operations and maintenance expenses. It even subsidized barge operations to encourage the barge industry's development in the 1940s and 1950s.

Problems of Regulation

Regulation prevented or discouraged the railroads from competing effectively, especially in rural areas. Other factors, including high labor costs, restrictive work rules, and questionable management choices, also contributed to the railroads' financial problems. Consequently, by the 1960s large portions of the railroad industry, and especially those serving rural areas, faced serious problems. Although competition from the other modes eroded markets, made much trackage obsolete and many services unprofitable, the ICC limited route and trackage abandonment. The railroads were allowed to stop their unprofitable intercity passenger services in 1970 when Congress established Amtrak. However, the railroad problems continued, resulting in the bankruptcies of many lines serving rural areas, and unprecedented numbers of applications to abandon trackage and service were made to the ICC. The miles of railroad track decreased to 179,000 miles in 1980, down from 206,000 miles in 1970 and 218,000 miles in 1960. Rail mileage had peaked at 254,000 in 1916. By 2005 there were just over 140,000 miles of track. Most of the abandonments were of low volume branch lines serving rural areas.

Congress attempted to assist the railroad industry in 1973 by passing the 3R Act (Regional Rail Reorganization Act) to reorganize the bankrupt railroads, but this was insufficient. In 1976, the 4R Act (Railroad Revitalization and Regulatory Reform Act) made fundamental changes in railroad regulations. However, the changes actually implemented by the ICC did not adequately free the railroads, improve their financial condition, or allow much improvement in service. Consequently in 1980, Congress deregulated the railroads with the Staggers Act of 1980.

Effects of the Staggers Act of 1980

These actions (Staggers Act of 1980, 3R Act, and 4R Act) along with ICC rulings during the 1970s, changed railroads from being one of the most regulated American industries to a market-oriented system. The Staggers Act (1) relaxed controls over rates, (2) allowed railroads to contract for specific services to individual firms and to enter into long-term contracts, and (3) made mergers between railroads and the abandonment of unprofitable branch lines easier. Railroads were not completely deregulated immediately as the ICC retained the ability to regulate maximum rates and other oversight powers. By the early 1990s, however, more than three-fourths of rail traffic was not subject to rate regulation either because rates were below threshold levels or because the ICC had exempted the traffic entirely. Exempted classes important to rural areas included boxcars, piggyback and container traffic, perishable agricultural products, lumber, wood, and transportation equipment. A major change from the long-standing principle of public and nondiscriminatory rate tariffs was the ability of the railroads to enter into confidential binding contracts for both rates and services. These contracts had to be filed with the ICC but were not made public. Many grain companies and other rural shippers took advantage of contracts to obtain improved or guaranteed services.

Railroad freight rates declined at an average rate of 1.5 percent annually between 1980 and 1994. However, there were significant differences in rate changes across commodities with many rates increasing after deregulation because of the greater market power of the railroads. However, by 1988, deregulation resulted in lower rates for most commodities, suggesting that increases in productivity and competition generally overcame the initial increases due to railroad market power. However, since the mid 1990s many railroads have had recurring capacity problems as the excess capacity of the pre-regulation era was scraped or utilized to meet the increased demand.

Major benefits to rural areas from rail deregulation included not only rate reduction, but also service improvements and increased reliability. Although railroad abandonments were of major concern to rural communities and shippers prior to, and immediately after, deregulation, most observers felt that rationalization of branch line track and service generally improved most rural rail service. The railroads abandoned thousands of miles of track, but the number of smaller railroads increased from 212 in 1980 to about 545 in 2002. Short lines now operate 46,000 miles of track or about one third of all track miles. Seventy two of the short line rail roads are "shipper owned." Many of these regional or short-line railroads that serve rural areas have done well financially because of regulatory reforms. Labor can be paid at local and not national wage levels, and work rules are relaxed so employees can do multiple tasks. This resulted in both reduced rail rates and the number of railroad employees. In addition, the regional and short line railroads are more responsive to local service needs that the urban-based nationally oriented railroads tended to ignore.

The rail crisis of the 1970s resulted in a growing realization of the failure of economic regulation in the face of changing technologies in a competitive economy. Consequently, several other deregulation bills for other transportation modes were passed prior to and after the Staggers Act. These included the Air Cargo Deregulation Act of 1977, the Airline Deregulation Act of 1978, the Motor Carrier Act of 1980, and the Bus Regulatory Reform Act of 1982. Although all of these had some impact on rural transportation industries, the most significant was the Motor Carrier Act of 1980.

Effects of the Motor Carrier Act of 1980

Trucking rates, service, and regulation had not received much attention in rural areas during the 1970s for two reasons. First, unlike rail, the availability of trucking service was not declining and trucks were frequently competing for rail's declining traffic base. The interstate highway system allowed trucks to lower costs and improve their reliability. Second, grain and unprocessed agricultural commodities truckers were exempt from ICC regulation. Back hauls to rural areas in exempt trucks were also exempt in many instances.

The Motor Carrier Act of 1980 (MCA) followed substantial liberalization of trucking regulation by the ICC in the late 1970s. These included reducing entry barriers, loosening restrictions on contract carriers, and allowing unregulated agricultural carriers to carry regulated commodities on back hauls. The MCA went further and allowed applicants to enter the industry when the service was found to meet a useful public purpose, reversing the previous burden of proof from the entrant to the existing carriers. The MCA permitted common carriers to raise and lower rates 10 percent annually without regulatory interference and the ICC was granted the discretion to permit even greater price freedom in the future. Antitrust immunity for voting on rates was reduced and eventually eliminated.

A major concern prior to motor truck deregulation in the U.S. was the possible loss of service to small communities. However, early studies showed little change in quality and availability of service and small benefits in lower rates. Eventually the results of trucking deregulation were substantial and far-reaching. Many new carriers entered the industry; the number of

trucking firms increased nationally from 16,000 in the mid-1970s to over 49,000 in 1992 and 117,000 in 2006. Many of these new carriers were formed to provide services to small- and medium-sized communities and markets. Previously, major firms ignored small-volume rural markets but always maintained that they were being adequately served. These established carriers protested against new applicants at ICC hearings and typically won, maintaining their status as a monopoly carrier. Many of the recent entrants are freight forwarders, brokers, or other third parties who expanded services to rural communities and provided innovative services such as small package pickup, package express, or air cargo.

Studies identified substantial cost reductions due to trucking deregulation through lower labor costs, route rationalization, and better equipment utilization. For example, Winston, et al. (1990) found lower operating costs for private trucking nation-wide generated $3 billion annually in benefits to shippers and $4 billion in rate reductions by commercial carriers. In addition, shippers received benefits in the form of more responsive and dependable service as a result of the new market discipline imposed by competition. These allowed shippers and customers to develop just-in-time inventory management by transporting smaller shipments more frequently, substantially reducing inventories and inventory carrying costs. This is especially important to shippers and firms in rural areas who would never have received the improved service under the old regulatory regime.

The Barge (Inland Waterway) Industry

The barge industry that operates on the inland waterway system is very important to rural America. Approximately 60 percent of U.S. grain and oilseed exports are shipped from Mississippi River terminals after traveling 700 to 1,200 miles by barge from the U.S. agricultural heartland. Since these distances are generally greater than those from international competitors' grain-producing areas to their ports, low-cost water transportation has been a major factor to maintain exports of U.S. agricultural products and bulk commodities. Waterway transportation is also important in moving bulk commodities like fertilizer, ores, and petroleum products from coastal areas to rural areas served by river terminals.

Unlike the other modes of transportation in the U.S., barges were not subject to extensive economic regulation. The Transportation Act of 1940 placed inland waterway barge transportation under the regulatory authority of the ICC but kept private carriage, most bulk carriage, and liquid cargo exempt from regulation. Consequently, shipments of bulk commodities such as grain, coal, chemicals, and petroleum products were all generally exempt from rate regulation, and although barges were technically deregulated in 1980, there were few direct impacts. The industry, however, was immediately impacted by competition from the deregulated railroads.

In spite of its low cost and energy efficiency, in recent years barge transportation in the U.S. has the disadvantage of being under continual attack by environmentalists, resulting in increased industry costs but limited environmental improvement. Fuel-user charges for commercial barges were instituted in 1980 as part of a compromise of the barge industry, shippers, and the U.S. Army Corps of Engineers (COE) with the railroads and environmentalists in order to remove a major bottleneck between the Upper Mississippi and Illinois Rivers and the Lower Mississippi. The commercial navigation fuel-user charge gradually increased to 20¢ per gallon in 1995 and reduced the cost advantage of water transportation over rail. Other compromises between the barge industry, the COE, and environmentalists on topics such as channel maintenance and dredging added to the industry's operating costs and underlying cost structure. The inland waterway's share of ton-miles has been declining in recent years.

Summary

The transportation services available to rural America have been expanded and improved in recent years. Deregulation of the transportation industries generally has been considered a success. In 1995 Congress passed the Interstate Commerce Commission Termination Act. Most of the ICC functions pertaining to rural transportation were assumed by the new Surface Transportation Board (STB) in the Department of Transportation. Rural areas ship a variety of goods and receive a full range of consumer goods and raw materials. Because of the volumes and distances required, a healthy transportation industry, providing low-cost and reliable transportation on a well-maintained infrastructure, is a necessity for rural America.

— *Jerry E. Fruin*

See also

Grain Elevators; History, Agricultural; History, Rural; Infrastructure; Public Services; River Engineering; Trade, Interregional; Trade, International

References

Glaskowsky, Nicholas A., Jr. *Effects of Deregulation on Motor Carriers*, 2nd edition. Westport, CT: Eno Foundation for Transportation, 1990.

Coyle, John J., Edward J. Bardi, and Robert A. Novack. *Transportation*, 6th edition. South-Western College Pub, 2005.

Locklin, D. Philip. *Economics of Transportation*, 7th edition. Homewood, IL: Richard D. Irvin, Inc., 1972.

Short Line and Regional Railroad Facts and Figures, American Short Line and Regional Railroad Association, 2007.

Smith, Frank A. "Historical Compendium 1939-1985." *Transportation in America: A Statistical Analysis of Transportation in the United States.* Westport, CT: Eno Foundation, 1989.

Teske, Paul, Samuel Best, and Michael Mintrom. *Deregulating Freight Transportation: Delivering the Goods.* Washington, DC: AEI Press, 1995.

Wilson, Rosalyn A. *Transportation in America: Statistical Analysis of Transportation in the United States,* 20th edition. Lansdowne, VA: Eno Foundation, 2006.

Trees

Joyce Kilmer in his poem "Trees" has captured the subject well through the eyes of a child and the sense of wonder.

"I think that I shall never see a poem as lovely as a tree;
A tree whose hungry mouth is prest against the earth's sweet flowing breast;
A tree that looks at God all day, and lifts her leafy arms to pray;
A tree that may in Summer wear a nest of robins in her hair;
Upon whose bosom snow has lain—Who intimately lives with rain.
Poems are made by fools like me, but only God can make a tree."

This poem in its simplicity presents an almost perfect description of a tree. Trees are among the largest members of the plant kingdom and are perennial, or grow and live and produce seed over many years of life. Trees are referred to as woody plants, as opposed to herbaceous plants, and occur in many orders and families of plants. The Plant Kingdom for trees is divided into two divisions, Coniferophyta and Anthrophyta. The Coniferophyta is also called Conifers or Gymnosperms, which means seeds borne naked in cones. The conifers include the families of Pinaceae (pines, spruce, firs, etc.), Taxaceae (yew, etc.) and Cypressaceae (junipers, arborvitaes, cypress, etc.). Most of these trees are considered evergreen trees because they retain their needles for several years. There are several genera of conifers that are deciduous such as larch and ginkgo trees. Deciduous trees are trees that drop their leaves in fall, are dormant over the winter and re-leaf in spring. The Anthrophyta is also called Flowering plants and Angiosperms, which means the seeds are enclosed in fruit (ovary). Most Angiosperms are deciduous trees with a few species that are considered evergreen such as some of the magnolia species. Angiosperms are further divided down into dicotyledons and monocotyledons. Dicotyledon plants or dicots germinate from a seed with two seed leaves at first, and another characteristic is that stem growth starts inside and continues outward. A few trees are moncotyledons or moncots like palm trees that germinate with one seed leaf and the stem cells grow inward.

Trees have a variety of growth forms, types of buds, leaves, flowers, seeds and other characteristics influenced by genetics and the environment. An example is the bur oak (*Quercus macrocarpa*), which produces two main types of leaves on each tree. One leaf form is called the fiddle-head leaf form and the other is more typical irregular lobes along the full length of the leaf. An oak having both leaves is the difference between bur oak and its cousin white oak, having only the leaves with irregular lobes. Environmental differences can be observed in the size of the acorns of bur oak. Acorns of bur oak grown in Missouri vary from 1.5 to two inches in diameter, whereas in Minnesota and the Dakotas acorns are only three-quarters to one inch in diameter.

Tree Structure

The understanding of the structure and how a tree functions has in the past been partial myth and, through recent research into these myths, has uncovered facts on how trees grow. The unseen root system is the most important role in keeping the tree alive and healthy. The roots have three main functions: 1) absorption of water and minerals; 2) anchorage of the trunk and branches, and 3) storage of carbohydrates or tree food. Try to visualize the size of an average tree's root system; the total amount of tissue above ground in its trunk, branches, twigs and leaves is equal to the amount in its roots. However in the past this illustration produced a myth that a tree's root system was a

Figure 1. *Bur Oak's fiddle-head leaf and acorn. U.S. Department of Agriculture Yearbook, 1949.*

Figure 2. *White oak's regularly lobed leaf and acorn. U.S. Department of Agriculture Yearbook, 1949.*

mirror image of its trunk and branch system. There was a deep tap root and root branches that extended downward along this tap root. Research has found that not all tree species have a tap root and that 90 percent of all important roots grow in the top two to three feet of the soil. Generally, most of the feeder roots in all soils will be in the top one to three feet of soil where oxygen levels are higher and most grow upward. In compacted soils, pore spaces are compressed, reducing porosity, which limits available oxygen and subsequently limits root growth. Under these conditions roots will be shallow where oxygen is more available. Research completed during the Depression years in North Dakota used relief workers to uncover tree roots and revealed that root growth varied by the species of tree and by soil type. Bur oak would set a tap root soon after germination, but most roots were in the top layers of the soil. American elm, typically a fibrous rooted species, was found to set a tap root in drier soils of the prairies. The study also found in deciduous trees, root spread was longer than one to two times the height of the tree from the trunk. Conifers generally were closer to one time the height of the tree from the trunk. More recent studies in urban areas confirm these results and show the importance of reducing compaction of soils in urban planting sites. An accurate picture of a tree would be that of a wine glass with a flat, wide, spreading base or root system and an upward branch system.

Another myth that is commonly said of tree roots is that they seek out water and minerals and grow out to where these are in great supply. Tree roots do not have noses that sniff out water, but rather grow out horizontally in all directions and continue until conditions are not favorable and then die back. When roots grow into soils with plenty of water, minerals and oxygen, they thrive until these conditions change. Large transfer roots that extend out from the trunk and from these roots, smaller branches root horizontally and upwards where oxygen and water are more available. Several smaller roots will grow downwards and in some species a tap root is developed under the trunk of the tree for anchoring the tree in the ground. Feeder roots that grow out produce tiny hair-like roots (called root hairs) extend out and absorb water and minerals into the cells of the root. The root hairs are ephemeral or short-lived roots, living and dying sometimes on a daily basis. Yet the root hairs will survive or re-grow as long as there are water and minerals available.

Research has also found that micro-organisms, primarily fungi, are beneficially associated with tree roots in the absorption of water and minerals. There are primarily two types of soil fungi that work in a symbiotic relationship. The ectomycorrhizal type of fungi grows on the outside of the root as an extended root system in a mass and thus increases the absorption area for water and minerals. The fungi release chemicals into the soil that dissolve minerals not normally available to tree roots. The second type is the endomycorrhizal type of fungi that grow into the root cells, form branched filaments and act as a bridge for water and minerals to flow within the root. Mycorrhizal fungi help reduce plant stress and disease by the formation and release of antibiotics. When a tree is of mature age, it may have as many as seven to eight different fungi associated with its root system.

The trunk and branches of the tree are made up mainly of two tissues xylem and phloem. The xylem or wood are cells that conduct water upward from the roots to the leaves. The phloem is located on the inner side of the bark and conducts the food manufactured in the leaves downward to the various parts of the tree and storage in the roots. The tree puts on growth annually and grows around each previous year's xylem or

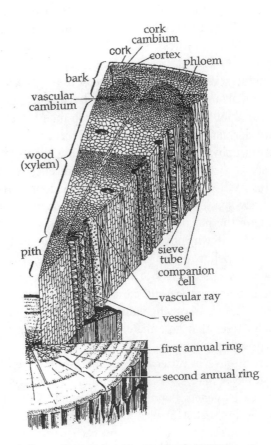

Figure 3. *Source: North Dakota Tree Handbook, NDSU Extension Service*

wood growth, which makes trees some of the largest creatures on Earth today. Growth in dicot trees can be explained as one tree that initiates cell growth over the previous growth and each year's growth is one more tree around the previous tree. If we cut a tree in half vertically, up and down, we can identify each tree within the larger tree; one can go back to the point where branches died and were covered over with each successive annual growth until they were absorbed into the trunk. Looking further, one can see and count the years when the branch was first initiated. If the tree is cut horizontally, across the trunk, one will see a bull's eye or a series of concentric circles at various widths around the center. Parts of the young branches and branch wounds can be identified and the buildup of callus rolls that eventually grew over the cut surface can be seen. Other occurrences seen can be injuries from forest fires or the movement of fungi growth and barriers the tree set up to protect itself. Years of drought and years of plenty can be discerned by narrower and wider annual rings. It is like turning back the page of history when looking at the cross-section of a tree.

Alex Shigo, a scientist with the U.S. Forest Service, uncovered more knowledge in recent years on how trees grow and how they defend themselves from attack from insect and disease pests. It is said that he dissected over 15,000 trees with a chainsaw and found the key to the strength of the tree in holding up its branches. He analyzed trees of many species and found a lamination process of the annual growth of the branches and the tree's trunk. As mentioned earlier, each year a new ring of wood is laid down around the trunk of the tree. There is a similar process in its branches and an overlapped area at the branch collar. So each year this lamination of trunk wood growing over the branch wood creates a stronger branch union.

After 40 years, a branch that has been on the tree for 20 years has a greater bond to the trunk than a two- to three-year-old branch has to the trunk. The practice of topping a tree is a shortcut method of so-called pruning done by less-than-competent people in control of chainsaws. Branches are pruned back to main branches many times larger than four to six inches in diameter. The goal is to create a denser ball-type canopy growth, similar to that gained by pinching back an herbaceous house plant. The problem is that a tree is not an herbaceous annual plant and its height requires a stronger branch and trunk union. If the tree does not die shortly afterward, it grows on to become a major safety hazard. Five to six years after, a topped tree will have tremendous branch growth almost equal to the original branch system but have fewer years of branch-to-trunk lamination and bond. This problem results in a high probability of weak branches falling in high winds.

Shigo (1995) and others also found that branches should be cut off at the branch collar, rather than flush next to the trunk. The branch collar is a natural zone of regrowth that produces a callus or cells that grow more quickly over the cut wound. The wound is also small and closes more quickly than a flush cut. It was also found that flush cuts next to the trunk cut back too far into the wound and destroyed natural barriers to invading fungi. This could create significant center heart rot in the trunk and cause the tree an early death and to become a safety hazard in high winds. Shigo also uncovered a unique set of barriers that the tree sets up when infected by a disease. These barriers are set up vertically by the annual ring growth that prevents movement horizontally, and tyloses are cells created to plug or seal off the pathogen from vertical movement in the xylem and ray tubes by forming a horizontal bar-

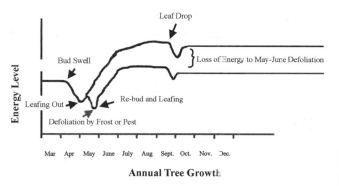

Table 1.
Energy Reserves and Annual Tree Growth

Source: Vernon Quam.

rier. This process is termed as CODIT or Compartmentalization of Decay in Trees.

The buds and leaves of a tree have just as important a function in the life of a tree as do the roots and trunk. It is in the buds that new stems and leaves or flowers and seed are formed. In some species these are developed in the growing season prior to their opening. The bud scale is a sheath that protects the bud physically, and some buds are protected by a dormancy that requires a period of cold temperature before the buds are allowed to open. This is a physiological protection that prevents buds from expanding and become subject to freezing injury in the middle of winter. As temperatures warm up in spring, flower buds can be injured by sudden periods of overnight frosts. Borderline hardy species meet their cold dormancy requirements earlier than native species of trees. Sometimes in a localized early spring heat wave, buds expand and start to grow. When the normal, cooler temperatures return, the new buds are damaged or killed. Many species of trees have subtending buds that are produced in case the initial buds are damaged. Subtending buds start growing to replace the first set of buds.

Early season damage to the buds or tender new growth means damage to the spring flowering and fruiting, and more so damage to the leaves and a delay in the tree's food production period. Table 1 shows tree growth and energy reserves within the tree during the growing season. Energy reserves would hold steady during the winter months when the tree is dormant. Then in spring when the buds start growing, there is a drop in energy reserves as energy is required to produce the stem and leaves and flower. This happens in April-May. As the tree leaves out, photosynthesis occurs, energy is produced in the leaves, and plant food is produced. Energy is used but much is stored and so the energy reserves increase. The goal of any tree is to build a profit of energy reserves to keep the tree in good health, build up defenses, and provide enough for next spring's startup. An early problem can be a major problem. A killing frost in May as the young leaves have just emerged and growing causes several problems. First, energy must be expended by the formation and growth of the damaged leaves. Second, additional energy must be used to push forth the subtended buds to take over. Third, the expense is the lost time of energy production and storage. And fourth, energy reserves are used to maintain other processes within the tree until new reserves are produced. If a tree experiences spring defoliation for several years in a row, it may end up with fewer energy reserves than it had in the spring. If the tree steadily loses energy reserves, it eventually becomes weakened and subject to more pest problems that will kill the tree.

The production of flowers is not only important aesthetically but important for fruit, nut and seed production. Fruit is usually accessory to the seed or pit of the tree or shrub. An example is the apple flesh surrounding the seed in the core or calyx of the total fruit. Plum flesh surrounds the pit or seed of the plum. The primary purpose of fruit is to attract wildlife and human feeding and dispersal of the seed away from the mother tree. Other protective covers of seeds include pods on honey locust, catalpa, etc.; inedible fleshy pulp like black walnut, hackberry, etc.; and wing attachments to be carried by winds like elm, ash, maple, etc. After finding a home, some seeds will germinate immediately, while others have dormancies built in to prevent the seed from germinating in hostile environments. Seed dormancies may require stratification periods of cold and/or warm treatments for as little as 30 days or over 120 days before germination can be attained. The seed coat surrounds the embryo and cotyledons of the seed and allows moisture, sunlight and oxygen into the seed to allow germination. A hard seed coat may require scarification or breaking the seed coat just enough to allow water, sunlight and oxygen into the inner seed. Scarification may require physically taking a file to each seed or soaking in warm water or sulfuric acid for a specific time. After dormancies are over, some seeds are placed in a light porous medium, not too wet and not dry, and with plenty of sunlight.

The transfer of water from the soil into the tree's roots is the process of water moving from a cell with high water pressure into a nearby cell with lower water pressure. This process is called osmosis and occurs from one root cell to the next. When water reaches the crown of the root system and collar of the trunk (approximately ground level), the cells start to specialize into xylem and phloem. The xylem cells carry the water up the tree to the leaves. The tensile strength of the water molecule is used to pull water upward like a magnet. The water molecule is referred to as a polar molecule in the electrical sense, having a positive side and a negative side. This can be readily seen by placing a drop of water on a table surface; the water will bead up. Water placed as a drop on a table can be stretched by touching it with a finger and moving it across the surface. It is like taking thousands of micro magnets and pulling them while they all hang on to each other. The water is then pulled up xylem cells molecule by molecule, but there still needs to be a pump to draw these water molecules. The third factor in water movement in the tree is transpiration. There are openings in the leaves that control the exchange of chemicals in and out of the leaf. When the sun is shining, water is given off by the leaves. The leaf becomes a suction pump that draws the water upward for use in chemical processes such as photosynthesis, a cooling agent, and a conveyer of carbohydrates after photosynthesis to other parts of the tree through the phloem cells downward.

During these same warm sunny days, the process of photosynthesis is in high gear. Water and minerals are added to a mixture of carbon dioxide drawn into the leaf through the stomata from the air. In the presence of chlorophyll, sunshine triggers a chemical reaction like a catalyst, carbohydrates (food) are produced, and oxygen is given off and released out of the stomata. During the evening hours the process of respiration is triggered. Respiration is a chemical process of fixing the carbohydrates for storage, and through this process oxygen is sucked from the air into the leaves.

Forests: A Community of Trees

Trees in nature are commonly found in association with other tree species, shrubs and vegetation as a dense stand of growth known as a forest. Trees are among the largest living plants on Earth and so a forest can be compared to a building or enlarged house. The vertical tree trunks form the walls or partitions, and the canopy forms the ceiling, with irregularly shaped skylights between the tree canopies. The forest floor is made of various types of shrubs and herbaceous plants (grasses, broadleaf plants, etc.). Mosses, growing on fallen tree trunks and branches, and herbaceous plants grow dependent on the patches of sunlight moving along the floor. Some plants prefer the shade and cool, moist conditions. In the fall, leaves drop to the floor, decay and form organic matter. Seeds are produced in the canopies and fall to the moist organic floor, germinate, and perpetuate the next forest. To complete this house, wildlife, animals and birds move in and out by streams, or fly among the tree branches. The associated plant and animal life will vary depending upon whether the forest is located along a river or on the slopes of a mountain. They will also differ by altitude and by latitude.

A forest can be thousands of acres in size or fewer than 100 acres along a river in a square mile area. A smaller forest of a few acres is called a grove of trees or a gallery forest spread out in a linear form along a river or windbreak planting on the prairie. The forests of North America can be divided into four general vegetation/forest regions. The Eastern forest covers the area from the East Coast of Canada and the United States west to the Mississippi River. The Northern boreal forest covers a large area from near the East Coast of the Northeastern United States and Canada to the Great Plains and up into northwestern Canada and Alaska. These forests are the northernmost in North America and meet the Arctic tundra. The prairie forest of the Great Plains in the United States and Canada is often glossed over because of the insignificance of its woodland acres relative to its predominant grassland vegetation. These native forests, although small in area, are important in their location along streams and rivers and in highly erodible sandy soils. Trees grow and survive best on the semi-humid plains, where there is moisture near rivers and in soils with a high or perched water table. Tree stands generally did not move out from these moist areas because prairie fires encouraged grassland development. The Western forest extends from the eastern edge of the Rocky Mountains to the West Coast. The native ranges of tree species in the West resemble spots or pockets of forest; they are divided physically by mountain ranges and climatically by cold temperatures in the upper altitudes.

To Great Lengths

Unlike humans and animals that shed their cells on a regular basis, trees continue to grow in height and width. Trees grow tall and wide and some species become the largest living creatures on Earth. There is a degree of appreciation when walking among trees that are 80-100 feet tall, but awesome describes a walk among the Coastal Redwoods along the Avenue of the Giants. Coastal Redwoods are the tallest trees in the world and are located in northern California along the Pacific Coast. The top four tallest trees in the U.S. are: first, Coastal Redwood (*Sequoia sempervirens*), 379.1 feet; second, Coastal Douglas-fir (*Pseudotsuga menziesii*), 326.1 feet; third, Sitka Spruce (*Picea sitchensis*), 317.3 feet; and fourth, Giant Sequoia (*Sequoiadendron giganteum*), 311.4 feet.

Trees also grow in girth or trunk width. Two types of measurements can be used to measure diameter or circumference of the trunk. The Giant Sequoias are more drought tolerant than the Coastal Redwoods and grow in the Sierra Nevada Mountains in northern California along the Nevada border. The Coastal Redwoods may be taller, but the Giant Sequoias are wider: Giant Sequoia (*Sequoiadendron giganteum*) General Grant Tree, 29 feet in diameter and Coastal Redwood (*Sequoia sempervirens*), 24.4 feet in diameter.

A few of the largest trees are measured by volume using both height and girth measurements. These measurements are a little more critical by taking the trunk and branch volume as well as consideration of the change in the trunk diameter as height increases: Giant Sequoia (*Sequoiadendron giganteum*) General Sherman Tree, 55,040 cubic feet; Coastal Redwood (*Sequoia sempervirens*), 35,890 cubic feet; and Western Redcedar (*Thuja plicata*), 17,650 cubic feet.

The oldest trees are usually measured by counting the annual rings when cut down or by taking a bore sample from the trunk and counting the rings. When looking at annual rings, one is looking at history. The General Sherman sequoia has been estimated between 2,500 and 3,000 years old, which means it was a seedling during King Solomon's reign. The Great Basin Bristlecone Pine can also be found in California's White Mountains and are over 4,000 years old—seedlings in the days of Abraham: Great Basin Bristlecone Pine (*Pinus longaevau*), 4,844 years; Giant Sequoia (*Sequoiadendron giganteum*), 3,266 years; and Rocky Mountain Bristlecone Pine (*Pinus aristata*), 2,435 years.

Many states have a Champion Trees program where the public is invited to nominate large specimens of various species. These nominations may be based on size or their association with historical events.

Trees and American History

Native Americans lived in harmony with forests. They cleared openings in the forests to provide enough sunshine to raise vegetable and fruit crops in the moist forest floor. The trees protected the crops from drying winds. Garden culture produced high-yielding crops such as corn, squash, tomatoes, peppers, potatoes, fruiting vines, and shrubs on small patches of ground. Trees were tapped for maple syrup, food and medicinal saps. Tree bark, leaves and fruit, along with native herbs, were harvested for medicine. The wildlife that used the forest for cover, shelter and food provided meat for the Native Americans. The skills used to harvest these resources were taught to early European colonists as basic survival skills.

The forest was a storehouse of natural resources for early colonists—lumber, tars, maple syrup, fruit, wild game and fresh water fish. Pitch pine was used as charcoal for smelting; tar and pitch as a wood preservatives for boats, ships and wharf piles; turpentine as a disinfectant; lumber for barn floors, bridges and mill water wheels; pitch for torches and axle grease for carts and wagons.

Trees and their byproducts played an important role in the lives of explorers and trappers. Canoes were made from hollowed logs or birch or larch bark. Frames of snow shoes were made from birch. Wagons and carts were built for the move West across wooden bridges, roadways and barges. Steam engines ran on wooden white pine rails. The clipper ships that sailed goods and passengers around South America to California were built with several species of pine.

The cider presses of the seventeenth and eighteenth centuries were used to extract juice from apples. Apple seeds were not damaged by this process, and it was from the debris of cider mills that John Chapman collected his seeds. Chapman was born in a log cabin in Leominster, Massachusetts, in 1774. At the age of 18 years, Johnny moved west to Pennsylvania and Ohio, planting apple seeds wherever he traveled. The seeds were planted in small nurseries scattered across Ohio, Indiana and Illinois. Chapman tended the nurseries and distributed apple seedlings to settlers moving west. Johnny Appleseed, as settlers called him, died in Indiana in 1845 of pneumonia he caught while traveling to one of his nurseries to fix a broken fence. His final will started "I, John Chapman by occupation a gatherer and planter of apple seeds…."

Forests became a hindrance to settlers as they traveled west to build settlements and clear for agricultural activities. The forest soils were shallow and not highly productive for long-term grain, cotton and tobacco farming. Settlers continued to move west until they reached the Great Plains. In his book, *The Great Plains*, historian Walter Prescott Webb wrote that there were three distinct characteristics of the region: an expansive, comparatively level surface; insufficient rainfall for intensive agriculture common to lands in humid climates; and a treeless, unforested area. Ironically, it was in the Great Plains that a new attitude toward trees began. The impression of the settler on this open sea of grass was almost agoraphobic. Trees were a rare occurrence, a landmark, and a place to hang on to in the wide open spaces. This was a quite different land from the forested East.

J. Sterling Morton, a Nebraska newspaper editor, disagreed with the idea that the Great Plains should be perceived as the Great American Desert. He believed in the productivity of the land and its people, and that tree planting was the key to survival against harsh environmental conditions. Morton, along with his newspaper colleagues, promoted the first Arbor Day observance on April 10, 1872, and is credited as the founder of Arbor Day. An estimated one million trees were planted in Nebraska on that first Arbor Day. One man alone planted 10,000 cottonwood, silver maple, Lombardy poplar, boxelder and yellow willow near Lincoln, Nebraska, that day. Nebraska Governor Furnas officially recognized Arbor Day as a holiday on April 8, 1874. All 50 states in the U.S., its possessions, and many other countries now recognize a day for planting trees.

The Timber Culture Act of 1873, sponsored by Nebraska Senator Phineas W. Hitchcock, encouraged tree planting to grow more timber, benefit the soil, and influence the climate. The Act included provisions to award 160 acres of land to settlers if they planted 40 acres of trees and cared for them for 10 years. The tree acreage later was reduced to 10 acres, and repealed in 1891.

The Clarke McNary Law in 1924 provided programs for fire protection of forests, distribution of tree seedlings, and planning assistance to landowner cooperators on new tree plantings, woodlots and shelterbelts. Many states had tree bounty programs that paid landowners to plant and care for trees on their land. Some states' laws reduced landowners' taxes instead of paying a set bounty per tree. New cities recognized the importance of trees. Hope, North Dakota, still has an ordinance requiring that all grazing animals be fenced to prevent feeding on young shade and boulevard trees.

Shelterbelt and Windbreaks

The concept of planting trees at close spacing in multiple rows for windbreaks has been credited to immigrants of various heritages. The windbreaks had their early use in England and Europe, and were referred to as hedgerows. Germans took this technology to the Russian steppes, and later carried it to the plains of Canada and the U.S. in the early part of the twentieth century. Dense plantings delineated property lines, and thorny tree species acted as a hedgerow fence for livestock. Hedgerows in France, Belgium and Holland were infamous during the World Wars as a hindrance to invading Allied troops, costing many lives.

The adaptation of hedgerows or windbreaks to North American agriculture provided many benefits, especially in the Great Plains. The drought of the 1930s and poor farming practices, such as continuous cropping, allowed the soil to blow. When dust storms were seen at the Capitol in Washington, DC, President Franklin Roosevelt became concerned and supported the Prairie States Forestry Project, the goal of which was to plant millions of windbreaks in the Great Plains. Together this series of windbreaks was to become a large national windbreak. Many tree plantings extend from North Dakota to Texas today as a result of this program. Trees planted in windbreaks became a valuable conservation tool.

Local Soil Conservation Districts were organized since the Great Depression. They provide trees for forest plantations and windbreaks to conserve soils, water and wildlife resources. The Agricultural Conservation Program in the past and currently the Conservation Reserve Program provided a cost-share incentive to landowners interested in tree planting. The National Arbor Day Foundation has several programs that encourage tree planting in rural and urban settings. Many private wildlife organizations also provide cost-share incentives.

Windbreaks provide a barrier against prevailing winds and create zones of protection on the leeward side of the tree planting. The winds are forced up and over the zone of protection. Soils are not exposed to wind erosion or desiccation within the zone of protection. More soil moisture is available to the crops in the zone, and yields are higher. However, crop yield is reduced immediately next to the windbreak. This zone of competition extends to a distance of only two to four times the height of the tallest trees. Yields dramatically increase from the zone of competition, and continue to the distance of 12 to 20 times the tree height. Past the

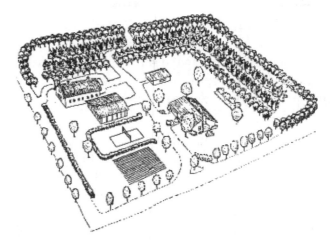

Figure 4. *Farmstead windbreak. Source: Kansas State University Extension Service*

zone of protection (or zone of increased crop yields), production gradually decreases to an average yield. The yield increase from windbreak protection in the zone of protection more than compensates for the yield loss in the zone of competition. Therefore, overall yields are higher in protected fields. Trees also provide protection to crops from wind damage, lodging and sandblasting.

Two main windbreak designs are based on tree density and number of tree rows. First, single-row windbreaks are designed with one row of trees, and are planted for field crop production. This windbreak design is highly valuable in winter; it allows snow to be blown evenly across fields. Farmers have fewer difficulties with snow pockets or wet areas at seeding time in the spring. The snow melt is more evenly distributed, adding more soil moisture to the field.

Second, multi-row windbreaks are planted around farmsteads, and commonly are called shelterbelts. Multi-row windbreaks collect snow in the tree planting and keep more snow out of the farmyard, driveways and working areas. The farmstead windbreaks reduce wind-chill factors and improve working conditions in the farmyard for people and animals. Energy costs to heat homes, barns and workshop buildings can be reduced by 20 to 40 percent with north and west protection by tree plantings.

Livestock need windbreak protection in winter or they will expend more energy to grow. This energy use is translated into increased feed requirements and weight loss. According to one Montana study, cattle protected by windbreaks gained an average 34 to 35 pounds more than those maintained in an open feedlot. During severe winters, protected cattle maintained 10.6 more pounds over unprotected cattle. Dairy cattle respond to lack of wind protection by lower milk production and increased feed requirements. Health can be reduced by cold temperatures along with freezing injury to reproductive parts and death in young animals. Swine are poorly adapted to cold temperature and require protection for weight gain and breeding stock.

Community Forests

Trees have traditionally played a major role in small rural and suburban communities for their aesthetic beauty with tree-lined streets, shaded parks and well-landscaped buildings and homes. In more recent years, trees have been used for many of the problems created by the increase in population of cities. In the past, trees were important for dressing up concrete buildings and asphalt parking lots. Now trees have become an important part of the sustainable landscape. A sustainable landscape in a word is efficient, wise decision-making in the use of energy, water, health and learning.

Tree plantings similar to rural shelterbelts can, by their height and density, force winds up and over neighborhoods. Many rural communities in the Great Plains established multi-row windbreaks on the north and west sides of their limits to assist in wind protection and snow control. Wind control reduces heat loss in the winter and improves working and play conditions outside of the homes. City snow management costs are reduced by collecting more snow outside the city and reducing ground drift that creates hazardous travel conditions. Tree plantings, or living snow fences, cost less than structural fences, and pay through reduced snow removal costs, improved travel conditions and saved lives.

A dual benefit of these community tree plantings is the use as a greenway in and around the town or suburban development. A greenway provides aesthetic beauty by using a wide variety of plant materials for colorful foliage, fragrant flowers, edible fruits, various textures and unique sounds such as shivering poplar leaves or whistling pine needles in the wind. Wildlife use plantings for food habitat, cover and travel lanes. Potential for recreational experience in these tree plantings is very high. Tree plantings provide wind protection for bike/hiking trails, camping areas, active sports fields, playgrounds and outdoor school classrooms.

Trees around homes and on boulevards that are not planted in dense windbreak designs can still be effective and beneficial, as described above. Additionally, shade trees planted on the east and west sides of houses reduce summertime cooling costs. The use of a single tree to shade an outdoor air conditioner can save as much as 10 or 15 percent in cooling costs. Trees in parks provide valuable shade and, if properly placed, can screen unsightly views. They can also muffle traffic noises and screen glare from the sun around ball fields and camping areas. The mixture of individual and group plantings in the collective yards of residential neighborhoods provides a wide variety of flowers, foliage, fruit, and forms year 'round aesthetic beauty and interest.

Water use is in many communities a critical concern in the finding of adequate water resources that will insure enough water for an increased number of homeowners and future development of business and industry. With the increased cost of water treatment, is there a way to reduce water use in the landscape? Xeriscaping is water conservation-minded landscaping. It is not a type of gardening like a rock garden, but uses several principles that apply to the whole landscape. One principle is grouping plants together of similar water requirements. Another principle is to limit high water use areas such as large expanses of turf grass. Shade trees to reduce the evapotranspiration rate (transpiration caused by heat and evaporation) from the grass and plants can benefit home cooling as well. The neighborhood shelterbelt along with other trees will reduce wind exposure and water loss from open turf grass areas and irrigation to sustain them.

Storm water is a concern that is facing many communities. Much of the non-point pollution comes from water runoff into area rivers or groundwater sources. These may be city's source for water and the cost increase for treatment of the pollution. The pollutants include fertilizers and pesticides from lawns; oil and gasoline products from streets and parking lots; along with other city wastes. Trees are a major solution to storm water runoff through the leaves, twigs, branches and trunk of the tree. Research has shown that in a light rain, duration one to five minutes, most of the water is held in the canopy of the tree and the collected water takes time before it is delivered down the trunk and into the exposed soil. Once in the soil, the water is readily used by the tree in growth. In heavy rains that last more than five minutes, trees and green spaces are still the answer in reducing storm water runoff.

The tree canopy also acts as an air filter. By the process of photosynthesis, oxygen is given off that helps in the diffusion of other air pollutants. Carbon dioxide is taken into the leaf and carbon is fixed as carbohydrates which the tree consumes as food. This process is called carbon sequestration. The tree in this pro-

Trees—Proceedings of the Fourth Urban Forestry Conference. St. Louis, MO, 1989.

Urban, C. John, Ciara Schlichting, Lorin Culver, Randy Neprash, and Corey Markfort. *City Trees: Sustainability Guidelines and Best Practices.* St. Paul, MN: Bonestroo Engineering and Twin City Tree Trust, 2007.

Webb, Walter Prescott. *The Great Plains.* New York, NY: Grosset and Dunlap, 1931. New York, NY: Ginn and Company, 1977.

Underemployment

Inadequate employment or employment-related hardship, such as employment that is less than full-time (including unemployment) and/or is inadequate with respect to training or economic returns (Lichter and Constanzo, 1987). Economic underemployment includes discouraged, unemployed, part-time for economic reasons, and working poor workers.

Who Are Underemployed

Nonmetropolitan areas are characterized by higher rates of underemployment than metropolitan areas. The most prevalent types of economic underemployment in rural areas are working poor and unemployed. A complex set of factors influence underemployment and include individual, family, structural and spatial characteristics. Underemployment directly affects the economic resources of many rural families and can disrupt family interaction processes, leading to increased stress and loss of community ties.

Level of underemployment in the U.S. in 1990 was about 22 percent of the civilian labor force. About 13 percent of the civilian labor force were economically underemployed. Although the level of economic underemployment in rural areas in 1990 decreased compared to its level in 1980 (Lichter and Constanzo, 1987), it remained slightly higher than that of metropolitan areas. About 13 percent of nonmetropolitan workers in 1990 were economically underemployed compared to 12 percent in metropolitan areas. In rural areas, four out of 10 full-time workers in rural areas in 1987 earned below poverty wages (Deavers and Hoppe, 1992). On farms, three out of four workers had poverty earnings (Gorham, 1992).

Women workers in nonmetropolitan areas are more likely to experience economic underemployment than their metropolitan counterparts. They are more likely than men to work part-time in absence of full-time jobs. Among those underemployed, men are more likely than women to be unemployed and work for poverty wages. Younger workers (less than 25 years of age) are more susceptible to unemployment than those aged 25 or more. In contrast, workers aged 25 and over are more likely than younger workers to be underemployed due to low income. Nonmetropolitan non-White residents are more likely than Whites to be unemployed, to work for poverty wages, or to work part-time in absence of full-time jobs.

Agriculture and extractive industries in rural areas have higher proportions of underemployed workers than manufacturing and service industries, particularly workers earning below poverty wages. In manufacturing industries, most underemployed workers are working poor and unemployed. In service industries, the working poor and part-time for economic reasons workers are the most frequent categories of underemployment.

The South is more likely to experience greater underemployment compared to other regions. The South has higher levels of unemployment and working poor rates compared to other regions. The Northeast has a lower rate of economic underemployment. The West and Northeast have a higher level of underemployment by occupational mismatch. The essential questions remain, Why is underemployment so prevalent in nonmetropolitan areas? and What social, economic, political and other factors have contributed to its higher levels in rural areas?

What Explains Underemployment

Research on rural underemployment examined the demographic, industrial and occupational positions of underemployed workers focusing on workers' characteristics, thus neglecting structural, institutional and organizational bases of underemployment. The challenge is to integrate individual, family, structural and spatial variations with multi-level analytical approaches to explain the social, economic organization, and spatial aspects of underemployment.

Determinants of rural underemployment include a limited opportunity structure which is the outcome of both past social and economic development policies and current economic transformation. Many rural areas lack stable employment, opportunities for upward mobility, investment in local communities, and diversity in the economy and other social institutions. Moreover, levels of underemployment are shaped by family organizations and individual characteristics. Finally, they are exacerbated by the fact that rural areas are increasingly socially and spatially isolated and particularly vulnerable to adverse effects from structural economic change.

Personal attributes and qualifications, such as age, skills and education, and work history, are important in that they represent investments in skills enhancement that are rewarded in the marketplace. Job skills and education are more poorly rewarded in rural areas with underemployment at each level of education higher in nonmetropolitan areas. These educational disadvantages are considerably higher among women and minorities (Swanson, 1988). Rural workers suffer deficits in education, cognitive skills and work experience.

Differences in earnings returns to education and workplace experience account for the largest portion of metropolitan-nonmetropolitan differences in earnings (McLaughlin and Perman, 1991). Although individual characteristics, especially educational factors, determine who receives low-paying or part-time jobs, as opposed to adequate employment, these characteristics alone cannot explain the persistent high poverty, unemployment and underemployment in rural areas or explain the poor rewards and persistent wage differentials in rural areas, especially among women and minorities (Lichter et al., 1993). The low skills and education of rural workers do not attract high-skilled jobs, so employment growth and industrial restructuring are not likely to benefit rural workers. Underemployment results from both skills gaps between rural workers and available jobs, and from a lack of good jobs available to rural workers.

Underemployment varies by demographic structure (age, sex and race) and by demographic processes, particularly life course, family structure, birth cohort and migration. Also, the demographic composition of the labor force has changed substantially since World War II. Metropolitan and nonmetropolitan differences in underemployment in part reflect differences in demographic composition by age, sex and race of their workforces.

Wages and employment are the main economic reasons for migration from nonmetropolitan areas. Those with higher human capital levels tend to migrate. Yet, many who remain in nonmetropolitan areas have higher education and continue to experience negative returns on their human capital investment. This implies that there are non-economic factors that influence the decision to migrate such that local communities provide residents with feelings of security and stability, along with strong ties to family and friends.

Poverty and Underemployment

Demographic evidence of poverty, unemployment and underemployment, especially in urban areas, shaped the debate about persistent poverty and its relationship to family structure and policy, especially welfare. The popular perception is that the poor in the U.S. are Black, urban, underclass and female-headed households. Poverty in female-headed households, especially for children, is much higher and lasts longer than that in married-couple households. Yet, changes in family structure have less causal influence on poverty than is commonly thought. In rural areas, traits often associated with families of urban poor—female-headed households, marginal parental attachment to workforce, and welfare dependency—are less in evidence (Lichter and Eggebeen, 1992). But, poverty in female-headed households is increasing in rural areas and the growing problem of rural poverty cannot be disassociated completely from changing family structure (Duncan and Tickamyer, 1988).

Childhood poverty and deep poverty both remain prevalent, especially in nonmetropolitan areas. Increasing rates of child poverty attributable to higher prevalence of female-headed households more than offset the economic improvements attributable to increases in female employment, rising levels of parental education and family size. Black children continuously living in two-parent families were as likely to experience poverty as White children who always lived in female-headed households.

Economic Organization and Underemployment

Underemployment is a structural problem that cannot be understood by reference to individual characteristics alone. The economic organization perspective or new structural perspective focuses on the nature of opportunities within the work place, including the quantity and quality of employment, but mainly the organization of work. Large work organizations offer higher wage rates. The relatively low earnings of rural workers is due in part to the disproportionate share of small firms in rural areas. The paternalistic organization of rural work may provide benefits such as personal loans for home improvements, automobile purchases, or to meet sudden financial crises. However, while paternalism implies commitment to reciprocal social relations between employers and loyal employees, the structure of interpersonal relationships involves unequal exchanges (Doeringer, 1984). Workers who quit their jobs generally have difficulty finding reemployment in the area because quitting is seen as evidence of a disloyal and unreliable worker. Opportunities for informal employment in rural areas offer low-wage jobs and are supplements for other sources of income. Low levels of remuneration for most informal work results because the products of such work are sold in highly competitive markets marked by uncertain demand.

Rural occupations have lower earnings potential. Farmers, for example, have one of the lowest earnings potentials as do rural services and semi-skilled manual jobs (Spenner et al., 1982). Thus, the persistence of rural poverty seems partially due to the prevalence of career lines in rural areas with limited earnings potential. For rural workers employed either in farm or service occupations, the option to switch careers in order to improve their earnings potential becomes more limited as they get older. The high poverty of many rural workers results from limitations in the earnings potential and exit portals of their career lines (Bloomquist et al., 1993).

The increased informalization in work is a strategy to reduce labor costs, not only in terms of wages but also in terms of benefit packages, maintenance of health and safety standards and other production costs related to the state regulation of economic organizations. Few analysts of informal activities, except Gringeri (1994), focused on rural social contexts in the U.S. or the resurgence of homework. Homework usually is paid by the piece or unit of production rather than labor-time, and offers limited if any fringe benefits or job security.

Studies of spatial division of labor focus on competitive advantages of different-sized places for the location of particular sustenance activities or industries. The advantages of rural areas from an ecological perspective are the relatively low cost for land and cheap labor availability, and access to natural resources and rural amenities (Bloomquist et al., 1993). Generally, ru-

ral areas serve as sites for routine, low-skilled work activities. Also, within most industries, routine production is located in rural areas while managerial and professional-technical jobs are concentrated in large metropolitan areas. The increase in rural working poor is related to these routine production jobs that pay low wages.

New industries attracted by rural areas' low labor costs and non-unions bring new jobs with low wages in peripheral and secondary sectors (Tickamyer, 1992). Few of these industries greatly assisted local economic growth and major financial transactions. In the rare case of industries that require higher skills and better paid jobs, they are usually performed by outside workers. Also, many rural plants quickly relocate operations in search of cheaper labor. Despite the fact that industrial growth in rural areas, particularly in depressed areas, improves the number of employment opportunities and the distribution of income across different groups, levels of underemployment may remain high. New jobs in peripheral industries and the secondary sector may create new forms of working poor (Tickamyer and Duncan, 1990).

Gender and Underemployment

Feminist perspectives note that women's economic opportunities are conditioned and shaped by their disadvantages in the wage labor market; by their high participation level in informal and unpaid labor, both productive and reproductive; and by state policies toward women, work and welfare (Tickamyer et al., 1993). Gender plays a central role in enabling, sustaining and integrating both relations of production and reproduction in a couple of ways. First, without women's domestic labor in social reproduction, waged labor geared toward production could never take place. Second, women engaged in waged labor are exploited not only as members of a particular class, but also as women. Rural women increasingly join the paid labor force. Yet, rural women have higher levels of underemployment than their urban counterparts. Underemployment among rural women has been a significant aspect of employment-related hardship in nonmetropolitan areas during the post-1970s period. One of every three rural female workers today experience some form of economic distress (Lichter, 1989). Women are less likely than men to become or stay adequately employed, a gender effect that cannot be explained by gender differences in human capital, job characteristics or spatial location (Lichter and Landry, 1991). Jobless and low wages are the greatest barriers for females seeking an adequate job. Overall, women are especially vulnerable to tight labor markets and limited opportunities (Tickamyer, 1992).

In formal employment, women tend to be concentrated in secondary occupations and peripheral industries with low wages and less prestige. Despite the increase in women's participation in the non-agricultural labor market, sex segregation has increased in rural communities. Women have much more limited employment opportunities and flatter earnings curves in areas dominated by agriculture and mining (Tickamyer and Bokemeier 1988). Women's wages and incomes are often the resources that sustain both family and farm in times of severe economic need. Yet family ties are more likely to constrain women than men; men are more likely to change jobs in order to improve their employment situation while women are more likely to change employment for reasons related to marriage, family or personal circumstances (Tickamyer and Bokemeier, 1989).

Women have always contributed to the survival of the family through paid and unpaid work in and out of the home. Rural women spend much time in domestic work, with major responsibility for child rearing and household chores, in work on farms and in gardens, and in other activities to sustain their families. Women's work both in the informal economy and households limit their opportunities to generate income, especially through jobs in the formal sector. Within many rural areas in the U.S., exploitative informalization has resulted in the development of unregulated enterprises and home-based industries targeted specifically to women (Gringeri, 1994).

Measuring Underemployment

The most commonly used indicator of economic hardship and employment marginality in prior research of labor market conditions has been the official unemployment rate. Yet the unemployment rate ignores workers who are marginally employed because it measures job seeking rather than true joblessness or job inadequacy. Underemployment indicators as developed by Clogg and Sullivan (1983) in the Labor Utilization Framework include six components: 1) Not in Labor Force; 2) Subunemployed; discouraged workers who are: a) persons not currently working because unable to find work, and b) part-year workers who are currently out of the labor force but looking for full-time work; 3) Unemployed, includes: a) persons without work but

who are seeking employment, and b) employed persons in the process of job transition or layoff; 4) Underemployed by Low Hours, the involuntary part-time and officially part-time for economic reasons who are working less than 35 hours a week, but who desire a full-time job; 5) Underemployment by Low Income, the working poor including those with earnings less than 1.25 times the individual poverty threshold; 6) Underemployed by Occupational Mismatch, refers to the overeducated, and workers whose completed schooling exceeds the educational level typical of persons holding a similar occupation; and 7) Adequately Employed Workers who are employed but not in any of the preceding categories. Voluntarily part-time workers are included among the adequately employed. The sum of categories 2, 3, 4 and 5 provides a composite measure of economic underemployment because of its direct link with individual labor-market earnings (Lichter and Constanzo, 1987).

Underemployed individuals are affected by changes in their economic resources and feeling about changes or losses of their jobs. For families, when a spouse is underemployed, both spouses may experience trouble in their communication, increasing conflicts and stress. Families adapt various employment strategies by seeking more than one job, increasing the number of earners, having irregular jobs, spending additional time in working activities, or opting for informal activities, both legal and illegal, for their survival. Family adaptive strategies require close-knit kinship and community structure based on solidarity.

— *Janet L. Bokemeier and Jean Kayitsinga*

See also
Division of Household Labor; Employment; Home-based Work; Income; Labor Force; Migrant Agricultural Workers; Policy, Rural Development; Policy, Socioeconomic; Poverty; Quality of Life; Social Class; Work; Welfare

References
Bloomquist Leonard E., Christina Gringeri, Donald Tomaskovic-Devey, and Cynthia Truelove. "Work Structures and Rural Poverty." Pp. 68-105 in *Persistent Poverty in Rural America*. Edited by the Rural Sociological Society Task Force on Persistent Rural Poverty. Boulder, CO: Westview Press, 1993.

Clogg, Clifford C. and Teresa A. Sullivan. "Labor Force Composition and Underemployment Trends, 1969-1980." *Social Indicators Research* 12 (1983): 117-152.

Deavers , Kenneth, and Robert Hoppe. "Overview of the Rural Poor in the 1980s." Pp. 3-20 in *Rural Poverty in*

America. Edited by Cynthia Duncan. New York, NY: New York Auburn House, 1992.

Doeringer, Peter B. "Internal Labor Markets and Paternalism in Rural Areas." Pp. 272-289 in *Internal Labor Markets.* Edited by Paul Osterman. Cambridge, MA: MIT Press, 1984.

Duncan, Cynthia M. and Ann R. Tickamyer. "Poverty Research and Policy for Rural America." *The American Sociologist* 19, no. 3 (1988): 243-259.

Gorham, Lucy. "The Growing Problem of Low Earnings in Rural Areas." Pp. 21-39 in *Rural Poverty in America.* Edited by Cynthia M. Duncan. New York, NY: Auburn House, 1992.

Gringeri, Christina E. *Getting By: Women Homeworkers and Rural Economic Development.* Lawrence, KS: University Press of Kansas, 1994.

Lichter, T. Daniel, Lionel J. Beaulieu, Jill L. Findeis, and Ruy A. Teixeira. "Human Capital, Labor Supply, and Poverty in Rural America." Pp. 39-67 in *Persistent Poverty in Rural America.* Edited by the Rural Sociological Society Task Force on Persistent Rural Poverty. Boulder, CO: Westview Press, 1993.

Lichter, Daniel T. and David J. Eggebeen. "Child Poverty and the Changing Rural Family." *Rural Sociology* 57, no. 2 (1992): 151-172.

Lichter Daniel T. and David J. Landry. "Labor Force Transition and Underemployment: The Stratification of Male and Female Workers." *Research in Social Stratification and Mobility* 10 (1991): 63-87.

Lichter, Daniel T. "The Underemployment of American Rural Women: Prevalence, Trends and Spatial Inequality." *Journal of Rural Studies* 5, no. 2 (1989): 199-208.

Lichter, T. Daniel and Janice Costanzo. "Non-metropolitan Underemployment and Labor-Force Composition." *Rural Sociology* 52, no. 3 (1987): 329-344.

McLaughlin, Diane K. and Lauri Perman. "Returns vs. Endowments in the Earnings Attainment Process for Metropolitan and Nonmetropolitan Men and Women." *Rural Sociology* 56, no. 3 (1991): 339-365.

Spenner, Kennneth I., Luther B. Otto, and Vaughn R. A. Call. *Career Lines and Careers: Entry into Career Series.* Volume 3. Lexington, MA: Lexington Books, 1982.

Swanson, Linda. "The Human Dimension of Rural South in Crisis." Pp. 87-98 in *The Rural South in Crisis: Change for the Future.* Edited by Lionel J. Beaulieu. Boulder, CO: Westview Press, 1988.

Tickamyer, Ann R., Janet L. Bokemeier, Shelly Feldman, Rosalind Harris, John Paul Jones, and DeeAnn Wenk. "Women and Persistent Rural Poverty." Pp. 201-229 in *Persistent Poverty in Rural America.* Edited by the Rural Sociological Society Task Force on Persistent Rural Poverty. Boulder, CO: Westview Press, 1993.

Tickamyer, Ann R. and Janet L. Bokemeier. "Alternative Strategies for Labor Market Analyses: Micro-Macro Models of Labor Market Inequality." Pp. 49-68 in *Inequality in Labor Market Areas.* Edited by Joachim Singelmann and Forrest A. Deseran. Boulder, CO: Westview Press, 1993.

Tickamyer, Ann R. "The Working Poor in Rural Labor Markets: The Example of the Southeastern United States." Pp. 41-62 in *Rural Poverty in America.* Edited by Cynthia M. Duncan. New York, NY: Auburn House, 1992.

Tickamyer, Ann R. and Cynthia M. Duncan. "Poverty and Opportunity Structure in Rural America." *Annual Review of Sociology* 16 (1990): 67-86.

Tickamyer, Ann R. and Janet L. Bokemeier. "Individual and Structural Explanations of Non-metropolitan Men and Women's Labor Force Experiences." In *Research in Rural Sociology and Development,* Volume 4. Edited by Falk W. Lyson. Greenwich, CT: JAI Press, 1989.

Tickamyer, Ann R. And Janet L. Bokemeier. "Sex Differences in Labor Market Experiences." *Rural Sociology* 53, no. 2 (1988): 166-189.

Urbanization

The conversion of rural land to urban uses that directly affects agriculture and other rural uses of land. This article looks at the rates of conversion of rural land to urban uses. It compares the areas of major land uses in the U.S. and the shifts between uses.

Population Growth: Rural-to-Urban Migration

Urbanization is the process of population expansion into rural areas. Urban expansion uses agricultural land, rangeland, forest land, and other rural land. The quantity and rate of urban conversion may affect national food and fiber production, rural economies, and environmental quality. Public concerns about urbanization include maintaining open space and retaining natural systems and processes. Other concerns include controlling public infrastructure costs, preserving local economies and protecting rural lifestyles and ethnic patterns, maintaining local specialty crops, and conserving energy.

State and local measures adopted to protect rural land uses include current use value assessment for property tax purposes, purchase or transfer of development rights, and agricultural districts. Right-to-farm laws, large-area land use planning and exclusive agricultural zoning also may serve to protect rural land (Vesterby and Buist 1994).

Population growth and demographic change are the primary forces shaping change in urban land use. The percentage of people living in urban areas has increased over time because of rural to urban migration. In 1950, the U.S. population was 151 million people, 64 percent of which lived in urban areas. By 2002, the U.S. population was 287 million people, with 227 million (79 percent) living in urban areas, which comprise less than three percent of the total U.S. land area.

Increases in population result in more housing, schools, shopping centers, offices, roads, recreation areas, utilities, and other infrastructure, which translates into demand for more land for urban uses (Lubowski 2006; U.S. Department of Commerce 2008). The number of metropolitan areas increased from 106 to 369 from 1950 to 2000. Over the same time period, population density in these areas went from 8.4 people per acre to 4 (U.S. HUD 2000). The growth in the number and size of metropolitan areas has been larger in the Southeast and Southwest reflecting the migration of the US population from the rustbelt to the sunbelt in recent decades (Vesterby, et al. 1994).

Population and Household Increases Compared

Population growth provides the major impetus for urban land use change. Two thirds of urban land is in residential use, which drives most of the conversion of land from rural-to-urban uses (Vesterby and Krupa 2002). These conversions directly relate to household formation and migration. Households make decisions that affect urban land use. Socioeconomic characteristics, such as age, marital status, and income, influence housing preference. These characteristics are more easily understood in terms of households than by general population characteristics. With smaller households at the same density, more land is needed per capita since more housing units must be built to serve the same number of people.

Household numbers increased by a greater percentage than population during the decades of the 1960s, 1970s, and 1980s due to decreases in persons per household. Average household size decreased from 3.40 persons per household in 1960 to 2.57 in 2006 (Vesterby, et al. 1994; U.S. Department of Commerce 2008).

Rates of Urbanization and Growth at the Urban Fringe

Urban land includes not only residential lots, but also streets, shopping centers, urban parks, recreation areas, and all other nonrural land. From 1982 to 2001, urban area increased by 1.7 million acres per year. The pace accelerated to 2.1 million acres per year in the later period from 1997 to 2001. In total, urban area expanded by 26% from 1982 to 1992 (13 million acres) and 33 percent (33 million acres) from 1992 to 2001 (Lubowski, et al. 2006). Despite the large percentage increase in urban area, the corresponding percentage decreases in rural area were small, about one-half of one percent for each decade. Rural area is much larger than urban area, which explains the difference in percentage changes. Accounting for all urban uses, the average amount of land used by each household has remained under one acre.

The major force shaping residential urban areas is the expansion of low-density housing at the intersection of urban and rural areas, called the urban fringe. While suburbanization refers to the growth of detached single family housing surrounding urban centers, the term "exurbanization" has been coined to refer to the trend towards even lower density growth of isolated large-lot housing developments beyond the urban fringe. From 1994 to 1997, 80 percent of land used for new housing development occurred in these exurban areas outside of the urban perimeter on lots greater than 1 acre (Heimlich and Anderson 2001).

Even though exurban areas are intimately linked with neighboring urban areas they are often not included as additions to urban area because population density is too low according to the definition used by the Bureau of the Census. Within urban areas the average lot size for new single-family homes decreased from 0.4 to 0.3 acres from the mid-1970s to the mid-1990s, which kept the rate of growth of land with lots below 1 acre flat. At the same time, growth in housing on 1 to 10 acres increased and accounted for a much larger total land area (Heimlich and Anderson 2001). Another factor causing an expansion of the urban rural fringe has been growth in service sector jobs, particularly within technology, in suburban areas. From 1992 to 1997, the percentage of metropolitan area jobs located in the suburbs grew from 39 percent to 57 percent (U.S. HUD 2000). This allows workers to move further into rural areas as they no longer need to commute to the city center.

Land Use

Of the almost 2.3 billion acres of U.S. land, 2.6 percent, or 60 million acres, was in urban uses in 2002 (see table). Land area used for cropland or pasture is nearly eight times larger than urban land area and is about

Table.
Major uses of land, United States, 2002

Land use	Acreage		Proportion of total	
	48 States	United States	48 States	United States
	Million acres		*Percent*	
Cropland[1]	441	442	23.3	19.5
Grassland pasture and range[2]	584	587	30.8	25.9
Forest-use land[3]	559	651	29.5	28.8
Special uses[4]	153	297	8.1	13.1
Urban	59	60	3.1	2.6
Miscellaneous other land[5]	97	228	5.1	10.1
Total land area[6]	1,894	2,264	100.0	100.0

[1]All land in the crop rotation, including cropland used for crops, idle cropland, and cropland used only for pasture. Alaska and Hawaii total less than 0.3 million acres (see table 5).

[2]Permanent grassland and other non-forested pasture and range.

[3]Total forest land as classified by the U.S. Forest Service, excluding an estimated 98 million acres used primarily for parks, wildlife areas, and other uses.

[4]Rural transportation areas, areas used primarily for recreation and wildlife purposes, various public installations and facilities, farmsteads, and farm roads, including about 98 million acres that overlap with forest land.

[5]Includes areas in miscellaneous uses not inventoried, and marshes, open swamps, bare rock areas, desert, tundra, and other land generally of low value for agricultural purposes. Does not include urban areas in contrast to previous reports on Major Land Uses.

[6]Includes streams and canals less than one eighth mile wide, and ponds, lakes and reservoirs covering less than 40 acres. Distributions by major use may not add to totals due to rounding.

Sources: Estimates are based primarily on reports and records of the Bureau of the Census (BOC, 1992, 2002, 2003) and Federal, State, and local land management and conservation agencies including BLM 2003; BTS, 2004; FAA, 2002; FHWA, 2002; FRA, 2004; FS 1989, 1998; FWS, 2001; GSA, 2001, 2005; GDT 2000; NASS 2004a, 2005; NPS, 2002; NRCS 2000, 2004; WI, 2002; and various unpublished data sources.

Table source: Lubowski, R.N., Vesterby, M., Bucholtz, S., Baez, A., Roberts, M.J. 2006. "Major Uses of Land in the United States, 2002" USDA Economic Research Service, Economic Information Bulletin Number 14, May 2006. www.ers.usda.gov/publications/eib14

one-fifth of all rural land. Rural land is primarily in forest, range, and other uses.

About 1.2 billion acres are classified as agricultural land. Less than one-half of all farmland is cropland and pasture (442 million acres in 2002). Whereas land in farms declined 17 percent (196 million acres) since 1945, land used for cropland and pasture remained remarkably stable fluctuating between 442 and 472 million acres (see table). Most of the farmland decline was from farm woodland, range, and other farmland uses, not from cropland. Woodland and forest, range, and other rural uses replaced much of the cropland lost to urbanization, illustrating the dynamics of shifting land uses (Lubowski, et al. 2006).

Distinction between Rural Land Uses

Rural land includes agricultural land, forest land, farmland, rangeland, and all other nonurban land. Agricultural land, farmland, and cropland are terms that often are used interchangeably, when in fact each have different meanings. Agricultural land includes farmland, non-federal rangeland, and any land not in farms that is used for crops or pasture, such as portions of wildlife refuges. Agricultural land excludes nonurban rural forest land, parks, roads, and wildlife refuge areas not in crops or pasture.

Farmland consists of land in farms, including cropland, pasture, and lands that are part of a farm but not used for producing crops or livestock. Cropland and pasture (95 percent), rangeland (59 percent), and some forest land (11 percent) constitutes "land in farms." Other (nonfarm) rural land includes public rangeland and forest land grazed on a permit basis and managed by the Bureau of Land Management and the Forest Service (Lubowski, et al. 2006). Some cropland and pasture are in wildlife refuges and are not classified as land in farms. Urban land includes residential, commercial, industrial, institutional, transportation, communications, utilities, and other built-up uses.

Acres Converted between Major Uses

Whereas most land stays in the same use over time, some land shifts between major uses. The number of acres that shift varies by use and by the length of the period under investigation. Shifts between cropland, rangeland, and forest land tend to be dynamic in the sense that increases and decreases occur to and from these major uses. Shifts to urban uses are usually smaller and permanent. Urban areas give up very little land to the other major uses although there is some shifting within the urban categories.

Research has shown that urbanization does not develop prime cropland faster than non-prime cropland in fast growth counties. Prime cropland is regarded as best suited to producing food and fiber. Forty-three percent of all cropland was classified as prime in fast-growth counties (compared to 49 percent nationally), but only 40 percent of cropland urbanized was prime (Vesterby, et al. 1994).

Urbanization can have both a negative and positive effect on agriculture. Close proximity to a large urban population provides part-time labor resources for high-value crops, expands markets for high-value crops through farmers' markets, and presents more off-farm employment opportunities. On the other hand, residential populations are likely to make it more difficult to engage in practices like livestock farming due to complaints about odors and water pollution. Transportation is also made more difficult by increased traffic on roads. An increase in land values from urbanization can also reduce farmers' propensity to invest in new technology if they believe there is a possibility that they will sell their land for urban development in the near future.

Average and Marginal Urban Acres per Household

Popular accounts of urbanization may prompt some to conclude that urban encroachment is converting all of the U.S. cropland and pasture to housing lots, shopping centers, and office parks. However, studies of land use change show that urban conversion of cropland is no threat to U.S. food and fiber production. Large increases in urban areas represent proportionately small decreases in rural areas. These studies have shown that total cropland and pasture in the U.S. remained almost constant since the early 1940s. Conversions from other major uses, such as rangeland and forest land, largely replaced cropland lost to urban uses.

Although urban encroachment is no threat to U.S. food and fiber production, there are many reasons to control urbanization at the local and regional levels. These include maintaining open space, maintaining traditional economic activities, preserving water and air quality, and conserving locally important farmland and specialty crops. Many different kinds of programs address farmland preservation, including use value assessment for property tax relief, zoning, agricultural districts, right-to-farm laws, and purchase of development rights.

— *Michael Brady and Marlow Vesterby*[1]

See also

Community; Future of Rural America; Impact Assessment; Land Ownership; Migration; Policy, Rural Development; Rural Demography; Rural, Definition of; Settlement Patterns

References

Bradshaw, T.K., and B. Muller. "Impacts of Rapid Urban Growth on Farmland Conversion: Application of New Regional Land Use Policy Models and Geographical Information Systems." *Rural Sociology* 63, no. 1 (1998): 1-25.

Daugherty, Arthur B. *Major Uses of Land in the United States: 1992*. AER-723. Washington, DC: U.S. Department of Agriculture, Economic Research Service, 1995.

Frey, H.T. *Expansion of Urban Area in the United States: 1960-80*. Staff Report AGES830615. Washington, DC: U.S. Department of Agriculture, Economic Research Service, 1983.

Heimlich, R.E. and W.D. Anderson. *Development at the Urban Fringe and Beyond: Impacts on Agriculture and Rural Land*. AER-803. Washington, DC: U.S. Department of Agriculture, Economic Research Service, 2001.

Krupa, K.S. and A.B. Daugherty. *Major Land Uses*. No. 89003, (computer file). Washington, DC: U.S. Department of Agriculture, Economic Research Service, 1990.

Theobald, D.M. "Land-Use Dynamics beyond the American Urban Fringe." *Geographical Review* 91, no. 3 (2001): 544-564.

Lubowski, R.N., M. Vesterby, S. Bucholtz, A. Baez, and M. J. Roberts. *Major Uses of Land in the United State, 2002*. EIB-14. Washington, DC: U.S. Department of Agriculture, Economic Research Service, 2006.

U.S. Department of Commerce, Bureau of the Census. *Statistical Abstract of the United States: 1994*. 114th edition. Washington, DC: U.S. Government Printing Office, 1994a.

U.S. Department of Commerce, Bureau of the Census. *1992 Census of Agriculture*. AC92-A-51. Washington, DC: U.S. Government Printing Office, 1994b.

U.S. Department of Commerce, Bureau of the Census. Population and Housing Unit Counts, U.S. Department of Commerce, Bureau of the Census. *1990 Census of Population and Housing*. CPH-2-1. Washington, DC: U. S. Government Printing Office, 1993.

U.S. Department of Commerce, Bureau of the Census. *Statistical Abstract of the United States: 1989*. 109th edition. Washington, DC: U.S. Government Printing Office, 1989.

U.S. Department of Commerce, Bureau of the Census. *County and City Data Book, 1956*. Statistical Abstract Supplement. Washington, DC: U.S. Government Printing Office, 1957.

U.S. Department of Commerce, Bureau of the Census. *Statistical Abstract of the United States: 2008, Section 1. Population*. Available online at: http://www.census.gov/compendia/statab/2008edition.html.

U.S. Department of Housing and Urban Development. *The State of the Cities 2000: Megaforces Shaping the Future of the Nation's Cities*, June 2000. Available online at: http://www.huduser.org/publications/polleg/soc2000_rpt.html.

---

[1]The views expressed are the author's and do not necessarily represent policies or views of the U.S. Department of Agriculture.

Vesterby, M. and H. Buist. "Land Use Planning in Agriculture." *Encyclopedia of Agricultural Science* 2 (1994): 645-655.

Vesterby, M., R.E. Heimlich, and K.S. Krupa. *Urbanization of Rural Land in the United States.* AER-673. Washington, DC: U.S. Department of Agriculture, Economic Research Service, 1994.

Vesterby, M. and K. Krupa. *Rural Residential Land Use: Tracking Its Growth.* Agricultural Outlook. Washington, DC: U.S. Department of Agriculture, Economic Research Service, August, 2002.

Value-added Agriculture

The set of issues related to processing raw agricultural commodities. Value-added agriculture is a multidimensional issue. This article addresses six of these dimensions. One dimension of value-added agriculture means building a manufacturing base in rural regions to process agricultural crops and livestock, which suggests a need to consider location economics and vertical integration. A second dimension involves close ties with agricultural industrialization and the new-generation farmer-owned cooperatives. Still another dimension suggests switching from the crops traditionally grown to niche market crops (like organic) or developing new commercial uses for crops and livestock. A final aspect of value-added agriculture for the foreseeable future is the emergence of biofuels.

The Scope of Value-added Agriculture

Value-added agriculture is widely acclaimed as a key strategy to revive and strengthen rural economies. Politicians from both parties and most farm organizations view value-added agriculture as the means for rural development and new job creation. Despite its broad appeal, there is no simple interpretation of value-added agriculture. This discussion of value-added agriculture includes its scope, rural economic development, industrial uses of crops, alternative crops, vertical integration and location economics.

To begin, the U.S. Commerce Department classifies the food manufacturing system using the North American Industry Classification System (NAICS) into 56 industry sectors. These sectors are classified as higher- or lower-value-added based on how much value is added by processing. Higher-value-added sectors manufacture retail-ready, packaged, consumer brand-name products of which at least 40 percent of the value is added by manufacturing. From 1988 to 1992, the average annual growth rate for higher-value-added agricultural sectors was 3.6 percent compared with only 2.1

percent for lower-value-added agricultural sectors. From 1997 to 2002, the growth rate for higher-value sectors stayed around the same at 3.8 percent, while lower-value sectors actually declined by 1.0 percent.

In 1992, both sectors employed around 500,000 workers, with those in the higher-value sector earning on average $11.87 per hour, compared with $9.26 per hour in the lower-value sector. Both sectors grew in terms of employment and wage rates during the 1990s. In 1997, production jobs in the higher-value sector grew to 625,000 jobs at $13.65 per hour and in the lower-value sector grew to 580,000 jobs at $12.95 per hour. While wage rates followed similar patterns from 1997 to 2002 (both growing to over $15.00 per hour), the number of production jobs dramatically shifted. Almost 200,000 more jobs were created in higher-value industries, while jobs shrank by 180,000 in lower-value agricultural sectors.

In 1997, half of the food industry shipments were of higher-value agricultural products. The growth in employment was accompanied by a growth in the value of shipments. By 2002, higher-value agricultural sectors accounted for 58 percent of the $561 billion in food industry shipments. In 2002, the three largest higher-value agricultural sectors by industry shipments were poultry processing ($37.6 billion), cigarettes ($34.6 billion) and commercial bakeries ($23.8 billion). The top three sectors for lower-value agricultural products were animal slaughter ($565.4 billion), soft drinks ($31.8 billion) and meat processing ($25.8 billion).

The "percent value-added" measures how much of an industry's final shipment value is added in processing. A larger value for percent value-added means that more value is added during processing. In 2002, the top three sectors in terms of percent value-added were cigarettes (88.1 percent), flavoring syrup and concentrates (84.5 percent) and ice (81.5 percent). The lowest three sectors were creamery butter (16.7 percent) animal slaughtering (17.0 percent) and cane sugar refining (21.6 percent).

Rural Economic Development

A second dimension of value-added agriculture is whether the industries developing in rural America are high or low value-added processing. A major impetus for such strategy is rural economic development. In the Great Plains, developmental efforts in the 1990s were led by a resurgence in new-generation farmer-owned cooperatives, along with involvement from rural electric cooperatives.

At least three reasons explain the continued efforts at rural development of value-added agriculture. First, rural development strategies that promote job creation are seen as critical to replacing jobs lost in farming since the 1970s. Providing additional opportunities for the youth in rural America reduces their incentive to migrate to metropolitan areas. In addition, these jobs are critical to maintain and expand the client bases for retail businesses on the main streets of rural towns and cities. Second, the creation of new value-added agriculture results in a more diversified economy, reducing rural states' historical reliance on production agriculture for tax revenues. Finally, while price supports are still a key component of the farm bill, increased emphasis is being placed on policies favoring market-based solutions. Thus, value-added agriculture is viewed as an important replacement for the expected eventual decline in federal payments to agriculture.

Industrial Uses of Crops

A third dimension of the growth in value-added agriculture considers industrial uses of crops. These efforts include new uses for traditional crops, such as corn and soybeans, as well as the introduction of new crops, such as crambe or switchgrass. Besides seeking new uses in food products, crops are being used to produce building materials, newsprint and ink, biopharmaceuticals, cosmetics, food colorings, plastics, and lubricants and hydraulic fluids. More recently, U.S. policy has focused on biofuels as one aspect of an energy policy more reliant on renewable fuels and less dependent on foreign oil.

Corn historically has been primarily used as a livestock feed. Yet even in the mid-1990s, 20 percent of corn was used in food, alcohol and industrial applications. The annual growth rate for industrial uses of corn from 1990 to 2001 was 3.5 percent. Since 2002, the annual growth rate for corn utilization as food, alcohol and industrial applications grew by 14.8 percent.

By 2007, 36 percent of the corn crop was used for value-added products. Examples of food and industrial uses of corn include ethanol, high fructose corn syrup, dextrose and glucose, and starch. In part, the industrial uses of corn reflect societal efforts to reduce pollution. Ethanol reduces air pollution, and corn starches are used in biodegradable plastics. Research at land-grant universities is investigating alternative uses for other traditional crops as well. Examples include using soybeans for ink, sunflower pectin in jelly, and wheat in ice cream.

Other public and private sector research is developing new industrial crops as substitutes for existing manufacturing inputs. Criteria for successful new industrial crops include 1) replacing an existing industrial input by being less expensive or more effective; 2) meeting a specific market niche requirement; 3) being compatible with the existing farming system; and 4) meeting quality standards and being produced in volumes sufficient to meet buyer requirements.

Alternative Crops

Yet another dimension of value-added agriculture suggests that different crops should be raised. Instead of growing commodities, such as corn, wheat or soybeans, individual producers might shift to specialty crops for niche markets. Two difficulties may prevent this as a viable strategy for many producers. First, the machinery complement designed for 2,000 acres of wheat probably does not adapt to growing 20 acres of carrots or garlic. Similarly the agronomic methods to raise alternative crops may require completely different production practices. Second, there may not be an established market, and size becomes critical. Until a certain minimum quantity is grown, building a processing plant is not feasible. Nevertheless, agricultural trade shows are filled with displays featuring niche market products, ranging from mustard to ostrich eggs to organic foods.

Consumption of organic foods has been growing at an annual rate of almost 20 percent over the past decade. One sign of organic foods' growing acceptance has been the allocation of shelf space by most major grocers for organic products. More recently, the emphasis has shifted from organic to local food, as eco-conscious consumers seek ways to lower their carbon footprint.

Vertical Integration

As a fifth dimension of value-added agriculture, the movement toward processing in rural America is a form of forward vertical integration. That is, farmers are taking ownership in forward assets, such as pasta plants, ethanol plants or buffalo slaughter-plants. These efforts are driven largely by farmer-owned cooperatives and individual farmer entrepreneurs. Their motivation is to capture the profit or value earned further up the value chain. Since production agriculture is a mature industry with slow growth, these new ventures become attractive to capture the returns earned by existing food processors.

Some large food companies, such as Conagra or Coors, are backwards vertically integrated. Reasons for vertical integration include capturing the profits or value in different stages of the value chain or ensuring a supply of critical raw materials. For example, Coors contracts with farmers in Colorado to grow malting barley. The malting barley is then processed in malting plants owned by Coors, before the malt is shipped to Coors breweries. In contrast, Miller Brewing concentrates on producing beer. Instead of vertically integrating, Miller buys all of its malt from independent suppliers such as Cargill or ADM.

Vertical integration is not without its difficulties. Studies in strategic management identify four disadvantages of vertical integration. First, vertical integration concentrates a firm's investment in a particular industry. Large financial commitments may make it more difficult to exit the industry or adapt new technology, despite changes in the industry that make it less attractive. Second, vertical integration may reduce flexibility in sourcing raw materials by linking the firm to particular suppliers. This is especially worrisome for farmer-owned cooperatives. Third, balancing capacity at each level of the supply chain might be difficult. For example, although a farmer-owned flour mill may be at an optimal size, its milling capacity may be more than is required at the next level of processing, say baking. Thus, the vertically integrated firm may be forced to sell its primary product to competitors. Finally, different business activities may require management with much different skills and business capabilities. Being a low-cost processor does not make one an effective manager of logistical or information technology issues.

Location Economics

Developers of new value-added agriculture also face pressure to build new processing plants in rural areas, despite firm economics. For example, traditional locational analyses suggest that weight-losing agricultural processes should locate near producing regions, whereas weight-gaining processes should locate near consuming regions. A further complication is a rail rate structure that heavily favors the movement of multiple-car shipments (70 to 110 rail cars) of bulk commodities. In contrast, processed products typically move in smaller rail shipments or by truck. The transportation cost difference can be enormous.

Thus, when promoting rural economic development, issues of altering the traditional description of firm objectives must be faced. Under traditional economic analysis, the objective is maximum profit, not location. However, a farmer-owned cooperative may opt for a lower return on their investment in exchange for the additional economic development in their community.

A final locational factor for the developers of new value-added agriculture is how to extend the definition of community. Large-scale value-added agriculture projects can require capital, labor and raw materials that can only be generated at a regional level. They may need to view several towns or even counties as their home rather than a specific town. Although all may benefit from cooperation, putting aside 100 years of rivalry among communities can be difficult.

Value-added agriculture is breathing new hope into many concerned with the future of rural America. The many sides of value-added agriculture make this a complex issue. Yet as U.S. agricultural policy increases its reliance on free markets and reduces government price support programs, new value-added agriculture will likely increase in importance.

— *Frank J. Dooley*

See also

Agricultural and Applied Economics; Agri/Food System; Cooperatives; Development, Community and Economic; Economic Development; Manufacturing Industry; Marketing; Markets; Policy, Rural Development

References

Boehlje, Michael. "Industrialization of Agriculture: What Are the Implications?" *Choices* 11 (1996): 30-33.

Boland, Michael A. and Gary W. Brester. "Vertical Integration in the Malting Barley Industry: A 'Silver Bullet' for Coors?" *Review of Agricultural Economics* 28 (2006): 272-282.

Conway, Roger K. and Marvin R. Duncan. "Bioproducts: Developing a Federal Strategy for Success." *Choices* 21 (2006).

Dicks, Michael R. and Katharine C. Buckley, eds. *Alternative Opportunities in Agriculture: Expanding Output Through Diversification.* Agricultural Economic Report No. 633. Washington, DC: U.S. Department of Agriculture, Economic Research Service, 1989.

Drabenstott, Mark. "Industrialization: Steady Current or Tidal Wave?" *Choices* 9 (1994):4-8.

Nelson, Paul N., James C. Wade, and Julie P. Leones. "The Economics of Commercializing New Industrial Crops." *Agribusiness: An International Journal* 11 (1995): 45-55.

Urban, Thomas N. "Agricultural Industrialization: It's Inevitable." *Choices* 6 (1991): 4-6.

Urban, Thomas N. "Beyond Industrialization: The Prescription Food System." *Choices* 13 (1998): 43-44.

U.S. Census Bureau *Economic Census—Industry Series Reports—Manufacturing.* Washington, DC: U.S. Census Bureau, 2005.

Values of Residents

In general, those things thought to be good, whether abstract or concrete. Personal security, for example, is a value that is abstract but often is associated with the material aspects of life, such as adequate food, shelter and clothing. But security has a psychological aspect as well. Some people can feel quite secure with much less wealth than others.

This entry discusses some of the historically distinct values associated with rural American life and begins with a brief contrast to those experienced by people living in urban settings. Then, two kinds of values are discussed in order to explain why some values are thought to be more important than others. In American literary and historical myth, values are reflected in moral character traits attributed to rural Americans. In turn, these rural values and virtues have been associated with broader community virtues and with the movement to sustainable agriculture. But these same American values also underlie economic efficiency and trends towards technological expansion that result in decline in the quality of life in rural America.

Rural Versus Urban Values

The moral and aesthetic values of people who live in rural areas are commonly thought to differ from those of their metropolitan or suburban counterparts. Certainly, the challenges and benefits of the two lifestyles differ so much in the U.S. today that people who move to small towns from large cities or vice versa almost always experience some culture shock that is associated with differences in tempo, intimacy and personal visibility in day-to-day life. The question of whether core values are unalterably different among populations who are raised and remain in rural areas from those more urban is a matter of continuing controversy and empirical uncertainty. But it is safe to say that the situations in which humans find themselves in rural versus urban settings contrast enough so that people behave differently in each setting. This means that in a rural setting, certain values and virtues become more apparent, but those same values or virtues may recede to the background for urban living.

Nevertheless, some values are thought to be more important than others regardless of the setting in which people live. To distinguish these more important values, usually a means-ends criterion is proposed, where ends are the values most important to humans and means are the various ways used to achieve those ends. In this way, values are respectively divided into those things that are intrinsically good and those that are good instrumentally. The former are sometimes described as "good in themselves" or "ends in themselves." Various intrinsic goods have been proposed—happiness, security, self-realization, enlightenment, nonviolence, love and oneness with nature, among them. Instrumental goods are desirable only because they help us to reach a more ultimate good. The linguistic usage of the term "instrumental" implies that such values are less important than the intrinsic ones. While intrinsically good things are desirable—people want them—not everything desirable is intrinsically good and may or may not be a means to such higher goods. In assessing the values of rural Americans, then, part of our task will be to think about whether the values associated with rural life are ultimately good for their own sakes or are good in certain contexts and situations as a means to some higher, unspoken, value that is shared by both rural and urban people alike.

Values and Virtues

Moral virtues are associated with values that may be instrumentally or intrinsically good, or both. A virtue is a character trait such as honesty, fidelity, courage, compassion, justice or self-reliance. People who are honest or faithful, brave or compassionate have a certain disposition to behave in recognizable ways, and they also are motivated for good and virtuous reasons to do what they do. A virtuous person will exhibit most or all of the good character traits and none of the bad ones.

Virtues often serve individuals or society by helping them to achieve a more ultimate intrinsic good. So, a society of people who tell the truth, keep their promises, admit mistakes, defend themselves against aggressors, and attend to the feelings of others would arguably be well on its way to achieving the higher ends of peace, harmony and security. Virtues are not solely instrumental, however. Becoming a virtuous person is a end in itself that no virtuous person could attain by seeking to be honest, faithful, self-reliant and courageous only as a means to virtuous integrity. In many instances, honesty, fidelity, justice and most other virtues are thought to be intrinsic goods, desirable as character traits of a truly good and happy person.

Virtues and American Mythology

Until the past few decades, the majority of the U.S. population lived in rural areas. Historically, American values were rural values. Most rural dwellers described in literature and research were farmers, ranchers, loggers, fishers and others who harvested renewable crops and owned small businesses that were family operated. Writing in Revolutionary times, Thomas Jefferson believed that a strong democracy depended on maintaining a nation of small landowners who make their livelihood from the land. According to Jefferson, such a populace would naturally exhibit the kind of self-reliance, independence and efficiency that is essential to a democratic way of life. Mythic tales about figures such as Paul Bunyan, Johnny Appleseed, the Lone Ranger, Davy Crockett, and Daniel Boone also signify the persona of hardiness that is closely associated with ideals of courage, liberty and individualism as American values. Henry David Thoreau articulated the virtue of self-reliance in his writings and life at Walden pond in the nineteenth century, and his ideas still symbolize the way many Americans believe we ought to view ourselves and our relationships to others.

Today, most Americans live in cities, but our cultural history and values are rooted in the images, stories and virtues of rural life. The stories that have been recorded and repeated and the virtues that are admired reflect only part of that rural culture. Although farmers, ranchers, loggers, fishers and other small business owners lived in rural America, large numbers of others live there, too. Most Native American populations live in rural areas. Many African Americans lived as slaves, sharecroppers or tenant farmers in the South during and after the Civil War. Chinese laborers were brought in to build the railways in the West, and immigrants from Mexico have been a staple in the labor force of Southwest farms and orchards since territorial days. The values of rural women have been assumed to be identical to those of the men in their families. Until recently, the contributions of all these and other groups to the quality of community life were downplayed or not recorded. Their values may be quite different from what many Americans perceive as central to the American way of rural life (see *Agriculture and Human Values,* Summer 1985, for a series of discussions).

Rural Values and Sustainable Agriculture

The values reflected in the mythology of pioneering America are largely those of people of European descent. With that vision in mind, recent commentators have claimed that the passing of traditional family farms signals the loss of important moral values from American life. Most urgent among them is community. The loss is both abstract and concrete. Small towns are disappearing as small farms sell out to larger farms and conglomerates. The sense of community has been lost, it is argued, and the quality of life thereby degraded. By this, writers usually refer to the feelings of trust and relationship, interdependence and unity that are prevalent in small towns. Small family farms have been extolled as places where these values arise. The land itself is sometimes said to be of intrinsic value. Small farmers should value a sustainable agriculture and should have better motivation to be good stewards than large profit-making corporations who have no intimate connection to the land and its surrounding communities.

The idea that small farmers are preservers of some important American values has been criticized in several ways. Most commonly, small farmers who must sell their farms to their neighbors because of debt load or low profit margin are said to be simply inefficient and by implication deserve to lose out because they have not worked hard enough or well enough. Efficiency and hard work are values these critics hold as more important than other values that might accompany the existence of small and medium-sized family farms, such as better communities and family integrity. Countering that attack, some economists note that economies of scale work to the advantage of medium-sized farms, many of which are family operated. Large farms are not necessarily better or more efficient farms.

Economic and Technological Impacts

Concerning the implication that inefficient farms somehow deserve their fates, many scholars point out that small farms are vulnerable to the technological treadmill. As new technologies are introduced to make farms more efficient, the earliest adopters benefit most from the cost savings that permit profits. Larger farms are more likely to be capable of adopting such technologies and thus reap the technological rewards. By the time small farmers are able to afford the innovations, commodity prices have dropped because the technology permits more production. If they adopt the innovations, their profit margin decreases because the technology is expensive and the drop in commodity prices only enables them to stay even or lag somewhat behind. If they do not adopt the technology at this later time, they face lower and lower returns on the crop or herds, which will eventually force them out of business. Thus, farmers on small and medium-sized farms have not earned their losses, but instead are victims of a system that has been arranged to benefit those who already have more wealth and power. Part of the system is funded by the public, and an affirmation of equality requires restructuring the system to benefit all citizens.

Many other aspects of the social structure of American life in transition from rural to urban majorities have contributed to the loss of rural community values. During the Farm Crisis of the 1980s, medium-size farms operated by a family or extended family on a full-time basis tended to disappear at an alarming rate. The causes of the decline lie in broad trends and policies that are not in themselves immoral or irresponsible. Mechanization, hybrid seed technology, chemicals, commodity programs, and a general tendency of Americans to encourage big business have been cited as the primary causes. The decline in world food production of the 1970s encouraged the U.S. to expand production to help feed the world. Farmers invested heavily in machinery and equipment and bought more land in a time of inflation. Bankers encouraged farmers to take high-leverage loans, but then the Federal Reserve raised interest rates to attack inflation, thereby increasing costs of production. Then exports began to decline and land values fell, pushing many family farmers to insolvency.

Rural community values were once argued as fostering conservationist virtues. Some scholars proposed that owners who live on and personally work the land develop a personal relationship to the land and would be more motivated to preserve the land as a bequest to their offspring. On the other hand, farms on the brink of profitability are less likely to exercise the restraint and self-sacrifice needed to insure good stewardship since they may need to plow fencerow-to-fencerow and be unable to exercise the conservation practices needed to preserve the quality of the soil.

Self-defeating Values?

Ironically, the values encoded in the traditional mythology of the American persona—independence, self-reliance, and individualism—may themselves be driving the decline in quality of rural life. Independence and individualism may lead to a so-called tragedy of the commons, wherein each person seeking his or her own good or self-interest is a collective cause of collapse of a community or common good. For example, each cattle rancher who places a herd along a river can reason that this single herd will do no irrevocable damage to the river, the fish population or the habitat of other animals. Each rancher abutting the river reasons that he or she has a right to use the water flowing by for the herds. But if each rancher reasons as if no other rancher matters or exists, then the river will be polluted, spawning beds destroyed and habitat lost.

Paradoxically, new champions of rural community as a lost value see interdependence as important. Some writers point to the Amish as exhibiting this kind of community where one could rely on one's neighbors in times of need. But in our culture, the writings traditionally taught in American literature, the heroes of American history, and the scions of American economics and politics have lived and admired independence and self-reliance and discouraged interdependence. Perhaps it is simply the small numbers living in rural towns that engender the trust and interdependence that people feel in living there. It is a condition of human life that each person can know only a limited number of people well enough for trust. A common theme in criticisms of urban life today involves loss of safety and the longing to see a familiar face in the endless crowds, for extended family and circles of friends with shared beliefs, among whom each of us can feel safe. In praising rural community virtues and values, their opposites are thereby logically excluded. Individualistic self-reliance and interdependent community are likely to be mutually exclusive in the American context.

— *Kathryn Paxton George*

See also
Agricultural Ethics; Animal Rights/Welfare; Culture; Environmental Ethics; Ethics; Land Stewardship; Religion; Theology of Land

References
Agriculture and Human Values. Special Issues: "Agrarianism, Agricultural Development, and the Farm Crisis." 2, no. 2 (Spring 1985); "Agriculture in the U.S.: Its Impact on Ethnic and Other Minority Groups." 2, no. 3 (Summer 1985); "The Land, the Agrarian Tradition,

This New Englander gathering sap from maple trees seems to exemplify the solid virtues thought to characterize farmers-hard work, efficiency, self-reliance, and independence. © *Bettmann / Corbis.*

and the Common Good." 2, no. 4 (Fall 1985); "Agriculture and the Social Sciences." 4, no. 1 (Winter 1987); "Ethical Values and Public Policy." 6, no. 4 (Fall 1989); "Agrarianism and the American Philosophical Tradition." 7, no. 1 (Winter 1990); "Rural Economic Development." 8, no. 3 (Summer 1991).

Berry, Wendell. *The Unsettling of America: Culture and Agriculture.* San Francisco, CA: Sierra Club Books, 1977.

Comstock, Gary, ed. *Is There a Moral Obligation to Save the Family Farm?* Ames, IA: Iowa State University Press, 1987.

Critchfield, Richard. *Trees, Why Do You Wait?* Washington, DC: Island Press, 1991.

Deaton, Brady J. and B.R. McManus, eds. *The Agrarian Tradition in American Society: A Focus on the People and the Land in an Era of Changing Values.* Proceedings of a Bicentennial Forum, June 16-18, 1976. Knoxville, TN: University of Tennessee, Institute of Agriculture, 1976.

George, Kathryn Paxton. "Do We Have a Moral Obligation to Practice a Sustainable Agriculture?" *Journal of Sustainable Agriculture* 1, no. 1 (1990): 81-96.

George, Kathryn Paxton. "Sustainability and the Moral Community." *Agriculture and Human Values* 9, no. 4 (Fall 1992): 48-57.

Goldschmidt, Walter. *As You Sow: Three Studies in the Social Consequences of Agribusiness.* Montclair, NJ: Allanheld, Osmun and Co., 1978

Montmarquet, James A. *The Idea of Agrarianism: From Hunter-Gatherer to Agrarian Radical in Western Culture.* Moscow, ID: University of Idaho Press, 1989.

Pollack, Norman. *The Populist Mind.* Indianapolis, IN: Bobbs-Merrill, 1967.

Sumner, Jennifer. *Sustainability and the Civil Commons: Rural Communities in the Age of Globalization.* Toronto, Ontario: University of Toronto Press, 2004.

Thoreau, Henry David. *Walden and Other Writings of Henry David Thoreau.* Edited by Brooks Atkinson. New York, NY: Random House, 1937.

Zube, Ervin H. and Margaret J. Zube. *Changing Rural Landscapes.* Amherst, MA: University of Massachusetts Press, 1977.

Vegetable Industry

Individuals and firms involved in the production, marketing, processing, handling, selling, or storage of vegetable plants grown primarily for human consumption. Vegetables are defined, in this article, by their common, culinary usage rather than their formal botanical meaning. For example, tomatoes, peppers, and eggplant are botanically classified as fruits but many consumers, producers, distributors, and industry analysts classify them as vegetables. Similarly, potatoes, sweet potatoes, melons, and mushrooms are frequently listed as vegetables so the broad definition of vegetables will be assumed in this article (for a complete list of included vegetables, please see various issues of the USDA's *Vegetables and Specialty Crops: Situation and Outlook Report*). This article examines trends that have occurred in the vegetable industry since the early 1990's. Important structural and organizational differences between the fresh market and processing sectors of the vegetable industry are noted and discussed. Production and marketing challenges faced by vegetable industry participants are also discussed.

For many Americans, an obvious link with their agrarian past is the planting and tending of a vegetable garden. The perishability of vegetables and the just-harvested taste of fresh produce motivate some individuals to spend hours planting and nurturing their gardens. For the modern family, however, it is more common to drive to a supermarket, select vegetables from several hundred or more types available, microwave a portion for that evening's meal, and repeat this process every few days. People are used to having fresh vegetables of all types available in the supermarket irrespective of season. Problems with out-of-season shortages, limited selection, and exorbitant prices are rarely constraints in buying. Sophisticated advances in genetics, production technology, and transportation have provided shoppers with a variety of high quality vegetables available throughout the year.

U.S. consumers have grown accustomed to the year-round availability of fresh market vegetables in grocery stores. In addition to traditional supermarkets, mass merchandisers such as Wal-Mart and Target expanded their sales items to include fresh produce and many canned food goods. Wal-Mart's annual produce sales rank them among the top retailers of produce in the U.S. Technological advances in transportation, storage, refrigeration, and communication systems allow retailers to obtain regular supplies of high quality vegetables from distant suppliers. The global nature of vegetable production allows supermarkets to obtain fresh vegetables from milder climates during lower domestic supply periods such as early spring, late fall, and winter. In addition to increases in off-season supply availability for vegetables, consumers also expanded and diversified their tastes and buying habits for vegetables.

Display of peppers for sale at a local market. Photo by Chris Gunter.

Supermarkets often offer over 400 types of fruits, vegetables, and specialty crops in their produce departments. Health, diet, and nutrition considerations often motivate consumers to experiment with new and different items such as yellow bell peppers and exotic mushrooms. Producers respond to the changing consumer preferences by expanding the set of traditional vegetables grown to include many specialty-type vegetables. The result has been steady growth in vegetable production and sales.

From 1980 through 2006, cash receipts for vegetables produced in the United States have grown by 146 percent. Harvested acreage grew over that period by only 5.5 percent. Greater output per farm was achieved through better utilization of resources and crop specialization in geographic areas where producers had a comparative advantage in growing vegetables. A reduction in trade barriers has been enormously important for rural vegetable farmers and residents. Although reductions in trade impediments made local vegetable producers more susceptible to foreign competitors (particularly fresh market imports from Mexico), lower

cost producers have additional opportunities to export vegetables. Economic growth associated with increased vegetable exports could expand small town employment, keep more people in the rural service base, and fund needed upgrades in rural services and infrastructure.

Trends

A number of important trends have influenced vegetable production over the last decade. The first is the concept of value-added. This is the conversion of raw vegetables into products of greater value. Value-added examples include bagging, packaging, bundling, and pre-cutting items. The purpose of adding value is twofold: 1) to make the item more attractive and more convenient for the buyer to use; and 2) to increase the value and usability of the commodity and thus make it easier for the producer to sell. Many value-added products are designed to save consumers preparation time. For example, a bagged salad mix may contain the prewashed lettuce and shredded vegetables in addition to a packet of salad dressing and a small bag of croutons.

The consumer simply needs to empty the contents of a fresh-cut salad mix into a bowl and it is ready to eat, saving preparation time. Many consumers are willing to pay for the convenience of products like these. Grocers have recognized the enormous added sales and added profit potential associated with fresh-cut and pre-packed vegetables so many have worked with producers to develop store brand labels for items such as partially-trimmed sweet corn instead of utilizing the grower's brand label.

A second trend in the vegetable industry revolves around heightened consumer awareness about health, diet, and nutrition. Consumers have become increasingly concerned about traditional production practices used in growing vegetable crops. This concern motivated producers to look for more sustainable methods of growing vegetables. This resulted in an economic incentive for growers to examine vegetable crop production using less synthetic pesticides and fertilizers. More sustainable production practices emphasize the use of renewable resources and the conservation of soil and water to enhance environmental quality. In 2000, a subset of production practices were formalized by USDA into a set of practices identified as the National Organic Standards program. These practices allowed growers using these techniques to become certified as organic growers following a specific set of allowable production practices. Certification allowed them to use the USDA label on their produce and identified their output as "Certified Organic" and this label alerted customers at the purchase point as to the set of production practices followed. Organic certification was important financially for many growers since oftentimes certified organic vegetables were sold for a 20% to 40% price premium compared with conventionally grown vegetables.

As consumer demand grew for this type of produce, small organic farms in California began to grow large and corporation run farms entered into organic production to allow supplies of organic produce to move through traditional distribution channels. Small organic growers were put at a marketing disadvantage when they tried to compete against larger corporate farms, often located hundreds or thousands of miles away. Consumers too were increasingly aware that the cost of transporting produce both in terms of fuel costs and air pollution were increasing over time and buying out-of-state corporate farming operations did not benefit local growers or alleviate environmental concerns associated with cross-country shipment of produce.

Top Ten Ranked Fresh-market Vegetables Measured via Shipment Volume and Per Capita Consumption in the U.S., 2006.

Fresh-use Vegetables	2006 Volume Shipped* (1000 cwt of product)	2006 U.S. per capita consumption (annual pounds per person)
Potatoes (tablestock)	170,324	43.6 pounds
Round Tomatoes	49,702	20.4 pounds
Onions (dry)	46,002	20.4 pounds
Watermelons	40,310	15.1 pounds
Lettuce (iceberg)	36,880	18.4 pounds
Muskmelon (cantaloupe)	27,378	9.6 pounds
Bell Pepper	17,643	7.8 pounds
Celery	16,770	5.8 pounds
Cucumbers	14,545	6.4 pounds
Lettuce (Romaine)	14,521	11.2 pounds

Source: *Vegetables and Melons Situation and Outlook Yearbook*, Gary Lucier and Alberto Jerardo, USDA-ERS, VGS-2007, July 26, 2007.

Over time, this awareness resulted in a desire by consumers to support and buy locally-grown fruits and vegetables. "Buy Local" marketing campaigns were started by growers and state departments of agriculture and increased in popularity. This trend benefitted smaller acreage producers and dramatically improved their local marketing prospects.

Third, aggregate vegetable consumption trends have been relatively flat for the past five years, increasing at about the annual U.S. net population growth rate. However, vegetable production yields per acre have increased in the field and in greenhouses because of intensive production practices such as increasing use of black plastic, drip irrigation, and high tunnels. As a result, aggregate U.S. vegetable harvested acreage has decreased, average yield per acre has increased, and farm-level sales value has increased. The re-emergence of community farmers markets as well as a modest sales growth has resulted in increased income for vegetable growers, especially many smaller to moderate-sized farm operations that depend on local and regional sales. This trend is likely to continue into the near future, especially since the latest version of the 2008 Farm Bill contains special funding for specialty crops (no other farm bill has included funding for fruits and vegetables).

A fourth trend in vegetable production is the sharp increase in production costs for the grower. Increased oil prices have led to higher costs of fertilizer, pest control products, tractor and transportation fuel, wages for labor, and higher prices for seed or transplants. Unlike some other industries, vegetable farmers operate in a very competitive marketplace (including imports from Mexico and South America where costs are often lower) and thus they cannot simply pass along higher costs to buyers. Increased production costs have forced producers to reduce profit margins for crops they produce. In the long run, industry-wide production costs will increase and higher costs will result in higher prices paid by consumers but it is likely there will be fewer domestic producers remaining in the U.S. produce industry.

Fresh Produce Safety

As mentioned earlier, consumers are increasing making fresh vegetable purchases based on a greater awareness of health, diet and nutrition. Most (70%) of all shopping trips are for an immediate need and average less than $11. Consumers have an expectation that the produce they demand will be readily available, fresh and safe to eat. Increasingly reports of illness related to fresh produce and other food commodities are making headlines. There are a number of reasons for this, including an increase in the consumption of fresh produce, better detection and communication by local health departments, increased interaction and coordination among grower organizations, local health departments, and the Centers for Disease Control, and increased media attention given to food safety issues. Growers must become increasingly aware of and utilize good agricultural practices (GAP) in the field, in their packing facility, and during transport (on-farm and off-farm). Having systems in place to ensure the traceability of produce is critical in the event of a food safety recall.

Fresh Vegetables

Production and consumption. Today, commercial fresh vegetable production is concentrated mostly in California, with growers there accounting for 41 percent cash receipts for vegetables and melons. Growers in Florida (nine percent), and Arizona (six percent), are also important suppliers of fresh vegetables, primarily during the fall, winter, and spring seasons. Growers and shippers located in Oregon, Washington, Michigan, and Georgia are seasonally important suppliers of commercially grown vegetables. Approximately 30 fresh market vegetable crops are grown commercially; the five most important vegetables measured by the amount shipped to market and per capita consumption are listed in the table.

Concerns. Fresh vegetables are expensive crops to grow and harvest. Although field corn or soybean production costs often range between $175 and $300 per acre, vegetable production costs typically range from $700 per acre for watermelons to nearly $10,000 per acre for fresh market staked tomatoes. Major expense categories include specialized machinery and equipment costs, hybrid seed or plant costs, disease and pest control, and harvesting expenses. Most fresh market vegetables must be harvested by hand, using hired workers or seasonal migrant laborers. Hand harvest expenses frequently account for 30 to 40 percent of total premarketing expenses. Because many vegetables are perishable and require extensive use of labor, most growers plant fewer than 50 acres of fresh market vegetables (although plantings can exceed 10,000 acres in certain states). Decentralized production of small-acreage quantities often result in insufficient volume for one grower to access mainstream marketing networks. Often, local marketing options, such as direct selling to consumers through community farmers' markets or pick-your-own operations, are the best marketing methods available. Alternatively, some rural growers have identified a "market window of opportunity" where market niches exist before or after vegetables are available from growers in competitive regions. The inability of many rural vegetable growers to successfully market their crop presents the greatest challenge to most rural vegetable growers.

Marketing. After harvest, activities shift from the field to central packing and shipping facilities. A small number of growers rely on field-pack operations where vegetables are harvested, sorted, graded, boxed, and palletized in the field. For example, California head lettuce is usually field packed. However, most vegetables are transported to nearby packing sheds where they are washed, graded, packed, and cooled prior to market shipment. Vegetables are graded according to USDA or customer standards using designated size, maturity, quality features, and then placed into standardized shipping containers. Most shed operators offer or arrange cooling as well as transportation to market. These firms are often identified as packer-shippers. Cooling vegetables maintains their field quality, preserves freshness, and extends product shelf life. Facilities can be owned by an individual grower or a group of growers such as a cooperative or marketing association. Alternatively, services can be provided by a firm who performs these tasks for a per unit fee. Often fee-based packers sell product for growers, providing payment to growers after the sales price is negotiated with a buyer and various service fees (e.g., packing, boxing, and selling) are deducted. Most vegetables are packed, graded, and sold from facilities owned by growers or grower groups.

After loading, the market destination is determined by the buyer or buyer's agent. If the buyer represents a chain store or wholesale company, the shipment will go to the company's central receiving warehouse. After arrival, vegetables are reinspected to ensure they meet company quality standards and resorted into smaller units for store distribution. If the buyer's agent is a broker or distributor, vegetables are shipped to a central market facility located in an urban area. It is difficult for rural, small-volume growers to access the chain, wholesale, and urban market networks because buyers often need larger quantities of product from few sources. Use of few suppliers tends to reduce buyer paperwork, per unit procurement costs, and handling time. For most rural growers, viable marketing options are limited to niche sales to local supermarkets and direct marketing to consumers such as pick-your-own, roadside stands, and community farmers markets. Successful niche and direct marketing strategies often ensure economic success and can result in long-term sustainability for farmers.

Processed Vegetables

Situation. The average American consumes nearly 215 pounds of processed vegetables each year, with processed potatoes (91 pounds per person), processed tomatoes (70 pounds per person), and processed sweet corn (18 pounds per person) among the most popular items. Canned or frozen vegetables are preferred by many consumers because of their stable shelf life and their convenience. Despite rapid increases in the amount of frozen vegetables consumed each year by Americans, the average consumer still eats nearly five times more canned vegetables than they consume frozen. Nearly two-thirds of all U.S. vegetable production for processing is raised in California. For some commodities, such as processing tomatoes, California growers supply nearly 90 percent of domestically grown product. Growers in other states are seasonally important suppliers of processing vegetables. The bulk of the processed green beans, sweet corn, sweet peas, and potatoes (for fries) are grown in Wisconsin, Michigan, Minnesota, Oregon, and Washington.

Procurement. Processing firms obtain vegetables in three principal ways. First, they can grow their own vegetables. Second, they can purchase vegetables on the open market; that is, at harvest time they make an offer to buy a grower's vegetables. And third, prior to planting processors can contract with an individual grower to purchase all or a portion of the grower's crop for a prearranged price. Most processors elect to acquire vegetables under the terms of a bilateral contract between the processing company and the grower or grower association. Contract terms typically include items such as planting dates, varieties planted, cultural practices, and a method for determining the price to be paid for the crop. Since processors require a consistent, steady flow of product to maintain efficient plant operations, contractual arrangements are advantageous. Vegetable processors perform many different tasks such as preservation (freezing broccoli), transforming raw product (making catsup, paste, or juice), and blending multi-ingredient food packages (canned soups or frozen dinners). In addition to processing vegetables for sale under their own brand name, many processors also freeze or can private label products such as store brands or cost cutter brands. Although the exact number of U.S. processing firms and plants is unknown, it is likely that there are fewer than 900 vegetable processing plants operating today.

Contracts. Because exact terms of a production contract are important to the success of both processors and growers, intense bargaining occurs. Contract terms are negotiated in two ways: (1) directly between an individual farmer and the processor; or (2) between the processor and a bargaining association who represents its grower members. Examples of successful bargaining associations include a group of processing tomato growers in central California and a group of sweet corn growers in central Washington. Contracting provides growers with relative price certainty and a definite sales outlet. In return for these advantages, however, negotiated prices for growers are usually below fresh market prices. Since most vegetables cannot be used in raw form directly (e.g., potatoes must be peeled and sliced for chips), processors often send raw product to preparation plants. Specific activities at prep facilities vary by location and the needs of the processor but generally the raw product must be washed, topped, skinned, cut or diced, and bulk-packed so they can be preserved in a shelf-stable form. Soup stock items such as celery and carrots, potatoes for chips, grapes for juice, and apple for sauce are prepared in this way. After commodities are frozen and bulk-packed at the prep plant, the commodities are stored for transport later to the final processing or blending plant facility.

Future Issues. Consumer demands for nutritious, convenient, and safe food produced in an environmentally sustainable way will continue to change basic production and distribution practices. An increasing focus on alternative fuels will turn attention towards the production of biofuels using high starch vegetables, such as sweet potatoes or other high starch vegetables. Integrated Pest Management, sustainable production methods, and environmentally-friendlier packages will be used more extensively by vegetable growers and marketers. Internationalization of markets will reduce the significance of border boundaries and will motivate growers to examine efficiency, cost, and resource use issues.

Labor issues will take on an increasingly important role in vegetable production in the future. Vegetable production is labor intensive in both production and handling. How we deal with the status of migrant farm laborers and the ease with which these laborers are available for use in this industry will play a critical role in whether production of fresh vegetables remains viable in the country or is moved to areas where labor is abundant. The issue of whether we import food or workers to grow the food will be critical in the future of vegetable production in the United States.

Rural farmers will provide the expertise, land, and entrepreneurial spirit needed to expand and diversify the mix of vegetables available to consumers. Rural communities and businesses will provide needed critical resources such as labor, operating inputs, and the financial capital to increase output. In the past, rural vegetable farmers discovered that the harder they worked, the more success they realized. In the future, accomplishments will depend on hard work and ability to work smarter.

— *Christopher C. Gunter and Edmund A. Estes*

See also

Agriculture, Hydroponic; Biodiversity; Food Safety; Genetically Modified Organisms; Greenhouses; Horticulture; Local Food Systems; Marketing; Organic Foods Industry

References

Estes, E.A. "Tomato Wars: A Discussion of How International Trade, Structural Changes, and Competitiveness Affect the North American Produce Industry." *Journal of Agricultural and Applied Economics* 35, no. 2 (August 2003): 313-319.

Gibson, Eric. *Sell What You Sow: The Grower's Guide To Successful Produce Marketing*. Carmichael, CA: New World Publishing, 1994.

Lucier, Gary and Alberto Jerardo. *Vegetables and Melons Situation and Outlook Yearbook*. VGS-2007 (July 26, 2007). Washington, DC: U.S. Department of Agriculture, Economic Research Service, 2007.

McLaughlin, Edward W. and D.J. Perosio. *Fresh Fruit and Vegetable Procurement Dynamics: The Role of the Supermarket Buyer*. Cornell Food Industry Management Program publication R.B. 94-1 (February). Ithaca, NY: Cornell University, Department of Agricultural, Resource, and Managerial Economics, 1994.

Produce Business. "The 20th Annual Mystery Shopper Report and Trends." Boca Raton, FL, Volume 23, No. 1-12, 2007. (Also see monthly issues.)

Powers, Nicholas J. *Marketing Practices for Vegetables*. Agricultural Information Bulletin No. 702 (August). Washington, DC: U.S. Department of Agriculture, Economic Research Service, 1994.

Voluntarism

Unpaid activity performed outside the home. Voluntarism has long been recognized as a hallmark of rural American life. The approach taken in this entry will be to provide a brief overview of the functions and dimensions of voluntarism within the larger society, followed by discussions of the rural voluntary tradition and contemporary issues and trends.

Dimensions

In the 1830s, the French scholar Alexis de Tocqueville returned from the U.S. convinced of the importance of the democratic experiment underway there. At the core of this new nation, he believed, was a commitment to the principle of voluntary association, which functioned not only as an efficient and egalitarian mechanism to organize communal life, but also as a bulwark against the potential excesses of government. He stated: "Americans of all ages, all stations in life, and all types of dispositions are forever forming associations. There are not only commercial and industrial associations in which all take part, but others of a thousand different types—religious, moral, serious, futile, very general and very limited, immensely large and very minute.... In every case, at the head of any new undertaking, where in France you would find the government or in England some territorial magnate, in the United States you are sure to find an association" (Tocqueville, 1969).

Voluntary activity continues to attract Americans today. Recent estimates are that some 38 million citizens, or just over 20 percent of the adult population, perform some type of unpaid service beyond their own homes and families (Hodgkinson and Weitzman, 1986). Most, although not all of this effort, occurs through organizations, with religious groups, schools, political or civic clubs, health care facilities, social welfare agencies, and sporting and recreational associations providing the primary outlets. All told, the dollar value of this donated labor is estimated at more than $100 billion annually. Although such participation is widespread, it tends to occur disproportionately among certain segments of the population, notably among those with higher levels of income and educational attainment, and among those between 35 and 54 years of age, and more among women and Whites than among men and members of minority groups. For present purposes, it should also be noted that small towns and rural areas often have been effective incubators of the voluntary spirit, and, more precisely, that nonmetropolitan residents have higher levels of voluntary participation than do city-dwellers and suburbanites.

The Voluntary Tradition in Rural Life

From colonial times onward, farmers and their neighbors relied on one another to carry out the routine tasks of the agrarian or village calendar and to provide assistance in the wake of disaster. Barn-raisings, state and county fairs, agricultural cooperatives, harvest festivals and volunteer fire companies remain among the best known of these rural traditions.

During the nineteenth and early twentieth centuries, the rural ethos of self-help and mutual aid provided the foundation for dozens of formal organizations of regional or national scope. Among the most influential of these groups was the Grange. Founded in 1867, the Grange gathered and disseminated information about promising agricultural practices and provided a framework to represent the political and economic interests of small farmers. Granges were among the first organizations to welcome the participation of women. Largely through the efforts of farm wives, the local Grange was often a focal point for social, cultural and recreational activity.

Later organizations that served broadly similar functions included the Farmers' Alliance, the Farmers' Union, and the Farm Bureau. Farmers and other rural groups provided support for both mainstream and radical political reformers, including the Populist movement that dominated the North Central states at the turn of the twentieth century. More recently, farm workers' unions were formed to advance the interests

of agricultural employees, many of whom are itinerants and who stand close to the bottom of the national income distribution. Similarly, when falling crop prices and rising interest rates combined to throw small farm owners into financial crisis in the 1980s, protest and self-help efforts were mounted across the country, including the benefit concert, Farm Aid.

Education is another institution with deep roots in the rural voluntary tradition. Prior to the establishment of the modern public school system in the mid-nineteenth century, families and churches were the principal sources of instruction for rural children and youth. In the more prosperous rural areas and townships, district schools and academies depended on a mixture of private and public support, and parents' donations to the local church often made it possible to employ a single man in the combined capacities of schoolmaster, church custodian and gravedigger. The enactment by Congress of the Morrill Act of 1862 gave rise to the land-grant university, which in turn provided the impetus for several voluntary organizations for rural youth, notably the 4-H Club and the Future Farmers of America. In addition, land-grant universities pioneered the Cooperative Extension movement, which offered professional and voluntary outreach activities in agriculture and related fields. During the 1930s, the federally organized Civilian Conservation Corps (CCC) trained thousands of young men to protect the natural environment. Although it ended with the onset of World War II, the CCC inspired some of the youth and adult environmental organizations that are now well established across rural America.

Contemporary Issues

Rural voluntarism today faces a variety of uncertainties, some of which stem from the ongoing decline of the rural population. Others are rooted in cultural and demographic transformations within the larger society. Most fundamentally, the migration from outlying regions to metropolitan areas poses the threat of nonsustainability for organizations that require a substantial recruitment base. In the case of service-oriented organizations, an additional difficulty is the enrollment of prospective clients. Compounding the rural organization's woes are the challenges that now confront voluntary associations everywhere. Several of these are consequences of the changing social roles of women, who have been the traditional mainstays of voluntarism in the U.S. Some feminist theoreticians, for instance, argue that voluntarism exploits women by denying them payment for their work and stigmatizing their efforts as lacking economic value. A related and more basic obstacle is the long-term erosion of workers' purchasing power, which forced many women to take paid employment who might otherwise prefer voluntary community service. Other demographic developments with crucial implications for voluntarism involve groups at opposite ends of the age spectrum. Older people represent the fastest-growing segment of the American population. Insofar as most no longer hold full-time jobs, they conceivably represent a fruitful source of recruits for voluntary organizations. On the other hand, the limited physical capacity and restricted financial resources that some senior citizens experience translate into a lower rate of volunteering and a greater reliance on the services provided by voluntary organizations. Young people ranging in age from 16 to 24 also have been comparatively reluctant to volunteer. One factor militating against their participation is the steady increase in the proportion of college and high school students now holding full- or part-time employment.

The challenge for rural voluntarism will be to make maximum use of dwindling human resources. Because they have been underrepresented thus far, the elderly and the young, together with the poor and the handicapped, are logical targets of any future recruitment drives. One set of obstacles that dependent populations encounter anywhere, but especially in rural areas, are physical isolation and the lack of adequate transportation facilities. Assuming, however, that technological advances continue to drive down the cost of telecommunications, it is possible to envision that voluntary activity increasingly will be conducted through computers, fax machines, and satellite and cable broadcasts rather than in person.

Another question that will impact the future of rural voluntarism involves the role of government. During the late 1980s and early 1990s, Congress passed a series of laws providing federal funding for community service activities. The most far-reaching of this legislation was the National and Community Service Trust Act of 1993 (NCSTA). Although the NCSTA is broad in scope, its centerpiece is AmeriCorps, an initiative that offers volunteers health benefits, a stipend, and an education voucher worth $4,725 that can be used to cover the costs of higher education or job training. To qualify for funding, projects must address at least one of four areas of human need: education, health care, public safety and environment. Several rural-based voluntary action programs, including those associated with the Co-operative State Research, Education, and Extension Service and 4-H, have been funded through AmeriCorps.

Rising concerns about budget deficits and the scope of government authority have cast a large shadow over AmeriCorps and other federally sponsored outreach efforts. Accordingly, the future of rural voluntarism ultimately will depend not on laws passed by governments but on the actions of ordinary citizens. Until fairly recently, the most common basis motive for voluntary participation was a well-developed sense of obligation that most women and men believed they owed to their communities, the nation, humanity or God. Although fulfillment of duty continues to be a driving force for many volunteers, recent studies conducted both among college students and adults indicate that it has been superseded by an ethos of self-fulfillment (Serow, 1991; Wuthnow, 1991). In other words, participating in various forms of voluntary activity permits some individuals to achieve personal goals that cannot be fulfilled through work, school or family life. The desire to live a complete, well-rounded life, and to make the most of one's talents, is not necessarily incompatible with a sense of neighborly obligation. Rather, organizations, particularly those drawing on relatively sparse population bases, should be prepared to take this new, more psychologically informed motivation into account when recruiting, training and evaluating their volunteers.

— *Robert C. Serow*

See also

Churches; Community; Community, Sense of; Cooperative State Research, Education, and Extension Service; Elders; Labor Force; Quality of Life; Rural Women; Social Movements

References

Coles, Robert. *The Call of Service: A Witness to Idealism.* Boston, MA: Houghton Mifflin. 1993.

Daniels, Arlene Kaplan. *Invisible Careers: Women Civic Leaders from the Volunteer World.* Chicago, IL: University of Chicago Press, 1988.

Ellis, Susan J. and Katherine H. Noyes. *By the People: A History of Americans as Volunteers.* New Century Edition. Philadelphia PA: Energize, Inc., 2006.

Hodgkinson, Virginia Ann, and Murray S. Weitzman. *Dimensions of the Independent Sector: A Statistical Profile,* 2nd ed. Washington, DC: Independent Sector, 1986.

Petrzelka, Peggy and Susan E. Mannon. "Keepin' This Little Town Going: Gender and Volunteerism in Rural America." *Gender & Society* 20, no. 2 (2006): 236-258.

Serow, R. "Students and Voluntarism: Looking into the Motives of Community Service Participants." *American Educational Research Journal* 28 (1991): 543-556.

Smith, David Horton and Burt R. Baldwin. "Voluntary Associations and Volunteering in the United States." Pp. 277-305 in *Voluntary Action Research*. Edited by David Horton Smith. Lexington, MA: Lexington Books, 1974.

Tocqueville, Alexis de. *Democracy in America*. Paris: C. Gosselin, 1835-1840. Garden City, NY: Doubleday, 1969.

Wuthnow, Robert. *Acts of Compassion: Caring for Ourselves and Others*. Princeton, NJ: Princeton University Press, 1991.

cess is a sink in which carbon is tied up until the tree decays. The tree's canopy, the leaves, twigs and branches, collect particulate matter such as dust and soot from industrial sources. Particulate matter is actually drawn through larger tree groves and filtered by the twigs, leaves and hairs on leaves. In a neighborhood shelterbelt, cool air moves out from the shaded areas and warm air replaces it. Trees are not only effective cost cutters and recyclers, but healthy to be around.

Fredrick Law Olmsted, designer of Central Park in New York City, stated that reproducing trees and nature into the city would bring "tranquility and rest to the mind." Studies have shown that settings with trees and other vegetation actually produce stress-reducing effects. There is also physiological evidence of stress reduction in one study involving 120 subjects using color/sound videotapes of different urban and natural settings. Studies in prisons and hospitals showed less stress-related illness and quicker healing if the prisoner or patient had a window view to a natural area with trees and shrubs than a view to other walls or buildings. The University of Illinois at Urbana-Champaign conducted a study of inhabitants of public housing and reactions to presence or lack of green space. Crowding, noise and danger can all contribute to chronic mental fatigue, whereas access to green spaces helped restore attention and relieved the everyday pressures of living in poverty. "Vegetation has been shown to alleviate mental fatigue, one of the precursors to violent behavior." The researchers also found that children who spend more time outside refreshed their ability to pay attention in school and had more creative play.

Voluntary planting activities of neighborhood residents and citywide volunteers are important in creating a sense of community and livability within the neighborhood and eventually throughout the city. Many activities to improve neighborhoods fail because the structure of renewal is top-down and the neighborhood residents have not bought into the idea. In cases where neighborhood residents were asked their opinions on Brownfield development, they worked together and there was more neighborhood pride and successful renewal projects. Trees are the major component of the green infrastructure and enhance the city by stimulating more livable neighborhoods not only by the benefits trees and shrub plantings provide, but also by the process of networking with residents, volunteer groups and the community as a whole.

Country Meets City

Trees in rural America can provide a unique rural-urban interface. Tree crops can open new ways to market and harvest natural products. Pick-your-own fruit tree or shrub orchards offer opportunities for urban dwellers to experience the country. Many pick-your-own orchards have special weekends of activities, such as apple grading demonstrations, juice and cider making, pie eating contests, and sack races. Such experiences with nature can be shared by adults and youth alike.

Another type of tree product marketing is the choose-and-cut Christmas tree operation. Urban families travel into the country to find their own tree, cut it, and bring it home—the start of a new family tradition. Nearby warming houses provide hot apple cider and fresh baked cookies; Christmas shops sell tree accessories, stands, wreaths, garlands, candles and floral and green arrangements. Misshapen or unsalable cull trees are salvaged for use as wreaths, garlands, and door swags. Christmas trees and fruit orchards require intensive cultural measures such as pruning, weed control, and insect and disease pest control. There is much work in providing the pick-your-own or choose-and-cut product including advertising and marketing, hiring personable employees, and providing a rewarding experience to customers.

As cities grow and develop, tree planting increases and availability and selection of nursery stock decreases for homeowners and developers. For the new homeowner, the desire is to have a larger thrifty-looking tree that will provide shade in a couple of years. The larger transplanting machines, also called tree spades, have made this dream a reality. Trees with a trunk diameter of five to six inches can be moved from a nursery farm to an urban lot in a matter of an hour or less. If the tree receives proper care, it will become established in three years. Tree survival can be high if done properly but quality is only insured if the homeowner checks on the operator's reputation. Tree nurseries just like pick-your-own fruit orchards and Christmas tree farms are gaining in popularity. It is important that a variety of tree selection is grown.

The Value of a Tree

It is difficult to place a monetary value on the benefits people derive from trees. Realtors have accessed landscaping accounts for 10-20 percent of the house and property value. The landscape value of a home valued at $150,000 is $3,000. Let's say there are trees valued at 5 percent of the home value, or $7,500. There are four large shade trees, two in the front and two in the back or $1,875-$2,000 a piece, which is not unreasonable. This is just the aesthetic value to the property, let alone the shading and energy reduction, etc. The price of a tree purchased at the nursery is based on the labor, materials, transportation and maintenance costs expended to produce it. Other factors involved in tree valuation include legal fees, insurance settlements, property value, timber value, and historical and sentimental values. A shade tree valuation formula was developed by the International Shade Tree Conference and National Arborists Association in 1951. The formula was tested and revised several times to meet new challenges, and the International Society of Arborists provides a handbook and teaching materials to assist tree assessors.

A true story that happened in the northern Great Plains occurred in the 1970s. A group of foresters from various professions got together to determine the value of a farmstead windbreak. A traditional forester examined the windbreak of about 40 years and came up with a value between $5,000 and $10,000. A windbreak forester examined the windbreak and looked at the value of the land and estimated a value of $15,000 and $20,000. The city forester had his way to estimate including the value of protection, the cost of maintenance over 40 years and used the ISA formula to come up with a value of $35,000 to $40,000. After a while they discussed how the city forester's formula was way out of range. They finally decided to ask the farmer who owned the windbreak to put his value on the tree planting. The farmer scratched his head thinking about the input in maintaining the trees, the wind protection provided, energy saved, and came up with a value of at least $50,000. He said, "If I buy a new tractor I have to pay that much at least and it doesn't hold up near as long as that windbreak."

Conclusion

Trees are valuable and seem to be more valuable each year. The National Agroforestry Center at Lincoln, Nebraska, developed the phrase "Working Trees" to change the passive view of trees just standing in the same spot for 100 years. A traditional saying in the rural community is "The farmer never fully appreciates the value of trees until he feels the sand between his teeth." Trees are silent workers, an investment for the future that always pays off and needs to be taught continually. A more preferable saying is: 'The best time to plant a tree was 20 years ago, the next best time is now!'

— *Vernon C. Quam*

See also

Conservation, Soil; Forest Products; Forestry Industry; Forests; History, Agricultural; History, Rural; Land Stewardship; Parks; Sawmilling

References

Brazell, Margaret. *Growing Trees on the Great Plains*. Golden, CO: Fulcrum Publishing, 1992.

Dirr, Michael and Charles Heuser. *The Reference Manual of Woody Plant Propagation, from Seed to Tissue Culture*. Athens, GA: Varsity Press, Inc., 1987.

Droze, Wilmon. *Trees, Prairies, and People*. Denton, TX: Texas Women's University, 1977.

Herman, Dale and Vernon Quam. *Trees and Shrubs for Northern Great Plains Landscapes*. Publication F-1309. Fargo, ND: North Dakota State University Extension Service, 2006.

McPherson, E. Gregory, James Simpson, Paula Peper, Scott Maco, Shelly Gardner, Shauna Cozad and Qingfu Xiao. *Midwest Community Tree Guide*. Report # NA-TP-05-05. Newtown Square, PA: U.S. Forest Service, 2005.

Moore, E.O. "A Prison Environment's Effect on Health Care Service Demands." *Journal of Environmental Systems* 11 (1981): 7-34.

Olson, James C. "Arbor Day—A Pioneer Expression of Concern for the Environment." *Nebraska History* 53, no. 1 (1972): 1-14.

Platt, Rutherford. *This Green World*, 2nd ed. New York, NY: Dodd, Mead and Company, 1988.

Quam, Vernon, Bruce Wight, and Harvey Hirning. *Farmstead Windbreak*. F-1055 (May). Fargo, ND: North Dakota State University Extension Service, 1993.

Quam, Vernon and Bruce Wight. *Protecting Fields with Windbreaks*. F-1054 (August). Fargo, ND: North Dakota State University Extension Service, 1993.

Quam, Vernon, John Gardner, James Brandle, and Teresa Boes. *Windbreaks in Sustainable Agricultural Systems*. EC91-1772-X. Lincoln, NE: University of Nebraska Extension Service, 1991.

Quam, Vernon and Jonnie Medina. *A Guide to Maintenance of Your Xeriscape*. Fargo, ND: City of Fargo and U. S. Bureau of Reclamation, 2001.

Shigo, Alex. *A New Tree Biology*, 2nd ed., 7th printing. Littleton, NH: Sherwin Dodge, Printer, 1995

Staley, Dan. *Casey Trees White Paper: Benefits of the Urban Forest Literature Review*. Washington, DC: Casey Trees Endowment Fund, 2004.

Ulrich, R. S. "The Role of Trees in Human Well-Being and Health." Pp. 25-30 in *Make Our Cities Safe for*

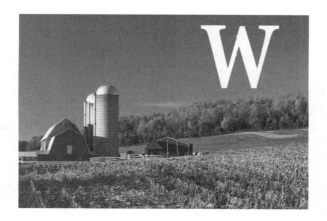

Water Policy

Heraclitus observed that it was not possible to "step into the same river twice, for fresh waters are ever flowing in upon you." At the present time in the United States, it is equally impossible to encounter the same water policy twice. The reasons are more complex than the mere fact that "fresh waters are ever flowing."

A primary reason for this complexity is the fact that there is no single water policy in the United States. Although federal policies exist in general terms at the national level, the more specific policies of various federal departments and agencies can differ greatly. On any particular matter, for example, the water policy of the Bureau of Reclamation may be substantially different from that of the Corps of Engineers.

Irrespective, one ongoing federal water policy has been deference to state water policies as long as those policies are consistent with the requirements of federal law. As a result, there are at least 50 state water policies. In many instances, however, water policies are as fragmented at the state level as they are at the federal level.

Consequently, what might be defined as *water policy in rural America* has as many definitions are there are actors involved in the policy process. In many instances, this absence of consistency is intentional as the *de facto* federal water policy appears to be a "policy of policies," both federal and state.

This chapter addresses water policy in rural America in generalized terms. First, it should be noted that "rural" water policy in many ways differs little from "urban" or "suburban" water policy. For example, federal and state policies protect groundwater regardless of location. At the federal level, these policies are reflected in the Safe Drinking Water Act, 42 U.S.C. §§ 300f–300j-26; the Resource Conservation and Recovery Act (RCRA), 42 U.S.C. §§ 6901–6992k; and the Comprehensive Environmental Response, Compensation and Liability Act (CERCLA), 42 U.S.C. §§ 9601–9657.

Similar statutes have been enacted in a number of states.

There are, of course, unique aspects of rural water policy. Chohin-Kuper et al. (2003) have identified four objectives to be served by rural water policy: 1) land improvement, 2) national security ("reduction of food dependency"), 3) prevention of rural depopulation, and 4) food production. Earlier in the history of the U.S., these objectives were served by a rural water policy that focused on providing water for agriculture. These policies are addressed in the following section, "Water *for* Agriculture."

In more recent years, however, rural water policy has begun to include improving the efficiency of agricultural water use so that additional supplies of water might be conserved or "saved" and then made available for expanding municipal, industrial and energy development. These more recent policy developments are addressed in the "Water *from* Agriculture" section. Conclusions are presented in the final section.

Water for Agriculture

At the federal level, water for agriculture in the Western states has been provided primarily by the Bureau of Reclamation since 1902. The Bureau's water supply policies, "including subsidized prices, long-term contracts, and restrictions on the sale of water by farmers—have resulted in a rigid allocation of major water resources to agriculture." (CBO, 1997)

At the state level, an excellent summary of water law and policy in the Eastern states is contained in the *Regulated Riparian Model Water Code* (the *Model Water Code*), which was adopted by the American Society of Civil Engineers as an ASCE Standard in 2003 (ASCE, 2004). More recently, the ASCE published an *Appropriative Rights Model Water Code* that contains an equally excellent summary of water law and policy in the Western states (Dellapenna, 2007).

The policy of providing water for agriculture is reflected in several provisions of the *Model Water Code*. For example, § 6R-3-04(1) of the *Model Water Code* establishes an agricultural preference for available water supplies:

> When the waters available from a particular water source are insufficient to satisfy all lawful demands upon that water source, water is to be allocated by permits up to the safe yield or other applicable limit of allocation of the resource according to the following preferences: (a) direct human consumption or sanitation in so far as necessary for human survival and health; (b) *uses necessary for the survival or health of livestock and to preserve crops* or physical plant and equipment from physical damage or loss in so far as it is reasonable to continue such activities in relation to particular water sources; and (c) other uses in such a manner as to maximize employment and economic benefits within the overall goal of sustainable development as set forth in the comprehensive water plan. (ASCE, 2004:110-111, emphasis added)

Similar legislation or constitutional provisions exist in at least 12 Eastern states (Sherk, 2003; Sherk, 1990) and 13 Western states (Dellapenna, 2007).

These preferences are reflected in other provisions of the *Model Water Code*. With regard to droughts or other water emergencies, for example, § 7R-3-01(3) provides that any emergency restrictions on water use permits "shall comply with the preferences provided in section 6R-3-04." Under §7R-3-05(2), the same preferences apply to emergency restrictions on water uses for which no permit was required. Similar legislation has been enacted in at least 15 Eastern states (ASCE, 2004; Sherk, 2003; Sherk, 1990) and four Western states (Dellapenna, 2007). With regard to preferences *among* agricultural water uses during droughts or other water emergencies, Cummings et al. (2003) noted that in Georgia the Flint River Drought Protection Act, *Official Code of Georgia*, §§ 12-5-540–12-5-550, adopts a rule of temporal priority by imposing a LIFO ("last-in-first-out") requirement.

An agricultural preference also may exist with regard to water use fees which are authorized by § 4R-1-08 of the *Model Water Code*. As noted in the Commentary, some of the states that instituted water use fees also provided exemptions for agricultural water uses (ASCE, 2004).

Water from Agriculture

Municipal, industrial and energy development throughout the U.S. is increasing demands for water. Given that the development of new water supplies is expensive, time-consuming and may have unacceptable environmental consequences, a great deal of attention has been focused on the reallocation of water from existing uses to the uses noted above. A primary source of the water to be reallocated is that presently being used for agricultural purposes.

Agriculture is *the* primary water user in the Western states. As noted by the Congressional Budget Office (CBO, 1997): "76 percent of all withdrawals of surface water are for agricultural purposes. That figure is much higher in many individual western states and river basins. For example, approximately 95 percent of the water diverted from the Rio Grande and the upper basin of the Colorado River is used for irrigating crops or for livestock. In only five of the 17 western states does agriculture account for less than 80 percent of the diversion of surface water." In addition, agricultural water use has continued to increase in the Eastern states.

An essential premise is that improving the efficiency of agricultural water uses will result in a substantial quantity of this water becoming available for reallocation. Irrigation efficiency can be increased, for example, by lining canals to prevent seepage or by converting a surface ditch-and-furrow system to a sprinkler system utilizing groundwater. An example relating to the production of citrus crops was provided by the Florida Department of Agriculture and Consumer Services (FDACS, 2003): "The transition from the older irrigation methods to micro-irrigation between 1991 and 2001 resulted in considerable reduction in per acre water use requirements for citrus. In 1991, there were about 770,000 acres of citrus being irrigated with 53% using micro-irrigation systems. The irrigated citrus acreage increased to about 830,000 acres in 2001 with 80% using micro-irrigation systems. Since the average micro-irrigation system saves about 140,000 gallons/acre/year, the annual water savings was 52 billion gallons in 1991 and 90 billion gallons in 2001."

With regard to the reallocation of agricultural water conserved by irrigation efficiency improvements, two critical water policy questions emerge (Cordua, 1998): "First, water users who contemplate investing in conservation are unsure whether they will have the right to use or transfer all the water saved due to their efforts. Second, transferors are uncertain whether they must account for any injuries to third parties that result from their conservation and transfer of agricultural water."

Rights to Conserved or "Saved" Waters. The question is deceptively simple: Does an irrigator have the right to transfer the amount of water conserved through improvements in irrigation efficiency? State responses to this question have been both varied and inconsistent. Some Western states allow an irrigator to claim supplies of water that result from improving irrigation efficiency, while other Western states specifically do not allow such claims. On a state-by-state basis, uncertainty regarding the legal availability of conserved or "saved" water inhibits the use of such supplies for future municipal, industrial and energy development purposes. In essence, while improving the efficiency of agricultural water uses may make water physically available, this does not mean that the water would be legally available.

In part, the need for certainty regarding rights to conserved or "saved" water stems from the cost of improvements necessary to increase agricultural water use efficiency. As Neuman (1998) noted: "[I]mproving efficiencies in western water use will be expensive. Changing from flood irrigation or other low-tech irrigation methods to pumps, pipes, sprinklers, or high-tech systems could cost thousands of dollars per acre for installation and ongoing operational costs; that would quickly add up to hundreds of thousands of dollars even for fairly small farms. Lining or enclosing over a hundred thousand miles of leaky ditches would add huge additional costs. A twenty year old estimate outlined total costs of nearly $ 15 billion to adopt conservation improvements in irrigated agriculture westwide, just to improve irrigation efficiencies from forty-one percent to fifty-eight percent."

In § 9R-1-02(1), the *Model Water Code* addresses the question of rights to water conserved:[1] "When a person holding a water right voluntarily undertakes conservation measures beyond those required by this Code, including beyond the terms and conditions of the person's permit, that result in significant quantifiable reductions in the water that person has been using other than during a period of water shortage or water emergency, that person shall receive approval of a modification of the permit to enable the person to use the water in other locations or for other purposes in preference to others who might apply for a permit to use the water conserved" (ASCE, 2004). Similar legislation has been enacted in California, Idaho, Indiana, Montana, New Mexico, Oregon, Utah and Washington (Dellapenna, 2007; Tarlock, 2005; ASCE, 2004; Fleming and Hall, 2000; Neuman, 1998; Morandi, 1994).

With regard to water supplied by federal projects, a policy model could be the Central Valley Project Improvement Act (CVPIA) enacted by Congress in 1992 (Title 34, Pub. Law No. 102-575). The provisions of the CVPIA are of note (Weinberg, 2002): "First, the act grants any CVP [Central Valley Project] contractor the right to sell water to any user for any (beneficial) use at any price. However, it places several constraints and conditions on those transfers, including directing the Bureau [of Reclamation] to charge full-cost rates for water transferred to urban uses.[2] Second, it creates an increasing block-rate pricing structure. The (subsidized) contract rate applies to the first 80% of a district's water allotment, the second tier applies to the next 10% of the water allotment, and is set midway between the contract and full-cost prices, and the final tier applies to the last 10% of the water allotment and is charged at the full-cost price. Third, it imposes a number of surcharges to finance a fish and wildlife restoration fund. The surcharges include a $25 per acrefoot (af) charge on water transfers for sales to non-CVP urban water users, charges of up to $6/af on all agricultural water users and $12/af on all urban water users (indexed to 1992 dollars), and an additional charge of $7/af on Friant Division water (eastern San Joaquin Valley)."

Amelioration of Third-Party Impacts. Transfers of water from existing agricultural uses to municipal, industrial and energy uses will have third-party impacts. These impacts fall into four general categories: 1) social and cultural impacts (e.g., unemployment, loss of rural community cohesion), 2) environmental consequences (e.g., reduced instream flows, diminished wetlands), 3) economic impacts (e.g., reduced sales of agricultural inputs such as seed, fertilizer, chemicals and equipment, reduced level of processing agricultural outputs, loss of tax base) and 4) jurisdictional conflicts (e.g., adverse downstream impacts triggering litigation).

---

[1] Similar language is contained in § 9A-1-02(1) of the *Appropriative Rights Model Water Code*. (Dellapenna 2007:356-357)

[2] As Weinberg has noted, prior to 1992, the Bureau of Reclamation was delivering water to Central Valley Project water districts "under the terms of forty-year contracts specifying fixed quantities of water (allotments) [at] a set, below-cost price. The legacy of that policy is that irrigation contract prices, typically set in the 1960s range from only $2/af to $31/af. In contrast, most urban water districts in the state [California] charge prices approaching or exceeding $1,000/af." (Weinberg 2002:545-546, citations omitted).

States allowing transfers of conserved or "saved" water also have promulgated "no injury" rules as one way to ameliorate third-party impacts. In essence, "no injury" rules mandate that no one be made worse off by the transfer of water. According to Gould, such a requirement "reflects the interdependency of water rights; one user's return flow is another user's source of supply" (Gould, 1995). Consequently, implementing the "no injury" rule may limit the quantity of water that is available for transfer to the historic consumptive use amount. For example, Howe et al. (1986) noted a case involving a proposed transfer by Boulder, Colorado. After all third-party impacts had been ameliorated, Boulder was able to transfer only 18 percent of the total quantity of the water right that it had attempted to transfer.

With regard to the "no injury" rule, Frederick stressed that "the full costs ... of a transfer must be borne by the buyers and sellers" (Frederick, 2001). A number of authors have called for strict regulation of agricultural water transfers in order to prevent or ameliorate third-party impacts (Gleick et al., 2002; Michelsen, 1994; Colby et al., 1993). Weber concurs, noting that the definition of "third-party impacts" is "expanding to include the public interest" and that "[s]tates which allow trades in water do so with many restrictions attached" (Weber, 2001).

The *Model Water Code* addresses third-party impacts by requiring compensation. With regard to permit modifications that would be required to facilitate water transfers, § 7R-2-02(3) provides that if a state "approves a modification even though some adversely affected water right holders have not consented to the modification, the State Agency shall condition approval of the modification upon the payment of adequate compensation to such adversely affected water right holders."[3] Legislation regarding the amelioration of third-party impacts has been enacted in 19 Eastern and Western states (Dellapenna, 2007; ASCE, 2003). Interestingly, Howe notes that California, Wyoming, New Mexico and Utah require community values to be considered in the water transfer review process (Howe, 2000).

Conclusions

The policy conflicts are clear. Water policy in rural America can best be described as inconsistent. In less charitable terms, "schizophrenic" may be the most applicable descriptor. Multiple federal and state water policies provide agriculture a priority in receiving available water supplies. Other federal and state water policies view agriculture as a source of future water supplies needed for municipal, industrial and energy development.

Despite this situation, however, these policy conflicts undoubtedly will be resolved in the future. Water supplies will be reallocated from agriculture to allow for municipal, industrial and energy development.

As noted above with regard to the Central Valley Project Improvement Act, it is quite likely that fees will be imposed on water transfers, and that these fees will be used to remediate the environmental and natural resource damages that resulted from decades of providing water for agriculture irrespective of cost. As Weinberg has noted, the water supply policies of the Bureau of Reclamation resulted in "well-documented allocation inefficiencies" as well as "environmental degradation" (Weinberg, 2002). Improving agricultural water use efficiency and imposing fees on the reallocation of conserved or "saved" water could provide the means to correct this degradation.

However, despite efficiency improvements, water will continue to be used for agricultural production. As the Florida Department of Agriculture and Consumer Services has noted, future rural water policy in America must "ensure that agriculture has access to an adequate quantity of water of sufficient quality to remain competitive in a dynamic global marketplace" (FDACS, 2003).

— *George William Sherk and Jonathan P. Deason*

See also

Conflict, Water; Groundwater; Hydrology; River Engineering; Water Use; Water, Value of; Watersheds; Wetlands

References

American Society of Civil Engineers (ASCE). *Regulated Riparian Model Water Code—ASCE Standard ASCE/EWRI 40-03.* Reston, VA: American Society of Civil Engineers, 2004.

Congressional Budget Office (CBO). *Water Use Conflicts in the West: Implications of Reforming the Bureau of Rec-*

---

[3]Section 1A-1-08 of *Appropriative Rights Model Water Code* provides: "The State shall encourage and enable the sale or other voluntary modification of water rights subject to the protection of third parties and the public interest." (Dellapenna 2007:16)

lamation's Water Supply Policies. Washington, DC: The Congress of the United States, 1997.

Chohin-Kuper, A., T. Rieu, and M. Montginoul. *Water Policy Reforms: Pricing Water, Cost Recovery, Water Demand and Impact on Agriculture. Lessons from the Mediterranean Experience* in *Water Pricing Seminar (June 30–July 2, 2003), Parallel Session C: The Impact of Cost Recovery on Agriculture.* Agencia Catalana del Agua and World Bank Institute, 2003.

Colby, B.G., K. Crandall, and D.B. Bush. "Water Right Transactions: Market Values and Price Dispersion." *Water Resources Research* 29, no. 6 (1993): 1,565-1,572.

Cummings, R.G., et al. *Changing Rules For Agricultural Water Use: Policy Options Related To Metering And Forfeiture For Non-use.* Atlanta, GA: Andrew Young School of Policy Studies, Georgia State University, 2001.

Dellapenna, J.W., ed. *Appropriative Rights Model Water Code.* Reston, VA: American Society of Civil Engineers, 2007.

Florida Department of Agriculture and Consumer Services (FDACS). *Florida's Agricultural Water Policy: Ensuring Resource Availability.* Tallahassee, FL: Florida Department of Agriculture and Consumer Services, 2003.

Fleming, W.M. and G.E. Hall. "Water Conservation Incentives for New Mexico: Policy and Legislative Alternatives." *Natural Resources Journal* 40 (2000): 69-91.

Frederick, K.D. "Water Marketing: Obstacles and Opportunities." *Forum for Applied Research and Public Policy* 19, no. 1 (2001): 54-62.

Gleick, P.H., et al. *The New Economy of Water: The Risks and Benefits of Globalization and Privatization of Fresh Water.* Oakland, CA: The Pacific Institute, 2002.

Gould, G.A. "Recent Developments in the Transfer of Water Rights." In *Water Law: Trends, Policies and Practice.* Edited by K.M. Carr and J.D. Crammond. Chicago, IL: American Bar Association, 1995.

Howe, C.W. "Protecting Public Values in a Water Market Setting: Improving Water Markets to Increase Economic Efficiency and Equity." *University of Denver Water Law Review* 3 (2000): 357-372.

Howe, C.W., D.R. Schurmeier, and W.D. Shaw, Jr. "Innovative Approaches to Water Allocation: The Potential for Water Markets." *Water Resources Research* 22, no. 4 (1986): 439-445.

Michelsen, A.M. "Administrative, Institutional and Structural Characteristics of an Active Water Market." *Water Resources Bulletin* 30, no. 6 (1994: 971-982).

Morandi, L., *Rethinking Western Water Policy: Assessing the Limits of Legislation.* Denver, CO: National Conference of State Legislatures, 1994.

Neuman, J.C. "Symposium on Water Law: Beneficial Use, Waste, and Forfeiture: The Inefficient Search for Efficiency in Western Water Use." *Environmental Law* 28 (1998): 919-996.

Sherk, G.W. "East Meets West: The Tale of Two Water Doctrines." *Water Resources Impact* 5, no. 2 (2003): 5-8.

Sherk, G.W., "Eastern Water Law: Trends in State Legislation." *Virginia Environmental Law Journal* 9 (1990): 287-321.

Tarlock, A.D. *§5:19. Waters subject to appropriation - Saved water* in *Law of Water Rights and Resources.* Eagan, MN: Thomson West, 2005.

Weber, M.L. "Markets for Water Rights under Environmental Constraints." *Journal of Environmental Economics and Management* 42 (2000): 53-64.

Weinberg, M. "Assessing a Policy Grab Bag: Federal Water Policy Reform." *American Journal of Agricultural Economics* 84, no. 3 (2002): 541-556.

Water Use

Water employed as an input to activities or products that people enjoy, including withdrawals from ground or surface water sources for use elsewhere or the enjoyment of water where it is found, such as by fishing or boating in a stream or lake. This article provides an overview of rural water use and associated economic values. Several concerns related to rural water management are described and key policy questions are raised.

Water Use in Rural America

Water is important to the vitality of families, businesses and communities in rural America. It is crucial to rural citizens' health and quality of life. Access to water is a key determinant of where rural people live, opportunities for employment and enjoyment of recreation. Agriculture and many other rural businesses and industries depend on the availability of a high-quality water supply for their survival and growth.

Although water is clearly important to almost every aspect of rural life, less than ideal information is available concerning its use and importance in different regions of the country. Major, regularly tracked rural water uses include domestic uses that are self-supplied by wells or other sources, livestock watering and irrigation of agricultural lands. The most recent effort to estimate water use in the U.S. (Solley et al., 1993) indicates that, first, about 42.8 million people, or about 17 percent of the nation's population, had their own individual water supply systems and withdrew about 3.4 billion gallons of water per day. Almost all (96 percent) of this water was taken from groundwater. Second, water used by livestock includes that associated with traditional products (e.g., meat, poultry, eggs and milk) and animal specialties, primarily fish farming. Such water use amounted to 4.5 billion gallons per day. About 60 percent of these withdrawals were from underground supplies. More than two-thirds of the water used for livestock purposes was for used for consumptive purposes and not returned to water bodies. Third, an estimated 137 billion gallons of water per day were used for irrigation purposes. Irrigation water use includes all water artificially applied to farms and water use in horticultural facilities and golf courses, which may not be located in rural areas. Sixty-three percent of this water came from surface water sources. Irrigation use was highest in the West followed by the Lower Mississippi River and Southern-Gulf regions.

Rural Water Infrastructure

Water is important to rural residents for both water supply and to dispose of domestic wastewater. Based on the 1990 Census, almost 50 percent of households in rural areas (places with 2,500 or fewer people) used individual drilled or dug wells to obtain water. Forty-six percent of rural households receive their water supply from a public or community water system, many of which were small and lacked economies of size in water treatment and distribution.

Generally, rural residents consume more water on average than their urban counterparts. This may be due to differences in needs (e.g., larger yards or gardens), lifestyles or water costs. Many smaller public water rural systems do not meter customers' usage. Metering and price increases are effective ways to increase residential water conservation. Several water demand studies have shown that rural customers are more sensitive to price changes than those in urban areas.

In addition to direct water withdrawal from ground or surface sources, rural residents and businesses use ambient water to dispose of or dilute their liquid wastes. In 1990, about three-quarters of rural households used a septic system or other individual method to treat sewage and other domestic wastewater. Collective or public sewer treatment of wastewater was used by the remaining rural households before discharge into waterways.

The Value of Water

The actual or expected use of water gives rise to its value. The values of water are often not reflected in its price due to imperfect or non-existent markets. Important rural water uses include domestic (either self-supplied or through a community/municipal system), agricultural (livestock and irrigation), industrial and recreational uses. Analysis of residential demand for water indicates that the value of water, at the margin, varies greatly among regions within the U.S. For example, Gibbons (1986) found that households were willing to pay as much as $5 more per year to avoid a 10 percent reduction in water use. For larger possible reductions, willingness to pay was found to be much greater. More recently, researchers documented the value of quality attributes of water supplies. A 1991 study conducted in rural Massachusetts, New York, and Pennsylvania communities found that households were willing to pay between $42 and $81 per year to protect their groundwater supplies (J. Powell, as cited in National Research Council, forthcoming 1997).

Most water used for agricultural purposes occurred on irrigated farms in the Western U.S. Researchers who assessed the extra value added to crop production from irrigation found values ranging from zero to $100 per acre-foot, according to the geographic area and the crop produced. This wide range of values indicates that scarce water has different productivity levels in different agricultural activities. Institutional arrangements that allow shifting water to higher-valued uses do not exist or are not functioning well. Legal and institutional barriers often prevent water reallocation and protect inefficient water uses. As markets for water develop and water rights become more transferable, it is likely that higher-valued uses will bid away water from lower-valued ones. In some populated areas of the West, municipal users purchased the rights of agricultural users leading to reduced irrigation.

The value of water for industrial use depends on the quantity and quality needs of the particular industry. Some industrial users in rural areas, such as cooling power generating plants, consume large water quantities and have the potential to impact other uses, such as recreation on rivers and streams. Contamination of water supplies can also impact industries that require high-quality supplies.

There are possible values of water that exist beyond current actual uses. People may have values for potential future use, or option value, of a water resource. In addition, some individuals are willing to pay to protect a water resource, although they have no intention to use it directly. This category of value is called existence value. Option and existence value for rural water resources may be held by both rural and urban residents.

Current Concerns and Issues

Drinking Water Availability and Safety. Many rural residents lack complete water facilities in their homes and reliable access to a safe water supply for domestic use. Information about rural water conditions is fragmented, so it is difficult to get an accurate overall picture of the problem. The USDA estimates that more than 500,000 rural households do not have complete indoor plumbing. Many such households are located in the poorest and most isolated areas of the U.S., including Appalachia, the lower Mississippi Delta, along the U.S.-Mexico border, and in several American Indian reservations and Alaskan villages. Problems include the need for technical and financial resources to develop water supplies, and the use of cheaper, innovative water treatment approaches. The USDA initiated a new program in 1994 to coordinate and focus public and private efforts on this problem with the goal of providing all rural residents with a reliable supply of clean water by the end of the century.

Rural residents, whether they have their own wells or are connected to a public water system, generally encounter more water quality problems than do urban water consumers. Private wells are generally shallower and often not as well built as public wells, leading to contaminants from the surface entering the well. In addition to natural substances such as iron and manganese found in groundwater, several important categories of human activities can contaminate well water. These include waste disposal, storage and handling of oil and other materials, mining and oil and gas production, and agricultural practices. The most common contaminants from human sources found in well water are bacteria and nitrates. Assessments of rural drinking water wells found that as many as 40 percent of private individual wells are contaminated with coliform bacteria, often due to improperly located or constructed wells. Based on a 1990 nationwide survey of water wells, the U.S. Environmental Protection Agency (EPA) estimated that 4.2 percent of rural domestic wells had detectable levels of commonly used agricultural chemicals, but generally not exceeding health-based standards, for the 10 commonly used pesticides. Nitrates were present in more than half of the well samples, but only in 2.5 percent of the cases did the levels exceed health guidelines (EPA, 1992).

Rural residents who receive water from public community systems also face water quality and reliability problems. Community systems that serve rural residents are smaller, older and in many cases lack the funds and expertise needed to be properly run and maintained. In a national assessment of rural infrastructure needs, nearly one-third of rural systems were found to have unacceptable levels of coliform bacteria (Stinson et al., 1989). Based on its 1990 survey, the EPA estimated that 10.4 percent of rural community wells have detectable levels of pesticides and about 50 percent contained nitrates. Only a very small percentage of wells exceeded the health risk standard for these contaminants.

Affordability. A major issue facing rural residents is the rising cost of water supply and sewage disposal. The 1986 amendments to the federal Safe Drinking Water Act created an expanding list of national safety standards that must be monitored by local water suppliers. These and other requirements pushed the costs of supplying water upward across the nation. The financial impacts of complying with these rules is greatest for small rural systems that lack economies of size and often have management and financial constraints. For example, customers of small water systems can expect to pay $360 to $600 more per year to filter surface water compared to only $72 more per year for large systems. Through the end of this century, small water systems are expected to incur costs of more than $3 billion to comply with new regulations and an additional $20 billion to refurbish and expand infrastructure to deliver safe drinking water (U.S. Government Accounting Office, 1994). Many small communities also have difficulty upgrading wastewater collection and treatment facilities to meeting federally established water quality goals contained in the federal Clean Water Act.

State and local concerns about the high costs to implement some federal laws give rise to local complaints about unfunded mandates. Affordability concerns are central to the debate over reauthorization of several national environmental laws, and influence the decisions of the EPA, USDA and other agencies. Efforts to revise the federal Safe Drinking Water Act have been made. Some of the proposals included increasing infrastructure financing through a state revolving loan fund allowing greater flexibility to states with respect to monitoring and use of alternative treatment technologies targeting financial and technical assistance to needy problem areas, promoting consolidation of small systems, and preventing new systems that are too small to be economically viable from being formed.

Protecting Water Resources. As the cost of the mistakes in water resource management has become evident, scientists and water resource managers developed proactive, comprehensive strategies to better manage the nation's water assets. Such approaches are aimed at both ground- and surface water protection.

Several attributes of groundwater have proven to be economically advantageous and have allowed people to live and work in rural areas. Groundwater can be obtained at the point of use, such as the farm or home. Unlike surface water, no expensive pipes are needed to transport water from the source to the point of use. Also, groundwater has been pure enough, at least in the past, to be used for drinking and cooking purposes with little or no treatment. In many cases, these advantages of groundwater are recognized too late, often only after the resource became contaminated. Actions by individuals who are more widely dispersed can degrade groundwater, although contamination events also may be concentrated at a specific locale. Prevention is a much wiser management approach since cleaning groundwater is very costly and, in some cases, impossible. Policies emerged to change practices that degrade groundwater as awareness of the costs of mistakes in managing groundwater increased. U.S. policy for groundwater quality protection presently is decentralized and largely voluntary in nature. The EPA encouraged states to develop comprehensive ground water protection programs. It encouraged public water suppliers in rural areas to delineate recharge areas for their wells and to manage land use within these areas through its promotion of wellhead protection programs. A critical challenge is the development of collaborative arrangements among local jurisdictions needed to protect groundwater resources since water flow does not respect political boundaries.

Water resources protection efforts are moving in the direction of being more proactive and comprehensive. One important development is the attempt to manage resources on a watershed basis. The existence of many autonomous jurisdictions is a barrier to such a strategy. But, efforts such as the Chesapeake Bay Program indicate that progress can be made to address water resources problems at a more comprehensive, systemic level. A second way water management is becoming more comprehensive is the emergence of consideration of in-stream and extractive water uses in public decisions. In the past, water managers emphasized protection of uses that involved withdrawals of water from surface or underground sources, such as municipal or agricultural uses. In-stream water uses, such as recreational lake fishing or viewing wildlife that depend on wetlands habitats, recently are being recog-

nized. These uses were overlooked because the products or services are often not marketed; therefore, prices are not readily available. Conflicts can occur between users who withdraw water and alter its condition or consume large quantities and those who enjoy in-stream water uses. Those who withdraw water have an advantage in these conflicts because of earlier usage and because such uses are easier to monetarily quantify. A significant challenge for public agencies and institutions is the development of management approaches to balance those of traditional extractive users and those of people who enjoy the in-stream benefits of water resources.

Key Policy Questions

Several underlying questions reappear in rural environmental issues. What should be the resource management goal (i.e., how clean is clean?). What is the appropriate role of government? Who bears the cost and who enjoys the benefits, and who decides? The answer to each question will change as rural areas change or public values shift toward natural and environmental resources (Batie and Diebel, 1990).

Defining the Management Goal. A question at the center of the rural water quantity and quality issue involves the desirable amount of water protection or conservation. In terms of water quality, how pure should water supplies be? In the case of water allocation issues, how much water should each user category be allowed when supplies become scarce? Since human health effects become a consideration in ground- and surface water management and water infrastructure decisions, discussions of management goals translate into the difficult area of defining an acceptable risk.

Role of Government. What is the appropriate role of government in rural water resource management? In a society that places a premium on individual rights and relies on markets to allocate goods and services, a central question involves under what situation is government intervention needed. This question of water use can be restated: do individuals' and firms' actions in response to incentives within the existing market rules result in the best resource use for society? If not, there may be a role for government to change public policies that determine the opportunities and constraints water users face to obtain a result more consistent with broader societal goals. The extent and degree of governmental action to protect water supplies must be balanced against a loss in individuals' rights to use land or water.

Who Bears the Cost? Few things can be obtained without a price; the goal of protecting and conserving rural water resources is not an exception. If rural water supplies are to be protected from farm chemicals contamination, changes in agricultural practices will be required. It can be expected that such changes will have a cost in most cases. Should farmers bear the costs of changes in practices to protect water supplies? If so, what will be the impact on rural businesses and neighbors should the added costs cause the farm to go out of business?

Who Decides? Rural water management policies will be influenced by the participants involved in the policy making process. The level of government that takes action affects who influences decisions. It determines whether the advantages of basin or watershed water management on a more comprehensive basis are realized. Federal officials previously took the lead in setting standards for drinking water provided by public water systems and guidelines for discharges into the nation's water. Other programs, such as the EPA's program to protect groundwater, put state and local authorities in the lead position. In the 1990s, the trend is toward giving more responsibility for decision making to the state and local leaders. In many cases, an attempt is made to balance the influence and interests of various publics and decision makers. With change and new information about impacts of government programs that affect water, the sharing of decision making authority will be renegotiated over time. In addition, the choice of which agency will make decisions about program details is crucial. This decision affects how water resources are used and resultant benefits and burdens for different rural and, in many cases, urban interests.

— *Charles W. Abdalla*

See also

Agriculture, Hydroponic; Aquaculture; Conservation, Water; Environmental Regulations; Groundwater; Hydrology; Irrigation; Natural Resource Economics; Policy, Environmental; River Engineering; Recreational Activities; Water, Value of; Watersheds; Wetlands

References

Batie, Sandra S. and Penelope L. Diebel. "Key Policy Choices in Groundwater Quality Management." *Journal of Soil and Water Conservation* 45, no. 2 (1990): 194-197.

Gibbons, Diana C. *The Economic Value of Water.* Washington, DC: Resources for the Future, 1986.

National Research Council. *Valuing Ground Water.* Washington, DC: Water Science and Technology Board, Commission on Geosciences, Environment and Resources (forthcoming 1997).

Solley, Wayne B., Robert R. Pierce, and Howard A. Perlman. *Estimated Use of Water in the United States in 1990.* Circular 1081. Alexandria, VA: U.S. Geological Survey, 1993.

Stinson, Thomas F., Patrick J. Sullivan, Barry Ryan and Norman A. Reid. *Public Water Supply in Rural Communities: Results from the National Rural Communities Facilities Assessment Study.* Staff Report No. AGES 89-4. Washington, DC: U.S. Department of Agriculture, 1989.

U.S. Bureau of the Census, *1990 Census of Housing, Detailed Housing Characteristics.* Washington, DC: U.S. Department of Commerce, Bureau of the Census, 1993.

U.S. Environmental Protection Agency. *Another Look: National Survey of Pesticides In Drinking Water Wells (Phase 2 Report).* Report No. 570/9-91-020 (January). Washington, DC: U.S. Environmental Protection Agency, Office of Water, 1992.

U.S. Government Accounting Office. *Drinking Water: Stronger Efforts Essential for Small Communities to Comply with Standards.* Report No. US GAO/RCED-94-40. Washington, DC: U.S. Government Accounting Office, 1994.

Water, Value of

Benefit gained when water is used to satisfy a variety of human needs. Rural America relies on groundwater and surface water for living, working and playing, but droughts, floods and geography lead to large variations in the supply of water over time and space. In order to make good decisions about water quantity and water quality issues, it is important to understand the value of water. Water is valuable because there is not enough water to simultaneously satisfy the many competing demands. The quantity and quality of fresh water resources, including both groundwater (e.g., underground aquifers) and surface water (e.g., lakes, rivers and streams), significantly impact life in rural America. At the same time, human activity often impacts the quantity and quality of water available in a given time and place. This entry identifies several important functions of water in rural America, defines the economic value of water, and describes several methods for estimating the value of a change in water quantity or quality.

The Demand for Water in Rural America

Often the first thing people think of when considering rural water demand is irrigation. The benefit of irrigation is obvious; it increases the amount of land suitable for agricultural production. Irrigation needs depend on climate, soil characteristics and the type of crop, but the need for irrigation water is often a key element of water resource discussions in rural areas. Irrigation water comes from both groundwater and surface water sources. Some small ponds and lakes are owned by a single farmer, but most sources must be shared by multiple users, increasing the potential for conflict. Regardless of ownership, diverting water for irrigation clearly reduces the quantity of water available for other needs. However, agricultural activity can also impact the quality of water. As water runs off fields and pasture, it carries fertilizer and animal waste into nearby lakes and streams. This increases nutrient levels (mainly nitrogen and phosphorous) and algae production which can have many negative effects on fish populations and human health.

Drinking water is another important element of rural water demand. Almost all drinking water in rural areas is groundwater, and much of this comes from individual wells. While municipal drinking water is generally treated and distributed from a central source, the quality of drinking water in rural areas is more difficult to assess and improve. Many organizations and agencies help rural residents test their well water for contaminants and provide information about activities that might degrade the water supply, such as inappropriate disposal of chemicals.

A third component of water demand that is important in some rural areas is industrial water use. Industries such as pulp and paper, food and beverage, mining, and petroleum refining use water directly or indirectly in their production process. In rural areas, a single factory or plant may constitute a large share of local economic activity, the loss of which would be difficult to recover from. The most common industrial water use is for power generation. In addition to hydropower generation, water is used for cooling in thermoelectric and nuclear power plants. While most of the water extracted for cooling purposes is returned to the watershed, there are some concerns related to pockets of increased water temperatures. While water for hydropower is not removed from the source, dams and reservoirs alter environments upstream and down. Whether these changes are benefits or costs depends on one's perspective; filling a reservoir might destroy wetland habitat but create recreational opportunities and stabilize agricultural water supplies.

Many Americans enjoy water-based recreation activities such as fishing, boating, swimming and waterfowl hunting. Maintaining water quantity and quality levels needed to sustain these activities is a fourth major element of water demand in rural areas. Recreational needs are an "instream" use, meaning water is not removed from the source. In the Western U.S. water rights were not historically granted for instream use, but this is changing. Increasingly, courts are recognizing the importance of water-based recreation and in some cases are granting rights to these types of users.

A fifth category of water demand relates to the importance of water in maintaining essential ecological functions and processes. Recent approaches to natural resource management have centered on the provision of ecosystem goods and services. These include both the material goods and the processes provided by nature that are of value to humans. Providing water for irrigation, drinking, industry and recreation are all examples of ecosystem goods and services, but these are not the only examples. Decisions that lead to changes in water quantity or water quality may threaten habitat for aquatic and wetland species, increase the risk of water-borne disease, impact the frequency of floods and related crop damage, and impact soil erosion rates and nutrient cycling processes. Though these water needs are not always transparent, they are no less important.

Defining the Economic Value of Water

The economic value of water, or improved water quality, is equal to the value of what we would be willing to give up to have more, or cleaner, water. There are many components to this definition of value. Part of the total value of water is a use value, or a value associated with all the consumptive and non-consumptive (or instream) uses of water described above. Consumptive use is any use that removes water from its source and does not return it in a relatively short amount of time. Drinking and irrigation are consumptive uses of water. Recreational boating provides non-consumptive, and also non-market, value. Even though the boater is not withdrawing the water or using it in the production of something with monetary value, the lake is a source of enjoyment and pleasure, and this is an important component of the total economic value of water.

In addition to use value, there are non-use values of water in some situations. Non-use (or passive use) value is the benefit provided by water even if the water is not used. Non-use value is often attributed to existence value, bequest value, or option value. Existence values capture the benefit from simply knowing that an environmental resource exists. For example, wetlands in the rural U.S. are an important habitat for many endangered species of birds. An individual might value the existence of these wetlands as an important bird habitat, though they will never visit the wetland or view the bird. Bequest value captures the value in knowing future generations will be able to enjoy a particular resource. Many people would like to protect their favorite fishing spot so their children and grandchildren might also be able to fish the same spot. Option value is related to the value of having the option to make a decision in the future. For example, building a dam to provide hydropower is an irreversible decision with uncertain benefits and costs. There may be value in waiting until the uncertainty is resolved to make a decision. In some cases, non-use values of water resources are a major component of the total economic value, but these values are more difficult to estimate and therefore more difficult to incorporate into water management decisions.

Estimating the Value of Changes in Water Quantity and Quality

The often competing demands of water make it difficult to determine the "best" use (or non-use) of our limited water resources. Private decisions and public policies often define the best decision as the one that maximizes the use and non-use value of the water, but it is difficult to compare the different water needs. Is the value of irrigation water less than the value of leaving water in a river to protect recreational fishing? Economists have developed several methods for water valuation, or estimating the value of water in monetary terms. A monetary value provides a common scale of measurement, making it easier to compare disparate values. Valuation methods are used to evaluate the change in value due to a change in water quantity or quality. That is, rather than estimating the "value of water" per se, these methods might estimate the loss in benefits due to a reduction in the amount of water used for irrigation. This is consistent with the main objective of economic valuation which is to evaluate proposed policies or decisions that will alter water quantity or quality.

In some cases, a market or market-like system exists in which the right to withdraw or use water can be traded. In these cases, the value of a small increase in water quantity may be inferred from the price of water or a water permit. This method of valuation requires complete understanding of initial water rights, a mechanism for exchanging these rights, and many buyers and sellers who are fully aware of their own value of the water. For example, in order for permit price to reflect the true value of water, farmers selling irrigation permits must know how forgoing irrigation water will affect crop values. Griffin (2006) describes how water marketing and water banks (market-like systems in which a public agency acts as a broker) work and provides several examples of water markets in the U.S.

In many cases there is no price from which the value of water can be inferred. In these situations, non-market valuation methods can be used. These methods are so named because they are used to estimate the value of goods that are not traded in markets. The remainder of this entry describes three general methods that are commonly used to estimate the value of changes in water quantity and water quality in the absence of market prices of water: production methods, revealed preference methods, and stated preference methods.

When water is used as an input in the production of another good, the value of water can be inferred from information about the production process. Consider the value of irrigation water. If the relationship between water use and crop production is fully understood, and the prices of the output (the crop) and all other inputs (e.g., labor, energy and fertilizer) are known, the value of water to crop production can be calculated even if the water is obtained for free. Young (2005) summarizes these methods and suggests ways of overcoming challenges associated with their application.

Revealed preference methods use observations of individuals or households in a market activity related to water resources to estimate the value of a change in water quantity or quality. The two most common revealed preference methods are the hedonic property method and the travel cost method. The hedonic property method uses property sales data to estimate the impact of water resource changes. If two properties are identical in every way except for the quantity or quality of water associated with the property, any difference in property sales price can be attributed to the value of the difference in water. Applications of the hedonic property method have found positive values associated with increased lake levels and improved water quality, as measured by water clarity, bacterial count and a variety of other criteria. The hedonic method has also been used to estimate the value of irrigation water by comparing the value of farms sold with irrigation permits to those sold without.

Another common revealed preference method is the travel cost method, which is frequently used to estimate the value of water for recreation. The travel cost method bases its value estimates on observations of individuals' recreation decisions. For example, if a boater is willing to travel to a more distant location to boat simply because the water quality is better, the value of the improved water quality is directly related to the value of the additional travel time and expense. Hundreds of travel cost studies have been conducted, with many of these estimating the value of water-based recreation in rural areas.

Another class of valuation methods is stated preference methods, including the contingent valuation method and stated choice (or conjoint analysis). These methods rely on data from carefully designed surveys to directly elicit individuals' willingness to pay for changes in water quantity or quality. These methods require the investigator to develop a hypothetical scenario that involves a change in water quantity or quality. After describing the scenario, the survey asks respondents one or more questions about how they would make decisions involving tradeoffs between the water resource and other things, including money, in the hypothetical scenario. Results are then analyzed to determine the expected willingness to pay per person. Stated preference methods were first developed over 50 years ago and have since been used in countless studies to estimate all types of water resource values, such as the value of quality and quantity improvements for recreation, aesthetics, existence value and drinking water.

Champ et al. (2003) and Freeman (2003) offer a more detailed description of revealed and stated preference methods. While the tendency in the literature appears to favor revealed preference methods over stated preference, both methods have advantages and limitations. For example, revealed preference studies do not require the researcher to develop a hypothetical scenario, but generally only capture the values attributable to property owners or recreational users. They cannot measure non-use values, which might comprise a large portion of the total value. When trying to estimate the value of a change in water quantity or quality, it is important to understand all of the inherent assumptions and limitations of each approach and choose the method that best matches the problem and data available.

— *Rebecca L. Moore*

See also

Agricultural and Applies Economics; Conflict, Water; Conservation, Water; Natural Resources Management; Water Policy; Water Use; Watersheds

References

Brown, Thomas C., John C. Bergstrom, and John B. Loomis. "Defining, Valuing, and Providing Ecosystem Goods and Services." *Natural Resources Journal* 47, no. 2 (2007): 329-376.

Champ, Patricia A., Kevin J. Boyle, and Thomas C. Brown. *A Primer on Nonmarket Valuation: The Economics of Non-Market Goods and Resources.* Boston, MA: Kluwer Academic Publishers, 2003.

Freeman, A. Myrick, III. *The Measurement of Environmental and Resource Values: Theory and Methods.* Washington, DC: Resources for the Future, 2003.

Griffin, Ronald C. *Water Resource Economics: The Analysis of Scarcity, Policies, and Project.* Cambridge, MA: MIT Press, 2006.

Mitchell, R., and R. Carson. *Using Surveys to Value Public Goods: The Contingent Valuation Method.* Washington, DC: Resources for the Future, 1989.

Shaw, W. Douglass. *Water Resource Economics and Policy: An Introduction.* Cheltenham, UK: Edward Elgar, 2005.

Young, Robert A. *Determining the Economic Value of Water: Concepts and Methods.* Washington, DC: Resources for the Future, 2005.

Watersheds

Topographically delineated units of land that is defined as the area above some point in a stream or river that drains to that point. Within the boundaries of a watershed, precipitation is transformed into a flowing stream that begins its journey to the ocean. Watersheds help us understand how people's use of the land influences soil and water and how these effects are connected to impacts on downstream areas. Recognizing this hydrologic connection is essential for understanding the importance and value of rural watersheds. Watershed boundaries and the upland-downstream connections are not always apparent to people living and working in rural uplands or in downstream areas. Through experience, however, we see that expanding populations in rural areas and their increasing demands on land and water resources can dramatically affect large numbers of people living in uplands and downstream areas alike. Watersheds, therefore, not only represent hydrologic units, but they are exceptionally well suited for determining environmental, financial and social consequences of people's use of land and water. As such, watersheds provide a unique system and framework suitable for planning, developing and managing land and water resources.

Watersheds vary in scale from small areas that drain into a headwater stream, lake or wetland, to large river basins, such as the Mississippi, Colorado and Columbia River basins. The term *catchment* is used often when describing small watersheds, such as the uppermost headwater catchments of rivers. The majority of flow in major rivers, as much as 70 to 80 percent, originates in headwater catchments. In describing watersheds and their relation to one another, they can be classified on the basis of their hierarchy within a river basin. A first order watershed is one that contains an unbranched stream, called a first order stream. The confluence of two first order streams form a second order stream; the confluence of two second order streams form a third order stream, and so forth. The watershed that contributes flow to a stream of a particular order has the same order number as its stream. As stream and watershed order increase, the size of each increases as well. River basins are large order watersheds representing the sum of all watersheds contributing flow to the river. As a result, the flow of water at the mouth of rivers represents the cumulative response from all its watersheds.

The amount, timing and quality of water flowing in a stream are the product of the climatic regime, geology, topography, soils, vegetative cover and uses of the land that occur within the watershed. Consequently, each watershed has its unique hydrologic and water quality *fingerprint*. The hydrologic fingerprints of watersheds vary considerably across rural America. However, a common thread that runs through these rural watersheds is people's dependence on them for goods and services. People living in the West depend on snowmelt runoff from mountainous watersheds for their water supply. Municipal watersheds in the East provide drinking water for most major cities. The Midwest is the nation's breadbasket, yet watershed transformations of prairies, forests and wetlands into productive croplands have brought environmental consequences. The cumulative effects of land conversions to intensive cropping and urbanization in the Mississippi River basin have contributed to hypoxia, or the dead zone, in the Gulf of Mexico. The export of nitrate nitrogen from rural agricultural watersheds is a major contributor to hypoxia in the Gulf. This is an example of how people's actions in rural watersheds can dramatically impact people living far downstream, in this case fishermen in the Gulf of Mexico. Similar connections between people's use of the land and their downstream consequences can be seen across America. States are faced with the imposing challenge of identifying and mitigating impaired waters in rural watersheds to meet the goals of the Clean Water Act. Furthermore, there are instances of expanding urban centers, transportation systems and home site development in rural watersheds that increase runoff, sediment transport and flooding of downstream communities. All of these reflect a changing rural landscape with downstream environmental consequences and economic impacts. A watershed perspective is needed if they are to be adequately addressed. In seeking solutions to such problems, or better yet, avoiding problems in the first place, natural processes and responses of watersheds must be understood. With this understanding, attention can be focused on modifying human behavior on the land that results in the impairment of land and water.

The hydrologic cycle operates in watersheds irrespective of human activities. Climate and precipitation regimes interact on watersheds to generate streamflow, the magnitude and character of which varies dramatically across rural watersheds. The amount, duration and intensity of rainfall and snowmelt largely determine the occurrence and magnitude of floods from any particular watershed. Importantly, the soils, vegetative cover, land slope and amount of impervious areas in a watershed play a role in mitigating the amount of precipitation that becomes runoff and streamflow. Floods occur when the flow in a stream channel exceeds its banks. When streamflow levels are at or exceed bank full conditions, the velocity and amount of flowing water has increasing power to pick up and transport sediment, rocks, debris and other material. It is important for people to realize that floods occur naturally and that most streams average at least one flood per year. Although floods are extreme events, they are not rare. Watershed inhabitants should expect, and plan for, the occurrence of floods when pursuing development in watersheds.

High flows, particularly at bank full levels or during floods, play an important role in moving sediment and thereby developing and shaping stream channels and their valleys. Runoff from storms erodes uplands, flood waters work to erode and transport sediment in channels. Sediment that is transported in the channel becomes deposited in floodplains and in locations where the stream gradient (slope) is low, such as the mouths of rivers. Sediment movement is episodic. Most sediment is transported during peak flood flows and deposited when flood waters recede. As flood waters leave their channels, new channels can be formed and old channels abandoned. This process is repeated over eons, lowering and widening valleys in the watershed. Land use in the watershed that changes the frequency or magnitude of flooding, or that modifies the stream channel, can affect the stability of stream channels. Unstable stream channels have excessive bank erosion and can contribute to high levels of sediment in streamflow.

Low flows that occur in a watershed, as with high flows, are the product of watershed characteristics and climate. Rural watersheds have varying streamflow responses during dry seasons. Streams that flow year round—perennial streams—are fed by groundwater and provide valuable aquatic habitat and a stable supply of water for human use. Stream channels in drylands typically have little or no flow during their prolonged dry seasons. Yet streams in drylands, with deeper groundwater commonly being present in adjacent floodplains, are heavily exploited to meet water supply needs in these water poor areas.

Whether flows are high or low, streams carry many forms of matter, including sediment, minerals, nutrients and chemicals associated with human activities on the land. Being an excellent solvent, water dissolves many of the minerals and nutrients that exist in a watershed. Because groundwater is in direct contact with soils and geologic strata over long time periods, it is richer in dissolved minerals than water that enters streams from surface runoff. As a result, dissolved minerals in streamflow vary seasonally in relation to changing magnitudes of flow. Interactions between streamflow, its channel, floodplain and its riparian area, influence suspended sediment and nutrient concentrations, water temperature, dissolved oxygen and aquatic habitat. As the transition area between land and water bodies, *riparian* areas provide valuable habitat and are particularly sensitive to land use activities. Consequently, riparian areas become the focus of programs aimed at protecting water quality and aquatic habitat.

Prior to European settlement in North America, rural watersheds were cloaked in native vegetation, with forests dominating the wettest areas, sparse plant cover in deserts, and prairie grasslands in the intermediate precipitation regimes. The amount, quality and pattern of flow from watersheds were strongly influenced by native vegetative cover and soils, yet also tempered by the local topography and geologic setting. Dryland watersheds, with sparse vegetation and thin soils, produce surface runoff and flash floods from high-intensity rainstorms, yet their channels are dry most of the year. In contrast, forested watersheds produce flow that is less erratic over the year, with their highest flows, or *peak* flows, being of a lower magnitude than those produced from watersheds in which forest cover has been removed and converted to crops, pastures or urban areas.

Rural watersheds in America have undergone considerable change since European settlement, as noted earlier. Yet rural Americans remain closely connected to their land and water resources—they perhaps see more clearly than their urban counterparts how their use of the land affects water and how water can impact the landscape. Farmers, ranchers and foresters are examples of people who depend directly on land and water and the sustainability of these resources for their livelihood. Creeping urbanization, increasing demands for resources and services, and climate change will undoubtedly change rural watersheds and the character of watershed inhabitants. Road construction, mining, timber harvesting, intensive agricultural practices, increasing demands for recreational opportunities, and urbanization are the agents of change. Changing rural landscapes and the uncertainty of climatic variability raise imposing challenges to people living in rural watersheds. The existence of upstream-downstream linkages and the likelihood of greater financial and environmental impacts caused by degraded watersheds make the case for planning and management resources through the "lens" of a watershed.

Managing land and water resources in a sustainable manner and with a watershed perspective is the essence of *integrated watershed management (IWM)*. Taking an IWM approach, resource use and development take place with the recognition that watersheds provide the goods and services that people need from the land, yet must be accomplished in a manner that does not harm the soil, water and aquatic ecosystems. Otherwise, uses of land and water can diminish the long-term productivity of uplands and adversely affect the flow and quality of water reaching people downstream. Integrated watershed management permits a comprehensive understanding of how people's use of land and water in uplands affects those living downstream. The question is, Who will perform this integrated watershed management? The answer must include all watershed inhabitants and those who depend on the products and services provided by watersheds.

Achieving IWM in most rural watersheds is constrained by the reality that communities and agencies responsible for managing land and/or water rarely are organized around watershed boundaries. Because water flows downhill and downstream regardless of political or property boundaries, conflicts have arisen among land users and downstream communities in the past. Resolving or avoiding such conflicts provides good justification for using watersheds as units for planning, developing and managing land and water resources.

Grassroots organizations in local communities, watershed management districts, and river basin commissions have been formed to resolve conflicts and reconcile political-watershed boundary issues. These organizations work with countless local, state and federal agencies that have varying degrees of responsibility for land and water management within and across watersheds. Cooperation and collaboration among the myriad of watershed inhabitants and organizations is essential to resolve conflicts and achieve the goals of improved land and water management. Inequities among those who pay for, and those who benefit from, improved watershed conditions need to be addressed in any watershed management arrangement. Ultimately, achieving the goals of healthy and productive watersheds and clean water resides with the people who work the land. They are the people who directly influence land use and the development of land and water. They are the true managers of watersheds in rural America whose actions will determine the sustainability of land and water resources for future generations.

— *Kenneth N. Brooks*

See also

Conflict, Water; Conservation, Water; Hydrology; Policy, Water; Regional Diversity; Water, Value of; Water Use; Wetlands

References

Black, Peter E. *Watershed Hydrology*. Englewood Cliffs, NJ: Prentice Hall, 1991.

Brooks, Kenneth N., Peter F. Ffolliott, Hans M. Gregersen and Leonard F. DeBano. *Hydrology and the Management of Watersheds*, 3rd ed. Ames, IA: Iowa State Press, 2003.

Calder, Ian R. *Blue Revolution—Integrated Land and Water Resource Management*. London: Earthscan, 2005.

Committee on Watershed Management/National Research Council (CWM/NRC). *New Strategies for America's Watersheds*. Washington DC: National Academies Press, 1999.

de la Cretaz, Avril L. and Paul K. Barten. *Land Use Effects on Streamflow and Water Quality in the Northeastern United States*. Boca Raton, FL: CRC Press, 2007.

Gregersen, Hans M., Peter F. Ffolliott, and Kenneth N. Brooks. *Integrated Watershed Management—Connecting People to Their Land and Water*. Oxfordshire, UK: CAB International, 2007.

Satterlund, Donald R. and Paul W. Adams. *Wildland Watershed Management*, 2nd ed. New York: John Wiley & Sons, 1992.

Weather

A set of global atmospheric phenomena that are, in many cases, of great importance to the biota of the rural U.S. This article includes a general description of atmospheric science, weather prediction, climate change and air pollution, biometeorology, biomicrometeorology, agricultural meteorology, microclimatology, and severe and unusual weather. Weather prediction, agricultural meteorology and biometeorology, are emphasized because these topics are especially relevant to rural areas.

Atmospheric Science

Numerous variables are used to quantify atmospheric science and describe the phenomena such as temperature, precipitation type and amount, humidity, radiation and others described below. The study of fluid dynamics and mechanics is used to describe and predict atmospheric flow patterns that determine day-to-day weather. The interaction among atmospheric flow patterns, heating and cooling of the Earth's surface by radiation, and evaporation and condensation of water is complex and still not fully understood. Supercomputers are needed to predict weather with reasonable accuracy, and can be used to predict detailed weather conditions on the regional scale. Severe weather such as tornadoes and hail can impact agricultural activities, as can less spectacular phenomena such as extremes in temperature and precipitation. Finally, human activities can result in alteration of the atmospheric composition, commonly thought of as air pollution, which can impact rural regions.

Biomicrometeorological tower with sensors measuring evapotranspiration, carbon dioxide exchange, wind speed, wind direction, turbulence, air temperature and humidity, run by the University of California, Davis, Department of Land, Air and Water Resources.

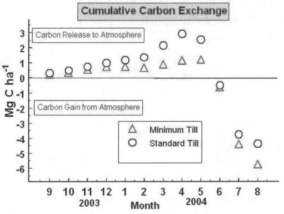

Estimates of cumulative carbon absorbed by a maize (Zea mays) agroecosystem under two different tillage regimes, minimum till and standard till. The minimum till treatment absorbs more carbon than the standard till, partly because of greater weed growth before crop planting absorbing carbon dioxide in the minimum till field.

The major variables used in atmospheric science are temperature, humidity, wind velocity (speed and direction), pressure, precipitation amount and type, radiation, sky cover, evaporation and composition of the atmosphere. In the U.S., temperature is frequently measured in units of degrees Fahrenheit (°F), humidity in units of dew point temperature (°F) or percent (relative humidity), precipitation and evaporation in inches falling on or evaporating from the ground, and radiation in Watts falling on a meter squared. Scientists and most countries except the U.S. use the units of degrees Celsius (°C) for air temperature and dew point temperature and millimeters or meters for precipitation and evaporation.

Weather is composed of 1) the fluid dynamics of the atmosphere, coupled with 2) the thermodynamics of evaporation, condensation and precipitation, and 3) heating and cooling by radiation. Evaporation uses some of the radiative (solar) energy gained by the Earth's surface. This energy is later released to the atmosphere when condensation occurs. Pressure differences, associated with differential heating by radiation (such as land-ocean differences), drive the wind patterns of weather.

Weather Prediction and Recent Technological Advances

Complex calculus equations (partial differential equations), which may be solved by computers, may be used to describe fluid flow at the scale of a field of crops or a forest (Meyers and Paw U, 1987) or at larger regional (Pyles et al., 2000) or even global scales. The numerical solution of equations describing the three main types of processes mentioned in the previous paragraph are used to predict weather. Predictions are made for a range of times in the future, from a few hours ranging to hundreds of years. The accuracy of such predictions, when made for less than a week in the future, is excellent. It improved over the past quarter century, when computers and satellites played an increasing role. However, because precipitation is highly variable on a horizontal area basis, frequently at scales smaller than resolvable by the numerical models, for any particular location in a rural area errors may occur even when regionally accurate forecasts are made.

Recent technological advances include Doppler radar, the National Weather Service's NEXt general RADar (NEXRAD) program, which has the capability to accurately observe precipitation and the wind velocity field. This allows NEXRAD radars to be used for increased accuracy in tornado warnings.

Several general methods are available for non-atmospheric scientists who wish to predict weather based on the type of information commonly available from the Internet, broadcast and print media. The first prediction method is based on assuming the weather tomorrow will be the same as today's; this method is called persistence forecasting. A related method is to assume that weather systems, which generally move from west to east, will continue to move at the same speed as they have in the past; this method is called continuity. Both these methods suffer from inaccuracy caused by the increase or decrease in intensity of pressure systems, which are not accounted for. Another popular method in rural areas is to use historical climatological records to predict the weather of any particular day.

Numerical forecasts, made up to a week in advance and disseminated by the National Weather Service, are usually more accurate than climatology. Forecasts made for longer periods in the future, by numerical methods or by individuals, are generally no more accurate than climatological predictions. Mathematical chaos theory indicates that limits exist on the ability of computers to predict weather too far into the future.

Climate Change and Air Pollution

Atmospheric pollution occurs mainly because of combustion processes and other human activities, although some biogenic chemicals are also released from microbes, plants and animals. The main pollutant problems in rural areas arise from secondary pollutants, which are transformed from the primary pollutants directly emitted into the atmosphere. Rural areas may be affected by acidic precipitation (acid rain), high ozone (O_3) concentrations close to the ground, and elevated particulate levels. Stratospheric ozone depletion by chlorofluorocarbons also impacts biota by letting in more damaging ultraviolet radiation. The stratospheric ozone depletion is greatest at high latitudes.

Computer simulations of the world's climate show that if the concentration of certain gases, such as carbon dioxide (CO_2), methane (CH_4), and nitrogen compounds, continue to increase, mainly because of human activities, the average temperature of the air near the surface of the globe will increase by several degrees Celsius over the next 100 years (IPCC, 2007). Climatological records confirm model simulations, indicating a warming trend of 0.7°C (1.3°F) in the last century (IPCC, 2007). Other predicted changes have been confirmed with observations, such as an increase in the sea level by melting glaciers and ice caps.

Specific rural localities may have much greater temperature changes, especially at higher latitudes, or little change at all, because of the complexities of local climatology and the statistical variability of weather. In general, it is predicted that the U.S. Grain Belt will become warmer and Canadian rural locations will become a more ideal location for certain crops. A number of studies have suggested some plants could increase their growth because of increased CO_2 concentrations (Tubiello et al., 2007), but it should be noted that the competition between weed and agricultural species, plant host-pest interactions, and nutrient limitations may be altered with increased CO_2 concentrations coupled with climate change, and plants may also adapt to the integrated climate changes such that there is no net increase, or even a decrease in plant growth and crop yield (Rosenberg et al., 1980; McKenney et al., 1992; Patterson et al., 1999; McMichael, 2001; Shaw et al., 2002; Fuhrer, 2003; Sehgal et al., 2006; Xiong et al., 2007). Phenological changes in the timing of different life stages of crop, orchard, other plants and animals are also predicted, including growing seasons and frost-free periods.

The models used in these global climatic simulations are called General Circulation Models (GCMs). These models have been shown to yield reasonable distributions of temperature and pressure, and less accurate distributions of precipitation, when used to simulate current climatology. They are based on very large numerical grids, such that only a few grid points are used to describe even a state as large as California. Therefore, topological effects and localized climatology are not well described by such models. Recent advances in computer power have allowed the coupling of regional scale and even field models with GCM output to allow some assessment of localized effects (Pyles et al., 2000), but the accuracy of these interpolations is not established.

Biometeorology, Biomicrometeorology and Agricultural Meteorology

The intimate interaction between biota (animals and plants) and the atmosphere is called biometeorology. When applied to agriculture, biometeorology is more specifically called agricultural meteorology, and when applied to small-scale interactions (for example, fields of crops) between biota and the atmosphere (such as turbulent exchange of water vapor and carbon dioxide between plants and the atmosphere), the term biomicrometeorology is used. For several millennia, people recognized the importance of weather and climate in controlling the location and abundance of plant and animal as food, building material, and tool sources (Tromp, 1980). It is generally recognized that atmospheric composition and its mean temperature have been influenced by biotic evolution. Atmospheric oxygen (O_2 is mainly the result of photosynthesis, and the greatly reduced carbon dioxide concentration compared to Venus is to some extent caused by photosynthetic activity. The net result is a moderate temperature ideal for life on Earth.

The importance of biometeorology has led to an extensive mythology in virtually all rural cultures. Many aspects of mythology appear to contain elements of scientific observations within them. One example is the counting of cricket chirps to obtain temperature, which is relatively accurate when calibrated for a particular cricket species. Other myths have little scientific support, such as Groundhog Day and woolly caterpillars having more fur before a harsh winter. Although many animals, including insects and small mammals, prepare for winter in a variety of physiological ways, this preparation is dependent on seasonality rather than some innate predictive ability.

Biometeorological indices that are used in rural regions include Growing Degree Days (GDD), which represent the linear integration of mean temperature above some threshold, with respect to time measured in days. GDDs are used to analyze and predict the stage (phenophase) of crop and plant growth and yield. A form of GDD is used by entomologists to predict the timing of insect plant pests and their populations. A related measure, Heating Degree Days, is used to determine energy usage in buildings. Other temperature-related indices include the first date of frost and thaw based on climatological records or long-term climatological predictions.

The hours of sunshine and intensity of visible light are linked closely to photosynthetic rates, and therefore plant growth. Areas where the growing season is relatively cloud-free, such as the Central Valley region of California, result in opportunities for large crop yields. Solar radiation in the ultraviolet range can be harmful not only to some plants, but also to plant diseases and pests.

The photoperiod of plants and some animals represents the daylength or change of daylength that is sensed by these organisms to cue into changes in season. The accumulated night length (scotophase) is biochemically measured by the plant chemical phytochrome. A long-day plant is one that senses a day is longer than some threshold, and a short-day plant is one that senses a day shorter than some threshold.

Some biometeorological indices are used to gauge the health of plants and animals. The potential evapotranspiration, defined as the water loss by evaporative processes from a short grass plant canopy with no water stress, is used to measure evaporative demand in rural areas, and therefore as an aid to irrigation scheduling and water management. Combined temperature and humidity indices are used to quantify the thermal stress to humans and animals. Increased thermal stress to animals, for example, can lead to reduced weight gain, increased morbidity and mortality, and reduced milk production.

One biometeorological index used for humans is the Wind Chill Index (WCI) and the Wind Chill Equivalent Temperature (WCET and WCT). The WCI is a dry heat (energy) loss index, indicating wind conditions under which metabolic rate cannot keep up with advective heat loss, resulting in frostbite and other detrimental cold damage to exposed human extremities. The WCET (also called the WCT) represents the temperature to which a thermostat in an almost wind-free room would have to be set for the heat loss from a human face to match the heat loss occurring for the face exposed to an ambient wind at the ambient air temperature (Osczevski and Bluestein, 2005). The WCI and WCET do not account for radiational effects or phase changes effects such as evaporative cooling of the skin (Steadman, 1971).

Microclimatology

The microclimatology of a locality is frequently unique. The typical profile with height or horizontal position of variables such as wind speed, air temperature, humidity and radiation may follow a similar diurnal pattern each day of a season, or may change because of changes in plant cover and atmospheric variables.

Microclimate modification may be accomplished to improve plant productivity. Irrigation is one of the oldest methods of modification, providing water where precipitation is not sufficient. Another well-known method is that of windbreaks, which shield crops from adverse wind speeds, and reduce eolian soil loss. Mulches are used to cover soil and crops to suppress weed formation and water loss. Frost protection methods use large fans, combustion heaters (smudge pots), sprinkler systems, and soil flooding and compaction (Rosenberg et al., 1980). The drift of aerial applications of agricultural chemicals represents modification of the local atmospheric chemistry.

Severe, Unusual and Extreme Weather

Severe weather and unusual events may seriously affect agricultural operations in the rural U.S. High winds, associated with severe storms, hurricanes, hail and tornadoes, may lodge or damage crops, injure or kill humans and other animals, blow trees over, and damage rural buildings. Frost occurrence may damage crops and trees. Excess precipitation may flood regions, cause the soil to be too wet for agricultural operations, and damage plant organs at critical phenophases, such as the flower bud stage. Too much snow may break branches of orchard or other trees. Excessive snow may also damage telephone lines and prevent driving on roads until the road is plowed. Too little precipitation may cause serious damage, also, when droughts are lengthy enough to cause plants to be stressed or even die. Lightning is the leading cause of weather-related deaths in the U.S., and causes forest fires.

— *Kyaw Tha Paw U*

See also

Drought; Solar Energy; Wind Energy

References

Fuhrer, J. "Agroecosystem Responses to Combinations of Elevated CO_2 Ozone, and Global Climate Change." *Agriculture Ecosystems and Environment* 97 (2003): 1-20.

Intergovernmental Panel on Climate Change (IPCC). *Climate Change 2007: Synthesis Report. Contribution of Working Groups I, II, and III to the Fourth Assessment Report of the Intergovernmental Panel on Climate Change.* Edited by Core Writing Team, R.K. Pachauri and E. Reisinger. Geneva, Switzerland: Intergovernmental Panel on Climate Change, 2007.

Jones, Hamlyn G. *Plants and Microclimate: A Quantitative Approach to Environmental Plant Physiology*, 2nd edition. New York, NY: Cambridge University Press, 1992.

McKenney, Mary S., W.E. Easterling, and N.J. Rosenberg. "Simulation of Crop Productivity and Responses to Climate Change in the Year 2030: The Role of Future Technologies, Adjustments and Adaptations." *Agricultural and Forest Meteorology* 59 (1992): 103-127.

McMichael, A.J. "Impact of Climatic and Other Environmental Changes on Food Production and Population Health in the Coming Decades." *Proceedings of the Nutrition Society* 60 (2001): 195-201.

Meyers, Tilden P. and K.T. Paw U. "Modeling the Plant Canopy Micrometeorology with Higher-order Closure Principles." *Agricultural and Forest Meteorology* 41 (1987): 143-163.

Osczevski, Randall and Maurice Bluestein. "The New Wind Chill Equivalent Temperature Chart." *Bulletin of the American Meteorological Society* 86 (2005): 1453-1458.

Patterson, D.T., Westbrook, J.K., Joyce, R.J.V., Lindren, P. D., and Rogasik, J. "Weeds, Insects and Diseases." *Climate Change* 43 (1999): 711-727

Pyles, R.D., Weare, B.C., and Paw U, K.T. "The UCD Advanced-Canopy-Atmosphere-Soil Algorithm (Acasa): Comparisons with Observations from Different Climate and Vegetation Regimes." *Quarterly Journal of the Royal Meteorological Society* 126 (2000): 2951-2980.

Rosenberg, Norman J., B.L. Blad, and S.B. Verma. *Microclimate: The Biological Environment.* 2nd ed. New York, NY: Wiley, 1983.

Sehgal, M., s. Das, S. Chander, and N. Kaira. "Climate Studies and Insect Pests: Implications for the Indian Context." *Outlook on Agriculture* 35 (2006): 33-40.

Shaw, M. Rebecca., Zavaleta, Erika J., Chiariello, Nona R., Cleland, Elsa E., Mooney, Harold A., and Field, Cristopher B. "Grassland Responses to Global Environmental Changes Suppressed by Elevated CO_2." *Science* 298 (2002):1987-1990.

Steadman, Richard G. "Indices of Windchill of Clothed Persons." *Journal of Applied Meteorology* 10 (1971): 674-683.

Tromp, Solco W. *Biometeorology: The Impact of the Weather and Climate on Humans and Their Environment (Animals and Plants)*. London, UK: Heyden Publishing, 1980.

Tubiello, Francesco N., Soussana, J-F., and S. Mark Howden. "Crop and Pasture Response to Climate Change." *Proceedings of the National Academy of Science* 104 (2007): 19686-19690.

Xiong, Wei, Matthews, Robin, Holman, Ian, Lin, Erda, and Yinglong Xu. "Modelling China's Potential Maize Production at Regional Scale Under Climate Change." *Climatic Change* 85 (2007): 433-451.

Welfare

Publicly funded provision of basic goods and services for families and individuals. In this entry we describe rural America's relationship with welfare. In describing this relationship, we identify the sources of variability in rural poverty and rural age structure because these two structural characteristics drive welfare eligibility. Knowledge about these two structural characteristics is foundational for understanding why welfare is an important institution in rural America.

Since President Franklin Roosevelt signed the Social Security Act in 1935, welfare has been defined by two components: 1) means-tested programs that serve the needy, including needy families with children, and 2) universal retirement programs for the elderly, primarily Social Security income transfers and medical insurance (e.g., "Medicare"). These two components are related to income differences where the elderly enjoy relative income security, versus young families who are relatively insecure and face higher poverty risk. How these programs play out within rural America has been analyzed in relation to the 1996 "welfare reform" act (The Personal Responsibility and Work Opportunity Reconciliation Act of 1996) signed by President Bill Clinton. This legislation modified means-tested programs established by the Social Security Act, but did not affect universal welfare for the elderly.

Means-Tested Welfare

Means-tested programs use the federal poverty level and related measures of income and asset deprivation to determine program eligibility. For example, Food Stamps became a federal program in 1964 as part of President Lyndon Johnson's War on Poverty. This program defines eligibility at approximately 130 percent of the federal poverty level; families and individuals above this income level are generally not eligible for food stamps. From the perspective of rural America, the extent of poverty is a key parameter for eligibility and participation in food stamps as well as for other types of means-tested welfare.

Poverty is highly variable across rural America, ranging from well below the national average in many rural counties adjacent to cities, to well above the national average in other areas, particularly subregions of the rural South. There are a number of high poverty counties that contain concentrations of rural minority populations, notably Native Americans in counties with Indian reservations, African Americans in the Old South, and Hispanics in the Southwest (Beale, 2004). Finally, there is a large region of non-Hispanic White poverty in the upland area of the Eastern United States known as Appalachia. Many of the counties in these areas have been labeled "persistently poor" because their county poverty rates have been persistently higher than 20 percent for several decades.

Spatial unevenness in rural poverty was initiated by capitalist development during the eighteenth and nineteenth centuries, primarily in connection with the British industrial revolution in textiles (North, 1965). Cotton cultivated by slaves in the rural South was a key input to British industry, and the profitability of this trade induced Southern planters to specialize. As a consequence, the South imported most of its clothing, foodstuffs and farm implements, and ultimately much of this from the non-South. This led to uneven rural development where high levels of poverty and social inequality became endemic to the rural South, but not to rural areas of the Northeast and Midwest. In addition, westward territorial expansion of the U.S. effectively impoverished indigenous Mexican and Native American populations. Many of these initial patterns of inequality persist to the present due to intuitional mechanisms and the failure of subsequent capitalist development to significantly diminish poverty (Duncan, 1999). The result is that some rural regions remain impoverished, and others are not. This uneven pattern of poverty leads to highly variable patterns of eligibility and participation in means-tested welfare across rural America.

A common ideological notion about means-tested welfare is that most Americans never use it. This notion may be stronger in rural communities which are sometimes believed to exemplify the virtues of hard work and self-reliance. However, if one looks at the evidence, this notion is revealed to be myth: when measured over the entire life course, two out of three Americans will use means-tested welfare defined as Medicaid, food stamps, emergency assistance, energy assistance, and family cash assistance (Rank and Hirschl, 2002). The majority of Americans are vulnerable to periods of poverty for at least one year during their life course, and will turn to means-tested programs for assistance.

There is evidence that the rural poor are, in fact, less likely to use welfare than the urban poor due to the structural characteristics of rural communities (Hirschl and Rank, 1992). Rural communities are smaller and less segregated by race and social class in comparison to their urban counterparts. This settlement pattern tends to suppress rural welfare participation which depends upon awareness of program options as well as specialized knowledge about eligibility criteria. There is evidence that this type of knowledge is less pervasive in rural versus urban communities because the rural poor are more isolated from each other. Second, means-tested welfare can be, and often is, socially stigmatized, and this stigma may exercise more behavioral control in rural communities where the poor are spatially diffuse and engaged in cross-class social networks. What is important about observed rural-urban differences in participation is not their magnitude (these are often in the 10 to 20 percent range), but rather what these differences imply about the relatively isolated quality of life among the rural poor.

Rural America and Welfare Reform

The Personal Responsibility and Work Opportunity Reconciliation Act of 1996 (hereafter simply "welfare reform") represents the latest chapter in the American government's policy tilt toward reliance upon labor markets as the solution to poverty. This bill ended family entitlements to cash assistance in favor of time limited "temporary assistance" while providing greater discretionary power to states in specifying program parameters. The bill also features moral language about the virtues of marriage in preventing poverty, and the role of out-of-wedlock births in causing poverty. Final-

ly, the bill contains language about "making work pay" by requiring welfare recipients to work while receiving welfare, and phasing out welfare income over time in favor of labor market earnings. Thus, an implicit intention of welfare reform is reduction in the welfare rolls.

The implications of welfare reform for rural America appear to be largely unintended due to the fact that the bill was not designed with rural conditions in mind. These conditions include the following: 1) compared to the urban poor, the rural poor are more likely to work (impoverished rural families often hold more than one job), 2) employment in rural communities is more likely to be seasonal due to the character of rural industries (e.g., agriculture and tourism), 3) average earnings are lower in rural communities, and 4) support services such as transportation and child care are less available in rural communities. One apparent result of welfare reform was identified in a survey of the research literature showing that the rural welfare rolls declined less than urban welfare rolls after welfare reform (Weber et al., 2001). Although this urban/rural difference is confounded by interstate differences in welfare reform implementation (Zimmerman, 2002), the evidence is consistent with the proposition that leaving welfare has higher costs for rural recipients because labor market opportunities and support services are less available in rural communities.

Welfare reform poses critical dilemmas for rural communities, especially those with high poverty rates (Zimmerman and Hirschl, 2003). Welfare reform emphasizes greater reliance upon labor market earnings in an environment where such earnings may not be readily available. It presumes the existence of adequate child care and transportation services where these may be lacking or inadequate. These dilemmas are particularly salient in light of the variability in rural poverty. In the absence of equitable community development within high poverty counties, welfare reform puts the poor at greater risk of the highly negative health and social costs of poverty.

Universal Retirement Welfare

Universal retirement welfare presents a different set of relationships with rural America. Although agricultural workers are excluded from participation, most other workers (including farm owners) are legally mandated to contribute to Social Security/Disability/Medicare payroll taxes, and to receive benefits upon retirement. Thus, the program is nearly universal for the employed workforce, and in addition provides social protection (income transfers) for surviving members of workers' families, and for disabled workers.

The universal character of retirement welfare is associated with different public perceptions in comparison to means-tested welfare. In promoting the Social Security Act, President Franklin Roosevelt stressed that Social Security is not "welfare," but rather a "trust fund" where benefits received in retirement are based upon payments made during the working years. This characterization turns out to be more ideological than substantive, and represents Roosevelt's effort to separate popular notions about Social Security from welfare stigma, and to build broad political and social support for the legislation. This effort has borne fruit in the politics of congressional lobbying by organizations such as the AARP (American Association of Retired Persons) and allied organizations that have successfully indexed Social Security benefits to inflation, and fended off attempts to downsize programs which paid benefits worth well over $800 billion in 2006 (Social Security plus Medicare).

Retirement welfare is especially significant to rural America because the rural age structure is older and aging faster than the age structure of urban and metropolitan America. The country as a whole is aging due to a declining birth rate and the aging of the Baby Boom generation. Rural America is aging faster than the country as whole due to young out-migration from rural areas, and because older rural residents are likely to stay in place. Thus, the retirement welfare benefits paid to elderly rural residents are relatively important for sustaining rural households and the rural economy.

In addition, there is evidence that retirement welfare can have developmental effects on rural communities. Attracting retirees to an area is thought to be a development strategy for rural America because many retirees are relatively affluent, and their incomes have been shown to boost local economies via a "multiplier effect" (Serow, 2003). This strategy is seen as particularly viable in areas with natural amenities such as lakes, mountains and related outdoor recreational opportunities. Universal welfare is one important component of elderly income, although retirees that enhance local economies typically have higher incomes more than their relatively modest welfare income. Nevertheless, retirement welfare is one component of elderly income, and should be thought of as an underlying factor in this type of community economic development.

Means-tested welfare and universal retirement welfare are the two major types of welfare in the United States, and each has critical implications for rural America. Because county poverty rates are highly variable across rural America, eligibility for, and participation in, means-tested welfare is highly variable. High poverty counties depend greatly upon means-tested welfare, and welfare reform puts these counties at greater risk of poverty's ill effects. Retirement welfare is driven by age composition, and rural America has a disproportionate share of persons age 65 and over; in addition, rural America is aging faster than the country as a whole. Thus, retirement welfare is highly significant for rural people and their households, and this significance will continue to increase over time as rural communities continue to age. Welfare was not designed with rural America in mind, yet it has become an important rural institution.

— *Thomas A. Hirschl and Julie N. Zimmerman*

See also
Family; Income; Policy, Rural Family; Policy, Socioeconomic; Poverty

References

Beale, Calvin L. "Anatomy of Nonmetro High-Poverty Areas: Common in Plight, Distinctive in Nature." *Amber Waves*, February 2004. Available online at: http://www.ers.usda.gov/AmberWaves/February04/Features/Anatomy.htm.

Duncan, Cynthia M. *Worlds Apart: Why Poverty Persists in Rural America*. New Haven: Yale University Press, 1999.

Hirschl, Thomas A. and Mark R. Rank. "The Effect of Population Density on Welfare Participation." *Social Forces* 70 (1991): 225-235.

North, Douglas C. *The Economic Growth of the United States 1790-1860*, 2nd edition. New York: WW Norton, 1966.

Rank, Mark R. and Thomas A. Hirschl. "Welfare Use as a Life Course Event: Toward a New Understanding of America's Safety Net." *Social Work* 47 (2002): 237-248.

Serow, William J. "Economic Consequences of Retiree Concentrations: A Review of North American Studies." *The Gerontologist* 43 (2003): 897-903.

Weber, Bruce, Greg J. Duncan, and Leslie A. Whitener. "Welfare Reform in Rural America: What Have We Learned?" *American Journal of Agricultural Economics* 83 (2001): 1282-1292.

Zimmerman, Julie N. "Contextualizing Cash Assistance and the South." Introduction to the Special Issue on Welfare Reform. *Southern Rural Sociology* 18, no. 1 (2002): 1-20.

Zimmerman, Julie N. and Thomas A. Hirschl. "Welfare Reform in Rural Areas: A Voyage Through Uncharted Waters." Pp. 363-374 in *Challenges for Rural America in the Twenty-First Century*. Edited by David L. Brown and Louis E. Swanson. University Park, PA: Pennsylvania State University Press, 2003.

Wetlands

The wide variety of areas from the shallow edge of open waters to areas that are often dry but are subject to seasonal flooding. After a history of developing these areas for commercial uses, policy makers increasingly recognize the importance of wetlands to Earth's ecological balance. Many federal and state programs have been established to promote the protection of wetlands and to reverse years of damage. Although there is little controversy over the goal of protecting wetlands and the functions they provide, wetland management has been the source of considerable debate. A renewed public debate emerged in the late 1980s over the question of how much wetland acreage is needed, how to balance economic and ecologic priorities, and how best to restore previously damaged areas. In the last decade, the debate intensified as questions surfaced about federal Clean Water Act jurisdiction over wetlands.

Overview

Wetlands are a significant component of our rural landscape. They played an important role in forming the geography of our settlement patterns by serving as a source of food, water and rich land that could often be easily brought under cultivation. It has been estimated that there were originally 220 million acres of wetlands in the 48 contiguous states and another 200 million acres in Alaska. As the country developed, approximately 53 percent of the original wetlands in the 48 states was converted to other uses such as farms, home sites, roads and ports. It was estimated that during the 1960s and 1970s more than 11 million acres of wetlands, an area twice the size of New Jersey, were drained and developed for various purposes (Thompson, 1983). Conversions of wetlands decreased in the 1980s and 1990s. One set of estimates suggests annual conversion of wetland acreage fell from approximately 730,000 from 1954 to 1974, to 446,000 from 1974 to 1982, to 156,000 from 1982 to 1992 (Heimlich et al., 1998).

Wetlands have been viewed as both wastelands, which served no beneficial purpose, and as critical natural resources deserving of protection. The understanding of the importance of wetlands has increased, but there is still controversy over how they should be managed.

Wetlands form a transition between sites that are permanently wet and those that are generally dry, and although they may have characteristics of both, they cannot be classified exclusively as either aquatic or terrestrial. There is not a consensus as to a single structure to classify wetlands. This is because they encompass such a wide variation in their physical and hydrologic characteristics and in the types of plant and animal communities they support (Finlayson and Moser, 1991). In general, they include the following six types:

Marshes are among the most productive ecosystems in the world. There are three major groups: freshwater marshes, tidal salt marshes, and tidal freshwater marshes. Collectively these account for over 90 percent of the wetlands within the contiguous 48 states. Dominant plants often include reeds, sedges and rushes. They are used by a variety of waterfowl, muskrats, beavers, turtles, fish and fur bearers.

Swamps differ from marshes in that they have saturated soils or are flooded for most of the growing season. They are dominated by woody plants such as the red maple in the Northeastern states and the bald cypress and tupelo in the South.

Peatlands occur most often in shallow lake basins, along sluggish streams, and on flat uplands. They support a spongy groundcover of mosses, horsetails, sedges and rushes. Their shape, thickness and dominant plant material varies widely depending in part on the hydrology and latitude.

Floodplains are the low areas bordering rivers and streams which are subject to periodic flooding, particularly during the spring.

Estuaries and lagoons are areas at the mouths of rivers that form a boundary between fresh and marine environments. The deltas that form from sediment-rich rivers provide necessary environments for spawning and feeding of many marine species of fish and habitat for shorebirds and waterfowl.

Lakes are wetlands that characterize the shallow margins of many large and deeper lakes, or the entire area of shallow bodies of open water. The types of wetlands and their productivity vary according to the water depth and shoreland gradient.

Functions

Wetlands of virtually all varieties have been subjected to alterations to make them more adaptable for grazing or cultivation, or by filling for roads, railways, buildings and other developments. It is possible to fly over coastal salt marshes and see the herringbone patterns of trenches that were dug in the 1800s in order to drain the soil, making it easier to harvest the grasses and other marsh plants for animal feed. Although wetlands were not ideal for development, they were relatively flat and easy to fill. For roughly the past 100 years federal and state policies encouraged the alteration and development of wetlands to provide services more highly valued by society at that time. Historically, agricultural use accounted for over 80 percent of the conversions (Weller, 1985). In the 1980s and 1990s, agriculture played a lesser role in conversions, making up 53 percent of conversions from 1974 to 1982 and 20 percent of conversions from 1982 to 1992 (Heimlich et al., 1998). From 1974 to 1992, the percent of conversions associated with urban or developed uses increased (Heimlich et al., 1998).

Over time the important ecological and social functions that wetlands provide in their natural state have been better understood. The loss of coastal wetlands to development and pollution has been linked to population declines in important fisheries that use them for spawning and nursery areas. In addition to providing wildlife and fishery habitat and flood protection, wetlands serve to stabilize shorelands and reduce soil erosion. The damage caused by Hurricane Katrina to New Orleans and the surrounding Gulf Coast area was more extensive than it might have otherwise been due to the long-term loss of wetlands in the Mississippi Delta and surrounding coastal wetlands. Louisiana has lost about 1,900 square miles of coastal wetlands since the 1930s (Burdeau, 2005). Hurricanes Katrina and Rita combined to wash away an additional 217 square miles of wetlands, which increases the likelihood of significant future damage from storms in the area (USGS, 2006).

Wetlands retain and absorb nutrients from surface runoff and thereby protect lake and river water quality. They often serve as a hydrologic link between surface waters and groundwater, at times as a source of recharge for depleted groundwater or as a discharge of groundwater to surface waters to maintain critical rates of stream flow. They may have forestry or agricultural potential in their natural state. Examples of commercial products from wetlands include cranberries and wild rice. Many people enjoy wetlands for their educational and recreational value.

Although wetlands vary significantly in size and character, each provides at least one or more of the above functions. The further conversion of wetlands entails a loss of their natural productive attributes. The type and magnitude of the impact will vary from site to site. Policies to protect wetlands have been difficult to establish and administer because of conflicting values about priorities. Most of the functions performed by wetlands are recognized as valuable to society and the environment, but they are functions that are not easily expressed in terms of market value. On the other hand, a wetland site that is converted to another use as a site for a road, homes or cultivated cropland will produce products that are more readily valued in a market economy. History demonstrates that Americans give greater weight to market-based alternatives. Only recently have significant efforts been made to develop policies and regulations to preserve or protect wetlands.

Regulation

Congress began to make the protection of wetlands a priority with the 1972 Water Pollution Control Act and the 1977 Clean Water Act. Section 404 of the Clean Water Act gave the U.S. Army Corps of Engineers the authority to regulate activities that affect wetlands through a permit process. Some argue that because agriculture and forestry are exempted from this process, there is a significant gap in the protection which the Clean Water Act provides. Others argue that the Corps has gone too far in their role and overstepped their authority (Wakefield, 1982). Two recent Supreme Court decisions (*Solid Waste Agency of Northern Cook County vs. U.S. Army Corps of Engineers* [2001] and *Rapanos vs. United States* [2006]) raise doubts related to federal Clean Water Act jurisdiction over isolated ponds and non-navigable waters (Environmental Law Institute, 2007).

Because agriculture was exempt from the Section 404 provisions, there was concern that other federal programs provided incentives for conversion of wetlands to agricultural uses. This led to the Swampbuster provisions of the 1985 Farm Bill, or the Food Security Act. The Swampbuster provisions sought to remove any incentives for the agricultural conversion of wetlands by denying farm program benefits to producers who filled, drained or otherwise converted wetlands for cropland use (McCullough, 1985; Heimlich and Langer, 1986). It made farmers ineligible for price-support payments, crop insurance, disaster payments, and insured or guaranteed loans for any year in which the crop was produced on lands that had been converted from wetlands. It did not prevent further conversions, but it removed significant incentives which had previously existed. Additional reductions in incentives for agricultural conversions of wetlands and increases in incentives for agricultural restoration of wetlands have emerged in the USDA's Conservation Reserve Program and Wetlands Reserve Program (Heimlich et al., 1998).

Recent policies under Presidents Bush and Clinton were motivated by a policy of "no net loss." This goal was based on the view that the point was reached where it was important to make every effort to protect all remaining wetlands. In those cases where it was determined to be essential to convert an area of wetland, the policy allowed the activity only if it was offset with the construction or rehabilitation of another site into a stable and functioning wetland comparable to the site that was being lost. This technique is commonly referred to as mitigation. The degree to which such efforts are technically successful or adequately replace the functions of the natural site remain very controversial.

Many, but not all, states established regulatory controls over wetlands that go beyond the protection afforded by federal programs. A recent survey of state programs indicates that most states enacted additional regulatory controls. Some states rely on an additional permit review process or a combination of other requirements such as mitigation or the permanent dedication of another wetland site by the developer to its natural state through acquisition or easements. Recent management efforts have benefited from improved data describing the location of wetlands and the rise in use of geographic information systems (GIS) for natural resource planning. Some states are shifting from focusing on individual wetlands to consideration of wetland systems at a watershed scale, acknowledging connectivity among wetlands and the importance of wetlands such as vernal pools. Much progress has been made, but there is more to be done to insure that wetland regulations are effective and targeted at the appropriate level of protection.

Information about local wetlands can be obtained from the Water Resources Institute at each state's land-grant university. Further information about regulations of wetlands may be obtained from the state's depart-

ment of natural resources, environmental protection, or inland fisheries and wildlife.

— *Gregory K. White and Kathleen P. Bell*

See also

Agricultural Programs; River Engineering; Conservation, Water; Environmental Protection; Environmental Regulations; Groundwater; Hydrology; Natural Resource Economics; Policy, Environmental; Water, Value of; Watersheds; Wildlife

References

Burdeau, Cain. "Hurricanes Take Bite Out of La. Wetlands." Associated Press article as reported in Washingtonpost.com, November, 2005. Available online at: http://www.washingtonpost.com/wp-dyn/content/article/2005/11/10/AR2005111000133_pf.html

Environmental Law Institute. *The Clean Water Act Jurisdictional Handbook*. Washington DC: Environmental Law Institute, 2007.

Heimlich, Ralph and L. Langer. *Swampbusting: Wetland Conversion and Farm Programs*. Agricultural Economics Report No. 51. Washington DC: U.S. Department of Agriculture, Natural Resource Economics Division, Economic Research Service, 1986.

Heimlich, Ralph, Weibe, K.D., Claasen, R., Gadsy, R., and R.M. House. *Wetlands and Agriculture: Private Interests and Public Benefits*. Washington DC: U.S. Department of Agriculture, Economic Research Service, 1998.

Klinko, Deborah and J. Bergstrom. "The Value and Regulation of Wetlands in the United States: A Review." Unpublished manuscript. Athens, GA: University of Georgia, Department of Agricultural Economics.

Larson, J.S. "North America." In *Wetlands*. Edited by M. Finalyson and M. Moser. Oxford, UK: International Waterfowl and Wetlands Research Bureau, Facts On File Limited, 1991.

Maltby, E. "Wetlands and Their Values." P. 8 in *Wetlands*. Edited by M. Finalyson and M. Moser. Oxford, UK: International Waterfowl and Wetlands Research Bureau, Facts On File Limited, 1991.

McCullough, Rose and D. Weiss. "An Environmental Look at the 1985 Farm Bill." *Journal of Soil and Water Conservation* 40, no.3 (1985): 267-270.

Thompson, Roger. "America's Disappearing Wetlands." *Congressional Quarterly Editorial Reports* 11 (1983): 615-632.

USGS. "USGS Reports Latest Land Change Estimates for Louisiana Coast" press release, Lafayette, LA: National Wetlands Research Center, 2005.

Wakefield, Penney. "Reducing the Federal Role in Wetlands Protection." *Environment* 24 (1982): 6-13, 30-33.

Weller, Milton W. "Reports on Reports." A review of "Wetlands of the United States: Current Status and Recent Trends" and "Wetlands: Their Use and Regulation." *Environment* 27 (1985): 25-27.

Woodward, Richard T., and Y. Wui. 'The economic value of wetland services: a meta-analysis.' *Ecological Economics* 37(2001): 257-270.

Wheat Industry

All individuals and companies involved in the production, transportation, marketing and sale of wheat to domestic and international consumers. This article provides an overview of the wheat industry, one of the most important sectors of U.S. agriculture. Individual sections discuss wheat production, marketing, selected government programs, supply and demand, economic impacts of wheat on rural economies, and recent industry trends.

Wheat ranks with rice as one of the world's most important food crops. Adapted to a variety of growing conditions, wheat has excellent storage qualities and is consumed worldwide in a variety of forms (e.g., bread and baked goods, cereals, noodles and pasta). The U.S. is a major wheat-producing country, with production exceeded only by China, the former Soviet Union and the European Union.

In recent years, wheat has ranked third among U.S. field crops in terms of planted acreage (behind corn and soybeans) and third in terms of gross farm receipts (behind corn and soybeans). Wheat is the primary food grain for U.S. consumers. Domestic demand has grown steadily for milled and baked products, fueling the expansion of diversified processing industries. Wheat is also a major export crop. About half of U.S. wheat production is exported (a larger fraction than for corn or soybeans). As a result, the wheat sector is influenced strongly by external market forces, with U.S. prices moving in response to shifts in global supply and demand.

U.S. wheat production is concentrated in the Great Plains, although significant quantities are also grown in other regions. Wheat has five separate classes, each with unique characteristics and suitability for different end products. Hard Red Winter (HRW) wheat accounts for about 40 percent of total production and is grown primarily in the Central and Southern Plains (Kansas, Oklahoma and Texas). HRW is principally used to make bread flour. Hard Red Spring (HRS) wheat accounts for about 25 percent of production and is grown primarily in the Northern Plains (North Dakota, Montana, Minnesota and South Dakota). HRS wheat is valued for high protein levels, which makes it suitable for specialty breads and blending with lower-protein flours. Soft Red Winter (SRW) wheat (15 to 20 percent of total production) is grown in Missouri, Illinois and Ohio and is used for cakes, cookies and crackers. White wheat (10 to 15 percent) is grown in Washington, Oregon and Idaho and is used for noodle products, crackers and cereals. Durum wheat (3 to 5 percent) is grown primarily in North Dakota and is used for pasta.

Production

Production practices vary throughout the U.S. due to differences in seasonal cropping patterns, growing conditions and farming systems (e.g., organic, no-till and conventional). Agronomic conditions are responsible for much of the regional variation. In the Northern Plains where winters are harsh, HRS and durum wheat are planted in the spring and harvested in the fall of the same year. In the Southern Plains where winters are generally mild, winter wheat is planted in the fall and harvested midway through the following summer. In response to dry conditions found in the western Dakotas and western Kansas, farmland is often summer-fallowed, a practice of idling portions of land each year to conserve top moisture and nutrients. Wheat production practices in other parts of the U.S. are influenced by general farming systems, such as double cropping and rotational considerations for row crops.

Farms in the Great Plains raise primarily small grains and tend to be larger than farms raising only row crops. In Kansas and North Dakota, top wheat-producing states, wheat accounts for 46 percent and 39 percent of all planted acres, respectively. In other regions of the country, particularly in the Corn Belt and Southeast, wheat is secondary to row crops, often raised to add flexibility in crop rotations and to provide enterprise diversification.

U.S. wheat production is highly mechanized. Pre-plant tillage operations include the use of disks, harrows and field cultivators to prepare the soil and apply fertilizer and pre-emergence herbicides. Wheat is predominantly planted using an air seeder. Some farming systems apply post-emergence herbicides to control weeds and some require occasional treatments to combat insects and plant diseases. Wheat is typically harvested using a combine, either alone in a process called straight-combining (a combine cuts and thrashes in one operation) or in conjunction with a swather.

Swathing cuts and places unthrashed wheat into windrows to be harvested later. At harvest, wheat normally is hauled directly to storage facilities either on the farm or at local elevators. Depending upon farming systems, post-harvest tillage will involve the use of discs, chisel plows or moldboard plows.

Yields vary according to agronomic factors, such as soil type, temperature, amount and timing of precipitation, plant pests, wheat variety limitations, and nutrient availability, and management-related factors, such as seeding rate, time of planting, fertilizer use, weed control and harvest efficiency. Wheat yields in the Southern Plains average 38 bushels/acre, while yields in the Northern Plains average 34 bushels/acre. Yields in the Corn Belt and Southeast average about 55 bushels/acre, with the highest yields, 60 bushels/acre, occurring in the Pacific Northwest.

Revenues from wheat production generally consist of cash crop sales and (for participating producers) payments from government programs. Most wheat is sold as cash deliveries to local elevators at harvest or stored and delivered in the months following harvest. Prices received by producers vary depending upon crop quality, global supply and demand, and seasonal factors. Gross revenues, not including government program payments, range from over $300 per acre in the Southern Plains to $420 per acre in the Pacific Northwest. Gross revenues from wheat production in the U.S. average about $320 per acre. Variable cash expenses average about 40 to 45 percent of gross revenues in the Northern Plains and up to 75 percent of gross revenues in the Southeast. Generally, fertilizer and fuel/lubrication expenses comprise the greatest portion of variable costs, followed by machinery repairs, pesticides and seed expenses. Fixed cash expenses average about 20 percent of gross revenues, with remaining returns applied toward noncash expenses.

Marketing

The marketing chain for wheat sometimes is described as the physical flow of grain from producers to processors. Seen in this way, the chain begins with the delivery of wheat (by truck) from farms to country elevators. The country elevators assemble grain for shipment (by truck or rail) to larger facilities, called subterminal or terminal elevators. From these elevators, the wheat can be shipped (by truck, rail or barge) to domestic millers or to port elevators, where it is loaded onto ocean vessels for export.

Alternatively, the chain can be identified with changes in ownership as wheat moves through the marketing system. The distinction is important because changes in physical location need not imply a purchase or sale. Some wheat-handling firms are highly integrated, owning elevators both at points of origin (wheat-producing regions) and points of destination (terminal markets or ports). Further, wheat may be bought or sold (and re-sold) well in advance of actual shipment. In this light, the market chain comprises a sequence of transactions linking producers to handlers and merchandisers, domestic millers and foreign buyers.

Wheat prices are determined in individual transactions between buyers and sellers. This may occur through private negotiations or through public and semipublic trading mechanisms. Prices received by producers are generally those bid by local elevators. These reflect quality factors (e.g., protein, test weight and dockage), costs of shipping to alternative markets, and daily changes in market conditions. In general, elevators and merchandisers seek to add value through blending and conditioning activities, grain storage, and efficiencies in shipping and handling.

Commodity futures play an essential role in the wheat marketing system. Futures are highly standardized contracts calling for delivery of fixed quantities (5,000 bushels per contact) at specified times and locations. Wheat futures contracts are traded on the Chicago Board of Trade (CBT), the Kansas City Board of Trade (KCBT), and the Minneapolis Grain Exchange (MGE). Prices at these three exchanges reflect locational differences and other differences in delivery specifications. MGE wheat futures pertain to HRS wheat and KCBT futures to HRW wheat. CBT wheat futures are more widely traded, with less restrictive delivery specifications (admitting several classes of wheat). Hence, the Chicago futures price provides the best barometer of national market conditions.

Futures provide standard reference prices for buyers and sellers. Grain traders commonly express their bids or offers in terms of basis values (cents above or below a specified futures price). Futures also provide a mechanism to reduce price risk via hedging. Producers, trading firms and processors can use futures contracts to establish a price in advance of an intended sale or purchase. This eliminates much of the risk associated with holding grain stocks, for example, or pending sale commitments. Relatively few wheat producers trade futures directly. However, elevators often act as intermediaries for producers. By using futures (or options based on futures) to offset their commitments, elevators can offer forward contracts to producers or other contracts that offer more pricing discretion.

Government Payments and Programs

The USDA played a significant role in the wheat sector for several decades. Policies have changed with farm legislation, which has been subject to renewal or revision in roughly five-year intervals.

Through the early 1990s, the government sought to support incomes of wheat farmers through a target-price mechanism. The target price for wheat is an administrative device used to calculate program payments to producers who participate in the program. Producers collect deficiency payments, equal to the difference between the target price and the national average wheat price multiplied by qualifying production. Participation is voluntary, but often has required producers to idle some portion of their base acreage. Acreage restrictions under the program have been used by the USDA to influence domestic supplies, wheat prices and (hence) the costs borne by taxpayers.

The 1996 farm bill changed the direction of federal support for agriculture because of high commodity prices. It allowed producers the freedom to plant based on market signals instead of historical production patterns. In addition, commodity payments were converted to transition payments which were to expire within seven years. After the transition period, the federal government would not support agriculture with financial payments. Commodity prices fell during 1997-2001, requiring ad hoc emergency funding for producers. In the 2002 farm bill, the ad hoc emergency funding measures were included in the farm bill as counter-cyclical payments, which supported and stabilized producer's income. Current versions of the 2007 farm bills continue with similar funding levels.

Apart from the budgetary cost, critics of the program have pointed to a skewed distribution of benefits. Most wheat deficiency and counter-cyclical payments are collected by larger-scale producers because payments are tied to base acres, which vary enormously across farms.

Factors Affecting Wheat Supply and Demand

Market fundamentals are essential to understanding wheat prices and how they change from year to year. U.S. supplies of wheat consist of current production, beginning stocks (wheat in storage) and imports (mainly from Canada). Production levels reflect producers' planting decisions, which, in turn, depend on farm program parameters, expected returns from alternative crops, and anticipated market conditions at the time of harvest. Weather conditions during the growing season can cause upward or downward revisions in expected production with immediate impacts on futures and cash prices.

Demand for wheat can be divided into domestic use, exports and ending stocks. Domestic use includes demand for food (i.e., millers and processors) and demand for livestock feed. Food use usually accounts for 75 to 80 percent of domestic use, and shows little variation around an upward, long-term trend. Feed use can vary markedly from year to year depending on crop conditions and prices of alternative feed crops. Feed use is a residual market for wheat, becoming important only with excess production or substandard crop quality. Exports accounted for half of the total use between 2001 and 2007. Shifts in export demand due to changes in market conditions or to the availability of U.S. subsidies can have pronounced price effects, particularly when stocks are low relative to total use.

Beyond these aggregate factors, wheat prices reflect other, more detailed market relationships. Buyers prefer different classes and grades of wheat for different end products. Prices are quoted for individual classes and grades, and most buyers apply premiums or discounts for specific quality factors, such as protein. The availabilities of different classes and qualities change through time, due to growing conditions and transitory demand pressures. Quality-related price differences are a critical feature of grain merchandising and, to varying degrees, are reflected in the net revenues of most wheat producers.

Economic Impacts of Wheat Production

Although wheat is produced throughout the U.S., production is concentrated in a few regions. This concentration has important economic implications. In several of the Great Plains states, wheat production comprises a substantial share of the economic base. Economic base activities bring new dollars into a region and generate personal income, retail sales, gross business volume, employment and tax revenue. Because there are few viable alternative crops in the Northern and Southern Plains, the dependence of these regions on wheat is accentuated.

Several studies have identified the economic contribution of wheat production to rural, agriculturally based economies (e.g., Bangsund and Leistritz, 2005). Economic impact estimates have included industry-wide expenditures and revenues associated with wheat activities and estimates of the spending and re-spending of industry outlays and returns. Results from recent studies of the wheat sector in North Dakota are indicative: total annual impacts from wheat production in North Dakota were estimated at $1.35 billion. Crop sales alone accounted for $1.14 billion annually. Other impacts in North Dakota included the indirect support of 35,000 full-time jobs and the generation of nearly $77 million in economy-wide tax revenue annually. Unquestionably, the wheat industry plays a similar role in other major wheat-producing states, such as Kansas, Minnesota, Oklahoma and Washington.

Trends in the Industry

Significant changes are underway in the industry. Among these are changes or pressures for change in production practices, which have traditionally relied on intensive chemical applications. As environmental and food safety concerns play a larger role in regulations and policy guidelines, wheat producers are being pressured to consider alternative farming methods.

In recent years, firm concentration in the wheat handling, merchandising and processing sectors has increased. Throughout the wheat growing regions, grain handling has become dominated by a small number of private firms and cooperatives. Similar trends are evident in the wheat export business, where a handful of integrated companies with elevators at ports and interior locations account for most U.S. export shipments. As a result of this consolidation and because of improved efficiency in grain transportation and logistics, there are fewer links in the wheat marketing chain (i.e., transactions between buyers and sellers). A parallel phenomenon has been the decline of centralized markets to trade cash grain (e.g., in Minneapolis). These trends pose a long-term challenge to market participants, including wheat producers, who rely on publicly disseminated price information.

Government programs for producers of wheat and other commodities are increasingly viewed as an unnecessary burden on taxpayers. In successive rounds of congressional farm legislation, changes have been implemented to reduce the outlays for crop subsidies and restore a market orientation in the decision making of wheat producers. Reductions in future farm subsidies appear likely and may have significant impacts on wheat producers. The exit of smaller, less efficient producers from the industry may be accelerated, and wheat production may become more concentrated. The move toward larger farms has long been evident in wheat, as in other sectors of U.S. agriculture.

Changes in the global marketplace will also impact the U.S. wheat sector. As a result of treaty obligations under the World Trade Organization, the U.S. and other wheat-exporting countries have begun to reduce export subsidies, reduce domestic subsidies and increase market access. Another important development has been the movement toward market reform in many importing countries, such as Russia and Mexico, where grain trade formerly was controlled by state monopolies. In this new trading environment, U.S. wheat exports will depend more heavily on competitive market forces.

— Won Koo, Richard Taylor, D. Demcey Johnson, and Dean A. Bangsund

See also

Agricultural Prices; Agricultural Programs; Crop Surplus; Dryland Farming; Futures Markets; Grain Elevators; Grain Farming; Markets; Marketing; Mechanization; Policy, Agricultural

References

Bangsund, Dean A. and F. Larry Leistritz. *Economic Contribution of the Wheat Industry to North Dakota*. Agricultural Economics Report No. 554. Fargo, ND: Department of Agricultural Economics, North Dakota State University, 2005.

Hoffman, Linwood A., Sara Schwartz, and Grace V. Chomo. *Wheat: Background for 1995 Farm Legislation*. Agricultural Economic Report No. 712. Washington, DC: U.S. Department of Agriculture, Economic Research Service, 1995.

Pasour, E.C. and Randal R. Rucker. *Plowshears & Pork Barrels: The Political Economy of Agriculture*. Oakland, CA: The Independent Institute, 2005

U.S. Department of Agriculture. *The Physical Distribution System for Grain*. Agricultural Information Bulletin No. 457. Washington, DC: U.S. Department of Agriculture, Office of Transportation, 1990.

U.S. Department of Agriculture. *Characteristics and Production Costs of U.S. Wheat Farms*. Statistical Bulletin No. 974-5. Washington, DC: U.S. Department of Agriculture, Economic Research Service, July 2002.

U.S. Department of Agriculture. *The Changing Face of the U.S. Grain System: Differentiation and Identity Preservation Trends*. Economic Research Report No. 35. Washington, DC: U.S. Department of Agriculture, Economic Research Service, July 2002.

U.S. Department of Agriculture. *Wheat Backgrounder*. Electronic Outlook Report, No., WHS-05k-01. Washington DC:U.S. Department of Agriculture, Economic Research Service, December 2005.

U.S. Department of Agriculture. *Wheat Situation and Outlook Report*. Washington, DC: U.S. Department of Agriculture, Economic Research Service, various issues.

U.S. Department of Agriculture. PS&D Data Base. Available online at: www.fas.usda.gov/psdonline.

Wilderness

Land retaining its primeval character and influence, without permanent human habitation, which is protected and managed so as to preserve its natural conditions. This discussion of wilderness is divided in two sections. First, the history of the concept of wilderness as it emerged in Europe and the U.S. is examined. The second section addresses the current status and amount of land devoted to wilderness in the U.S.

History of the Wilderness Idea in Europe and the U.S.

American ideas about wilderness are like some surprising mutant grain, new but deeply rooted. They combine and modify several western traditions. For most of their recorded history, European people have not regarded wilderness highly. Traditional Judeo-Christian thought portrayed wilderness as a dangerous place, home to savage and even demonic beasts, and no place for moral people. Many early Christians believed Cain had been banished from Eden to the wilderness, and wilderness still was home to Cain's infernal descendants. The Bible explicitly contrasts alien wilderness with the blessed and domesticated Garden of Eden (e.g., "The land is the Garden of Eden before them, and behind them a desolate wilderness." Joel 2:3). If a seventeenth-century European or American had trekked into the wilderness for enlightenment or pleasure, most contemporaries would have responded with puzzlement and some derision.

The past 250 years witnessed a radical transformation in the values Europeans attached to wilderness. This transformation, which is still going on, is one of the most dramatic turnabouts in the history of ideas. For Americans in the twenty-first century, it is also one of the most important.

The modern idea of wilderness evolved through three phases so far. The first phase occurred in the late eighteenth and early nineteenth century. Nature became a teacher. In England, this phase was romanticism. Writers like Edmund Burke, William Wordsworth and Lord Byron portrayed wild nature as a source of sublime awe, delight and inspiration. In France, it was primitivism. Jean Jacques Rousseau wrote of the noble savage, innocent of the corruption of court and city. In America, intellectuals absorbed both doctrines, romanticism and primitivism, and they added a third from the Far East; seafaring Yankees brought new ideas about the sanctity of nature.

The "Boston Brahmins" stirred all these doctrines together to produce the heady brew of transcendentalism. For transcendentalists, God dwelt in nature, and the natural world was a reliable guide to enlightenment. Two great writers, Ralph Waldo Emerson and Henry David Thoreau, took up the transcendental torch with revolutionary results. They turned the theology of two millennia upside-down. With Yankee brashness in his 1851 essay "Walking," Thoreau announced, "In wildness is the preservation of the World" (p. 275). Nature was not the problem but the solution. Thanks largely to Thoreau and Emerson, transcendentalism has influenced ideas of wilderness ever since.

In the first phase, romantic, primitivist, transcendental Anglo-Americans prized wilderness as a source of moral elevation. In the second phase, they saw more businesslike values. Scientists and other thinkers began to describe the practical benefits of wilderness, such as watershed protection. They argued that people had a responsibility to protect those benefits. George Perkins Marsh led this group with his brilliant, influential book, *Man and Nature* (1864). Marsh admonished that humans had a responsibility to care for nature, not simply consume it. He developed the important idea that civilization had fallen because of the waste of resources. As an example of practices that brought down great civilizations in the past, he pointed to indiscriminate logging. With the Adirondacks in mind, he argued that Americans should preserve large areas of undeveloped land. Economics joined aesthetics as a category of wilderness values. The modern wilderness movement had begun its erratic course.

Marsh's ideas were timely and influential. Other Americans agreed that the conservation of natural resources was good policy, and the U.S. began to protect special places. Usually, the reasons given were a mixture of aesthetic, spiritual, recreational and practical. For all those reasons, in 1872, President Grant set aside two million acres in northwestern Wyoming as Yellowstone, America's first national park. Largely for watershed protection, the state of New York established the 715,000-acre Adirondack Forest Preserve in 1885.

Still, the marriage of economics and aesthetics was not completely congenial. The transcendental gene was strong, and advocates of preservation for its own sake demanded to be heard. By far the most forceful was the naturalist John Muir. The first official act of preserving wilderness for its own sake was the creation of Yosemite National Park in 1890, thanks to John Muir's writing and organizing. Yet the struggle was just beginning.

In the third phase, the U.S. developed a unique, extensive system of protected wilderness areas and a complex set of laws and institutions surrounding them. In 1891, Congress gave the president authority to create forest reserves, which were later renamed national forests. President Harrison immediately created 15 reserves, comprising more than 13 million acres. Yet the Act left the purpose of the reserves unclear and opened the door for disagreement between those who advocated restricted timber production and those who wanted complete preservation. That issue was raised almost immediately, and is still a matter of intense debate.

Wilderness preservation came into its own as a twin to the idea of conservation. Gifford Pinchot defined conservation as the wise use of natural resources for the long-term benefit of society. With Pinchot, conservation became one of the key elements of the Progressive Movement's credo.

Well into the twentieth century, this utilitarian view of humankind's relationship to the rest of the natural world dominated virtually all official policy with regard to the public lands of the U.S. Meanwhile, however, John Muir and a few like-minded visionaries slowly began to develop the protocols of another way of thinking. Building on transcendentalism, they held that wild country had a value transcending any human use and deserved preservation for its own sake.

This was not a sentiment that the average public lands bureaucrat found appealing. People like Muir, the utilitarian said, were naive romantics. Ironically, the two men most responsible for beginning the long crusade that ultimately made wilderness preservation public policy were both veterans of the U.S. Forest Service, the definitive federal land-management bureaucracy: Aldo Leopold and Robert Marshall.

Both men had discovered in wild country values that deserved the respect, love and protection of human beings. Leopold persuaded his superiors to set aside more than half a million acres of New Mexico wild lands as the first official federal wilderness area in 1924. Marshall helped to formulate Forest Service regulations that established a system of protected primitive areas in the country's national forests—the beginning of today's National Wilderness Preservation System.

In 1930, Marshall called for "an organization of spirited people who will fight for the freedom of the wilderness" (p. 149). In 1935, Leopold and Marshall joined with a handful of other preservationists to found The Wilderness Society.

Two more veterans of the federal bureaucracy, Olaus Mure and Howard Zhaniser, led The Wilderness Society as it joined with such other organizations such as the Sierra Club and the Izaak Walton League to engineer the wilderness ideas' most important triumph. In 1964, after one of the longest and most sophisticated environmental campaigns ever launched, Congress passed the Wilderness Act. The Act established a National Wilderness Preservation System and thereby validated an idea once dismissed as impossibly romantic.

Current Status and Extent of Wilderness in the U.S.

Today, more than 115 million acres of federal land in 44 states enjoy protection as wilderness under the 1964 Wilderness Act. Only Connecticut, Rhode Island, Delaware, Maryland, Kansas and Iowa, states which have little federal land, do not currently have designated wilderness areas within their boundaries. Well over half (57 million acres) are located in Alaska, whereas only four million acres are located in states east of the Mississippi River. National parks account for 47 million acres of designated wilderness, followed by 39 million acres on national forests, 21 million acres on national wildlife refuges, and just 10 million acres on Bureau of Land Management lands, the largest manager of federal lands in the U.S. Government (Table 1). There is no inventory or reliable estimate of the area of federal land that could still be eligible for wilderness designation under the terms of the 1964 Act.

The Wilderness Act defines wilderness as land where "man is a visitor who does not remain." Going further, the Act states "an area of wilderness is further defined to mean in this Act an area of undeveloped federal land retaining its primeval character and influence, without permanent human habitation, which is protected and managed so as to preserve its natural conditions." These definitions have given rise to the view held by many that federal wilderness designation removes those lands from human use, and thus renders them of little economic value, and in fact, wilderness designation can be of significant detriment to local communities. The facts are quite different, however.

Table 1.
Designated Wilderness by State (in Acres), 2008.

State	National Forests	Wildlife Refuges	National Parks	Bureau of Land Management	Summed Total Acres
Alabama	41,367	0	0	0	41,367
Alaska	5,753,548	18,869,348	32,979,406	0	57,602,302
Arizona	1,351,708	1,383,944	444,055	1,482,766	4,662,473
Arkansas	121,367	2,144	34,933	0	158,444
California	5,049,171	32,988	6,314,074	5,064,536	16,460,769
Colorado	3,267,717	30,540	362,403	257,910	3,918,570
Florida	74,495	51,252	1,296,500	0	1,422,247
Georgia	142,195	362,107	9,886	0	514,188
Hawaii	0	0	155,509	0	155,509
Idaho	2,365,955	0	43,243	802	2,410,000
Illinois		28,732	4,050	0	0
Indiana	12,945	0	0	0	12,945
Kentucky	18,097	0	0	0	18,097
Louisiana	8,679	8,346	0	0	17,025
Maine	12,000	7,392	0	0	19,392
Massachusetts	0	3,244	0	0	3,244
Michigan	92,583	25,310	132,018	0	249,911
Minnesota	810,088	6,180	0	0	816,268
Missouri	63,423	7,730	0	0	71,153
Mississippi	6,046	0	4,080	0	10,126
Montana	4,490,845	11,366	0	6,000	4,508,211
Nebraska	7,795	4,634	0	0	12,429
Nevada	1,144,035	0	3,498,716	2,302,117	6,944,868
New Hampshire	137,432	0	0	0	137,432
New Jersey	10,341	0	0	0	10,341
New Mexico	1,388,262	39,908	56,392	150,464	1,635,026
New York	0	0	1,363	0	1,363
North Carolina	131,901	0	0	0	131,901
North Dakota	0	9,732	29,920	0	39,652
Ohio	0	77	0	0	77
Oklahoma	22,893	8,570	0	0	31,463
Oregon	2,308,751	387	0	426,287	2,735,425
Pennsylvania	9,031	0	0	0	9,031
South Carolina	22,086	29,000	15,010	0	66,096
South Dakota	13,426	0	64,144	0	77,570
Tennessee	115,268	0	0	0	115,268
Texas	38,483	0	46,850	0	85,333
Utah	772,894	0	0	302,439	1,075,333
Vermont	101,073	0	0	0	101,073
Virginia	100,356	0	79,579	0	179,935
Washington	2,635,766	805	1,739,763	7,140	4,383,474
West Virginia	89,166	0	0	0	89,166
Wisconsin	42,294	29	33,500	0	75,823
Wyoming	4,032,318	0	0	0	4,032,318
U.S. TOTAL	36,834,532	20,899,083	47,341,344	10,000,461	115,075,420

Source: Wilderness.net, 2008.

Wilderness in America provides substantial social and

economic benefits. These values are reflected by industries associated with wilderness recreation such as outfitters and guides. In addition, wilderness is increasingly used for personal growth, therapy, education and leadership development by businesses, educational organizations and a variety of nonprofit groups. Some estimates are that such commercial uses of wilderness generate over $100 million in revenues annually to entrepreneurs and even more to local communities as those dollars are re-spent in local businesses.

Wilderness lands, though protected from commercial logging, are open to commercial grazing and mining interests. Many grazing allotments exist on designated wilderness areas, and hardrock mining claims remain in force, although few mines are active, primarily due to low prices. Prospecting for new claims was ended with legislation passed in 1983.

Other economic values of wilderness include its contribution to property values of private land adjacent to designated wilderness. Studies in the Northern Rockies region, for example, have shown that population growth among counties along the front range of the Rocky Mountains is fastest in those with greater concentration of designated wilderness within their boundaries. That growth contributes to the value of local property and fuels the local economy. Yet given its economic, social and biological importance, wilderness management continues to receive little attention. The Forest Service, for example, spends just 1 percent of its total land management budget on wilderness management, even though wilderness represents 20 percent of the lands that it is charged to manage. The situation is the same or worse in the other federal agencies charged with wilderness management.

Today a broad consensus in the U.S. supports wilderness preservation. People's motives for preservation differ, but four values are common. First, Americans support protecting rare species and communities of species. The most common cause of extinction is the loss of habitat, and preserving wild land is essential for habitat protection. Second, Americans recognize the need to protect useful natural systems and processes. For example, the most efficient way to provide clean water is often the protection of natural watersheds. Third, wilderness provides unique opportunities for recreation and spiritual renewal. Fourth, many people accept an ethical responsibility to what Leopold called the land community. He argued that the idea of community should be expanded to include other species on whom humans depend, and ethical responsibilities to the larger community should be recognized.

— *G. Jon Roush and Jeffrey T. Olson*

See also

Biodiversity; Camps; Desert Landscapes; Environmental Protection; Forestry Industry; Mountains; National Resources Economics; Parks; Policy, Environmental; Tourism, Ecotourism; Watersheds; Wetlands; Wildlife

References

Babbitt, Bruce. *Cities in the Wilderness: A New Vision of Land Use in America*. Washington, DC: Island Press, 2005.

Callicott, J. Baird Callicott and Michael P. Nelson, eds. *The Great New Wilderness Debate*. Athens: University of Georgia Press, 1998.

David, Mark. *Dispossessing the Wilderness: Indian Removal and the Making of the National Parks*. New York: Oxford University Press, 2000.

Fox, Stephen. *John Muir and His Legacy*. Boston, MA: Little Brown, 1981.

Hendee, John C. and Chad P. Dawson. *Wilderness Management: Stewardship and Protection of Resources and Values*, 3rd. ed. Golden, CO: FulcrumPublishing, 2002.

Leopold, Aldo. *A Sand County Almanac and Sketches Here and There*. New York, NY: Oxford University Press, 1949.

Marsh, George P. *Man and Nature; or, Physical Geography as Modified by Human Action*. New York, NY: Charles Scribner, 1864.

Marshall, Robert. "The Problem of Wilderness." *Scientific Monthly* (1930): 142-148.

Nash, Roderick. *Wilderness and the American Mind*, 4th edition. New Haven, CT: Yale University Press, 2001.

Newton, Julianne Lutz. *Aldo Leopold's Odyssey: Rediscovering the Author of A Sand County Almanac*. Washington, DC: Island Press, 2006.

Thoreau, Henry David. "Walking" in *The Writings of Henry David Thoreau*, Volume 9. Boston, MA: Houghton Mifflin, 1893.

Wilderness.net. "Statistics Reports." Accessed February 2008. Available online at: http://www.wilderness.net/index.cfm.

Wildlife

Living creatures not directly under human control. The term usually excludes fish, and is associated with larger animals such as birds, mammals and reptiles. Wildlife represents a historic and contemporary source of rural-urban conflict. It is especially important to rural areas, as it provides recreation opportunities, economic benefits and costs, and symbolic meaning. However, social change in rural areas historically has affected and will continue to affect this linkage.

Background/History

Within the United States, rural people, through the mid-nineteenth century and in special instances today, depend on some species of wildlife for subsistence. Until recently, predator species were vilified and targeted for extermination because they represented potential economic loss through damage to livestock, competition for subsistence species and potential harm to humans. Many of these species (e.g., the wolf, grizzly bear mountain lion) were extirpated from many areas of the continental U.S. by the early twentieth century.

As a societal response to scarcity, urban sportsmen led the fight for scientific state-centered wildlife management. These interests demanded controlled hunting seasons, limits on hunting techniques deemed unsporting, prohibitions on the commercial sale of game, and required use of hunting licenses. Whereas some of these regulations proved useful to maintain wildlife populations, they marginalized the experience and interests of the poorer, more subsistence-oriented rural people. Although spectacularly successful for maintaining and increasing the populations of species valued by sport hunters (e.g., whitetail deer, Canada geese), this approach often did not prevent the extirpation of large predator species perceived to be in conflict with nongame species.

Wildlife Recreation

Wildlife recreation can be broadly classified as consumptive (the goal of which is to pursue and harvest an animal) and nonconsumptive (to observe, photograph or feed). The great majority of both types of recreation takes place in rural areas. According to the U.S. Fish and Wildlife Service (USFWS) reports, nonmetropolitan United States residents were more than twice as likely as the general population to have hunted in 2006 (12 percent versus 5 percent, respectively). In contrast, only 3 percent of those living in a large Metropolitan Standard Area (MSA) of one million or more hunted. Because so many Americans live in cities, however, 62 percent of all hunters reside in metropolitan areas. Regions of relatively low population density also have higher levels of hunting participation. For example, the Rocky Mountain and West Central regions show 2006 hunting participation rates of 6 percent and 12 percent, respectively. In contrast, only 3 percent of the population in the heavily populated New England region hunts.

Hunting in rural areas is fostered by greater opportunity, a more dominant hunting culture and active parental socialization (the process by which knowledge, attitudes, values, skills and motives are learned and internalized). Males who grow up in a rural area whose fathers hunted are much more likely than other demographic groups to begin and continue hunting. Rural socialization also fosters hunting participation among males without hunting fathers and—to a lesser degree—for females as well. Some researchers suggest that two types of hunters exist based on contrasting socialization mechanisms linked to urban versus rural areas. First, traditional hunters are socialized in rural areas by family members at a young age. This group obtains a broad base of satisfactions from their participation, is provided extensive social support and is committed to continuing participation. In contrast, the late adopter is socialized by friends at an older age and is more likely to have an urban residence. This type of hunter has less social support, is less committed to hunting and more likely to cease participation.

The USFWS classifies primary nonresidential, nonconsumptive recreation as travel one mile or more from the residence with the specific purpose of observing, feeding or photographing wildlife. Thirty-one percent of the total U.S. population participated in this activity in 2006, making it far more common than hunting. In contradistinction to hunting participation figures, rural people were only slightly more likely to participate. Thirty-eight percent of those not living in a metropolitan statistical area (MSA) participated compared to 25 percent of people living in a large MSA. Nonconsumptive recreation appears to depend neither on increased rural opportunity nor on rural socialization; participants are more likely than hunters to be self-initiated at older ages.

Wildlife in Rural Economies

Wildlife can have an important positive or negative economic impact on rural people and places. Economic value is not distributed evenly among wildlife species. Those that are important to recreation or subsistence provide much-needed redistribution of monies to rural areas. Expenditures related to consumptive use of animals (hunting) totaled $22.9 billion in 2006. Of these monies, $6.7 billion was spent on trip-related expenses, including food and lodging ($2.8 billion), and transportation ($2.7 billion). Many of these revenues may go di-

rectly to rural areas. To the degree that money is spent by urban dwellers in rural areas, this process can redistribute income from urban to rural areas.

Leasing and fee hunting are an increasingly important part of wildlife-related income. Although wildlife in the U.S. is owned by the state, the private landowner can regulate access and charge a fee if he or she wishes. About 7 percent of hunters hunted on leased land in 2005; the average price for leases was $861 per year. Great regional variation exists in these figures: leasing is most prevalent in the Southeast and South Central regions of the U.S. The prevalence of leasing and fee hunting is influenced by the relationship between buyers, sellers, and the amount and quality of game available. For example, if the rural landscape is characterized by small, dispersed parcels, or if regulations severely limit the amount of game that can be harvested, an individual landowner cannot command a high price.

Nonconsumptive wildlife-oriented recreation also accounted for high levels of expenditures. Primary nonresidential recreationists spent $12.9 billion on trip-related expenses in 2006. Of these, food and lodging alone accounted for $7.5 billion; transportation accounted for an additional $4.5 billion. Wildlife-oriented tourism is increasing, and wildlife represents a major factor in people's decisions to visit certain rural areas. The potential for capture of monies from this depends on the appeal and presence of the species, compatibility with other income-generating activities, local economic structure and sociocultural traditions.

From "Resource" to "Problem": Wildlife Conflict

Much of the historical policy development surrounding wildlife in the rural United States (i.e., regulations against market hunting, or the preservation of wildlife habitat) has been based on the idea of wildlife as a scarce and valued resource to be conserved. In some contexts and for some species, this is changing, and management is focused instead on minimizing conflict between people and wildlife by controlling wildlife populations. For example, hunting bag limits for species such as white-tailed deer or snow geese have become greatly liberalized in many places in recent years as managers have struggled with keeping populations in check. High populations of species such as these can result in ecological and economic damage, as well as concerns about human health related to the emergence of wildlife-based disease such as chronic wasting disease, Lyme disease, or avian influenza. Concern is also increasing in areas where interactions between humans and large predators, such as black bears and/or mountain lions, are becoming more common.

Wildlife on rural lands can thus represent a double-edged sword. Although the potential benefits are extensive, so too are the potential costs. Wildlife can have negative economic impacts through various types of property damage, or even represent physical hazards through contact with humans For example, multiple injuries and fatalities occur every year from deer-vehicle incidents, and the prevalence of these incidents continues to increase. Millions of dollars are lost annually through wildlife-related losses to agricultural production. Although mechanisms exist to compensate farmers for wildlife damage to crops and/or livestock, filing claims and receiving compensation may be complicated and time consuming. Nor may the compensation be adequate to cover damages. The extent or cause of damage may be disputed. For example, although there exists a pool of money to compensate ranchers for livestock killed by wolves, such claims may be disputed (was the animal killed by a wolf, or was the wolf merely feeding on an animal that died from other causes?). These problems have policy implications; surveys in many states show that those who are actively involved in farming or ranching are most strongly opposed to wolf restoration. Theoretically, the financial losses that rural people, particularly agriculturists, suffer from wildlife damage are offset by the revenues that wildlife provide to rural areas. In reality, with the exception of income from leasing and fee hunting, wildlife-related revenues usually do not accrue to the same people who suffer losses, but instead to business owners who may or may not be locally based. In short, those who sustain the costs of maintaining high populations of desired wildlife often do not reap the benefits. Mitigating wildlife damage and redistribution of revenues to those who suffer economic damage is important if high populations of wildlife are to be maintained in rural areas.

The growth of wildlife-human conflicts is based on multiple factors, including the success of past wildlife management efforts resulting in increased populations of some species; an increased tolerance of human presence by some species—tied to decreased hunting and increases in activities such as wildlife feeding—and the continued movement of people into wildlife habitat through the emergence and growth of the urban-rural interface in high-amenity rural places. As the density of human population increases, so do the opportunities for interaction. The effects can be positive, as manifested in increased recreational opportunities, or negative, as realized through negative encounters, perceived risk or economic impact.

Symbolic Importance of Wildlife

There can be strong differences in attitudes toward wildlife between urban and rural residents. Traditional rural residents are more likely than other groups to see animals as resources that can provide material, utilitarian benefits to humans, or see humans as superior to animals, with animal-human interactions providing opportunities for the exercise of human skill. These attitudes are manifested most strongly in traditional rural occupations; farmers are especially strong in these orientations. In contrast, urban residents tend to be of two primary types. First, those scoring highly on moralistic or humanistic scales express concern with the welfare and suffering of individual animals, based either on affection or general philosophical principles. Another type of urban orientation is neutral or negativistic; these people score high on scales that measure irrelevance, avoidance or intolerance of wildlife.

Rural places sometimes identify themselves with the presence of wildlife species characteristic to the area, particularly if these species are valued for their rarity, beauty or importance to humans. This identification may be particularly strong during hunting seasons. Small towns and rural areas are dominated by hunting-based totemic display, such as blaze orange and camouflage clothing in storefronts, "Welcome Hunters" signs on many places of business, "big buck" contests, high school classes and places of employment devoid of males on opening day, and special "Hunter's Breakfasts." Fitchen (1991), in her treatment of rural New York State, writes

> Deer hunting ... is above all a local cultural activity rooted in rural space ... an annual ritual, part of the annual cycle of seasons and events, that helps proclaim "who we are" and "what we do here" and that defines "the kind of life we lead in this rural county." ... The first day of deer season is surrounded by anticipatory events, opening-day breakfasts, and community camaraderie ... .As such, deer hunting is an activity that proclaims and reaffirms the relationship between people and land.

Wildlife-based identities are not limited to places. Individuals can develop personal identity-based interactions with wildlife. Interactions with wildlife, especially hunting, are mechanisms to transmit culture, skills, beliefs and attitudes representative of a particular

Ruffed Grouse at Park Falls, Wisconsin. Courtesy of the Park Falls Chamber of Commerce

group or area. Contact with wildlife extends beyond the actual participants. Other people are socialization agents, but also may participate in some aspects of the hunt, have positive beliefs about hunting, and perceive that they receive benefits from hunting. This extension of the hunting culture is especially common in rural areas.

It would be a mistake to think of rural as a stable entity and the relationships between rural people, places and wildlife as unchanging. There is widespread agreement that traditional rural orientations are changing. Urbanization resulted in a steady decline of people being socialized in rural areas. This phenomenon is reflected in declines in hunter participation. USFWS numbers show that hunter participation is declining steadily; 11.2 percent of the population hunted in 1960, 8.4 percent in 1985 (a 25 percent decline in 25 years). The pace of this decline is accelerating; only 7.4 percent reported in 1991 that they hunted, which dropped to 5.5 percent in 2006. An especially sharp drop has occurred in the recruitment of new, younger hunters: the hunter population is thus aging faster than society as a whole. The two most important causes of the decline in hunter numbers are linked to rural change: the percentage of people socialized in rural communities and current rural residence. Changing family structures and racial and ethnic composition of the U.S. population are part of this decline as well.

Urbanization is not the only factor salient to rural change. Remaining rural areas themselves are changing through immigration and linkages (information- and transportation- based) to urban areas. It is therefore important to have a realistic idea of what rural means: rural renaissance and high rates of urban-to-rural migration will not likely cause a return to the traditional rural attitudes and socialization mechanisms concerning wildlife.

— *Thomas A. Heberlein and Richard C. Stedman*

See also
Animal Rights/Welfare; Fisheries Management; Recreational Activities; Tourism, Ecotourism; Wildlife Management

References
Conover, Michael R. *Resolving Human-Wildlife Conflicts: The Science of Wildlife Damage Management.* Lewis Publishers, 2002.

Decker, Daniel J. and Gary R. Goff. *Valuing Wildlife: Economic and Social Perspectives.* Boulder, CO: Westview, 1987.

Fitchen, J. *Endangered Spaces, Enduring Places.* Boulder, CO: Westview, 1991.

Kellert, Steven R. *The Value of Life: Biological Diversity and Human Society.* Washington, DC: Island Press/Shearwater Books, 1996.

Marks, Stuart A. *Southern Hunting in Black and White.* Princeton, NJ: Princeton University Press, 1991.

Miller, John. *Deer Camp: Last Light in the Northeast Kingdom.* Cambridge, MA: MIT Press and Middlebury, VT: Vermont Folklife Center, 1992.

Stedman, R.C. and T.A. Heberlein. "Hunting and Rural Socialization." *Rural Sociology* 66, no. 4 (2001): 599-617.

Tober, James A. *Who Owns Wildlife?: The Political Economy of Conservation in Nineteenth Century America.* Westport, CT: Greenwood Press, 1981.

U.S. Department of the Interior and U.S. Department of Commerce. *2006 National Survey of Fishing, Hunting, and Wildlife-Associated Recreation.* Washington, DC: U.S. Department of the Interior, Fish and Wildlife Service, and U.S. Department of Commerce, U.S. Census Bureau, 2006.

Wildlife Management
Collecting information on animals, such as birds, mammals and reptiles, their habitats, behaviors and foods, and using this information in conjunction with the desires of people to manipulate (increase, decrease or sustain) populations. Wildlife managers are trained in wildlife biology, ecology, habitat management, criminal justice and conflict resolution. Game populations are managed for harvest based on information that can include population size, growth rate, survival and mortality factors. Rare animals are restored to native habitats by releasing animals into unoccupied habitats and evaluating population viability. Federal agencies (U.S. Fish and Wildlife Service, U.S. Department of Agriculture (USDA) Forest Service, National Park Service) and state wildlife agencies employ trained wildlife managers.

Wildlife management was formally recognized as a profession beginning in 1933 with the publication of *Game Management* by Aldo Leopold. Leopold defined game management as the art of making the land produce sustained annual crops of wild game for recreational use. Prior to this time, management largely involved the enforcement of game laws to protect game animals from over-harvest. In 1934, the Migratory Bird Hunting Stamp Act was passed. The act provided funds for the purchase and protection of waterfowl habitat, such as waterfowl production areas and refuges. In 1937, the passage of the Federal Aid to Wildlife Restoration Act, also known as the Pittman-Robertson Act, placed a 10 percent tax on firearms and ammunition to provide funds to restore wildlife populations that had been decimated by market hunting. These funds were, and continue to be, allotted to states based on a formula that includes land area and number of hunting licenses sold. Funds continue to be used to restock vacant range and to collect information on wildlife populations for the benefit of management agencies. Through time, game agencies saw the need to protect all wildlife species, not just game animals. Other acts, such as the Endangered Species Act of 1973, allowed for the listing of rare species, such as bald eagles, grizzly bears, and wolves, as threatened and endangered. More recently, the Teaming with Wildlife initiative was established by Congress to provide funds for the management of non-game wildlife, such as turtles and song birds.

Wildlife belongs to the people of the states and is protected, as well as managed, by the state management agencies and by federal agencies for those species that travel across state and federal borders. Ranchers may be concerned with pronghorn and prairie dog use of vegetation and how it will affect the ability of their cattle to gain weight. Farmers may be concerned with wetlands, depredation (consumption of crops by wildlife) by blackbirds, or killing of livestock by predators, such as coyotes.

Communities may be concerned with Canada geese use of golf courses. Furthermore, hunters may be concerned with the availability of trophy deer, which in some regions have been defined as males with greater than or equal to eight tines (four tines or points per antler). The wildlife manager's goal is to balance wildlife populations at levels that minimize concerns of local people while maximizing the benefits of wildlife. In some cases, harvest may be the best tool available to keep species at a level that diminishes concerns. In other instances, tools such as effigies (e.g., owls), fences or scare devices may constitute the best techniques for minimizing concerns (Conover, 2002). Managers collect information on populations using research studies and also on their constituents using surveys of attitudes of hunters and landowners toward wildlife. This information is used to determine the most acceptable strategy for manipulating a wildlife population.

Habitat evaluation is an important component of wildlife management. Habitat is defined as the place where an animal lives, and it includes both abiotic (climate) and biotic (other animals and plants) elements (Scalet et al., 1996). Wildlife requires water, food and cover to successfully survive and reproduce. Browse (tree and shrub leaves and stems), fruit, aquatic plants and agricultural crops are examples of foods consumed by herbivorous wildlife species. Deer, small mammals, birds, insects, fruit and vegetation are examples of foods consumed by predators. Cover can be further defined as escape cover, or cover that allows an animal to escape from a predator, and thermal cover, or cover that provides a microclimate that is beneficial to wildlife (shields animals from wind, and rain, or moderates ambient temperature). Wildlife research has been used to document habitat components associated with successful and unsuccessful wildlife populations. Techniques are available to improve habitat for wildlife species via manipulations that include vegetative plantings or food plots, fertilization, logging, brush removal and water developments. Depending on the species being managed, a variety of manipulations may be used that, either alone or in concert, could improve habitats for populations. For example, trees in close proximity to corn food plots have been associated with increased winter survival of pheasants. In addition, restoration of aspen stands have improved habitat for deer as well as elk. Some methods (e.g., wetland restoration) allow for increases in wildlife diversity and as such, improve conditions concurrently for birds, mammals and herptiles (reptiles and amphibians). Geographical Information Systems (mapping systems) are currently used to develop landscape approaches to habitat management.

Conversion of natural habitats to agriculture and urbanization have contributed to the fragmentation of wildlife habitats in rural landscapes. For example, large fields of corn can represent cover and food resources for some wildlife species. However, those habitats are eliminated in fall via crop harvest, which can result in major movements of animals in search of winter habitats that provide security. Habitats that remain likely are occupied by the species, which can result in large concentrations of animals that frequent farm yards in search of food. Deer in South Dakota have damaged stored hay due to urine and fecal contamination during severe winters. Managers have used late-season harvests to decrease and disperse deer concentrations when these conditions persist. Federal programs like the Conservation Reserve Program pay farmers to take agricultural lands out of production and replant those lands with native vegetation. This program is responsible for creating habitat for wildlife and has resulted in improved habitat conditions that help to disperse wildlife. The improved habitat conditions resulting from this program also have contributed to increased populations of species like pheasants and song birds.

Wildlife management in rural landscapes requires cooperation between state and federal agencies and private landowners. Much of the land (habitat) in rural areas is either forested or agricultural and in private ownership. Some landowners plant crops that have improved populations of many game species, such as white-tailed deer, pheasants and wild turkeys. If populations increase to the point where significant crop damage occurs, usually greater than about 10 percent, then landowner tolerance of game declines. Because human-related factors are responsible for up to 80 percent of annual mortality of game species, use of harvest is necessary to manage game species at densities that minimize crop damage in rural areas. Management of game is becoming more difficult due to increases in game populations and decreases in hunters; yet, in some regions, the proportion of recreationalists involved in hunting have stabilized (USFWS, 2007).

For game species that are harvested, information on population dynamics, which includes population size, growth rate, mortality factors, dispersal, survival and reproduction, is obtained by game managers when possible. Estimates of population size are obtained by counting animals using, for example, aerial surveys, and quantifying biases that impede a manager's ability to get a true count (observability; Lancia et al., 2005), such as vegetation that hides an animal from view. Even animals like pronghorn that occupy open prairies can have low observation rates in aerial surveys if they occur in small groups and are inactive. Managers use these observation rates to adjust estimates of population size. Growth rate is defined as the change in population size through time. It can be positive or negative and is calculated from estimates of population size over more than one time period (year) (Caughley, 1977). Examples of mortality factors affecting wildlife populations in rural areas include hunting, disease, predation and vehicles. These mortality factors can reduce survival and population size, whereas annual reproduction (young per female) adds to the population. For populations that are harvested, managers use this information in population models to predict sustained yield or the number of animals that can be removed from the population without decreasing annual population size. Size of the harvest is based on this information. In addition, information on landowner tolerance is used in harvest recommendations.

Dispersal is defined as movement away from a point of origin to where the animal reproduces or would have reproduced if it had survived (Caughley, 1977). Dispersal is a one-way movement, whereas migration includes movement back to the point of origin. Dispersal movements are important for the exchange of genetic material between populations and for expanding the distribution of species that may have undergone local extinctions. Dispersal of white-tailed deer has been linked to habitat conditions with dispersal distances increasing as forest cover declines. Longest dispersals have been documented in the Great Plains region with, for example, white-tailed deer dispersing over 200 kilometers. Other species, such as mountain lions, mountain goats and bighorn sheep also have traveled great distances in search of food and mates. In fact, the longest distance dispersed by a mountain lion began in the Black Hills of Wyoming and ended in Red Rock, Oklahoma (Thompson and Jenks, 2005), a straight-line distance of 1,067 kilometers. Wildlife managers use these movements, as well as topography and roads, to define unit boundaries within which populations are managed uniformly.

Human pathogens that are spread by wildlife are an important concern to wildlife management agencies. Examples of these pathogens include rabies, which is a virus spread by skunks, coyotes and other furbearers, and botulism, which can result in die-offs of large numbers of waterfowl. Most diseases are spread through contact between animals with potential for contact increasing with population size or density (animals per unit area). Furbearers in rural areas use abandoned farmsteads for refuge and consume agricultural crops during winter, which can maintain populations at high levels. When populations of these furbearers increase, animals come into close contact with humans, increasing the chances of infection and death. Management agencies use trapping as a tool to keep furbearers at densities that minimize the spread of these diseases. Information collected from trapped animals, such as age and sex, allow managers to set trapping seasons so that they can reduce populations to desired levels. Number of trappers that are actively involved in the capture of furbearers varies with fur prices. When prices are low, other tools are necessary to maintain these populations at levels below those where diseases become problematic. In some cases, such as with sarcoptic mange, a parasite affecting coyotes and foxes, the disease itself reduces the furbearer population.

The United States Fish and Wildlife Service manages animals, including ducks and geese, that cross international borders under the auspices of the Migratory Bird Treaty Act of 1918 (Scalet et al., 1996). Management occurs within waterfowl flyways, Atlantic, Mississippi, Central, and Pacific, which represent regions within which populations of ducks and geese migrate between wintering and breeding areas. Population size of these species has been linked to wetland conditions (abundance and condition). For example, aerial transect surveys (east-west strip 0.4 kilometers wide and up to 240 kilometers in length are conducted in the Prairie Pothole region of North America (Iowa, Minnesota and the Dakotas) annually to count both ponds and waterfowl. This information is used in an adaptive management framework (seasons are adjusted based on the best information available on populations) to set harvest seasons and bag limits (number of animals that can be harvested per day). If information on a particular species, for example canvasback ducks, indicates that the species is in decline, bag limits might be reduced. Alternatively, if wetland conditions and counts indicate expansion of waterfowl populations, harvest season length or bag limits might be increased.

Rare species, such as black-footed ferrets, also are managed by the United States Fish and Wildlife Service via the Endangered Species Act. Upon listing, management involves collecting information (population size), documenting habitat conditions, and developing restoration plans. In extreme situations where few animals remain in the wild, management may include transfer of those animals to a captive facility until conditions favorable for repatriation of animals back into the wild. These steps were taken for black-footed ferrets and California condors. Once restoration is initiated, monitoring programs are funded to ensure the long-term viability of these species. In regions such as the prairies of central North America, where rare species have been extirpated (are locally extinct), restoration programs have been instituted. Black-footed ferrets and swift fox have been restored to native prairies whereas bighorn sheep have been restored to regions that include isolated mountain ranges and prairies throughout central and western North America. For those species that have undergone local extinctions, individual animals from other regions have been captured and released back into the wild. Most restoration programs mark,

via radio collars, released animals and relocate them through the use of telemetry systems to evaluate the restoration program. Through the use of these techniques, movements and survival are evaluated to assess viability of the released animals and to determine if additional releases are necessary.

The long-term goal of restoration programs is viable populations occupying native habitats that are robust to extirpation. Because genetic problems, such as founder effects (low genetic diversity due to few released animals) and inbreeding (high genetic similarity between male and female pairs), have been associated with population declines, assessing genetic characteristics of populations is useful for determining population viability (long-term population persistence). Viability is generally calculated as the chance a species will remain on the landscape for 100 years. Viability has been increased in bighorn sheep populations in western states by selecting individuals from a variety of populations to augment local herds. For example, bighorns from New Mexico were transported to Badlands National Park and released into a region with a population that had declined due to a perceived reduction in genetic diversity. Restoration of grizzly bears, in the Yellowstone Ecosystem, and bald eagles, nationwide, has resulted in removal of these species from listing as threatened and endangered.

Modern wildlife agencies employ specialists for the management of large mammals, waterfowl, furbearers, non-game wildlife, habitat and human dimensions. Specialists are trained in subjects including animal life history, data collection, data analysis, population modeling, habitat suitability, as well as criminal justice and conflict resolution. Non-governmental organizations (NGOs) are requiring agencies to justify management decisions. Consequently, managers may need to testify in court to defend management decisions, especially those involving trapping and hunting seasons. Harvest management decisions have been brought to trial in Maine (moose harvest season), Massachusetts (trapping seasons), Colorado (black bear harvest), Arizona (trapping seasons), South Dakota (mountain lion harvest), and against the U.S. Fish and Wildlife Service (snow goose harvest and gray wolf delisting). Other issues that likely will affect management of wildlife in the future include global warming, urbanization, use of agricultural crops and grasslands for ethanol production, and the creation of large wind farms for the production of electricity.

— *Jonathan A. Jenks*

See also

Animal Rights/Welfare; Livestock Production; Natural Resources Management; Wildlife; Wildlife Value Orientations

References

Caughley, Graeme. *Analysis of Vertebrate Populations.* New York: John Wiley and Sons, 1977. Reprinted 2004.

Conover, Michael. *Resolving Human-Wildlife Conflicts: The Science of Wildlife Damage Management.* New York: Lewis Publishers, 2002.

Krausman, Paul. *Introduction to Wildlife Management: The Basics.* Upper Saddle River, NJ: Prentice Hall, 2002.

Lancia, Richard, William Kendall, Kenneth Pollock, and James Nichols. "Estimating the Number of Animals in Wildlife Populations." Pp. 106-153 in *Techniques for Wildlife Investigations and Management*, 6th ed. Edited by C.E. Braun. Bethesda, MD: The Wildlife Society, 2005.

Leopold, Aldo. *Game Management.* New York: Charles Scribner's Sons, 1933. Reprinted 1986.

Reynolds, John, Georgina Mace, Kent Redford, and John Robinson. *Conservation of Exploited Species.* Cambridge, UK: Cambridge University Press, 2001.

Scalet, Charles, Lester Flake, and David Willis. *Introduction to Wildlife and Fisheries: An Integrated Approach.* New York: W. H. Freeman and Company, 1996.

Thompson, Daniel, and Jonathan Jenks. "Long-Distance Dispersal by a Subadult Male Cougar (*Puma concolor*) From the Black Hills, South Dakota." *Journal of Wildlife Management* 69 (2005): 818-820.

United States Fish and Wildlife Service. *2006 National Survey of Fishing, Hunting and Wildlife-Associated Recreation: State Overview.* Washington DC: United States Department of the Interior, United States Fish and Wildlife Service, 2007.

Wildlife Value Orientations

The way people view and relate to wildlife. Rural Americans have always had a special connection to wildlife. Parents have traditionally taught their children how to hunt. People in general understand the relationship between harvesting game and putting food on the table. Local rural economies benefit from the influx of new dollars during hunting seasons. Much of this tradition is predicated on the assumption of a utilitarian value orientation between humans and animals. Some evidence, however, suggests that this traditional world view is changing. Declines in recreational hunting in North America and increases in animal rights groups have stimulated speculation about changing societal views toward wildlife. Manfredo and Zinn (1996) partially attribute the trend away from utilitarian value orientations to urbanization and intergenerational differences.

The loss of family-owned farms, decreasing acreage for wildlife habitat, and increasing out-migration to urban centers are all impacting rural communities and potentially changing the way rural Americans relate to wildlife. This chapter: 1) compares the values orientations of individuals who grew up in rural America against those of individuals who spent their childhood in more urban areas, and 2) examines potential value shifts among different generations of rural and non-rural Americans. The cognitive hierarchy (i.e., value orientations, attitudes, norms, behaviors) is used as the organizing theoretical framework for understanding these relationships.

The Cognitive Hierarchy

Popular media commonly assert that values influence environmental attitudes and behaviors, but empirical evidence showing direct predictive validity is sparse. For example, research suggests that values have limited effects on predicting support for specific wildlife management actions or for specific forms of environmental activism such as signing petitions (Vaske and Donnelly, 2007). Social-psychological theories offer explanations for these disparities, suggesting that attitudes and norms mediate the relationships between values and behavior (Whittaker et al., 2006). These theories distinguish stable but abstract values from more specific cognitions (e.g., attitudes and norms) that evaluate objects or situations encountered in daily life. Such cognitions are best understood as part of a "hierarchy" from general to specific. Specific attitudinal or normative variables are more likely to predict behaviors than more general measures like values. These elements build upon one another in what has been described as an inverted pyramid. Research has applied this "cognitive hierarchy" to evaluations and behavior associated with wildlife (Fulton et al., 1996; Manfredo et al., 2003; Vaske and Donnelly, 2007; Vaske and Needham, 2007).

Values and Value Orientations. *Values* represent the most basic social cognitions and differ from other elements in the cognitive hierarchy model in at least

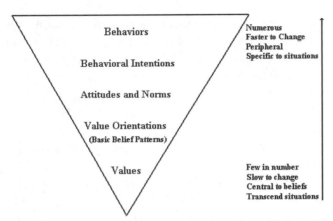

Figure 1. The cognitive hierarchy. Source: Vaske and Donnelly (1999).

three ways. First, values are learned early in life, are central to a person's belief system, and thus are difficult to change. Second, values are believed to transcend situations and issues. For example, a person who holds "honesty" as a value would be expected to be honest when completing IRS tax forms, conducting business deals or interacting with friends. Third, because values tend to be relatively constant within a culture, their predictive power in explaining specific cognitions or behavior is limited.

Value orientations refer to patterns of basic beliefs about general objects, which give meaning to more abstract values (Vaske and Donnelly, 1999; 2007). For example, while values measure the extent to which people identify with abstract concepts (e.g., honesty), value orientations reflect basic belief patterns about broad classes of objects (e.g., all wildlife), which link back to underlying values-level cognitions. Value orientations facilitate understanding differences in attitudes, norms and behavior among people who hold the same value. For example, the value "protecting wildlife" might be interpreted by some individuals as people should never harm wildlife under any circumstances. Others who value wildlife protection may take a different stance and believe that it is acceptable to kill wildlife for food.

Within the human dimensions literature, one wildlife value orientation focuses on a *protection-use* continuum that is measured by the degree of agreement with a series of statements about "wildlife rights," "wildlife use," and "hunting" (Fulton et al., 1996; Whittaker et al., 2006). Example statements include "Animals should have rights similar to the rights of humans" (rights), "Recreational use of natural environments is more important than protecting wildlife" (use), and "Hunting is cruel to animals" (hunting). A second wildlife value orientation is a *wildlife apprecia-*

tion continuum. Basic beliefs associated with this orientation are typically measured with statements about "wildlife benefits," appreciation of wildlife in "recreation" and "residential settings," "interest in learning about wildlife," and "wildlife existence" (Fulton et al., 1996; Whittaker et al., 2006). Although protection-use and appreciation reflect two primary orthogonal orientations, "protection-use" is a better predictor of specific attitudes and norms related to management actions (e.g., destroying nuisance wildlife, hunting urban wildlife, wildlife trapping) than "appreciation" (Gliner et al., 2001; Manfredo et al., 2003). In contrast, appreciation value orientations appear to predict wildlife learning and wildlife viewing recreation behavior better than protection-use (Fulton et al., 1996).

Attitudes and Norms. In the cognitive hierarchy, value orientations (i.e., protection-use, appreciation) shape variation in people's wildlife-related behaviors and their attitudes and norms toward wildlife (Fulton et al., 1996; Manfredo et al., 2003; Vaske and Donnelly, 2007). Attitudes are positive or negative evaluations of some object, while norms are judgments about what is appropriate in a specific situation or standards that individuals use to evaluate whether behavior or conditions should occur (Vaske and Whittaker, 2004). While there are measurement and conceptual distinctions between attitudes and norms, both are fundamentally evaluative variables that can vary considerably by the specificity of their object. For example, if the object is "wolves," the evaluation reflects the mix of cognitions that form a general attitude or norm. If the object is "wolf reintroduction in rural Colorado in 2008," the evaluation reflects a narrower context and time frame, and thus a more specific evaluation.

The specificity of the norm or the attitude is critical for determining whether they will accurately predict behavior (Vaske and Needham, 2007). For example, in a statewide sample of New Hampshire residents, Vaske and Donnelly (1995) found specific beliefs were better predictors of residents' reactions to a proposed moose hunt than either general beliefs or personal characteristics. The traditional socio-demographic variables were among the poorest predictors of respondents' attitude. Place of residence (rural vs. urban) did not statistically influence approval of the hunt in any of the models examined.

Rural-Urban Influences on Wildlife Value Orientations

Although variables such as place of residence often have limited predictive power in cognitive hierarchy models, rural-urban measures can be useful in describing and understanding trends in value orientations. Data from a 1996 survey ($n = 971$) of Alaska residents (Whittaker et al., 2006) and a 2007 survey ($n = 364$) of university students are used here to illustrate this relationship.

Following Fulton et al. (1996) and Whittaker et al. (2006), wildlife value orientations were computed in a two-step process. The first step used 27 belief variables to measure eight wildlife basic belief dimensions: 1) wildlife use, 2) hunting, 3) wildlife rights, 4) wildlife appreciation in recreation settings, 5) appreciation in residential settings, 6) importance of wildlife to life, 7) wildlife learning, and 8) wildlife existence and bequest value. Each of the basic belief dimensions contained three to four items (see Table 1 for actual question wording). Each variable was measured on a seven-point scale: (-3) strongly disagree, (0) neutral, and (+3) strongly agree. Reliabilities for the eight basic belief scales were all .70 or greater (Cronbach alpha range .70 to .88). The second step combined these eight variables to measure two value orientations: 1) wildlife protection-use, and 2) wildlife appreciation.

Because wildlife value orientations are formed early in life, the independent variable was the respondent's place of residence while growing up. The U.S. Office of Management and Budget categories were used to define: 1) rural (i.e., <5,000 people, $n = 418$), 2) micropolitan (i.e., 10,000 to 50,000 people, $n = 283$), and 3) metropolitan (i.e., >50,000 people, $n = 562$) areas.

Respondents who grew up in rural America were statistically more likely to hold a traditional utilitarian view of wildlife (i.e., wildlife use) and were more positive toward hunting than those who lived in a metropolitan area during their childhood. The strength of these differences, however, was "minimal" (see Gliner et al., 2001) with eta values of .155 and .074, respectively. There were no statistical differences for place of residence during childhood and the wildlife rights basic belief dimension. Individuals in all three rural to urban categories were "neutral" on wildlife rights.

Only one of the basic belief dimensions (i.e., residential appreciation) associated with the wildlife appreciation value orientation revealed statistical differences on the rural-urban variable. Individuals who lived in rural areas during their childhood appreciated the presence of wildlife near their residences more than those who grew up in metropolitan areas. None of the other four appreciation basic belief dimensions differed significantly by place of childhood residence.

Combined Rural-Urban and Age Influences on Wildlife Value Orientations

Because fundamental values change slowly, past research has suggested that shifts in wildlife value orientations should be evident in different age groups (Manfredo and Zinn, 1996). To examine this hypothesis, a series of two-way analyses of variance were conducted. The independent variables were: 1) a rural versus non-rural measure[1] and 2) a categorical age variable. The age categories included: 1) youth (i.e., <25 years old), 2) Gen X (i.e., 25 to 40), 3) baby boomers (i.e., 41 to 59), and 4) individuals 60 and older. As expected, these models explained less than 5 percent of the variability in any of the criterion variables. The general pattern of findings, however, illustrates some potential shifts in value orientation. For the wildlife use basic belief dimension, individuals who came from either a rural or non-rural background and who were less than 25 years old were least likely to report a utilitarian value orientation, while the oldest generation (60+) was most likely to agree with using wildlife for human benefit (Figure 2a). Differences between rural and non-rural respondents on wildlife use were only apparent for baby boomers and those over 60.

People who grew up in rural areas were consistently more favorable toward hunting than the non-rural respondents across all age groups. Gen X (age = 25 to 40) respondents from rural backgrounds, however, were most supportive of hunting, while non-rural respondents 60 and over were least likely to agree with the hunting basic belief dimension.

The appreciation wildlife value orientation was computed as the average of the five basic belief dimensions associated with the concept. Individuals who were less than 25 years old and who grew up in a rural area were more likely to appreciate wildlife than their non-rural counterparts. At the other end of the generation continuum (60+), non-rural respondents were more likely to hold an appreciation value orientation than the rural individuals.

---

[1]Given the general lack of statistical significance between the micropolitan and metropolitan sample, this variable combined these two categories into "non-rural."

Table 1.
Basic wildlife belief indices and value orientations

Wildlife value orientations and basic beliefs comprising each scale[1]	Description of residence while growing up[10]			F-value	p	η
	Rural <5,000 (n = 418)	Micropolitan 10,000 to 50,000 (n = 283)	Metropolitan >50,000 (n = 562)			
Protection-use Value Orientation						
Wildlife Use[2]	1.12[a]	0.95[ab]	0.86[b]	3.49	.031	.155
Hunting[3]	1.50[a]	−1.16[b]	0.86[c]	15.51	<.001	.074
Wildlife Rights[4]	0.009	−0.007	−0.053	0.16	.855	.016
Appreciation Value Orientation						
Recreation Appreciation[5]	2.34	2.28	2.29	0.44	.642	.027
Residential Appreciation[6]	1.72[a]	1.58[ab]	1.49[b]	3.27	.038	.072
Importance of Wildlife to Life[7]	1.72	1.70	1.62	0.75	.475	.034
Wildlife Learning[8]	2.44	2.40	2.37	1.07	.343	.038
Wildlife Existence/Bequest[9]	2.60	2.59	2.54	0.90	.405	.041

1. All variables and indices were coded on a seven-point scale (-3) strongly disagree, (0) neutral, and (+3) strongly agree.
2. The "wildlife use" basic belief index included four statements: (a) Humans should manage wild animal populations so that humans benefit, (b) It is acceptable for human use to cause the loss of some individual animals so long as animal populations are not jeopardized, (c) It is important for humans to manage populations of wildlife, and (d) If animal populations are not threatened, we should use wildlife to add to the quality of human life (Cronbach's α = .70).
3. The "hunting" basic belief index included three statements: (a) hunting is cruel to animals, (b) hunting makes people insensitive to suffering, and (c) I would be upset if I saw an animal injured/killed by a hunter (Cronbach's α = .88). These items were reverse coded.
4. The "wildlife rights" basic belief index included three statements: (a) The rights of wildlife are more important than human use of wildlife, (b) The needs of humans are more important than the rights that wildlife may have, and (c) The rights of people and rights of wildlife are equally important (Cronbach's α = .79).
5. The "recreation appreciation" basic belief index included three statements: (a) I enjoy watching wildlife when I take a trip outdoors, (b), Some of my most memorable outdoor experiences occurred when I saw wildlife that I did not expect to see, and (c) The opportunity to see wildlife is one of the reasons I take trips outdoors (Cronbach's α = .74).
6. The "residential appreciation" basic belief index included three statements: (a) I am interested in making the area around my home attractive to wildlife, (b) Having wildlife around my home is important to me, and (c) An important part of my community is the wildlife I see there (Cronbach's α = .85).
7. The "importance of wildlife to life" basic belief index included four statements: (a) I take pride in the amount of wildlife in my area, even if they cause some problems or hazards, (b) While wildlife cause some problems, these problems make life more special, (c) Although some wildlife encounters can be dangerous, they make life more interesting, and (d) People who live in my area should learn to live with some conflicts or problems associated with wildlife (Cronbach's α = .86).
8. The "wildlife learning" basic belief index included three statements: (a) It is important that we learn as much as we can about wildlife, (b) I enjoy learning about wildlife, and (c) It is important that all people have a chance to learn about wildlife in their area (Cronbach's α = .79).
9. The "wildlife existence/bequest" basic belief index included three statements: (a) We should be sure that future generations have an abundance of wildlife, (b) It is important to maintain wildlife so that future generations can enjoy them, and (c) It is important to me to know that there are healthy populations of wildlife in my area (Cronbach's α = .78).
10. Cell entries are means. Means with different superscripts differ statistically at $p < .05$.

Conclusions

Past research suggests that wildlife value orientations in the United States are moving away from a utilitarian value orientation. Most analyses conducted to date have consistently shown that: 1) attitudes and norms mediate the relationship between value orientations and behaviors, and 2) demographic indicators such as place of residence (rural vs. urban) and age are relatively weak predictors of value orientations, attitudes, norms, behaviors. Demographic variables, however, are useful in examining trends in wildlife value orientations. Rural Americans have traditionally held strong utilitarian values. The analyses in this chapter suggest that this trend continues today. Individuals who came from a rural background were more likely to agree with wildlife use and hunting basic beliefs than those from more urban areas. Because rural Americans are often still connected to the land where hunting and the consumption of harvested game are often an integral component of their lifestyle, traditional value structures appear to remain relatively stable. A change in rural Americans' relationships with wildlife may be occurring as the population ages, but at a rate slower than what is found in more urban sectors.

— *Jerry J. Vaske*

See also

Animal Rights/Welfare; Livestock Production; Natural Resources Management; Wildlife; Wildlife Management

References

Donnelly, Maureen. P. and Jerry J. Vaske. "Predicting Attitudes Toward a Proposed Moose Hunt." *Society and Natural Resources* 8, no. 4 (1995): 307-319.

Figure 2. Wildlife use, hunting and appreciation value orientations

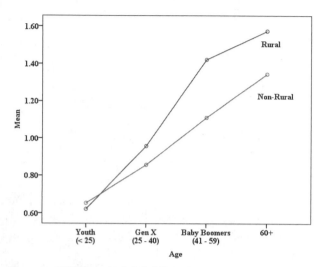

Figure 2a. Wildlife use basic belief dimension

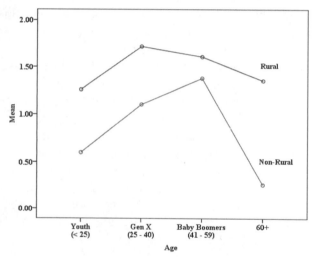

Figure 2b. Hunting basic belief dimension

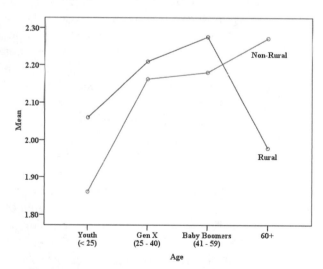

Figure 2c. Appreciation wildlife value orientation

Fulton, David. C., Michael J. Manfredo, and James Lipscomb. "Wildlife Value Orientations: A Conceptual and Measurement Approach." *Human Dimensions of Wildlife* 1 (1996): 24-47.

Gliner, Jeffery A., Jerry J. Vaske, and George A. Morgan. "Null Hypothesis Significance Testing: Effect Size Matters." *Human Dimensions of Wildlife* 6, no. 4 (2001): 291-301.

Manfredo, Michael J. and Harry C. Zinn. "Population Change and Its Implications for Wildlife Management in the New West: A Case Study of Colorado." *Human Dimensions of Wildlife* 1 (1996): 62-74.

Manfredo, Michael J., Tara L. Teel, and Alan D. Bright. "Why Are Public Values Toward Wildlife Changing?" *Human Dimensions of Wildlife* 3, no. 4 (2003): 287-306.

Vaske, Jerry J. and Maureen P. Donnelly. "A Value-Attitude-Behavior Model Predicting Wildland Preservation Voting Intentions." *Society and Natural Resources* 12, no. 6 (1999): 523-537.

Vaske, Jerry J. and Maureen P. Donnelly. *Public Knowledge and Perceptions of the Desert Tortoise.* (HDNRU Report No. 81). Report for the National Park Service. Fort Collins: Colorado State University, Human Dimensions in Natural Resources Unit, 2007.

Vaske, Jerry J. and Mark D. Needham. "Segmenting Public Beliefs about Conflict with Coyotes in an Urban Recreation Setting." *Journal of Park and Recreation Administration* 25, no. 4 (2007): 79-98.

Vaske, Jerry J. and Doug Whittaker. "Normative Approaches to Natural Resources." Pp. 283–294 in *Society and Natural Resources: A Summary of Knowledge.* Edited by Michael J. Manfredo, Jerry J. Vaske, Brett L. Bruyere, Donald R. Field, and Perry J. Brown. Jefferson, MO: Modern Litho, 2004.

Whittaker, Doug, Jerry J. Vaske, and Michael J. Manfredo. "Specificity and the Cognitive Hierarchy: Value Orientations and the Acceptability of Urban Wildlife Management Actions." *Society and Natural Resources* 19 (2006): 515:530.

Wind Energy

The conversion of the kinetic energy present in the air currents into mechanical energy for the production of electricity or some other use such as pumping water or grinding grains. Ultimately, wind energy is a product of solar energy in that wind currents around the world are a result of differential heating of Earth's surface by the sun.

Wind energy has been used by civilization since the nineteenth century. The technology of wind energy has advanced tremendously to become the wind energy industry that we have today, an industry of sophisticated wind turbines producing renewable energy in an ever-important energy sector.

Since the beginning of civilization, wind power has helped move people across water in sailboats, grind grains for food, and pump water for irrigation and consumption. Exploitation of wind by land-based machines began in Persia, China and Eastern Europe, moved to Western Europe, and since the late 1800s has been used in the United States. From the late 1800s through the mid-1900s, water-pumping wind machines saw extensive use in the developing American West, where the primary source of water was groundwater. In the late nineteenth century, the first wind power system for generating electricity was operating in Cleveland, Ohio (Righter, 1996).

By the 1920s, fossil fuel plants eliminated the need for small wind generators in the eastern United States. However, throughout the 1920s and 1930s, these machines were widely used across the Great Plains to power lights and charge batteries on rural American farms. In the 1930s and 1940s, small wind turbines were replaced by traditional electrical generation as the U.S. Government intervened to electrify rural America (Righter, 1996).

The wind does not blow all the time, nor is it consistently strong enough for wind turbines to generate full power all the time. The power output of a wind turbine generator depends on the area of the rotor, the density of the air and, most importantly, the speed of the wind. Power output is proportional to the cube of the wind speed, and small changes in wind speed result in large differences in power production. Hence, the measurement of the wind is important to characterize the wind resource prior to the installation of any wind turbines. Wind resource assessments usually require a minimum of one year and require the installation of anemometers and direction vanes on tall towers.

The wind resource maps categorize wind power into seven classes. Each class represents a range of mean wind power density or equivalent mean wind speed at a designated height above the ground. Wind power Class 3 or greater is considered suitable for wind energy development based on current technology. Wind resource mapping is now quite sophisticated, using modern computing power to develop detailed wind resource maps. Although occasionally debated, work by the Pacific Northwest Laboratory ranked the top 10 states for wind energy potential. With 1 being the high-

Wind Power Class	Resource Potential	Wind Power Density at 50 m W/m²	Wind Speed[a] at 50 m m/s	Wind Speed[a] at 50 m mph
2	Marginal	200–300	5.6–6.4	12.5–14.3
3	Fair	300–400	6.4–7.0	14.3–15.7
4	Good	400–500	7.0–7.5	15.7–16.8
5	Excellent	500–600	7.5–8.0	16.8–17.9
6	Outstanding	600–800	8.0–8.8	17.8–19.7
7	Superb	800–1600	8.8–11.1	19.7–24.8

[a]Wind speeds are based on a Welbull k value of 2.0.

Source: National Renewable Energy Laboratory wind resource classification system.

est, the following six states from the Midwest, along with their ranking, include Iowa (#10), Kansas (#3), Minnesota (#9), Nebraska (#6), North Dakota (#1), and South Dakota (#4) (Elliott et al., 1991).

Today's wind turbines are highly sophisticated machines generating electricity from the wind. The wind turbines that are being mass-produced and installed throughout the U.S. are called three-bladed upwind horizontal-axis machines: the axis of rotation is horizontal, the rotor is made up of three blades, and the rotor is upwind of the tower.

The main components of a wind turbine are the tower, nacelle (or enclosure for the power plant), and the rotor. The rotor comprises the blades and a hub. The nacelle houses a gearbox, generator, and braking system. Most commonly used wind turbines have blades that are either fixed pitch or variable pitch. The most important difference is that the blades on a fixed-pitch machine are bolted to the hub at a fixed angle and variable-pitch wind turbines have the ability to change depending on the wind.

Regardless of the type of wind turbine, the power curves of the generators that produce the electricity are comparable. The generator will typically start producing electricity at around eight or nine miles per hour (mph), or four meters per second (m/s). This is known as the cut-in speed. The generator output will increase with wind speed up to the generator's "rated speed," which is typically around 35 mph, or 15 m/s. At this point, the generator will be producing its maximum output, also known as rated output. As wind speeds increase, the wind turbine will continue to produce at or slightly above the rated output until the wind speed reaches the "cut-out speed" (approximately 55 mph, or 25 m/s), at which time the wind turbine will deploy tip brakes at the end of the turbine blades and apply the braking mechanism, stopping rotation of the blades and "parking" itself. (The reference to the cut-in, rated, and cut-out speeds of wind turbines were derived from

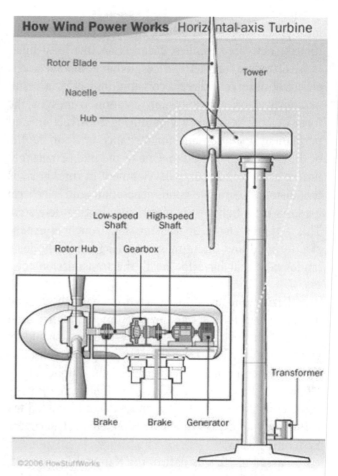

Wind Turbine Components. (Source: How Stuff Works Website)

Large Wind Turbine. (Source: Energy and Environmental Research Center)

a variety of published manufacturers' wind turbine power curves.)

Wind turbine performance and, ultimately, economic performance are based on how much time the wind turbine generator spends at different parts of the generator power curve. The relationship is called the capacity factor, which is defined as the actual production of the generator over a set time period divided by the theoretical 100 percent production over the same time period. Generally speaking, average wind generation sites will have an annual capacity factorbetween 30 percent and 35 percent, with some of the best sites achieving annual capacity factors greater than 40 percent (Nelson, 2003).

Generally speaking, the best wind resources exist in rural areas of the central United States. This creates both benefits to rural America and challenges for wind energy development. Wind energy development infuses rural America with new economic opportunity for landowners and creates much-needed jobs. Landowners can expect to receive royalty payments from wind energy developers for having wind turbines on their land, and local governments and school districts can realize significant new tax revenues. In addition, the local businesses (trades, contract services, lodging, food services, etc.) will observe a direct economic impact as a result of construction activities. Job creation comes in the form of both temporary jobs during construction and permanent operation and maintenance jobs for the life of the wind farm operation. One of the main challenges presented by wind energy development in rural areas is the distance between wind generation and electrical load, where a bulk of the electricity must be delivered. This requires electrical transmission, which is expensive to build and oftentimes not well received by local landowners that have to "host" the transmission towers.

Legislation has been enacted on both the federal and state level to foster and even promote the increased development of renewable energy sources, including wind energy. At the federal level, the primary legislation that has been enacted includes the Public Utility Regulatory Policy Act (PURPA), the Renewable Energy Production Tax Credit (PTC), and a lesser discussed tax law known as the Modified Accelerated Cost-Recovery System (MACRS).

Passed in 1978 as part of the National Energy Act, PURPA was meant to promote greater use of renewable energy by creating a market for non-utility electric power producers. At that time only utilities could own and operate electrical generation facilities, but PURPA required electric utilities to purchase electrical generation from non-utility power producers at the "avoided cost," which was the cost the utility would have incurred from generating electricity from its other sources. PURPA, although significant at the time of its passing, has had limited impact recently and has become somewhat outdated.

The PTC is probably the most well-known policy fostering wind energy development. Enacted as part of the Energy Policy Act of 1992, the PTC is an inflation-adjusted production tax credit (currently $0.02/kWh) against corporate tax liabilities for the first 10 years of operation of the wind plant. Since the PTC is a tax credit, only taxable corporations are eligible to claim it which excludes nonprofits, rural electric cooperatives, municipal utilities and tribal utilities. Since its enactment, the PTC legislative language has always included sunset clauses which have meant that the PTC has been allowed to expire several times before being reenacted as part of newer policies. The sporadic history has caused a great deal of disruption in the wind energy in-

dustry, resulting in a boom-and-bust pattern of development in the United States (Union of Concerned Scientists Website, Database of State Incentives for Renewables and Efficiency Website).

Enacted as part of the Tax Reform Act of 1986, MACRS replaced the Accelerated Cost Recover System for depreciating capital purchases. For wind energy installations, capital investments are allowed to be depreciated over five years. The Economic Stimulus Act of 2008 modified this incentive slightly by allowing 50 percent of the adjusted basis or the property to be deducted in the first year, with the remaining 50 percent to be depreciated over the ordinary depreciation schedule (Database of State Incentives for Renewables and Efficiency Website).

A variety of legislative policies have been enacted at the state level to promote wind energy development. Most notable are Renewable Portfolio Standards (RPS) which vary from state to state but typically require that a certain percentage of a utility's generating capacity or energy sales must be derived from renewable resources by a certain date (i.e., 20 percent by 2020). Not surprisingly, the enactment of an RPS has notably increased the amount of wind energy in states that have implemented such policies, and there have been discussions to implement an RPS at the federal level. Many other state incentives exist including state tax incentives, grant and loan programs, and public benefits funds, to name a few.

Wind turbines come in a wide range of sizes and are generally categorized as "small," "intermediate," and "large" based on the turbine's rated generating capacity. Each category of wind turbine typically performs a different function. Small wind is typically considered to be 20 kW or smaller turbines, which are installed for providing electricity for homes, farms and off-grid applications. Small wind turbines are not as tall as the larger counterparts, with tower heights ranging from 40 to 120 feet tall. Intermediate wind includes turbines between 20 kW and 250 kW and are typically installed to supply power to larger single loads, small villages or as distributed electrical generation projects. Many of these wind turbines were originally designed and manufactured as the first generation of large-scale wind turbines. Large wind turbines are greater than 660 kW and are installed as single units or in wind farms or parks for the purpose of wholesale electrical generation. The wind turbine industry continues to manufacture larger wind turbines with rated capacities exceeding 2 MW in size and tower heights of 200 feet

Small Wind Turbine (Source: U.S. Department of Energy)

and greater. (The wind turbine size categories are not strictly defined and are presented based on typical wind energy industry classifications.)

Not surprisingly, small wind systems are owned and operated by individuals for their own use. The larger wind turbines and wind farms, on the other hand, have typically been installed, owned, and operated by wind energy development companies with utilities being the off-taker/purchaser of the electricity. Electric utilities to a less degree have also owned and operated single turbine projects and larger wind farms. More recently, with creative financing and ownership structures, individuals or groups of individuals, municipalities, and corporations have become owners of wind turbines and small wind farms. These types of projects have been termed "community wind" by the wind industry and are usually smaller in total wind farm size than traditional wind farms.

There are two components to electrical generation, energy and capacity. All electrical generators are energy providers and can be compared directly on an energy production basis, but some electrical generators are also capacity producers. For an electrical generator to be a capacity producer, the operator must have the ability to call on the system to produce on demand, a characteristic known as dispatchable. Electrical generators that are dispatchable are also known as baseload generators and include traditional generation types such as coal plants, natural gas generators, nuclear reactors, and hydroelectric dams. Wind energy generation is not dispatchable and, therefore, has little or no capacity value.

Although the cost of wind energy projects has risen significantly in recent years, the technology has proven itself to be competitive with other new generation types, both renewable and fossil fuel-based, as an energy provider. Many factors influence the economic feasibility of wind energy projects, but since wind projects are front-end capital intensive, the most crucial are wind turbine and electrical transmission costs. Another critical component to the project's economic viability is the power purchase agreement, which is the contract that determines the terms of the sale of the produced electricity, both pricing structure and duration of the sales.

— *Bradley G. Stevens*

See also
Electrification; Environmental Protection; Environmental Regulations; Solar Energy; Technology; Weather

References

Database of State Incentives for Renewables and Efficiency. Website available online at: http://www.dsireusa.org.

Elliott, D. L., L.L. Wendell, and G.L. Grower. *An Assessment of the Available Windy Land Area and Wind Energy Potential in the Contiguous United States.* Richland, WA: Pacific Northwest National Laboratory, 1991.

Energy and Environmental Research Center, Grand Forks, ND. Website available online at: http://www.undeerc.org.

National Renewable Energy Laboratory, Golden, CO. Website available at: http://www.nrel.gov/wind.

Nelson, V. *Wind Energy and Wind Turbines.* Online course. Canyon, TX: Department of Physics, West Texas A&M University, 2003.

Righter, R.W. *Wind Energy in America: A History.* Norman, OK: University of Oklahoma Press, 1996.

Union of Concerned Scientists. Website available online at: http://www.ucsusa.org.

Wine Industry

All individuals and companies involved in the production, transportation, marketing and sale of wine grapes, wine and wine-related products to domestic and international consumers. The U.S. has a large, well-established wine industry, which, especially since the 1960s, emerged as a world-class producer of high-quality wine. The first section of this article is a general overview of American wine production and the types of wine produced. Next, the U.S. system of winery regulation is contrasted with that of France. This is followed by a brief discussion of the history of the American wine industry. The final two sections focus on the structure of the American wine industry and a discussion of the problems facing the industry.

Wine Production

As of 1990 the U.S. ranked sixth in the world in wine production, producing only about a quarter of the amount of wine as that of the largest producer, France. Although at least some wine from grapes is commercially produced in almost all 50 states, the industry is dominated by California, which accounts for about 90 percent of U.S. production. The U.S. wine and brandy production industries employ about 14,000 people; many more are involved in distribution and sales. An unknown and constantly fluctuating number of migrant farm workers tend vineyards, mostly in California.

Prior to the twentieth century in the eastern U. S., wine was made from the fruit of the native American *vitis labrusca* vine (the Muscadine in the South and the Niagara and Concord varieties in the Northeast). *Labrusca* grapes are now used mostly for jellies, juice and other non-wine grape products. American wine is now predominantly made in the European style from *vitis vinifera* (Eurasian) grape varieties. American wineries produce all of the commonly accepted wine types: red and white dry table wines, sparkling wines, and fortified wines. They also produce large quantities of flavored wines, such as vermouth and proprietary brands such as Boone's Farm, and wine coolers, although wine coolers increasingly use a malt-beverage base. Significant amounts of grape wine brandy are produced in California. Rootstock grafting, hybridization techniques, and more careful site selection has enabled the expansion of *vinifera* wine production to the Northeast and the South where it was formerly barred by climate. *Vinifera* grape wine is also produced in Canada and Mexico.

The most common red dry table wine varieties produced in the U.S. include Cabernet Sauvignon, Zinfandel, Pinot Noir, and Grenache; white varieties include Chardonnay, Chenin Blanc, and Colombard. There are three basic price/quality market segments for American wine. The premium segment consists of wines $12 and higher for a 750-milliliter bottle. Most of these wines are produced on a small scale by small wineries. However, several larger wineries also have premium product lines. At the other end of the spectrum are the low-priced, mass-produced wines, about $6 or less per 750 ml. Many of these wines are sold in large jugs, although the trend has been away from this

for some time. A third, mid-priced varietal market segment has emerged over the last two decades. These wines are produced on a relatively large scale and are marketed to consumers who are interested in quality wines at a reasonable price.

Regulation

American wine regulation is predicated on a varietal-entrepreneurial model that focuses on taxation, sanitation standards, minimum and maximum alcohol levels, marketing and distribution ordinances, etc. This contrasts with the French *Chateau*-appellation model in which wineries must not only conform to basic regulations, but must make their wine according to the stylistic dictates of their appellation (wine district). How an American winemaker chooses to adjust the character of his or her wine is of no concern to regulators. American wine is mostly labeled by grape variety, again contrasting with France in which a given wine carries the name of the *Chateau* that produced it. Most individual American wineries produce at least two or three different types of wine, usually some combination of red and white table wines, or table wines and sparkling wines. Wine is not a true niche product; wineries compete with each other based on their image and the popular acceptance of their product. From the perspective of the consumer, there are only marginal subjective differences between wines in the same price classification.

Bureau of Alcohol, Tobacco, and Firearms (BATF) regulations stipulate that at least 95 percent of a wine labeled with a vintage year be made from grapes harvested that year, that at least 90 percent of the wine be of the variety named on the label, and that at least 75 percent be produced from grapes grown within the appellation on the label. The BATF also allows the marketing of semi-generic wines using "borrowed" names such as champagne, Chianti, sherry or burgundy. Non-varietal blends with proprietary names such as Hearty Burgundy or Thunderbird also are permitted. Some premium wineries are beginning to follow the French *Chateaux* by giving their varietal blends proprietary names; a well-known example is Opus One, a Cabernet Sauvignon/Merlot blend produced by a Robert Mondavi, Baron Phillippe de Rothschild joint venture. BATF regulations also provide for a system of established American viticultural areas (AVAs) created through a petition process. As of 1986, there were 84 AVAs in the U.S., 49 in California. In an effort to heighten the exclusivity of their product, some California winemakers recently advocated the creation of sub-appellations within already established AVAs.

History

Vinifera grape varieties were introduced to California by Spanish missionaries in the seventeenth century. The so-called Mission variety, which made an inferior quality wine, dominated viniculture in the state up until the mid-nineteenth century. Prior to the Gold Rush period, commercial winemaking was centered in Los Angeles. A virulent vine disease, urban development, and the economic attraction of the prospering San Francisco area all helped move the industry's center of gravity to the more climatically hospitable northern coastal area. In 1870 California became the leading wine producing state, surpassing Missouri and Ohio. Industry growth was spectacular; from 1880 to 1910 vineyard area expanded 600 percent.

The onset of Prohibition in 1919 devastated the wine industry without completely destroying it. Home winemaking was still legal and large quantities of grapes and grape concentrates intended for winemaking, many of which shipped with packets of yeast, were exported east from California by rail. Although many wineries closed down, others survived by producing wine for sacramental and medicinal purposes, also still legal under Prohibition. Thus, at Repeal in 1932, at least some wine industry infrastructure existed and the industry gradually recovered.

Throughout its history the American wine industry underwent many cyclical fluctuations. The most recent boom began in the late 1960s in California. In 1960 there were approximately 200 wineries in the state, a post-Prohibition low. That number nearly tripled by the mid-1980s to over 700 (about the current number). While large-scale wine production grew during this period, the most significant growth was in small wineries. Many entrepreneurially minded investors, flush with capital from the state's booming economy and attracted to the rural idyll that winemaking seemed to promise, became winemakers. They encountered consumers who, for a series of economic and cultural reasons connected with postwar affluence, expressed increased interest in lifestyle-enhancing products such as wine. The American wine industry shifted from providing a relatively undifferentiated product to immigrants, housewives and the occasional wine connoisseur to a higher-quality product differentiated by winery image and popularity.

Industry Structure

The past two decades saw a national liberalization of winemaking regulation, spurring the revival of the small winery sector in New York, and the new development of small winery production in other states, most notably Oregon, Washington and Texas. It is legal for home winemakers to make up to 200 gallons of wine per year; many amateur winemakers are active in both rural and urban settings.

Most commercial wine in the U.S. is produced with grapes purchased from growers. This occurs across the winery size spectrum, although small wineries are more likely to grow their own grapes. Growers usually enter into long-term contracts with wineries which specify the type of grapes, growing methods and minimum quality standards. Often there are disputes between growers and wineries over quality and price, particularly with larger wineries that have significant market power.

Generally, the wine industry conforms to a standard tripartite production/distribution structure: winery to distributor to retailer. Most wineries bottle their own wine, some using the services of mobile bottling contractors, and then sell it to distributors who place it in retail outlets. Some boutique wineries market directly to restaurants and wine shops. U.S. law prohibits direct winery ownership of retail outlets, although on-site sales, which constitute a major source of revenues for many small wineries, are allowed.

It is possible to distinguish three distinct winery-size categories. About 10 percent of American wineries have storage capacities in excess of one million gallons. The 10 largest wineries account for about 80 percent of wine shipments. The largest American winery, E & J Gallo, produces about 25 percent of all wine consumed in the United States. Gallo operates its own glass bottle and aluminum screw cap factories and owns a trucking company that it uses both to haul grapes and distribute finished wines. Most large wineries market their own branded products, although several ship wine in bulk to other wineries who blend it with their own wines. The majority of American wineries fall into the medium-size category. These range from fairly large producers of premium wines to smaller producers fighting for a share of the mid-priced varietal market. Finally there are the microwineries who produce small quantities of premium quality wine. Many microwineries find it difficult to make a profit because of the rise in vineyard land costs, the high cost of equipment, the vagaries of weather, and the fickleness of consumers. Some of the wineries in this category consist of winemakers who buy grapes and rent excess production capacity from other winemakers. Many others are owned by affluent professionals or business executives for whom winemaking is a hobby.

Most American wineries are privately owned, often by a single family, or by a partnership. This includes wineries all across the size scale, from the gigantic Gallo, which is still owned by the Gallo family, to most smaller wineries. Wine and wine grape cooperatives are virtually nonexistent in the U.S. Foreign investment, which is in excess of about $1.5 billion, comes in two forms. The first consists of multinational beverage producers such as Seagram, Nestlé, and Heublein, who have portfolios of investments in both large and small wineries. Grand Metropolitan, a British firm with significant holdings in food processing, retailing and hotels, is the second largest producer of wine by volume in the U.S. The second main form of foreign investment in the American wine industry is European producers seeking to expand their wine production, but stymied by the lack of expansion potential in their home regions. This is best exemplified by sparkling wine producers like Taittinger, Moët-Hennessy (France), and Codorniu (Spain), who among others have established high-profile operations in the Napa and Sonoma areas of California. French interests, both individual and corporate, have also moved into other parts of the United States, most notably New Mexico, Texas, Oregon and Virginia.

Problems Facing the Wine Industry

Although overall alcohol consumption in America has declined, the shift in wine has been from quantity to quality; or in the words of wine industry analysts, Americans are drinking less, but drinking better. The decline in alcohol consumption coincided with the proliferation of small, premium wineries and mid-priced varietal producers. Larger producers responded by improving the quality of their wines, or in some cases, by repackaging their jug wines in smaller bottles with more attractive labels. Despite this seemingly benign quality-consumption shift, however, the widespread revival of anti-alcohol sentiment increased the pressure in what is already a brutally competitive market. Increasing urbanization and the natural limit of available land in appropriate climatological zones helped to force huge increases in vineyard land prices. Economic recession and banks unwilling to make loans to wineries led to numerous bankruptcies and sellouts to larger, better

capitalized interests. New winery startups in California declined every year from their peak in 1980. A recent outbreak of Phylloxera (a vine-destroying pest) in the Napa and Sonoma valleys placed an extra burden on many smaller wineries, forcing them to replace entire vineyards, which requires a three- to four-year production hiatus. Creeping suburban development and pressures caused by tourism and non-winery development stimulated years of acrimonious debate over the implementation of special agricultural protections in the Napa Valley.

— *James Curry*

See also
Addiction; Marketing; Migrant Agricultural Workers

References

Adams, Leon D. *The Wines of America*. 2nd ed. New York, NY: McGraw-Hill, 1990.

Blue, Anthony D. *American Wine: a Comprehensive Guide*. rev. ed. New York, NY: Harpercollins, 1992.

Eysberg, Cyees D. *The Californian Wine Economy: Natural Opportunities and Socio-Cultural Constraints*. Utrecht, Netherlands: Netherlands Geographical Studies, 1990.

Jackisch, Philip. *Modern Winemaking*. Ithaca, NY: Cornell University Press, 1985.

Johnson, Hugh. *Vintage: The Story of Wine*. New York, NY: Simon and Schuster, 1989.

Muscatine, Doris, Maynard A. Amerine, and Bob Thompson, eds. *The Book of California Wine*. Berkeley, CA: University of California Press/Sotheby, 1984.

Pinney, Thomas. *A History of Wine in America, Volume 1: From the Beginnings to Prohibition*. Berkeley: University of California Press, 2007.

Pinney, Thomas. *A History of Wine in America, Volume 2: From Prohibition to the Present*. Berkeley: University of California Press, 2007.

Stuller, Jay and Glen Martin. *Through the Grapevine: The Business of Wine in America*. New York, NY: Wynwood Press, 1989.

Teiser, Ruth and Catherine Harroun. *Winemaking in California*. New York, NY: McGraw-Hill, 1983.

Unwin, Tim. *Wine and the Vine: An Historical Geography of Viticulture and the Wine Trade*. London, UK: Routledge, 1996.

Wagner, Paul. M. *Grapes into Wine: The Art of Winemaking in New York*. New York, NY: Knopf, 1994.

Wool Industry

The production, processing and marketing of wool, a product of sheep. It is the purpose of this chapter to

Shearing wool from one of America's six million sheep. Photograph by Glen D. Whipple.

discuss the wool industry and its place in the rural U.S. Since it is not possible to understand the wool industry without considering aspects of lamb production and marketing, this chapter will first discuss lamb and wool production patterns and practices. U.S. wool policy is then considered, followed by a discussion of the demand for wool. The concluding section considers world markets and trade in wool.

Sheep Husbandry: Wool and Lamb Production

The sheep industry has been a mainstay of the rural economy for centuries. The sheep, domesticated around 12,000 years ago, is one of the first animals domesticated by humans. Providing both meat and fiber, it has been one of humanity's most useful domesticated animals. Based on current day wild sheep, it is likely that the ancestors of wild sheep had a hairy and colored coat and gave birth to single lambs. Over the centuries of domestication, shepherds selected lambs to retain in the breeding flock that possess the most desirable characteristics and thus altered the genetic base of the world's sheep population considerably. Wool production, carcass characteristics, hardiness and the prevalence of multiple births or twinning are desirable traits for commercial sheep production in the U.S. Sheep are used for meat, milk and fiber. All sheep breeds can produce these three products, but specialized breeds are used in commercial production of each.

Although some flocks are kept for milk production, the vast majority of sheep in the U.S. are used in lamb and wool production. There are about 10 commercially important sheep breeds in the U.S. Each of these produces both lambs and wool. However, each of these breeds is used to generate a particular mix of lamb and wool outputs or a particular quality of lamb or wool. For example, Rambouillet or Merino are used for high-quality, fine wool production, while Colombia, Corriedale, or Hampshire are used if lamb production is the primary objective. In most sheep operations both lambs and wool are produced for market from the same sheep flock.

There are generally two types of sheep operations in the U.S.: range flocks and farm flocks. Typically, range flocks are located in Texas, South Dakota, the Rocky Mountain states, and the Pacific Coast states, or the "territory states." Range flocks take most of their feed in the form of standing forage that could not be economically harvested by any other means. They usually represent a primary source of income for the ranching unit. Range flocks typically contain wool breeds, as they are hardy and excellent foragers. Wool from these areas called "territory wools" tends to be finer and is used to make apparel. It is not unusual for range operations to cross pure-bred, wool-breed ewes with meat-breed rams. This strategy results in high-quality wool from shearing the ewes and high-quality cross-bred lambs for meat production. About two-thirds (about four million sheep) of U.S. sheep and wool are managed in range flocks, but only about one-fifth of producers are range flock operators. The territory states, though dominated by range flocks, have some farm flocks. These states contain about 70 percent of the U.S. sheep.

Most other sheep are in Virginia, West Virginia, Pennsylvania, states north of the Ohio River and the Great Plains area ("fleece states"). Sheep in these areas are typically managed in farm flocks. Farm flocks are generally small flocks (less than 40 head) kept in farming areas. They are usually a supplementary source of income to the owner of the flock. They typically graze, generally in fenced areas, for only a part of the season and are more intensively managed. Farm flocks account for only about one-third (about two million sheep) of the sheep and wool production in the U.S. but most of the sheep producers. Sheep in these areas tend to be meat-breeds and most of the wool produced is medium grade, used to make coats, sweaters and blankets. Some farm flock operators use specialized breeds to produce colored or otherwise unusual fleeces for spinning and weaving by craftspeople.

The sheep industry has been in decline in terms of breeding flock size and lamb and wool production since the early 1960s. One explanation for this decline is that the sheep enterprise has been less profitable than other enterprises that the farmer or rancher could undertake. Among the reasons cited for this decline are the unavailability and high cost of herder labor in sheep production, large losses to predators in range flock areas, relatively low-cost imports, high marketing costs, and increasing marketing margins. Regardless of the reason, the U.S. sheep industry declined steadily for the past 40 years from over 33 million head in 1960 to just over six million head in 2008.

U.S. Wool Policy

The sheep industry has been supported by various U.S. Government programs since 1938. The wool incentive program supported wool production since 1955. It provides payments to sheep producers when the market price of wool falls below the wool incentive price, a price set under the federal farm bill. In recent years the incentive price has been more than twice the market wool price. However, Congress passed legislation in 1993 to phase out the wool incentive program. Payments were reduced in 1994 and 1995. After 1995, no incentive payment was received. The loss of the wool incentive program is a serious blow to the wool production in the U.S. During many years, incentive payments accounted for over one-fifth of producers' total receipts from the sheep enterprise. In 2003 Congress reinstituted federal support for wool making marketing assistance loans and loan deficiency payments available to wool producers through the 2007 crop year. Even so, U.S. wool production has declined 12 percent since 2003.

Wool Consumption

Wool is a natural fiber used for thousands of years. Wool is unique among most other natural fibers such as cotton, silk, flax, hemp and jute in that it is a result of livestock production. Along with other natural fibers, wool's position in the marketplace has been challenged by synthetic fibers. Wool is used in a variety of textile products including fine suits, sweaters, outerwear, carpets, blankets and decorative textile products.

Wool is classified into two categories: apparel wool and carpet wool. Carpet wool, with a fiber diameter of greater than 30 microns, is shorter and less uniform than apparel wool. Carpet wools are used in carpets. Most apparel wool is processed by the worsted or the woolen process. The worsted process uses the longer, finer fibers. The wool is carded, combed and drawn into a thin strand of apparel fibers spun together to form a strong, thin yarn. Under the woolen system, shorter wool is carded and drawn into long, softly twisted strands spun into a bulky yarn that lacks the strength of the worsted yarns. Tops and noils are intermediate products of the worsted and woolen processes. Tops are created by carding the longer wools and removing the shorter fibers called noils. Twisting top fibers together forms rovings, which are spun into worsted yarns.

Most wool produced in the United States is marketed as raw, uncleaned wool, much as it is shorn from the sheep. Over three-quarters of the wool produced in the U.S. is exported to processors and mills in other countries, because the world textiles and clothing industries are centered outside the U.S. There are small but growing local markets for specialty wools used in crafts; spinning, weaving and fiber art; and a developing organic wool market. U.S. consumers use an average of 1.4 pounds of wool each year in textile products. This is compared to about 38 pounds of cotton, and 48 pounds of synthetic fibers. Wool currently accounts for about 1.5 percent of each U.S. consumer's annual fiber consumption compared to 9 percent in 1939. It is synthetic fibers, rather than cotton, that have displaced wool in U.S. consumers' textile selections. Cotton and wool do not compete for most end uses, and they are rarely blended in fabrics. A major factor in the decline in wool use has been the loss of the carpet market to synthetic fibers, mainly nylon. Although synthetic fibers displaced wool, resulting in low consumption, synthetics have been unable to duplicate adequately the desirable properties of wool such as heat and flame resistance, excellent dying properties, resistance to soiling, and moisture absorption properties. Recent developments in wool processing enhanced wool fabric's ability to hold a crease and keep its shape.

World Markets for Wool

Australia is the world's leading wool producer and the world's largest wool exporter. The country produces over 590 million pounds of wool each year, about a fourth of the world's production. Australia often exports over 90 percent of its production. Approximately 70 percent of the wool traded in world wool markets is of Australian origin. New Zealand is the second largest wool exporter but third in wool production. Argentina, Uruguay and South Africa are also major wool producing and exporting countries. These five countries account for over 95 percent of the world's wool exports. Most of the world's exportable surplus of wool comes from the Southern Hemisphere.

The Russian Federation and China produce about a quarter of the world's wool, but because of large populations and consumptions, are wool importers. Over 60 percent of the world's raw wool is processed by the Chinese textiles industry. Half is consumed as apparel within China and the other half is exported as finished products primarily to Europe, the United States and Japan. Although the U.S. is not a large consumer or importer of wool by world standards, wool imports are important to U.S. textile consumers. Over 94 percent of the wool consumed in the U.S. in 2007 was imported. The U.S. imports about half the wool processed in U.S. textile mills. Most U.S. wool imports are already manufactured into textile products.

Because of the size of its industry and a heavy reliance on world markets to sell its wool crop, Australia has historically taken an active stance in the international wool market. The Australian Wool Corporation (AWC) was formed in 1972 to aid in the domestic and international marketing of Australian wool. Competition from synthetic fibers was recognized as a problem and the AWC worked to enhance the competitive qualities of wool. The AWC pioneered wool grading, objective measurement and improved presentation of raw wool. Objective measurement and sorting for consistency reduce the fiber users' costs and improve wool's competitiveness with other fibers. Carrying the burden of a large stock of wool to help stabilize prices, the Australian Wool Corporation suspended its activities in February 1991. Australian wool policy actions since that time have focused on selling down the large wool stock gathered in the 1980s, promoting the international sale of Australian wool and helping the Australian sheep industry adjust to freer and more competitive world markets. World wool markets are generally as free and unrestrained by government policy as any world agricultural markets.

— *Glen D. Whipple and Dale J. Menkhaus*

See also

Agricultural Programs; Clothing and Textiles; Livestock Industry; Livestock Production; Marketing; Pasture; Policy, Agricultural; Textile Industry; Trade, International

References

Botkin, M.P., R.A. Field and C.L. Johnson. *Sheep and Wool Science Production and Management*. Englewood Cliffs, NJ: Prentice Hall, 1988.

Purcell W.D., J. Reeves, and W. Preston. *Economics of Past, Current and Pending Change in the U.S. Sheep Industry with an Emphasis on Supply Response.* MB 363. Blacksburg, VA: Department of Agricultural Economics, Virginia Tech University, 1991.

Richardson, Bob. "The Politics and Economics of Wool Marketing, 1950-2000." *The Australian Journal of Agricultural Economics* 45, no. 1 (2001): 95-115.

Shapouri, Hosein. *Sheep Production in 11 Western States.* Staff Report No. AGES 9150. Washington, DC: U.S. Department of Agriculture, Economics Research Service, Commodity Economics Division, 1991.

Sheep Industry Development Program, Inc. *Sheep Industry Development (SID): Sheep Production Handbook.* Denver, CO: Sheep Industry Development Program, Inc, 1992.

U.S. Department of Agriculture. "Cotton and Wool Situation and Outlook Yearbook" *CWS-2007.* Washington, DC: U.S. Department of Agriculture, Markets and Trade Economics Division, Economics Research Service, November 2007.

U.S. Department of Agriculture. "Sheep and Wool Policy" *Briefing Rooms.* Washington, DC: U.S. Department of Agriculture, Economic Research Service, November 14, 2007.

U.S. Department of Agriculture. "Sheep and Wool: Background" *Briefing Rooms.* Washington, DC: U.S. Department of Agriculture, Economic Research Service, November 14, 2007.

Work

All activities that contribute to the material survival or livelihood of individuals and their households. The work that rural Americans do encompasses a wide variety of activities. Included are jobs or businesses in which rural people are formally employed, as well as other kinds of work they do as part of their household livelihood strategies, such as work in the informal economy and self-provisioning activities. Household maintenance, childcare and other domestic activities are included in this definition of work. Such a broad conception of work is necessary not only to describe the work that rural Americans do, but to understand how this work has changed in recent decades.

Recent changes in the structure of work in rural America are highlighted in this article, with special emphasis on how those changes are related to divisions of labor between rural and urban areas and between women and men. The article begins with a discussion of the economic restructuring that occurred both in the formal and informal sectors. The subsequent section relates this transformation to the gender division of labor in rural America. The restructuring of work in rural America is also related to other social divisions of labor, such as divisions by class, ethnicity and age. Special consideration is given to the gender division of labor because it is the primary basis for allocating work within households.

The Restructuring of Work in Rural America

Alphonse Karr's (1849) comment, *plus ça change, plus c'est la même chose* (the more things change, the more they remain the same) applies to the restructuring of work in rural America. Work in rural America was transformed by a profound economic and social restructuring during the later part of the twentieth century, but the hierarchical spatial division of labor between rural and urban areas remains, as does the gender division of labor within rural households. The restructuring of work in rural America began long before the economic and social restructuring that captured the nation's attention in the 1970s and 1980s. Central to the earlier restructuring in rural America was the transformation of agriculture. Agricultural work became highly mechanized, greatly reducing the number of farmers and farm laborers as tractor power fostered a move toward larger and fewer farms. As a consequence of this transformation of agriculture, less than 10 percent of rural Americans worked in agriculture in the 1990s. And among the rural Americans who do continue to farm, most rely upon off-farm work as part of their household livelihood strategies.

The shift away from agricultural work in rural America has produced an industry structure that is similar to the structure of industries in urban America. In 1992 over half of all rural workers employed in the formal economy worked in the service sector. In addition, another one-third worked in either the manufacturing or government sectors (U.S. Department of Agriculture, 1995). Whereas the industry structure of rural America became more like that of urban America, the division in the work done in rural and urban America remained very much the same through a persistent spatial division of labor. Similar to farmers' historical role of providing cheap food for urban populations, a primary role of rural workers in nonagricultural industries today is to provide cheap labor for urban-managed industries.

The general pattern of the spatial division of labor is for work in rural America to be concentrated in routine production activities, whereas a disproportionate share of the professional and managerial work within an industry is located in urban areas. A consequence of this spatial division of labor is that rural economies have become more vulnerable to downturns in the national and world economies as routine production jobs are often the first to be cut back during recessions. Moreover, rural workers are more likely to experience underemployment, and the resultant low hours and low earnings, than urban workers (McGranahan, 1983).

The restructuring of work in rural America involved more than changes in the kinds of work that rural people do in the formal economy. There also has been a restructuring in the informal and domestic spheres of work in rural America. The major change in the informal sphere is tied to the shift away from agriculture. Farm households have a long tradition of informal exchanges of labor and materials related to their farms' production. In the nonfarm household the informal work activities relate more to household reproduction, such as the informal exchange of personal services or commodities for household consumption (which is not to deny the significance of "egg money" to many farm households).

One implication of this shift is that the informal work activities of rural nonfarm households are similar to the informal work activities of urban households. Informal work is especially important to households in the most remote rural areas, where informal work activities compensate for the local lack of services and job opportunities in the formal economy (Jensen et al., 1995). With regard to the restructuring of work in the domestic sphere, the major change has involved the increased dependence of rural households on women who, in addition to their domestic work, have increased their participation in the formal economy. This aspect of the restructuring of work in rural America is related to a persistent gender division of labor in the formal economy and within households.

Restructuring Work and the Gender Division of Labor

Despite the profound economic and social restructuring of work in rural America, much about work in rural America remained the same. Considerable change occurred in the kinds of work that rural Americans do, but the relation of their work to the spatial and gender divisions of labor has not changed fundamentally. As a consequence, work opportunities for rural Americans remain tied to persistent divisions of labor in the organization of work. The spatial division of labor helped preserve a division in the kinds of work that rural and urban Americans do. Likewise, the gender division of labor has helped preserve a division in the kinds of work that rural women and men do. Women hold a wide range of positions in the work structure of rural America. Yet, their access to certain kinds of work and their control over the products of their labor is usually less than men's. And this gender inequality in work opportunities and power is related strongly to the household division of labor. Within rural and urban households, men usually have an inordinate control over the household's disposable income and any capital or means of production the household owns. Conversely, cooking, childcare, and other work in the domestic sphere is almost exclusively allotted to women.

Even within farm households, where women often do the bookkeeping and other clerical work for the farm enterprise and participate extensively in physical agricultural labor, it is men who usually control the technology that is incorporated into agricultural production. As the cost-price squeeze pushed more and more farms to part-time farming, farm women often found themselves not only entering the formal labor market, maintaining their own farm and domestic work, but also expanding their farm production duties to fill in for their male partners who work off the farm. Because much of household labor is indispensable, women are unable to adjust the time they spend on household labor to their paid labor demands. It does not appear that farm men have been contributing very extensively to the domestic sphere of their households' livelihood strategies. With more women entering the paid labor force, there has been an increase in household labor by men. Yet, this increase has been slight, especially when compared to the proportionate increase in women's paid labor time (Shelton, 1992).

A gender division of labor remains in the formal economy as well, with rural women being most likely to work in clerical, operative and personal service jobs, whereas rural men are more likely than women to work in skilled manual jobs. Semyonov (1983) points out the increased labor force participation by women in rural areas accentuates the general pattern of occupational segregation by gender, with women being even more concentrated in low-status, low-wage jobs than in areas where relatively few women work outside the home. Men in rural areas with high levels of women's participation in the formal economy also are more likely to receive low wages for the work they do in the formal economy (Tigges and Tootle, 1990). Therefore, the increased significance of women's participation in the formal economy to many rural household's livelihood strategies occurred in conjunction with a diminished earnings capacity of rural men and women. Whereas both rural men's and women's earnings capacities are adversely affected by women's increased labor force participation, gender earnings inequality remains. This gender gap in earnings has become even more critical for rural women in conjunction with the increased proportion of female-headed households in rural America.

The gender division of labor also is related to the allocation of informal work in rural America. Men's work in the informal sphere usually involves their physical labor, such as repair work or landscaping. Women's work is likely to be an extension of their domestic work, such as childcare for other households or the selling of food commodities produced in their home.

One aspect of the recent trends in the informalization of work has been for rural women to increasingly take on industrial homework as part of their household's livelihood strategy. Industrial homework refers to employers' contracting work out to households with the work usually performed by women for minimal wages and with few benefits. Gringeri (1993) argues that the acceptance of industrial homeworking as a rural economic development strategy has been facilitated by traditional beliefs about women's roles within the household and the labor market. The instability, low wages and limited benefits of industrial homework are justified through the assumption that these jobs are secondary and supplemental to the work of men in the household.

Women involved in industrial homeworking, much like women who work outside of their home, often find they are doing double the work as they remain primarily responsible for childcare, household maintenance and other forms of domestic work. This imbalance in work responsibilities within the rural household continues to be a dominant factor shaping gender divisions in both the formal and informal spheres of work in rural America.

To understand work in rural America, therefore, it is important to consider the various activities that rural Americans get involved in as they strive to meet their household's livelihood needs. It also is important to recognize that work opportunities for rural Americans

remained tied to the spatial and gender divisions of labor, despite the considerable change that occurred in the kinds of work that rural Americans do. The more things changed, the more they remained the same.

— *Leonard E. Bloomquist and Bridget E. Murphy*

See also
Careers in Agriculture; Division of Household Labor; Employment; Foresters; Labor Force; Miners; Underemployment; Rural Women

References
Burnell, Beverly A. "The 'Real World' Aspirations of Work-bound Rural Students." *Journal of Research in Rural Education* 18, no. 2 (Fall, 2003): 104-113.

Falk, William W., Michael D. Schulman, and Ann R. Tickamyer. *Communities of Work: Rural Restructuring in Local and Global Contexts.* Athens, OH: Ohio University Press, 2003.

Gringeri, Christina A. "Inscribing Gender in Rural Development: Industrial Homework in Two Midwestern Communities." *Rural Sociology* 58, no. 1 (1993): 30-52.

Jensen, Leif, Gretchen T. Cornwell, and Jill L. Findeis. "Informal Work in Nonmetropolitan Pennsylvania." *Rural Sociology* 60, no. 1 (1995): 67-107.

Karr, Alphonse. *Les Guêpes.* [Janvier, 1849].

McGranahan, David A. "Changes in the Social and Spatial Structure of the Rural Community." Pp. 163-178 in *Technology and Social Change in Rural Areas.* Edited by Gene F. Summers. Boulder, CO: Westview Press, 1983.

Semyonov, Moshe. "Community Characteristics, Female Employment and Occupational Segregation: Small Towns in a Rural State." *Rural Sociology* 48, no. 1 (1983): 104-119.

Shelton, Beth Anne. *Women, Work and Time: Gender Differences in Paid Work, Housework and Leisure.* New York, NY: Greenwood Press, 1992.

Tigges, Leann M. and Deborah M. Tootle. "Labor Supply, Labor Demand, and Men's Underemployment in Rural and Urban Labor Markets." *Rural Sociology* 55, no. 3 (1990): 328-356.

U.S. Department of Agriculture. *Understanding Rural America.* Washington, DC: U.S. Department of Agriculture, Economic Research Service, 1995.

Workers' Compensation

A state-administered program that provides employees with definite and sure compensation for injuries or death suffered in the course and scope of their employment. This article examines the duties agricultural employers owe their employees. It also explores the advantages and disadvantages of providing agricultural employees with workers' compensation benefits. It explains the compulsory nature of workers' compensation considering the agricultural exemption. It also reviews the advantages and disadvantages of buying liability insurance coverage for agricultural employees in place of workers' compensation coverage.

Employers' Duties to Employees

Employers must provide employees with a reasonably safe workplace and safe tools, and issue rules and warnings so employees work safely. Employers must ensure that all workers are reasonably competent. If the employer breaches any of those duties, and the breach causes an employee's injures, the employer is financially responsible. Agriculture ranks high on the list of most dangerous occupations as farm workers risk fatal and nonfatal injuries. They use dangerous machinery causing physical injuries and noise-induced hearing loss. They risk physical harm handling large, unruly animals. Agricultural workers often work in extreme weather and prolonged sun exposure. Exposure to dangerous chemicals and gases, such as methane, ammonia and hydrogen sulfide, can cause skin diseases, work-related lung diseases, certain cancers and death. If the employer does not have insurance to cover an employee's bodily injures and medical expenses, both the employer and employee may face devastating financial outcomes.

The Case for Workers' Compensation

Each state enacts its own workers' compensation statute, and benefits vary from state to state. All state workers' compensation systems, however, provide an injured worker with disability payments while medically unable to work. Injured workers receive some compensation for loss of earning capacity and degrees of permanent disability. Workers' compensation pays the injured workers' reasonable medical care costs related to the injury. Workers' compensation also pays some compensation to the survivors of a worker who dies of a work-related injury or illness.

To qualify for workers' compensation benefits, the claimant must qualify as an employee under the state's workers' compensation statute. The statute must cover the work performed, as state statutes exempt some work from coverage under the system. A connection must exist between the work performed and the worker's injury. The injury must arise out of and during employment.

Workers' compensation insurance offers both advantages and disadvantages to the employer and the employee. It is a quid pro quo program in which each of the parties gives up something for a stable and predictable means to handle work-related injuries.

For the employer, workers' compensation provides the exclusive remedy to claims filed by an employee. For example, a worker entitled to compensation under a state workers' compensation act cannot sue the employer under state products liability law, wrongful death statutes, or bring a negligence claim against the employer. The system protects employers from massive lawsuits. The state's workers' compensation act limits the employer's financial exposure to amounts set out in the state's act.

However, even workers' compensation will not prevent an action if an employer intentionally injures an employee. Similarly, few states have adopted the substantially certain doctrine. The doctrine allows an employee to sue an employer outside the workers' compensation remedy if the employer places the employee in a position where harm is substantially certain to occur, regardless of the employer's intent. For example, a group of workers repeatedly exposed to toxic fumes in a manufacturing plant successfully sued their employer outside the state's workers' compensation statute because the employer repeatedly failed to remove known toxic fumes.

For the employee, workers' compensation insurance guarantees the employee compensation and medical care, even if the employee was at fault. The employer cannot raise the employee's own negligence or fault as a defense. An insured worker should receive compensation for any personal injury caused by an accident or disease related to employment.

A benefits schedule determines an injured worker's compensation. Every injury, depending on whether the injury is permanent or temporary, pays the employee a fixed percentage of the worker's average weekly wage for a set number of weeks, up to a maximum amount. Workers' compensation also pays death benefits for fatal injuries.

In exchange for waiving their right to sue, workers' compensation automatically entitles employees to benefits. Employees also receive benefits more quickly. However, employees are rarely fully compensated for their injuries. Workers' compensation often does not provide compensation for impotency, pain and suffering, psychological damage, or disfigurement. Workers' compensation also does not compensate family members for loss of consortium or companionship.

Is Workers' Compensation Compulsory?

In analyzing insurance needs an agricultural employer must first discover whether state law mandates workers' compensation insurance coverage. Twelve states require that agricultural workers receive the same workers' compensation coverage as nonagricultural workers.

In those states, if an employer fails to buy the compulsory workers' compensation, he or she loses certain common law defenses in any lawsuit filed by an injured employee.

One example of a common law defense lost is contributory negligence. This defense looks at the employee's own carelessness. If the injury is more the employee's fault than the employer's, the court denies or reduces the employee's award.

A second example of a lost defense is assumption of risk. This defense applies if the employee was aware of the work's danger and voluntarily risked injury. In assuming the risk of injury, the employee forgoes compensation if injured. The employer who does not buy the required workers' compensation insurance loses both defenses. Also, the employer loses the benefit of any other liability insurance he or she might have. Liability policies commonly state there is no coverage under the policy for injured employees when state law requires coverage under workers' compensation insurance.

The Agricultural Exemption

Most states exempt some farm laborers from state workers' compensation statutes. However, there is much variation among states. Some states exclude all agricultural workers. Eleven states specifically exempt agricultural employees from workers' compensation. Those eleven states do not require agricultural employers to buy workers compensation insurance for their employees. Even those states that exclude agricultural workers from compensation coverage, however, usually give the employer the right to bring their agricultural workers under the state workers' compensation act.

Twenty-seven states partially restrict workers' compensation coverage for agricultural employees. For example, some states exclude the workers of farmers who employ less than a certain number of employees. Other states exempt agricultural employees if the employers' annual payroll is less than a fixed amount, or whose employees work less than a specified number of hours each year.

In interpreting the state exemption for agricultural workers, some courts have found concentrated poultry or hog operations to be commercial businesses outside the agricultural exemption. In those cases the courts found workers' compensation insurance compulsory.

Similarly, if an employee regularly shifts from strictly farm work to an assignment of some nonfarm work, workers' compensation must cover the worker regardless of any agricultural exemption. An employer who has an employee constantly running or repairing nonfarm machinery, or repairing other nonfarm equipment or buildings, may find the agricultural exemption inapplicable to an injured worker.

Undocumented Workers

A major issue today is whether state workers' compensation covers an estimated 11 to 12 million undocumented workers in the United States. Undocumented workers comprise possibly 4.7 percent of the total U.S. workforce, about 7.2 million workers, it says there are an estimated 11 to 12 million undocumented workers in the United States. In agriculture undocumented workers are an estimated 24 percent of the total workforce.

The Immigration Reform and Control Act of 1986 (IRCA) forbids employers from hiring undocumented workers. Although the IRCA makes it illegal for employers to hire undocumented workers, almost all state workers' compensation systems cover the work-related injuries and deaths of undocumented workers. They require coverage because a legal disability cannot preclude an injured worker from claiming benefits. The IRCA does not prohibit undocumented workers from making contracts.

Some state workers' compensation statutes, such as those of California, Florida and Virginia, clearly cover undocumented workers by including unlawfully employed workers in the statutory definition of an employee. In other states, such as Arkansas and Mississippi, their statutes implicitly cover undocumented workers by providing coverage for all workers under a contract of hire.

In states where statutory protection is unclear for undocumented workers, courts repeatedly find workers' compensation coverage for undocumented workers. For example, Oklahoma courts find undocumented workers covered because the state's workers' compensation statute does not explicitly exclude undocumented workers from coverage. Other state courts, such as those in New Jersey and Maryland, use similar reasoning to find coverage for undocumented workers.

Some states providing workers' compensation benefits for undocumented workers restrict the awards, sometimes severely. Pennsylvania, for example, awards undocumented workers only necessary medical benefits. Pennsylvania denies undocumented workers wage loss benefits because undocumented workers cannot legally gain employment. California allows wage loss benefits for undocumented workers, but not vocational rehabilitation.

Virginia denied any workers' compensation benefits to undocumented workers until 2000. In 2000 the Virginia legislature amended Virginia's workers' compensation statute so undocumented workers could receive some benefits. In Virginia, injured undocumented workers receive workers' compensation benefits, except for temporary partial disability benefits.

Nevada indirectly denies benefits to undocumented workers. The Nevada Supreme Court held that, once an employer knows of a worker's illegal status, the employer is no longer required to follow statutory requirements providing modified employment opportunities to an injured worker unlawfully employed.

Wyoming is the only state that does not provide workers' compensation coverage for undocumented workers. In recent years, however, legislators in Colorado, Maryland, New Jersey and South Carolina unsuccessfully tried to exclude undocumented workers from their state workers' compensation systems. Concern over undocumented workers in the U.S. could fuel more such efforts.

Regardless of state workers' compensation systems covering undocumented workers, most undocumented workers in agriculture remain uncovered because of the agricultural exemption, or other exemptions such as the one for day laborers.

Finding the Right Coverage

If employers choose to provide workers' compensation insurance for their employees, they must also decide what insurance is best for them. There are three basic ways to secure workers' compensation insurance under state workers' compensation acts. Many states allow self-insurance, which is simply a program whereby the employer regularly sets aside enough assets to cover potential liability claims. The states that do allow self-insurance have specific rules for setting up such programs.

For many employers, self-insurance is not a choice because of the large amounts of assets needed to cover potential claims. In some states it is possible to buy workers' compensation at competitive rates through a state fund. An insurance agent or the state's workers' compensation committee can provide information about such funds. For most employers, state law (as well as economics) requires buying workers' compensation coverage through a private insurance company. Employers should shop around because insurance company rates for workers' compensation vary. Employers should check insurance companies for reputation, reliability and financial stability.

There are services that rate insurance companies. A.M. Best, Standard & Poor's, Duffy & Phelps, and Moody's Service all rank insurance companies on reliability and are helpful in selecting an insurance company.

The cost of workers' compensation insurance varies with the nature of the agricultural business, number of employees and payroll size. More employees equal a greater payroll and higher insurance premiums. An agricultural business with a high risk of injury to workers demands a higher insurance premium. A business' safety record also impacts premiums.

Other Insurance Coverage

If state law allows an agricultural employer to not buy workers' compensation insurance, what other insurance best protects the employer and his or her employees?

The agricultural employer may already have a Farmer's Comprehensive Personal Liability (FCPL) policy or a Commercial General Liability (CGL) policy and believe that coverage is enough. If so, the employer is flirting with economic disaster. Most FCPL policies and CGL policies do not provide protection for injured employees. Instead, they specifically exclude coverage for bodily injuries and any medical payments for those employees.

Employers who already have other insurance may adapt their coverage to protect themselves and their employees. They can expand an FCPL policy or CGL policy to provide bodily injury coverage for employees and some medical compensation. They do so by adding an Employer's Liability and Employee's Medical Payments Endorsement to the standard liability policy. It is important, however, to understand what an endorsement does and does not cover.

An Employer's Liability and Employee's Medical Payments Endorsement does not provide coverage if workers' compensation should have covered the employee's injuries. It does not pay for injuries or medical expenses already covered by disability benefits, employment compensation, or similar laws. The endorsement does not cover injuries to a person illegally employed, if the employer knew of the illegal employment. For example, an agricultural employer's insurer did not pay for a 15-year-old boy's injures received while handling a defective manure spreader. State law banned anyone under 18 years old from cleaning moving machinery or working any dangerous job.

Similarly, the endorsement provides incomplete coverage for occupational diseases. The endorsement commonly excludes coverage of any claims or suits brought more than 36 months after the end of the policy period. However, unlike a physical injury, an occupational disease may not show itself until many years after the worker's exposure to the particular hazard.

The endorsement also excludes coverage for certain types of damages. The Employer's Liability and Employee's Medical Payment Endorsement does not pay for punitive damages. A wrongdoer must pay punitive damages as well as compensatory damages awarded an injured person. Courts award punitive damages to deter the wrongdoer from engaging in similar reckless and willful misconduct in the future. For example, suppose an agricultural employer must pay $50,000 to a worker with lungs injured by ammonia during work. In addition, the court orders the employer to pay $100,000 in punitive damages for unlawfully failing to warn the worker of the dangers associated with ammonia. The insurance company would pay the $50,000 in compensatory damages. It would not pay the $100,000 in punitive damages, even if the employer's liability policy contained coverage over $150,000.

Endorsements also exclude coverage for consequential damages sought by the spouse, child, parent or sibling of an injured farm employee. These are damages that other family members might be able to receive because of the injuries suffered by the family worker. A classic example would be a wife who sues for loss of consortium because her husband's injuries made him impotent.

If an agricultural employer decides to buy an Employer's Liability and Employee's Medical Payments Endorsement, the cost will depend on the number of people employed and whether they are full-time or part-time workers. For rating purposes, full-time employees are those who work 180 days or more a year. An endorsement divides part-time employees into those who work over 40, but fewer than 180 days a year; and those who work 40 or fewer days a year. An endorsement typically contains a schedule on the declarations page specifying the total number of employees in each classification. The schedule also lists those employees to whom the terms of the endorsements do not apply.

— *John D. Copeland*

See also
Agricultural Law; Employment; Fringe Benefits; Injuries; Insurance; Labor Force; Labor Unions; Work

References
Ark. Code Ann. 8 11-9-102 (Lexis Nexis, 2008) (any person covered whether lawfully or unlawfully employed).
Bureau of Labor Statistics, Department of Labor, National Census of Fatal Occupational Injuries in 2007 (2007) available at http://www.bls.gov/news.release/pdf/cfoi.pdf.
Cal. Lab. Code §3351 (Lexis Nexis, 2008) (workers' compensation covers lawfully or unlawfully employed workers, including aliens).
Colo. S.B. 98.4 at 2-4 (2006) (excluding unauthorized aliens from workers' compensation coverage).
Copeland, J.D. *Recreational Access to Private Lands: Liability Problems and Solutions.* Fayetteville, AR: National Center for Agricultural Law Research and Information, 1995.
Copeland, J.D. *Understanding the Farmers Comprehensive Personal Liability Policy: A Guide for Farmers' Attorneys and Insurance Agents.* Fayetteville, AR: National Center for Agricultural Law Research and Information, 1992.
Del Taco v. Workers' Comp. Appeals Bd. 94 Col. Rptr. 2d 825 (Cal. Ct. App. 2000) (Awarding vocational rehabilitation benefits to undocumented workers violates employers' rights under the Equal Protection Clause).
Felix v. State ex rel. Safety & Compensation Div., 986 O, 2d 671 (Colo. Ct. App. 1997) (Construing Wyo. Stat. Ann. §27-14-102 (a) (vii) to exclude undocumented workers).
Feltman, R. *Undocumented Workers in the United States: Legal, Political, and Social Effects,* 7 Rich. J. Global L. & Bus. 65, 66-71 (Winter 2008); see footnote 14 for a list of court decisions awarding workers' compensation benefits to undocumented workers.
Fla. Stat. §440.02 (Lexis Nexis, 2008) (lawfully or unlawfully employed workers, including aliens).
Granados v. Windson Dev. Corp., 509 S.E. 2d 290 (Va. Ct. App. 1999) (illegal aliens are not employees under workers' compensation law).

Immigration Reform and Control Act of 1986, 8 U.S.C. § 1324 a (a-h) (1986)

Jerry, II, Robert H. *Understanding Insurance Law.* New York, NY: M. Bender, 1987.

Klamut, J., *The Invisible Fence: De Facto Exclusion of Undocumented Workers from State Workers' Compensation Systems,* 16 Kan. J.L. § Pub. Pol'y 174 (Winter 2006/2007).

Larson, L.K. & Larson, A., 1 Larson's Workers' Compensation Law at §74.01 (2004) (describing state agricultural exemptions).

Larson, L.K. & Larson, A., 1 Larson's Workers Compensation Law §101, at 1-2 (2004) (describing the workers' compensation system).

Looney, J.W., J. Wilder, S. Brownback, and J. Wadley. *Agricultural Law: A Lawyer's Guide to Representing Farm Clients.* Chicago, IL: American Bar Association, Section of General Practice, 1990.

M.D. H.B. 37, 2 at 25 (2005) (undocumented immigrant is not a covered employee).

Miss. Code Ann. §71-3-3 (Lexis Nexis, 2008) (any person covered whether lawfully or unlawfully employed).

Morris Painting v. Workers Comp. Appeal Bd., 814 A. 2d 879 (Pa. Commaw. Ct. 2003) (Pennsylvania law denies wage loss benefits because an undocumented worker is not legally entitled to employment).

Nackley, J.V. *Primer on Workers' Compensation.* Washington, DC: Bureau of National Affairs, 1989.

Nat'l Inst. For Occupational Safety & Health, Ctr. For Disease Control, NIOSH Safety and Health Topic: Agriculture (2007) available at http://www.cdc.gov/niosh/topics/construction.

The National Underwriter Co. *Fire Casualty and Surety Bulletins.* Cincinnati, OH: The National Underwriter Co., 1990 and 1994-5.

N.J. A.B. 654, 2 at 24-29 (2006) (excluding employees not legally admitted or residing in the U.S.).

Passel, J. Pew Hispanic Ctr., "The size and characteristics of the unauthorized Migrant Population in the U.S. 1, 9 (2006), available at http://pewhispanic.org/files/execsum/61.pdf (last visited February 1, 2008).

S.C. H.B. 3288 (2005) (eliminating workers' compensation benefits if injured worker is an illegal alien).

Tarango v. State Indus. Ins. Sys., 25 P. 3d 175 (Nev. 2001).

Tramposh, A. *Avoiding the Cracks: A Guide to the Workers' Compensation System.* New York, NY: Praeger, 1991.

U.S. Department of Labor, Coverage of Agricultural Workers (2006) (describing agricultural exemptions), available at http://www.dol.gov/esa/regs/statutes/owcp/stwclaw/tables-pdf/table3.pdf

Va. Code Ann. §65.2-101 (Lexis Nexis, 2008) (aliens included whether lawfully or unlawfully employed).

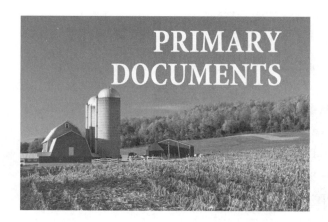

PRIMARY
DOCUMENTS

Table of Contents
Primary Documents: Visions for Rural America

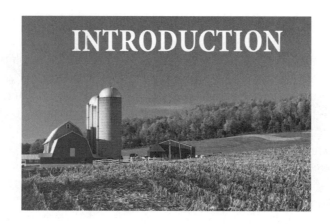

INTRODUCTION

Visions for Rural America

Rural America is at an uncertain crossroad. The uncertainties that rural America faces are not for the lack of innovative ideas regarding which direction to take. Rather, the uncertainties illustrate the lack of general consensus regarding which vision will determine rural America's future. How these uncertainties are resolved will directly impact not just *rural* Americans, but *all* Americans, as well as people across the globe. Critical decisions relating to a unified vision of rural America will affect the lives of millions of people for many years to come.

The diversity of visions for rural America can be illustrated by the variety of answers to the following questions: What do rural Americans want for themselves, their families, and their communities? What way of life would they prefer? What should rural America look like? The answers to these questions are shaped by people's "visions" for rural America, which are based on people's core values and beliefs about what is important, what is right, what is realistic, and what is best for the land and the people. These visions are more than just pleasant dreams for the future; they serve as the basis for policies and practices, and they offer a roadmap beyond the current crossroad. Despite the wide variety of visions for rural America, some common themes have emerged. These visions are clustered into three sets based on these common themes: Industrialized, Sustainable, and Alternative Visions.

The first two articles in this section of Primary Documents are intended to spark readers' own visions for rural America. In the first, "A Vision for Rural America," Cornelia Flora states, "My vision for rural America is one of constant change. It is a vision of constant growth. It is a vision of constant learning." Rural America has experienced constant change, growth, and learning, all of which require a vision of creativity. But

change and growth does not come without loss and wounding, which requires a vision of healing. Such are the themes of the second introductory article, John Ikerd's "Healing and Creativity: A Whole Vision for Rural America." Ikerd describes several trends and cycles that have wounded rural America, and he offers a visionary approach for its healing. He concludes by noting that "the people of a community must search for and find some common positive elements among their different visions to provide the nucleus for a shared vision of hope. Otherwise, the group is not really a community…"

Following the two introductory articles are sets of articles that represent several visions for rural America. The articles were selected because they were either written by authors who share a common perspective or who have shed light on the consequences of that perspective. Some articles are quite contemporary; others are "classic must-reads." Most of the articles pertain to agriculture or the environment. The agricultural and environmental themes were intentionally selected because of their articulated focus on visions for rural America. As readers examine the authors' visions, they will discover that these visions transcend agriculture and the environment and have profound implications for all facets of rural life.

Readers are invited to examine each article objectively and ask the following questions: What does this article say about rural America and where it is going? What are the core beliefs and values implied by the author of this article? What practices and polices logically stem from this author's vision for rural America? What solutions would this vision solve, and what problems would it create? How well does the vision illustrated by this author reflect my own vision for rural America?

Set I: Industrialized Visions

Articles in this first cluster—Industrialized Visions—place economic value on natural resources, forests, and the land as a way to better people's lives. This vision emphasizes technological advances (e.g., genetic modification, agrichemicals, and computers), globalization, market efficiencies, concentration of ownership, and vertical and horizontal integration of control (see *Neoliberal Economics* page 675). The notion held by those in the Industrialized Visions group is that such policies and practices are the most effective way in which to increase agricultural production and feed the growing number of people in the world. That notion is articulated by agronomist Norman Borlaug, the Nobel prize winner who founded the Green Revolution. In "Agriculture in the 21st Century: Vision for Research and Development," Borlaug and his co-author, Christopher Dowswell, describe the importance of biotechnological advances to further the Green Revolution.

In "Critical Dimensions of Structural Change", agricultural economist Michael Boehlje observes that increasing food production will require not only biotechnological solutions, but also changes in resource ownership and financial characteristics (see *Agriculture, Structure of* page 60 and *Agri/Food System* page 66). Boehlje argues, "Industrialization of production means the movement to large-scale production units that use standardized technology and management and are linked to the processor by either formal or informal arrangements."

The result of the industrialization of agriculture and natural resources is described in economist Steven Blank's article, "The End of the American Farm?" He assumes that the ownership of farms and other natural resource enterprises will become more concentrated, larger, and more capital intensive. Globalization will increase competition for these firms, and despite increased efficiency, their higher production costs will inevitably prevent them from remaining economically viable. Thus, American consumers will find cheaper food shipped into the U.S. from abroad, and American taxpayers will become increasingly unwilling to provide financial supports to ailing industries. In Blank's words, "The U.S. economy no longer needs agriculture and is rapidly outgrowing it." If farmers are being displaced as a result of industrialization and globalization, perhaps loggers, fishers, miners, and others in the natural resource industries will be affected in the same way.

Concentration in ownership is one outcome of Industrialized Visions. Although Mary Hendrickson and William Heffernan are not themselves proponents of these visions, these authors describe the growing concentration of various food sectors in their research, "Concentration of Agricultural Markets." They provide information on the "concentration ration" of the top four firms in specific food industries (CR4). For example, they show that the top four beef packing firms controlled 72 percent of that sector in 1990, and by 2005 the CR4 had jumped to 83.5 percent.

As farms and other natural resource industry firms have become larger, the result is that there are fewer farmers, loggers, fishers, miners, and their families. In turn, fewer business and services are needed to support those individuals and their families in rural communities, which reduce the population in rural communities. This observation led Deborah and Frank Popper ("The Great Plains: From Dust to Dust") to their provocative proposal for a "buffalo commons" as a way to manage depopulated lands.

Set II: Sustainable Visions

The word "sustainability" grew in popularity since the 1980s (see *Sustainable Agriculture* page 63, *Sustainable Rural Economies* page 945, and related articles). The concept meant that a practice or policy must be environmentally resilient, economically viable, and socially just. Proponents of this perspective often maintain a nearly sacred understanding of the environment, as illustrated by Liberty Hyde Bailey's classic 1915 book, *The Holy Earth*. Bailey was a horticultural scientist, agricultural college administrator, and proponent of rural life (see *Country Life Movement* page 213) who used a biblical perspective to advocate a sacred perspective of the earth.

The high view of the earth is evident in "Visions for Rural Kentucky" by the prolific poet, essayist, and Kentucky farmer, Wendell Berry. He is "really nervous about people who have visions for other people" because he does not want to live in "somebody else's political or economic or technological vision." Berry places more emphasis on local concerns than on globalized concerns, and is more comfortable with "small-scale, private, inexpensive visions of improvement." This would be his way to "hold securely in possession and in trust a beautiful countryside, producing a dependable, healthful supply of food and other necessities."

Just as Wendell Berry's vision of a sustainable rural America appears to be localized, other authors describe how that vision may be put into practice. One example is Frederick Kirschenmann—both a university professor and a North Dakota farmer—who authored "Agriculture's Uncertain Future: Unfortunate Demise or Timely Opportunity?" Kirschenmann points out that every farm has its own unique characteristics that require its own specific practices to achieve sustainability. He argues for agricultural products that have "an accompanying food story." Such agriculture is geared to produce public goods and provide a living wage, is produced locally or regionally, and preserves the identity where the foods are grown.

The efficacy of the transparent, local food production system described by Fred Kirschenmann was studied by rural sociologist Thomas Lyson, author of "A Promise of a More Civic Agriculture." He defines "civic agriculture" as "the emergence and growth of community-based agriculture and food production activities that not only meet consumer demands for fresh, safe, and locally produced foods, but create jobs, encourage entrepreneurship, and strengthen community identity." Lyson concludes that civic agriculture builds relationships among persons, social groups, and institutions in communities. Similarly, agricultural economist John Ikerd, author of "Sustainable Farming and Rural Community Development," studied the impact of industrialization on rural communities and residents, and examined what a "post-industrial agriculture" would look like. He concluded that post-industrialization will result in a renaissance for rural communities, and offered strategies for these communities' revitalization. Community revitalization can take place when a community builds on its assets or "capital." Various forms of community capital are described by Cornelia Butler Flora and her colleagues in "Community Capitals: A Tool for Evaluating Strategic Interventions and Projects."

Whereas many of the authors in this section emphasized local production and consumption as a key to sustainability, other authors maintain that a sustainable rural economy can include global components. In "Echoes of the Past: Lessons We Soon Forgot," agricultural economist Neil Harl states, "Peace and stability rarely coexist in areas of chronic food shortage. The surest way to success in addressing food availability, food safety and stability in the world is a global food and agriculture policy." In his article, Harl describes features of global food and agricultural policy that must be evident if those policies are to be sustainable and produce food justly.

Set III. Alternative Visions

Visions for rural America are multiple and varied. Although many people share commonalities with either the Industrialized Visions for rural America or the Sustainable Visions, others have uniquely different criteria for what they believe rural America should be. These Alternative Visions challenge the predominant paradigms because they offer a radically different perspective of the world and how it works. The paradigms of the Alternative Visions range from a distinctive understanding of the relationship between humans and the environment to a justice-oriented feminist perspective or indigenous people's traditions that stress harmonious interactions.

When forester and ecologist Aldo Leopold's *A Sand County Almanac* first appeared in 1949, few people considered land to be anything other than a commodity whose only value was economic or recreational. Leopold's "The Land Ethic" article describes land as having intrinsic value and rights in the same sense that human beings have intrinsic value and personal rights. His "land ethic" meant that, "A thing is right only when it tends to preserve the integrity, stability and beauty of the community; and the community includes the soil, water, fauna and flora, as well as the people." Leopold's land ethic was seen as benignly romantic by some, but as radically subversive by others. Just as Rachel Carson's *Silent Spring* became the explosive trigger for the modern environmental movement, Leopold's *A Sand County Almanac* served as its conscience.

Environmental sociologists William Catton and Riley Dunlap explore Aldo Leopold's reflections on the relationship between humans and the environment. They observe that an anthropocentric (i.e., human-centered) perspective of the human-environment relationship predominates in most people's thinking. They refer to the assumptions behind that perspective as the "Human Exceptionalism Paradigm" (HEP). Catton and Dunlap believe that policy makers, practitioners, and academics who maintain HEP assumptions will be unable to solve either environmental or social problems. Instead, they propose the "New Environmental Paradigm" (NEP) with radically different assumptions about humans' interdependence with other species, the linkages between humans' actions and the environment, and the earth's limitations.

Catton and Dunlap's NEP assumptions are evident in the last two articles of this section: Rosemary Radford Ruether's "Ecofeminism" and John Mohawk's "Wild and Slow: Nourished by Tradition." Theologian Rosemary Radford Ruether traces the connections between the domination of both women and nature that is evident throughout history. Provocatively she notes, "Nature does not need us to rule over it, but runs itself very well and better without humans. We are the parasites on the food chain of life, consuming more and more, and putting too little back to restore and maintain the life system that supports us." Radford Ruether describes several types of "conversions" as central to an ecofeminist ethic, which she believes is essential for social justice and environmental sustainability. She states, "Instead of salvation sought either in the disembodied soul or the immortalized body, in a flight to heaven or to the end of history, salvation should be seen as continual conversion to the center, to the concrete basis by which we sustain our relation to nature, and to one another."

Radford Ruether's earthy vision is shared by Seneca scholar John C. Mohawk. In his article, "Wild and Slow: Nourished by Tradition," Mohawk describes how Native people's shift from their localized, land-based traditions resulted in a pervasive malady facing an overwhelming number of these people—diabetes. He points out that the recognized cause of the diabetes epidemic is the modern, highly refined, carbohydrate intensive, "fast food" diet. Mohawk states that "the 'cure' for the malady, it turns out, has been with them all along. It lies in their own traditional foods..." Just as Radford Ruether's vision challenges Western culture's domination of women and nature, Mohawk's vision for rural America challenges the West's penchant for novelty and economic utility over indigenous traditions.

Conclusions

Rural America is at a tumultuous crossroads. Many voices continue to propose visions for what rural America could and should be. The articles in this section describe and critique a sample of these visions. No doubt, some of these visions will gain hegemony, at least for a while, and other alternatives will continue to be proposed. The visions, when implemented through policy and practice, have consequences not just for the land and people of rural America, but for *all* Americans, indeed for all who share the Earth.

A VISION FOR RURAL AMERICA

By Cornelia B. Flora

Our ability to shape the future depends in part on our visions of the future and our understanding of where we are and how we got here. Visions have an important basis in religious history. Native Americans have visions that connect them to land, to each other, and to the Creator. For a community of faith, narrative is particularly important, because it gives us a sense of a shared past. Through the liturgy we share the Judeo-Christian heritage of the wandering, the searching, the moving toward a vision. Liturgy also provides a sense of the present and presents the possibility of alternative futures. In this essay, I will lay out two "what if" scenarios. One will be, "What if we keep going as we are?" and the other, "What if we build on the assets and the people and the place to move forward?"

The European Americans who came after the Native Americans, often displacing them, also had visions—perhaps narrower ones. Some envisioned agriculture as it was in England, Germany, or Scandinavia. That past practice from a different place did not generate a sustainable agriculture on the harsh and arid environment of the Great Plains. Their struggle to impose that vision yielded human suffering and inappropriate treatment of the land.

I.   Institutional Trends

Visions are linked to action when we tell them through narratives and stories. And actions bring change when they are incorporated into institutions. Institutions are critical to the way we frame our past, present, and future. Plato laid out three important institutions that frame the individual's response to societal forces: the state, the market, and civil society.

The *state*, government at all levels, from international—such as the World Trade Organization (WTO)—to national to state to local, is a series of institutions that sets and enforces the formal rules. The government has a social contract with its citizens to attend to the common good. The *market* is the series of economic relationships that come about as we interchange goods and services for a price, though it can also include barter. It always involves exchange that is negotiated between buyer and seller—recognizing, however, that the negotiating power of one may bemuch greater than that of the other. *Civil society* is comprised of formal and informal groups of citizens that mediate between the market and the state. Churches are part of civil society, bringing the question of values to both government and market institutions.

Cornelia B. Flora is a faculty member in the department of Sociology and director of the North Central Regional Center for Rural Development, located at Iowa State. This center is one of four regional centers in the United States that combine research and outreach for rural development. It covers the twelve north central states. See page 1278 for more on author.

1. Government

Devolution (or decentralization) and privatization are major contemporary trends in government affairs. Worldwide, governments, particularly at the federal level, are saying, "Well, we can't afford this issue, and we aren't very effective in solving the real problems of people's lives, so let's give it to local governments." All of us have seen this occur in rural communities. Things that the federal government once did, states are now supposed to do—e.g., welfare programs—but then the states in turn pass this on to the counties.

The problem with devolution is that people are given the responsibility but often not the resources. With devolution local governments, which in rural areas are run by volunteers (a very interesting intersection between civil society and government institutions), are suddenly taking on huge responsibilities.

Privatization means that things that were once considered to be part of the social contract between state and citizen are being moved to the market, generally in the name of efficiency. That may be the case, for example (if political pressures are not part of the negotiating procedure), when the state hires a private firm to build and run prisons. The efficiencies of privatization cause some to wonder about continued equity of access for excluded members of society—for example, when recreation, parks, and education are privatized.

2. Civil Society

Polarization is a current trend in civil society. Rapid economic change, along with increased diversity in income, race, and ethnicity, are frightening to many people. Sometimes such people seek a single solution to the complexity of present problems. This can produce significant hostility. Fewer people are willing to run for public office, particularly at the local level. Many of those who do run are single-issue candidates. They seek to achieve a single goal—stopping the teaching of evolution in the schools, for example—and do not pay attention to the other parts of governing needed to create and maintain healthy schools and places.

With such polarization, people who do assume public responsibility are often bombarded with hate mail, making them want to resign or not run again. This polarizing aspect of civil society has major implications for the state.

3. The Market

Two key trends in the market are globalization and what I call post-Fordist industrialization. Fordism was the standardization of production brought by the assembly line, which created many products exactly alike of a guaranteed quality. Post-Fordist industrialization still produces guaranteed quality, but products are made to end-user specifications, using technology like CAD (computer aided design), which allows machines to be rapidly retooled to meet the exact specifications of the user.

Globalization brings, first of all, increased competition. There are more and more players in the market, producing greater supply and lower prices. Thus, all commodity prices are low. Rural Americans think primarily about the low prices of wheat, soybeans, corn, and various other grains. Beef prices are low, and hog prices are way out of sync. But, other prices are also depressed. Oil prices in 1998 and 1999 were as low, in real terms, as they have been since the '20s. Copper and timber prices are low. All of these prices are low, in part at least, because of the greatly increased competition brought about by globalization of the economy. Only when there is some sort of supply control, usually initiated by market institutions (as in the case of oil, where the Organization of Petroleum Exporting Countries [OPEC] limited supply at the end of 1999) or partnerships between state and market institutions (as in the case of sugar in the United States) have prices risen or been maintained.

Thus, commodity prices—by commodities I mean all of these raw materials that we use to make other things—are down. When commodity prices are down, profit margins get razor thin and the only way to compete is by volume. So a farmer raising commodities must raise more and more and get bigger and bigger in order to survive. These are not economies of scale, since often the small producer can be as cost-effective per unit produced as the large producer. But it is only by producing more and more of a commodity that sells for less and less that a producer can make enough money to continue in business.

Low profit margins lead to the next thing, which is the consolidation of enterprises. We are seeing huge consolidations among oil companies, the media, pharmaceutical companies, and seed and agro-chemical companies, among others. Farms are getting larger, and the number of operators smaller. Such consolidation brings an enormous increase in negotiating power, especially since the government in this time of devolution is declining to regulate in this area.

The *Baltimore Sun* recently published a depressing investigative report on chicken producers who work with integrators—the only way you can raise chickens these days, particularly in the south and the east. These farmers have no recourse with regard to their contracts. They cannot negotiate the terms that are in the contracts or even enforce the terms that are there. Every time farmers try a legal tactic or collective action, the power of the very few slaughter plants ensures that they lose. This may be a harbinger of things to come for the pork industry.

Post-Fordist industrialization shifts from producing commodities to producing products—products with controlled means of production and particular specifications regarding taste, convenience, and price. People who have found ways to produce quality ingredients for very specific products—rather than commodities—are pockets of optimistic survival in agriculture. We now see farmers joining with community members to form new alternative value chains. But so do multinational corporations, who own land and water rights, manure distribution rights, hogs, trucks, packing plants, and distribution networks.

Post-Fordist industrialization brings decreased numbers of linkages between producers and consumers. In the Fordist system, beef cattle can have as many as six owners before they get to the packing plant. The folks who are doing the cow/calf and the stocker/feeder operations are managing the *resource*—the complex interaction between the ruminant, uniquely able to utilize feed stuffs that are not digestible by non-ruminants, and the land. They figure out how much grass, how much pasture, how much corn stover, how much autumn wheat they have available, nature willing, and plan their number of animals accordingly. It is a very complex interrelation among humans, animals, and the environment. On the other hand, the packers and the folks who own the feed lots are managing the *market*. That is easiest done by ignoring nature and separating cattle from it in feedlots. These produce huge amounts of manure in one place and require corn, which is often irrigated, thus using up the ground water. Now folks are trying to shorten those value chains, because at every step, each owner takes a cut. Shortening the value chains in the proper way can accrue more to those early producers who manage the natural resource.

As a citizen, I have a great interest in the people who are managing and protecting the environment. I am much more interested in that piece going well than I am in whether feeders and pack yards do well. The struggle between those managing the resource and the packers, stockyards, and feed lots has gone on for a very long time. The history of beef production in this country shows the market concentrating control, while civil society organizes to promote justice, encouraging the government to care for the welfare of people in the sector of agriculture.

Industrialization also results in the separation of management from ownership. There are companies in Iowa that manage half a million acres. In this case, the land is not owned by foreign individuals or corporations but by the heirs of farmers, living in Florida and California, whose major concern about the land is their quarterly check. This kind of management encourages consolidation and short term profits. Linkages between rural and urban churches could provide contact between managers and landowners in a way that could raise questions of joint responsibility that go beyond a merely financial interest.

The present economy has brought a decreased number of core firms in the packing industry. The number of core firms has decreased in steel, car manufacturing, and grain processing as well. But the number of outsourcers is increasing, people who supply little pieces to those core firms.

II. A Different Vision

This is the setting—the present in our story. One vision for society's future is more of the same. But in the Bible, vision implies change. And for change to occur, civil society has to become more involved and more active—not only in telling congress what the government should do, but also in forming faith-based enterprises. And that is happening. One example is the formation of church-to-church distribution networks, where rural churches link with their urban counterparts, thus shortening the value chain between producers and consumers.

Vision requires that we know where we are going. In that regard, I would like to draw on the President's Council for Sustainability and talk about the three "e's": environment, equity, and economy. Equity is the hardest of these to measure. Frankly, it is difficult to get people interested in equity these days. We can get people quite concerned about the economy. But if they think about equity at all, they fall back on the statement, "A rising tide raises all boats." Yes, but if it is a tidal wave, a lot of small boats get sunk. Some people can get mildly enthusiastic about ecosystems and the environment, but they think it is inefficient to talk about equity. Concerns for justice are thought to take us away from our *real* business, which appears to be making sure that profits accumulate very rapidly for stockholders.

A biblical vision includes healthy ecosystems. We are to be stewards of the land. That concern is linked to intergenerational equity. We want to be sure that what we do today does not limit the opportunities of our children and our children's children. At the same time we are also concerned about intra-generational equity, which requires that we do not have a large number of very poor people and a few very rich people. Social equity would give everyone equal access to his or her congress people, where calls would be answered regardless of economic status.

Communities—communities of interest and communities of place—are absolutely vital to achieve a vision of equity, environment, and economy. All communities have resources available to them—human capital, social capital, natural capital, and financial capital.

Human capital is contained in individuals. It includes formal knowledge acquired through degrees and informal knowledge acquired through experience. It involves health, values, and leadership. Understanding and respecting the diversity of the human capital in a community is critical for a vision to be reached.

Second is *social capital*. Social capital involves mutual trust, networks of reciprocity, and shared symbols. Social capital provides ways of interacting, identifying ourselves communally—by what we do, how we believe, and how we treat one another—rather than identifying ourselves by what we consume. A collective identity implies a shared future. What happens to you matters to me. This ability to share joy in each other's success is an important part of social capital.

Next is *natural capital*, including air, soil, water, biodiversity (plants, animals, soil microbes, etc.), and landscape. A sociological truth requires the necessity of naming something in order to act toward it. We can impact something unintentionally, but unless we name it, we can't take intentional action toward it. Take air, for example, which we tend to take for granted: rural air is good; urban air is bad. But the situation is more complex. We produce greenhouse gases at an alarming rate, contributing to global warming. We pave things over, eliminating the carbon sinks we need to maintain air quality, reduce flooding, and protect water quality. Naming the realities involved with air permits informed action.

We don't even know about the extent of the earth's biodiversity. We may be destroying an invisible living world that is critical for our survival. We need science to help us name that world—and values to help us appreciate it. Landscape involves what we see, how we relate to it, and our necessary feeling of space. Do we feel comfortable with a chaotic environment, such as that provided in nature reserves or even shelter belts? Or do we require order—lots of the same thing in straight rows?

I grew up on a desert, so when I moved to Kansas I found it to be really green. Then I moved to Virginia and thought, "This is *too* green." While visiting us in Virginia, my father-in-law, who farmed in Kansas, said, "I feel a little closed in here in Virginia. The trees block the view." Our sense of landscape, our relation to the land, contributes to our sense of identity and is part of our social and human capital.

Financial capital involves money and its many instruments: stocks, bonds, tax abatements, derivatives, mutual funds. It is important because you can build things with it. You can construct school systems and roads. You can double your parking lot size and build an extra wing for the Sunday school. Financial capital is very useful, but only if it is viewed as a means, not as an end. Vital economies do not require huge rates of growth; vital economies generate a way for everyone to earn a living with dignity and to meet their needs rather than their wants.

We have good human capital in rural America. In the north central region, we believe in education and we have invested in it. So, we have a wealth of human capital available. However, we also have a problem, because our model of creating financial capital is based on the notion from the 1950s and '60s that what we really need is jobs.

The biggest barrier to economic vitality in rural America is lack of labor. We lack the needed labor force, in part because our model of development focused on bringing in low-wage jobs. Not surprisingly, the folks we trained so well have left for greener pastures. However, people can change that. In South Dakota, for example, a farmer set up a dairy cooperative, trying to take advantage of the social capital; but the members didn't think very hard about human capital. As a result, they paid only $7–$8 per hour and found that they were only able to attract students and others who couldn't find any other kind of job. Their dairy manager, whom they brought in from California, said, "Get me a good labor force or in three days, I will call my contacts in California and I will have some very hard working, excellent, experienced Mexican workers here." I hope the response was not due to racism, but the farmers who owned the co-op decided to offer $10 an hour, and they don't have a labor force problem anymore. By providing quality jobs at decent pay, they solved this major problem.

A second economic problem in rural America is the lack of housing. I just finished a study of the impact of bringing a large integrated industrial hog operation into rural Oklahoma. We found that the local, state, and federal governments found it more convenient to invest their financial capital in the corporation than in building housing for the workers. They wanted to create jobs, and they did. But that meant that the cost of housing in that county increased dramatically. The failure to invest in housing for the large number of new workers resulted in a decline in per capita income, an increased crime rate, and a rise in the number of civil suits filed. While retail sales shot up, the number of retail stores remained the same, as "big box" stores replaced local small businesses. Consumer loans went up, while business loans went down.

The corporation couldn't get any of the small producers who raise beef to integrate with them, so they became completely vertically integrated, building their own confinement operations and hog lagoons on land they purchased. They claimed to be agriculture so they could be exempt from anti-pollution and nuisance laws, and they claimed to be industry so they could get all the industrial incentives. A lot of manure lagoons were constructed with industrial revenue bonds.

In this case, the state (federal, state, and local) invested public dollars in a market effort that will probably have negative impacts on equity, definitely negative impacts on the environment, and variable impacts on the economy. The role of civil society in such situations is to understand that any change has winners and losers, and to make sure that the most vulnerable, particularly those without a voice through the market or the state, are not irreparably damaged in the process.

Our vision for the future of rural America is based on our incredible capital base. That human capital base involves people who have been here for a very long time, Native Americans. It involves people who have been here a pretty long time, including century farmers around the area, and it includes people who have been here not very long, who are often of Hispanic origin. These various groups are assets, not problems. In my vision, we come to understand the resource these people provide and our potential to move them up occupational ladders so they can replace the skilled labor force that is about to retire in our areas. They can be part of a dynamic community where, in terms of built capital, we will no longer have shuttered main streets and a few big box stores outside of town (so the corporations don't have to pay city taxes). Instead, we will have a main street that is vital and operating.

They will not necessarily be doing what main streets used to do—selling goods—but they will be providing services. We will see day-care centers and eldercare day care—sometimes together. There will be an appreciation of the different cultures that are increasingly coming together in rural communities.

We will be electronically connected so we can overcome the disadvantages of distance and dispersion, allowing us to build our own nuclei of market activity rather than merely recruiting branch plants. Entrepreneurial farm community partnerships will be an important part of that market activity. Farmers will no longer grow only corn and soybeans but use their incredibly rich soils to grow a wide variety of crops. They will constantly change what they produce, because community institutions will help them find emerging new markets. People will find that they are eating a lot more of what they grow directly rather then sending it out to other countries where the cattle are fed and then sent back here.

In my vision, our environment is in much better shape. Flooding has decreased because we understand that we don't have to pave everything to improve our quality of life. Since we are no longer exporting as many raw materials, we no longer need to put more locks on the Mississippi River. The channels are running freer. There is less siltation. The movement of the river is more natural, so it is better able to hold water.

Water quality is increasing, because we understand the ability of nature to deal with problems of nutrients when the water is allowed to stand where it is. Urban people are beginning to realize the importance of agriculture and rural areas, not just for providing food and fiber but for providing air and water. They are willing to pay for that benefit to the ecosystem as well as appreciate the quality ingredients that come through specific products.

The farming of the future will be among the most intellectually challenging of professions. Our new knowledge of plant genomics and specific microbial soil diversity will allow farmers to plant varieties that build on the local ecosystem, rather than attempting to overcome it. As we finish the genomemapping projects and are able to move genes more quickly, we will be able to move toward boutique crops. Alternatively, we can move to boutique crops through the seed saving that is already practiced by some farmers. People will be producing a lot of different things that will retain their identity from the field to the end-user consumer. Some people will want genetically modified organisms; others will not. We will be able to provide both, because we will have the organization at the social level that allows this to happen.

III. A Time for Change

In agriculture, farmers produce what they produce—a few commodities with very low prices—because we have established a series of institutions that support producing those commodities. Federal farm programs are based on a few commodities, elevators that do not segregate crops, and commodity associations that focus on producing more and more at less and less cost.

If we keep doing what we are already doing, we will get more of the same. With more of the same, we will face serious problems. Our human capital, social capital, environmental capital, and economic vitality are all at risk. Change is required—constant change.

Many of us are not very comfortable with constant change. We find it easy to make the non-risky shifts, like changing our brand of toothpaste or our variety of soybeans. But changing our farming system is a risky shift. Risky shifts threaten our comfort, but they might also mean that local businesses work to connect farmers to markets in new ways.

My vision for rural America is one of constant change. It is a vision of constant growth. It is a vision of constant learning. It is a vision where we learn how to relate better to the land, to each other, and to God.

Current trends in government, market, and society will continue to bring decline to the quality of life in rural America. But change is possible—change that risks defining and moving into an alternative future.

HEALING AND CREATIVITY: A WHOLE VISION FOR RURAL AMERICA

By John E. Ikerd

Most American rural communities have roots in agriculture. When Europeans arrived in the New World, they found a land of great natural wealth. Some of that wealth was in minerals and timber, but most of it lay in vast plains and winding valleys of fertile farmland. However, it took people to transform this wealth into material wellbeing. People cleared the land and tilled the soil bringing forth a bounty of food and fiber from the fertile fields. People cared for cattle and sheep as they grazed the vast plains. As these people, these farmers and ranchers, achieved surpluses beyond their own needs, they needed other people in towns and rural communities. Farmers needed people who would take their surpluses in exchange for things that farms could not produce. They needed blacksmiths, dry goods stores, livery stables, banks, and salons. They also needed schools, churches, and medical care, if they were to move beyond economic survival to achieve a more desirable quality of life.

Some of the early American communities built up around timber and mining towns, but most towns were farming and ranching towns. The number of people in these towns reflected the nature of agriculture on the surrounding farms and ranches. The larger the number of people needed to care for the land, the larger the number of people needed in town to support those farmers and ranchers. It is likely true that distance between most rural towns relate to a day's roundtrip by horse and wagon. However, the number of people in those towns was determined in large part by the nature of agriculture. For example, lands well suited for vegetables and row crops were farmed more intensively—supporting more families per acre or section. Lands suited only for small grains or pasture were farmed less intensively—supporting fewer families per section or township. Of course, town folks also had mouths to be fed with locally grown foods—greens, milk, eggs, and bacon. But, the density of population in most rural places reflected the nature of the surrounding agriculture.

At the turn of the 20th century, America was still an agrarian country—about 40 percent of its people were farmers and well over half lived in very rural areas. However, then came the second phase of the industrial revolution and the need to collect large numbers of people into cities to "man" the factories and offices of a growing manufacturing economy. The simultaneous industrialization of agriculture—mechanization, specialization, standardization—made it possible for fewer farmers to feed more people better at a lower cost to consumers. This "freed" farmers and other rural people to find work in the cities and freed consumer income to buy those things the industrial economy was to produce.

The same technologies that pulled rural people toward the cities pushed them off the farms and out of rural communities. These technologies increased production per person by substituting capital and generic knowledge for labor and individual management. As successful new farming technologies were developed, they invariably reduced production

John E. Ikerd is a faculty member emeritus in the department of Agricultural Economics at the University of Missouri. See page 1282 for more on author.

This paper was presented at the National Catholic Rural Life Conference, Des Moines, Iowa, November 5-6, 1999. Reprinted with permission.

costs—per bushel or per pound of production—but only if each farmer produced more. Thus, the incentive to realize greater profits by reducing costs was inherently an incentive to buy bigger equipment and more commercial inputs in order to farm more land and produce more output. As farmers individually responded to these incentives, production in total invariably expanded, market prices fell, and the promise of continuing profits vanished. The new technologies were then necessary—no longer for profits but now for survival. Those who adopted and expanded too little too late were unable to compete. They were "freed" from their farms to find jobs in the city.

The farms that survived grew larger and larger. In fact, with a limited population to feed and a limited amount of land to farm, it was possible for only fewer and fewer farmers to survive. In addition, large specialized farms often bypassed their local communities in purchasing inputs and marketing their products in order to remain competitive with other large farms. Their competitors were not just down the road or even across the country, but might be half way around the world.

Fewer farmers buying less locally meant less need for farm related businesses in small towns. Fewer farmers also meant fewer farm families to buy groceries, clothes, and haircuts in small towns. Fewer families also meant fewer people to fill the desks in rural schools, pews in rural churches, and the waiting rooms of rural doctors. Fewer people with a purpose for being in rural areas meant that many rural communities were losing their purpose for being as well.

Today, America is no longer an agrarian nation. Less that 2 percent of Americans call themselves farmers and most farm households earn most of their household income off the farm. Somewhere around 25 percent of the people live in non-metropolitan areas—but many if not most commute to a city to work. There are few people left in farming communities to move to town and no longer any social justification for moving them. Industries are "downsizing" and "outsourcing"—laying off workers by the thousands. As consumers, we spend on the average a little over a dime out of each dollar for food and the farmer only gets a penny of that dime. The rest goes to pay for commercial inputs and marketing services—packaging, advertising, transportation, etc. Society no longer has anything to gain from further industrialization of agriculture—yet it continues. In addition, rural communities in farming areas continue to wither and die.

Feeling the stress of an industrializing society, many small towns turned to industrial recruitment—trying to become a city rather than a town—as a means of survival. Others have tried to capture natural advantages in climate or landscapes to become destinations for tourists from the cities. Those near the growing industrial centers "rented out their communities" as bedrooms for those who are willing to commute to the city. However, most rural communities in agricultural areas have not been successful in their efforts to regain prosperity—or even to survive. Most rural communities have become and remain places in search of a purpose.

As the industrialization of agriculture moves into its final phase—the centralization of decision making among giant agribusiness corporations—there might seem little hope for either family farms or rural communities. The futures of both family farms and rural communities most certainly are at risk. The wounds of the past one hundred years will not be easy to heal. Nevertheless, there is still hope for the future. The industrial era appears to be nearing an end elsewhere in the economy, even as it continues to consume agriculture. The emergence of a new post-industrial era for human society may create opportunities for a new kind of American farm and new American communities. However, the wounds of the past will not heal themselves. Rural people must address their problems at their root causes, and must find the wisdom and courage to develop and pursue a new holistic vision for the future of rural America.

Removing the Sacred from Food and Farming

The wounding of rural America has several root causes, but none is more fundamental nor more important than the dehumanizing and desacralizing of food and farming. As we have specialized, standardized, and centralized control of agriculture to make it more efficient, we have forced living systems, including people, to behave as lifeless machines. Not only have we removed the life from agriculture—we have also removed its soul. We will never restore life to rural communities until we restore the live and health of agriculture. We can never restore its life and health until we first restore its soul. Before we can heal rural America, we must reclaim the sacred to food and farming.

Farming is fundamentally biological. All of life arises from the soil. The essence of agriculture begins with conversion of solar energy through the living process of photosynthesis carried out by plants that feed on the soil. The food that sustains our lives as people comes from other living things. If life itself is sacred, then food and farming must be sacred as well. In fact, people have considered food and farming to be sacred throughout nearly all of human history. Farmers prayed for rain, for protection from pestilence, and for bountiful harvests. People gave thanks to God for their "daily bread"—as well as for harvests at annual times of Thanksgiving. For many, farming and food are still sacred. But for many more, farming has become nothing more than another business and food just something else to buy. Those who still treat food and farming as something sacred, modern are labeled as old-fashion, strange, radical, or naïve.

However, the time to reclaim the sacred in food and farming may well be at hand. The trends that have desacralized farming have run, and overrun, their course. There is a growing skepticism concerning the claim that more "stuff"—be it larger houses, fancier cars, more clothes, or more food—will make us happier or more satisfied with life. There is growing evidence that when we took out the sacred, we took out the substance. As agriculture has been robbed of its natural productivity, our lives have been robbed of depth and meaning. But, people now are beginning to question the logic of our materialistic society. We have more "stuff" than any society has ever had but our wants seem as great as ever. How much is "enough?" Can anyone ever have "enough?"

The old question of how can I get more is being replaced with the question, how can my life be more fulfilling? The answer to this question, at least in part, is that we must reclaim the spiritual dimension of our lives. But, how can we reclaim the sacred? And, how will doing so change our farms and rural communities? We will address these questions later, but first we need to understand why we took spirituality out of food and farming in the first place and why we now need to put it back in.

Until some four hundred years ago, people considered nearly everything in life to be spiritual or sacred. The religious scholars were the primary source of knowledge in the intellectual segments of society. The uneducated masses accepted claims that kings, chiefs, and clan leaders—the people who other people looked to for wisdom—had special divine or spiritual powers. Only during the seventeenth century did the spiritual nature of the world come under serious challenge. Among the most notable challengers was Descartes, a Frenchman, who proposed the spirit/matter dualism. "The Cartesian division allowed scientists to treat matter as dead and completely separate from themselves, and to see the material world as a multitude of different objects assembled into a huge machine" (1983. p.22). Sir Isaac Newton, an Englishman, also held this mechanistic view of the universe and shaped it into the foundation for classical physics.

Over time, scientists expanded the mechanical model to include the living as well as the "dead." Scientists now treat plants, animals, and even people, as complex mechanisms with many interrelated, yet separable functioning parts. During the early part of this century, physicists developed fundamentally new theories they called quantum physics. The emergence of quantum physics challenges the old mechanistic worldview. Quantum physics views everything as interconnected—there is no separation of cause from effect. However, mechanical reductionism, which attempts to explain all biological processes as purely chemical and mechanical processes, still dominates the applied biological sciences from agriculture to medicine.

Scientists consider the spiritual realm, to the extent considered at all, to be in the fundamental nature of things—the unchanging relationships that they seek to discover. In science, there is no active spiritual aspect of life, only the passive possibility that spirituality was involved somehow in the initial creation of the universe that we are now exploring. The more we understood about the working of the universe, the less we needed to understand about the nature of God. The more we "knew" the less we needed to "believe." As we expanded the realm of the "factual" we reduced the realm of the "spiritual" until it became trivial, at least in matters of science.

Over time, the concept of science had shifted from a "science of understanding" to a "science of manipulation" (Schumacher). Over time, the goal of science had shifted from increasing "wisdom" to the goal of increasing "power." We did not want just to understand the universe; we wanted to dominate it. The purpose of science had become to enhance our ability to influence, direct, and control.

Farming was one of the last strongholds for the sacred in the world of science. "Mechanical" processes—using machines to manufacture things from "dead" matter—were relatively easy to understand and manipulate. But, "biological" processes—involving living organisms, including humans—proved much more difficult to understand and to manage. Farming and food are fundamentally biological in nature. So it took far longer to learn to manipulate and control agriculture. Farmers continued to pray for rain, and people continued to give thanks for food—although scientists would have advised us that both were either unnecessary or futile.

However, science eventually succeeded in taking the sacred out of farming—at least out of modern, industrialized farming. People tend to be difficult to understand and manipulate. But, machines took the laborers out of the fields, so farming became more manageable. Selective breeding brought genetic vagaries more or less under control. Genetically modified organisms (GMOs) are but the latest attempts by humans to manipulate and control other life forms. Commercial fertilizers gave farmers the power to cope with the uncertainties of organic-based nutrient cycling. Commercial pesticides provided simple scientific means of managing predator, parasites, and pests. Deep-well irrigation reduced the grower's dependence on rainfall. Processing, storage, and transportation—all mechanical processes—removed many of the previous biological constraints associated with form, time, and place of production.

Farms have become factories without roofs. Supermarkets and restaurants are but the final stages in long and complex assembly lines for food. Why pray for rain when we can drill a deep well and irrigate? Why thank God for food created by ConAgra? Who needs God when we have modern science and industrial technology?

The Inevitability of Change

Admittedly, if past trends affecting food and farming were to continue into the future, there will be little hope for rural agricultural communities. But, trends never continue, at least not indefinitely. A few years back, a couple of scientists proposed a list of the top twenty "great ideas in science" in *Science* magazine, one of the two most respected scientific journals in the world (Pool). They invited scientists from around the world to comment on their proposed list. Among the top twenty were such ideas as the relationship between electricity and magnetism, and the first and second laws of thermodynamics. The top twenty also included the proposition that "everything on the earth operates in cycles." Some scientists responding to the *Science* survey disagreed with the proposed theory of universal cycles, but most left it on their list of the top twenty great ideas in science (Culotta).

In essence, the theory of universal cycles claims that trends never continue forever. Trends are nothing more than phases on longer-term cycles. In reality, it's just common sense—everything that goes up eventually comes down, everything that goes around eventually comes around.

The theory of cycles implies that farms will neither get larger nor smaller forever, but instead will cycle between larger and smaller over time. If we think back over past centuries and around the globe, we can find examples where control of land became concentrated in the hands of a few, such as in feudal times, only later to be dispersed among the many. The most significant such occurrence in the U.S. may have been the development and later demise of plantation agriculture in the South. The most significant such occurrence in the world at present is taking place in what once was Communist Russia. These cyclical turning points have been associated with major historical events. However, large-scale, industrial agriculture is coming under increasing environmental and social challenges all around the globe. So, the trend toward fewer and larger farms in the U.S. is but a phase of a cycle that may well be nearing an end.

The theory of cycles implies that people will not migrate from the country to cities forever, but instead, cycle between rural to urban and urban to rural migration over time. In fact, human history is marked by such cycles in spatial dispersion and concentration of people in general. Anthropological evidence indicates that people have concentrated in large cities in centuries past, but later, for a variety of reasons, have abandoned those cities and dispersed themselves across the countryside. Thus, there is reason to believe that migration from rural areas to U.S. cities during the twentieth-century was simply a phase of a cycle rather than an unending trend.

Most large center-cities are already losing population as people move to the suburbs in increasing numbers. A further migration back to rural areas might be a logical continuation of the dispersion phase of this cycle. The phenomena we call urban sprawl today eventually may lose its ties to the city and evolve into patterns of dispersed rural resettlement. The most relevant question for rural communities might be, when will people abandon the cities and suburbs to resettle rural areas and why? There is nothing in cycle theory that dictates that people return to the same rural areas they left.

The Great Transition

Today, as in the seventeenth century, we are in a time of "great transition." "We are at that very point in time when a 400-year-old age is dying and another is struggling to be born—a shifting of culture, science, society, and institutions enormously greater than the world has ever experienced. Ahead, the possibility of the regeneration of individuality, liberty, community, and ethics such as the world has never known, and a harmony with nature, with one another, and with the divine intelligence such as the world has never dreamed." These are not the words of a priest of a philosopher but of Dee Hock, founder of the one of the largest financial institutions in the World, the VISA Corporation.

Hock is certainly not alone in this thinking. A whole host of futurists from the secular business community, including Alvin Toffler, Vaclav Havel, Tom Peters, Peter Drucker, John Naisbitt, Robert Reich, and others agree that we are in a time of fundamental change.

Capra, a physicist, writes about a "turning point," in scientific understanding that will shake the very foundations of science. They talk and write of a shift in worldview from the mechanistic, industrial era where people derive power from control of capital and the technical means of production to a post-industrial era where the source of human progress becomes knowledge. People will enhance their quality of life by learning to live better with what they have rather than by acquiring more "stuff." Knowledge is biological rather than mechanical in its fundamental nature—it changes, grows, and multiplies over time. Thus, the knowledge based era of human progress will require a new "science of understanding" to replace the old "science of manipulation."

The transitions in agriculture and rural communities are but small parts of *the great transition* that is taking place all across society. The questioning that is driving changes in agriculture, however, exemplifies the broader questioning of society that is fueling *the great transition*.

Questions concerning sustainability of agriculture and rural communities arise directly from our loss of spirituality. Using almost anyone's definition, concerns for sustainability imply concerns for intergenerational equity—meeting the needs of our current generation while leaving equal or better opportunities for those of generations to follow. The three corner stones of sustainable agriculture—ecological soundness, economic viability, and social responsibility—rest upon a foundation of intergenerational equity. Intergenerational equity, in turn, has its foundation in human spirituality. Sustainability applies the Golden Rule across generations.

Paraphrasing William James, a well-known religious philosopher, we may define spirituality as a "felt need to live in harmony with some unseen order of things." The sustainability issue ultimately is rooted in a perceived "need to be in harmony with the order of things"—in spirituality. Finding harmony with a higher order requires an understanding of that order—wisdom not power and control. Sustainable farming means farming in harmony with nature—nurturing nature rather than dominating or manipulating nature. Sustainable farming means farming in harmony among people—within families, communities, and societies. Sustainable farming means farming in harmony with future generations—being good stewards of finite resources. A life of quality is a spiritual life.

However, sustainable agriculture is also about economic viability. A farm is not sustainable unless it makes sufficient profits to stay in business financially. Sustainable farming systems generate profits by fitting farming to the farm, the farmer, and the community—not forcing either to fit some predefined prescription for productivity. Thus, sustainable farming must be knowledge-based—knowledge of how to work with nature rather than against it. Sustainable farmers must match their unique abilities and talents with their land, their community, and their markets. It requires a higher level of understanding of consumer tastes and preferences and the uniqueness of relationship markets. It requires greater sensitivity to sources of potential support, as well as sources of concern, within the community. Sustainable farming requires a higher level of understanding of the land and of nature's productive processes. Sustainable farming requires more intensive resource management—more thinking and creativity per acre or land or dollar of investment.

Sustainable agriculture, with attention to equity, stewardship, and high levels of management skills is consistent with post-industrial trends in the broader economy. The increased knowledge needed to manage resources sustainably suggests a trend toward smaller family farms that allows farm families to remain personally connected to the land. Sustainable agriculture strategies provide more opportunities for local ownership, hands-on management, and long term commitment to the local community. A high level of farming skill increases returns to management and leads to greater profitability for small farms. Farming becomes profitable for farmers and for rural communities as more dollars remain in the community.

Agricultural sustainability requires a systems approach to decision making which treats farms, families, and communities as parts of shared ecological systems. Such systems embody enormous complexity in simultaneous and dynamic linkages among a multitude of interrelated factors. Cognitive scientists have shown that humans can deal consciously with only a very small number of separate variables simultaneously. Yet humans can perform enormously complex tasks; such as driving a car in heavy traffic, playing a tennis match, or carrying on a conversation that baffles the most sophisticated computers. People are capable of performing such tasks routinely by using their well-developed subconscious minds.

The subconscious human mind appears to be virtually unlimited in its capacity to cope with complexity. As organizational theorist Charles Keifer puts it, "When the switch is thrown subconsciously, you become a systems thinker thereafter. Reality is automatically seen systemically as well as linearly. Alternatives that are impossible to see linearly are surfaced by the subconscious as proposed solutions. Solutions that were outside of our 'feasible set' become part of our feasible set. 'Systemic' becomes a way of thinking and not just a problem solving methodology" (as quoted in Senge, p. 366). The subconscious mind is capable of assimilating hundreds of feedback relationships simultaneously as it integrates detail and dynamic complexities together (Senge, p. 367). The human mind may be the only mechanism capable of dealing effectively with the systems complexities embodied in the concept of sustainable agriculture.

Wendell Berry, a Kentucky farmer, has clearly articulated the connections among people, quality of life, and a sustainable agriculture."...*if agriculture is to remain productive, it must preserve the land and the fertility and ecological health of the land; the land, that is, must be used well. A further requirement, therefore, is that if the land is to be used well, the people who use it must know it well, must be highly motivated to use it well, must know how to use it well, must have time to use it well, and must be able to afford to use it well*" (p. 147).

The words of Wendell Berry, the farmer and writer, are completely consistent with Peter Drucker, the industrial business consultant and writer, "*In the knowledge society into which we are moving, individuals are central. Knowledge is not impersonal, like money. Knowledge does not reside in a book, a databank, a software program; they contain only information. Knowledge is always embodied in a person, carried by a person; created, augmented, or improved by a person; applied by a person; taught by a person, and passed on by a person. The shift to the knowledge society therefore puts the person in the center (p. 210).*"

Sustainable agriculture, the new vision for the future of agriculture, is a knowledge-based approach to meeting the food and fiber needs of society that puts people at the center.

Human Creativity and Sustainable Rural Communities

Sustainable rural communities, like sustainable farms, must maintain the productivity of their local resources while protecting their physical and social environment. Sustainable communities must also provide an acceptable level of economic returns and otherwise enhance the quality of life of those who live and work in the community. Strategies that rely solely, or even primarily, on local natural resources are unlikely to fulfill these latter requirements. However, rural people can overcome the obstacle of limited local resources through a clear vision of the new realities of post-industrial development and a firm commitment to the concept of community. They can leverage limited natural resources—in much the same way as they might leverage equity capital in financing a business. As the local economy continues to grow, its natural resource "equity" will become a smaller proportion of its total economy, but no less important than is equity capital to a business in ensuring its survivability and sustainability.

Robert Reich, former Secretary of Labor, stresses that the economy is no longer local, or even national in scope, but is truly global. Neither communities nor nations can depend on capturing the benefits of local capital, local industries, or even locally developed technologies in a global economy. Money, jobs, and technology can and will move freely to anywhere on the globe where they can be used to the greatest advantage.

First, sustainable development must be linked to something that cannot easily be moved. Second, sustainable development strategies must give local workers and investors a logical reason for investing, working, and spending in the communities where they live. Communities cannot be sustained without strong economic interdependencies among those within communities. But, people must have strong logical reasons for developing interdependent relationships.

Reich outlines two fundamental strategies for national economic development in a global economy. First, he advocates investment in infrastructure, including such things as roads, bridges, airports, and telecommunications access systems. Infrastructure has two important development dimensions. First, it facilitates productivity by making production processes easier and more efficient. Second, infrastructure is fixed geographically. If producers want to use U.S. roads, bridges, airports and communications accesses, they have to use them where they are, in the country that built them. Fixed natural resources—such as agricultural land—achieve this same critical developmental impact without building anything. The challenge is to find ways to leverage the local land base to support more people better without degrading it.

Reich's second, and even more important, development strategy is to invest in people. People who work with their minds will be the fundamental source of productivity in a knowledge-based era of the twenty-first century. Human creativity provides the foundation for sustainable economic development in the post-industrial era. Creativity makes the local natural base less limiting, but no less important, than in the industrial era of development. If a nation is to be productive in the post-industrial economy, its people must be productive. If agriculture is to be a cornerstone for rural community development, it must employ the talents of thinking, innovative, productive people—it must be a sustainable agriculture. These thinking, innovative, productive people who can then leverage a limited resource base into vibrant, caring, sharing rural community.

Many people have strong ties to rural areas; however, rural communities cannot depend on an allegiance of rural residents to their communities to keep productive people from moving to town. People can and do move freely among communities within the U.S. Thus, it will be critically important for sustainable communities to be able to attract new mind workers, if there are to be places where "home-grown" mind workers will want to stay. The primary attraction of rural communities for current and future mind workers will be the promise of a desirable quality of life.

Quality of life is a product of human relationships—relationships among people and between people and their environment. Obviously, other things such as employment, income, personal safety, economic security, and access to health care are important aspects of quality of life. However, quality of life also includes peoples' subjective judgments regarding self-determination, freedom to participate, individual equity, freedom from discrimination, economic opportunity, ability to cope with change, social acceptance, and treatment according to accepted social principles of one's culture.

Rural communities that survive and prosper in the future will be culturally diverse. Successful rural communities will be made up of long-time rural residents, bright young people who choose to stay, returning rural residents, those born in urban areas of the U.S., and those born in other countries. They may also be Anglo American, Afro American, Asian, Mexican, and Canadian as well. Male and female, young and old, rich and poor, educated and less well educated, may be viewed as different, but they must be respected for their differences in the workplace and in the town halls of rural renaissance communities. This diversity will be an important source of creativity, innovation, and synergistic productivity, and will be an important aspect of quality of life in rural areas. In rural such communities, people will have an opportunity to know each other individually rather than simply accept the stereotypes of their cultural groups.

The most important single step toward success may be for those in the community to develop a shared vision of hope for their future—for a better way of life and a brighter future of their community. The vision of each person in the community will be different from the vision of others in many respects and not all will be hopeful. However, the people of a community must search for and find some common positive elements among their different visions to provide the nucleus for a shared vision of hope. Otherwise, the group is not really a community but rather a collection of people who happen to live in the same general area. A community that has found its shared vision has made its first critical step toward self-revitalization and community sustainability. Hope then can begin to transform reality. To paraphrase Jesse Jackson, the articulate civil rights leader, "if they can conceive it, and believe it, they can achieve it." The future of rural America belongs to those who have a vision of hope and courage to seize it.

References

Berry, Wendell. 1990. *What are People For*. San Francisco: North Point Press

Capra, Fritjof. 1983. *Tao of Physics*, Shambhala Publications, Boulder, CO.

Capra, Fritjof. 1982. *The Turning Point: Science, Society, and the Rising Culture*, Simon and Shuster, New York, NY.

Drucker, Peter. 1989. *The New Realities*. Harper and Row Publishers, Inc. New York, NY.

Drucker, Peter. 1994. *Post-Capitalist Society*, HarperBusiness, a Division of HarperCollins Publishing, New York, NY.

Hock, Dee. 1996. "The Trillion-Dollar Vision of Dee Hock," in SCSI Web Page, http://www. Fastcompany. com/fasco/5/well/deehocl.htm, by M. Michell Waldrop. December ,1996.

Hock, Dee W. 1995. "The Chaordic Organization: Out of Control and Into Order," World Business Academy Perspectives, Vol. 9, NO.1, Berrett-Koehler Publishers (pp. 5-21).

Hoval, Vaclav. 1994, "Transcending Modern," Columbia Daily Tribune, Columbia, Mo, July 10, 1994.

Naisbitt, John and Patricia Aburdene. *Megatrends 2000*. 1990. Avon Books, The Hearst Corporation, New York, NY.

Peters, Tom. 1994. *The Pursuit of WOW!*, Vantage Books, Random House, Inc. New York, NY.

Reich, Robert B. 1992, *The Work of Nations*. Vintage Books, Random House Publishing, New York, NY.

Schumacher, E. F. 1975. *Small is Beautiful*, Harper and Row, New York, NY.

Senge, Peter M. 1990. *The Fifth Discipline*. New York, New York: Doubleday Publishing Co.

Toffler, Alvin. 1990. *Power Shifts*. Bantam Books: New York, NY

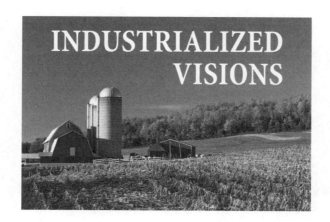

INDUSTRIALIZED VISIONS

THE END OF THE AMERICAN FARM?

By Steven C. Blank

Farming is an increasingly expensive lifestyle choice in the United States. As the nation turns to cheaper imported foods, smart farmers are selling their land to developers, but not happily.

Most Americans could not care less if farming and ranching disappear, as long as they get their burgers and fries. America will waddle on. The U.S. economy no longer needs agriculture and is rapidly outgrowing it. Voters support urban positions over rural interests. Taxpayers are tired of paying subsidies to farmers while surplus food sits in subsidized storage facilities. Suburbanites are fed up with the odors, dust, and toxins from the old farm down the road. No one is buying the farmer's sob story anymore. Instead, they are buying imported food.

American culture is no longer rural. Just like other rich countries, America has created alternate lifestyle choices in and around cities, and the population has flocked to them. Furthermore, in this stage of its economic development, the United States offers varied rural lifestyle choices. Family farming is not the only form of rural living available to the American population. People can live near cities and still have the ranchette of their dreams. As America develops further, information engineering and other new industries will enable a return to a rural lifestyle for many people if they desire it. It is already happening.

Part of the attachment to family farming comes from the "small is better" bias held by many Americans. There may or may not be some truth to this notion elsewhere in the economy, but it no longer applies to farming and ranching. Today, the only people who argue in favor of "saving the family farm" are former or current family farmers who have been or are being pushed out of business because they cannot compete with their larger, more profitable neighbors. Small, mom-and-pop operations cannot compete with larger firms, so family farms have become an expensive lifestyle that America cannot afford; it is an inefficient use of resources that is becoming a hobby that leads to bankruptcy.

Large-scale American farms and ranches will outlive family farms, but they will not survive indefinitely. Those big fish will feed on the little fish, but eventually they will fall prey to leaner, meaner foreign fish. The high costs of producing food in America, compared with the costs in poorer countries, are pushing American producers out of business as foreign competitors develop enough to serve the same markets. Foreign firms with lower cost levels will increasingly be able to underbid American producers. As a result, American agricultural firms will lose their profitability and be forced to shift into some other industry with better prospects. This is not a bad thing. This is life in a competitive world.

Steven C. Blank is a cooperative extension economist in the department of Agricultural and Resource Economics at the University of California, Davis. 530-752-0823; blank@primal.ucdavis.edu. He is author of *The End of Agriculture in the American Portfolio*, 1998.

Originally published in *THE FUTURIST*, April 1, 1999. Used with permission from the World Future Society, 7910 Woodmont Avenue, Suite 450, Bethesda, Maryland 20814. 301-656-8274; www.wfs.org

Abandoning Agriculture

Small, rich European countries were the first to be forced to face the end of their agriculture. Switzerland, Belgium, and the Netherlands are examples of countries that have nearly abandoned agriculture. They had no choice. They did not have much land, so their populations' food demands had outgrown their ability to produce long ago.

As the production of various food products was given up and reliance on imported products increased, the countries were able to pay for the imports with their incomes from the sale of other, more valuable products that were produced domestically. A lot of Swiss farmers found that making cuckoo clocks (and other manufactured goods) during the cold winters rewarded them with higher incomes and more-comfortable lives than did tending to snow-bound livestock. It was not difficult to convince many of those farmers to make the switch. Other Swiss farmers may have decided that they liked the rural life, but they now support their farming addiction by running winter ski resorts or other tourist businesses.

A few large European countries are also well on their way toward the end of agriculture. In 1995, Germany's agriculture minister said that the government was planning to in crease aid to rural Germany in order to develop commercial alternatives to the shrinking agriculture sector. Tourism and care for the elderly were alternatives to farming put forward by the ministry.

It must have been a shock to many farmers to hear the agriculture ministry recommend tourism over farming, but the message could not have been clearer: Get ready, the real world is coming.

Less Farming, More Food

Some people worry that leaving agriculture behind and shifting to imported commodities may cause Americans to miss a meal or two. But the United States has been importing an increasing amount of food for years, and Americans' waistlines are growing, not shrinking.

The alarmists are starting to worry about the future, but their view is limited and isolationist. For example, according to a panel of experts at the 1995 national meeting of the American Association for the Advancement of Science, energy shortages, exhausted land, scarce water, and a doubling in population will combine to radically change the American diet by the year 2050. The panel said that American lands are already pushed nearly to the limit of production and that crop yield increases are not going to keep up with population growth. These experts predicted that by the year 2050 arable American farmland would decrease to 290 million acres from the present 470 million. They also said that water will become less available for agriculture, forcing a shift of farmers to regions where rainfall is plentiful, and that the United States will cease to be a food exporter. The new diet, they said, will have less meat and dairy products, more grains and beans, and a sparser variety of vegetables. They concluded that, by then, Americans could be spending up to half their income on food instead of the present 13%.

The shortcoming of all these predictions is that they ignore food imports. The experts suffer from the "America must be self-feeding" bias. It is time for these people to wake up and smell the (imported) coffee. America has' not been completely self-sufficient in food supplies since the days of the Boston Tea Party. U.S. imports of food commodities have increased constantly and will continue to do so.

Some people fear agriculture's loss of economic importance. But the decline of agriculture is a national phenomenon. Even in the Midwest, where agribusiness remains a powerful economic force, manufacturing is the main engine of the region's economic boom. Figures on farming's recent success hide a problem: Farmers themselves did not fare so well because the ratio of prices they received to prices they paid is at an all-time low. Agriculture's poor profitability is its downfall. There is no plot against farmers. No one is doing anything to purposely hurt agriculture. Agriculture in America is simply losing its economic competitiveness as other industries develop and offer investors a better return.

So, what do farmers—the group with the biggest investment in agriculture—want? Surprisingly, many want the government to quit helping them through federal commodity programs, price-support loans, cash deficiency payments, federally subsidized storage, and other programs. Studies reveal that farm programs are not improving the profitability of agriculture as an industry—they just improve the bank accounts of selected people. And, unfortunately, many of those lucky people are not farmers or ranchers. One study found that farm payments tend to be based on land ownership, not land stewardship. In Kansas City, for example, the largest recipient was a real estate investment group.

Loss of subsidies would have a greater relative effect on small farms than on large operations, according to U.S. Department of Agriculture economists. The biggest impact of a loss of federal subsidies would be in the Corn Belt and the Northern Plains, which together get half of federal outlays. But this weaning process is a good thing. Good farmers want bad farmers out of the way. That is why so many farmers want an end to government meddling.

The number of American farms is shrinking, but those that remain are more productive. In 1994, USDA economists described this as a long-term structural trend that is likely to continue into the next century. In fact, farm numbers have been declining for over 60 years. The economists report that the decline in the number of farms continued steadily into the early 1990s at a rate similar to that of the mid-1980s. Census of Agriculture figures showed a total of 1.9 million farms in 1992, down from 2.7 million in 1969 and 2.09 million in 1987, a drop of about 33,000 farms per year. If trends continue, the number of farms will fall by around 39,000 a year between 1997 and 2002, then the rate will begin to slow.

Is this decline in farm numbers something to fear? No, it is an improvement in the efficiency of America's economy. Is it a scary thing? Yes, it is very traumatic for those farmers and ranchers facing the end of their small businesses. But the demise of a family farm is no more important than the end of a family business of some other sort. All small businesses are important to their owners, but insignificant to the economy. America will still be all right.

Are Factory Farms the Enemy?

Protesters claim that large-scale or "factory" farms are threatening rural communities. The fight in American agriculture is a rural-vs.-urban clash. It is a producer-vs.-environmentalist clash. It is a big-vs.-little clash. It is a public-vs.-private clash. It is also a clash between fact and opinion. For example, two rural Sociologists—from the University of Missouri and Iowa State University—said that farmers raising commodities are "getting the short end of the stick." Large food companies are getting a 20% return on their investment, but even the top third of family farmers only make 3%-5% on their investment.

The decline in family farms, these sociologists said, goes beyond agriculture and is really a question about the food system and the socioeconomic fabric of rural America. "Will consumers," they asked, "have a better quality, more available, more wholesome food system under a corporate, integrated model than what they've enjoyed under the family farm?" The sociologists are so busy worrying about the institution of family farming that they ignore the bottom line: There is no "rural America" anymore, and the people trying to hang on to the outdated version of farming are simply holding on to a bad investment.

The Last Roundup

American agriculture is heading for the last roundup. The rural countryside is heading into the final stage of its economic development. Looking out across that countryside, many will find it impossible to imagine the United States without farms and ranches. Especially at this point in history, when American agriculture leads the world in almost every way, it is startling to think that the country will not need farmers or ranchers for much longer. But it is true.

To understand and appreciate the changes, we need to place farming into context. We need to strip away the romance and nostalgia surrounding agriculture and see it for what it is: a business. It is a type of business that has limited potential for long-run profits because of its competitive nature. The whole world can do it. In America, the cost of doing it has risen to the point where it is not very profitable compared with alternative types of businesses. Thus, the people, money, and other resources invested in agriculture currently will be forced to leave for greener pastures.

In the transition, America's green pastures are going to have a bumpy ride. Prices of farmland increased 6.4% nationally in 1994 and increased again in 1995 and 1996. An economist in Ohio said that the price protection provided by federal farm subsidies, combined with high production, has farmers feeling good. Demand for farmland is high, with urban dwellers contributing to the price pressures because of desires to escape the cities.

Unfortunately, demand from city folks will grow slower than the rate at which farm subsidies will be reduced in this era of tight budgets. Less cash income (or subsidy payments) from farming makes farmland less valuable. For example, land values in Kansas could plummet 53% if Congress completely eliminates farm subsidy programs, according to an official with the Kansas Wheat Growers Association, quoted in the Wichita Eagle. Citing a Kansas State University study, the official told a Senate committee that even a 30% cut in the programs could reduce the state's land values by 9%. He said that small towns and rural communities would be hurt.

In the long run, however, city folks will ride to the rescue. A growing number of Americans are using telecommunications to bring their high-salaried urban jobs into rural America. In one example, using a Small Business Administration grant of $680,000, a Nebraska business developer set up two telebusiness centers with the aim of ending the exodus of rural Americans from the region.

It is ironic that many farmers and ranchers retiring in the future will be thankful for the flood of city folks into rural America. At the end of a farmer's career, virtually all of the money he or she has been able to accumulate is in the form of farmland. Thus, the farmer needs to sell to get the money into spendable form. If it were not for buyers from the city, many farmers would not get anything near the price they expect for their land.

That irony is lost on many Defenders of the Farm. Several groups, such as the American Farmland Trust (AFT), still strive to preserve the nation's farmland. They hate the fact that the United States is losing at least 1.4 million acres of farmland per year to development. AFT says that, more important than the acreage figure, much of the land being lost tends to be the most productive and nearest to consumers.

But it should surprise no one that the land closest to consumers is consumed first! So Defenders of the Farm have in many cases become Defenders of the Farmer. For example, in some places where the economic pressure to develop farmland is strong, the AFT has created a "Purchase of Development Rights" program to help farmers reap some of the development value of their land without selling to developers. In other words, when the value of land is too high to justify farming it, AFT will buy it at market prices so that land can sit idle instead of being developed into something useful. This is an example of shooting yourself in the foot.

People on the other side of the fight over land haven't exactly got the story figured out either. In 1995, a Des Moines Register columnist argued against sweeping laws to protect prime agricultural land. He noted that, although "vanishing croplands" has always been a popular headline, we are paying farmers to take land out of cultivation. He said that residential developments like the one he lives in near Des Moines have resulted in "urban forests" that support a wide variety of wildlife. Who would have believed it years ago—someone in Iowa defending urban sprawl because it was a source of wildlife habitat?

Clearly the end of agriculture in America is near, but some people refuse to see the signs and are hurting themselves in an effort to resist the inevitable. A classic example of this comes from reports that retiring farmers are passing their livelihoods on to young enthusiasts through a growing number of programs that match retiring farmers with younger ones in order to keep alive a family farm and a way of life. The idea of "matching services" was developed in 1990 by a think tank in Nebraska and has spread to more than a dozen states across the country. Yet, all the analysts agree that these programs are not going to change the face of agriculture because most farmers will always choose to sell out rather than commit several years to a transaction that requires working closely with a stranger.

The good sense and bad bank balances of American farmers and ranchers will win out over their hopes and dreams. As farms in Montgomery County, Maryland; Fresno County, California; and elsewhere in America continue to be shoved to the outer reaches of the county, and the urban sprawl continues to spawn new regulations with which to check growth, farm families are having a hard time figuring out how to fit in and maintain their way of life. They want to maintain something that they enjoy and do well, but they are bright people with families to protect, so they must do the prudent thing. As painful as it might be, the prudent thing is to manage their portfolio of assets with their head, not their heart.

As a nation, the United States must do the same. Americans can still listen to country music, but they have to drive their pickups into town. They must learn to let go of farming and ranching. In the short run, this means eliminating the subsidies that delay the inevitable development of the nation out of agriculture and into more-profitable industries. In the long run, this means becoming citizens of the world, dependent on others for food commodities while Americans produce the marvels and the know-how for the future.

America has to do these things to remain competitive, but the nation has shown that it can do anything to which it sets its mind. The first step is to accept that farming, although it enabled America to move into its dynamic future, is part of a proud past.

Job well done.

CRITICAL DIMENSIONS OF STRUCTURAL CHANGE

By Michael Boehlje

The U.S. food production and distribution industry is in the midst of major structural change—changes in product characteristics, in worldwide production and consumption, in technology, in size of operation, in geographic location. And the pace of change seems to be increasing. Production is changing from an industry dominated by family-based, small-scale, relatively independent firms to one of larger firms that are more tightly aligned across the production and distribution value chain. Food retailing is increasingly more customer responsive, more service focused and more global in ownership. And the input supply and product processing sectors are becoming more consolidated more concentrated, more integrated.

There are a number of drivers of and contributors to these changes including pressures from consumers and end-use markets, increasing competition from global market participants, economies of size and scope in production and distribution, risk mitigation and management strategies of buyers and suppliers, changes in government policy and regulation of the agricultural industries, strategic positioning and market power/control strategies of individual businesses and private sector R&D information and technology transfer initiatives and policies.

Changes in the structure of an industry or sector are typically dimensioned in terms of size, financial characteristics, resource ownership, technology and similar characteristics. But the most dramatic changes occurring in agriculture might best be described in terms of changes in the fundamental business proposition and the ways of doing business.

Development of Differentiated Products

One of the most important changes in the business proposition in agriculture is the development of differentiated products. The transformation of crop and livestock production from commodity to differentiated product industries will be driven by consumers' desire for highly differentiated food products; their demands for food safety and trace-back ability; from continued advances in technology; and from the need to minimize to total costs of production, processing, and distribution. Food systems will attempt to differentiated themselves and their products by science and/or through marketing. Ways to differentiate through science include gaining exclusive rights to genetics through patentable biotechnology discoveries; by exclusive technology in processing systems; and by superior food safety integrity. Differentiation will occur not only in terms of the attributes of the product, but also in terms of process. Agricultural raw materials will be different because they are grown in different ways (for example free-range poultry) or with different technologies (for example non-GMO corn or organic vegetables) as well as their nutritional value or chemical composition. Marketing may include: branding, advertising, packaging, food safety, product quality, product attributes, bundling with other food products for holistic nutritional packages, and presentation of products in non-traditional formats.

Michael Boehlje is a faculty member in the department of Agricultural Economics at Purdue Univertisy. See page 1274 for more on author.

Article is reprinted with permission.

For example, in the grain industries, high oil corn acreage has been growing rapidly, and new crops such as high oil soybeans, high protein wheat, and specific amino acid composition soybeans are expanding. In pork, differentiation on lean content is increasingly common. In the future at least two types of pork sire lines will likely be developed for different markets. One sire line will be selected to produce extremely lean and efficient pigs, with an objective of least-cost for reasonably acceptable lean pork. Other lines with higher intramuscular lysine content destined for export and restaurant markets will be selected for high pork quality.

Product differentiation is an important and particularly unique phenomena for the production sector of agriculture. Much of the production sector has focused on commodity products in the past and these commodity products are typically produced in large volumes by numerous producers in an increasing number of geographic locales in the world. Consequently, margins in commodity production are under constant pressure because of market forces that encourage increased production when prices and margins increase even slightly. In contrast differentiated products are sufficiently unique that they can not be produced everywhere by everyone. And differentiated products generally have more intrinsic value because they have additional attributes that consumers and end-users want. So the margins for differentiated products are generally higher and are less easily eroded by market forces compared to commodity products.

Finally, the science of biology is profoundly changing agriculture's role as a raw material supplier for a broader set of industries. The agriculture of the past 100 years has been a raw material supplier for the food and nutrition industry and, to a limited degree, the fiber and textile industry. But biotechnology and advances in biochemistry expand dramatically the potential uses for agricultural products. In fact, some are suggesting that in the future agriculture will be a significant supplier of raw materials for: (1) food and nutrition products, (2) health and pharmaceutical products, and (3) industrial products including synthetic fibers, plastics, wall coverings, and other products that have historically been derived from petrochemical raw materials. This significant broadening of the economic sectors that will use agricultural products as raw materials increases agriculture's importance in the overall economy. It also provides a broader base for the demand for biologically-based raw materials (i.e., agricultural products) as well as an opportunity to think of agriculture as a core source of integration of the total economy. The end result is that agriculture and the biological sciences that create agricultural products have the potential to not only redefine the sector's role in overall economic systems, but to substantially expand that role.

Implementation of Biological Manufacturing

A second significant change in agriculture is the implementation of biological manufacturing. Adoption of process control technology and a manufacturing mentality throughout the entire food chain, but particularly in production agriculture, has profound implications for the structure of the industry. Agriculture is being transformed from an industry that produces and processes commodities to one that manufactures specific attribute products for unique end-use markets. Farming is being transformed from *growing stuff* to *manufacturing biological based specific attribute raw materials*.

Biological manufacturing is characterized by industrialized production that uses modern business principles and manufacturing approaches including procurement, inventory management and process control technologies and techniques. Three types of process control technology are critical in biological manufacturing:

- *Monitoring/measuring and information technology* to real time monitor and trace the development and/or deterioration of attributes throughout the food chain.

- *Biotechnology and nutritional technology* to manipulate the attribute development and deterioration process in plant and animal production and product processing.

- *Intervention technology* to intervene with the proper adjustments or controls (in many cases using automatic or servo adjustment mechanisms) that will close the gap any time actual performance of a process deviates from potential performance.

This technological transformation is significantly different than the mechanical and even biological transformations of the past. In essence implementation of the three components of process control technology in production agriculture as well as in the input supply manufacturing and product processing and retailing sectors eliminates the disconnect that has previously occurred at the farm gate in the assembly line from genetic material to the retail food store.

Biological manufacturing has characterized much of the fruit and vegetable and poultry sectors for a number of years (Drabenstott; Perry, Banker and Green). Industrialized pork production and distribution is becoming the norm for most expanding firms in that industry. In many cases, this industrialized model of production and distribution will foster much larger scale firms; in 1988, approximately 5 percent of total pork production was concentrated in the hands of the 40 largest firms whereas, the 50 largest firms in 1999 are expected to produce approximately 50 percent of the total U.S. pork output (Freese).

The poultry industry moved to an industrialized model from the 1940s through the 1960s. Cattle feeding moved to the industrialized model in the 1960s and 1970s. The brood cow industry continues to be much less affected by industrialization, as technologies have yet to be found that can greatly increase the productivity of the brood cow through confinement and intensive management. Specialty crops have or are rapidly adopting industrialized production systems. The grain industry is moving more slowly to this type of agriculture, but segments of the commodity markets are increasingly adopting a biological manufacturing approach.

Industrialization of production means the movement to large-scale production units that use standardized technology and management and are linked to the processor by either formal or informal arrangements. Size and standardization are important characteristics in lowering production costs and in producing more uniform crop products and animals that fit processor specifications and meet consumers' needs for specific product attributes, as well as food safety concerns. Smaller operations not associated with an industrialized system will have increasing difficulty gaining the economies of size and the access to technology required to be competitive except perhaps in niche markets. Smaller operations can however remain in production for a number of years since they may have facilities that have low debt and are able to utilize family labor. Technological advances combined with continued pressures to control costs and improve quality are expected to provide incentives for further industrialization of agriculture.

Formation of Food Supply Chains

A third profound structural change in agriculture is the adoption and implementation of common industrial procedures for organizing business activity—tightly aligned value or supply chains. This supply chain approach from genetics to end user/consumer is expected to improve efficiency through better flow scheduling and resource utilization, increase the ability to manage and control quality throughout the chain, reduce risks and especially the risk associated with food safety and contamination through traceback, and increase the ability of the agricultural industries to respond quickly to changes in consumer demand for food attributes.

A supply chain structure and approach begins with a different premise than traditionally used in most approaches to managing agricultural businesses—the focus is on the function performed, not on the firm or the economic agents that perform it. A supply or value chain increases the interdependence among the various stages in the food chain by using strategic alliances, networks and other governance structures to improve logistics, product flow, and information flow. Competition or rivalry occurs not in the form of individual firms competing with one another for market share within a stage, but in the form of supply chains competing for their share of the consumer's food expenditures. Supply chain thinking will also impact investment decisions—it will increase the interdependence of decisions concerning size, location, technology, and so on of food product production, processing, and distribution systems. The benefits of an integrated system are likely to result in the development of interdependent food production-processing centers as the optimal strategy for growth and expansion in the agricultural industries, similar to the location strategy of expansion in European manufacturing industries.

Food safety is a major driver in the formation of chains. One way to manage food safety risk is to monitor the production/distribution process all the way from final product back through the chain to genetics. A trace-back system combined with HACCP (Hazard Analysis Critical Control Points) quality assurance procedures facilitates control of the system to minimize the chances of a food contaminant, or to quickly and easily identify the sources of contamination.

A Final Comment

The evolution of the new agriculture is being profoundly impacted by the simultaneous emergence of the new economy—an economy characterized by knowledge, information and intangibles as the key strategic resources; integration and networking; virtual linkages and virtual reality; miniaturization and nanotechnology, molecularization and the new biology of genomics and proteinics, disintermediation; digitization; globalization; real time immediacy, rapid change and innovation; increased economic disparity; new (revenue growth) valuation, etc. The end result will be an agricultural industry that is much more fully integrated into the overall economy in terms of not only ways of doing business, but also in terms of sourcing and rewarding resources—particularly capital and human resources. In fact, this more complete integration of the food production and distribution system into the industrial economy is quite possibly the most important structural change that has or will occur in the agricultural industry.

AGRICULTURE IN THE 21ST CENTURY: VISION FOR RESEARCH AND DEVELOPMENT

By Norman E. Borlaug & Christopher Dowswell

Introduction

It is a pleasure to visit southeast Asia again, to participate with scientists and national policy makers in discussions about the prospects and future of biotechnology in Thailand and the Philippines. The majority of agricultural scientists—myself included—anticipate great benefits from biotechnology in the coming decades to help meet our future food and fiber needs. Indeed, the commercial adoption by farmers of transgenic crops has been one of the most rapid cases of technology diffusion in the history of agriculture. Between 1996 and 1999, the area planted commercially to transgenic crops has increased from 1.7 to 39.9 million hectares (James, 1999).

I am now in my 56th year of continuous involvement in agricultural research and production in the low-income, food-deficit developing countries. I have worked with many colleagues, political leaders, and farmers to transform lower-yielding food production systems into higher-yielding ones.

Great progress has been achieved in Asian agriculture since the early 1960s (FAOSTAT, 1998). Between 1961 and 1998, cereal production in Developing Asia has increased more than three-fold, due largely to the widespread adoption during the 1960s and 1970s of high-yielding rice and wheat production technology (and later in maize and other crops). The core technological components were management-responsive varieties, fertilizers, and irrigation.

Poverty Still Haunts Asia

Despite the successes of smallholder Asian farmers in applying Green Revolution technologies to triple cereal production since 1961, the battle to ensure food security for hundreds of million miserably poor Asian people is far from won, especially in South Asia. Of the roughly 1.3 billion people in this sub-region, 500 million live on less than US$ 1 per day, 400 million are illiterate adults, 264 million lack access to health services, 230 million to safe drinking water, and 80 million children under 4 are malnourished (*Eliminating World Poverty*. UK White Paper, 1997). Mushrooming populations and inadequate poverty intervention programs have eaten up many of the gains of the Green Revolution.

These statistics point out two key problems of feeding the world's people. The first is the complex task of producing sufficient quantities of the desired foods to satisfy needs, and to accomplish this Herculean feat in environmentally and eco-

Norman E. Borlaug has pursued fighting hunger through scientific research for most of his 94 years. He was awarded the Nobel Peace Prize in 1970 for his "Green Revolution" which helped Pakistan, India and other countries improve their food production. He is president of the Sasakawa Africa Association and continues to work in his laboratories at CIMMYT (International Maize and Wheat Improvement Center) in Mexico.

Christopher Dowswell, an African National who lives in Mexico, has spent the past 15 years in various positions at the Sasakawa Africa Association. He is involved in strategic planning in agriculture, and continues to write on agriculture, rural development and natural resource management.

Article appeared in *AgBioWorld*, March 21, 2000. Reprinted with permission.

nomically sustainable ways. The second task, equally or even more daunting, is to distribute food equitably. Poverty is the main impediment to equitable food distribution, which, in turn, is made more severe by rapid population growth.

Future Food Demand

IFPRI's 2020 projections indicate that Asian cereal demand (for food and feed) will increase considerably, both because of expected population growth and rising incomes (Rosegrant, et. al., 1995).

Most Asian societies today are still primarily rural, with more than half their labor forces engaged in agriculture. But the region is urbanizing rapidly, at roughly twice the rate of national population growth. In a number of countries non-farm employment (rural and urban) already exceeds agricultural employment. By the year 2020 most Asian countries are likely to have more people living in urban centers than in rural areas.

Higher incomes and urbanization are leading to major changes in dietary patterns. While per capita rice consumption is declining wheat consumption is increasing in most Asian countries, an indication of rising incomes and westernization of diets (Pingali and Rosegrant, 1998). Per capita consumption of fish, poultry and meat products is on the rise., and this expanding poultry and livestock demand will, in turn, require growing quantities of high quality feeds to supply its needs.

The migration of rural Asians to urban areas will affect farm production in several ways. First, with an out-migration of labor, more farm activities will have to be mechanized to replace labor-intensive practices of an earlier day. Second, large urban populations, generally close to the sea, are likely to increasingly buy food from the lowest-price producer, which for certain crops may very well mean importing from abroad. Domestic producers, therefore, will have to compete—in price and quality—with these imported foodstuffs.

Production Potential

Total cereal production (milled rice equivalent used) in the developing Asian nations has increased from 248 to 795 million tonnes between 1961 and 1998. During this period, most Asian countries achieved—or nearly achieved—food self-sufficiency in the basic grains. During the next 20 years, Asian farmers will have to meet this current level of production plus produce several hundred million additional tonnes of cereals more than they do today. Even with significant new production growth, Asian wheat imports, for example, are likely to increase from 30 to 75 million tonnes by 2020 (Pingali and Rosegrant, 1998).

Over the past 35 years, FAO reports that in Developing Asia the irrigated area has nearly doubled—to 169 million nutrient hectares, and fertilizer consumption has increased more than 30-fold over, and is now stands at about 70 million tonnes of nutrients. During the next century, Asia's food supply will be produced on a shrinking land base. While there are still opportunities to bring irrigation to some new lands, rainfed agriculture will become increasingly more important for expanding future supplies of cereals. Here, the spread of modern varieties in rainfed areas has begun is growing rapidly. (Morris and Byerlee, 1998).

Most Asian farmers have adopted modern varieties. HYVs already cover almost all of the irrigated rice and wheat areas, and a fair portion of the rainfed areas. But varietal replacement is too slow, with farmers often only changing varieties (with the exception of India) every 10 years or so. There are important gains to be made from more rapid varietal replacement, in which farmers have early access to the newer varieties with higher yield potential and resistance to a greater range of biotic and abiotic stresses.

There is still considerable scope to increase cereal yields, especially in rainfed areas but also in many irrigated areas as well. Significant increases in 'technical efficiency' are possible by using more purchased inputs and capital to substitute for increasingly scarce land and labor (Byerlee, 1992). Among the growing proportion of farmers who already have achieved high cereal yields, the interest in using more precise information and management skills to improve the efficiency of input use, mainly to reduce production costs.

Future Crop Research Challenges

Agricultural researchers and farmers in Asia face the challenge during the next 25 years of developing and applying technology that can increase the cereal yields by 50-75 percent, and to do so in ways that are economically and environmentally sustainable. Much of the near-term yield gains will come from applying technology "already on the shelf". But there will also be new research breakthroughs—especially in plant breeding to improve yield stability and, hopefully, maximum genetic yield potential—if science is permitted to work as it should be.

Genetic improvement—Continued genetic improvement of food crops—using both conventional as well as biotechnology research tools¾ is needed to shift the yield frontier higher and to increase stability of yield. In rice and wheat, three distinct, but inter-related strategies are being pursued to increase genetic maximum yield potential: changes in plant architecture, hybridization, and wider genetic resource utilization (Rajaram and Borlaug, 1996; Pingali and Rajaram, 1997). Significant progress has been made in all three areas. IRRI remains optimistic that it will be successful in developing the new "super rice," with fewer—but highly productive—tillers. While still probably 10-12 years away from widespread impact on farmers' fields, IRRI claims that this new plant type, in association with direct seeding, could increase rice yield potential by 20-25 percent (Kush, 1995).

In wheat, new plants with an architecture similar to the "super rices" (larger heads, more grains, fewer tillers) could lead to an increase in yield potential of 10-15% above the spring x winter *Veery* descendants (Rajaram and Borlaug, 1997). Introducing genes from related wild species into cultivated wheat¾ can introduce important sources of resistance for several biotic and abiotic stresses, and perhaps for higher yield potential as well, especially if the synthetic wheats are used as parent material in the production of hybrid wheats (Kazi and Hettel, 1995).

The success of hybrid rice in China (now covering more than 50 percent of the irrigated area) has led to a renewed interest in hybrid wheat, when most research had been discontinued for various reason, mainly low heterosis which trying to exploit cytoplasmic male sterility, and high seed production costs. However, recent improvements in chemical hybridization agents, advances in biotechnology, and the emergence of the new wheat plant type have made an assessment of hybrids worthwhile. With better heterosis and increased grain filling, the yield frontier of the new plant material could be 25-30 percent above the current germplasm base.

Maize production has really begun to take off in many Asia countries, especially China. It now has the highest average yield of all the cereals in Asia, with much of the genetic yield potential yet to be exploited. Moreover, recent developments with high-yielding quality protein maize (QPM) varieties and hybrids stand to improve the nutritional quality of the grain without sacrificing yields. This achievement—which was delayed nearly a decade because of inadequate funding—offers important nutritional benefits for livestock and humans. With biotechnology tools, it is likely that we see a range of nutritional "quality" improvements incorporated into the cereals in years to come.

There is growing evidence that genetic variation exists within most cereal crop species for genotypes that are more efficient in the use of nitrogen, phosphorus, and other plant nutrients than are the currently available in the best varieties and hybrids. In addition, there is good evidence that further heat and drought tolerance can be built into high-yielding germplasm.

Crop management—Crop productivity depends both on the yield potential of the varieties and the crop management employed to enhance input and output efficiency. Crop management productivity gains can be made all along the line—in tillage, water use, fertilization, weed and pest control, and harvesting.

An outstanding example of new Green/Blue Revolution technology in wheat production is the "bed planting system," which has multiple advantages over conventional planting systems. Plant height and lodging are reduced, leading to 5-10 percent increase in yields and better grain quality. Water use is reduced 15-20 percent, a spectacular savings! Input efficiency (fertilizers and crop protection chemicals) is also greatly improved, which permits total input reduction by 25 percent. After growing acceptance in Mexico and other countries, Shandong Province and other parts of China are now preparing to extend this technology rapidly (personal communications, Prof. Xu Huisan), President, Shandong Academy of Agricultural Science, July 7, 1999). Think of the water use and water quality implications of such technology!!

Conservation tillage (no-tillage, minimum tillage) is spreading rapidly in the agricultural world. The Monsanto Company estimated that there were 75.3 million ha using conservation tillage in 1996 and this area is projected to grow to 95.5 million ha by the year 2000 (1997 Annual Report).

Conservation tillage offers many benefits. By reducing and/or eliminating the tillage operations, turnaround time on lands that are double- and triple-cropped annually can be significantly reduced, especially rotations like rice/wheat and cotton/wheat. This leads to higher production and lower production costs. Conservation tillage also controls weed populations and greatly reduce the time that small-scale farm families must devote to this backbreaking work. Finally, the mulch left on the ground reduces soil erosion, increases moisture conservation, and builds up the organic matter in the soil—all very important factors in natural resource conservation.

Water Resource Development

Water covers about 70 percent of the Earth's surface. Of this total, only about 2.5 percent is fresh water. Most of the Earth's fresh water is frozen in the ice caps of Antarctica and Greenland, in soil moisture, or in deep aquifers not readily accessible for human use. Indeed, less than 1 percent of the world's freshwater—that found in lakes, rivers, reservoirs, and underground aquifers shallow enough to be tapped economically—is readily available for direct human use (World Meteorological Organization, 1997). This only represents about 0.007 percent of all the water on Earth!

Agriculture accounts for 93 percent of the global consumptive use of water (rainfall and irrigation). Rainfed agriculture, covering 83 percent of the world's farmland, accounts for about 60 percent of global food production. Irrigated agriculture—which accounts for 70 percent of global water withdrawals—covers some 17 percent of cultivated land (about 270 million ha) and contributes nearly 40 percent of world food production.

How can we continue to expand food production for a growing world population within the parameters of likely water availability? The inevitable conclusion is that humankind in the 21st Century will need to bring about a "Blue Revolution—more crop for every drop" to complement the so "Green Revolution" of the 20th Century. Water use productivity must be wedded to land use productivity. Science and technology will be called upon to show the way.

The UN's 1997 Comprehensive Assessment of the Freshwater Resources of the World estimates that, "about one third of the world's population lives in countries that are experiencing moderate-to-high water stress, resulting from increasing demands from a growing population and human activity. By the year 2025, as much as "two-thirds of the world's population could be under stress conditions" (WMO, 1997).

"Water shortages and pollution are causing widespread public health problems, limiting economic growth and agricultural development, and harming a wide range of ecosystems. They may put global food supplies in jeopardy, and lead to economic stagnation in many areas of the world."

The world irrigated area—with of it located in Asia—doubled between 1961 and 1996, from 139 to 268 million ha. In most of these schemes, proper investments were not made in drainage systems to maintain water tables from rising too high and to flush salts that rise to the surface back down through the soil profile. We all know the consequences—serious salinization of many irrigated soils, especially in drier areas, and waterlogging of irrigated soils in the more humid area. In particular, many Asian irrigation schemes—which account for nearly two-thirds of the total global irrigated area—are seriously affected by both problems. The result is that most of the funds going into irrigation end up being used for stopgap maintenance expenditures for poorly designed systems, rather than for new irrigation projects. Government must invest in drainage systems in ongoing irrigation schemes, so that the current process of salinization and waterlogging is arrested. In new irrigation schemes, water drainage and removal systems should be included in the budget from the start of the project. Unfortunately, adding such costs to the original project often will result in a poor return on investment. Society then will have to decide how much it is willing to subsidize new irrigation development.

There are many technologies for reducing water use. Wastewater can be treated and used for irrigation. This could be an especially important source of water for peri-urban agriculture, which is growing rapidly around many of the world's mega-cities. Water can be delivered much more efficiently to the plants and in ways to avoid soil waterlogging and salinization. Changing to new crops requiring less water (and/or new improved varieties), together with more efficient crop sequencing and timely planting, can also achieve significant savings in water use.

Proven technologies, such as drip irrigation, which saves water and reduces soil salinity, are suitable for a much larger area than currently used. Various new precision irrigation systems are also on the horizon, which will supply water to plants only when they need it. There is also a range of improved small-scale and supplemental irrigation systems to increase the productivity of rainfed areas, which offer much promise for smallholder farmers.

Clearly, we need to rethink our attitudes about water, and move away from thinking of it as nearly a free good, and a God-given right. Pricing water delivery closer to its real costs is a necessary step to improving use efficiency. Farmers and irrigation officials (and urban consumers) will need incentives to save water. Moreover, management of water distribution networks, except for the primary canals, should be decentralized and turned over to the farmers. Farmers' water user associations in the Yaqui valley in northwest Mexico, for example, have done a much better job of managing the irrigation districts than did the Federal Ministry of Agriculture and Water Resources previously.

What Can We Expect from Biotechnology?

During the 20th Century, conventional breeding has produced a vast number of varieties and hybrids that have contributed immensely to higher grain yield, stability of harvests, and farm income. There has been, however, important improvements in resistance to diseases and insects, and in tolerance to a range of abiotic stresses, especially soil toxicities, but we also must persist in efforts to raise maximum genetic potential, if we are to meet with the projected food demand challenges before us.

What began as a biotechnology bandwagon nearly 20 years ago has developed invaluable new scientific methodologies and products which need active financial and organizational support to bring them to fruition in food and fiber production systems. So far, biotechnology has had the greatest impact in medicine and public health. However, there are a number of fascinating developments that are approaching commercial applications in agriculture. In animal biotechnology, we have Bovine somatatropin (BST) now widely used to increase milk production, and Porcine somatatropin (PST) waiting in the wings for approval.

Transgenic varieties and hybrids of cotton, maize, potatoes, containing genes from *Bacillus thuringiensis,* which effectively control a number of serious insect pests, are now being successfully introduced commercially in the United States. The use of such varieties will greatly reduce the need for insecticide sprays and dusts. Considerable progress also has been made in the development of transgenic plants of cotton, maize, oilseed rape, soybeans, sugar beet, and wheat, with tolerance to a number of herbicides. This can lead to a reduction in overall herbicide use through much more specific interventions and dosages. Not only will this lower production costs; it also has important environmental advantages.

Good progress has been made in developing cereal varieties with greater tolerance for soil alkalinity, free aluminum, and iron toxicities. These varieties will help to ameliorate the soil degradation problems that have developed in many existing irrigation systems. They will also allow agriculture to succeed into acid soil areas, such as the *Cerrados* in Brazil and in central and southern Africa, thus adding more arable land to the global production base. Greater tolerance of abiotic extremes, such as drought, heat, and cold, will benefit irrigated areas in several ways. First, we will be able to achieve "more crop per drop" through designing plants with reduced water requirements and adoption of between crop/water management systems Recombinant DNA techniques can speed up the development process.

There are also hopeful signs that we will be able to improve fertilizer use efficiency as well. Scientists from the University of Florida and the Monsanto company have been working on the development through genetic engineering of wheat and other crops that have high levels of glutamate dehydrogenase (GDH). Transgenic wheats with high GDH, for example, yielded up to 29 percent more with the same amount of fertilizer than did the normal crop (Smil, 1999).

Transgenic plants that can control of viral and fungal diseases are not nearly so developed. Nevertheless, there are some promising examples of specific virus coat genes in transgenic varieties of potatoes and rice that confer considerable protection. Other promising genes for disease resistance are being incorporated into other crop species through transgenic manipulations.

Recently, IRRI scientists, in collaboration with other researchers, have succeeded in transferring genes to increase the quantity of Vitamin A, iron, and other micronutrients contained in rice. This could have profound impact for millions of people with deficiencies of Vitamin A and iron, causes of blindness and aenemia, respectively.

Since most of this research is being done by the private sector, which patents its inventions, agricultural policy makers must face up to a potentially serious problem. How will these resource-poor farmers of the world be able to gain access to the products of biotechnology research? How long, and under what terms, should patents be granted for bio-engineered products? Further, the high cost of biotechnology research is leading to a rapid consolidation in the ownership of agricultural life science companies. Is this desirable? These issues are matters for serious consideration by national, regional and global governmental organizations.

National governments need to be prepared to work with—and benefit from—the new breakthroughs in biotechnology. First and foremost, government must establish a regulatory framework to guide the testing and use of genetically modified crops. These rules and regulations should be reasonable in terms of risk aversion and cost effective to implement. Let's not tie science's hands through excessively restrictive regulations. Since much of the biotechnology research is underway in the private sector, the issue of intellectual property rights must be addressed, and accorded adequate safeguards by national governments.

Standing up to the Anti-Science Crowd

Science and technology are under growing attack in the affluent nations where misinformed environmentalists claim that the consumer is being poisoned out of existence by the current high-yielding systems of agricultural production. While I contend this isn't so, I often ask myself how it is that so many supposedly "educated" people are so illiterate about science? There seems to be a growing fear of science, per se, as the pace of technological change increases. The breaking of the atom and the prospects of a nuclear holocaust added to people's fear, and drove a bigger wedge between the scientist and the layman. The world was becoming increasingly unnatural, and science, technology and industry were seen as the culprits. Rachel Carson's *Silent Spring*, published in 1962, reported that poisons were everywhere, killing the birds first and then humans—struck a very sensitive nerve.

Of course, this perception was not totally unfounded. By the mid 20th century air and water quality had been seriously damaged through wasteful industrial production systems that pushed effluents often literally into "our own backyards." Over the past 30 years, we all owe a debt of gratitude to environmental movement in the industrialized nations, which has led to legislation to improved air and water quality, protect wildlife, control the disposal of toxic wastes, protect the soils, and reduce the loss of biodiversity.

Yet, in almost every environmental category far more progress is being made than most in the media are willing to admit–at least in the industrialized world. Why? I believe that it's because "apocalypse sells." Sadly, all too many scientists, many who should and do know better, have jumped on the environmental bandwagon in search of research funds.

When scientists align themselves with anti-science political movements, like the anti-biotechnology crowd, what are we to think? When scientists lend their names to unscientific propositions, what are we to think? Is it any wonder that science is losing its constituency? We must be on guard against politically opportunistic, pseudo-scientists like T.D. Lysenko, whose bizarre ideas and vicious persecution of anyone who disagreed with him, contributed greatly to the collapse of the former USSR.

I often ask the critics of modern agricultural technology what the world would have been like without the technological advances that have occurred? For those whose main concern is protecting the "environment," let's look at the positive impact that the application of science-based technology has had on the land.

Had Asia's 1961 average cereal yields (930 kg/ha) still prevailed today, nearly 600 million ha of additional land—of the same quality—would have been needed to equal the 1997 cereal harvest (milled rice adjusted) (Figure 1). Obviously, such a surplus of land was not available in populous Asia. Moreover, even if it were available, think of soil erosion, loss of forests and grasslands, wildlife species that would have ensured had we tried to produce these larger harvests with the low-input technology!

In his writings, Professor Robert Paarlberg, who teaches at Wellesley College and Harvard University in the United States, has sounded the alarm about the consequences of the debilitating debate between agriculturalists and environmentalists over what constitutes so-called "sustainable agriculture" in the Third World. This debate has confused–if not paralyzed–many in the international donor community who, afraid of antagonizing powerful environmental lobbying groups, have turned away from supporting science-based agricultural modernization projects still needed in much of smallholder Asia, sub-Saharan Africa, and Latin America. This deadlock must be broken. We cannot lose sight of the enormous job before us to feed 10-11 billion people, many¾ indeed probably most¾ of whom will begin life in abject poverty. Only through dynamic agricultural development will there be any hope to alleviate poverty and improve human health and productivity.

Farmers need to be motivated to adopt many of the desired improvements in input use efficiency (irrigation water, fertilizers, crop protection chemicals). This will require a two-pronged-strategy, in which reductions in subsidies are linked to aggressive and effective extension education programs to increase the efficiency of input use. Many agricultural research and extension organizations need to be decentralized, more strongly farmer-oriented, and more closely linked within the technology-generation and dissemination process. Universal primary education in rural areas—for both boys and girls—is imperative and must be given the highest priority. Ways must also be found to improve access to information by less-educated farmers—because of equity reasons and also to facilitate accelerated adoption of the newer knowledge-intensive technologies.

Closing Comments

Thirty years ago, in my acceptance speech for the Nobel Peace Prize, I said that the Green Revolution had won a temporary success in man's war against hunger, which if fully implemented, could provide sufficient food for humankind through the end of the 20th century. But I warned that unless the frightening power of human reproduction was curbed, the success of the Green Revolution would only be ephemeral.

I now say that the world has the technology—either available or well advanced in the research pipeline—to feed a population of 10 billion people. The more pertinent question today is whether farmers and ranchers will be permitted to use this new technology?

Extreme environmental elitists seem to be doing everything they can to stop scientific progress in its tracks. Small, well-financed, vociferous, and anti-science groups are threatening the development and application of new technology, whether it is developed from biotechnology or more conventional methods of agricultural science.

I agree fully with a petition written by Professor C.S. Prakash of Tuskegee University, and now signed by several thousand scientists worldwide, in support of agricultural biotechnology, which states that "no food products, whether produced with recombinant DNA techniques or more traditional methods, are totally without risk. The risks posed by foods are a function of the biological characteristics of those foods and the specific genes that have been used, not of the processes employed in their development."

While the affluent nations can certainly afford to adopt elitist and positions, and pay more for food produced by the so-called "natural" methods, the one billion chronically undernourished people of the low-income, food-deficit nations cannot. It is access to new technology that will be the salvation of the poor, and not, as some would have us believe, maintaining them wedded to outdated, low-yielding, and more costly production technology.

Most certainly, agricultural scientists and leaders have a moral obligation to warn the political, educational, and religious leaders about the magnitude and seriousness of the arable land, food and population problems that lie ahead, even with breakthroughs in biotechnology. If we fail to do so, we will be negligent in our duty and inadvertently may be contributing to the pending chaos of incalculable millions of deaths by starvation. But we must also speak to policy makers—unequivocally and convincingly—that global food insecurity will not disappear without new technology; to ignore this reality will make future solutions all the more difficult to achieve.

References

Byerlee, D. 1992. Technical change, productivity, and sustainability in irrigated cropping systems of South Asia: Emerging issues in the post-Green Revolution era. *Journal of International Development 4(5)*: 477-496.

Byerlee, D. 1996. Knowledge-Intensive Crop Management Technologies: Concepts, Impacts, and Prospects in Asian Agriculture. *International Rice Research Conference*, Bangkok, Thailand, 3-5 June, 1996.

James, Clive. 1999. Global Review of Commercialized Transgenic Crops: 1999. ISAAA Briefs No.12 Preview. ISAAA:Ithaca, NY

Khush, G.S. 1995. Modern varieties—their real contribution to food supply and equity. *Geojournal* 35(3), 275-284.

Morris, M. and D.Byerlee. 1998. "Maintaining Productivity Gains in Post-Green Revolution Asian Agriculture. *In* International Agricultural Development 3rd Edition, Eds:Carl K. Eicher and John Staatz. Johns Hopkins University Press,: Baltimore and London.

Mujeeb-Kazi, A., and G.P. Hettel, eds. 1995. Utilizing Wild Grass Biodiversity in Wheat Improvement—15 Years of Research in Mexico for Global Wheat Improvement. Wheat Special Report No. 29. Mexico, DF: CIMMYT.

Pingali, P.L. and S. Rajaram. 1997. "Technological Opportunities for Sustaining Wheat Productivity Growth,": paper presented at the World Food and Sustainable Agriculture Program Conference:*Meeting the Demand for Food in the 21stCentury: Challenges and Opportunities for Illinois Agriculture*, Urbana, Illinois, May 27, 1997.

Rajaram, S. and N.E. Borlaug. 1997. "Approaches to Breeding for Wide Adaptation, Yield Potential, Rust Resistance and Drought Tolerance," paper presented at *Primer Simposio Internacional de Trigo*, Cd. Obregon, Mexico, April 7-9, 1997.

Rosegrant, M.W., Mercedita Agcaoili-Sombilla, and Nicostrato D. Perez. 1995. Global Food Projections to 2020. Washington DC:IFPRI.

Smil, Vaclav. 1999. Long-Range Perspectives on Inorganic Fertilizers in Global Agriculture. Travis P. Hignett Memorial Lecture, IFDC, Muscle Shoals, Alabama United Kingdom. 1997. Eliminating World Poverty: A Challenge for the 21st Century. White Paper presented to Parliament by the Secretary of State for International Development.

World Meteorological Organization. 1997. Comprehensive Assessment of the Freshwater Resources of the World.

CONCENTRATION OF AGRICULTURAL MARKETS

By Mary Hendrickson and William Heffernan

CR4 is the concentration ratio (relative to 100%) of the top four firms in a specific food industry.

BEEF PACKERS   CR4 = 83.5%*

	Daily Slaughter Capacity**
1. Tyson	36,000 head
2. Cargill	28,300 head
3. Swift & Co.	16,759 head
4. National Beef Packing Co.	13,000 head

Historical CR4

1990	1995	1998	2000	2005
72%	76%	79%	81%	83.5%

Source: *Cattle Buyer's Weekly: Steer and Heifer Slaughter reported in *Feedstuffs* 6/16/03.
**Feedstuffs Reference Issue 2006 (9/13/06) as reported in *Feedstuffs* 1/29/07.
Note: Smithfield Foods is the 5th largest beef packer after a series of acquisitions.

BEEF FEEDLOTS

Capacity	One-time
1. Five Rivers (Smithfield and ContiBeef)	811,000
2. Cactus Feeders Inc.	510,000
3. Cargill (Caprock Cattle Feeders)	330,000
4. Friona Industries	275,000

Top Cattle Feedlots 1998

1. Continental Grain Cattle Feeding	405,000
2. Cactus Feeders Inc.	350,000
3. ConAgra Cattle Feeding	320,000
4. National Farms Inc.	274,000
5. Caprock Industries (Cargill)	263,000

Source: *Beef Today,* Nov-Dec. 1998

Source: *Feedstuffs* Reference Issue 9/13/06 as quoted in *Feedstuffs* 10/23/06

PORK PACKERS   CR4 = 66% (Estimated)*

	Daily Capacity**
1. Smithfield Foods	102,900
2. Tyson Foods	72,800
3. Swift & Co.	46,000
4. Cargill	36,000

Historical CR4

1987	1989	1990	2001**	2005***
37%	34%	40%	59%	64%

** *Feedstuffs Reference Issue* 2001.
*** 2007 *Feedstufs* Reference Issue

Source: *Smithfield is reported to process 27 million hogs per year and account for 26% of the total market. From this figure, we estimated the CR 4. *New York Times* 1/26/07 ** Daily Capacity from 2007 *Feedstuffs* Reference Issue.

PORK PRODUCTION

	Number of Sows*
1. Smithfield Foods	1,200,115
2. Triumph Foods	399,800
3. Seaboard Corporation	213,600
4. Iowa Select Farms	150,000

Number of Sows In 2001**

Smithfield Foods	710,000
PSF	211,100
Seaboard	185,000
Triumph	140,000

** *Successful Farming Pork Powerhouses* (October 2001)

Source: * *Successful Farming Pork Powerhouses* (October 2006). Notes: Smithfield includes sow numbers from PSF that is pending acquisition. Triumph markets pork through Seaboard.

Mary Hendrickson is a faculty member in the department of Rural Sociology at the University of Missouri. She is a coordinator for the Food Circles Networking Project. HendricksonM@missouri.edu

William Heffernan is a faculty member emeritus in the Rural Sociology department at the University of Missouri and involved in the Food Circles Networking Project. HeffernanW@missouri.edu

This report was prepared with financial assistance from the National Farmers Union. All rights reserved. Reprinted with permission of the authors and the National Farmers Union.

BROILERS   CR4 = 58.5%*

1. Pilgrim's Pride
2. Tyson
3. Perdue
4. Sanderson Farms

	Historical CR4			
1986	1990	1994	1998	2001
35%	44%	46%	49%	50%

Source: *Feedstuffs 1/15/07
Note: The CR2 in this sector is 47%.

TURKEYS   CR4 = 55%*

	Slaughter Capacity
1. Butterball LLC**	1,420 Million #s
2. Hormel Foods (Jennie-O Turkey Store)	1,265 Million #s
3. Cargill	961 Million #s
4. Sara Lee	260 Million #s

	Historical CR4			
1988	1992	1996	2000	2005
31%	35%	40%	45%	51%

Source: *Feedstuffs 10/9/06 (CR 4 is extrapolated from market share of new company.)
** Butterball LLC was created through a joint venture between Smithfield (49%) and Maxwell Foods (51%) that bought ConAgra's turkey operations.

ANIMAL FEED PLANTS   ANNUAL CAPACITY*

1. Land O'Lakes LLC/Purina Mills	12.5 million tons
2. Cargill Animal Nutrition (Nutrena)	8.0 million tons
3. ADM Alliance Nutrition	3.2 million tons
4. J.D. Heiskell & Co.	2.8 million tons

Source: * 2007 Feedstuffs Reference Issue (9/13/06)

FLOUR MILLING CR4 = unknown

	Daily Milling Capacity*
1. Cargill/CHS (Horizon Milling)	291,500 cwts
2. ADM } CR3=55%**	277,800 cwts
3. ConAgra	248,600 cwts

	Historical CR4		
1982	1987	1990	2005
40%	44%	61%	63%

Source: * Milling and Baking News 10/10/06 and 2006 Grain and Milling Annual
** Total US 24-Hour Milling Capacity is 1,492,456 cwts (Milling and Baking News 6/20/06)

SOYBEAN CRUSHING   CR4 = 80%*

Historical CR4		
1977	1982	1987
54%	61%	71%

1. ADM
2. Bunge } CR3=71%**
3. Cargill
4. Ag Processing Inc.

Census of Manufacturing

Source: *2002 Census of Manufacturing (released 6/06); **Wall Street Journal 7/22/02

ETHANOL PRODUCTION   CR4 = 31.5%

Million Gallons/Year (Capacity)

1.	ADM	1070
2.	US Biofuels	250
3.	VeraSun Energy Corporation	230
4.	Hawkeye Renewables	220

Historical CR4

1987	1995	1999	2002
73%	73%	67%	49%

Source: http://www.ethanolrfa.org/industry
Note: Farmer owned ethanol plants accounted for 39% of total capacity.

TOP DAIRY PROCESSORS IN U.S. AND CANADA

Annual Sales*

1.	Dean Foods	$10,106 Million
2.	Kraft Foods (Majority owner is Philip Morris)	$ 4,400 Million
3.	Land O'Lakes	$ 3,901 Million
4.	Saputo Inc.**	$ 3,461 Million

Source: *Dairy Foods: Dairy 100 (2006)
Notes: ** Over 40% of Saputo Inc. plants are in Canada.

INPUT MARKET NOTES
Corn Seed: CR2=58%*

The CR2 in the U.S. corn seed market has remained relatively stable, changing little from a CR2 of 56%** that existed in 1997. However, while Pioneer dominated the market 10 years ago, now DuPont (Pioneer) and Monsanto have roughly equal shares.
Source: *Wall Street Journal, 1/22/2007; ** Jorge Fernandez-Cornejo, 2004, USDA-ERS, The Seed Industry in the US.

Globally, Monsanto has its genetically modified seeds for corn, cotton, soybeans and canola on more than 90% of acreage that uses GMO seeds. By comparison, Syngenta is in 2nd place with about 4% of global biotech acreage using its seed.
Source: Financial Times, 11/16/2006.

Globally, four seed firms, DuPont (Pioneer), Monsanto, Syngenta and Limagrain have about 29% of the world market for commercial seeds.
Source: Tracing the Trend Towards Market Concentration. UN Conference on Trade and Development. 2006.

Global Phosphate, Nitrogen, Potash and Feed Phosphate Fertilizer Companies
1. Yara (6% of world's fertilizer market)*
2. Mosaic (Cargill owns 67% with ICM owning 33%)
3. Potash Corp

Source: * Dow Jones Commodities Service 2/14/07

U.S. FOOD RETAILING   CR5 = 48%*

Supermarket	Sales in Thousands			Change '04-'06
	2006	2005	2004	
1)Wal-Mart	$ 98,745,400	$ 79,704,300	$66,465,100	48.57%
2)Kroger	$ 58,544,668	$ 54,161,588	$46,314,840	26.41%
3)Albertson's**	$ 36,287,940	$ 36,733,840	$31,961,800	13.54%
4)Safeway	$ 32,732,960	$ 29,359,408	$29,572,140	10.69%
5)Ahold	$ 23,848,240	$ 21,052,200	$25,105,600	-5.01%

Historical CR5		
1997	2001	2004
24%	38%	46%

Source: * *Progressive Grocer's Super 50* (5/1/05) *Progressive Grocer* reports only grocery sales from supermarkets and does not report general merchandise, drug or convenience sales. **Note the CR5 is from 2005, and has most likely grown larger given the rates of change from 2004 to 2005.** In February 2005, the top 50 supermarkets accounted for 82% of total supermarket sales nationally.
** Supervalu completed their acquisition of 60% of Albertsons in June 2006. The remaining 40% was sold to Cerebus Capital Management. **Supervalu is now the 3rd largest supermarket**. *Progressive Grocer* 2/1/07.

WORLD'S TOP GROCERY RETAILERS 2006

1.	Wal-Mart Stores (United States)	$312.4 billion annual sales
2.	Carrefour (France)	$ 92.6
3.	Tesco (United Kingdom)	$ 69.6
4.	Metro Group (Germany)	$ 69.3
5.	Kroger (United States)	$ 60.6
6.	Ahold (The Netherlands)	$ 55.3
7.	Costco (United States)	$ 52.9
8.	Rewe (Germany)	$ 51.8
9.	Schwarz Group (Germany)	$ 45.8
10.	Aldi (Germany)	$ 45.0

Source: *Supermarket News* 5/29/06

TOP U.S. FOOD PROCESSING COMPANIES:

	Company (Fiscal year in parentheses if different from calendar year)	2005 Food Sales ($ millions)	2002 Food Sales ($ millions)
1.	Tyson Foods Inc. (10/1/05)	23,899	21,285
2.	Kraft Foods Inc.	23,293	21,485
3	Pepsico Inc.	21,186	17,363
4.	Nestle (US & Canada)	19,941	13,110
5.	Anheuser-Busch Cos. Inc.	11,546	10,574
6.	Dean Foods Co.	10,505	8,992
7.	General Mills (5/28/06)	9,803	9,206
8.	Smithfield Foods Inc. (4/30/06)	9,614	7,356
9.	ConAgra Foods Inc. (5/28/05)	8,195	22,521
10.	Swift & Company (5/29/05)	7,847	8,476

Source: Food Processing, Vol. 67(8):34-48, August 2006.

THE GREAT PLAINS: FROM DUST TO DUST

A daring proposal for dealing with an inevitable disaster

By Deborah Epstein Popper and Frank J. Popper

At the center of the United States, between the Rockies and the tallgrass prairies of the Midwest and South, lies the shortgrass expanse of the Great Plains. The region extends over large parts of 10 states and produces cattle, corn, wheat, sheep, cotton, coal, oil, natural gas, and metals. The Plains are endlessly windswept and nearly treeless; the climate is semiarid, with typically less than 20 inches of rain a year.

The country is rolling in parts in the north, dead flat in the south. It is lightly populated. A dusty town with a single gas station, store, and house is sometimes 50 unpaved miles from its nearest neighbor, another three-building settlement amid the sagebrush. As we define the region, its eastern border is the 98th meridian. San Antonio and Denver are on the Plains' east and west edges, respectively, but the largest city actually located in the Plains is Lubbock, Texas, population 179,000. Although the Plains occupy one-fifth of the nation's land area, the region's overall population, approximately 5. 5 million, is less than that of Georgia or Indiana.

The Great Plains are America's steppes. They have the nation's hottest summers and coldest winters, greatest temperature swings, worst hail and locusts and range fires, fiercest droughts and blizzards, and therefore its shortest growing season. The Plains are the land of the Big Sky and the Dust Bowl, one-room schoolhouses and settler homesteads, straight-line interstates and custom combines, prairie dogs and antelope and buffalo. The oceans-of-grass vistas of the Plains offer enormous horizons, billowy clouds, and somber-serene beauty.

During America's pioneer days and then again during the Great Depression, the Plains were a prominent national concern. But by 1952, in his book *The Great Frontier*, the Plains' finest historian, the late Walter Prescott Webb of the University of Texas, could accurately describe them as the least-known, most fateful part of the United States. We believe that over the next generation the Plains will, as a result of the largest, longest-running agricultural and environmental miscalculation in American history, become almost totally depopulated. At that point, a new use for the region will emerge, one that is in fact so old that it predates the American presence. We are suggesting that the region be returned to its original pre-white state, that it be, in effect, deprivatized.

Deborah Epstein Popper is a faculty member at the City University of New York's College of Staten Island, where she teaches Geography and participates in the Environmental Science, International Studies and American Studies programs. She is also a visiting professor at the Environmental Institute at Rutgers University.

Frank J. Popper is on the faculty in the Bloustein School of Planning and Public Policy at Rutgers University, where he also participates in the departments of American Studies, Geography and Human Ecology.

Last settled

As the U.S. spread into Indian territory in the late nineteenth century, the Plains became the last part of the nation to be settled by whites. The 1862 Homestead Act marked the beginning of sharp cycles of growth and decline, boom and bust. Federally subsidized settlement and cultivation repeatedly led to overgrazing and over-plowing (sodbusting, in Plains terms). When nature and the economy turned hostile again, many of the farmers and ranchers were driven out-and the cycle began anew. Most of the post-Civil War homesteaders succumbed to the blizzards of the 1880s and the drought and financial panic of the 1890s. Homesteading flourished again in the early 1900s, crested during World War I as European agricultural productivity fell, and once more slumped in the early 1920s when drought and locusts hit.

For much of the Plains, the Great Depression began before it struck Wall Street. By 1925, Montana had suffered 214 bank failures, and the average value of all its farm and ranch land had dropped by half. As the depression intensified, the Plains were perhaps the most afflicted part of the country. In 1935, the five states with the largest percentage of farm families on relief were New Mexico, South Dakota, North Dakota, Oklahoma, and Colorado, and conditions were far worse in the Plains portions of each of those states.

Thus the Plains had undergone a dozen years of depression before the onset of the Dust Bowl in 1934, which in turn was the ecological consequence of earlier decades of too-assertive agriculture. The shortgrass Plains soil in places was destroyed by an excess of cattle and sheep grazing and of cultivation of corn, wheat, and cotton. When drought hit with its merciless cyclically, the land had no defenses. By the late 1930s, the Dust Bowl covered nearly a third of the Plains. It kicked up dirt clouds five miles high and tore the paint off houses and cars. It sent the Okies west to California, inspiring both John Steinbeck's famous novel, *The Grapes of Wrath*, and Dorothea Lange's stark photographs.

The federal government responded by abolishing homesteading in 1934. The next year it established the Agriculture Department's Soil Conservation Service, which built windbreaks and shelter belts. Beginning in 1937, the federal government bought up 7.3 million acres of largely abandoned farm holdings of the Plains (an area bigger than Maryland), replanted them, and designated them "national grasslands." Today the national grasslands, which are administered by the Agriculture Department's Forest Service, are used primarily for low-intensity grazing and recreation. Often thick with shortgrass, they rank among the most successful types of federal landholdings.

After the Dust Bowl

After the trauma of the Dust Bowl, much of the recent history of the Plains seems anti-climactic. A measure of agricultural prosperity returned during World War II and after, although the Plains remained a poor region, falling further behind most of the rest of the country economically and continuing to suffer depopulation. To some extent, the picture looked rosier. New technologies came in—custom combines, ever-larger irrigation pumps, center-pivot irrigation sprayers—and the average size of farms and ranches grew steeply. Droughts persisted; after one in the 1970s, the National Oceanic and Atmospheric Administration estimated that, had it continued another month, the Dust Bowl might have returned.

The federal government found new ways to intervene. The crop subsidy programs introduced experimentally in the thirties were greatly expanded in the forties and fifties. The dam and irrigation projects begun in 1902, primarily in the intermountain West, accelerated in 1944 with the adoption of the $6 billion, 100-dam, Pick-Sloan plan for the Missouri River, an effort aimed primarily at the Plains portion of the watershed. It meant that Plains farmers and ranchers could, like their competitors farther west, get federal water at below-market prices.

With the creation in 1934 of the Interior Department's Grazing Service and its evolution after the war into the Bureau of Land Management, the federal government established public land grazing districts that rented grazing rights to ranchers at below-market rates.

More recently, the Plains benefited from the energy boom of the middle and late 1970s, which quintupled prices for oil and natural gas. Some 200 energy boomtowns suddenly sprouted in the Dakotas, Montana, Wyoming, and Colorado. The lessons of the 1930s were forgotten as agricultural commodity prices rose rapidly. Plains farmers and ranchers once again chopped down their windbreaks, planted from fencepost to fencepost, and sodbusted in the classic 1880s-1910s manner. This time, though, the scale was much larger, often tens of thousands of acres at a time.

A crisis looms

The 1980s punctured the illusion of prosperity. Today the pressures on the Plains and their people are as ominous as at any time in American history. The region's farm, ranch, energy, and mineral economies are in deep depression. Many small towns are emptying and aging at an all-time high rate, and some are dying. The 1986 outmigration from West and Panhandle Texas, for instance, helped make the state a net exporter of population for the first time ever.

Soil erosion is approaching Dust Bowl rates. Water shortages loom, especially atop the Ogallala Aquifer, a giant but essentially nonrenewable source of groundwater that nourishes more than 11 million acres of agriculture in Plains Colorado, Kansas, Nebraska, New Mexico, Oklahoma, and Texas. Important long-term climatic and technological trends do not look favorable. Government seems unable to react constructively to these trends, much less to anticipate them.

In fact, the agricultural crisis is more serious on the Plains than in its more publicized neighbor region to the east, the Midwest's Corn Belt. Plains farmers and ranchers have always operated under conditions that their counterparts elsewhere would have found intolerable, and now they are worse. Farm bankruptcy and foreclosure rates are higher in the Plains than in other rural areas, as are many of the indices of resulting psychological stress: family violence, suicide, mental illness. In 1986, there were 138 bank collapses in the U.S., the largest number since the Depression. Texas had the most, 26, followed by Oklahoma with 16 and Kansas with 14. In contrast, the two Midwestern states in the most agricultural difficulty, Iowa and Missouri, had 10 and nine, respectively.

A series of mid-1980s federal agricultural initiatives—new subsidies, such as the Payment in Kind (PIK) program; additional tax breaks; a national conservation reserve where farmers and ranchers are paid not to cultivate erodible soil (that is, not to sod-bust)—seem to have little impact in the Plains. The national conservation reserve, for instance, can at most cover a quarter of any one county. The only federal measure that appears effective is a 1985 law that makes it easier for farmers and ranchers to declare bankruptcy.

The situation is comparable in the energy sector. Oil prices have fallen drastically since 1983. Many large Plains oil and natural gas companies have laid off most of their employees. The energy boomtowns have long gone bust. Between 1985 and 1986, the number of active oil rigs in West Texas's Permian Basin dropped from 298 to 173, reducing local income by an estimated $50 million.

Ripple effect

The local collapses reverberate. When local banks fail or are endangered, the remaining ones lend more conservatively and charge higher interest. When a heavily agricultural county's farmers and ranchers cannot make a living, neither can its car dealers, druggists, restaurants, and clothing stores. Local public services, which have never been exactly generous in the Plains, fall off. Items like schools, roads, law enforcement, and welfare are always relatively expensive to provide and administer in large, lightly populated areas; they are especially expensive because of the traditional Plains pattern of many comparatively small local governments, which cannot take advantage of economies of scale.

Faced with a choice between higher local taxes and fewer services, most Plains localities chose the latter. In the late 1970s, for example, Oklahoma towns rode the oil boom to become early leaders in school reform; now a tenth of the state's teachers have lost their jobs, many others have had their salaries frozen, classroom size has grown, buses are not repaired, and textbooks go unreplaced.

The quality of life also declines. The service cutbacks fall hardest on the poor: Montana farm laborers, South Dakota Indians, Mexican-Americans along the Rio Grande, clients of social work and public health agencies across the Plains. Agricultural market towns get smaller, older, and poorer. Already modest downtowns become gap-toothed streets of increasingly marginal businesses. Entire counties lack a single doctor or a bank, and many more are about to lose them.

The long-term outlook is frightening. Climatologists note that, over the last 50 years, rainfall in the Plains has actually been comparatively stable. Future droughts are inevitable, and they're likely to hit harder and more often. The greenhouse effect—the buildup in the atmosphere of carbon dioxide from fossil-fuel combustion—is expected to warm the Plains by an average of at least two to three degrees, making the region even more vulnerable to drought. The longstanding attempts to seed clouds or otherwise artificially induce rain continue to be unavailing.

Water supplies are diminishing throughout the Plains, primarily because of agricultural overuse. Farmland has already been abandoned for lack of water in the Pecos River Valley of New Mexico and between Amarillo and Lubbock in Texas. In 1950, the Kansas portion of the Ogallala Aquifer was 58 feet deep; today in many places it may be less than six feet. As parts of the aquifer approach exhaustion within a decade or so, Plains water prices are sure to rise steeply. Moreover, our huge national and regional agricultural surpluses argue against further irrigation initiatives to stimulate yet more agriculture.

Some farmers and ranchers and some localities are undertaking serious water- and soil-conservation measures, but it may already be too late to halt the erosion. Such counties as Gaines in Texas and Crowley and Kiowa in Colorado appear to be nearing Dust Bowl conditions. The federal Council on Environmental Quality has classified the desertification of West Texas and eastern New Mexico and parts of Colorado, Kansas, and Oklahoma as "severe."

Already today, when Plains farmers and ranchers, small or large, give up land, the big agribusiness corporations are usually unwilling to buy it, even at a bargain price. Because the big companies are not interested—in clear contrast to their behavior elsewhere in the country—the price of Plains land drops lower still. The brute fact is that most Plains land is simply not competitive with land elsewhere. The only people who want it are already on it, and most of them are increasingly unable to make a living from it.

The tragedy of the commons

"Grass no good upside down," said a Pawnee chief in northeast Colorado as he watched the late-nineteenth-century homesteaders rip through the shortgrass with their steel plows. He mourned a stretch of land where the Indians had hunted buffalo for millennia. It grew crops for a few years, then went into the Dust Bowl; farmers abandoned it. Today, it is federal land, part of the system of national grasslands. Like most of the Plains, it is an austere monument to American self-delusion. Three separate waves of farmers and ranchers, with increasingly heavy federal support, tried to make settlement stick on the Plains. The 1890s and 1930s generations were largely uprooted, as the 1980s one soon will be.

Our national experience in the Plains represents a spectacular variant on the tragedy of the commons, Garrett Hardin's famous ecological fable of how individual short-term economic rationality can lead to collective long-term environmental disaster. To the Indians and the early cattlemen, all of the Plains was a commons. The Homestead Act and the succeeding federal land subsidies for settlers amounted to attempts to privatize the Plains, to take them out of the federal domain and put them permanently in individual or corporate hands. Today's subsidies for crops, water, and grazing land amount to attempts to buttress the privatization.

But private interests have proved unable to last for long on the Plains. Responding to nationally based market imperatives, they have overgrazed and overplowed the land and overdrawn the water. Responding to the usually increasing federal subsidies, they have overused the natural resources the subsidies provided. They never created a truly stable agriculture or found reliable conservation devices. In some places, private owners supplemented agriculture with inherently unstable energy and mineral development.

Now that both the market imperatives and federal subsidies seem inadequate to keep the private interests on the Plains, these interests are, as Hardin would have predicted, rapidly degrading the land and leaving it, in many places perhaps forever. As a nation, we have never understood that the federally subsidized privatization that worked so well to settle most of the land west of the Appalachians is ineffective on the Plains. It leads to overproduction that then cannot be sustained under the Plains' difficult economic and climatic conditions.

Bleak future

It is hard to predict the future course of the Plains ordeal. The most likely possibility is a continuation of the gradual impoverishment and depopulation that in many places go back to the 1920s. A few of the more urban areas may pull out of their decline, especially if an energy boom returns. And a few cities—Lubbock and Cheyenne, for example—may hold steady as self-contained service providers. But the small towns in the surrounding countryside will empty, wither, and die. The rural Plains will be virtually deserted. A vast, beautiful characteristically American place will go the way of the buffalo that once roamed it in herds of millions.

Little stands in the way of this outcome. New mineral or energy sources might discovered on the Plains. New crops might be developed, such as the cereal triticale (a high-protein cross between wheat and rye) or a Plains equivalent of the Southwest's jojoba bush, whose oil is now finding applications ranging from facial creams to industrial lubrication. Several groups in Kansas are exploring uses for oils from amaranth and rapeseed plants. Other Plains states are trying to create a llama or donkey industry that will meet the demand for horse substitutes, unconventional pets, or exotic wool. But most conceivable replacement crops for the Plains do not yet exist or are more economically and abundantly produced elsewhere, usually in the Midwest.

For some parts of the Plains, tourism and recreation might be plausible options. Growing numbers of ranchers offer their land for hunting, wildlife photography, backpacking trips, and wilderness expeditions in addition to the usual dude-and-tenderfoot packages. In places within three or four hours' drive of big cities—most noticeably in West Texas—ranches are being carved into ranchettes for weekend cowboys. But tourism cannot offer much to the Plains as a whole. Farmers typically cannot tap the recreation market, and many ranchers feel that tourism demeans them, compromises their independence.

Bring back the commons

The most intriguing alternative would be to restore large parts of the Plains to their pre-white condition, to make them again the commons the settlers found in the nineteenth century. This approach, which would for the first time in U.S. history treat the Plains as a distinct region and recognize its unsuitability for agriculture, is being proposed with increasing frequency. Bret Wallach, a University of Oklahoma geographer and MacArthur fellow, has suggested that the Forest Service enter into voluntary contracts with Plains farmers and ranchers, paying them the full value of what they would cultivate during each of the next 15 years but requiring them not to cultivate it. During this time, they would instead follow a Forest Service-approved program of planting to reestablish the native shortgrasses. Afterwards, the service would, as part of the original contract, buy out their holdings except for a 40-acre homestead.

Similarly, Charles Little, former editor of *American Land Forum*, suggests that by expanding the national grasslands, the grazing districts operated by the Bureau of Land Management, and the anti-sodbusting national conservation reserve, we could retire enough agricultural land to slow the depletion of the Ogallala Aquifer. Robert Scott of the Institute of the Rockies in Missoula, Montana, urges that 15,000 square miles of eastern Montana, about a tenth of the state, be transformed into an East African-style game preserve called the Big Open. With state and federal help, fences would come down, domestic animals would be removed, and game animals stocked. According to Scott, the land could support 75,000 bison, 150,000 deer, 40,000 elk, 40,000 antelope. A ranch of 10,000 acres (nearly 16 square miles), by now a normal size for the area, would net at least $48,000 a year from the sale of hunting licenses alone. Some 1,000 new jobs—for outfitters, taxidermists, workers in gas stations, restaurants, motels—would develop in this sparsely settled area.

Scott's approach, unlike Wallach's and Little's, lets ranchers and farmers keep all their land by treating it as free range. Yet all three proposals would be costly and provoke great resistance from the landowners because they would constrain their property rights.

We believe that despite history's warnings and environmentalists' proposals, much of the Plains will inexorably suffer near-total desertion over the next generation. It will come slowly to most places, quickly to some; parts of Montana, New Mexico, South Dakota, and Texas, especially those away from the interstates, strike us as likely candidates for rapid depopulation. The overall desertion will largely run its course. At that point, the only way to keep the Plains from turning into an utter wasteland, an American Empty Quarter, will be for the federal government to step in and buy the land—in short, to deprivatize it.

If the federal government intervenes late rather than early—after the desertion instead of before it—the buy-back task will, ironically, be easier. The farmers and ranchers will already have abandoned large chunks of land, making it simpler for the government to reassemble the commons (and to persuade the holdouts to sell). Those parts of the Plains where agriculture, energy development, mining, or tourism remains workable will have become clear, and here government would make no deprivatization attempts. We suspect, however, that there won't be many such places.

In practical terms, a federal deprivatization program would have two thrusts, one for Plains people, the other for Plains land. On the people side, government would negotiate buy-backs from landowners—often under distress-sale circumstances. Some of the landowners will be in a position to insist on phased sales or easements that allow them to hold on to their land somewhat longer.

It will be up to the federal government to ease the social transition of the economic refugees who are being forced off the land. For they will feel aggrieved and impoverished, penalized for staying too long in a place they loved and pursuing occupations the nation supposedly respected but evidently did not. The government will have to invent a 1990s version of the 1930s Resettlement Administration, a social work-finance-technical assistance agency that will find ways and places for the former Plains residents to get back on their feet.

On the land side, the government will take the newly emptied Plains and tear down the fences, replant the shortgrass, and restock the animals, including the buffalo. It will take a long time. Even if large pieces of the commons can be assembled quickly, it will be at least 20 to 30 years before the vegetation and wildlife reassert themselves in the semiarid Plains settings, where the land changes so slowly that wagon-trail ruts more than a century old are still visible. There may also be competing uses for the land. In South Dakota, several Sioux tribes are now bringing suit for 11,000 square miles, including much of the Black Hills. The federal government might settle these and other longstanding Plains Indian land claims by giving or selling the tribes chunks of the new commons.

Recreating the commons

The federal government's commanding task on the Plains for the next century will be to recreate the nineteenth century, to reestablish what we would call the Buffalo Commons. More and more previously private land will be acquired to form the commons. In many areas, the distinctions between the present national parks, grasslands, grazing lands, wildlife refuges, forests, Indian lands, and their state counterparts will largely dissolve. The small cities of the Plains will amount to urban islands in a shortgrass sea. The Buffalo Commons will become the world's largest historic preservation project, the ultimate national park. Most of the Great Plains will become what all of the United States once was—a vast land mass, largely empty and unexploited.

Creating the Buffalo Commons represents a substantial administrative undertaking. It will require competent land-use planning to identify acquisition areas, devise fair buyout contracts, and determine permitted uses. It will demand compassionate treatment for the Plains' refugees and considerable coordination between huge distant, frequently obtuse federal agencies, smaller state agencies whose attention often goes primarily to the non-Plains parts of their states, and desperate local governments. To accomplish these tasks, the federal government will, for the first time, have to create an agency with a Plains-specific mandate—a regional agency like the Tennessee Valley Authority or a public-land agency like the Bureau of Land Management, but with much more sweeping powers.

By creating the Buffalo Commons, the federal government will, however belatedly, turn the social costs of space—the curse of the shortgrass immensity—to more social benefit than the unsuccessfully privatized Plains have ever offered.

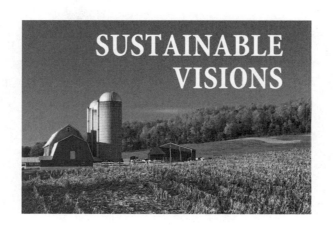

SUSTAINABLE VISIONS

THE HOLY EARTH

By Liberty Hyde Bailey

First, the Statement

So BOUNTIFUL hath been the earth and so securely have we drawn from it our substance, that we have taken it all for granted as if it were only a gift, and with little care or conscious thought of the consequences of our use of it; nor have we very much considered the essential relation that we bear to it as living parts in the vest creation.

It is good to think of ourselves-of this teeming, tense, and aspiring human race-as a helpful and contributing part in the plan of a cosmos, and as participators in some far-reaching destiny. The idea of responsibility is much asserted of late, but we relate it mostly to the attitude of persons in the realm of conventional conduct, which we have come to regard as very exclusively the realm of morals; and we have established certain formalities that satisfy the conscience. But there is some deeper relation than all this, which we must recognize and the consequences of which we must practise. There is a directer and more personal obligation than that which expends itself in loyalty to the manifold organizations and social requirements of the present day. There is a more fundamental co-operation in the scheme of things than that which deals with the proprieties or which centres about the selfishness too often expressed in the salvation of one's soul.

We can be only onlookers on that part of the cosmos that we call the far heavens, but it is possible to co-operate in the processes on the surface of the sphere. This co-operation may be conscious and definite, and also useful to the earth; that is, it may be real. What means this contact with our natural situation, this relationship to the earth to which we are born, and what signify this new exploration and conquest of the planet and these accumulating prophecies of science? Does the mothership of the earth have any real meaning to us?

All this does not imply a relation only with material and physical things, nor any effort to substitute a nature religion. Our relation with the planet must be raised into the realm of spirit; we cannot be fully useful otherwise. We must find a way to maintain the emotions in the abounding commercial civilization. There are two kinds of materials,-those of the native earth and the idols of one's hands. The latter are much in evidence in modern life, with the conquests of engineering, mechanics, architecture, and all the rest. We visualize them everywhere, and particularly in the great centres of population. The tendency is to be removed farther and farther from the everlasting backgrounds. Our religion is detached.

We come out of the earth and we have a right to the use of the materials; and there is no danger of crass materialism if we recognize the original materials as divine and if we understand our proper relation to the creation, for then will gross selfishness in the use of them be removed. This will necessarily mean a better conception of property and of one's obli-

Liberty Hyde Bailey (1858–1954) was an American horticulturist, botanist and co-founder of the American Society for Horticultural Science. He is the author of many books and articles, was instrumental in the creation of the 4-H movement, parcel post, agricultural extension services, and is considered the father of rural sociology and journalism.

From *The Holy Earth*. New York: C. Scribner Sons, pp. 1-12, 1915. First published by Comstock Publishing Co., Ithaca, NY

gation in the use of it. We shall conceive of the earth, which is the common habitation, as inviolable. One does not act rightly toward one's fellows if one does not know how to act rightly toward the earth.

Nor does this close regard for the mother earth imply any loss of mysticism or of exaltation: quite the contrary. Science but increases the mystery of the unknown and enlarges the boundaries of the spiritual vision. To feel that one is a useful and co-operating part in nature is to give one kinship, and to open the mind to the great resources and the high enthusiasms. Here arise the fundamental common relations. Here arise also the great emotions and conceptions of sublimity and grandeur, of majesty and awe, the uplift of vast desires, when one contemplates the earth and the universe and desires to take them into the soul and to express oneself in their terms; and here also the responsible practices of life take root.

So much are we now involved in problems of human groups, so persistent are the portrayals of our social afflictions, and so well do we magnify our woes by insisting on them, so much in sheer weariness do we provide antidotes to soothe our feelings and to cause us to forget by means of many empty diversions, that we may neglect to express ourselves in simple free personal joy and to separate the obligation of the individual from the irresponsibilities of the mass.

In the beginning

It suits my purpose to quote the first sentence in the Hebrew Scripture: In the beginning God created the heaven and the earth.

This is a statement of tremendous reach, introducing the cosmos; for it sets forth in the fewest words the elemental fact that the formation of the created earth lies above and before man, and that therefore it is not man's but God's. Man finds himself upon it, with many other creatures, all parts in some system which, since it is beyond man and superior to him, is divine.

Yet the planet was not at once complete when life had appeared on it. The whirling earth goes through many vicissitudes; the conditions on its fruitful surface are ever-changing; and the forms of life must meet the new conditions: so does the creation continue, and every day sees the genesis in process. All life contends, sometimes ferociously but more often bloodlessly and benignly, and the contention results in momentary equilibrium, one set of contestants balancing another; but every change in the outward conditions destroys the equation and a new status results. Of all the disturbing living factors, man is the greatest. He sets mighty changes going, destroying forests, upturning the sleeping prairies, flooding the deserts, deflecting the courses of the rivers, building great cities. He operates consciously and increasingly with plan aforethought; and therefore he carries heavy responsibility.

This responsibility is recognized in the Hebrew Scripture, from which I have quoted; and I quote it again because I know of no other Scripture that states it so well. Man is given the image of the creator, even when formed from the dust of the earth, so complete is his power and so real his dominion: And God blessed them: and God said unto them, Be fruitful, and multiply, and replenish the earth, and subdue it; and have dominion over the fish of the sea, and over the fowl of the air, and over every living thing that moveth upon the earth.

One cannot receive all these privileges without bearing the obligation to react and to partake, to keep, to cherish, and to co-operate. We have assumed that there is no obligation to an inanimate thing, as we consider the earth to be: but man should respect the conditions in which he is placed; the earth yields the living creature; man is a living creature; science constantly narrows the gulf between the animate and the inanimate, between the organized and the inorganized; evolution derives the creatures from the earth; the creation is one creation. I must accept all or reject all.

The earth is good

It is good to live. We talk of death and of lifelessness, but we know only of life. Even our prophecies of death are prophecies of more life. We know no better world: whatever else there may be is of things hoped for, not of things seen. The objects are here, not hidden nor far to seek: And God saw everything that he had made, and, behold, it was very good.

These good things are the present things and the living things. The account is silent on the things that were not created, the chaos, the darkness, the abyss. Plato, in the "Republic," reasoned that the works of the creator must be good because the creator is good. This goodness is in the essence of things; and we sadly need to make it a part in our philosophy of life. The earth is the scene of our life, and probably the very source of it. The heaven, so far as human beings know, is the source only of death; in fact, we have peopled it with the dead. We have built our philosophy on the dead.

We seem to have overlooked the goodness of the earth in the establishing of our affairs, and even in our philosophies. It is reserved as a theme for preachers and for poets. And yet, the goodness of the planet is the basic fact in our existence.

I am not speaking of good in an abstract way, in the sense in which some of us suppose the creator to have expressed himself as pleased or satisfied with his work. The earth is good in itself, and its products are good in themselves. The earth sustains all things. It satisfies. It matters not whether this satisfaction is the result of adaptation in the process of evolution; the fact remains that the creation is good.

To the common man the earth propounds no system of philosophy or of theology. The man makes his own personal contact, deals with the facts as they are or as he conceives them to be, and is not swept into any system. He has no right to assume a bad or evil earth, although it is difficult to cast off the hindrance of centuries of teaching. When he is properly educated he will get a new resource from his relationships.

It may be difficult to demonstrate this goodness. In the nature of things we must assume it, although we know that we could not subsist on a sphere of the opposite qualities. The important consideration is that we appreciate it, and this not in any sentimental and impersonal way. To every bird the air is good; and a man knows it is good if he is worth being a man. To every fish the water is good. To every beast its food is good, and its time of sleep is good. The creatures experience that life is good. Every man in his heart knows that there is goodness and wholeness in the rain, in the wind, the soil, the sea, the glory of the sunrise, in the trees, and in the sustenance that we derive from the planet. When we grasp the significance of this situation, we shall forever supplant the religion of fear with a religion of consent.

We are so accustomed to these essentials-to the rain, the wind, the soil, the sea, the sunrise, the trees, the sustenance-that we may not include them in the categories of the good things, and we endeavor to satisfy ourselves with many small and trivial and exotic gratifications; and when these gratifications fail or pall, we find ourselves helpless and resourceless. The joy of sound sleep, the relish of a sufficient meal of plain and wholesome food, the desire to do a good day's work and the recompense when at night we are tired from the doing of it, the exhilaration of fresh air, the exercise of the natural powers, the mastery of a situation or a problem,- these and many others like them are fundamental satisfactions, beyond all pampering and all toys, and they are of the essence of goodness. I think we should teach all children how good are the common necessities, and how very good are the things that are made in the beginning.

It is kindly

We hear much about man being at the mercy of nature, and the literalist will contend that there can be no holy relation under such conditions. But so is man at the mercy of God.

It is a blasphemous practice that speaks of the hostility of the earth, as if the earth were full of menaces and cataclysms. The old fear of nature, that peopled the earth and sky with imps and demons, and that gave a future state to Satan, yet possesses the minds of men, only that we have ceased to personify and to demonize our fears, although we still persistently contrast what we call the evil and the good. Still do we attempt to propitiate and appease the adversaries. Still do we carry the ban of the early philosophy that assumed materials and "the flesh" to be evil, and that found a way of escape only in renunciation and asceticism.

Nature cannot be antagonistic to man, seeing that man is a product of nature. We should find vast joy in the fellowship, something like the joy of Pan. We should feel the relief when we no longer apologize for the creator because of the things that are made.

It is true that there are devastations of flood and fire and frost, scourge of disease, and appalling convulsions of earthquake and eruption. But man prospers; and we know that the catastrophes are greatly fewer than the accepted bounties. We have no choice but to abide. No growth comes from hostility. It would undoubtedly be a poor human race if all the pathway had been plain and easy.

The contest with nature is wholesome, particularly when pursued in sympathy and for mastery. It is worthy a being created in God's image. The earth is perhaps a stern earth, but it is a kindly earth.

Most of our difficulty with the earth lies in the effort to do what perhaps ought not to be done. Not even all the land is fit to be farmed. A good part of agriculture is to learn how to adapt one's work to nature, to fit the crop-scheme to the climate and to the soil and the facilities. To live in right relation with his natural conditions is one of the first lessons that a wise farmer or any other wise man learns. We are at pains to stress the importance of conduct; very well: conduct toward the earth is an essential part of it.

Nor need we be afraid of any fact that makes one fact more or less in the sum of contacts between the earth and the earthborn children. All "higher criticism" adds to the faith rather than subtracts from it, and strengthens the bond between. The earth and its products are very real.

Our outlook has been drawn very largely from the abstract. Not being yet prepared to understand the conditions of nature, man considered the earth to be inhospitable, and he looked to the supernatural for relief; and relief was heaven. Our pictures of heaven are of the opposites of daily experience,-of release, of peace, of joy uninterrupted. The hunting-grounds are happy and the satisfaction has no end. The habit of thought has been set by this conception, and it colors our dealings with the human questions and to much extent it controls our practice.

But we begin to understand that the best dealing with problems on earth is to found it on facts of earth. This is the contribution of natural science, however abstract, to human welfare. Heaven is to be a real consequence of life on earth; and we do not lessen the hope of heaven by increasing our affection for the earth, but rather do we strengthen it. Men now forget the old images of heaven, that they are mere sojourners and wanderers lingering for deliverance, pilgrims in a strange land. Waiting for this rescue, with posture and formula and phrase, we have overlooked the essential goodness and quickness of the earth and the immanence of God.

This feeling that we are pilgrims in a vale of tears has been enhanced by the wide-spread belief in the sudden ending of the world, by collision or some other impending disaster, and in the common apprehension of doom; and lately by speculations as to the aridation and death of the planet, to which all of us have given more or less credence. But most of these notions are now considered to be fantastic, and we are increasingly confident that the earth is not growing old in a human sense, that its atmosphere and its water are held by the attraction of its mass, and that the sphere is at all events so permanent as to make little difference in our philosophy and no difference in our good behavior.

I am again impressed with the first record in Genesis in which some mighty prophet-poet began his account with the creation of the physical universe.

So we do not forget the old-time importance given to mere personal salvation, which was permission to live in heaven, and we think more of our present situation, which is the situation of obligation and of service; and he who loses his life shall save it.

We begin to foresee the vast religion of a better social order.

The earth is holy

Verily, then, the earth is divine, because man did not make it. We are here, part in the creation. We cannot escape. We are under obligation to take part and to do our best, living with each other and with all the creatures. We may not know the full plan, but that does not alter the relation. When once we set ourselves to the pleasure of our dominion, reverently and hopefully, and assume all its responsibilities, we shall have a new hold on life.

We shall put our dominion into the realm of morals. It is now in the realm of trade. This will be very personal morals, but it will also be national and racial morals. More iniquity follows the improper and greedy division of the resources and privileges of the earth than any other form of sinfulness.

If God created the earth, so is the earth hallowed; and if it is hallowed, so must we deal with it devotedly and with care that we do not despoil it, and mindful of our relations to all beings that live on it. We are to consider it religiously: Put off thy shoes from off thy feet, for the place whereon thou standest is holy ground.

The sacredness to us of the earth is intrinsic and inherent. It lies in our necessary relationship and in the duty imposed upon us to have dominion, and to exercise ourselves even against our own interests. We may not waste that which is not ours. To live in sincere relations with the company of created things and with conscious regard for the support of all men now and yet to come, must be of the essence of righteousness.

This is a larger and more original relation than the modern attitude of appreciation and admiration of nature. In the days of the patriarchs and prophets, nature and man shared in the condemnation and likewise in the redemption. The ground was cursed for Adam's sin. Paul wrote that the whole creation groaneth and travaileth in pain, and that it waiteth for the revealing. Isaiah proclaimed the redemption of the wilderness and the solitary place with the redemption of man, when they shall rejoice and blossom as the rose, and when the glowing sand shall become a pool and the thirsty ground springs of water.

The usual objects have their moral significance. An oak tree is to us a moral object because it lives its life regularly and fulfills its destiny. In the wind and in the stars, in forest and by the shore, there is spiritual refreshment: And the spirit of God moved upon the face of the waters.

I do not mean all this, for our modern world, in any vague or abstract way. If the earth is holy, then the things that grow out of the earth are also holy. They do not belong to man to do with them as he will. Dominion does not carry personal ownership. There are many generations of folks yet to come after us, who will have equal right with us to the products of the globe. It would seem that a divine obligation rests on every soul. Are we to make righteous use of the vast accumulation of knowledge of the planet? If so, we must have a new formulation. The partition of the earth among the millions who live on it is necessarily a question of morals; and a society that is founded on an unmoral partition and use cannot itself be righteous and whole.

VISIONS FOR RURAL KENTUCKY

By Wendell Berry

A vision for rural Kentucky...is a subject I approach with a good deal of uneasiness, for I know something of the history of visions in rural Kentucky. The Bible says that where there is no vision the people perish. It is also true that where the vision is wrong the people perish.

In Kentucky we know that the important question is, "Who has the vision?" The coal companies have had a vision of the Kentucky coalfields. The timber companies have had a vision of Kentucky forests. The tobacco companies have had a vision of Kentucky farms, and so have the packing houses and the grain dealers. The great agribusiness, timber, and coal corporations still have a vision of rural Kentucky, and in their vision the bottom dollar is always passing from the strong to the weak, and the top dollar from the weak to the strong. And of course rural Kentucky is always shrinking because of the visions of subdividers and developers.

The fact of the matter is that rural Kentucky is now more endangered than it has ever been. We are losing our farmers; the old are dying, the young are leaving. We have serious soil erosion. We are losing land to "development." We are in depression, and under threat. If you look for the money made from the products and the labor of one of our rural counties, you will see that very little of it is retained within the county line and not much more within the boundaries of the state. The story of these losses—of soil, land, farmers, economic resources and opportunities—is an ongoing story. We are going to be living with that story and its consequences for a long time.

I'm far from believing that rural Kentucky is a place for optimists. It would be unwise to risk underestimating the difficulties we are in. On the other hand, I do believe that rural Kentucky is a place for hope. I'm hopeful because I know, I have seen for myself, that we have people who are doing a good job, both as producers and as stewards of the land. And so I know that things can be better; we have good examples in front of us; abuse is not the inevitable consequence of use.

What I'm really nervous about is people who have visions for other people. Generally, I don't mind advice that begins, "Not bossing you or anything, but you could do it this way." But I would mind living in somebody else's political or economic or technological vision. I don't want to live next-door to a hog factory or chemical plant. I don't want to live where my community's fate and future will be determined by people who don't care about it. I know that some economies reduce freedom and economic opportunity.

Wendell Berry has farmed Kentucky soils and grown crops and abundant poetry, fiction, and essays—totalling now over thirty books. His is the superbly-crafted voice of rural America, especially its farmers; his clarity allows the toughest truths to be drunk with the greatest ease and pleasure. *A Timbered Choir* is a collection of his poems. This essay is from a speech at the Family Farms Agricultural Roundtable. Originally printed in *Foresight*, a publication of the Kentucky Long-term Policy Research Center (800/853-2851).

Whole Earth Review, Winter 1998 issue. Reprinted with permission.

The visions I am comfortable with are small-scale, private, inexpensive visions of improvement. There are no good farmers, probably, who do not see visions of the ways their farms could be improved: their farms could be more diverse, more productive, better fenced; there could be a wider margin between carrying capacity and numbers of livestock, giving comfort in dry years; there are scars that could be healed, woodlands that could be protected—and so on. I'm comfortable too with consumers' visions of fresher, healthier, more trustworthy produce from the local countryside, of farmers' markets, of ways in which local citizens could invest their money and work in a community-conserving and land-conserving local economy. I like visions that come from the spirit of neighborliness and care and thrift.

But even small, modest visions can be wrong. I know this from experience. If you visited my very marginal farm, you would see that I have had some visions that were right, and some that were wrong. I have had some visions that I could not have had if I had not been ignorant.

Our political principles of democracy and liberty are meant to protect our visions about how we want to live and work, and they're meant to protect us against other people's visions. But our political principles can't protect us from having the wrong visions about land use.

There is no doubt that we need a vision for rural Kentucky. We need, I think, a lot of visions for rural Kentucky. But if those visions are not to be (again) destructive and too costly, then we must take the trouble to know rural Kentucky and all its great diversity of landscapes, soil, economies, and natural and human communities. We must learn together to think from the ground up. We can't find the best ways of using and caring for our land just by forcing our visions and ideas upon it. The real question is how to fit in. How can human economies be fitted into nature's economies without finally destroying both? There's a thread of wisdom running through our cultural inheritance that says that everything depends on knowing where we are. It says that farmers and gardeners and foresters must consult the nature of the place. It says that in any given place there are certain things that nature will permit us to do without damage, certain things that nature will help us to do, and certain things that nature will penalize or punish us for doing.

To hold securely in possession and in trust a beautiful countryside, producing a dependable, healthful supply of food and other necessities, would be good for everybody. We don't have to destroy our land in order to live from it. We don't have to defeat and damage one another in order to prosper. There is a better way, and I think we're beginning to find it.

COMMUNITY CAPITALS: A TOOL FOR EVALUATING STRATEGIC INTERVENTIONS AND PROJECTS

By Cornelia Butler Flora, Mary Emery, Susan Fey, and Corry Bregendahl

Article begins on the following page.

Cornelia B. Flora is a faculty member in the department of Sociology and director of the North Central Regional Center for Rural Development, located at Iowa State. This center is one of four regional centers in the United States that combine research and outreach for rural development. It covers the twelve north central states. See page 1278 for more on author.

Reprinted with permission from the North Central Regional Center for Rural Development, Iowa State University, 107 Curtiss Hall, Ames, IA 50011-1050 (515) 294-8321, (515) 294-3180 fax, www.ncrcrd.iastate.edu

Community Capitals: A Tool for Evaluating
Strategic Interventions and Projects

by Cornelia Butler Flora, Mary Emery, Susan Fey and Corry Bregendahl

North Central Regional Center for Rural Development,
Iowa State University, 107 Curtiss Hall, Ames, IA 50011-1050
(515) 294-8321, (515) 294-3180 fax, www.ncrcrd.iastate.edu

To understand how communities function, Flora and Flora (2004) developed the Community Capitals framework. Based on their analyses of entrepreneurial communities, they determined that the communities that were successful in supporting healthy sustainable community and economic development (CED) paid attention to seven types of capital: natural, cultural, human, social, political, financial and built. Beyond identifying the capitals and their role in community economic development, this approach focuses on the interaction among these seven capitals and how they build upon one another.

This framework is used not only as a tool for analysis, but also as a way to assist project managers in identifying key boundary partners. By identifying which agencies or organizations link to each of the community capitals, project managers can determine which organizations with which to partner. Once partners are identified, the framework can then be employed to determine what each partner may need to do in order for the partnership to be successful.

Using the Community Capitals framework, project managers and evaluators can trace how an investment in human capital, for example leadership training, might impact financial capital as leaders use their skills to acquire new funds and better manage existing funds. Social capital may then be impacted as members of the leadership program develop new bonds among themselves

and new bridges among the groups with whom they interact. The same leadership course might consequently expand political capital by providing information about how the political system works and how to access resources within the community; it could also help participants develop key linkages to other sources of political power.

Finally, the interaction with representatives from different community groups may expand the cultural capital in the community as people learn to value the voices and heritages of others.

The Community Capitals model has become an invaluable tool in the North Central Regional Center for Rural Development's work with the National Rural Funders' Collaborative.

This framework helps project staff and funders better understand the strategic nature of the funded programs and their impact on reducing poverty, creating wealth, supporting family self-sufficiency, and expanding local leadership. NCRCRD's research focus with the Benedum Foundation addresses the question: Is CED possible in rural communities with populations less than 10,000 people? By measuring the investments in each of the capitals and the changes resulting from that investment, the framework provides a means by which researchers begin to understand the impact of CED on rural people and places.

COMMUNITY CAPITALS

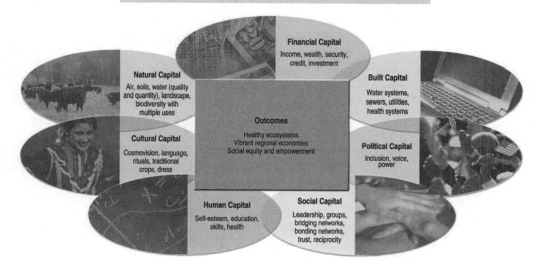

Context	Process	Outputs and Outcomes
Context → Pre-existing conditions and structures	**Process** → Actions, investments, intervention	**Outputs and Outcomes** Results of Actions

Community Characteristics—Impetus for Community Economic Development (CED) Efforts

Natural Capital:
Air quality, land, water and water quality, natural resources, biodiversity, scenery

Cultural Capital:
Values, heritage recognition and celebration

Human Capital:
Population, education, skills, health, creativity, youth, diverse groups

Social Capital:
Trust, norms of reciprocity, network structure, group membership, cooperation, common vision and goals, leadership, depersonalization of politics, acceptance of alternative views, diverse representation

Political Capital:
Level of community organization through the use of government; ability of government to garner resources for the community

Financial Capital:
Tax burden/savings, state and federal tax monies, philanthropic donations, grants, contracts, regulatory exemption, investments, reallocation, loans, poverty rates

Built Capital:
Housing, transportation infrastructure, telecommunications infrastructure and hardware, utilities, buildings

---

CED Investments in Seven Capitals to Change Community Characteristics

What: CED projects focus on strengthening capitals
Who: Actors (groups involved)
How: Actions to address CED
When: Year effort initiated; duration of CED effort

Natural Capital Investments:
Preserving, restoring, enhancing, conserving environmental features in the CED effort

Cultural Capital Investments:
Sharing cultural identities (heritage, history, ethnicity, etc.) to drive CED effort

Human Capital investments:
Work expertise contributed to CED effort

Social Capital investments:
Risks taken to express differences of opinion on CED issues; organizations involved in CED effort; involving youth in CED; public participation/input in CED effort; organizational link with non-local involvement; actions linking community to the outside; local and non-local organizations involved in CED effort; organizational representative on CED decision-making board; number of different groups on CED board

Political Capital Investments:
Relationship presence and nature of relationship between CED board and local, county, state, federal, tribal, regional governments

Financial Capital Investments:
Type of materials contributed to CED effort; presence and sources of both local and external financial support; mechanisms used for leveraging financial support

Built Capital Investments
Infrastructure used for CED effort

Positive Changes in Community Characteristics

Changes in Natural Capital:
Indicator: Healthy ecosystems with multiple community benefits

Measures: Landscape, scenery, outdoor recreation opportunities, soils, air quality, water quality, wildlife, vegetation preserved, conserved or restored; land development policies adopted

Changes in Cultural Capital:
Indicator: Cultural consciousness

Measure: New community festivals

Changes in Human Capital:
Indicators: Increased use of the skills and abilities of local people (critical thinking, innovation, problem solving); increased initiative, responsibility and innovation

Measures: New skills acquired, new training programs established; health care improved; childcare improved; youth and adult education improved; workforce improved; community population and median age changes post-CED effort

Changes in Social Capital:
Indicators: Increased networks, communication, cooperation, trust

Measures: New groups involved and partners in CED; new groups formed from CED effort; more community cooperation; increased local and non-local participation; local strategic plan formed; new leaders; more effective leaders

Changes in Political Capital:
Indicator: Increased ability to secure resources for the community through elected officials
Measures: New community and government connections at various levels

Changes in Financial Capital:
Indicator: Appropriately diverse and vital economies

Measures: New financial instruments established, new bond issues passed; outside funding obtained to improve infrastructure and business development; poverty reduction

Changes in Built Capital:
Indicator: Appropriately diverse and vital economies

Infrastructure improved and strengthened (including telecommunications, education facilities; government buildings; community buildings; transportation; business district; health care facilities; industrial park; indoor rec facilities; cultural facilities; housing; churches; city services; energy services, etc.)

:

ECHOES OF THE PAST: LESSONS WE SOON FORGOT

By Neil E. Harl

The end of the 2002 Farm Bill marks 75 years under a national food and agriculture policy, which was a radical idea in 1933. Although the farm policy legislation during much of this period was shaped by the Agricultural Adjustment Act of 1938, the entire period has been characterized by legislation designed to bring a modicum of stability to the agricultural sector by focusing heavily on the so-called program crops.

During the last dozen years, under the 1996b and 2002 farm bills, stability was sought by drawing upon the U.S. Treasury to replace part of the lost income from low prices, which proved to be costly. Indeed, the cost is now widely viewed as politically and fiscally unacceptable against a backdrop of $425 to $500 billion deficits and a serious WTO challenge.

For the period of more than half a century before that dramatic shift, stability was sought by commissioning the Secretary of Agriculture, within statutory authority, to be the surrogate CEO of the agricultural sector with powers to seek a balance in demand and supply of program crops by idling land, administering on-farm and commercial commodity storage programs and participating in various commodity disposal programs on a reduced cost or no-cost basis.

Before turning to a discussion of the lessons we should have learned from the past 85 years, I want to shift our sights slightly and look ahead a few decades and attempt to make the case for a global food and agriculture policy for the next century.

A Global Food and Agriculture Policy

Eighty years ago, the Congress and the country were locked in a rancorous debate; is there a place for a national food and agriculture policy in this country? It was a pressing matter at the time-the prosperity of the pre-World War I era had given way to sharply lower commodity prices, leading to the 1919 crash in land values. Congress in 1921 had moved cautiously to enact legislation cracking down on futures trading abuses; to pass the Packers and Stockyards Act in 1921 which addressed anti-competitive practices in meat packing and processing; and to adopt the Capper-Volstead Act in 1922 which, for the first time, provided a framework for farmers to bargain collectively in producing and marketing their products.

But efforts to raise commodity prices and stabilize the sector were fruitless until the 1930s. By that time, the well-known head of the Bureau of Agricultural Economies, H.C. Taylor, had been fired for speaking out on the need for a new farm policy and the country had been through lengthy and boisterous debates about the McNary-Haugen bill and other proposals to raise commodity prices domestically.[1]

Neil E. Harl is Charles F. Curtiss Distinguished Professor in Agriculture and Emeritus Professor of Economics at Iowa State University.

This paper was presented at the Agricultural Policy Summit, Iowa State University, Ames, Iowa, July 7, 2005. Reprinted with permission.

[1] See Taylor, H.C., *A Farm Economist in Washington: 1919-1925* (1992).

The 1930s brought a sea change in thinking about farm policy. The desperate economic state of the country (as well as the decade-old economic problems of the agricultural sector) generated enough political support for a bold shift in farm policy. The Secretary of Agriculture, Henry A. Wallace, was given unprecedented power to attempt to balance demand and supply, soil conservation legislation was passed, bills to provide credit for agriculture were enacted and rural electrification was given a huge boost.

U.S. agriculture was at a crossroads in 1932 and the country chose to move aggressively toward a national food and agriculture policy.

Need for a global food and agriculture policy

Today, U.S. agriculture and the agricultural sector around the world stand at a different crossroads. The pressing question now is whether there is a place for a global food and agriculture policy. It is our firm belief that the answer to that question must be yes. The most pressing reason is that the United States (and the world), having grown much wealthier over the past century, now have the means at hand to move toward ending the biggest problem facing the human family since the beginning of time-death from starvation and malnutrition. To achieve that goal, which has eluded every generation since the dawn of civilization, will require an enormous effort.[2] The place to begin is with adoption and implementation of a global food and agriculture policy. The Seattle, Doha and Cancun World Trade Organization (WTO) meetings are markers in what can be a long march toward an era of adequate diets for everyone on the planet.

Also, not only has the world become wealthier in the past half century, it has become dramatically more integrated through trade, the emergence of transnational firms involved with input supply and output handling and processing and a burgeoning capital market that tends to knit the world together through a myriad of commercial transactions on a daily basis.

Components of a global food and agriculture policy

To be assured of any measure of success, a global food and agriculture policy should address several key policy problems.

Third World economic development. The three greatest barriers to eliminating starvation in the world are income, income and income. Inadequate food production has not been a problem for several decades. The problem now is that food, understandably, is produced and distributed almost universally in a market economy and those without an adequate income cannot access the market for available food. If food production were doubled, there would be substantial numbers of poor families that still could not afford an adequate diet.

Studies have shown that in Third World countries as much as 70 to 75 percent of additional income is spent on food. It is truly the last frontier for increasing food demand. That's why boosting Third World development makes sense for the major food producing countries as well as for the low-income peoples of the world.

For these reasons, strong support for Third World economic development is viewed as the most critical of the components for a global food and agriculture policy. It is in the interests of First World countries, as well as Third World developing economies, for global attention to be focused on Third World economic development. Unfortunately, some countries, notably those in Central Africa, are unable to position themselves in the development queue that has allowed several other countries to make better use of their scarce resources, particularly labor, to boost incomes and move to a higher level of nutritional adequacy.

In *a New York Times* article examining the causes of hunger, "Why Famine Persists" (July 13, 2003), Barry Bearak noted that "Families starve because families lack money. In most cases, it is that simple."

Food safety. Even though food supplies have probably never been safer, there is more concern today about food safety than at any time in the modern era. Much of the concern in the United States relates to imported food.

---

[2] International Policy Council on Agriculture Food and Trade, *Attaining Global Food Security by 2025.* Position Paper No. 3, November 1996.

But, globally, concerns about mad cow disease (BSE), hoof and mouth disease, E. *coli,* dioxin, pesticide and herbicide residues and feed additives for livestock have all registered with consumers. In countries where there is a high level of confidence in regulatory agencies, the concerns have been relatively less. It is in the global interest for food production and handling practices to be consistent with a policy of providing a safe and nutritious food supply for everyone. Clearly, we need a global reach to assure that foodstuffs are safe regardless of where they are produced.

Food security. The United States has not suffered periods of food inadequacy for a very long time. The nation's food producing potential and the presence of rational food distribution policies have allowed us to sidestep the food security issue.

But other parts of the world have not been as fortunate. Many areas have known food shortages, sometimes exacerbated by interruptions in food imports at times of reduced production. Indeed, there are numerous countries in the world that have faced food shortages within the memories of the living. An even greater number of countries have experienced periods of food scarcity to the point of widespread hunger within the past century and a half.

Clearly, political and economic instability have caused many countries (including some that have not experienced serious hunger problems in recent decades) to pursue food and agriculture policies with food security in mind.

Sharing germ plasm. Some countries, mostly in the tropics, are concerned about loss of germ plasm to the rest of the world. That problem is complicated and amplified by the concentration occurring among firms producing improved varieties of seed. Moreover, the concerns also relate to the ability of aggressive commercializing firms to seek and obtain intellectual property rights protection which may have the effect of denying access to germ plasm except on a licensing basis.

Conservation and the environment. Concerns are voiced regularly over the impacts of industrial food production on the environment. The effects of the use of commercial fertilizers on water supplies (such as hypoxia in the Gulf of Mexico) are a highly visible example of that problem. The consequences often spread well beyond the country in which the farming practices in question are carried on. Farming practices are helping to drive deforestation, air and water pollution, ocean degradation and species loss which some characterize as a serious long-term environmental threat.

International trade. The gradual demolition of trade barriers, which is far from complete, has contributed to the "globalization" of economic activity on the planet. There are sound, widely accepted reasons for encouraging the reduction of trade barriers with each country pursuing the production of foodstuff and fiber products for which that country has the greatest comparative advantage. While there are unquestioned economic gains from freer trade, there are pressing issues relating to the economic adjustments necessitated by freer trade, compensation for those displaced in the process and the question of whether the gains are absorbed disproportionately by firms that dominate commodity trading worldwide.

An economic theorem holds that if capital can flow freely across national boundaries, if goods can pass without limitation or restriction across national boundaries and if technology is equally available everywhere, the returns to labor and land (of the same quality) should be the same everywhere. This "leveling" in terms of returns to labor and land is profoundly disturbing, particularly to countries seeking to maintain a premium standard of living.[3] Many concede that a premium standard of living is only possible by-(1) generating a steady stream of technology that is "milked" for its income-boosting features (which is becoming increasingly difficult as commercializing firms seek to maximize their worldwide revenues from new technologies as soon as possible); and (2) investing in education for their population such that the quality of the labor force justifies premium compensation.

Coping with excess supply. Occasionally, production worldwide exceeds the market demand for food products. The predictable result is low world prices. Part of the problem contributing to the breakdown of discussions in Cancun was that all-out production in the United States, coupled with a robust stream of technology, boosted production and dropped commodity prices well below the cost of production not only in the United States but worldwide. Generous subsidies replaced part of the lost income for U.S. producers but in food producing countries where the government is unwilling or unable to provide such subsidies, land values decline and returns to farm workers drop to the point where farm families

[3] Learner, Edward, *Sources of International Comparative Advantage: Theory and Evidence.* Chapter 1, 1984.

cannot subsist. Workers then leave the land and exacerbate social problems in the large cities, often stunting the economic development which frequently begins with improved agricultural productivity. The U.S. market share increases, but partly at the expense of Third World development.

Other reasons. There are numerous other reasons for a global food, agriculture and energy policy. Much of modern agriculture is dependent on fossil fuels, yet these fuels are in limited (even dwindling) supply and their use has been linked to environmental problems, including global climate change. Agriculture in many areas relies on water supplies that could be threatened with rationing or restrictions. Many countries have trouble not only with the quantity, but also the quality of existing water supplies. Finally, recently there have been disturbing signs of an increase in infectious diseases. This includes an increase in the incidence of such diseases as well as a rise in resistance to common treatment methods and added examples of the transfer of diseases from animals to humans.

Summing up

Food is clearly the most basic need for survival and social stability. Assuring an opportunity for access to an adequate diet is in everyone's interest and should be a win-win for food producers as well as those who would benefit through better diets. Moreover, it is a critically important security issue. Peace and stability rarely coexist in areas of chronic food shortage.

The surest way to success in addressing food availability, food safety and stability in the world is a global food and agriculture policy. It generally has been believed that a country that is well fed, prosperous and populated with individuals who see a brighter future in the decades ahead is far less likely to be a mischief maker in the world.

The challenge of this generation, perhaps the first generation to have the means and the inclination in terms of political support to implement such a global food and agriculture policy, is to begin now by laying a foundation for international support for a global food and agriculture policy.

The authors of this paper do not presume to propose agricultural policy changes for every country. That task falls to those who are familiar with the conditions that exist in each nation. We only offer suggestions for changes in U.S. policy that might become part of a larger global dialogue. But we do believe that the objectives and components outlined above offer food for thought within the global agriculture community. These components might be the basis for international policy actions that coincide with what we will propose for future U.S. policy. These thoughts could provide the impetus for a summit to develop a truly global food and agriculture policy for the planet.

II.   Lessons We Should Have Learned (and Soon Forgot)

Permit me now to identify a half dozen lessons we should have learned during the past 85 years, and to examine the relevance of those lessons for the next farm bill and beyond.

Lesson 1: It has been painfully obvious that farmers, acting individually, do not adjust to low commodity prices as neoclassical economics would suggest. This was clear in the 1920s, when the prevailing view was that there was no room in the pantheon of federal policies for a national food and agriculture policy. It was also clear in the late 1990s and the early years of the twenty-first century under a farm bill that assumed exports would boost demand sufficiently so that there was no need for downside protection. We learned a very important lesson in 1998 and 1999—in Congress, low commodity prices trump ideology every time. The result was ad hoc funding to replace part of the lost income, boosting federal spending for agriculture to record levels.

Lesson 2: If an objective is to replace part or all of the lost income of producers when commodity prices fall to low levels, it is exceedingly responsive for commodities with an inelastic demand, where an increase in supply rewards the producers with a disproportionate drop in price and in profitability.

Lesson 3: Any attempt to stabilize the sector runs the risk of distorting resource allocation, but stabilizing the sector through replacement of *part* of the lost income is massively distortive as the outcome in some years is production and sale of commodities well below the cost of production.

Lesson 4: We have learned that all-out production coupled with a commitment by government to replace part or all of the lost income with tax dollars lowers world commodity prices, puts pressure on land values in countries that cannot or will not match the largess of the U.S. government, reduces returns to labor in those countries, and enlarges the U.S. market share but at a cost of stunting economic development in other countries and at a cost to the U.S. taxpayer.

Lesson 5: We have learned that the agricultural sector in this country is vulnerable to unstable fiscal and monetary policies. In the 1970s and early 1980s, the problem was instability in monetary policy which resulted in sharp increases in interest rates, especially for short-term credit, which jeopardized about one-third of the producers. Going forward, the greatest risk factor is in an unstable fiscal policy as a high and growing federal budget deficit and a large and growing trade deficit could eventually result in significantly higher interest rates to keep non-U.S. creditors in a happy and cheerful state. Loss of confidence by non U.S. creditors in the United States as a debtor nation could have devastating consequences.

Lesson 6: The experience with massive subsidies under the 1996 and 2002 farm bills indicates that the benefits of federal farm programs (to the extent such programs continue) should be shaped to eliminate the advantage of the largest operations in using their economies of scale to bid up cash rents and land values, to the detriment of midsize and smaller operators. Gains from efficiency from the largest operations are not passed along to consumers. Gains from bigness go heavily to acquire additional land. Thus, federal funds are being used to help the largest operators become even larger, and there's little public interest in that.

III.   Conclusion

The pressing task for interest groups and the Congress is to seek a modicum of agreement on the precise objectives to be served by the next farm bill. The architecture of that legislation should reflect a clear, transparent message to the non-farm world as to why commodity programs should continue to merit $10 billion or more per year.

Calls are being heard for Congress to pull the plug on spending, with land values declining to a new plateau well below current levels. Some argue that would make U.S. producers competitive with South American producers. That is clearly wrong-headed. The lesson was learned a century and a half ago that land values are price determined, not price determining. In every country, producers bid available profits into cash rents with capitalization ultimately into land values. U.S. land values are higher because of expected profitability from production plus the net present value of expected government payments.

A key issue that should help shape U.S. farm policy is how best to achieve a modicum of stability in an unstable world and avoid massive economic losses in times of great instability.

SUSTAINABLE FARMING AND RURAL COMMUNITY DEVELOPMENT

By John E. Ikerd

"Every few hundred years in Western history there occurs a sharp transformation. Within a few short decades, society rearranges itself—its worldview; its basic values; its social and political structure; its arts; its key institutions. Fifty years later, there is a new world. We are currently living through just such a transformation." (Peter Drucker, *Post-Capitalistic Society*, p. 1)

Rural Communities: Places Without a Purpose

The roots of most American rural communities are in agriculture. The land that is now the United States was a land of great natural wealth. Some of that wealth was in minerals and timber, but most of it lay in vast plains and winding valleys of fertile farmland. However, it took people to transform this wealth into wellbeing. People had to clear the land and till the soil to bring forth the bounty of food and fiber from the fertile fields. It took people to care for the cattle and sheep that grazed the vast plains. And as these people—these farmers and rancher—achieved surpluses beyond their own needs, they came to need other people in towns and rural communities. They needed people with whom they could trade their surpluses for the things they couldn't produce. They needed blacksmiths, dry goods stores, livery stables, banks, and salons. But they also needed schools, churches, and medical care if they were to move beyond economic survival to achieve a desirable quality of life.

Some of the early American communities were built around timber and mining towns, but most towns were farming and ranching towns. And the more people needed to care for the land, the more people needed in town to support those farmers and ranchers. It's likely true that distances between many towns were determined by a day's round trip by horse and wagon. But, the number of people in those towns was determined in large part by the nature of agriculture. For example, lands well suited for vegetables and row crops could be farmed more intensively—supporting more families per acre or section. Lands suited only for small grains or pasture were farmed less intensively—supporting fewer families per section or township. Of course, town folks also had mouths to feed with locally grown foods—greens, milk, eggs, and bacon. But, the density of population in most rural places reflected the nature of their agriculture.

At the turn of the 20th century, America was still an agrarian country—about 40 percent of its people were farmers and well over half lived in very rural areas. But, then came the second phase of the industrial revolution and the need to collect large numbers of people into cities to "man" the large factories and offices of a growing manufacturing economy.

John E. Ikerd is a faculty member emeritus in the department of Agricultural Economics at the University of Missouri. See page 1282 for more on author.

This paper was presented at the Annual Conference of the Northern Plains Sustainable Agriculture Society, Bismarck, ND in 1999. Reprinted with permission.

The simultaneous industrialization of agriculture—mechanization, specialization, routinization,—made it possible for fewer farmers to feed more people better—"freeing" farmers and other rural people to find work in the cities.

The same technologies that pulled rural people toward the cities pushed them off the farms and out of rural communities. These technologies increased production per person by substituting capital and generic knowledge for labor and individual management. As successful new farming technologies were developed, they invariably reduced production costs—per bushel or per pound of production—but only if each farmer produced more. Thus, the incentive to realize greater profits by reducing costs was inherently an incentive to buy bigger equipment and more commercial inputs in order to farm more land and produce more output. As farmers individually responded to these incentives, production in total invariably expanded, market prices fell, and the promise of continuing profits vanished. The new technologies were now necessary—no longer for profits but now for survival. Those who adopted and expanded too little too late were unable to compete. They were "freed" from their farms to find a job in the city.

Farms were forced to get larger and larger just to survive. In fact, with a limited population to feed and a limited amount of land to farm, fewer and fewer farmers could possibly survive. In addition, large specialized farms often had to bypass the local community in purchasing inputs and marketing their products in order to remain competitive with other large farms. Their competitors were not down the road or across the country, but might be half way around the world.

Fewer farmers buying less locally meant less need for farm related businesses in small towns. Fewer farmers also meant fewer farm families to buy groceries, clothes, and haircuts in small towns. Fewer families also meant fewer people to fill the desks in rural schools, pews in rural churches, and the waiting rooms of rural doctors. Fewer people with a purpose for being in rural areas meant that many rural communities were losing their purpose as well.

Today, America is no longer an agrarian nation. Less that 2 percent of Americans call themselves farmers and even those earn more than half of their income off the farm. Somewhere around 25 percent of the people live in non-metropolitan areas—but many if not most commute to a city to work. There are few people left in farming communities to move to town and no longer any social benefit in moving them. Industries are "downsizing" and "outsourcing"—laying off workers by the thousands. As consumers we spend on the average a little over a dime out of each dollar for food and the farmer only gets a penny of that dime. The rest goes to pay for commercial inputs and marketing services—packaging, advertising, transportation, etc. Society no longer has anything to gain from further industrialization of agriculture, but yet it continues. And rural communities in farming areas continue to wither and die.

Feeling the stress of an industrializing society, many small towns turned to industrial recruitment—trying to become a city rather than a town—as a means of survival. Others have tried to capture natural advantages in climate or landscapes to become destinations for tourists from the cities. Those near the growing industrial centers "rented out their communities" as bedrooms for those who are willing to commute to the city. But, most rural communities in agricultural areas have not been successful in their efforts to regain prosperity—or even to survive. Most rural communities have become and remain places in search of a purpose.

Farming: A Profession without a Future

As rural communities have lost their purpose, farming—at least farming, as it is known today—has lost its future. There is no future in farming—at least not in the kind of farming that requires ever-increasing amounts of capital and commercial inputs to produce basic commodities for processing into food and fiber for global markets. By definition, if the trend toward larger, more specialized production units continues there will be room for fewer and fewer of these units until only a handful remains.

As capital requirements continue to grow, a corporate share-holding organizational structure will be required to finance agricultural enterprises. Giant corporate entities already control the processing and distribution sectors for most agricultural commodities. As corporations gain control of agricultural production—through outright ownership or through contractual arrangements with individual producers—those who refuse to contract will find they have no markets for their products. The surviving "farmers" will, in fact, become corporate "hired hands." Thus, there is no future in farming—as long as the only options farmers are given are to get big, give in, or get out.

One need only look to corporate structure of the poultry industry as a model for future livestock production. Corporate domination of cattle feeding has been a fact of life for years and the farm cattle feeder has become a rarity. Corporate control of hog production is becoming a reality—with recent attempts by large operators to gain market share forcing hog prices to their lowest levels since the Great Depression. Corporate contractual control of ranching operations is likely not far in the future.

Corporate control of fresh fruits and vegetable production has been around for decades, but may not be the model for the future of field crops. Genetic engineering instead is the key to corporate control of crop production. Genetically modified organisms (GMOs) can be patented—giving the patent holder exclusive rights to their utilization. The corporations who hold the patents on the seed stock will either control or contract with those who control processing and distribution of the resulting farm commodities. Thus, the only viable markets will be for commodities from organisms that have been genetically modified in some way—and are produced under contract for the patent holder. This same strategy will likely be employed by livestock operations as well—as corporate consolidation of firms in both the crop and livestock sectors continues.

The publicly stated justifications for the demise of farming will be to "ensure that the public continues to have an adequate supply of safe and healthful food at a reasonable price"—the same as the oft-stated justification for the industrialization of agriculture. However, the true motivation for the corporate take-over of agriculture is pure economic power. Those corporations that have been able to gain control of significant sectors of agriculture have been able to reap large profits in return. If a handful of corporations gain control of the global food supply—they will have more economic power than has ever been seen. It is a prize they are willing to pursue at any risk.

Can farmers compete head-to-head with the big corporations by forming cooperative organizations and networks? Perhaps, for a while, but the longer-term outlook for farmer collectives is doubtful at best. Will farmer groups grow big enough, fast enough to keep up with the consolidation of corporate power? This game is not just about economic efficiency, or minimizing costs of production, it is about raw market power. Will farmer groups be willing to rape the environment and gut rural communities—if necessary—to pursue their economic goals? If they are, is society any better served by a group of such farmers than by a group of similar minded businessmen?

Farming as we know it is coming to an end. There is no future for farming, and no future for most rural communities, unless we are willing to embrace a new and different kind of farming and a new and different vision for rural communities.

The Inevitability of Change

There might seem to be little hope for farming, or for many rural communities. But, current trends, toward industrialization and corporate domination, will not continue. Trends never continue, at least indefinitely. And these too will come to an end—maybe far sooner than might now seem reasonable.

A couple of scientists proposed a list of the top twenty "great ideas in science" in *Science* magazine, and invited scientists from around the world to comment (Pool, 1991). Among their top twenty were such well known ideas as the universal laws of motion, the first and second laws of thermodynamics, and the proposition that all life is based on the same genetic code. But, the top twenty included another proposition—that "everything on the earth operates in cycles." A few scientists responding to the *Science* survey disagreed with the proposed theory of universal cycles. But most who responded left "everything operated in cycles" on their list of the top twenty great ideas in science (Culotta, 1991).

Based on this theory of universal cycles, any observed trend is, in fact, just a phase of a cycle. This theory of cycles implies that farms will not continue to get either larger or smaller, at least indefinitely, but instead will cycle between growing larger and smaller over time. History provides numerous examples where land became concentrated in the hands of a few only later to be dispersed and controlled by the many. For example, vast feudal land holdings once dominated much of Europe, only to be replaced by independent land ownership. In the U.S., large plantations grew to dominate the South—only to later be dispersed among many individual landholders. In what once was the Soviet Union, giant communal farms are now being divided into smaller individual plots. It seems ironic that many of the advisors sent to the former U.S.S.R to facilitate this process of dispersion are deeply involved in the consolidation of independent farms into large-scale corporate production units in the U.S.

There have been similar cycles in the collecting and scattering of people. Anthropological evidence indicate that people who have concentrated in large cities in centuries past, have later—for a variety of reasons—abandoned those cities and dispersed themselves across the countryside. There is reason to believe that migration from rural areas to U.S. cities during the twentieth-century was simply a phase of a similar cycle rather than an unending trend. Most large center-cities have been losing population for decades as people move to the suburbs in increasing numbers. The current trend is called "urban sprawl"—people now abandoning the suburbs for a few acres in the country. Even further migration to more isolated rural areas might be a logical continuation of the dispersion phase of this cycle. The most relevant question for rural communities might be when, and for what reasons, will people abandon the cities and suburbs to resettle rural areas? They won't necessarily come back to the same places abandoned by people before.

Toward A Post-Industrial Economy

Alvin Toffler, in his book *Powershift*, points out that many forecasters make the mistake of simply projecting unrelated trends into the future, as if they would continue indefinitely. Such forecasts provide no insight regarding how the trends are interconnected or what forces are likely to reverse current trends and move them in opposite directions.

Toffler contends that the forces of industrialization have run their course and have already begun to reverse. He believes the Industrial models of economic progress are becoming increasingly obsolete, and the old notions of efficiency and productivity are no longer valid. The new "modern" model is to produce customized goods and services aimed at niche markets, to constantly innovate, to focus on value-added products, and specialized production. Innovations that tailor products to the wants and needs of specific customers are replacing cost cutting as a source of profits and growth.

He goes on to state that "the most important economic development of our lifetime has been the rise of a new system of creating wealth, based no longer on muscle but on the mind" (p. 9). He contends that "the conventional factors of production—land, labor, raw materials, and capital—become less important as knowledge is substituted for them" (p. 238). "Because it reduces the need for raw material, labor, time, space, and capital, knowledge becomes the central resource of the advanced economy (p. 91).

Peter Drucker, a time-honored consultant to big business, talks of the "Post Business Society," in his book, *The New Realities*. He states "the biggest shift—bigger by far than the changes in politics, government or economics—is the shift to the knowledge society. The social center of gravity has shifted to the knowledge worker. All developed countries are becoming post-business, knowledge societies" (p. 173).

Knowledge-based production embodies enormous complexity in simultaneous and dynamic linkages among a multitude of interrelated factors. Cognitive scientists have shown that humans can deal consciously with only a very small number of separate variables simultaneously. Yet humans can perform enormously complex tasks; such as driving a car in heavy traffic, playing a tennis match, or carrying on a conversation—tasks that baffle the most sophisticated computers. In fact, people are capable of performing such tasks routinely by using their well-developed subconscious minds.

The subconscious human mind appears to be virtually unlimited in its capacity to cope with complexity. The human mind is capable of assimilating hundreds of feedback relationships simultaneously as it integrates detail and dynamic complexities together (Senge, p. 367). In fact, the human mind may be the only mechanism capable of dealing effectively with the systems complexities embodied in the production concepts that will dominate economic development in the future.

Drucker points out also that there is an important, fundamental difference between knowledge work and industrial work. Industrial work is fundamentally a mechanical process whereas the basic principle of knowledge work is biological. He related this difference to determining the "right size" of organization required to perform a given task. "Greater performance in a mechanical system is obtained by scaling up. Greater power means greater output: bigger is better. But this does not hold for biological systems. Their size follows their function. It would surely be counterproductive for a cockroach to be big, and equally counterproductive for the elephant to be small. As biologists are fond of saying, 'The rat knows everything it needs to know to be a successful rat.' Whether the rat is more intelligent that the human being is a stupid question; in what it takes to be a successful rat, the rat is way ahead of any other animal, including human beings" (p. 259).

Differences in organizing principles may be critically important in determining the future size and organizational structure of economic enterprises and ultimately in determining their optimum geographic location. Other things being equal, the smallest effective size is best for enterprises based on information and knowledge work. "'Bigger' will be 'better' only if the task cannot be done otherwise" (Drucker, p. 260). Small enterprises can be located almost anywhere.

When there is no longer any economic justification for bigness, there will no longer be any economic justification for corporations. The only societal motivation for chartering corporations was to make it easier to raise the capital necessary to finance enterprises larger than could be financed by individuals or partnerships of investors. Corporations have been subsidized by various means, providing additional incentives for businesses to become larger, under the assumption that larger organizations would be more efficient, and would pass along their cost savings to consumers. There are serious questions concerning whether corporations today serve any positive public purpose—even in cases where large operations might be more cost efficient. In an era where "smaller is better," corporations will have lost even their original claim to special treatment. Corporations exist only at the consent of the people—the public granted their original charters, and the public can revoke those charters. The practical question for the future is whether corporations have gained so much political power that they may continue to exist, and even be subsidized, long after they have lost any societal purpose for being. But once they have lost their purpose, the era of corporations eventually will come to an end—regardless of their political power at the present.

Robert Reich, former U.S. Secretary of Labor, addresses future trends in the global economy in his book, *The Work of Nations*. He identifies three emerging broad categories of work corresponding to emerging competitive positions within the global economy: routine production service, in-person service, and symbolic-analytic services (Reich, p. 174). He calls routine service workers the old foot soldiers of American capitalism in high-volume enterprises. They include low- and mid-level managers—foremen, line managers, clerical supervisors, etc.—in addition to traditional blue-collar workers. Production workers typically work for large industrial organizations. These workers live primarily by the sweat of their brow, or their ability to follow directions and carry out orders, rather than by using their minds.

In-person service, like production service, entails simple and repetitive tasks. The big difference is that these services must be provided person-to-person. They include people such as retail sales workers, waiters and waitresses, janitors, cashiers, child-care workers, hairdressers, flight attendants, and security guards. Like routine production work, most in-person service work is closely supervised and requires relatively little education. In-person service providers utilize a diversity of organizational structures, ranging from individual providers to large franchised organizations. Unlike routine production work, individual personality can be a big plus, or minus, for in-person service workers.

Symbolic-analysts are the "mind workers" in Reich's classification scheme. They include all the problem-solvers, problem-identifiers, and strategic-brokers. They include scientists, design engineers, public relations executives, investment bankers, doctors, lawyers, real estate developers, and consultants of all types. They also include writers and editors, musicians, production designers, teachers, and even university professors. He points out that symbolic analysts often work alone or in small teams, which are frequently connected only informally and flexibly with larger organizations. Like Toffler and Drucker, Reich believes that power and wealth of the future will be created by symbolic-analysis, by mind work, rather than by routine production or in-person service.

John Naisbitt and Patricia Aburdene in their book, *Megatrends 2000*, call the triumph of the individual the great unifying theme at the conclusion of this century. They talk about greater acceptance of individual responsibility as new technologies extend the power of individuals. Their "mind workers" are called individual entrepreneurs. They point out that small-time entrepreneurs have already seized multibillion-dollar markets from large, well-heeled businesses—successes of small "upstart" in microcomputers and microbreweries provide a couple of examples (p. 324).

They point out, that the industrial revolution built the great cities of Europe, America, and Japan. But today's cities are based on technologies of 100 years ago such as indoor plumbing, electric lighting, steel frame buildings, elevators, subways, and the telephone. Railroads and waterways made it easy and inexpensive to move raw materials and finished goods over long distances, but it was much more expensive then to move people even short distances.

But, the cities have already lost much of their purpose as places for people to live. Multi-lane freeways and extended mass transit systems have allowed people to retreat to the suburbs by making it easier for them to get to and from work. Naisbitt and Aburdene contend that "In many ways, if cities did not exist, it now would not be necessary to invent them" (p. 332). Drucker adds that the real-estate boom, and the associated new skyscrapers, in big cities in the seventies and eighties were not signs of health. They were instead the signals of the beginning of the end of the central city. "The city might become an information center rather than a center of work—a place from which information (news, data, music) radiates. It might resemble the medieval cathedral where the peasants from the surrounding countryside congregated once or twice a year at the great feast days; in between it stood empty except for the learned clerics and its cathedral school" (Drucker, p. 259).

People are abandoning the cities for the suburbs for quality of life reasons: lower crime rates, quality housing at a lower cost, and recreational opportunities. Many people are now free to abandon the suburbs for rural area for quality of life reasons as well: more living space, a cleaner environment, prettier landscapes, and, perhaps most important, for a place to regain a sense of community, a sense of belonging.

Many knowledge workers, while working alone or in small groups, are choosing not to face the world alone but rather are seeking community—the free association among people. Large business organizations, government bureaucracies, labor unions, and other collectives have provided hiding places for avoiders of responsibility. In a community there is no place to hide. Everyone knows who is contributing and who is not. In communities, individual differences are recognized and rewarded. Enlightened individuals may well choose to restore a sense of community—all but destroyed by corporate industrialism. These people are not looking for a place to hide but rather for a place to be recognized—a place to belong.

Toward A Post-Industrial Agriculture

If the rest of society is moving toward a post-industrial economy, why are some sectors of the agricultural economy, specifically swine and dairy, continuing to experience rapid industrialization? In Joel Barker's book: *Paradigms*, he points out that new paradigms (including developmental models) tend to emerge while, in the minds of most people, the old paradigm is doing quite well.

Typically, "a new paradigm appears sooner than it is needed" and "sooner than it is wanted." Consequently the logical and rational response to a new paradigm by most people is rejection (Barker, p. 47). New paradigms emerge when it becomes apparent to some people, not necessarily many, that the old paradigm is incapable of solving some important problems of society. Paradigms may also create new problems, while providing poor solutions to the old ones, when they are applied in situations where they are not well suited.

American agriculture provides a prime example of both over application and misapplication of the industrial paradigm. The early gains of appropriate specialization in agriculture lifted people out of subsistence living and made the American industrial revolution possible. But, the potential societal benefits from agricultural industrialization were probably largely realized by the late 1960s. More recent "advances" in agricultural technologies may well have done more damage to the ecological and social resources of rural areas than any societal benefit they may have created from more "efficient" food production.

Industrialization of agriculture probably lagged behind the rest of the economy because its biological systems were the most difficult to industrialize. Agriculture, due to its biological nature, doesn't fit industrialization; it is being forced to conform. Consequently, the benefits are less, the problems are greater, it is being industrialized last, and it likely will remain industrialized for a shorter period of time.

A new post-industrial paradigm for American agriculture is already emerging to replace the industrial model of agriculture. The new paradigm is emerging under the conceptual umbrella of sustainable agriculture. A sustainable agriculture must meet the needs of the current generation while leaving equal or better opportunities for those of future generations. To achieve sustainability, farming systems must be ecologically sound, economically viable, and socially responsible. All are necessary and none alone or in pairs is sufficient. Sustainable agriculture cannot be defined as a set of farming practices or methods, but instead must be defined in terms of its purpose—sustaining people across generations through agriculture—and the ecological, economic, and social principles that must be followed in achieving that purpose.

The sustainable agriculture paradigm has emerged to address the problems created by the industrial model, primarily pollution of the natural environment and degradation of the natural resource base. This new paradigm seems capable also of creating benefits that are inherently incompatible with the industrial model—such as greater individual creativity, greater dignity of work, and more attention to issues of social equity. It is conceivable that industrial agricultural systems might be developed that appear to be both profitable and ecologically sound—at least in the short run. But, industrial systems inherently degrade the human resources—the people they employ—they simply cannot meet the sustainability test for social responsibility.

The sustainable agriculture paradigm is consistent with the visions of Toffler, Drucker, Reich and others of a post-industrial era of human progress. Sustainable agriculture is management intensive, rather than management extensive. Sustainable farms must be managed holistically as a living organism—with consideration given to multitudes of interdependencies and feed back loops among their interrelated parts or organs. Sustainable systems must be individualistic, site-specific, and dynamic. They must be capable of responding to the every changing capacities and abilities of both the farmer and the land. Thus, sustainable farming is inherently information, knowledge, and management intensive.

Complexity, interdependency, and simultaneous processes are fundamental elements of the sustainable model, which is clearly biological rather than mechanical in nature. For such systems, size and form must follow function. In biological systems, individual elements must conform to their ecological and social niche. Big, specialized farms will be sustainable only if their "niche" is equally large and homogeneous. Most conventional commercial farming operations have already outgrown their niches. That's the basic source of their ecological, social, and economic problems.

The sustainable agriculture paradigm in agriculture is at about the same stage of development as was agricultural industrialization in the days of steam-driven threshing machines and steel wheeled tractors. In other words, a few sustainable agriculture pioneers are out on the frontier of knowledge, but this new frontier of farming is still far from being settled. Much remains to be learned about this new paradigm and only time will reveal how it is to be implemented in sustaining a desirable quality of life for farmers and for society as a whole. Some current examples of its application include: organic production of vegetables, grains, and meats; low-input production for local, direct markets; community supported agriculture (CSAs); farmers' markets and other niche market for ecologically grown products; management intensive grazing of livestock and seasonal dairies; free range and pastured poultry; and organic cotton. The USDA is supporting a project to develop mini case studies of one thousand successful sustainable farmers. This project quite likely will illustrate a thousand different approaches to sustaining agriculture—as many as there are farmers who pursue it. But, the project will also illustrate a common dedication to the same basic purpose and to the fundamental principles of sustainability.

It will take knowledge, "mind work," not physical or economic muscle, for farmers of the future to find a niche where they carry out farming by means that are ecologically sound, economically viable, and socially responsible. Returning to Peter Drucker's *Post-Capitalistic Society*: "In the knowledge society into which we are moving, individuals are central. Knowledge is not impersonal, like money. Knowledge does not reside in a book, a databank, a software program; they contain only information. Knowledge is always embodied in a person, carried by a person; created, augmented, or improved by a person; applied by a person; taught by a person, and passed on by a person. The shift to the knowledge society therefore puts the person in the center" (p. 210). People are at the key to farming sustainably. People—not new technologies—are the key to the future of farming and of rural communities.

The Renaissance of Rural Communities

Community economic development strategies are already changing to reflect knowledge-based approaches to economic development. As large companies and branch plants leave rural areas and move overseas for cheaper labor, communities are beginning to concentrate on improving the quality of jobs remaining. Rural people—if not community leaders—are beginning to question the old strategies of industrial recruitment, industrial parks, and tax breaks for new industries. The new strategies for community self-development are in line with the business theories of Reich and others. These strategies invest in mind-workers by encouraging entrepreneurs within the community to build small businesses and strengthen the local economy. Local buyer-supplier projects are encouraged to plug the loss in dollars leaving the community by replacing imports with locally produced goods and services.

However, most communities still seem to be lacking a clear vision of a new fundamental purpose for their existence. They know they can no longer depend on agriculture as the primary engine of rural economic development. They realize that industry recruitment is destined to fail for most rural communities—there simple won't be enough American based industries in the future to go around. They see promotion of small-scale projects; such as niche markets, bed and breakfasts, and local festivals; as piecemeal, stop-gap strategies with limited long run potential for developing their community.

Rural communities that have no development strategies of their own essentially forfeit the rights to develop their communities to others—others from outside the community. Those "others" already have their own vision of the future in mind for rural areas—as places to dump whatever they don't want in "their back yards" in urban areas. They see rural areas as open spaces where they can build prisons, garbage dumps, landfills, toxic waste incinerators, and large confinement animal feeding operations. They are looking for open spaces housed by a few desperate people who will accept almost anything that offers a minimum wage job or a chance to sell out and move to town.

Rural communities need positive development strategies of their own—strategies that will create economic opportunity without degrading either the land or the people. They need strategies for "sustainable" development. They need development that is linked to local resources, that maintains the productivity of those resources, and protects their physical and social environment. However, sustainable development must also provide an acceptable level of economic returns and otherwise enhance the quality of life of those who live and work in the community. Development strategies that rely solely, or even primarily, on local natural resources are unlikely to fulfill these latter requirements. However, the obstacle of limited local resources can be overcome by those who have a clear vision of the new realities of economic development and a firm commitment to make their community a part of the coming rural renaissance. Limited natural resources will be leveraged—in much the same way as equity capital is leveraged in financing a business. As the local economy continues to grow, its natural resource "equity" will become a smaller proportion of its total economy, but no less important than is equity capital to a business in ensuring its survivability and sustainability.

Robert Reich stresses that the economy is no longer local, or even national in scope, but is truly global. Neither communities nor nations can depend on capturing the benefits of local capital, local industries, or even locally developed technologies in a global economy. Money, jobs, and technology can and will move freely to anywhere on the globe where they can be used to the greatest advantage. First, sustainable development must be linked to something that cannot easily be moved. And second, sustainable development strategies must give local workers and investors a logical reason for investing, working, and spending in the communities where they live. Communities cannot be sustained with out strong economic interdependencies among those within communities. But, people must have strong logical reasons for developing interdependent relationships.

Reich outlines two fundamental strategies for national economic development in a global economy. First, he advocates investment in infrastructure, including such things as roads, bridges, airports, and telecommunications access systems. Infrastructure has two important development dimensions. First, it facilitates productivity by making production processes easier and more efficient. Second, infrastructure is geographically fixed in the country where it is built. If producers want to use U.S. roads, bridges, airports and communications accesses, they have to use them where they are, in the country that built them. Fixed natural resources—such as agricultural land—can be used to achieve this same critical developmental impact without building anything. The challenge is to find ways to leverage the local land base to support more people better without degrading the resource—to develop a more sustainable agriculture.

Reich's second, and even more important, development strategy is to invest in people. People who work with their minds will be the fundamental source of productivity in a knowledge-based era of the twenty-first century. This makes the local natural base less limiting, but no less important, than in previous eras of development. If a nation is to be productive in the post-industrial economy, its people must be productive. Reich apparently depends heavily on national allegiance to keep productive people working in the nation that helped them develop their minds. If agriculture is to be a cornerstone for rural community development, it must be the type of agriculture that employs the talents of thinking, innovative, productive people—it must be a sustainable agriculture. These are the types of people who can leverage a limited resource base into a vibrant, sustainable community.

With one important added element, Reich's strategy for national economic development—investing in infrastructure and local people—becomes a logical strategy for rural community development. However, rural communities cannot depend on an allegiance of rural residents to their communities to keep productive people in rural areas. People can and do move freely among communities within the U.S. During the rural renaissance, it will be critically important for communities to be able to attract new mind workers, if there are to be places where "home-grown" mind workers will want to stay. The primary attraction of rural communities for current and future mind workers will be the promise of a desirable quality of life.

Quality of life is a product of human relationships—relationships among people and between people and their environment. Obviously, other things such as employment, income, personal safety, economic security, and access to health care are important aspects of quality of life. However, quality of life also includes peoples' subjective judgments regarding self-determination, freedom to participate, individual equity, freedom from discrimination, economic opportunity, ability to cope with change, social acceptance, and treatment according to accepted social principles of one's culture.

Communities that survive and prosper during the rural renaissance will be culturally diverse. Diversity will be an important source of creativity, innovation, and synergistic productivity, and will be an important aspect of quality of life in rural areas. In rural communities people will have an opportunity to know each other individually rather than simply accept the stereotypes of their cultural groups.

Successful rural communities will be made up of long-time rural residents, bright young people who choose to stay, returning rural residents, those born in urban areas of the U.S., and those born in other countries. They may also be Anglo American, Afro American, Asian, Mexican, and Canadian as well. Male and female, young and old, rich and poor, educated and less well educated, may be viewed as different, but they must be respected for their differences in the workplace and in the town halls of rural renaissance communities. Communities that fail to meet the challenges of the cultural renaissance will be unlikely to provide the quality of life necessary to participate in the economic renaissance as well.

Basic Strategies for Rural Revitalization

Successful rural revitalization strategies for the future will be unique to each community that succeeds. Standard operating procedures, best practices, and recipes for success were characteristics of the industrial era but not of the post-industrial era of knowledge-based development. However, the fundamental principles and concepts outlined above can provide some guidance for those who have the vision of a rural renaissance and the determination to participate in this historic process. The following are a few of the more obvious elements of a successful rural revitalization strategy.

- Invest in people: People are the basic source of productivity in a knowledge-based era of economic development. The "virtuous cycle" of education, increased innovation, increased investment, increased value, and higher wages offers an alternative to the vicious cycle of industrial recruitment, low wages, declining emphasis on education, declining communities, and resulting downward spiral (Reich, 1991). The common practice of preparing the "best and the brightest" to leave rural areas will have to be reversed to meet the cultural and economic needs. "Home-grown" mind workers have a sense of the quality of rural life that immigrants from urban areas will be seeking. Quality life-long education will be equally critical to prepare people to succeed in the new, dynamic era of economic development.

- Invest in infrastructure: Good roads and access to airports will be important. However, modern telecommunications systems will be the key element in making rural areas competitive with urban and suburban areas in an information driven, knowledge-based society. A national initiative to bring twenty-first century communications systems to rural communities may be more important to rural areas today than was the rural free mail delivery and rural electrification programs of times past. Invest in facilities that will bring people together. A good farmers' market may be more effective than a recreation facility in helping people within the community understand each other's way of life.

- Invest in quality of life: Help people make the most of local climate, landscapes and recreational opportunities. Land use planning and zoning can make and keep quality spaces in rural communities providing quality places for people to live. However, farming, residential, and recreation land uses can be compatible—and must be compatible—in a sustainable rural community. Make health care an investment in the future. Provide maternity wards and pediatricians not just cardiac units and nursing homes. Make personal security and safety a top priority. This, as much as any single factor, will enhance the perception of rural communities a quality place to live.

- Make a commitment of understanding, accepting, and valuing diversity: Quality of life is about relationships among people. Thinking, learning, behaving, and working alike was necessary for success in the industrial era of development. Thinking, learning, behaving, and working differently, but working in harmony, will be the key to success in the knowledge-based era of development. Communities that fail to understand, accept, and value diversity among people are unlikely to succeed in a knowledge-based era of development.

- Link development to local resources: This is the key to making development sustainable in any given place. Natural resources such as land, minerals, landscapes, and climates must be utilized, at least initially, in the geographic locations where they exist. Agricultural land is still the most valuable geographically fixed resource for many rural communities. Large scale, industrial agriculture provides little local community support. Sustainable agriculture, on the other hand, is a knowledge-based system of farming that depends on the productivity of local people. Wendell Berry points out, "…if agriculture is to remain productive, it must preserve the land and the fertility and ecological health of the land; the land, that is, must be used well. A further requirement, therefore, is that if the land is to be used well, the people who use it must know it well, must be highly motivated to use it well, must know how to use it well, must have time to use it well, and must be able to afford to use it well" (p. 147). Agricultural mind-work can multiply the value to agricultural products before they leave rural areas and replace many agricultural inputs that are brought in from elsewhere. Investments that sustain local agriculture may well be the most important investment many rural communities can make to sustain their local economies.

- Share the vision: A community must share its vision of the future rural America, and what it is doing to shape its own future with others, if it is to share in the rural renaissance. There may be a great-untapped demand for what rural communities have, or can have, to offer. Productive people who desire a better quality of life may simply be locked into an old vision of rural communities as places of depression, decline, and decay.

The most important single step toward success may be for those in the community to develop a shared vision of hope—for a better way of life and a brighter future of their community. The vision of each person in the community will be different from the vision of others in many respects and not all will be hopeful. However, the people of a community must search for and find some common positive elements among their different visions to provide the nucleus for a shared vision of hope. Otherwise, the group is not really a community but rather a collection of people who happen to live in the same general area. A community that has found its shared vision has made its first critical step toward self-revitalization. Hope then can begin to transform reality. To paraphrase Jesse Jackson, the articulate civil rights leader, "if they can conceive it, and believe it, they can achieve it." The future of rural America belongs to those who have the courage to seize it.

References

Barker, Joel. 1993. *Paradigms: The Business of Discovering the Future*, HarperBusiness, a Division of HarperCollins Publishing, New York, New York.

Berry, Wendell. 1990. *What are People For*. North Point Press, San Francisco, CA.

Culotta, Elizabeth. 1991. "Science's 20 greatest hits take their lumps," *Science*, American Academy of Science, March 15, 251:4999, p. 1308.

Drucker, Peter. 1989. *The New Realities*. Harper and Row, Publishers, Inc. New York, New York.

Drucker, Peter, 1993. *Post-Capitalist Society*, HarperCollins Publishers, Inc. New York, New York.

Naisbitt, John and Patricia Aburdene. *Megatrends 2000*. 1990. Avon Books, The Hearst Corporation, New York, New York.

Pool, Robert. 1991. "Science Literacy: The Enemy is Us," *Science*, American Academy of Science, March 15, 251: 4991, p. 267.

Reich, Robert B. 1992, *The Work of Nations*. Vintage Books, Random House Publishing, New York, New York.

Senge, Peter M. 1990. *The Fifth Discipline*. Doubleday Publishing Co. New York, New York.

Toffler, Alvin, *Powewshift*, Bantam Books, New York, NY, 1990.

AGRICULTURE'S UNCERTAIN FUTURE: UNFORTUNATE DEMISE OR TIMELY OPPORTUNITY?

By Frederick Kirschenmann

The farm is a place to live. The criterion of success is a harmonious balance between plants, animals, and people; between the domestic and the wild; between utility and beauty.—Aldo Leopold

Perhaps the single greatest challenge facing us as we enter the 21st century is the need to articulate a vision for agriculture that meets the requirements of the new world in which we find ourselves. No one would argue that the vision for agriculture that captured the imagination of U.S. citizens for most of the 20th century was unsuccessful. Our industrial vision spawned an array of new technologies to control nature for the purpose of making agriculture more productive. In many respects we succeeded beyond the wildest dreams of our grandparents. It was the goal of industrial agriculture to produce all of the food and fiber required to fulfill the nation's domestic and export needs while using a dramatically reduced labor force. This is turn would free people to work in the industrial and professional arts in order to improve our common quality of life. The farm population has plummeted from more than 30 million in the 1940s to less than 2 million today, yet until very recently we continued to overproduce essential food commodities.

But successful industrialization also yielded a host of new questions that now confront agriculture. Many of these problems were articulated in a report by the Institute of Food and Agricultural Sciences (IFAS) at the University of Florida. In the process of "Focusing IFAS Resources on Solutions for Tomorrow (FIRST)," the university's voices sound some common themes:

1. they are concerned about the impact that expanded government regulations will have on Florida's agriculture;

2. they are uncertain about their ability to deal with the constant influx of new pests while the number of pesticides available to treat their crops is declining;

3. they face serious water quality and usage issues, especially given the continuing dramatic increase in the state's population;

4. they worry about the impact of urban encroachment on agricultural and fragile lands in Florida; and

5. they fear negative effects on Florida's agriculture from the economic pressures of foreign markets.

These concerns are among the challenges of the new world in which we live. They compel us to develop a new vision for agriculture.

Frederick Kirschenmann is Distinguished Fellow at the Leopold Center for Sustainable Agriculture at Iowa State University in Ames, Iowa. Mary Adams, editor at the Leopold Center for Sustainable Agriculture, assisted with the research and the revision of this paper.

This paper is from a June 2001 keynote address to the University of Florida's Institute of Food and Agricultural Sciences. Reprinted with permission.

New World Characteristics

There are at least four characteristics of our 21st century world that affect agriculture–and encourage us to develop a new vision for agriculture.

1. The Earth as Community

First, we now know that our world is a *community*, not a collection of objects that we can manipulate solely for the benefit of the human species. Our industrial worldview was based on scientific analyses that date back to the 17th century. That scientific outlook assumed that nature conferred on us a collection of raw materials that the human species had to shape into a functioning world exclusively to serve humans. We now know that nature is made up of a complex, interconnected, interdependent array of organisms that are constantly creating their own environment by continually modifying it. The way each species modifies its surrounding environment creates opportunities and challenges for every species in that community.

Such modifications do not automatically result in a harmonious balance among species. The fact that 99.9 percent of all species that have existed on this planet are now extinct belies such a romantic view of nature. In fact each species is engaged, to some extent, in destroying its own environment. All species use resources that are in short supply and transform them into forms that cannot be used again by individuals of the same species. But this act of destruction serves up resources for other species. The waste created by the activity of one species becomes food for another–hence the communal, interdependent nature of the planet.

This awareness of the way in which species interact offers important lessons for agriculture. It suggests, on one hand, that any effort to create an agriculture that seeks to dominate nature while ignoring this complex, dynamic and interactive process is doomed to ultimate failure. It also means, conversely, that any effort to create an agriculture that seeks to "leave nature alone," or to achieve some kind of sustained equilibrium in nature, also is destined to fail. What we can and must do is develop an agriculture that seeks to sustain human life in a constantly changing environment. And that, of necessity, requires that we pay closer attention to all of the other complex dynamic interactions occurring in the environment on which we depend.

It follows that agriculture, to be successful in the 21st century, must employ "adaptive" rather than "control" management strategies. The problem with control management is at least twofold. First, given the dynamic, complex and interactive nature of the universe, there simply is no mechanism we can devise to effectively control even small enclaves of an ecosystem. Second, control management tends to narrow the focus of the problem in an effort to reduce it to a manageable equation and then design a solution that fits the problem. Defining problems this way readily lends them to industrial solutions. Our industrial society is well equipped to deal with problems in this manner–it is technologically, economically and administratively geared for such an approach.

Unfortunately, this approach to solving production problems in agriculture fails to acknowledge that the environment is changing constantly. Since all species are continually modifying their environments, often in response to solutions that other species have imposed, the whole system remains dynamic and interactive. The result is that our industrial solutions are almost always short-lived and often may exacerbate the problems they were designed to solve.

Joe Lewis, who worked with the Agriculture Research Service's Insect Biology and Population Management Research Laboratory in Tifton, Georgia, suggested that given these dynamic systems in nature we need to change our paradigm for dealing with agricultural pest management. He proposed that we shift from our "therapeutic intervention" approach, which seeks to eliminate an undesirable organism in our farming systems by applying a "direct counter force against it," to a natural systems approach that seeks to understand and shore up "the full composite of inherent plant defenses, plant mixtures, soil, natural enemies, and other components of the system."

Such ecological approaches to solving agriculture's production problems are proving successful in many parts of the world. A study by Jules Pretty and Rachel Hine at the University of Essex looked at 208 cases from 52 countries, involving almost 9 million farmers managing 28.82 million hectares. These farms all employed "nature's goods and services as functional inputs" to achieve production goals. In other words, they used natural systems approaches. The study revealed that these farms experienced yield increases of 50 to 100 percent on rain-fed crops and 5 to 10 percent increases on irrigated crops.

The October 1999 issue of the *Ecologist* magazine reported similar results from using these ecological approaches to solve production problems. Takao Furuno, a farmer in Japan, has developed such a system on his two-hectare farm. He devotes 1.4 hectares of his farm to rice paddies and the rest to organic vegetable production. A few years ago Mr. Furuno decided to incorporate ducks into his rice paddies. He discovered that the ducks ate the insects and snails that normally attack the rice. The ducks dine on the weed seeds and weed seedlings so he no longer needs to weed his rice paddies, and the activity of the ducks also appears to oxygenate the water "encouraging the roots of the rice plants to grow." Other species of plants and animals in his paddies provide plant nutrients. Farmers who have adopted this method in various parts of the world report a 20 to 50 percent increase in rice yields in the first year. According to the report, Furuno's small farm now annually produces "seven tonnes of rice, 300 ducks, 4,000 ducklings and enough vegetables to supply 100 people." From the perspective of the farmer's bottom line it is worth noting that Furuno not only has dramatically increased his rice yield but once he has finished with the inputs (namely the ducks) they also become a source of income.

Such ecologically driven solutions could help deal with several of the agriculturally- related problems outlined in IFAS's "Florida FIRST" project. If the Florida scientific community were to perform research that could uncover the ecological equivalent of Mr Furuno's method for Florida agriculture, it could simultaneously reduce the need for government regulation. It also could alleviate some of Florida's pest and water quality problems, improve the net income of farmers, and potentially support more people on Florida's farmland, reducing at least some of the pressure of urban encroachment.

2. It's a "Full" World

A second characteristic of our 21st century world is that we no longer possess unlimited natural resources to fuel our industrial enterprises, nor do we have unlimited sinks to absorb their wastes. This leaves us with no choice but to begin internalizing more of the costs of our industrial agriculture systems.

Industrial agriculture's success during the past century was largely due to readily available natural resources that we used to fuel our industrial agriculture enterprises. Among those natural resources were cheap fuel (especially petroleum); fertile, virgin soils; and readily available mineral deposits that could be cheaply mined and used as synthetic fertilizers. All of these natural resources are now in short supply and predictably will increase the cost of sustaining industrial agriculture.

Even more troubling is the fact that the earth's sinks which have been used to absorb the wastes of industrial agriculture are now filled to near capacity and are beginning to cause serious disruptions in the healthy functioning of the earth's ecosystems. Nitrogen pollution serves as a telling example. The five-part series on "Feeding the World, Poisoning the Planet," published in the *Baltimore Sun*, predicted an "ecological calamity" if we continue adding nitrogen to the environment at current rates. Given today's projections, nitrogen pollution will double in the next 25 years. We already have 50 dead zones on the planet due to eutrophication caused by excess nitrogen.

While 22 million tons of nitrogen are added to the environment annually by unearthing fossil fuels, the major nitrogen source is industrial farming. Fertilizer production is the primary cause of nitrogen pollution. Large-scale, concentrated production of animals, both terrestrial livestock and poultry and farmed fish, is rapidly becoming an additional major contributor to nitrogen pollution. These animal systems generate an accumulation of manure that cannot be cycled back to the fields where the grain to feed the animals was produced, creating a double nitrogen pollution problem. More synthetic nitrogen then has to be manufactured to fertilize the grain to feed the animals, and the animal manure cannot be disposed of without polluting the environment with excess nitrogen.

Further difficulties may be lurking in an unsolved nitrogen mystery. Experts have determined that only about one-fifth of all the nitrogen "leaking from human activities appears to end up in waterways. The rest is unaccounted for." While some of the excess is recycling into the atmosphere, experts suspect that some also is accumulating in soils. This raises the question of whether "soils are becoming so saturated that millions of tons of nitrogen soon will begin leaking out to further taint our waters?"

As our industrial systems continue to load the environment with these and other wastes, they increasingly invite draconian regulations and add substantially to production costs. The Netherlands, which harbors the world's highest concentration of farm animals, may serve as an example of what farmers in other parts of the world will be facing if we fail to adopt more ecologically sound farming practices. The Dutch Levy Bureau now monitors animal manure with the same vigilance and sophisticated techniques that are used to track drug money launderers. A Dutch farmer can be taxed thousands of dollars a year for livestock manure excesses.

3. Markets as Conversations

A third characteristic of our 21st century world can be found in the marketplace. A fundamental shift is taking place in the way we communicate with one another. We have moved from a broadcast era to a conversation era thanks to the Internet. As a book, *The Cluetrain Manifesto*, points out, the Web is not simply a new medium of communication, it is a "global set of conversations–people talking together, in their own voices, about what they care about."

This shift in the way we obtain our information likely will have a profound effect on the way people do business, and therefore on the way our food and agriculture enterprises are organized. The day of "broadcasting" information to prospective buyers through high-powered media campaigns, aimed at getting people to buy food products, is rapidly coming to a close. These marketing strategies were designed to keep people from knowing what went on in the production and processing of food, and focused entirely on convincing people to buy the end product. People were treated like "consumers"—passive objects of media campaigns intent on cajoling them into making a purchase.

But the 21st century food buyer has grown up with the Internet and will have experienced the world as a set of intimate conversations, not as a billboard broadcasting marketing slogans. Today people can have an informed conversation about anything they wish with almost anyone they choose. So, increasingly, food shoppers will want to have a conversation about the food they buy. Where was it produced? Who grew it? How were the animals treated? What was the impact on the environment? How were the workers treated? Did they get a fair share of the profits? Increasingly, food customers will seek for and find the answers to their questions. This will have a profound effect on the way food is grown and marketed. Food will have to be sold with a story, and the story will have to meet the expectations of the customer–and it had better be authentic.

Marketing as conversation will create opportunities to decentralize the food system. Different people in different cultures want to buy their food with different stories. That will provide opportunities for small and midsize farms to partner with midsize processors and retailers to market their food products with the kind of story that their particular customers want to support. New technologies will enable food customers to access the story of their food in the grocery store. In Denmark, computer scanners already in stores are connected to food stories via barcode tracking systems. By placing a food item under the scanner, the computer shows pictures of the family that raised the food, the environment in which it was produced, and the processing facility where it was processed.

This new way of looking at food is a golden opportunity to develop an assortment of regional food value chains that create partnerships among farmers who use sound ecological practices, processors that maintain high food quality and retailers that operate locally owned businesses.

4. The Global Economy

The 20th century has been dominated by an economic theory that assumes all human activity is determined by economic incentives. That paradigm has created two serious problems for agriculture.

First, it perpetuates, as William Rees at the University of British Columbia puts it, an economic mindset that is totally "money-based." And a money-based economy ignores "both the biophysical basis of the economic process and the behavioral dynamics of the ecosystems within which it takes place." Accordingly, our economic system has ignored the facts that farms are biological organisms which exist within ecosystems and therefore function within certain biological constraints, and that agriculture exists within human communities, making the health of both the community and the farm dependent on one another.

Since specialization and routinization increase processing efficiency, industrial food systems–operating solely on a money-based economy–require that processing operations be simplified by using as few commodities as possible. Farmers, in such an industrial system, therefore are reduced to being raw materials suppliers of only one or two commodities. Farms, accordingly, have become huge monoculture factories. Yet, biodiversity is the key to the resilience of any biological system, including farms. The result is that the specialization demanded by "efficient" processing systems has turned farms into biologically dysfunctional operations that can remain productive only by introducing an ever increasing quantity of exogenous inputs–and, increasingly, by bolstering them with huge infusions of taxpayer subsidies. As a consequence, farmers continue to go bankrupt, the environment continues to deteriorate, and local communities continue to decline.

Secondly, economic determinism inevitably fosters social and environmental decline since it always seeks to obtain labor and raw materials as cheaply as possible, and to externalize as much risk as possible. Capital, accordingly, will flow to the lowest common denominator. This is why Florida farmers are experiencing pressures from foreign markets. Global markets will always require raw materials for food products to be produced wherever these materials can be accessed most cheaply. And given the dramatically lower land and labor costs in other parts of the world, markets will inevitably source raw materials from those locations. Steven Blank, agricultural economist at the University of California-Davis, following the rationale of this economic paradigm to its logical conclusion, has suggested that the United States should just get out of the farming business altogether and concentrate its labor force on higher value- producing activity. From a strict economic determinist point of view, that makes perfect sense. What it fails to do, however, is to take into consideration the values of food security, vibrant rural communities, and well-managed local ecologies, none of which can be measured by a strict money-based economy.

A related cost of our global economy also is being experienced by Florida agriculture. The concern expressed in the Florida FIRST papers over introduction of new pests is likely to increase with our current food and agriculture system. As the sourcing of raw materials for food and fiber from distant ecologies intensifies, alien species from those ecologies increasingly will hitchhike along for the ride, and be introduced into our farming neighborhoods. Past experience has taught us that such alien species introduced into ecologies where they did not evolve can be devastating to agriculture. Yvonne Baskin, renowned ecologist, reported that such invader species cost the United States between $5.5 and $7.5 billion annually, with most of the cost falling to agriculture. That figure does not include the harm invader species cause native species and ecosystems, damage which eventually also affects agriculture.

As industrial food systems, driven by economic determinism, expand the practice of sourcing raw materials from distant ecologies, local ecologies become increasingly vulnerable to pests and diseases which can be devastating to agriculture, especially in places like Florida which provide ideal breeding grounds for alien pests and diseases. And as our own ecologies become more brittle, owing to specialized monoculture production, the problem will intensify. The threat of hoof and mouth disease may be only a symptom of a much larger, systemic problem in this regard.

An Alternative Vision

Land grant universities are in a good position to explore an alternative vision for agriculture that is economically viable, ecologically resilient, and socially vibrant. To be effective, the new vision must take into account the characteristics of the world in which we now live. The old paradigms and the old structures will become increasingly dysfunctional.

What will the new agriculture look like? Farms couldl look a lot like Takao Furuno's farm. Not that all the farms will be five acres in size, but they will be more ecology driven and less technology dependent. Biodiversity will be the key to their economic and ecological resilience. All waste in the system will be food for another part of the system, and most of the energy will be "current"-derived from solar sources. And the communities in which the farms exist will be more vibrant economically and socially. This will occur because more of the value of the agricultural enterprises will be retained on farms and in local communities. Less farm income will be spent on exogenous inputs, and therefore more of the earned income will be retained in the farm operation and be available for investment in improved local enterprises and social institutions.

What will agricultural policy look like? It will be less commodity based and more community based. Public support for agriculture will be geared more to producing public goods, like better soil and water quality, more resilient wild landscapes and habitat for wild species. It will be aimed at helping young farmers get started in economically vibrant regional food production systems, rather than subsidizing the production of raw materials for an industrial, global food system. It might include a living wage scheme for farmers and farm workers to improve the quality of life for rural families, and therefore for rural communities.

What will the food market look like? Increasingly food will be sold with an accompanying food story. Those food stories will create many new opportunities for small and medium-size farms to partner with regional food processing and retail enterprises to produce and preserve the identity of food produced in an identifiable manner. Hogs raised in hoop barns (where they are free to roam and root, where no antibiotics or growth hormones are used, and where the manure and urine are captured in deep litter and then composted to be applied to fields as a source of natural fertilizer) will be processed in locally owned processing facilities and marketed in regional retail stores. Computer scanners at the stores will allow local food shoppers to run their package of pork ribs by the scanner and view the family that raised the hogs, see the pigs playing in the hoop barns, see the pork being processed in the locally-owned facility, and have complete access to information describing how the waste from each part of the system was recycled. And if they wish, they can have a conversation with any of the parties involved by accessing the information available to them on the Internet.

Most food products will be sold with similar stories. The entire process will be transparent. Increasingly food entrepreneurs will work to earn the trust of the people who buy their products and everyone in the food chain will work to keep their food story authentic, because if the conversations their customers have reveal that the story is not authentic, their market will evaporate. The story is the market.

New policies designed to support communities instead of commodities, new production systems that make the best use of nature's goods and services, and new markets that invite conversations–these innovations can alter today's food and agriculture systems to make them compatible with our 21st century world.

Transitions from one world-view to another are always difficult and sometimes painful. Certainly we face many uncertainties as we study the problems of our 20th century food and agriculture system and seek to redesign it to suit the realities of our 21st century world. Standing on the threshold of such transitions always affords us the choice of viewing the future as the unfortunate demise of an old, but troubled system, or a timely opportunity to participate in the birth of a new and more functional system.

I believe that the vision I have tried to offer here is compatible with the commitment that the University of Florida's Institute of Food and Agricultural Sciences has made in its "Florida FIRST" initiative. Hopefully this paper can provide an overarching framework to help guide that important work.

A PROMISE OF A MORE CIVIC AGRICULTURE

By Thomas A. Lyson, Ph. D.

The term *civic agriculture* has jumped onto the food policy scene in response to recent discussions over the future of food and agricultural systems in the U.S. While the American food and agricultural system continues to follow a decades-old path of industrialization and globalization, a counter trend toward localizing some agricultural and food production has appeared. I have labeled this rebirth of locally-based agricultural and food production civic agriculture. Civic agriculture references the emergence and growth of community-based agriculture and food production activities that not only meet consumer demands for fresh, safe, and locally produced foods, but create jobs, encourage entrepreneurship, and strengthen community identity. Civic agriculture brings together production and consumption activities within communities and offers consumers real alternatives to the commodities produced, processed, and marketed by large agribusiness firms.

Based on an extensive review of the literature, I have identified several characteristics associated with civic agriculture in the United States. Civic agriculture producers are oriented toward local markets and meeting the needs of local consumers rather than national or international mass markets. Civic agriculture is viewed as an integral part of rural communities, not merely as production of commodities. Civic agriculture farmers are concerned more with high quality and value added products than with quantity (yield) and least cost production practices. Production at the farm-level is often more labor intensive and land intensive and less capital intensive and land extensive. Civic farm enterprises tend to be considerably smaller in scale and scope than industrial producers. Farmers more often rely on indigenous, site-specific knowledge and less often on a uniform set of "best management practices." Producers forge direct market links to consumers rather than indirect links through middlemen, such as wholesalers, brokers, processors, and the like.

Civic agriculture enterprises are visible in many forms on the local landscape. *Farmers' markets* provide immediate, low-cost, direct contact between local farmers and consumers and are an effective economic development strategy for communities seeking to establish stronger local food systems. *Community* and *school gardens* provide fresh produce to under served populations, teach food production skills to people of all ages, and contribute to agricultural literacy. *Small-scale organic farmers* across the country have pioneered the development of local marketing systems and formed 'production networks' that are akin to manufacturing industrial districts. *Community Supported Agriculture* (CSA) operations forge direct links between non-farm households and their CSA farms. New *grower-controlled marketing cooperatives* are forming, especially in peri-urban areas, to more effectively tap emerging regional markets for locally produced food and agricultural products. *Agricultural districts* organized around particular commodities (such as wine) have served to

---

Thomas A. Lyson (1948–2006) was Liberty Hyde Bailey Professor in the department of Sociology at Cornell University. He served as director of Cornell's Farming Alternative Program, as a researcher for the Center of Economic Studies of the U.S. Census Bureau, and as a senior Fulbright research fellow in sociology at the University of Canterbury, Christchurch, New Zealand.

stabilize farms and farmland in many areas of the country. *Community kitchens* provide the infrastructure and technical expertise necessary to launch new food-based enterprises. *Specialty producers* and *on-farm processors* of products for which there are not well developed mass markets (deer, goat/sheep cheese, free range chickens, organic dairy products, etc.) and *small scale, off-farm, local processors* add value in local communities and provide markets for farmers who cannot or choose not to produce bulk commodities for the mass market. What these civic agriculture efforts have in common is that they have the potential to nurture local economic development, maintain diversity and quality in products, and provide forums where producers and consumers can come together to solidify bonds of community.

Civic agriculture then, is the embedding of local agricultural and food production in the community. Civic agriculture is not only a source of family income for farmers and food processors, but civic agricultural enterprises contribute to community health and vitality in a variety of social, economic, political and cultural ways. For example, civic agriculture increases agricultural and food literacy by directly linking consumers to producers. Likewise, civic agricultural enterprises have a much higher local economic multiplier than farms or processors that are producing for the global mass-market.

Civic agriculture should not be confused with civic farmers. Farmers who vote in local elections, sit on school boards, are active members of local service clubs such as Rotary, Lions, or Kiwanis, and otherwise participate in the civic affairs of their communities may be seen as 'good citizens.' However, a farm or food operation that is unconnected from the local community, that produces for the export market, that relies on non-local hired labor, and that provides few benefits for its workers is not a civic enterprise, regardless of the civic engagement of its operator.

Obviously, no agricultural or food enterprise is without some civic merit. However, large-scale, contract poultry and hog operations would probably lie at the far outside end of civicness. Likewise, large-scale, absentee-owned or operated, industrial-like, fruit and vegetable farms that rely on large numbers of migrant workers and export their products around the world would not be deemed very civic.

The conventional approach to production agriculture has been to treat the farm operator as a manager and as an individual 'problem solver.' The role of Cooperative Extension has been to provide the farmer with the 'tools' (skills, information, technology) necessary to make the best decisions within the parameters of his or her own farm. The farm operator, not the local community, has been the sole locus of attention, program development, and action. Farmers who 'failed' to make a profit and subsequently went out of business were deemed 'bad managers' by the agricultural establishment.

Civic agriculture is a locally organized system of agriculture and food production characterized by networks of producers who are bound together by place. Civic agriculture embodies a commitment to developing and strengthening an economically, environmentally, and socially sustainable system of agriculture and food production that relies on local resources and serves local markets and consumers. The economic imperative to earn a profit is filtered through a set of cooperative and mutually supporting social relations. Community problem solving, rather than individual competition, is the foundation of civic agriculture.

The Global Food System

In order to effect a shift to civic agriculture, it is critical that we recognize and address the fact that control of today's food system rests primarily with powerful and highly concentrated economic interests, and not with local communities or even government. Large-scale, well-managed, capital intensive, technologically sophisticated, industrial-like farm operations have become tightly tied into a network of national and global food producers. Industrial farms produce large quantities of highly standardized bulk commodities that are fed into large national and multinational integrators and processors. A few thousand very large farms account for most of the gross agricultural sales, but these farms are not representative of the majority of individual farm income. There are about two million farms in the U.S. today and over half of these farms sell less than $10,000 a year of agricultural products. Yet these farms account for only 1.5% of all sales in the country. On the other side of the spectrum, about 1% of the farms in the U.S. report sales over $1 million a year. However, this one percent of farms accounts for almost 42% of all sales. Taken further, the largest one-tenth of 1% of all farms, those with sales over $5 million a year, account for 20.5% of all sales—and this segment is growing. Looked at another way, there are about 2,800 farms in the U.S. today with sales over $5 million a year. These 2,800 farms account for almost fourteen times the sales of the nearly one million smallest farms, those with sales less than $10,000 a year.

The task of organizing and coordinating the production, processing and distribution of food has fallen into the hands of very large multinational agribusiness firms. Today, mass-production food processors and distributors along with mass market retailers have become dominant fixtures in the American food economy. These large-scale producers and retailers provide abundant quantities of relatively inexpensive, standardized goods. The degree of concentration has reached the point where the ten largest U.S. based multinational corporations control about 60 percent of the food and beverages sold in the United States. According to *Prepared Foods*, the leading trade publication for the food and beverage industry, total sales of food and beverage products in the U.S. for 1999/2000 amounted to over $260 billion. The ten largest publicly traded U.S. corporations and their 1999/2000 sales (in $billions) were Phillip Morris ($31.1), Pepsico ($20.4), Coca Cola ($19.8), Conagra ($19.0), IBP Inc. ($14.1), Sara Lee ($10.6), Anheuser Busch ($9.7), H.J. Heinz ($9.4), Best Foods ($8.6), and Nabisco ($8.3). Several international corporations, also with annual sales in the billions of dollars, such as Diageo (UK), Nestle (Switzerland), Unilever N.V. (Netherlands and UK), and Danone (France) also control a substantial portion of the U.S. food dollar through their subsidiaries.

In a similar vein, Bill Heffernan (1999) recently identified three "food chain clusters" 1) Cargill/Monsanto, 2) Conagra, and 3) Novartis/ADM that have emerged as dominant political and economic forces in American agriculture. The large-scale, industrial-like farms that produce the bulk commodities that are processed by large food processors are becoming mere cogs in a large agribusiness machine. On the one hand, farmers who produce for the mass market must now rely on the genetically modified seeds and the special fertilizers and pesticides produced by the large multinational input suppliers. On the other hand, their marketing choices are restricted to the small number of large multinational food processors who control most of the market.

Turning Toward Civic Agriculture

While corporate interests are likely to continue to influence the food system in the direction of increased economic globalization, there are options available for communities, groups, and local governments. Last fall, Brother David Andrews (2000), writing in *Catholic Rural Life*, posed the following challenge. "In a country which increasingly takes for granted what we eat, who grew it, how it was grown, how its growth affected the environment and the local community, how it got to us, and how it affects our bodies, it is paramount to raise the questions about our food system and to search for more positive alternatives. (*Catholic Rural Life*, pg) I believe that local governments, community organizations, and even churches have many tools which can be used to effect change and move toward a more civic agriculture. Some of these tools include encouraging local economic development efforts to support community-based food processing activities; fostering land use policies that protect active farm areas from random residential development; enacting and enforcing zoning codes that allocate land into areas of non-farm development, areas of natural preservation, and areas for agricultural production; instituting institutional food acquisition practices that integrate local food production directly into the community; and developing educational programs to increase agricultural literacy among both children and adults including school and community gardens, summer internship programs, and community-farm days. The Catholic Church has always had ties to agriculture and farming. Indeed, many orders, schools, colleges, universities and even parishes have operated their own farms for generations, providing food for themselves and those in nearby communities. And in recent years, church related organizations have provided the moral basis for the movement to a more sustainable agriculture.

As the NCRLC (1996) recently noted in their publication *Religious Congregations on the Land*, "There is a growing consensus today, recovered from our religious traditions, of what is needed in the way of a sacramental worldview and a spirituality sustaining environmental ethic." However, despite a sound moral foundation, the NCRLC noted "What is still lacking are demonstrable examples of how to integrate these practices, especially at the level of the household and local economies. What is needed are viable economic alternatives that can be put into place today in a way that simultaneously produces spiritual, environmental, and community renewal."

Developing and nurturing civic agriculture is one way that the NCRLC challenge can be met. An agricultural development agenda organized around civic agriculture principles can link sustainable agriculture, sustainable communities/economies, and spiritual identity. Already there is evidence of a growing, though as yet unorganized, church-based Community Supported Agriculture (CSA) movement. The Poor Handmaids of Jesus Christ in Donaldson, IN; the Heartland Farm and Spirituality Center in Pawnee Rock, KS; the Sisters of Saint Joseph in Kalamazoo, MI; and the Passionist Nuns in Clarks

Summit, PA are some of the Catholic communities that have established CSA's on their farms. Other orders and communities have organized farmers' markets. For example, a group of nuns working through Catholic Charities in central New York has operated a bi-weekly farmers' market in Cincinnatus, NY since 1989. And many parishes across the country provide space and assistance for farmers' markets.

Civic agriculture, then, as one aspect of the civic community, becomes a powerful template around which to build non- or extra-market relationships between persons, social groups, and institutions which have been distanced from each other. Indeed a growing number of community groups, including churches, across the U.S. are recognizing that creative new forms of community development, built around the regeneration of local food systems, may eventually generate sufficient economic and political power to mute the more socially and environmentally destructive manifestations of the global marketplace. A turn toward a more civic agriculture is both theoretically and practically possible. Indeed, the seeds have been sown and are taking root throughout the United States. Civic agriculture represents a promising economic alternative that can nurture community businesses, save farms, and preserve farmland by providing consumers with fresh, locally produced agricultural and food products.

Endnotes

Andrews, David. 2000. "The Lord's table, the world's food." *Catholic Rural Life* 43(1):36-42.

Heffernan, William. 1999. Consolidation in the Food and Agriculture System. Report to the National Farmers Union (http://nfu.org/).

National Catholic Rural Life Conference. 1996. *Religious Congregations on the Land*. Des Moines, IA.

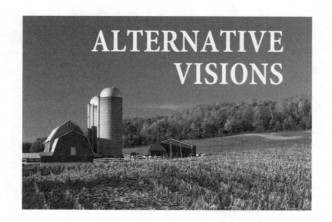

ALTERNATIVE
VISIONS

ENVIRONMENTAL SOCIOLOGY: A NEW PARADIGM

By William R. Catton, Jr. and Riley E. Dunlap

Ostensibly diverse and competing theoretical perspectives in sociology are alike in their shared anthropocentrism. From any of these perspectives, therefore, much contemporary and future social experience has to seem anomalous. Environmental sociologists attempt to understand recent societal changes by means of a nonanthropocentric paradigm. Because ecosystem constraints now pose serious problems both far human societies and for sociology, three assumptions quite different from the prevalent Human Exceptionalism Paradigm (HEP) have become essential. They form a New Environmental Paradigm (NEP). Sociologists who accept this New Environmental Paradigm have no difficulty appreciating the sociological relevance of variables traditionally excluded from sociology. The core of environmental sociology is, in fact, study of interactions between environment and society. Recent work by NEP-oriented

Sociology appears to have reached an impasse. Efforts of sociologists to assimilate into their favorite theories some of the astounding events that have shaped human societies within the last generation have sometimes contributed more to the fragmentation of the sociological community than to the convincing explanation of social facts. But as Thomas Kuhn (1962:76) has shown, such an impasse often signifies "that an occasion for retooling has arrived."

The rise of environmental problems, and especially apprehensions about "limits to growth," signalled sharp departures from the exuberant expectations most sociologists had shared with the general public. Environmental problems and constraints contributed to the general uneasiness in American society brought about by events in the sixties. Sociologists, no less than other thinking people, are still grappling with the dramatic shift from the calmer fifties, when the American dreams of social progress, upward mobility, and societal stability seemed secure.

William R. Catton, Jr. is a faculty member emeritus in the department of Sociology at Washington State University. He is a recipient of the WSU College of Arts and Sciences Distinguished Faculty Achievement Award (1989) and participated in the Environmental Science Program. His research interests include the division of labor and the ecological basis of revolutionary change.

Riley E. Dunlap is a faculty member in the department of Sociology at Oklahoma State University. He has served as Gallup Scholar in the Environment for the Gallup Organization since 1999 and as past chairs of the American Sociological Association and the Society for the Study of Social Problems. His research interests include environmental sociology, political sociology and survey research methods.

The authors contributed equally to the preparation of this paper, and are listed alphabetically. At various times we have had the benefit of stimulating discussions, for which we are grateful, with the following colleagues or graduate students: Don A. Dillman, Viktor Gecas, Dennis L. Peck, Kenneth R. Tremblay, Jr., Kent D. Van Liere, John M. Wardwell, and Robert L. Wisniewski. We are especially indebted to Don Dillman for his critical reading of an earlier draft of this paper. Dunlap's contribution to the paper was supported by Project 0158, Department of Rural Sociology, Washington State University, and this is Scientific Paper No. 4933, College of Agriculture Research Center, Washington State University, Pullman, WA 99164.

In 1976 the American Sociological Association, following precedents set a few years earlier in the Rural Sociological Society and in the Society for the Study of Social Problems, established a new "Section on Environmental Sociology."[1] In this paper we shall try to account for the development of environmental sociology by showing how it represents an attempt to understand recent societal changes that are difficult to comprehend from traditional sociological perspectives. We contend that, rather than simply representing the rise of another speciality within the discipline, the emergence of environmental sociology reflects the development of a new paradigm, and that this paradigm may help to extricate us from the impasse referred to above.

The "New Environmental Paradigm" (NEP) implicit in environmental sociology is, of course, only one among several current candidates to replace or amend the increasingly obsolescent set of "domain assumptions" which have defined the nature of social reality for most sociologists. Environmental sociologists, no less than the advocates of the very different alternatives Gouldner (1970) has described, are attempting to come to grips with a changed "sense of what is real." Further, we believe the NEP may contribute to a better understanding of contemporary and future social conditions than is possible with previous sociological perspectives. To illustrate the power of this paradigm to shed new light on important sociological issues, we shall briefly describe some recent NEP-based examinations of problems in stratification. But first we must contrast the old and new sets of assumptions.

The "Human Exceptionalism Paradigm"

The numerous competing theoretical perspectives in contemporary sociology—e.g., functionalism, symbolic interactionism, ethnomethodology, conflict theory, Marxism, and so forth—are prone to exaggerate their differences from each other. They purport to be paradigms in their own right, and are often taken as such (see, e.g., Denisoff, *et al.*, 1974, and Ritzer, 1975). But they have also been construed simply as competing "preparadigmatic" perspectives (Friedrichs, 1972). We maintain that their apparent diversity is not as important as the fundamental anthropocentrism underlying *all* of them.

This mutual anthropocentrism is part of a basic sociological worldview (Klausner, 1971:10–11). We call that worldview the "Human Exceptionalism Paradigm" (HEP). We contend that acceptance of the assumptions of the HEP has made it difficult for most sociologists, regardless of their preferred orientation, to deal meaningfully with the social implications of ecological problems and constraints. Thus, the HEP has become increasingly obstructive of sociological efforts to comprehend contemporary and future social experience.

The HEP comprises several assumptions that have either been challenged by recent additions to knowledge, or have had their optimistic implications contradicted by events of the seventies. Accepted explicitly or implicitly by all existing theoretical persuasions, they include:

1. Humans are unique among the earth's creatures, for they have culture.

2. Culture can vary almost infinitely and can change much more rapidly than biological traits.

3. Thus, many human differences are socially induced rather than inborn, they can be socially altered, and inconvenient differences can be eliminated.

4. Thus, also, cultural accumulation means that progress can continue without limit, making all social problems ultimately soluble.

Sociological acceptance of such an optimistic worldview was no doubt fostered by prevalence of the doctrine of progress in Western culture, where academic sociology was spawned and nurtured. It was under the American branch of Western culture that sociology flourished most fully, and it has been clear to foreign analysts of American life, from Tocqueville to Laski, that most Americans (until recently) ardently believed that the present was better than the past and the future would improve upon the present. Sociologists could easily share that conviction when natural resources were still so plentiful that limits to progress remained unseen. The historian, David Potter (1954:141), tried to alert his colleagues to

---

[1] In the late sixties a Natural Resources Research Group was formed in the RSS, and in 1973 SSSP established an Environmental Problems Division.

some of the unstated and unexamined assumptions shaping their studies; his words have equal relevance for sociologists: "The factor of abundance, which we first discovered as an environmental condition and which we then converted by technological change into a cultural as well as a physical force, has... influenced all aspects of American life in a fundamental way."[2]

Not only have sociologists been too unmindful of the fact that our society derived special qualities from past abundance; the heritage of abundance has made it difficult for most sociologists to perceive the possibility of an era of uncontrived scarcity. For example, ecological concepts such as "carrying capacity" are alien to the vocabularies of most sociologists (Catton, 1976a; 1976b), yet disregard for this concept has been tantamount to assuming an environment's carrying capacity is always enlargeable as needed—thus denying the possibility of scarcity.

Neglect of the ecosystem-dependence of human society has been evident in sociological literature on economic development (e.g., Horowitz, 1972), which has simply not recognized biogeochemical limits to material progress. And renewed sociological attention to a theory of societal evolution (e.g., Parsons, 1977) has seldom paid much attention to the resource base that is subjected to "more efficient" exploitation as societies become more differentiated internally and are thereby "adaptively upgraded." In such literature, the word "environment" refers almost entirely to a society's "symbolic environment" (cultural systems) or "social environment" (environing social systems).[3]

It is the habit of neglecting laws of other sciences (such as the Principle of Entropy and the Law of Conservation of Energy)[4]—as if human actions were unaffected by them—that enables so distinguished a sociologist as Daniel Bell (1973: 465) to assert that the question before humanity is "not subsistence but standard of living, not biology, but sociology," to insist that basic needs "are satiable, and the possibility of abundance is real," to impute "apocalyptic hysteria" to "the ecology movement," and to regard it as trite rather than questionable to expect "compound interest" growth to continue for another hundred years. Likewise, this neglect permits Amos Hawley (1975:8-9) to write that "there are no known limits to the improvement of technology" and the population pressure on nonagricultural resources is neither "currently being felt or likely to be felt in the early future." Such views reflect a staunch commitment to the HEP.

Environmental Sociology and the "New Environmental Paradigm"

When public apprehension began to be aroused concerning newly visible environmental problems, the scientists who functioned as opinion leaders were not sociologists. They included such Individuals as Rachel Carson, Barry Commoner, Paul Ehrlich and Garrett Hardin—biologists. Leadership in highlighting the precariousness of the human condition was mostly forfeited by sociologists, because until recently, most of us had been socialized into a worldview that makes it difficult to recognize the reality and full significance of the environmental problems and constraints we now confront. Due to our acceptance of the HEP, our discipline has focused on humans to the neglect of habitat; consideration of our *social* environment has crowded out consideration of our physical circumstances (Michelson, 1976:17). Further, we have had unreserved faith that equilibrium between population and resources could and would be reached in noncatastrophic ways, since technology and organization would mediate the relations between a growing population and its earthly habitat (see, e.g., Hawley, 1975).

But, stimulated by troubling events, some sociologists began to read such works as Carson (1962), Commoner (1971), Ehrlich and Ehrlich (1970), and Hardin (1968), and began to shed the blinders of the HEP. As long-held assumptions began to lose their power over our perceptions, we began to recognize that the reality of ecological constraints posed serious problems for human societies *and* for the discipline of sociology (see, e.g., Burch, 1971). It began to appear that, in order to make sense of the world, it was necessary to rethink the traditional Durkheimian norm of sociological purity—i.e., that social facts can be explained *only* by linking them to other *social* facts. The gradual result of such rethinking has been the development of environmental sociology.

---

[2] For an early warning that this exuberance-producing force could be temporary, see Sumner (1896). Few twentieth century sociologists have taken the warning seriously.

[3] Even sociological human ecologists have limited their attention primarily to the *social* or *spatial* environment, rather than the *physical* environment (see Michelson, 1976:17-23), reflecting their adherence to the HEP.

[4] See Miller (1972) for a lucid discussion of these laws.

Environmental sociology is clearly still in its formative years. At the turn of the decade rising concern with "environment" as a social problem led to numerous studies of public attitudes toward environmental issues and of the "Environmental Movement" (see Albrecht and Mauss, 1975). A coalition gradually developed between sociologists with such interests and sociologists with a range of other concerns—including rather established interests such as the "built" environment, natural hazards, resource management and outdoor recreation, as well as newer interests such as "social impact assessment" (mandated by the National Environmental Policy Act of 1969). After the energy crisis of 1973, numerous sociologists (including many with prior interests in one or more of the above areas) began to investigate the effects of energy shortages in particular, and resource constraints in general, on society: the stratification system, the political order, the family, and so on. (For an indication of the range of interests held by environmental sociologists see Dunlap, 1975, and Manderscheid, 1977; for reviews of the literature see Dunlap and Catton, forthcoming, and Humphrey and Buttel, 1976.)

These diverse interests are linked into an increasingly distinguishable specialty known as environmental sociology by the acceptance of "environmental" variables as meaningful for sociological investigation. Conceptions of "environment" range from the "manmade" (or "built") environment to the "natural" environment, with an array of "human-altered" environments—e.g., air, water, noise and visual pollution—in between. In fact, *the study of interaction between the environment and society is the core of environmental sociology*, as advocated several years ago by Schnaiberg (1972).[5] This involves studying the effects of the environment on society (e.g., resource abundance or scarcity on stratification) and the effects of society on the environment (e.g., the contributions of differing economic systems to environmental degradation).[6]

The study of such interaction rests on the recognition that sociologists can no longer afford to ignore the environment in their investigations, and this in turn appears to depend on at least tacit acceptance of a set of assumptions quite different from those of the HEP. From the writings of several environmental sociologists (e.g., Anderson, 1976; Burch, 1971, 1976; Buttel, 1976; Catton, 1976a, 1976b; Morrison, 1976; Schnaiberg, 1972, 1975) it is possible to extract a set of assumptions about the nature of social reality which stand in stark contrast to the HEP. We call this set of assumptions the "New Environmental Paradigm" or NEP (see Dunlap and Van Liere, 1977 for a broader usage of the term, referring to emerging public beliefs):

1. Human beings are but one species among the many that are interdependently involved in the biotic communities that shape our social life.

2. Intricate linkages of cause and effect and feedback in the web of nature produce many unintended consequences from purposive human action.

3. The world is finite, so there are potent physical and biological limits constraining economic growth, social progress, and other societal phenomena.

Environmental Facts and Social Facts

Sociologists who adhere to the NEP readily accept as factual the opening sentences of the lead article (by a perceptive economist) in a recent issue *of Social Science Quarterly* devoted to "Society and Scarcity": "We have inherited, occupy, and will bequeath a world of scarcity: resources are not adequate to provide all of everything we want. It is a world, therefore, of limitations, constraints, and conflict, requiring the bearing of costs and calling for communal coordination" (Allen, 1976:263). Persistent adherents of the HEP, on the other hand, accustomed to relying on endless and generally benign technological and organizational breakthroughs, could be expected to discount such a statement as a mere manifestation of the naive presumption that the "state of the arts" is fixed (see, e.g., Hawley, 1975:6–7).

Likewise sociologists who have been converted to the assumptions of the NEP have no difficulty appreciating the sociological relevance of the following fact: the $36 billion it now costs annually to import oil to supplement depleted Ameri-

---

[5] This does not mean that environmental sociologists focus only on bi-variate relationships between social and environmental variables, as illustrated by Schnaiberg's (1975) "societal-environmental dialectic" (to be discussed below).

[6] For an alternative and narrower view of the domain of environmental sociology see Zeisel (1975: Chap 1)

can supplies is partially defrayed by exporting $23 billion worth of agricultural products—grown at the cost of enormous soil erosion (van Bavel, 1977). Environmental sociologists expect momentous social change if soil or oil, or both are depleted. But sociologists still bound by the HEP would probably ignore such topics, holding that oil and soil are irrelevant variables for sociologists. However, we believe that only by taking into account such factors as declining energy resources can sociologists continue to understand and explain "social facts." We will attempt to demonstrate this by examining some work by NEP-oriented sociologists in one of the areas they have begun to examine—social stratification.

Usefulness of the NEP: Recent Work in Social Stratification

The bulk of existing work in stratification appears to rest on the Human Excep- tionalism Paradigm, as it "... does not adequately consider the context of resource constraints or lack thereof in which the stratification system operates..." (Morrison, 1973:83). We will therefore describe recent work in the area by environmental sociologists, in an effort to illustrate the insights into stratification processes provided by the NEP. We will limit the discussion to three topics: the current decline in living conditions experienced by many Americans; contemporary and likely future cleavages in our stratification system; and the problematic prospects for ending self-perpetuating poverty.

Recent decline in standard of living: A majority of Americans are concerned about their economic situation (Strumpet, 1976:23), and in *Food, Shelter and the American Dream*, Aronowitz (1974) exemplifies the growing awareness that *something* is not going according to expectation—that old ideals of societal progress, increasing prosperity and material comfort, and individual and intergenerational mobility for *all* segments of society are *not* being realized (also see Anderson, 1976:1–3). Yet, even a "critical sociologist" such as Aronowitz seems impeded by the HEP in attempting to understand these changes. He views recent shortages in food, gasoline, heating oil, and so on, entirely as the result of "manipulations" by large national and supranational corporations, and is skeptical of the idea that resource scarcities may be real. Thus, his solution to the decline in the American standard of living would apparently be solely political—reduce the power of large corporations.

Although many environmental sociologists would not deny that oil companies have benefited from energy shortages, their acceptance of the NEP leads to a different explanation of recent economic trends. Schnaiberg (1975:6-8), for instance, has explicated a very useful "societal-environmental dialectic." Given the *thesis* that "economic expansion is a social desideratum" and the *antithesis* that "ecological disruption is a necessary consequence of economic expansion," a dialectic emerges with the acceptance of the proposition that "ecological disruption is harmful to human society." Schnaiberg notes three alternative *syntheses* of the dialectic: (1) an *economic synthesis* which ignores ecological disruptions and attempts to maximize growth; (2) *a managed scarcity synthesis*[7] which deals with the most obvious and pernicious consequences of resource-utilization by imposing controls over selected industries and resources; and (3) an *ecological synthesis* in which "substantial control over both production and effective demand for goods" is used to minimize ecological disruptions and maintain a "sustained yield" of resources. Schnaiberg (1975:9-10) argues that the synthesis adopted will be influenced by the basic economic structure of a society, with "regressive" (inequality-magnifying) societies most likely to maintain the "economic" synthesis and "progressive" (equality-fostering) societies least resistive to the "ecological" syntehsis.[8] Not surprisingly, therefore, the U.S., with its "non-redistributive" economy, has increasingly opted for "managed scarcity" as the solution to environmental and resource problems.[9]

Managed scarcity involves, for example, combating ecological disruptions by forcing industries to abate pollution, with resultant costs passed along to consumers via higher prices, and combating resource shortages via higher taxes (and thus higher consumer prices) on the scarce resources. There is growing recognition of the highly regressive impacts of both mechanisms (Morrison, 1977; Schnaiberg, 1975), and thus governmental reliance on "managed scarcity" to cope with

---

[7] Schnaiberg's term was "planned scarcity," but because adherents of the HEP might suppose that phrase referred to scarcity *caused* by planners—rather than scarcities (and their costs) *allocated* by planners—we prefer to speak of "managed scarcity."

[8] Thus, e.g., among industrialized nations Sweden appears to have come closest to the ecological synthesis, while China represents the closest approximation to it by any developing nation (Anderson, 1976:242–251). In contrast, highly regressive developing nations such as Brazil seem strongly committed to the economic synthesis.

[9] The U.S. economy is "non-redistributive" because overall patterns of inequality (i.e., relative shares of wealth) have been altered very little by growth, even though all strata have improved their lot via growth (Schnaiberg, 1975:9; Zeitlin, 1977: Part 2).

pollution and resource shortages at least partly accounts for the worsening economic plight of the middle-, working, and especially lower-classes—a plight in which adequate food and shelter are often difficult to obtain. Unfortunately, these economic woes cannot simply be corrected by returning to the economic synthesis. The serious health threats posed by pollutants, the potentially devastating changes in the ecosystem wrought by unbridled economic and technological growth (e.g., destruction of the protective ozone layer, alteration of atmospheric temperature), and the undeniable reality of impending shortages in crucial resources such as oil, all make reversion to the traditional economic synthesis impossible in the long run (see, e.g., Anderson, 1976; Miller, 1972). Of course, as Morrison (1976) has noted, the pressures to return to this synthesis are great, and understanding them provides insights into contemporary and future economic cleavages.

Cleavages within the stratification system: Schnaiberg's ecological synthesis amounts to what others have termed a "stationary" or "steady-state" society, and it is widely agreed that such a society would need to be far more egalitarian than the contemporary U.S. (Anderson, 1976:58–61; Daly, 1973:168–170).[10] Achieving the necessary redistribution would be very difficult, and opposition to it would be likely to result in serious, but unstable cleavages within the stratification system. In the long run, as environmental constraints become more obvious, ecologically aware "haves" are likely to opt for increased emphasis on managed scarcity to cope with them. The results would be disastrous for the "have nots," as slowed growth and higher prices would reverse the traditional trend in the U.S. in which *all* segments of society have improved their material condition—not because they obtained a larger slice of the "pie," but because the pie kept growing (Anderson, 1976:28-33; Morrison, 1976). Slowed growth *without* increased redistribution will result in real (as well as relative) deprivation among the "have nots," making class conflict more likely than ever before.[11] As Morrison (1976:299) notes, "Class antagonisms that are soothed by general economic growth tend to emerge as more genuine class conflicts when growth slows or ceases." Thus, in the long run the NEP suggests that Marx's predictions about class conflict may become more accurate, although for reasons Marx could not have foreseen.

In the short run, however, a very different possibility seems likely. The societal pressures resulting from managed scarcity are such that large portions of *both* "haves" and "have nots" will push for a reversion to the economic (growth) synthesis. In fact, Morrison (1973) has predicted the emergence of a Dahrendorfian (i.e., non-Marxian) cleavage: "growthists vs. nongrowthists," with *all* those highly dependent upon industrial growth (workers *and* owners) coalescing to oppose environmentalists (who typically hold positions—in the professions, government, education, for example—less directly dependent on growth). The staunch labor union support for growth, and the successful efforts of industry to win the support of labor and the poor in battles against environmentalists, both suggest the emergence of this coalition. Somewhat ironically, therefore, support for continued economic growth has united capitalists and the "left" (used broadly to include most labor unions, advocates for the poor, and academic Marxists). Not only does this support reveal the extent to which most of the left has abandoned hopes for real *redistribution* in favor of getting a "fair share" of a growing pie, but it also reveals a misunderstanding of the distribution of costs and benefits of traditional economic growth.

The "Culture of Poverty" solidified: Sociologists guided by the NEP have not only questioned the supposed universal benefits of growth, but they consistently point to the generally neglected "costs" of growth—costs which tend to be very regressive (Anderson, 1976:30-31; Schnaiberg, 1975:19). Thus, it is increasingly recognized that the workplace and inner city often constitute serious health hazards, and that there is generally a strong inverse relationship between SES and exposure to environmental pollution (Schnaiberg, 1975:19). Further, in his study of the SES-air pollution relationship, Burch (1976:314) has gone so far as to suggest that, "Each of these pollutants when ingested at certain modest levels over continuing periods, is likely to be an important influence upon one's ability to persist in the struggle for improvement of social position... These exposures, like nutritional deficiencies, seem one mechanism by which class inequalities are re-

---

[10] For example, wasteful consumption due to excess wealth and economic growth stemming from the investment of excess capital (for profit) would need to be halted, as would pressure for economic growth stemming from the unmet needs of the lower strata (see, e.g., Anderson, 1976:58-61; Daly, 1973:168-171).

[11] Managed scarcity and slowed growth are also likely to exacerbate tensions between developed and developing nations. This leads NEP-oriented sociologists (e.g., Anderson, 1976:258-269; Morrison, 1976) to see the future of international development quite differently than sociologists bound by the HEP (see, e.g., Horowitz, 1972).

inforced." This leads him to suggest that efforts to eradicate poverty which do not take into account the debilitating impact of environmental insults are likely to fail.

Conclusion

We have attempted to illustrate the utility of the NEP by focusing on issues concerning stratification, for we believe this is one of many aspects of society that will be significantly affected by ecological constraints. As noted above, in the short run we expect tremendous pressure for reverting to the economic growth synthesis, for such a strategy seeks to alleviate societal tensions at the expense of the environment. Of course, the NEP implies that such a strategy cannot continue indefinitely (and the evidence seems to support this—see, e.g., Miller, 1972). Thus we are faced with the necessity of choosing between managed scarcity and an ecological synthesis.[12] The deleterious effects of the former are already becoming obvious; they help account for the trends described by Aronowitz and others. However, the achievement of a truly ecological synthesis will require achieving a steady-state society, a very difficult goal. As students of social organization, sociologists should play a vital role in delineating the characteristics of such a society, feasible procedures for attaining it, and their probable social costs. (See Anderson, 1976 for a preliminary effort.) Until sociology extricates itself from the Human Exceptionalism Paradigm, however, such a task will be impossible.

References

Albrecht, Stan L. and Armand L. Mauss 1975 "The environment as a social problem." Pp. 556–605 in A. L. Mauss, Social Problems as Social Movements. Philadelphia: Lippincott.

Allen, William R. 1976 "Scarcity and order: The Hobbesian problem and the Humean resolution." Social Science Quarterly 57:263–275.

Anderson, Charles H. 1976 The Sociology of Survival: Social Problems of Growth. Homewood, Illinois: Dorsey.

Aronowitz, Stanley 1974 Food, Shelter and the American Dream. New York: Seabury Press.

Bell, Daniel 1973 The Coming of Post-Industrial Society. New York: Basic Books.

Burch, William R., Jr. 1971 Daydreams and Nightmares: A Sociological Essay on the American Environment. New York: Harper and Row. 1976 "The peregrine falcon and the urban poor: Some sociological interrelations." Pp. 308-316 in P.J. Richerson and J. McEvoy III (eds.), Human Ecology: An Environmental Approach. North Scituate, Mass.: Duxbury.

Buttel, Frederick H. 1976 "Social science and the environment: Competing theories." Social Science Quarterly 57:307–323.

Carson, Rachel 1962 Silent Spring. Boston: Houghton-Mifflin.

Catton, William R., Jr. 1976a "Toward prevention of obsolescence in Sociology." Sociological Focus 9:89–98 1976b "Why the future isn't what it used to be (and how it could be made worse than it has to be)." Social Science Quarterly 57:276-291.

Commoner, Barry 1971 The Closing Circle. New York: Knopf.

Daly, Herman E. 1973 "The steady-state economy: Toward a political economy of biophysical equilibrium and moral growth." Pp. 149–174 in H.E. Daly (ed.), Toward a Steady-State Economy. San Francisco: W. H. Freeman.

Denisoff, R. Serge, Orel Callahan, and Mark H. Levine (eds.) 1974 Theories and Paradigms in Contemporary Sociology. Itasca, Illinois: Peacock.

Dunlap, Riley E. (ed.) 1975 Directory of Environmental Sociologists. Pullman: Washington State University, College of.Agriculture Research Center, Circular No. 586.

Dunlap, Riley E. and William R. Catton, Jr. 1979 "Environmental sociology." Annual Review of Sociology. Palo Alto, Calif.: Annual Reviews, Inc.

Dunlap, Riley E. and Kent D. Van Liere 1977 "The 'new environmental paradigm': A proposed measuring instrument and preliminary results." Paper presented at the Annual Meeting of the American Sociological Association, Chicago.

Ehrlich, Paul R and Anne H. Ehrlich 1970 Population, Resources, Environment. San Friedrichs, Robert W. 1972 A Sociology of Sociology. New York: Free Press

Gouldner, Alvin W. 1970 The Coming Crisis of Western Sociology. New York: Basic Books.

Hardin, Garrett 1968 "The tragedy of the commons." Science 162:1243–1248.

Hawley, Amos H. (ed.) 1975 Man and Environment. New York: New York Times Company.

---

[12] A point implicit in our discussion is worth making explicit: the NEP suggests that resource scarcities are unavoidable, but—as Schnaiberg's work indicates—societies may react to them in a variety of ways. Thus, as Schnaiberg (1975:17) suggests, sociologists should begin to examine the social impacts (especially distributional impacts) of alternatives.

Horowitz, Irving L. 1972 Three Worlds of Development: The Theory and Practice of International Stratification. 2nd ed. New York: Oxford University Press.

Humphrey, Craig R. and Frederick H. Buttel 1976 "New directions in environmental sociology." Paper presented at the Annual Meeting of the Society for the Study of Social Problems, New York.

Klausner, Samuel Z. 1971 On Man in His Environment. San Francisco: Jossey-Bass.

Kuhn, Thomas S. 1962 The Structure of Scientific Revolutions. Chicago: University of Chicago Press

Manderscheid, Ronald W. (ed.) 1977 Annotated Directory of Members: Ad Hoc Committee on Housing and Physical Environment. Adelphi, Maryland: Mental Health Study Center, NIMH.

Michelson, William H. 1976 Man and His Urban Environment. 2nd ed. Reading, Mass.: Addison-Wesley.

Miller G. Tyler Jr. 1972 Replensih the Earth: A Primer in Human Ecology. Belmont, Calif.:Wadsworth.

Morrison, Denton E. "The environmental movement: Conflict dynamics." Journal of Voluntary Action Research 2:74-85. 1976 "Growth, environment, equity and scarcity." Social Science Quarterly 57:292-306. 1977 "Equity impacts of some major energy alternatives." Paper presented at the Annual Meeting of the American Sociological Association, Chicago.

Parsons, Talcott 1977 The Evolution of Societies (ed. by Jackson Toby). Englewood Cliffs, NJ: Prentice-Hall.

Potter, David M. 1954 People of Plenty. Chicago: University of Chicago Press.

Ritzer, George 1975 Sociology: A Multiple Paradigm Science. Boston: Allyn and Bacon.

Schnaiberg, Allan 1972 "Environmental sociology and the division of labor." Department of Sociology, Northwestern University, mimeograph. 1975 "Social syntheses of the societal-environmental dialectic: The role of distributional impacts." Social Science Quarterly 56: 5–20.

Strumpel, Burkhard (ed.) 1976 Economic Means for Human Needs. Ann Arbor: Institute for Social Research, University of Michigan.

Sumner, William Graham 1896 "Earth hunger or the philosophy of land grabbing." Pp. 31-64 in A.G. Keller (ed.), Earth Hunger and Other Essays. New Haven: Yale University Press, 1913. van Bavel, Cornelius H.M. 1977 "Soil and oil" Science 197:213.

Zeisel, John 1975 Sociology and Architectural Design. New York: Russell Sage Foundation.

Zeitlin, Maurice (ed.) 1977 American Society, Inc. 2nd ed. Chicago: Rand McNally

THE LAND ETHIC

By Aldo Leopold

When GOD-LIKE Odysseus returned from the wars in Troy, he hanged all on one rope a dozen slave-girls of his household whom he suspected of misbehavior during his absence.

This hanging involved no question of propriety. The girls were property. The disposal of property was then, as now, a matter of expediency, not of right and wrong.

Concepts of right and wrong were not lacking from Odysseus' Greece: witness the fidelity of his wife through the long years before at last his black-prowed galleys clove the wine-dark seas for home. The ethical structure of that day covered wives, but had not yet been extended to human chattels. During the three thousand years which have since elapsed, ethical criteria have been extended to many fields of conduct, with corresponding shrinkages in those judged by expediency only....

The first ethics dealt with the relation between individuals; the Mosaic Decalogue is an example. Later accretions dealt with the relation between the individual and society. The Golden Rule tries to integrate the individual to Society; democracy to integrate social organization to the individual.

There is as yet no ethic dealing with man's relation to land and to the animals and plants which grow upon it. Land, like Odysseus' slave-girls, is still property. The land-relation is still strictly economic, entailing privileges but no obligations.

The extension of ethics to this third element in human environment is, if I read the evidence correctly, an evolutionary possibility and an ecological necessity. It is the third step in a sequence. The first two have already been taken. Individual thinkers since the days of Ezekiel and Isaiah have asserted that the despoliation of land is not only inexpedient but wrong. Society, however, has not yet affirmed their belief. I regard the present conservation movement as the embryo of such an affirmation....

The Community Concept

All ethics so far evolved rest upon a single premise: that the individual is a member of a community of interdependent parts. His instincts prompt him to compete for his place in that community, but his ethics prompt him also to co-operate (perhaps in order that there may be a place to compete for).

Aldo Leopold (1887-1948) was an outdoor enthusiast, conservationist, forester, philosopher, educator, and prolific writer. He is considered by many to be the father of wildlife management and was instrumental in 1922 in developing the proposal to designate the Gila National Forest as a wilderness area, the first such official designation. *A Sand County Almanac* is a collection of essays, geared for general audiences examining humanity's relationship to the natural world.

The land ethic simply enlarges the boundaries of the community to include soils, waters, plants, and animals, or collectively: the land.

This sounds simple: do we not already sing our love for and obligation to the land of the free and the home of the brave? Yes, but just what and whom do we love? Certainly not the soil, which we are sending helter-skelter downriver. Certainly not the waters, which we assume have no function except to turn turbines, float barges, and carry off sewage. Certainly not the plants, of which we exterminate whole communities without batting an eye. Certainly not the animals, of which we have already extirpated many of the largest and most beautiful species. A land ethic of course cannot prevent the alteration, management, and use of these 'resources,' but it does affirm their right to continued existence, and, at least in spots, their continued existence in a natural state.

In short, a land ethic changes the role of *Homo sapiens* from conqueror of the land-community to plain member and citizen of it. It implies respect for his fellow-members, and also respect for the community as such....

The Ecological Conscience

Conservation is a state of harmony between men and land. Despite nearly a century of propaganda, conservation still proceeds at a snail's pace; progress still consists largely of letterhead pieties and convention oratory. On the back forty we still slip two steps backward for each forward stride.

The usual answer to this dilemma is 'more conservation education.' No one will debate this, but is it certain that only the *volume* of education needs stepping up? Is something lacking in the *content* as well?

It is difficult to give a fair summary of its content in brief form, but, as I understand it, the content is substantially this: obey the law, vote right, join some organizations, and practice what conservation is profitable on your own land; the government will do the rest.

Is not this formula too easy to accomplish anything worth-while? It defines no right or wrong, assigns no obligation, calls for no sacrifice, implies no change in the current philosophy of values. In respect of land-use, it urges only enlightened self-interest. Just how far will such education take us?...

No important change in ethics was ever accomplished without an internal change in our intellectual emphasis, loyalties, affections, and convictions. The proof that conservation has not yet touched these foundations of conduct lies in the fact that philosophy and religion have not yet heard of it. In our attempt to make conservation easy, we have made it trivial....

The Outlook

It is inconceivable to me that an ethical relation to land can exist without love, respect, and admiration for land and a high regard for its value. By value, I of course mean something far broader than mere economic value; I mean value in the philosophical sense.

Perhaps the most serious obstacle impeding the evolution of a land ethic is the fact that our educational and economic system is headed away from, rather than toward, an intense consciousness of land. Your true modern is separate from the land by many middlemen, and by innumerable physical gadgets. He has no vital relation to it; to him it is the space between cities on which crops grow. Turn him loose for a day on the land, and if the spot does not happen to be a golf links or a 'scenic' area, he is bored stiff. If crops could be raised by hydroponics instead of farming, it would suit him very well. Synthetic substitutes for wood, leather, wool, and other natural land products suit him better than the originals. In short, land is something he has 'outgrown.'

Almost equally serious as an obstacle to a land ethic is the attitude of the farmer for whom the land is still an adversary, or a taskmaster that keeps him in slavery. Theoretically, the mechanization of farming ought to cut the farmer's chains, but whether it really does is debatable.

One of the requisites for an ecological comprehension of land is an understanding of ecology, and this is by no means co-extensive with 'education'; in fact, much higher education seems deliberately to avoid ecological concepts. An understanding of ecology does not necessarily originate in courses bearing ecological labels; it is quite as likely to be labeled geography, botany, agronomy, history, or economics. This is as it should be, but whatever the label, ecological training is scarce.

The case for a land ethic would appear hopeless but for the minority which is in obvious revolt against these 'modern' trends.

The 'key-log' which must be moved to release the evolutionary process for an ethic is simply this: quit thinking about decent land-use as solely an economic problem. Examine each question in terms of what is ethically and esthetically right, as well as what is economically expedient. A thing is right when it tends to preserve the integrity, stability, and beauty of the biotic community. It is wrong when it tends otherwise.

It of course goes without saying that economic feasibility limits the tether of what can or cannot be done for land. It always has and it always will. The fallacy the economic determinists have tied around our collective neck, and which we now need to cast off, is the belief that economics determines *all* land-use. This is simply not true. An innumerable host of actions and attitudes, comprising perhaps the bulk of all land relations, is determined by the land-users' tastes and predilections, rather than by his purse. The bulk of all land relations hinges on investments of time, forethought, skill and faith rather than on investments of cash....

The evolution of a land ethic is an intellectual as well as emotional process. Conservation is paved with good intentions which prove to be futile, or even dangerous, because they are devoid of critical understanding either of the land or of economic land-use. I think it is a truism that as the ethical frontier advances from the individual to the community, its intellectual content increases.

The mechanism of operation is the same for any ethic: social approbation for right actions: social disapproval for wrong actions.

By and large, our present problem is one of attitudes and implements. We are remodeling the Alhambra with a steam shovel, and we are proud of our yardage. We shall hardly relinquish the shovel, which after all has many good points but we are in need of gentler and more objective criteria for its successful use.

WILD AND SLOW: NOURISHED BY TRADITION

By John C. Mohawk

It has been apparent for well over a decade that when indigenous peoples shift from their traditional diet to a "modern," highly refined, carbohydrate diet, they become exposed to a range of degenerative diseases. The most pervasive is diabetes mellitus.

This disease is epidemic among all indigenous peoples in North America (and many other parts of the world) and seems especially destructive among desert populations. A population that is introduced to a radical food—a food that either does not appear in nature or is probably not intended for human consumption—can require long periods of exposure before becoming physically adapted to it. No one knows for certain how long this might take, but it is clear, from the current health profiles of native populations, that not enough time has passed to render these foods safe for indigenous consumption.

In Mexico, some 3.8 million people suffer from the direct and related effects of diabetes. This is also true throughout indigenous America, where a range of groups such as Native Seeds/SEARCH's Desert Foods for Diabetes <www.nativeseeds.org> and Tohono O'odham Community Action <www.tocaonline.org> in Arizona, has been mobilized to promote a new message of nutrition education among native peoples.

The "cure" for the malady, it turns out, has been with them all along. It lies in their own traditional foods that include, for desert people, such traditional favorites as cacti and prickly pear, and an impressive list of foods gathered from the desert.

Diabetes is so prevalent in some communities that up to 65 percent of the adult population have been diagnosed with it. Given that a pathway to health is known, as represented by a return to traditional, nutrient-dense foods, one might expect it would be easy to make changes that could reverse the unhealthy trend. But the problem can be daunting. One of the most powerful traditional garden foods, tepary beans, is known to provide dramatic positive results. People who include such high-fiber beans have been known to reverse their disease symptoms. But knowing what to do isn't the same as being able to do it. Young people, raised on a diet of fast-food restaurants, complain they don't like tepary (or any other) beans.

This situation is at the crux of behavioral science. What causes people to change their food habits? No one knows, but one thing is certain: attitudes and behaviors toward food are formed early in life, and it's not easy to change people's eat-

John C. Mohawk, Ph.D (1945-2006) was a faculty member in the department of American Studies and director of Indigenous Studies at the State University of New York at Buffalo. As a leading scholar of Seneca culture and history, he was a columnist for *Indian Country Today* and received the Native American Journalism Association Best Historical Perspective of Indigenous People Award in 2000 and 2001. He founded and directed the Iroquois White Corn Project and the Pinewoods Cafe, promoting Iroquois white corn products and foods.

ing patterns once they are formed. The list of health issues related to diabetes is daunting: circulatory ailments, stroke, kidney failure, obesity, and so forth. The preferred lifestyle changes that would help reverse the trends are predictable: traditional foods, increased exercise, and avoidance of harmful foods and habits.

Traditional foods have qualities that are somewhat rare in a contemporary grocery store. All foods that are gathered from the natural world, such as cacti and wild berries, are what have been designated "slow foods." They are wild foods that have not been cultivated. Cultivated foods rely on human activity to protect them from enemies such as weeds and even drought. They reward the agriculturalist with high yields, but they differ nutritionally and otherwise from their wild relatives.

One way in which cultivated foods are different is that they are generally easier to digest and to cook. As a rule, the more a plant is hybridized, and the more its fruit is refined by machinery or chemistry, the more rapidly its carbohydrates are likely to be absorbed in the bloodstream. For people who are in a hurry, foods that speed up the digestive process seem to be a good thing. But for native and indigenous peoples and others who are sensitive to rapidly absorbed carbohydrates, these foods produce a higher level of blood sugar than do the wild foods, leading to increased risk for diet-related diseases.

Some indigenous peoples have survived on the wild foods growing in their homelands for centuries. Those foods once saved them from hunger. Today, they can help save them from degenerative diseases.

I once heard that culture is what one does without thinking about it. This was mentioned in regard to the foods people eat, as well as the customs they follow. There was a time when Indian people didn't need to think about what they needed to do. It was a given that people would get enough exercise because there wasn't much choice. There were no cars and, in most cases, few horses, so unless one was going to just lie around, one had to walk. And since food stamps or hunger relief programs were unknown, people who wanted to eat had to do something: hunt, fish, garden—all good exercise.

A healthy diet was fairly easy to come by, as well. Indeed, there were few alternatives to healthy foods. If you wanted to eat junk food, you were out of luck.

In the contemporary world, doing things without thinking about them is not working out. This is true for all people, because the same issues are impacting all populations worldwide. We are seeing an unprecedented growth of the same kinds of diet-related diseases, even among affluent suburban populations. The antidote may require some organizing.

The first step is nutrition education, but simply telling people about the problem is not enough. Something like a mini cultural revolution needs to happen in order to change behaviors. People who are motivated to change are going to need to find alternatives to unhealthy diets and lifestyles. They will need to support one another, share ideas and, in this case, recipes.

They need to share experiences about which available foods are "slow foods" or act on the metabolism as slow foods do. Many of these highly nutritious foods are found in the fresh fruits and vegetables section, but people can't live on fruits and vegetables alone. They want and need variety—treats and comforts foods—with all the dangers that modern, cultivated foods represent.

It would help if people could organize themselves into support groups to help each other. This is actually consistent with the "societies" indigenous cultures often created of people who were committed to helping one another. In this case, the help might come in the form of shared recipes and information about how some foods are beneficial and others are dangerous. Regular meetings could offer information about the traditional culture, and provide information about sourcing traditional slow foods. There might even be a way to share foods, recipes, and success stories.

Such a movement should appeal to, be open to, and focused on, children and young adults, as well as the general public. Every day in public schools, a new message could be served along with new meals made from highly nutritious slow foods. The message is that exercise is important, food is important; self-esteem and a long list of other healthy things are important; and sharing a path toward healing is the most important of all. The ancient Indians knew that, and contemporary Indians need to learn it and practice it. There can be a way to cultural as well as physical health.

ECOFEMINISM

Symbolic and Social Connections of the Oppression of Women and the Domination of Nature

By Rosemary Radford Ruether

What is ecofeminism? Ecofeminism represents the union of the radical ecology movement, or what has been called "deep ecology," and feminism. The word "ecology" emerges from the biological science of natural environmental systems. It examines how these natural communities function to sustain a healthy web of life and how they become disrupted, causing death to the plant and animal life. Human intervention is obviously one of the main causes of such disruption. Thus ecology emerged as a combined socioeconomic and biological study in the late sixties to examine how human use of nature is causing pollution of soil, air, and water, and destruction of the natural systems of plants and animals, threatening the base of life on which the human community itself depends (Ehrlich et al. 1973).

Deep ecology takes this study of social ecology another step. It examines the symbolic, psychological, and ethical patterns of destructive relations of humans with nature and how to replace this with a life-affirming culture (Devall and Sessions 1985).

Feminism also is a complex movement with many layers. It can be defined as only a movement within the liberal democratic societies for the full inclusion of women in political rights and economic access to employment. It can be defined more radically in a socialist and liberation tradition as a transformation of the patriarchal socioeconomic system, in which male domination of women is the foundation of all socioeconomic hierarchies (Eisenstein 1979). Feminism can be also studied in terms of culture and consciousness, charting the symbolic, psychological, and ethical connections of domination of women and male monopolization of resources and controlling power. This third level of feminist analysis connects closely with deep ecology. Some would say that feminism is the primary expression of deep ecology (see Doubiago 1989, 40–44).

Yet, although many feminists may make a verbal connection between domination of women and domination of nature, the development of this connection in a broad historical, social, economic, and cultural analysis is only just beginning. Most studies of ecofeminism, such as the essays in *Healing the Wounds: The Promise of Ecofeminism*, are brief and evocative, rather than comprehensive (Plant 1989).

Fuller exploration of ecofeminism probably goes beyond the expertise of one person. It needs a cooperation of a team that brings together historians of culture, natural scientists, and social economists who would all share a concern for the

Rosemary Radford Ruether is a visiting faculty member in the department of Feminist Theology at Claremont Graduate School. She serves as the Carpenter Emerita Professor of Feminist Theology at Pacific School of Religion and GTU, as well as the Georgia Harkness Emerita Professor of Applied Theology at the Garrett Evangelical Theological Seminary in Evanston, Illinois. She is the author and editor of more than 30 books including *Gaia and God: An Eco-feminist Theology of Earth Healing* (1992) and *Sexism and God-Talk: Toward a Feminist Theology, New Women/New Earth* (1983, 1993).

This article is reprinted with permission from the author.

interconnection of domination of women and exploitation of nature. It needs visionaries to imagine how to construct a new socioeconomic system and a new cultural consciousness that would support relations of mutuality, rather than competitive power. For this, one needs poets, artists, and liturgists, as well as revolutionary organizers, to incarnate more lifegiving relationships in our cultural consciousness and social system.

Such a range of expertise certainly goes beyond my own competence. Although I am interested in continuing to gain working acquaintance with the natural and social sciences, my primary work lies in the area of history of culture. What I plan to do in this essay is to trace some symbolic connections of domination of women and domination of nature in Mediterranean and Western European culture. I will then explore briefly the alternative ethic and culture that might be envisioned, if we are to overcome these patterns of domination and destructive violence to women and to the natural world.

Pre-Hebraic Roots

Anthropological studies have suggested that the identification of women with nature, and males with culture, is both ancient and widespread (Ortner 1974, 67–88). This cultural pattern itself expresses a monopolizing of the definition of culture by males. The very word "nature" in this formula is part of the problem, because it defines nature as a reality below and separated from "man," rather than one nexus in which humanity itself is inseparably embedded. It is, in fact, human beings who cannot live apart from the rest of nature as our life-sustaining context, while the community of plants and animals both can and, for billions of years, did exist without humans. The concept of humans outside of nature is a cultural reversal of natural reality.

How did this reversal take place in our cultural consciousness? One key element of this identification of women with nonhuman nature lies in the early human social patterns in which women's reproductive role as childbearer was tied to making women the primary productive and maintenance workers. Women did most of the work associated with child care, food production and preparation, production of clothing, baskets, and other artifacts of daily life, cleanup, and waste-disposal (French 1985, 25–64).

Although there is considerable variation of these patterns cross-culturally, generally males situated themselves in work that was both more prestigious and more occasional, demanding bursts of energy, such as hunting larger animals, war, and clearing fields, but allowing them more space for leisure. This is the primary social base for the male monopolization of culture, by which men reinforced their privileges of leisure, the superior prestige of their activities, and the inferiority of the activities associated with women.

Perhaps for much of human history, women ignored or discounted these male claims to superiority, being entirely too busy with the tasks of daily life and expressing among themselves their assumptions about the obvious importance of their own work as the primary producers and reproducers (Murphy and Murphy 1974, 111–41). But, by stages, this female consciousness and culture was sunk underneath the growing male power to define the culture for the whole society, socializing both males and females into this male-defined point of view.

It is from the perspective of this male monopoly of culture that the work of women in maintaining the material basis of daily life is defined as an inferior realm. The material world itself is then seen as something separated from males and symbolically linked with women. The earth, as the place from which plant and animal life arises, became linked with the bodies of women, from which babies emerge.

The development of plow agriculture and human slavery very likely took this connection of woman and nature another step. Both are seen as a realm, not on which men depend, but which men dominate and rule over with coercive power. Wild animals which are hunted retain their autonomy and freedom. Domesticated animals become an extension of the human family. But animals yoked and put to the plow, driven under the whip, are now in the new relation to humans. They are enslaved and coerced for their labor.

Plow agriculture generally involves a gender shift in agricultural production. While women monopolized food gathering and gardening, men monopolize food production done with plow animals. With this shift to men as agriculturalists comes a new sense of land as owned by the male family head, passed down through a male line of descent, rather than communal landholding and matrilineal descent that is often found in hunting-gathering and gardening societies (Martin and Voorhies 1975, 276–332). The conquest and enslavement of other tribal groups created another category of humans, beneath the familiar community, owned by it, whose labor is coerced. Enslavement of other people through military conquest typically took the form of killing the men and enslaving the women and their children for labor and sexual service. Women's work becomes identified with slave work (Lemer 1986, ch. 4). The women of the family are defined as a higher type of slave over a lower category of slaves drawn from conquered people. In patriarchal law, possession of women, slaves, animals, and land all are symbolically and socially linked together. All are species of property and instruments of labor, owned and controlled by male heads of family as a ruling class (see Herlihy 1988, 1–28).

As we look at the mythologies of the Ancient Near Eastern, Hebrew, Greek, and early Christian cultures, one can see a shifting symbolization of women and nature as spheres to be conquered, ruled over, and finally, repudiated altogether.

In the Babylonian Creation story, which goes back to the third millennium B.C.E., Marduk, the warrior champion of the gods of the city states, is seen as creating the cosmos by conquering the Mother Goddess Tiamat, pictured as a monstrous female animal. Marduk kills her, treads her body underfoot, and then splits it in half, using one half to fashion the starry firmament of the skies, and the other half the earth below (Mendelsohn 1955,17–46). The elemental mother is literally turned into the matter out of which the cosmos is fashioned (not accidentally, the words *mother* and *matter* have the same etymological root). She can be used as matter only by being killed; that is, by destroying her as "wild," autonomous life, making her life-giving body into 'stuff' possessed and controlled by the architect of a male-defined cosmos.

The Hebraic World

The view of nature found in Hebrew Scripture has several cultural layers. But the overall tendency is to see the natural world, together with human society, as something created, shaped, and controlled by God, a God imaged after the patriarchal ruling class. The patriarchal male is entrusted with being the steward and caretaker of nature, but under God, who remains its ultimate creator and Lord. This also means that nature remains partly an uncontrollable realm that can confront human society in destructive droughts and storms. These experiences of nature that transcend human control, bringing destruction to human work, are seen as divine judgment against human sin and unfaithfulness to God (see Isaiah 24).

God acts in the droughts and the storms to bring human work to naught, to punish humans for sin, but also to call humans (that is, Israel) back to faithfulness to God. When Israel learns obedience to God, nature in turn will become benign and fruitful, a source of reliable blessings, rather than unreliable destruction. Nature remains ultimately in God's hands, and only secondarily, and through becoming servants of God, in male hands. Yet the symbolization of God as a patriarchal male and Israel as wife, son, and servant of God, creates a basic analogy of woman and nature. God is the ultimate patriarchal Lord, under whom the human patriarchal lord rules over women, children, slaves, and land.

The image of God as single, male, and transcendent, prior to nature, also shifts the symbolic relation of male consciousness to material life. Marduk was a young male god who was produced out of a process of theogony and cosmogony. He conquers and shapes the cosmos out of the body of an older Goddess that existed prior to himself, within which he himself stands. The Hebrew God exists above and prior to the cosmos, shaping it out of a chaos that is under his control. Genesis 2 gives us a parallel view of the male, not as the child of woman, but as the source of woman. She arises out of him, with the help of the male God, and is banded over to him as her Master.[1]

The Greek World

When we turn to Greek philosophical myth, the link between mother and matter is made explicit. Plato, in his creation myth, the *Timaeus*, speaks of primal, unformed matter as the receptacle and "nurse" (Plato, 29). He imagines a disembodied male mind as divine architect, or Demiurgos, shaping this matter into the cosmos by fashioning it after the intellectual blueprint of the Eternal Ideas. These Eternal Ideas exist in an immaterial, transcendent world of Mind, separate from and above the material stuff that he is fashioning into the visible cosmos.

---

[1] Phyllis Trible (1973) views the story of Eve's creation from Adam as essentially egalitarian. For an alternative view from the Jewish tradition, see Reik 1960.

The World Soul is also created by the Demiurgos, by mixing together dynamics of antithetical relations (the Same and the Other). This world soul is infused into the body of the cosmos in order to make it move in harmonic motion. The remnants of this world soul are divided into bits, to create the souls of humans. These souls are first placed in the stars, so that human souls will gain knowledge of the Eternal Ideas. Then the souls are sown in the bodies of humans on earth. The task of the soul is to govern the unruly passions that arise from the body.

If the soul succeeds in this task, it will return at death to its native star and there live a life of leisured contemplation. If not, the soul will be reincarnated into the body of a woman or an animal. It will then have to work its way back into the form of an (elite) male and finally escape from bodily reincarnation altogether, to return to its original disincarnate form in the starry realm above (Plato, 23). Plato takes for granted an ontological hierarchy of being, the immaterial intellectual world over material cosmos, and, within this ontological hierarchy, the descending hierarchy of male, female, and animal.

In the Greco-Roman era, a sense of pessimism about the possibility of blessing and well-being within the bodily, historical world deepened in Eastern Mediterranean culture, expressing itself in apocalypticism and gnosticism. In apocalypticism, God is seen as intervening in history to destroy the present sinful and finite world of human society and nature and to create a new heaven and earth freed from both sin and death.[2] In gnosticism, mystical philosophies chart the path to salvation by way of withdrawal of the soul from the body and its passions and its return to an immaterial realm outside of and above the visible cosmos.[3]

Christianity

Early Christianity was shaped by both the Hebraic and Greek traditions, including their alienated forms in apocalypticism and gnosticism. Second-century Christianity struggled against gnosticism, reaffirming the Hebraic view of nature and body as God's good creation. The second century Christian theologian Irenaeus sought to combat gnostic anticosmism and to synthesize apocalypticism and Hebraic creationalism. He imaged the whole cosmos as a bodying forth of the Word and Spirit of God, as the sacramental embodiment of the invisible God.

Sin arises through a human denial of this relation to God. But salvific grace, dispensed progressively through the Hebrew and Christian revelations, allows humanity to heal its relation to God. The cosmos, in turn, grows into being a blessed and immortalized manifestation of the divine Word and Spirit, which is its ground of being (Richardson 1953, 1: 387–98).

However, Greek and Latin Christianity, increasingly influenced by Neoplatonism, found this materialism distasteful. They deeply imbibed the platonic eschatology of the escape of the soul from the body and its return to a transcendent world outside the earth. The earth and the body must be left behind in order to ascend to another, heavenly world of disembodied life. Even though the Hebrew idea of resurrection of the body was retained, increasingly this notion was envisioned as a vehicle of immortal light for the soul, not the material body, in all its distasteful physical processes, which they saw as the very essence of sin as mortal corruptibility.[4]

The view of women in this ascetic Christian system was profoundly ambivalent. A part of ascetic Christianity imagined women becoming freed from subordination, freed both for equality in salvation and to act as agents of Christian preaching and teaching. But this freedom was based on woman rejecting her sexuality and reproductive role and becoming symbolically male. The classic Christian "good news" to woman as equal to man in Christ was rooted in a misogynist view of female sexuality and reproduction as the essence of the sinful, mortal, corruptible life (see Vogt, 1990).

For most male ascetic Christians, even ascetic woman, who had rejected her sexuality and reproductive role, was too dangerously sexual. Ascetic women were increasingly deprived of their minor roles in public ministry, such as deaconess, and locked away in convents, where obedience to God was to be expressed in total obedience to male ecclesiastical authority. Sexual woman, drawing male seminal power into herself, her womb swelling with new life, became the very es-

---

[2] For the major writings of inter-testamental apocalyptic, see Charles 1913.
[3] For the major gnostic literature, see Robinson 1977.
[4] Origen (1966, Bk. 2, ch. 3, 83–94). Also Nyssa, 464–65.

sence of sin, corruptibility, and death, from which the male ascetic fled. Eternal life was disembodied male soul, freed from all material underpinnings in the mortal bodily life, represented by woman and nature.

Medieval Latin Christianity was also deeply ambivalent about its view of nature. One side of medieval thought retained something of Irenaeus's sacramental cosmos, which becomes the icon of God through feeding on the redemptive power of Christ in the sacraments of bread and wine. The redeemed cosmos as resurrected body, united with God, is possible only by freeing the body of its sexuality and mortality. Mary, the virgin Mother of Christ, assumed into heaven to reign by the side of her son, was the representative of this redeemed body of the cosmos, the resurrected body of the Church (Semmelroth 1963, 166–68).

But the dark side of Medieval thought saw nature as possessed by demonic powers that draw us down to sin and death through sexual temptation. Women, particularly old crones with sagging breasts and bellies, still perversely retaining their sexual appetites, are the vehicles of the demonic power of nature. They are the witches who sell their souls to the Devil in a satanic parody of the Christian sacraments (Summers 1928).

The Reformation and the Scientific Revolution

The Calvinist Reformation and the Scientific Revolution in England in the late sixteenth and seventeenth centuries represent key turning points in the Western concept of nature. In these two movements, the Medieval struggle between the sacramental and the demonic views of nature was recast. Calvinism dismembered the Medieval sacramental sense of nature. For Calvinism, nature was totally depraved. There was no residue of divine presence in it that could sustain a natural knowledge or relation to God. Saving knowledge of God descends from on high, beyond nature, in the revealed Word available only in Scripture, as preached by the Reformers.

The Calvinist reformers were notable in their iconoclastic hostility toward visual art. Stained glass, statues, and carvings were smashed, and the churches stripped of all visible imagery. Only the disembodied Word, descending from the preacher to the ear of the listener, together with music, could be bearers of divine presence. Nothing one could see, touch, taste, or smell was trustworthy as bearer of the divine. Even the bread and wine were no longer the physical embodiment of Christ, but intellectual reminders of the message about Christ's salvific act enacted in the past.

Calvinism dismantled the sacramental world of Medieval Christianity, but it maintained and reinforced its demonic universe. The fallen world, especially physical nature and other human groups outside of the control of the Calvinist church, lay in the grip of the Devil. All who were labeled pagan, whether Catholics or Indians and Africans, were the playground of demonic powers. But, even within the Calvinist church, women were the gateway of the Devil. If women were completely obedient to their fathers, husbands, ministers, and magistrates, they might be redeemed as goodwives. But in any independence of women lurked heresy and witchcraft. Among Protestants, Calvinists were the primary witch-hunters (Perkins 1590, 1596; see also Carlsen 1980).

The Scientific Revolution at first moved in a different direction, exorcizing the demonic powers from nature in order to reclaim it as an icon of divine reason manifest in natural law (Easlea 1980). But, in the seventeenth and eighteenth centuries, the more animist natural science, which unified material and spiritual, lost out to a strict dualism of transcendent intellect and dead matter. Nature was secularized. It was no longer the scene of a struggle between Christ and the Devil. Both divine and demonic spirits were driven out of it. In Cartesian dualism and Newtonian physics, it becomes matter in motion, dead stuff moving obediently, according to mathematical laws knowable to a new male elite of scientists. With no life or soul of its own, nature could be safely expropriated by this male elite and infinitely reconstructed to augment its wealth and power.

In Western society, the application of science to technological control over nature marched side by side with colonialism. From the sixteenth to the twentieth centuries, Western Europeans would appropriate the lands of the Americas, Asia, and Africa, and reduce their human populations to servitude. The wealth accrued by this vast expropriation of land and labor would fuel new levels of technological revolution, transforming material resources into new forms of energy and mechanical work, control of disease, increasing speed of communication and travel. Western elites grew increasingly optimistic, imagining that this technological way of life would gradually conquer all problems of material scarcity and even push back the limits of human mortality. The Christian dream of immortal blessedness, freed from finite limits, was translated into scientific technological terms (Condorcet 1794).

Ecological Crisis

In a short three-quarters of a century, this dream of infinite progress has been turned into a nightmare. The medical conquest of disease, lessening infant mortality and doubling the life span of the affluent, insufficiently matched by birth limitation, especially among the poor, has created a population explosion that is rapidly outrunning the food supply. Every year 10 million children die of malnutrition! The gap between rich and poor, between the wealthy elites of the industrialized sector and the impoverished masses, especially in the colonized continents of Latin America, Asia, and Africa, grows ever wider (Wilson and Ramphele 1989).[5]

This Western scientific Industrial Revolution has been built on injustice. It has been based on the takeover of the land, its agricultural, metallic, and mineral wealth appropriated through the exploitation of the labor of the indigenous people. This wealth has flowed back to enrich the West, with some for local elites, while the laboring people of these lands grew poorer. This system of global affluence, based on exploitation of the land and labor of the many for the benefit of the few, with its high consumption of energy and waste, cannot be expanded to include the poor without destroying the basis of life of the planet itself. We are literally destroying the air, water, and soil upon which human and planetary life depend.

In order to preserve the unjust monopoly on material resources from the growing protests of the poor, the world became more and more militarized. Most nations have been using the lion's share of their state budgets for weapons, both to guard against one another and to control their own poor. Weapons also become one of the major exports of wealthy nations to poor nations. Poor nations grow increasingly indebted to wealthy nations while buying weapons to repress their own impoverished masses. Population explosion, exhaustion of natural resources, pollution, and state violence are the four horsemen of the new global apocalypse.

The critical question of both justice and survival is how to pull back from this disastrous course and remake our relations with one another and with the earth.

Toward an Ecofeminist Ethic and Culture

There are many elements that need to go into an ecofeminist ethic and culture for a just and sustainable planet. One element is to reshape our dualistic concept of reality as split between soulless matter and transcendent male consciousness. We need to discover our actual reality as latecomers to the planet. The world of nature, plants, and animals existed billions of years before we came on the scene. Nature does not need us to rule over it, but runs itself very well, even better, without humans. We are the parasites on the food chain of life, consuming more and more, and putting too little back to restore and maintain the life system that supports us.

We need to recognize our utter dependence on the great life-producing matrix of the planet in order to learn to reintegrate our human systems of production, consumption, and waste into the ecological patterns by which nature sustains life. This might begin by revisualizing the relation of mind, or human intelligence, to nature. Mind or consciousness is not something that originates in some transcendent world outside of nature, but is the place where nature itself becomes conscious. We need to think of human consciousness not as separating us as a higher species from the rest of nature, but rather as a gift to enable us to learn how to harmonize our needs with the natural system around us, of which we are a dependent part.

Such a reintegration of human consciousness and nature must reshape the concept of God, instead of modeling God after alienated male consciousness, outside of and ruling over nature. God, in ecofeminist spirituality, is the immanent source of life that sustains the whole planetary community. God is neither male nor anthropomorphic. God is the font from which the variety of plants and animals well up in each new generation, the matrix that sustains their life-giving interdependency with one another (McFague 1987, 69–77).

---

[5] Cited in a talk in London, May 29, 1989, by Dr. Nafis Sadik, head of the United Nations Fund for Population Activities. See Broder, 1989.

In ecofeminist culture and ethic, mutual interdependency replaces the hierarchies of domination as the model of relationship between men and women, between human groups, and between humans and other beings. All racist, sexist, classist, cultural, and anthropocentric assumptions of the superiority of whites over blacks, males over females, managers over workers, humans over animals and plants, must be discarded. In a real sense, the so-called superior pole in each relation is actually the more dependent side of the relationship.

But it is not enough simply to humbly acknowledge dependency. The pattern of male female, racial, and class interdependency itself has to be reconstructed socially, creating more equitable sharing in the work and the fruits of work, rather than making one side of the relation the subjugated and impoverished base for the power and wealth of the other.

In terms of male-female relations, this means not simply allowing women more access to public culture, but converting males to an equal share in the tasks of child nurture and household maintenance. A revolution in female roles into the male work world, without a corresponding revolution in male roles, leaves the basic pattern of patriarchal exploitation of women untouched. Women are simply overworked in a new way, expected to do both a male workday, at low pay, and also the unpaid work of women that sustains family life.

There must be a conversion of men to the work of women, along with the conversion of male consciousness to the earth. Such conversions will reshape the symbolic vision of salvation. Instead of salvation sought either in the disembodied soul or the immortalized body, in a flight to heaven or to the end of history, salvation should be seen as continual conversion to the center, to the concrete basis by which we sustain our relation to nature and to one another. In every day and every new generation, we need to remake our relation with one another, finding anew the true nexus of relationality that sustains, rather than exploits and destroys, life (Ruether 1984, 325–35).

Finally, ecofeminist culture must reshape our basic sense of self in relation to the life cycle. The sustaining of an organic community of plant and animal life is a continual cycle of growth and disintegration. The western flight from mortality is a flight from the disintegration side of the life cycle, from accepting ourselves as part of that process. By pretending that we can immortalize ourselves, souls and bodies, we are immortalizing our garbage and polluting the earth. In order to learn to recycle our garbage as fertilizer for new life, as matter for new artifacts, we need to accept our selfhood as participating in the same process. Humans also are finite organisms, centers of experience in a life cycle that must disintegrate back into the nexus of life and arise again in new forms.

These conversions, from alienated, hierarchical dualism to life-sustaining mutuality, will radically change the patterns of patriarchal culture. Basic concepts, such as God, soul-body, and salvation will be reconceived in ways that may bring us much closer to the ethical values of love, justice, and care for the earth. These values have been proclaimed by patriarchal religion, yet contradicted by patriarchal symbolic and social patterns of relationship.

These tentative explorations of symbolic changes must be matched by a new social practice that can incarnate these conversions in new social and technological ways of organizing human life in relation to one another and to nature. This will require a new sense of urgency about the untenability of present patterns of life and compassionate solidarity with those who are its victims.

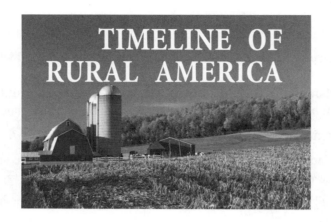

TIMELINE OF RURAL AMERICA

Items for the timeline were selected to reflect the various emphases of the *Encyclopedia of Rural America*, 2nd edition, some of which include agriculture and other natural resource based industries, natural resource management, care for the land, community life, and the wide diversity of residents in rural America.

1700s

1748	Commercial coal mining begins in Virginia
1775	Committee on Indian Affairs established by the Continental Congress to study unique problems of the American Indian peoples and propose legislation
1776	Land grants are offered to the Soldiers in Continental Army by the Continental Congress Public Land Act passed, allowing federal land to be sold to the public
1785	Basic Land Ordinance Act passed, that reserved land in every township in the Western Territory for the maintenance of public schools
1794	Invention of the cotton gin Year of the Whiskey Rebellion, an uprising against a tax on whiskey that directly affected the many farmers who traditionally converted excess grain into liquor
1797	Invention of the cast-iron plow

1800s

1803	Year of the Louisiana Purchase
1804-1806	The transcontinental expedition of Lewis and Clark
1819	Acquisition of Florida from Spain Start of the food canning industry
1820	Agriculture Committee of the U.S. House of Representatives established to give agricultural issues the same weight as commerce and manufacturing
1824	Bureau of Indian Affairs established by the U.S. War Department similar to agencies that were established as far back as 1775

1825	Agriculture Committee of the U.S. Senate established; see 1820 entry
1830	McCormick Reaper patented, a machine said to be responsible for the global shift of labor from farmlands to cities, due to making farming more efficient
	Commercial train locomotive manufacture begins
	Indian Removal Act passed, allowing states to put pressure on American Indian leaders to remove their tribes from state land
	"Trail of Tears" as Cherokees were forced to resettle west of the Mississippi River
1837	John Deere and Leonard Andrus begin the manufacture of steel plows
1839	Invention of the steam shovel for surface coal mining
1840	Farmers are 69% of labor force
1841	The grain drill is patented
1845	U.S. annexed Texas from Mexico
1847	George Perkins Marsh's *Man and Nature or The Earth as Modified by Human Action* published
1848	Coal miners union formed in Pennsylvania
	Year of the Mexican Cession, ceding land (12% of the current US territory) from Mexico to the US
1849	Chemical fertilizers sold commercially
	Department of the Interior established for the management and conservation of federal land
1850	Farmers are 64% of labor force; 1.4 million farms; average acres, 203
1853	Year of the Gadsden Purchase, the U.S. purchase of 29,670 square miles from Mexico to allow the construction of the southern railroad route
1854	Henry David Thoreau's *Walden; or, Life in the Woods* published
1860	Farmers are 58% of labor force; 2.0 million farms; average acres, 199
1861-1865	American Civil War
1865-1870	Sharecropping system in the South replaced the slave plantation system
1862	U.S. Department of Agriculture established
	Morrill Land Grant College Act passed, allowing for the creation of land-grant colleges that would teach military tactics, as well as agriculture and engineering (see entries for 1890 and 1994)

Homestead Act passed, giving qualified applicants, in exchange for improving the land, 160 acres outside the original 13 colonies

Pacific Railroad Act passed, which enabled the government to construct a railroad and telegraph line from the Missouri River to the Pacific Ocean

1863   Year of the Emancipation Proclamation

1867   Year of the Alaska Purchase

1868   First use of steam tractors

1869   First use of spring-tooth harrow for quick, efficient seedbed preparation

1870   Farmers are 53% of labor force; 2.7 million farms; average acres, 153

First use of silos and deep-well drilling

U.S. Weather Bureau established

1871   U.S. Commission of Fish and Fisheries established to research the cause of decreasing commercial fish

1872   Yellowstone became the first National Park

Arbor Day established, an annual holiday encouraging the planting and caring of trees

1873   Timber Culture Act passed as a follow up to the Homestead Act (see 1862 entry), giving homesteaders another 160 acres if they planted trees on 25% of the land

1874   Georgia State Department of Agriculture was established, the first state agriculture department in the nation

Invention of barbed wire

1876   National Grange of the Order of Patrons of Husbandry (the Grange) was founded to encourage farm families to work together for economic and political success, growing to over 1 million members

1877   Desert Land Act passed, allowing 640-acre parcels of arid land to be sold for $1.25 an acre and the promise to irrigate

1879   U. S. Geological Survey established as part of the Department of the Interior

1880   Farmers are 49% of labor force; 4.0 million farms; average acres, 134

1881   Hybridized corn first produced

1886   Founding of the Audubon Society, which is dedicated to conservancy

1887   Hatch Experiment Station Act passed, which gave federal land grants in exchange for the creation of agricultural experiment stations in the areas of soil mineral, plant growth, etc.

Dawes Act passed, dividing Indian tribal lands into individual allotted tracts

1890   Farmers are 43% of labor force; 4.6 million farms; average acres, 136

Morrill Act broadened to fund Black land-grant colleges (see 1862 entry)

First use of cream separators

United Mine Workers of America founded

1890-1891   Federal Meat Inspection Act passed

1891   Forest Reserve Act passed, establishing the National Forest System

1892   Invention of gasoline tractors

The Sierra Club founded as an environmental and conservancy group, by professors at UC Berkeley and Stanford University, with John Muir as president

1896   The beginning of Rural Free Delivery (RFD), which built the roads necessary to deliver mail to rural residents

1898   The annexation of Hawaii to the United States

1900s

1900   Farmers are 38% of labor force; 5.7 million farms; average acres, 147

46.0 million people live in rural America—60.4% of the American population

George Washington Carver became director of agricultural research at the Tuskegee Institute

1902   Reclamation Act passed, which funded irrigation projects for arid areas in the western part of the U.S.

4-H (Head, Heart, Hands, Health) clubs started through Ohio State University, to "engage youth to reach their fullest potential," now 6.5 million strong

National Farmers Union founded

1905   Forest Service created

International Workers of the World ("Wobblies") organized, considered one of the most important events of the American labor movement

Upton Sinclair's *The Jungle* published, exposed unsanitary conditions of the nation's meatpacking industry

1906   Food and Drug Act passed, to encourage food safety

Meat Inspection Act passed, to encourage food safety

Act for the Preservation of American Antiquities passed, protecting Indian remains and artifacts

1907   Country Life Commission established by President Theodore Roosevelt to determine how to improve rural living conditions

1910   Farmers are 31% of labor force; 6.4 million farms; average acres, 138

50.2 million live people in rural America—54.4% of the American population

1912   Plant Quarantine Act passed

1913   USDA Office of Markets established

1914-1918   World War I

1914   Smith-Lever Extension Act passed, establishing cooperative extension services connected to land-grant universities designed to educate the public about agriculture (see 1862 entry)

Cotton Futures Act passed, authorizing the USDA to establish standards for the cotton industry

1915   Liberty Hyde Bailey's *The Holy Earth* published

1916   Stock Raising Homestead Act passed, allowing ranchers to take over federal land whose only value was seen as livestock grazing; currently, over 70 million acres have been affected

Federal Farm Loan Act passed, establishing regional Farm Loan Banks to provide competitive loans to small farmers and business owners

National Park Service Act created the National Park Service within the Department of the Interior

1917   Lever Food Control Act authorized the U.S. President to regulate food, feed, and fuel prices during World War I

1918   Migratory Bird Act (Weeks-McLean Act) passed, designed to protect birds migrating between the U.S. and Canada

1919   American Farm Bureau founded

1920   Farmers are 27% of labor force; 6.5 million farms; average acres, 148

51.8 million people live in rural America—48.8% of the American population

1920-1940   Shift occurs in agriculture from animal powered equipment to mechanized equipment

1922   Capper-Volstead Act passed, providing legal status to agricultural cooperatives

1923   National Catholic Rural Life Conference founded, with Father Edwin V. O'Hara as its first executive secretary

1924   Indian Citizenship Act passed, granting citizenship to Native Americans

Clark-McNary Act passed, to assist states with forest fire control and fund forestry extension work

1925   Purnell Act passed, to fund socio-economic research at the state Experiment Stations

1928
Future Farmers of America, now with over one-half million members in 7,358 chapters

1929-1939
The Great Depression

1930
Farmers are 21% of labor force; 6.3 million farms; average acres, 157

54.0 million people live in rural America—43.9% of the American population

Introduction of all-purpose, rubber-tired tractor with complementary machinery

1933
Agricultural Adjustment Act passed, paying farmers subsidies to idle their crop land, thus raising crop values and increasing farmers' incomes

New Deal programs created, including the Farm Credit Administration to help farmers refinance their mortgages, and the Commodity Credit Corporation, to help stabilize agricultural commodity prices

Tennessee Valley Authority created, providing flood control and generating electricity in the Tennessee Valley

1934
Indian Reorganization Act passed, ending allotment policies of the Dawes Act of 1887

Taylor Grazing Act passed, regulating the grazing of private livestock on public lands

Southern Tenant Farmers Union (later the National Farm Labor Union) formed

Mid-1930s
"Dust Bowl" in the Plains region

1935
New Deal programs created, including the Work Progress Administration to provide employment through the construction of public projects, and the Resettlement Administration, to relocate families to government-planned communities

Soil Conservation and Domestic Allotment Act passed, establishing the Soil Conservation Service

Wilderness Society founded

1936
Rural Electrification Act passed, forming member-owned cooperative power companies that provide electricity to farms and small towns

1937
New Deal created Farm Security Administration, to improve incomes and living conditions of sharecroppers and tenant farmers

1939
Food Stamp Program started, allowing states to administer benefits to those living in poverty

DDT (dichlorodiphenyltrichloroethane) introduced as a chemical pesticide to control insects

1939-1945
World War II

1940	Farmers are 18% of labor force; 6.1 million farms; average acres, 175
	57.5 million people live in rural America—43.5% of the American population

1941   National Victory Garden Program initiated, encouraging citizens to plant gardens for food to support the war effort

1942-1949   Price controls and food rationing in place as a wartime emergency

1946   Nation School Lunch Act passed, providing reduced cost/free lunches to school students

Research and Marketing Act passed, funding research to improve the marketing and distribution of agricultural commodities

1947   General Agreement on Tariffs and Trade (GATT) established to enhance economic recovery after World War II through a reduction in trade barriers

1949   Agricultural Act passed, whereby price supports for farmers and donated surplus foods provided aid to needy nations

Aldo Leopold's *A Sand County Almanac* published

1950   Farmers are 12.2% of labor force; 5.4 million farms; average acres, 216

54.5 million people live in rural America—36.0% of the American population

Anhydrous ammonia used as a source of nitrogen fertilizer starting in this decade

1950-1956   Korean War

1954   Agricultural Trade Development and Assistance Act passed, re-establishing flexible price supports to farms, including support payments on wool

1955   National Farmers Organization founded, noted for its 1964 15-day milk "withholding action"

1956   Soil Bank Program created, retiring land from crop production in exchange for subsidies

Federal–Aid Highway Act (or the National Interstate and Defense Highways Act) passed, designed to construct 41,000 miles of highway over 20 years

1957   Poultry Products Inspection Act passed

1958   Humane Methods of Slaughter Act passed, amended in 1978

1959   Mechanical tomato harvester first used

1960   Farmers are 8.3% of labor force; 3.7 million farms; average acres, 303

54.1 million people live in rural America—30.1% of the American population

1961   Coal becomes primary fuel used to generate electricity

1962   Rachel Carson's *Silent Spring* published on the harmful effects of DDT (see 1939 entry)

United Farm Workers of America co-founded by Dolores Huerta and César Estrada Chávez

1964   Food Stamp Act passed to provide food assistance to low income people

War on Poverty, declared by President Johnson, including programs such as Job Corps, Head Start, Volunteers in Service to America, and Community Action Programs

Agricultural Act passed, authorizing voluntary control programs for the cotton and wheat industries

Wilderness Act established National Wilderness Preservation System

1964-1973   Vietnam War

1965   Appalachian Regional Development Act created the Appalachian Regional Commission for economic development

1966   Fair Labor Standards Act extended to agricultural workers

Wholesome Meat Act imposed federal inspection standards of beef and poultry in slaughterhouses

1967   National Wild and Scenic Rivers Act designated select waterways to be preserved in "free-flowing condition"

National Trails System Act created a system of scenic and recreational trails

1968   American Indian Movement founded, whose demonstrations included taking over the Bureau of Indian Affairs offices in 1972 and the Wounded Knee incident in 1973

1969   National Environmental Policy Act passed (amended in 1970), establishing the Environmental Protection Agency and requiring environmental impact statements for federal projects

1970   Farmers are 4.6% of labor force; 2.8 million farms; average acres, 390

53.6 million people live in rural America—26.4% of the American population

Clean Air Act passed (amended the 1963 Act), designed to reduce smog and air pollution

No-tillage agriculture in use during this decade

1972   Federal Water Pollution Control Act (Clean Water Act) passed, introducing a permit system to regulate point of source water pollution from municipalities, industry, and agriculture

Rural Development Act passed, designed to develop rural communities

Wheat sales to Russia results in higher agricultural commodity prices

1973   Agriculture and Consumer Protection Act passed, placing emphasis on increasing agriculture production rather than controlling it

Endangered Species Act passed, designed to protect species from extinction

1973-1974   Organization of Petroleum Exporting Countries (OPEC) oil embargo

1977   American Agriculture Movement founded, whose demonstrations included the "tractorcade" in Washington, DC in 1978, protesting farm foreclosures

Surface Mining Control and Reclamation Act passed, regulating coal mining industry's actions that impacted the environment, and creating the Department of the Interior's Office of Surface Mining

1978   Forest and Rangeland Renewable Resources Research Act passed, authorizing funds for research on fish, wildlife, and their habitats

1979   Grain embargo imposed against the USSR for its invasion of Afghanistan

1980   Farmers are 3.4% of labor force; 2.4 million farms; average acres, 426

59.5 million people live in rural America—26.3% of the American population

Alaska National Interest Lands Conservation Act passed

1980-1985   "Farm crisis" resulted in high rate of farm foreclosures caused by low prices and high debt

1983   USDA implements payment-in-kind (PIK) programs to reduce the number of acres devoted to agricultural production

1985   Food Security Act passed, establishing the Conservation Reserve Program, lowering government farm supports, and encouraging agricultural exports

1989   Start of low input sustainable agriculture (LISA) to reduce the use of pesticide, herbicide, synthetic fertilizers, and other agrichemicals

1990   Farmers are 2.6% of labor force; 2.1 million farms; average acres, 461

61.7 million people live in rural America—24.8% of the American population

Food, Agriculture, Conservation and Trace Act passed, increasing the flexibility of planting decisions for farmers who participate in government programs

Organic Food Production Act passed, establishing a nationwide definition for organic food

1993   Revised GATT and North American Free Trade Agreement (NAFTA) established

1994   Federal Crop Insurance Reform and Department of Agriculture Reorganization Act establishes the Natural Resources Conservation Service

Department of Agriculture Reorganization Act consolidated several USDA offices to increase efficiency

Satellite and remote sensing technology is used in farming for field equipment operation and more accurate agrichemical application

FDA grants approval for FLAVRSAVR® tomato, produced through biotechnology, or genetic modification

Congressional Equity in Educational Land-Grant Status Act created the Tribal Land-Grant College system

1996   Federal Agriculture Improvement and Reform Act (FAIR or "Freedom to Farm" Act) passed, revising direct payment programs for commodity crops, and eliminating milk price supports

1997   Soybeans and cotton become commercially available as weed and insect resistant biotechnology crops

"New Leaf Superior" potato developed by biotechnology that carries a beetle-killing gene

2000s

2000   Farmers are less than 2% of work force; 2.1 million farms; average acres, 441

59 million people live in rural America—21.0% of the American population

USDA established organic standards and official organic seal

2005   Energy Policy Act passed, designed to upgrade the generation, transmission, and distribution of energy

2008   Food, Conservation and Energy Act passed, designed to ensure national food security, promote renewable energy sources, reform farm programs, protect the environment, and strengthen international food aid

Sources:

American Coal Foundation. "Timeline of Coal in the United States." 2005. Available online at: http://www.teach-coal.org/lessonplans/pdf/coal_timeline.pdf.

Danbom, David. *Born in the Country: A History of Rural America.* Baltimore, MD: Johns Hopkins University Press, 1995.

Economic Research Service. *A History of American Agriculture, 1607-2000.* ERS-POST-12. Washington, DC: U.S. Department of Agriculture, Economic Research Service, 2000. Available online at: http://www.agclassroom.org/gan/timeline/farmers_land.htm.

Food Safety and Inspection Service. "100 Years Since the Federal Meat Inspection Act (FMIA): A Timeline." Washington, DC: Food Safety and Inspection Service, U.S. Department of Agriculture, 2006. Available online at: http://www.fsis.usda.gov/About_FSIS/100_Years_Timeline/index.asp.

Library of Congress. "The Evolution of the Conservation Movement." Washington, DC: Library of Congress, 2002. Available online at: lcweb2.loc.gov/ammem/amrvhtml/cnchron1.html.

Northeast Fisheries Science Center. "Fisheries Historical Page." National Oceanic and Atmospheric Administration, 2007. Available online at: http://www.nefsc.noaa.gov/history.

Steiner, F.R. "Table 1. Chronology of federal soil and water conservation involvement." In *Soil Conservation in the United States: Policy and Planning.* Baltimore, MD: Johns Hopkins University Press, 1990. Available online at: http://ciesin.org/docs/002-475/002-475.html.

U.S. Census Bureau. "Table 1. Urban and Rural Population: 1900 to 1990." Washington, DC: U.S. Census Bureau, 1995. Available online at: http://www.census.gov/population/censusdata/urpop0090.txt.

U.S. Department of Agriculture. "A Condensed History of American Agriculture: 1776-1999." Washington, DC: U.S. Department of Agriculture. Available online at: http://www.usda.gov/news/pubs/99arp/timeline.pdf.

U.S. Department of Agriculture. "Historical Highlights, 2002 and Earlier Census Years." Washington, DC: U.S. Department of Agriculture. Available online at: http://www.agcensus.usda.gov/Publications/2002/Volume_1,_Chapter_1_US/st99_1_001_001.pdf.

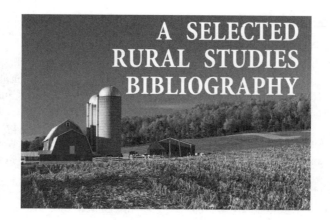

A SELECTED RURAL STUDIES BIBLIOGRAPHY

The following books and monographs, written between 1980 ansd 2008, pertain to various aspects of life in rural America. These interdisciplinary references were selected by the editor and the authors of the encyclopedia articles, and represent the variety of topics addressed in this 2nd edition.

Adams, Jane. *The Transformation of Rural Life: Southern Illinois, 1890-1990.* Chapel Hill: University of North Carolina Press, 1994.

Adams, M.A. and R.W. McLellan. *Use of Nonindustrial Private Land for Public Recreation: An Annotated Bibliography.* Clemson, SC: Clemson University, U.S. Department of Agriculture, Soil Conservation Service and Department of Parks, Recreation, and Tourism Management, nd.

Agency for Health Care Policy and Research. *Delivering Essential Health Care Services in Rural Areas: An Analysis of Alternative Models.* AHCPR Pub. No. 91–0017 (May). Washington, DC: U.S. Department of Health and Human Services, Agency for Health Care Policy and Research, 1991.

Agency for Healthcare Research and Quality. *Health Care Disparities in Rural Areas: Selected Findings from the 2004 National Healthcare Disparities Report Agency for Healthcare Research and Quality.* AHRQ Pub No. 05-P022 (May). Rockville, MD: Agency for Healthcare Research and Quality, 2005.

Agriculture and Biosystems Engineering Department. *Conservation Tillage Systems and Management, Crop Residue Management with No-till, Ridge till and Mulch till.* Midwest Plains Service, MWPS-45, First Edition. Ames: Agriculture and Biosystems Engineering Department, Iowa State University, 1992.

Agrios, G.N. Plant Pathology, 5th edition. Academic Press, Burlington, MA, 2004.

Albin, R.C. and G.B. Thompson. *Cattle Feeding: A Guide to Management,* 2nd edition. Amarillo, TX: Trafton Printing, 1996.

Albrecht, Don E. and Steve H. Murdock. *The Sociology of U.S. Agriculture: An Ecological Perspective.* Ames: Iowa State University Press, 1990.

Allen, James P. and Eugene J. Turner. *We the People: An Atlas of America's Ethnic Diversity.* New York: Macmillan, 1988.

Allen, John C. and Don A. Dillman. *Against All Odds: Rural Community in the Information Age.* Boulder, CO: Westview Press, 1994.

Allen, Patricia, ed. *Food for the Future: Conditions and Contradictions.* New York: John Wiley and Sons, 1993.

Allen, Patricia. *Together at the Table: Sustainability and Sustenance in the American Agrifood System.* University Park, PA: Penn State University Press, 2004.

Altieri, M.A. *Agroecology: The Science of Sustainable Agriculture,* 2nd edition. Boulder, CO: Westview Press, 1995.

Altieri, Miguel A., ed. *Crop Protection Strategies for Subsistence Farmers.* Boulder, CO: Westview Press, 1993.

Altieri, Miguel A., Richard B. Norgaard, Susanna B. Hecht, John G. Farrell, and Matt Liebman. *Agroecology: The Scientific Basis of Alternative Agriculture.* Boulder, CO: Westview Press, 1987.

Ambler, Marjane. *Breaking the Iron Bonds: Indian Control of Energy Development.* Lawrence: University Press of Kansas, 1990.

American Farmland Trust. *Farming on the Edge: A New Report on the Importance and Vulnerability of Agriculture near American Cities.* Washington, DC: American Farmland Trust, 1993.

American Indian Higher Education Consortium and The Institute for Higher Education Policy. *Tribal College Contributions to Local Economic Development.* Alexandria, VA: American Indian Higher Education Consortium, February 2000

American Poultry Historical Society. *American Poultry History, 1823–1973.* Madison, WI: American Printing and Publishing, 1974.

American Poultry Historical Society. *American Poultry History, 1974–1993.* Mt. Morris, IL: Watt, 1996.

Andreas, Carol. *Meatpackers and Beef Barons: Company Town in a Global Economy.* Niwot, CO: University Press of Colorado, 1994.

Andrews, David. *Ministry in the Small Church.* Kansas City, MO: Sheed and Ward, 1988.

Appalachian Land Ownership Task Force. *Who Owns Appalachia?* Lexington, KY: University of Kentucky Press, 1983.

Arendt, Randall. *Rural by Design.* Chicago: APA Planners Press, 1994.

Arno, Stephen F. and Ramona P. Hammerly. *Timberline: Mountain and Arctic Forest Frontiers.* Seattle, WA: The Mountaineers, 1984.

Arntzen, Charles J. and Ellen M. Ritter, eds. *Encyclopedia of Agricultural Science.* 4 volumes. San Diego, CA: Academic Press, 1994.

Arthur, Eric and Dudley Witney. *The Barn: A Vanishing Landmark in North America.* New York: Arrowood Press, 1988.

Association of State and Territorial Health Officials. *Rural Public Health Preparedness Challenges: An Ongoing Dialogue Issue.* ASTHO Report (June) 2006. Arlington, VA: Association of State and Territorial Health Officials, 2006.

Audirac, Ivonne. *Rural Sustainable Development in America.* New York: John Wiley & Sons, 1997.

Axton, W.F. *Tobacco and Kentucky.* Lexington: University Press of Kentucky, 1975.

Ayres, J. S., R. Cole, C. Hein, S. Huntington, W. Kobberdahl, W. Leonard, D. Zetocha. *Take Charge: Economic Development in Small Communities.* Ames, IA: North Central Regional Center for Rural Development, 1990.

Ayres, Janet, F. Larry Leistritz, and Kenneth E. Stone. *Revitalizing the Retail Trade Sector in Rural Communities: Lessons from Three Midwestern States.* Ames, IA: North Central Regional Center for Rural Development, 1989.

Baharanyi, Ntam, Robert Zabawa, and Walter Hill, eds. *New Directions in Local and Rural Development.* Tuskegee, AL: Tuskegee University, 1992.

Ball, Donald M., Carl S. Hoveland, and Garry D. Lacefield. *Southern Forages: Modern Concepts for Forage Crop Management,* 4th edition. Norcross GA: Potash and Phosphate Institute, 2007.

Barkley, David L. *Economic Adaptation: Alternatives for Nonmetropolitan Areas.* Boulder, CO: Westview Press, 1993.

Barnes, Robert F, C. Jerry Nelson, Michael Collins, and Kenneth J. Moore. *Forages: An Introduction to Grassland Agriculture,* 6th edition. Vol. I. Ames, IA: Iowa State Press, 2003.

Barnes, Robert F, C. Jerry Nelson, Kenneth J. Moore, and Michael Collins. *Forages: The Science of Grassland Agriculture,* 6th edition. Vol. II. Ames, IA: Blackwell, 2007.

Barkley, David L., ed. *Economic Adaptation: Alternatives for Nonmetropolitan Areas.* Boulder, CO: Westview Press, 1993.

Barkley, Paul W. and Gene Wunderlich. *Rural Land Transfers in the United States.* AIB 574. Washington, DC: Economic Research Service, U.S. Department of Agriculture, 1989.

Barlett, Peggy F. *American Dreams, Rural Realities: Family Farms in Crisis.* Chapel Hill: University of North Carolina Press, 1993.

Barnard, Freddie L. *Banker's Agricultural Lending Manual.* Austin, TX: Sheshunoff Information Services, Inc., 1993.

Barritt, Bruce H. and K. Bert van Dalfsen. *Intensive Orchard Management: A Practical Guide to the Planning, Establishment, and Management of High Density Apple Orchards.* Yakima, WA: Goodfruit Grower, 1992.

Barry, Peter J., Paul N. Ellinger, C.B. Baker, and John A. Hopkin. *Financial Management in Agriculture.* 5th ed. Danville, IL: Interstate Publishers, Inc., 1995.

Barry, Robert D., Luigi Angelo, Peter J. Buzzanell, and Fred Gray. *Sugar: Background for the 1990 Farm Legislation.* Staff Report No. AGES 9006. Washington, DC: U.S. Department of Agriculture, Economic Research Service, Commodity Economics Division, 1990.

Bartlett, Richard A. *Rolling Rivers: An Encyclopedia of America's Rivers.* New York: McGraw Hill, 1984.

Bath, D.L., F.N. Dickinson, H.A. Tucker, and R.D. Appleman. *Dairy Cattle: Principles, Practices, Problems, Profits.* 3rd ed. Philadelphia. PA: Lea and Febiger, 1985.

Baumgardt, Bill R. and Marshall A. Martin, eds. *Agricultural Biotechnology: Issues and Choices.* West Lafayette, IN: Purdue University Agricultural Experiment Station, 1991.

Baur, Donald, et al. *Natural Resources Law Handbook.* Rockville, MD: Government Institutes, Inc., 1991.

Bazzaz, Fakhri A. *Plants in Changing Environments: Linking Physiological, Population, and Community Ecology.* Cambridge, UK: Cambridge Press, 1998.

Beaulieu, Joyce E. and David E. Berry, eds. *Rural Health Services: A Management Perspective.* Ann Arbor, MI: Aupha Press, 1994.

Beaulieu, Lionel J., ed. *The Rural South in Crisis: Challenges for the Future.* Boulder, CO: West View Press, 1988.

Beaulieu, Lionel J. and David Mulkey. *Investing in People: The Human Capital Needs of Rural America.* Boulder, CO: Westview Press, 1995.

Beeton, Sue. *Ecotourism: A Practical guide for Rural Communities.* Collingwood, Australia: Landlinks Press, 1998.

Bell, Edward L. *Vestiges of Mortality and Remembrance: A Bibliography on the Historical Archaeology of Cemeteries.* Metuchen, NJ: Scarecrow, 1994.

Bell, G. *The Permaculture Way: Practical Steps to Create a Self-Sustaining World.* East Meon, UK. Permanent Publications, 2004.

Bender, Lloyd D., Bernal L. Green, Thomas F. Hady, John A. Kuehn, Marlys K. Nelson, Leon B. Perkinson, and Peggy J. Ross. *The Diverse Social and Economic Structure of Nonmetropolitan America,* U.S.D.A.-E.R.S. Rural Development Research Report No. 49. Washington, DC: U.S. Government Printing Office, 1985.

Bennett, John. *Of Time and the Enterprise: North American Family Farm Management in a Context of Resource Marginality.* Minneapolis, MN: University of Minnesota Press, 1982.

Berardi, G.M. and C.C. Geisler. *The Social Consequences and Challenges of New Agricultural Technologies.* Boulder, CO: Westview Press, 1984.

Berman, David. *County Governments in an Era of Change.* Westport, CT: Greenwood Press, 1993.

Berry, Brian, John B. Parr, Bart J. Epstein, Avjit Ghosh, and Robert H.T. Smith. *Market Centers and Retail Location: Theory and Applications.* Englewood Cliffs, NJ: Prentice-Hall, 1988.

Berry, Wendell. *What Are People For?* San Francisco, CA: North Point Press, 1990.

Beveridge, Malcolm. *Cage Aquaculture,* 3rd edition. Hoboken, NJ: John Wiley and Sons, Inc., 2004.

Bhat, Mahadev G., Burton C. English, Anthony F. Turhollow and Herzon O. Nyangito. *Energy in Synthetic Fertilizers and Pesticides: Revisited.* Oak Ridge, TN: Oak Ridge National Laboratory, 1994.

Billingsley, A. *Mighty Like a River: The Black Church and Social Reform.* New York: Oxford University Press, 1999.

Billington, Ray Allen. *Westward Expansion: A History of the American Frontier,* 6th edition. Albuquerque, NM: University of New Mexico Press, 2001.

Bird, Elizabeth Ann R., Gordon L. Bultena, and John C. Gardner, eds. *Planting the Future. Developing an Agriculture That Sustains Land and Community.* Ames: Iowa State University Press, 1995.

Blackburn, William R. *The Sustainability Handbook: The Complete Management Guide To Achieving Social, Economic, and Environmental Responsibility.* Washington DC: Environmental Law Institute, 2007.

Blank, Steven. *The End of Agriculture in the American Portfolio.* Quorum Books. 1998.

Blank, Steven C., Colin A. Carter, and Brian H. Schmiesing. *Futures and Options Markets: Trading in Commodities and Financials.* Englewood Cliffs, NJ: Prentice Hall, 1991.

Blatz, Charles V., ed. *Ethics and Agriculture: An Anthology on Current Issues in World Context.* Moscow, ID: University of Idaho Press, 1991.

Blevins, Winfred. *Dictionary of the American West.* New York: Facts on File, 1993.

Boardman, John, John A. Dearing, and Ian D.L. Foster. *Soil Erosion on Agricultural Lands.* New York: John Wiley and Sons, 1990.

Boehlje, Michael D. and Vernon R. Eidman. *Farm Management.* New York: John Wiley & Sons, 1984.

Bolen, Eric G. and William L. Robinson. *Wildlife Ecology and Management,* 3rd edition. Englewood Cliffs, NJ: Prentice Hall, 1995.

Bollier, D. *The Importance of Communications and Information Systems to Rural Development in the United States. Report of an Aspen Institute Conference.* Turo, MA: Aspen Institute for Humanistic Studies, 1988.

Bonanno, Alessandro, Lawrence Busch, William Friedland, Lourdes Gouveia, and Enzo Mingione. *From Columbus to ConAgra: The Globalization of Agriculture and Food.* Lawrence: University Press of Kansas, 1994

Boodley, J.W. *The Commercial Greenhouse.* Albany, NY: Delmar Publishers Inc., 1981.

Botkin, M.P., R.A. Field and C.L. Johnson. *Sheep and Wool Science Production and Management.* Englewood Cliffs, NJ: Prentice Hall, 1988.

Brady, N.C. and R. R. Weil. *The Nature and Properties of Soils,* 14th edition. New York, NY: MacMillan, 2007.

Brickell, Christopher, Elvin McDonald, and Trevor Cole, eds. *The American Horticultural Society Encyclopedia of Gardening.* New York: Dorling Kindersley, 1993.

Bridwell, R. *Hydroponic Gardening.* Santa Barbara, CA: Woodbridge Press, 1990.

Briody, Elizabeth K. *Household Labor Patterns Among Mexican Americans in South Texas.* New York: AMS Press, 1986.

Brown, David, et al., eds. *Rural Economic Development in the 1980's: Preparing for the Future.* Rural Development Research Report No. 69 (September). Washington, DC: U.S. Department of Agriculture, Agriculture and Rural Economy Division, Economic Research Service, 1988.

Brown, David L. and Louis E. Swanson, eds. *Challenges for Rural America in the Twenty-First Century.* University Park, PA: The Pennsylvania State University Press, 2003.

Brown, D.L., D.R. Field, and J.J. Zuiches. *The Demography of Rural Life.* University Park PA: Northeast Regional Center for Rural Development, 1993.

Brown, John Gary. *Soul in the Stone: Cemetery Art from America's Heartland.* Lawrence: University Press of Kansas, 1994.

Brown, Linda Keller and Kay Mussell, eds. *Ethnic and Regional Foodways in the United States.* Knoxville, TN: University of Tennessee Press, 1984.

Brown, T.D. *Quality Control in Lumber Manufacture.* San Francisco, CA: Miller Freeman Publications, Inc., 1982.

Browne, William P. *Cultivating Congress.* Lawrence: University Press of Kansas, 1995.

Browne, William P., Jerry R. Skees, Louis E. Swanson, Paul B. Thompson, and Laurian J. Unnevehr. *Sacred Cows and Hot Potatoes: Agrarian Myths in Agricultural Policy.* Boulder, CO: Westview Press, 1992.

Brulle, Robert J. *Agency, Democracy, and Nature: The U.S. Environmental Movement from a Critical Theory Perspective.* Cambridge, MA: MIT Press, 2000.

Brunvand, Jan Harold. *The Study of American Folklore: An Introduction.* 3rd edition. New York: W.W. Norton & Company, 1986.

Bruyn, Severyn T. and James Meehan. *Beyond the Market and the State: New Directions in Community Development.* Philadelphia, PA: Temple University Press, 1987.

Bryan, Frank. *Politics in the Rural States: People, Parties and Processes.* Boulder, CO: Westview Press, 1981.

Bull, C. Neil and Share D. Bane, eds. *The Future of Aging in Rural America.* Kansas City, MO: National Resource Center for Rural Elderly, University of Missouri, Kansas City, 1992.

Bull, C. Neil, ed. *Aging in Rural America.* Newbury Park, CA: SAGE Publications, Inc., 1993.

Burns, Shirley Stewart. *Bringing Down the Mountains: The Impact of Mountaintop Removal on Southern West Virginia.* Morgantown, WV: West Virginia University, 2007.

Burt, Brian A., and Stephen A. Eklund, eds. *Dentistry, Dental Practice and the Community,* 4th edition. Philadelphia, PA: W.B. Saunders Company, 1992.

Busch, Lawrence and William B. Lacy. *Science, Agriculture and the Politics of Research.* Boulder, CO: Westview, 1983.

Busch, Lawrence, and William B. Lacy, eds. *The Agricultural Scientific Enterprise: A System in Transition.* Boulder, CO: Westview, 1986.

Butler, Margaret A. *The Farm Entrepreneurial Population, 1988–1990.* Washington, DC:, Economic Research Service, 1993.

Butler, Sandra S. and Lenard W. Kaye. *Gerontological Social Work in Small Towns and Rural Communities.* New York: The Haworth Press, Inc., 2003.

Buttel, Frederick H., Olaf F. Larson, and Gilbert W. Gillespie, Jr. *The Sociology of Agriculture.* Westport, CT: Greenwood Press, Inc., 1990.

Buzzanell, Peter and Ron Lord. *Sugar and Corn Sweetener: Changing Demand and Trade in Mexico, Canada, and the United States.* Agriculture Information Bulletin Number 655, (April). Washington, DC: U.S. Department of Agriculture, Economic Research Service, 1993.

C.K. Winter, J. Seiber and C.F. Nuckton. *Chemicals in the Human Food Chain.* New York: Van Nostrand Reinhold, 1990.

Calkins, Peter H. and Dennis D. DiPietre. *Farm Business Management: Successful Decisions in a Changing Environment.* New York: MacMillan Publishing Co., Inc., 1983.

Callicott, J. Baird. *In Defense of the Land Ethic: Essays on Environmental Policy.* Albany: State University of New York Press, 1989.

Callicott, J. Baird. *Beyond the Land Ethic: More Essays in Environmental Philosophy.* Albany, NY: State University of New York Press, 1999.

Callicott, J. Baird and Michael P. Nelson, eds. *The Great New Wilderness Debate.* Athens: University of Georgia Press, 1998.

Canton, Lucien G. *Emergency Management: Concepts and Strategies for Effective Programs.* Hoboken, NJ: Wiley, 2007.

Carlson, Allan. *The New Agrarian Mind: The Movement Toward Decentralist Thought in Twentieth-Century America.* New Brunswick, N.J.: Transaction, 2000.

Carlson, Robert V. *A Case Study of the Impact of a State-Level Policy Designed to Improve Rural Schools in the State of Vermont.* Occasional Paper No. 36. Charleston, WV: Appalachia Educational Laboratory, February, 1994.

Carney, Cary Michael. *Native American Higher Education in the United States.* New Brunswick, NJ: Transaction Publishers, 1999.

Carpenter, J. and L. Gianessi. *Agricultural Biotechnology: Updated Benefit Estimates.* Washington, DC: National Center for Food and Agriculture Policy, 2001.

Carroll, C.R.. J.H. Vandermeer, and P.M. Rosset. *Agroecology.* New York: McGraw-Hill Publishing Company, 1990.

Carroll, Matthew S. *Community & the Northwestern Logger: Continuities and Changes in the Era of the Spotted Owl.* Boulder, CO: Westview, 1995.

Carter, Harold O., Henry J. Vaux, Jr., and Ann F. Scheuring, eds. *Sharing Scarcity: Gainers and Losers in Water Marketing.* Davis, CA: University of California Agricultural Issues Center, 1994.

Carter, M.R. *Conservation Tillage in Temperate Agroecosystems.* Baco Raton, FL: Lewis Publishers, CRC Press Inc., 1994.

Carter, Timothy J., G. Howard Phillips, Joseph F. Donnermeyer, and Todd N. Wurschmidt. *Rural Crime: Integrating Research and Prevention.* Totowa, NJ: Allanheld, Osmund and Company, Publishers, Inc., 1983.

Carroll, Matthew S. *Community and the Northwestern Logger: Continuities and Change in the Era of the Spotted Owl.* Boulder, CO: Westview Press, 1994.

Cassidy, Frederic G. *The Dictionary of American Regional English,* Volumes I, II, and III. Cambridge, MA: Harvard University Press, 1985, 1991, 1996.

Castle, Emery N., ed. *The American Countryside: Rural People and Places.* Lawrence: University Press of Kansas, 1995.

Chalk, Peter. *Hitting America's Soft Underbelly: The Potential Threat of Deliberate Biological Attacks against the U.S. Agricultural and Food Industry.* Santa Monica, CA: RAND Corporation, 2004.

Chan, Sucheng. *This Bittersweet Soil: The Chinese in California Agriculture, 1860–1910.* Berkeley: University of California Press, 1986.

Cheeke, Peter R. *Impacts of Livestock Production on Society, Diet/Health and the Environment.* Danville, IL: Interstate Publishers, 1993.

Chibnik, Michael. *Farm Work and Fieldwork: American Agriculture in Anthropological Perspective.* Ithaca, NY: Cornell University Press, 1987.

Childs, Alan W. and Gary B. Melton., eds. *Rural Psychology.* New York: Plenum Press, 1983.

Chicago Board of Trade, Education and Marketing Services Department. *Introduction to Agricultural Hedging.* Chicago: Chicago Board of Trade, 1988.

Chicago Board of Trade. *Commodity Trading Manual.* Chicago: Chicago Board of Trade, 1989.

Chicago Board of Trade. *GRAINS, Production, Processing and Marketing.* Chicago: Chicago Board of Trade, 1982.

Chicago Mercantile Exchange. *Self Study Guide to Hedging With Livestock Futures.* Chicago: Chicago Mercantile Exchange, 1986.

Childs, Alan W. and Gary B. Melton, eds. *Rural Psychology.* New York: Plenum Press, 1983.

Christenson, James, Richard C. Maurer, and Nancy L. Strang. *Rural Data, People, and Policy: Information Systems for the 21st Century.* Bolder, CO: Westview Press, 1994.

Christenson, James A. and Cornelia B. Flora. *Rural Policies for the 1990s.* Boulder, CO: Westview Press, 1991.

Church, D.C. *Livestock Feeds and Feeding,* 3rd edition. Englewood Cliffs, NJ: Prentice Hall, 1991

Clark, E.H. II, J.A. Haverkamp, and W. Chapman. *Eroding Soils: The Off-Farm Impacts.* Washington, DC: The Conservation Foundation, 1985.

Clay, Daniel C. and Harry K. Schwarzweller. *Household Strategies. Research in Rural Sociology and Development,* Volume 5. Edited by. Greenwich, CT: JAI Press, 1991.

Claytor, Diana L., coord. *Bibliography of Fruit, Vegetable, Tree Nut, and Ornamental Publications.* U.S. Department of Agriculture handout prepared for the 1994 Produce Marketing Association Convention and Exposition, San Antonio, TX, October 1994.

Cleland, Charles L., Will Fontanez, and Brian S. Williams. *Rurality Scores for U.S. Counties, 1994.* (map). Agricultural Experiment Station Bulletin 689. Knoxville, TN: University of Tennessee, 1994.

Cloke, Paul J., Terry Marsden, and Patrick Mooney, eds. *Handbook of Rural Studies.* London: Sage Publications, 2006.

Coastal Georgia Regional Development Center. *Rural Solid Waste Management: Regional Planning User Guide.* Brunswick, GA: Coastal Georgia Regional Development Center, 1994.

Cobia, David W., ed. *Cooperatives in Agriculture.* Englewood Cliffs, NJ: Prentice Hall, 1989.

Coburn, Andrew, Sam Cordes, Robert Crittenden, J. Patrick Hart, Keith Mueller, Wayne Myers, and Thomas Ricketts. *The Rural Perspective on National Health Reform Legislation: What are the Critical Issues?* Prepared for The House Committee on Agriculture. Columbia: Rural Policy Research Institute, University of Missouri, 1994.

Coburn, Carol K. *Life at Four Corners: Religion, Gender, and Education in a German-Lutheran Community, 1868-1945.* Lawrence: University Press of Kansas, 1992.

Cocklin, Chris, Barry Smit, and Tom Johnston, eds. *Demands on Rural Lands: Planning for Resource Use.* Boulder, CO: Westview Press, 1987.

Cochrane, Willard W. *The Development of American Agriculture, A Historical Analysis.* 2nd edition. Minneapolis, MN: University of Minnesota Press, 1993.

Cochrane, Willard W. *A Food and Agricultural Policy for the 21st Century.* Minneapolis, MN: Institute for Agriculture and Trade Policy, 2000.

Coff, Christian. *The Taste for Ethics. An Ethic of Food Consumption.* Dordrecht: Springer, 2006.

Commission on Agricultural Workers. *Report of the Commission on Agricultural Workers.* Washington, DC: U.S. Government Printing Office, 1993.

Comstock, Gary, ed. *Is There a Moral Obligation to Save the Family Farm?* Ames: Iowa State University Press, 1987.

Comstock, Gary L. *Vexing Nature? On the Ethical Case Against Agricultural Biotechnology.* Norwell: Kluwer Academic Publishers, 2000.

Conger, Rand D. and Glen H. Elder, Jr. *Families in Troubled Times: Adapting to Change in Rural America.* New York: Aldine de Gruyter, 1994.

Congressional Budget Office. *Water Use Conflicts in the West: Implications of Reforming the Bureau of Reclamation's Water Supply Policies.* Washington, DC: United States Congress, 1997.

Conover, Michael R. *Resolving Human-Wildlife Conflicts: The Science of Wildlife Damage Management.* Lewis Publishers, 2002.

Contrat, Maisie and Richard Conrat. *The American Farm: A Photographic History.* San Francisco, CA: California Historical Society and Boston, MA: Houghton Mifflin Company, 1977.

Cook, Peggy J. and Karen L. Mizer. *The Revised ERS County Typology: An Overview,* Rural Development Research Report No. 89. Washington, DC: U.S. Department of Agriculture, Economic Research Service, 1994.

Cook, Roberta L. *North American Free Trade Agreement: Fruit and Vegetable Issues, Volume IV.* Park Ridge, IL: American Farm Bureau Research Foundation Project, 1991.

Copeland, J.D. *Recreational Access to Private Lands: Liability Problems and Solutions.* Fayetteville, AR: National Center for Agricultural Law Research and Information, 1995.

Copeland, J.D. *Understanding the Farmers Comprehensive Personal Liability Policy: A Guide for Farmers' Attorneys and Insurance Agents.* Fayetteville, AR: National Center for Agricultural Law Research and Information, 1992.

Corbin, David. *Life, Work and Rebellion in the Coal Fields: The Southern West Virginia Miners, 1880-1922.* Urbana: University of Illinois Press, 1981.

Cotterill, Ronald W. *Competitive Strategy Analysis for Agricultural Marketing Cooperatives.* Boulder, CO: Westview Press, 1994.

Council for Agricultural Science and Technology (CAST). *Effective Use of Water in Irrigated Agriculture.* Ames, IA: Council for Agricultural Science and Technology, 1988.

Cowan, Tadlock. *The Changing Structure of Agriculture and Rural America: Emerging Opportunities and Challenges.* Washington, DC: Congressional Research Service, Library of Congress, 2001.

Coward, Raymond T., C. Neil Bull, Gary Kukulka, and James M. Galliher, eds. *Health Services for Rural Elders.* New York: Springer Publishing Company, Inc., 1994.

Coward, Raymond T. and Gary R Lee, eds. *The Elderly in Rural Society: Every Fourth Elder.* New York: Springer Publishing Company, Inc., 1985.

Coward, Raymond T. and Jeffrey W. Dwyer. *Health Programs and Services for Elders in Rural America: A Review of the Life Circumstances and Formal Services that Affect the Health and Well-Being of Elders.* Kansas City MO: National Resource Center for Rural Elderly, University of Missouri, Kansas City, 1991.

Coward, Raymond T., Gary R. Lee, Jeffrey W. Dwyer, and Karen Seccombe. *Old and Alone in Rural America.* Washington, DC: American Association of Retired Persons, 1993.

Coward, Raymond T. and William M Smith, Eds. *The Family in Rural Society.* Boulder, CO: Westview Press, 1981.

Cramer, Gail L. and Eric J. Wailes, eds. *Grain Marketing.* 2nd edition. Boulder, CO: Westview Press, 1993.

Crispeels, M. J., and D. E. Sadava. *Plants, Genes, and Agriculture.* Boston: Jones and Bartlett Publishers, 1994.

Critchfield, Richard. *Trees, Why Do You Wait?* Washington, DC: Island Press, 1991.

Cronon, William. *Changes in the Land: Indians, Colonists, and the Ecology of New England*, 20th Anniversary edition. New York: Hill & Wang, 2003.

Conover, Michael. *Resolving Human-Wildlife Conflicts: The Science of Wildlife Damage Management*. New York: Lewis Publishers, 2002.

Dacquel, Laami T. and Donald C. Dahmann. *Residents of Farms and Rural Areas: 1991*, Bureau of the Census, Current Population Reports, P20-472. Washington, DC: U.S. Government Printing Office, 1993.

Daly, Herman E. *Ecological Economics and Sustainable Development*. Cheltenham, Edward Elgar, 2007.

Daly, Herman E. and John B. Cobb. *For the Common Good: Redirecting the Economy Toward Community, the Environment and a Sustainable Future*, 2nd edition. Boston, MA: Beacon Press, 1994.

Daly, Herman E. and Joshua Farley. *Ecological economics: Principles and Applications*. Washington DC: Island Press, 2004.

Dana, S.T. and S.K. Fairfax. *Forest and Range Policy*. New York: McGraw-Hill, 1980.

Danbom, David B. *Born in the Country: A History of Rural America*, 2nd edition. Baltimore, MD: Johns Hopkins University Press, 2006.

Daniel, Pete. *Breaking the Land: The Transformation of Cotton, Tobacco, and Rice Cultures since 1880*. Urbana: University of Illinois Press, 1985.

Daniels, Steven E. and Greg B. Walker. *Working Through Environmental Conflict: The Collaborative Learning Approach*. Westport, CT: Praeger, 2001.

Dary, David. *Cowboy Culture: A Saga of Five Centuries*. New York: Knopf, 1981. Paperbound edition. Lawrence: University Press of Kansas, 1989.

Daugherty, Arthur B. *Major Uses of Land in the United States: 1992*. AER-723. Washington, DC: U.S. Department of Agriculture, Economic Research Service, 1995.

David, Mark. *Dispossessing the Wilderness: Indian Removal and the Making of the National Parks*. New York: Oxford University Press, 2000.

Davidson, Osha Gray. *Broken Heartland*. New York: The Free Press, 1990.

Davidson, R.H. and W.F. Lyon. *Insect Pests of Farm, Garden, and Orchard*. 8th edition. New York: Wiley, 1987.

Davis, R.C., ed. *Encyclopedia of American Forest and Conservation History*. 2 vols. New York: Macmillan Co., 1983.

Davis, Robert Murray. *Playing Cowboys: Low Culture and High Art in the Western*. Norman: University of Oklahoma Press, 1992.

DeBraal, J. Peter. *Foreign Ownership of U.S. Agricultural Land*. Statistical Bulletin No. 879. Washington, DC: U.S. Department of Agriculture, Economic Research Service, 1994.

DeBraal, J. Peter. *Taxes on U.S. Agricultural Real Estate, 1890-1991, and Methods of Estimation*. SB-866. Washington, DC: U.S. Department of Agriculture, Economic Research Service, 1993.

deBuys, William. *Enchantment and Exploitation: The Life and Hard Times of a New Mexico Mountain Range*. Albuquerque: University of New Mexico Press, 1985.

Decker, Daniel J. and Gary R. Goff. *Valuing Wildlife: Economic and Social Perspectives*. Boulder, CO: Westview, 1987.

DeGregori, Thomas R. *Agriculture and Modern Technology*. Ames, IA: Iowa State University Press, 2001.

DeGrove, John M. and Deborah A. Miness. *The New Frontier for Land Policy: Planning and Growth Management in the States*. Cambridge, MA: Lincoln Institute of Land Policy, 1992.

Dellapenna, J.W., ed. *Appropriative Rights Model Water Code*. Reston, VA: American Society of Civil Engineers, 2007.

Deloria, Vine Jr. and Daniel Wildcat. *Power and Place:Indian Education in America*. Golden, CO: Fulcrum Resources, 2001.

Dethloff, Henry C. *A History of the American Rice Industry, 1685–1985*. College Station, TX: Texas A&M University Press, 1988.

Detomasi, Don D. and John W. Gartrell, eds. *Resource Communities: A Decade of Disruption*. Boulder, CO: Westview Press, 1984.

DeYoung, Alan J. *Rural Education Issues and Practices*. New York and London, UK: Garland Publishing, 1991.

DeYoung, Alan J. *The Life and Death of a Rural American High School: Farewell, Little Kanawha*. New York: Garland Publishing, 1995.

Dicks, Michael R. and Katharine C. Buckley, eds. *Alternative Opportunities in Agriculture: Expanding Output through Diversification*. Agricultural Economic Report No. 633. Washington, DC: U.S. Department of Agriculture, Economic Research Service, 1989.

Dillman, Don and Daryl Hobbs. *Rural Society in the U.S.: Issues for the 1980s*. Boulder, CO: Westview Press, 1982.

D'Intino, Robert. *Volunteer Firefighter Recruitment and Retention in Rural Pennsylvania*. Harrisburg, PA: The Center for Rural Pennsylvania, 2006.

Doeksen, Gerald A., et al. *A Guidebook for Rural Solid Waste Management Services*. Mississippi State, MS: Southern Rural Development Center, 1993.

Dolbeare, Cushing N. *Conditions and Trends in Rural Housing. A Home in the Country: The Housing Challenges Facing Rural America*. FannieMae Office of Housing Research. October 30, 1995.

Donahue, Brian. *Reclaiming the Commons: Community Farms and Forests in a New England Town*. New Haven: Yale University Press, 1999.

Doppelt, B., M. Scurlock, C. Frissell, and J. Karr. *Entering the Watershed: A New Approach to Save America's River Ecosystems*. Covelo, CA: The Pacific Rivers Council, 1993.

Dorman, Robert L. *Revolt of the Provinces: The Regionalist Movement in America, 1920–1945*. Chapel Hill: University of North Carolina Press, 1993.

Du Bry, Travis. *Immigrants, Settlers, and Laborers: The Socioeconomic Transformation of a Farming Community*. New York: LBF Scholarly Publishing, 2007.

Duhart, Detis T. *Urban, Suburban, and Rural Victimization, 1993–98.* U.S. Department of Justice, Bureau of Justice Statistics Special Report. Washington, DC: U.S. Department of Justice, October 2000.

Dunayer, Joan. *Animal Equality: Language and Liberation.* Derwood, MD: Ryce Publishing, 2001.

Duncan, Cynthia M., ed. *Rural Poverty in America.* New York: Auburn House, 1992.

Duncan, Cynthia M. *Worlds Apart: Why Poverty Persists in Rural America.* New Haven, CT: Yale University Press, 1999.

Duncan, Dayton. *Miles from Nowhere: Tales from America's Contemporary Frontier.* New York: Viking, 1993.

Dunlap, R.E. and A.G. Mertig, eds. *American Environmentalism: The U.S. Environmental Movement, 1979-1990.* Philadelphia, PA: Taylor & Francis, 1992.

Durham, Weldon B. *American Theater Companies, 1888–1930.* New York: Greenwood Press, 1987.

Durrenberger, E. Paul and Kendall Thu. *Pigs, Profits, and Rural Communities.* State University of New York, 1997.

Dyson, Lowell K. *Farmers' Organizations.* Westport, CT: Greenwood Press, 1986.

Edid, Maralyn. *Farm Labor Organizing: Trends and Perspectives.* Ithaca, NY: Cornell University Press, 1994.

Edwards, Franklin R. and Cindy W. Ma. *Futures and Options.* New York: McGraw-Hill, Inc., 1992.

Egerstrom, Lee. *Make No Small Plans.* Rochester, MN: Lone Oak Press, Ltd., 1994.

Eidman, Vernon R. *The 2002 Farm Bill: a Step Forward or a Step Backward?* St. Paul, MN: University of Minnesota, Center for International Food and Agricultural Policy, 2002.

Elliott, D. L., L.L. Wendell, and G.L. Grower. *An Assessment of the Available Windy Land Area and Wind Energy Potential in the Contiguous United States.* Richland, WA: Pacific Northwest National Laboratory, 1991.

Elliott, R.L., and M.E. Jensen, eds. *Design and Operation of Farm Irrigation Systems.* 2nd edition. ASAE Monograph No. 3. St. Joseph, MI: American Society of Agricultural Engineering, 1997.

Ensminger, M.E. *Animal Science.* 9th edition. Danville, IL: Interstate Publishers, 1991.

Ensminger, M.E., *Dairy Cattle Science.* 3rd edition. Danville, IL: Interstate Publishers, 1993.

Ensminger, Robert F. *The Pennsylvania Barn: Its Origin, Evolution, and Distribution in North America.* Baltimore, MD: Johns Hopkins University Press, 1992

Epstein, Howard. *Jews in Small Towns: Legends and Legacies.* Santa Rosa, CA: Vision Books, 1997.

Erickson, Duane E. and John T. Scott, eds. *Farm Real Estate,* NCR No. 51. Urbana: University of Illinois, 1990.

Estes, E.A., ed. *Look Through the 90's: The U.S. Fruit and Vegetable Industry.* Proceedings of the S-222 Regional Research Committee Workshop on the U.S. Fruit and Vegetable Industry. Overland Park, KS: The Packer, Vance Publications, June 1990.

Estrée, Tamra, and Bonnie Colby. *Braving the Currents: Evaluating Environmental Conflict Resolution to the River Basins of the American West.* Norwell, MA: Kluwer Academic Publishers, 2004.

Evans, Bernard and Greg Cusack, eds. *Theology of the Land.* Collegeville, MN: The Liturgical Press, 1987.

Evans, J. Warren. *Horses: A Guide to Selection, Care, and Enjoyment,* 3rd edition. New York: Macmillan, 2002.

Ewert, Alan W., Deborah J. Chavez, and Arthur W. Magill. *Culture, Conflict, and Communication in the Wildland-Urban Interface.* Boulder, CO: Westview Press, 1993.

Eysberg, Cyees D. *The Californian Wine Economy: Natural Opportunities and Socio-Cultural Constraints.* Utrecht, Netherlands: Netherlands Geographical Studies, 1990.

Fahl, R.J. *North American Forest and Conservation History: A Bibliography.* Santa Barbara, CA: Forest History Society, 1977. Updated annually in computerized database by Forest History Society, Durham, NC.

Fairbanks, Carol, and Sara Brooks Sundberg. *Farm Women on the Prairie Frontier: A Sourcebook for Canada and the United States.* Metuchen, NJ: The Scarecrow Press, Inc., 1983.

Fairchild, Deborah M., ed. *Groundwater Quality and Agricultural Practices.* Chelsea, MI: Lewis Pub., 1987.

Falk, William W. and Thomas A. Lyson. *High Tech, Low Tech, No Tech: Recent Occupational and Industrial Changes in the South.* Albany: State University of New York Press, 1988.

Falk, William W. and Thomas A. Lyson. *Rural Labor Markets.* Research in Rural Sociology and Development. Greenwich, CT: JAI Press, Inc., 1989.

Fanning, D.S. and M.C.B. Fanning. *Soil Morphology, Genesis, and Classification.* New York: Wiley, 1989.

Faust, Miklos. *Physiology of Temperate Zone Fruit Trees.* New York: John Wiley and Sons, Inc. 1989.

Federal Emergency Management Administration. *Are You Ready: A Guide to Citizen Preparedness.* Washington, DC: Department of Homeland Security, Federal Emergency Management Administration, Citizen Corps Programs, 2004.

Fennell, David. *Ecotourism,* 2nd edition. New York: Routledge, 2003.

Ferleger, Lou. *Agricultural and National Development: Views on the Nineteenth Century.* The Henry A. Wallace Series. Ames: Iowa State University Press, 1990.

Ferriss, Susan and Ricardo Sandoval. *The Fight in the Fields: Cesar Chavez and the Farmworkers Movement.* New York: Harcourt Brace & Company, 1997.

Fett, John. *Sources and Use of Agricultural Information: A Literature Review.* Madison, WI: Department of Agricultural Journalism, University of Wisconsin, 1993.

Fink, Deborah. *Agrarian Women: Wives and Mothers in Rural Nebraska, 1880–1940.* Chapel Hill: University of North Carolina Press, 1992.

Finalyson M. and M. Moser. *Wetlands.* Oxford, UK: International Waterfowl and Wetlands Research Bureau, Facts On File Limited, 1991.

Fishback, Price. *Soft Coal, Hard Choices: The Economic Welfare of Bituminous Coal Miners, 1890-1930*. New York: Oxford University Press, 1992.

Fitchen, Janet M. *Endangered Spaces, Enduring Places: Change, Identity, and Survival in Rural America*. Boulder, CO: Westview Press, 1991.

Fitchen, Janet M. *Poverty in Rural America: A Case Study*. Boulder, CO: Westview, 1981.

Fite, Gilbert C. *American Farmers: The New Minority*. Bloomington. IN: Indiana University Press, 1981.

Fleisher, B. *Agricultural Risk Management*. Boulder, CO: Lynne Rienner Publishers, 1990.

Flint, M.L. and R. Van den Bosch. *Introduction to Integrated Pest Management*. New York: Plenum Press, 1981.

Flora, Cornelia B. and James A. Christenson, eds. *Rural Policies for the 1990s*. Boulder, CO: Westview Press, 1991.

Flora, Cornelia B. and Jan L. Flora. *Rural Communities: Legacy and Change, 3rd edition*. Boulder, CO: Westview Press, 2008.

Florida Department of Agriculture and Consumer Services (FDACS). *Florida's Agricultural Water Policy: Ensuring Resource Availability*. Tallahassee, FL: Florida Department of Agriculture and Consumer Services, 2003.

Fluck, Richard C., ed. *Energy in Farm Production. Vol. 6, Energy in World Agriculture*. B.A. Stout, editor-in-chief. Amsterdam: Elsevier, 1992.

Follett, R.F. and B.A. Stewart. *Soil Erosion and Crop Productivity*. Madison, WI: American Society of Agronomy, 1985.

Fossett, Mark A. and M. Therese Seibert. *Long Time Coming: Racial Inequality in the Nonmetropolitan South, 1940-1990*. Boulder, CO: Westview Press, 1997.

Foster, S. *No Place to Hide: Substance Abuse In Mid-Size Cites and Rural America*. New York: National Center on Addiction and Substance Abuse, 2000.

Foth, H.D. *Fundamentals of Soil Science*. 8th edition. New York: Wiley, 1990.

Francavighia, Richard V. *Hard Places: Reading the Landscape of America's Historic Mining Districts*. Iowa City: University of Iowa Press, 1991.

Fraser, Andrew F. and Donald M. Broom. *Farm Animal Behavior and Welfare*. 3rd edition. Philadelphia, PA: Bailliere Tindall, 1990.

Fraser, James. *The American Billboard: 100 Years*. New York: Harry N. Abrams, Inc., 1991.

Free, John B. *Insect Pollination of Crops*. London, England: Academic Press, Inc., 1992.

Freier, George D. *Weather Proverbs: How 600 Proverbs, Sayings and Poems Accurately Explain Our Weather*. Tucson, AZ: Fisher Books, 1989.

Frenzen, Paul D. *The Medicare and Medicaid Programs in Rural America: A Profile of Program Beneficiaries and Health Care Providers*. Staff Paper No. AGES9604. Washington, DC: U.S. Department of Agriculture, Rural Economy Division, Economic Research Service, 1996.

Freudenberger, C. Dean. *Food for Tomorrow?* Minneapolis, MN: Augsburg Publishing House, 1984.

Freyfogle, Eric T. *Agrarianism and the Good Society: Land, Culture, Conflict, and Hope*. Lexington: University Press of Kentucky, 2007.

Friedland, William H., Amy E. Barton, and Robert J. Thomas. *Manufacturing Green Gold: Capital, Labor, and Technology in the Lettuce Industry*. New York: Cambridge University Press, 1981.

Fuguitt, Glenn V., David L. Brown, and Calvin L. Beale. *Rural and Small Town America*. New York: Russell Sage, 1989.

Fuller, Varden. *Hired Hands in California's Farm Fields*. Giannini Foundation Special Report. Davis, CA: University of California, Davis, June 1991.

Fuller, Wayne E. *One-room Schools of the Middle West: An Illustrated History*. Lawrence: University Press of Kansas, 1994.

Fuller, Wayne E. *The Old Country School: The Story of Rural Education in the Middle West*. Chicago: University of Chicago Press, 1982.

Galaty, John G. and Douglas L. Johnson, eds. *The World of Pastoralism: Herding Systems in Comparative Perspective*. New York: Guilford Press, 1990.

Galbraith, Michael W., ed. *Education in the Rural American Community: A Lifelong Process*. Melbourne, FL: Krieger Publishing Co., 1992.

Galeski, Boguslaw and Eugene Wilkening. *Family Farming in Europe and America*. Boulder, CO: Westview Press, 1987.

Galston, William A. and Karen J. Baehler. *Rural Development in the United States: Connecting Theory, Practice, and Possibilities*. Washington, DC: Island Press, 1995.

Gamboa, Erasmo. *Mexican Labor and World War II: Braceros in the Pacific Northwest, 1942- 1947*. Austin: University of Texas Press, 1990.

Gard, Robert and Kolhoff, Ralph. *The Arts in the Small Community: A National Plan*. Washington DC: National Assembly of Local Arts Agencies, reprinted 1984.

Garreau, Joel. *The Nine Nations of North America*. Boston, MA: Houghton Mifflin Company, 1981.

Gaventa, John. *Power and Powerlessness: Quiescence and Rebellion in an Appalachian Valley*. Urbana: University of Illinois Press, 1980.

Geisler, Charles C. and Frank J. Popper, eds. *Land Reform, American Style*. Totawa, NJ: Rowan and Allanheld, 1984.

Gendel, Steven M., A. David Kline, D. Michael Warren, and Faye Yates, eds. *Agricultural Bioethics: Implications of Agricultural Biotechnology*. Ames: Iowa State University Press, 1990.

General Accounting Office. *U.S. Agriculture: Status of the Farm Sector*, GAO/RCEDB95–104FS. Washington, DC: General Accounting Office, March 1995.

General Accounting Office. *Pesticides: A Comparative Study of Industrialized Nations' Regulatory Systems*. Washington, DC: Program Evaluation and Methodology Division, GAO, July 1993.

George, Henry. *The Land Question*. New York, NY: Robert Shalkenbach Foundation, 1881/1982.

Ghelfi, Linda M., ed. *Rural Conditions and Trends: Special Census Issue* 4, no. 3. Washington, DC: U.S. Department of Agriculture, Economic Research Service, 1993.

Gibbons, Diana C. *The Economic Value of Water*. Washington, DC: Resources for the Future, 1986.

Gibson, Eric. *Sell What You Sow: The Grower's Guide To Successful Produce Marketing*. Carmichael, CA: New World Publishing, 1994.

Gilbert, Jess, ed. Special Issue, Minorities in Rural Society. *Rural Sociology* 56 (1991): 175- 298.

Gilbert, Richard, J., ed. *The Environment of Oil*. Norwell, MA: Kluwer Academic Publishers, 1993.

Gilford, Dorothy M., Glen L. Nelson, and Linda Ingram, eds. *Rural America in Passage: Statistics for Policy*. Washington, DC: National Academy Press, 1981.

Ginsberg, Leon H., ed. *Social Work in Rural Communities*, 4th edition. Alexandria, VA: Council on Social Work Education, 2005.

Glasmeier, Amy K. *Rural America in the Age of High Technology*. New Brunswick, NJ: Center for Urban Policy Research, Rutgers University Press, 1991.

Glasmeier, A.K. *The High-Tech Potential: Economic Development in Rural America*. New Brunswick, NJ: Center for Urban Policy Research, Rutgers University Press, 1991.

Glasmeier, Amy K. and Michael E. Conroy. *Global Squeeze on Rural America: Opportunities, Threats, and Challenges From NAFTA, GATT, and Processes of Globalization*. A Report of The Institute for Policy Research and Evaluation, Graduate School of Public Policy and Administration. College Park, PA: Pennsylvania State University, 1994.

Glenn, George D. and Poole, Richard L. *The Opera Houses of Iowa*. Ames: Iowa State University Press, 1993.

Gliessman, Stephen R. *Agroecology: The Ecology of Sustainable Food Systems*. Boca Raton, FL: CRC Press, 2007.

Goldman, Robert and Stephen Papson. *Sign Wars: The Cluttered Landscape of Advertising*. New York: Guilford, 1996.

Goodwin, John W. *Agricultural Price Analysis and Forecasting*. New York: John Wiley and Sons, Inc., 1994.

Gopalakrishnan, Chennat. *The Economics of Energy in Agriculture*. Aldershot, UK: Avebury, 1994.

Gordon, Robert B. and Patrick M. Malone. *The Texture of Industry: An Archaeological View of the Industrialization of North America*. New York: Oxford, 1994.

Gordon, Jeffrey, ed. *Solar Energy—The State of the Art*. London, UK: James and James, 2001.

Gore, Al. *An Inconvenient Truth: The Planetary Emergency of Global Warming and What We Can Do About It*. New York, NY: Rodale Books, 2006.

Goreham, Gary. *The Rural Church in America: A Century of Writings—A Bibliography*. New York: Garland, 1990.

Goreham, Gary A., David L. Watt, and Roy Jacobsen. *The Socioeconomics of Sustainable Agriculture: An Annotated Bibliography*. New York: Garland Publishing Company, 1993.

Gottlieb, Robert. *Environmentalism Unbound: Exploring Pathways for Change*. Boston, MA: MIT Press, 2001.

Government Accounting Office. *Wool and Mohair Program, Need for Program Still in Question*. GAO/RCED-90–51 (March). Washington, DC: Government Accounting Office, 1990.

Graf, William L., ed. *Geomorphic Systems of North America*. Boulder, CO: The Geological Society of America, 1987.

Graham, J.M., ed. *The Hive and the Honey Bee*. Hamilton, IL: Dadant and Sons, 1992.

Green, Gary Paul, Steven C. Deller, and David W. Marcouiller, eds. *Amenities and Rural Development: Theory, Methods, and Public Policy*. Cheltenham, UK and Northhampton, MA: Edward Elgar Publishing, 2005.

Green, Gary Paul and Anna Haines. *Asset Building and Community Development*, 2nd edition. Thousand Oaks, CA: Sage Publications, 2007.

Gregory, James Noble. *American Exodus: The Dust Bowl Migration and Okie Culture in California*. New York: Oxford University Press, 1989.

Grey, Gene and Gregory Smith. *So You Want to Be in Forestry*. Bethesda, MD: The American Forestry Association and The Society of American Foresters, 1989.

Griffin, Ronald C. *Water Resource Economics: The Analysis of Scarcity, Policies, and Project*. Cambridge, MA: MIT Press, 2006.

Griffith, David and Ed Kissam. *Working Poor: Farmworkers in the United States*. Philadelphia, PA: Temple University Press, 1995.

Grigg, David. *The Dynamics of Agricultural Change: The Historical Experience*. New York: St. Martin's Press, 1982.

Gringeri, Christina E. *Getting By: Women Homeworkers and Rural Economic Development*. Lawrence: University Press of Kansas, 1994.

Groom, M., G. Meffe, C.R. Carroll. *Principles of Conservation Biology*, 3rd edition. Sunderland, MA: Sinauer Associates, 2006.

Gulliford, Andrew. *Boomtown Blues: Colorado Oil Shale, 1885-1985*. Niwot, CO: University Press of Colorado, 1989.

Gunn, Christopher and Hazel Dayton Gunn. *Reclaiming Capital: Democratic Initiatives and Community Development*. Ithaca, NY: Cornell University Press, 1991.

Gursky, Elin A. *Hometown Hospitals: The Weakest Link? Bioterrorism Readiness in America's Rural Hospitals*. ANSER Institute for Homeland Security. Report Commissioned by the National Defense University, Center for Technology and National Security Policy, 2004.

Hadwiger, Don F. *The Politics of Agricultural Research*. Lincoln: University of Nebraska Press, 1982.

Hahamovitch, Cindy. *The Fruits of Their Labor: Atlantic Coast Farmworkers and the Making of Migrant Poverty, 1870-1945*. Chapel Hill: University of North Carolina Press, 1997.

Hahn, Steven and Jonathan Prude, eds. *The Countryside in the Age of Capitalist Transformation: Essays in the Social History of Rural America*. Chapel Hill: University of North Carolina Press, 1985.

Halcrow, H.G., E.O. Heady, and M.L. Cotner, eds. *Soil Conservation Policies, Institutions, and Incentives.* Ankeny, IA: Soil Conservation Society Press, 1982.

Hale, Lorraine. *Native American Education: A Reference Handbook. Contemporary Education Issues.* Santa Barbara, CA: ABC-CLIO, 2002.

Hall, Carl W., Nelson E. Hay, and Walter Vergara. *Natural Gas: Its Role and Potential in Economic Development.* Boulder, CO: Westview Press, 1990.

Hall, J.D., J. Leloudis, R. Korstad, M. Murphy, L. Jones, and C.B. Daly. *Like a Family: The Making of a Southern Cotton Mill World.* Chapel Hill: University of North Carolina Press, 1987.

Hallam, Arne. *Size, Structure, and the Changing Face of American Agriculture.* Boulder, CO: Westview Press, 1993.

Hallberg, Milton C. *The U.S. Agricultural and Food System: A Postwar Historical Perspective,* Publication # 35. University Park, PA: Northeast Center for Rural Development, Pennsylvania State University, 1988.

Hallberg, Milton C., Robert F.G. Spitze, and Daryll E. Ray. *Food, Agriculture, and Rural Policy into the Twenty-first Century: Issues and Trade-offs.* Boulder, CO: Westview Press, 1993.

Hammerman, Donald R., William M. Hammerman, and Elizabeth L. Hammerman. *Teaching in the Outdoors.* Danville, IL: Interstate Printing, 1985.

Hammerman, William H., ed. *Fifty Years of Resident Outdoor Education.* Martinsville, IN: American Camping Association, 1981.

Haney, Wava G. and Donald R. Field. *Agriculture and Natural Resources: Planning for Educational Priorities for the Twenty-first Century.* Boulder, CO: Westview Press, 1991.

Haney, Wava G. and Jane B. Knowles, eds. *Women and Farming: Changing Roles, Changing Structures.* Boulder, CO: Westview Press, 1988.

Hanou, John. *A Round Indiana: Round Barns in the Hoosier State.* West Lafayette, IN: Purdue University Press, 1993

Hanson, Victor Davis. *Fields without Dreams: Defending the Agrarian Ideal.* New York: Free Press, 1996.

Hargett, N.L. and J.T. Berry. *Commercial Fertilizers 1990.* TVA Bulletin Y-216. Muscle Shoals, AL: Tennessee Valley Authority, National Fertilizer, and Environmental Research Center, 1990.

Harl, Neil E. *The Farm Debt Crisis of the 1980s.* Ames: Iowa State University Press, 1990.

Harper, Sarah. *The Greening of Rural Policy: Perspectives from the Developed World.* London, UK and New York: Guilford Press, 1993.

Harsh, Stephen B., Larry J. Connor, and Gerald D. Schwab. *Managing The Farm Business.* Englewood Cliffs, NJ: Prentice-Hall, Inc., 1981.

Hart, G.L., R.A. Rosenblatt, and B.A. Amundson. *Rural Hospital Utilization: Who Stays and Who Goes?* WAMI Rural Health Research Center working paper series, March, 1989.

Hart, John. *Sacramental Commons.* Lanham: Rowman & Littlefield, 2006.

Hartel, Peter G., Kathryn Paxton George, and James Vorst, eds. *Agricultural Ethics: Issues for the 21st Century.* ASA Special Publication no. 57. Madison, WI: Soil Science Society of America, American Society of Agronomy, Crop Science Society of America, 1994.

Hartley, C., J. Gale, and D. Lambert. *Substance Abuse Among Rural Youth.* Muskie School of Public Service: Research & Policy Brief, 2007.

Harvey, Mark. *A Symbol of Wilderness: Echo Park and the American Conservation Movement.* Seattle: University of Washington Press, 2000.

Hassebrook, Chuck and Gabriel Hegyes. *Choices for the Heartland: Alternative Directions in Biotechnology and Implications for Family Farming, Rural Communities, and the Environment.* Ames: Iowa State University, Technology and Social Change Program, and Walthill, NE: Center for Rural Affairs, 1989.

Hassinger, Edward W., John S. Holik, and J. Kenneth Benson. *The Rural Church: Learnings from Three Decades of Change.* Nashville, TN: Abingdon Press, 1988.

Hatch, Upton and Henry Kinnucan, eds. *Aquaculture: Models and Economics.* Boulder, CO: Westview Press, 1993.

Havir, Linda Marie. *But Will They Use It? Social Service Utilization by Rural Elderly.* New York: Garland Publishing, 1995.

Havlin, John, Alan Schlegel, Kevin C. Dhuyvetter, James P. Shroyer, Hans Kok, and Dallas Peterson. *Enhancing Agricultural Profitability and Sustainability: Great Plains Dryland Conservation Technologies.* S-81. Manhattan, KS: Cooperative Extension Service, Kansas State University, 1995.

Hawley, Amos H. and Sara Mills Maize, eds. *Nonmetropolitan America in Transition.* Chapel Hill: University of North Carolina Press, 1981.

Hayenga, Marvin, James MacDonald, Kyle Steigert, and Brian L. Buhr. *The 2007 Farm Bill: Policy Options and Consequences; Concentration, Mergers and Antitrust.* Oak Brook, IL: Farm Foundation, 2007.

Hayes, Robert G., ed. *Early Stories from the Land: Short-Story Fiction from Rural American Magazines 1900–1925.* Ames: Iowa State University Press, 1995.

Hays, Samuel P. *Beauty, Health, and Permanence: Environmental Politics in the United States, 1955-1988.* New York: Cambridge University Press, 1987.

Haynes, Richard W. *An Analysis of the Timber Situation in the United States: 1989-2040.* USDA General Technical Report RM-199. Washington, DC: U.S. Department of Agriculture, Forest Service, 1990.

Heady, Harold F. and R. Dennis Child. *Rangeland Ecology and Management.* Boulder, CO: Westview Press, 1995.

Health Resources and Services Administration. *Rural Communities and Emergency Preparedness.* Washington, DC: Office of Rural Health Policy, HRSA, U.S. Department of Health and Human Services, 2002.

Hedges, Elaine, and William Hedges. *Land and Imagination: The Rural Dream in America.* Rochelle Park, NJ: Hayden Book Company, 1980.

Heffernan, William, Douglas Constance, Robert Gronski, and Mary Hendrickson. *Concentration of Agricultural Markets.* Columbia: Department of Rural Sociology, University of Missouri - Columbia, 1996.

Heimlich, R.E. and W.D. Anderson. *Development at the Urban Fringe and Beyond: Impacts on Agriculture and Rural Land.* AER–803. Washington, DC: U.S. Department of Agriculture, Economic Research Service, 2001.

Heimlich, Ralph and L. Langer. *Swampbusting: Wetland Conversion and Farm Programs.* Agricultural Economics Report No. 51. Washington DC: U.S. Department of Agriculture, Natural Resource Economics Division, Economic Research Service, 1986.

Heiser, Charles B., Jr. *Seed to Civilization. The Story of Food.* San Francisco, CA: W.H. Freeman and Company Press, 1981.

Heitschmidt, Rodney K. and Jerry W. Stuth, eds. *Grazing Management: An Ecological Perspective.* Portland, OR: Timber Press, Inc., 1991.

Helge, D., guest editor. Special Topical Issue: Rural Special Education. *Journal of Exceptional Children* 50, no. 4 (1984): 293–369.

Helsel, Zane R., ed. *Energy in Plant Nutrition and Pest Control. Vol. 2, Energy in World Agriculture.* B.A. Stout, editor-in-chief. Amsterdam: Elsevier, 1987.

Hendee, John C. and Chad P. Dawson. *Wilderness Management: Stewardship and Protection of Resources and Values*, 3rd. ed. Golden, CO: Fulcrum Publishing, 2002.

Herz, D.C. *Drugs in the Heartland: Methamphetamine Use in Rural Nebraska.* National Institute of Justice, 2000.

Hewitt, Marcia E. *Defining "Rural" Areas: Impact on Health Care Policy and Research.* Staff Paper, Office of Technology Assessment. Washington, DC: Government Printing Office, 1989.

Heywood, V.H., ed. *Global Biodiversity Assessment.* New York: Cambridge University Press, 1995.

Hickman, John, Jeff Jacobsen, and Drew Lyon. *Best Management Practices for Wheat: A Guide to Profitable and Environmentally Sound Production.* Washington, DC: Cooperative Extension Service and The National Association of Wheat Growers Foundation, 1994.

Hickey, Joseph V. *Ghost Settlement on the Prairie: A Biography of Thurman, Kansas.* Lawrence: University Press of Kansas, 1995.

Hillel, Daniel. 1991. *Out of the Earth: Civilization and the Life of the Soil.* Berkeley: University of California Press.

Hinrichs, C. Clare and Thomas A. Lyson, eds. *Remaking the North American Food System: Strategies for Sustainability.* Lincoln, NB: University of Nebraska Press, 2007

Hirschfelder, Arlene and Martha Kreipe de Montano. *The Native American Almanac, A Portrait of Native America Today.* New York: Prentice Hall General Reference, 1993.

Hoban, Thomas J. and Patricia A. Kendall. *Consumer Attitudes about Food Biotechnology.* Raleigh, NC: North Carolina Cooperative Extension Service, 1993.

Hodgson, John. *Grazing Management Science into Practice.* New York: John Wiley and Sons, Inc., co-published with Longman Scientific and Technical, 1990.

Hoffman, G.J., T.A. Howell, and K.H. Solomon, eds. *Management of Farm Irrigation Systems.* ASAE Monograph. St. Joseph, MI: American Society of Agricultural Engineering, 1990.

Hoffman, Linwood A., Sara Schwartz, and Grace V. Chomo. *Wheat: Background for 1995 Farm Legislation.* Agricultural Economic Report No. 712. Washington, DC: U.S. Department of Agriculture, Economic Research Service, 1995.

Holechek, Jerry, Rex Pieper, and Carlton Herbel. *Range Management: Principles and Practices*, 5th edition. Englewood Cliffs, NJ.: Prentice Hall, 2004

Holland, I.I., G.L. Rolfe, and D.A. Anderson. *Forests and Forestry.* Danville, IL: Interstate Publishers, 1990.

Holmgren, D. *Permaculture: Principles and Pathways beyond Sustainability.* Victoria, Australia: Holmgren Design Services, 2002.

Hopkin and Associates. *Transition in Agriculture: A Strategic Assessment of Agricultural Banking.* Washington, DC: American Bankers Association, 1986.

Hoppe, R. *The Role of the Elderly's Income in Rural Development.* Rural Development Research Report 80. Washington, DC: U.S. Department of Agriculture, ERS, 1991.

Horan, Patrick M. and Charles M. Tolbert II. *The Organization of Work in Rural and Urban Labor Markets.* Boulder, CO: Westview Press, 1984.

Housing Assistance Council. *Rural Homelessness: A Review of the Literature.* Washington, DC: The author, 1991.

Housing Assistance Council. *Homeownership as an Asset in Rural America.* Washington DC: Housing Assistance Council, March 2005.

Howell, F.M., Y. Tung, and C.W. Harper. *The Social Cost of Growing-up in Rural America: A Study of Rural Development and Social Change During the Twentieth Century.* Mississippi State, MS: Social Science Research Center, Mississippi State University, October, 1995.

Hoxie, Frederick E. *A Final Promise. The Campaign to Assimilate the Indian, 1880–1920.* Lincoln: University of Nebraska Press, 1984.

Hubka, Thomas C. *Big House, Little House, Back House, Barn: The Connected Farm Buildings of New England.* Hanover, NH: University Press of New England, 1984.

Hughes, Dean W., Stephen C. Gabriel, Peter J. Barry, and Michael D. Boehlje. *Financing the Agricultural Sector.* Boulder, CO: Westview Press, 1986.

Humstone, Mary. *BARN AGAIN!: A Guide to Rehabilitation of Older Farm Buildings.* Denver, CO: Meredith Corporation and The National Trust for Historic Preservation, 1988.

Hunter, Kent R. *The Lord's Harvest and the Rural Church.* Kansas City, MO: Beacon Hill Press, 1993.

Hurley, Andrew. *Diners, Bowling Alleys and Trailer Parks: Chasing the American Dream in Postwar Consumer Culture.* New York: Basic Books, 2001.

Hurt, R. Douglas. *The Dust Bowl: An Agricultural and Social History.* Chicago: Nelson- Hall, 1981.

Hurt, R. Douglas. *American Agriculture: A Brief History,* Revised edition. West Lafayette, IN: Purdue University Press, 2002.

Huquenin, J.E. and J. Colt, eds. *Design and Operating Guide for Aquaculture Seawater System*s, 2nd edition. Elsevier Science, 2002.

Ilic, Pedro. *Southeast Asian Farmers in Fresno County: Status Report 1992.* Fresno, CA: Fresno County Office of University of California Cooperative Extension, 1992.

Inge, M. Thomas, ed. *Agrarianism in American Literature.* New York: The Odyssey Press, 1969.

Isenberg, Andrew. *Destruction of the Bison.* Cambridge: Cambridge University Press, 2000.

Isern, Thomas D. *Bull Threshers and Bindlestiffs: Harvesting and Threshing on the North American Plains.* Lawrence: University Press of Kansas, 1990.

Iwata, Masakazu. *Planted in Good Soil: A History of the Issei in United States Agriculture.* New York: P. Lang, 1992.

Jackson, Kenneth and Camillo José Vergara. *Silent Cities: The Evolution of the American Cemetery.* New York: Princeton Architectural Press, 1989.

Jain, R.K., L.V. Urban, G.S. Stacey, and H.E. Balbach. *Environmental Assessment.* New York: McGraw-Hill, Inc., 1993.

Janick, Jules. *Horticultural Science.* 4th edition. New York: W.H. Freeman and Co., 1986.

Jansson, AnnMari, Monicao Hammer, Carl Folke, and Robert Costanza, eds. *Investing in Natural Capital: The Ecological Economics Approach to Sustainability.* Covelo, CA: Island Press, 1994.

Jarvis, Lovel S. *The Potential Effect of Two Biotechnologies on the World Dairy Industry.* Boulder, CO: Westview Press, 1994.

Jasper, James M. and Dorothy Nelkin. *The Animal Rights Crusade: The Growth of a Moral Protest.* New York: The Free Press, 1992.

Jellison, Katherine. *Entitled to Power: Farm Women and Technology.* Chapel Hill: University of North Carolina Press, 1993.

Jenkins, J. Craig. *The Politics of Insurgency: The Farm Worker Movement of the 1960's.* New York: Columbia University Press, 1985.

Jensen, M.E., ed. *Design and Operation of Farm Irrigation Systems.* ASAE Monograph No. 3. St. Joseph, MI: American Society of Agricultural Engineering, 1983.

Johannessen, S. and Hastorf, C.A., eds. *Corn and Culture in the Prehistoric New World.* Boulder, CO: Westview Press, 1994.

Johanson, Harley E. and Glenn V. Fuguitt. *The Changing Rural Village: Demographics and Rural Trends Since 1950.* Cambridge, MA: Ballinger Publishing Co., 1984.

Johnson, Kenneth M. *The Impact of Population Change on Business Activity in Rural America.* Boulder, CO: Westview Press, 1985.

Johnson, Thomas, Brady J. Deaton, and Eduardo Segarra. *Local Infrastructure Investment in Rural America.* Boulder, CO: Westview Press, 1988.

Jones, Hamlyn G. *Plants and Microclimate: A Quantitative Approach to Environmental Plant Physiology,* 2nd edition. New York: Cambridge University Press, 1992.

Judy, Marvin. *From Ivy Tower to Village Spire.* Dallas, TX: Southern Methodist University Printing, 1984.

Jung, Shannon. *We Are Home: A Spirituality of the Environment.* Mahwah, NJ: Paulist Press, 1993.

Jung, Shannon, Pegge Boehm, Deborah Cronin, Gary Farley, Dean Freudenberger, Judy Heffernan, Sandy LaBlanc, Ed Queen, and Dave Ruesink. *Rural Ministry: The Shape of the Renewal to Come.* Nashville, TN: Abingdon Press, 1997.

Jung, Shannon and Mary A. Agria. *Rural Congregational Studies: A Guide for Good Shepherds.* Nashville, TN: Abingdon, 1997.

Kabacher, J. and Oliveira, V. *Structural and Financial Characteristics of U.S. Farms, 1992: 17th Annual Family Farm Report to Congress.* Agriculture Information Bulletin Number 72. Washington, DC: Rural Economy Division, Economic Research Service, U.S. Department of Agriculture, 1995.

Kandel, William and David L. Brown. *Population Change and Rural Society.* The Netherlands: Springer, 2006.

Kader, Adel A., ed. *Postharvest Technology of Horticultural Crops.* Oakland, CA: University of California, Division of Agriculture and Natural Resources, 1992.

Kadlec, John E. *Farm Management: Decisions, Operation, Control.* Englewood Cliffs, NJ: Prentice-Hall, Inc., 1985.

Kann, Kenneth L. *Comrades and Chicken Ranchers: The Story of a California Jewish Community.* Ithaca, NY: Cornell University Press, 1993.

Kay, Ronald D. and William M. Edwards, *Farm Management.* 3rd edition. New York: McGraw-Hill, Inc., 1994.

Keith, Jeanette. *Country People in the New South: Tennessee's Upper Cumberland.* Chapel Hill: University of North Carolina Press, 1995.

Keizer, Garrett. *No Place but Here: A Teacher's Vocation in a Rural Community.* New York: Viking Penguin, Inc., 1988.

Keller, Peter A. and J. Dennis Murray, eds. *Handbook of Rural Community Mental Health.* New York: Human Services Press, 1982.

Kellogg, Robert L., Margaret Stewart Maizel, and Don W. Goss. *Agricultural Chemical Use and Groundwater Quality: Where are the Potential Problem Areas?* Washington, DC: U.S. Department of Agriculture, Soil Conservation Service, 1992.

Kelly, Eric Damian and Gary J. Raso. *Sign Regulation for Small and Midsize Communities.* Planning Advisory Service Report No. 419. Chicago: American Planning Association, 1989.

Kenny, Martin F. *Biotechnology: The University-Industrial Complex.* New Haven, CT: Yale University Press, 1986.

Kephart, William M. and William W. Zellner. *Extraordinary Groups: An Examination of Unconventional Life-Styles.* 4th edition. New York: St. Martin's Press, 1991.

Kerr, Norwood A. *The Legacy: A Centennial History of the State Agricultural Experiment Stations 1887–1987.* Columbia: Missouri Agricultural Experiment Station, University of Missouri, 1987.

Killian, M.S., L.E. Bloomquist, S. Pendleton, and D.A. McGranahan, eds. *Symposium on Rural Labor Market Research Issues.* Staff Report AGES860721. Washington, DC: U.S. Department of Agriculture, Economic Research Service, 1986.

Kingsolver, Barbara. *Holding the Line: Women in the Great Arizona Mine Strike of 1983.* Ithaca, NY: ILR Press, 1989.

Kirschenman, Frederick. *Switching to a Sustainable System Strategies for Converting from Conventional/Chemical to Sustainable/Organic Farm Systems.* Windsor, ND: The Northern Plains Sustainable Agriculture Society, 1988; Emmaus, PA: Rodale Press, Inc., Holding Library, 1996.

Kline, R.R. *Consumers in the Country: Technology and Social Change in Rural America.* Baltimore: Johns Hopkins University Press, 2000.

Kloppenburg, Jack R., Jr. *First the Seed: The Political Economy of Plant Biotechnology, 1492-2000.* New York: Cambridge University Press, 1988.

Knobloch, Frieda. *The Culture of Wilderness: Agriculture as Colonization in the American West.* Chapel Hill: University of North Carolina Press, 1996.

Knutson, R.D., J.B. Penn, W.T. Boehm, and J. L. Outlaw. *Agricultural and Food Policy.* 4th edition. Englewood Cliffs, NJ: Prentice Hall, 2007.

Knutson, Ronald D., C. Robert Taylor, John B. Penson, and Edward G. Smith. *Economic Impacts of Reduced Chemical Use.* College Station, TX: Knutson and Associates, 1990.

Kohl, David M. *Weighing the Variables: A Guide to Ag Credit Management.* Washington, DC: American Bankers Association, 1992.

Kohler, C.C., and W.A. Hubert, eds. *Inland Fisheries Management in North America,* 2nd edition. Bethesda, MD: American Fisheries Society, 1999.

Kohls, Richard L. and Joseph N. Uhl. *Marketing of Agricultural Products,* 9th edition. New York: Macmillan Publishing Company, 2002.

Korsching, Peter F., Timothy O. Borich, and Julie Stewart, eds. *Multicommunity Collaboration: An Evolving Rural Revitalization Strategy.* Ames, IA: North Central Regional Center For Rural Development, July 1992.

Kraenzel, Carl. *The Social Cost of Space in Yonland.* Bozeman, MT: Big Sky Press, 1980.

Krause, Tina B., ed. *Care of the Earth: An Environmental Resource Manual for Church Leaders.* Chicago: Lutheran School of Theology at Chicago, 1994.

Krausman, Paul. *Introduction to Wildlife Management: The Basics.* Upper Saddle River, New Jersey: Prentice Hall, 2002.

Kromm, David E. and Stephen E. White, eds. *Groundwater Exploitation in the High Plains.* Lawrence: University Press of Kansas, 1992.

Krout, J.A. *The Aged in Rural America.* New York: Greenwood Press, 1986.

Krout, J.A., ed. *Providing Community Based Services to the Rural Elderly.* Thousand Oaks, CA: SAGE Publications, Inc., 1994.

Lampkin, Nicolas. *Organic Farming.* Ipswich, UK: Farming Press Books, 1980.

Land, Aubrey, ed. *Bases of the Plantation Society.* Columbia: University of South Carolina Press, 1969.

Langhans, Robert W. *Greenhouse Management: A Guide to Structures, Materials Handling, Crop Programming, and Business Analysis.* 3rd edition. Ithaca, NY: Halcyon Press of Ithaca, 1990.

Lapping, Mark B., Thomas L. Daniels, and John W. Keller. *Rural Planning and Development in the United States.* London, UK and New York: Guilford Press, 1989.

LaRoe, Edward T, Gaye S. Farris, Catherine E. Puckett, Peter D. Doran, Michael J. Macs, eds. *Our Living Resources: A Report to the Nation on the Distribution, Abundance, and Health of U.S. Plants, Animals, and Ecosystems.* Washington, DC: U.S. Department of the Interior, National Biological Service, 1995.

Larson, Olaf F., Edward O. Moe, and Julie N. Zimmerman. *Sociology in Government: A Bibliography of the Work of the Division of Farm Population and Rural Life, U.S. Department of Agriculture, 1919-1953.* Boulder, CO: Westview Press, 1992.

Lasley, F.A. *The U.S. Poultry Industry: Changing Economics and Structure,* A.E. Report No. 502 (July). Washington, DC: U.S. Department of Agriculture, Economic Research Service, 1983.

Lasley, F.A., H.B. Jones, E.E. Easterling, and L.A. Christensen. *The U.S. Broiler Industry,* A.E. Report No. 591 (November). Washington: U.S. Department of Agriculture, Economic Research Service, 1988.

Lasley, F.A., W.L. Henson, and H.B. Jones. *The U.S. Turkey Industry.* A.E. Report No. 525 (March). Washington, DC: U.S. Department of Agriculture, Economic Research Service, 1985.

Lasley, Paul, F. Larry Leistritz, Linda M. Lobao, and Katherine Meyer. *Beyond the Amber Waves of Grain: An Examination of Social and Economic Restructuring in the Heartland.* Boulder, CO: Westview Press, 1995.

Lee, Warren F., Michael D. Boehlje, Aaron G. Nelson, and William G. Murray. *Agricultural Finance.* 8th edition. Ames: Iowa State University Press, 1988.

Leeuwis, Cees and Anne van den Ban. *Communication for Rural Innovation: Rethinking Agricultural Extension.* Ames, Iowa: Iowa State University Press, 2004.

Leifeld, Jessica. *An Exploration of the National Incident Management System (NIMS) Mandate in Rural America: Through the Eyes of Emergency Management Practitioners.* Master's thesis. Fargo, ND: North Dakota State University, 2007.

Leistritz, F. Larry and Steven H. Murdock. *The Socioeconomic Impact of Resource Development: Methods for Assessment.* Boulder, CO: Westview Press, 1981.

Lekang, Odd-Ivar. *Aquaculture Engineering.* Hoboken, NJ: Wiley-Blackwell, 2007.

Leopold, Aldo. *Sand County Almanac.* New York, NY: Oxford University Press, 1949

Lesser, William H. *Marketing Livestock and Meat.* Binghamton, NY: Food Products Press, 1993.

Lester, James P. *Environmental Politics and Policy: Theories and Evidence*, 2nd edition. Durham, NC: Duke University Press, 1995.

Leukefeld, Carl, Godlaski, Thomas, Clark, J, Brown, C, and Lon Hays. *Behavioral Therapy for Rural Substance Abusers*. Lexington, KY: The University Press of Kentucky, 2000.

Leuthold, Raymond M., Joan C. Junkus, and Jean E. Cordier. *The Theory and Practice of Futures Markets*. Lexington: Lexington Books, 1989.

Lewis, Ronald L. *Black Coal Miners in America: Race, Class and Community Conflict*. Lexington: University Press of Kentucky, 1987.

Lewis, Steven. *The Wisdom of the Spotted Owl*. Covelo, CA: Island Press, 1994.

Libbin, James D., Lowell B. Catlett, and Michael L. Jones. *Cash Flow Planning in Agriculture*. Ames: Iowa State University Press, 1994.

Lieb, Robert C. *Transportation*. 4th edition. Houston, TX: Dame Publications, Inc. 1994.

Lincoln, C. Eric and Lawrence H. Mamiya. *The Black Church in African-American Experience*. Durham, NC: Duke University Press, 1990.

Lindell, M., C. Prater, C., and R. Perry. *Introduction to Emergency Management*. Hoboken, NJ: Wiley, 2007.

Linder, Marc. *Migrant Workers and Minimum Wages*. Boulder, CO: Westview Press, 1992.

Lingeman, Richard. *Small Town America: A Narrative History, 1620-The Present*. Boston, MA: Houghton Mifflin, 1980.

Lobao, Linda M. *Locality and Inequality: Farm and Industry Structure and Socioeconomic Conditions*. Albany: State University of New York Press, 1990.

Logsdon, Gene. *At Nature's Pace: Farming and the American Ideal*. New York: Pantheon, 1994.

Lohman, Nancy and Roger A. Lohman. *Rural Social Work Practice*. New York, NY: Columbia University Press, 2005.

Lohr, L. *Factors Affecting International Demand and Trade in Organic Food Products: Changing Structure of Global Food Consumption and Trade* (WRS-01-1). Washington, DC: U.S. Department of Agriculture, Economic Research Service, 2001.

Long, Patrick, Jo Clark, and Derek Liston. *Win, Lose, or Draw? Gambling With America's Small Towns*. Washington, DC: The Aspen Institute, 1994.

Longstreth, Richard. *The Buildings of Main Street: A Guide to American Commercial Architecture*. Washington, DC: The Preservation Press, 1987.

Looney, J.W., J. Wilder, S. Brownback, and J. Wadley. *Agricultural Law: A Lawyer's Guide to Representing Farm Clients*. Chicago: American Bar Association, Section of General Practice, 1990.

Lovejoy, Stephen B. and Ted L. Napier, eds. *Conserving Soil: Insights From Socioeconomic Research*. Ankeny, IA: Soil Conservation Society Press, 1986.

Lovell, Tom, ed. *Nutrition and Feeding of Fish*, 2nd edition. Boston, MA: Kluwer Academic Publishers, 1998.

Lucas, John S. and Paul C. Southgate, eds. *Aquaculture: Farming Aquatic Animals and Plants*. Wiley-Blackwell, 2003.

Lucier, Gary, coord. *Vegetables and Specialties: Situation and Outlook Report*. TVS-263 (July). Washington, DC: U.S. Department of Agriculture, Economic Research Service, 1994.

Luebke, Frederick, ed. *Ethnicity on the Great Plains*. Lincoln: University of Nebraska Press, 1980.

Luh, Bor S., ed. *Rice: Production and Utilization*. 2nd edition. Vol. 2. New York: Van Nostrand Reinhold, 1991.

Luloff, A.E. and Louis E. Swanson. *American Rural Communities*. Boulder, CO: Westview Press, 1990.

Lyle, John Tillman. *Regenerative Design for Sustainable Development*. Wiley Series in Sustainable Design. New York: John Wiley and Sons, 1994.

Lyson, Thomas A. *Two Sides of the Sunbelt: The Growing Divergence between the Rural and Urban South*. New York: Praeger, 1989.

Lyson, Thomas. *Civic Agriculture. Reconnecting Farm, Food, and Community*. Medford, MA: Tufts University Press, 2004.

Lyson, Thomas A. and William W. Falk, eds. *Forgotten Places: Uneven Development in Rural America*. Lawrence: University Press of Kansas, 1993.

MaCC Group. *Waste Reduction Strategies for Rural Communities*. Washington, DC: American Plastics Council, with support from the Tennessee Valley Authority, 1994.

MacDonald, June Fessenden. *Agricultural Biotechnology and the Public Good*. Ithaca, NY: National Agricultural Biotechnology Council, 1994.

MacDonald, June Fessenden. *Agricultural Biotechnology: A Public Conversation about Risk*. Ithaca, NY: National Agricultural Biotechnology Council, 1993.

Maher, Neil M. *Nature's New Deal: The Civilian Conservation Corps and the Roots of the American Environmental Movement*. New York: Oxford University Press, 2008.

Majka, Linda C. and Theo J. Majka. *Farm Workers, Agribusiness and the State*. Philadelphia, PA: Temple University Press, 1982.

Malia, James E. and Janice Morrisey. *Rural Communities and Subtitle D: Problems and Solutions*. Knoxville, TN: Tennessee Valley Authority, 1994.

Malone, Bill. *Country Music, USA*. rev. edition. Austin: University of Texas Press, 1985.

Manchester, Alden. *Rearranging the Economic Landscape*, AER-660. Washington, DC: U.S. Department of Agriculture, Economic Research Service, 1992.

Marcus, Alan I. *Agricultural Science and the Quest for Legitimacy: Farmers, Agricultural Colleges, and Experiment Stations, 1870–1890*. Ames: Iowa State University Press, 1985.

Manning, Richard. *Grassland: The History, Biology, Politics and Promise of the American Prairie*. Penguin, 1997.

Maril, Robert Lee. *The Bay Shrimpers of Texas*. Lawrence: University Press of Kansas, 1995.

Marotz-Baden, Ramona, Charles B. Hennon, and Timothy H. Brubaker. *Families in Rural America: Stress, Adaptation, and*

Revitalization. St. Paul, MN: National Council on Family Relations, 1988.

Marshall, Robert, ed. *Standard Methods for the Examination of Dairy Products.* 16th edition. Washington, DC: American Public Health Association, 1992.

Marti, Donald B. *Women of the Grange: Mutuality and Sisterhood in Rural America, 1866-1920.* New York: Greenwood Press, 1991.

Martin, Guy R., Traci J. Stegemann, and Karen Donovan. *Water Conservation: The Federal Role.* Washington, DC: American Water Works Association, 1994.

Martin, Lee R. *A Survey of Agricultural Economics Literature: Economics of Welfare, Rural Development and National Resources in Agriculture, 1940's to 1970's.* Volume 3. Minneapolis: University of Minnesota Press, 1981.

Martin, Philip L. *Promise Unfulfilled: Unions, Immigration, and the Farm Workers.* Ithaca, NY: Cornell University Press, 2003.

Martin, Philip L. and David A. Martin. *The Endless Quest: Helping America's Farm Workers.* Boulder, CO: Westview Press, 1993.

Martin, Russell. *Cowboy: The Enduring Myth of the Wild West.* New York: Stewart, Tabori, and Chang, 1983.

Mason, J. *Commercial Hydroponics.* Kenthurst, NSW, Australia: Kangaroo Press, 1990.

May, Roy. *The Poor of the Land: A Christian Case for Land Reform.* Maryknoll, NY: Orbis Books, 1991.

Mayberry, B.D. *A Century of Agriculture in the 1890 Land-grant Institutions and Tuskegee University-1890–1990.* New York: Vantage Press Inc., 1991.

McCarthy, Tom. *Auto Mania: Cars, Consumers, and the Environment.* New Haven: Yale University Press, 2007.

McCloskey, Amanda H. and John Luehrs. *State Initiatives to Improve Rural Health Care.* Washington, DC: Center for Policy Research, National Governors' Association. Published in cooperation with Office of Rural Health Policy, Health Resources and Services Administration, Public Health Service, U.S. Dept. of Health and Human Services, 1990.

McCoy, John H. and M.E. Sarhan. *Livestock and Meat Marketing.* 3rd edition. New York: Van Nostrand Reinhold Company, 1988.

McDonald, Thomas D., Robert A. Wood, and Melissa A. Pflug. *Rural Criminal Justice.* Salem, WI: Sheffield Publishing Co., 1996.

McEntire, David A. *Disaster Response and Recovery: Strategies and Tactics for Resilience.* NJ: Wiley, 2007.

McEowen, R. and Harl, N. *Principles of Agricultural Law.* Eugene, OR: Ag Law Press, 1996.

McFague, Sallie. *The Body of God: An Ecological Theology.* Minneapolis, MN: Fortress Press, 1993.

McFate, Kenneth L., ed. *Electrical Energy in Agriculture. Vol. 3, Energy in World Agriculture.* B.A. Stout, editor-in-chief. Amsterdam: Elsevier, 1989.

McGranahan, David A., J. Hession, F. Hines, et al. *Social and Economic Characteristics of the Population in Metro and Nonmetro Counties, 1970–1980.* Rural Development Research Report No. 58. Washington, DC: U.S. Department of Agriculture, Economic Research Service, 1985.

McHughen, A. *Pandora's Picnic Basket.* New York, NY: Oxford University Press, 2000.

McKibben, Bill. *Hope, Human and Wild: True Stories of Living Lightly on the Earth.* Boston, MA: Little, Brown, and Co., 1995.

McLaughlin, Edward W. and D.J. Perosio. *Fresh Fruit and Vegetable Procurement Dynamics: The Role of the Supermarket Buyer.* Cornell Food Industry Management Program publication R.B. 94–1 (February). Ithaca, NY: Cornell University, Department of Agricultural, Resource, and Managerial Economics, 1994.

McMichael, Philip. *Food and Agrarian Orders in the World Economy.* Westport, CT: Greenwood Press, 1995.

McMurry, Sally. *Families and Farmhouses in Nineteenth Century America.* New York: Oxford University Press, 1988.

McNall, Scott G. and Sally Ann McNall. *Plains Families: Exploring Sociology through Social History.* New York: St. Martin's Press, 1983.

Meffe, Gary K. and C. Ronald Carroll. *Principles of Conservation Biology.* Sunderland, MA: Sinauer Associates, Inc., 1994.

Meier, Matt S. and Feliciano Ribera. *Mexican Americans/ American Mexicans: From Conquistadors to Chicanos.* New York: Hill and Wang, 1993.

Meinig, Donald. W., et al., ed. *The Interpretation of Ordinary Landscapes.* New York: Oxford University Press, 1979.

Meinig, Donald W. *The Shaping of America: A Geographical Perspective on 500 Years of History. Volume 1: Atlantic America, 1492–1800.* New Haven, CT: Yale University Press, 1986.

Meinig, Donald W. *The Shaping of America: A Geographical Perspective on 500 Years of History. Volume 2: Continental America, 1800–1867.* New Haven, CT: Yale University Press, 1993.

Metcalf, R.L. and R.A. Metcalf. *Destructive and Useful Insects: Their Habits and Control.* 5th edition. New York: McGraw-Hill, 1993.

Metcalf, R.L. and W.H. Luckman. *Introduction to Insect Pest Management.* 3rd edition. New York: Wiley, 1994.

Metcalf, R.L., B.M. Francis, D.C. Fischer, and R.M. Kelly. *Integrated Pest Management for the Home and Garden.* 3rd edition. Urbana-Champaign, IL: Institute for Environmental Studies, University of Illinois, 1994.

Meyer, Richard E., ed. *Cemeteries and Gravemarkers: Voices of American Culture.* Logan, UT: Utah State University Press, 1992.

Meyer, Richard E., ed. *Ethnicity and the American Cemetery.* Bowling Green, OH: Bowling Green State University Press, 1993.

Michrina, Barry P. *Pennsylvania Mining Families: The Search for Dignity in the Coalfields.* Lexington: University Press of Kentucky, 1993.

Milbrath, Lester W. *Envisioning a Sustainable Society.* Albany: State University of New York Press, 1989.

Miller, Char, ed. *Fluid Arguments: Five Centuries of Western Water Conflict*. Tucson, AZ: University of Arizona Press, 2001.

Miller, Char, and Hal K. Rothman, eds. *Out of the Woods: Essays in Environmental History*. Pittsburgh, PA: University of Pittsburgh Press, 1997.

Miller, James P. *Survival and Growth of Independent Firms and Corporate Affiliates in Metro and Nonmetro America*. Washington, DC: U.S. Department of Agriculture, Economic Research Service, 1990.

Miller, John. *Deer Camp: Last Light in the Northeast Kingdom*. Cambridge, MA: MIT Press and Middlebury, VT: Vermont Folklife Center, 1992.

Miller, S. *The Economic Benefits of Open Space*. Portland, ME: Maine Coast Heritage, 1992.

Miller, Sandra E., Craig W. Shinn, and William R. Bentley. *Rural Resource Management: Problem Solving for the Long Term*. Ames: Iowa State University Press, 1994.

Mohatt, D.F., M.M. Bradley, S.J. Adams, and C.D. Morris, eds. *Mental Health and Rural America: 1994-2005*. Rockville, MD: Health Resources and Services Administration, Office of Rural Health Policy, 2005.

Mollison, B.C. *Permaculture: a Practical Guide for a Sustainable Future*. Washington, DC: Island Press, 1990.

Molnar, Joseph J. and Henry Kinnucan, eds. *Biotechnology and the New Agricultural Revolution*. Boulder, CO: Westview Press, 1989.

Moltmann, Jurgen. *God in Creation: A New Theology of Creation and the Spirit of God*. San Francisco, CA: Harper and Row, 1985.

Monk, David H. *Disparities in Curricular Offerings: Issues and Policy Alternatives for Small Rural Schools*. Paper prepared for the Appalachia Educational Laboratory. Ithaca, NY: Cornell University, Department of Education, February, 1988.

Monk, David H. and Emil Haller. *Organizational Alternatives for Small Rural Schools*. Ithaca, NY: Cornell University, Department of Education, 1986.

Monke, Jim. *Agroterrorism: Threats and Preparedness*. (CRS Report RL32521) Washington, DC: Library of Congress, Congressional Research Service, 2004.

Montmarquet, James A. *The Idea of Agrarianism: From Hunter-Gatherer to Agrarian Radical in Western Culture*. Moscow, ID: University of Idaho Press, 1989.

Mooney, Patrick H. *My Own Boss? Class, Rationality and the Family Farm*. Boulder, CO: Westview Press, 1988.

Mooney, Patrick H. and Theo J. Majka. *Farmers' and Farm Workers' Movements: Social Protest in American Agriculture*. New York: Twayne Publishers, 1995.

Moore, R., ed. *The Hidden America: Social Problems in Rural America in the 21st Century*. Cranbury, NJ: Associated University Presses, 2001.

Morandi, L., *Rethinking Western Water Policy: Assessing the Limits of Legislation*. Denver, CO: National Conference of State Legislatures, 1994.

Morrison, Peter A., ed. *A Taste of the Country: A Collection of Calvin Beale's Writings*. University Park, PA: Pennsylvania State University Press and The RAND Corporation, 1990.

Morse, R.A. & T. Hooper, eds. *The Illustrated Encyclopedia of Beekeeping*. New York: E.P. Dutton, 1985.

Morse, R.A. and K. Flottum, eds. *The ABC & XYZ of Bee Culture*, 40th edition. Medina, OH: A.I. Root Co., 1990.

Mortensen, Viggo, ed. *Region and Religion: Land, Territory and Nation from a Theological Perspective*. International Consultation, Brazil, 1993. LWF Studies No.4. Geneva, Switzerland: The Lutheran World Federation, 1994.

Muckle, M.E. *Basic Hydroponics*. Princeton, BC, Canada: Growers Press, 1982.

Muir, John. *My First Summer in the Sierra*. Mariner Books, 1998 (First published 1911).

Murphy, Dennis. *Safety and Health for Production Agriculture*. St. Joseph, MI: American Society of Agricultural Engineers, 1992.

Murray, J. Dennis and Peter A. Keller, eds. *Innovations in Rural Community Mental Health*. Mansfield, PA: Mansfield University Rural Services Institute, 1986.

Muse, Ivan and Ralph B. Smith, with Bruce Barker. *The One-teacher School in the 1980s*. Ft. Collins, CO: ERIC Clearinghouse on Rural Education and Small Schools, 1987.

Nachtigal, Paul M. *Rural Education: In Search of a Better Way*. Boulder, CO: Westview Press, Inc., 1982.

Napier, Ted L., ed. *Implementing the Conservation Title of the Food Security Act of 1985*. Ankeny, IA: Soil Conservation Society Press, 1990.

Napier, Ted L., ed. *Outdoor Recreation Planning, Perspectives and Research*. Dubuque, IA: Kendall/Hunt Publishing Company, 1981.

Napier, Ted L., Silvana M. Camboni, and Samir A. El-Swaify. *Adopting Conservation on the Farm: An International Perspective on the Socioeconomics of Soil and Water Conservation*. Ankeny, IA: Soil and Water Conservation Society Press, 1994.

Napier, Ted L., Donald F. Scott, William K. Easter, and Raymond J. Supalla, eds. *Water Resources Research: Problems and Potentials for Agriculture and Rural Communities*. Ankeny, IA: Soil and Water Conservation Society of America Press.

Nash, Roderick. *Wilderness and the American Mind*, 4th edition. New Haven: Yale University Press, 2001.

National Academy of Sciences. *Measuring our Nation's Natural Resources and Environmental Sustainability*. Washington, DC: Government Accountability Office, 2007.

National Advisory Committee on Rural Health and Human Services. *The 2004 Report to the Secretary: Rural Health and Human Service Issues*. Report to the U.S. Secretary of Health and Human Services, April 2004.

National Center for Health Statistics. *Common Beliefs about the Rural Elderly: What Do National Data Tell Us?* Hyattsville, MD: U.S. Dept. of Health and Human Services, Public Health

Service, Centers for Disease Control, National Center for Health Statistics, 1993.

National Center for Education Statistics. *Status of Education in Rural America*. Washington, DC: U.S. Department of Education, Institute of Education Sciences, 2007.

National Geographic Society. *Life in Rural America*. Washington, DC: National Geographic Society, Special Publication Division, 1978.

National Research Council, Board on Agriculture. *Alternative Agriculture*. Washington, DC.: National Academy Press, 1989.

National Research Council. *Managing Global Genetic Resources: Livestock*. Washington, DC: National Academy Press, 1993.

National Research Council. *Valuing Ground Water*. Washington, DC: Water Science and Technology Board, Commission on Geosciences, Environment and Resources,1997.

National Research Council (NRC). *Environmental Effects of Transgenic Plants: The Scope and Adequacy of Regulation*. Washington, DC: National Academies Press, 2002.

National Research Council (NRC). *Safety of Genetically Engineered Foods: Approaches to Assessing Unintended Health Effects*. Washington, DC: National Academies Press, 2004.

National Rural Health Association. *Study of Models to Meet Rural Health Care Needs Through Mobilization of Health Professions Education and Services Resources*. Volume I. Washington, DC: Health Resources Services Administration, 1992.

National Telecommunications Information Infrastructure. *Survey of Rural Information Infrastructure Technologies*. Washington, DC: U.S. Department of Commerce, September 1995.

Nelson, P.V. *Greenhouse Operation and Management*, 6th edition. Upper Saddle River, NJ: Prentice Hall, 2003.

Neth, Mary. *Preserving the Family Farm: Women, Community, and the Foundations of Agribusiness in the Midwest, 1900–1940*. Baltimore, MD: Johns Hopkins University Press, 1995.

Nettl, Bruno. *Folk and Traditional Music of the Western Continents*. 3rd edition. Englewood Cliffs, NJ: Prentice-Hall, 1989.

Neyland, Leedell. *Historically Black Land-Grant Institutions and the Development of Agriculture and Home Economics 1890-1990*. Tallahassee, FL: Florida A&M University Foundation, Inc., 1990.

Noble, Allen G. *Wood, Brick, and Stone: The North American Settlement Landscape*. 2 vols. Amherst, MA: University of Massachusetts Press, 1984.

Noble, Allen. *Barns of the Midwest*. Athens, OH: Ohio University Press, 1995.

Norris, Kathleen. *Dakota: A Spiritual Geography*. Boston, MA: Houghton Mifflin, 1993.

Norton, B. G. *Sustainability: A Philosophy of Adaptive Ecosystem Management*. Chicago: The University of Chicago Press: Chicago, 2005.

Nugent, J. and J. Boniface. *Permaculture Plants: a Selection*. Hampshire, UK: Permanent Publications, 2004.

Oberholtzer, L., C. Dimitri, and C. Greene. *Price Premiums Hold on as Organic Produce Market Expands*. Outlook Report VGS-308-01. Washington, DC: U.S. Department of Agriculture, Economic Research Service, 2005.

O'Brien, Sharon. *American Indian Tribal Governments*. Norman: University of Oklahoma Press, 1989.

O'Leary, Rosemary and Lisa B. Bingham, eds. *The Promise and Performance of Environmental Conflict Resolution*. Washington, DC: Resources for the Future, 2003.

O'Neill, John, Alan Holland, and Andrew Light. *Environmental Values*. Oxford, New York: Routledge. 2008.

O'Rourke, A. Desmond. *The World Apple Market*. Binghamton, NY: Haworth Press, 1994.

Oelschlaeger, Max. *The Idea of Wilderness: From Prehistory to the Age of Ecology*, New Haven, CT: Yale University Press, 1991.

Office of Technology Assessment. *A New Technological Era for American Agriculture*. Washington, DC: U.S. Government Printing Office, 1992.

Office of Technology Assessment. *Health Care in Rural America*, OTA-H-434 (September). Washington, DC: U.S. Congress, Office of Technology Assessment, 1990.

Office of Technology Assessment. *Technology, Public Policy and the Changing Structure of American Agriculture*. Washington, DC: U.S. Government Printing Office, 1986.

Olkowski, N., S. Door and H. Olkowski. *Common-sense Pest Control*. Newton, CT: Tauton, 1991.

Orloff, Tracey M. and Barbara Tymann. *Rural Health: An Evolving System of Accessible Services*. Washington, DC: National Governors' Association, 1995.

Ortolano, Leonard. *Environmental Planning and Decision Making*. New York: John Wiley and Sons, 1984.

Osborne, Diana, and Lise Fondren, eds. *National Rural Health Policy Atlas*. Chapel Hill: University of North Carolina, 1991.

Osteen, Craig D., and Philip I. Szmedra. *Agricultural Pesticide Use Trends and Policy Issues*, Agricultural Economic Report No. 622 (September). Washington, DC: U.S. Department of Agriculture, Economic Research Service, 1989.

Ostler, Jeffrey. *Prairie Populism: The Fate of Agrarian Radicalism in Kansas, Nebraska, and Iowa, 1880-1892*. Lawrence: University Press of Kansas, 1993.

Overton, Patrick. *Grassroots & Mountain Wings: The Arts in Rural and Small Communities*. Columbia, MO: Columbia College, 1992.

Overton, Patrick. *Rebuilding the Front Porch of America: Essays on the Art of Community Making*. Columbia, MO: Columbia College, 1996.

Paarlberg, Don. *Farm and Food Policy: Issues of the 1980s*. Lincoln: University of Nebraska Press, 1980.

Palerm, Juan Vicente. *Farm Labor Needs and Farm Workers in California, 1970–1989*. Sacramento, CA: California Agricultural Studies, Employment Development Department, 1991.

Palmer, Tim. *Lifelines: The Case for River Conservation*. Washington, DC: Island Press, 1994.

Parker, Blaine F., ed. *Solar Energy in Agriculture. Vol. 4, Energy in World Agriculture*. B.A. Stout, editor-in-chief. Amsterdam: Elsevier, 1991.

Parker, Edwin B., Heather Hudson, and Don A. Dillman. *Rural America in the Information Age*. Boston, MA: University Press of America, 1989.

Parker, Edwin B., Heather E. Hudson, Don A. Dillman, Sharon Strover, and Frederick Williams. *Electronic Byways: State Policies for Rural Development through Telecommunications*, 2nd edition. Washington, DC: The Aspen Institute, 1995.

Parker, Rick. *Aquaculture Science*, 2nd edition. Florence, KY: Delmar CENGAGE Learning, 2000.

Parks, Arnold G. *Black Elderly in Rural America: A Comprehensive Study*. Bristol, IN: Wyndham Hall Press, 1988.

Parlin, Bradley W. and Mark W. Lusk. *Farmer Participation and Irrigation Organization*. Boulder, CO: Westview Press, 1991.

Patton, Larry. *The Rural Homeless.* Washington, DC: Health Resources and Services Administration, 1987.

Peart, Robert M. and Roger C. Brook, eds. *Analysis of Agricultural Energy Systems. Vol. 5, Energy in World Agriculture.* B.A. Stout, editor-in-chief. Amsterdam: Elsevier, 1992.

Peat, Marwick, and Mitchell, & Co. *The Economic Impact of the U.S. Horse Industry*. Washington, DC: American Horse Council, 1987.

Pedigo, L.P. *Entomology and Pest Management*. New York: Macmillan. 1989.

Pellow, David N. *Resisting Global Toxics: Transnational Movements for Environmental Justice*. Cambridge, MA: MIT Press, 2007.

Pence, Richard A. *The Next Greatest Thing*. Washington, DC: The National Rural Electrical Cooperative Association, 1984.

Penson, John B. Jr. and David A. Lins. *Agricultural Finance: An Introduction to Micro and Macro Concepts*. Englewood Cliffs, NJ: Prentice-Hall, Inc., 1980.

Perez, Agnes M. *Changing Structure of U.S. Dairy Farms*. Agricultural Economics Report 690, July. Washington, DC: U.S. Department of Agriculture, Economic Research Service, 1994.

Perlin, John. *A Forest Journey: The Role of Wood in the Development of Civilization*. Cambridge, MA: Harvard University Press, 1991.

Peterson, Fred W. *Homes in the Heartland: Balloon Frame Farmhouses of the Upper Midwest, 1850-1920*. Lawrence: University of Kansas Press, 1992.

Peterson, George L., Cindy Sorg Swanson, Daniel W. McCollum, and Michael H. Thomas. *Valuing Wildlife Resources in Alaska*. Boulder, CO: Westview Press, 1991.

Petulla, Joseph M. *American Environmental History*, 2nd edition. Columbus, OH: Merrill Publishing Co., 1988.

Phillips, R.E. and S.H. Phillips, eds. *No-Tillage Agriculture: Principles and Practices*. New York: Van Nostrand Reinhold Co., Inc., 1984.

Phillips, Willard and Barton D. Russell. *Rural Government: A Time of Change*. Washington, DC: U.S. Department of Agriculture, 1982.

Physicians Task Force on Hunger in America. *Hunger in America: The Growing Epidemic*. Middletown, CT: Wesleyan University Press, 1985.

Pickering, Kathleen, Mark H. Harvey, Gene F. Summers, and David Mushinski. *Welfare Reform in Persistent Rural Poverty: Dreams, Disenchantments, and Diversity*. University Park, PA: Pennsylvania State University Press, 2006.

Pigg, Kenneth E. *The Future of Rural America*. Boulder, CO: Westview Press, 1991.

Pillay, T.V.R. *Aquaculture and the Environment*, 2nd edition. Hoboken, NJ: Wiley-Blackwell, 2004.

Pillay, T.V.R. and M.N. Kutty. *Aquaculture: Principles and Practices*, 2nd edition. Hoboken, NJ: Wiley-Blackwell, 2005.

Pimentel, David. *The Handbook on Pest Management in Agriculture*. Boca Raton, FL: CRC Press, 1991.

Pimentel, David. *Handbook of Energy Utilization in Agriculture*. Boca Raton, FL: CRC Press, Inc., 1980.

Pimentel, David and H. Lehman. *The Pesticide Question*. New York: Champman and Hall, 1993.

Pinchot, Gifford. *The Fight for Conservation*. New York: Harcourt Brace, 1901.

Plater, Zygmunt J.B., Robert H. Abrams, and William Goldfarb. *Environmental Law and Policy: A Coursebook on Nature, Law, and Society*. St. Paul, MN: West Publications, 1992.

Platt, Rutherford. *This Green World*. 2nd edition. New York: Dodd, Mead and Company, 1988.

Poincelot, Raymond P. *Toward a More Sustainable Agriculture*. Westport, CT: AVI Publishing Co., Inc., 1986.

Ponting, Clive. *A Green History of the World: The Environment and the Collapse of Great Civilizations*. New York: St. Martin's Press, 1991.

Powell, D.S., J.L. Faulkner, D.R. Darr, Z. Zhu, and D.W. MacCleery. *Forest Resources of the United States, 1992*, General Technical Report RM-234. Washington, DC: U.S. Department of Agriculture, Forest Service, 1994.

Powers, Nicholas J., *Marketing Practices for Vegetables*. Agricultural Information Bulletin No. 702 (August). Washington, DC: U.S. Department of Agriculture, Economic Research Service, 1994.

Price, Larry W. *Mountains and Man: A Study of Process and Environment*. Berkeley: University of California Press, 1981.

Public Law 97–470. *Migrant and Seasonal Agricultural Act, 1983*. Ninety-Seventh Congress of the United States of America, January 14, 1983.

Public Law 99–603. *Immigration Reform and Control Act of 1986*. Ninety-Ninth Congress of the United States of America, November 6, 1986.

Purcell W.D., J. Reeves, and W. Preston. *Economics of Past, Current and Pending Change in the U.S. Sheep Industry with an Emphasis on Supply Response*. MB 363. Blacksburg, VA: Department of Agricultural Economics, Virginia Tech University, 1991.

Purcell, Wayne D and Stephen R. Koontz. *Agricultural Futures and Options: Principles and Strategies*, 2nd edition. Upper Saddle River, NJ: Prentice- Hall, Inc., 1999.

Quinn, Bernard. *The Small Rural Parish.* New York: Glenmary Home Missioners, 1980.

Rasmussen, Wayne D. *Taking the University to the People: Seventy-five Years of Cooperative Extension*. Ames: Iowa State University Press, 1989.

Reeder, Richard J. and Dennis M. Brown. *Recreation, Tourism, and Rural Well-being*. ERS Report No. 7. Washington, DC: U.S. Department of Agriculture, Economic Research Service, August 2005.

Reeder, Richard and Anicca A. Jansen. *Rural Governments-Poor Counties 1962–1987*. Washington, DC: U.S. Department of Agriculture, 1995.

Regan, Tom. *The Case for Animal Rights*. Berkeley: University of California Press, 1983.

Relf, Diane, ed. *The Role of Horticulture in Human Well-Being and Social Development*. Portland, OR: Timber Press, 1992.

Resh, H.M. *Hydroponic Food Production*. 5th edition. Santa Barbara, CA: Woodbridge Press, 1995.

Resh, H.M. *Hydroponic Home Food Gardens*. Santa Barbara, CA: Woodbridge Press, 1990.

Resh, H.M. *Hydroponic Tomatoes for the Home Gardener*. Santa Barbara, CA: Woodbridge Press, 1993.

Reyhner, Jon Allan and Jeanne Eder. *American Indian Education: A History*. Norman, OK: University of Oklahoma Press, 2004.

Rheingold, Howard. *The Virtual Community: Homesteading on the Electronic Frontier*. Reading, MA: Addison Wesley, 1993.

Ricketts, T.C. *Rural Health in the United States*. New York, NY: Oxford University Press, 1999.

Riebsame, William E., Stanley Changnon, Jr., and Thomas Karl. *Drought and Natural Resources Management in the United States: Impacts and Implications of the 1987–1989 Drought*. Boulder, CO: Westview Press, 1991.

Rifkin, Jeremy. *Beyond Beef: the Rise and Fall of the Cattle Culture*. New York: Dutton 1992.

Righter, R.W. *Wind Energy in America: A History*. Norman, OK: University of Oklahoma Press, 1996.

Riney-Kehrburg, Pamela. *Rooted in Dust: Surviving Drought and Depression in Southwestern Kansas*. Lawrence: University Press of Kansas, 1994.

Roberts, Lesley and Derek Hall. *Rural Tourism and Recreation: Principles to Practice*. New York: CABI Publishing, 2001.

Rodgers, Harrell R., Jr. and Gregory Weiher. *Rural Poverty: Special Causes and Policy Reforms*. Prepared under the auspices of the Policy Studies Organization. New York: Greenwood Press, 1989.

Roe, Keith E. *Corncribs in History, Folklife & Architecture*. Ames: Iowa State University Press, 1988.

Rogers, Carolyn C. *Rural Children at a Glance*. Economic Information Bulletin No. 1. Washington, DC: U.S. Department of Agriculture, Economic Research Service, March 2005.

Rogers, Denise and Gene Wunderlich. *Acquiring Farmland in the United States*. AIB 682. Washington, DC: U.S. Department of Agriculture, Economic Research Service, 1993.

Rogers, Denise M. *Leasing Farmland in the United States*. AGES-9159. Washington, DC: U.S. Department of Agriculture, Economic Research Service, 1991.

Rogers, Everett M. *The Diffusion of Innovations*, 5th edition. New York: Free Press, 2003.

Rogers, Everett M., Rabel J. Burdge, Peter F. Korsching, and Joseph F. Donnermeyer. *Social Change in Rural Societies: An Introduction to Rural Sociology*. 3rd edition. Englewood Cliffs, NJ: Prentice Hall, 1988.

Rolfe, G.L., J.M. Edgington, I.I. Holland, and G.C. Fortenberry. *Forests and Forestry*, 6th edition. Lebanon, IN: Pearson Education, 2003.

Rollin, B.E. *Farm Animal Welfare: Social, Bioethical, and Research Issues*. Ames: Iowa State University Press, 1995.

Rome, Adam. *The Bulldozer in the Countryside: Suburban Sprawl and the Rise of Environmentalism*. Cambridge: Cambridge University Press, 2001.

Rooney, John F. Jr., Wilbur Zelinsky, Dean R. Louder, eds. *This Remarkable Continent: An Atlas of the United States and Canadian Society and Cultures*. College Station, TX: Texas A&M University Press, 1982.

Rose, Peter I., with Liv Olson Pertzoff. *Strangers in Their Midst: Small-Town Jews and Their Neighbors*. Merrick, NY: Richwood, 1977.

Rosenbaum, Walter. *Environmental Politics and Policy*. 2nd edition. Washington DC: Congressional Quarterly Inc., 1991.

Rosenblatt, Paul C. *Farming Is in Our Blood: Farm Families in Economic Crisis*. Ames: Iowa State University Press, 1990.

Rosenblatt, Roger A. and Ira S. Moscovice. *Rural Health Care*. New York: John Wiley and Sons, 1982.

Rosenblum, Jonathon D. *Copper Crucible: How the Arizona Miners' Strike of 1983 Recast Labor-Management Relations in America*. Ithaca, NY: ILR Press, 1995.

Rosenfeld, Rachel Ann. *Farm Women: Work, Farm, and Family in the United States*. Chapel Hill: University of North Carolina Press, 1985.

Ross, M.R. *Fisheries Conservation and Management*. Upper Saddle River, NJ: Prentice Hall, 1997.

Rothenberg, Daniel. *With These Hands: The Hidden World of Migrant Farmworkers Today*. New York, Harcourt Brace, 1998.

Rowles, Graham D., Joyce E. Beaulieu, and Wayne W. Myers, eds. *Long-Term Care for the Rural Elderly*. New York: Springer Publishing Company, Inc., 1996.

Rowley, D. Thomas and Peter L. Sternberg. *A Comparison of Military Base Closures Metro and Nonmetro Counties, 1961–90*. (Staff Report No. AGES 9307, April). Washington, DC: U.S. Department of Agriculture, Agriculture and Rural Economy Division, Economic Research Service, 1993.

Royer, J.P. and C.D. Risbrudt, eds. *Nonindustrial Private Forests: A Review of Economic and Policy Studies*. Durham, NC: School of Forestry and Environmental Studies Duke University, 1983.

Rubin, Claire B., ed. *Emergency Management: The American Experience 1900-2005*. Fairfax: Public Entity Risk Institute, 2007.

Rural Policy Research Institute. *Block Grants and Rural America* P95–4 (November), Iowa State University, University of Missouri, University of Nebraska. Columbia: University of Missouri November, 1995.

Rural Policy Research Institute. *Opportunities for Rural Policy Reform: Lessons Learned from Recent Farm Bills*, P95-2 (April), Iowa State University, University of Missouri, University of Nebraska. Columbia: University of Missouri, 1995.

Rural Sociological Society. *Persistent Poverty in Rural America.* Rural Sociological Society Taskforce on Persistent Rural Poverty. Boulder, CO: Westview Press, 1993.

Russell, Howard S. *A Long, Deep Furrow: Three Centuries of Farming in New England.* Hanover, NH: University Press of New England, 1982.

Ruttan, Vernon W., ed. *Health and Sustainable Agricultural Development: Perspectives on Growth and Constraints.* Boulder, CO: Westview Press, 1994.

Ryugo, Kay. *Fruit Culture: Its Science and Art.* New York: John Wiley and Sons, Inc., 1988.

Sachs, Carolyn E. *Gendered Fields: Rural Women, Agriculture, and Environment.* Boulder, CO: Westview Press, 1996.

Salamon, Sonya. *Newcomers to Old Towns: Suburbanization of the Heartland.* Chicago: University of Chicago Press, 2003.

Salamon, Sonya. *Prairie Patrimony: Family Farming and Community in the Midwest.* Chapel Hill: University of North Carolina Press, 1992.

Sanders, H.C. *The Cooperative Extension Service.* Englewood Cliffs, NJ: Prentice-Hall, Inc., 1966.

Sapontzis, Steve F. *Food for Thought. The Debate over Eating Meat.* Amherst, NY: Prometheus, 2004.

Sargent, Frederic O., Paul Lusk, José A. Rivera, and María Varela. *Rural Environmental Planning for Sustainable Communities.* Washington, DC: Island Press, 1991.

Savory, Allan. *Holistic Resource Management.* Washington, DC: Island Press, 1988.

Scales, T. Laine and Calvin L. Streeter, eds. *Rural Social Work: Building and Sustaining Community Assets.* New York: Wadsworth Publishing Company, 2003.

Schmandt, J. F. Williams, R. H. Wilson, and S. Strover, eds. *Telecommunications and Rural Development: A Study of Business and Public Service Applications.* New York: Praeger, 1991.

Schmidt, G.H., L.D. VanVleck, and M.F. Hutjens. *Principles of Dairy Science.* 2nd edition. Englewood Cliffs, NJ: Prentice Hall, 1988.

Schmuck, Richard A. and Patricia A. Schmuck. *Small Districts Big Problems: Making Schools Everybody's House.* Newbury Park, CA: Corwin Press, Inc., 1992.

Schnaiberg, Allan and Kenneth Allan Gould. *Environment and Society: The Enduring Conflict.* New York: St. Martins, 1994.

Schoenrich, Lola. *Case Studies of Seven Rural Programs Cooperatively Marketing Recyclables.* St. Paul, MN: The Minnesota Project, 1994.

Schor, Joel. *Agriculture in the Black Land-grant System to 1930.* Tallahassee, FL: Florida A&M University, 1982.

Schrimper, Ronald A. *Economics of Agricultural Markets.* Prentice Hall, 2001.

Schultz, LeRoy G. *Barns, Stables and Outbuildings: A World Bibliography in English, 1700–1983.* Jefferson, NC: McFarland and Company, Inc., 1986.

Schwager, Jack D. *A Complete Guide to the Futures Market.* New York: John Wiley & Sons, Inc., 1984.

Schwartzweller, H.K. *Research in Rural Sociology and Development: Volume I, Focus on Agriculture.* Greenwich, CT: JAI Press Inc., 1984.

Scott, Shaunna L. *Two Sides to Everything: The Cultural Construction of Class Consciousness in Harlan County, Kentucky.* Albany: State University of New York Press, 1995.

Sears, David W. and J. Norman Reid. *Rural Development Strategies.* Chicago: Nelson-Hall, 1995.

Senate Committee on Environment and Public Works. *Rural Transportation Issues: Hearings Before the Subcommittee on Water Resources, Transportation, and Infrastructure of the Committee on Environment and Public Works* (August 20, 1990, Boise, Idaho). 101st Congress, Second Session, 1990.

Senauer, Ben and Jean Kinsey, eds. *Final Report by the Food and Consumer Issues Working Group, 1995 Farm Bill Project.* Washington DC: National Center for Food and Agricultural Policy and St. Paul, MN: University of Minnesota, Hubert H. Humphrey Institute of Agricultural Policy, March 1995.

Seroka, Jim. *Rural Public Administration: Problems and Prospects.* Westport, CT: Greenwood Press, 1986.

Setia, Parveen, Nathan Childs, Eric Wailes, and Janet Livezey. *The U.S. Rice Industry.* Washington, DC: U.S. Department of Agriculture, Economic Research Service, 1994.

Shallat, Todd. *Structures in the Stream: Water, Science, and the Rise of the U.S. Army Corps of Engineers.* Austin: University of Texas Press, 1994.

Shapouri, Hosein. *Sheep Production in 11 Western States.* Staff Report No. AGES 9150. Washington, DC: U.S. Department of Agriculture, Economics Research Service, Commodity Economics Division, 1991.

Sheldon, Ian M. and Philip C. Abbott. *Industrial Organization and Trade in the Food Industries.* Boulder, CO: Westview Press, 1994.

Sherman, Arloc. *Falling by the Wayside: Children in Rural America.* Washington, DC: The Children's Defense Fund, 1992.

Shifflett, Crandall. *Coal Towns: Life, Work, and Culture in Company Towns of Southern Appalachia, 1880–1960.* Knoxville, TN: University of Tennessee Press, 1991.

Shinagawa, Larry Hajime and Michael Jang. *Atlas of American Diversity.* Newbury Park, CA: Sage Publications/Altamira Press, 1996.

Shuman, Michael H. *Going Local. Creating Self-Reliant Communities in a Global Age.* New York, NY: The Free Press, 1998.

Schumann, G.L., and D'Arcy, C.J. *Essential Plant Pathology.* 1st Edition. St. Paul, MN: The American Phytopathological Society, 2006.

Singer, Peter. *Animal Liberation.* New York: Avon Books, 1990.

Singer, Peter, ed. *In Defense of Animals: The Second Wave.* Malden. MA: Blackwell Publishing Ltd, 2006.

Slatta, Richard W. *Cowboys of the Americas.* New Haven, CT: Yale University Press, 1990. Paperbound edition 1994.

Slatta, Richard W. *The Cowboy Encyclopedia.* Santa Barbara, CA: ABC-CLIO, 1994.

Sloan, David Charles. *The Last Great Necessity: Cemeteries in American History.* Baltimore: Johns Hopkins University Press, 1991.

Smil, Vaclav, Paul Nachman, and Thomas V. Long II. *Energy Analysis and Agriculture.* Boulder, CO: Westview Press, 1983.

Smith, C. Wayne, Javier Betran, and E.C.A. Runge, eds. *Corn: Origin, History, Technology, and Production.* Hoboken: Wiley, 2004.

Smith, Duane A. *Mining America: The Industry and The Environment, 1800-1980.* Niwot, CO: University Press of Colorado, 1993.

Smith, Duane A. *Rocky Mountain Mining Camps: The Urban Frontier.* Niwot, CO: University Press of Colorado, 1992.

Smith, R.K., E.J. Wailes, and G.L. Cramer. *The Market Structure of the U.S. Rice Industry.* Bulletin 921. Fayetteville, AR: University of Arkansas, Arkansas Agricultural Experiment Station, 1990.

Smith, W.B., P.D. Miles, J.S. Vissage, and S.A. Pugh. *Forest Resources of the United States, 2002,* General Technical Report NC–241. St. Paul, MN: U.S. Department of Agriculture, Forest Service, North Central Research Station, 2003.

Snipp, C. Matthew. *American Indians: The First of This Land.* New York: Russell Sage Foundation, 1989.

Society of American Foresters. *Task Force Report on Sustaining Long-Term Forest Health and Productivity.* Bethesda, MD: Society of American Foresters, 1993.

Soil and Water Conservation Society. *Journal of Soil and Water Conservation.* Special issue on conservation tillage in different geographic regions of North America. 32, no. 1 (1977): 3–65.

Solid Waste Association of North America. *Rural Solid Waste Management Series.* Silver Spring, MD: Solid Waste Association of North America, 1994.

Sooby, J. *State of the States: Organic Farming Systems Research at Land Grant Institutions 2001-2003,* 2nd edition. Santa Cruz, CA: Organic Farming Research Foundation, 2003.

Soule, Judith D. and Jon K. Piper. *Farming in Nature's Image: An Ecological Approach to Agriculture.* Washington, DC: Island Press, 1992.

Southern Rural Development Center. *Decision Aids for Municipal Solid Waste Management in Rural Areas: An Annotated Bibliography.* Mississippi State, MS: Southern Rural Development Center, 1995.

Speth, James Gustave. *The Bridge at the Edge of the World Capitalism, the Environment, and Crossing from Crisis to Sustainability.* New Haven: Yale University Press, 2008.

Stam, Jerome M. and Bruce L. Dixon. *Farmer Bankruptcies and Farm Exists in the United States, 1899-2002.* Agriculture Information Bulletin No. 788. Washington, DC: U.S. Department of Agriculture, Economic Research Service, March 2004.

Stam, Jerome M., Steven R. Koenig, Susan E. Bentley, and H. Frederick Gale, Jr. *Farm Financial Stress, Farm Exits, and Public Sector Assistance to the Farm Sector in the 1980's.* Agricultural Economic Report No. 645 (April). Washington, DC: U.S. Department of Agriculture, Economic Research Service, 1991.

Steinberg, Ted. *Down to Earth: Nature's Role in American History,* 2nd edition. New York: Oxford University Press, 2008.

Steiner, Frederick R. *Soil Conservation in the United States: Policy and Planning.* Baltimore, MD: Johns Hopkins University Press, 1990.

Steiner, Frederick. *The Living Landscape.* New York: McGraw-Hill, 1991.

Stern, Joyce D. *The Condition of Education in Rural Schools.* Washington, DC: U.S. Department of Education, Office of Educational Research and Improvement Programs for the Improvement of Practice, 1994.

Stewart, B.A., and D.R. Nielsen, eds. *Irrigation of Agricultural Crops.* Agronomics Series No. 30. Madison, WI: American Society of Agronomy, 1990.

Stewart, James B. and Joyce E. Allen-Smith, eds. *Blacks in Rural America.* New Brunswick, NJ: Transaction Publishers, 1995.

Still, Donald, Michael J. Broadiway, and David Griffith. *Any Way You Cut It: Meat Processing and Small Town America.* Lawrence: University Press of Kansas, 1995.

Stinson, Thomas F., Patrick J. Sullivan, Barry Ryan and Norman A. Reid. *Public Water Supply in Rural Communities: Results from the National Rural Communities Facilities Assessment Study.* Staff Report No. AGES 89-4. Washington, DC: U.S. Department of Agriculture, 1989.

Stock, Catherine McNicol. *Main Street in Crisis: The Great Depression and the Old Middle Class on the Northern Plains.* Chapel Hill: University of North Carolina Press, 1992.

Stokes, Samuel N., A. Elizabeth Watsor, Genevieve P. Keller, and J. Timothy Keller. *Saving America's Countryside.* Baltimore, MD: Johns Hopkins University Press, 1989.

Stokowski, Patricia A. *Riches and Regrets: Betting on Gambling in Two Colorado Mountain Towns.* Niwot, CO: University Press of Colorado, 1996.

Stoll, Steven. *Larding the Lean Earth: Soil and Society in Nineteenth-Century America.* New York: Hill & Wang, 2002.

Stone, Kenneth E. *Competing With the Retail Giants: How to Survive in the New Retail Landscape.* New York: John Wiley and Sons, 1995.

Stone, Lynn. *Old America Plantations.* Vero Beach, FL: Rourke Publishing, Inc, 1993.

Stone, Michael E. *Shelter Poverty.* Philadelphia, PA: Temple University Press, 1993.

Stone, Ted, ed. *100 Years of Cowboy Stories.* Roundup Series. Red Deer, Alberta: Red Deer College Press, 1994.

Storer YMCA Camps. *Nature's Classroom: A Program Guide for Camps and Schools.* Martinsville, IN: American Camping Association, 1988.

Strange, Marty. *Family Farming: A New Economic Vision.* Lincoln: University of Nebraska Press, 1988.

Strover, S. and F. Williams. *Rural Revitalization and Information Technologies in the United States.* Report to the Ford Foundation. New York: Ford Foundation, 1990.

Stull, Donald, Michael Broadway, and David Griffith. *Any Way You Cut It: Meat Processing and Small-Town America.* Lawrence: University Press of Kansas, 1995.

Summers, Gene F., et al., eds. *Agriculture and Beyond: Rural Economic Development.* Madison: University of Wisconsin-Madison, Department of Agricultural Journalism, 1987.

Summers, Gene F., ed. *Technology and Social Change in Rural Areas: A Festschrift for Eugene A. Wilkening.* Boulder, CO: Westview Press, 1983.

Summers, A. J. Schriver, P. Sundet, and R. Meinert. *Social Work in Rural Areas: The Past, Charting the Future, Acclaiming a Decade of Achievement. Proceedings of the 10th National Institute of Rural Areas.* Columbia: University of Missouri at Columbia, School of Social Work, 1987.

Sun, Ren Jen and John B. Weeks. *Bibliography of Regional Aquifer-system Analysis Program of the U. S. Geological Survey, 1978–91.* Water-Resources Investigations Report 91–4122. Reston, VA: U.S. Geological Survey, 1991.

Sunstein, Cass R. and Martha C. Nussbaum, eds. *Animal Rights: Current Debates and New Directions.* Oxford, UK: Oxford University Press, 2004.

Surrey, Peter. *The Small Town Church.* Nashville, TN: Abingdon Press, 1981.

Suter, Robert C. *The Appraisal of Farm Real Estate.* 3rd edition. Lafayette, IN: Retus Inc., 1992.

Swanson, Linda L. and David L. Brown, ed. *Population Change and the Future of Rural America*, Staff Report No. AGES 9324. Washington, DC: U.S. Department of Agriculture, Economic Research Service, Agriculture and Rural Economy Division, 1993.

Swanson, Louis, ed. *Agriculture and Community Change in the U.S.: The Congressional Research Reports.* Boulder, CO: Westview Press, 1988.

Sweeten, J.M. *Cattle Feedlot Waste Management Practices for Water and Air Pollution Control.* B-1671. College Station, TX: Texas Agricultural Extension Service, Texas A&M University, 1990.

Tanzer, Michael. *The Race for Resources: Continuing Struggles over Minerals and Fuels.* New York: Monthly Review Press, 1980.

Taylor, Harold H. *Fertilizer Use and Price Statistics, 1960-93.* Statistical Bulletin No. 893 (September). Washington, DC: U.S. Department of Agriculture, Economic Research Service, 1994.

Teiser, Ruth and Catherine Harroun. *Winemaking in California.* New York: McGraw-Hill, 1983.

Teske, Paul, Samuel Best, and Michael Mintrom. *Deregulating Freight Transportation: Delivering the Goods.* Washington, DC: AEI Press, 1995.

Thomas, M.G. and D.R. Schumann. *Income Opportunities in Special Forest Products.* Agriculture Information Bulletin No. 666. Washington, DC: U.S. Department of Agriculture, Forest Service, 1993.

Thompson, Paul B. *The Spirit of the Soil: Agriculture and Environmental Ethics.* London: Routledge, 1995.

Thompson, Paul and William Stout, eds. *Beyond the Large Farm.* Boulder CO: Westview Press, 1991.

Thornton, Russell. *American Indian Holocaust and Survival: A Population History Since 1492.* Norman: University of Oklahoma Press, 1987.

Thu, Kendell M. and E. Paul Durrenbgerger, eds. *Pigs, Profits and Rural Communities.* New York: State University of New York Press, 1998.

Thurston, H. David. *Sustainable Practices for Plant Disease Management in Traditional Farming Systems.* Boulder, CO: Westview, Press, 1991.

Tichi, Cecelia. *High Lonesome: The American Culture of Country Music.* Chapel Hill: University of North Carolina Press, 1994.

Tin, Jan S. *Housing Characteristics of Rural Households: 1991.* Bureau of the Census Current Housing Reports, Series H121/93-5. Washington, DC: U.S. Government Printing Office, 1993.

Tisdale, Samuel L., Werner L. Nelson, James D. Beaton, and John L. Havlin. *Soil Fertility and Fertilizers.* 5th edition. New York: Macmillan Publishing Co., 1993.

Tober, James A. *Who Owns Wildlife?: The Political Economy of Conservation in Nineteenth Century America.* Westport, CT: Greenwood Press, 1981.

Todd, David Keith. *Groundwater Hydrology.* New York: John Wiley, 1980.

Tomek, William G. and Kenneth L. Robinson. *Agricultural Product Prices.* 3rd edition. Ithaca, NY: Cornell University Press, 1990.

Tooch, D.E. *Successful Sawmill Management.* Old Forge, NY: Northeastern Loggers Association Inc., 1992.

Troeh, F.R., J.A. Hobbs, and R.L. Donahue. *Soil and Water Conservation,* 4th edition. Englewood Cliffs, N.J: Prentice-Hall, 2004.

Troeh, F.R., and L.M. Thompson. *Soils and Soil Fertility,* 6th edition. Ames, IA: Blackwell Publishing, 2005.

Tromp, Solco W. *Biometeorology: The Impact of the Weather and Climate on Humans and Their Environment (Animals and Plants).* London, UK: Heyden Publishing, 1980.

Tullis, F.L. and W.L. Hollist. *Food, the State, and International Political Economy.* Lincoln: University of Nebraska Press, 1985

Tweeten, Luther G. and Stanley R. Thompson. *Agriculture Policy for the 21st Century.* Ames, IA: Iowa State Press, 2002.

U.S. Commission on Civil Rights. *The Decline of Black Farming in America: A Report of the United States Commission on Civil Rights.* Washington, DC: United States Commission on Civil Rights, 1982.

U.S. Congress. Senate. Committee on Agriculture, Nutrition, and Forestry. *Circle of Poison: Impact on American Consumers.* 102nd Cong., 1st Sess., September 20, 1991.

U.S. Congress, Office of Technology Assessment. *A New Technological Era for American Agriculture*, OTA-F-474. Washington, DC: U.S. Government Printing Office, 1992.

U.S. Congress, Office of Technology Assessment. *Agriculture, Trade, and Environment: Achieving Complementary Policies.* Washington, DC: U.S. Government Printing Office, 1995.

U.S. Congress, Office of Technology Assessment. *Health Care in Rural America*, OTA-H-434 (September). Washington, DC: U.S. Government Printing Office, 1990.

U.S. Congress, Office of Technology Assessment. *Rural America at the Crossroads: Networking for the Future.* Washington DC: U.S. Government Printing Office, 1992.

U.S. Congress. *Hunger in Rural America, Hearing before the Subcommittee on Domestic Marketing, Consumer Relations, and Nutrition of the Committee on Agriculture House of Representatives*, 101 Congress, May 17, 1989, Serial No. 101–15. Washington, DC: Government Printing Office, 1989.

U.S. Department of Agriculture. *Agricultural Income and Finance: Situation and Outlook Report.* USDA-ERS, AIS-52, February. Washington, DC: U.S. Department of Agriculture, Economic Research Service, 1994.

U.S. Department of Agriculture. *Agricultural-Food Policy Review: Commodity Program Perspective*, Agricultural Economic Report No. 530 (July). Washington, DC: U.S. Department of Agriculture, Economic Research Service, 1985.

U.S. Department of Agriculture, Forest Service. *An Analysis of the Timber Situation in the United States: 1989–2070.* General Technical Report RM-199. Ft. Collins, CO: Rocky Mountain Forest and Range Experiment Station, 1990.

U.S. Department of Agriculture, National Agriculture Library. *Sustainable Agriculture in Print: Current Books.* Beltsville, MD: Alternative Farming Systems Information Center, 1993.

U.S. Department of Agriculture, National Agriculture Library. *Periodicals Pertaining to Alternative Farming Systems.* Beltsville, MD: Alternative Farming Systems Information Center, 1993.

U.S. Department of Agriculture, Soil Conservation Service. *SEEPPAGE: A System for Early Evaluation of the Pollution Potential of Agricultural Groundwater Environments.* Engineering Geology Technical Note 5. Chester, PA: Northeastern National Technical Center, 1988.

U.S. Department of Agriculture. *A Time to Choose: Summary Report on the Structure of Agriculture.* Washington, DC: U.S. Department of Agriculture, 1981.

U.S. Department of Agriculture. *Agricultural Conservation Program: 1993 Fiscal Year Statistical Summary.* Washington, DC: U.S. Department of Agriculture, Agricultural Stabilization and Conservation Service 1994.

U.S. Department of Agriculture. *Agricultural Resources and Environmental Indicators.* Agricultural Handbook No. 705. Washington, DC: U.S. Department of Agriculture, Economic Research Service, 1994.

U.S. Department of Agriculture, Natural Resources Conservation Service. *Agricultural Waste Management Field Handbook–Part 651.* Washington DC: U.S. Department of Agriculture, Natural Resources Conservation Service, 2000.

U.S. Department of Agriculture. *Economic Indicators of the Farm Sector: Costs of Production, 1993-Major Field Crops and Livestock and Dairy.* Report No. ECIFS 13–3. Washington, DC: U.S. Department of Agriculture, Economic Research Service, 1995.

U.S. Department of Agriculture. *Education and Rural Economic Development: Strategies for the 1990s*, ERS Staff Report No. AGES 9153 (September). Washington, DC: U.S. Department of Agriculture, Agriculture and Rural Economy Division, Economic Research Service, 1991.

U.S. Department of Agriculture. *Focusing on the Needs of the Rural Homeless.* Washington, DC: Rural Housing Service, 1996.

U.S. Department of Agriculture. *Labor Market Areas for the United States.* Washington, DC: U.S. Department of Agriculture, Economic Research Division, 1987.

U.S. Department of Agriculture. *Organic Production/Organic Food: Information Access Tools.* Washington, DC: U.S. Department of Agriculture, 2007.

U.S. Department of Agriculture. *Report and Recommendations on Organic Farming.* Washington, DC: U.S. Department of Agriculture, July 1980.

U.S. Department of Agriculture. *Rural Poverty at a Glance.* Rural Development Research Report Number 100. Washington DC: U.S. Department of Agriculture, 2004.

U.S. Department of Agriculture. *Rural Urban Continuum Codes* 2003. Washington, DC: U.S. Department of Agriculture, 2008.

U.S. Department of Agriculture. *Sugar and Sweetener: Situation and Outlook Yearbook.* USDASSRV18N2 (June). Washington, DC: U.S. Department of Agriculture. Economic Research Service, 1993.

U.S. Department of Agriculture. *The Basic Mechanisms of U.S. Farm Policy*, Miscellaneous Publication No. 1479 (January). Rockville, MD: U.S. Department of Agriculture, Economic Research Service, National Agricultural Statistics Service, 1990.

U.S. Department of Agriculture. *The Physical Distribution System for Grain.* Agricultural Information Bulletin No. 457. Washington, DC: U.S. Department of Agriculture, Office of Transportation, 1990.

U.S. Department of Agriculture. *The Second RCA Appraisal: Soil, Water, and Related Resources on Nonfederal Land in the United States.* USDA Misc. Publ. No. 1482. Washington, DC: U.S. Department of Agriculture, 1989.

U.S. Department of Agriculture. *Understanding Rural America.* Washington, DC: U.S. Department of Agriculture, Economic Research Service, 1995.

U.S. Department of Agriculture. *USDA Plant Hardiness Map*, Agricultural Research Service. Washington, DC: U.S. Government Printing Office, 1990.

U.S. Department of Agriculture. *Yearbook of Agriculture.* Washington, DC: Superintendent of Documents, various years.

U.S. Department of Health and Human Services, Office of Rural Health Policy. *Mental Health and Rural America: 1980–1993.* Washington, DC: U.S. Government Printing Office, 1993.

U.S. Department of the Interior and U.S. Department of Commerce. *2006 National Survey of Fishing, Hunting, and Wildlife-Associated Recreation.* Washington, DC: U.S. Department of the Interior, Fish and Wildlife Service, and U.S. Department of Commerce, U.S. Census Bureau, 2006.

U.S. Environmental Protection Agency. *Another Look: National Survey of Pesticides In Drinking Water Wells* (Phase 2 Report). Report No. 570/9–91–020 (January). Washington, DC: U.S. Environmental Protection Agency, Office of Water, 1992.

U.S. Environmental Protection Agency. *National Water Quality Inventory.* Report EPA 440–4–90–003. Washington, DC: Environmental Protection Agency, Office of Water, 1990.

U.S. Environmental Protection Agency. *Risk Assessment, Management and Communication of Drinking Water Contamination.* Report EPA 625–4–89–024. Washington, DC: Environmental Protection Agency, Office of Water, 1990.

U.S. Environmental Protection Agency. *The United States' Experience with Economic Incentives to Control Environmental Pollution,* Report 230BRB92–001. Washington, DC: U.S. Environmental Protection Agency, Office of Planning, Policy and Evaluation, July 1992.

U.S. Environmental Protection Agency. *National Water Quality Inventory: 1988 Report to Congress,* EPA 440–4B90–003, U.S. EPA, Washington, D.C., April 1990.

U.S. Environmental Protection Agency. *The Worker Protection Standard for Agricultural Pesticides: How to Comply.* EPA 7354-B-93–001. Washington, DC: U.S. Environmental Protection Agency, 1993.

U.S. Fish and Wildlife Service. *2006 National Survey of Fishing, Hunting and Wildlife-Associated Recreation: State Overview.* Washington D.C.: United States Department of the Interior, United States Fish and Wildlife Service, 2007.

U.S. Geological Survey. *Concepts for National Assessment of Water Availability and Use.* USGS Circular 1223. Washington, DC: U.S. Geological Survey, 2005.

U.S. Geological Survey. *Ground Water Atlas of the United States.* Washington, DC: U.S. Geological Service, 2007.

U.S. Geological Survey. *Ground Water Resources Program.* Washington, DC: U.S. Geological Service, 2007.

U.S. Government Accounting Office. *Drinking Water: Stronger Efforts Essential for Small Communities to Comply with Standards.* Report No. US GAO/RCED-94-40. Washington, DC: U.S. Government Accounting Office, 1994.

U.S. Senate Committee on Agriculture, Nutrition, and Forestry. *Farm Structure: A Historical Perspective on Changes in the Number and Size of Farms.* 96th Cong., 2nd sess. Washington, DC: Government Printing Office, 1980.

U.S. Travel and Tourism Administration. *Rural Tourism Handbook: Selected Case Studies and Development Guide.* Washington, DC: U.S. Department of Commerce, U.S. Travel and Tourism Administration, 1994.

Upton, Dell, ed. *America's Architectural Roots: Ethnic Groups that Built America.* Washington, DC: The Preservation Press, 1986.

Upton, Dell and John Michael Vlach. *Common Places: Readings in American Rural Architecture.* Athens: University of Georgia Press, 1982.

Utley, Robert M. *The Indian Frontier of the American West, 1846–1890.* Albuquerque: University of New Mexico Press, 1984.

Vachal, Kimberly and Denver Tolliver. *Regional Elevator Survey: Grain Transportation and Industry Trends for Great Plains Elevators.* Fargo, ND: Upper Great Plains Transportation Institute North Dakota State University, 2001.

Valente, C. and W. Valente. *Introduction to Environmental Law and Policy.* St. Paul, MN: West Publications, 1995.

Valle, Isabel. *Fields of Toil: A Migrant Family's Journey.* Pullman, WA: Washington State University Press, 1994.

van Kooten, Cornelis G. *Land Resource Economics and Sustainable Development.* Vancouver, Canada: UBC Press, 1993.

Vandeman, Ann, Jorge Fernandez-Cornejo, Sharon Jans, and Bi-ing-Hwan Lin. *Adoption of Integrated Pest Management in U.S. Agriculture,* Agriculture Information Bulletin No. 707. Washington, DC: U.S. Department of Agriculture, Economic Research Service, September 1994.

Vasey, Daniel E. *An Ecological History of Agriculture, 10,000 B.C.-A.D. 10,000.* Ames: Iowa State University Press, 1992.

Vavrek, Bernard. *Assessing the Role of the Rural Public Library.* Clarion, PA: Department of Library Science, Center for the Study of Rural Librarianship, Clarion University of Pennsylvania, 1993.

Vavrek, Bernard. *Assessing the Information Needs of Rural Americans.* Clarion, PA: College of Library Science, Center for the Study of Rural Librarianship, Clarion University of Pennsylvania, 1990.

Vesterby, M., R.E. Heimlich, and K.S. Krupa. *Urbanization of Rural Land in the United States.* AER-673. Washington, DC: U.S. Department of Agriculture, Economic Research Service, 1994.

Vitek, William and Wes Jackson. *Rooted in the Land : Essays on Community and Place.* New Haven, CT: Yale University Press, 1996.

Vroomen, Harry, and Harold Taylor. *Fertilizer Trade Statistics, 1970-91,* Statistical Bulletin No. 851. Washington, DC: U.S. Department of Agriculture, Economic Research Service, January 1993.

Wagenfeld, Morton O., J. Dennis Murray, Dennis Mohatt, and Jeanne C. DeBruyn. *Mental Health in Rural America: 1980–1993.* Washington, DC: National Institute of Mental Health, 1993.

Wagner, Paul. M. *Grapes into Wine: The Art of Winemaking in New York.* New York: Knopf, 1982.

Wahl, Richard W. *Markets for Federal Water: Subsidies, Property Rights, and the Bureau of Reclamation.* Washington, DC: Resources for the Future, 1989.

Wallace, Henry A. and Brown, William L. *Corn and Its Early Fathers*. Rev. edition. Ames: Iowa State University Press, 1988.

Walzer, Norman. *Rural Community Economic Development*. New York: Praeger Publishers, 1991.

Ward, Fay E. *The Cowboy at Work*. Norman: University of Oklahoma Press, 1958, 1987.

Warman, Arturo. *Corn and Capitalism: How a Botanical Bastard Grew to Global Dominance*. Translated by Nancy L Westrate. Chapel Hill, NC: University of North Carolina Press, 2003.

Warner, Paul D. and James A. Christenson. *The Cooperative Extension Service: A National Assessment*. Boulder, CO: Westview Press, 1984.

Weber, David J., ed. *Biotechnology: Assessing Social Impacts and Policy Implications*. New York: Greenwood, 1990.

Weissbach, Lee Shai. *Jewish Life in Small-Town America: A History*. New Haven, CT: Yale University Press, 2005.

Weisheit, Ralph A., David N. Falcone, and L. Edward Wells. *Crime and Policing in Rural and Small–Town America*, 3rd edition. Prospect Heights, IL: Waveland Press, 2006.

Welsh, Roger L. *Of Trees and Dreams: the Fiction, Fact, and Folklore of Tree-Planting on the Northern Plains*. 2nd printing. Lincoln: University of Nebraska Press, 1988.

Westman, Walter. *Ecology, Impact Assessment, and Environmental Planning*. New York: John Wiley and Sons, 1985.

Westwood, Melvin N. *Temperate-Zone Pomology, Physiology and Culture*. 3rd edition. Portland, OR: Timber Press, 1993.

Weyler, Rex. *Blood of the Land: The Government and Corporate War against the American Indian Movement*. New York: Everest House, 1982.

White, Robert H. *Tribal Assets: The Rebirth of Native America*. New York: Henry Holt and Co., 1990.

Whitefield, P. *The Earth Care Manual: a Permaculture Handbook for Britain and Other Temperate Climates*. Portsmouth, UK: Permanent Publications, 2004.

Wilhite, Donald and William Easterling, eds. *Planning for Drought: Toward a Reduction of Societal Vulnerability*. Boulder, CO: Westview Press, 1987.

Wilhite, Donald. *Drought Assessment, Management, and Planning: Theory and Case Studies*. Dordrecht, Netherlands: Kluwer Academic Publishers, 1993.

Wilkinson, Alec. *Big Sugar: Seasons in the Cane Fields of Florida*. New York: Alfred A. Knopf, 1989.

Wilkinson, Charles F. *Crossing the Next Meridian: Land, Water, and the Future of the West*. Washington, DC: Island Press, 1992.

Wilkinson, Kenneth P. *The Community in Rural America*. New York: Greenwood Press, 1991.

Williams, M. *Americans and Their Forests: A Historical Geography*. Cambridge, MA: Cambridge University Press, 1989.

Willis, D.W., C.G. Scalet, and L.D. Flake. *Introduction to Wildlife and Fisheries: An Integrated Approach*, 2nd edition. New York: W.H. Freeman and Company, 2008.

Wimberley, Ronald C. and Libby V. Morris. *The Southern Black Belt: A National Perspective*. Lexington: TVA Rural Studies and The University of Kentucky, 1997.

Wirzba, Norman, ed. *The Art of the Commonplace: The Agrarian Essays of Wendell Berry*. Washington, D.C.: Counterpoint, 2002.

Wirzba, Norman, ed. *The Essential Agrarian Reader: The Future of Culture, Community, and the Land*. Lexington: University Press of Kentucky, 2003.

Wojtkowski, P.A. *Introduction to Agroecology: Principles and Practices*. New York: Food Product Press, 2006.

Wondolleck, Julia M. and Steven L. Yaffee. *Making Collaboration Work: Lessons from Innovation in Natural Resource Management*. Washington, D.C: Island Press, 2000.

Worldwatch Institute. *Biofuels for Transport: Global Potential and Implications for Energy and Agriculture*. London: Earthscan, 2006.

Worster, Donald. *Dust Bowl: The Southern Plains in the 1930s*, 25th Anniversary edition. New York: Oxford University Press, 2004.

Wright, John B. *Rocky Mountain Divide: Selling and Saving the West*. Austin: University of Texas Press, 1993.

Wright, R. Dean and Susan E. Wright. *Homeless Children and Adults in Iowa: Addressing Issues and Options in Education, Services and the Community*. Des Moines, IA: State of Iowa, Department of Education, 1993.

Wunderlich, Gene. *American Country Life: A Legacy*. Lanham, MD: University Press of America, 2003.

Wunderlich, Gene. *Land Ownership and Taxation in American Agriculture*. Boulder, CO: Westview Press, 1992.

Wunderlich, Gene. *Owning Farmland in the United States*. AIB 637. Washington, DC: U.S. Department of Agriculture, Economic Research Service, 1991.

Wunderlich, Gene and John Blackledge. *Taxing Farmland in the United States*. Agricultural Economics Report No. 679. Washington, DC: U.S. Department of Agriculture, 1994.

Wyckoff, William and Larry M Dilsaver. *The Mountainous West: Explorations in Historical Geography*. Lincoln: University of Nebraska Press, 1995

Yarborough, Paul. *Information Technology and Rural Economic Development: Evidence from Historical and Contemporary Research*. Washington, DC: Office of Technology Assessment, U.S. Congress, 1990.

Yoder, Don. *Discovering American Folklife: Studies in Ethnic, Religious, and Regional Culture*. Ann Arbor, MI: UMI Research Press, 1990.

Yoder, Don. *Discovering American Folklife: Essays on Folk Culture and the Pennsylvania Dutch*. Mechanicsburg, PA: Stackpole Books, 2001.

Young, John A. and Jan M. Newton. *Capitalism and Human Obsolescence: Corporate Control vs. Individual Survival in Rural America*. Montclair, NJ: Allanheld, Osmun, 1980.

Young, Robert A. *Determining the Economic Value of Water: Concepts and Methods*. Washington, DC: Resources for the Future, 2005.

Zabawa, Robert, Ntam Baharanyi, and Walter Hill, eds. *Challenges in Agriculture and Rural Development*. Tuskegee, AL: Tuskegee University, 1993.

Zeitlin, Steven J., Amy J. Kotkin, and Holly Cutting Baker. *A Celebration of American Family Folklore: Tales and Traditions from the Smithsonian Collection*. New York: Pantheon Books, 1982.

Zelinsky, Wilbur. *The Cultural Geography of the United States*. Englewood Cliffs, NJ: Prentice-Hall, 1992.

ABOUT THE CONTRIBUTORS

Charles W. Abdalla is Associate Professor, Department of Agricultural Economics and Rural Sociology, Pennsylvania State University. His research and extension work involves economic assessments of water management technologies; groundwater values; environmental, groundwater, and farm policy; and community conflict over pollution from animal agriculture.

Marcel Aillery is an agricultural economist with the Economic Research Service, U.S. Department of Agriculture. His research interests include water resource management, animal agriculture, and conservation policy.

Don E. Albrecht is Professor, Department of Recreation, Park and Tourism Sciences, Texas A&M University. He specializes in poverty, inequality, natural resources, and community development. Dr. Albrecht is the co-author of *The Sociology of U.S. Agriculture: An Ecological Perspective* (with Steve H. Murdock, 1990).

Ralph Alcock is the former Chair, Department of Agricultural Engineering, South Dakota State University, Brookings.

John C. Allen is Professor of Sociology, Department of Sociology, Social Work and Anthropology, Utah State University. Professor Allen's research focuses on rural community response to change, social network structure and its influence on rural development and natural resource management. He has worked in rural communities for over twenty years facilitating locally led development efforts.

Patricia Allen is Director, Center for Agroecology and Sustainable Food Systems, Oakes Academic Services, University of California, Santa Cruz. She works on issues such as labor, gender, and access to food. Dr. Allen wrote *Together at the Table: Sustainability and Sustenance in the American Agrifood System* (2004).

Kim Anderson is Professor and Extension Economist, Department of Agricultural Economics, Oklahoma State University. His research interests include international marketing, agricultural sales, and risk management.

Marilyn Aronoff is an emeritus faculty, Department of Sociology, Michigan State University. She specializes in community theory and research, collective action, qualitative field methods, and community responses to economic and environmental cri-

ses. Dr. Aronoff's research examines reactions to toxic waste contamination in Michigan Superfund site communities.

Donald E. Arwood is Professor, Department of Rural Sociology, and Associate Director, Census Data Center, South Dakota State University. His research examines the agricultural, social, and demographic characteristics of South Dakota and the Upper Great Plains. His current research focuses on rural-urban differences in low birth weight, suicide, and crime.

Julian H. Atkinson is Professor Emeritus, Department of Agricultural Economics, Purdue University. Dr. Atkinson conducted annual studies of land values in Indiana for many years and assisted in similar studies at Auburn University and the University of Florida.

Ivonne Audirac is Associate Professor in the Department of Urban and Regional Planning at Florida State University in Tallahassee. Her research focused on social aspects of urban design and urban form, growth management, sustainable development, and postindustrial change in rural and metropolitan regions.

Carmen Bain is Assistant Professor, Department of Sociology at Iowa State University. Her research interests include the political economy of global agrifood systems, and rural development and social change. Currently, her research is focused on examining the social and economic implications of biofuels development in Iowa.

Dean A. Bangsund is Research Associate, Department of Agribusiness and Applied Economics, North Dakota State University. He is currently assessing the economics of noxious weed control methods.

Peggy F. Barlett is Professor, Department of Anthropology, Emory University. Her current interests focus on economic development theory and the globalization of culture. She is active in rethinking ways to teach these issues in anthropology. She is the author of *American Dreams, Rural Realities: Family Farms in Crisis* (1993).

Freddie L. Barnard is Professor, Department of Agricultural Economics at Purdue University. His Extension interests include agricultural finance and farm management. Professor Barnard's responsibilities include serving as director of the Midwest Agricultural Banking School, which is cosponsored by the Illinois, Indiana, Michigan, and Ohio Bankers Associations and held at Purdue University.

C. Phillip Baumel is Emeritus Professor, Department of Economics, and Charles F. Curtiss Distinguished Professor in Agriculture and Life Sciences, Iowa State University, Ames. He specializes in the economics of grain transportation and distribution systems, genetically modified corn and soybeans, and ethanol production.

Jaishree Beedasy is a Research Assistant Professor, Institute of Rural Health at Idaho State University. Her research areas include spatial analysis and visualization of environmental and health data, distance learning technologies and collaborative virtual environments. She leads the evaluation of the Idaho Bioterrorism Awareness and Preparedness Program.

Michael M. Bell is Professor, Department of Rural Sociology, University of Wisconsin, Madison. Dr. Bell co-edited *Country Boys: Masculinity and Rural Life* (with H. Campbell and M. Finney, 2006). He co-authored *Farming for Us All: Practical Agriculture and the Cultivation of Sustainability* (with S. Jarnagin, G. Peter, and D. Bauer, 2004).

Kathleen P. Bell is Associate Professor, School of Economics at the University of Maine. Dr. Bell's research interests include the economics of land use change and the interactions between land use change and the environment.

Kathleen J. Bergseth is a doctoral student in the Department of Criminal Justice and Political Science, North Dakota State University. Her interests include juvenile delinquency, adult/juvenile reentry, female criminality, criminal justice processing and women's lives, and rural justice; her articles have been published in the *Journal of Criminal Justice* and *Youth Violence and Juvenile Justice*.

G. Andrew Bernat, Jr., is Chief, Analysis Branch, Regional Economic Analysis Division, Bureau of Economic Analysis, U.S. Department of Commerce. His research includes regional input-output modeling, econometric modeling, and economic growth particularly with the role of manufacturing.

Rick Bevins is Professor of Psychology, University of Nebraska-Lincoln. His research concentrated on drug addiction and learning processes and the etiology of drug addiction. His current research uses preclinical models to understand the learning processes involved in addiction and relapse, and to develop better pharmacotherapy and immunotherapy treatments.

M. Deborah Bialeschki is Senior Researcher for the American Camp Association (ACA). She was on the faculty at the University of North Carolina-Chapel Hill for 20 years until she retired in 2005 as Professor Emeritus. Her research interests at ACA included youth development, the value of outdoor experiences, gender perspectives, quality improvement, and staff training.

Chris Biga is Assistant Professor, Department of Sociology, Anthropology, and Emergency Management, North Dakota State University. His research emphasizes sociological social psychology theory to study individuals' behaviors regarding the envi-

ronment, aging, family caregivers of Alzheimer's disease patients, and training programs for family members, paraprofessionals, and professionals who care for individuals with dementia.

Sampson Lee Blair is Associate Professor of Sociology, State University of New York—Buffalo. Dr. Blair is a family sociologist whose research interests include marriage and marital relationships, parenting and child development, and gender issues in the family. He served as the senior editor of *Sociological Inquiry*, and has served on the editorial boards of *Journal of Family Issues*, *Marriage & Family Review*, and *Social Justice Research*.

Anita D. Bledsoe is Research Assistant, University of Akron, and a doctoral student studying sociology and social psychology.

Leonard E. Bloomquist is Associate Professor, Department of Sociology, Anthropology and Social Work, Kansas State University. His research interests include rural work structures, the organization of rural communities, and the impacts of economic and social restructuring on rural localities.

Michael D. Boehlje is Distinguished Professor in the Department of Agricultural Economics and the Center for Food and Agricultural Business, Purdue University. His research and teaching focus is on agricultural finance, farm and business strategy, and management and structural change in the agricultural industries.

Rosemarie Bogal-Allbritten is Professor, Department of Sociology, Anthropology, and Social Work, Murray State University. Her research interests include service delivery to victims of domestic violence and rape, the use of self-help groups (Parents Anonymous) to work with abusive parents, and campus efforts to address date rape and dating violence.

Janet L. Bokemeier is Professor, Department of Sociology, Michigan State University. She specializes in studies of gender, work, family, and agriculture in rural America. Her current research involves multiple jobholding and underemployment, how changes in the dairy industry affect farm families and communities, children, rural poverty, and school readiness.

David O. Born is Professor and Chair, Division of Health Ecology, University of Minnesota School of Dentistry. He directs research and training programs on rural dental health issues, focusing on health professional recruitment, retention, and placement programs. He served on the National Health Council's Task Force on Health Manpower Distribution.

Michael Brady is an agricultural economist with the Economic Research Service in the U.S. Department of Agriculture. His research concentrates on land-use with a focus on how technology and policy influence the relative competitiveness of agriculture to compete for land based resources.

Bonnie Braun is Vice-Chair of the Rural Maryland Council and Chair of its Health Working Committee. She is a W.K. Kellogg Foundation Leadership Fellow and is the 2007-08 President of the American Association of Family & Consumer Sciences. Dr. Braun held Cooperative Extension appointments at Oklahoma State University, Virginia Tech, the University of Minnesota, and the University of Maryland.

Gene A. Brewer is Adjunct Associate Professor, Department of Public Administration and Policy, University of Georgia. Dr. Brewer's research involves public sector reform, governmental performance, and bureaucratic accountability in democratic political systems. He is on the editorial board of the *Public Administration Review*.

Kenneth N. Brooks is Professor of Forest Hydrology and Watershed Management, Department of Forest Resources, University of Minnesota, St. Paul. His teaching and research concentrated on watershed management, wetland, and forest hydrology. His publications include *Hydrology and the Management of Watersheds* (2003) and *Integrated Watershed Management—Connecting People to their Land and Water* (2007).

Michael L. Brown is Professor in the Department of Wildlife and Fisheries Sciences, South Dakota State University. His primary research interests include quantitative fisheries science and fisheries management.

Ralph B. Brown is Professor of Sociology and Director of the International Development Minor, Brigham Young University. His research centered on social change and development in rural communities and Southeast Asia.

Robert J. Brulle is an Associate Professor, Drexel University in Philadelphia. His research focuses on the dynamics of the U.S. environmental movement. Among his publications are *Agency, Democracy, and Nature: U.S. Environmental Movements from a Critical Theory Perspective* (2000), and editor (with David Pellow) of *Power, Justice and the Environment: A Critical Appraisal of the Environmental Justice Movement* (2005).

Jodi Burkhardt Bruns serves as an Extension Agent and community coach with the North Dakota State University Extension Service. Her research focus is social capital and its impact on rural communities, and the study of adequate housing trends in those communities.

Carolyn Junior Bryant was Assistant Professor of Social Work, Department of Sociology, Anthropology, and Social Work, Mississippi State University. She pursued an international research agenda, studying Ghanaian women living with HIV and AIDS.

Steven T. Buccola is Professor of Agricultural and Resource Economics at Oregon State University. He teaches microeconomic theory and conducts research in the economics of biotechnology, productivity and technical change, and farmer cooperatives. He formerly edited the *American Journal of Agricultural Economics*, and serves as a Fellow and Past-President of the American Agricultural Economics Association.

William W. Budd is Professor, Program in Environmental Science and Regional Planning at Washington State University. He examines environmental regulations and policies, including the carrying capacity of the land.

Gary Burkart is Director, Center for the Rural and Small Town Church, and Chair, Department of Sociology, Benedictine College, Atchison, Kansas. He advises the North American Forum on the process of faith formation (Catechumenate) regarding rural parishes, and completed a needs-assessment for the Catholic Archdiocese of Kansas City, Kansas to facilitate long-range planning.

R. Jeffrey Burkhardt is Professor, Institute of Food and Agricultural Sciences, Department of Food and Resource Economics, University of Florida. He teaches courses on agricultural and natural resource ethics. His research interests focus on the ethical implications of new technologies in agriculture with emphasis on new biotechnology.

Lowell Bush is Professor, Department of Agronomy, University of Kentucky. He conducts research on alkaloid biosynthesis in tobacco, which examines the enzymes and chemical intermediates in the biosynthetic pathways, genetic and geologic regulation of formation, and use of nicotine by the plant.

Terry F. Buss is Project Director at the National Academy of Public Administration. He published 12 books and more than 300 articles on economic development, entrepreneurship, and unemployment. His latest book is *Haiti in the Balance* (Brookings 2008), a study on foreign aid failure.

Frederick H. Buttel was the William H. Sewell Professor of Rural Sociology at the University of Wisconsin until 2005. A recognized and respected researcher on issues related to the interconnection of environment, agriculture, economics, and technology, Buttel published more than 215 articles and book chapters. He co-edited nine volumes, and his work fundamentally changed rural sociology, powerfully influenced environmental sociology, and has a prominent place in science and technology studies.

Erick T. Byrd is Assistant Professor in the Department of Recreation, Parks and Tourism, University of North Carolina at Greensboro. His research interests include sustainable tourism development and community involvement.

Sang-Eun Byun is Assistant Professor, College of Human Sciences at Auburn University. Dr Byun's teaching and research focuses on apparel retailing, consumer behavior, and global sourcing.

Robert V. Carlson is Professor Emeritus, Department of Education at the University of Vermont. Dr. Carlson continues to teach, consult, and advise doctoral students on topics related to rural education. His publications include *Reframing and Reform: Perspectives on Organization, Leadership, and School Change* (1995).

Dewey M. Caron is Professor of Entomology and Wildlife Ecology, University of Delaware. He teaches introductory courses in Entomology and Beekeeping, and serves as Extension Entomologist in Delaware. Dr. Caron's research interests include Integrated Pest Management of bee mites, pollination of crops and native plants by bees, Africanized honey bees, and pests/predators/diseases of bees.

C. Ronald Carroll is Professor and Associate Director, Institute of Ecology, and Director of the Conservation Ecology and Sustainable Development graduate training program, University of Georgia. His research projects include integrated pest management in Guatemala, restoration ecology training in Ecuador, and southeastern ultisols native community restoration.

Lisa Chase is Natural Resources Specialist with the University of Vermont Extension, and Director of the Vermont Tourism Data Center. Her research focuses on tourism and recreation that enhance environmental conservation and sustainable development.

Peter R. Cheeke is Emeritus Professor, Department of Animal Sciences, Oregon State University. His studies include contemporary issues in animal agriculture, and comparative animal nutrition. He is the author of *Contemporary Issues in Animal Agriculture* (3rd edition, 2003).

Robbin Christianson is Cooperative Research Network Operations Manager, National Rural Electric Cooperatives Association, Arlington, VA.

Neale R. Chumbler is Research Scientist at the VA Rehabilitation Outcomes Research Center, Gainesville, Florida, and Associate Professor, Department of Health Services Research, Management, and Policy at the University of Florida. His research involves developing, implementing, and evaluating tele-health models for veterans with disabling, chronic diseases.

Kimberly Chung is Associate Professor of Community, Agriculture, Recreation, and Resource Studies, Michigan State University, East Lansing, MI. Her areas of specialization are Community Food Security, Participatory Development, and Mixed Methods, including Qualitative and Participatory Methods. Dr. Chung has authored multiple publications on these areas.

Rodney L. Clouser is Professor and Extension Public Policy Specialist, Food and Resource Economics, University of Florida. His research and extension interests involve public policy related to growth, land use, and taxation.

David W. Cobia is Professor Emeritus, Department of Agricultural Economics, and Director, Quentin N. Burdick Center for Cooperatives, North Dakota State University, Fargo. He conducted research on new, emerging value-adding contract agricultural cooperatives, and edited *Cooperatives in Agriculture* (1989).

Jack T. Cole is Professor and Director of Special Education, Department of Special Education/Communication Disorders, New Mexico State University. He worked in rural regular and special education for 30 years, was the Director of the ERIC Clearinghouse on Rural Education and Small Schools, and is Executive Editor of *Rural Special Education Quarterly*.

Dennis R. Cooley is Associate Director of the Northern Plains Ethics Institute and Associate Professor of Philosophy and Ethics at North Dakota State University, Fargo. His research interests include environmental ethics, bioethics, business ethics, and technology.

John D. Copeland is a Professor, Division of Business, John Brown University and an Executive-in-Residence for the Soderquist Center for Leadership and Ethics. Dr. Copeland conducts research and teaches undergraduate and graduate courses in corporate governance; business ethics; insurance and risk management; and mission, vision, and values.

Sam M. Cordes is Professor, Department of Agricultural Economics, and Director, Center for Rural Community Revitalization and Development, University of Nebraska. His research studies concentrate on community economic development with emphasis on rural health care delivery. He served on the U.S. Department of Health and Human Services' National Advisory Committee on Rural Health. His publications include *Recreational Access to Private Lands: Liability Problems and Solutions* (1995) and *Understanding the Farmers Comprehensive Personal Liability Policy: A Guide for Farmers' Attorneys and Insurance Agents* (1992).

Arthur G. Cosby is Professor of Sociology and Director, Social Science Research Center, Mississippi State University. He conducts societal monitoring, policy research and futuring, and focuses on the visualization of social and economic phenomena and the growth of legalized gaming and gambling in the United States. He led the 1995 U.S. Survey of Gaming and Gambling.

Connie Coutellier was Director, Professional Development, and Past President, American Camping Association. She directed camps in Ohio, California, and Michigan and is integrating camp director education courses into a development plan for camping professionals. She is author of *Management Risks and Emergencies* and the Camp Fire Boys and Girls *Outdoor Book*.

Raymond T. Coward is Professor of Health Policy and Epidemiology, Affiliate Professor of Sociology, and Director, Institute for Gerontology, University of Florida. His research focuses on the affect of race and residence on the process of aging and on health and human services delivery to older adults and their families. He is coauthor of *Health Programs and Services for Elders in Rural American: A Review of the Life Circumstances and Formal Services That Affect the Health and Well-Being of Elders* (1991) and *Old and Alone in Rural America* (1993).

Cynthia M. Cready is a doctoral student in sociology, Texas A&M University. Her dissertation examines African American population size and the impact of desegregation on public school finances and White enrollment in the nonmetropolitan South. Additional research involves the effect of mate availability on African American family structure and minority group intermarriage.

Susan J. Crockett is Vice President and Senior Technology Officer with the General Mills Bell Institute of Health and Nutrition, Minneapolis, MN.

John B. Cromartie is a geographer with the Economic Research Service, U.S. Department of Agriculture. His research studies pertain to rural migration, settlement patterns, and minority populations. His current studies involve examining post-1990 rural migration and labor market changes and mapping national settlement patterns using census tracts.

James Curry teaches at the Departamento de Estudios Norteamericanos (Department of North American Studies), El Colegio de la Frontera Norte, Tijuana, B.C., Mexico. His publications pertain to the California wine industry and the restructuring of agri-industry.

Carol L. Cwiak teaches in North Dakota State University's Emergency Management Program, Fargo. She serves as the program's Internship Coordinator and is a member of FEMA's Emergency Management Roundtable. Her interests include emergency management identity, professionalization, higher education initiatives, business continuity, the seamless integration between education and experience, and the sustainability paradigm.

David B. Danbom is Professor, Department of History and Religion, North Dakota State University. His recent publications include *Born in the Country: A History of Rural America*, 2nd edition (2006) and an upcoming manuscript entitled "Making Farms/Making Lives: Farm-Making on the Great Plains, 1870-1915."

Jacqueline M. Davis-Gines is Membership Specialist, Girl Scouts of Northeast Georgia. Previously, Dr. Davis-Gines was a faculty member in the Department of Sociology, University of Memphis.

Jonathan Deason is a Professor and Director of the Environmental and Energy Management program, George Washington University. His research interests include environmental policy and management and renewable energy. He served as Director, Office of Environmental Policy and Compliance, U.S. Department of the Interior.

Lesley Deem-Dickson is a graduate student in the Department of Entomology, University of Illinois at Urbana-Champaign. She is studying pest management.

Steven C. Deller is Professor, Agricultural and Applied Economics, University of Wisconsin, Madison. His research pertains to modeling community and small regional economies in order to better understand the changing dynamics of the economy, assess the impact of those changes, and identify local economic strengths, weaknesses, opportunities and threats.

Janaan Diemer is Special Education Coordinator, supervising programs for the Seriously Emotionally Disordered Students, Psychology, and Social Work Department, Las Cruces Public Schools, Las Cruces, New Mexico. She taught regular and special education for 14 years, served as administrator for six years, and is pursuing a doctorate in educational administration.

David M. Diggs is Coordinator, University of Northern Colorado's Laboratory for Geographic Information Science, and Associate Professor of Geography at UNC. Dr. Diggs has a background in geographic information science (GIS) technologies and GIS applications for natural resource issues. His projects include research for the Colorado Geography Education Fund via the National Geographic Society and for the British Broadcasting Corporation.

Otto C. Doering III is Professor, Department of Agricultural Economics, Purdue University, and a public policy specialist focusing on agricultural and resource issues. He coordinated environmental policy research through the School of Agriculture for the state and federal government.

Frank J. Dooley is Professor and Teaching Coordinator, Department of Agricultural Economics, Purdue University. His research studies focus on logistics and supply chain management, the economic and legal aspects of the rail, motor carrier, airline, and country grain elevator industries.

Rodrigo Salcedo Du Bois is a doctoral candidate in the Department of Agricultural Economics and Rural Sociology at Pennsylvania State University, and is affiliated with the Population Research Institute at the University. He is pursuing dual doctoral degrees in Agricultural, Environmental and Regional Economics, as well as Demography.

Stacy Duffield is Assistant Professor, School of Education, North Dakota State University, Fargo. Her research pertains to teacher preparation, adolescent and adult literacy, and middle level education.

Michael Duffy is Associate Professor in the Department of Economics, Iowa State University. His research focuses on natural resource and environmentally related agricultural concerns such as agrichemical use on farms.

Lauren Duffy is a graduate student in the Department of Recreation, Parks and Tourism at the University of North Carolina, Greensboro. Her research interests include sustainable tourism, ecotourism, and globalization.

Joshua M. Duke is Associate Professor, Department of Food and Resource Economics, the Legal Studies Program, and the Department of Economics, University of Delaware. His research interests address economics of land use and land preservation. He instructs courses in environmental economics, sustainable development, and environmental law.

Thomas J. Durant, Jr. is Professor of Sociology and African American Studies at Louisiana State University in Baton Rouge. His research interests include rural sociology, ethnic minorities, and southern culture.

Ron Durst is tax team leader and senior economist in the Rural Economy Division, Economic Research Service, U.S. Department of Agriculture. He holds degrees in agricultural economics, law, and taxation. His research pertains to taxation and related topics.

Jamieson L. Duvall is a Post-Doctoral Fellow, Department of Behavioral Science, University of Kentucky, with an appointment at the Center on Drug and Alcohol Research. His primary research interests include rural substance use, alcohol misuse, and risky decision making.

Terri L. Earnest is Assistant Professor of Sociology at Francis Marion University. She instructs courses in race relations, criminology, juvenile delinquency, and drugs and society. Her research interests include gender/race differences in deterrent effects on decisions to reoffend, society's responses to the methamphetamine epidemic, and the evolving social definitions of crime.

Clyde Eastman is a development sociologist with the Department of Agricultural Economics and Agricultural Business, New Mexico State University. He conducts research on small-scale irrigation systems, farms, and farm labor in its various dimensions.

Michael L. Elliott is Associate Professor, Department of City and Regional Planning, Georgia Institute of Technology. His research interests include environmental dispute resolution and public participation processes. Dr. Elliot co-edited *Making Sense of Intractable Environmental Conflicts* (with Roy Lewicki and Barbara Gray, 2003).

Lowell J. Endahl served as donated equipment manager, National Rural Electric Cooperative Association, International Foundation. He managed power plants, developed marketing, technological, and member relations programs. Endahl traveled extensively in Europe, Africa, South America, and Asia for the United Nations' Working Party on Rural Electrification.

Robert D. Espeseth is Professor Emeritus, Office of Recreation and Tourism Development and Department of Leisure Studies, University of Illinois, Champaign-Urbana. His research concentrates on the Ohio River National Heritage Corridor, East St. Louis Cultural Heritage District, and the Economic Impact of Park and Recreation Areas for the National Society for Park Resource.

Edmund A. Estes is Associate Department Head, Departmental Extension Leader, and Professor in the Department of Agricultural and Resource Economics, North Carolina State University. His research and extension interests include fruit and vegetable marketing analysis, supply chain and agribusiness management, cost of production estimates, postharvest handling technologies, niche and specialty crop marketing, organic vegetables, economic analysis of cultural practices including drip irrigation and plastic mulch, and direct marketing.

D. Merrill Ewert is President, Fresno Pacific University, Fresno, CA. Previously, he served as Director, Cornell Cooperative Extension, and as faculty in the Department of Education, Cornell University. He studied the link between rural literacy education and community development in New York.

Gary Farley is retired Director of the Town and County Program of the Southern Baptist Convention. He currently serves as the Director of Missions for the Pickens Baptist Association of West Alabama.

Frank L. Farmer is Professor of Rural Sociology in the School of Human Environmental Science at the University of Arkansas. His current research focus is population structure and change in rural areas with a particular focus on Hispanic in-migration. He also studies the impact of population change on an array of environmental indicators.

Shingairai A. Feresu is Assistant Professor of Epidemiology in the Department of Epidemiology, College of Public Health, University of Nebraska Medical Center. Her current research interests include rural substance abuse treatment, reproductive health as it relates to prenatal outcomes, HIV infection, health care disparities in health outcomes, including breast and cervical cancer screening, cardiovascular diseases, diabetes, and obesity as it relates to maternal and infant outcomes.

William E. Field is Professor, Department of Agricultural and Biological Engineering, Purdue University, West Lafayette. Dr. Field teaches and conducts research and extension programs related to agricultural health and safety. He supervises Purdue University's Breaking New Ground Outreach Program that assists farmers with physical handicaps.

Jill L. Findeis is Distinguished Professor of Agricultural, Environmental and Regional Economics and Demography at State University. She is a faculty member in the Department of Agricultural Economics and Rural Sociology and is Faculty Associate in the Population Research Institute.

Price V. Fishback is Professor, Department of Economics, University of Arizona, Tucson. He has authored reports about insurance rationing and worker's compensation for the National Bureau of Economic Research and is the author of *Soft Coal, Hard Choices: The Economic Welfare of Bituminous Coal Miners: 1890-1993* (1992).

Emmett P. Fiske is Extension Organizational Effectiveness Specialist, Department of Rural Sociology, Washington State University. His research studies pertain to resolution of environmental conflicts.

Harrison L. Flint is Professor, Department of Horticulture, Purdue University. He has published several books and journal articles on landscape plants.

Cornelia Butler Flora is the Charles F. Curtiss Distinguished Professor of Agriculture and Life Sciences and Sociology at Iowa State University and Director of the North Central Regional Center for Rural Development. A Fellow of the American Association for the Advancement of Science, she served as President of the Rural Sociological Society, the Community Development Society, and the Agriculture and Human Values Association.

Richard C. Fluck is Professor, Department of Agricultural and Biological Engineering, University of Florida. His research projects concentrate on the Florida Agricultural Energy Consumption Model, educational materials on energy use in sustainable agriculture, and budgets to evaluate energy productiveness of alternative production practices for North Florida commodities. He is the editor of *Energy in Farm Production. Volume 6, Energy in World Agriculture* (1992).

Charles A. Francis is Professor and Director, Center for Sustainable Agricultural Systems, University of Nebraska, Lincoln. His areas of research study and expertise include intercropping systems in Columbia, Philippines, and the Midwest United States. He is currently developing and testing innovative learning environments and designing diverse, resource-efficient farming systems.

C. Dean Freudenberger was professor, Christian Social Ethics and Rural Ministry, Luther Seminary. His emphasis of research study pertains to agricultural ethics, hunger, poverty, and the integration of theology and ecology, and is the author of *Food for Tomorrow?* (1984).

Eric T. Freyfogle is Max L. Rowe Professor of Law at the University of Illinois College of Law. His publications concentrate on nature, culture, and land use, with particular reference to private rights in nature and to the conservation movement as a critique of modern culture. He published *On Private Property: Finding Common Ground on the Ownership of Land* (2007) and *Why Conservation Is Failing and How It Can Regain Ground* (2006).

Jerry E. Fruin is Associate Professor of Marketing and Transportation in the Department of Applied Economics, and an Extension Specialist in Transportation at the University of Minnesota. His research interests include the costs and adequacy of all modes of transportation serving Minnesota and the Upper Midwest including roads, railroads, the Mississippi River System and the Great Lakes and the Seaway System.

Isao Fujimoto is Professor Emeritus, Department of Applied Behavioral Science and Department of Asian American Studies, University of California, Davis. His research study concentrates on Asian Pacific Americans and Japanese rural community revitalization.

Wayne E. Fuller is Professor Emeritus, Department of History, University of Texas at El Paso. He has written on rural history, including the Rural Free Delivery mail system. He published *The Old Country School: The Story of Rural Education in the Middle West* (1982) and *One-room Schools of the Middle West* (1994).

D. Linda Garcia is Adjunct Professor, School of Foreign Service and Program on Communications, Culture, and Technology, Georgetown University, and School of Advanced International Studies, Johns Hopkins University. Her research studies focus on telecommunications.

Melanie Gardner conducts research at the Rural Information Center, National Agricultural Library, Beltsville, Maryland.

Charles C. Geisler is Professor, Development Sociology, Cornell University. His research interests include the evolution of property in changing state, community, and global contexts, development-induced displacement, the social dimensions of home-land securitization, and the environmental effects of war and everyday militarization.

Jack M. Geller is Professor and Head of the Department of Arts, Humanities and Social Sciences at the University of Minnesota, Crookston. He has been professionally active in the area of rural health care delivery for years, having previously served as Professor of Community Medicine & Rural Health at the University of North Dakota School of Medicine and Health Sciences. A current member of the Minnesota Board of Medical Practice, he also currently serves on the board of the Minnesota Rural Health Association.

Kathryn Paxton George is Emerita Professor of Philosophy, Department of Philosophy, University of Idaho. Her area of expertise focuses on ethics in agriculture and her publications include *Animal, Vegetable or Woman? A Feminist Argument against Ethical Vegetarianism*. She also co-edited *Readings in the Development of Moral Thought* (1992) and *Agricultural Ethics: Issues for the 21st Century* (1994).

Erick Gibbs is Manager of Business Development and Project Analysis, National Rural Electric Cooperative Association International.

Duane A. Gill is Associate Director for Research on Society and Environment and Research Professor at the Social Science Research Center and Professor of Sociology, Department of Sociology, Anthropology and Social Work at Mississippi State University. His research interests pertain to disasters, their interconnections with community and the environment and their human impacts.

Nancy J. Gladwell is Associate Professor and the Director of the Recreation and Parks Management Program, University of North Carolina, Greensboro. Her research interests focus on management issues in recreation and parks and the impact of family caregiving on leisure travel.

Leland L. Glenna is Assistant Professor of Rural Sociology, Department of Agricultural Economics and Rural Sociology, Pennsylvania State University. His current research studies pertain to the social and environmental impacts of agricultural science and technologies and the role of ideology and science in policy making.

Nancy K. Glomb is Assistant Professor, Department of Special Education and Rehabilitation and Director, Mild/Moderate Distance Learning Degree and Licensure Program, Utah State University. She acquired grant funding for A Distance Education Program to Prepare Special Education Teachers for Students with Mild/Moderate Disabilities from the Utah State Office of Education. Dr. Glomb has published many educational articles, book chapters, and books.

Theodore Godlaski is Assistant Professor of Psychiatry, Multidisciplinary Research Center on Drug and Alcohol Abuse University of Kentucky, Lexington. His research studies concentrate on patients who received treatment in Kentucky drug and alcohol programs and future planning for additional capacity management across the state.

Stephen J. Goetz is Associate Professor, Department of Agricultural Economics, University of Kentucky, Lexington. He identifies determinant of economic growth in rural areas, such as human capital, labor force, and government policy and studies food manufacturing industry location and that industry's potential to preserve farms in rural areas.

Robert Goodland is the independent environmental commissioner for the EIR, a World Mining Commission, and former Chief of the Environmental Department of the World Bank. As a tropical ecologist, Dr. Goodland is involved in the assessment of social and environmental impacts of development projects.

Chennat Gopalakrishnan is Professor of Natural Resource Economics, University of Hawaii. He directed several research projects dealing with water institutions, water markets and pricing, and water conservation and management.

Gary A. Goreham is Professor of Sociology in the Department of Sociology, Anthropology, and Emergency Management, North Dakota State University. His teaching and research interests include community economic development, environmental sociology, sociology of agriculture, sociology of religion, and cooperatives.

Kathleen M. Grant is Staff Physician on the Substance Use Disorders Program, VA Nebraska Western Iowa Health Care System, Omaha. She is Assistant Professor of Internal Medicine at the University of Nebraska Medical Center. Her current research interests pertain to rural substance abuse treatment, health care disparities, methamphetamine treatment, and treatment of nicotine dependence in persons with alcoholism.

Craig R. Grau is Vaughan-Bascom Professor of Plant Pathology, Department of Plant Pathology, University of Wisconsin, Madison. His research focuses on crop diseases in Wisconsin and neighboring states, developing methods to identify, assess, and manage disease problems in alfalfa, soybean, pea, snap bean, small grains, and corn crops.

Phyllis Gray-Ray is Professor of Sociology at Florida A & M University. Other positions she held included Vice President for Research at Florida A & M University, Chief Research Officer in the University of North Carolina System for Winston-Salem State University, and Dean of the School of Graduate Studies and Research at Winston-Salem State University.

Gary P. Green is Professor, Department of Rural Sociology, University of Wisconsin-Madison and Co-director, Center for Community and Economic Development, University of Wisconsin-Extension. Green's research, teaching, and outreach interests involve community and economic development in the U.S., New Zealand, South Korea, Uganda, and Ukraine. He served as Editor of *Rural Sociology* (2003-2005).

John J. Green is Research Assistant, Social Science Research Center, Department of Sociology, Anthropology, and Social

Work, Mississippi State University. His publications pertain to plantations in the rural South.

Clyde S. Greenlees is Instructor, Department of Sociology, South Texas College, McAllen, Texas. His research pertains to the employment patterns of Mexican immigrant women.

Charles L. Griffin is Professor, School of Family Studies and Human Services, Kansas State University. He is a marriage and family therapist who has worked with a wide range of farm family, rural community, and rural mental health concerns involving crisis response, communication, stress management, conflict resolution and mediation, and community and organizational change.

Christina E. Gringeri is Associate Professor, Graduate School of Social Work, and Director, Women's Study Program, University of Utah. Her research focus is rural poverty and women, work, and development in the Intermountain West and she is the author of *Getting By: Women Homeworkers and Rural Economic Development* (1994).

Charles F. "Fritz" Gritzner is Distinguished Professor of Geography, Department of Geography, South Dakota State University. A cultural geographer, Gritzner is a former President of the National Council for Geographic Education and a recipient of the Council's George J. Miller Award for Distinguished Service.

Robert Gronski is Policy Director, National Catholic Rural Life Conference, Des Moines, Iowa. His policy work covers the U.S. farm bill, land stewardship, international trade, biofuels, and impacts of climate change on agriculture and rural communities.

James L. Groves works in the School of Hotel and Restaurant Management, Oklahoma State University. His writings concentrate on restaurants and their role in rural communities.

Robert W. Groves is Professor of Music, Division of Fine Arts, North Dakota State University. His areas of expertise include piano literature and performance, oral histories and American music history, and the relief of tendon stress syndrome in computer keyboard use.

Carolyn E. Grygiel is Director, Natural Resources Management Interdisciplinary Program and Associate Professor, Rangeland Ecology in the School of Natural Resource Sciences at North Dakota State University. Her current research interest focuses on developing new methodologies for restoring tall grass prairies.

H. Irene Hall is Chief of the Surveillance Research Section, Cancer Surveillance Branch, Centers for Disease Control and Prevention, Atlanta, GA. Her research is focused on skin cancer prevention: the problem, responses, and lessons learned.

Susan Hamburger is the Manuscripts Cataloging Librarian at Pennsylvania State University. She authored "On the Land for Life: Black Tenant Farmers on Tall Timbers Plantation," *Florida Historical Quarterly*; essays in *American National Biography*; "We Take Care of Our Womenfolk: The Home for Needy Confederate Women in Richmond, Virginia" in *Before the New*

Deal: Southern Social Welfare History, 1830-1930; and essays in *African Americans in Sports*

Neil D. Hamilton is Distinguished Professor and Director, Agricultural Law Center, Drake University. His research examines how people and forces shape America's food and agricultural system.

Wava G. Haney is Professor Emerita, Department of Anthropology and Sociology, University of Wisconsin Colleges and the Professional Development Coordinator for the University of Wisconsin Colleges. She spent a sabbatical year at the Centre for Rural Affairs, University of Trondheim, Norway, where she pursued her long-term interest in rural women and rural community development.

Rosalind Harris is Associate Professor in the Department of Sociology and Department of Community and Leadership Development, University of Kentucky. Her research examines the dynamics of collaborative efforts between universities and community-based organizations in addressing the needs of persistently poor communities within the Black Belt region of the Southern U.S.

Mark Harvey, Professor of History, North Dakota State University. Dr. Harvey teaches and writes about environmental and American West history. His scholarship focuses on national parks and monuments and wilderness preservation within the United States during the middle– and late–20th century.

Upton Hatch is Professor, Department of Agricultural Economics, Auburn University. He teaches and conducts research on the economics of aquaculture, natural resources, and the environment. He is developing instructional materials for aquaculture curricula and for estimates of the economic value of water.

Richard P. Haynes is Emeritus Associate Professor of Philosophy, University of Florida. He is founding editor of the journal *Agriculture and Human Values* and editor-in-chief of the *Journal of Agricultural and Environmental Ethics*. His book, *Animal Welfare: Competing Conceptions and Their Ethical Implications* will be published by Springer in 2008.

Thomas Heberlein served as Chair of the Department of Rural Sociology and Director of the Center for Resource Policy Studies at the University of Wisconsin-Madison where he is Professor Emeritus. He assisted in founding Human Dimensions of Wildlife and published widely in the area. He is currently Professor, Department of Wildlife, Fish, and Environmental Studies, Swedish University of Agricultural Sciences. He divides his time between Stockholm and Wisconsin.

William D. Heffernan is Professor Emeritus, Department of Rural Sociology, University of Missouri, Columbia. His studies focus on the changes in the structure of agriculture and the concentration in agribusiness, or the agro/food complex, with special emphasis on the poultry sector. He co-authored *Concentration of Agricultural Markets* (1996).

David A. Henderson works at the Piketon Research and Extension Center, Ohio State University. His research studies include expenditure patterns between rural elderly residents and rural-to-urban elderly migrants, with particular emphasis on previous occupation.

Shida Rastegari Henneberry is Professor of International Agricultural Trade, Department of Agricultural Economics, Oklahoma State University. Dr. Henneberry teaches and conducts research in the areas of agricultural market development and factors affecting U.S. competitiveness in global markets. She also conducts research in the areas of teaching and advising effectiveness.

Lawrence J. Hill is Head, Department of Communication and Theater Arts, Western Carolina University. He received grant funding from the North Dakota Humanities Council and the National Endowment for the Humanities to research 19th century scenic design and preservation projects. Dr. Hill is treasurer of the United States Institute for Theater Technology.

Clare Hinrichs is Associate Professor of Rural Sociology at Pennsylvania State University. Her research and teaching addresses broad issues of social change and development in food and agricultural systems, with particular focus on transitions to sustainability.

Thomas A. Hirschl is Professor in the Department of Developmental Sociology, Cornell University. His focus is on social class differentiation in contemporary societal development and is working on a new, adequate method for measuring social class.

Thomas J. Hoban is Professor, Department of Sociology and Anthropology, North Carolina State University. He focuses on how people accept new products and respond to change. Dr. Hoban studies the impacts of biotechnology on agriculture and the environment as well as American and Japanese consumers' attitudes about food produced through biotechnology.

Daryl J. Hobbs is Professor, Department of Sociology, and Director, Office of Social and Economic Data Analysis, University of Missouri. He teaches, gives presentations, and conducts research on the problems and opportunities that pertain to rural schools, health care, and community development.

David W. Hughes is Professor and Rural Development (Extension) Economist in the Department of Applied Economics and Statistics and Community Development Extension Program Leader in the Clemson Institute for Economic and Community Development, Sandhill Research and Education Center, Clemson University. His research interests include regional, rural, and community economic development, economic impact analysis, public service provision, and workforce development.

Teresa Hughes is a graduate research assistant in the Department of Plant Pathology, University of Wisconsin-Madison. Her research focuses on elucidating the role pathogen and host variability have on disease development in order to develop control methods that minimize economic loss and environmental impact.

Craig R. Humphrey is Associate Professor Emeritus of Sociology and Demography at Pennsylvania State University. He co-authored *Environment, Energy and Society: A New Synthesis* (with T.L. Lewis and the late F.H. Buttel, 2002) and *Environment, Energy, And Society: Exemplary Works* (with T.L. Lewis and the late F.H. Buttel, 2003). His research focuses on the relationships between social theory, the environment and population, and the relationship between international energy politics and the environment.

Mary Humstone is Research Scientist, American Studies Program, University of Wyoming. She teaches architectural history and historic preservation, and coordinates outreach activities in the American Studies Program. Dr. Humstone was Assistant Director, Mountains/Plains Office of the National Trust for Historic Preservation, where she co-founded BARN AGAIN! Her research interests include the study, interpretation, and preservation of cultural landscapes.

Chris A. Hurt is Professor and Extension Economist, Department of Agricultural Economics, Purdue University. He teaches agricultural marketing to undergraduates and grain and livestock marketing to farmers and agribusiness managers. His research is focused on marketing problems of family farms.

Ronald J. Hustedde is Professor, Department of Community and Leadership Development at the University of Kentucky. He specializes in rural community development, public policy deliberation, public conflict resolution, and building entrepreneurial cultures.

John E. Ikerd is Professor Emeritus, Agricultural Economics, University of Missouri. For the past three decades, his work has focused on issues of economic sustainability with an emphasis on agriculture and rural communities. He is author of *Sustainable Capitalism*, *A Return to Common Sense*, *Small Farms are Real Farms*, and *Crisis and Opportunity: Sustainability in American Agriculture*.

Thomas D. Isern is Professor of History and University Distinguished Professor at North Dakota State University. A specialist in the history of agriculture and the history of the Great Plains, Dr. Isern is the author of two books on the history of wheat harvesting.

Harvey M. Jacobs is Professor in the Department of Urban and Regional Planning and in the Gaylord Nelson Institute for Environmental Studies, University of Wisconsin-Madison. His work focuses on public policy and political economy of land use and environmental management, how societies define property, and institutions that manage the relationship between private and public rights in property.

Harvey S. James, Jr. is Associate Professor of Agribusiness in the Department of Agricultural Economics, University of Missouri, Columbia. His research interests include business ethics, the organization of agricultural production, and the economics of trust. Dr. James is editor-in-chief of the journal *Agriculture and Human Values*, and serves on the editorial board of *Business Ethics Quarterly*.

Jonathan A. Jenks is Distinguished Professor and Director of Graduate Programs, Department of Wildlife and Fisheries Sciences, South Dakota State University, Brookings. Dr. Jenks' research involves large mammal ecology and management, wild ruminant nutrition, wildlife management, and population dynamics.

Eric B. Jensen is a doctoral student in Rural Sociology and Demography, Pennsylvania State University. His dissertation research focuses on the occupational trajectories of Mexican-origin farm workers in the United States.

Leif Jensen is Professor of Rural Sociology and Demography, Pennsylvania State University. He studies poverty and economic survival strategies among rural and urban households, including work on underemployment and participation in the informal economy. He also studies immigration to the United States with emphasis on immigrant groups in new destinations.

Marvin E. Jensen is a consultant on irrigation issues. He was Director of the Colorado Institute for Irrigation Management, Colorado State University, and the National Program Leader of the Water Management Research, Agricultural Research Service, U.S. Department of Agriculture.

Edward J. Jepson, Jr. is Assistant Professor in the Master of Science in Planning program in the Department of Political Science, University of Tennessee, Knoxville. His primary research interests include planning for sustainable development, land use management tools and regulations, and analytical methods and techniques.

Patrick C. Jobes was Professor, Department of Sociology, Montana State University. His studies focus on crime and delinquency, demography and human ecology, and environmental and energy concerns of the western United States.

Chandice M. Johnson, Jr., retired in 1999 after serving five years as the founding director of the North Dakota State University Center for Writers. His interest is freelance editing with private individuals and a consortium of Communication professors across the nation producing scholarly works. He serves as editor for *The Proceedings of the Linguistic Circle of Manitoba and North Dakota*.

D. Demcey Johnson was Assistant Professor, Department of Agricultural Economics, North Dakota State University. His research interests included agricultural price analysis, agricultural trade with focus on commodities produced in the Northern Plains, and economics of grain quality.

L. Shannon Jung is Professor of Town and Country Ministries, Saint Paul School of Theology in Kansas City, Missouri. His research interests include a collaborative volume and website on *Practicing Care in Rural Congregations and Communities* (with Jeanne Hoeft and Joretta Marshall) and writing on the theology and ethics of eating.

Raymond A. Jussaume, Jr. is Professor and Chair in the Department of Community and Rural Sociology, Washington State University. He has conducted extensive research on the political sociology of the community dimensions of international agricultural trade, particularly in the United States, Europe and East Asia, and sustainability issues surrounding local food systems.

Adel A. Kader is Professor Emeritus of Postharvest Physiology in the Department of Plant Sciences, University of California at Davis. For 36 years, he conducted research on postharvest biology and technology of fruits, taught several courses, and mentored graduate students and postdoctoral researches. He served as the President of the American Society for Horticultural Science in 1996.

Aileen A. Kader is a Master Gardener who is interested in the interactions between people and plants. She teaches photography and woodworking at the Crafts Center of the University of California at Davis.

Cathy D. Kassab is Research Associate, Institute for Policy Research and Evaluation, Pennsylvania State University. Her research focuses on changes in job quality, strategies used by low-income households to enhance economic well-being, and barriers to health care services use among non-metropolitan populations.

Lenard W. Kaye is Director of the University of Maine Center on Aging and Professor in the University of Maine School of Social Work. Dr. Kay has lectured and written extensively on rural social work practice and aging-related health and social service issues. He is the co-editor of *Gerontological Social Work in Small Towns and Rural Communities* (2003).

Jean Kayitsinga is a doctoral student in the Department of Sociology, Michigan State University. His research interests include rural families, sociology, demography, and statistical methodologies.

Eric Damian Kelly is Dean, College of Architecture and Planning, Ball State University. His writing focuses on issues in planning law and planning implementation, and he has coauthored *Sign Regulation for Small and Midsized Communities* (with G.J. Raso, 1989), a Planning Advisory Service Report of the American Planning Association.

Philip Kenkel is Professor in the Agricultural Economics Department, Oklahoma State University and holds the Bill Fitzwater Cooperative Chair in that department. His research activities include assessment of value-added cooperative venture feasibility, and the development of decision aids to enhance the cooperative business performance.

Jean Kinsey is Professor and Director of the Food Industry Center, Department of Applied Economics at the University of Minnesota where she teaches "Economics of Food Marketing" and "Information and Behavioral Economics." Her research interests include consumer behavior and food choices, food companies' strategies to protect against food terrorism, and food accessibility.

Frederick L. Kirschenmann is Distinguished Fellow at the Leopold Center for Sustainable Agriculture, and Professor of Religion and Philosophy, Iowa State University. Dr. Kirschen-

mann manages a certified organic farm in North Dakota and assisted in founding the Farm Verified Organic, Inc. and the Northern Plains Sustainable Agriculture Society.

Daniel J. Klenow is Professor and Chair of the Department of Sociology, Anthropology, and Emergency Management, North Dakota State University. His emergency management interests include special populations, rural issues, terrorism, and natural disasters. He participated in research funded by the National Science Foundation, Natural Hazards Center, and the Federal Emergency Management Agency.

James B. Kliebenstein is Professor of Agricultural Economics at Iowa State University. His research interests are in the areas of economic evaluation of livestock production systems which are environmentally sound, socially acceptable, and profitable; economic assessment of animal health management; and structural adjustment in the livestock industry. His teaching responsibilities focus on farm business management.

Timothy J. Kloberdanz is Associate Professor, Department of Sociology, Anthropology, and Emergency Management, North Dakota State University. His research includes folklore of the Great Plains and Rocky Mountain regions, genetic Alzheimer's disease, and ethnic persistence in the major grassland regions of the European steppes, North American prairies, and South American pampas.

Peter F. Korsching is Professor, Department of Sociology, Iowa State University. His work pertains to adoption, diffusion, and impacts of new technologies on farming populations and rural communities. His studies involve sustainable agriculture practices and technologies and the potential of new telecommunications technologies for rural community development.

Won W. Koo is Chamber of Commerce Distinguished Professor and Director of Center for Agricultural Policy and Trade Studies, North Dakota State University. He has been an educator and researcher in international trade and agricultural marketing.

Dianne T. Koza, Auburn University, developed training materials to teach computer skills to apparel students and plant employees, and is developing software for the apparel and textiles industries.

John A. Krout is Professor of Gerontology and Director of the Gerontology Institute, Ithaca College, Ithaca, New York. He conducted national studies on rural-urban differences of senior centers and other services for older adults. Other research interests include service knowledge and utilization, elder migration, housing, intergenerational programming, and creativity and aging.

Fred M. Lamb is Professor Emeritus in the Department of Wood Science and Forest Products, Virginia Tech, Blacksburg, Virginia. His focus is on teaching, research, and continuing education in wood processing technology, product manufacturing, and material utilization for the wood products industries throughout the U.S. and internationally.

Christopher Lant is Chair, Department of Geography, Southern Illinois University, Carbondale, and Editor, *Water Resources Bulletin*. His research interests include projects to determine farmers' willingness to enroll cropland in the Conservation Reserve Program and the Wetlands Reserve Program as ways to improve water quality in agricultural watersheds.

Paul Lasley is Professor and Chair, Department of Sociology at Iowa State University. He provides leadership to research and extension programs on the changing nature of agriculture and the implications for rural communities and farm families.

William F. Lazarus is Extension Economist and Professor, Department of Applied Economics at the University of Minnesota. His research interests include crop and livestock production economics, farm machinery management, renewable energy, structural change in the agricultural sector, and agricultural policy.

Chiwon W. Lee, Professor of Horticulture, Department of Plant Sciences, North Dakota State University, has taught horticulture science, plant propagation, floriculture, and greenhouse management for many years. His research involves plant nutrition and growing media for greenhouse crops.

Irene K. Lee is Extension Family and Child Development Specialist, University of Arkansas at Pine Bluff. She implemented a statewide teenage pregnancy prevention program in Arkansas that resulted in a decrease in teenage birth rate. Her teen suicide and stress prevention program contributed to a 20 percent decline in the teen suicide rate in the state.

Irene E. Leech is State Coordinator, Women's Financial Information Program, Virginia Polytechnic Institute, Blacksburg. Her programs are offered with the American Association of Retired Persons and the High School Financial Program. She offers training and educational support for financial counseling volunteer programs.

Jessica Leifeld is a doctoral student at North Dakota State University's Emergency Management Program, Department of Sociology, Anthropology, and Emergency Management. She holds a M.S. in Emergency Management and a B.A. in Political Science.

F. (Fredrick) Larry Leistritz is a Distinguished Professor of Agribusiness and Applied Economics at North Dakota State University, Fargo. His research interests include teaching, and his outreach activities focus on economic assessments of agricultural and natural resource development initiatives, including the effects on the regional economy, the population, and infrastructure of affected communities.

Carl G. Leukefeld is Professor and Chair, Department of Behavioral Science and Director of the Center on Drug and Alcohol Research, University of Kentucky, Lexington. His research interests include treatment outcomes, HIV, criminal justice, health services, and rural populations.

Harriet Light was Professor, Child Development and Family Science Department, North Dakota State University, and editor, *Journal of Family and Consumer Sciences*. She is past Board of Directors president of the American Home Economics Association.

Linda M. Lobao is Professor of Rural Sociology, Sociology, and Geography in the Department of Human and Community Resource Development, Ohio State University. Her research centers on state and market changes and their impacts on regions, communities, and social groups. She is the co-author of *Beyond the Amber Waves of Grain* (1995) and co-editor of *The Sociology of Spatial Inequality* (2007).

Wayne Loescher is Professor, Department of Horticulture, Program in Plant Breeding and Genetics, Michigan State University, East Lansing, MI. His research focuses on photosynthesis and carbohydrate metabolism, in part on tree fruits, and in stress physiology, especially in how plants tolerate abiotic environmental stresses, and developing an understanding of the molecular mechanisms.

Robert Luedeman is a graduate of Drake University School of Law. He is attending the University of Arkansas agricultural law program.

Katherine MacTavish is an Assistant Professor in Human Development and Family Sciences at Oregon State University. Her research is on child development and family well being in the context of rural communities. Dr. MacTavish has examined child and youth development in the often high-risk context of rural trailer parks.

Wilbur R. Maki is Professor Emeritus, Department of Applied Economics, University of Minnesota. Dr. Maki's research included analysis and construction of decision support systems for state and regional resource management and new business ventures. He served as the Minnesota State Economist.

Allan P. Marsinko is professor of Forest Management Economics, Department of Forestry and Resources, Clemson University. He teaches forest economics, forest valuation and an introductory course for non-foresters, and conducts research on non-timber values of forest and the economic/marketing aspects of human dimensions as they relate to forests.

Steve C. Martens is Associate Professor, Department of Architecture and Landscape Architecture, North Dakota State University. He teaches architecture and historic preservation, and has research interests in architectural heritage of distinct culture groups, commonplace building types like cooperative creamery buildings, and the enduring architectural legacy of the Progressive Era and Great Depression.

Lee Mason is a doctoral student in the Department of Special Education and Rehabilitation, Utah State University.

William J. (Jim) McAuley is Professor of Communication and Gerontology at George Mason University. He also serves as Editor-in-Chief of *The Gerontologist*, an interdisciplinary journal addressing issues in aging. His research interests include rural-urban aging, long-term care, and end of life services.

Cynthia McCall is Professor, Department of Animal Sciences at Auburn University, where she teaches equine science courses and serves as the Extension Horse Specialist for Alabama. She breeds and shows Dutch Warmblood horses from her farm, Ceres Farm, in Alabama.

Cynthia M. McCready is Assistant Professor in the Department of Sociology, University of North Texas. Dr. McCready has expertise in research methodology and is studying the impacts of self-managed work teams on nurse aides' attitudes, absenteeism, and turnover in nursing home facilities.

Megan McCutcheon is a Research Instructor at George Mason University and the Managing Editor of *The Gerontologist*. She manages research and service projects for the older adult population, including health-related issues and caregiving.

Thomas D. McDonald is a Professor of Criminal Justice, North Dakota State University. Research interests include analysis of policy and program innovations in policing and corrections with a special focus on unique challenges in rural criminal justice. His publications have appeared in *Western Sociological Review*, *Sociological Practice Review*, *Adolescence*, *The Great Plains Sociologist*, and *Sociology and Social Research*.

Alan McHughen is Biotechnology Specialist and Geneticist, University of California, Riverside, and a public sector educator, scientist and consumer advocate. His interests in crop improvement and environmental sustainability helped develop U.S. and Canadian regulations on genetically engineered crops and foods. He published *Pandora's Picnic Basket: The Potential and Hazards of Genetically Modified Foods* (2000).

Walter G. McIntire is Director, Center for Research and Evaluation, and Professor, College of Education, University of Maine, Orono. He is a retired high school science teacher, school board member, consultant, and researcher and has three decades of experience in rural and small schools. He also edited the *Journal of Research in Rural Education*.

Gregory James McKee is Assistant Professor and Director, Quentin Burdick Center for Cooperatives in the Department of Agribusiness and Applied Economics, North Dakota State University. His interests include management, marketing activities, and financial performance of cooperatives. He studies contracting and vertical integration in agribusinesses, and agribusiness' relationships with their customer base.

James R. McKenna is Associate Professor, Department of Crop and Soil Environmental Sciences, Virginia Polytechnic Institute and State University. His teaching and research are in the area of crop science with special interests in sustainable agriculture and the history of American agriculture.

John C. McKissick is Extension Economist, Department of Agricultural and Applied Economics, University of Georgia. He develops marketing and farm management educational programs for farmers and writes about agricultural pricing alternatives, futures markets, option markets, and cash markets.

Dale J. Menkhaus is Professor of Agricultural and Applied Economics at the University of Wyoming. His research focuses on how alternative trading institutions, methods of delivery, policies, and structure impact market outcomes using experimental economics methods.

Joyce M. Merkel is Clinical Information Specialist for the International Bibliographic Information on Dietary Supplements clinical database, a project of the National Institutes of Health's Office of Dietary Supplements and the U.S. Department of Agriculture's National Agricultural Library. She served as Nutrition Information Specialist, National Agricultural Library Food and Nutrition Information Center.

Robert L. Metcalf is Professor Emeritus, Department of Entomology, University of Illinois at Urbana-Champaign. His research focus is on pest management and he has authored *Introduction to Pest Management*, 3d edition (with W.H. Luckman, 1994).

Richard E. Meyer is Professor, Department of English, Western Oregon State College, Monmouth. He edited three books on cemeteries, serves as chair of the Cemeteries and Gravemarkers Section, American Culture Association, and edited *Markers: Journal of the Association for Gravestone Studies*.

DeMond Shondell Miller is Associate Professor of Sociology and Director of the Liberal Arts and Sciences Institute for Research and Community Service at Rowan University (Glassboro, New Jersey). His primary areas of specialization are environmental sociology, disaster studies, social construction of place, community development, and social impact assessment.

Eleanor Miller works with media relations at the National Rural Electric Cooperative Association in Arlington, VA.

Lee M. Miller is Assistant Professor, Sociology Department, Sam Houston State University. Her research focuses on the sociology of disaster, particularly why some communities effectively prepare for, and respond to, disaster and others do not. How people are connected within communities is seen as the key to understanding disaster responses.

Vicki L. Miller is a doctoral student in Emergency Management in the Department of Sociology, Anthropology, and Emergency Management, North Dakota State University. Her research focuses on the Emergency Assistance Compact (EMAC). She served as Program Manager for Idaho's Bureau of Hazardous Materials, Operations Specialist for the Idaho Bureau of Disaster Services, and Planner for the Idaho Bureau of Homeland Security.

Vikram V. Mistry is Professor and Head of the Dairy Science Department, South Dakota State University. His primary research interest is in the area of dairy products processing.

Melody S. Mobley was Forest Health Specialist, Forestry Management Staff, U.S. Department of Agriculture. She was the first African American woman forester employed by the Forest Service and served in numerous positions in her 19 years with the Forest Service.

Joseph J. Molnar is Professor of Rural Sociology, Department of Agricultural Economics and Rural Sociology at Auburn University. He is a Fellow of the American Association for the Advancement of Science and Past President of the International Rural Sociology Association. He studies animal agriculture industrialization, sustainable agricultural practice adoption, and Conservation Security Program implementation.

Zola K. Moon is Program Technician and doctoral student in the Rural Sociology Program, Arkansas State University. Her specialties include spatial analyses, demography, natural resources, poverty, and health issues.

Patrick H. Mooney is Professor and Chair of the Department of Sociology, University of Kentucky. His research focuses on rural social movements and class analysis in the U.S. and Poland and food security and comparative rural regional development.

Rebecca Moore is Assistant Professor of Natural Resource Economics, University of Georgia, Warnell School of Forestry and Natural Resources. Her primary research interests include integrating economic and ecological models, water resources, economic valuation, and applied econometrics.

Libby V. Morris is Professor of Higher Education and Director of the Institute of Higher Education, University of Georgia. Her research interests include the Black Belt South, dependence and socioeconomic well being, needs assessments for health professions education, and various topics in higher education. She is the editor of *Innovative Higher Education*, and is a past president of the Southern Rural Sociological Association.

Keith J. Mueller is Associate Dean, College of Public Health, University of Nebraska Medical Center, and Director of the Rural Policy Research Institute, Center for Rural Health Policy Analysis. He serves on the Advisory Panel on Medicare Education for the Centers for Medicare and Medicaid Services. Dr. Mueller's research interests include access to care in rural areas, Medicare managed care and health policy.

David Mulkey is Professor of Food and Resource Economics at the University of Florida. His research interests are in regional economics, community development and economic impact analysis.

Bridget E. Murphy is a graduate student in the Department of Sociology, Anthropology and Social Work, Kansas State University. Her research interests include rural community organization, divisions of labor based on gender, race, and ethnicity, social movements, and environmental sociology.

Ted L. Napier is Professor, Department of Agricultural Economics and Rural Sociology, Ohio State University. His research focuses on soil conservation and the adoption of soil and water quality protection practices by Ohio farmers. He is coauthor of *Adopting Conservation on the Farm: An International Perspective on the Socioeconomics of Soil and Water Conservation* (1994).

C. Jerry Nelson is Curators' Distinguished Professor of Plant Science at the University of Missouri. Dr. Nelson served as President of the Crop Science Society of America, the American Society of Agronomy, and the International Crop Science Society. His research focused on forages and grasslands.

Craig J. Newschaffer is Research Assistant Professor of Medicine, Jefferson Medical College, Thomas Jefferson University, Philadelphia, and Adjunct Assistant Professor, St. Louis University, Prevention Research Center. His research includes epidemiologic investigations of breast and prostate cancer and HIV, as well as chronic disease prevention in rural populations.

Bailey Norwood is Associate Professor, Department of Agricultural Economics at Oklahoma State University. Dr. Norwood teaches economics and focuses his research on livestock policy, farm animal welfare, and the determinants of student success in college.

Garrett J. O'Keefe is Professor of Journalism and Technical Communication, Colorado State University. His work has involved the uses and effects of public information programs related to environmental risk and public health and safety among rural publics.

Dave Olivier is Manager, Strategic Analysis Information, National Rural Electric Cooperative Association (NRECA) in Arlington, VA. He conducts research for the NRECA staff and manages NRECA databases.

Jeffrey T. Olson was Program Officer in the Ford Foundation's Rural Poverty and Resources Program, New York. Prior to joining the Ford Foundation in 1994, he was Director of the Bolle Center for Ecosystem Management at the Wilderness Society and has been a member of the Society of American Foresters since 1978.

Dan Otto was Economics Professor and Extension Economist at Iowa State University for over 25 years. He specialized in rural economic development and regional policy analysis issues.

Patrick Overton is Director of the Front Porch Institute in Astoria, Oregon. Prior, he was Associate Professor, Department of Communication and Cultural Studies, Columbia College, Missouri. He wrote *Rebuilding the Front Porch of America: Essay on the Art of Community Making* (1996).

Deborah Larson Padamsee is a research assistant in the Department of Education, Cornell University. Her doctoral dissertation examines rural literacy and community development issues.

Juan-Vicente Palerm is Professor of Anthropology at the University of California Santa Barbara, received his Ph.D. in Social Anthropology at the Universidad Iberoamericana, Mexico. His research interests are in agricultural and rural change, and migration studies, and he maintains active ethnographic field research in Spain, Mexico and the United States.

Debra Pankow is Extension Family Economic Specialist, Department of Child Development and Family Sciences and North

Dakota State University Extension Service. Dr. Pankow's research and extension interests include family economics, rural and women's economic issues, retirement preparation, and youth spending.

Domenico "Mimmo" Parisi is Associate Professor of Sociology in the Department of Sociology, Anthropology, and Social Work, and Co-Director of the Unit for Community and Environmental Studies at Mississippi State University. He specializes in rural sociology, community development, and public welfare policy.

William M. Park is Professor, Department of Agricultural Economics and Rural Sociology, and Senior Fellow, Waste Management Research and Education Institute, University of Tennessee. His studies focus on several aspects of rural solid waste management, including the economics of rural collection, drop-off recycling, regional cooperation, and unit pricing.

John G. Parsons is Professor Emeritus, Department of Dairy Science, South Dakota State University. He oversaw the university's 160-cow dairy farm and milk processing plant, and conducted dairy projects through the Agricultural Experiment Station and in conjunction with the State Dairy Lab.

Kyaw Tha Paw U is Professor of Atmospheric Science and Biometeorologist, California Agricultural Experiment Station, Department of Land, Air and Water Resources, University of California, Davis. His research studies focus on the exchange of water, carbon dioxide, other trace gases, and heat between plant ecosystems and the atmosphere; and on turbulence in air flow influenced by plants and other roughness elements.

Chuck W. Peek is a postdoctoral fellow, Agency for Health Care Policy and Research, Center for Rural Health and Aging and Department of Health Policy and Epidemiology, University of Florida. He investigates changes in caregiving networks of elders over time and race and residence variation in health, household composition, and long-term care.

Gina G. Peek is a doctoral student in the Housing and Consumer Economics in the College of Family and Consumer Sciences at the University of Georgia. Her research interests include rural housing, housing as it relates to health, and consumer behaviors related to rural housing.

David N. Pellow is Professor of Ethnic Studies, University of California, San Diego. His focus is environmental justice issues in communities of color in the U.S. and globally. His books include: *Resisting Global Toxics: Transnational Movements for Environmental Justice* (2007); *The Silicon Valley of Dreams: Environmental Injustice, Immigrant Workers, and the High-Tech Global Economy* (with L.S. Park, 2002); and *Garbage Wars: The Struggle for Environmental Justice in Chicago* (2002)

Judy E. Perkin is Chair and Professor, Department of Public Health, University of North Florida. Her areas of specialty include nutritional epidemiology, health education, food and culture/the arts, and public health nutrition.

Gary A. Peterson is Professor, Department of Soil and Crop Sciences, Colorado State University. He is the principal investigator of the Dryland Agroecosystem Project, which involves water and soil conservation and efficient use of precipitation. His research focuses on interactions of climate, soil, and crop rotation variables and he team-teaches courses in crop and soil management systems.

Ann E. Preston is Professor and Chair of the Department of Communication at St. Ambrose University, Davenport, Iowa. Her interest in rural film is inspired by her background in geography and the small, but steady stream of heartland students who pursue their dreams of becoming filmmakers. She is particularly interested in how the popular culture represents the underrepresented.

J. Walter Prevatt is Professor in the Department of Agricultural Economics and Rural Sociology at Auburn University. His extension and research responsibilities include livestock management and market, futures marketing, and farm real estate.

Mark A. Purschwitz is Research Scientist, National Farm Medicine Center, Marshfield Clinic Research Foundation, Marshfield, Wisconsin. His areas of interest include agricultural engineering focusing on prevention of traumatic farm injuries, farm equipment safety and hazard control, and farm injury surveillance.

Vernon C. Quam is consultant, Forestry Department, City of Fargo, North Dakota. He served as horticulture/forestry specialist, North Dakota State University Extension Service, and editor, *Windbreak Demonstrator Newsletter*. He writes articles and circulars on tree care and provides educational presentations to adults and youths on trees, their care and management.

Ramesh Ramloll is a Research Assistant Professor at the Institute of Rural Health, Idaho State University. His research interests include human computer interface design, computer supported cooperative work, telemedicine applications, computer based assistive technology applications, distance learning and simulation technologies. He is currently leading the implementation of simulation and distance learning technologies under the Idaho Bioterrorism Awareness and Preparedness Program.

Ronald D. Randel is a Professor, Regents Fellow, and Senior AgriLife Research Fellow in the Texas A&M System located at Overton, Texas. His research interests are reproductive management of exotic deer and cattle including the impact of nutrition on reproduction.

Wayne D. Rasmussen was a historian for 50 years at the U.S. Department of Agriculture. He wrote numerous books about the USDA and changes in the structure of agriculture, including *Taking the University to the People: Seventy-five Years of Cooperative Extension* (1989).

William O. Rasmussen is Associate Professor, Department of Agricultural and Biosystems Engineering at University of Arizona, Tucson. His research interests are developing web based water resources courses.

Richard W. Rathge is Professor in the Department of Sociology, Anthropology, and Emergency Management and the Department of Agribusiness and Applied Economics. He is the Director of the State Data Center. Dr. Rathge's research focuses on the consequences of continuous population decline in rural areas of the Great Plains and the implications of the new federalism for rural communities.

Melvin C. Ray is Associate Vice President for Economic Development and Associate Professor of Sociology, Mississippi State University. His research areas include race and society, rural economic development, and sociology of entrepreneurship.

Larry Redmon is Professor, Department of Soil and Crop Sciences, Texas A&M University, and State Forage Specialist for the Texas AgriLife Extension Service and offices in College Station. His programs include reducing winter feeding costs through the use of year-round grazing, increased use of forage legumes in pasture systems, the importance of forage analysis, the use of appropriate stocking rates, and wildlife forages.

Donald C. Reicosky is a soil scientist with the USDA-ARS, North Central Soil Conservation Research Laboratory in Morris, MN, and Adjunct Professor, Department of Soil, Water, and Climate Science, University of Minnesota, St. Paul. His research focuses on carbon cycling, tillage, and residue management with emphasis on tillage-induced carbon loss and carbon sequestration.

Ann Reisner is Associate Professor of Agricultural and Environmental Communications, Department of Human and Community Development, University of Illinois at Urbana-Champaign. Her research interests include environmental communications, environmental social movements and organizations, the sociology of mass media, and community mobilizing.

C. Matthew Rendleman is Associate Professor, Department of Agribusiness Economics, Southern Illinois University in Carbondale. His research interests include agricultural policy, ethanol production, and chemical use in agriculture.

Howard M. Resh is an international consultant and full-time contractor in development projects and has worked on hydroponic projects in North America, South America, the Middle East, and the Far East. He is the author of three books on greenhouse management and hydroponics; the most recent is *Hydroponic Tomatoes for the Home Gardener* (1993).

Matt Rhoades is Senior Speech Writer and Strategic Communications Manager, National Rural Utilities Cooperative Finance Corporation, Herndon, Virginia.

Marc O. Ribaudo is an agricultural economist with the Economic Research Service, U.S. Department of Agriculture. His research interests include water quality policy, conservation policy, and markets for environmental services.

James W. Richardson is Co-director of the Agricultural and Food Policy Center, Regents Professor in the Department of Agricultural Economics, and AgriLife Senior Faculty Fellow, at Texas A&M University. He developed the Simulation & Econo-metrics to Analyze Risk (Simetar©) add-in for Microsoft® Excel to facilitate risk analysis and probabilistic forecasting.

Don Roach II, as a graduate student, Department of Forest Resources, Clemson University, assisted Dr. Allan Marsinko on a survey of forest industry hunt lease programs in the South.

Robert A. Robertson is Assistant Professor and Coordinator, Tourism Program, Department of Resource Economics and Development, University of New Hampshire. He conducts research on tourism and the human dimensions of recreation resource management issues.

Ardath Harter Rodale is Chief Inspiration Officer of Rodale Inc., Co-Chairman of the Board of the Rodale Institute. She is the author of four books: *Climbing Toward the Light* (1989); *Gifts of the Spirit* (1997); *Reflections: Finding Love, Hope, and Joy in Everyday Life* (2002); and *Everyday Miracles: Meditations on Living an Extraordinary Life* (2007).

George B. Rogers served at the University of New Hampshire and wrote extensively on production, marketing, and processing in the poultry industry.

Debra J. Romberger is Professor of Internal Medicine and College of Public Health, Vice Chair of Research, Department of Internal Medicine at University of Nebraska Medical Center and Associate Chief of Staff, Research at the Omaha VAMC. Her research interests include agriculture occupational exposures and lung disease and smoking cessation in substance use disorder treatment.

Paul C. Rosenblatt is Professor, Department of Family Social Science, University of Minnesota, St. Paul. His research focus is rural families and how families and marriages react to tension and stress, bereavement, and economic crisis. He is co-author of *Rural Health Care* (with I.S. Moscovice, 1982).

Carol Meeks Roskey is Professor Emerita and former Dean of the College of Family and Consumer Sciences at Iowa State University, Ames, Iowa. Dr. Meeks is retired and lives in Green Valley, Arizona where she is a member of the Sherriff's Auxiliary Volunteers and is creating stained glass.

Daniel Rothenberg is Managing Director of International Projects, DePaul University's International Human Rights Law Institute, Chicago. He studies transitional justice issues, truth commissions, amnesty laws, and tribunals and reparations. He is the author of *With These Hands: The Hidden World of Migrant Farmworkers Today* (1998) and editor of the forthcoming *Guatemala: Memory of Silence*.

G. Jon Roush is a consultant to environmental organizations, government agencies, and businesses. He served as President of the Wilderness Society, Washington, DC, and executive vice president and chairman of the board of governors of the Nature Conservancy.

David C. Ruesink is Professor Emeritus and Extension Rural Sociologist, Department of Rural Sociology, Texas A&M University, and project director, Rural Social Science Education. He assists rural communities and churches with community development programs and helps denominations and seminaries with rural ministry education programs.

Julie A. Rursch is a doctoral student in computer engineering at Iowa State University. She previously held information technology positions in private industry, and holds a doctorate in Mass Communications from the University of Wisconsin-Madison.

Cathy A. Rusinko is Assistant Professor of Management, School of Business Administration, Philadelphia University, and has worked in the U.S. Department of Agriculture. Her research interests include technology transfer in agriculture and manufacturing.

Sandra Rutland is a former graduate research assistant, Mississippi Crime and Justice Research Unit, Social Science Research Center, Mississippi State University, and now works with the Mississippi State Probation and Parole. Her interests include conjugal visitations in state prisons, race relations, and juvenile delinquency.

Rogelio Saenz is Professor, Department of Rural Sociology, Texas A&M University. He studies demography and racial, race and ethnic relations, Latina/Latino sociology, and social inequality. His projects included analyses of Mexican American entrepreneurship and interregional migration patterns and Latino demographic and socioeconomic trends.

Sonya Salamon is Research Professor, School of Economic, Political and Policy Sciences, University of Texas at Dallas, and since 2006, Professor of Community Studies Emeritus, University of Illinois at Urbana-Champaign. Her research studies focus on how culture shapes family farming and rural and small town community change. She is the author of two books: *Prairie Patrimony: Family, Farming and Community in the Midwest* and *Newcomers to Old Towns; Suburbanization of the Heartland.*

Divya Saxena is Extension Associate in the Department of Child Development and Family Sciences and the North Dakota Extension Service, North Dakota State University.

Peter V. Schaeffer is Professor, Economic Policy in the Resource Management program, West Virginia University, Morgantown. Dr. Schaeffer's research interests pertain to regional economics and development, labor markets, human capital, geographic and occupational mobility, and demographic change. He is currently the President of Southern Regional Science Association.

Harwood Schaffer is Research Associate with the Agricultural Policy Analysis Center at the University of Tennessee. His doctorate research is in sociology at the University of Tennessee with an emphasis in agricultural and economic policy. Schaffer began his work in agricultural policy as a rural parish pastor in the 1970s.

Kai A. Schafft is Assistant Professor in the Department of Education Policy Studies at Pennsylvania State University where he

directs the Center on Rural Education and Communities and serves as editor for the *Journal of Research in Rural Education.*

Neill Schaller was Associate Director, Henry A. Wallace Institute for Alternative Agriculture, Greenbelt, MD. He holds degrees in agricultural economics and sociology and has worked in the U.S. Department of Agriculture. The Henry A. Wallace Institute is a national, nonprofit organization dedicated to increasing the understanding and adoption of sustainable agriculture.

Clifford W. Scherer is Associate Professor, Social and Behavioral Research Unit, Department of Communication, Cornell University, Ithaca, New York. His research concentrates on strategies for effective communication of complex science, and how lay audiences make decisions about science-based problems.

Shaunna L. Scott is Associate Professor of Sociology at the University of Kentucky, and President, Appalachian Studies Association. Her research interests include social stratification, social movements, environmental sociology, politics, and the scholarship of teaching and learning.

Joan P. Sebastian is Professor, Department of Special Education, National University, LaJolla, California. She is involved with special educator preparation throughout the state of California. Her research interests include a focus on preparing highly qualified rural special educators through the use of online technologies.

Jim Seroka is Professor of Political Science and Public Administration, Auburn University. His research interests include state and local political, administration, and public policy analysis.

Robert C. Serow is Professor, Department of Educational Leadership and Program Evaluation, North Carolina State University. His research focuses on the integration of community service programs in American colleges and universities. He is a member of the North Carolina Commission on National and Community Service.

Todd Shallat directs the Center for Idaho History and Politics at Boise State University. His environmental writings include *Structures in the Stream: Army, Science, and the Rise of the U.S. Army Corps of Engineers* (1994), *Snake: The Plain and its People* (1994), and *Secrets of the Magic Valley* (2002).

George William (Jerry) Sherk is Adjunct Professor, University of Denver College of Law, and Associate Research Professor in the Division of Environmental Science and Engineering, Colorado School of Mines, and a practicing attorney. His research focuses on interstate water conflicts, and the location of future energy production facilities in the western United States.

William C. Sherman was Associate Professor, Department of Sociology/Anthropology, North Dakota State University, and served as parish priest at St. Michael's Catholic Church, Grand Forks, ND. He wrote *African-American in North Dakota* and is studying Arab-Americans in North Dakota and Eastern European folk housing on the Northern Plains.

Larry Hajime Shinagawa is Associate Professor and Director of Asian American Studies, University of Maryland, College Park. Dr. Shinagawa studies the social demography of racial groups, intermarriage, multiracial identity, and Asian American culture and community. He is the author of *Atlas of American Diversity* (1997).

R. Luke Shouse is a medical officer at the Centers for Disease Control and Prevention, Atlanta, Georgia. Dr. Shouse focuses his research on the epidemiology of HIV in the United States with special emphasis on the HIV epidemic in the south.

Jim P. Shroyer is Professor of Agronomy and Extension Crops Specialist, Kansas State University. He conducts applied, on-farm research trials and demonstrations with farmer assistance, and works primarily with wheat production and cropping systems.

Carol L. Simmons was an Environmental Protection Agency fellow and graduate student in the Department of Entomology, Iowa State University.

Rhonda Skaggs is Professor, Department of Agricultural Economics and Agricultural Business, New Mexico State University, Las Cruces. Dr. Skaggs's research interests include food and agricultural policy, structure, and ethics. She is involved in projects pertaining to attitudes toward agriculture, government, and the environment in New Mexico, and the chile pepper industry in the Southwest.

Richard W. Slatta is Professor, Department of History, North Carolina State University, Raleigh. He is the author of *Cowboys of the Americas* (1990) and *The Cowboy Encyclopedia* (1994) and is a staff writer for *Cowboys & Indians* magazine.

Duane A. Smith is Professor of History, Fort Lewis College, Durango, CO. He is writing a fourth-grade text on Colorado history and researching the Colorado mining man and politician, Henry Teller. He conducted a comparative study of a mining camp and farming town in the 1890s. He is the author of *Mining America: The Industry and the Environment, 1800-1980* (1993).

Nathan B. Smith is Assistant Professor and Extension Economist in the Department of Agricultural and Applied Economics, University of Georgia, Tifton. His concentration is production marketing and policy for peanuts, agricultural marketing and consumer demand agribusiness, production economics, and risk management.

C. Matthew Snipp is Professor of Sociology, Stanford University. His research interests include stratification and mobility, demography, and race, ethnic, and minority relations. He is the author of *American Indians: The First of This Land* (1989).

Jane Sooby is the organic research specialist with the Organic Farming Research Foundation, which funds organic agricultural research to, 1. help organic farmers make production decisions based on science and, 2. assist other farmers make the transition to organic farming.

Michael T. Southern is Senior Architectural Historian and GIS Coordinator for the State Historic Preservation Office, North Carolina Department of Cultural Resources. He participated in field studies of historic buildings in all 100 of North Carolina's counties. He is co-author of three field guides to the historic architecture of Eastern, Piedmont, and Western North Carolina published between 1997 and 2003.

Jerome M. Stam is a finance team leader, Rural Economy Division, Economic Research Service, U.S. Department of Agriculture. He studies regional economics, economic development, public finance, and agricultural finance issues. He has served as secretary, National Agricultural Credit Committee since 1984. He is a coauthor of *Farm Financial Stress, Farm Exits, and Public Sector Assistance to the Farm Sector in the 1980s* (1991).

B. Hudnall Stamm is Director of the Idaho State University Institute of Rural Health. She was recognized by the International Society for Traumatic Stress Studies for making fundamental contributions to the international public understanding of trauma.

Bernard F. Stanton is a Professor Emeritus of Agricultural Economics, Cornell University. He is a former department chairman (1968-76), and former president and fellow of the American Agricultural Economics Association. His work has been in production economics, farm management, and structural change in agriculture. He is the author of *George F. Warren, Farm Economist* (2007.).

Richard C. Stedman is Assistant Professor, Department of Natural Resources at Cornell University. His research and teaching focuses on the relationship between social and environmental change, community well-being, and sense of place.

Philip H. Steele is Professor, Department of Forest Products, College of Forest Resources, Mississippi State University. His research areas are production economics of lumber manufacturing operations, detection of wood characteristics with radio frequency signals and development of bio-fuels from woody biomass.

Frederick W. Steiner is Professor and Director, School of Panning and Landscape Architecture, Arizona State University. He helps the U.S. Department of Agriculture refine agricultural land evaluation and site assessment systems, assists Arizona in riparian area protection efforts, and works with rural communities on environmental protection, land-use planning, and the growth management projects.

Joyce D. Stern worked for the National Education Association, the Appalachia Regional Education Laboratory, and the U.S. Department of Education. She served as guest editor of the National Rural Education Association's journal, *The Rural Educator*, and authored *The Condition of Education in Rural Schools* (1994).

Bradley G. Stevens is Research Manager, Energy and Environmental Research Center (EERC), University of North Dakota, and Wind Energy Program Manager in EERC's Center for Renewable Energy and Biomass Utilization. His areas of expertise include soil, groundwater, and industrial process water remediation; process instrumentation and control; wind power generation, and hydrogen production.

Thomas F. Stinson is a Professor, Department of Applied Economics at the University of Minnesota. He also serves as the Minnesota State Economist where he supervises preparation of the state revenue forecast. His current research interests include the impact of baby boom retirements on state and local revenues.

Patricia A. Stokowski is Associate Professor and Assistant Dean, University of Vermont. She conducts research on the social, cultural, and institutional effects of rural community tourism development. Her publications include *Riches and Regrets: Betting on Gambling in Two Colorado Mountain Towns* (1996).

Janis Stone was Extension Professor, Department of Textiles and Clothing, Iowa State University. Her work involved development of personal protective clothing for farmers and greenhouse workers to prevent pesticide exposure.

Kenneth E. Stone is Professor Emeritus of Economics at Iowa State University. He formally retired from the University in 2004 after serving on the faculty for 28 years. He continues to study trade areas and other aspects of retail trade and continues to act as a consultant.

William W. Stoops is Assistant Professor, Department of Behavioral Science, University of Kentucky College of Medicine. His primary interest lies in understanding the behavioral pharmacology of stimulants and opioids in humans.

Tim Stratton is Associate Professor of Pharmacy Practice, University of Minnesota College of Pharmacy, Duluth. Dr. Stratton is a member of the Board of Directors of the Minnesota Rural Health Association, chairs the Section Advisory Group on Small and Rural Hospitals for the American Society of Health-System Pharmacists, and serves on the Faculty Leadership Council of the University of Minnesota AHEC.

Trista A. Strauch is the Coordinator of the Captive Wild Animal Management minor at the University of Missouri. Her research focuses on improving overall animal management for domestic and wild species, with a specific interest in the effects of nutrition on reproduction.

Louis E. Swanson is Vice Provost for Outreach and Strategic Partnerships, Colorado State University. His research emphasizes agricultural environmental and rural development policy. He served as the editor of *Agriculture and Community Change in the U.S.: The Congressional Research Reports* (1988).

Anne L. Sweaney is Professor and Head, Department of Housing and Consumer Economics, University of Georgia. She also serves as the Director of the Housing and Demographics Research Center. Her research interests include the effect of public policy on housing for families and consumers, housing needs of older adults, and the role of technology in adapting housing for the life span.

John M. Sweeten is Resident Director and Professor, Texas AgriLife Research and Extension Center, Amarillo. He conducts research on cattle feedlots and on their waste management practices for water and air pollution control. His publications include *Cattle Feedlot Waste Management Practices for Water and Air Pollution Control* (1990).

Franklyn L. Tate works for the Department of Corrections, Jackson, MS. He was previously employed at the Department of Public Administration, Mississippi State University.

Courtney E. Taylor is a graduate student in Natural Resources Management at North Dakota State University. Her research interests are ecotourism, environmental sustainability, and emergency management.

Dawn Thilmany is Professor and Extension Economist, Colorado State University. She specializes in alternative food systems and marketing and economic development through entrepreneurial agriculture. Dr. Thilmany served as the Organic Program Leader for USDA-CSREES from 2006-07 and is a current Farm Foundation Fellow for Rural Community Vitality.

Leann Tigges is Professor and Chair, Department of Rural Sociology, University of Wisconsin, Madison. Dr. Tigges studies labor market inequality, employment issues related to gender, and family and work. She served as editor of the *American Behavioral Scientist* special edition "Community Cohesion and Place Attachment" (October 2006).

Ernest W. Tollner is Professor, Department of Biological and Agricultural Engineering, University of Georgia. His research interests include: use of X-ray scanning to quantify soils, biological materials, and water; ecological process engineering; and watershed assessment.

William (Bill) G. Tomek is Professor Emeritus, Department of Applied Economics and Management, Cornell University. He is a past president and fellow of the American Agricultural Economics Association.

Frederick R. Troeh is Professor Emeritus, Iowa State University. Since retiring in 1995, he has remained involved in writing projects, including *Soils and Soil Fertility, Soil and Water Conservation for Productivity and Environmental Protection,* and *Dictionary of Agricultural and Environmental Science.*

Ronnie B. Tucker is Associate Professor of Political Science at Shippensburg University, Shippensburg PA. His research interests include Affirmative Action, African American politics, public policies relating to elderly abuse and neglect, and ethics in public administration.

Pamela Ulrich is Professor in the College of Human Sciences at Auburn University with a teaching and research focus on the historical development of the textile, apparel and retail industries and apparel product development.

Gary L. Vacin is Professor, Department of Agricultural Leadership, Education, and Communication, University of Nebraska, Lincoln. He develops computer solutions to rural issues.

Jerry J. Vaske is Professor, Department of Natural Resource Recreation and Tourism, Colorado State University. Dr. Vaske applies social psychological theories and methods to address conflicts. His studies have included hunters' responses to Chronic Wasting Disease, recreationists' attitudes toward endangered or threatened species, and urban residents' beliefs about human-wildlife conflicts.

Bernard Vavrek is Professor of Library Science and Director, Center for the Study of Rural Librarianship, Clarion University of Pennsylvania. He is regularly involved in organizing national conferences on bookmobile services and conducting opinion surveys of public library users attempting to determine the impact the library has on their lives. He is the author of *Assessing Information Needs of Rural Americans* (1990).

Marlow Vesterby was an agricultural economist in the Natural Resource Conservation and Management Branch, Economic Research Service, U.S. Department of Agriculture. His research involved urbanization, farmland preservation, land-use change issues, land condition, national capital expenditures, depreciation, and imports and exports of farm machinery. He coauthored *Urbanization of Rural Land in the United States* (1994).

Frank Vignola is Director of the University of Oregon Solar Energy Center and has worked in the solar energy field since 1977. Dr. Vignola is a Fellow of the American Solar Energy Society and an associate editor for solar resource of the *Solar Energy Journal*. He operates a 30-station solar monitoring network in the Pacific Northwest that monitors both the solar resource and performance of photovoltaic systems.

Morton O. Wagenfeld is Professor of Sociology and Community Health Services, Western Michigan University. His studies pertain to rural mental health services and policy and drug and alcohol epidemiology. He is a coauthor of *Mental Health in Rural America: 1980-1993* (1993).

Eric J. Wailes is the L.C. Carter Professor of Rice and Soybean Marketing, Department of Agricultural Economics and Agribusiness, University of Arkansas, Fayetteville. His research interests include U.S. and international agricultural trade policy, global rice economy, adoption and acceptability of biotechnology, and environmental and sustainability policy.

Gilson A.C. Waldkoenig is Associate Professor of Church in Society, B.B. Maurer Chair for Town and Country Church Ministry, and Director of the Town and Country Church Institute, Lutheran Theological Seminary at Gettysburg. Dr. Waldkoenig co-authored *Cooperating Congregations: Profiles in Mission Strategies* (with William O. Avery, 2000).

Katey Walker was Professor and Extension Specialist, School of Family Studies and Human Services, Kansas State University. She worked in leadership development for beginning and emerging leaders interested in community action and public policy. She has served as president, Association of Leadership Educators.

Rodney B. Warnick is Associate Professor of Recreation Resources Management, Department of Hotel, Restaurant and Travel Administration, University of Massachusetts at Amherst. He conducts research on recreation and tourism trends and consumer behavior and marketing issues in recreation resource management.

Bruce Weber is Professor of Agricultural and Resource Economics, and Extension Economist, Oregon State University. His research focuses on the impacts of changes in federal and state fiscal and regulatory policy on rural and urban economies and income distribution. He is a member of the National Rural Studies Committee and the Oregon Rural Development Council.

Christina D. Weber is Assistant Professor, Department of Sociology, Anthropology, and Emergency Management, North Dakota State University. Her focus is on qualitative studies that emphasize the sociology of memory and trauma in relation to war and gender relations. Her research focuses on the experiences of women soldiers and veterans, examining how their war and post-war experiences compare with men's experiences.

Ralph Weisheit is Distinguished Professor of Criminal Justice, Illinois State University. He has written extensively about rural crime, and drugs and crime. He is currently conducting research on methamphetamine, with a particular emphasis on its impact on rural areas

Lee Shai Weissbach is Professor of History, University of Louisville, and served as Department Chair and Associate Dean in the College of Arts and Sciences. Among Dr. Weissbach's publications are *The Synagogues of Kentucky: Architecture and History* (1995), *Jewish Life in Small-Town America: A History* (2005), and articles in journals such as *Jewish History*, the *Journal of Social History*, *Shofar*, *American Jewish History*, and *The American Jewish Archives Journal*.

Glen Whipple is Professor of Agricultural and Applied Economics, University of Wyoming, and Associate Dean and Director, University of Wyoming Cooperative Extension Service. His research interests focus on markets, rural economy, and policy.

Gregory K. White is Professor, School of Economics, University of Maine. He is a past Director of the Maine Water Research Institute. His research focuses on marketing issues facing small and mid-sized farms.

Katherine Whiting serves as an Assistant County Agent with the Georgia Cooperative Extension Service.

Frederick Williams is Professor, Center for Research on Communication Technology and Society, University of Texas at Austin. His research examines the information highway and the relationship between telecommunications and rural development.

David W. Willis is Distinguished Professor and Department Head for the Department of Wildlife and Fisheries Sciences at

South Dakota State University. His primary research interests include fish ecology and sport fisheries management.

Ronald C. Wimberley is William Neal Reynolds Distinguished Professor of Sociology, North Carolina State University. His research interests are in the Black Belt South, rural development and quality of life, spatial sociology, the globalization of food, and civil religiosity and voting behavior. He is a past president of both the Rural Sociological Society and the Southern Sociological Society.

Robert N. Wisner is Professor, Department of Agricultural Economics, Iowa State University, Ames. He conducts research on grain, corn, and soybean futures and option marketing strategies.

Francis W. Wolek is Professor of Management, College of Commerce and Finance, Villanova University. He served as deputy assistant secretary for science and technology, U.S. Department of Commerce. His research pertains to management of technological innovation.

Sam Wortman is a graduate student at the University of Nebraska-Lincoln working toward a M.S. degree in Agronomy. His research interests include soil fertility and weed management in long-term crop rotations.

Mike D. Woods is Professor, Department of Agricultural Economics, Oklahoma State University. He evaluates local economic development efforts, such as small business incubators and downtown revitalization efforts, and he provides technical assistance and training to local communities to aid in strategic planning efforts.

Susan K. Woodward is Research Associate, Center for Research and Evaluation, College of Education, University of Maine, Orono. She researches and analyzes policy materials for local educational leaders and is the manuscript editor for the *Journal for Research in Rural Education.*

D. Wynne Wright is Assistant Professor of Community, Food, and Agriculture at Michigan State University and adjunct faculty in the Department of Sociology. Her research interests focus on the contested nature of agrofood restructuring in global and local contexts. She is editor of *The Fight Over Food: Producers, Consumers, and Activists Challenge the Global Food System* (with G. Middendorf, 2007).

John B. Wright is Associate Professor, Department of Geography, New Mexico State University. His focus is on land conservation issues, land trusts, and the changing cultural landscapes of the Rocky Mountain West. He is the author of *Registered Places of Montana: Big Sky Country and Rocky Mountain Divide: Selling and Saving the West* (1993).

R. Dean Wright is Ellis and Nelle Levitt Professor Emeritus of Sociology at Drake University, Des Moines, Iowa. In conjunction with Susan Wright, he studies issues of homelessness related to death and dying. He co-authored, with William Du Bois, *Politics in the Human Interest: Applying Sociology in the Real World* (2007) and *Applying Sociology: Making a Better World* (2001).

Susan E. Wright is Professor of Sociology and Associate Provost at Drake University. She continues to work with R. Dean Wright on issues of homelessness related to death and dying. Most recently, her research focused on issues related to higher education.

Laura C. Yancer is President of L&T Associates, a public policy consulting firm. She also works with the National Academy of Public Administration and the Advisory Council on Intergovernmental Relations to evaluate infrastructure benchmarking practices by state and local governments across the United States.

D.K. (Dong Keun) Yoon is Assistant Professor in the Department of Sociology, Anthropology, and Emergency Management at North Dakota State University. His research interests encompass planning and policy for natural hazards, risk and vulnerability analysis, community-based disaster management, and Geographic Information Systems.

George A. Youngs, Jr. is Professor of Sociology and Emergency Management in the Department of Sociology, Anthropology, and Emergency Management at North Dakota State University, Fargo, ND. He studies rural emergency management issues and the sociology of disaster from a social psychological perspective.

William Zawacki is a graduate student, Department of Forest Resources, Clemson University. He works with Dr. Allan Marsinko on valuation of non-consumptive wildlife recreation based on a travel cost model.

Julie N. Zimmerman is Associate Extension Professor, Department of Community and Leadership Development, University of Kentucky. Her research interests include rural development, inequality, and rural poverty. She served as a member of the Rural Policy Research Institute Rural Welfare Reform Initiative, the National Rural Development Partnership's Welfare Reform Task Force, and the Kentucky Welfare Reform Assessment Project.

Ervin H. Zube is Professor, Department of Renewable Natural Resources and Department of Geography and Regional Development, University of Arizona, Tucson. He has written on environmental design, quality, assessment, evaluation, and policy and changing rural landscapes.

INDEX

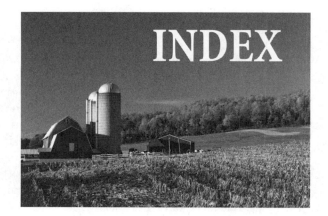

S

So Big (Ferber), 581
Social capital, 151–152, 158–159
Social capital theory, 138
Social change, 156–157 4
Social Class, **893–897**
 agricultural, 895
Social costs, 19, 332
Social impact assessment (SIA), 501
Social infrastructure, 152–153
Social Movements, **898–902**
 for agricultural sustainability, 937–941
 globalization and biotechnology, 902
 role of, 937
 rural, 900–901
 types of, 898
Social order, 134, 162, 214, 539
Social relationships
 and social class, 893, 894
Social Security Act (1935), 904, 1082, 1084
Social Security income, 1082
Social services, 882
 faith-based, **903–906**
 social workers and, 907, 908
Social sustainability, 349 (table)
Social Work, **907–910**
 NASW policy statement, 907
Society of American Foresters, 406
Society of equity, 899
Socioeconomic inequality, 508
Socioeconomic policy, 759–762
Sociologists, 160, 726, 761, 918
Sociology for the South; or, the Failure of Free Society (Fitzhugh), 580
Sod houses, 472
Sodium, 378
Soft Red Winter (SRW) wheat, 1088
Softwoods, 403, 873, 874, 876, 877
Soil, **910–913**
 acid, 703
 analysis of, 703
 bacteria, 119
 biological properties, 913
 chemical properties, 912–913
 chemistry, 550
 classification, 911
 color and temperature, 912
 compaction, 912
 conservation, 183–190, 913
 drainage, 912
 in dryland farming, 283
 erosion, 56, 76, 150, 183–189, 225, 664–665. *See also* Erosion control
 fertility, 63, 703
 formation, 805

 management, 673
 moisture, 1031
 nutrients, 703
 organic matter contents, 913
 permeability criteria, 377, 912
 prairie, 78
 profile, 910–911
 salinity, 913
 stirring, 283
 structure, 912
 taxonomy, 911, 914 (table)
 temperature, 912, 985
 testing, 182
 texture, 912
 tillage, 912
 types, 911
 water management, 193–194
The Soil and Health (book), 63
Soil and Water District Boards, 753
Soil Bank Program, 184
Soil Conservation Act (1933), 184, 341
Soil Conservation and Domestic Allotment Act (1936), 441
Soil Conservation Districts, 151
Soil Conservation Service (SCS), 184, 281, 341, 342, 346, 376, 441, 471, 738
Soil Erosion Service (1933), 281
Soilless agriculture. *See* Hydroponic agriculture
Soil Science Journal, 80
Soil Science Society of America (SSSA), 80
Soil Taxonomy, 911, 914 (table)
Solar electricity, 916
Solar Energy, **914–917**
Solar thermal collectors, 915
Solid Waste Association of North America, 655
Solid wastes, 653
 disposal, 761
 dumps, 647, 958
 See also Municipal Solid Waste Management (MSWM)
Somatotropins, 120
Songbirds, 115
Songs, 658, 660
A Son of the Middle Border (Garland), 581
Sonoran Desert, 114, 262
Sons of Norway, 358
Sorenson, Ray, 380
Sorghum, 449 (photo)
 hybrid, 447, 450
 production, 208
 yields, 450
Sorokin, Pitirim, 833
South Africa, 432

South America, 59, 91, 567, 693
South Carolina, 465, 473, 844
 cotton, 78
 farmland value, 547
 land, 886
 Latino agriculture in, 568
 plantation, 725
 rice production, 823
 tobacco production in, 992
Southcentral Alaska, 717
South Dakota, 427, 744
 corn, 210
 cowboys, 216
 electrification, 313
 gambling, 425
 gross cash rent for cropland in, 547–548
 Jewish agricultural colonies in, 529
 rural pharmacy, 854
 volunteer fire departments, 387
Southeast Asia, 693
Southeastern Theater Conference, Inc., 979
Southern Agrarians, 470
Southern Christian Leadership Conference, 10
Southern Corn Leaf Blight (SCLB), 212, 719, 720
Southern Pacific Railroad, 263
Southern Rural Development Center, 655
Southern Tenant Farmers' Union (STFU), 31, 540, 900
Southern University, 556
Southern University and A&M College, 555 (table)
South Korea, 823
South/southeast
 Appalachian and strip mining, 957
 apparel production in, 975
 drought, 279
 farmers, 527
 farm value, 547 (table)
 household income, 896
 manufacturing, 598
 plantations, 722–725
 plantations and settlements, 886
 sharecropping, 900
 underemployment in, 1037
Southwest
 desert, 261
 farmland, loss of, 508
 farm operators, 864
 farm workers' movements, 901
 folklore, 659
 population decline in, 838

Business Information ◆ **Ratings Guides** ◆ **General Reference** ◆ **Education** ◆ **Statistics** ◆ **Demographics** ◆ **Health Information** ◆ **Canadian Information**

The Directory of Business Information Resources, 2008

With 100% verification, over 1,000 new listings and more than 12,000 updates, *The Directory of Business Information Resources* is the most up-to-date source for contacts in over 98 business areas – from advertising and agriculture to utilities and wholesalers. This carefully researched volume details: the Associations representing each industry; the Newsletters that keep members current; the Magazines and Journals - with their "Special Issues" - that are important to the trade, the Conventions that are "must attends," Databases, Directories and Industry Web Sites that provide access to must-have marketing resources. Includes contact names, phone & fax numbers, web sites and e-mail addresses. This one-volume resource is a gold mine of information and would be a welcome addition to any reference collection.

"This is a most useful and easy-to-use addition to any researcher's library." –The Information Professionals Institute

Softcover ISBN 978-1-59237-193-8, 2,500 pages, $195.00 | Online Database $495.00

Hudson's Washington News Media Contacts Directory, 2008

With 100% verification of data, Hudson's Washington News Media Contacts Directory is the most accurate, most up-to-date source for media contacts in our nation's capital. With the largest concentration of news media in the world, having access to Washington's news media will get your message heard by these key media outlets. Published for over 40 years, Hudson's Washington News Media Contacts Directory brings you immediate access to: News Services & Newspapers, News Service Syndicates, DC Newspapers, Foreign Newspapers, Radio & TV, Magazines & Newsletters, and Freelance Writers & Photographers. The easy-to-read entries include contact names, phone & fax numbers, web sites and e-mail and more. For easy navigation, Hudson's Washington News Media Contacts Directory contains two indexes: Entry Index and Executive Index. This kind of comprehensive and up-to-date information would cost thousands of dollars to replicate or countless hours of searching to find. Don't miss this opportunity to have this important resource in your collection, and start saving time and money today. Hudson's Washington News Media Contacts Directory is the perfect research tool for Public Relations, Marketing, Networking and so much more. This resource is a gold mine of information and would be a welcome addition to any reference collection.

Softcover ISBN 978-1-59237-393-2, 800 pages, $289.00

Nations of the World, 2009 A Political, Economic and Business Handbook

This completely revised edition covers all the nations of the world in an easy-to-use, single volume. Each nation is profiled in a single chapter that includes Key Facts, Political & Economic Issues, a Country Profile and Business Information. In this fast-changing world, it is extremely important to make sure that the most up-to-date information is included in your reference collection. This edition is just the answer. Each of the 200+ country chapters have been carefully reviewed by a political expert to make sure that the text reflects the most current information on Politics, Travel Advisories, Economics and more. You'll find such vital information as a Country Map, Population Characteristics, Inflation, Agricultural Production, Foreign Debt, Political History, Foreign Policy, Regional Insecurity, Economics, Trade & Tourism, Historical Profile, Political Systems, Ethnicity, Languages, Media, Climate, Hotels, Chambers of Commerce, Banking, Travel Information and more. Five Regional Chapters follow the main text and include a Regional Map, an Introductory Article, Key Indicators and Currencies for the Region. As an added bonus, an all-inclusive CD-ROM is available as a companion to the printed text. Noted for its sophisticated, up-to-date and reliable compilation of political, economic and business information, this brand new edition will be an important acquisition to any public, academic or special library reference collection.

"A useful addition to both general reference collections and business collections." –RUSQ

Softcover ISBN 978-1-59237-273-7, 1,700 pages, $155.00

The Directory of Venture Capital & Private Equity Firms, 2008

This edition has been extensively updated and broadly expanded to offer direct access to over 2,800 Domestic and International Venture Capital Firms, including address, phone & fax numbers, e-mail addresses and web sites for both primary and branch locations. Entries include details on the firm's Mission Statement, Industry Group Preferences, Geographic Preferences, Average and Minimum Investments and Investment Criteria. You'll also find details that are available nowhere else, including the Firm's Portfolio Companies and extensive information on each of the firm's Managing Partners, such as Education, Professional Background and Directorships held, along with the Partner's E-mail Address. *The Directory of Venture Capital & Private Equity Firms* offers five important indexes: Geographic Index, Executive Name Index, Portfolio Company Index, Industry Preference Index and College & University Index. With its comprehensive coverage and detailed, extensive information on each company, The Directory of Venture Capital & Private Equity Firms is an important addition to any finance collection.

"The sheer number of listings, the descriptive information and the outstanding indexing make this directory a better value than ...Pratt's Guide to Venture Capital Sources. Recommended for business collections in large public, academic and business libraries." –Choice

Softcover ISBN 978-1-59237-272-0, 1,300 pages, $565/$450 Library | Online Database $889.00

Business Information ♦ Ratings Guides ♦ General Reference ♦ Education ♦
Statistics ♦ Demographics ♦ Health Information ♦ Canadian Information

Grey House
Publishing

The Encyclopedia of Emerging Industries

*Published under an exclusive license from the Gale Group, Inc.

The fifth edition of the *Encyclopedia of Emerging Industries* details the inception, emergence, and current status of nearly 120 flourishing U.S. industries and industry segments. These focused essays unearth for users a wealth of relevant, current, factual data previously accessible only through a diverse variety of sources. This volume provides broad-based, highly-readable, industry information under such headings as Industry Snapshot, Organization & Structure, Background & Development, Industry Leaders, Current Conditions, America and the World, Pioneers, and Research & Technology. Essays in this new edition, arranged alphabetically for easy use, have been completely revised, with updated statistics and the most current information on industry trends and developments. In addition, there are new essays on some of the most interesting and influential new business fields, including Application Service Providers, Concierge Services, Entrepreneurial Training, Fuel Cells, Logistics Outsourcing Services, Pharmacogenomics, and Tissue Engineering. Two indexes, General and Industry, provide immediate access to this wealth of information. Plus, two conversion tables for SIC and NAICS codes, along with Suggested Further Readings, are provided to aid the user. *The Encyclopedia of Emerging Industries* pinpoints emerging industries while they are still in the spotlight. This important resource will be an important acquisition to any business reference collection.

"This well-designed source…should become another standard business source, nicely complementing Standard & Poor's Industry Surveys. It contains more information on each industry than Hoover's Handbook of Emerging Companies, is broader in scope than The Almanac of American Employers 1998-1999, but is less expensive than the Encyclopedia of Careers & Vocational Guidance. Highly recommended for all academic libraries and specialized business collections." –Library Journal

Hardcover ISBN 978-1-59237-242-3, 1,400 pages, $325.00

Encyclopedia of American Industries

*Published under an exclusive license from the Gale Group, Inc.

The Encyclopedia of American Industries is a major business reference tool that provides detailed, comprehensive information on a wide range of industries in every realm of American business. A two volume set, Volume I provides separate coverage of nearly 500 manufacturing industries, while Volume II presents nearly 600 essays covering the vast array of services and other non-manufacturing industries in the United States. Combined, these two volumes provide individual essays on every industry recognized by the U.S. Standard Industrial Classification (SIC) system. Both volumes are arranged numerically by SIC code, for easy use. Additionally, each entry includes the corresponding NAICS code(s). The *Encyclopedia's* business coverage includes information on historical events of consequence, as well as current trends and statistics. Essays include an Industry Snapshot, Organization & Structure, Background & Development, Current Conditions, Industry Leaders, Workforce, America and the World, Research & Technology along with Suggested Further Readings. Both SIC and NAICS code conversion tables and an all-encompassing Subject Index, with cross-references, complete the text. With its detailed, comprehensive information on a wide range of industries, this resource will be an important tool for both the industry newcomer and the seasoned professional.

"Encyclopedia of American Industries contains detailed, signed essays on virtually every industry in contemporary society. ... Highly recommended for all but the smallest libraries." -American Reference Books Annual

Two Volumes, Hardcover ISBN 978-1-59237-244-7, 3,000 pages, $650.00

Encyclopedia of Global Industries

*Published under an exclusive license from the Gale Group, Inc.

This fourth edition of the acclaimed *Encyclopedia of Global Industries* presents a thoroughly revised and expanded look at more than 125 business sectors of global significance. Detailed, insightful articles discuss the origins, development, trends, key statistics and current international character of the world's most lucrative, dynamic and widely researched industries – including hundreds of profiles of leading international corporations. Beginning researchers will gain from this book a solid understanding of how each industry operates and which countries and companies are significant participants, while experienced researchers will glean current and historical figures for comparison and analysis. The industries profiled in previous editions have been updated, and in some cases, expanded to reflect recent industry trends. Additionally, this edition provides both SIC and NAICS codes for all industries profiled As in the original volumes, *The Encyclopedia of Global Industries* offers thorough studies of some of the biggest and most frequently researched industry sectors, including Aircraft, Biotechnology, Computers, Internet Services, Motor Vehicles, Pharmaceuticals, Semiconductors, Software and Telecommunications. An SIC and NAICS conversion table and an all-encompassing Subject Index, with cross-references, are provided to ensure easy access to this wealth of information. These and many others make the *Encyclopedia of Global Industries* the authoritative reference for studies of international industries.

"Provides detailed coverage of the history, development, and current status of 115 of "the world's most lucrative and high-profile industries." It far surpasses the Department of Commerce's U.S. Global Trade Outlook 1995-2000 (GPO, 1995) in scope and coverage. Recommended for comprehensive public and academic library business collections." -Booklist

Hardcover ISBN 978-1-59237-243-0, 1,400 pages, $495.00

Business Information ♦ **Ratings Guides** ♦ **General Reference** ♦ **Education** ♦
Statistics ♦ **Demographics** ♦ **Health Information** ♦ **Canadian Information**

The Directory of Mail Order Catalogs, 2008

Published since 1981, *The Directory of Mail Order Catalogs* is the premier source of information on the mail order catalog industry. It is the source that business professionals and librarians have come to rely on for the thousands of catalog companies in the US. Since the 2007 edition, *The Directory of Mail Order Catalogs* has been combined with its companion volume, *The Directory of Business to Business Catalogs*, to offer all 13,000 catalog companies in one easy-to-use volume. Section I: Consumer Catalogs, covers over 9,000 consumer catalog companies in 44 different product chapters from Animals to Toys & Games. Section II: Business to Business Catalogs, details 5,000 business catalogs, everything from computers to laboratory supplies, building construction and much more. Listings contain detailed contact information including mailing address, phone & fax numbers, web sites, e-mail addresses and key contacts along with important business details such as product descriptions, employee size, years in business, sales volume, catalog size, number of catalogs mailed and more. Three indexes are included for easy access to information: Catalog & Company Name Index, Geographic Index and Product Index. *The Directory of Mail Order Catalogs*, now with its expanded business to business catalogs, is the largest and most comprehensive resource covering this billion-dollar industry. It is the standard in its field. This important resource is a useful tool for entrepreneurs searching for catalogs to pick up their product, vendors looking to expand their customer base in the catalog industry, market researchers, small businesses investigating new supply vendors, along with the library patron who is exploring the available catalogs in their areas of interest.

"This is a godsend for those looking for information." –Reference Book Review

Softcover ISBN 978-1-59237-202-7, 1,700 pages, $350/$250 Library | Online Database $495.00

Sports Market Place Directory, 2008

For over 20 years, this comprehensive, up-to-date directory has offered direct access to the Who, What, When & Where of the Sports Industry. With over 20,000 updates and enhancements, the *Sports Market Place Directory* is the most detailed, comprehensive and current sports business reference source available. In 1,800 information-packed pages, *Sports Market Place Directory* profiles contact information and key executives for: Single Sport Organizations, Professional Leagues, Multi-Sport Organizations, Disabled Sports, High School & Youth Sports, Military Sports, Olympic Organizations, Media, Sponsors, Sponsorship & Marketing Event Agencies, Event & Meeting Calendars, Professional Services, College Sports, Manufacturers & Retailers, Facilities and much more. The Sports Market Place Directory provides organization's contact information with detailed descriptions including: Key Contacts, physical, mailing, email and web addresses plus phone and fax numbers. *Sports Market Place Directory* provides a one-stop resources for this billion-dollar industry. This will be an important resource for large public libraries, university libraries, university athletic programs, career services or job placement organizations, and is a must for anyone doing research on or marketing to the US and Canadian sports industry.

"Grey House is the new publisher and has produced an excellent edition...highly recommended for public libraries and academic libraries with sports management programs or strong interest in athletics." -Booklist

Softcover ISBN 978-1-59237-348-2, 1,800 pages, $225.00 | Online Database $479.00

Food and Beverage Market Place, 2008

Food and Beverage Market Place is bigger and better than ever with thousands of new companies, thousands of updates to existing companies and two revised and enhanced product category indexes. This comprehensive directory profiles over 18,000 Food & Beverage Manufacturers, 12,000 Equipment & Supply Companies, 2,200 Transportation & Warehouse Companies, 2,000 Brokers & Wholesalers, 8,000 Importers & Exporters, 900 Industry Resources and hundreds of Mail Order Catalogs. Listings include detailed Contact Information, Sales Volumes, Key Contacts, Brand & Product Information, Packaging Details and much more. *Food and Beverage Market Place* is available as a three-volume printed set, a subscription-based Online Database via the Internet, on CD-ROM, as well as mailing lists and a licensable database.

"An essential purchase for those in the food industry but will also be useful in public libraries where needed. Much of the information will be difficult and time consuming to locate without this handy three-volume ready-reference source." –ARBA

3 Vol Set, Softcover ISBN 978-1-59237-198-3, 8,500 pages, $595 | Online Database $795 | Online Database & 3 Vol Set Combo, $995

The Grey House Performing Arts Directory, 2007

The Grey House Performing Arts Directory is the most comprehensive resource covering the Performing Arts. This important directory provides current information on over 8,500 Dance Companies, Instrumental Music Programs, Opera Companies, Choral Groups, Theater Companies, Performing Arts Series and Performing Arts Facilities. Plus, this edition now contains a brand new section on Artist Management Groups. In addition to mailing address, phone & fax numbers, e-mail addresses and web sites, dozens of other fields of available information include mission statement, key contacts, facilities, seating capacity, season, attendance and more. This directory also provides an important Information Resources section that covers hundreds of Performing Arts Associations, Magazines, Newsletters, Trade Shows, Directories, Databases and Industry Web Sites. Five indexes provide immediate access to this wealth of information: Entry Name, Executive Name, Performance Facilities, Geographic and Information Resources. *The Grey House Performing Arts Directory* pulls together thousands of Performing Arts Organizations, Facilities and Information Resources into an easy-to-use source – this kind of comprehensiveness and extensive detail is not available in any resource on the market place today.

"Immensely useful and user-friendly ... recommended for public, academic and certain special library reference collections." –Booklist

Business Information ♦ **Ratings Guides** ♦ **General Reference** ♦ **Education** ♦
Statistics ♦ **Demographics** ♦ **Health Information** ♦ **Canadian Information**

Softcover ISBN 978-1-59237-138-9, 1,500 pages, $185.00 | Online Database $335.00

New York State Directory, 2008/09

The New York State Directory, published annually since 1983, is a comprehensive and easy-to-use guide to accessing public officials and private sector organizations and individuals who influence public policy in the state of New York. *The New York State Directory* includes important information on all New York state legislators and congressional representatives, including biographies and key committee assignments. It also includes staff rosters for all branches of New York state government and for federal agencies and departments that impact the state policy process. Following the state government section are 25 chapters covering policy areas from agriculture through veterans' affairs. Each chapter identifies the state, local and federal agencies and officials that formulate or implement policy. In addition, each chapter contains a roster of private sector experts and advocates who influence the policy process. The directory also offers appendices that include statewide party officials; chambers of commerce; lobbying organizations; public and private universities and colleges; television, radio and print media; and local government agencies and officials.

> *"This comprehensive directory covers not only New York State government offices and key personnel but pertinent U.S. government agencies and non-governmental entities. This directory is all encompassing... recommended." -Choice*

New York State Directory - Softcover ISBN 978-1-59237-358-1, 800 pages, $145.00
New York State Directory with *Profiles of New York* – 2 Volumes, Softcover ISBN 978-1-59237-359-8, 1,600 pages, $225.00

The Grey House Homeland Security Directory, 2008

This updated edition features the latest contact information for government and private organizations involved with Homeland Security along with the latest product information and provides detailed profiles of nearly 1,000 Federal & State Organizations & Agencies and over 3,000 Officials and Key Executives involved with Homeland Security. These listings are incredibly detailed and include Mailing Address, Phone & Fax Numbers, Email Addresses & Web Sites, a complete Description of the Agency and a complete list of the Officials and Key Executives associated with the Agency. Next, *The Grey House Homeland Security Directory* provides the go-to source for Homeland Security Products & Services. This section features over 2,000 Companies that provide Consulting, Products or Services. With this Buyer's Guide at their fingertips, users can locate suppliers of everything from Training Materials to Access Controls, from Perimeter Security to BioTerrorism Countermeasures and everything in between – complete with contact information and product descriptions. A handy Product Locator Index is provided to quickly and easily locate suppliers of a particular product. This comprehensive, information-packed resource will be a welcome tool for any company or agency that is in need of Homeland Security information and will be a necessary acquisition for the reference collection of all public libraries and large school districts.

> *"Compiles this information in one place and is discerning in content. A useful purchase for public and academic libraries." –Booklist*

Softcover ISBN 978-1-59237-196-6, 800 pages, $195.00 | Online Database $385.00

The Grey House Safety & Security Directory, 2008

The Grey House Safety & Security Directory is the most comprehensive reference tool and buyer's guide for the safety and security industry. Arranged by safety topic, each chapter begins with OSHA regulations for the topic, followed by Training Articles written by top professionals in the field and Self-Inspection Checklists. Next, each topic contains Buyer's Guide sections that feature related products and services. Topics include Administration, Insurance, Loss Control & Consulting, Protective Equipment & Apparel, Noise & Vibration, Facilities Monitoring & Maintenance, Employee Health Maintenance & Ergonomics, Retail Food Services, Machine Guards, Process Guidelines & Tool Handling, Ordinary Materials Handling, Hazardous Materials Handling, Workplace Preparation & Maintenance, Electrical Lighting & Safety, Fire & Rescue and Security. Six important indexes make finding information and product manufacturers quick and easy: Geographical Index of Manufacturers and Distributors, Company Profile Index, Brand Name Index, Product Index, Index of Web Sites and Index of Advertisers. This comprehensive, up-to-date reference will provide every tool necessary to make sure a business is in compliance with OSHA regulations and locate the products and services needed to meet those regulations.

> *"Presents industrial safety information for engineers, plant managers, risk managers, and construction site supervisors..." –Choice*

Softcover ISBN 978-1-59237-205-8, 1,500 pages, $165.00

Business Information ✦ **Ratings Guides** ✦ **General Reference** ✦ **Education** ✦
Statistics ✦ **Demographics** ✦ **Health Information** ✦ **Canadian Information**

The Grey House Transportation Security Directory & Handbook

This is the only reference of its kind that brings together current data on Transportation Security. With information on everything from Regulatory Authorities to Security Equipment, this top-flight database brings together the relevant information necessary for creating and maintaining a security plan for a wide range of transportation facilities. With this current, comprehensive directory at the ready you'll have immediate access to: Regulatory Authorities & Legislation; Information Resources; Sample Security Plans & Checklists; Contact Data for Major Airports, Seaports, Railroads, Trucking Companies and Oil Pipelines; Security Service Providers; Recommended Equipment & Product Information and more. Using the *Grey House Transportation Security Directory & Handbook*, managers will be able to quickly and easily assess their current security plans; develop contacts to create and maintain new security procedures; and source the products and services necessary to adequately maintain a secure environment. This valuable resource is a must for all Security Managers at Airports, Seaports, Railroads, Trucking Companies and Oil Pipelines.

"Highly recommended. Library collections that support all levels of readers, including professionals/practitioners; and schools/organizations offering education and training in transportation security." -Choice

Softcover ISBN 978-1-59237-075-7, 800 pages, $195.00

The Grey House Biometric Information Directory

This edition offers a complete, current overview of biometric companies and products – one of the fastest growing industries in today's economy. Detailed profiles of manufacturers of the latest biometric technology, including Finger, Voice, Face, Hand, Signature, Iris, Vein and Palm Identification systems. Data on the companies include key executives, company size and a detailed, indexed description of their product line. Information in the directory includes: Editorial on Advancements in Biometrics; Profiles of 700+ companies listed with contact information; Organizations, Trade & Educational Associations, Publications, Conferences, Trade Shows and Expositions Worldwide; Web Site Index; Biometric & Vendors Services Index by Types of Biometrics; and a Glossary of Biometric Terms. This resource will be an important source for anyone who is considering the use of a biometric product, investing in the development of biometric technology, support existing marketing and sales efforts and will be an important acquisition for the business reference collection for large public and business libraries.

"This book should prove useful to agencies or businesses seeking companies that deal with biometric technology. Summing Up: Recommended. Specialized collections serving researchers/faculty and professionals/practitioners." -Choice

Softcover ISBN 978-1-59237-121-1, 800 pages, $225.00

The Environmental Resource Handbook, 2008/09

The Environmental Resource Handbook is the most up-to-date and comprehensive source for Environmental Resources and Statistics. Section I: Resources provides detailed contact information for thousands of information sources, including Associations & Organizations, Awards & Honors, Conferences, Foundations & Grants, Environmental Health, Government Agencies, National Parks & Wildlife Refuges, Publications, Research Centers, Educational Programs, Green Product Catalogs, Consultants and much more. Section II: Statistics, provides statistics and rankings on hundreds of important topics, including Children's Environmental Index, Municipal Finances, Toxic Chemicals, Recycling, Climate, Air & Water Quality and more. This kind of up-to-date environmental data, all in one place, is not available anywhere else on the market place today. This vast compilation of resources and statistics is a must-have for all public and academic libraries as well as any organization with a primary focus on the environment.

"…the intrinsic value of the information make it worth consideration by libraries with environmental collections and environmentally concerned users." –Booklist

Softcover ISBN 978-1-59237-195-2, 1,000 pages, $155.00 | Online Database $300.00

Business Information ♦ Ratings Guides ♦ General Reference ♦ Education ♦
Statistics ♦ Demographics ♦ Health Information ♦ Canadian Information

The Rauch Guide to the US Adhesives & Sealants, Cosmetics & Toiletries, Ink, Paint, Plastics, Pulp & Paper and Rubber Industries

The Rauch Guides save time and money by organizing widely scattered information and providing estimates for important business decisions, some of which are available nowhere else. Within each Guide, after a brief introduction, the ECONOMICS section provides data on industry shipments; long-term growth and forecasts; prices; company performance; employment, expenditures, and productivity; transportation and geographical patterns; packaging; foreign trade; and government regulations. Next, TECHNOLOGY & RAW MATERIALS provide market, technical, and raw material information for chemicals, equipment and related materials, including market size and leading suppliers, prices, end uses, and trends. PRODUCTS & MARKETS provide information for each major industry product, including market size and historical trends, leading suppliers, five-year forecasts, industry structure, and major end uses. Next, the COMPANY DIRECTORY profiles major industry companies, both public and private. Information includes complete contact information, web address, estimated total and domestic sales, product description, and recent mergers and acquisitions. *The Rauch Guides* will prove to be an invaluable source of market information, company data, trends and forecasts that anyone in these fast-paced industries.

> *"An invaluable and affordable publication. The comprehensive nature of the data and text offers considerable insights into the industry, market sizes, company activities, and applications of the products of the industry. The additions that have been made have certainly enhanced the value of the Guide." –Adhesives & Sealants Newsletter of the Rauch Guide to the US Adhesives & Sealants Industry*

Paint Industry: Softcover ISBN 978-1-59237-127-3 $595 | Plastics Industry: Softcover ISBN 978-1-59237-128-0 $595 | Adhesives and Sealants Industry: Softcover ISBN 978-1-59237-129-7 $595 | Ink Industry: Softcover ISBN 978-1-59237-126-6 $595 | Rubber Industry: Softcover ISBN 978-1-59237-130-3 $595 | Pulp and Paper Industry: Softcover ISBN 978-1-59237-131-0 $595 | Cosmetic & Toiletries Industry: Softcover ISBN 978-1-59237-132-7 $895

Research Services Directory: Commercial & Corporate Research Centers

This ninth edition provides access to well over 8,000 independent Commercial Research Firms, Corporate Research Centers and Laboratories offering contract services for hands-on, basic or applied research. Research Services Directory covers the thousands of types of research companies, including Biotechnology & Pharmaceutical Developers, Consumer Product Research, Defense Contractors, Electronics & Software Engineers, Think Tanks, Forensic Investigators, Independent Commercial Laboratories, Information Brokers, Market & Survey Research Companies, Medical Diagnostic Facilities, Product Research & Development Firms and more. Each entry provides the company's name, mailing address, phone & fax numbers, key contacts, web site, e-mail address, as well as a company description and research and technical fields served. Four indexes provide immediate access to this wealth of information: Research Firms Index, Geographic Index, Personnel Name Index and Subject Index.

> *"An important source for organizations in need of information about laboratories, individuals and other facilities." –ARBA*

Softcover ISBN 978-1-59237-003-0, 1,400 pages, $465.00

International Business and Trade Directories

Completely updated, the Third Edition of *International Business and Trade Directories* now contains more than 10,000 entries, over 2,000 more than the last edition, making this directory the most comprehensive resource of the worlds business and trade directories. Entries include content descriptions, price, publisher's name and address, web site and e-mail addresses, phone and fax numbers and editorial staff. Organized by industry group, and then by region, this resource puts over 10,000 industry-specific business and trade directories at the reader's fingertips. Three indexes are included for quick access to information: Geographic Index, Publisher Index and Title Index. Public, college and corporate libraries, as well as individuals and corporations seeking critical market information will want to add this directory to their marketing collection.

> *"Reasonably priced for a work of this type, this directory should appeal to larger academic, public and corporate libraries with an international focus." –Library Journal*

Softcover ISBN 978-1-930956-63-6, 1,800 pages, $225.00

Business Information ◆ <u>**Ratings Guides**</u> ◆ General Reference ◆ Education ◆
Statistics ◆ Demographics ◆ Health Information ◆ Canadian Information

TheStreet.com Ratings Guide to Health Insurers

TheStreet.com Ratings Guide to Health Insurers is the first and only source to cover the financial stability of the nation's health care system, rating the financial safety of more than 6,000 health insurance providers, health maintenance organizations (HMOs) and all of the Blue Cross Blue Shield plans – updated quarterly to ensure the most accurate information. The Guide also provides a complete listing of all the major health insurers, including all Long-Term Care and Medigap insurers. Our *Guide to Health Insurers* includes comprehensive, timely coverage on the financial stability of HMOs and health insurers; the most accurate insurance company ratings available–the same quality ratings heralded by the U.S. General Accounting Office; separate listings for those companies offering Medigap and long-term care policies; the number of serious consumer complaints filed against most HMOs so you can see who is actually providing the best (or worst) service and more. The easy-to-use layout gives you a one-line summary analysis for each company that we track, followed by an in-depth, detailed analysis of all HMOs and the largest health insurers. The guide also includes a list of TheStreet.com Ratings Recommended Companies with information on how to contact them, and the reasoning behind any rating upgrades or downgrades.

> *"With 20 years behind its insurance-advocacy research [the rating guide] continues to offer a wealth of information that helps consumers weigh their healthcare options now and in the future." -Today's Librarian*

Issues published quarterly, Softcover, 550 pages, $499.00 for four quarterly issues, $249.00 for a single issue

TheStreet.com Ratings Guide to Life & Annuity Insurers

TheStreet.com Safety Ratings are the most reliable source for evaluating an insurer's financial solvency risk. Consequently, policy-holders have come to rely on TheStreet.com's flagship publication, *TheStreet.com Ratings Guide to Life & Annuity Insurers*, to help them identify the safest companies to do business with. Each easy-to-use edition delivers TheStreet.com's independent ratings and analyses on more than 1,100 insurers, updated every quarter. Plus, your patrons will find a complete list of TheStreet.com Recommended Companies, including contact information, and the reasoning behind any rating upgrades or downgrades. This guide is perfect for those who are considering the purchase of a life insurance policy, placing money in an annuity, or advising clients about insurance and annuities. A life or health insurance policy or annuity is only as secure as the insurance company issuing it. Therefore, make sure your patrons have what they need to periodically monitor the financial condition of the companies with whom they have an investment. The TheStreet.com Ratings product line is designed to help them in their evaluations.

> *"Weiss has an excellent reputation and this title is held by hundreds of libraries. This guide is recommended for public and academic libraries." -ARBA*

Issues published quarterly, Softcover, 360 pages, $499.00 for four quarterly issues, $249.00 for a single issue

TheStreet.com Ratings Guide to Property & Casualty Insurers

TheStreet.com Ratings Guide to Property and Casualty Insurers provides the most extensive coverage of insurers writing policies, helping consumers and businesses avoid financial headaches. Updated quarterly, this easy-to-use publication delivers the independent, unbiased TheStreet.com Safety Ratings and supporting analyses on more than 2,800 U.S. insurance companies, offering auto & homeowners insurance, business insurance, worker's compensation insurance, product liability insurance, medical malpractice and other professional liability insurance. Each edition includes a list of TheStreet.com Recommended Companies by type of insurance, including a contact number, plus helpful information about the coverage provided by the State Guarantee Associations.

> *"In contrast to the other major insurance rating agencies...Weiss does not have a financial relationship worth the companies it rates. A GAO study found that Weiss identified financial vulnerability earlier than the other rating agencies." -ARBA*

Issues published quarterly, Softcover, 455 pages, $499.00 for four quarterly issues, $249.00 for a single issue

TheStreet.com Ratings Consumer Box Set

Deliver the critical information your patrons need to safeguard their personal finances with *TheStreet.com Ratings' Consumer Guide Box Set*. Each of the eight guides is packed with accurate, unbiased information and recommendations to help your patrons make sound financial decisions. TheStreet.com Ratings Consumer Guide Box Set provides your patrons with easy to understand guidance on important personal finance topics, including: *Consumer Guide to Variable Annuities, Consumer Guide to Medicare Supplement Insurance, Consumer Guide to Elder Care Choices, Consumer Guide to Automobile Insurance, Consumer Guide to Long-Term Care Insurance, Consumer Guide to Homeowners Insurance, Consumer Guide to Term Life Insurance, and Consumer Guide to Medicare Prescription Drug Coverage*. Each guide provides an easy-to-read overview of the topic, what to look out for when selecting a company or insurance plan to do business with, who are the recommended companies to work with and how to navigate through these often-times difficult decisions. Custom worksheets and step-by-step directions make these resources accessible to all types of users. Packaged in a handy custom display box, these helpful guides will prove to be a much-used addition to any reference collection.

Issues published twice per year, Softcover, 600 pages, $499.00 for two biennial issues

**Business Information ♦ Ratings Guides ♦ General Reference ♦ Education ♦
Statistics ♦ Demographics ♦ Health Information ♦ Canadian Information**

Grey House
Publishing

TheStreet.com Ratings Guide to Stock Mutual Funds

TheStreet.com Ratings Guide to Stock Mutual Funds offers ratings and analyses on more than 8,800 equity mutual funds – more than any other publication. The exclusive TheStreet.com Investment Ratings combine an objective evaluation of each fund's performance and risk to provide a single, user-friendly, composite rating, giving your patrons a better handle on a mutual fund's risk-adjusted performance. Each edition identifies the top-performing mutual funds based on risk category, type of fund, and overall risk-adjusted performance. TheStreet.com's unique investment rating system makes it easy to see exactly which stocks are on the rise and which ones should be avoided. For those investors looking to tailor their mutual fund selections based on age, income, and tolerance for risk, we've also assigned two component ratings to each fund: a performance rating and a risk rating. With these, you can identify those funds that are best suited to meet your - or your client's – individual needs and goals. Plus, we include a handy Risk Profile Quiz to help you assess your personal tolerance for risk. So whether you're an investing novice or professional, the *Guide to Stock Mutual Funds* gives you everything you need to find a mutual fund that is right for you.

> *"There is tremendous need for information such as that provided by this Weiss publication. This reasonably priced guide is recommended for public and academic libraries serving investors." -ARBA*

Issues published quarterly, Softcover, 655 pages, $499 for four quarterly issues, $249 for a single issue

TheStreet.com Ratings Guide to Exchange-Traded Funds

TheStreet.com Ratings editors analyze hundreds of mutual funds each quarter, condensing all of the available data into a single composite opinion of each fund's risk-adjusted performance. The intuitive, consumer-friendly ratings allow investors to instantly identify those funds that have historically done well and those that have under-performed the market. Each quarterly edition identifies the top-performing exchange-traded funds based on risk category, type of fund, and overall risk-adjusted performance. The rating scale, A through F, gives you a better handle on an exchange-traded fund's risk-adjusted performance. Other features include Top & Bottom 200 Exchange-Traded Funds; Performance and Risk: 100 Best and Worst Exchange- Traded Funds; Investor Profile Quiz; Performance Benchmarks and Fund Type Descriptions. With the growing popularity of mutual fund investing, consumers need a reliable source to help them track and evaluate the performance of their mutual fund holdings. Plus, they need a way of identifying and monitoring other funds as potential new investments. Unfortunately, the hundreds of performance and risk measures available, multiplied by the vast number of mutual fund investments on the market today, can make this a daunting task for even the most sophisticated investor. This Guide will serve as a useful tool for both the first-time and seasoned investor.

Editions published quarterly, Softcover, 440 pages, $499.00 for four quarterly issues, $249.00 for a single issue

TheStreet.com Ratings Guide to Bond & Money Market Mutual Funds

TheStreet.com Ratings Guide to Bond & Money Market Mutual Funds has everything your patrons need to easily identify the top-performing fixed income funds on the market today. Each quarterly edition contains TheStreet.com's independent ratings and analyses on more than 4,600 fixed income funds – more than any other publication, including corporate bond funds, high-yield bond funds, municipal bond funds, mortgage security funds, money market funds, global bond funds and government bond funds. In addition, the fund's risk rating is combined with its three-year performance rating to get an overall picture of the fund's risk-adjusted performance. The resulting TheStreet.com Investment Rating gives a single, user-friendly, objective evaluation that makes it easy to compare one fund to another and select the right fund based on the level of risk tolerance. Most investors think of fixed income mutual funds as "safe" investments. That's not always the case, however, depending on the credit risk, interest rate risk, and prepayment risk of the securities owned by the fund. TheStreet.com Ratings assesses each of these risks and assigns each fund a risk rating to help investors quickly evaluate the fund's risk component. Plus, we include a handy Risk Profile Quiz to help you assess your personal tolerance for risk. So whether you're an investing novice or professional, the *Guide to Bond and Money Market Mutual Funds* gives you everything you need to find a mutual fund that is right for you.

> *"Comprehensive... It is easy to use and consumer-oriented, and can be recommended for larger public and academic libraries." -ARBA*

Issues published quarterly, Softcover, 470 pages, $499.00 for four quarterly issues, $249.00 for a single issue

TheStreet.com Ratings Guide to Banks & Thrifts

Updated quarterly, for the most up-to-date information, *TheStreet.com Ratings Guide to Banks and Thrifts* offers accurate, intuitive safety ratings your patrons can trust; supporting ratios and analyses that show an institution's strong & weak points; identification of the TheStreet.com Recommended Companies with branches in your area; a complete list of institutions receiving upgrades/downgrades; and comprehensive coverage of every bank and thrift in the nation – more than 9,000. TheStreet.com Safety Ratings are then based on the analysts' review of publicly available information collected by the federal banking regulators. The easy-to-use layout gives you: the institution's TheStreet.com Safety Rating for the last 3 years; the five key indexes used to evaluate each institution; along with the primary ratios and statistics used in determining the company's rating. *TheStreet.com Ratings Guide to Banks & Thrifts* will be a must for individuals who are concerned about the safety of their CD or savings account; need to be sure that an existing line of credit will be there when they need it; or simply want to avoid the hassles of dealing with a failing or troubled institution.

> *"Large public and academic libraries most definitely need to acquire the work. Likewise, special libraries in large corporations will find this title indispensable." -ARBA*

Issues published quarterly, Softcover, 370 pages, $499.00 for four quarterly issues, $249.00 for a single issue

Business Information ✦ <u>**Ratings Guides**</u> ✦ **General Reference** ✦ **Education** ✦
Statistics ✦ **Demographics** ✦ **Health Information** ✦ **Canadian Information**

TheStreet.com Ratings Guide to Common Stocks

TheStreet.com Ratings Guide to Common Stocks gives your patrons reliable insight into the risk-adjusted performance of common stocks listed on the NYSE, AMEX, and Nasdaq – over 5,800 stocks in all – more than any other publication. TheStreet.com's unique investment rating system makes it easy to see exactly which stocks are on the rise and which ones should be avoided. In addition, your patrons also get supporting analysis showing growth trends, profitability, debt levels, valuation levels, the top-rated stocks within each industry, and more. Plus, each stock is ranked with the easy-to-use buy-hold-sell equivalents commonly used by Wall Street. Whether they're selecting their own investments or checking up on a broker's recommendation, TheStreet.com Ratings can help them in their evaluations.

"Users... will find the information succinct and the explanations readable, easy to understand, and helpful to a novice." -Library Journal

Issues published quarterly, Softcover, 440 pages, $499.00 for four quarterly issues, $249.00 for a single issue

TheStreet.com Ratings Ultimate Guided Tour of Stock Investing

This important reference guide from TheStreet.com Ratings is just what librarians around the country have asked for: a step-by-step introduction to stock investing for the beginning to intermediate investor. This easy-to-navigate guide explores the basics of stock investing and includes the intuitive TheStreet.com Investment Rating on more than 5,800 stocks, complete with real-world investing information that can be put to use immediately with stocks that fit the concepts discussed in the guide; informative charts, graphs and worksheets; easy-to-understand explanations on topics like P/E, compound interest, marked indices, diversifications, brokers, and much more; along with financial safety ratings for every stock on the NYSE, American Stock Exchange and the Nasdaq. This consumer-friendly guide offers complete how-to information on stock investing that can be put to use right away; a friendly format complete with our "Wise Guide" who leads the reader on a safari to learn about the investing jungle; helpful charts, graphs and simple worksheets; the intuitive TheStreet.com Investment rating on over 6,000 stocks — every stock found on the NYSE, American Stock Exchange and the NASDAQ; and much more.

"Provides investors with an alternative to stock broker recommendations, which recently have been tarnished by conflicts of interest. In summary, the guide serves as a welcome addition for all public library collections." -ARBA

Issues published quarterly, Softcover, 370 pages, $499.00 for four quarterly issues, $249.00 for a single issue

TheStreet.com Ratings' Reports & Services

- Ratings Online — An on-line summary covering an individual company's TheStreet.com Financial Strength Rating or an investment's unique TheStreet.com Investment Rating with the factors contributing to that rating; available 24 hours a day by visiting www.thestreet.com/tscratings or calling (800) 289-9222.
- Unlimited Ratings Research — The ultimate research tool providing fast, easy online access to the very latest TheStreet.com Financial Strength Ratings and Investment Ratings. Price: $559 per industry.

Contact TheStreet.com for more information about Reports & Services at www.thestreet.com/tscratings or call (800) 289-9222

TheStreet.com Ratings' Custom Reports

TheStreet.com Ratings is pleased to offer two customized options for receiving ratings data. Each taps into TheStreet.com's vast data repositories and is designed to provide exactly the data you need. Choose from a variety of industries, companies, data variables, and delivery formats including print, Excel, SQL, Text or Access.

- Customized Reports - get right to the heart of your company's research and data needs with a report customized to your specifications.
- Complete Database Download – TheStreet.com will design and deliver the database; from there you can sort it, recalculate it, and format your results to suit your specific needs.

Contact TheStreet.com for more information about Custom Reports at www.thestreet.com/tscratings or call (800) 289-9222

Business Information ◆ Ratings Guides ◆ <u>General Reference</u> ◆ Education ◆
Statistics ◆ Demographics ◆ Health Information ◆ Canadian Information

Grey House Publishing

The Value of a Dollar 1600-1859, The Colonial Era to The Civil War

Following the format of the widely acclaimed, *The Value of a Dollar, 1860-2004*, *The Value of a Dollar 1600-1859, The Colonial Era to The Civil War* records the actual prices of thousands of items that consumers purchased from the Colonial Era to the Civil War. Our editorial department had been flooded with requests from users of our *Value of a Dollar* for the same type of information, just from an earlier time period. This new volume is just the answer – with pricing data from 1600 to 1859. Arranged into five-year chapters, each 5-year chapter includes a Historical Snapshot, Consumer Expenditures, Investments, Selected Income, Income/Standard Jobs, Food Basket, Standard Prices and Miscellany. There is also a section on Trends. This informative section charts the change in price over time and provides added detail on the reasons prices changed within the time period, including industry developments, changes in consumer attitudes and important historical facts. This fascinating survey will serve a wide range of research needs and will be useful in all high school, public and academic library reference collections.

"The Value of a Dollar: Colonial Era to the Civil War, 1600-1865 will find a happy audience among students, researchers, and general browsers. It offers a fascinating and detailed look at early American history from the viewpoint of everyday people trying to make ends meet. This title and the earlier publication, The Value of a Dollar, 1860-2004, complement each other very well, and readers will appreciate finding them side-by-side on the shelf." -Booklist

Hardcover ISBN 978-1-59237-094-8, 600 pages, $145.00 | Ebook ISBN 978-1-59237-169-3 www.gale.com/gvrl/partners/grey.htm

The Value of a Dollar 1860-2004, Third Edition

A guide to practical economy, *The Value of a Dollar* records the actual prices of thousands of items that consumers purchased from the Civil War to the present, along with facts about investment options and income opportunities. This brand new Third Edition boasts a brand new addition to each five-year chapter, a section on Trends. This informative section charts the change in price over time and provides added detail on the reasons prices changed within the time period, including industry developments, changes in consumer attitudes and important historical facts. Plus, a brand new chapter for 2000-2004 has been added. Each 5-year chapter includes a Historical Snapshot, Consumer Expenditures, Investments, Selected Income, Income/Standard Jobs, Food Basket Standard Prices and Miscellany. This interesting and useful publication will be widely used in any reference collection.

"Business historians, reporters, writers and students will find this source... very helpful for historical research. Libraries will want to purchase it." –ARBA

Hardcover ISBN 978-1-59237-074-0, 600 pages, $145.00 | Ebook ISBN 978-1-59237-173-0 www.gale.com/gvrl/partners/grey.htm

Working Americans 1880-1999
Volume I: The Working Class, Volume II: The Middle Class, Volume III: The Upper Class

Each of the volumes in the *Working Americans* series focuses on a particular class of Americans, The Working Class, The Middle Class and The Upper Class over the last 120 years. Chapters in each volume focus on one decade and profile three to five families. Family Profiles include real data on Income & Job Descriptions, Selected Prices of the Times, Annual Income, Annual Budgets, Family Finances, Life at Work, Life at Home, Life in the Community, Working Conditions, Cost of Living, Amusements and much more. Each chapter also contains an Economic Profile with Average Wages of other Professions, a selection of Typical Pricing, Key Events & Inventions, News Profiles, Articles from Local Media and Illustrations. The *Working Americans* series captures the lifestyles of each of the classes from the last twelve decades, covers a vast array of occupations and ethnic backgrounds and travels the entire nation. These interesting and useful compilations of portraits of the American Working, Middle and Upper Classes during the last 120 years will be an important addition to any high school, public or academic library reference collection.

"These interesting, unique compilations of economic and social facts, figures and graphs will support multiple research needs. They will engage and enlighten patrons in high school, public and academic library collections." –Booklist

Volume I: The Working Class Hardcover ISBN 978-1-891482-81-6, 558 pages, $145.00 | Volume II: The Middle Class Hardcover ISBN 978-1-891482-72-4, 591 pages, $145.00 | Volume III: The Upper Class Hardcover ISBN 978-1-930956-38-4, 567 pages, $145.00 | Ebooks www.gale.com/gvrl/partners/grey.htm

Working Americans 1880-1999 Volume IV: Their Children

This Fourth Volume in the highly successful *Working Americans* series focuses on American children, decade by decade from 1880 to 1999. This interesting and useful volume introduces the reader to three children in each decade, one from each of the Working, Middle and Upper classes. Like the first three volumes in the series, the individual profiles are created from interviews, diaries, statistical studies, biographies and news reports. Profiles cover a broad range of ethnic backgrounds, geographic area and lifestyles – everything from an orphan in Memphis in 1882, following the Yellow Fever epidemic of 1878 to an eleven-year-old nephew of a beer baron and owner of the New York Yankees in New York City in 1921. Chapters also contain important supplementary materials including News Features as well as information on everything from Schools to Parks, Infectious Diseases to Childhood Fears along with Entertainment, Family Life and much more to provide an informative overview of the lifestyles of children from each decade. This interesting account of what life was like for Children in the Working, Middle and Upper Classes will be a welcome addition to the reference collection of any high school, public or academic library.

Hardcover ISBN 978-1-930956-35-3, 600 pages, $145.00 | Ebook ISBN 978-1-59237-166-2 www.gale.com/gvrl/partners/grey.htm

Business Information ✦ Ratings Guides ✦ <u>General Reference</u> ✦ Education ✦
Statistics ✦ Demographics ✦ Health Information ✦ Canadian Information

Grey House
Publishing

Working Americans 1880-2003 Volume V: Americans At War

Working Americans 1880-2003 Volume V: Americans At War is divided into 11 chapters, each covering a decade from 1880-2003 and examines the lives of Americans during the time of war, including declared conflicts, one-time military actions, protests, and preparations for war. Each decade includes several personal profiles, whether on the battlefield or on the homefront, that tell the stories of civilians, soldiers, and officers during the decade. The profiles examine: Life at Home; Life at Work; and Life in the Community. Each decade also includes an Economic Profile with statistical comparisons, a Historical Snapshot, News Profiles, local News Articles, and Illustrations that provide a solid historical background to the decade being examined. Profiles range widely not only geographically, but also emotionally, from that of a girl whose leg was torn off in a blast during WWI, to the boredom of being stationed in the Dakotas as the Indian Wars were drawing to a close. As in previous volumes of the *Working Americans* series, information is presented in narrative form, but hard facts and real-life situations back up each story. The basis of the profiles come from diaries, private print books, personal interviews, family histories, estate documents and magazine articles. For easy reference, *Working Americans 1880-2003 Volume V: Americans At War* includes an in-depth Subject Index. The Working Americans series has become an important reference for public libraries, academic libraries and high school libraries. This fifth volume will be a welcome addition to all of these types of reference collections.

Hardcover ISBN 978-1-59237-024-5, 600 pages, $145.00 | Ebook ISBN 978-1-59237-167-9 www.gale.com/gvrl/partners/grey.htm

Working Americans 1880-2005 Volume VI: Women at Work

Unlike any other volume in the *Working Americans* series, this Sixth Volume, is the first to focus on a particular gender of Americans. *Volume VI: Women at Work*, traces what life was like for working women from the 1860's to the present time. Beginning with the life of a maid in 1890 and a store clerk in 1900 and ending with the life and times of the modern working women, this text captures the struggle, strengths and changing perception of the American woman at work. Each chapter focuses on one decade and profiles three to five women with real data on Income & Job Descriptions, Selected Prices of the Times, Annual Income, Annual Budgets, Family Finances, Life at Work, Life at Home, Life in the Community, Working Conditions, Cost of Living, Amusements and much more. For even broader access to the events, economics and attitude towards women throughout the past 130 years, each chapter is supplemented with News Profiles, Articles from Local Media, Illustrations, Economic Profiles, Typical Pricing, Key Events, Inventions and more. This important volume illustrates what life was like for working women over time and allows the reader to develop an understanding of the changing role of women at work. These interesting and useful compilations of portraits of women at work will be an important addition to any high school, public or academic library reference collection.

Hardcover ISBN 978-1-59237-063-4, 600 pages, $145.00 | Ebook ISBN 978-1-59237-168-6 www.gale.com/gvrl/partners/grey.htm

Working Americans 1880-2005 Volume VII: Social Movements

Working Americans series, Volume VII: Social Movements explores how Americans sought and fought for change from the 1880s to the present time. Following the format of previous volumes in the Working Americans series, the text examines the lives of 34 individuals who have worked -- often behind the scenes --- to bring about change. Issues include topics as diverse as the Anti-smoking movement of 1901 to efforts by Native Americans to reassert their long lost rights. Along the way, the book will profile individuals brave enough to demand suffrage for Kansas women in 1912 or demand an end to lynching during a March on Washington in 1923. Each profile is enriched with real data on Income & Job Descriptions, Selected Prices of the Times, Annual Incomes & Budgets, Life at Work, Life at Home, Life in the Community, along with News Features, Key Events, and Illustrations. The depth of information contained in each profile allow the user to explore the private, financial and public lives of these subjects, deepening our understanding of how calls for change took place in our society. A must-purchase for the reference collections of high school libraries, public libraries and academic libraries.

Hardcover ISBN 978-1-59237-101-3, 600 pages, $145.00 | Ebook ISBN 978-1-59237-174-7 www.gale.com/gvrl/partners/grey.htm

Working Americans 1880-2005 Volume VIII: Immigrants

Working Americans 1880-2007 Volume VIII: Immigrants illustrates what life was like for families leaving their homeland and creating a new life in the United States. Each chapter covers one decade and introduces the reader to three immigrant families. Family profiles cover what life was like in their homeland, in their community in the United States, their home life, working conditions and so much more. As the reader moves through these pages, the families and individuals come to life, painting a picture of why they left their homeland, their experiences in setting roots in a new country, their struggles and triumphs, stretching from the 1800s to the present time. Profiles include a seven-year-old Swedish girl who meets her father for the first time at Ellis Island; a Chinese photographer's assistant; an Armenian who flees the genocide of his country to build Ford automobiles in Detroit; a 38-year-old German bachelor cigar maker who settles in Newark NJ, but contemplates tobacco farming in Virginia; a 19-year-old Irish domestic servant who is amazed at the easy life of American dogs; a 19-year-old Filipino who came to Hawaii against his parent's wishes to farm sugar cane; a French-Canadian who finds success as a boxer in Maine and many more. As in previous volumes, information is presented in narrative form, but hard facts and real-life situations back up each story. With the topic of immigration being so hotly debated in this country, this timely resource will prove to be a useful source for students, researchers, historians and library patrons to discover the issues facing immigrants in the United States. This title will be a useful addition to reference collections of public libraries, university libraries and high schools.

Hardcover ISBN 978-1-59237-197-6, 600 pages, $145.00 | Ebook ISBN 978-1-59237-232-4 www.gale.com/gvrl/partners/grey.htm

Business Information ✦ Ratings Guides ✦ <u>General Reference</u> ✦ Education ✦
Statistics ✦ Demographics ✦ Health Information ✦ Canadian Information

The Encyclopedia of Warrior Peoples & Fighting Groups

Many military groups throughout the world have excelled in their craft either by fortuitous circumstances, outstanding leadership, or intense training. This new second edition of *The Encyclopedia of Warrior Peoples and Fighting Groups* explores the origins and leadership of these outstanding combat forces, chronicles their conquests and accomplishments, examines the circumstances surrounding their decline or disbanding, and assesses their influence on the groups and methods of warfare that followed. Readers will encounter ferocious tribes, charismatic leaders, and daring militias, from ancient times to the present, including Amazons, Buffalo Soldiers, Green Berets, Iron Brigade, Kamikazes, Peoples of the Sea, Polish Winged Hussars, Teutonic Knights, and Texas Rangers. With over 100 alphabetical entries, numerous cross-references and illustrations, a comprehensive bibliography, and index, the *Encyclopedia of Warrior Peoples and Fighting Groups* is a valuable resource for readers seeking insight into the bold history of distinguished fighting forces.

"Especially useful for high school students, undergraduates,
and general readers with an interest in military history." –Library Journal

Hardcover ISBN 978-1-59237-116-7, 660 pages, $135.00 | Ebook ISBN 978-1-59237-172-3 www.gale.com/gvrl/partners/grey.htm

The Encyclopedia of Invasions & Conquests, From the Ancient Times to the Present

This second edition of the popular *Encyclopedia of Invasions & Conquests*, a comprehensive guide to over 150 invasions, conquests, battles and occupations from ancient times to the present, takes readers on a journey that includes the Roman conquest of Britain, the Portuguese colonization of Brazil, and the Iraqi invasion of Kuwait, to name a few. New articles will explore the late 20th and 21st centuries, with a specific focus on recent conflicts in Afghanistan, Kuwait, Iraq, Yugoslavia, Grenada and Chechnya. In addition to covering the military aspects of invasions and conquests, entries cover some of the political, economic, and cultural aspects, for example, the effects of a conquest on the invade country's political and monetary system and in its language and religion. The entries on leaders – among them Sargon, Alexander the Great, William the Conqueror, and Adolf Hitler – deal with the people who sought to gain control, expand power, or exert religious or political influence over others through military means. Revised and updated for this second edition, entries are arranged alphabetically within historical periods. Each chapter provides a map to help readers locate key areas and geographical features, and bibliographical references appear at the end of each entry. Other useful features include cross-references, a cumulative bibliography and a comprehensive subject index. This authoritative, well-organized, lucidly written volume will prove invaluable for a variety of readers, including high school students, military historians, members of the armed forces, history buffs and hobbyists.

"Engaging writing, sensible organization, nice illustrations, interesting and
obscure facts, and useful maps make this book a pleasure to read." –ARBA

Hardcover ISBN 978-1-59237-114-3, 598 pages, $135.00 | Ebook ISBN 978-1-59237-171-6 www.gale.com/gvrl/partners/grey.htm

Encyclopedia of Prisoners of War & Internment

This authoritative second edition provides a valuable overview of the history of prisoners of war and interned civilians, from earliest times to the present. Written by an international team of experts in the field of POW studies, this fascinating and thought-provoking volume includes entries on a wide range of subjects including the Crusades, Plains Indian Warfare, concentration camps, the two world wars, and famous POWs throughout history, as well as atrocities, escapes, and much more. Written in a clear and easily understandable style, this informative reference details over 350 entries, 30% larger than the first edition, that survey the history of prisoners of war and interned civilians from the earliest times to the present, with emphasis on the 19th and 20th centuries. Medical conditions, international law, exchanges of prisoners, organizations working on behalf of POWs, and trials associated with the treatment of captives are just some of the themes explored. Entries are arranged alphabetically, plus illustrations and maps are provided for easy reference. The text also includes an introduction, bibliography, appendix of selected documents, and end-of-entry reading suggestions. This one-of-a-kind reference will be a helpful addition to the reference collections of all public libraries, high schools, and university libraries and will prove invaluable to historians and military enthusiasts.

"Thorough and detailed yet accessible to the lay reader.
Of special interest to subject specialists and historians; recommended for public and academic libraries." - Library Journal

Hardcover ISBN 978-1-59237-120-4, 676 pages, $135.00 | Ebook ISBN 978-1-59237-170-9 www.gale.com/gvrl/partners/grey.htm

The Encyclopedia of Rural America: the Land & People

History, sociology, anthropology, and public policy are combined to deliver the encyclopedia destined to become the standard reference work in American rural studies. From irrigation and marriage to games and mental health, this encyclopedia is the first to explore the contemporary landscape of rural America, placed in historical perspective. With over 300 articles prepared by leading experts from across the nation, this timely encyclopedia documents and explains the major themes, concepts, industries, concerns, and everyday life of the people and land who make up rural America. Entries range from the industrial sector and government policy to arts and humanities and social and family concerns. Articles explore every aspect of life in rural America. *Encyclopedia of Rural America*, with its broad range of coverage, will appeal to high school and college students as well as graduate students, faculty, scholars, and people whose work pertains to rural areas.

"This exemplary encyclopedia is guaranteed to educate our
highly urban society about the uniqueness of rural America. Recommended for public and academic libraries." -Library Journal

Two Volumes, Hardcover, ISBN 978-1-59237-115-0, 800 pages, $250.00

Business Information ✦ Ratings Guides ✦ <u>**General Reference**</u> ✦ Education ✦
Statistics ✦ Demographics ✦ Health Information ✦ Canadian Information

The Religious Right, A Reference Handbook

Timely and unbiased, this third edition updates and expands its examination of the religious right and its influence on our government, citizens, society, and politics. From the fight to outlaw the teaching of Darwin's theory of evolution to the struggle to outlaw abortion, the religious right is continually exerting an influence on public policy. This text explores the influence of religion on legislation and society, while examining the alignment of the religious right with the political right. A historical survey of the movement highlights the shift to "hands-on" approach to politics and the struggle to present a unified front. The coverage offers a critical historical survey of the religious right movement, focusing on its increased involvement in the political arena, attempts to forge coalitions, and notable successes and failures. The text offers complete coverage of biographies of the men and women who have advanced the cause and an up to date chronology illuminate the movement's goals, including their accomplishments and failures. This edition offers an extensive update to all sections along with several brand new entries. Two new sections complement this third edition, a chapter on legal issues and court decisions and a chapter on demographic statistics and electoral patterns. To aid in further research, *The Religious Right*, offers an entire section of annotated listings of print and non-print resources, as well as of organizations affiliated with the religious right, and those opposing it. Comprehensive in its scope, this work offers easy-to-read, pertinent information for those seeking to understand the religious right and its evolving role in American society. A must for libraries of all sizes, university religion departments, activists, high schools and for those interested in the evolving role of the religious right.

" Recommended for all public and academic libraries." - Library Journal

Hardcover ISBN 978-1-59237-113-6, 600 pages, $135.00 | Ebook ISBN 978-1-59237-226-3 www.gale.com/gvrl/partners/grey.htm

From Suffrage to the Senate, America's Political Women

From Suffrage to the Senate is a comprehensive and valuable compendium of biographies of leading women in U.S. politics, past and present, and an examination of the wide range of women's movements. Up to date through 2006, this dynamically illustrated reference work explores American women's path to political power and social equality from the struggle for the right to vote and the abolition of slavery to the first African American woman in the U.S. Senate and beyond. This new edition includes over 150 new entries and a brand new section on trends and demographics of women in politics. The in-depth coverage also traces the political heritage of the abolition, labor, suffrage, temperance, and reproductive rights movements. The alphabetically arranged entries include biographies of every woman from across the political spectrum who has served in the U.S. House and Senate, along with women in the Judiciary and the U.S. Cabinet and, new to this edition, biographies of activists and political consultants. Bibliographical references follow each entry. For easy reference, a handy chronology is provided detailing 150 years of women's history. This up-to-date reference will be a must-purchase for women's studies departments, high schools and public libraries and will be a handy resource for those researching the key players in women's politics, past and present.

"An engaging tool that would be useful in high school, public, and academic libraries
looking for an overview of the political history of women in the US." –Booklist

Two Volumes, Hardcover ISBN 978-1-59237-117-4, 1,160 pages, $195.00 | Ebook ISBN 978-1-59237-227-0
www.gale.com/gvrl/partners/grey.htm

An African Biographical Dictionary

This landmark second edition is the only biographical dictionary to bring together, in one volume, cultural, social and political leaders – both historical and contemporary – of the sub-Saharan region. Over 800 biographical sketches of prominent Africans, as well as foreigners who have affected the continent's history, are featured, 150 more than the previous edition. The wide spectrum of leaders includes religious figures, writers, politicians, scientists, entertainers, sports personalities and more. Access to these fascinating individuals is provided in a user-friendly format. The biographies are arranged alphabetically, cross-referenced and indexed. Entries include the country or countries in which the person was significant and the commonly accepted dates of birth and death. Each biographical sketch is chronologically written; entries for cultural personalities add an evaluation of their work. This information is followed by a selection of references often found in university and public libraries, including autobiographies and principal biographical works. Appendixes list each individual by country and by field of accomplishment – rulers, musicians, explorers, missionaries, businessmen, physicists – nearly thirty categories in all. Another convenient appendix lists heads of state since independence by country. Up-to-date and representative of African societies as a whole, An African Biographical Dictionary provides a wealth of vital information for students of African culture and is an indispensable reference guide for anyone interested in African affairs.

"An unquestionable convenience to have these concise, informative biographies gathered into
one source, indexed, and analyzed by appendixes listing entrants by nation and occupational field." –Wilson Library Bulletin

Hardcover ISBN 978-1-59237-112-9, 667 pages, $135.00 | Ebook ISBN 978-1-59237-229-4 www.gale.com/gvrl/partners/grey.htm

Business Information ✦ Ratings Guides ✦ <u>General Reference</u> ✦ Education ✦
Statistics ✦ Demographics ✦ Health Information ✦ Canadian Information

American Environmental Leaders, From Colonial Times to the Present

A comprehensive and diverse award winning collection of biographies of the most important figures in American environmentalism. Few subjects arouse the passions the way the environment does. How will we feed an ever-increasing population and how can that food be made safe for consumption? Who decides how land is developed? How can environmental policies be made fair for everyone, including multiethnic groups, women, children, and the poor? *American Environmental Leaders* presents more than 350 biographies of men and women who have devoted their lives to studying, debating, and organizing these and other controversial issues over the last 200 years. In addition to the scientists who have analyzed how human actions affect nature, we are introduced to poets, landscape architects, presidents, painters, activists, even sanitation engineers, and others who have forever altered how we think about the environment. The easy to use A–Z format provides instant access to these fascinating individuals, and frequent cross references indicate others with whom individuals worked (and sometimes clashed). End of entry references provide users with a starting point for further research.

"Highly recommended for high school, academic, and public libraries needing environmental biographical information." –Library Journal/Starred Review

Two Volumes, Hardcover ISBN 978-1-59237-119-8, 900 pages $195.00 | Ebook ISBN 978-1-59237-230-0
www.gale.com/gvrl/partners/grey.htm

World Cultural Leaders of the Twentieth & Twenty-First Centuries

World Cultural Leaders of the Twentieth & Twenty-First Centuries is a window into the arts, performances, movements, and music that shaped the world's cultural development since 1900. A remarkable around-the-world look at one-hundred-plus years of cultural development through the eyes of those that set the stage and stayed to play. This second edition offers over 120 new biographies along with a complete update of existing biographies. To further aid the reader, a handy fold-out timeline traces important events in all six cultural categories from 1900 through the present time. Plus, a new section of detailed material and resources for 100 selected individuals is also new to this edition, with further data on museums, homesteads, websites, artwork and more. This remarkable compilation will answer a wide range of questions. Who was the originator of the term "documentary"? Which poet married the daughter of the famed novelist Thomas Mann in order to help her escape Nazi Germany? Which British writer served as an agent in Russia against the Bolsheviks before the 1917 revolution? A handy two-volume set that makes it easy to look up 450 worldwide cultural icons: novelists, poets, playwrights, painters, sculptors, architects, dancers, choreographers, actors, directors, filmmakers, singers, composers, and musicians. *World Cultural Leaders of the Twentieth & Twenty-First Centuries* provides entries (many of them illustrated) covering the person's works, achievements, and professional career in a thorough essay and offers interesting facts and statistics. Entries are fully cross-referenced so that readers can learn how various individuals influenced others. An index of leaders by occupation, a useful glossary and a thorough general index complete the coverage. This remarkable resource will be an important acquisition for the reference collections of public libraries, university libraries and high schools.

"Fills a need for handy, concise information on a wide array of international cultural figures."-ARBA

Two Volumes, Hardcover ISBN 978-1-59237-118-1, 900 pages, $195.00 | Ebook ISBN 978-1-59237-231-7
www.gale.com/gvrl/partners/grey.htm

Political Corruption in America: An Encyclopedia of Scandals, Power, and Greed

The complete scandal-filled history of American political corruption, focusing on the infamous people and cases, as well as society's electoral and judicial reactions. Since colonial times, there has been no shortage of politicians willing to take a bribe, skirt campaign finance laws, or act in their own interests. Corruption like the Whiskey Ring, Watergate, and Whitewater cases dominate American life, making political scandal a leading U.S. industry. From judges to senators, presidents to mayors, *Political Corruption in America* discusses the infamous people throughout history who have been accused of and implicated in crooked behavior. In this new second edition, more than 250 A–Z entries explore the people, crimes, investigations, and court cases behind 200 years of American political scandals. This unbiased volume also delves into the issues surrounding Koreagate, the Chinese campaign scandal, and other ethical lapses. Relevant statutes and terms, including the Independent Counsel Statute and impeachment as a tool of political punishment, are examined as well. Students, scholars, and other readers interested in American history, political science, and ethics will appreciate this survey of a wide range of corrupting influences. This title focuses on how politicians from all parties have fallen because of their greed and hubris, and how society has used electoral and judicial means against those who tested the accepted standards of political conduct. A full range of illustrations including political cartoons, photos of key figures such as Abe Fortas and Archibald Cox, graphs of presidential pardons, and tables showing the number of expulsions and censures in both the House and Senate round out the text. In addition, a comprehensive chronology of major political scandals in U.S. history from colonial times until the present. For further reading, an extensive bibliography lists sources including archival letters, newspapers, and private manuscript collections from the United States and Great Britain. With its comprehensive coverage of this interesting topic, *Political Corruption in America: An Encyclopedia of Scandals, Power, and Greed* will prove to be a useful addition to the reference collections of all public libraries, university libraries, history collections, political science collections and high schools.

"...this encyclopedia is a useful contribution to the field. Highly recommended." - CHOICE
"Political Corruption should be useful in most academic, high school, and public libraries." Booklist

Two Volumes, Hardcover ISBN 978-1-59237-297-3, 500 pages, $195.00

Business Information ◆ Ratings Guides ◆ <u>General Reference</u> ◆ Education ◆
Statistics ◆ Demographics ◆ Health Information ◆ Canadian Information

Religion and Law: A Dictionary

This informative, easy-to-use reference work covers a wide range of legal issues that affect the roles of religion and law in American society. Extensive A–Z entries provide coverage of key court decisions, case studies, concepts, individuals, religious groups, organizations, and agencies shaping religion and law in today's society. This *Dictionary* focuses on topics involved with the constitutional theory and interpretation of religion and the law; terms providing a historical explanation of the ways in which America's ever increasing ethnic and religious diversity contributed to our current understanding of the mandates of the First and Fourteenth Amendments; terms and concepts describing the development of religion clause jurisprudence; an analytical examination of the distinct vocabulary used in this area of the law; the means by which American courts have attempted to balance religious liberty against other important individual and social interests in a wide variety of physical and regulatory environments, including the classroom, the workplace, the courtroom, religious group organization and structure, taxation, the clash of "secular" and "religious" values, and the relationship of the generalized idea of individual autonomy of the specific concept of religious liberty. Important legislation and legal cases affecting religion and society are thoroughly covered in this timely volume, including a detailed Table of Cases and Table of Statutes for more detailed research. A guide to further reading and an index are also included. This useful resource will be an important acquisition for the reference collections of all public libraries, university libraries, religion reference collections and high schools.

Hardcover ISBN 978-1-59237-298-0, 500 pages, $135.00

Human Rights in the United States: A Dictionary and Documents

This two volume set offers easy to grasp explanations of the basic concepts, laws, and case law in the field, with emphasis on human rights in the historical, political, and legal experience of the United States. Human rights is a term not fully understood by many Americans. Addressing this gap, the new second edition of *Human Rights in the United States: A Dictionary and Documents* offers a comprehensive introduction that places the history of human rights in the United States in an international context. It surveys the legal protection of human dignity in the United States, examines the sources of human rights norms, cites key legal cases, explains the role of international governmental and non-governmental organizations, and charts global, regional, and U.N. human rights measures. Over 240 dictionary entries of human rights terms are detailed—ranging from asylum and cultural relativism to hate crimes and torture. Each entry discusses the significance of the term, gives examples, and cites appropriate documents and court decisions. In addition, a Documents section is provided that contains 59 conventions, treaties, and protocols related to the most up to date international action on ethnic cleansing; freedom of expression and religion; violence against women; and much more. A bibliography, extensive glossary, and comprehensive index round out this indispensable volume. This comprehensive, timely volume is a must for large public libraries, university libraries and social science departments, along with high school libraries.

> *"...invaluable for anyone interested in human rights issues ... highly recommended for all reference collections."*
> *- American Reference Books Annual*

Two Volumes, Hardcover ISBN 978-1-59237-290-4, 750 pages, $225.00

The Comparative Guide to American Elementary & Secondary Schools, 2008

The only guide of its kind, this award winning compilation offers a snapshot profile of every public school district in the United States serving 1,500 or more students – more than 5,900 districts are covered. Organized alphabetically by district within state, each chapter begins with a Statistical Overview of the state. Each district listing includes contact information (name, address, phone number and web site) plus Grades Served, the Numbers of Students and Teachers and the Number of Regular, Special Education, Alternative and Vocational Schools in the district along with statistics on Student/Classroom Teacher Ratios, Drop Out Rates, Ethnicity, the Numbers of Librarians and Guidance Counselors and District Expenditures per student. As an added bonus, *The Comparative Guide to American Elementary and Secondary Schools* provides important ranking tables, both by state and nationally, for each data element. For easy navigation through this wealth of information, this handbook contains a useful City Index that lists all districts that operate schools within a city. These important comparative statistics are necessary for anyone considering relocation or doing comparative research on their own district and would be a perfect acquisition for any public library or school district library.

"This straightforward guide is an easy way to find general information.
Valuable for academic and large public library collections." –ARBA

Softcover ISBN 978-1-59237-223-2, 2,400 pages, $125.00 | Ebook ISBN 978-1-59237-238-6 www.gale.com/gvr/partners/grey.htm

The Complete Learning Disabilities Directory, 2008

The Complete Learning Disabilities Directory is the most comprehensive database of Programs, Services, Curriculum Materials, Professional Meetings & Resources, Camps, Newsletters and Support Groups for teachers, students and families concerned with learning disabilities. This information-packed directory includes information about Associations & Organizations, Schools, Colleges & Testing Materials, Government Agencies, Legal Resources and much more. For quick, easy access to information, this directory contains four indexes: Entry Name Index, Subject Index and Geographic Index. With every passing year, the field of learning disabilities attracts more attention and the network of caring, committed and knowledgeable professionals grows every day. This directory is an invaluable research tool for these parents, students and professionals.

"Due to its wealth and depth of coverage, parents, teachers and others… should find this an invaluable resource." -Booklist

Softcover ISBN 978-1-59237-207-2, 900 pages, $145.00 | Online Database $195.00 | Online Database & Directory Combo $280.00

Educators Resource Directory, 2007/08

Educators Resource Directory is a comprehensive resource that provides the educational professional with thousands of resources and statistical data for professional development. This directory saves hours of research time by providing immediate access to Associations & Organizations, Conferences & Trade Shows, Educational Research Centers, Employment Opportunities & Teaching Abroad, School Library Services, Scholarships, Financial Resources, Professional Consultants, Computer Software & Testing Resources and much more. Plus, this comprehensive directory also includes a section on Statistics and Rankings with over 100 tables, including statistics on Average Teacher Salaries, SAT/ACT scores, Revenues & Expenditures and more. These important statistics will allow the user to see how their school rates among others, make relocation decisions and so much more. For quick access to information, this directory contains four indexes: Entry & Publisher Index, Geographic Index, a Subject & Grade Index and Web Sites Index. *Educators Resource Directory* will be a well-used addition to the reference collection of any school district education department or public library.

"Recommended for all collections that serve elementary and secondary school professionals." –Choice

Softcover ISBN 978-1-59237-179-2, 800 pages, $145.00 | Online Database $195.00 | Online Database & Directory Combo $280.00

Business Information ✦ **Ratings Guides** ✦ **General Reference** ✦ **Education** ✦
<u>**Statistics** ✦ **Demographics**</u> ✦ **Health Information** ✦ **Canadian Information**

Profiles of New York | Profiles of Florida | Profiles of Texas | Profiles of Illinois | Profiles of Michigan | Profiles of Ohio | Profiles of New Jersey | Profiles of Massachusetts | Profiles of Pennsylvania | Profiles of Wisconsin | Profiles of Connecticut & Rhode Island | Profiles of Indiana | Profiles of North Carolina & South Carolina | Profiles of Virginia | Profiles of California

The careful layout gives the user an easy-to-read snapshot of every single place and county in the state, from the biggest metropolis to the smallest unincorporated hamlet. The richness of each place or county profile is astounding in its depth, from history to weather, all packed in an easy-to-navigate, compact format. Each profile contains data on History, Geography, Climate, Population, Vital Statistics, Economy, Income, Taxes, Education, Housing, Health & Environment, Public Safety, Newspapers, Transportation, Presidential Election Results, Information Contacts and Chambers of Commerce. As an added bonus, there is a section on Selected Statistics, where data from the 100 largest towns and cities is arranged into easy-to-use charts. Each of 22 different data points has its own two-page spread with the cities listed in alpha order so researchers can easily compare and rank cities. A remarkable compilation that offers overviews and insights into each corner of the state, each volume goes beyond Census statistics, beyond metro area coverage, beyond the 100 best places to live. Drawn from official census information, other government statistics and original research, you will have at your fingertips data that's available nowhere else in one single source.

"The publisher claims that this is the 'most comprehensive portrait of the state of Florida ever published,' and this reviewer is inclined to believe it...Recommended. All levels." –Choice on Profiles of Florida

Each Profiles of… title ranges from 400-800 pages, priced at $149.00 each

America's Top-Rated Cities, 2008

America's Top-Rated Cities provides current, comprehensive statistical information and other essential data in one easy-to-use source on the 100 "top" cities that have been cited as the best for business and living in the U.S. This handbook allows readers to see, at a glance, a concise social, business, economic, demographic and environmental profile of each city, including brief evaluative comments. In addition to detailed data on Cost of Living, Finances, Real Estate, Education, Major Employers, Media, Crime and Climate, city reports now include Housing Vacancies, Tax Audits, Bankruptcy, Presidential Election Results and more. This outstanding source of information will be widely used in any reference collection.

"The only source of its kind that brings together all of this information into one easy-to-use source. It will be beneficial to many business and public libraries." –ARBA

Four Volumes, Softcover ISBN 978-1-59237-349-9, 2,500 pages, $195.00 | Ebook ISBN 978-1-59237-233-1
www.gale.com/gvrl/partners/grey.htm

America's Top-Rated Smaller Cities, 2008/09

A perfect companion to *America's Top-Rated Cities, America's Top-Rated Smaller Cities* provides current, comprehensive business and living profiles of smaller cities (population 25,000-99,999) that have been cited as the best for business and living in the United States. Sixty cities make up this 2004 edition of America's Top-Rated Smaller Cities, all are top-ranked by Population Growth, Median Income, Unemployment Rate and Crime Rate. City reports reflect the most current data available on a wide-range of statistics, including Employment & Earnings, Household Income, Unemployment Rate, Population Characteristics, Taxes, Cost of Living, Education, Health Care, Public Safety, Recreation, Media, Air & Water Quality and much more. Plus, each city report contains a Background of the City, and an Overview of the State Finances. *America's Top-Rated Smaller Cities* offers a reliable, one-stop source for statistical data that, before now, could only be found scattered in hundreds of sources. This volume is designed for a wide range of readers: individuals considering relocating a residence or business; professionals considering expanding their business or changing careers; general and market researchers; real estate consultants; human resource personnel; urban planners and investors.

"Provides current, comprehensive statistical information in one easy-to-use source… Recommended for public and academic libraries and specialized collections." –Library Journal

Two Volumes, Softcover ISBN 978-1-59237-284-3, 1,100 pages, $195.00 | Ebook ISBN 978-1-59237-234-8
www.gale.com/gvrl/partners/grey.htm

Profiles of America: Facts, Figures & Statistics for Every Populated Place in the United States

Profiles of America is the only source that pulls together, in one place, statistical, historical and descriptive information about every place in the United States in an easy-to-use format. This award winning reference set, now in its second edition, compiles statistics and data from over 20 different sources – the latest census information has been included along with more than nine brand new statistical topics. This Four-Volume Set details over 40,000 places, from the biggest metropolis to the smallest unincorporated hamlet, and provides statistical details and information on over 50 different topics including Geography, Climate, Population, Vital Statistics, Economy, Income, Taxes, Education, Housing, Health & Environment, Public Safety, Newspapers, Transportation, Presidential Election Results and Information Contacts or Chambers of Commerce. Profiles are arranged, for ease-of-use, by state and then by county. Each county begins with a County-Wide Overview and is followed by information for each Community in that particular county. The Community Profiles within the county are arranged alphabetically. *Profiles of America* is a virtual snapshot of America at your fingertips and a unique compilation of information that will be widely used in any reference collection.

A Library Journal Best Reference Book "An outstanding compilation." –Library Journal

Four Volumes, Softcover ISBN 978-1-891482-80-9, 10,000 pages, $595.00

To preview any of our Directories Risk-Free for 30 days, call (800) 562-2139 or fax (518) 789-0556
www.greyhouse.com books@greyhouse.com

Business Information ◆ Ratings Guides ◆ General Reference ◆ Education ◆
Statistics ◆ Demographics ◆ Health Information ◆ Canadian Information

Grey House
Publishing

The Comparative Guide to American Suburbs, 2007/08

The Comparative Guide to American Suburbs is a one-stop source for Statistics on the 2,000+ suburban communities surrounding the 50 largest metropolitan areas – their population characteristics, income levels, economy, school system and important data on how they compare to one another. Organized into 50 Metropolitan Area chapters, each chapter contains an overview of the Metropolitan Area, a detailed Map followed by a comprehensive Statistical Profile of each Suburban Community, including Contact Information, Physical Characteristics, Population Characteristics, Income, Economy, Unemployment Rate, Cost of Living, Education, Chambers of Commerce and more. Next, statistical data is sorted into Ranking Tables that rank the suburbs by twenty different criteria, including Population, Per Capita Income, Unemployment Rate, Crime Rate, Cost of Living and more. *The Comparative Guide to American Suburbs* is the best source for locating data on suburbs. Those looking to relocate, as well as those doing preliminary market research, will find this an invaluable timesaving resource.

"Public and academic libraries will find this compilation useful…The work draws together figures from many sources and will be especially helpful for job relocation decisions." – Booklist

Softcover ISBN 978-1-59237-180-8, 1,700 pages, $130.00 | Ebook ISBN 978-1-59237-235-5 www.gale.com/gvrl/partners/grey.htm

The American Tally: Statistics & Comparative Rankings for U.S. Cities with Populations over 10,000

This important statistical handbook compiles, all in one place, comparative statistics on all U.S. cities and towns with a 10,000+ population. *The American Tally* provides statistical details on over 4,000 cities and towns and profiles how they compare with one another in Population Characteristics, Education, Language & Immigration, Income & Employment and Housing. Each section begins with an alphabetical listing of cities by state, allowing for quick access to both the statistics and relative rankings of any city. Next, the highest and lowest cities are listed in each statistic. These important, informative lists provide quick reference to which cities are at both extremes of the spectrum for each statistic. Unlike any other reference, *The American Tally* provides quick, easy access to comparative statistics – a must-have for any reference collection.

"A solid library reference." -Bookwatch

Softcover ISBN 978-1-930956-29-2, 500 pages, $125.00 | Ebook ISBN 978-1-59237-241-6 www.gale.com/gvrl/partners/grey.htm

The Asian Databook: Statistics for all US Counties & Cities with Over 10,000 Population

This is the first-ever resource that compiles statistics and rankings on the US Asian population. *The Asian Databook* presents over 20 statistical data points for each city and county, arranged alphabetically by state, then alphabetically by place name. Data reported for each place includes Population, Languages Spoken at Home, Foreign-Born, Educational Attainment, Income Figures, Poverty Status, Homeownership, Home Values & Rent, and more. Next, in the Rankings Section, the top 75 places are listed for each data element. These easy-to-access ranking tables allow the user to quickly determine trends and population characteristics. This kind of comparative data can not be found elsewhere, in print or on the web, in a format that's as easy-to-use or more concise. A useful resource for those searching for demographics data, career search and relocation information and also for market research. With data ranging from Ancestry to Education, *The Asian Databook* presents a useful compilation of information that will be a much-needed resource in the reference collection of any public or academic library along with the marketing collection of any company whose primary focus in on the Asian population.

"This useful resource will help those searching for demographics data, and market research or relocation information… Accurate and clearly laid out, the publication is recommended for large public library and research collections." -Booklist

Softcover ISBN 978-1-59237-044-3, 1,000 pages, $150.00

The Hispanic Databook: Statistics for all US Counties & Cities with Over 10,000 Population

Previously published by Toucan Valley Publications, this second edition has been completely updated with figures from the latest census and has been broadly expanded to include dozens of new data elements and a brand new Rankings section. The Hispanic population in the United States has increased over 42% in the last 10 years and accounts for 12.5% of the total US population. For ease-of-use, *The Hispanic Databook* presents over 20 statistical data points for each city and county, arranged alphabetically by state, then alphabetically by place name. Data reported for each place includes Population, Languages Spoken at Home, Foreign-Born, Educational Attainment, Income Figures, Poverty Status, Homeownership, Home Values & Rent, and more. Next, in the Rankings Section, the top 75 places are listed for each data element. These easy-to-access ranking tables allow the user to quickly determine trends and population characteristics. This kind of comparative data can not be found elsewhere, in print or on the web, in a format that's as easy-to-use or more concise. A useful resource for those searching for demographics data, career search and relocation information and also for market research. With data ranging from Ancestry to Education, *The Hispanic Databook* presents a useful compilation of information that will be a much-needed resource in the reference collection of any public or academic library along with the marketing collection of any company whose primary focus in on the Hispanic population.

"This accurate, clearly presented volume of selected Hispanic demographics is recommended for large public libraries and research collections."-Library Journal

Softcover ISBN 978-1-59237-008-5, 1,000 pages, $150.00

Business Information ✦ Ratings Guides ✦ General Reference ✦ Education ✦
Statistics ✦ **Demographics** ✦ Health Information ✦ Canadian Information

Grey House Publishing

Ancestry in America: A Comparative Guide to Over 200 Ethnic Backgrounds

This brand new reference work pulls together thousands of comparative statistics on the Ethnic Backgrounds of all populated places in the United States with populations over 10,000. Never before has this kind of information been reported in a single volume. Section One, Statistics by Place, is made up of a list of over 200 ancestry and race categories arranged alphabetically by each of the 5,000 different places with populations over 10,000. The population number of the ancestry group in that city or town is provided along with the percent that group represents of the total population. This informative city-by-city section allows the user to quickly and easily explore the ethnic makeup of all major population bases in the United States. Section Two, Comparative Rankings, contains three tables for each ethnicity and race. In the first table, the top 150 populated places are ranked by population number for that particular ancestry group, regardless of population. In the second table, the top 150 populated places are ranked by the percent of the total population for that ancestry group. In the third table, those top 150 populated places with 10,000 population are ranked by population number for each ancestry group. These easy-to-navigate tables allow users to see ancestry population patterns and make city-by-city comparisons as well. This brand new, information-packed resource will serve a wide-range or research requests for demographics, population characteristics, relocation information and much more. *Ancestry in America: A Comparative Guide to Over 200 Ethnic Backgrounds* will be an important acquisition to all reference collections.

> *"This compilation will serve a wide range of research requests for population characteristics … it offers much more detail than other sources." –Booklist*

Softcover ISBN 978-1-59237-029-0, 1,500 pages, $225.00

Weather America, A Thirty-Year Summary of Statistical Weather Data and Rankings

This valuable resource provides extensive climatological data for over 4,000 National and Cooperative Weather Stations throughout the United States. Weather America begins with a new Major Storms section that details major storm events of the nation and a National Rankings section that details rankings for several data elements, such as Maximum Temperature and Precipitation. The main body of Weather America is organized into 50 state sections. Each section provides a Data Table on each Weather Station, organized alphabetically, that provides statistics on Maximum and Minimum Temperatures, Precipitation, Snowfall, Extreme Temperatures, Foggy Days, Humidity and more. State sections contain two brand new features in this edition – a City Index and a narrative Description of the climatic conditions of the state. Each section also includes a revised Map of the State that includes not only weather stations, but cities and towns.

> *"Best Reference Book of the Year." –Library Journal*

Softcover ISBN 978-1-891482-29-8, 2,013 pages, $175.00 | Ebook ISBN 978-1-59237-237-9 www.gale.com/gvrl/partners/grey.htm

Crime in America's Top-Rated Cities

This volume includes over 20 years of crime statistics in all major crime categories: violent crimes, property crimes and total crime. *Crime in America's Top-Rated Cities* is conveniently arranged by city and covers 76 top-rated cities. Crime in America's Top-Rated Cities offers details that compare the number of crimes and crime rates for the city, suburbs and metro area along with national crime trends for violent, property and total crimes. Also, this handbook contains important information and statistics on Anti-Crime Programs, Crime Risk, Hate Crimes, Illegal Drugs, Law Enforcement, Correctional Facilities, Death Penalty Laws and much more. A much-needed resource for people who are relocating, business professionals, general researchers, the press, law enforcement officials and students of criminal justice.

> *"Data is easy to access and will save hours of searching." –Global Enforcement Review*

Softcover ISBN 978-1-891482-84-7, 832 pages, $155.00

Business Information ◆ Ratings Guides ◆ General Reference ◆ Education ◆
Statistics ◆ Demographics ◆ **Health Information** ◆ Canadian Information

The Complete Directory for People with Disabilities, 2008

A wealth of information, now in one comprehensive sourcebook. Completely updated, this edition contains more information than ever before, including thousands of new entries and enhancements to existing entries and thousands of additional web sites and e-mail addresses. This up-to-date directory is the most comprehensive resource available for people with disabilities, detailing Independent Living Centers, Rehabilitation Facilities, State & Federal Agencies, Associations, Support Groups, Periodicals & Books, Assistive Devices, Employment & Education Programs, Camps and Travel Groups. Each year, more libraries, schools, colleges, hospitals, rehabilitation centers and individuals add *The Complete Directory for People with Disabilities* to their collections, making sure that this information is readily available to the families, individuals and professionals who can benefit most from the amazing wealth of resources cataloged here.

"No other reference tool exists to meet the special needs of the disabled in one convenient resource for information." –Library Journal

Softcover ISBN 978-1-59237-194-5, 1,200 pages, $165.00 | Online Database $215.00 | Online Database & Directory Combo $300.00

The Complete Learning Disabilities Directory, 2008

The Complete Learning Disabilities Directory is the most comprehensive database of Programs, Services, Curriculum Materials, Professional Meetings & Resources, Camps, Newsletters and Support Groups for teachers, students and families concerned with learning disabilities. This information-packed directory includes information about Associations & Organizations, Schools, Colleges & Testing Materials, Government Agencies, Legal Resources and much more. For quick, easy access to information, this directory contains four indexes: Entry Name Index, Subject Index and Geographic Index. With every passing year, the field of learning disabilities attracts more attention and the network of caring, committed and knowledgeable professionals grows every day. This directory is an invaluable research tool for these parents, students and professionals.

"Due to its wealth and depth of coverage, parents, teachers and others… should find this an invaluable resource." -Booklist

Softcover ISBN 978-1-59237-207-2, 900 pages, $145.00 | Online Database $195.00 | Online Database & Directory Combo $280.00

The Complete Directory for People with Chronic Illness, 2007/08

Thousands of hours of research have gone into this completely updated edition – several new chapters have been added along with thousands of new entries and enhancements to existing entries. Plus, each chronic illness chapter has been reviewed by a medical expert in the field. This widely-hailed directory is structured around the 90 most prevalent chronic illnesses – from Asthma to Cancer to Wilson's Disease – and provides a comprehensive overview of the support services and information resources available for people diagnosed with a chronic illness. Each chronic illness has its own chapter and contains a brief description in layman's language, followed by important resources for National & Local Organizations, State Agencies, Newsletters, Books & Periodicals, Libraries & Research Centers, Support Groups & Hotlines, Web Sites and much more. This directory is an important resource for health care professionals, the collections of hospital and health care libraries, as well as an invaluable tool for people with a chronic illness and their support network.

"A must purchase for all hospital and health care libraries and is strongly recommended for all public library reference departments." –ARBA

Softcover ISBN 978-1-59237-183-9, 1,200 pages, $165.00 | Online Database $215.00 | Online Database & Directory Combo $300.00

The Complete Mental Health Directory, 2008/09

This is the most comprehensive resource covering the field of behavioral health, with critical information for both the layman and the mental health professional. For the layman, this directory offers understandable descriptions of 25 Mental Health Disorders as well as detailed information on Associations, Media, Support Groups and Mental Health Facilities. For the professional, The Complete Mental Health Directory offers critical and comprehensive information on Managed Care Organizations, Information Systems, Government Agencies and Provider Organizations. This comprehensive volume of needed information will be widely used in any reference collection.

"… the strength of this directory is that it consolidates widely dispersed information into a single volume." –Booklist

Softcover ISBN 978-1-59237-285-0, 800 pages, $165.00 | Online Database $215.00 | Online & Directory Combo $300.00

Business Information ◆ Ratings Guides ◆ General Reference ◆ Education ◆
Statistics ◆ Demographics ◆ <u>Health Information</u> ◆ Canadian Information

Grey House
Publishing

The Comparative Guide to American Hospitals, Second Edition

This new second edition compares all of the nation's hospitals by 24 measures of quality in the treatment of heart attack, heart failure, pneumonia, and, new to this edition, surgical procedures and pregnancy care. Plus, this second edition is now available in regional volumes, to make locating information about hospitals in your area quicker and easier than ever before. The Comparative Guide to American Hospitals provides a snapshot profile of each of the nations 4,200+ hospitals. These informative profiles illustrate how the hospital rates when providing 24 different treatments within four broad categories: Heart Attack Care, Heart Failure Care, Surgical Infection Prevention (NEW), and Pregnancy Care measures (NEW). Each profile includes the raw percentage for that hospital, the state average, the US average and data on the top hospital. For easy access to contact information, each profile includes the hospital's address, phone and fax numbers, email and web addresses, type and accreditation along with 5 top key administrations. These profiles will allow the user to quickly identify the quality of the hospital and have the necessary information at their fingertips to make contact with that hospital. Most importantly, The Comparative Guide to American Hospitals provides easy-to-use Regional State by State Statistical Summary Tables for each of the data elements to allow the user to quickly locate hospitals with the best level of service. Plus, a new 30-Day Mortality Chart, Glossary of Terms and Regional Hospital Profile Index make this a must-have source. This new, expanded edition will be a must for the reference collection at all public, medical and academic libraries.

"These data will help those with heart conditions and pneumonia make informed decisions about their healthcare and encourage hospitals to improve the quality of care they provide. Large medical, hospital, and public libraries are most likely to benefit from this weighty resource."-Library Journal

Four Volumes Softcover ISBN 978-1-59237-182-2, 3,500 pages, $325.00 | Regional Volumes $135.00 |
Ebook ISBN 978-1-59237-239-3 www.gale.com/gvrl/partners/grey.htm

Older Americans Information Directory, 2008

Completely updated for 2008, this sixth edition has been completely revised and now contains 1,000 new listings, over 8,000 updates to existing listings and over 3,000 brand new e-mail addresses and web sites. You'll find important resources for Older Americans including National, Regional, State & Local Organizations, Government Agencies, Research Centers, Libraries & Information Centers, Legal Resources, Discount Travel Information, Continuing Education Programs, Disability Aids & Assistive Devices, Health, Print Media and Electronic Media. Three indexes: Entry Index, Subject Index and Geographic Index make it easy to find just the right source of information. This comprehensive guide to resources for Older Americans will be a welcome addition to any reference collection.

"Highly recommended for academic, public, health science and consumer libraries..." –Choice

1,200 pages; Softcover ISBN 978-1-59237-357-4, $165.00 | Online Database $215.00 | Online Database & Directory Combo $300.00

The Complete Directory for Pediatric Disorders, 2008

This important directory provides parents and caregivers with information about Pediatric Conditions, Disorders, Diseases and Disabilities, including Blood Disorders, Bone & Spinal Disorders, Brain Defects & Abnormalities, Chromosomal Disorders, Congenital Heart Defects, Movement Disorders, Neuromuscular Disorders and Pediatric Tumors & Cancers. This carefully written directory offers: understandable Descriptions of 15 major bodily systems; Descriptions of more than 200 Disorders and a Resources Section, detailing National Agencies & Associations, State Associations, Online Services, Libraries & Resource Centers, Research Centers, Support Groups & Hotlines, Camps, Books and Periodicals. This resource will provide immediate access to information crucial to families and caregivers when coping with children's illnesses.

"Recommended for public and consumer health libraries." –Library Journal

Softcover ISBN 978-1-59237-150-1, 1,200 pages, $165.00 | Online Database $215.00 | Online Database & Directory Combo $300.00

The Directory of Drug & Alcohol Residential Rehabilitation Facilities

This brand new directory is the first-ever resource to bring together, all in one place, data on the thousands of drug and alcohol residential rehabilitation facilities in the United States. The Directory of Drug & Alcohol Residential Rehabilitation Facilities covers over 1,000 facilities, with detailed contact information for each one, including mailing address, phone and fax numbers, email addresses and web sites, mission statement, type of treatment programs, cost, average length of stay, numbers of residents and counselors, accreditation, insurance plans accepted, type of environment, religious affiliation, education components and much more. It also contains a helpful chapter on General Resources that provides contact information for Associations, Print & Electronic Media, Support Groups and Conferences. Multiple indexes allow the user to pinpoint the facilities that meet very specific criteria. This time-saving tool is what so many counselors, parents and medical professionals have been asking for. The Directory of Drug & Alcohol Residential Rehabilitation Facilities will be a helpful tool in locating the right source for treatment for a wide range of individuals. This comprehensive directory will be an important acquisition for all reference collections: public and academic libraries, case managers, social workers, state agencies and many more.

"This is an excellent, much needed directory that fills an important gap..." –Booklist

Softcover ISBN 978-1-59237-031-3, 300 pages, $135.00

Business Information ◆ Ratings Guides ◆ General Reference ◆ Education ◆
Statistics ◆ Demographics ◆ **Health Information** ◆ Canadian Information

Grey House
Publishing

The Directory of Hospital Personnel, 2008

The Directory of Hospital Personnel is the best resource you can have at your fingertips when researching or marketing a product or service to the hospital market. A "Who's Who" of the hospital universe, this directory puts you in touch with over 150,000 key decision-makers. With 100% verification of data you can rest assured that you will reach the right person with just one call. Every hospital in the U.S. is profiled, listed alphabetically by city within state. Plus, three easy-to-use, cross-referenced indexes put the facts at your fingertips faster and more easily than any other directory: Hospital Name Index, Bed Size Index and Personnel Index. *The Directory of Hospital Personnel* is the only complete source for key hospital decision-makers by name. Whether you want to define or restructure sales territories... locate hospitals with the purchasing power to accept your proposals... keep track of important contacts or colleagues... or find information on which insurance plans are accepted, *The Directory of Hospital Personnel* gives you the information you need – easily, efficiently, effectively and accurately.

"Recommended for college, university and medical libraries." -ARBA

Softcover ISBN 978-1-59237-286-7, 2,500 pages, $325.00 | Online Database $545.00 | Online Database & Directory Combo, $650.00

The Directory of Health Care Group Purchasing Organizations, 2008

This comprehensive directory provides the important data you need to get in touch with over 800 Group Purchasing Organizations. By providing in-depth information on this growing market and its members, *The Directory of Health Care Group Purchasing Organizations* fills a major need for the most accurate and comprehensive information on over 800 GPOs – Mailing Address, Phone & Fax Numbers, E-mail Addresses, Key Contacts, Purchasing Agents, Group Descriptions, Membership Categorization, Standard Vendor Proposal Requirements, Membership Fees & Terms, Expanded Services, Total Member Beds & Outpatient Visits represented and more. Five Indexes provide a number of ways to locate the right GPO: Alphabetical Index, Expanded Services Index, Organization Type Index, Geographic Index and Member Institution Index. With its comprehensive and detailed information on each purchasing organization, *The Directory of Health Care Group Purchasing Organizations* is the go-to source for anyone looking to target this market.

"The information is clearly arranged and easy to access...recommended for those needing this very specialized information." –ARBA

1,000 pages; Softcover ISBN 978-1-59237-287-4, $325.00 | Online Database, $650.00 | Online Database & Directory Combo, $750.00

The HMO/PPO Directory, 2008

The HMO/PPO Directory is a comprehensive source that provides detailed information about Health Maintenance Organizations and Preferred Provider Organizations nationwide. This comprehensive directory details more information about more managed health care organizations than ever before. Over 1,100 HMOs, PPOs, Medicare Advantage Plans and affiliated companies are listed, arranged alphabetically by state. Detailed listings include Key Contact Information, Prescription Drug Benefits, Enrollment, Geographical Areas served, Affiliated Physicians & Hospitals, Federal Qualifications, Status, Year Founded, Managed Care Partners, Employer References, Fees & Payment Information and more. Plus, five years of historical information is included related to Revenues, Net Income, Medical Loss Ratios, Membership Enrollment and Number of Patient Complaints. Five easy-to-use, cross-referenced indexes will put this vast array of information at your fingertips immediately: HMO Index, PPO Index, Other Providers Index, Personnel Index and Enrollment Index. *The HMO/PPO Directory* provides the most comprehensive data on the most companies available on the market place today.

"Helpful to individuals requesting certain HMO/PPO issues such as co-payment costs, subscription costs and patient complaints. Individuals concerned (or those with questions) about their insurance may find this text to be of use to them." -ARBA

Softcover ISBN 978-1-59237-204-1, 600 pages, $325.00 | Online Database, $495.00 | Online Database & Directory Combo, $600.00

Medical Device Register, 2008

The only one-stop resource of every medical supplier licensed to sell products in the US. This award-winning directory offers immediate access to over 13,000 companies - and more than 65,000 products – in two information-packed volumes. This comprehensive resource saves hours of time and trouble when searching for medical equipment and supplies and the manufacturers who provide them. Volume I: The Product Directory, provides essential information for purchasing or specifying medical supplies for every medical device, supply, and diagnostic available in the US. Listings provide FDA codes & Federal Procurement Eligibility, Contact information for every manufacturer of the product along with Prices and Product Specifications. Volume 2 - Supplier Profiles, offers the most complete and important data about Suppliers, Manufacturers and Distributors. Company Profiles detail the number of employees, ownership, method of distribution, sales volume, net income, key executives detailed contact information medical products the company supplies, plus the medical specialties they cover. Four indexes provide immediate access to this wealth of information: Keyword Index, Trade Name Index, Supplier Geographical Index and OEM (Original Equipment Manufacturer) Index. *Medical Device Register* is the only one-stop source for locating suppliers and products; looking for new manufacturers or hard-to-find medical devices; comparing products and companies; know who's selling what and who to buy from cost effectively. This directory has become the standard in its field and will be a welcome addition to the reference collection of any medical library, large public library, university library along with the collections that serve the medical community.

"A wealth of information on medical devices, medical device companies... and key personnel in the industry is provide in this comprehensive reference work... A valuable reference work, one of the best hardcopy compilations available." -Doody Publishing

Two Volumes, Hardcover ISBN 978-1-59237-206-5, 3,000 pages, $325.00

To preview any of our Directories Risk-Free for 30 days, call (800) 562-2139 or fax (518) 789-0556
www.greyhouse.com books@greyhouse.com

Business Information ◆ Ratings Guides ◆ General Reference ◆ Education ◆
Statistics ◆ Demographics ◆ Health Information ◆ __Canadian Information__

Grey House
Publishing

Canadian Almanac & Directory, 2008

The Canadian Almanac & Directory contains sixteen directories in one – giving you all the facts and figures you will ever need about Canada. No other single source provides users with the quality and depth of up-to-date information for all types of research. This national directory and guide gives you access to statistics, images and over 100,000 names and addresses for everything from Airlines to Zoos - updated every year. It's Ten Directories in One! Each section is a directory in itself, providing robust information on business and finance, communications, government, associations, arts and culture (museums, zoos, libraries, etc.), health, transportation, law, education, and more. Government information includes federal, provincial and territorial - and includes an easy-to-use quick index to find key information. A separate municipal government section includes every municipality in Canada, with full profiles of Canada's largest urban centers. A complete legal directory lists judges and judicial officials, court locations and law firms across the country. A wealth of general information, the *Canadian Almanac & Directory* also includes national statistics on population, employment, imports and exports, and more. National awards and honors are presented, along with forms of address, Commonwealth information and full color photos of Canadian symbols. Postal information, weights, measures, distances and other useful charts are also incorporated. Complete almanac information includes perpetual calendars, five-year holiday planners and astronomical information. Published continuously for 160 years, *The Canadian Almanac & Directory* is the best single reference source for business executives, managers and assistants; government and public affairs executives; lawyers; marketing, sales and advertising executives; researchers, editors and journalists.

Hardcover ISBN 978-1-59237-220-1, 1,600 pages, $315.00

Associations Canada, 2008

The Most Powerful Fact-Finder to Business, Trade, Professional and Consumer Organizations
Associations Canada covers Canadian organizations and international groups including industry, commercial and professional associations, registered charities, special interest and common interest organizations. This annually revised compendium provides detailed listings and abstracts for nearly 20,000 regional, national and international organizations. This popular volume provides the most comprehensive picture of Canada's non-profit sector. Detailed listings enable users to identify an organization's budget, founding date, scope of activity, licensing body, sources of funding, executive information, full address and complete contact information, just to name a few. Powerful indexes help researchers find information quickly and easily. The following indexes are included: subject, acronym, geographic, budget, executive name, conferences & conventions, mailing list, defunct and unreachable associations and registered charitable organizations. In addition to annual spending of over $1 billion on transportation and conventions alone, Canadian associations account for many millions more in pursuit of membership interests. *Associations Canada* provides complete access to this highly lucrative market. *Associations Canada* is a strong source of prospects for sales and marketing executives, tourism and convention officials, researchers, government officials - anyone who wants to locate non-profit interest groups and trade associations.

Hardcover ISBN 978-1-59237-277-5, 1,600 pages, $315.00

Financial Services Canada, 2008/09

Financial Services Canada is the only master file of current contacts and information that serves the needs of the entire financial services industry in Canada. With over 18,000 organizations and hard-to-find business information, Financial Services Canada is the most up-to-date source for names and contact numbers of industry professionals, senior executives, portfolio managers, financial advisors, agency bureaucrats and elected representatives. Financial Services Canada incorporates the latest changes in the industry to provide you with the most current details on each company, including: name, title, organization, telephone and fax numbers, e-mail and web addresses. *Financial Services Canada* also includes private company listings never before compiled, government agencies, association and consultant services - to ensure that you'll never miss a client or a contact. Current listings include: banks and branches, non-depository institutions, stock exchanges and brokers, investment management firms, insurance companies, major accounting and law firms, government agencies and financial associations. Powerful indexes assist researchers with locating the vital financial information they need. The following indexes are included: alphabetic, geographic, executive name, corporate web site/e-mail, government quick reference and subject. *Financial Services Canada* is a valuable resource for financial executives, bankers, financial planners, sales and marketing professionals, lawyers and chartered accountants, government officials, investment dealers, journalists, librarians and reference specialists.

Hardcover ISBN 978-1-59237-278-2, 900 pages, $315.00

Directory of Libraries in Canada, 2008/09

The Directory of Libraries in Canada brings together almost 7,000 listings including libraries and their branches, information resource centers, archives and library associations and learning centers. The directory offers complete and comprehensive information on Canadian libraries, resource centers, business information centers, professional associations, regional library systems, archives, library schools and library technical programs. *The Directory of Libraries in Canada* includes important features of each library and service, including library information; personnel details, including contact names and e-mail addresses; collection information; services available to users; acquisitions budgets; and computers and automated systems. Useful information on each library's electronic access is also included, such as Internet browser, connectivity and public Internet/CD-ROM/subscription database access. The directory also provides powerful indexes for subject, location, personal name and Web site/e-mail to assist researchers with locating the crucial information they need. *The Directory of Libraries in Canada* is a vital reference tool for publishers, advocacy groups, students, research institutions, computer hardware suppliers, and other diverse groups that provide products and services to this unique market.

Hardcover ISBN 978-1-59237-279-9, 850 pages, $315.00

Canadian Environmental Directory, 2008 /09

The Canadian Environmental Directory is Canada's most complete and only national listing of environmental associations and organizations, government regulators and purchasing groups, product and service companies, special libraries and more! The extensive Products and Services section provides detailed listings enabling users to identify the company name, address, phone, fax, e-mail, Web address, firm type, contact names (and titles), product and service information, affiliations, trade information, branch and affiliate data. The Government section gives you all the contact information you need at every government level – federal, provincial and municipal. We also include descriptions of current environmental initiatives, programs and agreements, names of environment-related acts administered by each ministry or department PLUS information and tips on who to contact and how to sell to governments in Canada. The Associations section provides complete contact information and a brief description of activities. Included are Canadian environmental organizations and international groups including industry, commercial and professional associations, registered charities, special interest and common interest organizations. All the Information you need about the Canadian environmental industry: directory of products and services, special libraries and resource, conferences, seminars and tradeshows, chronology of environmental events, law firms and major Canadian companies, *The Canadian Environmental Directory* is ideal for business, government, engineers and anyone conducting research on the environment.

Softcover ISBN 978-1-59237-224-9, 900 pages, $315.00

Canadian Parliamentary Guide, 2008

An indispensable guide to government in Canada, the annual *Canadian Parliamentary Guide* provides information on both federal and provincial governments, courts, and their elected and appointed members. The Guide is completely bilingual, with each record appearing both in English and then in French. The Guide contains biographical sketches of members of the Governor General's Household, the Privy Council, members of Canadian legislatures (federal, including both the House of Commons and the Senate, provincial and territorial), members of the federal superior courts (Supreme, Federal, Federal Appeal, Court Martial Appeal and Tax Courts) and the senior staff for these institutions. Biographies cover personal data, political career, private career and contact information. In addition, the Guide provides descriptions of each of the institutions, including brief historical information in text and chart format and significant facts (i.e. number of members and their salaries). The Guide covers the results of all federal general elections and by-elections from Confederations to the present and the results of the most recent provincial elections. A complete name index rounds out the text, making information easy to find. No other resources presents a more up-to-date, more complete picture of Canadian government and her political leaders. A must-have resource for all Canadian reference collections.

Hardcover ISBN 978-1-59237-310-9, 800 pages, $184.00

Figure 1. *Rural/Urban Maps. Data source for the maps in Figure 1A, 1B, 1C : U.S. Census Bureau; RUCA codes: USDA Economic Research Service and the WWAMI Rural Health Research Center, http://depts.washington.edu/uwruca/index.html.*

A

Average Size of Farms in Acres - 2002

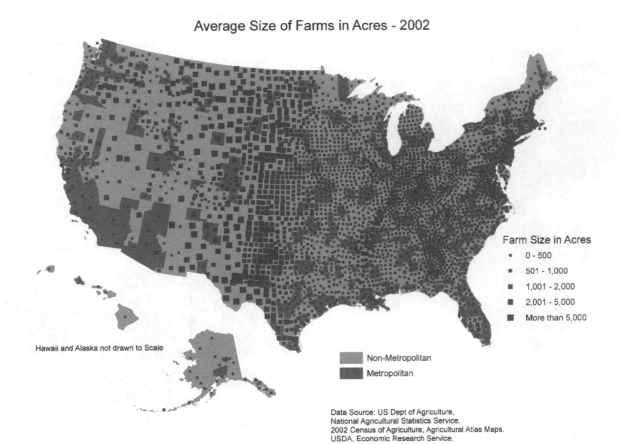

Farm Size in Acres
- ▪ 0 - 500
- ▪ 501 - 1,000
- ■ 1,001 - 2,000
- ■ 2,001 - 5,000
- ■ More than 5,000

Hawaii and Alaska not drawn to Scale

Non-Metropolitan
Metropolitan

Data Source: US Dept of Agriculture,
National Agricultural Statistics Service,
2002 Census of Agriculture, Agricultural Atlas Maps.
USDA, Economic Research Service.

B

Market Value of Agricultural Products Sold - 2002

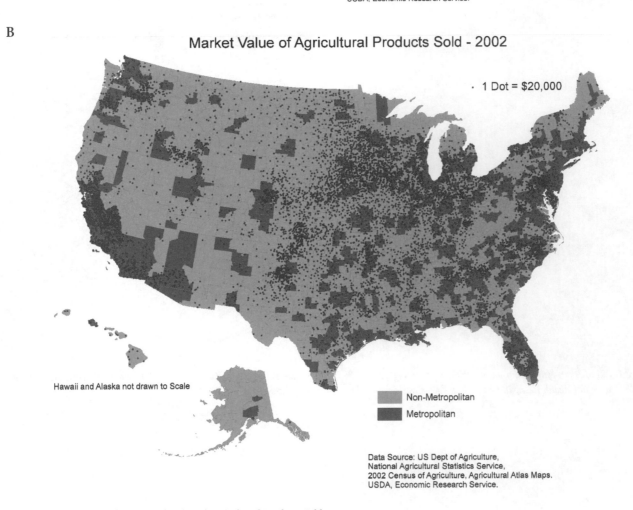

· 1 Dot = $20,000

Hawaii and Alaska not drawn to Scale

Non-Metropolitan
Metropolitan

Data Source: US Dept of Agriculture,
National Agricultural Statistics Service,
2002 Census of Agriculture, Agricultural Atlas Maps.
USDA, Economic Research Service.

Figure 2. *Average Size of Farms and Value of Agricultural Products Sold*

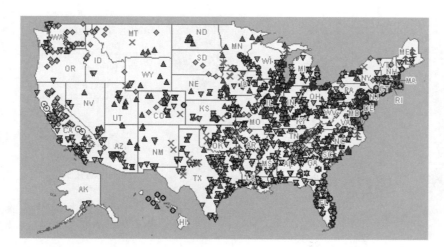

Electric Power Plants

Min. net sumer capacity of
100 megawatts
(Values below are U.S. totals)

▽ Natural Gas (731)
▲ Coal (401)
◆ Hydro (183)
⬢ Petroleum (108)
⊕ Nuclear (66)
✕ Wind (31)
🌲 Wood (8)
⊙ Geothermal (4)
⬤ Biomass (2)
✹ Solar (2)

Figure 3. *Electric Power Plants. Source: U.S. Department of Energy, Energy Information Administration, "State Energy Profiles," Online: http://tonto.eia.doe.gov/state.*

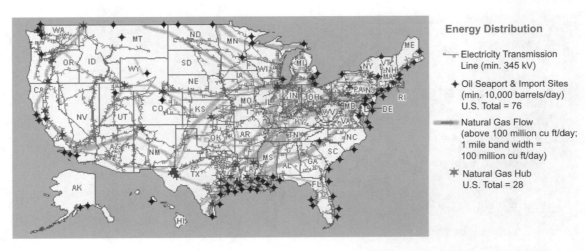

Figure 4. *Energy Distribution. Source: U.S. Department of Energy, Energy Information Administration, "State Energy Profiles," Online: http://tonto.eia.doe.gov/state.*

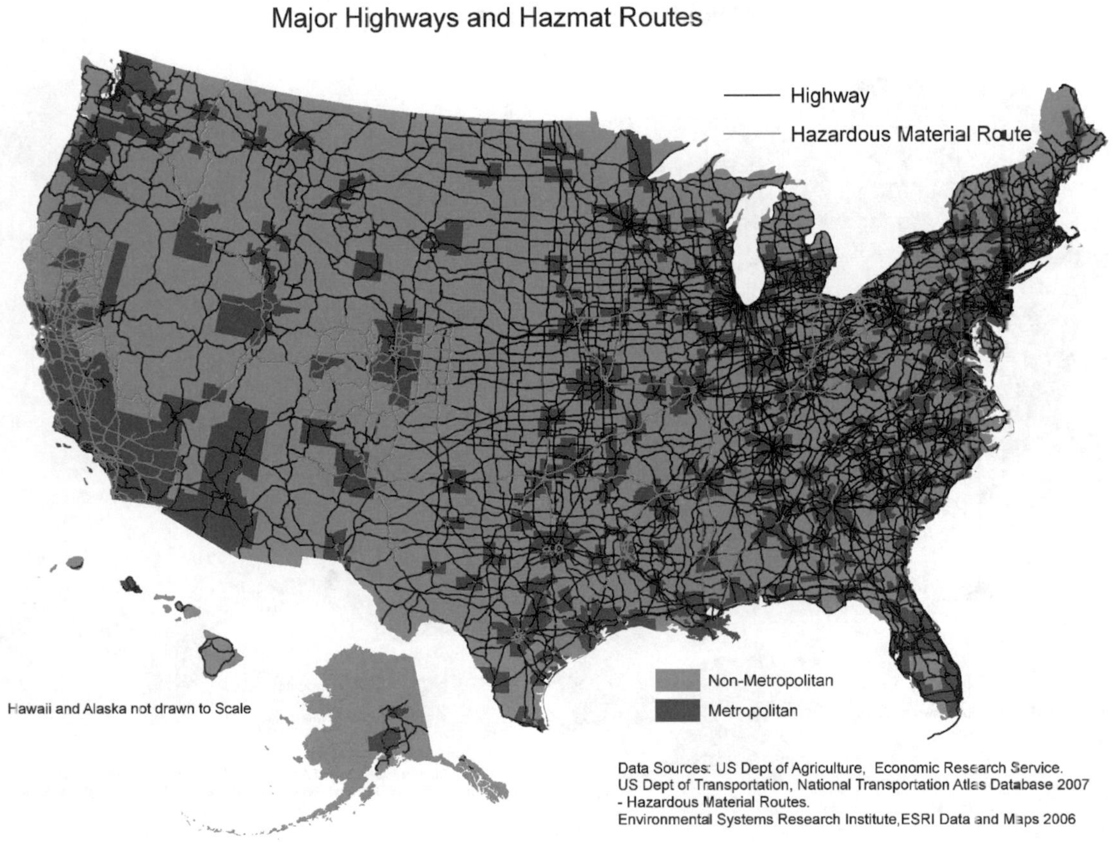

Major Highways and Hazmat Routes

— Highway
— Hazardous Material Route

Hawaii and Alaska not drawn to Scale

Non-Metropolitan
Metropolitan

Data Sources: US Dept of Agriculture, Economic Research Service.
US Dept of Transportation, National Transportation Atlas Database 2007
- Hazardous Material Routes.
Environmental Systems Research Institute,ESRI Data and Maps 2006

Figure 5. *Major Highways and Hazmat Routes*

Major Rivers and Dams

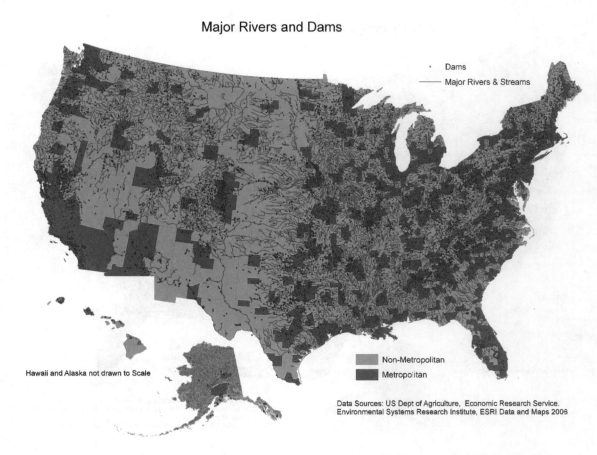

Hawaii and Alaska not drawn to Scale

Non-Metropolitan

Metropolitan

Data Sources: US Dept of Agriculture, Economic Research Service.
Environmental Systems Research Institute, ESRI Data and Maps 2006

Figure 6. *Major Rivers and Dams in the U.S.*

Hospitals

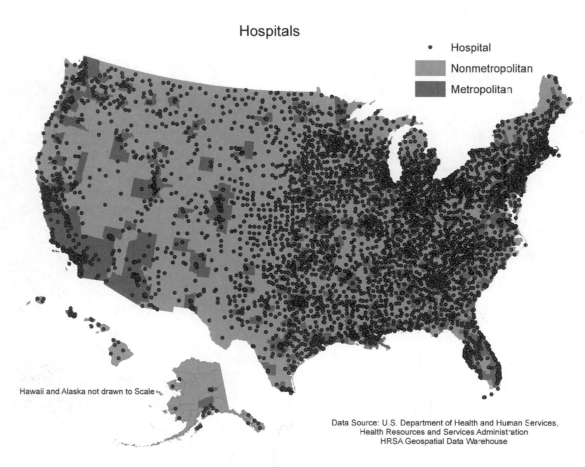

Hawaii and Alaska not drawn to Scale

Data Source: U.S. Department of Health and Human Services,
Health Resources and Services Administration
HRSA Geospatial Data Warehouse

Figure 7. Hospitals in the U.S.